Psychology

The Science of Mind and Behaviour

4th edition

by **Richard Gross**

Dedication

To Jan, whose life has been on hold for the last year while this book has been written. With love and thanks.

British Library Cataloguing in Publication Data
A catalogue record for this title is available from the British Library

ISBN 0 340 79061 X

First published 2001

Impression number	10	9	8	7	6	5	4	3	2	1
Year			2005	2004	2003	2002	2001			

Typeset by GreenGate Publishing Services, Tonbridge, Kent.

Printed and bound in Italy for Hodder and Stoughton Educational, a division of Hodder Headline plc, 338 Euston Road, London NW1 3BH, by Printer Trento.

Contents

Part 6: Individual Differences 587

Part 7: Issues and Debates 695

Preface to the fourth edition

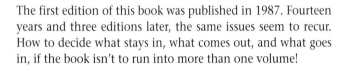

The first edition of this book was published in 1987. Fourteen years and three editions later, the same issues seem to recur. How to decide what stays in, what comes out, and what goes in, if the book isn't to run into more than one volume!

So, what were my guiding principles?
- The overriding aim was to provide a general introduction to psychology, which means that all the major topic areas are covered.
- Within each topic, some of the material from the third edition has been retained, some removed or pruned, some given greater emphasis and extended; moreover, some completely new material has been added (e.g. face recognition; internet relationships).
- Another major aim was to give the book a more contemporary feel by including chapters on some of the major applied areas of psychology (such as health, sport, and criminological psychology).
- Similarly, certain research areas make an appearance, for the first time, such as parapsychology, substance abuse, and exceptional development (another of the applied areas, covering giftedness, autism and learning disability, including dyslexia).
- Some material has been redistributed. For example, stress has come out of Emotion and Stress and moved into Health Psychology, and eyewitness testimony has moved from Memory to Psychology and the Law (another applied chapter).
- The applied chapters come at the end of each of the major sections. Their aim is to demonstrate how the theory and research discussed in the preceding chapters have been used in attempts to understand current real-life issues and problems and implement practical interventions (such as interviewing eyewitnesses, preventing crime and re-offending, enhancing the performance of sports teams, and trying to help people lead safer and healthier lives).

So, what else is new?
- There's been an increase in the number of chapters, which are shorter on the whole, making them more accessible.
- The chapter contents are clearly shown in the panel at the beginning of each chapter.
- The text is more reader-friendly, with shorter blocks of text and more headings and subheadings interspersed throughout. A more colloquial style has also been used.
- The end-of-chapter summaries are more condensed.
- Throughout each chapter there are 'Ask yourself ...' breaks. These are designed to encourage you to think about the text that follows, to have questions in your mind (if not always answers) to help you understand and digest the studies and theories that you read about. So, instead of just reading in a fairly passive way, you'll adopt a more critical approach, equipped with some idea of what to expect and what to look out for.

  Sometimes the questions will be quite specific, and the answers will be given, quite directly, in the text that immediately follows. At other times, the questions will be more general and abstract, and the answers will unfold only throughout the next few paragraphs. Another kind of question will require you to think about your own experiences and views on a particular issue – in these cases, there'll be no standard answer as such.

  In all cases, the aim is to engage you, to make the process of reading the text more active and interactive, and, consequently, more interesting. Sometimes, the questions can easily be used as the basis for a seminar or class debate.
- A completely re-designed, two-colour page, with more boxes, more pictures and diagrams, means, overall, a more attractive book that will make reading easier and more pleasurable.
- Web addresses appear at the end of each chapter, plus a revamped, annotated *Further reading* box.

What's gone?
- Instead of the end-of-chapter *Glossary*, page numbers in bold in the index indicate where key terms are defined.

Hopefully, all that was good about the previous edition is still here, mixed in with much that is different. The appeal of the previous edition was perhaps that it catered for the needs of students on a wide range of courses, without being written specifically or exclusively for any one group. I hope – and trust – that the same can be said of this present edition. As before, please let me know what you think of my efforts (via the publisher).

Good luck – and enjoy!

Acknowledgements

I'd like to thank everyone at GreenGate involved in this project, especially Anna Churchman for her expert, and often challenging, editing of the text. Special thanks too to (the now departed from Hodder) Greig Aitken, for his co-ordination of the project and his artwork suggestions. Thanks also to everyone else at Hodder & Stoughton, including Tim Gregson-Williams: less hands-on, perhaps, but still very much 'there'. I'd also like to thank Jill Hodges for sharing with me some of her as yet unpublished findings regarding the effects of early institutionalisation, and Barbara Woods for her help with the chapter on Sport.

The publishers would like to thank the following for permission to reproduce photographs, other illustrations and text in this book:

p.3, © ADAGP, Paris and DACS, London 2001; p.10, Reproduced with permission of www.CartoonStock.com p.12, ©Roger Ressmeyer/CORBIS; p.13, CORBIS; p.15, CORBIS; p.16, CORBIS (a, b, & d), The Robert Hunt Library; p.17, NI Syndication; p.19, CORBIS; p.20, CORBIS; p.29 Cambridge University Press; p.30, CORBIS (left & right); p.31, CORBIS (top & bottom); p.38, William Vandivert, Dennis, MA, USA/Scientific American; p.43, Eye of Science/Science Photo Library; p.49, From Penfield, W. & Boldrey, E. (1937): Journal – Brain, 60, 389–442, Oxford University Press; p.50 (left) Guardian Newspaper, 1996; p.53, Figure 4.10, reproduced from Phantoms in the Brain, by V.S. Ramachandran & S. Blakeslee, 1998, with permission from HarperCollins Publishers Ltd; p.65, © ADAGP, Paris and DACS, London 2001; p.69, Figure 5.3, from Matlin & Foley, Sensation & Perception, Copyright © 1992 by Allyn & Bacon. Adapted by permission; p.70, Alan Hobson/Science Photo Library; p.78, Popperfoto/Reuters; p.79, The Moviestore Collection; p.80, Figure 6.1, 'Visions from a Dying Brain', reproduced by permission of Liz Pyle; p.82, Jeremy Walker/Science Photo Library; p.87, David Parker/Science Photo Library; p.88, The Bridgeman Art Library, © Kingdom of Spain, Gala – Salvador Dali Foundation, DACS, London 2001; p.95, The Image Bank; p.104, The Ronald Grant Archive; p.105, the cover of ADDICTED by Tony Adams & Ian Ridley, HarperCollinsWillow, 1999; p.108, Popperfoto; pp.109–110, Figure 8.2 (and Box text), from 'Young people are drinking to "get trolleyed" like never before' by Rosie Waterhouse, Mark Macaskill and Senay Boztas, © Times Newspapers Ltd, 23 July 2000, reproduced by permission; p.110, Rex Features Ltd; p.113, Figure 8.3, reproduced from 'Substance use, abuse and dependence' by R. Hammersley in Psychology and Social Care (1999), D. Messer and F. Jones (Eds), with permission from Jessica Kingsley Publishers; p.115, The Bridgeman Art Library; p.117, © Hulton-Deutsch Collection/CORBIS; p.121, 'Unmasking the Face' by P. Ekman and W. V. Friesen, Consulting Psychologists Press, 1984; p.124, from Psychology: Science, Behaviour & Life, 2nd Edition, by Robert Crooks, permission of Holt, Rinehart & Winston; p.125, The Advertising Archives; p.126, Scientific American; p.127, University of Wisconsin Primate Laboratory; p.132, The Bridgeman Art Library; p.133, from Unmasking the Face, by P. Ekman & W.V. Friesen, Consulting Psychologists Press; p.140, Robert Estall Photo Library; p.142, Reproduced with permission of www.CartoonStock.com; p.144, The Bridgeman Art Library; p.146, Science Photo Library; p.149, Hulton Getty Picture Collection; p.158, The Bridgeman Art Library; p.160, Figure 12.1, from Health Psychology: A Textbook, 2nd edition, by Jane Ogden, Open University Press, 2000; p.161, The Ronald Grant Archive; p.164, The Advertising Archives; p.168, Popperfoto/Reuters; p.170, Will & Deni Mcintyre/Science Photo Library; p.175, Claire Paxton & Jacqui Farrow/Science Photo Library; p.183, © Kelly Harriger/CORBIS; p.184, Professor Harold Egerton/Science Photo Library; p.193, Paul Thompson/Ace Photo Library; p.203 (left), Dr Helmut Leder, Freie Universität Berlin; p.204, 'Gazzaker', reproduced with permission from Dr Derek Carson, University of Abertay, Dundee; p.209, Cordon Art/Baarn/Holland; p.216 (bottom right), Cordon Art/Baarn/Holland; p.223, Eastern Counties Newspapers Ltd; p.228, BSIP, LECA/Science Photo Library; p.229, Barnaby's Picture Library; p.236, Figure 16.8, Professor Mark Johnson, Centre for Brain and Cognitive Development; p.237 (bottom right), Francoise Sauze/Science Photo Library; p.243, © Philip James Corwin/CORBIS; p.250, Eve Lucas; p.252, Dr. Fred. Espenak/Science Photo Library; p.253, Press Association; p.257 (bottom) from Cognitive Psychology, Volume 3, Wollen, K.A., Weber, A. & Lowry, D.H., Copyright ©1972 Academic Press; p.266, Hubertus Kanus/Barnaby's Picture Library; p.268, Robert Estall Photo Library; p.270, The Bridgeman Art Library; p.277, Georgia State University/Enrico Ferrorreli/Colorific!; p.278, © Graham Rawle/The Agency (London) Ltd; p.284, Popperfoto; p.290, © Bettmann/CORBIS; p.293, Science Photo Library; p.298, CORBIS; p.301, Hulton Getty Picture Collection; p304, Figure 20.6, adapted by permission of George Retseck; p.305, Peter Menzel/Science Photo Library; p.308, The Ronald Grant Archive; p.325, © R.W. Jones/CORBIS; p.329, Press Association; p.334, © Reuters

x

Acknowledgements

NewMedia Inc./CORBIS; p.335, The Ronald Grant Archive; p.340, The Ronald Grant Archive; p.344, Neil Tingle/Action Plus; p.346, Glyn Kirk/Action Plus; p.349, © Robert Maass/CORBIS; p.350, from *Attitude, Organisation and Change*, Holland & Rosenburg (Eds), 1960, Yale University Press; p.354, Popperfoto/Reuters; p.356, Karen Hoddle/Barnaby's Picture Library; p.357, Health Education Authority; p.366, Barnaby's Picture Library; p.368, Poster reproduced by permission of The Commission for Racial Equality; p.370, Press Association; p.371, Associated Press; p.374, David Roger/Allsport; p.377, Concord Video & Film Council; p.379, Bob Thomas/Popperfoto;p.382, Scientific American; p.387, The Ronald Grant Archive; p.388, Associated Press/Itsuo Inovye; p.391, The Ronald Grant Archive; p.393 (right), Copyright 1965 by Stanley Milgram from the film *Obedience*, distributed by Pennsylvania State University, Audio Visual Services; p.395, © Barry Lewis/CORBIS; p.398, From Psychology & Life by Philip Zimbardo, permission of Philip Zimbardo; p.405, Based on Brehm, S.S. (1992) *Intimate Relationships*, 2nd Edition, New York, McGraw Hill; p.409, Professor J. Langlois, University of Texas at Austin; p.413, © Hulton-Deutsch Collection/CORBIS; p.414, Based on Brehm, S.S. (1992) *Intimate Relationships*, 2nd Edition, New York, McGraw Hill; p.415 (top left), Based on Brehm, S.S. (1992) *Intimate Relationships*, 2nd Edition, New York, McGraw Hill; p.416, The Moviestore Collection; p.419, Science Photo Library; p.421, Popperfoto/Reuters; p.424, from *American Psychological Association Journal of Personality & Social Psychology, 7*, 202–7, Berkowitz, L. & LePage, A.; p.426, Key Study 29.4 (text) from 'Getting a kick from TV violence', by Alexandra Frean, © Times Newspapers Ltd, reproduced by permission; p.427, The Ronald Grant Archive; p.430, © Reuters NewMedia Inc./CORBIS; p.433, Popperfoto/Reuters; p.437, Popperfoto/Reuters; p.439, Rex Features Ltd; p.442, Associated Press; p.445, Neil Tingle/Action Plus; p.447, © Reuters NewMedia Inc./CORBIS; p.451, Glyn Kirk/Action Plus; p.453, © Hulton-Deutsch Collection/CORBIS; p.459, A. Bruce/Barnaby's Picture Library; p.461, Harlow Primate Laboratory, University of Wisconsin (left and right); p.462, Science Photo Library; p.468, Concord Films Council/Joyce Robertson; p.474, © Reuters NewMedia Inc./CORBIS; p.476, Glyn Kirk/Action Plus; p.479, The Bridgeman Art Library; p.481, © Mitchell Gerber/CORBIS; p.482, © Horace Bristol/CORBIS; p.490, The Bridgeman Art Library; p.505, The Ronald Grant Archive; p.507, The Ronald Grant Archive; p.509, ZEFA; p.510, Eric Bretagnon/Action Plus; p.541, Figure 37.3. Coleman J.C. and Hendry L. (1990) *The Nature of Adolescence*, 2nd ed., London: Routledge; p.516, Albert Bandura, Stanford University; p.517, Albert Bandura, Stanford University; p.520; Science Photo Library; p.521, Popperfoto; p.527, Life File/Nicola Sutton (top), Sally & Richard Greenhill (bottom); p.523 (left & right), from *Man & Woman, Boy & Girl*, Money, J. & Ehrhardt, A. (1972), John Hopkins University Press; p.529, Press Association; p.532, The Bridgeman Art Library, © Munch Museum/Munch – Ellingsen Group, BONO, Oslo, DACS, London 2001; p.533, The Kobal Collection; p.536, Superstock; p.537, Popperfoto/Reuters; p.540, The Ronald Grant Archive; p.541, from *The Nature of Adolescence*, 2nd edition, Routledge; p.543, ©Roger Ressmeyer/CORBIS; p.546, © S.I.N./CORBIS; p.548, The Ronald Grant Archive; p.552, Sally & Richard Greenhill; p.554, © Reuters NewMedia Inc./CORBIS; p.555, Popperfoto (left & right); p.559, The Bridgeman Art Library; p.560, Popperfoto/Reuters; p.563, BSIP Ducloux/Science Photo Library; p.564, © Paul A. Soulders/CORBIS; p.565, Topham Picturepoint (top), Sally & Richard Greenhill (bottom); p.567, BBC; p.572, Popperfoto; p.573, © Reuters NewMedia Inc./CORBIS; p.576, The Bridgeman Art Library; p578, Figure 40.1, reproduced by permission of the National Autistic Society; p580, Figure 40.2, reprinted from *Cognition*, Vol 21, Baron-Cohen, S., Leslie, A.M., & Frith, U. 'Does the autistic child have a theory of mind?' pp 37–46 (1985), with permission from Elsevier Science; p.590, Barnaby's Picture Library; p.602, Rex Features Ltd; p.604, Tek Image/Science Photo Library; p.609, The Ronald Grant Archive; p.611, UPI/Bettmann Archive; p.613, © Reuters NewMedia Inc./CORBIS; p.623, The Bridgeman Art Library; p.630, The Bridgeman Art Library EXTRA COPYRIGHT BY-LINE TO FOLLOW; p.631, © Bettmann/CORBIS; p.632, The Bridgeman Art Library; p.644, The Bridgeman Art Library; p.645, Science Photo Library; p.653, © Bethlem Royal Hospital Archives and Museum; p.658, Rex Features Ltd; p.659, © Mitchell Gerber/CORBIS; p.661, Mary Evans Picture Library; p.666, Science Photo Library; p.668, Freud Museum Publications; p.671, The Ronald Grant Archive; p.682, The Ronald Grant Archive; p.683, © Reuters NewMedia Inc./CORBIS; p.683, Figure 46.1, reproduced from 'Crime and crime prevention' by Hollin, in *Psychology and Social Care* (1999), D. Messer and F. Jones (Eds), with permission from Jessica Kingsley Publishers; p.685, © Hulton-Deutsch Collection/CORBIS; p.690 (left), The Ronald Grant Archive; p.690 (right), © Reuters NewMedia Inc./CORBIS; p.697, St. Bartholemew's Hospital/Science Photo Library; p.699, Bailey-Cooper Photography; p.702, first published in *The Psychologist, The Bulletin of the British Psychological Society*, Vol. 11, November 1998, © The Purcell Team/CORBIS; p.703, Wellesley College (Mary Calkins) p.707, © Bettmann/CORBIS; p.709, Rex Features Ltd; p.721, © Jeffry W. Myers/CORBIS; p.722, AKG, London; p.723, Popperfoto/Reuters; p.726, The Ronald Grant Archive; p.732, Prof. K. Seddon & Dr. T. Evans, Queen's University, Belfast/Science Photo Library; p.738, The Ronald Grant Archive

Every effort has been made to obtain necessary permission with reference to copyright material. The publishers apologise if inadvertently any sources remain unacknowledged and will be glad to make the necessary arrangements at the earliest opportunity.

The Nature and Scope
of Psychology

Chapter 1

What Is This Thing Called Psychology?

Introduction and overview

When a psychologist meets someone for the first time at, say, a party and replies truthfully to the standard 'opening line', 'What do you do for a living?', the reaction of the newly-made acquaintance is likely to fall into one of the following categories:

- 'Oh, I'd better be careful what I say from now on' (partly defensive, partly amused);

- 'I bet you meet some right weirdos in your work' (partly intrigued, partly sympathetic);

- 'What exactly *is* psychology?' (partly inquisitive, partly puzzled).

What these reactions betray – especially the first two – is an inaccurate and incomplete understanding of the subject. The first seems to imply that psychologists are mindreaders and have access to other people's thoughts (they *don't*), while the second seems to imply that psychologists work only or largely with people who are 'mentally ill' or 'mad' (again, they *don't*, although many do). The third reaction perhaps implies that the boundaries between psychology and other subject disciplines aren't clearly drawn (they *aren't*), but what this chapter aims to do is make them sufficiently clear to enable you, the reader, who may be 'visiting' psychology for the first time, to find your way around this book – and the subject – relatively easily.

The opening chapter in any textbook is intended to 'set the scene' for what follows, and this normally involves defining the subject or discipline. In most disciplines, this is usually a fairly simple task. With psychology, however, it's far from straightforward. Definitions of psychology have changed frequently during its relatively short history as a separate field of study. This reflects different, and sometimes conflicting, theoretical views regarding the nature of human beings and the most appropriate methods for investigating them.

A brief history

The word psychology is derived from the Greek *psyche* (mind, soul or spirit) and *logos* (discourse or study). Literally, then, psychology is the 'study of the mind'. The emergence of psychology as a separate discipline is generally dated at 1879, when Wilhelm Wundt opened the first psychological laboratory at the University of Leipzig in Germany. Wundt and his co-workers were attempting to investigate 'the mind' through *introspection* (observing and analysing the structure of their own conscious mental processes). Introspection's aim was to analyse conscious thought into its basic elements and perception into its constituent sensations, much as chemists analyse compounds into elements. This attempt to identify the structure of conscious thought is called *structuralism*.

Wundt and his co-workers recorded and measured the results of their introspections under controlled conditions, using the same physical surroundings, the same 'stimulus' (such as a clicking metronome), the same verbal instructions to each participant, and so on. This emphasis on measurement and control marked the separation of the 'new psychology' from its parent discipline of philosophy.

Philosophers had discussed 'the mind' for thousands of years. For the first time, scientists (Wundt was actually a physiologist by training) applied some of scientific investigation's basic methods to the study of mental processes. This was reflected in James's (1890) definition of psychology as:

> '... the Science of Mental Life, both of its phenomena and of their conditions ... The Phenomena are such things as we call feelings, desires, cognition, reasoning, decisions and the like'.

However, by the early twentieth century, the validity and usefulness of introspection were being seriously questioned, particularly by an American psychologist, John B. Watson. Watson believed that the results of introspection could never

be proved or disproved, since if one person's introspection produced different results from another's, how could we ever decide which was correct? *Objectively*, of course, we cannot, since it's impossible to 'get behind' an introspective report to check its accuracy. Introspection is *subjective*, and only the individual can observe his/her own mental processes.

Consequently, Watson (1913) proposed that psychologists should confine themselves to studying *behaviour*, since only this is measurable and observable by more than one person. Watson's form of psychology was known as *behaviourism*. It largely replaced introspectionism and advocated that people should be regarded as complex animals, and studied using the same scientific methods as chemistry and physics. For Watson, the only way psychology could make any claims to being scientific was to emulate the natural sciences, and adopt its own objective methods. He defined psychology as:

> ' ... that division of Natural Science which takes human behaviour – the doings and sayings, both learned and unlearned – as its subject matter' (Watson, 1919).

The study of inaccessible, private, mental processes was to have no place in a truly scientific psychology.

Especially in America, behaviourism (in one form or another) remained the dominant force in psychology for the next 40 years or so. The emphasis on the role of learning (in the form of *conditioning*) was to make that topic one of the central areas of psychological research as a whole (see Chapter 2, pages 13–15 and Chapter 11).

| Box 1.1 | **Psychoanalytic theory and Gestalt psychology** |

In 1900, Sigmund Freud, a neurologist living in Vienna, first published his *psychoanalytic theory* of personality in which the *unconscious* mind played a crucial role. In parallel with this theory, he developed a form of psychotherapy called *psychoanalysis*. Freud's theory (which forms the basis of the *psychodynamic* approach) represented a challenge and a major alternative to behaviourism (see Chapter 2, pages 15–18).

A reaction against both structuralism and behaviourism came from the *Gestalt* school of psychology, which emerged in the 1920s in Austria and Germany. Gestalt psychologists were mainly interested in perception, and believed that perceptions couldn't be broken down in the way that Wundt proposed (see Chapter 3) and behaviourists advocated for behaviour (see Chapters 3 and 11). Gestalt psychologists identified several 'laws' or principles of perceptual organisation (such as 'the whole is greater than the sum of its parts'), which have made a lasting contribution to our understanding of the perceptual process (see Chapter 15 for a detailed discussion).

In the late 1950s, many British and American psychologists began looking to the work of computer scientists to try to understand more complex behaviours which, they felt, had been either neglected altogether or greatly oversimplified by learning theory (conditioning). These complex behaviours were what Wundt, James and other early scientific psychologists had called '*mind*' or mental processes. They were now called *cognition* or *cognitive processes* and refer to all the ways in which we come to know the world around us, how we attain, retain and regain information, through the processes of perception, attention, memory, problem-solving, language and thinking in general.

Cognitive psychologists see people as *information-processors*, and cognitive psychology has been heavily influenced by computer science, with human cognitive processes being compared with the operation of computer programs (the *computer analogy*). Cognitive psychology now forms part of *cognitive science*, which emerged in the late 1970s (see Figure 1.1). The events which together constitute the 'cognitive revolution' are described in Box 3.3 (page 32).

Although mental or cognitive processes can only be *inferred* from what a person does (they cannot be observed literally or directly), mental processes are now accepted as being valid subject-matter for psychology, provided they can be made 'public' (as in memory tests or problem-solving tasks). Consequently, what people say and do are perfectly acceptable sources of information about their cognitive processes, although the processes themselves remain inaccessible to the observer, who can study them only indirectly.

The influence of both behaviourism and cognitive psychology is reflected in Clark & Miller's (1970) definition of psychology as:

> ' ... the scientific study of behaviour. Its subject matter includes behavioural processes that are observable, such as gestures, speech and physiological changes, and processes that can only be inferred, such as thoughts and dreams'.

Similarly, Zimbardo (1992) states that:

> 'Psychology *is formally defined as the scientific study of the behaviour of individuals and their mental processes'*.

Classifying the work of psychologists

Despite behaviourist and cognitive psychology's influence on psychology's general direction in the last 80 years or so, much more goes on within psychology than has been outlined so far. There are other theoretical approaches or orientations, other aspects of human (and non-human) activity that constitute the special focus of study, and different kinds of work that different psychologists do.

A useful, but not hard and fast, distinction can be made between the *academic* and *applied* branches of psychology (see Figure 1.2, page 9). Academic psychologists carry out research in a particular area and are attached to a university or research establishment, where they'll also teach undergraduates and supervise the research of postgraduates. Research is both *pure* (done for its own sake and intended, primarily, to increase our knowledge and understanding) and *applied* (aimed at solving a particular problem). Applied research is usually funded by a government institution like the Home Office or the Department of Education and Employment, or by some commercial or industrial institution. The range of topics that may be investigated is as wide as psychology itself, but they can be classified as focusing either on the *processes* or *mechanisms* underlying various aspects of behaviour, or more directly on the *person* (Legge, 1975).

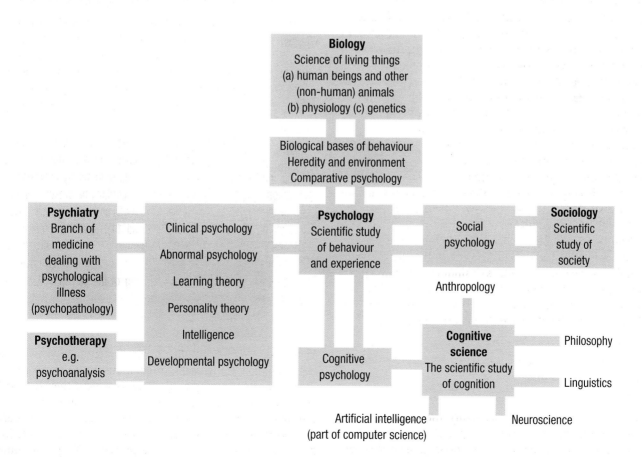

Figure 1.1 *The relationship between psychology and other scientific disciplines*

The process approach

This is divided into three main areas: *physiological psychology*, *cognitive processes* and *comparative psychology*.

Physiological (or bio-)psychology (Chapters 4–12)

Physiological (or bio-)psychologists are interested in the physical basis of behaviour, how the functions of the *nervous system* (in particular the *brain*) and the *endocrine* (hormonal) system are related to and influence behaviour *and* mental processes. For example, are there parts of the brain specifically concerned with particular behaviours and abilities (*localisation of brain function*)? What role do hormones play in the experience of emotion and how are these linked to brain processes? What is the relationship between brain activity and different *states of consciousness* (including sleep)?

A fundamentally important biological process with important implications for psychology is genetic transmission. The *heredity and environment* (or *nature–nurture*) issue draws on what geneticists have discovered about the characteristics that can be passed from parents to offspring, how this takes place and how genetic factors interact with environmental ones (see Chapters 41, 44 and 50). Other topics within physiological psychology include motivation and stress (an important topic within health psychology: see Chapter 12), and sensory processes, which are closely connected with perception (see Chapter 15).

Cognitive psychology (Chapters 13–21)

As we saw earlier (page 5), cognitive (or mental) processes include *attention*, *memory*, *perception*, *language*, *thinking*, *problem-solving*, *reasoning* and *concept-formation* ('higher-order' mental activities). Although these are often studied for their own sake, they may have important practical implications too, such as understanding the memory processes involved in *eyewitness testimony* (see Chapter 21). Much of social psychology (classified here as belonging to the person approach) is cognitive in flavour, that is, concerned with the mental processes we use, for example, to explain people's behaviour, and is known as *social cognition*. Also, Piaget's theory (again, belonging to the person approach) is concerned with *cognitive development*.

Comparative psychology

Comparative psychology is the study of the behaviour of animals, aimed at identifying similarities and differences between species. It also involves studying non-human animal behaviour to gain a better understanding of human behaviour. The basis of comparative psychology is *evolutionary theory*. Research areas include classical and operant conditioning (see Chapter 11), animal communication, language and memory (see Gross *et al.*, 2000), and evolutionary explanations of human behaviour (see Chapter 2, pages 24–27, and Clamp, 2001).

The person approach

Social psychology (Chapters 22–31)

Some psychologists would claim that 'all psychology is social psychology', because all behaviour takes place within a social context and, even when we're alone, our behaviour continues to be influenced by others. However, other people usually have a more immediate and direct influence upon us when we're actually in their presence (as in conformity and obedience: see Chapters 26 and 27).

Social psychology is also concerned with interpersonal perception (forming impressions of others), interpersonal attraction and social relationships, prejudice and discrimination, and pro- and anti-social behaviour (especially aggression). Chapter 31 looks at the social psychology of sport.

Developmental psychology (Chapters 32–40)

Developmental psychologists study the biological, cognitive, social and emotional changes that occur in people over time. One significant change within developmental psychology during the past 25 years or so is the recognition that development isn't confined to childhood and adolescence, but is a lifelong process (the *lifespan approach*). It's now generally accepted that adulthood is a developmental stage, distinct from childhood, adolescence and old age.

Developmental psychology isn't an isolated or independent field, and advances in it depend on progress within psychology as a whole, such as behavioural genetics, (neuro)physiological psychology, learning, perception and motivation. Although Piaget's theory of cognitive development was meant to map the changes that take place up to about 15 years of age, he's considered to have made a major contribution to psychology as a whole (see Chapter 34). While the focus is on normal development, Chapter 40 is concerned with *exceptional/atypical* development.

Individual differences (Chapters 41–46)

This is concerned with the ways in which people can differ from one another, including *personality*, *intelligence*, and *psychological abnormality*. Major *mental disorders* include schizophrenia, depression, anxiety disorders and eating disorders. Abnormal psychology is closely linked with *clinical psychology*, one of the major *applied* areas of psychology (see below, page 7). Psychologists who study abnormality and clinical psychologists are also concerned with the effectiveness of different forms of treatment and therapies. Each major theoretical approach has contributed to both the explanation and treatment of mental disorders (see Chapters 2 and 45).

Another source of individual differences is *criminal behaviour*, which is discussed in Chapter 46.

Comparing the process and person approaches

In practice, it's very difficult to separate the two approaches, even if it can be done theoretically. However, there are important relative differences between them.

> **Box 1.2** **Some important differences between the process and person approaches**
>
> - **The process approach** is typically confined to the laboratory (where experiments are the method of choice). It makes far greater experimental use of non-human animals and assumes that psychological processes (particularly learning) are essentially the same in all species and that any differences between species are only *quantitative* (differences of degree).

• **The person approach** makes much greater use of field studies (such as observing behaviour in its natural environment) and of non-experimental methods (e.g. correlational studies: see Coolican, 1999). Typically, human participants are studied, and it's assumed that there are *qualitative* differences (differences in kind) between humans and non-humans.

Areas of applied psychology

Discussion of the person/process approaches has been largely concerned with the *academic* branch of psychology. Since the various areas of *applied* psychology are all concerned with people, they can be thought of as the applied aspects of the person approach. According to Hartley & Branthwaite (1997), most applied psychologists work in four main areas: *clinical*, *educational* and *occupational psychology* and *government service* (such as prison psychologists). Additionally, Coolican *et al.* (1996) identifies *criminological* (or *forensic*), *sports*, *health* and *environmental* psychologists. Hartley and Branthwaite argue that the work psychologists do in these different areas has much in common: it's the *subject matter* of their jobs which differs, rather than the skills they employ. Consequently, they consider an applied psychologist to be a person who can deploy specialised skills appropriately in different situations.

Box 1.3	Seven major skills (or roles) used by applied psychologists

• **The psychologist as counsellor:** helping people to talk openly, express their feelings, explore problems more deeply and see these problems from different perspectives. Problems may include school phobia, marriage crises and traumatic experiences (such as being the victim of a hijacking), and the counsellor can adopt a more or less *directive* approach (see Chapter 2, pages 18–20, and Chapter 45, page 676).
• **The psychologist as colleague:** working as a member of a team and bringing a particular perspective to a task, namely drawing attention to the human issues, such as the point of view of the individual end-user (be it a product or a service of some kind).
• **The psychologist as expert:** drawing upon psychologists' specialised knowledge, ideas, theories and practical knowledge to advise on issues ranging from incentive schemes in industry to appearing as an 'expert witness' in a court case.
• **The psychologist as toolmaker:** using and developing appropriate measures and techniques to help in the analysis and assessment of problems. These include questionnaire and interview schedules, computer-based ability and aptitude tests and other *psychometric* tests (see Chapters 41 and 42).
• **The psychologist as detached investigator:** many applied psychologists carry out evaluation studies to assess the evidence for and against a particular point of view. This reflects the view of psychology as an objective science, which should use controlled experimentation whenever possible. The validity of this view is a recurrent theme throughout psychology (see, in particular, Chapter 3).

• **The psychologist as theoretician:** theories try to explain observed phenomena, suggesting possible underlying mechanisms or processes. They can suggest where to look for causes and how to design specific studies which will produce evidence for or against a particular point of view. Results from applied psychology can influence theoretical psychology and vice versa.
• **The psychologist as agent for change:** applied psychologists are involved in helping people, institutions and organisations, based on the belief that their work will change people and society for the better. However, some changes are much more controversial than others, such as the use of psychometric tests to determine educational and occupational opportunities, and the use of behaviour therapy and modification techniques to change abnormal behaviour (see Chapter 45).

(Based on Hartley & Branthwaite, 2000)

Clinical psychology

Clinical psychologists are the largest single group of psychologists, both in the UK (Coolican *et al.*, 1996) and the USA (Atkinson *et al.*, 1990). A related group is 'counselling psychologists', who tend to work with younger clients in colleges and universities rather than in hospitals.

Box 1.4	The major functions of the clinical psychologist

Clinical psychologists have had three years post-graduate training and their functions include:

• assessing people with learning difficulties, administering psychological tests to brain-damaged patients, devising rehabilitation programmes for long-term psychiatric patients, and assessing the elderly for their fitness to live independently;
• planning and carrying out programmes of therapy, usually *behaviour therapy/modification* (both derived from learning theory principles), or *psychotherapy* (group or individual) in preference to, or in addition to, behavioural techniques (see Chapter 45);
• carrying out research into abnormal psychology, including the effectiveness of different treatment methods ('outcome' studies). Patients are usually adults, many of whom will be elderly, in psychiatric hospitals, psychiatric wards in general hospitals and psychiatric clinics;
• involvement in community care, as psychiatric care in general moves out of the large psychiatric hospitals;
• teaching other groups of professionals, such as nurses, psychiatrists and social workers.

Psychotherapy is usually carried out by *psychiatrists* (medically qualified doctors specialising in psychological medicine) or *psychotherapists* (who've undergone special training, including their own psychotherapy). In all its various forms, psychotherapy is derived from Freud's psychoanalysis (see Chapters 2 and 45) and is distinguished both from behavioural treatments and physical (somatic) treatments (those based on the medical model: see Chapters 43 and 45).

Criminological (or forensic) psychology

This is a branch of psychology which attempts to apply psychological principles to the criminal justice system. It's rooted in empirical research and draws on cognitive, developmental, social and clinical psychology. One main focus is the study of criminal behaviour and its management, but in recent years research interests have expanded to include other areas, most notably those with a high media profile (such as stalking: see Chapter 46).

Box 1.5 Some recent areas of research interest among criminological psychologists

- Jury selection
- The presentation of evidence
- Eyewitness testimony (see Chapter 21)
- Improving the recall of child witnesses
- False memory syndrome and recovered memory (see Chapter 21)
- Offender profiling (see Chapter 46)
- Crime prevention (see Chapter 46)
- Devising treatment programmes (such as anger management: see Chapter 46)
- Assessing the risk of releasing prisoners (see Chapter 46)

(From Coolican *et al.*, 1996)

Criminological psychologists work in a wide range of contexts, including psychiatric hospitals and special hospitals for the criminally insane (such as Broadmoor and Rampton), young offender institutions and prisons. Like clinical psychologists, a crucial part of their work involves research and evaluation of what constitutes successful treatment.

Educational psychology

Educational psychologists have had at least two years teaching experience and gained a postgraduate qualification in educational or child psychology.

Box 1.6 Some of the responsibilities of the educational psychologist

- administering psychometric tests, particularly intelligence (or IQ) tests, as part of the assessment of learning difficulties (see Chapters 40 and 41);
- planning and supervising remedial teaching; research into teaching methods, the curriculum (subjects taught), interviewing and counselling methods and techniques;
- planning educational programmes for those with mental and physical impairments (including the visually impaired and autistic), and other groups of children and adolescents who aren't attending ordinary schools (special educational needs: see Chapter 40);
- advising parents and teachers how to deal with children and adolescents with physical impairments, behaviour problems or learning difficulties;
- teacher training.

Educational psychologists are usually employed by a Local Education Authority (LEA) and work in one or more of the following: child and family centre teams (previously called 'child guidance'), the Schools Psychological Service, hospitals, day nurseries, nursery schools, special schools (day and residential) and residential children's homes. Clients are aged up to 18 years, but most fall into the five to 16 age group.

Occupational (work or organisational) psychology

Occupational psychologists are involved in the selection and training of individuals for jobs and vocational guidance, including administration of aptitude tests and tests of interest. (This overlaps with the work of those trained in *personnel management*.)

Box 1.7 Other responsibilities of the occupational psychologist

- helping people who, for reasons of illness, accident or redundancy, need to choose and re-train for a new career (industrial rehabilitation);
- designing training schemes, as part of '*fitting the person to the job*'. Teaching machines and simulators (such as an aeroplane cockpit) often feature prominently in these schemes;
- 'fitting the job to the person' (*human engineering/engineering psychology* or *ergonomics*), wherein applications from experimental psychology are made to the design of equipment and machinery in order to make the best use of human resources and to minimise accidents and fatigue. Examples include telephone dialling codes (memory and attention) and the design of decimal coinage (tactile and visual discrimination);
- advising on working conditions in order to maximise productivity (another facet of *ergonomics* – the study of people's efficiency in their working environments). Occupational groups involved include computer/VDU operators, production line workers, and air traffic controllers;
- helping the flow of communication between departments in government institutions, or 'industrial relations' in commerce and industry (*organisational psychology*). The emphasis is on the social, rather than the physical or practical aspects of the working environment;
- helping to sell products and services through advertising and promotions. Many psychologists are employed in the advertising industry, where they draw on what experimental psychologists have discovered about human motivation, attitudes, cognition and so on (see Chapter 24).

Ask yourself ...

- What, if anything, has come as a surprise to you regarding what goes on in the name of 'psychology'?

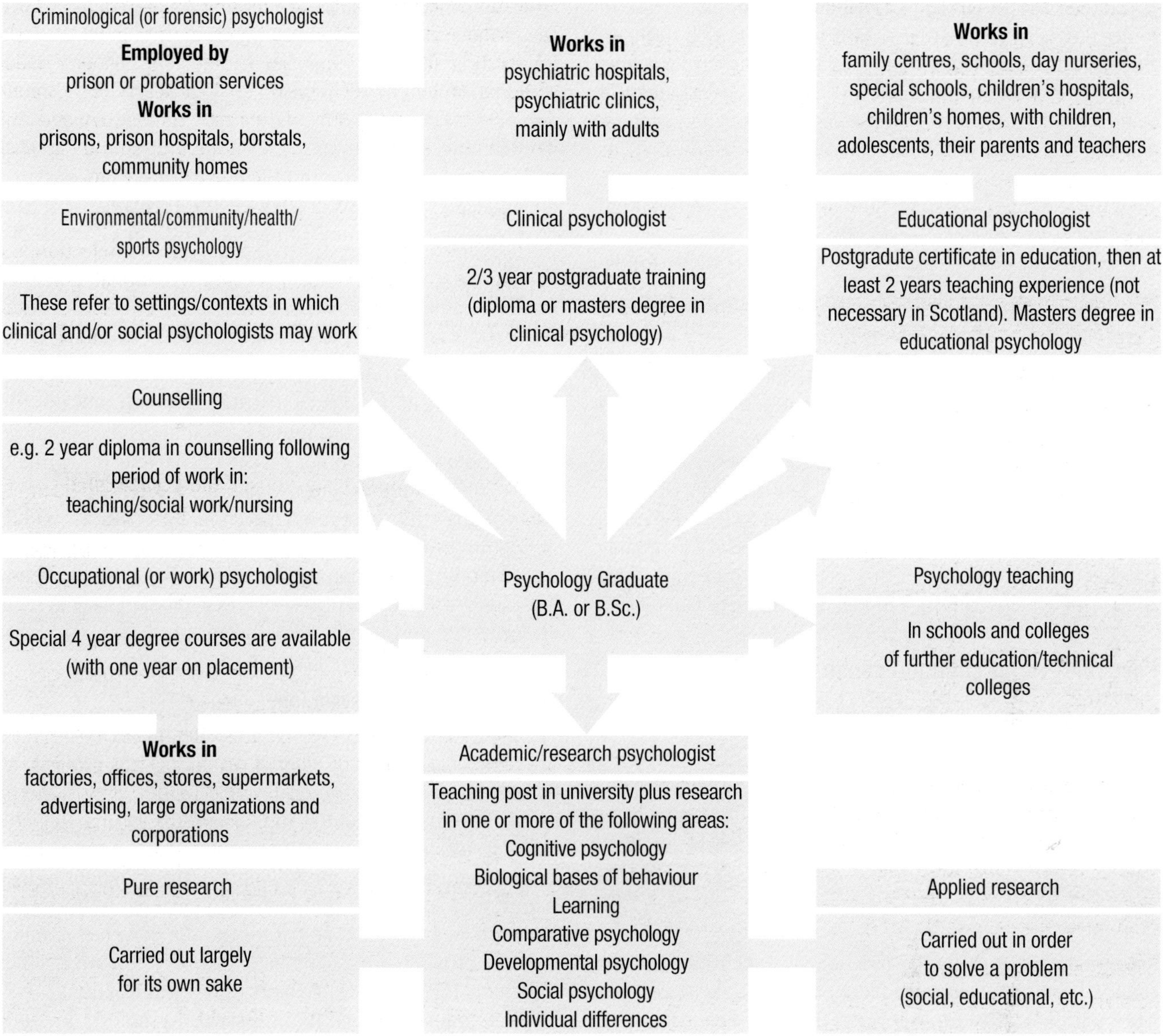

Criminological (or forensic) psychologist

Employed by
prison or probation services
Works in
prisons, prison hospitals, borstals,
community homes

Environmental/community/health/
sports psychology

These refer to settings/contexts in which
clinical and/or social psychologists may work

Counselling

e.g. 2 year diploma in counselling following
period of work in:
teaching/social work/nursing

Occupational (or work) psychologist

Special 4 year degree courses are available
(with one year on placement)

Works in
factories, offices, stores, supermarkets,
advertising, large organizations and
corporations

Pure research

Carried out largely
for its own sake

Works in
psychiatric hospitals,
psychiatric clinics,
mainly with adults

Clinical psychologist

2/3 year postgraduate training
(diploma or masters degree in
clinical psychology)

Psychology Graduate
(B.A. or B.Sc.)

Academic/research psychologist

Teaching post in university plus research
in one or more of the following areas:
Cognitive psychology
Biological bases of behaviour
Learning
Comparative psychology
Developmental psychology
Social psychology
Individual differences

Works in
family centres, schools, day nurseries,
special schools, children's hospitals,
children's homes, with children,
adolescents, their parents and teachers

Educational psychologist

Postgradute certificate in education, then at
least 2 years teaching experience (not
necessary in Scotland). Masters degree in
educational psychology

Psychology teaching

In schools and colleges
of further education/technical
colleges

Applied research

Carried out in order
to solve a problem
(social, educational, etc.)

Figure 1.2 *The main areas of academic and applied psychology open to psychology graduates*

Chartered psychologists

Since 1987, the British Psychological Society (BPS), the only professional body for British psychologists incorporated by Royal Charter, has been authorised under its Charter to keep a Register of Chartered Psychologists. Entry to the Register is restricted to members of the Society who've applied for registration and who have the necessary qualifications or experience to have reached a standard sufficient for professional practice in psychology without supervision (Gale, 1990).

The language of psychology

As in all sciences, there's a special set of technical terms (jargon) to get used to, and this is generally accepted as an unavoidable feature of studying the subject. But over and above this jargon, psychologists use words that are familiar to us from everyday speech *in a technical way*, and it's in these instances that 'doing psychology' can become a little confusing.

Some examples of this are 'behaviour' and 'personality'. For parents to tell their child to 'behave yourself' is meaningless to a psychologist's ears: behaving is something we're all doing all the time (even when asleep). Similarly, to say that someone 'has no personality' is meaningless because, as personality refers to what makes a person unique and different from others, you cannot help but have one!

Other terms which denote large portions of the research of experimental psychology, such as memory, learning and intelligence, are called *hypothetical constructs*, that is, they don't refer to anything that can be directly observed but which can be *inferred* only from observable behaviour (see above, page 5). They seem to be necessary in order to account for the behaviour being observed, but there's a danger of thinking of them as 'things' or 'entities' (this is called *reification*), rather than as a way of trying to make sense of behaviour.

Another way in which psychologists try to make sense of something is by comparing it with something else using an *analogy*. (Often something complex is compared with something more simple). Since the 1950s and the development of computer science, the *computer analogy* has become very popular as a way of trying to understand how the mind works. As we saw earlier, the language of computer science has permeated the cognitive view of human beings as information processors (see Chapter 2, pages 20–22).

A *model* is a kind of *metaphor*, involving a single, fundamental idea or image; this makes it less complex than a theory (although sometimes the terms are used interchangeably). A *theory* is a complex set of inter-related statements which attempt to *explain* certain observed phenomena. But in practice, when we refer to a particular theory (for example, Freud's or Piaget's), we often include *description* as well. Thomas (1985) defines a theory as 'an explanation of how the facts fit together', and he likens a theory to a lens through which to view the subject matter, filtering out certain facts and giving a particular pattern to those it lets in. A *hypothesis* is a testable statement about the relationship between two or more variables, usually derived form a model or theory (see Chapter 3).

Psychology and common sense

Ask yourself ...

- What do you understand by the term 'common sense'?
- In what ways are we all psychologists?
- How might a 'common sense' understanding of human behaviour and experience differ from that of professional psychologists?

A common reaction among psychology students, when discussing the findings of some piece of research, is to say, 'but we knew that already' (implying that it's mere 'common sense'). Alternatively, they might say, 'but that's not what we normally understand by such-and-such', implying that the research is in some way wrong. So psychology often seems to be in a no-win position – either it merely confirms common sense or it contradicts it, in which case psychology seems to be the less credible of the two.

"Ok, let's try reverse psychology.
Andrew... don't eat all your dinner up!"

Reproduced with permission of www.CartoonStock.com

We all consider we know something about people and why they behave as they do, and so there's a sense in which we're all psychologists! (see Chapters 22 and 23). This is a theme explored at length by Joynson in *Psychology and Common Sense* (1974). He begins by stating that human beings aren't like the objects of natural science – we understand ourselves and can already predict and control our behaviour to a remarkable extent. This creates for the psychologist a paradoxical task: what kind of understanding can you seek of a creature which already understands itself?

For Joynson, the fundamental question is, 'If the psychologist did not exist, would it be necessary to invent him?'. Conversely, for Skinner (1971), 'it is a science or nothing' and Broadbent (1961) also rejects the validity of our everyday understanding of ourselves and others (Joynson calls this 'the behaviourists' prejudice'). Yet we cannot help but try to make sense of our own and other people's behaviour (by virtue of our cognitive abilities and the nature of social interaction), and to this extent we're all psychologists. Heather (1976) points to ordinary language as embodying our 'natural' understanding of human behaviour: as long as human beings have lived they've been psychologists, and language gives us an 'elaborate and highly refined conceptual tool, developed over thousands of years of talking to each other'.

Formal vs informal psychology

Legge (1975) and others resolve this dilemma by distinguishing between *formal* and *informal* psychology (or professional versus amateur, scientific versus non-scientific). Our common sense, intuitive or 'natural' understanding is unsystematic, and doesn't constitute a body of knowledge. This makes it very difficult to 'check' an individual's 'theory' about human nature, as does the fact that each individual has to learn from his/her own experience. So part of the aim of formal psychology is to provide such a systematic body of knowledge, which represents the unobservable bases of our 'gut reactions'.

Yet it could be argued that informal psychology does provide a 'body of knowledge' in the form of proverbs or sayings or folk wisdom, handed down from generation to generation (for example, 'Birds of a feather flock together', 'Too many cooks spoil the broth' and 'Don't cross your bridges before you come to them'). While these may contain at least a grain of truth, for each one there's another proverb which states the opposite ('Opposites attract', 'Many hands make light work' and 'Time and tide wait for no man' or 'Nothing ventured, nothing gained').

However, formal psychology may help us reconcile these contradictory statements. For example, there's evidence to support both proverbs in the first pair (see Chapter 28). Formal psychology tries to identify the conditions under which each statement applies, and they *appear* contradictory if we assume that only one or the other can be true! In this way, scientific psychology throws light on our everyday, informal understanding, rather than negating or invalidating it.

Legge (1975) believes that most psychological research should indeed be aimed at demonstrations of 'what we know already', but that it should also aim to go one step further. Only the methods of science, he believes, can provide us with the public, communicable body of knowledge that we're seeking. According to Allport (1947), the aim of science is

'Understanding, prediction and control above the levels achieved by unaided common sense', and this is meant to apply to psychology as much as to the natural sciences (see Chapters 3 and 42).

Conclusions

Psychology is a diverse discipline. Psychologists investigate a huge range of behaviours and mental or cognitive processes. There's a growing number of applied areas, in which theory and research findings are brought to bear in trying to improve people's lives in a variety of ways. During the course of its life as a separate discipline, definitions of psychology have changed quite fundamentally, reflecting the influence of different theoretical approaches. Rather than having to choose between our common sense understanding of people and the 'scientific' version, psychology as a scientific discipline can be seen as complementing and illuminating our 'everyday' psychological knowledge.

- While the process approach is largely confined to laboratory experiments using non-humans, the person approach makes greater use of field studies and non-experimental methods involving humans. The two approaches see species differences as **quantitative** or **qualitative** respectively.
- Most **applied** psychologists work in **clinical, educational, occupational** or **government service**, with newer fields including **criminological/forensic, sports, health** and **environmental psychology**.
- There's a sense in which we're all psychologists, creating a dilemma for psychologists: are they necessary? One solution is to distinguish between **informal/commonsense** and **formal/scientific psychology**. The latter aims to go beyond commonsense understanding and to provide a public, communicable body of knowledge.

CHAPTER SUMMARY

- Early psychologists, such as Wundt, attempted to study the mind through **introspection** under controlled conditions, aiming to analyse conscious thought into its basic elements (**structuralism**).
- Watson rejected introspectionism's subjectivity and replaced it with **behaviourism**. Only by regarding people as complex animals, using the methods of natural science and studying observable behaviour, could psychology become a true science.
- **Gestalt** psychologists criticised both structuralism and behaviourism, advocating that 'the whole is greater than the sum of its parts'. Freud's **psychoanalytic theory** was another major alternative to behaviourism.
- Following the **cognitive revolution**, people came to be seen as **information-processors**, based on the **computer analogy**. Cognitive processes, such as perception and memory, became an acceptable part of psychology's subject matter.
- **Academic** psychologists are mainly concerned with conducting **research** (**pure** or **applied**), which may focus on underlying processes/mechanisms or on the person.
- The **process approach** consists of physiological psychology, cognitive processes and comparative psychology, while the **person approach** covers developmental and social psychology and individual differences.

Web addresses

www.bps.org.uk

http://altavista.digital.com/

http://www.psych.bangor.ac.uk/deptpsych/BIPsychDepts/BIPsychDepts .html

http://www.gasou.edu/psychweb/psychweb.htm

http://www.unipissing.ca/psyc/psycsite.htm

Further reading

Benson, N.C. & Grove, G. (1998) *Psychology for Beginners*. Cambridge: Icon Books. Psychology through cartoons, part of an excellent series, which includes many titles relevant to psychology. Just as relevant to Chapter 2.

Butler, G. & McManus, F. (1998) *Psychology: A Very Short Introduction*. Oxford: Oxford University Press. As the title indicates, a short but very handy, pocket-sized account of many of the major areas.

Danziger, K. (1990) *Constructing the Subject: Historical Origins of Psychological Research*. Cambridge: Cambridge University Press. Recommended to the more dedicated student.

Fancher, R.E. (1996) *Pioneers of Psychology* (3rd edition). New York: Norton. An excellent account of the key figures in the history of psychology (including the philosophical background), just as relevant (if not more so) to Chapter 2. Also includes a useful chapter on artificial intelligence (see Chapter 20).

Chapter 2

Theoretical Approaches to Psychology

Introduction and overview

Different psychologists make different assumptions about what particular aspects of a person are worthy of study, and this helps to determine an underlying model or image of what people are like. In turn, this model or image determines a view of psychological normality, the nature of development, preferred methods of study, the major cause(s) of abnormality, and the preferred methods and goals of treatment.

An approach is a perspective which isn't as clearly outlined as a theory and which:

> ' … *provides a general orientation to a view of humankind. It says, in effect, we see people as operating according to these basic principles and we therefore see explanations of human behaviour as needing to be set within these limits and with these or those principles understood'.* (Coolican *et al.*, 1996)

As we shall see, all the major approaches include two or more distinguishable theories, but within an approach, they share certain basic principles and assumptions which give them a distinct 'flavour' or identity. The focus here is on the *behaviourist, psychodynamic, humanistic, cognitive, social constructionist* and *evolutionary* approaches.

The behaviourist approach

Basic principles and assumptions

As we saw in Chapter 1 (page 4), Watson (1913) revolutionised psychology by rejecting the introspectionist approach and advocating the study of observable behaviour. Only by modelling itself on the natural sciences could psychology legitimately call itself a science. Watson was seeking to transform the very subject matter of psychology (from 'mind' to 'behaviour') and this is often called *methodological behaviourism*. According to Skinner (1987):

> '"*Methodological*" *behaviourists often accept the existence of feelings and states of mind, but do not deal with them because they are not public and hence statements about them are not subject to confirmation by more than one person'.*

In this sense, what was revolutionary when Watson (1913) first delivered his 'behaviourist manifesto' (see Box 3.2, page 32) has become almost taken for granted, 'orthodox' psychology. It could be argued that *all* psychologists are methodological behaviourists (Blackman, 1980). Belief in the importance of empirical methods, especially the experiment, as a way of collecting data about humans (and non-humans), which can be quantified and statistically analysed, is a major feature of mainstream psychology (see Chapter 3). By contrast, as Skinner (1987) asserts:

> '"*Radical*" *behaviourists … recognise the role of private events (accessible in varying degrees to self-observation and physiological research), but contend that so-called mental activities are metaphors or explanatory fictions and that behaviour attributed to them can be more effectively explained in other ways'.*

For Skinner, these more effective explanations of behaviour come in the form of the principles of reinforcement derived from his experimental work with rats and pigeons. What's 'radical' about Skinner's *radical behaviourism* is the claim that feelings, sensations and other private events cannot be used to explain behaviour but are to be *explained* in an analysis of behaviour. While methodological behaviourism proposes to ignore such inner states (they're *inaccessible*), Skinner rejects them as variables which can explain behaviour (they're *irrelevant*) and argues that they can be translated into the language of reinforcement theory (Garrett, 1996).

According to Nye (2000), Skinner's ideas are also radical because he applied the same type of analysis to *covert* behaviour (thoughts and feelings) occurring 'within the skin' as he did to *overt*, publicly observable behaviours. He stressed the importance of identifying *functional relations* (cause-and-effect connections) between environmental conditions and behaviours. As Nye (2000) points out:

> '*Radical behaviourists are able to describe with considerable detail various observable factors that affect learning, thereby buttressing the arguments that human behaviour is controlled in many ways by circumstances that can be objectively specified and manipulated'.*

Given this important distinction between methodological and radical behaviourism, we need to consider some principles and assumptions that apply to behaviourism in general.

Box 2.1 **Basic principles and assumptions made by the behaviourist approach**

- Behaviourists emphasise the role of environmental factors in influencing behaviour, to the near exclusion of innate or inherited factors: see Chapter 50. This amounts essentially to a focus on learning. The key form of learning is *conditioning*, either *classical* (*Pavlovian* or *respondent*), which formed the basis of Watson's behaviourism, or *operant* (*instrumental*), which is at the centre of Skinner's radical behaviourism. Classical and operant conditioning are often referred to (collectively) as *learning theory*, as opposed to 'theories of learning' (which usually implies theories other than conditioning theories, that is, non-behaviourist theories: see Chapter 11).

B.F. Skinner (1904–90)

- Behaviourism is often referred to as 'S–R' psychology ('S' standing for 'stimulus' and 'R' for 'response'). While classical and operant conditioning account for observable behaviour (responses) in terms of environmental events (stimuli), the stimulus and response relationship is defined in fundamentally different ways. Only in classical conditioning is the stimulus seen as triggering a response in a predictable, automatic way, and this is what's conveyed by 'S–R' psychology. It's, therefore, a mistake to describe operant conditioning as a 'S–R' approach (see Chapter 11).

- Both types of conditioning are forms of *associative learning*, whereby associations or connections are formed between stimuli and responses that didn't exist before learning took place. This reflects the philosophical roots of behaviourism, namely the *empiricist* philosophy of John Locke, which was a major influence on the development of science in general, as well as on behaviourism in particular (see Chapter 3).

- Part of Watson's rejection of introspectionism was his belief that it invoked too many vague concepts that are difficult, if not impossible, to define and measure. According to the *law of parsimony* (or 'Occam's razor'), the fewer assumptions a theory makes the better (more 'economical' explanations are superior).

- The mechanisms proposed by a theory should be as simple as possible. Behaviourists stress the use of *operational definitions* (defining concepts in terms of observable, measurable, events).

- The aim of a science of behaviour is to *predict* and *control* behaviour. This raises both *conceptual* questions (about the nature of science, in particular the role of theory: see Chapter 3) and *ethical* questions (for example, about power and the role of psychologists as agents of change: see Chapter 48).

Theoretical contributions

Behaviourism made a massive contribution to psychology, at least up to the 1950s, and explanations of behaviour in conditioning terms recur throughout this book. For example, apart from a whole chapter on learning and conditioning (Chapter 11), imagery as a form of organisation in memory and as a memory aid is based on the principle of association, and the interference theory of forgetting is largely couched in stimulus–response terms (Chapter 17). Language, moral and gender development (Chapters 19, 35 and 36) have all been explained in terms of conditioning, and some influential theories of the formation and maintenance of relationships focus on the concept of reinforcement (Chapter 28). The behaviourist approach also offers one of the major models of abnormal behaviour (Chapter 45). Finally, Skinner's notorious views on free will are discussed in detail in Chapter 49.

As with Freud's psychoanalytic theory (see below), theorists and researchers critical of the original, 'orthodox' theories have modified and built on them, making a huge contribution in the process. Noteworthy examples are Tolman's (1948) *cognitive behaviourism* (see Chapter 11) and *social learning theory* (see Chapters 29, 35 and 36).

Ask yourself ...

- Dip into some of these chapters, just to familiarise yourself with the range of topic areas to which the behaviourist approach has been applied (and to help you find your way round the book).

Practical contributions

We may think of *methodological behaviourism*, with its emphasis on experimentation, operational definitions, and the measurement of observable events (see Box 2.1), as a major influence on the practice of scientific psychology in general (what Skinner, 1974, called the 'science of behaviour'). This is quite unrelated to any views about the nature and role of mental events. Other, more 'tangible' contributions include:

- *behaviour therapy and behaviour modification* (based on classical and operant conditioning respectively) as major approaches to the treatment of abnormal behaviour (see Chapter 45) and one of the main tools in the clinical psychologist's 'kit bag' (see Box 1.4, pages 5–6);
- *biofeedback* as a non-medical treatment for stress-related symptoms, derived from attempts to change rats' autonomic physiological functions through the use of operant techniques (see Chapter 12);
- *teaching machines and programmed learning*, which now commonly take the form of *computer assisted learning* (CAL).

An evaluation of behaviourism

In addition to the criticisms – both general and specific – which occur in the particular chapters where behaviourist explanations are presented, two evaluative points will be made here. The first concerns the famous 'Skinner box', the 'auto-environmental chamber' in which rats' and pigeons' environments can be totally controlled by the experimenter (see Chapter 11). Since pressing the lever was intended to be equivalent to a cat operating an escape latch in Thorndike's puzzle box, counting the number of lever presses (frequency of response) became the standard measure of operant learning. Despite Skinner's claims to not having a *theory*, 'the response' in operant conditioning has largely considered *only* the frequency of behaviour, ignoring intensity, duration and quality. As Glassman (1995) observes:

> 'While the focus on frequency was a practical consideration, it eventually became part of the overall conceptual framework as well – a case of research methods directing theory'.

But in everyday life, frequency isn't always the most meaningful aspect of behaviour. For example, should we judge an artist's worth by how many paintings s/he produces, rather than their content?

Ask yourself ...

- Do you agree with Skinner's claim that thoughts and other 'covert behaviours' don't *explain* our behaviour (because they cannot *determine* what we do)?

The second criticism relates to Skinner's claim that human behaviour can be predicted and controlled in the same way as the behaviour of non-humans. Possessing language allows us to communicate with each other and to think about 'things' that have never been observed (and may not even exist), including rules, laws and principles (Garrett, 1996). While these can only be expressed in words or thought about by means of words, much of people's behaviour is governed by these thoughts. According to Garrett, when this happens:

' ... behaviour is now shaped by what goes on inside their [people's] heads ... and not simply by what goes on in the external environment'.

What people *think* is among the important variables determining what they do and say, the very opposite of what Skinner's radical behaviourism claims.

The psychodynamic approach

The term 'psychodynamic' denotes the active forces within the personality that motivate behaviour, and the inner causes of behaviour (in particular the unconscious conflict between the different structures that compose the whole personality). While Freud's was the original psychodynamic theory, the approach includes all those theories based on his ideas, such as those of Jung (1964), Adler (1927) and Erikson (1950). Freud's *psychoanalytic theory* is psychodynamic, but the psychodynamic theories of Jung and so on, aren't psychoanalytic. So the two terms *aren't* synonymous. However, because of their enormous influence, Freud's ideas will be emphasised in the rest of this section.

Basic principles and assumptions

Freud's concepts are closely interwoven, making it difficult to know where their description should begin (Jacobs, 1992). Fortunately, Freud himself stressed the acceptance of certain key theories as essential to the practice of *psychoanalysis*, the form of psychotherapy he pioneered and from which most others are derived (see page 17).

Box 2.2 **The major principles and assumptions of psychoanalytic theory**

- Much of our behaviour is determined by *unconscious* thoughts, wishes, memories and so on. What we're consciously aware of at any one time represents the tip of an iceberg: most of our thoughts and ideas are either not accessible at that moment (*pre-conscious*) or are totally inaccessible (*unconscious*: see Chapter 7). These unconscious thoughts and ideas can become conscious through the use of special techniques, such as *free association*, *dream interpretation* and *transference*, the cornerstones of psychoanalysis (see Chapter 45).
- Much of what's unconscious has been made so through *repression*, whereby threatening or unpleasant experiences are 'forgotten' (see Chapter 21, pages 318–321). They become inaccessible, locked away from our conscious awareness. This is a major form of *ego defence* (see Chapter 42). Freud singled it out as a special cornerstone 'on which the whole structure of psychoanalysis rests. It is the most essential part of it' (Freud, 1914). Repression is closely related to *resistance*, interpretation of which is another key technique used in psychoanalysis (see Chapter 45).
- According to the *theory of infantile sexuality*, the sexual instinct or drive is active from birth and develops through a series of five *psychosexual stages*. The most important of these is the *phallic stage*

(spanning the ages 3–5/6), during which all children experience the Oedipus complex (see Chapter 35). In fact, Freud used the German word '*Trieb*', which translates as 'drive', rather than '*Instinkt*', which was meant to imply that experience played a crucial role in determining the 'fate' of sexual (and aggressive) energy (see Box 50.2, page 734).

- Related to infantile sexuality is the general impact of early experience on later personality (see Chapter 32). According to Freud (1949):

'It seems that the neuroses are only acquired during early childhood (up to the age of six), even though their symptoms may not make their appearance until much later ... the child is psychologically father of the man and ... the events of its first years are of paramount importance for its whole subsequent life'.

Sigmund Freud (1896–1939)

Theoretical contributions

As with behaviourist accounts of conditioning, many of Freud's ideas and concepts have become part of mainstream psychology's vocabulary. You don't have to be a 'Freudian' to use concepts such as 'repression', 'unconscious' and so on, and many of the vast number of studies of different aspects of the theory have been conducted by critics hoping to discredit it (such as Eysenck, 1985; Eysenck & Wilson, 1973).

Like behaviourist theories, Freud's can also be found throughout psychology as a whole. His contribution is extremely rich and diverse, offering theories of motivation (see Chapter 9), dreams and the relationship between sleep and dreams (Chapter 7), forgetting (Chapter 21), attachment and the effects of early experience (Chapter 32), moral and gender development (Chapters 35 and 36), aggression (Chapter 29) and abnormality (Chapter 45). Psychoanalytic theory has also influenced Gould's (1978, 1980) theory of the evolution of adult consciousness (Chapter 38) and Adorno *et al.'s* (1950) theory of the authoritarian personality (a major account of prejudice: see Chapter 25).

Finally, and as noted earlier, Freud's theories have stimulated the development of alternative theories, often resulting from the rejection of some of his fundamental principles and assumptions, but reflecting his influence enough for them to be described as psychodynamic.

Ask yourself ...

• Repeat the exercise suggested for the behaviourist approach (see page 14).

Some major alternative psychodynamic theories

■ *Ego psychology*, promoted by Freud's daughter, Anna, focused on the mechanisms used by the ego to deal with the world, especially the ego defence mechanisms. Freud, by contrast, stressed the influence of the id's innate drives (especially sexuality and aggression) and is often described as an instinct theorist (but see Box 2.2, third point). The ego, as well as the id, originates in basic human inheritance and has its own developmental course. It uses neutralised (non-sexual) energy, which makes possible an interest in objects and activities that aren't necessarily related to underlying sexual and aggressive drives.

According to Nye (2000), the increased attention given to an independent ego has probably resulted partly from a change in the types of patients psychoanalysts are treating. In recent years, patients tend more often to be troubled by the problems of an increasingly complex society (vague anxieties, insecurities and dissatisfaction), and are seeking ways to find meaning and value in work, family and social roles:

> 'Since the ego is the part of the personality that must deal with the external world in some rational, decision-making way, it seems natural that more emphasis should be given to it. Perhaps for the contemporary patient .it is important to focus more attention on conscious thought processes and coping mechanisms; he or she is less likely to be plagued by unconscious guilt and repressed sexuality than by the uncertainties and rootlessness of modern society that requires the ego to grapple with existential problems'. (Nye, 2000)

■ Erik Erikson, trained by Anna Freud as a child psychoanalyst, also stressed the importance of the ego, as well as the influence of social and cultural factors on individual development. He pioneered the *lifespan approach* to development, proposing eight *psychosocial stages*, in contrast with Freud's five *psychosexual stages* that end with physical maturity (see Chapters 37 and 38).

■ Two of Freud's original 'disciples', Carl Jung and Alfred Adler, broke ranks with Freud and formed their own 'schools' (*analytical psychology* and *individual psychology* respectively). Jung attached relatively little importance to childhood experiences (and the associated *personal* unconscious) but considerable importance to the *collective* (or *racial*) unconscious, which stems from the evolutionary history of human beings as a whole (see Chapter 42).

■ Like Jung, Adler rejected Freud's emphasis on sexuality, stressing instead the *will to power* or *striving for superiority*, which he saw as an attempt to overcome feelings of inferiority faced by all children as they grow up. He also shared Jung's view of the person as an indivisible unity or whole, and Erikson's emphasis on the social nature of human beings.

■ Melanie Klein (1932) is often seen as a key transitional figure between Freud's instinct theory and the object relations school (see Box 2.3). Like Anna Freud, she adapted Freud's techniques (such as pioneering *play therapy*) in order to tap a young child's unconscious, and maintained that the superego and Oedipus complex appear as early as the first and second years of life (see Chapter 35).

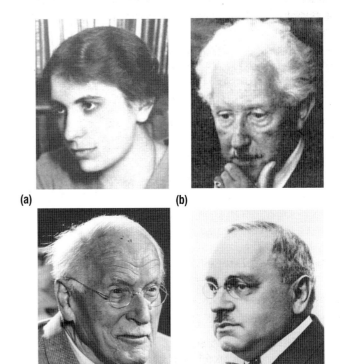

(a) (b)

(c) (d)

a Anna Freud (1895–1982)   b Erik Erikson (1902–1994)
c Carl Gustav Jung (1875–1961)   d Alfred Adler (1870–1937)

Box 2.3 Object relations theory

The *object relations school* (the 'British school') was greatly influenced by Klein's emphasis on the infant's earliest (pre-Oedipal) relationships with its mother. It places far less emphasis on the role of instincts and more on the relationship with particular love objects (especially the mother), seeing early *relationships* as crucial for later patterns of relationships with others. Fairbairn (1952), for example, saw the aim of the libido as object-seeking (as opposed to pleasure-seeking), and this was extended by Bowlby (1969) in his *attachment theory* (see Chapter 32).

According to Nye (2000):

'Although both object relations theory and Freudian theory are concerned with childhood experiences and the inner world of the person, the former puts more emphasis on discrepancies between inner-world and real-world persons and situations. The latter puts more emphasis on the role of factors such as instinctual drives and unresolved Oedipus conflicts ...'.

Object relations theory isn't a single, widely accepted theory. Rather, it refers to a number of separate ideas proposed by different theorists. However, they all stress that internal images ('representations') of one's self and of 'objects' (a technical term usually denoting another person toward whom we direct emotion and action: significant others) can have powerful effects on our relationships with others.

Mahler (1975) and Winnicott (1965) stress the movement from the newborn's absolute dependence to the independence and autonomy of adults as the primary and lifelong developmental task. Development proceeds from symbiotic fusion with the mother, through various stages of partial differentiation of the self and other, to a state of increased individuation and independence (see Chapter 38). The internalised images of others (objects) in the infant (and the psychotic adult: see Chapter 44) are primitive, engulfing, devouring and otherwise menacing. Only when separation from the mother has been successfully achieved, are we capable of empathising with others and seeing them as they really are (rather than projections of our primitive fantasies).

(Based on Holmes, 1993; Nye, 2000; Zeldow, 1995)

Practical contributions

The current psychotherapy scene is highly diverse, with only a minority using Freudian techniques (see Chapter 45), but, as Fancher (1996) points out:

'Most modern therapists use techniques that were developed either by Freud and his followers or by dissidents in explicit reaction against his theories. Freud remains a dominating figure, for or against whom virtually all therapists feel compelled to take a stand'.

Both Rogers, the major humanistic therapist (see below) and Wolpe, who developed *systematic desensitisation* (a major form of behaviour therapy: see Chapter 45), were originally trained in Freudian techniques. Perls, the founder of *Gestalt therapy*, Ellis, the founder of *rational emotive therapy* (RET) (see Chapter 45) and Berne, who devised *transactional analysis* (TA) were also trained psychoanalysts.

Even Freud's fiercest critics concede his influence, not just within world psychiatry but in philosophy, literary criticism, history, theology, sociology, and art and literature generally. Freudian terminology is commonly used in conversations between therapists well beyond Freudian circles, and his influence is brought daily to therapy sessions as part of the cultural background and experience of nearly every client (Jacobs, 1992).

Many mental health practitioners (including psychotherapists, counsellors and social workers), although not formally trained as psychoanalysts, have incorporated elements of Freudian thought and technique into their approaches to helping their patients (Nye, 2000).

An evaluation of the psychodynamic approach

Falsifiability and testability

A criticism repeatedly made of Freudian (and other psychodynamic) theories is that they're unscientific because they're *unfalsifiable* (incapable of being disproved). For example, if the Freudian prediction that 'dependent' men will prefer big-breasted women is confirmed, then the theory is supported. However, if such men actually prefer small-breasted women (Scodel, 1957), Freudians can use the concept of *reaction formation* (an ego defence mechanism: see Table 42.5, page 624) to argue that an unconscious fixation with big breasts may manifest itself as a conscious preference for the opposite, a clear case of 'heads I win, tails you lose' (Popper, 1959; Eysenck, 1985).

Hans J. Eysenck (1916–1997)

However, it's probably a mistake to see reaction formation as typical of Freudian theory as a whole. According to Kline (1984, 1989), for example, the theory comprises a collection of hypotheses, some of which are more easily tested than others, some of which are more central to the theory than others, and some of which have more supporting evidence than others. Also, different parts of the theory have been tested using different methods (see Chapter 42, pages 625–626).

According to Zeldow (1995), the history of science reveals that those theories that are the richest in explananatory power have proved the most difficult to test empirically. For example, Newton's Second Law couldn't be demonstrated in a reliable, quantitative way for 100 years, and Einstein's general theory of relativity is still untestable. Eysenck, Popper and others have criticised psychoanalytic theory for being untestable. But even if this were true:

'... the same thing could (and should) be said about any psychological hypotheses involving complex phenomena and worthy of being tested...psychoanalytic theories have inspired more empirical research in the social and behavioural sciences than any other group of theories ...'.
(Zeldow, 1995)

Box 2.4	Evidence supporting Freudian theory

- Fisher & Greenberg (1996) conducted an extensive reappraisal of studies of psychoanalytic theory carried out up to the early 1990s. Along with Kline (1989), they argue that Freud's theory should be evaluated in terms of a series of specific hypotheses (or mini-theories), rather than as a whole. They also believe that what should be considered are *overall trends* across studies.

    Fisher and Greenberg concluded that there's evidence to support Freud's notion of oral and anal personality tendencies (see Chapter 42), and some aspects of his ideas on the origins of depression and paranoia (see Chapters 44 and 45). But they found only weak and indirect support for the notion of the Oedipal conflict, and no support for their impact on later development or for his views on women's sexuality and how their development differs from men's (see Chapter 35).

    While their review is extremely broad, it's not comprehensive (for example, it doesn't cover repression and other defence mechanisms, or transference). The strength of the evidence presented is variable and sometimes indirect, and where it's supportive it rests on Fisher and Greenberg's interpretation of the results (Andrews & Brewin, 2000). However, for Zeldow (1995) the mere existence of such reviews:

    '... gives the lie to the notion that all psychoanlaytic ideas are too vague or abstruse to be tested scientifically'.

- According to Andersen & Miranda (2000), *transference* is a normal, non-pathological process that's part of our normal mechanisms of social interaction. They claim that their research represents the first experimental demonstration of transference. Within the framework of *social cognition* they've shown that mental representations of significant others, developed in one's family and elsewhere, are linked to representations of self in memory. These representations are 'heavily laden with affect and motivation', and are often activated and used in responding to new people that resemble a significant other. Their experimental procedure in effect assesses transference in terms of how much participants 'go beyond the information given' (Bruner, 1957) about the new person (see Chapters 15, 22 and 23).

- According to Reason (2000), Freud was probably not right in asserting that (nearly) all slips (of the tongue) are in some way intended. But he was certainly correct in claiming that 'Freudian slips' represent minor eruptions of unconscious processing (see Chapter 42). Instead of taking a strictly psychoanalytic interpretation of 'unconscious', Reason prefers one that relates to processes that aren't directly accessible to consciousness, i.e. automatic processing or habitual performance (see Chapter 13).

- Similarly, much of modern cognitive psychology and neuropsychology (see Chapter 4) is consistent with the Freudian view that behaviour isn't dependent on conscious experience (Power, 2000). For example, modern theories of the display of facial affect explicitly recognise a role for the conscious and unconscious control of behaviour (Ekman, 1986: see Chapter 10). Another example is *blindsight* (Weiskrantz, 1986: see Case Study 5.1, page 72). According to Power (2000):

'...Whereas cognitive psychology has emphasised the co-operation between conscious and automatic processes (essential, for example, whilst driving), psychoanalysis has always emphasised conflict instead. The most recent models in psychology have come to consider both co-operation and conflict between conscious and unconscious processes'.

Furthermore, Freud's theory provides methods and concepts which enable us to interpret and 'unpack' underlying meanings (it has great *hermeneutic strength*). Popper's and Eysenck's criticism above helps to underline the fact that these meanings (both conscious and unconscious) cannot be measured in any precise way. Freud offers a way of understanding that's different from theories that are easily testable, and it may actually be more appropriate for capturing the nature of human experience and action (Stevens, 1995: see Chapter 3). According to Fancher (1996):

'Although always controversial, Freud struck a responsive chord with his basic image of human beings as creatures in conflict, beset by irreconcilable and often unconscious demands from within as well as without. His ideas about repression, the importance of early experience and sexuality, and the inaccessibility of much of human nature to ordinary conscious introspection have become part of the standard Western intellectual currency'.

Reason (2000) believes that it's time to reacknowledge Freud's greatness as a psychologist. Like James, he had a rare gift for describing and analysing the phenomenology of mental life. Perhaps Freud's greatest contribution was in recognising that apparent trivia that we now commonly call 'Freudian slips' are 'windows on the mind'. According to Kline (1998):

'... after 100 years, Freudian theory cannot be uncritically accepted just as it cannot be totally rejected. However ... Freudian theory contains some profound observations and understanding of human behaviour. These must be incorporated into any adequate human psychology, not only its theory but also its methods ...'.

The humanistic approach

Basic principles and assumptions

As we noted earlier, Rogers, a leading humanistic psychologist (and therapist) was trained as a psychoanalyst. Although the term 'humanistic psychology' was coined by Cohen (1958), a British psychologist, this approach emerged mainly in the USA during the 1950s. Maslow (1968), in particular, gave wide currency to the term 'humanistic' in America, calling it a 'third force' (the other two being behaviourism and Freudianism). However, Maslow didn't reject these approaches but hoped to unify them, thus integrating both subjective and objective, the private and public aspects of the person, and providing a complete, holistic psychology.

Box 2.5 Some basic principles and assumptions of the humanistic approach

- Both the psychoanalytic and behaviourist approaches are *deterministic*. People are driven by forces beyond their control, either unconscious forces from within (Freud) or reinforcements from without (Skinner). Humanistic psychologists believe in *free will* and people's ability to *choose* how they act (see Chapter 49).

- A truly scientific psychology must treat its subject matter as fully human, which means acknowledging individuals as interpreters of themselves and their world. Behaviour, therefore, must be understood in terms of the individual's *subjective experience*, from the perspective of the actor (a *phenomenological* approach, which explains why this is sometimes called the 'humanistic-phenomenological' approach). This contrasts with the *positivist* approach of the natural sciences, which tries to study people from the position of a detached observer. Only the individual can explain the meaning of a particular behaviour and is the 'expert' – not the investigator or therapist.

- Maslow argued that Freud supplied the 'sick half' of psychology, through his belief in the inevitability of conflict, neurosis, innate self-destructiveness and so on, while he (and Rogers) stressed the 'healthy half'. Maslow saw *self-actualisation* at the peak of a hierarchy of needs (see below and Chapter 9), while Rogers talked about the *actualising tendency*, an intrinsic property of life, reflecting the desire to grow, develop and enhance our capacities. A fully functioning person is the ideal of growth. Personality development naturally moves towards healthy growth, unless it's blocked by external factors, and should be considered the norm (see Chapter 42).

- Maslow's contacts with Wertheimer and other Gestalt psychologists (see Chapter 15) led him to stress the importance of understanding the *whole person*, rather than separate 'bits' of behaviour.

(Based on Glassman, 1995)

gestalt, constantly in the process of forming and reforming' (Rogers, 1959: see Chapter 42). This view contrasts with many other self theorists who see it as a central, unchanging core of personality (see Chapter 33 and Gross *et al.*, 1997).

Abraham H. Maslow (1908–1970)

Ask yourself ...

- Repeat the exercise as for the behaviourist and psychodynamic approaches.

Theoretical contributions

Maslow's *hierarchy of needs* (see Chapter 9, pages 118–119) distinguishes between motives shared by both humans and non-humans and those that are uniquely human, and can be seen as an extension of the psychodynamic approach. Freud's id would represent physiological needs (at the hierarchy's base), Horney (a major critic of the male bias in Freud's theory: see Chapter 35) focused on the need for safety and love (corresponding to the next two levels), and Adler (see above, page 16) stressed esteem needs (at the fourth level). Maslow added self-actualisation to the peak of the hierarchy (Glassman, 1995).

According to Rogers (1951), while awareness of being alive is the most basic of human experiences, we each fundamentally live in a world of our own creation and have a unique perception of the world (the *phenomenal field*). It's our *perception* of external reality which shapes our lives (not external reality itself). Within our phenomenal field, the most significant element is our sense of *self*, 'an organised consistent

Practical contributions

By far the most significant practical influence of any humanistic psychologist is Rogers' *client-* (or *person-*) *centred therapy* (see Chapter 45). Originally (in the 1950s) it was called 'client-centred' (CCT), but since the mid-1970s it's been known as 'person-centred' therapy (PCT):

> '... *psychotherapy is the releasing of an already existing capacity in a potentially competent individual*'. (Rogers, 1959)

The change in name was meant to reflect more strongly that the *person*, in his/her full complexity, is the centre of focus. Also, Rogers wanted to convey that his assumptions were meant to apply broadly to almost all aspects of human behaviour – not just to therapeutic settings. For example, he saw many parallels between therapists and teachers: they're both 'facilitators' of an atmosphere of freedom and support for individual pursuits (Nye, 2000). For Nye:

> '*At the level at which Rogers' ideas were developed originally, in therapy and counselling situations, his impact certainly has been significant and far-reaching. A wide range of individuals – psychotherapists, counsellors, social workers, clergy and others – have been influenced by Rogers' assumptions that, if one can be a careful and accurate listener, while showing acceptance and honesty, one can be of help to troubled persons*'.

Less well known is the prolific research that Rogers undertook during the 1940s, '50s and '60s into this form of therapy. According to Thorne (1992):

'This body of research constituted the most intensive investigation of psychotherapy attempted anywhere in the world up to that time ... The major achievement of these studies was to establish beyond all question that psychotherapy could and should be subjected to the rigours of scientific enquiry'.

Rogers helped develop research designs (such as Q-sorts) which enable objective measurement of the self-concept, ideal self, and their relationship over the course of therapy, as well as methodologies (such as rating scales and the use of external 'consultants') for exploring the importance of therapist qualities. These innovations continue to influence therapeutic practice, and many therapists are now concerned that their work should be subjected to research scrutiny. Research findings are now more likely than ever before to affect training procedures and clinical practice across many different therapeutic orientations (Thorne, 1992: see Chapter 45).

By emphasising the therapist's personal qualities, Rogers opened up psychotherapy to psychologists and contributed to the development of therapy provided by non-medically qualified therapists (*lay therapy*). This is especially significant in the USA, where psychoanalysts (until recently) had to be psychiatrists (medically qualified). Rogers originally used the term 'counselling' as a strategy for silencing psychiatrists who objected to psychologists practising 'psychotherapy'. In the UK, the outcome of Rogers' campaign has been the evolution of a counselling profession whose practitioners are drawn from a wide variety of disciplines, with neither psychiatrists nor psychologists dominating. Counselling skills are used in a variety of settings throughout education, the health professions, social work, industry and commerce, the armed services and international organisations (Thorne, 1992).

Carl Rogers (1902–1987)

Evaluation of the humanistic approach

According to Wilson *et al.* (1996), the humanistic approach isn't an elaborate or comprehensive theory of personality, but should be seen as a set of uniquely personal theories of living created by humane people optimistic about human potential. It has wide appeal to those who seek an alternative to the more mechanistic, deterministic theories. However, like

Freud's theory, many of its concepts are difficult to test empirically (such as self-actualisation), and it cannot account for the origins of personality. Since it describes but doesn't explain personality, it's subject to the *nominal fallacy* (Carlson & Buskist, 1997).

Nevertheless, for all its shortcomings, the humanistic approach represents a counterbalance to the psychodynamic (especially Freud) and the behaviourist approaches, and has helped to bring the 'person' back into psychology. Crucially, it recognises that people help determine their own behaviour and aren't simply slaves to environmental contingencies or to their past. The self, personal responsibility and agency, choice and free will are now legitimate issues for psychological investigation.

The cognitive approach

Basic principles and assumptions

Despite its undoubted influence within psychology as a whole (see below and Chapter 3), it's more difficult to define the boundaries of cognitive psychology compared with the other major approaches. Its identity isn't as clearly established, and it cannot be considered to be a specific, integrated set of assumptions and concepts. It has several contemporary forms, with many theories, research programmes and forms of psychotherapy having a 'cognitive tilt' (Nye, 2000).

Also, there's no specific figure who can be identified as being central to its development in the same way as Watson, Freud, Rogers can with their respective approaches. As Wade & Tavris (1990) say:

'Cognitive psychology does not yet have a unifying theory, and unlike other 'brands' of psychology...it lacks an acknowledged spokesperson'.

Box 2.6	**Some basic principles and assumptions of the cognitive approach**

- According to Parkin (2000), psychologists in general, and cognitive psychologists in particular, face a problem not faced by other scientists:

   'The human brain is not like other organs of the body in that looking at its structure does not reveal anything about how it functions. We can see that the wall of the small intestine acts as an absorptive surface, the heart as a pump, and the kidney as a filter. The brain, however, is a large mass of cells and fibres which, no matter how clearly we look at it, gives no indication of how we think, speak and remember...'.

   For these reasons, cognitive psychologists are forced to seek *analogies* and *metaphors* when trying to describe a construct within the brain: that is, how the brain works is compared with the operation of something we already understand.
- Many different analogies have been used in cognitive psychology. By far the most dominant is that internal mental abilities are *information processing systems* (drawing on ideas from telecommunications and computer science : the *computer analogy*).

Included within this overall analogy are several central ideas or concepts, such as *coding*, *channel capacity*, and *serial/parallel processing* (see Chapter 20).

- Every telecommunication system uses some form of *coding*. For example, a telephone receives and translates our voice into an electromagnetic code, which is then decoded back into our voice at the other end. Cognitive psychologists realised that the concept of coding was central to understanding the representations used by the brain. When we see a picture, for example, we extract information from it which forms a code, which is, therefore, a *symbol* of the original stimulus (see Chapters 5 and 15).

- *Channel capacity* is the idea that any transmission system has a finite limit to the amount of information it can hold. Nowadays, with the advent of optic fibres, channel capacity can be huge – but it's still limited. This is also true of human beings: most of our mental activities are capacity-constrained, such as our attentional processes (see Chapter 13). But compared with physical communication devices, human coding is more flexible, and can take account of the form of the input in order to reduce the amount and nature of information that's actually formed into a code (as demonstrated in *span of apprehension experiments* and *chunking* (see Chapter 17). Unlike humans, physical systems reduce all information to fundamental units ('bits'), which in turn allows the absolute capacity of the system to be defined (which is impossible for human information processing).

(Based on Parkin, 2000)

Theoretical contributions

We noted earlier (see page 12) that two major modifications to 'orthodox' learning theory are Tolman's *cognitive behaviourism* and *social learning theory* (associated primarily with Bandura). Both these theories stress the central role of cognitive processes in the learning process. The influence of the information-processing approach is obvious in relation to attention, pattern recognition, and memory (see Box 2.6), but it has permeated many other areas of psychology. As we noted in Chapter 1, *social cognition* is now a commonly used term to refer to many aspects of the perception of people (see Chapter 22), attribution (see Chapter 23), attitudes and attitude change (including prejudice: see Chapters 24 and 25), and other areas of social psychology.

The information-processing approach also represents an increasingly influential view of cognitive development (see Chapter 34) and of the nature of intelligence (see Chapter 41). Cognitive behaviour therapy also represents a major approach to the treatment of mental disorders (see Chapter 45 and *Practical contributions* below).

Ask yourself ...

- Repeat the exercise as for the behaviourist, psychodynamic, and humanistic approaches.

Practical contributions

In relation to counselling and psychotherapy, Ellis's *rational emotive behaviour therapy* (REBT: previously just called rational emotive therapy or RET) deserves special attention (Nye, 2000). According to Rorer (1998), 'the *cognitive* revolution in psychotherapy began with the publication of [Ellis's 1962 book] *Reason and Emotion in Psychotherapy*'. REBT is the predecessor of the current cognitive and cognitive-behaviour therapies (see Chapter 45) and continues to evolve and gain in popularity. His emphasis on the primacy of cognition in psychopathology are at the forefront of practice and research in clinical psychology (Nye, 2000).

REBT attempts directly and actively to get clients to dispute their irrational and unscientific beliefs, and replace them with rational beliefs, which are less likely to be associated with extremely negative emotional states or maladaptive behaviours. The key concept underlying REBT (and other cognitive approaches) is that people are disturbed *not* by events but by their *perception* of them.

Although Ellis (1987) believes that people have a biological tendency to think irrationally, REBT is an optimistic approach. It emphasises that:

'... people have enormous power to think about their thinking, to use rationality and the scientific method, and to radically control and change their emotional destiny – providing they really work at doing so'. (Ellis, 1987)

An evaluation of the cognitive approach

The parallels between human beings and computers are compelling (Parkin, 2000). According to Lachman *et al.* (1979):

'Computers take a symbolic input, recode it, make decisions about the recoded input, make new expressions from it, store some or all of the input, and give back a symbolic input. By analogy that is what most cognitive psychology is about. It is about how people take in information…recode and remember it, how they make decisions, how they transform their internal knowledge states, and how they translate these states into behavioural outputs'.

Box 2.7	Some other similarities between computers and humans as information processors

- Computers operate in terms of information-streams, which flow between different components of the system. This is conceptually similar to how we assume symbolic information flows through human information channels (for example, see Atkinson and Shiffrin's multi-store model of memory, Chapter 17, page 248).

- All computers have a *central processing unit*, which carries out the manipulation of information. At the simplest level, a central processor might take a sequence of numbers and combine them according to a particular rule in order to compute an average. This was seen by many as analogous to the mechanism that would be responsible for the same type of mental operation.

- Computers have *databases* and *information stores*, which are permanent representations of knowledge the computer has acquired. In many ways this is comparable to our permanent (long-term) memory.
- Information sometimes needs to be held for a period of time while some other operation is performed. This is the job of the *information buffer*, which is a feature of computers and information-processing models of human attention (see Chapter 13) and memory (again see the multi-store model in Chapter 17).

(Based on Parkin, 2000)

Ask yourself ...

- Can you think of some limitations of the computer analogy? (See Box 2.10 and Chapter 20, pages 303–306.)

Information-processing accounts invariably address some specific aspect of mental processing, rather than being all-embracing accounts of cognition. A good example (in addition to those given in Box 2.7) is Bruce & Young's (1986) model of face recognition (see Chapter 14, pages 205–206). A *model* is more than a mere analogy (see Chapter 1, page 10): the proposed information-processing system is specified in sufficient detail to enable clear predictions to be made about how humans would behave in certain situations.

Cognitive psychologists implicitly adopted, at least initially, a strong *nomothetic* view of human mental processes, that is, they assumed that any information-processing model would apply equally to everyone (see Chapter 42, page 611). But the influence of *individual differences* soon became apparent. The general rule is that, the more complex the cognitive process, the more likely there are to be individual differences (Parkin, 2000).

Until the mid-1980s, mainstream cognitive psychologists took little interest in the study of how brain damage affects subsequent cognitive and behavioural functioning. *Cognitive neuropsychologists* now study people with acquired cognitive deficits in order to learn about the nature and organisation of cognitive functioning in normal people (the *cognitive architecture* of mental processes: see Chapter 4).

The social constructionist approach

Basic principles and assumptions

Social constructionism has played a central role in the various challenges that have been made to mainstream, academic psychology (see Chapter 3) during the last 30 years or so. The emergence of social constructionism is usually dated from Gergen's (1973) paper 'Social psychology as history'. In this, he argued that all knowledge, including psychological knowledge, is historically and culturally specific, and that we therefore must extend our enquiries beyond the individual into social, political and economic realms for a proper understanding of the evolution of present-day psychology and social life. Since the only constant feature of social life is that it's continually *changing*, psychology in general, and social psychology in particular, becomes a form of historical undertaking: all we can ever do is try to understand and account for how the world appears to be *at the present time*.

The paper was written at the time of 'the crisis in social psychology'. Starting in the late 1960s and early 1970s, some social psychologists were becoming increasingly concerned that the 'voice' of ordinary people was being omitted from social psychological research. By concentrating on *decontextualised* laboratory behaviour, it was ignoring the real-world contexts which give human action its meaning. Several books were published, each proposing an alternative to positivist science and focusing on the accounts of ordinary people (e.g. Harré & Secord, 1972). These concerns are clearly seen today in social constructionism.

Ask yourself ...

- Try to formulate some arguments for and against the view that people are basically the same, regardless of culture and historical period (the *universalist assumption*).

While there's no single definition of social constructionism that would be accepted by all those who might be included under its umbrella, we could categorise as social constructionist any approach which is based on one or more of the following key attitudes (as proposed by Gergen, 1985). Burr (1995) suggests we might think of these as 'things you would absolutely have to believe in order to be a social constructionist':

- *A critical stance towards taken-for-granted knowledge*: our observations of the world don't reveal in any simple way the true nature of the world, and conventional knowledge isn't based on objective, unbiased 'sampling' of the world (see Table 3.1, page 34). The categories with which we understand the world don't necessarily correspond to natural or 'real' categories/distinctions. Belief in such natural categories is called *essentialism*, so social constructionists are *anti-essentialism*.
- *Historical and cultural specificity*: how we commonly understand the world, and the categories and concepts we use, are historically and culturally *relative*. Not only are they specific to particular cultures and historical periods, they're seen as *products* of that culture and history, and this must include the knowledge generated by the social sciences. The theories and explanations of psychology thus become time- and culture-bound, and cannot be taken as once-and-for-all descriptions of human nature:

  'The disciplines of psychology and social psychology can therefore no longer be aimed at discovering the 'true' nature of people and social life ...'. (Burr, 1995)

CRITICAL DISCUSSION 2.1

Trans-cultural and cross-cultural psychology, and the universalist assumption

If knowledge is culturally created, then we shouldn't assume that our ways of understanding are necessarily any better (i.e. closer to 'the truth') than other ways. Yet this is precisely what mainstream (social) psychology has done. According to Much (1995), a new *(trans)cultural psychology* has emerged in North America (e.g. Bruner, 1990; Cole, 1990; Shweder, 1990) as an attempt to overcome the bias of *ethnocentrism* that has too often limited the scope of understanding in the social sciences (see Chapter 47, pages 702–705).

Shweder (1990) makes the crucial distinction between *cultural psychology* and *cross-cultural psychology*, which is a branch of experimental social, cognitive and personality psychology. Most of what's been known as 'cross-cultural' psychology has presupposed the categories and models that have been based on (mostly experimental) research with (limited samples of) Euro-American populations. It has mostly either 'tested the hypothesis' or 'validated the instrument' in other cultures or 'measured' the social and psychological characteristics of members of other cultures with the methods and standards of Western populations, usually assumed as a valid universal norm. The new 'cultural psychology' rejects this *universalist* model (Much, 1995). It's become almost a 'standing joke' that experimental (social) psychology is really the psychology of the American undergraduate/psychology major (see Chapter 47, page 703). Apart from their accessibility, the argument commonly assumed to justify the practice of studying mostly student behaviour is based upon a sweeping and gratuitous universalist assumption: since we're all human, we're all fundamentally alike in significant psychological functions, and cultural/social contexts of diversity don't affect the important 'deep' or 'hard-wired' structures of the mind. The corollary of this assumption is that the categories and standards developed on Western European/North American populations are suitable for 'measuring', understanding and evaluating the characteristics of other populations.

By contrast, a genuinely transcultural psychology ('the interplay between the individual and society and [symbolic] culture'; Kakar, 1982, quoted in Much, 1995) would base its categories, discriminations and generalisations upon empirical knowledge of the fullest possible range of existing human forms of life, without privileging one form as the norm or standard for evaluation. This is related to the *emic–etic* distinction: see Chapter 47, page 704).

■ *Knowledge is sustained by social processes*: our current accepted way of understanding the world ('truth') doesn't reflect the world as it really is (objective reality), but is constructed by people through their everyday interactions. Social interaction of all kinds, and particularly language, is of central importance for social constructionists: it's other people, both past and present, who are the sources of knowledge.

'We are born into a world where the conceptual frameworks and categories used by the people of our culture already exist. These concepts and categories are acquired by all people as they develop the use of language and are thus reproduced every day by everyone who shares a culture and language ... the way people think, the very categories and concepts that provide a framework of meaning for them, are provided by the language that they use. Language therefore is a necessary pre-condition for thought as we know it ...'. (Burr, 1995)

By giving a central role to social interactions and seeing these as actively producing taken-for-granted knowledge of the world, it follows that language itself is more than simply a way of expressing our thoughts and feelings (as typically assumed by mainstream psychology). When people talk to each other, they (help to) construct the world, such that language use is a form of *action*, that is, it has a '*performative*' role (see Chapter 18).

■ *Knowledge and social action go together*: these 'negotiated' understandings could take a wide variety of forms, so that there are many possible 'social constructions' of the world. But each different construction also brings with it, or invites, a different kind of action: how we account for a particular behaviour (what caused it) will dictate how we react to and treat the person whose behaviour it is (see Chapter 23).

Mainstream psychology looks for explanations of social phenomena inside the person, for example, by hypothesising the existence of attitudes, motives, cognitions, and so on (*individualism*: see Box 47.1, page 698). This can also be seen as *reductionist* (see Chapter 49, pages 727–730). Social constructionists reject this view: explanations are to be found neither inside the individual psyche, nor in social structures or institutions (as advocated by sociologists), but in the *interactive processes* that take place routinely between people. For Burr (1995):

'Knowledge is therefore seen not as something that a person has (or does not have), but as something that people do together ...'.

Theoretical contributions and an evaluation of social constructionism

Social constructionism and social representation theory

According to *social representation theory* (SRT), people come to understand their social world by way of images and social representations (SRs) shared by members of a social group. These representations act like a map which makes a baffling or novel terrain familiar and passable, thereby providing evaluations of good and bad areas. Attitudes are secondary phenomena, underpinned by SRs. SRT tries to provide a historical account of people's understanding of the world (Potter, 1996).

During the 1950s, the French psychologist, Moscovici, conducted one of the classic pieces of research on SRs. He was interested in how the ideas/concepts of psychoanalytic theory could be absorbed within a culture (post-Second World War France), based on women's magazines, church publications and interviews. He concluded that psychoanalytic theory had trickled down from the analytic couch and learned journals into both 'high' culture and popular common sense: people 'think' with psychoanalytic concepts, without it seeming as if they are doing anything theoretical at all. But rather than the general population of Paris being conversant with/conversing with psychoanalytic theory in all its complexities, they were working with a simplified image of it, with some concepts having a wide currency (such as repression), and others not (such as libido) (Potter, 1996: see Chapter 22, pages 328–330).

SRT is a constructionist theory: instead of portraying people as simply perceiving (or misperceiving) their social worlds, it regards these worlds as constructed, and a SR is a device for doing this construction. It allows someone to make sense of something potentially unfamiliar and to evaluate it. For Moscovici, all thought and understanding is based on the working of SRs, each of which consists of a mixture of concepts, ideas and images; these are both in people's minds and circulating in society.

Box 2.8 **What's social about social representations (SRs)?**

According to Potter (1996), SRs are truly social because:

- They're *generated in communication*. When people interact through gossip, argue with one another or discuss political scandals, they're building up shared pictures of the world: 'social representations are the outcome of an increasing babble and a permanent dialogue between individuals' (Moscovici, 1985). The media play a major role in sustaining, producing and circulating SRs, which cannot be reduced to images inside people's heads.
- They *provide a code for communication*. As a consequence of people sharing SRs, they can clearly understand each other and have free-flowing conversations, since they share a stable version of the world. Communication between people with different SRs is likely to produce conflict.
- They *provide a way of distinguishing social groups*. According to Moscovici, one way of defining a group is in terms of a shared set of SRs, which provide a crucial homogenising force for groups.

SRT wasn't published in English until the early 1980s; since then research has snowballed, especially in Europe, Australia and South America (though it's been largely ignored by mainstream North American social psychologists in the experimental cognitive tradition). Potter (1996) suggests that one reason for this may be that the latter's pursuit of general laws and processes is directly challenged by SRT's emphasis on the specific content of a culture's or group's SR as the main object of analysis.

Social constructionism and feminist psychology

For Stainton Rogers *et al.* (1995),

> '… there is no conceptual vacuum we can occupy where we can be 'outside' the pressing 'social facts' that constitute our understanding of the world. All we can ever do is … begin to recognise the illusions which constitute our 'social realities' as illusions and not as really-real realities'.

Feminist scholars are concerned with trying to identify and challenge those illusory aspects of our social realities that specifically relate to women. According to Nicolson (1995), they've been consistently developing critiques of *positivist* science (see Chapter 3) for the past 100 years, with momentum and influence gathering especially since the early 1970s.

Part of this feminist critique involves demonstrating how positivist science, far from being value-free, displays a clear bias towards the 'pathologisation' of women (see Chapters 36, 43, 44 and 47). Nicolson (1995) argues that *the scientific method is gender-biased* (see Chapters 3 and 47). Nicolson believes that the priority Western society attaches to science is more problematic today than ever before, because of the relationship of science to the media which influences human socialisation (cf. the role of the media in circulating SRs – see above). She argues that:

> 'Psychology relies for its data on the practices of socialised and culture-bound individuals, so that to explore 'natural' or 'culture-free' behaviour (namely that behaviour unfettered by cultural, social structures and power relations) is by definition impossible, which is a state of affairs that normally goes unacknowledged …'.

'Normally' denotes mainstream psychology. Social constructionism, in its various forms, is concerned with acknowledging this 'state of affairs'. The view that 'science as knowledge is fabricated rather than discovered' (Fox, 1993) is gaining popularity amongst feminist psychologists.

Although within feminism itself there are many different 'voices', feminism is essentially a reaction to and a product of *patriarchal* culture (or *patriarchy*), and one of its significant roles has been to account for women's subordination. Patriarchy commonly refers to the context and processes through which men and male-dominated institutions (including universities and other organisations that foster scientific endeavour) promote male supremacy. Feminist psychologists seek to *contextualise* women's lives and to explain the constraints, attributed by some to biology, within a social framework: women's lack of social power is made to seem 'natural' by the practice of academic psychology. They also offer a critical challenge to psychological knowledge on gender issues by drawing on other disciplines (such as sociology and anthropology). This rarely occurs in psychology, because, traditionally, it's 'jealous' of its boundaries (Nicolson, 1995).

The evolutionary approach

Basic principles and assumptions

Sociobiology (Wilson, 1975) grew out of the work of evolutionary biologists in the 1960s. Wilson set out to explain all non-human and human social behaviour in terms of evolution and other biological principles. It concentrated on the evolutionary origins of behaviour, and tended to imply *rigid genetic control* (Archer, 1996). Since then, many of these principles have been used to study topics covered by the social sciences – including psychology.

Evolutionary psychology (Buss, 1995) is a development of sociobiology (and is often referred to as 'neo- or modern

Darwinism'). According to evolutionary psychology (EP), evolutionary principles are used to link the original function of behaviour to current psychological mechanisms, and *flexibility of responding* is central to those mechanisms. Starting with the principle of natural selection (see Gross *et al.*, 2000), evolutionary psychologists construct a theory of human nature, that is, an overall view of how we should expect humans to behave. From this, they derive and test more specific theories and hypotheses (Archer, 1996).

According to Rose (2000):

'The declared aim of evolutionary psychology is to provide explanations for the patterns of human activity and the forms of organisation of human society which take into account the fact that humans are animals, and like all other currently living organisms, are the present-day products of some four billion years of evolution …'.

Box 2.9 **Some basic principles and assumptions of evolutionary psychology (EP)**

- EP rejects the *Standard Social Science Model* (SSSM), which makes two broad assumptions about human beings: (a) there's no such thing as human nature, or if there is, it has so little effect on people's social lives that it can be ignored; (b) explanations of social behaviour can be derived from considering only social roles, socialisation, and culture.

- Human social behaviour, like that of non-humans, can be understood in terms of its past contribution to survival and reproduction. For example, instead of regarding young males' proneness to violence in terms of social learning (modelling) or frustration (Berkowitz, 1993), EP views it as the result of its past contributions to obtaining resources, status, and access to women (Daly & Wilson, 1988: see Chapter 29).

- While acknowledging their debt to sociobiology, evolutionary psychologists contend that sociobiologists often ignored the role of *mind* in mediating links between genes and behaviour. According to Barkow, Cosmides and Tooby (1992), the mind consists of a collection of specialised, independent mechanisms or modules, designed by natural selection to solve problems that faced our hunter-gatherer ancestors, such as acquiring a mate, raising children and dealing with rivals. The solutions often involve such emotions as lust, fear, affection, jealousy and anger. Together, these modules and the related emotions constitute *human nature*.

- EP is, in general, about universal features of the mind. Insofar as individual differences exist, the default assumption is that they're expressions of the same universal human nature as it encounters different environments. *Gender* is the crucial exception to this rule. Natural selection has constructed the mental modules of men and women in very different ways as a result of their divergent reproductive roles (*sexual dimorphism*).

- EP *isn't* a form of *genetic determinism* (or *nativism*: see Chapter 50). Like most modern biologists and social scientists, evolutionary psychologists argue that 'nature or nurture' is a false dichotomy, and they distinguish themselves from behaviour geneticists.

(Based on Horgan, 1995; Rose, 2000)

Theoretical contributions

As indicated in Box 2.9, EP (and sociobiological) explanations can be found throughout psychology. For example, fear is commonly regarded as an adaptive response to threatening stimuli and events, while anxiety is an 'aberration' (see Chapter 44). Similarly, the harmful effects of stress have been explained in evolutionary terms. While the body's stress response evolved to help us cope with life-threatening situations (emergencies), most 'modern-day' stressors aren't like this. Consequently, our bodies react in an inappropriate, and potentially life-threatening way to 'chronic' stress (see Chapter 12).

Rather more controversially, Buss (1994) claims that men, because they can in principle father a virtually infinite number of children, are much more inclined towards promiscuity than women are. Women, because they can average only one child per year, are choosier in selecting a mate. Men in all cultures place greater emphasis on youth and physical attractiveness, while women look to men's 'resources' (see Chapter 28). Similarly, because men can never be sure that a child is theirs, their jealousy tends to be triggered by fears of a mate's sexual infidelity. Women, on the other hand, become more upset at the thought of losing a mate's emotional commitment – and thus his resources. In turn, women make greater 'parental investment' in their children than men do (see Chapter 32).

Perhaps the best-known, and also one of the most controversial, claims of *sociobiology* is Dawkins' (1976) 'selfish-gene' theory (see Chapter 30, and Gross *et al.*, 2000).

Is language an instinct?

According to Pinker (1994), a linguist 'converted' to EP, language is far too complex to be learned: it must stem from an innate programme hardwired into our brains. Language almost certainly arose, he claims, because it was adaptive, that is, it conferred benefits on our hunter-gatherer ancestors. It would have allowed early hominids to share learned toolmaking, hunting and other skills, and those especially adept at language could manipulate others, and form alliances which would increase their chances of producing offspring.

Ironically, these claims are *denied* by Chomsky, a fellow linguist and colleague of Pinker's. Chomsky first argued in the 1950s that language represents a distinct mental module (or 'language organ') unique to human beings and independent of general cognitive ability, and that we all possess an innate Language Acquisition Device (LAD: see Chapter 19). In this way, he laid the foundation for EP, and evolutionary psychologists are, in a sense, his heirs (Horgan, 1995; Kohn, 1998).

However, Chomsky disputes the assumption that language is a 'selected trait': just because language is adaptive now, doesn't mean that it *arose* in response to selection pressures. Given the enormous gap between human language and the relatively simple communication systems of other species, and given our fragmentary knowledge of our evolutionary past, science can tell us little about how language evolved. It may have been an incidental/accidental by-product of a spurt in intelligence or of the human brain's large size (Horgan, 1995; Kohn, 1998). The same may be true of other properties of the human mind.

An evaluation of EP

Our hunter–gatherer past

EP is based on the belief that the human mind is adapted to cope with life as a Pleistocene hunter–gatherer (which we were for about two million years before the ancient Chinese, Indian, Egyptian and Suimerian civilisations: Abdulla, 1996). Forms of behaviour and social organisation which evolved adaptively over many generations in human hunter–gatherer society may or may not be adapive in modern industrialised society, but have become to a degree fixed by humanity's evolutionary experience in the palaeolithic *Environment of Evolutionary Adaptation* (EEA), thought to be the African savannah (Rose, 2000).

However, just as Chomsky's argument with Pinker concerned *how* language evolved (rather than whether or not it evolved), so the story of our human hunter–gatherer ancestors is, inevitably, partly a work of fiction (Turney, 1999). According to Rose (2000), the descriptions offered by EP of what hunter–gatherer societies were like read little better than 'Just so' accounts:

> 'There is a circularity about reading this version of the present into the past, and then claiming that this imagined past explains the present'.

In other words, based on what human beings are capable of *now*, evolutionary psychologists imagine how these abilities may have evolved, then propose this constructed past as the cause of these current abilities.

Evolutionary psychologists also claim that the timescale of human history has been too short for evolutionary selection pressures to have produced significant change. But we know very little about just how quickly such change can occur (Rose, 2000). Evolutionarily modern humans appeared 100,000 years ago. Allowing 15–20 years for each generation, there have been 5000–6600 generations between human origins and modern times. We really have no idea whether these generations are 'time enough' for substantial evolutionary change:

> 'However, granted the very rapid changes in human environment, social organisation, technology, and mode of production that have clearly occurred over that period, one must assume significant selection pressures operating ... the automatic assumption that the palaeolithic was an EEA in which fundamental human traits were fixed, and that there has not been time since to alter them, does not bear serious inspection'. (Rose, 2000)

Box 2.10 EP, computers and emotion

Drawing heavily on the jargon and conceptual framework of computer science and artificial intelligence (see Chapter 20), evolutionary psychologists see the mind as a cognitive machine, an information-processing device that's 'run' by the brain. It's not a general-purpose computer, but is composed of several specific modules (see Box 2.9). But for Rose (2000):

> '... it is not adequate to reduce the mind/brain to nothing more than a cognitive 'architectural' information-processing machine. Brains/minds do not just deal with information. They are concerned with living meaning ... the key feature which distinguishes brains/minds from computers is their/our capacity to experience emotion. Indeed, emotion is primary – which may be why Darwin devoted an entire book to it rather than to cognition'. (Rose, 2000)

Several neuroscientists have devoted considerable attention to the mechanisms and survival advantages of emotion (e.g. LeDoux, 1998: see Chapter 44). This makes it all the more surprising that evolutionary psychologists give so much emphasis to cognitive functions. For Rose:

> '... affect and cognition are inextricably engaged in all brain and mind processes, creating meaning out of information – just one more reason why brains aren't computers'.

Most remarkable of all is the phrase used by Cosmides, Tooby and others, namely the 'architecture of the mind', implying a static, stable structure, built to a blueprint. Nothing could be less appropriate for capturing the fluid, dynamic process whereby our minds/brains develop, creating '... order out of the blooming buzzing confusion of the world which confronts us moment by moment' (Rose, 2000).

Phylogeny and ontogeny

According to Karmiloff-Smith (2000), developmental psychologists see *plasticity* during brain growth as the rule, rather than the exception or a response to brain injury (see Chapter 4). Cosmides & Tooby (1994) compare the newborn brain to a Swiss army knife, crammed with independent functional tools, each designed for a specific problem that faced our hunter–gatherer ancestors (see Box 2.9). But even if we set aside the problem of knowing just what the problems faced by our ancestors were (and, therefore, what tools they needed), Karmiloff-Smith believes that it's just as plausible that, unlike the gross macro-structure of the brain, cortical micro-circuitry *isn't* innately specified by evolution but is progressively constructed by the postnatal experience of different kinds of input.

She argues that:

> 'Evolution has helped to guarantee human survival by raising the upper limits on complexity and avoiding too much prespecification of higher cognitive functions ...'.

Development requires both evolution (*phylogeny*) and *ontogeny* (individual development):

'A multitude of different learning mechanisms which may have emerged from evolution might, during ontogeny, each discover inputs from the environment that are more or less suited to their form of processing. Gradually, with development and with trying to process different kinds of input, each mechanism would become progressively more domain-specific'.

Hence:

'Evolutionary psychology's Swiss army knife view of the brain is inappropriate for understanding higher cognitive functions, particularly for children ... '. (Karmiloff-Smith, 2000)

Violent stepfathers and the problem of unfalsifiability

According to Daly & Wilson (1988a and b), children under the age of two were at least 60 times more likely to be killed by a stepparent – and almost always a stepfather – than by a natural parent. This is exactly what evolutionary theory would predict, since step-parents and step-children are genetically unrelated, while a child inherits half its genes from each biological parent. However, most stepfathers *don't* kill or abuse, and a minority of biological fathers do: these findings are difficult to square with any explanation based on shared/non-shared genes.

More seriously, in discussing women who kill their newborn babies, Pinker (1997b) claimed that when such an act takes place in conditions of poverty, it could be regarded as an *adaptationist* response. The psychological module which normally induces protectiveness in mothers of newborns is switched off by the challenge of an impoverished environment. This means that both killing *and* protecting are explained by evolutionary selection. As Hilary Rose (2000) says, this explains everything, and therefore, nothing.

Conclusions

The focus of this discussion of various theoretical approaches within psychology has been on how each conceptualises human beings. Freud's 'tension-reducing person', Skinner's 'environmentally controlled person', and Rogers' 'growth-motivated person really are quite different from each other (Nye, 2000). The person-as-information-processor, and the person-as-shaped-by-our-evolutionary-past are different again – both from each other and from the first three approaches. Social constructionism's image of the person is rather less concrete and more elusive: what people are like and what they do is *relative* to their culture, historical period and so on.

However, we've also noted some important similarities between different approaches, such as the deterministic nature of Freud's and Skinner's theories, and the influence of the information-processing approach on evolutionary psychology. As we shall see throughout this book, each approach has something of value to contribute to our understanding of ourselves – even if it is only to reject the particular explanation it offers. The diversity of approaches reflects the complexity of the subject-matter, so, usually, there's room for a diversity of explanations.

CHAPTER SUMMARY

- Different theoretical **approaches/perspectives** are based on different models/images of the nature of human beings.
- **Methodological behaviourism** focuses on what can be quantified and observed by different researchers. Skinner's **radical behaviourism** regards mental processes as both inaccessible and irrelevant for explaining behaviour.
- The behaviourist approach stresses the role of environmental influences (learning), especially classical and operant **conditioning**. Psychology's aim is to predict and control behaviour.
- Tolman's **cognitive behaviourism** and **social learning theory** represent modifications of 'orthodox' learning (conditioning) theory.
- Methodological behaviourism has influenced the practice of scientific psychology in general. Other practical contributions include **behaviour therapy** and **modification**, and **biofeedback**.
- The **psychodynamic approach** is based on Freud's **psychoanalytic theory**. Central aspects are the **unconscious** (especially **repression**), **infantile sexuality** and the impact of early experience.
- Freud's ideas have become part of mainstream psychology, contributing to our understanding of motivation, sleep and dreams, forgetting, attachment, aggression and abnormality.
- Major modifications/alternatives to Freudian theory include **ego psychology**, Erikson's **psychosocial** theory, and the **object relations school**.
- All forms of **psychotherapy** stem directly or indirectly from **psychoanalysis**. Many trained psychoanalysts have been responsible for developing radically different therapeutic approaches, including Rogers, Perls and Wolpe.
- Maslow called the **humanistic approach** the 'third force' in psychology. It believes in free will, adopts a **phenomenological perspective**, and stresses the positive aspects of human personality.
- Rogers was a prolific researcher into the effectiveness of his client/person-centred therapy, opened up psychotherapy to psychologists and other non-medically qualified practitioners, and created a counselling profession that operates within a wide diversity of settings.
- The **cognitive approach** lacks both a central figure and a unifying theory. It uses **analogies** and **metaphors** when trying to describe what's going on inside the brain, in particular the **computer analogy** and the view of people as **information processors**.
- Other important features include the concepts of **coding**, **channel capacity** and **serial/parallel processing**.
- A major application of the cognitive approach has been **cognitive behaviour therapy**, as in Ellis's REBT.
- While the computer analogy is a useful way of understanding cognitive processes, there are also some important differences between how computers and people process information.

- One of the goals of **social constructionism** is to correct the tendency of **mainstream** psychology to **decontextualise** behaviour. Related to this is the **universalist assumption**, which is challenged by **(trans)cultural** (as distinct from **cross-cultural**) **psychology**.
- **Social representation theory** is a social constructionist theory, and many **feminist psychologists** adopt a social constructionist approach in challenging maintream psychology.
- **Evolutionary psychology** (EP) grew out of **sociobiology**. Unlike the latter, EP puts the mind in centre stage, identifying several independent mental mechanisms or **modules**. These form the core of **human nature**.
- A major assumption of EP is that these mental modules have become fixed by our hunter–gatherer ancestors' experience in the palaeolithic **Environment of Evolutionary Evolution** (EEA). But knowledge of the EEA is largely speculative, and there's good reason to believe that human traits have changed since that time.
- The notion of the 'architecture of the mind' is contradicted by the dynamic nature of brain activity and development, which requires both evolution (**phylogeny**) and individual development (**ontogeny**).

Self-assessment questions

1 Critically assess the contributions of any **two** major theoretical approaches.
2 Discuss the strengths and weaknesses of **two or more** major theoretical approaches.
3 Critically consider the claim that the existence of several theoretical approaches reflects the complexity of psychology's subject matter.

Web addresses

http://evolution.humb.univie.ac.at/jump.html
http://www.indian.educ/~kinsey
http://www.liv.ac.uk/
www/evolpsych/main.htm
http://www.bga.org
http://www.cogsci.soton.ac.uk
www.psychoanalysis.org.uk
www.ipa.org
www.freud.org

Further reading

Glassman, W.E. (1995) *Approaches to Psychology* (2nd edition) Buckingham: Open University Press. This discusses the biological, behaviourist, cognitive, psychodynamic and humanistic approaches in relation to development, social and abnormal behaviour. Useful as a general introductory text.

Nye, R.D. (2000) *Three Psychologies: Perspectives from Freud, Skinner, and Rogers* (6th edition). Belmont, C.A.: Wadsworth/Thomson Learning. A thorough but readable account and evaluation of the key ideas of these 'big three'.

Rose, H. & Rose, S. (Eds) (2000) *Alas, Poor Darwin: Arguments Against Evolutionary Psychology*. London: Jonathan Cape. Separate chapters by eminent critics, including the editors, who also offer a useful introduction.

Chapter 3

Psychology as a Science

Introduction and overview

As we saw in Chapter 1, psychology is commonly defined as the *scientific* study of behaviour and cognitive processes (or mind or experience). In effect, this book as a whole looks at how different psychologists have put this definition into practice, through their use of various investigative methods to study a wide variety of behaviours and cognitive processes.

This chapter turns the spotlight once more on the definition of psychology given above. It does this by examining the nature of science (including the major features of scientific method), and by tracing some of the major developments in psychology's history as a scientific discipline. This enables us to address the question of how appropriate it is to use scientific method to study human behaviour and cognitive processes, and to assess the validity of this widely accepted definition.

Some philosophical roots of science and psychology

The seventeenth-century French philosopher Descartes was the first person to distinguish formally between mind and matter (*philosophical dualism*: see Chapter 49), which had an enormous impact on the development of both psychology as a science and science in general. Dualism allowed scientists to treat matter as inert and completely distinct from human beings, which meant that the world could be described *objectively*, without reference to the human observer. *Objectivity* became the ideal of science, and was extended to the study of human behaviour and social institutions in the mid-1800s by Comte, who called it *positivism*.

Descartes also promoted *mechanism,* the view that the material world comprises objects which are assembled like a huge machine and operated by mechanical laws. He extended this view to living organisms, including, eventually, humans. Because the mind is non-material, Descartes believed that, unlike the physical world, it can be investigated only through *introspection* (observing one's own thoughts and feelings: see Chapter 1, page 4). He was also one of the first advocates of *reductionism* (see Chapter 49).

Empiricism refers to the ideas of the seventeenth- and eighteenth-century British philosophers, Locke, Hume and Berkeley. They believed that the only source of true knowledge about the world is sensory experience (that which comes to us through our senses or what can be inferred about the relationship between such sensory facts). Empiricism is usually contrasted with *nativism* (or *rationalism*), according to which knowledge of the world is largely innate or inborn (see, for example, Chapters 16, 19, 29, 32, 36, 41, 44 and 50).

The word '*empirical*' ('through the senses') is often used to mean 'scientific', implying that what scientists do, and what distinguishes them from non-scientists, is carry out experiments and observations as ways of collecting data or 'facts' about the world (hence, 'empirical methods' for 'scientific methods'). Empiricism proved to be one of the central influences on the development of physics and chemistry.

Empiricism and psychology

Prior to the 1870s, there were no laboratories devoted specifically to psychological research, and the early scientific psychologists had trained mainly as physiologists, doctors, philosophers or some combination of these. The two professors who set up the first two psychological laboratories deserve much of the credit for the development of academic psychology. They were Wundt (1832–1920) in Germany, and James (1842–1910) in the USA (Fancher, 1979).

Wundt's contribution

A physiologist by training, Wundt is generally regarded as the 'founder' of the new science of experimental psychology, or what he called 'a new domain of science' (1874). Having worked as Helmholtz's assistant (see Chapter 15), Wundt eventually became professor of 'scientific philosophy' at Leipzig University in 1875, illustrating the lack of distinct boundaries between the various disciplines which combined to bring about psychology's development (Fancher, 1979).

Wilhelm Wundt (1832–1920)

In 1879, Wundt converted his 'laboratory' at Leipzig into a 'private institute' of experimental psychology. For the first time, a place had been set aside for the explicit purpose of conducting psychological research, and hence 1879 is widely accepted as the 'birth date' of psychology as a discipline in its own right. From its modest beginnings, the institute began to attract people from all over the world, who returned to their own countries to establish laboratories modelled on Wundt's.

René Descartes (1596–1650)

Box 3.1 Wundt's study of the conscious mind: introspective psychology and structuralism

Wundt believed that conscious mental states could be scientifically studied through the systematic manipulation of antecedent variables (those that occur before some other event), and analysed by carefully controlled techniques of *introspection*. Introspection was a rigorous and highly disciplined technique for analysing conscious experience into its most basic elements (*sensations* and *feelings*). Participants were always advanced psychology students, who'd been carefully trained to introspect properly.

Sensations are the raw sensory content of consciousness, devoid of all 'meaning' or interpretation, and all conscious thoughts, ideas, perceptions and so on were assumed to be combinations of sensations. Based on his experiment in which he listened to a metronome beating at varying rates, Wundt concluded that *feelings* could be analysed in terms of *pleasantness–unpleasantness*, *tension–relaxation*, and *activity–passivity*.

Wundt believed that introspection made it possible to cut through the learned categories and concepts that define our everyday experience of the world, and so expose the 'building blocks' of experience. Because of introspection's central role, Wundt's early brand of psychology was called *introspective psychology* (or *introspectionism*), and his attempt to analyse consciousness into its elementary sensations and feelings is known as *structuralism*.

(Based on Fancher, 1979)

Ask yourself ...

- Consider the difficulties that might be involved in relying on introspection to formulate an account of the nature of conscious experience (i.e. an account that applies to *people in general*).
- In what ways is structuralism *reductionist*? (See Chapter 49.)
- Which major theory of perception rejects this structuralist approach, and what are its principal features? (See Chapter 15.)

James's contribution

James taught anatomy and physiology at Harvard University in 1872, and by 1875 was calling his course *The Relations Between Physiology and Psychology*. In the same year, he established a small laboratory, used mainly for teaching purposes. In 1878, he dropped anatomy and physiology, and for several years taught 'pure psychology'.

His view of psychology is summarised in *The Principles of Psychology* (1890), which includes discussion of instinct, brain function, habit, the stream of consciousness, the self (see Chapter 33), attention (Chapter 13), memory (Chapter 17), perception (Chapters 15 and 16), free will (Chapter 49) and emotion (Chapter 10).

The Principles of Psychology provided the famous definition of psychology as 'the science of mental life' (see Chapter 1). But ironically, James was very critical both of his book and of

William James (1842–1910)

what psychology could offer as a science. He became increasingly interested in philosophy and disinterested in psychology, although in 1894 he became the first American to call favourable attention to the recent work of the then little known Viennese neurologist, Sigmund Freud (Fancher, 1979).

James proposed a point of view (rather than a theory) that directly inspired *functionalism*, which emphasises the purpose and utility of behaviour (Fancher, 1979). Functionalism, in turn, helped to stimulate interest in *individual differences*, since they determine how well or poorly individuals adapt to their environments. These attitudes made Americans especially receptive to Darwin's (1859) ideas about individual variation, evolution by natural selection, and the 'survival of the fittest' (see Chapter 2).

Watson's behaviourist revolution

Watson took over the psychology department at Johns Hopkins University in 1909, and immediately began cutting psychology's ties with philosophy and strengthening those with biology. At that time, Wundt's and James's studies of consciousness were still the 'real' psychology, but Watson was doing research on non-human animals and became increasingly critical of the use of introspection.

John Broadus Watson (1878–1958)

In particular, Watson argued that introspective reports were unreliable and difficult to verify. It's impossible to check the accuracy of such reports, because they're based on purely private experience, to which the investigator has no possible means of access. As a result, Watson redefined psychology in his famous 'behaviourist manifesto' of 1913.

Box 3.2 Watson's (1913) 'behaviourist manifesto'

Watson's article 'Psychology as the behaviourist views it' is often referred to as the 'behaviourist manifesto', a charter for a truly scientific psychology. It was behaviourism which was to represent a rigorous empiricist approach within psychology for the first time. According to Watson:

'Psychology as the behaviourist views it is a purely objective natural science. Its theoretical goal is the prediction and control of behaviour. Introspection forms no essential part of its methods, nor is the scientific value of its data dependent upon the readiness with which they lend themselves to interpretation in terms of consciousness. The behaviourist … recognises no dividing line between man and brute. The behaviour of a man … forms only a part of the behaviourist's total scheme of investigation'.

Three features of this 'manifesto' deserve special mention:

- Psychology must be purely objective, excluding all subjective data or interpretations in terms of conscious experience. This redefines psychology as the 'science of behaviour' (rather than the 'science of mental life').
- The goals of psychology should be to predict and control behaviour (as opposed to describing and explaining conscious mental states), a goal later endorsed by Skinner's *radical behaviourism* (see Chapter 2).
- There's no fundamental (*qualitative*) distinction between human and non-human behaviour. If, as Darwin had shown, humans evolved from more simple species, then it follows that human behaviour is simply a more complex form of the behaviour of other species (the difference is merely *quantitative* – one of degree). Consequently, rats, cats, dogs and pigeons became the major source of psychological data. Since 'psychological' now meant 'behaviour' rather than 'consciousness', non-humans that were convenient to study, and whose environments could be controlled easily, could replace people as experimental subjects.

(Based on Fancher, 1979; Watson, 1913)

Ask yourself …

- Try to formulate arguments for and against Watson's claim that there's only a *quantitative* difference between the behaviour of humans and non-humans.

In his 1915 presidential address to the American Psychological Association, Watson talked about his recent 'discovery' of Pavlov's work on conditioned reflexes in dogs. He proposed that the conditioned reflex could become the foundation for a full-scale human psychology.

The extreme environmentalism of Locke's empiricism (see page 30) lent itself well to the behaviourist emphasis on learning (through the process of Pavlovian or classical conditioning). While Locke had described the mind at birth as a *tabula rasa* ('blank slate') on which experience writes, Watson, in rejecting the mind as suitable for a scientific psychology,

simply swapped mind for behaviour: it's now behaviour that's shaped by the environment.

According to Miller (1962), empiricism provided psychology with both a *methodology* (stressing the role of observation and measurement) and a *theory*, including analysis into elements (such as stimulus–response units) and *associationism* (which explains how simple elements can be combined to form more complex ones).

Behaviourism also embodied positivism, in particular the emphasis on the need for scientific rigour and objectivity. Humans were now conceptualised and studied as 'natural phenomena', with subjective experience, consciousness and other characteristics (traditionally regarded as distinctive human qualities) no longer having a place in the behaviourist world.

The cognitive revolution

Academic psychology in the USA and the UK was dominated by behaviourism for the next 40 years. However, criticism and dissatisfaction with it culminated in a number of 'events', all taking place in 1956, which, collectively, are referred to as the 'cognitive revolution'.

Box 3.3 The 1956 'cognitive revolution'

- At a meeting at the Massachusetts Institute of Technology (MIT), Chomsky introduced his theory of language (see Chapter 19), Miller presented a paper on the 'magical number seven' in short-term memory (see Chapter 17), and Newell and Simon presented a paper on the logical theory machine (or logic theorist), with a further paper by Newell *et al.* (1958), which Newell & Simon (1972) extended into the *general problem solver* (GPS: see Chapter 20).
- The first systematic attempt to investigate concept formation (in adults) from a cognitive psychological perspective was reported (Bruner *et al.*, 1956).
- At Dartmouth College, New Hampshire (the 'Dartmouth Conference'), ten academics met to discuss the possibility of producing computer programs that could 'behave' or 'think' intelligently. These academics included McCarthy (generally attributed with having coined the term 'artificial intelligence'), Minsky, Simon, Newell, Chomsky and Miller (see Chapter 20).

(Based on Eysenck & Keane, 1995)

This new way of thinking about and investigating people was called the *information-processing approach*. At its centre is the *computer analogy*, the view that human cognition can be understood by comparing it with the functioning of a digital computer. It was now acceptable to study the mind again, although its conceptualisation was very different from that of Wundt, James and the other pioneers of the 'new psychology' prior to Watson's 'behaviourist revolution'.

Science, scientism and mainstream psychology

Despite this major change in psychology after 1956, certain central assumptions and practices within the discipline have remained essentially the same, and these are referred to as *mainstream psychology*. Harré (1989) refers to the mainstream as the 'old paradigm', which he believes continues to be haunted by certain 'unexamined presuppositions', one of which is *scientism*, defined by Van Langenhove (1995) as:

> *'… the borrowing of methods and a characteristic vocabulary from the natural sciences in order to discover causal mechanisms that explain psychological phenomena'.*

Scientism maintains that all aspects of human behaviour can and should be studied using the methods of natural science, which claims to be the sole means of establishing 'objective truth'. This can be achieved by studying phenomena removed from any particular context (*'context-stripping'* exposes them in their 'pure' form), and in a *value-free* way (there's no bias on the investigator's part). The most reliable way of doing this is through the laboratory experiment, the method providing the greatest degree of control over relevant variables (see Box 3.7, page 38). As noted earlier, these beliefs and assumptions add up to the traditional view of science known as positivism.

Ask yourself …

- Try to find examples of experimental studies of human behaviour that fit the definition of 'context-stripping' given above. Probably the 'best' examples will come from social psychology, which in itself should suggest criticisms of this approach to studying behaviour. (See also Chapter 47, page 699.)

Although much research has moved beyond the confines of the laboratory experiment, the same positivist logic is still central to how psychological enquiry is conceived and conducted. Method and measurement still have a privileged status:

> *'Whether concerned with mind or behaviour (and whether conducted inside or outside the laboratory), research tends to be constructed in terms of the separation (or reduction) of entities into independent and dependent variables and the measurement of hypothesised relationships between them'.* (Smith *et al.*, 1995)

Despite the fact that since the mid-1970s the natural sciences model has become the subject of vigorous attacks, psychology is still to a large extent dominated by it. The most prominent effect of this is the dominance of experiments (Van Langenhove, 1995). This has far-reaching effects on the way psychology *pictures* people as more or less passive and mechanical information-processing devices, whose behaviour can be split up into variables. It also affects the way psychology *deals* with people. In experiments, people aren't treated as single individuals, but as interchangeable 'subjects'. There's no room for individualised observations.

What do we mean by 'science'?

The major features of science

Most psychologists and philosophers of science would probably agree that for a discipline to be called a science, it must possess certain characteristics. These are summarised in Box 3.4 and Figure 3.1.

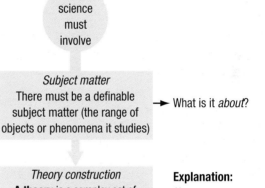

Box 3.4 The major features of science

- **A definable subject matter:** This changed from conscious human thought to human and non-human behaviour, then to cognitive processes, within psychology's first 80 years as a separate discipline.
- **Theory construction:** This represents an attempt to explain observed phenomena, such as Watson's attempt to account for (almost all) human and non-human behaviour in terms of classical conditioning, and Skinner's subsequent attempt to do the same with operant conditioning (see Chapters 2 and 11).
- **Hypothesis testing:** This involves making specific predictions about behaviour under certain conditions (for example, predicting that by combining the sight of a rat with the sound of a hammer crashing down on a steel bar just behind his head, a small child will learn to fear the rat, as in the case of Little Albert: see Key Study 11.1, page 148).
- **Empirical methods:** These are used to collect data (evidence) relevant to the hypothesis being tested.

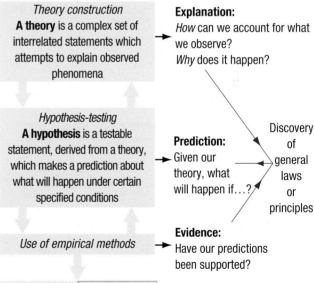

A science must involve

Subject matter
There must be a definable subject matter (the range of objects or phenomena it studies) → What is it *about*?

Theory construction
A theory is a complex set of interrelated statements which attempts to explain observed phenomena

Explanation:
How can we account for what we observe?
Why does it happen?

Hypothesis-testing
A hypothesis is a testable statement, derived from a theory, which makes a prediction about what will happen under certain specified conditions

Prediction:
Given our theory, what will happen if…?

Discovery of general laws or principles

Use of empirical methods

Evidence:
Have our predictions been supported?

1. Experiments	Laboratory
	Field
2. Observation	Natural
(a) naturalistic	
(b) controlled	
(c) participant	
3. Tests	
(a) standardised/objective	
(b) projective	
4. Surveys and questionnaires	
5. Case studies	

How is the data collected?

Figure 3.1 *A summary of the major features of a science*

What is 'scientific method'?

The account given in Box 3.4 and Figure 3.1 of what constitutes a science is non-controversial. However, it fails to tell us how the *scientific process* takes place, the sequence of 'events' involved (such as where the theory comes from in the first place, and how it's related to observation of the subject matter), or the exact relationship between theory construction, hypothesis testing and data collection.

Collectively, these 'events' and relationships are referred to as (the) *scientific method*. Table 3.1 summarises some common beliefs about both science and scientific method together with some alternative views.

Box 3.5   The inner world of scientists

According to Richards & Wolpert (1997), scientists, outside their own habitat, are a poorly understood species. If they feature in popular awareness at all, it's through a limited set of media stereotypes. With a few exceptions, if scientists aren't mad or bad, they're perceived as personality-free, their measured tones and formal reports implying ways of thinking and working far removed from the intellectual and emotional 'messiness' of other human activities.

Richards and Wolpert engaged in a series of conversations with several eminent scientists (including chemists, immunologists, biologists, biochemists, neuro- and evolutionary biologists) in an attempt to redress the balance, and give a rare glimpse of the human reality of scientific life.

Scientists think and feel about their work using the same psychological apparatus as the rest of us. The human qualities of science come over very strongly: its energy and imaginative richness, the frustration, love and despair which enslaves its practitioners.

For example, Mitchison (an immunologist) says that experiments start with 'the act of creation':

'Not all experiments you think of are good experiments, but thinking of one is just wonderful, eureka! It's fantastic'.

According to Edelman (an immunologist and neurobiologist), stumbling upon the solution to a problem when you least expect to find it is a '... remarkable pleasure'. Some scientists are like voyeurs, with '... almost a lustful feeling of excitement when a secret of nature is revealed'.

(Adapted from Richards & Wolpert, 1997)

Table 3.1 *Some common beliefs, and alternative views about, 'science' and 'scientific method'*

Common beliefs	Alternative views
● Scientific discovery begins with simple, unbiased, unprejudiced observation (i.e. the scientist simply 'samples' the world without any preconceptions, expectations or predetermined theories)	● There's no such thing as 'unbiased' or 'unprejudiced' observation. Observation is always selective, interpretative, prestructured and directed (i.e. we must have at least some idea of what we're looking for, otherwise we cannot know when we've found it). Goldberg (2000) cites a philosophy professor who asserted that what we call 'data' (that which is given) should more accurately be called 'capta' (that which is taken).
■ From the resulting sensory evidence ('data'/sense-data), generalised statements of fact will take shape (i.e. we gradually build up a picture of what the world is like based on a number of separate 'samples').	■ 'Data' do not constitute 'facts': evidence usually implies measurement, numbers, recordings and so on which need to be interpreted in the light of a theory. Facts don't exist objectively and cannot be discovered through 'pure observation'. 'Fact' = Data + Theory (Deese, 1972).
▲ The essential feature of scientific activity is the use of empirical methods, through which the sensory evidence is gathered (i.e. what distinguishes science from non-science is performing experiments and so on).	▲ Despite the central role of data collection, data alone don't make a science. Theory is just as crucial, because without it data have no meaning (see point above).
▼ The truth about the world (the objective nature of things, what the world is 'really like') can be established through properly controlled experiments and other ways of collecting 'facts' (i.e. science can tell us about reality as it is *independently* of the scientist or the activity of observing it).	▼ Scientific theory and research reflect the biases, prejudices, values and assumptions of the individual scientist, as well as of the scientific community to which s/he belongs. Science *isn't* value-free (see Chapter 47).
◆ Science involves the steady accumulation of knowledge, so that each generation of scientists adds to the discoveries of previous generations.	◆ Science involves an endless succession of long, peaceful periods ('normal science') and 'scientific revolutions' (Kuhn, 1962: see Table 3.3, page 35).
	❈ Science has a warm, human, exciting, argumentative, creative 'face' (Collins, 1994: see Box 3.5).

(Based on Medawar, 1963 and Popper, 1972)

As a result of the first two beliefs identified in Table 3.1, Popper (1972) has revised the stages of the scientific process as proposed by the classical view (the *inductive method*). This, together with Popper's revised version, is shown in Table 3.2.

Table 3.2 *Comparison between the classical, inductive view of science and Popper's revised version*

Inductive method	Popper's version
Observation and method	Problem (usually a refutation of an existing theory or prediction)
Inductive generalisation	Proposed solution or new theory
Hypothesis	Deduction of testable statements (hypotheses) from the new theory. This relates to the *hypothetico-deductive method*, which is usually contrasted with/opposed to the inductive method. In practice, both approaches are involved in the scientific process and are complementary
Attempted verification of hypothesis	Tests or attempts to refute by methods including observation and experiment
Proof or disproof	Establishing a preference between competing theories
Knowledge	

(Based on Popper, 1972)

Can psychology be a science if psychologists cannot agree what psychology is?

As we noted earlier, definitions of psychology have changed during its lifetime, largely reflecting the influence and contributions of its major theoretical approaches or orientations. In this chapter (and Chapter 2) we've seen that each approach rests upon a different image of what people are like, which in turn determines what is important to study, as well as the methods of study that can and should be used. Consequently, different approaches can be seen as self-contained disciplines, as well as different facets of the same discipline (Kuhn, 1962; Kline, 1988).

> *Ask yourself ...*
>
> - What is the underlying image of the person associated with each of the major theoretical approaches within psychology?
> - Which of these do you consider captures your own experience, and your experience of others, most accurately, and why? (You might find it helpful to refer to both Chapters 2 and 45.)

Kuhn argues that a field of study can only legitimately be considered a science if a majority of its workers subscribe to a common, global perspective or *paradigm*. According to Kuhn, this means that psychology is *preparadigmatic*: it lacks a paradigm, without which it's still in a state (or stage) of *prescience*. Whether psychology has, or has ever had, a paradigm, is hotly debated.

Table 3.3 *Stages in the development of a science (▲) and their application to psychology (■)*

▲ *Prescience*: No paradigm has evolved, and there are several schools of thought or theoretical orientations.

■ Like Kuhn, Joynson (1980) and Boden (1980) argue that psychology is preparadigmatic. Kline (1988) sees its various approaches as involving different paradigms.

▲ *Normal science*: A paradigm has emerged, dictating the kind of research that's carried out and providing a framework for interpreting results. The details of the theory are filled in, and workers explore its limits. Disagreements can usually be resolved within the limits allowed by the paradigm.

■ According to Valentine (1982), behaviourism comes as close as anything could to a paradigm. It provides: (a) a clear definition of the subject matter (behaviour as opposed to 'the mind'); (b) fundamental assumptions, in the form of the central role of learning (especially conditioning), and the analysis of behaviour into stimulus–response units, which allow prediction and control; (c) a methodology, with the controlled experiment at its core.

▲ *Revolution*: A point is reached in most established sciences where the conflicting evidence becomes so overwhelming that the old paradigm has to be abandoned and is replaced by a new one (*paradigm shift*). For example, Newtonian physics was replaced by Einstein's theory of relativity. When this paradigm shift occurs, there's a return to normal science.

■ Palermo (1971) and LeFrancois (1983) argue that psychology has already undergone several paradigm shifts. The first paradigm was *structuralism*, represented by Wundt's introspectionism. This was replaced by Watson's *behaviourism*. Finally, *cognitive psychology* largely replaced behaviourism, based on the computer analogy and the concept of information processing. Glassman (1995) disagrees, claiming that there's never been a complete reorganisation of the discipline, as has happened in physics.

Is a theoretical approach the same as a paradigm?

As Table 3.3 shows, Kuhn (a philosopher of science), along with some psychologists, maintains that psychology is still a prescience. Others believe that psychology has already undergone at least two revolutions, and is in a stage of normal science, with cognitive psychology the current paradigm. A third view, which represents a blend of the first two, is that psychology currently, and simultaneously, has a number of paradigms.

For example, Smith & Cowie (1991) identify psychoanalysis, behaviourism, sociobiology, and the information-processing, and cognitive–developmental approaches as paradigms, with the last being the most important as far as child development is concerned (see Chapters 34 and 35). For Davison & Neale (1994) there are 'four major paradigms of contemporary abnormal psychology', namely, the biological, psychoanalytic, learning (behaviourist) and cognitive (see Chapter 45).

Lambie (1991) believes it's a mistake to equate 'paradigm' with 'approach'. As noted in Table 3.2, while theory is an essential part of a paradigm, there's much more involved than this. For example, different theories can coexist within the same overall approach, such as classical and operant conditioning within 'learning theory' (the behaviourist approach), and Freud's and Erikson's theories within the psychodynamic approach.

One of the 'ingredients' that makes a paradigm different from an approach is its *social psychological* dimension. Paradigms refer to assumptions and beliefs held in common by most, if not all, the members of a given scientific community. This issue is discussed further in the following section.

The scientific study of human behaviour

The social nature of science: The problem of objectivity

'Doing science' is part of human behaviour. When psychologists study what people do, they're engaging in some of the very same behaviours they're trying to understand (such as thinking, perceiving, problem-solving and explaining). This is what's meant by the statement that psychologists are part of their own subject matter, which makes it even more difficult for them to be objective than other scientists.

According to Richards (1996b):

'Whereas in orthodox sciences there is always some external object of enquiry – rocks, electrons, DNA, chemicals – existing essentially unchanging in the non-human world (even if never finally knowable "as it really is" beyond human conceptions), this is not so for psychology. "Doing psychology" is the human activity of studying human activity; it is human psychology examining itself – and what it produces by way of new theories, ideas and beliefs about itself is also part of our psychology!'.

Knowable 'as it really is' refers to objectivity, and Richards is claiming that it may be impossible for any scientist to achieve complete objectivity. One reason for this relates to the social nature of scientific activity. As Rose (1997) says:

'How biologists – or any scientists, perceive the world is not the result of simply holding a true reflecting mirror up to nature: it is shaped by the history of our subject, by dominant social expectations and by the patterns of research funding'.

Does this mean that 'the truth' only exists 'by agreement'? Does science tell us not about what things are 'really' like, but only what scientists happen to believe is the truth at any particular time?

Ask yourself ...

- Given what was said earlier about the sometimes very intense feelings aroused in individual scientists during the course of their work (see Box 3.5), in what ways do you think science can be described as a social activity? (It might be useful to think about why you do practical work/labs – other than because you have to!)

According to Richardson (1991), whatever the *logical* aspects of scientific method may be (deriving hypotheses from theories, the importance of refutability and so on), science is a very *social* business. Research must be qualified and quantified to enable others to replicate it, and in this way the procedures, instruments and measures become standardised, so that scientists anywhere in the world can check the truth of reported observations and findings. This implies the need for universally agreed conventions for reporting these observations and findings (Richardson, 1991).

Collins (1994) takes a more extreme view, arguing that the results of experiments are more ambiguous than is usually assumed, while theory is more flexible than most people imagine:

'This means that science can progress only within communities that can reach consensus about what counts as plausible. Plausibility is a matter of social context so science is a "social construct"'. (Collins, 1994)

Kuhn's concept of a paradigm also stresses the role of agreement or consensus among scientists working within a particular discipline. Accordingly, 'truth' has more to do with the popularity and widespread acceptance of a particular framework within the scientific community than with its 'truth value'. The fact that revolutions do occur (paradigm shifts: see Table 3.3) demonstrates that 'the truth' can and does change.

For example, the change from Newtonian to Einsteinian physics reflected the changing popularity of these two accounts. For Planck, who helped to shape the 'Einsteinian revolution':

'A new scientific theory does not triumph by convincing its opponents and making them see the light, but rather because its opponents eventually die, and a new generation grows up that is familiar with it'. (Cited in Kuhn, 1970)

The popularity or acceptability of a theory, however, must be at least partly determined by how well it explains and predicts the phenomena in question. In other words, *both* social and 'purely' scientific or rational criteria are relevant.

However, even if there are widely accepted ways of 'doing science', 'good science' doesn't necessarily mean 'good psychology'. Is it valid to study human behaviour and experience as part of the natural world, or is a different kind of approach needed altogether? After all, it isn't just psychologists who observe, experiment and theorise (Heather, 1976).

The psychology experiment as a social situation

To regard empirical research in general, and the experiment in particular, as objective involves two related assumptions:

- researchers only influence the participants' behaviour (the outcome of the experiment) to the extent that they decide what hypothesis to test, how the variables are to be operationalised, what design to use, and so on;
- the only factors influencing the participants' performance are the objectively defined variables manipulated by the experimenter.

Ask yourself ...

- Try to formulate some arguments against these two assumptions. What do the experimenter and participant bring with them into the experimental situation that isn't directly related to the experiment, and how may this (and other factors) influence what goes on in the experimental situation? (See Chapter 47.)

Experimenters are people too: the problem of experimenter bias

According to Rosenthal (1966), what the experimenter is *like* correlates with what s/he does, as well as influencing the participant's perception of, and response to, the experimenter. This is related to *experimenter bias*.

Box 3.6	Some examples of experimenter bias

According to Valentine (1992), experimenter bias has been demonstrated in a variety of experiments, including reaction time, psychophysics, animal learning, verbal conditioning, personality assessment, person perception, learning and ability, as well as in everyday life situations.

What these experiments consistently show is that if one group of experimenters has one hypothesis about what it expects to find and another group has the opposite hypothesis, both groups will obtain results that support their respective hypotheses. The results *aren't* due to the mishandling of data by biased experimenters, but the experimenter's bias somehow creates a changed environment, in which participants actually behave differently.

When experimenters were informed that rats learning mazes had been specially bred for this ability ('maze-bright'), they obtained better learning from their rats than did experimenters who believed their rats were 'maze-dull' (Rosenthal & Fode, 1963; Rosenthal & Lawson, 1964). In fact, both groups of rats were drawn from the *same* population and were *randomly* allocated to the 'bright' or 'dull' condition. The crucial point is that the 'bright' rats did actually learn faster. The experimenters' expectations in some way concretely changed the situation, although how this happened is far less clear.

In a natural classroom situation, children whose teachers told them they'd show academic 'promise' during the next academic year showed significantly greater IQ gains than children for whom such predictions weren't made (although this latter group also made substantial improvements). The children were, in fact, *randomly* allocated to the two conditions, but the teachers' expectations actually produced the predicted improvements in the 'academic promise' group, that is, there was a *self-fulfilling prophecy* (Rosenthal & Jacobson, 1968).

(Based on Valentine, 1992 and Weisstein, 1993)

Ask yourself ...

- How could you explain the findings from the studies described in Box 3.6? How could experimenter expectations actually bring about the different performances of the two groups of rats and children?

Participants are psychologists too: demand characteristics

Instead of seeing the person being studied as a passive responder to whom things are done ('subject'), Orne (1962) stresses what the person *does*, implying a far more active role. Participants' performance in an experiment could be thought of as a form of problem-solving behaviour. At some level, they see the task as working out the true purpose of the experiment and responding in a way which will support (or not support, in the case of the unhelpful participant) the hypothesis being tested.

In this context, the cues which convey the experimental hypothesis to participants represent important influences on their behaviour, and the sum total of those cues are called the *demand characteristics* of the experimental situation. These cues include:

> '... the rumours or campus scuttlebut [gossip] about the research, the information conveyed during the original situation, the person of the experimenter, and the setting of the laboratory, as well as all explicit and implicit communications during the experiment proper'. (Orne, 1962)

This tendency to identify the demand characteristics is related to the tendency to play the role of a 'good' (or 'bad') experimental participant.

KEY STUDY 3.1

The lengths that some people will go to to please the experimenter (Orne, 1962)

Orne points out that if people are asked to do five push-ups as a favour, they'll ask 'Why?', but if the request comes from an experimenter, they'll ask 'Where?'. Similarly, he reports an experiment in which people were asked to add sheets of random numbers, then tear them up into at least 32 pieces. Five-and-a-half hours later, they were still doing it, and the experimenter had to tell them to stop !

This demonstrates very clearly the strong tendency of people to want to please the experimenter, and not to 'upset the experiment'. Its mainly in this sense that Orne sees the experiment as a social situation, in which the people involved play different but complementary roles. In order for this interaction to proceed fairly smoothly, each must have some idea of what the other expects of him or her.

The expectations referred to in Key Study 3.1 are part of the culturally shared understandings of what science in general, and psychology in particular, involves and without which the experiment couldn't 'happen' (Moghaddam *et al.*, 1993). So, not only is the experiment a social situation, but science itself is a *culture-related phenomenon*. This represents another respect in which science cannot claim complete objectivity.

The problem of representativeness

Traditional, mainstream experimental psychology adopts a *nomothetic* ('law-like') approach. This involves generalisation from limited samples of participants to 'people in general', as part of the attempt to establish general 'laws' or principles of behaviour (see Figure 3.1 and Chapter 42, pages 610–611).

Despite the fact that Asch's experiments were carried out in the early 1950s, very little has changed as far as participant samples are concerned. In American psychology, at least, the typical participant is a psychology undergraduate, who's obliged to take part in a certain number of studies as a course requirement, and who receives 'course credits' for so doing (Krupat & Garonzik, 1994).

Mainstream British and American psychology has implicitly equated 'human being' with 'member of Western culture'. Despite the fact that the vast majority of research participants are members of Western societies, the resulting findings and theories have been applied to 'human beings', as if culture made no difference (they are 'culture-bound and culture-blind': Sinha, 1997). This Anglocentric or Eurocentric bias (a form of *ethnocentrism*) is matched by the androcentric or masculinist bias (a form of *sexism*), according to which the behaviours and experiences of men are taken as the standard against which women are judged (see Chapter 47).

In both cases, while the bias remains implicit and goes unrecognised (and is reinforced by psychology's claim to be objective and value-free), research findings are taken as providing us with an objective, scientifically valid, account of what 'women/people in general are like'. Once we realise that scientists, like all human beings, have prejudices, biases and values, their research and theories begin to look less objective, reliable and valid than they did before (see Chapter 47).

The problem of artificiality

Criticisms of traditional empirical methods (especially the laboratory experiment) have focused on their *artificiality*, including the often unusual and bizarre tasks that people are asked to perform in the name of science (see Key Study 3.1). Yet we cannot be sure that the way people behave in the laboratory is an accurate indication of how they're likely to behave outside it (Heather, 1976).

What makes the laboratory experiment such an unnatural and artificial situation is the fact that it's almost totally structured by one 'participant' – the experimenter. This relates to *power differences* between experimenters and their 'subjects', which is as much an ethical as a practical issue (see Chapter 48).

Traditionally, participants have been referred to as 'subjects', implying something less than a person, a dehumanised and depersonalised 'object'. According to Heather (1976), it's a small step from reducing the person to a mere thing or object (or experimental 'subject'), to seeing people as machines or machine-like ('mechanism' = 'machine-ism' = mechanistic view of people). This way of thinking about people is reflected in the popular definition of psychology as the study of 'what makes people tick' (see Chapter 1 and page 30).

The problem of internal versus external validity

If the experimental setting (and task) is seen as similar or relevant enough to everyday situations to allow us to generalise the results, we say that the study has high *external* or *ecological validity*. But what about *internal validity*? Modelling itself on natural science, psychology attempts to overcome the problem of the complexity of human behaviour by using experimental control (what Rose, 1997, calls *reductionism as methodology*: see Box 49.6, page 728). This involves isolating an independent variable (IV) and ensuring that extraneous variables (variables other than the IV likely to affect the dependent variable) don't affect the outcome (see Coolican, 1999). But this begs the crucial question: *how do we know when all the relevant extraneous variables have been controlled?*

Box 3.7	Some difficulties with the notion of experimental control

- While it's relatively easy to control the more obvious *situational variables*, this is more difficult with *participant variables* (such as age, gender and culture), either for practical reasons (such as the availability of these groups), or because it isn't always obvious exactly what the relevant variables are. Ultimately, it's down to the experimenter's judgement and intuition: what s/he believes is important (and possible) to control (Deese, 1972).

- If judgement and intuition are involved, then control and objectivity are matters of degree, whether in psychology or physics (see Table 3.1).

- It's the *variability/heterogeneity* of human beings that makes them so much more difficult to study than, say, chemicals. Chemists don't usually have to worry about how two samples of a particular chemical might be different from each other, but psychologists need to allow for individual differences between participants.

- We cannot just assume that the IV (or 'stimulus' or 'input') is identical for every participant, definable in some objective way, independent of the participant, and exerts a standard effect on everyone. The attempt to define IVs (and DVs) in this way can be regarded as a form of *reductionism (see* Chapter 49).

- Complete control would mean that the IV alone was responsible for the DV, so that experimenter bias and the effect of demand characteristics were irrelevant. But even if complete control were possible (in other words, if we could guarantee the *internal validity* of the experiment), a fundamental dilemma would remain. The greater the degree of control over the experimental situation, the more different it becomes from real-life situations (the more artificial it gets and the lower its *external validity*).

As Box 3.7 indicates, in order to discover the relationships between variables (necessary for understanding human behaviour in natural, real-life situations), psychologists must 'bring' the behaviour into a specially created environment (the laboratory), where the relevant variables can be controlled in a way that's impossible in naturally occurring settings. However, in doing so, psychologists have constructed an artificial environment and the resulting behaviour is similarly artificial. It's no longer the behaviour they were trying to understand!

Conclusions

Psychology as a separate field of study grew out of several other disciplines, both scientific (such as physiology), and non-scientific (in particular philosophy). For much of its life as an independent discipline, and through what some call revolutions and paradigm shifts, it has taken the natural sciences as its model (scientism). This chapter has highlighted some of the major implications of adopting methods of investigating the natural world and applying them to the study of human behaviour and experience. In doing this, the chapter has also examined what are fast becoming outdated and inaccurate views about the nature of science. Ultimately, whatever a particular science may claim to have discovered about the phenomena it studies, scientific activity remains just one more aspect of human behaviour.

CHAPTER SUMMARY

- **Philosophical dualism** enabled scientists to describe the world objectively, which became the ideal of science. Its extension by Comte to the study of human behaviour and social institutions is called **positivism**. Descartes extended **mechanism** to the human body, but the mind remained accessible only through **introspection**.

- **Empiricism** emphasises the importance of sensory experience, as opposed to **nativism's** claim that knowledge is innate. 'Empirical' implies that the essence of science is collecting data/facts through experiments and observations.

- Wundt is generally regarded as the founder of the new science of experimental psychology. He used **introspection** to study conscious experience, analysing it into its basic elements (**structuralism**).

- James is the other pioneer of scientific psychology. As well as helping to make Freud's ideas popular in America, he influenced **functionalism** which, in turn, stimulated interest in **individual differences**.

- Watson argued that for psychology to be objective, it must study **behaviour** rather than mental life, its goals should be prediction and control, and there are only **quantitative** differences between human and animal behaviour.

- Dissatisfaction with behaviourism culminated in the 1956 'cognitive revolution'. At the centre of this new **information-processing approach** lay the **computer analogy**.

- **Scientism** maintains that all aspects of human behaviour can and should be studied using the methods of natural science. It involves 'context-stripping' and the **value-free**, **objective** use of **laboratory experiments** in particular.

- A science must possess a definable **subject matter**, involve **theory construction** and **hypothesis testing**, and use **empirical methods** for data collection. However, these characteristics fail to describe the **scientific process** or **scientific method**.

- While the classical view of science is built around the **inductive method**, Popper's revised view stresses the **hypothetico–deductive method**. The two methods are complementary.

- Different theoretical **approaches** can be seen as self-contained disciplines, making psychology **pre-paradigmatic** and so still in a stage of **prescience**. Only when a discipline possesses a paradigm has it reached the stage of **normal science**, after which **paradigm shifts** result in **revolution** (and a return to normal science).

- Science is a very **social** activity. Consensus among the scientific community is paramount, as shown by the fact that revolutions involve redefining 'the truth'.

- Environmental changes are somehow produced by experimenters' expectations (**experimenter bias**), and **demand characteristics** influence participants' behaviours by helping to convey the experimental hypothesis. The experiment is a social situation and science itself is **culture-related**.

- The **artificiality** of laboratory experiments is largely due to their being totally structured by experimenters. Also, the higher an experiment's **internal validity**, the lower its **external validity** becomes.

Self-assessment questions

1 a Define the term 'science'.
   b Outline the development of psychology as a separate discipline.
   c With reference to **two** areas/branches of psychology (e.g. physiological, developmental), assess the extent to which psychology can be regarded as a science.

2 Describe and evaluate arguments for and against the claim that psychology is a science.

Web addresses

http://elvers.stjoe.udayton.edu/history/people/Wundt.html
http://mfp.es.emory.edu/james.html
http://www.users.csbsju.edu/~tcredd/pb/pbnames.html
http://www.lucknow.com/horus/guide/cm106.html

Further reading

Deese, J. (1972) *Psychology As Art and Science*. New York: Harcourt Brace Jovanovich. A short, very readable, but thorough examination of many of the issues discussed in this chapter.

Rosnow, R.L. & Rosenthal, R. (1997) *People Studying People: Artifacts and Ethics in Behavioural Research*. New York: W.H. Freeman & Co. A discussion of how psychology falls short of being an objective science, including experimenter bias, self-fulfilling prophecies, and demand characteristics.

Smith, J.A., Harré, R. & van Langenhove, L. (Eds) (1995). *Rethinking Psychology*. London: Sage. A critical account of mainstream, positivist psychology. Chapter 2 is particularly relevant, but most chapters are relevant to other parts of *this* book.

Two

The Biological Basis of Behaviour and Experience

Chapter 4

The Nervous System

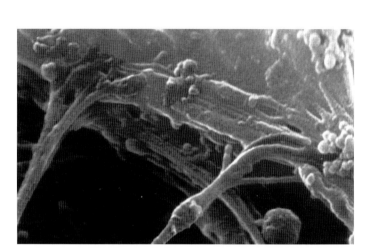

Introduction and overview

*B*iopsychology is the study of the biological bases (or physiological correlates) of behaviour. It's a branch of neuroscience (the 'brain sciences') – the study of the nervous system. While biopsychology is sometimes referred to as 'psychobiology', 'behavioural neuroscience', and 'physiological psychology', Pinel (1993) prefers 'biopsychology', because it denotes a biological approach to the study of psychology, where psychology 'commands centre stage'. According to Pinel: '... biopsychology's unique contribution to neuroscientific research is a knowledge of behaviour and of the methods of behavioural research ... the ultimate purpose of the nervous system is to produce and control behaviour'.

In other words, biopsychologists aren't interested in biology for its own sake, but for what it can tell them about behaviour and mental processes. In general terms:

- the kind of behaviour an animal is capable of depends on the kind of body it possesses. For example, humans can flap their arms as much as they like, but they'll never fly (unaided): arms are simply not designed for flying, while wings are. But we're very skilled at manipulating objects (especially small ones), because that's how our hands and fingers have evolved;
- the possession of a specialised body is of very little use unless the nervous system is able to control it. Of course, evolution of the one usually mirrors evolution of the other;
- the kind of nervous system also determines the extent and nature of the learning a species is capable of. Moving along the *phylogenetic* (evolutionary) scale, from simple, one-celled amoebae, through insects, birds and mammals, to primates (including *Homo sapiens*), the nervous system gradually becomes more complex and behaviour becomes increasingly the product of learning and environmental influence, rather than instinct and other innate (genetically determined) factors.

Biopsychology and other disciplines

According to Pinel (1993), biopsychology draws together knowledge from the other neuroscientific disciplines, in particular:

- *neuroanatomy*: the study of the structure of the nervous system (NS);
- *developmental neurobiology*: the study of how the NS changes as the organism matures and ages;
- *neurochemistry*: the study of the chemical bases of neural activity, especially those underlying the transmission of signals through and between neurons (nerve cells);
- *neuroendocrinology*: the study of the interactions between the NS and the endocrine (hormonal) system (see pages 61–62);
- *neuropathology*: the study of NS disorders. Related to this is *neuropsychology*, the study of the behavioural deficits produced in people by brain damage;
- *neuropharmacology*: the study of the effects of drugs on the NS, especially those influencing neural transmission. Related to this is *psychopharmacology*, which is concerned with the effects of drugs on behaviour (see pages 47–48 and Chapter 8);
- *neurophysiology*: the study of the responses of the NS, particularly those involved in transmission of electrical signals through and between neurons. This is related to (a) *physiological psychology*, which involves manipulation of the NS through surgical, electrical and chemical means under strictly controlled experimental conditions (*invasive methods*, using mainly non-human animals), and (b) *psychophysiology*, which uses *non-invasive methods*, mainly with human participants, to study the physiology of psychological processes such as attention, emotion, information-processing and, increasingly, major mental disorders (especially schizophrenia: see Chapter 44).

An overview of the human nervous system (NS): Structure and function

As Figure 4.1 (page 45) shows, the NS involves a number of subdivisions. Before looking at these in detail, we need to look at some of the general characteristics of the NS.

Neurons and glial cells

The NS as a whole comprises between ten and twelve billion (i.e. ten to twelve thousand million) nerve cells or *neurons*, the basic structural units or building blocks of the NS. Other kinds of cell in the NS include *glial* ('glue') cells.

Box 4.1   Glial cells

Glial cells are mostly smaller than neurons and ten times more numerous. They come in different forms, the most important being *astrocytes* and *oligodendrocytes*. It used to be thought that they merely 'fill in the space' between neurons, but they're increasingly being seen as capable of passing signals to each other, receiving signals from neurons, and perhaps even passing signals to neurons. They also play a vital role in brain development. Not only do they supply nutrients and structural support to the neurons and provide a barrier to certain substances from the bloodstream, but oligodendrocytes provide the insulating myelin sheath around the axon of the neuron (see Figure 4.2, page 46).

(Based on Young, 1994)

About 80 per cent of all neurons are found in the brain, particularly in the *cerebral cortex*, the topmost outer layer. Information is passed from neuron to neuron in the form of *electrochemical impulses*, which constitute the 'language' of the NS. Neurons are of three main kinds:

- *sensory* (or *afferent*), which carry information from the sense organs to the central nervous system (CNS);
- *motor* (or *efferent*), which carry information from the CNS to the muscles and glands;
- *interneurons* (or *connector* neurons), which connect neurons to other neurons and integrate the activities of sensory and motor neurons. Interneurons are the most numerous, constituting about 97 per cent of the total number of neurons in the CNS.

Although no two neurons are identical, most share the same basic structure, and they work in essentially the same way (see Figure 4.2, page 46).

The cell body (or *soma*) houses the *nucleus* (which contains the genetic code), the *cytoplasm* (which feeds the nucleus), and the other structures common to all living cells. The *dendrites* branch out from the cell body, and it's through the dendrites that the neuron makes electrochemical contact with other neurons, by receiving incoming signals from neighbouring neurons. The *axon* is a thin cylinder of protoplasm, which projects away from the cell body and carries the signals received by the dendrites to other neurons. The *myelin sheath* is a white, fatty substance, which insulates the axon and speeds up the rate of conduction of signals down the axon and towards the *terminal buttons* (or *synaptic knobs*). The myelin sheath isn't continuous, but is interrupted by the *nodes of Ranvier*.

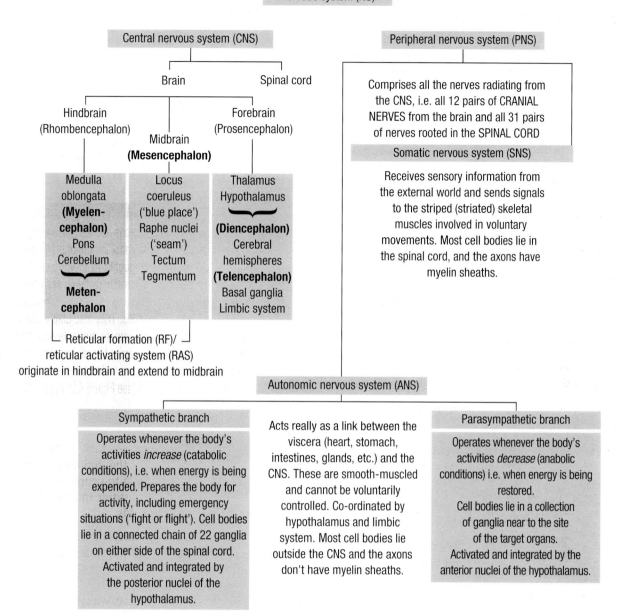

Figure 4.1 *Major subdivisions of the human nervous system (including the main subdivisions of the brain)*

In the spinal cord, a neuron may have an axon two to three feet long, running from the tip of the spine down to the big toe, while in the brain, neurons are only a few one-thousandths of an inch long. Axons of motor neurons which terminate in muscles end in a series of branches, tipped by *motor endplates*, each of which is attached to a single muscle fibre. Impulses at the motor endplate cause the muscle to contract (as in raising the arm).

A *nerve* is a bundle of elongated axons belonging to hundreds or thousands of neurons. Nerves spread out to every part of the body, connecting with sense receptors, skin, muscles and internal organs. Twelve pairs of *cranial nerves* leave the brain through holes in the skull, and 31 pairs of *spinal nerves* leave the spinal cord through the vertebrae. Together, they constitute the nerves of the *peripheral nervous system* (PNS: see Figure 4.1).

Communication between neurons

As Figure 4.3 (page 46) shows, the terminal buttons house a number of tiny sacs or *synaptic vesicles*, which contain between

ten and 100,000 molecules of a chemical messenger, called a *neurotransmitter*. When an *electrochemical impulse* has passed down the axon, it arrives at a terminal button and stimulates the vesicles to discharge their contents into the minute gap between the end of the terminal button (the *presynaptic membrane*) and the dendrite of the receiving neuron (the *postsynaptic membrane*). This is called the *synaptic cleft* (or *gap*).

The neurotransmitter molecules cross the synaptic gap and combine with special receptor sites in the postsynaptic membrane of the dendrite of the receiving neuron. So, the term 'synapse' refers to the *junction* between neurons (though there's no actual physical contact between them), at which signals are passed from a sending to a receiving neuron through the release of neurotransmitters. Although this *synaptic transmission* is the most common form of communication between neurons (Iversen, 1979), 20 per cent of the brain is completely devoid of neurons. Rather than forming a solid mass, the neurons are interspersed with a convoluted network of fluid-filled

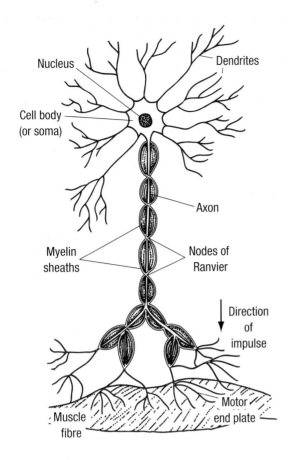

Figure 4.2 *A typical motor neuron*

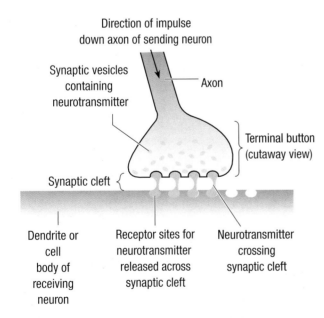

Figure 4.3 *The synapse*

spaces or cavities. According to Mitchell (1999), there's a growing body of opinion that neurons can communicate with large regions of the brain by releasing chemicals into these watery spaces. This is called *volume transmission*, which is seen as *complementary* to synaptic transmission.

Box 4.2 **What evidence is there for 'volume transmission'?**

Fuxe, Agnati and colleagues (1998, cited in Mitchell, 1999) tracked a neurotransmitter (*neuropeptide Y*) in rats' brains and found receptors that were sometimes several millimetres (a million times the width of a synaptic gap) away from the source of the neurotransmitter. Synaptic transmission couldn't work on this sort of scale – but volume transmission could.

Receptors for *serotonin* and *dopamine* (see Table 4.1, page 47) have also been identified away from their most likely locations. For example, Zhou *et al.* (1998, cited in Mitchell, 1999) found serotonin receptors on axons: only if serotonin could travel via volume transmission would you expect to find receptors there.

Although not everyone accepts the idea of volume transmission, there are certain global patterns of activity which are very difficult to explain in any other way. For example, Parkinson's disease sufferers seem to lose neurons in the substantia nigra, a brain region which normally supplies the neighbouring striatum with dopamine (which initiates and controls signalling to the muscles: see Table 4.1). However, sufferers don't develop symptoms until a massive 80 per cent of the dopamine-producing neurons have been lost, so signalling must have continued during this period of neuron-loss. Volume transmission would account for this far better than synaptic transmission.

Sleep is another good example of why the brain needs volume transmission (see Chapter 7). A molecule called *prostaglandins D2* sends us off to sleep, whereas *prostaglandins E2* helps to wake us up. The enzyme that produces D2 comes mainly from non-neuronal cells in the brain; it may reach its target by diffusing through the cerebrospinal fluid (CSF), which surrounds and bathes the neurons.

(Based on Mitchell, 1999)

Electrochemical impulses

The electrochemical signal which passes down the axon is called an *action potential*. Before an action potential occurs, an inactive neuron contains positively charged potassium (K^+) ions (electrically charged potassium atoms) and large, negatively charged protein molecules. Outside the neuron, in the surrounding fluid, there are concentrations of positively charged sodium ions (Na^+) and negatively charged chloride ions (Cl^-). The large, negatively charged, protein ions are trapped inside the neuron, while the positively charged sodium ions are kept out by the action of the *sodium–potassium pumps* in the cell membrane, which allow potassium (and chloride) ions to move in and out fairly freely.

The overall effect of this uneven distribution of ions is that the inside of the cell is electrically negative relative to the outside. The neuron is said to be *impermeable* to the positively charged sodium ions (its resting state or *resting potential*). When an action potential occurs, the inside of the neuron momentarily changes from negative to positive, the sodium channels are opened (for one millisecond), and sodium ions flood into the neuron (it's now permeable to sodium ions). This sets off a chain reaction, whereby the sodium channels open at adjacent membrane sites all the way down the axon. But almost as soon as the sodium channels are opened, they close again: potassium channels are opened instead, allowing potassium ions out through the membrane and restoring the negative resting potential.

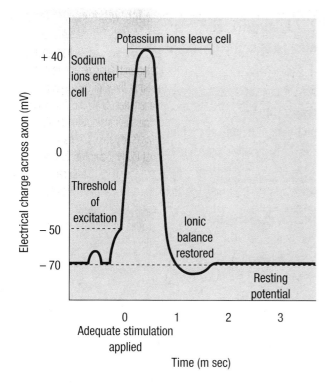

Figure 4.4 *The sequence of events when a neuron 'fires'. The small 'bump' on the left represents an incoming message that was not strong enough to cause the neuron to fire*

Because the myelin sheath isn't continuous but segmented (so that at the nodes of Ranvier the axon is actually exposed: see Figure 4.2), the action potential jumps from one node to another down the axon. This is called *saltatory conduction*, and is actually faster than if the sheaths were continuous.

Response threshold

The stimulus to the neuron must be intense enough to produce an action potential (it must exceed the *threshold of response*), but once this has occurred, it always travels at the same speed to the end of the axon. So, an impulse is either present or absent (the *all-or-none rule*). Action potentials are all of the same strength (*amplitude*), so the intensity of the stimulus is measured by:

- the frequency of firing: the stronger the stimulus, the more often the neuron will fire (a very strong stimulus producing a volley of impulses);
- the number of neurons stimulated: the stronger the stimulus, the greater the number of neurons stimulated.

However strong the stimulus, there's always a very short interval after each firing (one to two milliseconds), during which no further impulse can pass (the *absolute refractory period*). This is followed by a *relative refractory period*: the stronger the stimulus, the shorter the interval between the absolute refractory period and the next impulse.

Different types of synapses

Some synapses are *excitatory* (they 'instruct' the receiving neuron to 'fire', i.e. to conduct an action potential), while others are *inhibitory* (they 'instruct' the receiving neuron not to 'fire'). Because each neuron may have between 1000 and 10,000

synapses, both excitatory and inhibitory, the 'decision' to fire or not will depend on the combined effect of all its receiving synapses. If enough excitatory synapses are active, their combined effect may add up to exceed the threshold for firing of the receiving neuron (this is called *summation*).

Inhibitory synapses are important because they help control the spread of excitation through the highly interconnected NS, keeping activity channelled in appropriate networks or 'circuits'. Epileptic seizures (fits), for example, may be caused by excitation of many different brain circuits at the same time. If it weren't for inhibition, we might all be having seizures much of the time.

Different types of neurotransmitters

What makes a synapse either excitatory or inhibitory is the particular neurotransmitter(s) contained within the vesicles of the synaptic button. A region on the surface of the receptor site is

Table 4.1 *Major transmitters and their effects*

Neurotransmitter	Effect on receiving neuron	Related behaviour
Acetylcholine (ACh)	Generally *excitatory*, but can be *inhibitory*, depending on the type of receptor molecule involved	Voluntary movement of muscles, behavioural inhibition, drinking, memory. In Alzheimer's disease, there's a degeneration of ACh-producing neurons
Noradrenaline (norepinephrine)*	*Inhibitory* (in CNS); *excitatory* (in ANS)	Wakefulness and arousal (behavioural and emotional), eating, depression and mania (see Chapters 44 and 45)
Dopamine*	*Inhibitory* and *excitatory*	Voluntary movement, emotional arousal. Parkinson's disease involves degeneration of dopamine-releasing neurons. Schizophrenia is associated with excess of dopamine (see Chapter 44)
Serotonin*	*Inhibitory* and *excitatory*.	Sleep (see Chapter 7), temperature regulation.
GABA (gamma aminobutyric acid)	*Inhibitory* (the most common inhibitor in CNS)	Motor behaviour. Huntington's chorea may result from degeneration of GABA cells in the corpus striatum
Glycine	*Inhibitory* (found in spinal cord)	Spinal reflexes and other motor behaviour
Neuromodulators (neuropeptides; e.g. enkephalins and endorphins)	*Inhibitory* and *excitatory*	Sensory transmission, especially pain (see Chapter 12)

* Monoamine (MAO) transmitters

precisely tailored to match the shape of the transmitter molecule (in a lock-and-key fashion). The effect of the transmitter is brought to an end either by *deactivation* (it's destroyed by special enzymes) or by *reuptake* (it's pumped back into the presynaptic axon, either for destruction or recycling).

According to Iversen (1979), there are at least 30 different neurotransmitters in the brain, each with its specific excitatory or inhibitory effect on certain neurons. The various chemicals aren't randomly distributed throughout the brain, but are localised in specific groups of neurons and pathways. As a general rule, a single neuron will store and release the same neurotransmitter in all its axon terminals. So, *cholinergic, noradrenergic, dopaminergic,* and *serotonergic* neurons use ACh, noradrenaline, dopamine and serotonin respectively. However, there's some evidence that more than one kind of transmitter may be released from the same synaptic button depending on the pattern of action potentials reaching it (Lloyd *et al.*, 1984).

While neurotransmitters have a fairly direct influence on receiving neurons, *neuromodulators* 'tune' or 'prime' neurons, enabling them to respond in a particular way to later stimulation by a neurotransmitter. Included among the neuromodulators are certain *neuropeptides* (see Table 4.1), notably the *enkephalins* ('in the head') and the *endorphins* ('morphine-within').

Box 4.3 Opioids: the brain's natural painkillers?

The enkephalins and endorphins are also known as *opioids*, because functionally they resemble the opium drugs morphine, heroin and opium itself (see Chapter 8). Morphine is commonly used for the relief of severe, intractable pain, and the discovery of 'opiate receptors' in the neurons strongly suggested that the brain creates its own powerful painkiller. Enkephalins and endorphins seemed to fit the bill, and they may work by interfering with the release of transmitters from the presynaptic membrane of neurons which transmit information about pain. It's thought they're released during acupuncture and hypnosis, producing a reduction in perceived pain, although pain information probably still reaches the brain (the pain receptors aren't directly influenced: see Chapter 12). It's also believed that *placebos* ('dummy drugs') work by influencing the release of endorphins in response to the belief that an active drug was given (Hamilton & Timmons, 1995: see Chapters 12 and 45).

Other neuropeptides are founds as hormones, including:

- *vasopressin*, which is thought to play a role in memory;
- *corticosteroids* ('stress hormones') and *adrenocorticotrophic hormone* (ACTH), which are involved in stress reactions and emotional arousal (see Chapter 12);
- *androgens* (male sex hormones), which regulate sex drive in both sexes (see pages 61–62 and Table 36.1, pages 521–522).

The central nervous system (CNS)

Methods of studying the brain

Box 4.4 A classification of methods used to study the brain

- **Clinical/anatomical methods**: studying the effects on behaviour of accidental injury to the brain or brain disease in human beings, or patients who've undergone brain surgery for the treatment of disorders such as epilepsy (in particular, 'split-brain' patients: see text, pages 58–60).
- **Invasive methods**: surgically removing areas of brain tissue (*ablation*) or causing damage or injury (*lesions*) to particular brain sites or stimulation of the brain, either electrically or chemically. Also included is the recording of the electrical activity of very small areas of the brain, or even single neurons, through the insertion of very fine electrodes (*microelectrode recording*). These methods involve non-human animals.
- **Non-invasive methods**: either the brain's electrical activity is recorded by attaching electrodes to the scalp, or *computerised scanning/imaging techniques* are used to study the living human brain. In either case, the brain isn't interfered with in any way, and there's no risk of damage or injury.

Clinical/anatomical methods

One of the earliest methods used to study the CNS involved patients who'd suffered brain damage, as the result of an accident, stroke or tumour. A famous and early example is Broca's discovery of a specialised area of the brain for speech. In 1869, Broca reviewed evidence from a number of cases of brain damage and concluded that injury to a certain part of the left cerebral hemisphere (the left half of the brain) caused the patient's speech to become slow and laboured, but that the ability to understand speech was almost completely unaffected. What's now called *Broca's area* seems to control the ability to produce speech, and damage to it causes *motor* (or *expressive*) *aphasia*. In 1874, Wernicke reported that injury to a different part of the left hemisphere caused *receptive aphasia*, the inability to understand speech (one's own or someone else's).

These clinical studies of the brain have normally been conducted in parallel with anatomical studies, usually during the course of postmortem examinations. Studying structure and function in a complementary way is essential for an adequate understanding of such a complex organ as the brain. *Split-brain patients* are people with severe epilepsy who've undergone surgery (*commissurotomy*), which involves cutting the tissue which connects the two halves of the brain (the *corpus callosum*). Sperry and his colleagues in the 1960s and 1970s made full use of the unique opportunity to study these 'split brains'. Their work is discussed in detail later in the chapter (see pages 58–60).

Invasive methods

As noted in Box 4.4, parts of the brain may be surgically removed (*ablated*) or an area of the brain may be damaged (rather than removed: the *lesion method*). An early user of the first method was Lashley, working with rats in the 1920s, and it's been used extensively to study the role of the brain in eating (see Chapter 9). To destroy areas or structures located deep within the brain, a *stereotaxic apparatus* is used, which allows the researcher to operate on brain structures that are hidden from view (see Figure 4.5). While the subjects are exclusively non-human animals, stereotaxic surgery is also used with humans, including psychiatric patients (see Chapter 45).

Ask yourself ...

- Is it ethically acceptable to use invasive methods with non-human animals?
- How could you justify their use?
  (See Chapter 48, pages 714–717.)

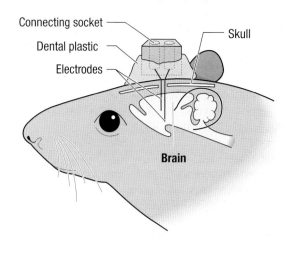

Figure 4.6 *Electrical stimulation of the brain*

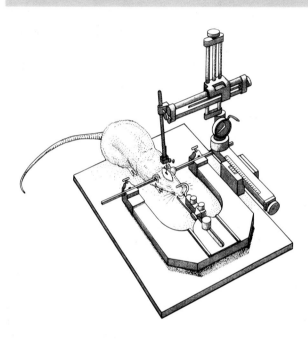

Figure 4.5 *A stereotaxic apparatus, used to insert an electrode into a specific portion of an animal's brain (from N. Carlson, 1992,* Foundations of Physiological Psychology, *2nd edition, Boston, Allyn & Bacon)*

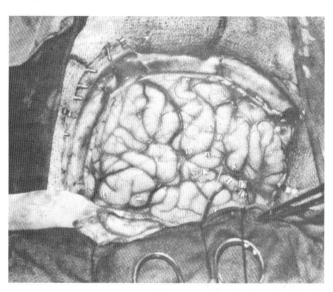

Photograph taken during surgery carried out by Penfield. The numbers refer to the parts of the cortex stimulated (Oxford University Press)

Instead of surgically removing or damaging the brain, it can be stimulated, either *chemically* or, more commonly, *electrically*, using microelectrodes, whereby precise locations can be stimulated. Again, it's usually non-human animals that are involved (see Figure 4.6 and Chapter 9), but sometimes patients already undergoing surgery for a brain tumour or some other abnormality (such as epilepsy) are studied. Here, the neurosurgeon takes advantage of the fact that the patient is conscious, alert and able to report memories, sensations and so on produced by the stimulation. Penfield pioneered this kind of research in the 1950s (and through it discovered the 'Penfield homunculus': see Figure 4.9, page 53).

Microelectrodes are also used to record the electrical activity in individual neurons when the subject (usually a cat or monkey) is presented with various kinds of stimuli. This method was used by Hubel and Wiesel in the 1960s to study visual feature detectors (see Chapters 5 and 14).

Non-invasive methods

The electroencephalogram (EEG)

The electrical activity of the brain can also be recorded from the outside, by fitting electrodes (passive sensors) to the scalp. The activity can be traced on paper, and typical brainwave patterns associated with various states of arousal have been found. The EEG records action potentials for large groups of neurons, and has been used extensively in the study of states of consciousness, including sleep. Related to this is the *electromyogram* (EMG), which records the electrical activity of muscles, and the *electro-oculogram* (EOG), which records eye movements, both of which are, like the EEG, used in sleep research (see Chapter 7).

Average evoked potentials (AEPs)

A brief change in the EEG may be produced by the presentation of a single stimulus, but the effect may well be lost (or obscured) in the overall pattern of waves. However, if the stimulus is presented repeatedly and the results averaged by a computer, other waves cancel out and the evoked response can be detected. This technique has shown that an identical visual stimulus yields different AEPs depending on the *meaning* the participant attaches to it.

EEG imaging and the geodesic net

While the EEG involves a small number of electrodes, EEG *imaging* records the brain's electrical activity using 32 electrodes. This is fed to a computer, which translates it into coloured moving images on a TV monitor. While originally developed for investigating convulsive seizures, it's been adapted in the form of a *geodesic net* for studying brain development in babies. This consists of 64 or 132 electrodes, whose combined output produces a map of the active regions across the baby's head. The computer then calculates the likely brain areas that generated the voltages observed on the scalp. While the geodesic net is unlikely to rival the spatial accuracy of adult scanning methods (see below), its resolution over time is far superior, allowing the study of brain events 'at the speed of thought' (Johnson, 2000). One area of research that has made use of the geodesic net is infants' perception of faces (see Chapter 16).

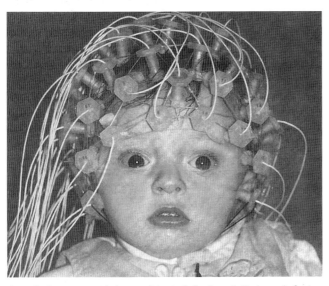

A geodesic sensor net being used to study brain activity in an infant

Radioactive labelling

This is a relatively recent method of studying the CNS, which takes advantage of the brain's flexible use of bloodborne oxygen. A radioactive isotope is added to the blood, causing low levels of radioactivity, which increase as greater blood flow occurs in more active areas of the brain. A scanner next to the head feeds radiation readings to a computer, which produces a coloured map of the most and least active brain regions: different regions change colour as the subject attempts a variety of tasks or is presented with a variety of stimuli.

Computerised axial tomography (CAT)

A moving X-ray beam takes pictures from different positions around the head, and these are converted by the computer into 'brain slices' (apparent cross-sections of the brain). CAT scanning is used primarily for the detection and diagnosis of brain injury and disease.

Positron emission tomography (PET)

This uses the same computer-calculation approach as CAT, but uses radiation for the information from which the brain slices are computed. A radioactive tracer is added to a substance used by the body (such as oxygen or glucose). As the marked substance is metabolised, PET shows the pattern of its use. For example, greater or less use of glucose could indicate a tumour, and changes are also revealed when the eyes are opened or closed. PET diagnoses brain abnormalities more efficiently than CAT.

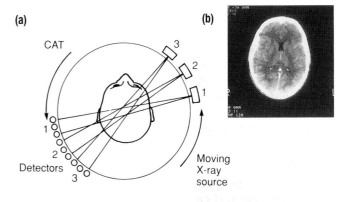

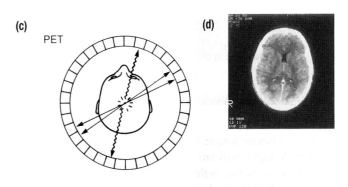

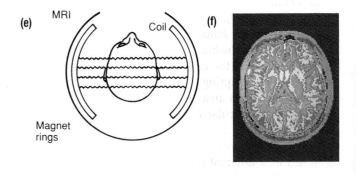

Figure 4.7 *Non-invasive techniques (a), (c) and (e) used to study detailed sections of the living human brain (b), (d) and (f)*

Magnetic resonance imaging (MRI)

This is like a CAT scan, but instead of using radiation, it passes an extremely strong magnetic field through the head and measures its effects on the rotation of atomic nuclei of some element in the body. Again, a computerised cross-sectional image is produced. So far only hydrogen nuclei have been used. Because hydrogen molecules are present in substantially different concentrations in different brain structures, the MRI can use the information to prepare pictures of brain slices which are much clearer (higher resolution) than CAT pictures.

Functional MRI (fMRI)

Despite the MRI's ability to identify the smallest tumour, or the slightest reduction in blood flow in a vein or artery, it shares with CAT the limitation of providing only *still* images of brain slices. This tells us very little about brain function. To remedy this, fMRI monitors blood flow in the brain over time as people perform different kinds of task, so it's used as much to study the normal as the damaged/diseased brain.

SPECT and SQUID

The most recent imaging techniques are *single-photon/positron emission computerised tomography* (SPECT), which, like PET, tracks blood flow through the brain, and *superconducting quantum imaging/interference device* (SQUID), which detects tiny changes in magnetic fields. Their main advantage is that they can focus on tiny areas of the brain. SPECT has revealed significant loss of functioning in the front part of the brain in patients with *Korsakoff's syndrome*, caused by prolonged and heavy use of alcohol (see Chapter 8).

An evaluation of scanning/imaging techniques: What they can and cannot tell us

Ask yourself ...

- What would you say are the main advantages of using scanning/imaging techniques compared with other methods?

Neuroscientists no longer have to rely on laboratory animals or brain-damaged patients requiring surgery to view what's happening inside the brain as it happens. We can now peer into a healthy living brain and observe the moment-to-moment changes that occur in relation to mental activity. But this *doesn't* mean that we can literally look inside someone's mind (see Chapter 49).

As we noted in the *Introduction and overview*, psychologists aren't interested in the brain for its own sake, but for what it can tell them about the control of psychological functions and abilities. It's tempting to infer that if damage to (or loss of) a particular brain area is associated with the loss of (or reduction in) a particular ability, then that part of the brain normally controls that ability. Unfortunately, there are other possibilities. For example, the damaged area might itself be controlled by a different (undamaged) area, or the damage may have disrupted the normal functioning of nearby, or related, intact areas. (See the discussion of split-brain patients below, pages 58–60.)

How does the brain develop?

One of the most remarkable things about the human brain is the staggering complexity of the *interconnections* between the neurons. Given that there are eight to ten billion neurons in the brain, each of which may have between 1000 and 10,000 synaptic connections with other neurons, it's been estimated that there are more possible ways in which the neurons of a single human brain can be interconnected than there are atoms in the known universe!

At birth, the baby has almost its full complement of neurons, and the brain is closer to its adult size than any other organ. It represents ten per cent of the baby's total body weight compared with two per cent of the adult's. At six months, the brain is already half its eventual adult weight; at twelve months, 60 per cent; at five years, 90 per cent, and at ten years 95 per cent. The brain reaches its maximum weight by about 20 years.

Box 4.5   Major aspects of infant brain development

While the major development *before* birth is the growth of neurons, brain growth *after* birth is the result of four major changes:

- The growth of *synaptic connections* between neighbouring neurons accounts for much of the increase in brain volume. However, there are also *regressive/subtractive events*, whereby the density of synapses increases until it's even greater than in adults (usually about 150 per cent of adult levels), followed by the death of many synapses. This reduces the overall number to those normally observed in adults. It seems that the less useful connections are 'pruned'. A similar pattern is found for complexity of dendrites and for measures of energy used by the brain (Johnson, 2000).
- Neurons *increase in size* (but not in number), as do synapses.
- *Glial cells* develop (see Box 4.1, page 44).
- The oligodendrocytes produce the *myelin sheaths*, which grow around the axons to insulate the neuron and speed up the conduction of action potentials (see text, page 46).

If the absolute size of brains determined level of intelligence, then humans would certainly be surpassed by many species, and even if we take brain size:body size ratio, house mice, porpoises, tree shrews and squirrel monkeys would still come higher in the intelligence league than ourselves. Clearly, it's the *kind* of brain that's important. What seems to be unique about the human brain is the proportion of it which isn't devoted to particular physical and psychological functions, and so which is 'free' to facilitate our intelligence, our general ability to think, reason, use language and learn.

The major structures and functions of the brain

As Figure 4.8 (page 52) shows, during the first five weeks of foetal life, the neural tube changes its shape to produce five bulbous enlargements which are generally accepted as the basic divisions of the brain. These are the *myelencephalon* (the medulla oblongata), the *metencephalon* (the pons and cerebellum), the *mesencephalon* (the tectum and tegmentum), the *diencephalon* (thalamus and hypothalamus) and the *telen-*

cephalon (the cerebral hemispheres or cerebrum, basal ganglia, and limbic system). 'Encephalon' means 'within the head'.

As shown in Figure 4.1, the myelencephalon and metencephalon together make up the *hindbrain*, the mesencephalon constitutes the *midbrain*, and the diencephalon and telencephalon make up the *forebrain*.

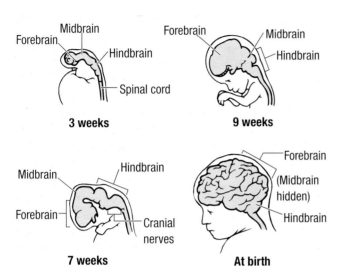

Figure 4.8 *The human brain at four stages of development*

The forebrain

The cerebral hemispheres (or cerebrum)

The cerebral hemispheres are the two largest structures at the top of the brain, which enfold (and, therefore, conceal from view) most other brain structures. If you were to remove an intact brain, its appearance would be dominated by the massive hemispheres, with just the cerebellum showing at the back.

The top layer of the cerebrum (about 1 cm at its deepest) is the *cerebral cortex* (usually just called 'cortex', which means 'bark'). It's highly wrinkled and convoluted (folded), which is necessary in order to pack its 2½ square foot surface area into the relatively small space inside the skull. The cortex is pinkish-grey in colour (hence 'grey matter'), but below it the cerebrum consists of much thicker white matter, composed of myelinated axons (the cortex consists of cell bodies).

There's a large crevice running along the cerebrum from front to back (the *longitudinal fissure/sulcus*), which divides the two hemispheres. But they're connected further down by a dense mass of commissurial ('joining') fibres, called the *corpus callosum* (or 'hard body').

There are two other natural dividing lines in each hemisphere: the *lateral fissure* (or *fissure of Sylvius*) and the *central fissure* (or *fissure of Rolando*). The lateral fissure separates the *temporal lobe* from the *frontal lobe* (anteriorly: towards the front) and from the *parietal lobe* (posteriorly: from the back), while the central fissure separates the frontal and parietal lobes. The *occipital lobe* is situated behind the parietal lobe and is at the back of the head. This division of the cortex into four lobes – named after the bones beneath which they lie – is a feature of *both* hemispheres, which are mirror-images of each other.

The *primary visual cortex* is found in the occipital lobe, the *primary auditory cortex* in the temporal lobe, the *primary somatosensory* (or *body-sense*) cortex in the parietal lobe, and the *primary motor cortex* in the frontal lobe (see Chapter 5). The somatosensory cortex and motor cortex are perhaps the most well-defined areas, both showing *contralateral control*: areas in the right hemisphere receive information from, and are concerned with the activities of, the left side of the body and vice versa. The crossing over (*corticospinal decussation*) takes place in the medulla (part of the brainstem). These areas represent the body in an upside-down fashion, so information from the feet, for example, is received by neurons at the top of the area.

Furthermore, the amount of cortex devoted to different parts of the body is related to their *sensitivity* and *importance* – *not* their size. So fingers, for example, have much more motor cortex devoted to them than the trunk, and the lips have a

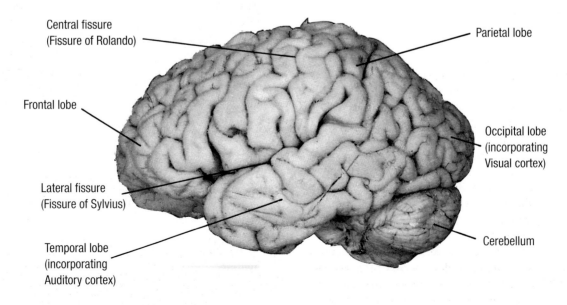

Lateral (side-on) view of the human brain (left cerebral hemisphere)

very large representation in the somatosensory cortex (see Figure 4.9). Broca's area is found in the frontal lobe and Wernicke's area borders the temporal and parietal lobes, but *only* in the left hemisphere. (We shall say more about this in the section on localisation and lateralisation of brain function: see pages 57–59.)

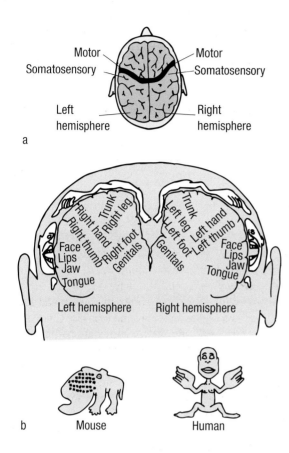

a

b   Mouse   Human

Figure 4.9 *Animunculi and homunculi showing how much cortical tissue is devoted to each body area. The mouse explores with its nose and each whisker has its own cortical area. We can use our hands for sensing, although we normally rely more on vision. The large face of the homunculus reflects the large cortical areas necessary for the control of speech. This is sometimes called the Penfield homunculus, after Wilder Penfield who discovered it*

The cortex and body image

The *homunculus* ('little man') in Figure 4.9 depicts how the body is represented by the brain. We each have a 'body image', which forms a fundamental part of our overall sense of ourselves as a stable, embodied 'self'. Usually, we just 'know' what our arms and legs are doing without having to look, they do what we 'ask' them to, and the 'body map' represented by the homunculus may appear to be 'hard-wired' into our brains. But our body image can become distorted, and when it does the disability it causes can be every bit as devastating as injuring the equivalent part of the body. If a stroke or accident damages the brain region housing the body map, patients may lose the use of perfectly healthy limbs – even though the brain areas that directly control movement remain intact (Phillips, 2000). Conversely, amputees can continue to experience their missing arms or legs as if they were still attached: this is the *phantom limb phenomenon*.

As Ramachandran & Blakeslee (1998) point out, the Penfield 'map' doesn't represent precisely the body's basic organisation. For example, the face isn't near the neck where it 'should be', but is below the hand. The genitals, instead of being between the thighs, are located *below the foot* (they cite the case of a female leg amputee, who had strange sensations in her phantom foot after sex!). This lack of a perfect match can help explain at least some cases of phantom limbs.

Box 4.6 **The case of the phantom hand**

Tom Sorenson lost a hand in car accident, after which his arm was amputated just above the elbow. When his *face* was touched in various places, he experienced sensations in his phantom thumb, index finger, little finger and so on. The whole surface of his hand was mapped out beautifully on his cheek. As Figure 4.10 shows, Tom also had a second 'map' of the missing hand, tucked into his left upper arm a few inches above the amputation line. Stroking the skin surface on this second map also produced precisely localised sensations on individual fingers.

How can we explain this apparently bizarre phenomenon? Ramachandron and Blakeslee believe the secret lies in the peculiar mapping of body parts in the brain. On the Penfield map, the hand area in the brain is flanked below by the face area and above by the upper arm/shoulder area. Sensory fibres originating from his face (which normally activate *only* the face area in the cortex) presumably invaded space left vacant by the amputated hand. The same must have happened with fibres originating in the upper arm/shoulder. The brain generated the feeling of the hand from the signals coming from another part of the body.

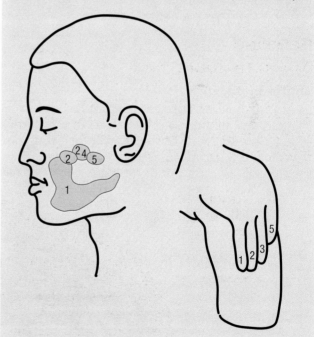

Figure 4.10 *Points on the body surface that produced referred sensations in the phantom hand (from Ramachandran & Blakeslee, 1998, reproduced with permission from HarperCollins Publishers Ltd)*

Ask yourself ...

- What conclusions can you draw from the case of Tom's phantom hand as to the potential for change in brain circuitry in adulthood?

According to Ramachandran and Blakeslee, cases such as Tom's contradict the widely held belief that once neurological circuitry is laid down in the foetus or early infancy, little modification is possible in adulthood. They argue that the phantom doesn't reside in the stump, but in the cortex, where the re-mapping has occurred. As they say:

'... every time Tom smiles or moves his face and lips, the impulses activate the 'hand' area of his cortex, creating the illusion that his hand is still there. Stimulated by all these spurious signals, Tom's brain literally hallucinates his arm and perhaps this is the essence of the phantom limb ...'.

Box 4.7 Demonstrating the flexibility of your brain's body image

Sit at a table and recruit a helper. Hide one hand under the table, resting palm down on your knee. Then ask your helper to tap, touch and stroke with his/her fingertips the back of your hidden hand and the table top directly above the hand with an identical pattern of movements, for a minute or two.

It's important to concentrate on the table, where your helper is touching, and to make sure you can't see your hand or your helper's hand under the table. The more irregular the pattern, and the more synchronised the touches you can see and feel, the more likely you are to feel something very strange. The table starts to feel like part of your body – as though the hand is transferred into the table!

According to Ramachandran and Blakeslee, just as an amputee might experience a phantom limb, so our entire body image is a phantom, something the brain constructs for convenience.

(Based on Phillips, 2000)

Can the brain repair itself?

If Ramachandran and Blakeslee's explanation of phantom limbs is correct, then the adult brain seems capable of compensating for damage or loss quite well, by making new connections between *existing* neurons. However, this is very different from the claim that the brain can *repair* itself (i.e.

produce new neurons to replace damaged ones). Until very recently, most neurobiologists firmly believed that the brain lacks the remarkable *stem cells*, which account for much of the repair involved in skin, bone and other body cells. However, Kempermann & Gage (1999) cite research showing that the mature human brain *does* produce new neurons in at least one site – the hippocampus (see below, page 56). According to Kempermann and Gage:

'Current data suggest that ... the adult brain, which repairs itself so poorly, might actually harbour great potential for neuronal regeneration ...'.

If we can learn how to induce existing stem cells to produce useful numbers of functioning neurons in selected brain regions, the practical benefits for people suffering from Alzheimer's and Parkinson's disease, and disabilities caused by strokes and trauma, would be enormous (Kempermann & Gage, 1999).

Association areas in the cortex

The primary motor and sensory areas account for only about 25 per cent of the cortex's surface area, leaving about 75 per cent without an obvious sensory or motor function. This *association cortex* is where the 'higher mental functions' (cognitive processes, such as thinking, reasoning, planning, and deciding) probably 'occur'. However, much less is known about where these functions are localised, compared with certain aspects of memory, perception, and language.

What's clear is that the cortex isn't necessary for biological survival (which is controlled by various *subcortical* structures). Some species (birds, for example) don't have a cortex to begin with, and in those that do, surgical removal doesn't prevent an animal from displaying a wide range of behaviour (although it becomes much more automatic and stereotyped). The human brain has a greater proportion of association cortex than any other species.

The thalamus ('deep chamber')

There are actually two thalami, situated deep in the forebrain (between the brainstem and the cerebral hemispheres). Each is an egg-shaped mass of grey matter, representing a crucial link between the cerebrum and the sense organs. All sensory

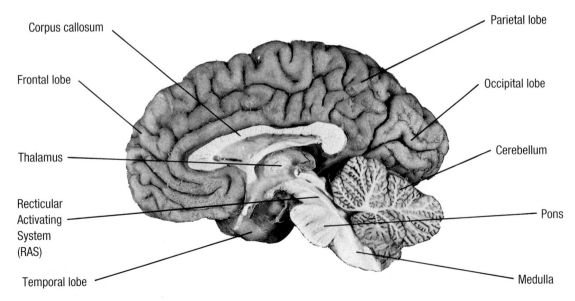

Front-to-back cross-section of the right cerebral hemisphere

signals pass through the thalami, which serve as a relay station or major integrator of information flowing in from the sense organs to the cortex. Each contains nuclei which are specialised to handle particular types of signal:

- the *ventrobasal complex*, which takes information fed in from the body via the spinal cord;
- the *lateral geniculate* ('bent') *body* (LGB), which processes visual information (see Chapter 5);
- the *medial geniculate body* (MGB), which processes auditory information.

The thalamus also receives information from the cortex, mainly dealing with complex limb movements, which are directed to the cerebellum. Another part of the thalamus plays a part in sleep and waking (see Chapter 7).

> ### Ask yourself ...
> - What role does the thalamus play in theories of emotion? (See Chapter 10, pages 134–141.)

The hypothalamus ('under the thalamus')

For its size (about equal to the tip of your index finger), the hypothalamus is a remarkable and extremely important part of the brain. It plays a major part in homoeostasis (control of the body's internal environment) and motivation, including eating and drinking (see Chapter 9), sexual behaviour, emotional arousal, and stress (see Chapter 12). Seven areas can be identified, each with its own special function: *posterior* (sex drive), *anterior* (water balance), *supraoptic* (also water balance), *presupraoptic* (heat control), *ventromedial* (hunger), *dorsomedial* (aggression), and *dorsal* (pleasure).

The hypothalamus works basically in two ways:

- by sending electrochemical signals to the entire ANS (see Figure 4.1), so that it represents a major link between the CNS and the ANS;
- by influencing the *pituitary gland*, to which it's connected by a network of blood vessels and neurons.

The pituitary gland is situated in the brain, just below and to one side of the hypothalamus. However, it's actually part of the endocrine (hormonal) system (see pages 61–62).

Basal ganglia ('nerve knots')

These are embedded in the mass of white matter of each cerebral hemisphere. They are themselves small areas of grey matter, comprising a number of smaller structures:

- the *corpus striatum* ('striped body'), composed of the *lentiform nucleus* and *caudate nucleus*;
- the *amygdala* ('almond');
- the *substantia nigra* (which is also part of the tegmentum, usually classified as part of the midbrain).

These structures are closely linked to the thalami, and they seem to play a part in muscle tone and posture by integrating and co-ordinating the main voluntary muscle movements, which are the concern of the great descending motor pathway (the pyramidal system). Information from the cortex is relayed to the brainstem and cerebellum.

The limbic system ('bordering')

This isn't a separate structure, but comprises a number of highly inter-related structures which, when seen from the side, seem to nest inside each other, encircling the brainstem in a 'wishbone' (see Figure 4.11). The major structures are: (i) the thalami bodies; (ii) hypothalamus; (iii) mamillary bodies;

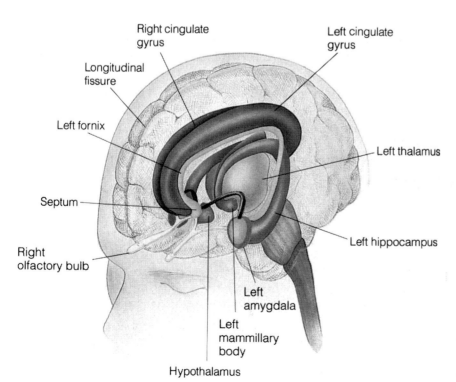

Figure 4.11 *The major structures of the limbic system: the thalami bodies, the hypothalamus, the mammillary bodies, the hippocampus, the amygdala, the septum, the fornix and the cingulate gyrus. Also illustrated are the olfactory bulbs, which are connected to several limbic structures (from J. Pine, 1993,* Biopsychology, *Boston, Allyn & Bacon)*

(iv) septum pellucidum; (v) cingulate gyrus; (vi) hippocampus; (vii) amygdala; (viii) fornix; and (ix) olfactory bulbs.

The human limbic system is very similar to that of primitive mammals, and so is often called 'the old mammalian brain'. It's also sometimes called the 'nose brain', because much of its development seems to have been related to the olfactory sense. It's closely involved with behaviours which satisfy certain motivational and emotional needs, including feeding, fighting, escape and mating.

The limbic system as a whole serves as a meeting place between the cortex (or 'neocortex', in evolutionary terms the most recent part of the brain to have developed), and older parts of the brain, such as the hypothalamus. From the cortex it receives interpreted information about the world, and from the hypothalamus information about the body's internal state. These are integrated, and the 'conclusions' are fed back to the cortex and to the older, subcortical areas.

The midbrain

This is really an extension of the brainstem, connecting the forebrain to the spinal cord. The main structure is the *reticular activating system* (RAS) or *reticular formation* (RF), which ascends from the spinal cord to the forebrain carrying mainly sensory information (the ascending reticular activating system/ARAS) and descends from the forebrain to the spinal cord carrying mainly motor information. Since it begins in the spinal cord and passes through the brainstem, it's often classified as part of the hindbrain in addition to the midbrain.

> **Box 4.8 Major functions of the ARAS**
>
> The ARAS is vitally important in maintaining our general level of arousal or alertness (the *consciousness switch*), and plays an important part (but by no means the only one) in the sleep–wake cycle (see Chapter 7). It also plays a part in selective attention (see Chapter 13). Although it responds unselectively to all kinds of stimulation, it helps to screen extraneous sensory information by, for example, controlling *habituation* to constant sources of stimulation, and making us alert and responsive mainly to *changes* in stimulation. Sleeping parents who keep 'one ear open' for the baby who might start to cry are relying on their ARAS to let only very important sensory signals through, so it acts as a kind of sentry for the cortex. Damage can induce a coma-like state of sleep.

The midbrain also contains important centres for visual and auditory reflexes, including the *orienting reflex*, a general response to a novel stimulus. Other structures include the *locus coeruleus* (see Chapter 7), the raphe nuclei, the tectum, and the tegmentum.

The hindbrain

Cerebellum ('little brain')

Like the cerebrum, the cerebellum consists of two halves or hemispheres, and is even more convoluted than the cortex. It plays a vital role in the co-ordination of voluntary (skeletal) muscle activity, balance and fine movements (such as reaching for things). Motor commands which originate in higher

brain centres are processed here before transmission to the muscles. Damage to the cerebellum can cause hand tremors, drunken movements and loss of balance. An impaired inability to reach for objects (*ataxia*) and hand tremors are quite common amongst the elderly.

The cerebellum also controls the intricate movements involved in playing a musical instrument or driving a car. Once learned, complex movements like those involved in picking up a glass, walking and talking seem to be 'programmed' into the cerebellum, so that we can do them 'automatically' without having to think consciously about what we're doing.

The cerebellum accounts for about eleven per cent of the brain's entire weight, and only the cerebrum is larger. Its grey matter consists of three layers of cells, the middle layer of which – the Purkinje cells – can link each synapse with up to 100,000 other neurons, more than any other kind of brain cell.

The pons ('bridge')

This is a bulge of white matter which connects the two halves of the cerebellum. It's an important connection between the midbrain and the medulla, and is vital in integrating the movements of the two sides of the body. Four of the twelve cranial nerves (which originate in the brain) have their nuclei ('relay stations') here, including the large trigeminal nerve. It's the middle portion of the brainstem.

The medulla oblongata ('rather long marrow')

This is a fibrous section of the lower brainstem (about 2 cm long), and is really a thick extension of the spinal cord. In evolutionary terms, it's the oldest part of the brain, and it's where the major nerve tracts coming up from the spinal cord and coming down from the brain cross over. It contains vital reflex centres, which control breathing, cardiac function, swallowing, vomiting, coughing, chewing, salivation and facial movements. The midbrain, pons and medulla together make up the *brainstem*.

The spinal cord

About the thickness of a little finger, the spinal cord passes from the brainstem down the whole length of the back and is encased in the vertebrae of the spine. The spinal cord is the main communication 'cable' between the brain (CNS) and the peripheral nervous system (PNS), providing the pathway between body and brain.

Messages enter and leave the spinal cord by means of 31 pairs of spinal nerves. Each pair innervates a different and fairly specific part of the body, containing both *motor neurons* (carrying information from the NS to the muscles) and *sensory neurons* (carrying information from the sensory receptors to the NS) for most of their length. But at the junction with the cord itself, the nerves divide into two roots – the *dorsal root* (towards the back of the body), which contains sensory neurons, and the *ventral root* (towards the front of the body), which contains motor neurons.

The basic functional unit of the NS is the *spinal reflex arc*, such as the knee-jerk reflex. This involves just two kinds of neurons: a sensory neuron conveys information about stimulation of the patella tendon (knee cap) to the spinal cord, and this information crosses a single synapse within the grey

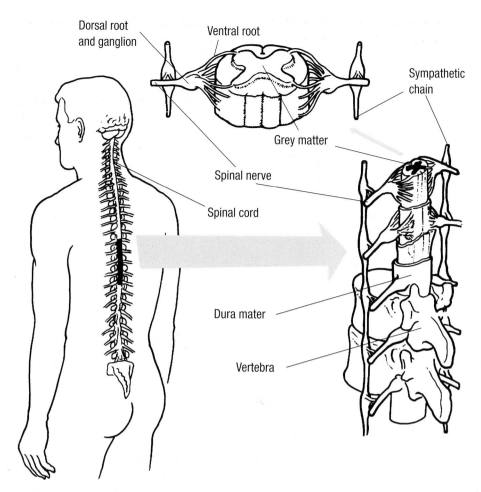

Dorsal root and ganglion

Ventral root

Sympathetic chain

Grey matter

Spinal nerve

Spinal cord

Dura mater

Vertebra

Figure 4.12 *The spinal cord and spinal nerves (from Rosenzweig & Leiman, 1989). The left diagram shows a general view of the spinal column with a pair of nerves emerging from each level. The right diagram shows how the spinal cord is surrounded by bony vertebra and enclosed in a membrane, the dura mater. Each vertebra has an opening on each side through which the spinal nerves pass. The top diagram shows the location of the spinal cord grey matter and the white matter that surrounds it. In the grey matter are interneurons and the motor neurons that send axons to the muscles. The white matter consists of myelinated axons that run up and down the spinal column*

'butterfly' (which runs inside the centre of the cord). This causes a motor neuron to stimulate the appropriate muscle groups in the leg, which causes the leg to shoot up in the air.

However, most spinal reflexes are more complex than this. For example, withdrawing your hand from a hot plate will involve an interneuron (as well as a sensory and motor neuron) and two synapses. Commonly, the experience of pain follows one to two seconds after you've withdrawn your hand – this is how long it takes for sensory information to reach the cortex.

The localisation and lateralisation of brain function

Ask yourself ...

• What do you understand by these two terms? How are they different?

When describing the cortex earlier (see pages 52–54), we saw that different functions, such as vision, hearing, movement, and sensation are *located* in different lobes (occipital, temporal, parietal, and frontal respectively). Remember also that all four lobes are found in both cerebral hemispheres, so, in this respect, the hemispheres can be regarded as mirror-images of each other. We also noted that there are distinct areas dealing with speech production and comprehension (Broca's area and

Wernicke's area, respectively), again illustrating *functional localisation*. However, these are found *only* in the left hemisphere, illustrating *functional lateralisation* (or *hemispheric asymmetry*).

Lateralisation, language and handedness

Much of the discussion of lateralisation has focused on language. From studies of stroke victims in particular, it's generally agreed that for the majority of right-handed people, the left hemisphere is dominant for speech (and language ability in general). People paralysed down their *right* side must have suffered damage to the *left* hemisphere and, if they've also suffered aphasia (see page 48), then we can infer that language is normally controlled by the *left* hemisphere.

One of the difficulties associated with generalisations in psychology (even with something as 'biological' as cerebral function) is the existence of *individual differences*. Some people seem to have much more lateralised brains than others, while others have language more or less equally represented on *both* sides (*bilateral representation*: Beaumont, 1988). The left hemisphere seems to be dominant for language for 95 per cent of right-handed patients, while only five per cent had their right hemispheres dominant. But with left-handers, things are much less clear-cut: 75 per cent had their left hemispheres dominant, none had the right dominant, but 25 per cent showed bilateral representation (based on a review by Satz, (1979), of all studies between 1935 and 1975; cited in Beaumont, 1988).

Are women really superior when it comes to language?

Over and above this left–right-handed difference, women show *less lateralisation* than men for both linguistic and other abilities. This means that left hemisphere damage would produce greater deficits in language ability for men (at least, most right-handed men) than it would in (most right-handed) women. This difference is thought to underlie females' advantage over males on a variety of linguistic tasks, from detection of dichotic syllables (where different auditory signals are presented to the two ears) to the generation of synonyms.

However, neuro-imaging studies using fMRI (see page 51) have shown that men and women can perform identical language processes with the same degree of functional capacity but, apparently, using very differently organised brain systems. One attempt to replicate these findings (Frost *et al.*, 1999) found that both sexes showed very similar, strongly left-lateralised activation patterns. Although sex differences may exist at a microscopic neural level, these aren't detectable using currently available fMRI methods.

(Based on Esgate, 1999)

The effects of brain damage: Is it 'where' or 'how much' that matters?

According to Zaidel (1978), the two hemispheres are fairly equal up until about age five. In general, a child's brain is much more *plastic* (flexible) than an adult's (Rose, 1976). For example, in children up to three years old, brain trauma produces similar effects regardless of which site is damaged. Provided the lesion isn't too severe, or that it occurs on one side only, considerable recovery is possible: the corresponding area on the other side takes over the function of the damaged area, and this seems to be especially true of language (see Chapter 19).

This seems to support the conclusions of Lashley, who (in the 1920s) studied the effects of brain destruction on rats' learning ability. His *law of mass action* (1929) states that the learning of difficult problems depends upon the *amount of damage* to the cortex, and not on the position or site of the damage. In other words, the greater the cortical damage, the greater the learning difficulty. However, Lashley couldn't find specific neural circuits related to the learning of, or memory for, particular types of problem. The *law of equipotentiality* states that corresponding parts of the brain are capable of taking over the function normally performed by the damaged area.

Similarly, the *principle of multiple control* maintains that any particular part of the brain is likely to be involved in the performance of many different types of behaviour. For example, rats with lesions to the lateral hypothalamus show deficits in certain learning situations, as well as impaired feeding (see Chapter 9). Conversely, the same behaviour (such as aggression or emotion) normally involves a number of brain sites, and the logical conclusion of this seems to be that the brain functions as a complete unit, an integrated whole. We shall return to this issue below.

Split-brain patients

Remember that split-brain patients have undergone surgery to cut the corpus callosum. While the surgery may relieve epilepsy, it has a major side-effect: the two hemispheres become functionally separate (they act as two separate, independent brains). Sperry (based on a number of studies in the 1960s and 1970s, for which he was awarded the Nobel Prize for Medicine in 1981) and Ornstein (1975) believe that split-brain studies reveal the 'true' nature of the two hemispheres, and that each embodies a different kind of consciousness (see Chapter 7). A typical split-brain experiment is described in Key Study 4.1.

KEY STUDY 4.1

When the left brain literally doesn't know what the left hand is doing (Sperry, 1968)

Participants sit in front of a screen, their hands free to handle objects behind the screen, but which are obscured from sight. While fixating on a spot in the middle of the screen, a word (for example, 'key') is flashed onto the *left* side of the screen for a tenth of a second (this ensures that the word is 'seen' only by the *right* hemisphere).

If asked to select the key from a pile of objects with the *left* hand (still controlled by the *right* hemisphere), this can be done quite easily. However, the participant is unable to *say* what word appeared on the screen (because the left hemisphere doesn't receive the information from the right as it normally would), and literally doesn't know why s/he chose the key.

Next, a word (for example, 'heart') is flashed on the screen, with 'he' to the left and 'art' to the right of the fixation point. If asked to name the word, participants will say 'art', because this is the portion of the word projected to the *left* hemisphere. However, when asked to *point with the left hand* to one of two cards on which 'he' and 'art' are written, the left hand will point to 'he', because this is the portion projected to the *right* hemisphere.

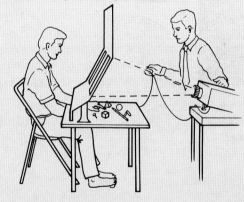

Figure 4.13 *Apparatus for studying lateralisation of visual, tactile, lingual and associated functions in the surgically separated hemispheres (from Sperry, 1968)*

Ask yourself ...

- What do these examples suggest regarding the right hemisphere's linguistic abilities?

These examples show that the right hemisphere isn't completely without language ability – otherwise participants couldn't successfully point or select. However, it clearly lacks the left hemisphere's ability to name and articulate what's been experienced. In the second example, both hemispheres are handicapped if information isn't conveyed from one to the other: the whole word ('heart') isn't perceived by either!

A similar but perhaps more dramatic example involved sets of photographs of different faces. Each photo was cut down the middle, and the halves of two different faces were pasted together. They were then presented in such a way that the left side of the photo would be visible only to the right hemisphere and vice versa.

Ask yourself ...

- If a picture of an old man were presented to the right and a young boy to the left, and participants were asked to *describe what they'd seen* (the *left hemisphere* responding), what would they have said?
- If asked to *point with their left hands* to the complete photo of the person they'd seen (the *right hemisphere* responding), which picture would they have pointed to?

In the first case, they said 'an old man', and in the second case, they pointed to the young boy. It seems that two completely separate visual worlds can exist within the same head!

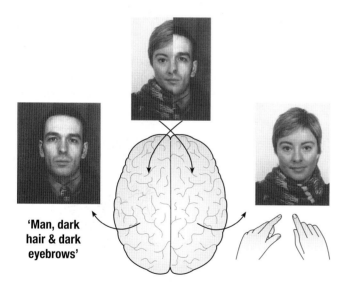

'Man, dark hair & dark eyebrows'

Figure 4.14 *Responses given by the left and right hemispheres to a chimeric*

One brain or two? One mind or two?

These and many more, equally dramatic experiments led Sperry, Ornstein and others to conclude that each of the separated hemispheres has its own private sensations, perceptions, thoughts, feelings and memories. In short, they constitute two separate minds, two separate spheres of consciousness (Sperry, 1964: see Figure 4.15). Levy-Agresti & Sperry (1968) concluded that the:

'... *mute, minor hemisphere is specialised for Gestalt perception, being primarily a synthesist in dealing with*

information input. The speaking, major hemisphere, in contrast, seems to operate in a more logical, analytic, computer-like fashion ...'.

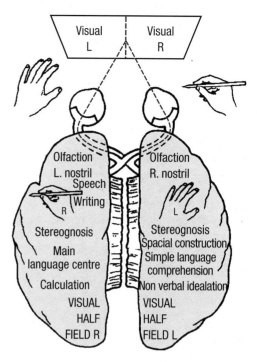

Figure 4.15 *Schematic outline of the functional lateralisation evident in behavioural tests of patients with forebrain commissurotomy (from Sperry, 1968)*

> **Box 4.10** **The major differences between the left and right hemispheres**
>
> Ornstein (1986) summarises the differences like this:
>
> - The *left* is specialised for *analytic and logical thinking* (breaking things down into their component parts), especially in verbal and mathematical functions, processes information *sequentially* (one item at a time), and its mode of operation is primarily *linear* (straight line).
> - The *right* is specialised for *synthetic thinking* (bringing different things together to form a whole), particularly in the area of spatial tasks, artistic activities, crafts, body image and face recognition, processes information more *diffusely* (several items at once), and its mode of operation is much *less linear* (more *holistic*).

Ask yourself ...

- Should we generalise about hemispheric differences from studies of split-brain patients?

Cohen (1975) argues that long-standing presurgical pathology might have caused an abnormal reorganisation of the brains of these split-brain patients, so that generalising to normal people might not be valid. Several attempts have been made to move beyond the simplistic left hemisphere–right hemisphere, verbal–non-verbal distinction, both in normal participants and in split-brain patients. In a review of research, Annett (1991) says that ' ... it is evident that each hemisphere has some role in the functions assigned to the other'. For example, the right hemisphere has a considerable understanding of language (see above), and it's been suggested that it might be responsible for semantic errors made by deep dyslexics (see Chapter 40). Similarly, the left hemisphere is almost certainly responsible for the production of imagery, 'which is likely to be required in much spatial thinking'.

According to Gazzaniga (1985), the brain is organised in a *modular fashion*; that is, relatively independent functioning units, which work in parallel. Many of the modules operate at a non-conscious level, in parallel to our conscious thought, with the left hemisphere interpreting the processing of these modules. So, brains are organised such that many mental systems coexist in a 'confederation'.

Sternberg (1990) believes that Gazzaniga's view isn't widely accepted by neuropsychologists, but many would also reject the degree of separation between the hemispheres suggested by Sperry and his co-workers. An alternative view is one of *integration*: the two hemispheres should be seen as playing different parts in an integrated performance (Broadbent, 1985, cited in Sternberg, 1990). Cohen (1975) agrees that, when normal participants are studied, the two sides of the brain don't function in isolation but form a highly integrated system. Most everyday tasks involve a mixture of 'left' and 'right' skills. For example, in listening to speech, we analyse both the words and the intonation pattern. Far from doing their own things, the two hemispheres work very much together (Cohen, 1975).

McCrone (1999) concludes that researchers have come to see the distinction between the two hemispheres as a subtle one of processing style, with every mental faculty shared across the brain, and each side contributing in a complementary, not exclusive, fashion. Evidence from imaging studies suggests that the left hemisphere 'prefers' (or pays more attention to) detail (such as grammar and specific word production), while the right prefers the overall meaning of what's being said (as conveyed by intonation and emphasis). This is consistent with the finding that people with right hemisphere stroke damage become much more literal in their interpretation of language. However, a 'smart' brain is one that responds in both ways. As McCrone says:

> '... whatever the story about lateralisation, simple dichotomies are out. It is how the two sides of the brain complement and combine that counts'.

The autonomic nervous system (ANS)

As shown in Figure 4.1; the ANS is the part of the PNS, which controls the internal organs and glands of the body over which we have little (or no) voluntary control. It comprises two branches:

- the *sympathetic*, which takes over whenever the body needs to use its energy (as in emergencies: the 'fight or flight' syndrome), and
- the *parasympathetic*, which is dominant when the body is at 'rest' and energy is being built up.

Table 4.2 *Major sympathetic and parasympathetic reactions*

	Organ or function affected	Sympathetic reaction	Parasympathetic reaction
1	Heart rate	Increase	Decrease
2	Blood pressure	Increase	Decrease
3	Secretion of saliva	Suppressed (mouth feels dry)	Stimulated
4	Pupils	Dilate (to aid vision)	Contract
5	Limbs (and trunk)	Dilation of blood vessels of the voluntary muscles (to help us run faster, for example)	Contraction of these blood vessels
6	Peristalsis (contraction of stomach and intestines)	Slows down (you don't feel hungry in an emergency)	Speeds up
7	Galvanic skin response (GSR) (measure of the electrical resistance of the skin)	Decreases (due to increased sweating associated with increased anxiety)	Increases
8	Bladder muscles	Relaxed (there may be temporary loss of bladder control)	Contracted
9	Adrenal glands	Stimulated to secrete more adrenaline and noradrenaline	Reduced secretion
10	Breathing rate	Increased (through dilation of bronchi)	Decreased
11	Liver	Glucose (stored as glycogen) is released into the blood to increase energy	Sugar is stored
12	Emotion	Experience of strong emotion	Less extreme emotions

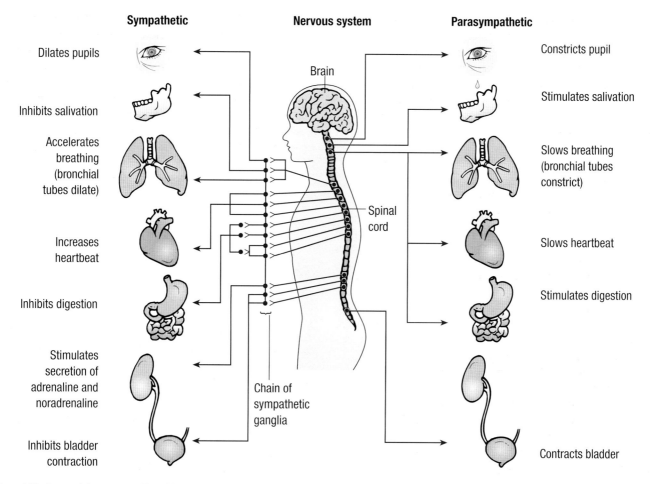

Figure 4.16 *Some of the organs affected by the two branches of the ANS (from Hassett & White, 1989)*

Although the two branches work in essentially opposite ways, they're both equally necessary for *homoeostasis* (see Chapter 9). Sometimes, a sequence of sympathetic and parasympathetic activity is required. For example, in sexual arousal in men, erection is primarily parasympathetic while ejaculation is primarily sympathetic. The ANS produces its effects in two ways:

- by direct neural stimulation of body organs;
- by stimulating the release of hormones from the endocrine glands (see below).

In both cases, the *hypothalamus* is the orchestrator. The ANS will be discussed further in Chapter 10 in relation to emotion and Chapter 12 in relation to stress.

The endocrine system

Endocrine glands secrete *hormones* (chemical messengers) which, unlike neurotransmitters, are released directly into the bloodstream and are carried throughout the body. While an electrochemical impulse can convey a message in a matter of milliseconds, it may take several seconds for a hormone to be stimulated, released, and reach its destination. Consequently, where an immediate behavioural reaction is required (for example, a reflex action), the NS plays a major role. Hormones are better suited to communicating steady,

relatively unchanging messages over prolonged periods of time (for example, the body changes associated with puberty: see Chapter 37).

> **Box 4.11   The pituitary gland**
>
> The major endocrine gland is the *pituitary gland*, which is physically (but not functionally) part of the brain (situated just below the hypothalamus). It's often called the 'master gland', because it produces the largest number of different hormones, and also because it controls the secretion of several other endocrine glands. The pituitary comprises two independently functioning parts, the *posterior* and the *anterior*. The former transmits hormones which are thought to be manufactured in the hypothalamus, while the latter is stimulated by the hypothalamus to produce its own hormones. The major hormones of the posterior and anterior lobes of the pituitary are shown, with their effects, in Table 4.3, page 62.

Other important endocrine glands are the *adrenals* (situated just above the kidneys), each of which comprises the *adrenal medulla* (inner core) and the *adrenal cortex* (outer layer). As Table 4.3 shows, the medulla secretes *adrenaline* and *noradrenaline*, which are the transmitter substances for the sympathetic branch of the ANS.

Table 4.3 *Major pituitary hormones and their effects*

Hormone	Endocrine gland or organ stimulated	Effects
Growth hormone (somatotrophin)	Body tissues	Increases growth of bones and muscles, particularly in childhood and adolescence. Too little produces pituitary dwarfism and too much gigantism
Gonadotrophic hormones **1 Luteinising hormone (LH)**	Gonads (Testes–male, Ovaries–female)	Development of sex (germ) cells: Ova (female), Sperm (male). Production of sex hormones: Oestrogen and progesterone (female), Testosterone (male)
2 Follicle-stimulating hormone (FSH)	Ovaries	Production of follicles in ovary during ovulation
Thyrotrophic hormone (TTH)	Thyroid gland	Secretion of thyroxin which controls metabolic rate – too little causes lethargy and depression, too much causes hyperactivity and anxiety
Lactogenic hormone (Prolactin)	Breasts	Milk production during pregnancy
Adrenocorticotrophic hormone (ACTH)	Adrenal glands **1** Adrenal medulla **2** Adrenal cortex	Secretion of adrenaline and noradrenaline. Secretion of adrenocorticoid hormones (or corticosteroids), e.g. cortisol and hydrocortisone (important in coping with stress) (see Chapter 12)
Oxytocin	Uterus (womb)	Causes contractions during labour and milk release during breast feeding
Vasopressin (also a neurotransmitter)	Blood vessels	Causes contraction of the muscle in the walls of the blood vessels and so raises blood pressure
Antidiuretic hormone (ADH)	Kidneys	Regulates the amount of water passed in the urine

Anterior pituitary (Growth hormone through Adrenocorticotrophic hormone)

Posterior pituitary (Oxytocin through Antidiuretic hormone)

Other endocrine glands include:

(a) Thymus – situated in the chest; functions unknown, but thought to involve production of antibodies (see Chapter 12)

(b) Pancreas – secretes insulin (anti-diabetic hormone), given in the treatment of diabetes. Controls the body's ability to absorb glucose and fats

(c) Pineal body/gland – situated near corpus callosum, functions unknown but may play a role in sleep–waking cycle (see Chapter 7)

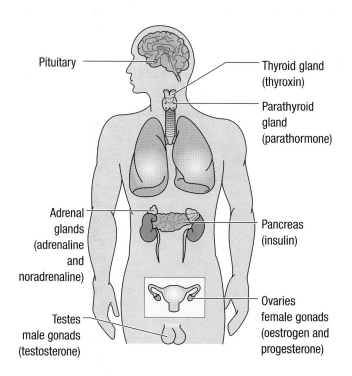

Figure 4.17 *Some major glands of the endocrine system and the hormones they produce*

CHAPTER SUMMARY

- **Biopsychology** is the branch of neuroscience that studies the biological bases of behaviour. Biopsychologists are interested in biology only for what it can tell them about behaviour and mental processes.

- The **nervous system** (NS) comprises ten to twelve billion **neurons**, 80 per cent of which are found in the brain, mainly in the cerebral cortex. There are ten times as many **glial cells**. Neurons are either **sensory/afferent**, **motor/efferent** or **interneurons/connector**.

- A **nerve** is a bundle of **elongated axons**. Twelve pairs of **cranial nerves** leave the brain through holes in the skull, while 31 pairs of **spinal nerves** leave the spinal cord through the vertebrae. Together, they constitute the nerves of the **peripheral nervous system** (PNS).

- When an **electrochemical signal/action potential** occurs, the inside of the neuron momentarily changes from negative to positive. The **resting potential** is almost immediately restored. Once the **threshold of response** has been exceeded, action potentials travel according to the **all-or-none rule**.

- **Synapses** are either **excitatory** or **inhibitory**, depending on the particular **neurotransmitter** contained within the **synaptic button**. Whether or not a particular neuron will fire depends on the combined effect of all its receiving synapses (**summation**). Once the transmitter molecules have crossed into the **postsynaptic membrane**, their effect is ended either by **deactivation** or **reuptake**.

- **Neuromodulators** 'prime' receiving neurons for later stimulation by neurotransmitters. Neuromodulators include **neuropeptides**, in particular the enkephalins and endorphins.

- **Clinical/anatomical methods** of studying the brain involve patients who've suffered accidental brain damage or disease, or **split-brain patients**.

- **Invasive methods** involve **ablation**, **stimulating** the brain (either electrically or chemically), and **microelectrode recording**.

- **Non-invasive methods** include the **electroencephalogram** (EEG), **electromyogram** (EMG), **electro-oculogram** (EOG) and **average evoked potentials** (AEPs).

- Computers are also used in a number of **scanning/imaging devices**. These include **computerised axial tomography** (CAT), **positron emission tomography** (PET), **magnetic resonance imaging** (MRI), **single-photon/positron emission computerised tomography** (SPECT) and **superconducting quantum imaging/interference device** (SQUID). These techniques provide access to processes associated with mental activity inside the healthy living brain as they happen.

- The **cerebral hemispheres/cerebrum** enfold and conceal most other brain structures. The top layer is the highly convoluted **cortex**. Each hemisphere is naturally divided into the **occipital lobe** (which houses the **visual cortex**), the **temporal lobe** (**auditory cortex**), the **parietal lobe** (**somatosensory/body-sense cortex**) and the **frontal lobe** (**motor cortex**).

- Highly sensitive parts of the body, and those over which we have precise motor control have much more cortex devoted to them than other parts. The whole body is represented on the surface of the cortex as a 'body map' (**homunculus**).
- The cerebral hemispheres are part of the **forebrain**, together with the **thalamus**, **hypothalamus**, **basal ganglia**, and the **limbic system**.
- The **midbrain** is an extension of the brainstem and connects the forebrain to the spinal cord. The **reticular activating system** (RAS) begins in the spinal cord and passes through the brainstem.
- The **hindbrain** consists of the **medulla oblongata**, the **pons**, and the **cerebellum**.
- The **spinal cord** is encased in the vertebrae and is the main communication cable between the CNS and the PNS. Messages enter and leave via 31 pairs of **spinal nerves**.
- There's considerable evidence for both **functional localisation** and **lateralisation**. The left hemisphere is dominant for language in most right-handed people, but some people seem to have much more lateralised brains than others, while others display bilateral representation.
- Children's brains show considerable **plasticity**, which supports Lashley's **laws of mass action** and **equipotentiality**. The **phantom limb** phenomenon suggests that the adult brain is also very malleable, and neurons may be capable of regeneration.
- The findings from **split-brain studies** have led to the view that each hemisphere constitutes a separate sphere of consciousness. An alternative interpretation is that the brain is organised in the form of **modules**, which work in parallel. A third view is that the two hemispheres differ in their **processing styles**, yet represent a highly **integrated** system.
- The **autonomic nervous system** (ANS) comprises the **sympathetic** and **parasympathetic branches**. It works either by direct neural stimulation of body organs, or by stimulating the release of hormones from the **endocrine system**.
- The **pituitary gland** produces the largest number of different hormones and controls the secretion of several other endocrine glands, such as the **adrenal glands**.

Self-assessment questions

1 Discuss how information is passed between neurons.
2 Discuss any **two** methods used to investigate the brain.
3 Describe and evaluate research into the lateralisation of function in the cerebral cortex.
4 Critically assess the claim that the two cerebral hemispheres constitute two minds.

Web addresses

httpp:/www.hhmi.org/sense/e/e110.htm

http:/www.brain.com/

http:/www.maclestr.edu/~psych/whathap/UBNRP/Imaging/pet/html

http:/www-hbp.scripps.edu/

http:/www.nmi.mcgill.ca./

http:/www.lsacd.org.uk/index.html [While these are genuine addresses, I'm unsure at the moment how many to include]

Further reading

Pinel, J.P.J. (1993) *Biopsychology* (2nd edition). Boston: Allyn and Bacon. An excellent, detailed, but very readable text, with excellent illustrations.

Ramachandran, V.S. & Blakeslee, S. (1998) *Phantoms in the Brain*. London: Fourth Estate. A highly readable, at times very funny, and extremely informative account of some of the relationships between mind and brain. Full of fascinating case studies.

Chapter 5

Sensory Processes

Introduction and overview

When we move our eyes or our heads, the objects we see around us remain stable. Similarly, when we follow a moving object, we attribute the movement to the object and not to ourselves. When we walk towards people in the street, we don't experience them as gradually growing 'before our eyes', and we recognise objects seen from various angles.

These examples of how we experience the world may seem mundane and obvious, until we realise what's actually taking place physically. If we compare what we experience (a world of objects that remain stable and constant) with what our sense organs receive in the form of physical stimulation (a world in an almost continuous state of flux), it's almost as if there were two entirely different worlds involved. The one we are aware of is a world of objects and people (*perception*), and the one we're not aware of is a world of sense data (*sensation*).

While perception cannot occur without sensation (the physical stimulaton of the sense organs), the sense data constitute only the 'raw material' from which our awareness of objects is constructed. Although we feel we're in direct and immediate contact with the world as it really is, in fact our awareness of things is the end-product of a long and complex process. This begins with physical energy stimulating the sense organs (light in the case of vision, sound waves in the case of hearing), and ends with the brain intepreting the information received from the sense organs.

This chapter concentrates on sensation, the physical processes necessary for the psychological process of perception (see Chapters 15 and 16). However, when we talk about *vision*, for example, we're referring not just to the eyes, but to the whole *visual system*. The system also includes pathways between the eyes and the brain, as well as the brain itself.

The senses: Providing the raw material of perception

According to Ornstein (1975), we don't perceive objective reality but, rather, our *construction* of reality. Our sense organs gather information, which the brain modifies and sorts, and this 'heavily filtered input' is compared with memories, expectancies and so on until, finally, our consciousness is constructed as a 'best guess' about reality.

In a similar vein, James (1902) maintained that '... the mind, in short, works on the data it receives much as the sculptor works on his block of stone'. However, different artists use different materials, and, similarly, different sensory systems provide different kinds of sense data for the perceiver–sculptor to 'model'. Each of our various sensory systems is designed to respond to only a particular kind of stimulation, but a related and equally important point (often overlooked) is that our sensory systems also function as *data reduction systems* (Ornstein, 1975).

If something cannot be sensed (because our senses aren't responsive or sensitive to it), *it doesn't exist for us*. While we normally regard our senses as our 'windows' to the world, a major job they perform is to discard 'irrelevant' information and to register only what's likely to be of practical value (something which has occurred as a result of evolutionary forces). We'd be overwhelmed if we responded to the world as it is: different forms of energy are so diverse that they're still being discovered, and each species has developed particular sensitivities to certain of these, which has aided their survival. According to Bruce & Green (1990):

'*Sensitivity to diffusing chemicals and to mechanical energy gives an animal considerable perceptual abilities but leaves it unable to obtain information rapidly about either its inan-*

imate world or about silent animals at a distance from itself ... The form of energy that can provide these kinds of information is light, and consequently most animals have some ability to perceive their surroundings through vision ...'.

Box 5.1 The nature of light

Light is one form of *electromagnetic radiation*, which includes radio waves, microwaves, infrared and ultraviolet light, as well as the visible spectrum. Although the entire spectrum ranges from less than 1 billionth of a metre to more than 100 metres, the human eye, by design, responds only to the tiny portion between 380 and 780 billionths of a metre (380–780 nanometres), which we call light. (Although pressure on the eyeball produces sensations of light, it's *external* sources of light which normally produce the sensation: see Figure 5.1, page 67.)

(Based on Bruce & Green, 1990)

Classifying sensory systems

The senses have been classified in several ways. For example, Sherrington (1906) identified three kinds of receptors:

- *exteroceptors*, which tell us about the external environment;
- *interoceptors*, which tell us about the internal environment;
- *proprioceptors*, which deal with the position of our body in space and its movement through space.

Exteroception includes the five 'traditional' senses of sight (*vision*), hearing (*audition*), smell (*olfaction*), taste (*gustation*) and touch (*cutaneous* or *skin senses*). Interoception includes the internal receptors for oxygen, carbon dioxide, blood glucose and so on. Proprioception is usually subdivided into: (a) the *kinaesthetic sense*, which monitors movements of the limbs, joints and muscles; and (b) the *vestibular sense*, which responds to gravity and the movements of the head.

Gibson (1966) rejected proprioception as a distinct sensory system (and saw taste and smell as representing the same system), and Legge (1975) includes proprioception under the general heading of interoception.

Characteristics of sensory systems

However we classify them, all sensory systems (or modalities) share certain characteristics:

- They each respond to particular forms of energy or information.
- They each have a *sense organ* (or *accessory structure*), which is the first 'point of entry' for the information that will be processed by the system (the sense organ, as it were, 'catches' the information).
- They each have *sense receptors* (or *transducers*). These are specialised cells which are sensitive to particular kinds of energy, and which then convert it into electrical nerve impulses (the only form in which this physical energy can be dealt with by the brain: see Chapter 4).
- They each involve a *specialised part of the brain* which interprets the messages received from the sense receptors and (usually) results in perception of an object, a person, a word, a taste, etc.

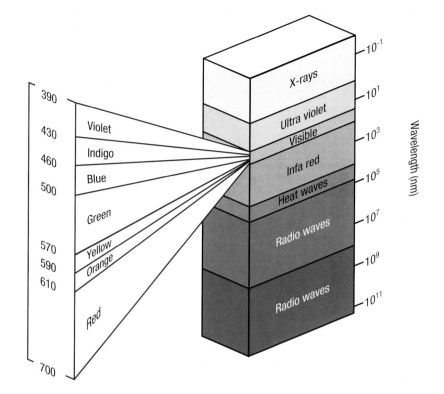

Figure 5.1 *The spectrum of electromagnetic radiation. Wavelengths are given in nanometres (1 nm = 10⁻⁹ m). The visible part of the spectrum is shown on the left, with the colours of different wavelengths of light (redrawn from Bruce & Green, 1990)*

These characteristics for the six major sense modalities are described in Table 5.1 below.

Table 5.1 *Sense organs, sense receptors and brain areas for the six major sense modalities*

Sense modality	Sense organ (accessory structure)	Sense receptor (transducer)	Brain area
Vision (sight)	Eye (in particular, the *lens*)	*Rods* and *cones* (in the retina)	*Occipital lobe* (striate cortex, extrastriate/ prestriate cortex) (via optic nerve)
Audition (hearing)	Outer ear (*pinna*), middle ear (*eardrum* and *ossicles*), inner ear (*cochlea*)	Specialised hair cells in *organ of Corti* (in cochlea)	*Temporal lobe* (via auditory nerve)
Gustation (taste)	Tongue (in particular the *taste buds* and *papillae*, the ridges around the side of the tongue)	Specialised receptors in taste buds, which connect with sensory neurons	*Temporal lobe* (via gustatory nerve)
Olfaction (smell)	Nose (in particular the *olfactory mucosa* of nasal cavity)	Transducers in the olfactory mucosa	*Temporal lobe* and *limbic system* (via olfactory bulb and olfactory tracts)
Skin/cutaneous senses (touch)	Skin	There are about 5 million sensors, of at least 7 types, including: • *Meissner's corpuscles* (touch); • *Krause end bulbs* (cold)	*Parietal lobe* (somatosensory cortex) and *cerebellum*
Proprioception (kinaesthetic and vestibular senses)	Inner ear (*semicircular canals*, *vestibular sacs*)	Vestibular sensors (*otoliths* or 'earstones'), tiny crystals attached to hair cells in vestibular sacs which are sensitive to gravity	*Cerebellum* (via vestibular nerve)

■ A certain *minimum stimulation* of the sense receptors is necessary before any sensory experience will occur (the *absolute threshold*). In practice, instead of there being a single intensity value below which people never detect the stimulus and above which they always detect it, a range of values is found, and the absolute threshold is taken to be the value at which the stimulus is detected 50 per cent of the time.

Sensory thresholds

Not only does the absolute threshold vary from individual to individual, but it varies for the same individual at different times, depending on his/her physical state, motivation, physical conditions of presentation, and so on.

The *difference threshold* is the minimum amount of stimulation necessary to discriminate between two stimuli, and is also known as the *just noticeable difference* (jnd). *Weber's law* states that the jnd is a constant value, but this, of course, will differ from one sense modality to another. For example, 1/133 is the value needed to tell apart the pitch of two different tones, and 1/5 for discriminating between saline solutions.

| Box 5.2 | Psychophysics and the Weber–Fechner law |

Fechner (1860) reformulated Weber's law. The Weber–Fechner law (as it's come to be known) states that large increases in the intensity of a stimulus produce smaller, proportional increases in the perceived intensity. Fechner's was one of the first attempts to express mathematically a psychological phenomenon, and was an important contribution to *psychophysics*, which studies the relationship between physical stimuli and the subjective experience of them. Psychophysics is of enormous historical importance in the development of psychology as a science (see Chapters 2 and 3).

The Weber–Fechner law holds only approximately through the middle ranges of stimulus intensities, and an alternative approach is *signal detection theory*, which rejects the notion of thresholds altogether. Each sensory channel always carries *noise* (any activity which interferes with the detection of a signal): the stronger the stimulus, the higher the *signal-to-noise ratio* and the easier it is to detect the stimulus. The detection of a stimulus, therefore, then becomes a question of *probabilities*.

The visual system

The fundamental job of a single-chambered eye (such as the human eye) is to map the spatial pattern in the *optic array* (the pattern of light reaching a point in space from all directions; Gibson, 1966: see Chapter 15) onto the retina by forming an *image*. All light rays striking the eye from one point in space are brought to a focus at one point on the retina (Bruce & Green, 1990). *Visual acuity* is a way of describing the efficiency with which the eye does this. Pinel (1993) defines acuity as '... the ability to see the details of objects ...'. Acuity is limited by several processes, in particular:

■ the efficiency with which the optical apparatus of the *eye* maps the spatial pattern of the optic array onto the retina;
■ the efficiency with which the *receptor cells* convert that pattern into a pattern of electrical activity;

■ the extent to which information available in the pattern of receptor cell activity is detected by the neural apparatus of the retina and the *brain*.

We'll now look at each of these aspects of acuity in turn.

The sense organ: the eye

Ask yourself ...

• Why do you think vision is considered to be the most important of the human sense modalities?

Ornstein (1975) describes the eye as 'the most important avenue of personal consciousness', and it's estimated that 80 per cent of the information we receive about the external world reaches us through vision (Dodwell, 1995). Research interest has focused largely on vision, both as a sensory system and a perceptual system. The sense organ of vision is the eye and its major structures are shown in Figure 5.2 (page 69).

The *conjunctiva* is a transparent membrane, covering the inside of the eyelids and the front of the eye. It contains nerves and many tiny blood vessels, which dilate (expand) if the eye is irritated or injured (the eye becomes bloodshot). The *cornea* is also a transparent membrane, which protects the lens and through which light enters the eye.

| Box 5.3 | The pupil and the ANS |

The *pupil* (the hole in the iris) regulates the amount of light entering the eye via the iris (the coloured part of the eye), which has tiny sets of muscles that dilate and contract the pupil. (Pupil size is also regulated by the ciliary muscles.) In bright light, the pupil contracts to shut out some of the light rays; when light is dim or we're looking at distant objects, the pupils dilate to let more light in. It's *sensitivity* rather than acuity which is crucial.

Ultimately, pupil size is controlled by the *autonomic nervous system* (ANS), and so is outside conscious control. The *parasympathetic branch* of the ANS controls change in pupil size as a function of change in illumination, while the *sympathetic branch* dilates the pupils under conditions of strong emotional arousal, as in an 'emergency' situation when we need to see 'better' (see Chapters 9, 10 and 12).

The *lens*, situated just behind the iris, is enclosed in a capsule held firmly in place by the *suspensory ligaments*. It focuses light on the retina as an *inverted* (upside-down) image, and its shape is regulated by the ciliary muscles. As with certain reptiles, birds and other mammals, the lens of the human eye thickens and increases its curvature (and the ciliary muscles contract) when focusing on nearby objects. When viewing more distant objects, it becomes flatter (and the ciliary muscles are fully relaxed). This process is called *accommodation* (see Figure 5.3, page 69).

Between the cornea and the lens is the anterior chamber filled with *aqueous humour*, a clear, watery fluid, and behind the lens is the larger posterior chamber filled with *vitreous humour*, a jellylike substance. Both fluids give the eyeball its shape and help to keep it firm.

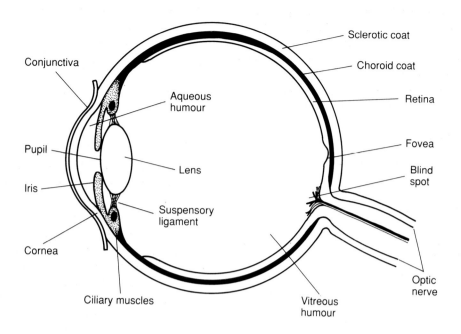

Figure 5.2 *The major structures of the human eye*

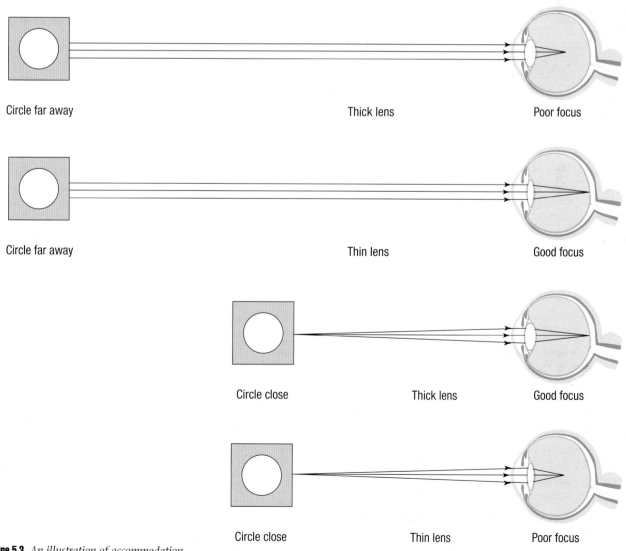

Figure 5.3 *An illustration of accommodation*
(from Matlin & Foley, Sensation & Perception, Copyright © 1992 by Allyn & Bacon. Adapted by permission)

The *sclerotic coat* is the thickest layer of the eyeball and forms the outer, white part of the eye. It consists of a strong, fibrous membrane, except in the front where it bulges to form the *cornea*. The *choroid coat* is a dark layer containing black-coloured matter, which darkens the chamber of the eye and prevents reflection of light inside the eye. In front, it becomes the *iris*, which can be seen through the transparent cornea.

Primates' eyes make the largest, most rapid and most precisely controlled movements of all animals except the chameleon. The human eye is held in position by a dynamic balance between three pairs of antagonistic muscles, and instability in this balance produces a continuous, small-amplitude tremor, which means that the retinal image is in constant motion.

Box 5.4 **Different types of eye movements**

Sampling the optic array is achieved by three kinds of movement:

- Sudden, intermittent jumps of eye position (*saccades*) occur while trying to fixate an object when looking directly at it (*foveal vision*). Even when we think we're looking steadily at something, or when we read or look at a picture, our eyes make several saccades each second to scan it.
- Once an object has been fixated, smooth and continuous *pursuit movements* keep it in foveal vision as the object or the observer moves.
- If the distance of the object from the observer changes, smooth and continuous *convergence movements* keep it fixated by the foveas of both eyes.

(Based on Bruce & Green, 1990)

According to Bruce & Green (1990), at any instant the human eye samples a relatively large portion of the optic array (the *peripheral visual field*) with low acuity, and a much smaller portion (the *central* or *foveal visual field*) with high acuity. Beaumont (1988) believes that constant alteration of the retinal image serves three useful purposes:

- it allows more time for the pigments to replace themselves after bleaching (see below).
- nervous tissue, that becomes less responsive with repeated stimulation, is also given a chance to recover.
- it helps reduce the possibility that parts of the retina will become obscured by blood vessels, by allowing slightly different parts of the stimulus to be viewed by different sets of receptors.

Is the eye a camera?

Ask yourself ...

- In what ways can the eye be compared with a camera, and how are they different?

In a camera, light striking each light-sensitive grain in the film comes from a narrow segment of the optic array, and this is also true of the retinal image (Bruce & Green, 1990). Both have a lens, which projects the image onto the film in a camera, or the retina in the case of the eye. So the camera is a useful analogy for understanding the optics of the eye.

The eye as a camera?

However, Bruce and Green point out a number of important differences:

- If judged by the same standards as a camera, even the most sophisticated eye forms an image of an extremely poor quality. Optical aberrations produce 'blur', aberrations of the lens and cornea cause distortions in the image, and the curvature of the retina means that images of straight lines are curved, and metrical relations in the image don't correspond to those in the world.
- A camera which moved as much as the eye does would produce blurred pictures.
- The retinal image has a yellowish cast, particularly in the macular region, and contains shadows of the blood vessels which lie in front of the receptor cells in the retina.
- While the purpose of a camera is to produce a static picture for people to look at, the purpose of the eye and brain is to extract the information from the changing optic array needed to guide a person's actions, or to specify important objects or events. The extraction of information about pattern begins in the retina itself. The optic nerve doesn't transmit a stream of pictures to the brain (as a TV camera does to a TV set), but instead transmits information about the *pattern* of light reaching the eyes. The brain then has to interpret that information.

The retina is the innermost layer of the eyeball, formed by the expansion of the optic nerve, which enters at the back and a little to the nasal side of the eye.

- *rods* and *cones*, photosensitive cells which convert light energy into electrical nerve impulses (and which form the rear layer of the retina);
- *bipolar cells*, connected to the rods, cones and ganglion cells;
- *ganglion cells*, whose fibres (axons) form the beginning of the optic nerve leading to the brain.

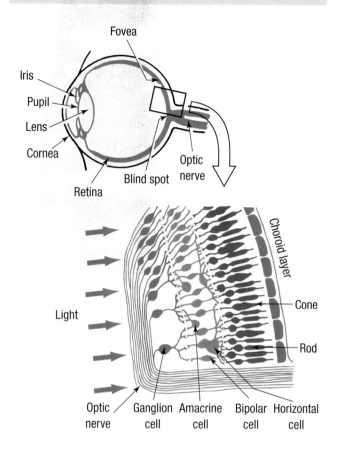

Figure 5.4 *A diagrammatic section through the eye and a section through the retina at the edge of the blind spot (from Atkinson et al., 1983)*

The receptors: rods and cones

Gregory (1966) has estimated that only about ten per cent of the light entering the eye actually reaches the *transducers* (*rods* and *cones*), the rest being absorbed by the *accessory structures* (the rest of the eye). See Figure 5.4.

The rods are 1000 times more sensitive than cones, that is, they're far more likely to respond to *low levels* of illumination. They're also far more numerous: in each retina there are 120 million rods and 7 million cones. Their distribution around the retina also differs. Cones are much more numerous towards the *centre* of the retina. The *fovea*, a pitlike depression, is part of a cone-rich area (the *macula lutea*), where there's a concentration of about 50,000 cones. By contrast, the rods are distributed fairly evenly around the *periphery* (but aren't found in the fovea).

What do rods and cones do?

The *rods* are specialised for vision in dim light (including night-time vision) and contain a photosensitive chemical (*rhodopsin*), which changes structure in response to low levels of illumination. They help us see black, white and intermediate greys (*achromatic colour*), and this is referred to as *scotopic vision*. The *cones* are specialised for bright light vision (including daylight) and contain *iodopsin*. They help us see *chromatic colour* (red, green, blue, and so on) and provide *photopic vision* (from 'photon', the smallest particle of light which travels in a straight line). The chemical difference between the rods and cones explains the phenomenon of *dark adaptation*. If you go into a dark cinema from bright sunlight, you'll experience near blindness for a few seconds, because the rods need a little time to take over from the cones, which were responding outside in the daylight. The rhodopsin in the rods is being regenerated (resynthesised), having been 'bleached' by the bright sunlight. It takes 30 minutes for the rods to reach their maximum level of response.

Rods, cones and adaptation

Human vision, like that of most species, is adapted to operate in a range of light intensities, and this is reflected in the structure of the retina. A photon passing through a rod is less likely to come out the other end, making rods far more sensitive than cones (see Box 5.6). According to Bruce & Green (1990), this difference explains the correlation between the rod:cone ratio in an animal's retina and its ecology. *Diurnal animals* (those which are active by day and sleep at night) have a *higher proportion of cones* than *nocturnals* (which are active by night and sleep by day: see Chapter 7). Pure-cone retinas are rare (mostly confined to lizards and snakes), as are pure-rod retinas (confined to deep-sea fish and bats, which never leave their dark habitats).

When focusing on an object in bright light, the most sharply defined image is obtained by looking *directly* at it, thereby projecting the light onto the fovea (which, remember, is packed with cones). In night light, however, the sharpest image is actually produced by looking slightly *to one side* of the object (for example, at a star in the sky), thereby stimulating the rods (which are found in the periphery of the retina).

The dense packing of cones helps explain *acuity*: the more densely packed the receptors, the finer the details of a pattern of light intensity which can be transformed into differences in electrical activity. The difference between a human's acuity and, say, a falcon's, is the result of a difference in receptor packing, with receptors being three times more densely packed in the falcon (Bruce & Green, 1990).

Rods, cones, and ganglion cells

The 127 million rods and cones in the human eye are 'reduced' to 1 million ganglion cells, which make up the optic nerve. This means that information reaching the brain has already been 'refined' to some extent compared with the relatively 'raw' information received from other sensory nerves. However, the degree of reduction (or summation) differs considerably for different areas of the retina. In the *periphery*, up to 1200 rods may combine to form a single ganglion cell, and so connect to a single axon in the optic nerve. This provides only *very general visual information*. At the *fovea*, only ten to twelve cones may be summed for each ganglion cell, providing *much more detailed information*.

Two other kinds of cell, *horizontal* and *amacrine*, interconnect with groups of the other cells and connect them together. This further increases the degree of information processing which takes place in the retina itself. Horizontal cells connect receptors and bipolar cells, while amacrine cells connect bipolar and ganglion cells (see Figure 5.4).

Ganglion cells and receptive fields

Each ganglion cell has a *receptive field*, a (usually) roughly circular region of the retina, in which stimulation affects the ganglion cell's *firing rate*. There are (at least) three kinds of ganglion cell, each with a different kind of receptive field:

1 *on-centre cells* are more neurally active when light falls in the centre of the receptive field, but less active when it falls on the edge;
2 *off-centre cells* work in the opposite way;
3 *transient cells* have larger receptive fields and seem to respond to movements, especially sudden ones.

The combined activity of on-centre and off-centre cells provides a clear definition of *contours* ('edges'), where there's a sudden change in brightness. These contours are essential in defining the shape of objects to be perceived (Beaumont, 1988). Further analysis of contours takes place in the *striate cortex* by simple, complex and hypercomplex cells (see below).

Box 5.8   Is the retina back-to-front?

As Beaumont (1988) points out, the retina appears to be built back-to-front: the receptors don't point to the source of the light, but towards the supporting cells at the back of the eye. Before light arrives at the receptors, it must pass through the layers of retinal cells and blood vessels inside the eye (see Figure 5.4). In view of this, it's surprising that such high-quality vision can still be achieved.

If you've ever looked directly at a flash of lightning, you may well have experienced a treelike after-image, which is the shadows of the blood vessels thrown upon the retina. Or when you look up at the sky, especially a cloudless blue sky, you sometimes see small transparent bubbles floating in front of you: these are red blood cells.

Visual pathways: from eye to brain

Ask yourself ...

- What are the important brain structures and areas as far as vision is concerned? (See Chapter 4, pages 52–53.)

As Figure 5.5 (page 73) shows, the pathways from the half of each retina closest to the nose cross at the *optic chiasma* (or *chasm*) and travel to the *opposite hemisphere* (crossed pathways). The pathways from the half of each retina furthest from the nose (uncrossed pathways) travel to the hemisphere on the same side as the eye. So, when you fixate on a point straight ahead (such that the eyes converge), the image of an object to the *right* of fixation falls on the *left* half of each retina, and information about it passes along the *crossed pathway* from the right eye to the left hemisphere and along the *uncrossed pathway* from the left eye to the left hemisphere. No information is passed directly to the right hemisphere.

All these relationships are reversed for an object to the *left* of the fixation point. It follows that any damage to the visual area of just one hemisphere will produce blind areas in both eyes; however, the crossed pathway ensures that complete blindness in either eye won't occur.

Before reaching the cortex, the optic nerve travels through the *lateral geniculate nucleus* (LGN), which is part of the thalami. Optic nerve fibres terminate at synapses with LGN cells arranged in layers (*laminae*), each lamina containing a *retinooptic map* of half the visual field.

LGN cells have concentric receptive fields similar to those of retinal ganglion cells, and the axons of LGN cells project to the *occipital lobe*. In monkeys, all LGN cells project to area 17, which is the *visual* or *striate cortex* (called the *geniculostriate path*).

CASE STUDY 5.1

D.B. and blindsight

In humans, the *geniculostriate path* must be intact for conscious experience of vision to be possible. People with damage to their visual cortex will report complete blindness in part or all of the visual field. Even so, they'll show some ability to locate or even identify objects which they cannot consciously see: Weiskrantz (1986) called this *blindsight*.

The most thoroughly investigated patient is D.B., who had an operation to reduce the number of severe migraines he suffered. Despite being left with an area of subjective blindness, he could detect whether or not a visual stimulus had been presented to the blind area and also identify its location. However, he seemed to possess only a rudimentary ability to discriminate shapes. This suggests that, while most visual functions rely on the 'primary' geniculostriate path, the 'secondary' *retinotectal path* (some ganglion cells are projected to the paired superior colliculi structures in the midbrain) carries enough information to guide some actions in an unconscious way. In the intact brain, these two paths function interdependently: the *corticotectal path* provides the superior colliculi with input from the cortex.

Hubel and Wiesel's studies of cortical cells

The first recordings from single cells in the striate cortex of cats and monkeys were made by Hubel & Wiesel (1959, 1962, 1968). They identified three kinds of cortical cells.

Box 5.9   Simple, complex and hypercomplex cells

- *Simple cells* respond only to particular features of a stimulus (such as straight lines, edges and slits) in particular orientations and in particular locations in the animal's visual field. For example, a bar presented vertically may cause a cell to 'fire', but if the bar is moved to one side or out of vertical, the cell will not respond.
- *Complex cells* also respond to lines of particular orientation, but location is no longer important. For example, a vertical line detector

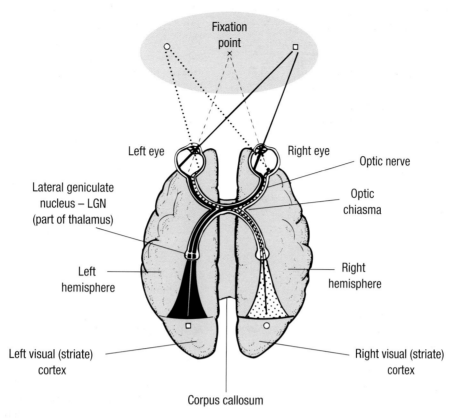

Figure 5.5 *The visual system*

will respond wherever the line is in the visual field. It seems that complex cells receive inputs from larger numbers of simple cells sharing the same orientation sensitivity.

- *Hypercomplex cells* are 'fed' by large numbers of complex cells and are similar to complex cells, except that they take length into account too (that is, they're most responsive to a bar or edge not extending beyond their receptive field).

Although some researchers have questioned the separate existence of hypercomplex cells (Bruce & Green, 1990), Hubel and Wiesel's research demonstrates that the visual cortex isn't a homogeneous mass of tissue, with randomly scattered cells of different kinds. Rather, it shows an astonishingly precise and regular arrangement of different cell types, which Hubel & Wiesel (1962) called the *functional architecture* of the visual cortex.

The six main layers of the striate cortex can be recognised under the microscope. The cortical area devoted to the central part of the visual field is proportionately larger than that devoted to the periphery. Hubel & Wiesel (1977) suggest that the cortex is divided into roughly square blocks of tissue (about 1 mm square), extending from the surface down to the white matter (*hypercolumns*).

The extrastriate (prestriate) cortex

Single-cell recordings have revealed many regions of the *extrastriate* (or *prestriate*) cortex, to the front of the striate, which can be considered 'visual areas'. However, it's proved more difficult to map these, compared with the striate cortex.

Maunsell & Newsome (1987) reviewed studies involving macaque monkeys. They concluded that there are 19 visual areas, covering large areas of the occipital, temporal and parietal lobes (see Figure 5.7). The deep folding of the cortex means that some areas, lying within folds (*sulci*), aren't visible from the exterior. This is why two important areas aren't shown in Figure 5.7, namely V3 (lying between V2 and V4) and the middle temporal area (MT: in front of V4).

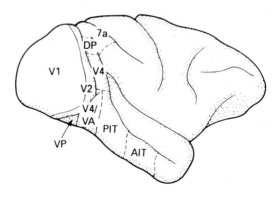

Figure 5.6 *Side view of the right cerebral hemisphere of a macaque monkey. Area VI is the striate cortex (from Maunsell & Newsome, 1987)*

Each area sends output to several others and most, if not all, connections are matched by reciprocal connections running in the opposite direction. Van Essen (1985) lists 92 pathways linking the visual areas. Most can be classified as either *ascending* (leading away from V1) or *descending* (leading towards V1). When the pathways are classified in this way, a consistently hierarchical pattern emerges, with areas placed at different levels (see Figure 5.7, page 74).

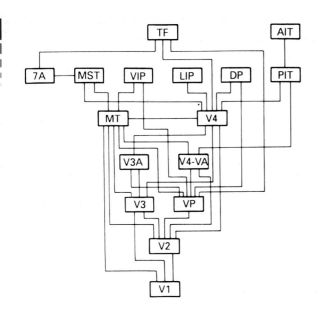

Figure 5.7 *The hierarchical organisation of extrastriate visual areas in the macaque monkey as proposed by Maunsell and Newsome (from Maunsell & Newsome, 1987)*

Does each area have its own specified function?

Zeki (1978) proposed a 'parcelling model', whereby the simple representation of the visual field in V1 and V2 is 'parcelled out' to be analysed by a number of areas working in parallel. For example, V3 analyses form, V4 colour, and V5 motion. However, Maunsell & Newsome (1987) and Van Essen (1985) believe that there might be two main pathways operating in parallel, one concerned with the analysis of motion and spatial layout, the other with colour, form and object recognition. Some of the evidence regarding processing of colour is discussed in the next section. Zeki himself later came to cast doubt on the parcelling model.

CASE STUDY 5.2

G.Y. and motion detection in the blind

Zeki (1992, 1993) studied G.Y., a man blinded in an accident when he was seven. He could detect fast-moving objects, such as cars, and the direction in which they were travelling. Scans confirmed that G.Y.'s V5 was active when he was 'seeing' fast motion, but his V1 wasn't. This suggests that fast movements are first processed by V5, while signals from *slow* movements arrive initially in V1. In Zeki's view, signals must go through V1 to see clearly, but even the blind can sometimes see through other areas in a rudimentary way.

The case of G.Y. still supports the view that different aspects of visual processing occur in different parts of the brain. This view is further supported by other examples of very specific visual impairments caused by brain damage. For example, V5 damage produces *akinetopsia*, in which moving objects appear invisible, even though the same objects can be seen quite clearly when stationary. Patients with *chromatopsia* (caused by widespread damage due to carbon monoxide poisoning) have intact colour vision, but almost all other visual abilities are

impaired. Similarly, P.B. awoke from a four-month coma to find he was blind, *except* for the ability to make out colours (Zeki, cited in Highfield, 1999). The converse of this is *achromatopia*. Following a stroke, E.H. reported that everything looked grey, although all other visual abilities were normal. A MRI scan revealed damage to V4 (Shuren *et al.*, 1996).

Colour vision and colour blindness

Ask yourself ...

- Try to define colour.
- What is colour blindness?

Light can be described physically by its *energy spectrum* (intensities at different wavelengths) or phenomenologically by three dimensions:

- *brightness* (perceived intensity);
- *hue* (perceived colour);
- *saturation* (the purity of hue: how much colour or how much white).

Although both hue and saturation are aspects of 'colour', hue is what theories of colour vision and discussion of colour vision defects are concerned with.

As we've seen, the cones are the photoreceptors responsible for chromatic vision, and rods and cones contain photosensitive pigments (which change their chemical constitution on exposure to light, namely, rhodopsin and iodopsin respectively).

Rushton & Campbell (1954; cited by Rushton, 1987) were the first to measure the visual pigments in the living human eye, applying the familiar observation that a cat's eye will reflect back light shone in it. Instead of the cat's shining *tapetum lucidium*, we have a very black surface behind the retina (the choroid coat) which reflects very faint light. Rushton and Campbell identified rhodopsin, plus red and green pigments. However, insufficient blue light is reflected to measure the blue cone pigment (Rushton, 1987).

Later, Marks *et al.* (1964; cited by Rushton, 1987) used fresh retinas from monkeys and human eyes removed during surgery, to measure visual pigments in single cones. They found the blue-, green- and red-sensitive cones, thus supporting the Young–Helmholtz trichromatic theory (see below). Rushton and Campbell's findings were also confirmed using living colour-blind participants, who possessed only one of the two pigments measured by them.

Theories of colour vision

The Young–Helmholtz trichromatic theory

The *trichromatic theory* (Young, 1801) claims that colour is mediated by three different kinds of cone, each responding to light from a different part of the visible spectrum. *Blue-sensitive*, *green-sensitive* and *red-sensitive* cones are maximally responsive to short, medium and long wavelengths respectively. While the sum of the three wavelengths (B + G + R) determines brightness, their *ratio* or pattern (B:G:R) determines colour. This is essentially what's believed today (Rushton, 1987).

This explains the painter's experience that mixing a few paints will produce a whole range of colours. It also implies that every colour (including white) should excite B, G and R cones in a characteristic set of ratios, such that a mixture of red and green and blue lights, adjusted to produce this same set of ratios, should appear white or whatever the initial colour was. Maxwell (1854) found that every colour can be matched by a suitable mixture of blue, green and red 'primaries' (the *trichromacy of colour*), and this was later confirmed by Helmholtz (Rushton, 1987). Hence, this is often called the *Young–Helmholtz trichromatic theory*.

The opponent process theory

While the Young–Helmholz theory can explain the effects of mixing colours of different wavelengths, it has difficulty explaining *colour blindness* and the phenomenon of *negative after-images* (see Box 5.10). Both of these can be explained more easily by the *opponent process* (*tetrachromatic*) theory (Hering, 1878). This claims that colour analysis depends on the action of two types of detector, each having two modes of response. One signals red *or* green, the other signals yellow *or* blue. A third type of detector, black–white, contributes to the perception of brightness and saturation.

Evidence for the opponent process theory

■ If you stare at a coloured surface (for example, red) and then look at a plain surface, you'll perceive an after-image which is coloured in the 'opposite direction' (i.e. green). This is called a *complementary* (or *negative*) after-image.

■ While the retina encodes in terms of three constituent components (a blue–green–red 'component' system: *stage one* of colour vision), output through the bipolar and ganglion cells and onto the LGN (*stage two*) becomes recoded in terms of opponent processes (DeValois & Jacobs, 1984). There seem to be *four* kinds of LGN cells: those which increase activity to red light but decrease with green (R+ G–), those which increase activity to green light but decrease with red (G+ R–), and similarly for blue and yellow (B+ Y–) and yellow and blue (Y+ B–). Still other LGN cells simply respond to black and white (Beaumont, 1988).

Box 5.10 Colour blindness

People with defective colour vision (often called '*colour blind*') usually fail to distinguish between *red and green*. This is the most common form of defect, caused by a recessive sex-linked gene which affects more males (about eight per cent) than females (about 0.4 per cent). Sufferers have *dichromatic* vision (normal vision is *trichromatic*): they possess only red- *or* green-sensitive cone pigments, but they can match every colour of the rainbow exactly with a suitable mix of only two coloured lights (for example, red and blue). Most people need the green primary as well if every colour is to be matched.

Next most common is true colour blindness, which involves an absence of any cones at all (*monochromatic vision*), and least common of all is *yellow–blue* blindness. These findings are clearly consistent with the opponent process theory.

Must we choose between the two theories?

Evidence such as this has led to the generally held view that a complete theory of colour vision must draw on elements from *both* theories. Indeed, Helmholtz himself showed that a simple transformation could change the three receptor outputs to two different signals, plus one additive signal (Troscianko, 1987). According to Harris (1998), both theories are compatible, and neurophysiological evidence exists for both.

Colour constancy

Any chromatic light hitting the retina is composed of different amounts of the three primary colours (for example, turquoise might be 70 per cent blue, 30 per cent green), so blue-sensitive cones would 'fire' quite quickly, and green-sensitive ones quite slowly (and red-sensitive wouldn't fire at all). However, perceived colour isn't solely determined by the wavelength composition of the light reflected from the object (the *spectral reflectance* of the object).

Box 5.11 Factors influencing the perception of colour

The perception of colour is affected by:

• the relative proportions of different wavelengths in the light falling on the object (the *spectral composition* of the illumination);
• prior stimulation of the retina (as shown by complementary or negative after-images);
• the nature of the surroundings, such as the simultaneous contrast created by adjacent areas of different colour or brightness. For example, a grey square will look brighter set against a black background than against a white background);
• our familiarity with, and knowledge of, an object's colour, which is part of the psychological phenomenon of *colour constancy*.

According to McCann (1987), our visual system is built to tell us about the permanent colours of objects, as opposed to the spectral composition of the light falling on a local area of the retina. Land (1977), the inventor of the Polaroid camera, provided a powerful demonstration of colour constancy.

KEY STUDY 5.1

Land's (1977) 'Mondrian' experiment

Land used a *colour Mondrian*, a patchwork of different-coloured matt papers, randomly arranged so that each colour was surrounded by several others. The display was illuminated by mixed light from projectors with red, green and blue filters. Each projector also had an independent brightness control.

Observers then selected one of the papers (for example, white) and Land measured the amounts of red, green and blue light coming from the white paper. They then selected a second paper (for example, red), and again the amounts of red, green and blue light were measured.

Land then changed the illumination so that the red light from the red paper was exactly equal to the red light from the white paper. This required only a small change, since roughly equal amounts of red light are reflected from a red and a white paper. However, a substantial change was required to adjust the other projectors to produce exactly the same amounts of green and blue (much less green and blue are reflected from a red than a white paper).

When all three projectors were turned on together, each observer reported 'red', despite the fact that the physical properties of the light from the red paper *were the same* as the light from the white paper. Using this method with other pairs of coloured papers, Land showed that almost the full range of colour sensations could be produced from a single mixture of red, green and blue light (thus supporting the trichromatic theory).

Retinex theory

If perceived colour were determined solely by the spectral composition of the reflected light, the first and second colours would have been seen as *the same*. The fact that they weren't, means that the observers were displaying *colour constancy*. To explain this, Land proposed the *retinex theory of colour constancy* ('retinex' is a combination of 'retina' and 'cortex'). According to the theory, there are three separate visual systems or retinexes, responsive primarily to long-, medium-, and short-wavelength light. Each produces a separate lightness image, and a comparison of these images is made. The comparison determines the colour that's perceived.

The three lightnesses provide the coordinates of a three-dimensional space. Whereas a colour space based on the *absolute* absorptions in the three classes of receptor predicts only whether two stimuli will *match*, a space based on the three lightnesses predicts how colours actually *look*. This is because between them they give the reflectance of the object in different parts of the spectrum (that is, a measure of their *relative absorptions*). Land's theory implies that the formation of lightnesses could occur in the retina *or* cortex, and that the *retina-cortical structure* acts as a whole.

Cells with suitable properties for retinex theory exist in the LGN, and Zeki (1980) found that the response of individual cells in V4 of macaque monkeys mirrored his own perception of surface colour as opposed to the physical composition of the light. These V4 cells seem to be genuinely colour- (rather than wavelength-) selective (Harris, 1998).

CHAPTER SUMMARY

- **Sensation** is necessary for **perception**, since sense data represent the 'raw material' from which conscious awareness of the world is constructed.
- Each **sense modality** is sensitive to a particular form of physical energy, but each also acts as a **data reduction system**.

- **Light** is one form of **electromagnetic radiation**. The human eye responds to only a tiny fraction of the visible electromagnetic spectrum.
- **Exteroceptors** include the five traditional senses of sight, hearing, smell, taste and touch, **interoceptors** include receptors for the internal environment, and **proprioceptors** are usually subdivided into the **kinaesthetic** and **vestibular senses**.
- Every sense modality comprises a **sense organ/accessory structure**, sense **receptors/transducers**, a **specialised brain area** that processes the sensory messages, and an **absolute threshold**.
- The **Weber–Fechner law** attempts to predict **difference threshold/jnd** and is an important part of **psychophysics**.
- **Signal detection theory** rejects the notion of thresholds, and instead uses the concept of **signal-to-noise ratio**.
- The fundamental job of the human eye is to focus an image of the **optic array** onto the retina with maximum **acuity**.
- The **pupil** regulates the amount of light entering the eye by contracting or dilating. Pupil size is controlled by the ciliary muscles and by the ANS.
- The **lens** focuses light on the retina as an inverted image, and its shape is regulated through **accommodation**. The retinal image is continuously moving, and other kinds of movement include **saccades**, **pursuit movements** and **convergence**.
- The camera is a useful analogy for understanding the optics of the eye. However, what's sent to the brain is information about the pattern of light reaching the eyes, which must then be interpreted.
- The **retina** contains **rods** and **cones**, the **photosensitive cells** which convert light energy into electrical nerve impulses. It also comprises **bipolar** and **ganglion cells**.
- The rods help us see **achromatic colour** (**scotopic vision**), and the cones help us see **chromatic colour** (**photopic vision**). The **fovea** is densely packed with cones.
- Cases of **blindsight** suggest that the **retinotectal path** carries enough information to allow some 'unconscious' vision. Normally, this and the **geniculostriate path** work together.
- **Simple**, **complex** and **hypercomplex** cells in the striate cortex of cats and monkeys respond to particular stimulus features. Large areas of the occipital, temporal and parietal lobes are involved in vision.
- The **Young–Helmholtz trichromatic theory of colour vision** stresses the ratio or pattern of the three wavelengths of light, while the **opponent process/tetrachromatic theory** is based on the two modes of response of two types of detector.
- Some of the evidence supporting the opponent process theory comes from the study of **colour-blind** people. Both theories are seen as valid and complementary.
- According to **retinex theory**, perceived colour isn't solely determined by the wavelength of the light reflected from the object, but also by a number of other factors, including **colour constancy**.

Self-assessment questions

1 Describe and evaluate research into the nature of visual information processing (e.g. the processing of colour).
2 **a** Outline the structure and functions of the visual system.
  b Assess the extent to which knowledge of the visual system's structure and functions helps us to understand visual information processing.

Web addresses

http:// vision.arc.nasa.gov./VisionScience/

http://www.socsci.uci.edu/cogsi/vision.html

http://minerva.acc.virginia.edu/~mklab

http://www.med.uni-muenchen.de/medpsy/vis/nvi/infpro.html

Further reading

Gregory, R.L. & Colman, A.M. (Eds) (1995) *Sensation and Perception*. London: Longman. Four of the five chapters in this book are relevant here: 'Fundamental Processes in Vision' (Dodwell); 'Hearing' (Moore); 'The Skin, Body and Chemical Senses' (Schiffman); 'Psychophysics' (Laming).

Chapter 6

Parapsychology

Introduction and overview

At least for most psychologists, the sensory systems described in Chapter 5 are the *only* means by which we can acquire information about our environment (both physical objects and other people). However, there are some phenomena which seem to involve meaningful exchanges of information between organisms and their environment, and yet at the same time, appear somehow to exceed the capacities of the sensory and motor systems as they're currently understood (Rao & Palmer, 1987). For these reasons, such phenomena are considered to be *anomalous*, and are commonly referred to as *paranormal* (or 'psi', short for 'psychic ability').

Such phenomena include 'extrasensory perception' (ESP). The term unambiguously implies that there *are* ways of acquiring information about the world that *don't* depend on vision, hearing and so on. So, 'paranormal' is used for phenomena apparently lying outside the range of normal scientific explanations and investigations. However, most parapsychologists consider themselves to be scientists applying the usual rules of scientific enquiry to admittedly unusual phenomena. Indeed, the term 'parapsychology' was first introduced in the 1930s to refer to the scientific investigation of paranormal phenomena (Evans, 1987a).

Parapsychology and science

Ask yourself ...

- How is it possible to believe in paranormal phenomena and be a scientist at the same time?

Perhaps the crucial phrase in the previous paragraph is 'apparently lying outside'. Parapsychologists who apply 'normal' scientific methods are following a long tradition of scientists investigating phenomena that *at the time* seemed mysterious (Utts & Josephson, 1996), or that were given what we'd now consider bizarre, 'unscientific', explanations. Gregory (1987a) gives the example of thunder and lightning:

'... once considered to be the wrath of the Gods, but now understood as the same electricity that we generate and use for wonders of our technology'.

In other words, 'paranormal' is a convenient label for certain aspects of human behaviour and experience, which can be investigated scientifically and are subject to 'scientific' explanations. Once they've been accounted for scientifically, they'll no longer be called 'paranormal':

'... Yet the phenomena of psi are so extraordinary and so similar to what are widely regarded as superstitions that some scientists declare psi to be an impossibility and reject the legitimacy of parapsychological inquiry ...'. (Atkinson et al., 1990)

Sometimes, 'extraordinary' can be construed as 'not real', and the history of parapsychology is littered with accusations of fraud on the part of 'believers' by those who, for whatever reason, reject their claims. However, if psi 'really exists', what does this imply for many of our fundamental scientific beliefs about the world? While strong opposition to parapsychology is understandable, prejudgements about the impossibility of psi are inappropriate in science. Many psychologists who aren't yet convinced psi has been demonstrated are nevertheless open to the *possibility* that new evidence may emerge that would be more compelling. Many parapsychologists believe that the case for psi has already been 'proven', or that experimental procedures exist which have the potential for doing so (Atkinson et al., 1990).

Agents Mulder and Scully in a scene from The X Files. *While Scully believes there is a 'scientific' explanation for everything, Mulder believes in the existence of other life-forms*

The historical roots of parapsychology (PP)

According to Evans (1987a), the history of PP can be conveniently divided into three overlapping phases or periods: *spiritualistic research/spiritualism*, *psychical research*, and *modern PP*.

Spiritualistic research/spiritualism

Most Victorian scientists brought up as orthodox Christians were expected to believe in the reality of an immortal, non-physical soul. So, a substantial number of them became involved in the minority religion of *spiritualism*: if souls or spirits survived death of the physical body, they must exist *somewhere* in the universe and should, in principle, be contactable (for example, through mediums). Some of the outstanding brains of the time, including physicists, biologists and anthropologists, solemnly tried to induce spirit forms to materialise in their laboratories. The Society for Psychical Research was founded in London in 1882, and soon afterwards, the *Journal of the Society for Psychical Research*.

Other, more critical or sceptical colleagues conducted their own experiments. Medium after medium was exposed as fraudulent, and the pioneers were shown to be gullible, incompetent, or both. By 1900, scientific interest was moving away from séances and towards 'more plausible' aspects of the paranormal.

Psychical research

This was the era of the 'ghost hunter'. Scientists and affluent amateurs turned to such phenomena as manifestations in haunted houses, poltergeist activity, demonic possession, apparitions, and premonitions. There was also a growing number of casual (i.e. uncontrolled) studies of telepathy and precognitive dreams.

Modern PP

According to Blackmore (1995), credit for the founding of PP (in the 1930s) was almost entirely due to J.B. Rhine and Louisa Rhine (although Louisa is often not mentioned, as in Evans', 1987a, account). They were biologists who wanted to find evidence against a purely materialist view of human nature (see Chapter 49). Despite sharing the same objectives, they wanted to dissociate themselves from spiritualism and bring their new science firmly into the laboratory. They renamed their research 'parapsychology', established a department of PP at Duke University in the USA, began to develop new experimental methods, and defined their terms operationally.

Varieties and definitions of parapsychological phenomena

Ask yourself ...

- What do you understand parapsychological/paranormal phenomena to be?
- Do you believe they exist as real phenomena (regardless of how you might explain them)?

J.B. Rhine introduced the term 'extrasensory perception' (ESP) in 1934. This was a general term used to cover three types of communication that supposedly occur without the use of the senses, namely, *telepathy*, *clairvoyance*, and *precognition*.

Box 6.1   The four types of psi

- **Telepathy:** '... the transmission of information from one mind to another, without the use of language, body movements, or any of the known senses ...' (Evans, 1987b). It was previously called 'thought transference'.
- **Clairvoyance:** '... the acquisition by a mind or brain of information which is not available to it by the known senses, and, most important, which is *not known at the time to any other mind or brain* ...' (Evans, 1987b).
- **Precognition:** '... the apparent ability to access information about future events before they happen ...' (Morris, 1989).

These are all forms of **extra-sensory perception** (ESP). In all cases, the direction of influence is from environment to person.

- **Psychokinesis (PK):** '... the supposed power of the mind to manipulate matter at a distance without any known physical means ...' (Evans, 1987b), or the apparent ability to '... influence events simply by a direct volitional act of some sort, by wanting the event to happen in a certain way ...' (Morris, 1989).

The direction of influence is from person to environment (the reverse of ESP).

One consequence of definitions such as those in Box 6.1 is that the field of PP is ever-shrinking. For example, hypnosis, hallucinations, and lucid dreams used to be considered part of PP, until psychologists made progress in understanding them. As Boring (1966) said, a scientific success is a failure for psychical research; in other words, PP is concerned with those phenomena that 'mainstream' or 'regular' psychology cannot explain with its currently available models and theories (see above).

Other paranormal experiences which are increasingly becoming part of mainstream psychology are *near-death* and *out-of-body experiences*. The title of an article by Blackmore (1988), a British parapsychologist, illustrates this 'shrinkage' of PP very well: *'Visions from the dying brain – Near-death experiences may tell us more about consciousness and the brain than about what lies beyond the grave'*. In it, Blackmore discusses near-death experiences and considers alternative explanations in terms of known or hypothesised physiological processes, in particular those relating to brain mechanisms. While seeing such experiences as deserving of serious study (they are real, powerful experiences), she rejects the claim that they're evidence of life-after-death (the occult/supernatural explanation). Instead, she argues that they should be understood in terms of brain function (neuropsychological explanations). Not only can we apply what we already know (about the brain) to these experiences, but they can also teach us much about the brain.

Figure 6.1 *A representation of near-death experience (NDE) (© Liz Pyle, 1988)*

Methods used to study psi

According to Alcock (1981), definitions of ESP and PK are all negative, in the sense that they depend on ruling out 'normal' communication before the paranormal can be assumed. Progression in PP's experimental methods have necessarily been designed to exclude the 'normal' with even greater confidence. However, this inevitably leaves it open for critics to argue for even more devious ways in which sensory communication or outright fraud might occur (Blackmore, 1995).

ESP and Zener cards

The Rhines were convinced that the supposedly paranormal powers of the mind were essentially psychological phenomena, and so should be investigated with the tools of traditional psychological research. Throughout the 1930s, they conducted a lengthy series of *telepathy* experiments, in which a receiver had to guess the identity of a target being looked at by an *agent*. To make the task as easy as possible, a set of simple symbols was developed and made into *Zener cards* (named after their designer) or 'ESP cards'. They come as a pack of 25 cards, consisting of five circles, five squares, five crosses, five stars, and five wavy lines.

Figure 6.2 *Zener card symbols*

The rationale for these studies was that they allowed the experimenter to compare the results achieved with what would be expected by chance. So, in a pack of 25 cards comprising five of each of five distinct symbols, we'd expect, on average, five to be *guessed* correctly (i.e. by chance alone). If receivers repeatedly scored above chance over long series of trials, this would suggest that they were 'receiving' some information about the cards. This would, in turn, imply that, if the experiments had been sufficiently tightly controlled as to exclude all normal or known sensory cues, then the information must be coming via ESP (Evans, 1987a). In *clairvoyance* experiments, the cards were randomised out of sight of anyone, and in *precognition* experiments, the card order was determined only *after* the receiver had made his/her guesses.

The order was determined initially by shuffling, and later by the use of random number tables. Only if the targets in ESP experiments are properly randomised can any kind of systematic biases be excluded: shuffling isn't adequate (Blackmore, 1995).

What were the Rhines' findings?

The technique seemed to be successful, and the Rhines reported results that were way beyond what could be expected by chance (Blackmore, 1995). They claimed that they'd established the existence of ESP. However, these claims produced considerable opposition from the psychological establishment.

For example, were the Rhines' receivers completely physically isolated from the experimenter, so that information couldn't be passed unwittingly (for example, by unconsciously whispering or other non-deliberate cues)? Were

checks on the data records precise enough to ensure minor errors weren't made (unconsciously or deliberately) to bias the results in a pro-ESP direction?

The Rhines tightened up their procedures on both counts by (a) separating receiver and experimenter in different buildings, and (b) arranging independent verification and analysis of the results. As a consequence, the above-chance results became more rare, although they remained sufficiently common to constitute apparently indisputable evidence for ESP. However, then came another, more fundamental criticism. When psychologists not committed to a belief in ESP tried to replicate the Rhines' findings in their own laboratories, they simply failed to produce any positive results.

In response to this potentially fatal blow, parapsychologists argued that a significant factor in ESP might be the *experimenter's attitude* to the phenomenon under investigation: sceptical or dismissive experimenters ('goats') might have a 'negative effect' on the results (the Rhines, and other believers, being 'sheep'). This argument seems to imply that only believers are fit to investigate ESP, which is contrary to the spirit of scientific research (Evans, 1987a: see Chapter 3). The director of research at the Duke University Laboratory (the Rhines themselves had retired) was later caught flagrantly modifying some experimental data in a pro-ESP direction. Fortunately or unfortunately (depending on whether you're a goat or a sheep), this wasn't an isolated example.

> ### Ask yourself ...
> - Are you (still) a sheep or a goat?

Box 6.2 The problem of fraud

According to Colman (1987), the history of PP is ... disfigured by numerous cases of fraud involving some of the most 'highly respected scientists', their colleagues and participants ...'. For example, Soal (Soal & Bateman, 1954), a mathematician at Queen Mary College, London, tried to replicate some of the Rhines' telepathy experiments using Zener cards. Despite his rigid controls and the involvement of other scientists as observers throughout, accusations of fraud resulted in a series of re-analyses of the data. Marwick, a member of the Society for Psychical Research in London, finally proved (in 1978) that Soal *had* cheated (Blackmore, 1995).

Against this, it's misleading to suggest that experimenter fraud is rife in PP, or even that it's more common here than in other disciplines. According to Roe (personal communication), books such as *Betrayers of the Truth* (Broad & Wade, 1982) show that fraud is more likely when the rewards are high and the chances of being caught (publicly exposed) are low. This characterises mainstream science (especially medicine), and is certainly *not* characteristic of PP.

Free-response ESP

One drawback of the early Rhine research was that guessing long series of cards is extremely boring. By contrast, reports of psychic dreams, premonitions and other cases of spontaneous psi abounded. The challenge was to capture this under laboratory conditions (Blackmore, 1995). *Free-response ESP* represents the most important attempts to meet this challenge.

Remote viewing

Free-response methods include *remote viewing* (RV) *studies* (Targ & Puthoff, 1974, 1977). RV is a form of *clairvoyance*, in which an individual is able to 'see' a specific location some distance away, without receiving any information about it through the usual sensory channels. Targ and Puthoff reported a series of field studies involving Pat Price, a former California police commissioner, which sparked a debate between researchers as to whether Price's successes constituted genuine clairvoyance. Despite the controversy, the research was sufficiently convincing for the US military to fund a substantial research programme. The CIA declassified this information and released details of more than 20 years of RV research (Blackmore, 1996). RV has been put to practical use in 'psychic archaeology' (finding lost sites), criminal investigations (see Chapter 46), and, most controversially, to predict price fluctuations of silver futures on the stock market!

The Ganzfeld

The most successful free-response method has been the *Ganzfeld* ('ganz' = 'whole'; 'Feld' = 'field'), first used for psi research by Honorton in 1974. He argued that the reason ESP occurs in dreams, meditation and reverie is that they're all states of reduced sensory input and increased internal attention. He tried to find a way of producing such a 'psi-conducive' state without the expense of a dream laboratory (see Chapter 7).

A receiver in the Ganzfeld

Box 6.3 The Ganzfeld

Halved ping-pong balls are taped over the *receiver's* eyes, and red light is shone into them, so all that can be seen is a pinkish glow. Soothing sea-sounds or hissing 'white noise' (like a radio that's not properly tuned in) is played through headphones while the participant lays on a comfortable couch or reclining chair. While this doesn't constitute total sensory deprivation (see Chapter 9), the Ganzfeld deprives receivers of patterned input, encouraging internal imagery. They typically report a pleasant sensation of being immersed in a 'sea of light'.

A *sender* (an experimenter acting as an agent) is situated in a separate, acoustically isolated room. A visual stimulus (a picture, slide, or brief video sequence) is randomly selected from a large pool of similar stimuli to serve as the *target*. While the sender concentrates on the target (for about 15 minutes), the receiver tries to describe it by providing a continuous verbal report of his/her ongoing imagery and free associations. The sender stays in the room for another ten minutes. From a separate room, the experimenter can both hear (via a microphone) and see (via a one-way mirror) the receiver, and is blind to the target (doesn't know what the target is).

At the end of the experimental session, the receiver is presented with four stimuli (one of which is the target), and is asked to rate the degree to which each one matches the imagery and associations experienced during the session. A 'direct hit' is recorded if the receiver assigns the highest rating to the target. The sender is then called in and reveals the target. A typical experiment involves about 30 sessions.

The 'Ganzfeld debate'

Honorton (1985) analysed 28 studies using the Ganzfeld procedure (totalling 835 sessions, conducted in ten different laboratories). He reported a 38 per cent correct selection of the target, which compares with a 25 per cent success rate by chance alone (i.e. by guessing). Statistically, this is highly significant: the chances of obtaining a 38 per cent success rate by chance alone is less than one in a billion (Honorton, 1985).

However, a critical review by Hyman (in the *Journal of Parapsychology*, 1985) pointed out discrepancies in the scoring systems used, and procedural flaws (such as the failure to use proper randomisation for selecting the targets). Hyman also claimed to have found correlations between the quality ratings for studies and outcome, with the sloppier studies giving the 'better' results. However, in the same journal, Honorton claimed to have found *no* evidence of such a correlation. Rosenthal provided a commentary on the debate, generally regarded as favouring Honorton's interpretation (Blackmore, 1995).

Hyman and Honorton issued a joint 'communique' (Hyman & Honorton, 1986), in which they agreed that the studies as a whole fell short of ideal, but that something beyond selective reporting, or inflated significance levels, seemed to be producing the non-chance outcomes. They also agreed that the significant outcomes had been produced by several different researchers. Further replication would decide which of their interpretations was correct.

This debate, which Morris (1989) describes as '... an outstanding example of productive interaction between critic and researcher ...', brought parapsychologists and sceptics together to try to agree what would constitute an acceptable experiment. As a consequence, Honorton designed a *fully automated* Ganzfeld experiment, leaving little scope for human error or deliberate fraud. Several experiments produced significant results, which were published in the *Psychological Bulletin* in 1994. This is one of the world's most prestigious psychology journals, and meant that 'The Ganzfeld had achieved respectability ...' (Blackmore, 1997). However, despite many parapsychologists believing that the Ganzfeld is a genuinely repeatable experiment, most other scientists seem to reject the evidence:

> '"Unfair" say the parapsychologists. But we still do not know who is right'. (Blackmore, 1997)

Clairvoyance vs telepathy

Some Ganzfeld experiments didn't use a sender, so that the target images could be acquired through *clairvoyance* (telepathy would require the involvement of another mind – the sender's). Honorton (1985) reported that where a sender was involved (*telepathy condition*), the results were generally more positive – but only when the experimenters were already experienced in using both sender and no-sender methods. Where experimenters consistently used one or other method, the no-sender/clairvoyance condition produced slightly more positive results.

Some recurring issues in ESP research

In our discussion of ESP research so far, we've seen just how divided opinion is between those who believe in the reality of ESP ('sheep') and those who don't ('goats'). We've also seen that accusations of fraud – the deliberate invention or modification of procedures or results – have been a feature of the history of PP research. Arguably, this makes the study of psi unique as an area of psychological enquiry. At least as far as goats are concerned, parapsychologists are guilty unless proven innocent. In other words, if psi doesn't exist (as goats maintain), then any claims by sheep that it does must be based on fraudulent (or, at best, unreliable and/or invalid) data. So, rather than simply trying to produce evidence that supports the existence of psi, parapsychologists are constantly having to show that they're *not cheating*! But how can you prove a negative?

The history of PP also seems to highlight a number of methodological issues which, while they recur throughout all areas of psychological research, assume a more exaggerated or extreme form in relation to psi. These include:

- the question of *the 'conclusive 'experiment*;
- the *replication problem*;
- *publication bias* (or the *file-drawer problem*);
- the *inadequacy of controls*;
- *experimenter* and *participant effects*.

The question of the 'conclusive' experiment

According to Abelson (1978), then editor of *Science*, 'extraordinary claims require extraordinary evidence' (quoted in Rao & Palmer, 1987). This implies that the strength of evidence needed to establish a new phenomenon is directly proportional to how incompatible the phenomenon is with our current beliefs about the world. If we reject the possibility of this new phenomenon (its *subjective probability* is zero), then no amount of empirical evidence will be sufficient to establish the claim. Rao and Palmer point out that:

> 'In serious scientific discourse, however, few would be expected to take a zero-probability stance because such a stance could be seen to be sheer dogmatism, and the very antithesis of the basic assumption of science's open-endedness'.

Abelson's 'extraordinary evidence' sometimes means, in practice, demands for a 'foolproof' experiment that would control for all conceivable kinds of error, including experimenter fraud. This assumes that at any given time, one can identify all possible sources of error and how to control for them.

> ### Ask yourself ...
> - Is this assumption valid? (See Box 3.7, page 38.)

The demand for controls against fraud are unique to discussion of evidence for what are perceived as extraordinary claims, and as Rao & Palmer (1987) observe:

> 'The concept of a "conclusive" experiment, totally free of any possible error or fraud and immune to all skeptical doubt, is a practical impossibility for empirical phenomena. In reality, evidence in science is a matter of degree ... a "conclusive" experiment [should] be defined more modestly as one in which it is highly improbable that the result is artifactual ...'.

In other words, there are no *absolutes* in science (no certainty, no once-and-for-all 'proof'), only *probabilities* (see Chapter 3). In *this* sense, Rao and Palmer believe that a case can be made for 'conclusive' experiments in PP.

> ### Box 6.4   Schmidt's (1969) random event generator (REG)
>
> Schmidt was a physicist at the Boeing Scientific Research Laboratories in the USA, designed to test for the possibility of ESP. A specially built machine seemed to rule out all artefacts arising from recording errors, sensory cues, or receiver cheating. The machine randomly selected targets with equal probability, and recorded both target selections and receivers' responses. The receiver's task was to guess which of four lamps would light, and press the corresponding button if aiming for a high number of hits (or to avoid pressing if aiming for a low number).
>
> Random lighting of the lamps was achieved by a sophisticated electronic *random event generator* (REG), which was extensively tested in control trials and found not to deviate significantly from chance.

The REG experiments:

- represent one of the major experimental paradigms in contemporary PP;
- are regarded by most parapsychologists as providing good evidence for psi;
- have been subjected to detailed scrutiny by critics.

Despite this, and almost inevitably, they've been criticised. For example, Hansel (1980) claimed that Schmidt's highly significant results haven't been replicated by other researchers (see below), and these criticisms are routinely taken as valid by most sceptics (such as Alcock, 1981). Although Hyman (1981) is one of the few psi goats who's questioned Hansel's basic reasoning, he still agrees with Hansel's claim that the REG experiments don't provide an adequate case for the existence of psi. However, according to Hyman (in Rao & Palmer, 1987):

'There is no such thing as an experiment immune from trickery … Even if one assembles all the world's magicians and scientists and puts them to the task of designing a fraud-proof experiment, it cannot be done'.

The replication problem

Rao & Palmer (1987) argue that science is concerned with establishing general laws, not unique events (this relates to the *idiographic–nomothetic debate*: see Chapter 42). Like other psychological phenomena, psi as a laboratory effect must be reasonably capable of being observed repeatedly if it's to be studied effectively and understood.

However, even Hansel (1980) conceded that the importance of a foolproof experiment recedes as the phenomenon becomes increasingly replicable. But replicability doesn't necessarily mean that a finding must be reproducible on demand. An experiment isn't either replicable or not replicable, but rather it's on a continuum:

'In this sense of statistical replication, an experiment or an effect may be considered replicated if a series of replication attempts provides statistically significant evidence for the original effect when analysed as a series'. (Rao & Palmer, 1987)

In other words, does the evidence *overall* support the existence of the effect being investigated? On *balance*, does the accumulated evidence, based on a large number of replication attempts, point towards the existence of psi, or not?

At the very least, 'reproducibility on demand' could only occur if one had perfect understanding of the critical variables and had control over them (see above). However, in practice:

'… perfect duplication of conditions is impossible to achieve. This is especially true in behavioural science experiments, where the causes of an effect are likely to be complex and difficult to pin down'. (Rao & Palmer, 1987)

Since a major goal of scientific investigation is to understand these crucial variables, it's inappropriate to demand absolute or even strong replicability of a phenomenon as a prerequisite for further research. If we already knew what those crucial variables were, there'd be no need to do the research in the first place – or the knowledge has come from research that's already been done!

Rao and Palmer argue that, once we give up the idea of absolute replication, we can see that parapsychological phenomena are replicated in a statistically significant sense.

As Atkinson *et al.* (1990) claim, experimenter effects (see below) may be even more acute in PP than in other research areas. Psi effects may legitimately depend on the motivational atmosphere created by the experimenter, which may reflect his/her attitudes towards psi and even his/her own psi abilities. However, even if we accept these potential difficulties, replicability of the Ganzfeld effect, for example, doesn't seem to depend on the significant results reported by just one or two researchers. For example, Palmer, Honorton & Utts (1988)

reviewed 28 Ganzfeld studies and found that significant results were reported by six out of the ten investigators. Even if all the 14 studies conducted by the two most successful are removed from the analysis, the results remain significant.

Publication bias (or the 'file-drawer' problem)

The so-called *file-drawer problem* refers to the claim that non-significant results may systematically go unreported: if a study fails to find evidence of psi, it's 'consigned to the filing-cabinet drawer', so that no one except the researchers who conducted the study knows of its existence. This would mean that those that are published (the database of known studies) may not accurately reflect the true state of affairs: they'll be strongly biased in favour of psi.

According to Rao & Palmer (1987), close scrutiny of the field suggests that the file-drawer problem cannot explain away the significant number of replications in PP. But isn't it impossible ever to establish how many studies may have been 'binned'?

Box 6.5 Solving the file-drawer problem

Parapsychologists are more sensitive to the possible impact of unreported negative results than most other scientists. In the USA, the Parapsychological Association (PA) has advocated publishing all methodologically sound experiments, regardless of the outcome. Since 1976, this policy has been reflected in publications of all affiliated journals (such as the *Journal of Parapsychology*) and in papers accepted for presentation at annual PA conventions.

There are relatively few parapsychologists, and most are aware of ongoing work in the various laboratories around the world. When conducting a meta-analysis (a special statistical technique which allows diverse studies to be compared on a single measure, called an *averaged effect size*: see Chapter 45), parapsychologists actively seek out unpublished negative studies at conventions and through personal networks.

A technique exists which makes it possible to estimate the number of unpublished, non-significant experiments that would be necessary to reduce an entire database to non-significance. For example, Honorton (1985) estimated that 423 non-significant Ganzfeld studies would be needed to reduce the direct-hit studies to a non-significant level (the equivalent of 12,000 sessions: see Box 6.3).

'Given the complex and time-consuming nature of the Ganzfeld procedure, it is unreasonable to suppose that so many experiments exist in the "file drawer" …'. (Rao & Palmer, 1987)

There are also some areas where we can be reasonably certain we have access to all the experiments conducted, for example, research into the relationship between ESP performance and ratings obtained on the defence mechanism test (DMT). Because the administration and scoring of the test requires specialised training available only to a few individuals, Johnson (at the University of Utrecht and a leading authority on DMT) has been able to keep track of the relevant experiments, conducted by qualified people. In all ten experiments identified by Johnson & Haraldsson (1984, cited in Rao & Palmer, 1987), the less defensive participants scored higher on ESP tests, seven studies proving significant at the 0.05 level.

(Based on Rao & Palmer, 1987; Atkinson *et al.*, 1990)

The inadequacy of controls

According to Alcock (1981), replication of an experimental result by other experimenters:

'... does not assure that experimental artifacts were not responsible for the results in the replication as well as in the original experiment'.

This is like saying that 'two wrongs don't make a right'. While it's true that replicating an effect implies nothing directly about its cause, it's also a basic premise of experimental science that replication reduces the probability of *some* causal explanations, particularly those related to the honesty or competence of individual experimenters (Rao & Palmer, 1987). As Alcock (1981) himself says in another context:

'It is not enough for a researcher to report his observations with respect to a phenomenon; he could be mistaken, or even dishonest. But if other people, using his methodology, can independently produce the same results, it is much more likely that error and dishonesty are not responsible for them'.

Some more specific criticisms of ESP research relating to inadequacy of controls were discussed in the sections on Methods used to study psi above (see pages 80–82).

Experimenter and participant effects

Alcock (1981) and others have argued that replications must be conducted by investigators *unsympathetic to psi* (goats). This would exclude most – but not all – parapsychologists (Blackmore being a good example of one who would 'qualify'). Researchers' personal beliefs are rarely reported and may often be difficult to determine reliably. Rao & Palmer (1987) believe that if such a criterion were to be applied retrospectively to published research in psychology as a whole, there wouldn't be much left. Why should parapsychologists be singled out in this way, and why haven't critics suggested that negative results from 'disbelievers' in psi also be rejected? It's impossible to know how many 'disbelievers' have obtained positive results, nor can we assume that such results would necessarily be acknowledged as such.

However, one of the most consistent findings in parapsychological research is that some experimenters, using well-controlled methods, repeatedly produce significant results, while others, using exactly the same methods, consistently produce non-significant results. As we saw in Chapter 3 (see Box 3.6, page 37), experimenters can affect the outcome of experiments, unwittingly, through tone of voice and other forms of bodily communication, which can subtly (and unconsciously) convey expectations to the participants. These experimenter effects have long been recognised and discussed in PP.

Box 6.6	Psi-permissive, psi-inhibitory, and psi-conducive experimenters

Some experimenters seem capable of creating a climate in which participants' psi abilities are allowed to express themselves (*psi-permissive* experimenters), while others have the opposite effect and produce consistently negative results (*psi-inhibitory* results). These differences seem to be related to:

- the pleasantness/unpleasantness of the experimental setting for the participant, such that a relaxed participant is more likely to display psi abilities (Crandall, 1985);
- the experimenter's expectations, such that participants are more likely to display psi abilities if the experimenter expects positive results (Taddonio, 1976).

According to Schmiedler (1997), some experimenters have produced particularly high levels of positive results with participants who fail to repeat their performance later. This could be explained in terms of a highly motivated experimenter, who has strong psi abilities him/herself. S/he may somehow *transfer* these abilities to participants during the course of the experiments (but not beyond). These are referred to as *psi-conducive* experimenters. This transfer can distort the experimental findings.

People with particular personality characteristics may be more likely to display psi abilities. For example, extroverts tend to score more highly in free-response Ganzfeld studies (Honorton *et al.*, 1990), although Morris *et al.* (1995: cited in Hayes, 1998) found a slight positive correlation between *introversion* and psi success with an artistic population (see Chapter 42). Also correlated with positive results are:

- having participated in other psi experiments (perhaps by reducing anxiety: Honorton, 1992);
- having practised yoga or meditation (which both induce an enhanced state of relaxation);
- being highly creative, especially musically (Dalton, 1997; Schlitz & Honorton, 1992).

Paranormal phenomena and the mind–brain relationship

Ask yourself ...

- What implications do paranormal phenomena have for belief in the existence of mind as separate from the body (or brain)?
- Do you believe that the mind exists separately from the body (or brain)?

As we noted earlier, PP grew out of spiritualism and psychical research. What seems to underlie accounts of psi is the notion of mind affecting other minds (as in ESP) or matter (as in PK), but this is exactly what most of us believe happens whenever we do anything at all, such as waggling a finger. 'Common sense' seems to assume *dualism*, the philosophical theory according to which mind and body (or mind and brain) are distinct. This contrasts with *identity theories* of the mind–body/brain relationship, which maintain that there is only 'matter' (see Chapter 49). According to Gregory (1987a):

'Clear-cut paranormal phenomena demonstrating disembodied mind might conceivably show identity theories to be untenable. So paranormal accounts do have empirical consequences, even though ... we may seriously doubt whether there are any such phenomena'.

Similarly, if it could be shown that psi exists:

> 'Not only would strictly mechanistic models of psychology – such as … Skinnerian behaviourism … have to be scrapped, but many of the assumptions and theories of physical science would need at least to be thoroughly overhauled …'. (Evans, 1987b)

According to Beloff (1987), not all parapsychologists are necessarily dualists, just as they're not necessarily 'believers'. Blackmore is a good example of a parapsychologist who regards psi as a function of the brain (see above, page 80).

Box 6.7   Psi and consciousness

According to Blackmore (1996), the popular view is that if ESP exists, it proves that mental phenomena are *non-local* (independent of space and time). If PK exists, it proves that mind can reach out beyond the brain to affect things at a distance. If you equate mind with consciousness, then, hey presto, ESP and PK prove the power of consciousness. She argues that it's a desire for this 'power of consciousness' that fuels much of the enthusiasm for the paranormal.

However, the more we look into the workings of the brain, the less it looks like a machine run by a conscious self. There's no place inside the brain where consciousness 'resides', where mental images are 'viewed', or where instructions are 'issued'. There's just massive parallel processing throughout and no centre (see Chapter 4). Indeed, she argues, there are even a few crucial experiments suggesting that conscious experience takes some time to build up, and is much too slow to be responsible for making things happen (see Chapter 7):

> '… the brain seems to be a machine that runs itself very well and produces an illusion that there is someone in charge …'.

PP is trying to prove that consciousness really does have power, that our minds really can reach out and 'do' things, not only within our own bodies but beyond.

Conclusions: The controversy goes on

Beloff (1987) considers it astonishing that:

> '… a century after the founding of the Society for Psychical Research, there is still a total lack of consensus regarding the actuality of any parapsychological phenomenon …'.

Similarly, Scott (1987) maintains that:

> 'Perhaps the only non-controversial statement that can be made about the present position is that the controversy continues …'.

Eysenck & Sargent (1993), two psychologists known for being hard-nosed scientists, who demand rigorous, objective standards of experimentation, conclude that:

> 'Human beings do seem to use sensory abilities beyond their "conventional" senses. They do seem to influence distant events and objects through will alone.'

Some parapsychologists and physicists are working actively on possible meeting points between PP and the 'new physics'

(*quantum theory/mechanics*). For example, there's evidence that the conscious act of making an experimental observation can directly influence the random events in the apparatus (Simpson, 2000). The new physics represents a major revolution in science since the beginning of the twentieth century, which, according to Morgan (2000):

> '… has challenged the very basis of classical materialism and caused a fundamental re-examination of the traditional division between mind and matter …'.

Perhaps the real significance of psi and of PP as areas of research, is that they force us to question some of our basic beliefs and assumptions about the world and ourselves. Both scientists and non-scientists are capable of prejudice and closed-mindedness, and PP can be seen as a case-study in 'doing science', which isn't the unbiased, objective activity which many scientists take it to be (see Chapters 3 and 47).

CHAPTER SUMMARY

- **Parapsychology** (PP) is the scientific study of paranormal phenomena (or 'psi'). Many psychologists have denied the possibility of their existence, and the history of PP is littered with accusations of fraud.

- Modern PP grew out of **spiritualistic research/spiritualism** and **psychical research** dating back to the 1880s.

- **Extrasensory perception** (ESP) consists of **telepathy**, **clairvoyance**, and **precognition**. The direction of influence is from environment to person. In **psychokinesis** (PK), the influence is from person to environment.

- PP is concerned with phenomena that mainstream psychology cannot explain. As psychological understanding increases, so the field of PP shrinks.

- Early ESP research used **Zener cards**, which allowed the experimenter to compare the results with what would be expected by chance (i.e. guessing).

- In **telepathy** experiments, a **receiver** had to guess the identity of a **target** symbol being looked at by an **agent/sender**. In **clairvoyance** experiments, the cards were randomised out of sight of everyone, and in **precognition** experiments, card order was determined only **after** the receiver had made his/her guesses.

- **Free-response** methods include **remote-viewing**, and the **Ganzfeld**. The so-called **Ganzfeld debate** brought parapsychologists and sceptics together in an effort to define an acceptable experiment. This resulted in a **fully automated Ganzfeld**, but the dispute between '**sheep**' and '**goats**' continues.

- Several methodological issues assume a more extreme form in relation to psi. These include the issue of the '**conclusive' experiment**, the **replication problem**, **publication bias** (the **file-drawer problem**), the **inadequacy of controls**, and **experimenter/participant effects**.

- The **random event generator** (REG) is regarded by many parapsychologists as constituting a 'conclusive' experiment, but critics disagree. The safest conclusion is that there's no such thing as a fraud-proof experiment.

- One of the most consistent findings concerns the consistency with which different experimenters produce positive or negative results (**psi-permissive**, **psi-inhibitory**, and **psi-conducive**). Important individual differences between participants relevant to psi abilities have also been identified.

- Belief in psi supports a **dualist** theory of the **mind-body/brain relationship**, as opposed to **identity theories**. But not all parapsychologists are necessarily dualists, and mind or consciousness can be explained in terms of brain processes alone.

- **Quantum theory/mechanics** challenges the traditional division between mind and matter, and may offer a revolutionary way of thinking about the world which could accommodate paranormal phenomena.

Self-assessment questions

1 Discuss some of the major methodological issues that have arisen in relation to parapsychological research.

2 a Explain what is meant by the Ganzfeld technique.
b Critically assess the significance of the 'Ganzfeld debate' within parapsychology as a whole.

3 Describe and evaluate parapsychological evidence for the existence of psi.

Web addresses

moebius.psy.ed.ac.uk/

www.ed.ac.uk/~ejua35/parapsy.htm

www.parapsychology.org/

www.rhine.org/

www.psiresearch.org/para1.html

www.xs4all.nl/~wichm/paraps.html

Further reading

Blackmore, S. (1995) Parapsychology. In A.M. Colman (Ed.) *Controversies in Psychology*. London: Longman. A very useful overview of the whole field, covering many of the issues raised in this chapter, sometimes in more detail than is possible here (such as the history of PP).

Gross, R. (1999) *Key Studies in Psychology* (3rd edition). London: Hodder & Stoughton. Chapter.27 provides a very detailed summary – and evaluation – of Blackmore's article on near-death experiences (referred to in this chapter – page 80).

Radin, D.I. (1997) *The Conscious Universe: The Scientific Truth of Psychic Phenomena*. New York: Harper Edge. A useful and detailed assessment of all the research described in this chapter – and lots more that isn't.

Chapter 7

States of Consciousness and Bodily Rhythms

Introduction and overview

For the first 30 or so years of its life as a separate discipline, pioneered by figures such as William James and Wilhelm Wundt, psychology took conscious human experience as its subject matter. As we saw in Chapter 1, *introspection* – the observation of one's own mind – was the primary method used to study it. This interest in consciousness shouldn't come as a surprise, given how fundamental it is to everything we do (Rubin & NcNeill, 1983).

Yet it's the very subjectivity of our experience that led Watson to reject introspectionism in favour of a truly scientific (i.e. objective) approach to the study of psychology, namely behaviourism. Writing from the perspective of a modern neuroscientist, Greenfield (1998) states that:

'Any scientific explanation of consciousness must be objective and embrace physical properties of the brain: but at the same time it must, nonetheless, somehow take account of the subjective. This is why consciousness has been such an anathema to scientists, because the whole essence of science is objectivity. And yet we are going to deal with a phenomenon that is subjective ...'.

However, as part of the 'cognitive revolution' in the 1950s, 'the mind' once more became an acceptable, focus of psychological research. Reflecting the current interest in consciousness by neuroscientists, philosophers, and psychologists, one of the questions we'll be asking here is: how might the brain generate consciousness?

There has been a considerable amount of research into *sleep* as a state of consciousness since the 1950s, much of it trying to find correlations between objective measures of physiological activity and subjective experience, in particular *dreaming*. Sleep is increasingly being discussed in relation to *bodily rhythms*, disruption of which through our modern life-style, is more and more being seen as a risk to health. According to Hobson (1995), the rhythm of rest and activity, '... the primordial of sleeping and waking ...', represents one of the most universal and basic features of life. So, the study of sleep is of interest to biologists as well as to psychologists.

What is 'consciousness'?

Are only human beings 'conscious'?

Ask yourself ...

- In what sense could non-human animals be described as conscious?

If being conscious means having sensations of pain, cold, hunger, fear, and so on, most species can be said to be conscious (see Chapter 48). Perhaps *sentient* would be a better term than 'conscious'.

If by conscious we mean having *self-consciousness*, then humans may be unique (with the possible exception of some higher primates: see Chapters 19 and 33). According to Singer (1998), *self-awareness* (normally used synonymously with 'self-consciousness') is the experience of one's own individuality, the ability to experience oneself as an autonomous individual with subjective feelings. It's considered to be '... the result of social interactions, and hence of cultural evolution'. This suggests that it's a rather human thing to have.

Singer also claims that when we say we're conscious, we usually mean that we perceive and remember in a way that makes it possible to report about the perceived and remembered content, or to make it the object of intentional deliberations. Given the crucial role of language in these processes, and given that language is regarded by many as unique to humans (but see Chapter 19), the rest of this chapter will focus on consciousness as a characteristic of human beings.

Some other definitions

- When we're awake we're *conscious*, but when we're asleep, in a coma, or we've been 'knocked out' by a punch to the head, we're *unconscious*. The term 'unconscious' is often reserved for the last two examples (but see below).
- When we do something *consciously*, we do it deliberately or knowingly, but to do something *unconsciously* means doing it automatically or without having to think about it (for example, an experienced driver or typist: see Chapter 13)
- Public-health campaigns (such as those promoting safe sex) are aimed at increasing *public consciousness* or awareness of the dangers of certain types of behaviour (see Chapters 12 and 24).

Freud saw consciousness as a whole comprising three levels:

- the *conscious*: what we're fully aware of at any one time;
- the *preconscious*: what we could become aware of quite easily if we switched our attention to it;
- the *unconscious*: what we've pushed out of our conscious minds, through repression, making it extremely inaccessible, although it continues to exert an influence on our thoughts, feelings and behaviour (see Chapters 2 and 42).

Most psychologists would agree that thoughts, feelings, memories, and so on, differ in their degree of accessibility. But most wouldn't accept Freud's formulation of the unconscious (based on repression). Indeed, other psychodynamic theorists, in particular Jung, disagreed fundamentally with Freud's view of the unconscious (see Chapter 42).

Rubin & McNeil (1983) define consciousness as 'our subjective awareness of our actions and of the world around us'. So, consciousness points *inwards*, towards our thoughts, feelings, actions and so on, and *outwards*, towards external, environmental events (including other people). This mirrors the 'mental' orientation of Wundt and James and cognitive psychologists since the mid-1950s, and Watson's (and Skinner's) behaviourist orientation respectively.

Consciousness, arousal and alertness

Objective physiological measures, such as electroencephalograms (EEGs), electromyograms (EMGs), electro-oculograms (EOGs) (see Chapter 4), breathing and heart rates, and other correlates of consciousness, are often described as measures of level of *arousal* or *alertness*. Both subjectively and in terms of overt behaviour, there's an obvious difference between being sleepy and being wide awake in terms of degree of arousal or alertness. Less obvious are the smaller changes which occur during normal wakefulness, and which are of two kinds – *tonic* and *phasic* – mediated by different brain systems (Lloyd *et al.*, 1984).

Tonic alertness

Changes in *tonic alertness* reflect intrinsic (and usually quite slow) changes of the basic level of arousal throughout a 24-hour period (or even across a lifetime), and so are closely related to various *biological rhythms*, in particular the *circadian rhythm* (see below). It was originally thought that the reticular activating system (RAS) was solely responsible for prompting and maintaining consciousness (in Chapter 4, the RAS was described as a 'consciousness switch'). For instance, if the brainstem is severed *below* the RAS, the animal will be paralysed but will remain fully alert when awake and will show normal sleep–wake EEG patterns. However, if it's severed *above* the RAS, it will fall into a state of continuous slow-wave sleep (see below).

KEY STUDY 7.1

Moruzzi & Magoun's (1949) study of cats' RAS

Moruzzi and Magoun found that electrical stimulation of the RAS of sleeping cats woke them up, in anaesthetised cats it produced long-lasting signs of arousal in their EEGs, and in cats that weren't anaesthetised, the effect of RAS stimulation was to produce behavioural signs of arousal, alertness and attention. According to Moruzzi and Magoun, sleep occurs when the activity of the RAS falls below a certain critical level.

In sleep, sensory input to the RAS is reduced, and the electrical activity sweeping from the RAS up through the cortex drops below the level required to keep us awake (Diagram Group, 1982).

It's now known that other brain structures (both in the thalamus and hypothalamus) are involved in the sleep-wake cycle, and the co-ordination of all these systems is necessary for the initiation and maintenance of conscious awareness. Both during wakefulness and sleep, there are periodic, fairly predictable changes in the degree of alertness: the daytime changes are governed by a *diurnal rhythm* and the sleep (nighttime) changes by an *ultradian rhythm*.

Phasic alertness

Changes in *phasic alertness* involve short-term, temporary variations in arousal, over a period of seconds, initiated by novel and important environmental events. An important component of these changes is the *orienting response* to arousing stimuli. It involves a decrease in heart rate and breathing rate, pupil dilation, tensing of the muscles and characteristic changes in the EEG, which becomes desynchronised.

If the stimuli are continuously presented, the orienting response is replaced by *habituation*, whereby the person or non–human animal stops responding to them. Habituation is, in fact, a form of *adaptation*. It's more important from a survival point of view to respond to novel stimuli, and since most stimuli are relatively constant, we need to be able to attend selectively to those which are different and/or unexpected. It's the *changing* aspects of the environment which demand, and usually receive, our attention, and nervous systems have evolved so as to make them especially responsive to change.

Consciousness and attention

Although consciousness is difficult to describe because it's fundamental to everything we do (Rubin & McNeil, 1983), one way of trying to 'pin it down' is to study what we're paying attention to, what's in the forefront of our consciousness. According to Allport (1980a), 'attention is the experimental psychologist's code name for consciousness'.

Focal attention

Focal attention/awareness is what we're currently paying deliberate attention to, and what's in the centre of our awareness (this corresponds to Freud's conscious). All those other aspects of our environment, or our own thoughts and feelings, which are on the fringes of our awareness, but which could easily become the object of our focal attention, are within our *peripheral attention/awareness* (corresponding to Freud's preconscious).

We seem to be capable of doing many things quite unconsciously or automatically (without having to think about what we're doing), and a good illustration of this is perception. It's difficult to imagine what it would be like if we were aware of how we perceive.

Box 7.1 | **Perception as an automatic process: doing what comes naturally**

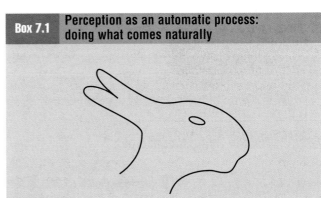

Figure 7.1

To select *consciously* one version of the ambiguous duck/rabbit figure above, we must *either* know that there's a duck and a rabbit 'in' the picture, *or* we must have already perceived both versions (in which case, how did the original perception come about?). You may have had difficulty yourself perceiving the duck if your immediate perception was of the rabbit, even though you consciously 'searched' for, and tried to see, the alternative version. This illustrates the very important difference between *conception* and *perception*: most of the time, perception is something we 'just do' (see Chapter 15).

Conversely, something we normally do quite automatically, such as walking down stairs, might be disrupted if we try to bring it into focal awareness (for example, thinking about each step as we take it: don't try this at home!). In general, being able to do things automatically makes sense in terms of freeing us to attend to those environmental events which are unfamiliar or threatening in some way. If we had to think about our bodily movements when walking, this would add to the long list of sources of stimulation competing for our attention! (see Chapter 13).

Even with skills which definitely do require focal attention when first acquired (such as driving or playing the piano), once they've been mastered, they become automatic. As Lloyd *et al.* (1984) put it, unconscious processes seem to be 'precipitates' of earlier conscious processes.

Nisbett & Wilson (1977) go so far as to claim that all psychological activities (including social behaviour) are governed by processes *of which we're unaware*. If people are asked what they think governed their behaviour after participating in a social psychology experiment, the answers they give don't usually correspond very well with the explanations which psychologists offer for the same behaviour (and which they believe are the *real reasons*).

Nisbett and Wilson argue that our belief that we can account for our own behaviour ('commonsense' or *intuitive explanations*) is illusory, because what *really* guides our behaviour is unavailable to consciousness (compare this with Freud's distinction between 'our' reasons and 'the reasons': see Chapter 42). We don't have direct or 'privileged' access to our cognitive processes themselves, only to the *products/outputs* of those processes. Joynson (1974), Heather (1976) and other psychologists present an opposing view, arguing that people are psychologists, and that commonsense explanations may be as valid as theoretical, scientific ones (see Chapter 1).

> **Ask yourself ...**
>
> - Do you lean towards Nisbett and Wilson on this issue, or Joynson and Heather?
> - How might you try to choose between them?

Consciousness and brain activity

Passingham at Oxford University and his colleagues from the Institute of Neurology in London (1998, in McCrone, 1999) conducted a finger-tapping experiment, which may have revolutionary implications for our understanding of what it means to experience something consciously.

> **Box 7.2 Could finger-tapping be the key to conscious experience?**
>
> Participants positioned their heads into the heart of a brain scanner and rested one of their hands on a keypad. Then, by trial-and-error, they started to work out an unknown sequence of eight finger taps. A tick would flash up on a screen whenever they pressed the correct key. Once they knew the sequence, their instruction was to keep drumming out the pattern until it became an unthinking rhythm. After an hour, their fingers were skipping through the complex routine almost of their own accord, and they were barely conscious of what they were doing.
>
> In the learning phase, while having to remember what they'd just discovered and simultaneously groping for the next step, regions all over the brain were clearly very active. These included a range of high-level cognitive areas in the forebrain (such as those involved with planning and memory), as well as other, lower brain areas that regulate movements (such as the basal ganglia and the cerebellum: see Chapter 4). Yet, within minutes of 'getting' the sequence, this 'wash' of activity began to fade. The job of moving the fingers became confined to just a small set of motor areas. According to McCrone (1999):

> 'It seems, having used the whole brain consciously to establish the individual finger movements, just the bare bones of the routine are left. The brain now has a template, or habit that can produce the same behaviour 'as if' it were still going through all the hoops of being consciously aware'.

McCrone believes that Passingham *et al.*'s results aren't especially surprising. After all, we'd expect the brain to be capable of 'automating' motor tasks, such as typing or riding a bike. However, he refers to other imaging studies, which have shown that a similar process occurs when we learn more cognitive skills, such as matching verbs to nouns (e.g. 'hammer' and 'hit'), learning to play a computer game, and learning a path through a drawn maze. What these studies show is that:

> '... paying focal, effortful attention to something calls large regions of the brain into action. The brain does not behave like a collection of isolated pathways, each doing their own thing, but as a coherent system'. (McCrone, 1999)

There seem to be general-purpose planning centres that come into play whenever the brain deals with any kind of novel or difficult mental situation. These guide the more specialist language and motor centres to an appropriate output. Once the brain has found an optimal way to respond to a certain situation, the 'wider scaffolding' quickly falls away. It's not a case of practice making more efficient use of the pathways that were active during conscious learning, but rather the response can be reduced to its bare essentials. When Passingham *et al.* asked their participants to pay close attention to their finger-tapping rhythms (after this had become automatic), their pre-frontal cortices immediately became active again. Just as significantly, their actual performance became more ragged, as if their brains were being put back into exploratory mode.

How might the brain generate consciousness?

Greenfield (1998) suggests that consciousness may have three properties:

- Where might a 'consciousness centre' in the brain be? A recurring problem in neuroscience in general is the difficulty of 'location of function' (see Chapter 4). Vision, memory, movement and other brain/mind functions seem almost certainly *not* to be related in a modular way to single respective brain regions. Many different regions play *parallel* roles, analysing the outside world in various ways and reintegrating it into a connected whole. This is likely to be true of consciousness: it could be spatially multiple, but also temporally unitary (that is, we're usually only conscious of any one state at a time). This view is consistent with Passingham *et al.*'s research discussed above.

- Rather than being all-or-nothing (either you're conscious or you're not), a more plausible scenario is that consciousness is more like the light on a dimmer switch that grows as the brain does. The more complex the brain, the greater the consciousness, with a continuum running from minimal to profound. This view can accommodate non-human animal consciousness, children's consciousness, as well as differences between the same individuals on different occasions (for example, changes in consciousness induced by drugs – see Chapters 8 and 45 – religious experience, or listening to music).

■ We're always conscious *of something*: there's always some kind of focus, epicentre or trigger.

Box 7.3 Epicentres and neuronal connectivity

The circuitry of the brain changes with learning and development. As we noted in Chapter 4, it's connections between neurons, rather than neurons themselves, that are established as a result of postnatal experience. This *plasticity* is especially marked in humans, and the brain remains adaptable and sensitive to life experiences even in adults (see Ramachandran's explanation of phantom limbs in Chapter 4, pages 53–54). Experience changes the connectivity of neurons according to whatever circuits are most stimulated, and hence the most active.

The *epicentre* is like a stone thrown into a pond, causing ripples to spread out over the surface of the water. The extent of these neuronal 'ripples' would affect the degree of consciousness at any one time. The epicentre that's going to trigger consciousness at any one moment is mediated by a group of neurons with relatively long-lasting connections between them. The activated hub of neurons generates the ripples in the brain which constitute consciousness.

(From Greenfield, 1998)

How might this happen? Greenfield cites an experiment by Libet, in which he pricked participants' skin and recorded the activity of large parts of the brain surface using the EEG. There was a huge amount of activity in the somatosensory cortex, but participants reported *no* conscious experience of tingling or any other sensations. They felt nothing, although their brain was registering signals of the touch to the skin, via the spinal cord. In Greenfield's model, it's this early component in the response that's equivalent to the 'epicentre'. But then, after about 500 m/sec, the activity evoked by the skin prick spread away from the somatosensory cortex to a much larger area of the brain. Only at this stage did participants report feeling a tingle.

Because we never have the same conscious experience on two separate occasions, the same number of neurons will never be stimulated to exactly the same extent or in exactly the same way more than once. Greenfield's model, therefore, needs a neuronal mechanism that can bias a large number of neurons to become activated simultaneously, and she believes that *neuromodulators* fit the bill. We saw in Chapter 4 that these chemicals 'prime' (*bias* or *modulate*) neurons for stimulation by neurotransmitters.

The functions of consciousness: What is it for?

Like perception, many cases of problem-solving seem to involve processes which are 'out of consciousness'. For example, answers often seem to 'pop into our heads', and we don't know how we reached them. If what's important is the solution (as opposed to the process involved in reaching it), then consciousness may be seen as *incidental* to information-processing (consistent with Nisbett and Wilson's view: see above, page 91). But while perception and other basic cognitive and

behavioural processes may not *require* consciousness, they're usually at least *accompanied* by consciousness. Assuming that most other species lack our kind of consciousness, then we can infer that it evolved in human beings for some purpose.

The complexity of our nervous systems which makes our consciousness possible provided our ancestors with the flexibility of behaviour which helped them survive. However, it's less obvious whether consciousness was itself adaptive or simply a side-effect or by-product of a complex nervous system. Some psychologists and biologists believe that consciousness is a powerful agent for controlling behaviour, which has evolved *in its own right*. Accordingly, non-conscious problem-solving systems are seen as the *servants of consciousness* (Ruch, 1984).

Box 7.4 Evolution of the 'inner eye'

Humphrey (1986, 1993) argues that if consciousness (the 'inner eye') is the answer to anything at all, it must be to a biological challenge which human beings have had to meet, namely, the human need to understand, respond to and manipulate the behaviour of other human beings:

'The first use of human consciousness was – and is – to enable each human being to understand what it feels like to be human and so to make sense of himself and other people from the inside'. (Humphrey, 1993)

This inner eye allowed our ancestors to raise social life to a new level, so that consciousness is essential for human social activity. We're natural psychologists in a way that species lacking consciousness cannot be (see Gross, 1995).

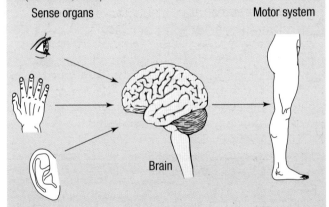

Figure 7.2a *How an animal without insight works (from Humphrey, 1986)*

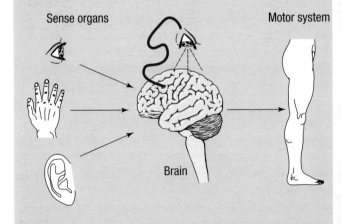

Figure 7.2b *How the addition of an 'inner eye' affects the animal (from Humphrey, 1986)*

Two kinds of consciousness

According to Hilgard's (1977) *'neodissociation' theory of hypnosis* (see Gross, 1999), the consciousness which solves a problem may be different from that which reports the solution: neither is 'higher' or 'lower' than the other, they're simply different. This is consistent with the work on *split-brain patients*. As we saw in Chapter 4, some psychologists believe that the two cerebral hemispheres are specialised (although they share the potential for many functions and both participate in most psychological activities), so that each is dominant with respect to particular functions.

Ornstein (1986) believes that these two modes of operation represent two distinct modes of consciousness. In daily life, we normally just alternate between them and, although they might complement each other, they don't readily substitute for one another (as when you try to describe a spiral staircase or how to tie a shoelace). Is there any evidence to support these claims?

KEY STUDY 7.2

Alpha rhythms and hemispheric lateralisation (Galin & Ornstein, 1972)

Galin and Ornstein (cited in Ornstein, 1986) recorded changes in participants' EEGs when presented with either verbal or spatial tasks. On verbal tasks, *alpha rhythms* (associated with a waking adult with the eyes closed) in the *right* hemisphere *increased* relative to the left, while on spatial tasks, the reverse was true. The appearance of alpha rhythms indicates a 'turning off' of information-processing in the area of the brain involved so, on verbal tasks, information-processing is being turned off in the right hemisphere. This is the side of the brain not being used (as if to reduce the interference between the two conflicting modes of operation of the two hemispheres).

Similarly, people with damage to the left hemisphere have greater problems with consciously executed writing, while those with right-hemisphere damage have greater problems with more automatic writing, such as signing their names. This suggests that the left hemisphere may be more involved in highly conscious processes which require intentional behaviour and the focusing of attention, while the right may be more involved with automatic or unconscious actions, and more sensitive to material outside the conscious focus of attention.

Consciousness and the electroencephalogram (EEG)

As we saw in Chapter 4, a major method (since the 1930s) of studying the working of the brain is to monitor its electrical activity. Exactly the same information can be used to throw light on consciousness, because particular patterns of electrical activity are correlated with other measures of arousal and alertness.

Electroencephalography (literally, 'electric-in-head writing') detects the output of minute electrical 'ripples', caused by changes in the electrical charges in different parts of the brain (usually the synchronised activity of large groups of neurons). Although there are characteristic patterns common to all individuals of a particular age or developmental stage, individuals' brain activity is as unique and distinctive as their fingerprints.

The electroencephalogram (EEG) has wires, an amplifier, electromagnetic pens and paper revolving on a drum. One end of each wire is attached to the scalp (with the help of special jelly), and the other to the amplifier, which can register impulses of 100 microvolts (1/10,000 of a volt) or less and magnifies them a million times. The impulses are traced on paper by pens and appear as rows of oscillating waves.

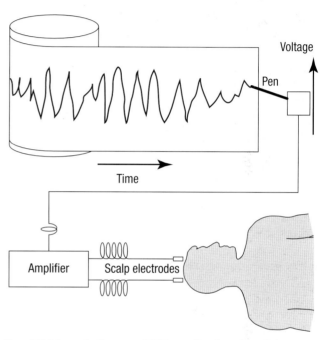

Figure 7.3 *Schematic diagram of EEG recording (based on Gleitman, 1981)*

The waves vary in frequency and amplitude:

- *Frequency* is measured as the number of oscillations per second – the more oscillations, the higher the frequency. One complete oscillation is a cycle, and the frequency is expressed as cycles per second (cps) or hertz (Hz).
- *Amplitude* is measured as half the height from the peak to the trough of a single oscillation. Frequency is the more important of the two measures.

Box 7.5	The four major types of brain wave (measured in frequency)

- **Delta (1–2 Hz):** found mainly in infants, sleeping adults, or adults with brain tumours.
- **Theta (3–7 Hz):** found mainly in children aged two to five years, and in psychopaths (see Chapter 46). May be induced by frustration.
- **Alpha (8–12 Hz):** found mainly in adults who are awake, relaxed, and whose eyes are closed. Most reliably recorded from the back of the scalp.

- **Beta (13 Hz and over):** found mainly in adults who are awake and alert, whose eyes are open, and who may be concentrating on some task or other. These brain waves are most reliably recorded from the middle of the scalp, and are related to activity in the somatosensory and motor cortices.

(See Table 7.1, page 97.)

Computerised electroencephalography has recently been used to detect evoked potentials, minute voltage changes induced in the brain by fairly specific visual and auditory stimuli. The average of a number of responses to similar kinds of stimuli is often used (the *average evoked potential*/AEP) in order to amplify the signal:noise ratio. AEPs are used to study newborns, some children with learning difficulties, patients in a coma, stroke victims, tumour patients and patients with multiple sclerosis. However, for certain brain conditions, brain scanning has largely replaced the EEG (Diagram Group 1982: see Chapter 4).

Sleep

Sleep and the circadian rhythm

Ask yourself ...

- Blakemore (1988) asks what would happen if we removed all the external cues to the nature of time (*Zeitgebers*), both natural (day and night) and manufactured (clocks, mealtimes). Would our bodies still have their own rhythmic existence?

CASE STUDY 7.1

Siffre and the 25-hour day

In 1972, Michel Siffre, a young French cave explorer, spent seven months underground with no cues as to the time of day. He had adequate food, water, books and exercise equipment, and his only contact with the outside world was via a telephone which was permanently staffed. He was linked up to a computer and video camera, by which scientists on the surface could monitor his physiological functions and state of mind. He organised his life into a fairly normal pattern of alternating periods of activity and sleep, and his 'day' was broken up by a normal meal pattern. The remarkable finding was that he chose to live a 25-hour day (not 24). For every real day that passed, he rose an hour later – the clock in his brain was running a little slow.

(From Blakemore, 1988)

According to Blakemore (1988):

'For all the advances of modern society, we cannot afford to ignore the rhythms of the animal brain within us, any more than we can neglect our need to breathe or eat. Without the biological clocks in our brains, our lives would be chaotic, our actions disorganised. The brain has internalised the rhythms of Nature, but can tick on for months without sight of the sun ...'.

Most animals display a *circadian rhythm* (from the Latin *circa dies* = 'about one day'), a periodicity or rhythmical alternation of various physiological and behavioural functions, synchronised to the 24-hour cycle of light and dark. So, during a 24-hour period, there's a cycle of several physiological functions (heart rate, metabolic rate, breathing rate, body temperature, hormonal secretion, urine excretion, immune function, alertness, and so on), which all tend to reach maximum values during the late afternoon and early evening, and minimum values in the early hours of the morning. (The disruption of circadian rhythms is discussed in Chapter 12 as a source of stress.)

The internal or biological clock

Rats, like humans, have an inherent rhythm of about 25 hours, which dictates their cycle of sleep and waking if they're put in the dark. This internal clock is as reliable and regular as most manufactured ones – the rhythm deviates by no more than a few minutes over several months. So how is the internal (biological) clock reset each day to the cycle of the real world, and where is the clock to be found?

It's thought to be a tiny cluster of neurons, the *suprachiasmatic nucleus* (SCN), situated in the medial hypothalamus. For example, damage to the SCN in rats produces complete disappearance of the circadian rhythm: the sleep–wake cycle, eating and drinking, hormone secretion, and so on, become completely random during the course of the 24-hour period. Although most of what's known about the SCN is based on experiments with non-human animals using ablation (see Chapter 4), and although we cannot make direct electrophysiological recordings from the human brain, anatomical studies show that humans have an SCN (Empson, 1993). The function of the SCN is to synchronise all the bodily functions governed by the circadian rhythm.

The SCN is situated directly above the optic chiasma (the junction of the two optic nerves en route to the brain: see Chapter 5). A tuft of thin nerve fibres branches off from the main nerve and penetrates the hypothalamus above, forming synaptic connections with cells in the SCN. This anatomically insignificant pathway is the link between the outside world and the brain's own clock (Blakemore, 1988). So the retina projects directly onto the SCN, which ensures that the sleep–wake cycle is tuned to the rhythm of night and day. If this connection with the retina is severed, the cycle goes 'haywire'.

The effects of disrupting the biological clock

So, in human adults at least, it appears that the circadian rhythm doesn't depend primarily on external cues, although it's surprisingly easy to outsmart our body clocks by external means such as alarm clocks.

Ask yourself ...

- What's an average night's sleep for you?
- Is this as much as you really need?

According to Melton (2000), scientists are warning that we ignore our natural bodily rhythms at our peril:

> 'Fighting our natural sleep tendencies ... may be grinding away at our health, triggering a string of maladies ... Giving up the late nights and weekend lie-ins in favour of a strict daily routine and a regular bedtime might be as important to our health as quitting smoking or cutting back on saturated fat'.

So, how much sleep do we need?

According to Maas (1998), we're biologically ill-prepared to function on minimal sleep: our prehistoric genetic blueprint for sleep hasn't evolved fast enough to keep up with the pace of twentieth-century life. Humans are more likely to need an average of ten hours of sleep a night than the four which Margaret Thatcher famously claimed to get by on. In the sleep laboratory, people who average eight hours a night, and maintain that they're fully alert during the day, and who then get an extra hour's sleep at night, find their productivity levels increase by 25 per cent.

Whatever happened to lunch-breaks? Our work-hungry society demands that we eat at our work-stations

Maas also claims that each of us maintains a personal sleep bank account. We need enough sleep in the account to be able to function properly during the day. This means at least eight hours for most people, in order to cancel out the sleep debt incurred by 16 hours of continuous alertness. Similarly, Dement (2000), one of the pioneers of sleep research and the founder of the world's first sleep disorders centre (see below), proposes a rough rule of thumb: most people require about an hour's sleep for every two waking hours.

Maas, Williams (1998), Folkard (in Melton, 2000), and others, argue that we're living in a *sleep-deprived society*. For example, Maas notes that in the past 20 years, we've added about 158 hours to our annual working and commuting time – equal to a full month of working hours. Young mothers with

children have added an astonishing 241 working hours since the 1960s (see Chapter 38). The British work longer hours than any other nation in Europe, and we sleep one-and-a-half hours less every night than our grandparents did. The pace of life is becoming faster and harder, and the stresses and pressures of work are leading to longer working hours and disrupted sleep.

How does sleep deprivation produce negative effects on health?

Dement (2000) believes that most of us carry a heavy 'sleep debt', a deficit of sleep built up over days, weeks and months. Sleep debt is dangerous, and potentially lethal. Examples are drivers who fall asleep at the wheel, pilots who're too sleepy to land planes safely, and surgeons who botch surgical procedures because they're exhausted. Both the Exxon Valdez disaster and the Challenger space shuttle disaster were attributed to human error caused by extreme sleep deprivation. Dement also links high blood pressure, heart attacks and strokes to *sleep apnea*, a chronic failure to sleep well because of problems breathing during sleep.

Moldofsky (in Melton, 2000) has observed dramatic changes in the *immune system* between waking and sleeping. *Natural killer cells* circulate in greater numbers during the day, while *T cells* are more active at night, as is the immune regulator *interleukin-1* (the immune system is discussed more fully in Chapter 12). Disruption of this pattern can explain the infections that often plague shift-workers. Morgan (in Melton, 2000) has reported that upsetting a person's natural circadian settings will keep their levels of glucose and some lipids in their blood dangerously high after a meal – which may explain why cardiovascular disease is shift workers' number one hazard.

Box 7.6   Are you a lark or an owl?

Larks (*morning types/early birds*) wake early, ready to face the day, while owls (*night-adepts/night-birds*) wake later, struggle to wake up, and stay up later at night. There's some evidence that owls' circadian rhythms are longer than 24 hours, while larks' cycles are much closer to the 'classic' 24 hours (see Case Study 7.1). However, Folkard (in Melton, 2000) believes that only between five to ten per cent of the population falls at either end of this spectrum, with most of us falling somewhere in between.

Nevertheless, morning types actually endure the punishing schedule of late shifts better, and suffer fewer physical problems than evening types. Why? According to Folkard, the crucial factor is how easily a person's body clock can be reset. Because morning people's clocks are stable and need no tuning – because they're almost bang on 24 hours – the clock remains constant even while working shifts.

These findings suggest that night-workers should try to orient their whole lives towards being daytime people, who just occasionally stay up all night to work. Shifts should be broken into units of just a few days to minimise circadian disruption. For example, working two successive nights is preferable to working four or five in a row. By contrast, most *chronobiologists* (who study biological rhythms) recommend that the way to maintain alertness and reduce the risk of accidents is to try adapting the body clock to suit the new work pattern fully, making shift changes *less* frequent, not more (see Chapter 12). According to Folkard:

Evening types on regular day jobs are also prone to mistreating their body clocks. An innocent lie-in at the weekend will throw their clock forwards. Come Monday, they'll have to get up earlier than their internal rhythm dictates, and this is likely to make them irritable and fed up ('Monday morning blues', which can often begin the night before!). According to Folkard (in Melton, 2000):

'… after millions of years of evolution, we can't suddenly ignore the body clock and become members of the 24-hour society without incurring penalties'.

The physiology of sleep

When darkness falls, the eyes indirectly inform the *pineal gland* (the 'third eye'), a tiny structure at the top of the brainstem which keeps track of the body's natural cycles and registers external factors such as light and darkness. The pineal gland secretes *melatonin* in response to darkness, making us drowsy. Downing (1988) calls melatonin 'nature's sleeping draught'. It's a hormone that affects brain cells which produce serotonin, a sleep-related transmitter substance. In turn, serotonin is concentrated in the *raphe nuclei* (situated near the pons), which secrete a substance that acts on the RAS to induce light sleep. Jouvet (1967) found that lesions of the raphe nuclei in cats produced severe insomnia, and naturally occurring lesions in humans seem to have a very similar effect.

Another important sleep centre is the *locus coeruleus* (LC), a tiny structure on each side of the brainstem whose cells are rich in noradrenaline, thought to be involved in inducing active (or rapid eye movement/REM) sleep (see below). The LC may well serve many of the functions previously attributed to the RAS. Although it has only two inputs (one excitatory, one inhibitory), LC outputs spread to all parts of the brain. Studies with rats suggest that its function might be to regulate the animal's level of *vigilance* to environmental stimuli (Empson, 1993).

There's also evidence that a substance called *factor S* accumulates gradually in the brains of animals while they're awake and that, if this is removed from the fluid surrounding the brain and transferred into another animal, sleep will be induced. It's likely that factor S contributes to our feelings of sleepiness (Diagram Group, 1982).

Varieties of sleep and the ultradian rhythm

In the typical sleep laboratory, a volunteer settles down for the night with not only EEG wires attached, but also wires from an electro-oculogram (EOG) ('oculo' meaning eye) and an electromyogram (EMG) ('myo' meaning muscle).

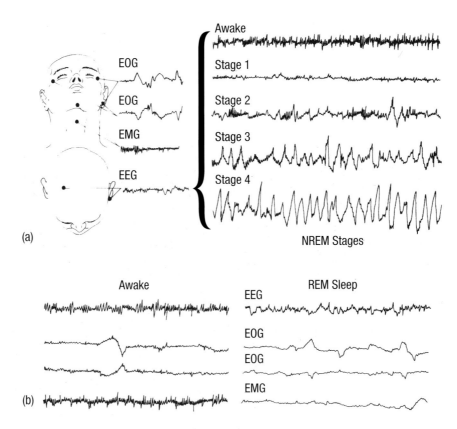

Figure 7.4 *Comparison of physiological measures for different types of sleep. (a) The non-rapid eye movement (NREM) stages are represented in typical order of appearance; in reality each one gradually blends into the next. (b) Rapid eye movement (REM) sleep is in some ways similar to waking but in others quite different; the EEG is more similar to waking than to that of any NREM stage and REMs are present, but the body muscles are deeply inhibited*

Table 7.1 *A typical night's sleep: The four stages of non-rapid eye movement (NREM) sleep*

After we shut our eyes and prepare to sleep, *alpha waves* begin to punctuate the high frequency *beta waves* of active wakefulness. The transition from being awake to entering stage 1 sleep is called the *hypnagogic period*, and is sometimes included in stage 1.

Stage 1: When we first fall asleep, the EEG is irregular and lacks the pattern of alpha waves which characterises the relaxed waking state. At first, there's a reduction in frequency of alpha waves, which are then replaced by low voltage, slow theta waves, accompanied by slow rolling eye movements. Heart rate begins to slow down, the muscles relax, but we can still be woken up easily.

Stage 2: This is a deeper state of sleep, but we can still be woken fairly easily. The EEG shows bursts of activity called *sleep spindles* (one–to two–second waxing and waning bursts of 12–14 Hz waves). There are also occasional sharp rises and falls in amplitude of the whole EEG (*K complexes*), which last up to two seconds.

Stage 3: Sleep becomes deeper, the spindles disappear and are replaced by long, slow *delta waves* for up to 50 per cent of the EEG record. We're now quite unresponsive to external stimuli, and so it's difficult to wake us up. Heart rate, blood pressure, and body temperature all continue to drop.

Stage 4: We now enter *delta sleep* (deep or 'quiet sleep': 50 per cent and more of the record consists of delta waves) and will spend up to 30 minutes in stage 4. About an hour has elapsed since stage 1 began. As in stage 3, it's difficult to wake us, unless something happens that's of great personal significance (such as our baby crying).

Stages 2–4 collectively are called *slow-wave sleep* (SWS). As we pass from stages 1 to 4, the frequency of the waves decreases, and the amplitude/voltage increases. Also, muscle tone steadily declines.

A typical night's sleep comprises a number of *ultradian cycles* (lasting approximately 90 minutes), and each cycle consists of a number of stages.

The cycle then goes into reverse, so we re-enter stage 3 and then stage 2, but instead of re-entering stage 1, a different kind of sleep (*active sleep*) appears. Pulse and respiration rates increase, as does blood pressure, and all three processes become less regular. EEGs begin to resemble those of the waking state, showing that the brain is active, supported by increases in oxygen consumption, blood flow and neural firing in many brain structures. But it's even *more* difficult to wake us from this kind of sleep than the deep stage 4 sleep, which is why it's called *paradoxical sleep* (Aserinsky & Kleitman, 1953).

Another characteristic of active sleep are the rapid eye movements (the eyeballs moving back and forth, up and down, together) under the closed lids (hence *rapid eye movement*/REM *sleep*). Finally, while the brain may be very active, REM sleep is characterised by muscular *paralysis* (especially the muscles of the arms and legs), so that all the tossing and turning and other typical movements associated with sleep in fact occur only during stages 1–4 (non-rapid eye movement/NREM sleep). The distinction between REM and NREM sleep was originally made by Dement & Kleitman (1957).

Another feature of REM sleep is the appearance of *pontine-geniculo-occipital* (PGO) *spikes/waves*, which are generated in the pons and travel through the lateral geniculate nucleus (LGN: see Chapter 5). Discovered in the 1960s by Jouvet working with cats, PGO spikes typically occur in bursts, often preceding individual eye movements. According to the activation-synthesis model of dreaming (see below), PGO activity is the prime source of the dreaming experience (Empson, 1993).

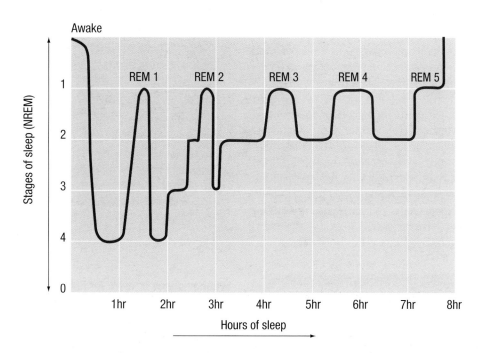

Figure 7.5 *A typical night's sleep (note the disappearance of stages 3 and 4 and the relative increase in the length of REM periods)*

Ask yourself ...

- Construct a summary table of differences between REM and NREM sleep.

After 15 minutes or so in REM sleep, we re-enter NREM sleep (stages 2–4), and so another ultradian cycle begins. However, with each 90-minute cycle (of which there are four to five on average per night), the duration of the REM sleep *increases* and that of NREM sleep *decreases*. The first cycle normally provides the deepest sleep and the shortest REM period and, as the night goes on, we spend relatively more time in REM and less in NREM sleep. In later cycles, it's quite common to go from REM to stage 2, and then straight back into REM sleep (bypassing stages 3 and 4). Natural waking usually occurs during a period of REM sleep (see Figure 7.5 on page 95).

According to Empson (1993):

'While most all-night recording experiments are over brief periods (of up to a week), some very extended studies have been done and there is no evidence that the patterns of sleep we observe over short periods (after the first night) are in any way peculiar to the unfamiliarity of the laboratory environment'.

Sleep and dreaming

Rapid eye movements and dreams

About 80 per cent of the time, sleeping volunteers woken during REM sleep will report that they've been dreaming. Being woken from NREM sleep produces only a 15 per cent 'dreaming rate'. So, REMs seem to be a very reliable indicator that someone is dreaming. To some extent, the nature of the REMs reflects the content of the dream (for example, dreaming about a tennis match and a back-and-forth movement of the eyes, as would happen in waking life). Although there's no one-to-one correspondence between dream action and eye movement, cues about the general nature of the dream can often be gleaned from the REM record. For example, if the eye movements are small and sparse, we're probably having a peaceful, fairly passive dream, whereas larger and more continuous REMs suggest a more active and emotional dream (Faraday, 1972).

The *kind* of mental activity associated with NREM and REM sleep is also very different. Participants woken from NREM sleep tend to report dreams which are shorter, less vivid and less visual than REM dreams and, in fact, they often describe themselves as having been 'thinking' rather than dreaming. NREM sleep is also associated with sleepwalking (*somnambulism*), sleeptalking and some types of nightmare. REM sleep has been called 'dream sleep' or the 'D-state' and some have gone as far as to call it the 'third state of existence': it's in many ways as different from NREM sleep (the 'S-state') as it is from waking.

Box 7.7 Are REM dreams simply more easily recalled?

Is it possible that the difference between dreams in REM and NREM sleep is actually an artefact of the ability to recall dreams following the 'rude awakening'? Beaumont (1988) argues that being woken from NREM sleep may lead to the dream being forgotten before the partici-

pant is sufficiently awake to report it (since this is a deeper kind of sleep in which the brain is much less active). By contrast, being woken from REM sleep may allow the ongoing dream to be remembered and then reported (because the brain is much more active).

The effects of sleep deprivation

As far as rats are concerned, long-term sleep deprivation is definitely not good for their health: it causes impaired thermoregulation, metabolic dysfunction and eventually death (Hobson, 1995). For example, Rechtschaffen *et al.* (1989a, b) selectively deprived rats of either REM or both REM and NREM sleep. After a week of total deprivation, they showed progressive weight loss even in the face of increased food intake. This became more pronounced after two weeks, and after four weeks they died. During this time, body weight plummeted, while food consumption soared and body temperature became progressively more unstable.

However, in the case of human beings, studies have been remarkably consistent in failing to show any marked changes in heart and breathing rates, blood pressure, skin conduction, body temperature, EMG or EEG, even when deprivation continues for up to 200 hours (Pinel, 1993). Webb & Bonnet (1979) limited participants to two hours' sleep on one particular night; they suffered no ill effects the following day, but that night they fell asleep more quickly and slept longer than usual. Longer periods of sleep deprivation may result in some unpleasant psychological effects, but people are remarkably able to do without sleep. Webb and Bonnet gradually reduced the length of sleep in a group of volunteers from eight to four hours per night over a two-month period, with no detectable effect.

Box 7.8 The REM rebound

When sleep is *abruptly* reduced (as, for example, in the case of hospital doctors, who may be on duty for 72 hours at a stretch), the effects are rather more serious. These effects include irritability, intellectual inefficiency, and an intense fatigue and need for sleep, which mirror those produced by depriving participants of approximately two hours of REM sleep (but otherwise allowing them to sleep normally). The following night, there's an increase in REM sleep (so as to compensate for the previous night's loss), which is called the REM *rebound.*

When volunteers are able to get by on greatly (but gradually) reduced amounts of sleep, it's probably because they pack their two hours of REM tightly into their sleeping time (thus reducing the amount of NREM sleep in between their dreams). When sleep is abruptly reduced, there's no time to adopt this alternative dreaming–sleep pattern.

What evidence is there for the REM rebound?

Dement (1960) woke participants from their REM sleep on five successive nights (while a control group was woken only during NREM sleep periods). When they were allowed to sleep uninterruptedly, they did 60 per cent more dreaming until they'd made up their lost REM time. For as many as five nights following their REM deprivation, they spent more time in REM sleep than usual, and on some nights they doubled their REM time.

In cats too, it seems that NREM alone is inadequate. Jouvet (1967) placed cats on a small island surrounded by water and allowed them either to remain awake or to go into NREM sleep. But whenever they entered REM sleep, they tended to slip into the water and so woke up. Prolonged deprivation of REM sleep produced abnormal behaviour, including hyper-sexuality, and, eventually death.

According to Pinel (1993), the most convincing evidence that REM sleep deprivation *isn't* severely debilitating comes from the study of the effects of tricyclic antidepressants (see Chapter 45). These selectively block REM sleep, but patients who regularly take large doses, and so get little REM sleep for months at a time, experience no serious side-effects that can be attributed to their REM loss.

Theories of sleep

According to Blakemore (1988):

> 'Our planet is a dangerous place; there is ruthless competition for limited resources and only the fittest survive. And yet all the most advanced animals, normally alert, shrewd, watchful, drop their defences to sleep. Even human beings, the most spectacularly successful species, spend one-third of their lives more or less paralysed and senseless. If sleep is so risky, it must bestow a huge benefit on animals that indulge in it, or it would have been eliminated by the powerful forces of natural selection. Animals that did not need sleep would surely have evolved and prevailed over their sleepy competitors ... sleep must surely be valuable ... '.

Empson (1993) maintains that even though physiologists have made great strides in understanding sleep mechanisms, this hasn't greatly helped in understanding what sleep is *for*. While sleep has the features of a primary drive (such as hunger and sex), what makes it unique as a primary biological drive is that the need for sleep is reflected in *decreased levels of arousal*, and its satisfaction (i.e. sleep) is associated with further decreases. Sleep, therefore, represents a serious exception to the view that organisms seek a single optimal level of (non-specific) arousal (Lloyd *et al.*, 1984: see Chapter 9).

The restoration theory

Oswald (1966) maintains that both REM and NREM sleep serve a restorative function. NREM restores bodily processes which have deteriorated during the day, while REM sleep is a time for replenishing brain processes, through the stimulation of protein synthesis.

Box 7.9   REM sleep and the developing brain

Restoration theory helps explain the large proportion of babies' sleeping time spent in REM sleep. During much of their first year, babies are sleeping for about 18 hours per 24, and by about twelve months they have two periods of sleep every 24 hours (one daytime and one night-time). Not until about five years has an 'adult' pattern become established, probably as a result of both environmental and maturational factors.

Within these changing patterns, the relative proportions of REM and NREM sleep change quite dramatically. Whereas newborns spend half their 18 hours in REM sleep, adults usually spend only one-quarter of their eight hours in REM sleep. The developing brain needs a great deal of protein synthesis for cell manufacture and growth, and REM sleep helps to achieve this.

An evaluation of restoration theory

■ Patients who survive drug overdoses and withdrawal, and other brain 'insults', such as intensive electroconvulsive therapy (see Chapter 45), experience prolonged increases in REM sleep. These increases are consistent with the estimated time for the half-life of proteins in the brain; that is, in a six-week period, about half the brain's total protein is replaced, and this is the approximate length of the increased REM period.

■ Nocturnal secretion of growth hormone (which produces bodily protein synthesis) depends on uninterrupted stage 4 sleep. In adults, a chronic lack of normal stage 4 is found in fibrositis sufferers, whose EEG during sleep is characterised by 'alpha–delta' patterns, a mixture of sleeping and waking EEG (typically experienced as fitful, 'unrestorative sleep'). The disturbance of stage 4 in healthy volunteers produces the symptoms of fibrositis.

■ According to Empson (1993), all this evidence is consistent with a general *anabolic function* for sleep: REM sleep underlies brain growth, repair and memory functions, and slow-wave (stage 4) sleep promotes bodily growth and repair. However, cell repair goes on 24 hours a day (even though it reaches a peak at night).

■ A more serious objection is that REM sleep is an active state (at least as far as the brain is concerned), and probably burns up a substantial amount of energy. Indeed, blood flow to the brain *increases* during REM sleep, and this would actually *prevent* high levels of protein synthesis. In view of this kind of evidence, Oswald (1974) maintains that *both* types of sleep are involved in the process of restoring *bodily tissue*.

Evolutionary theory

Different species characteristically sleep for different periods. Those at risk from predators, which cannot find a safe place to sleep, or which spend large parts of each day searching for and consuming food and water (such as herd animals), sleep very little (for example, zebras sleep for only two to three hours per day). Predators that sleep in safe places, and can satisfy their food and water needs fairly quickly, sleep for much of the day. Lions, for example, often sleep more or less continuously for two to three days after gorging themselves on a kill.

Box 7.10   Is evolutionary theory falsifiable?

The *evolutionary theory of sleep* (Meddis, 1975) maintains that sleep is an advantage, because it keeps the animal immobilised for long periods, making it less conspicuous to would-be predators and, therefore, safer. The safer the animal from predators, the longer it's likely to sleep.

However, as we noted above, a preyed-upon species may sleep for *shorter* periods, because of the constant need to stay on guard against predators. This means that whatever sleep pattern a species has, it can be explained in 'evolutionary' terms:

- *Long sleep* could serve *both* the function of needing to stay alert/staying out of the way of predators, *and* not needing to stay alert because the animal has no natural predator.
- *Short sleep* can also serve the function of protection against possible predators.

This is an example of *non-falsifiability* (see Chapter 3), and represents a serious limitation of evolutionary theory.

Meddis also argues that the long sleep periods of babies have evolved to prevent exhaustion in their mothers and, in this sense, sleep is still functional – at least for mothers of babies and small children! As to the need for immobilisation, this no longer seems viable as an explanation of sleep in humans, and so may be regarded as a remnant of our evolutionary past.

A variant of the evolutionary theory is *hibernation theory*: elaborate mechanisms of sleep have evolved solely to keep us quiet in the dark. Animals hibernate to conserve energy and to stay out of possible danger during the winter months.

An evaluation of evolutionary theory

- Empson (1993) believes that Meddis's 'waste of time' theory is contradicted by the fact that it's universal among animals, as well as by the finding that sleep deprivation can be fatal (Kleitman, 1927; Rechtschaffen *et al.*, 1989a, b).
- A weaker version of the 'waste of time' theory was proposed by Horne (1988), who distinguishes between *core sleep* (which is necessary) and *optional sleep* (which isn't). Evidence from sleep deprivation experiments (both partial and total) shows that accumulated sleep 'debts' are made up to some extent on recovery nights, but never entirely. For example, REM rebound accounts for approximately 50 per cent of the REM sleep lost during selective awakenings. This suggests that only the first three hours of sleep are truly necessary (core sleep), and the rest is optional (having no physiological function). In animals which sleep longer than three hours, it seems to reduce energy expenditure and keep them immobile. But most of us eat more than is biologically necessary (both in variety and quantity), yet no biologist would say that feeding was only partly functional (Empson, 1993).
- Empson (1993) concludes by saying:

'… sleep appears to be ubiquitous and necessary; it is a complex function of the brain involving far-reaching changes in body physiology as well as brain physiology. It is difficult to believe that it does not have an important function and the restorative theories provide a coherent account of what this might be'.

Hobson's levels

Although not a discrete theory, Hobson (1995) proposes that the function of sleep can be analysed at different levels:

- At the *behavioural level*, sleep suppresses activity at a time (night-time/darkness) when the chances of finding food or a mate are relatively low. Also, such activities have a high energy cost in warm-blooded animals when the temperature is low. This makes sleep behaviourally very efficient. In addition, the enforced nature of sleep, and its relation to resting activity, serves to unite animals in a family or pair-bonded situation, which may encourage sexual behaviour and promote care and development of the young. Hobson finds it incredible that ethologists have failed to recognise and study sleep systematically as a form of behaviour (see Chapter 2).
- At the *developmental level*, a function of REM sleep for developing organisms (see Box 7.9) could be the guaranteed activation of neural circuits underlying crucial, survival behaviours. From an evolutionary point of view, there would be great advantages gained from ensuring the organised activation of the complex systems of the brain before the organism has developed the ability to test them in the real world. In both the developing and the adult animal, REM sleep could constitute a form of *behavioural rehearsal*.
- At the *metabolic level*, the recurring cycles of NREM/REM sleep are accompanied by major changes in all the body's physiological systems. NREM involves decreased blood pressure, heart and breathing rates, as well as the release of growth and sex hormones from the pituitary (consistent with the restoration theory), while REM involves increased blood pressure, heart and breathing rates, as well as penile erection and clitoral engorgement.

Dreaming

Ask yourself …

- How do dreams differ from waking consciousness?

While psychologists have developed reliable techniques for establishing when people are likely to be dreaming, there's been no equivalent progress in understanding the nature of dreams. According to Empson (1993), a starting point must be to establish clearly how dreaming differs from waking consciousness. Empson identifies four such differences:

- Dreams *happen to us* as opposed to being a product of our conscious control:

'When dreaming we are the spectators of an unfolding drama, and only rarely does one have the impression of being in control …'.

Lucid dreaming, in which the dreamer 'knows' s/he is dreaming and decides how the dream plot should develop, is very rare.
- The *logic* of waking consciousness is suspended (see Freud's theory, Chapter 42).
- Dreams reported in the laboratory tend to be mundane and lack the *bizarre quality* of 'normal' dreams, probably because only the strangest experiences are remembered when we wake normally after a night's sleep.

- Dreams have a *singlemindedness*: the imagery of the dream totally dominates the dreamer's consciousness. When awake, however, we normally reflect on the stream of consciousness as it goes on, and can be aware of one thing but simultaneously imagine something else. However, Greenfield (1998) claims that waking consciousness is single-minded (see above, page 91).

Hobson (1995) describes dreams as typically including:

- *hallucinations* (predominantly visual, although auditory, tactile and movement sensations are also prominent, with taste and smell under-represented and pain extremely rare);
- *delusions* (believing that the events are real);
- *cognitive abnormalities* (such as the occurrence of events that would be physically impossible in the real world);
- *emotional intensification* and *amnesia* (we forget over 95 per cent of our dreams),

These characteristics have led to a comparison between dreams and abnormal states of mind, as in schizophrenia and organic mental disorders, in particular delirium (see Chapter 44).

Theories of dreaming

Ask yourself ...

- What's dreaming for? Why do we dream?

Reorganisation of mental structures

According to Ornstein (1986), REM sleep and dreaming may be involved in the reorganisation of our *schemas* (mental structures), so as to accommodate new information. People asked to perform difficult tasks for four hours just prior to sleep, spend longer in REM sleep than normal. REM time also increases after people have had to learn complex tasks.

This may explain why REM sleep decreases with age. As we've seen, newborns spend 50 per cent of their 18 hours of sleep in REM sleep, compared with 25 per cent spent by adults in their eight hours. Oswald suggested that babies' brains need to process and assimilate the flood of new stimuli pouring in from the outside world, and that this is (partly) achieved through REM sleep.

Activation-synthesis model (Hobson & McCarley, 1977; McCarley, 1983)

The cortex is highly active during REM sleep, although it receives little external stimulation. While the motor cortex is highly active (generating activity which would normally produce bodily movement), these commands don't reach the muscles of the limbs but are 'switched off' at a relay station at the top of the spinal column, so we're effectively paralysed (*output blockade*).

Not only is the cortex isolated (unable to control muscles), but there's also inhibition of incoming signals produced by the sensory systems. Consequently, perceptions of the 'real' world are selectively attenuated (*input blockade*). Hindbrain and midbrain structures, normally associated with relaying sensory information to the cortex, spontaneously generate signals (*PGO waves*: see page 97) responsible for cortical activation.

These are indistinguishable from signals which would normally have been relayed from the eyes/ears. This activity is under the control of a periodic triggering mechanism in the *pontine brainstem* (top of the spinal column, at the base of the brain).

So the brain is very active during REM (*activation*) and dreams are a conscious interpretation (*synthesis*) of all this activity. The cognitive system, which organises sensory information into the simplest meaningful interpretation when we're awake, processes all the internally generated signals *as if* they came from the outside world. In combination with oculomotor activity, PGO waves are sent to the visual and association cortex and the thalamus.

What we call a dream is the simplest way of interpreting these internally produced signals, by combining them into some meaningful whole. It's the unusual intensity and rapidity of brain stimulation (often involving simultaneous activation of areas not usually activated together when we're awake), which account for the highly changeable and sometimes bizarre content of dreams. According to Hobson (1995):

> '... the now autoactivated and autostimulated brain processes these signals and interprets them in terms of information stored in memory'.

Many dream experiences do seem to reflect the brain's and body's states, and so can be thought of as interpretations of these physical states. For example, being chased, locked up or frozen with fear may well reflect the blocked motor commands to the muscles, floating, flying and falling experiences may reflect vestibular activation (see Chapter 5), and the sexual content of dreams may reflect vaginal engorgement and penile erection (Ornstein, 1986).

Evaluation of the activation-synthesis model

- In a sense, we dream instead of acting (perhaps suggesting the need for rest/restoration for the body). Cats with brainstem injury act out their dreams by, for example, chasing the mice of their dreams while ignoring the real mice in their cages: they're not paralysed in the normal way during REM sleep.
- Crick & Mitchison (1983) proposed a modified version of the model, which they called *reverse learning*. The basic idea is that we dream in order to forget! The cortex (unlike other parts of the brain) is composed of richly interconnected neuronal networks. The problem with such a network system is that it malfunctions when there's an overload of incoming information. To deal with such overload, the brain needs a mechanism to 'debug' or 'clean up' the network, and REM sleep is that mechanism. In this way, we awake with a cleaned-up network, and the brain is ready for new input. According to Crick and Mitchison, trying to remember our dreams may not be a good idea: they're the very patterns of thought the system is trying to tune out.
- For others, especially psychoanalysts and other psychodynamic psychologists, it's essential that we *do* remember our dreams, so that we can try to understand their meaning. For example, Freud saw dreams as *wish fulfilments*. Both he and Jung saw *symbolism* as being of central importance in dreams, putting the dreamer in touch with parts of the self

usually inaccessible during waking life (see Chapter 42). Hall (1966) saw dreams as 'a personal document, a letter to oneself' and, like Jung, advocated the study of *dream series*, rather than single isolated dreams.

Conclusions: Integrating neurobiological, evolutionary, and psychological accounts of dreaming

Winson (1997), a neuroscientist, argues that neural and psychological theories of dreams *aren't* mutually exclusive. While Crick and Mitchison argue that we need to forget our dreams, Winson claims that:

> '… dreams may reflect a memory-processing mechanism inherited from lower species, in which information important for survival is reprocessed during REM sleep. This information may constitute the core of the unconscious'.

According to Winson, to maintain sleep locomotion has to be suppressed by inhibiting motor neurons. But suppressing *eye movements* isn't necessary, because this doesn't disturb sleep. With the evolution of REM sleep, each species could process the information most needed for its survival, such as the location of food, and means of predation or escape. In REM sleep, this information may be re-accessed and integrated with past experience to provide an ongoing strategy for behaviour.

Because non-humans have no language, the information processed during their REM sleep is necessarily *sensory*. Consistent with our early mammalian origins, our dreams are also sensory (mainly visual): they don't *need* to take the form of verbal narration. While there's no functional need in non-humans for this material to become conscious, in humans there's no reason for it *not* to become conscious: we *can* remember our dreams. Winson argues that, consistent with evolutionary and neuroscientific evidence, as well as people's reports:

> '… dreams reflect an individual's strategy for survival. The subjects of dreams are broad-ranging and complex, incorporating self-image, fears, insecurities, strengths, grandiose ideas, sexual orientation, desire, jealousy and love'.

Dreams clearly have a deep psychological core. Although the topic 'chosen' for consideration during a night's sleep is unpredictable, certain of life's difficulties so engage psychological survival that they're selected for REM processing. Freud's dream theory contains a profound truth: there *is* an unconscious and dreams are indeed the 'royal road' to its understanding (see Chapter 45). However, Winson rejects Freud's view of the unconscious as a cauldron of untamed passions and destructive wishes in favour of one in which:

> '… the unconscious is a cohesive, continually active mental structure that takes note of life's experiences and reacts according to its own scheme of interpretation … Their [dreams] unusual character is a result of the complex associations that are called from memory'.

CHAPTER SUMMARY

■ Most psychologists don't accept Freud's view of the unconscious as based on repression, but they would accept that there's a **continuum of consciousness**.

■ **Arousal/alertness** can be defined objectively in terms of various physiological measures, such as EEGs, EOGs, EMGs, breathing and heart rates. These are **correlates** of consciousness.

■ Changes in **tonic alertness** are closely linked to various biological rhythms, especially the circadian rhythm. Alertness changes in fairly predictable ways both during wakefulness (controlled by a **diurnal rhythm**) and sleep (**ultradian rhythm**).

■ Changes in **phasic alertness** involve changes in the **orienting response** to arousing stimuli. This is complemented by **habituation**, a form of adaptation.

■ Most animals display a **circadian rhythm**, which is synchronised to the 24-hour cycle of light and dark. The internal/**biological clock** is thought to be the **suprachiasmatic nucleus** (SCN).

■ Modern living increases the likelihood that the circadian rhythm will be disrupted, and people are sleeping less than human beings were designed for by evolution. This is having harmful effects on people's mental and physical health.

■ A typical night's sleep comprises four to five **ultradian cycles**, each consisting of several stages. Stages 2–4 are collectively called **slow-wave sleep** (SWS) or 'deep' sleep; stages 1–4 are collectively called **non-rapid eye movement** (NREM) sleep.

■ In **rapid eye movement** (REM) or active sleep, physiological processes increase and EEGs begin to resemble those of the waking state. Yet it's more difficult to wake someone from REM than from stage 4 sleep (making it **paradoxical**).

■ Depriving people of REM sleep produces the **REM rebound**, suggesting that dreaming associated with REM sleep is perhaps the most important function of sleep.

■ According to Oswald's **restoration theory**, REM and NREM sleep help replenish bodily and brain processes respectively. However, the fact that cell repair goes on 24 hours a day, and that the brain is highly active during REM sleep, led Oswald to claim that **both** REM and NREM sleep are involved in restoration of bodily tissue.

■ Meddis's **evolutionary theory** claims that sleep keeps the animal immobilised and safer from predators. But the theory is **unfalsifiable**. **Hibernation theory** is a variant of evolutionary theory.

■ According to the **activation-synthesis model**, dreams are the simplest way of interpreting all the internal, brain-produced signals that occur during REM sleep. Psychological theories of dreams, such as those of Freud, Jung and Hall, focus on the **synthesis** component, stressing their significance for the dreamer.

■ According to Crick and Mitchison's **reverse learning theory**, dreams are a way of 'cleaning up' the cortex's neural networks and preparing them for new input.

- Different theories of dreaming **aren't** mutually exclusive. REM sleep may have evolved to help animals' biological survival, but they continue to serve a vital function for individuals, helping them to survive psychologically.

Self-assessment questions

1 Discuss the concept of consciousness as it has been used in psychology.
2 Discuss **two** theories relating to the functions of sleep.
3 **a** Outline the nature of dreams.
  b Outline and evaluate **one** theory of the functions of dreaming.
4 Describe and evaluate the relationship between sleep and dreaming.

Web addresses

http://bisleep.medsch.ucla.edu/

http://faculty.washington.edu/chudler/sleep.html

http://www.lboro.ac.uk/departments/hu/groups/sleep/karger.htm

http://www.iag.net/~hutchib/.dream

http://www.spiritonline.com/dreams/why.html

http://dreamemporium.com/

www.sleepnet.com

www.stanford.edu/~dement

Further reading

Humphrey, N. (1986, 1993) *The Inner Eye*. London: Vintage.

An excellent, very slim, book, which discusses various aspects of consciousness. By the same author, *A History of the Mind* (1992) is a more challenging, but just as readable, journey around the study of consciousness.

Empson J. (1993) *Sleep and Dreaming* (2nd edition). Hemel Hempstead: Harvester Wheatsheaf.

A very thorough discussion of all the major aspects of the topic, including sleep disorders and sleep in animals.

Gross, R. (1999) *Key Studies in Psychology* (3rd edition). London: Hodder & Stoughton.

Chapter 24 provides a detailed summary of Dement & Kleitman's (1957) classic article on REM sleep and dreaming, plus an evaluation. Similarly, Chapter 26 summarises a classic article by Martin Orne (1966) on hypnosis.

Chapter 8

Substance Dependence and Abuse

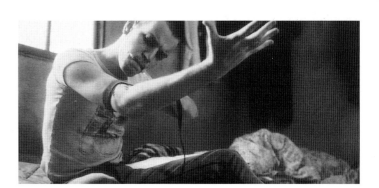

Introduction and overview

For thousands of years, people have taken substances to alter their perception of reality, and societies have always restricted the substances they've allowed their members to take. These substances, which we usually call drugs, are *psychoactive*, denoting a chemical substance that alters conscious awareness through its effect on the brain. Most drugs fit this definition. Some, for example aspirin, are *indirectly* psychoactive: their primary purpose is to remove pain, but being headache-free can lift our mood. Others, however, are *designed* to change mood and behaviour, and when used in medicine are collectively referred to as *psychotherapeutic* drugs, such as those used in the treatment of anxiety, depression, and schizophrenia (see Chapter 45).

This chapter is concerned with psychoactive drugs used to produce a temporarily altered state of consciousness for the purpose of *pleasure*. These include *recreational drugs*, which have no legal restrictions (such as alcohol, nicotine, and caffeine), and *drugs of abuse*, which are illegal. However, just as recreational drugs can be abused (such as alcohol), so illegal drugs are taken recreationally (such as ecstasy). 'Substance abuse', therefore, doesn't imply particular types of drug, but the extent to which the drug is used, and the effects – emotional, behavioural, and medical – it has on the (ab)user.

What is considered a recreational drug or a drug of abuse changes over time within a particular society, as well as between societies. For example, cocaine had been freely available over the counter in a huge variety of tonics and pick-me-ups before the 1930s, and was an ingredient of the original blend of Coca-Cola in the 1890s. At that time, it was seen as a harmless stimulant (Plant, 1999): now it's a Class A drug. Conversely, cannabis is currently a Class B drug (still illegal but seen as less dangerous and carrying a more lenient punishment), but its therapeutic (medical) use is likely to become legalised within a few years (Bennetto, 2000). According to Veitia & McGahee (1995):

> 'Cigarette smoking and alcohol abuse permeate our culture and are widespread enough to be considered ordinary addictions … The degree to which these drugs permeate our culture and the extent to which they are accepted by our society distinguish them from other addictive but illegal substances such as heroin and cocaine'.

Defining abuse

The concept of addiction

Ask yourself …
- What do you understand by the term 'addiction'?

Until recently, the study and treatment of drug problems were organised around the concept of addiction: people with drug problems have problems, because they're addicted to the drug (Hammersley, 1999). Addicts are compelled by a physiological need to continue taking the drug, experience horrible physical and psychological symptoms when trying to stop, and will continue taking it despite these symptoms because of their addictive need. Their addiction will also change them psychologically for the worse, they'll commit crimes to pay for the drug, neglect their social roles and responsibilities, and even harm the people around them. In addition, some drugs are considered inherently much more addictive than others (see below), and substance users can be divided into addicts and non-addicts.

Criticisms of the concept

■ It's an oversimplification. Most professionals who deal with people with any kind of problem – medical, criminal, educational, social – will have seen many clients who aren't exactly addicts, but whose drug use seems to have

contributed to, or worsened, their other problems (Hammersley, 1999).

■ It's based on the *addiction-as-disease* model. While medical models such as this are generally persuasive, because they offer a diagnosis, definition and a pathology, they also appear to relieve the 'addict' of responsibility for his/her behaviour (Baker, 2000: see Chapter 43).

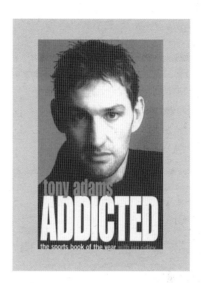

According to Hammersley (1999), the more modern view is to see drug problems as two-fold: *substance abuse and substance dependence* (hence the title of this chapter). This view is adopted in the American Psychiatric Association's (1994) *Diagnostic and Statistical Manual of Mental Disorders* (DSM-IV: see Boxes 8.1 and 8.2, page 106). 'Addiction' is now usually used to refer to a field of study, covering substance use, abuse, and dependence, rather than to a theory of why people become dependent.

Is there more to addiction than drugs?

Rather than rejecting the concept of addiction, some researchers argue that the concept should be *broadened*, in order to cover certain recent forms of 'addictive' behaviour which don't involve chemical substances at all. According to Shaffer *et al.* (1989):

> '*Addictive behaviours typically serve the addict in the short run at the price of longer-term destructiveness. Physical dependence is not a requisite for addiction … addictive behaviours organise the addict's life. All of life's other activities fit in the gaps that the addictive behaviour permits*'.

The addiction can be to a substance or an experience: shopping, gambling, or eating (or abstaining from eating: see Chapter 44) could all equally fit this definition. Drawing on current definitions of substance dependence, pathological gambling, and eating disorders, Walters (1999) suggests that addiction may be defined as 'the persistent and repetitious enactment of a behaviour pattern', which includes:

■ *progression* (increase in severity);
■ *preoccupation* with the activity;
■ *perceived loss of control*;
■ *persistence* despite negative long-term consequences.

Similarly, Griffiths (1999b) maintains that addiction isn't confined to drugs. Several other behaviours, including gambling, watching TV, playing amusement machines, overeating, sex, exercise, computer games, and using the Internet, are potentially addictive. Social pathologies are beginning to surface in cyberspace in the form of *technological addictions*, which are:

'… non-chemical (behavioural) addictions that involve human–machine interaction. They can be either passive (e.g. television) or active (e.g. computer games). The interaction usually contains inducing and reinforcing features (e.g. sound effects, colour effects …) that may promote addictive tendencies'. (Griffiths, 1995)

Griffiths (1996) argues that these behaviours display the same core components of addiction (complementing Walters' 'four Ps' above), namely:

- *salience:* the activity becomes the most important one in the person's life. It dominates thinking (preoccupations), feelings (cravings), and behaviour (socialised behaviour deteriorates);
- *mood modification*: for example, the activity produces an arousing 'buzz' or 'high';
- *tolerance*: increasing amounts of the activity are needed to achieve the same effects;
- *withdrawal symptoms*: discontinuation or sudden reduction of the activity produces unpleasant feelings and physical effects;
- *conflict*: this may be between the addict and those around him/her, with other activities (such as work, social life, and other interests), or within the individual him/herself;
- *relapse:* the addict reverts to earlier patterns of the activity soon after a period of abstinence or self-control.

Substance use and abuse

According to Hammersley (1999), abuse is the use of a substance in a harmful or risky manner, without medical sanction. The concept is something of a compromise, because it's debatable whether any use of a substance can be entirely risk-free. It also suggests that some risks are negligible, while others are substantial. Hammersley claims that:

'The health risks of tobacco smoking now seem so substantial that all smoking is probably abuse – there is no negligible-risk use of tobacco …'.

But he believes that most other drugs *can* be used in ways that make risks negligible.

> **Box 8.1 The DSM-IV criteria for substance abuse**
>
> - A maladaptive pattern of substance use leading to clinically significant impairment or distress, as manifested by one (or more) of the following, occurring within a twelve-month period:
>
>   1 recurrent substance use resulting in a failure to fulfil major role obligations at work, school or home (e.g. repeated absences or poor work performance related to substance use; substance-related absences, suspensions, or expulsions from school; neglect of children or household);

> 2 recurrent substance use in situations where it is physically hazardous (e.g. driving an automobile or operating a machine when impaired by substance use);
> 3 recurrent substance-related legal problems (e.g. arrests for substance-related disorderly conduct);
> 4 continued substance use despite having persistent or recurrent social or interpersonal problems caused or exacerbated by the effects of the substance (e.g. arguments with spouse about consequences of intoxication, physical fights).
>
> - The symptoms have never met the criteria for substance dependence for this class of substance.

Dependence

How does dependence differ from abuse?

> **Box 8.2 DSM-IV criteria for substance dependence**
>
> - A maladaptive pattern of substance use leading to clinically significant impairment or distress, as manifested by three (or more) of the following, occurring at any time in the same twelve-month period:
>
>   1 Tolerance, as defined by either of the following: (a) a need for markedly increased amounts of the substance to achieve intoxication or desired effect; (b) markedly diminished effect with continued use of the same amount of the substance.
>   2 Withdrawal, as manifested by either of the following: (a) the characteristic withdrawal syndrome for the substance (varies from substance to substance); (b) the same (or a closely related) substance is taken to relieve or avoid withdrawal symptoms.
>   3 The substance is often taken in larger amounts and over a longer period than was intended.
>   4 There is a persistent desire or unsuccessful efforts to cut down or control substance use.
>   5 A great deal of time is spent in activities necessary to obtain the substance (e.g. visiting multiple doctors or driving long distances), to use the substance (e.g. chain-smoking), or recover from its effects.
>   6 Important social, occupational, or recreational activities are given up or reduced because of substance use.
>   7 The substance use is continued despite knowledge of having a persistent physical or psychological problem that is likely to have been caused or exacerbated by the substance (e.g. current cocaine use despite recognition of cocaine-induced depression, or continued drinking despite recognition that an ulcer was made worse by alcohol consumption).
>
> Specify if:
>
> - with physiological dependence: evidence of tolerance or withdrawal (i.e. either item 1 or 2 is present);
> - with psychological dependence: no evidence of tolerance or withdrawal (i.e. neither item 1 or 2 is present).

The concept of dependence is based around a constellation of symptoms and problems, not just on the idea of physiological need for a drug. Only items 1 and 2 in Box 8.2 refer to physiological dependence. Anyone who fits three or more of these criteria would be diagnosed as substance dependent. Dependence, therefore, is quite varied, and few people fit all seven criteria (Hammersley, 1999).

Most substance-dependent people have tried to give up several times, always returning to use after weeks, months or even years. They often report strong craving or desire for the substance, and are at particular risk of resuming use when stressed, anxious, depressed, angry, or even happy. They also often feel they have difficulty controlling the amount they take, once they start. When they relapse, they often return very quickly to their old, often destructive, habits.

Physiological vs psychological dependence

As Box 8.2 shows, *physiological dependence* is related to *withdrawal* and/or *tolerance* (which relates to the traditional concept of *addiction*: see Figure 8.1), while *psychological dependence* isn't. However, being deprived of a substance that's highly pleasurable can induce anxiety. Since the symptoms of anxiety (rapid pulse, profuse sweating, shaking, and so on) overlap with withdrawal symptoms, people may mistakenly believe they're physiologically dependent. Psychological dependence is, though, part of the overall *dependence syndrome*.

A good way to explain the difference between the two types of dependence is by looking at imipramine, used to treat depression (see Chapter 45). When it's stopped after prolonged use, there may be nausea, muscle aches, anxiety, and difficulty in sleeping, but *never* a compulsion to resume taking it (Lowe, 1995). However, Lowe claims that 'psychological' dependence has little scientific meaning beyond the notion that drug taking becomes part of one's habitual behaviour. Giving it up is very difficult, because the person has become *habituated* to it:

> 'Habituation is the repeated use of a drug because the user finds that use increases pleasurable feelings or reduces feelings of anxiety, fear, or stress. Habituation becomes problematic when the person becomes so consumed by the need for the drug-altered state of consciousness that all his or her energies are directed to compulsive drug-seeking behaviour ...'. (Lowe, 1995)

Physiologically addictive drugs, such as heroin and alcohol, typically cause habituation *as well*. Most widely used recreational drugs, including cannabis, cocaine, LSD, PCP and *methylenedioxymethamphetamine* (MDMA: otherwise known as 'ecstasy'), *don't* cause physiological dependence – but people *do* become habituated (see Table 8.1, page 108).

Some dependent people can stay dependent for long periods *without* suffering any other problems. This applies particularly to people who otherwise fit well into society, and who haven't experienced financial, legal, or health problems as a result of their substance use – such as many smokers. Some very heavy drinkers 'only' damage their livers, and even some heroin or cocaine users fit this pattern. Nevertheless:

> '... one of the most striking things about the counselling of substance-dependent people is that they will continue to use the substance even when they have suffered very severe problems as a result ...'. (Hammersley, 1999)

Some of these severe problems are discussed in the section on the effects of drugs.

Classifying drugs

Psychoactive drugs have been classified in several different ways. For example, Hamilton & Timmons (1995) identify three broad groups:

- *stimulants* temporarily excite neural activity, arouse bodily functions, enhance positive feelings, and heighten alertness. In high doses, they cause overt seizures;
- *depressants* (or *sedatives*) depress neural activity, slow down bodly functions, induce calmness, and produce sleep. In high doses, they cause unconsciousness;
- *hallucinogens* produce distortion of normal perception and thought processes. In high doses, they can cause episodes of psychotic behaviour (see Chapters 43 and 44).

A fourth category is *opiates*. These also depress activity in the CNS, but have *analgesic* properties; that is, they reduce sensitivity to pain without loss of consciousness. The Royal College of Psychiatrists (1987) identify *minor tranquillisers* as a separate category, but in Table 8.1 these have been included under the general category of depressants. *Cannabis* doesn't fall easily into any of these other categories.

The effects of drugs

According to Greenfield (in Ahuja, 2000):

> 'As a person, you are the configuration of your brain cells... Drugs are specifically designed to alter that configuration. So when you blow your mind on drugs, you really are blowing your mind. They may not kill you, but they may dramatically alter the person you are ...'.

Children and teenagers, whose relatively malleable brains are still being moulded, are particularly vulnerable (see Chapter 4). It's teenagers who, for various social and cultural reasons, are especially likely to take drugs, including those which pose the greatest threat to physical and mental health.

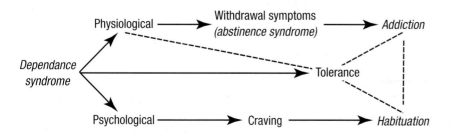

Figure 8.1 *Summary of major components of dependence syndrome*

Table 8.1 *Some examples of the major categories of psychoactive drugs*

Major category	Examples	Slang name(s)
Depressants (sedatives)	alcohol	
	barbiturates:	'downers', 'barbs', various other names derived from names or colour of pill/capsule (e.g. 'blueys').
	tranquillisers:	'tranx'
	solvents	
Stimulants	caffeine	
	nicotine	
	amphetamines :	'uppers', 'speed', 'sulphate', 'sulph', 'whizz'.
	MDMA:	'ecstasy', 'E', and many names derived from shape/colour of drugs
	cocaine:	'coke', 'snow', 'crack', 'freebase', 'base', 'wash', 'rock'.
Opiates	morphine:	
	heroin	'junk', 'skag', 'H', 'smack'
	codeine	
	methadone:	'amps' (injectable), 'linctus' (oral)
Hallucinogens	lysergic acid diethylamide (LSD):	'acid'
	mescaline:	
	psilocybin:	'magic mushrooms', 'mushies'.
	phencyclidine (PCP):	'angel dust'
Cannabis	cannabis sativa:	'pot', 'dope', 'blow', 'draw', 'smoke'.
	herbal cannabis:	'grass', 'marijuana', 'ganja'.
	cannabis resin:	'weed', 'the herb', 'skunk'.
	cannabis oil:	'hash', 'hashish'

(Based on Cooper, 1995)

Depressants

Alcohol

Despite the difficulties in assessing the relationship between level of intake of alcohol and its harmful effects, certain 'safe levels' are widely accepted (Gelder *et al.*, 1999). These are expressed in terms of *units* of alcohol, one of which is equal to eight grammes of ethanol (the equivalent of half a pint of beer, a small glass of wine, a glass of sherry, or a standard [pub] measure of spirits).

For *men*, up to *21 units* per week, and for *women*, up to *14 units* is considered safe, provided the whole amount isn't taken all at once and that there are occasional drink-free days. Anything over 50 and 35 units, respectively, is considered '*dangerous*'. The British legal driving blood alcohol limit is 80 mg per 100 ml (equivalent to two or three drinks).

How does alcohol affect us?

> *Ask yourself ...*
>
> • Either from your own experience, or from observing others, how would you describe the effects of alcohol?

According to Motluk (1999), it's possible to identify a number of stages, based on the amount of alcohol consumed:

■ With our first drink, and with blood alcohol levels remaining fairly low, *stimulation* is the first effect. At these low levels, alcohol sensitises one of the brain's major excitatory message pathways, the *N*-methyl-*D*-aspartate (NMDA) system (not to be confused with ecstasy!). This makes certain NMDA receptors more readily activated by the brain's main neurotransmitter, glutamate. Some of the most sensitised brain regions are the cortex (thinking), hippocampus (remembering), and nucleus accumbens (pleasure-seeking), and our inhibitions begin to decrease.

■ After two or three drinks, alpha rhythms (see Chapter 7) increase, extra blood flows to the prefrontal and right temporal cortices. Mood is heightened and we may even feel euphoric.

■ After three or four drinks, a turning point is reached, reflecting the complex 'biphasic' relationship with alcohol. With our blood now awash with alcohol, the very NMDA receptors that helped to perk us up after just one drink are refusing to respond. Also, the brain's *gamma-aminobutyric acid* (GABA) *system* becomes activated. GABA is an *inhibitory* neurotransmitter (see Table 4.1, page 47), which dulls activity (it's the system activated by benzodiazepines, such as *Valium*: see Chapter 45). From this point, alcohol begins to act more like a *depressant/sedative*. The hippocampus and thalamus are both slowed down.

■ Any more drinks, and our speech and other motor functions begin to fail us. The cerebellum seems to be most affected by this stage. A common experience is that the room is spinning. This is called *positional alcohol nystagmus*, a booze-induced version of an eye reflex normally triggered by the inner ear's balance organs when they detect head rotation (see Chapter 5).

■ A blood alcohol concentration of 500 mg per 100 ml is considered lethal. At that concentration, the brain centres that keep us breathing shut down.

Oliver Reed, well-known actor and alcoholic

> ### Box 8.3 Some physiological effects of alcohol
>
> - Ethanol is a *diuretic*, so you end up *expelling* more water than you drink. It acts on the pituitary gland, blocking production of the hormone *vasopressin*, which directs the kidneys to reabsorb water that would otherwise end up in the bladder. So, the body borrows water from other places, including the brain, which shrinks temporarily. Though the brain itself cannot experience pain, dehydration may shrivel the *dura* (a membrane covering the brain). As this happens, it tugs at pain-sensitive filaments connecting it to the skull. Water loss might also account for pains elsewhere in the body.
> - Frequent trips to the toilet also result in loss of essential sodium and potassium ions, which are central to how nerves and muscles work (see Chapter 4). Subtle chemical imbalances caused by ion depletion could account for a cluster of symptoms, including headaches, nausea, and fatigue.
> - Alcohol also depletes our reserves of sugar, leading to hypoglycaemia. The body's store of energy-rich glycogen in the liver is broken down into glucose; this quickly becomes another constituent of urine. This can account for feelings of weakness and unsteadiness the morning after.
>
> (Based on *New Scientist*, 1999)

Heavy drinkers suffer malnutrition. Since alcohol is high in calories, appetite is suppressed. It also causes vitamin deficiency, by interfering with absorption of vitamin B from the intestines. Long-term, this causes brain damage. Other physical effects include liver damage, heart disease, increased risk of a stroke, and susceptibility to infections due to a suppressed immune system (see Chapter 12). Women who drink while pregnant can give birth to babies with *foetal alcohol syndrome* (see Chapter 40).

Alcohol and memory

Alcohol interferes with normal sleep patterns. Although it causes sedation, alcohol also suppresses REM sleep by as much as 20 per cent (see Chapter 7). There also appears to be a link between alcohol-induced sleepiness and memory loss. Roehrs (cited in Motluk, 1999) observed that people who get drunk and then forget what happened have memory impairments similar to those suffered by people with sleep disorders, such as daytime sleepiness.

In both cases, the person cannot recall how they got home, or what happened while at work or at the pub. It seems to be the *transfer* of information into long-term memory that's disturbed. Roehrs believes that the GABA signals that induce the sleepiness can interfere with both the early and late stages of memory formation (*stimulus registration* and *consolidation*, respectively). Chemicals that mimic GABA can do this, and there are many GABA receptors in the hippocampus. An extreme memory disorder associated with chronic alcohol consumption is *Korsakoff's syndrome* (see Chapter 17).

Alcohol and sex

Alcohol lowers levels of testosterone, the male sex hormone, in the blood. One of testosterone's functions is to maintain and regulate sex drive, so excessive drinking can explain loss of sexual appetite and/or the inability to 'perform' (that is, get an erection – otherwise known as 'brewer's droop'). While sexual function returns after blood alcohol levels have fallen again, habitual overindulgence over a five- to ten-year period can permanently damage a man's virility (erectile dysfunction and impotence). Even more worrying, alcohol can actually reduce the size of a man's genitalia! (Burke, 1999).

In women, the reverse seems to happen: even a couple of drinks can very quickly *increase* testosterone levels in the blood, thus increasing their libido (making them *more* randy). This is especially marked in women on the Pill and non-Pill users who are ovulating. But as with men, chronic heavy women drinkers can suffer loss of libido and performance, and infertility (Burke, 1999).

Who drinks, and why?

The heaviest drinkers are men in their late teens and early 20s, but there have been recent increases among 15–16-year-olds. Fewer women than men drink dangerous amounts, but the rates among women are rising faster than in men, especially those in professional and managerial jobs (Gelder *et al.*, 1999).

A recent Mori poll (in Waterhouse *et al.*, 2000) showed that 17 per cent of those under 25 say they drink in order to get 'trolleyed'. A forthcoming European School Survey Project on Alcohol and Other Drugs indicates that more than half of 15–16-year-old British teenagers admitted 'binge drinking' in the previous month. The UK survey by the Alcohol and Health Research Centre in Edinburgh of more than 2600 school students revealed that 57 per cent of boys and 54.8 per cent of girls had drunk five or more drinks in a row in the previous 30 days. Among 16–24-year-olds, 38 per cent of men, and 21 per cent of women regularly drink twice the recommended daily limit (Waterhouse *et al.*, 2000: see above).

> ### Box 8.4 The influence of socio-economic changes on alcohol consumption
>
> Alcohol is much more affordable than it used to be. Although the cost of alcohol has increased 22 per cent more than house prices generally since 1976, households' disposable income has risen by 81 per cent in real terms. As Figure 8.2 (page 110) shows, in the 1960s, the British drank the equivalent of about 4.5 litres of pure alcohol per head per year; the figure for 1998 was 7.5 litres.
>
> According to Brain (in Waterhouse *et al.*, 2000), the alcohol industry is at least partly to blame for the increase in drinking among young people. Responding to a decline in traditional beer drinking, it has created a 'post-modern market' tempting young people to drink strong, designer drinks in glitzy theme bars. The number of applications for new drinking licences is running at 3000 a year, a 38 per cent increase since 1995. From 1978–1998, the number of pubs and bars in England and Wales rose by 16 per cent to 78,000, and nightclubs by 25 per cent to 4000.
>
> Another reason for the increase is the trend towards 'extended youth'. Puberty starts earlier (see Chapter 37), men and women are postponing both marriage and having children, creating a state of 'perpetual adolescence' (see Chapter 38).

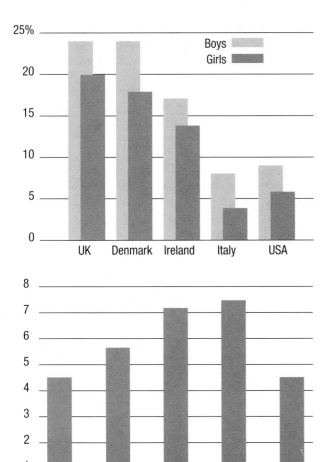

Figure 8.2 *(above) Percentages of boys and girls drunk three times in the last 30 days (below) Litres of pure alcohol drunk per head per year (UK) (from Waterhouse et al., 2000)*

Stimulants

Amphetamines

These were first synthesised in the 1920s. Their general effect is to increase energy, and enhance self-confidence. For this reason, they were used extensively by the military in World War II to reduce fatigue and increase the confidence of soldiers going into battle. Amphetamines also suppress appetite, and are hence the main ingredient of 'slimming pills' such as *Methedrine*, *Dexedrine* and *Benzedrine*.

Amphetamines are swallowed in pill form, inhaled through the nose in powder form, or injected in liquid form. Small amounts cause increased wakefulness, alertness, and arousal. Users experience a sense of energy and confidence, and feel that any problem can be solved and any task accomplished. Once the drug wears off, the user experiences a 'crash' or 'hangover', characterised by extreme fatigue and depression, irritability, disorientation, and agitated motor activity. This can be counteracted by taking the drug again. Large amounts can cause restlessness, hallucinations, and *paranoid delusions* (or *amphetamine psychosis*), which is virtually indistinguishable from *paranoid schizophrenia* (see Chapter 44). Long-term use has also been linked with severe depression, suicidal tendencies, disrupted thinking, and brain damage.

Tolerance and *psychological dependence* develop quickly. The amphetamine 'hangover' is indicative of *withdrawal*, suggesting *physiological dependence*.

Cocaine

Cocaine hydrochloride is a powerful CNS stimulant extracted from the leaves of the coca shrub, native to South America. The Peruvian Indians originally discovered that chewing the leaves could increase stamina, and relieve fatigue and hunger. While they still chew the leaves, elsewhere in the world it's inhaled in powder form, injected into the veins in liquid form, or smoked. When smoked, the drug reaches the brain in five to ten seconds, much faster than the other methods. It can also be swallowed, rubbed on the gums, or blown into the throat.

In general the effects of cocaine are similar to those of amphetamines, but they tend to last only 15–30 minutes (compared with several hours). Typically, the user experiences a state of euphoria, deadening of pain, increased self-confidence, energy and attention. There's a 'crash' when the drug wears off.

Even in small amounts, the stimulating effects can cause cardiac arrest and death. Recent research suggests that young people who use cocaine (and amphetamines) may be increasing their risks of having a stroke (brain haemorrhage) (Laurance, 2000). The growing pandemic of cocaine use in Western society is overshadowing the traditional risk factors for stroke, such as high blood pressure. While strokes are much more common in older people, it's becoming increasingly common for people under 30 to suffer strokes after taking drugs.

Cocaine (and amphetamines) appear to produce a surge in blood pressure. People with abnormal blood vessels in their brains, such as cerebral aneurysms, are at greatest risk. But it's also possible that the drug-taking caused the deformed blood vessels (Laurance, 2000). Repeated inhalation constricts the blood vessels in the nose. The nasal septum may become perforated, necessitating cosmetic surgery.

Daniella Westbrook's septum was said to have been perforated through repeated inhalation of cocaine

Formication refers to the sensation that 'insects' ('coke bugs') are crawling beneath the skin. Although this is merely random neural activity, users sometimes try to remove the imaginary insects by cutting deep into their skin. Cocaine definitely produces *psychological dependence*, but there's much more doubt regarding *physiological dependence, tolerance*, and *withdrawal*.

Both amphetamines and cocaine increase ANS activity. Increased brain activation is probably due to secretion of increased levels of noradrenaline and dopamine, whose reuptake is then inhibited (see Chapter 4). This results in an excess of these neurotransmitters, which increases neuronal activity, producing a persistent state of arousal. Dopamine probably accounts for the euphoric effect, while noradrenaline explains the increased energy. Cocaine stimulates neural circuits that are normally triggered by reinforcing events, such as eating or sex. The 'crash' is caused by the fairly sudden depletion of dopamine and noradrenaline.

> **Box 8.5   Crack**
>
> *Crack* is a form of cocaine, which first appeared in the 1980s. It's made using cocaine hydrochloride, ammonia or baking soda, and water. When heated, the ammonia or baking soda produces a 'cracking' sound. The result is a crystal, which has had the hydrochloride base removed (hence *'free basing'* to describe its production). Its effects are more rapid and intense than cocaine's, but the 'crash' is also more severe.

Unlike heroin-dependent people, most cocaine users will get over their drug problem *without* professional help (Hammersley, 1999).

MDMA

MDMA or 'ecstasy' is chemically related to amphetamine, first synthesised in 1912, and later patented as an appetite suppressant (but never marketed). It's swallowed in pill or tablet form, and sometimes taken with other mood-altering drugs. Small amounts produce a mild euphoric 'rush', which can last for up to ten hours. Self- and sexual confidence are increased. Serotonin and dopamine are the neurotransmitters affected.

Ecstasy causes extreme dehydration and hyperthermia, which induces a form of heatstroke. This can produce convulsions, collapse, and death. Blood pressure also rises dangerously, which can induce a stroke and permanent brain damage. Over 50 deaths in Britain alone have been attributed to the drug (Parrott, 1997), including the much publicised case of Leah Betts in 1995.

For a small minority, the side-effects can include severe depression, anxiety, paranoia, hallucinations, psychosis, and panic attacks. However, it's difficult in practice to establish a cause-and-effect link between ecstasy and these mental and physical reactions. The drug is taken mainly at raves and in clubs, where large numbers of sweaty people are in close proximity for hours on end. These conditions make heatstroke more likely, without any drug-taking being involved. Clubbers take impure drugs, and they take cocktails of drugs (that may include amphetamines: Naylor, 1998). Clubbers

have been warned recently against the use of GBH (ganmma hydroxybutyrate), also called 'liquid ecstasy', especially when mixed with alcohol. It's not actually illegal and is relatively cheap. Overdoses are common, and it can cause convulsions and coma (Laurance, 2000).

Brain cells die after taking the drug, meaning that they can no longer produce serotonin. This can account for the depression, which is quite commonly reported by users. Greenfield (in Ahuja, 2000) is more concerned about this long-term, irreversible, brain damage, than the deaths that occur from taking ecstasy. But not everyone agrees that these brain changes necessarily constitute damage, and the drug may induce depression (and other mental health problems) only in those who already have emotional difficulties (Naylor, 1988). According to the Department of Health (1994), *tolerance* occurs, but not *physiological dependence*.

Opiates

These are derived from the unripe seed pods of the opium poppy ('plant of joy'). One constituent of opium is *morphine*, from which *codeine* and *heroin* can be extracted.

Morphine and heroin

In general, the opiates depress neural functioning and suppress physical sensations and responses to stimulation. In Europe, *morphine* was first used as an analgesic during the Franco-Prussian War (1870–1). However, it quickly became apparent that it produced physiological dependence (the 'soldier's disease'). The German Bayer Company developed *heroin* (the 'hero' that would cure the 'soldier's disease') in order to prevent this dependence, but, unfortunately, it also causes physiological dependence and has many unpleasant side-effects.

Heroin can be smoked, inhaled, or injected intravenously. The immediate effects (the 'rush') are described as an overwhelming sensation of pleasure, similar to sexual orgasm but affecting the whole body. Such effects are so pleasurable that they override any thoughts of food or sex. Heroin rapidly decomposes into morphine, producing feelings of euphoria, well-being, relaxation, and drowsiness.

In long-term users, there's an increase in aggressiveness and social isolation, plus a decrease in general physical activity. Opiates in general may damage the body's immune system, leading to increased susceptibility to infection. The impurity of the heroin used, users' lack of adequate diet, and the risks from contaminated needles, all increase health risks. Overdoses are common.

Heroin produces both *physiological* and *psychological dependence. Tolerance* develops quickly. *Withdrawal symptoms* initially involve flu-like symptoms, progressing to tremors, stomach cramps and alternating chills and sweats. Rapid pulse, high blood pressure, insomnia, and diarrhoea also occur. The skin often breaks out into goose bumps resembling a plucked turkey (hence *'cold turkey'* to describe attempts to abstain). The legs jerk uncontrollably (hence *'kicking the habit'*). These symptoms last about one week, reaching a peak after about 48 hours.

Box 8.6 Heroin and endorphins

As we saw in Chapter 4, the brain produces its own opiates (*opioid pep-tides* or *endorphins*). When we engage in important survival behaviours, endorphins are released into the fluid that bathes neurons. Endorphin molecules stimulate *opiate receptors* on some neurons, producing an intensely pleasurable effect just like that reported by heroin users.

Regular use of opiates overloads endorphin sites in the brain, and the brain stops producing its own endorphins (Snyder, 1977). When the user abstains, neither the naturally occurring endorphins nor the opiates are available. Consequently, the internal mechanism for regulating pain is severely disrupted, producing some of the withdrawal symptoms described earlier.

Methadone

This is a synthetic opiate (or opioid) created to treat *physiological dependence* on heroin and other opiates. Methadone acts more slowly than heroin, and doesn't produce the heroin 'rush'. While heroin users may be less likely to take heroin if they're on methadone, they're likely to become at least *psychologically dependent* on it. By the early 1980s, long-term prescribing of methadone (methadone maintenance) began to be questioned, both in terms of effectiveness and the message it conveyed to users.

However, the HIV/AIDS epidemic has made harm minimisation a priority. Dispensing of injecting equipment and condoms in 'needle exchange' schemes has been combined with attempts to persuade users to substitute oral methadone for intravenous heroin. This reduces the risk of transmitting both HIV and other blood-borne viruses, such as hepatitis B (Lipsedge, 1997a).

Hallucinogens

These produce the most profound effects on consciousnsss, which is why they're sometimes called *psychedelics* ('mind expanding'). *Mescaline* comes from the peyote cactus, while *psilocybin* is obtained from the mushroom *psilocybe mexicana*. LSD and PCP are both chemically synthesised (see Table 8.1).

LSD

First produced in the 1940s, LSD was used during the 1960s for a variety of medical purposes, including pain relief for the terminally ill. But it became widely known during that period – and widely used – as a recreational drug. This use of LSD was largely inspired by Timothy Leary, a Harvard University psychologist, who coined the slogan 'turn on, tune in, and drop out'. LSD, peace and love were central to the 1960s hippy movement ('flower power').

LSD is usually impregnated on blotting paper and swallowed. Unlike other drugs, its effects may not appear until an hour or so after being taken. These include:

■ distorted sensory experiences, such as the intensification of sights and sounds, and changing form and colour. This can be pleasurable or terrifying (a 'bad trip'), depending on mood and expectations;
■ dramatic slowing down of subjective time;
■ *synaesthesia*: the blending of different sensory experiences (for example, music may be experienced visually);

■ *depersonalisation*: the body is perceived as being separate from the self. Users report being able to see themselves from afar, similar to out-of-body experiences (see Chapter 6);
■ *flashbacks*: some long-term users experience distorted perceptions or hallucinations days or weeks after the drug was taken.

There's no evidence of *physiological dependence* or *withdrawal*, but *tolerance* can develop quickly. If taken repeatedly, there are few effects until a week or so after it was last taken. Whether LSD produces *psychological dependence* is disputed.

PCP

First synthesised in the 1950s for use as a surgical anaesthetic, this was stopped once its psychoactive side-effects became apparent. It's usually combined with tobacco and smoked, producing distortions in body image and depersonalisation.

Used in small amounts, it induces euphoria, heightened awareness, and a sense that all problems have disappeared. In larger quantities, it has stimulant, depressant, and (not surprisingly given its original purpose), analgesic properties. Effects include violence, panic, psychotic behaviour, disrupted motor activity, and chronic depression. These may persist for weeks after the drug was last taken.

Long-term use is associated with the four 'Cs' (Smith *et al.*, 1978):

■ *combativeness*: agitated or violent behaviour;
■ *catatonia*: muscular rigidity of the body (see Chapter 44);
■ *convulsions*: epileptic-type seizures;
■ *coma*: a deep, unresponsive sleep.

Although PCP doesn't produce *physiological dependence*, users may become *psychologically dependent*.

Cannabis

This is second only to alcohol in popularity. The *cannabis sativa* plant's psychoactive ingredient is *delta-9-tetrahydrocannabinil* (*THC*). THC is found in the branches and leaves of the male and female plants (*marijuana*), but is highly concentrated in the resin of the female plant. *Hashish* is derived from the sticky resin and is more potent than marijuana (see Table 8.1).

Cannabis is usually smoked with tobacco, or eaten. When smoked, THC reaches the brain within seven seconds. Small amounts produce a mild, pleasurable 'high', involving relaxation, a loss of social inhibition, intoxication, and a humorous mood. Speech becomes slurred, and co-ordination is impaired. Increased heart rate, reduced concentration, enhanced appetite, and impaired short-term memory are also quite common effects. Some users report fear, anxiety, and confusion.

Large amounts produce hallucinogenic reactions, but these aren't full-blown as with LSD. THC remains in the body for up to a month, and both male sex hormones and the female menstrual cycle can be disrupted. If used during pregnancy, the foetus may fail to grow properly, and cannabis is more dangerous to the throat and lungs than cigarettes. *Reverse tolerance* has been reported, in which regular use leads to a *lowering* of the amount needed to produce the initial effects. This could be due to a build-up of THC, which takes a long time to be metabolised. Alternatively, users may become more efficient inhalers, and so perceive the drug's effects more quickly. *Withdrawal* effects (restlessness, irritability, and insomnia) have been reported, but they seem to be associated only with continuous use of very large amounts. *Psychological dependence* almost certainly occurs in at least some people.

Ask yourself ...

- Try to formulate arguments for and against the legalisation of cannabis.

CRITICAL DISCUSSION 8.1

Cannabis and the drugs debate

According to Skelton (in Naylor, 1998), coordinator of Edinburgh drugs agency Crew 2000:

> '*Up until a few years ago, if anybody went to a drugs project and said they had a problem with cannabis then they wouldn't be taken seriously ... This has changed quite a bit. People are recognising that there are side-effects, particularly for people who've got any sort of mental illness*'.

Greenfield (in Ahuja, 2000) considers cannabis to be very potent. It takes 0.3 mg to induce the same kind of effects as 7000 mg of alcohol, primarily feelings of well-being and relaxation. This potency suggests that specific cannabis receptors exist in the brain.

This is very much at odds with a recently published report (by the Police Federation, a charitable research organisation), which calls for major reform to drug laws. The laws on cannabis came in for particular criticism. Alcohol and tobacco are seen as much more harmful, both to the individual and society. While not denying the significant physical and psychological risks involved in using cannabis, the report rates alcohol and cocaine as equally dangerous (and top of the danger league table), followed by heroin, tobacco, ecstasy and LSD (all equally dangerous), with cannabis at the bottom. Specifically, it wants to change the present classification to:

- *cannabis* (class B): should be C;
- *ecstasy* (class A): should be B;
- *heroin* (class A): should remain A, but reduce penalty for possession;
- *LSD* (class A): should be B;
- *cocaine/crack* (class A): should remain A, but reduce penalty for possession.

According to the Report:

> 'We have concluded that the most dangerous message of all is the message that all drugs are equally dangerous'.

Downing Street and the Home Office rejected the proposals to reclassify ecstasy, LDS and cannabis, warning that they might encourage more people to experiment with drugs (Bennetto, 2000).

Theories of dependence

According to Lowe (1995):

> '*It is now generally agreed that addictive behaviours are multiply determined phenomena, and should be considered as biopsychosocial entities*'.

Similarly, Hammersley (1999) maintains that dependence is a complex behaviour that takes several years to develop. So, it's unlikely that one theory or factor could account for all of it. Most researchers believe that social, personal, family and lifestyle factors are important, as well as the action of the drug itself. However, it's not yet understood fully how these work and interact. According to Hammersley (1999), theories of dependence are concerned with the extent to which dependence is:

- supposedly caused by *biological*, as opposed to *social*, factors;
- the result of *abnormal/pathological* processes, as opposed to the *extreme end* of *normal* processes.

In the rest of this section, we'll consider one major theory (*addiction as a disease*) of one particular case of substance dependence (*alcohol dependence*).

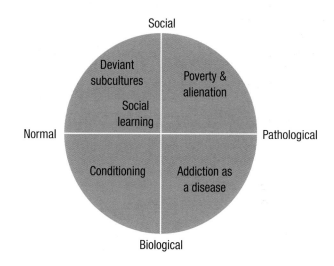

Figure 8.3 *Five main theories of addiction (from Hammersley, 1999)*

Theories of alcohol dependence

The disease model

Rush, widely regarded as the father of American psychiatry, is commonly credited with being the first major figure to conceptualise alcoholism as a 'disease', in the early 1800s. At about the same time, the British doctor, Trotter, likened alcoholism to a mental disorder. Both men saw it as a product of a distinct biological defect or dysfunction, much like cancer, diabetes, or TB (Lilienfeld, 1995).

In 1935, a doctor and former alcoholic, Smith, and Wilson (a stockbroker) founded Alcoholics Anonymous (AA) in the USA. AA assumes that certain individuals possess a physiological susceptibility to alcohol analogous to an allergy: a single drink is sufficient to trigger an unquenchable desire for more, resulting in an inevitable loss of control.

Perhaps the most influential champion of the disease model was Jellinek, a physiologist. Based on questionnaire data with AA members, Jellinek (1946, 1952) proposed that alcoholism was a biological illness with a highly characteristic and predictable course. It comprises four major stages:

- *pre-alcoholic phase*: alcohol provides a means of reducing tension and increasing self-confidence;
- *prodromal phase*: the alcoholic begins to drink secretly and heavily, and to experience *blackouts*;
- *crucial phase*: the alcoholic begins to lose control, engages in 'benders', and experiences severe withdrawal symptoms;
- *chronic phase*: the alcoholic drinks almost constantly and neglects almost all social and occupational responsibilities.

Jellinek (1960) also distinguished five 'species' of alcoholics:

- *alpha*: they drink to minimise tension;
- *beta*: they experience physical damage from drinking, such as cirrhosis of the liver, but aren't alcohol-dependent;
- *delta*: they're unable to abstain;
- *epsilon*: they lose control of their drinking and go on periodic benders;
- *gamma*: they lose control of their drinking, experience withdrawal symptoms, and are physically dependent.

Evaluating the disease model

According to Lilienfeld (1995), the course of alcoholism appears to be far more variable than this, and many drinkers don't fit into any of Jellinek's 'species'. Nevertheless, Jellinek's research was instrumental in persuading many scientists that alcoholism is best regarded as a physiological illness with a distinctive natural history.

This was the single most influential theory for much of the twentieth century. It's still the dominant view underlying psychiatric and other medically oriented treatment programmes, but is much less influential among psychologically based programmes since the 1980s.

Peele (1989) lists six major assumptions made by the disease model:

- Alcoholics drink too much, not because they intend to, but because they can't control their drinking.
- Alcoholics inherit their alcoholism, and so are born as alcoholics.
- Alcoholism as a disease can strike any individual, from any sociocultural background (it's an 'equal-opportunity destroyer').
- Alcoholism always gets worse without treatment; alcoholics can never cut back or quit on their own.
- Treatment based on the AA principles (see Box 8.7) is the *only* effective treatment.
- Those who reject the AA principles, or observers who reject any of the above, are in denial.

Peele argues that there's no evidence to support any of these assumptions. Regarding assumption 2, Lilienfeld (1995) observes that it implies that all individuals drink heavily for the same – or at least very similar – reasons. That is:

'Alcoholism is often viewed ... as a homogeneous entity resulting from a single set of causal influences ...'.

However, Cloninger (1987) proposed that *group 1* alcoholics are at risk for 'type 1' alcoholism:

- they drink primarily to reduce tension, are predominantly female, are prone to anxiety and depression, and tend to have relatively late onset of problem drinking.

By contrast, *group 2* alcoholics are at risk for 'type 2' alcoholism:

- they drink primarily to relieve boredom, to give free rein to their tendency towards risk-taking and sensation-seeking, are predominantly male, prone to antisocial and criminal behaviour, and tend to have relatively early onset of drinking behaviour (see Chapter 46).

Although the evidence for Cloninger's model is tentative and indirect, it challenges the disease model in a quite fundamental way. If he's correct, alcoholism may represent the culmination of two very different (and, in fact, essentially opposite), pathways (Lilienfeld, 1995).

Alcohol dependence syndrome (ADS: Edwards, 1986) is a later version of the disease model. It grew out of dissatisfaction with 'alcoholism' and with the traditional conception of alcoholism as disease. 'Syndrome' adds flexibility, suggesting a group of concurrent behaviours that accompany alcohol dependence. They needn't always be observed in an individual, nor observable to the same degree in everyone. For example, instead of loss of control or inability to abstain, ADS describes 'impaired control'. This implies that people drink heavily because, at certain times and for a variety of psychological and physiological reasons, they choose not to exercise control (Lowe, 1995). Lowe maintains that:

'Simple disease models have now been largely replaced by a more complex set of working hypotheses based, not on irreversible physiological processes, but on learning and conditioning, motivation and self-regulation, expectations and attributions'.

Treating alcohol dependence

The AA approach

According to Powell (2000), the more general concept of addiction as a 'disease of the will' has become popular. It's been broadly applied to other forms of addiction, and is adopted by the AA's 'sister' organisations, Narcotics Anonymous (NA) and Gamblers Anonymous (GA), Workaholics Anonymous (WA), Sex Addicts Anonymous (SAA), and even Survivors of Incest Anonymous.

Strictly, what AA offers isn't 'treatment' at all. Nor does it advocate any particular approach to treatment. Instead, it adopts a spiritual framework, requiring alcoholics to surrender their will to a 'higher power' (or God), confess their wrongs, and try to rectify them. This requires some spiritual feeling, an acceptance of abstinence as a goal, and usually works better for those who are heavily dependent (Hammersley, 1999). The AA philosophy is embodied in their famous twelve-step approach.

Absinthe, by Degas

Box 8.7 The Twelve Steps of Alcoholics Anonymous

1 We admitted that we were powerless over alcohol – that our lives had become unmanageable;

2 came to believe that a Power greater than ourselves could restore us to sanity;

3 made a decision to turn our will and our lives over to the care of God as we understood Him;

4 made a searching and fearless moral inventory of ourselves;

5 admitted to God, to ourselves, and to another human being, the exact nature of our wrongs;

6 were entirely ready to have God remove all these defects of character;

7 humbly asked Him to remove our shortcomings;

8 made a list of all persons we had harmed, and became willing to make amends to them all;

9 made direct amends to such people whenever possible, except when to do so would injure them or others;

10 continued to take personal inventory and when we were wrong promptly admitted it;

11 sought through prayer and meditation to improve our conscious contact with God as we understood Him, praying only for knowledge of His will for us and the power to carry that out;

12 having had a spiritual awakening as the result of these steps, we tried to carry the message to alcoholics, and to practise these principles in all our affairs.

At meetings, new members are introduced to the Twelve Steps and the Big Book (of guidance and member stories). They are allocated a sponsor for one-to-one support, listen to other members' stories, and tell their own. In addition to the weekly group meetings, there are professional residential programmes that use the twelve-step approach (the 'Minnesota Model'). This involves progression through a very structured programme, and movement through levels of seniority in a rigid hierarchy. Deviation from the rules is systematically and severely punished by, for example, 'demotion', or even expulsion. Half-way houses are also available to help the person's transition to an alcohol-free life in the community.

Evaluating the AA approach

- The twelve steps seem to work best for those who attend meetings regularly and get actively involved in the organisation. Indeed, this is part of the AA ethos (Hammersley, 1999). Extreme 'twelve-steppers' (recovered AA members) believe that 'it's abstinence or nothing', but the basic philosophy is *neutral* about the issue of whether abstinence is for everyone. Many have benefited from AA, and there are affiliated support groups for spouses (AL-ANON) and for teenage children (AL-TEEN). However, it's certainly not the only treatment available (Hammersley, 1999).

- In recent years, several ex-members and dependence treatment professionals have accused AA of having cult-like qualities, and using brainwashing and bullying methods to which weak and vulnerable people are particularly susceptible. The anti-AA lobby is especially strong in the US, and there's also a support group on the Internet called Recovery From Twelve Steps.

- In the UK, where there are 3350 AA groups, research by Hore (in Kenny, 1998) has found that the twelve-step approach has a 70 per cent success rate. One criticism of the approach is that members are encouraged to stay in AA *for life*: once an alcoholic, always an alcoholic. In AA, you can never move on. According to James (in Kenny, 1998):

  'After a year with AA, you're like a Moonie and you're probably in a relationship with another AA member ... By the end of your second year, you are definitely cured of your physical addiction, but not the underlying causes – and AA does nothing about this. It merely replaces one dependency with another ...'.

  James describes the AA approach as authoritarian and fascistic. This is very effective when it's getting you to stop taking the drug of your choice. That's clearly the most urgent need initially – you must stop killing yourself. But at some stage, perhaps after being clean for two years, you should move on to therapy. The paternalistic structure is designed to make this break very difficult.

- The issue of complete abstinence is also highly contentious. For some people, this may be appropriate, while others may be able to return to drinking safely and in moderation (Kenny, 1998).

CHAPTER SUMMARY

- Drugs are **psychoactive** substances. They may be used **therapeutically** or for **pleasure**, the latter being subdivided into **recreational** and **drugs of abuse**.

- Cigarette smoking and alcohol abuse are so widespread that they may be considered 'ordinary addictions'.

- The concept of **addiction** has been criticised for being oversimplified and for reflecting the **disease model**. The more modern view is to see drug problems as involving **substance abuse** and **dependence**. This view is adopted by DSM-IV.

- Some researchers argue that the concept of addiction should be **broadened**, so as to cover forms of addictive behaviour which don't involve chemical substances at all.

- **Dependence** can be either **psychological** or **physiological**, the latter indicated either by **tolerance** or **withdrawal**. Both types of dependence are part of the **dependence syndrome**.
- Physiologically addictive drugs, such as alcohol and heroin, typically also cause **habituation**. Most widely used recreational drugs, including cannabis, cocaine and ecstasy, produce habituation without causing physiological dependence.
- **Alcohol** is a **depressant**, although its initial effect is apparently to stimulate the brain. With increasing amounts, the brain generally slows down, and the breathing centres may eventually shut down.
- Alcohol can cause several life-threatening physical diseases, and impairs **memory** function, an extreme form being found in **Korsakoff's syndrome**.
- **Stimulants** include **amphetamines** and **MDMA** (or **ecstasy**).
- **Morphine** and **heroin** are **opiates**. It's thought that regular use of opiates causes the brain to stop producing its own **endorphins**.
- **Methadone** is an orally taken synthetic opiate created to treat physiological dependence on heroin and other opiates. Users may well become psychologically dependent.
- **LSD** and **PCP** are **hallucinogens**, which may produce psychological dependence. Neither produces physiological dependence.
- **Cannabis** doesn't fit neatly into the other categories. There's some evidence of **reverse tolerance**, and psychological dependence is likely for some people. Cannabis is at the centre of a current debate regarding changes to the UK drug laws.
- **Theories of dependence** differ according to whether they see the causes as **biological** or **social**, and whether dependence is seen as **pathological** or the **extreme end** of **normal processes**.
- The **disease model** of alcohol dependence assumes that everyone is dependent for the same reasons. The definition of **alcohol dependence syndrome** (ADS) draws on a more flexible version of the disease model.
- The twelve-steps philosophy of **Alcoholics Anonymous** (AA) has also been applied to other forms of 'addiction'. While it boasts a high success rate, its methods have been accused of being authoritarian and cult-like. Its core belief that alcoholics cannot be cured discourages people from becoming independent.

Self-assessment questions

1 Discuss the concept of drug addiction.
2 Describe and evaluate the disease model of alcohol dependence.

Web addresses

www.acsu.buffalo.edu/~gessner/abuse.html

www.mftsource.com/Treatment.substance.htm

alt.recovery.from-12-steps

www.independent.co.uk/links/

http://silk.nih.gov/silk/niaaa1/

publication/alalerts.htm

www.britishlivertrust.org.uk/research

Further reading

Griffiths. M. (1999) Internet addiction: Fact or fiction? *The Psychologist*, 12(5), 246–250. An up-to-date review of this serious area of research, which gets behind the 'media hype'.

Baker, A. (Ed.) (2000) *Serious Shopping: Essays in Psychotherapy and Consumerism*. London: Free Association Books. Chapter 2 (by Baker) discusses many of the issues regarding definitions and the nature of 'addiction' covered in this chapter. Chapter 6 (by Corbett) discusses shopping addiction in relation to women's body image, and so is relevant to eating disorders (Chapter 44 – of this book).

Powell, J. (2000) 'Drug and alcohol dependence'. In L. Champion & M. Power (Eds) *Adult Psychological Problems: An Introduction* (2nd edition). Hove: Psychology Press. Covers models of dependence not dealt within this chapter.

Chapter 9

Motivation

Introduction and overview

Trying to define motivation is a little like trying to define psychology itself. Taking as a starting point the layperson's view of psychology as the study of 'what makes people tick', motivation is concerned with why people act and think the way they do. 'Why' questions – and related 'how' questions – usually imply *causes* and *underlying mechanisms* or *processes*.

Each of the major theoretical approaches we discussed in Chapter 2 (namely the *behaviourist, psychodynamic, humanistic, cognitive, evolutionary,* and *social constructionist* approaches) tries to identify the key processes and mechanisms. This is also true of the neurobiological/biogenic approach (see Chapter 4).

At the heart of each approach lies an image of human beings which, in essence, is a theory of the causes of human behaviour.

Motivated behaviour is *goal-directed*, purposeful behaviour. It's difficult to think of any behaviour, human or non-human, which isn't motivated in this sense. However, just how the underlying motives are conceptualised and investigated depends very much on the persuasion of the psychologist. For example:

■ a *psychodynamic* psychologist tries to discover internal, *unconscious* drives and motives (see Chapter 42 for a discussion of Freud's psychoanalytic theory);

■ a *behaviourist* psychologist looks for environmental *schedules of reinforcement*, which can explain the behaviour of rats and pigeons as effectively as that of human beings (see Chapter 11). As a *radical behaviourist*, Skinner rejects the claim that mental or other internal events or processes – conscious or unconscious – can influence behaviour in any way. For him, 'motivation' and other mentalistic terms are 'explanatory fictions';

■ a *humanistic* psychologist, such as Maslow, will try to understand a person's behaviour in terms of a hierarchy of motives, with *self-actualisation* at the top of the hierarchy;

■ for a *biopsychologist*, what's of central importance are bodily events and processes taking place in the CNS, the ANS, the endocrine system, or *interactions* between these different systems (see Chapter 4). These events and processes are related to the person's or animal's biological survival.

Although we shall consider a range of different motives, this chapter has a very 'biological' flavour. Maslow's *hierarchy of needs* is useful as a general framework for examining other approaches. *Homeostatic drive theories* try to explain hunger and thirst. But even in the case of such basic biological motives as these, *cognitive* and other individual factors, as well as *social*, *cultural*, and other environmental factors, play a crucial role.

We shall also consider *non-homeostatic* needs and drives, including electrical self-stimulation of the brain (ES-SB), competence and cognitive motives, and some important *social* motives.

What is motivation?

According to Rubin & McNeil (1983), motives are a special kind of cause which '... energise, direct and sustain a person's behaviour (including hunger, thirst, sex and curiosity)'. Similarly:

'Motivation refers, in a general sense, to processes involved in the initiation, direction, and energisation of individual behaviour ...'. (Geen, 1995)

The word 'motive' comes from the Latin for 'move' (*movere*), and this is captured in Miller's (1962) definition:

'The study of motivation is the study of all those pushes and prods – biological, social and psychological – that defeat our laziness and move us, either eagerly or reluctantly, to action'.

As we noted in the *Introduction and overview*, different schools of thought within psychology look for the causes of behaviour in very different 'places'. These differences indicate that motives may vary with regard to a number of features or dimensions, including:

1 internal or external;
2 innate or learned;
3 mechanistic or cognitive;
4 conscious or unconscious.

Several attempts have been made to classify different kinds of motives. For example, Rubin & McNeil (1983) classify motives into two major categories:

■ survival or physiological motives;
■ competence or cognitive motives.

Social motives represent a third category. Clearly, humans share survival motives with all other animals, as well as certain competence motives (see below). But other motives are peculiarly and uniquely human, notably *self-actualisation*, which lies at the peak of a 'hierarchy of needs' in Maslow's (1954) humanistic theory.

Maslow's hierarchy of needs

Although Maslow's theory is commonly discussed in relation to personality (see Chapter 42), its focus on needs makes it equally relevant to motivation. (The book in which he first proposed his hierarchy was called *Motivation and Personality*.) According to Maslow, we're subject to two quite different sets of motivational states or forces:

1 those that ensure survival by satisfying basic physical and psychological needs (physiological, safety, love and belongingness, and esteem); and
2 those that promote the person's self-actualisation, that is, realising one's full potential, 'becoming everything that one is capable of becoming' (Maslow, 1970), especially in the intellectual and creative domains.

As Maslow states:

'We share the need for food with all living things, the need for love with (perhaps) the higher apes, [and] the need for Self-Actualisation with [no other species]'.

While behaviours that relate to survival or deficiency needs (*deficiency* or *D-motives*) are engaged in because they satisfy those needs (a *means to an end*), those that relate to self-actualisation are engaged in for their own sake, because they're intrinsically satisfying (*growth, being or B-motives*). The latter include the fulfilment of ambitions, the acquisition of admired skills, the steady increase of understanding about people, the universe or oneself, the development of creativeness in whatever field or, most important, the ambition to be simply a good human being. Unlike D-motives, it's inaccurate to speak in such instances of tension reduction, which implies the overcoming of an annoying state, for these states aren't annoying (Maslow, 1968). Another term for tension reduction is *drive reduction*, which is discussed later in the chapter. Maslow's argument is that to reduce the full range of human motives to drives that must be satisfied or removed, is simply mistaken.

The hierarchical nature of Maslow's theory is intended to highlight the following points:

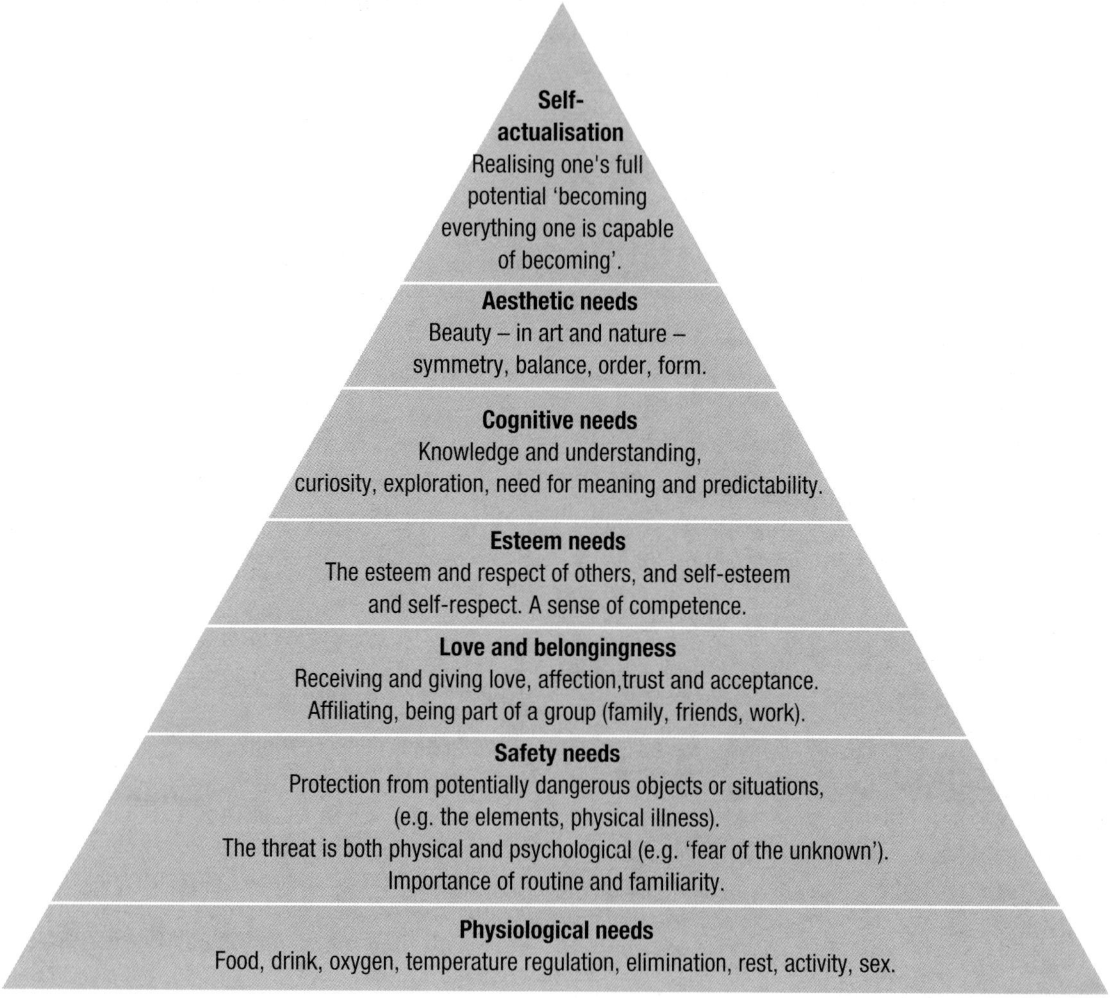

Self-actualisation
Realising one's full potential 'becoming everything one is capable of becoming'.

Aesthetic needs
Beauty – in art and nature – symmetry, balance, order, form.

Cognitive needs
Knowledge and understanding, curiosity, exploration, need for meaning and predictability.

Esteem needs
The esteem and respect of others, and self-esteem and self-respect. A sense of competence.

Love and belongingness
Receiving and giving love, affection, trust and acceptance. Affiliating, being part of a group (family, friends, work).

Safety needs
Protection from potentially dangerous objects or situations, (e.g. the elements, physical illness). The threat is both physical and psychological (e.g. 'fear of the unknown'). Importance of routine and familiarity.

Physiological needs
Food, drink, oxygen, temperature regulation, elimination, rest, activity, sex.

Figure 9.1 *Maslow's heirarchy of needs (based on Maslow, 1954)*

■ Needs lower down in the hierarchy must be satisfied before we can attend to needs higher up. For example, if you're reading this while your stomach is trying to tell you it's lunchtime, you probably won't absorb much about Maslow. Similarly, if you're tired or in pain. Yet you can probably think of exceptions, such as the starving artist who finds inspiration despite hunger, or the mountain climber who risks his/her life for the sake of adventure (what Maslow would call a 'peak' experience – if you'll forgive the pun).

■ Higher level needs are a later evolutionary development: in the development of the human species (*phylogenesis*), self-actualisation is a fairly recent need. This applies equally to the development of individuals (*ontogenesis*): babies are much more concerned with their bellies than with their brains. But it's always a case of one need *predominating* at any one time, not excluding all other needs.

■ The higher up the hierarchy we go, the more the need becomes linked to life experience, and the less 'biological' it becomes. Individuals will achieve self-actualisation in different ways, through different activities and by different routes. This is related to experience, not biology:

'A musician must make music, an artist must paint, a poet must write, if he is to be ultimately at peace with himself. What a man can be, he must be'. (Maslow, 1968)

This captures nicely the *idiographic* nature of Maslow's theory, that is, the view that every individual is unique (see Chapter 42).

■ The higher up the hierarchy we go, the more difficult it becomes to achieve the need at that level. Many human goals are remote and long term, and can only be achieved in a series of steps. This pursuit of aims/goals that lie very much in the future is unique to human beings, although individuals differ in their ability to set and realise such goals.

Ask yourself ...

• Do you consider Maslow's hierarchy to be a useful way of thinking about human motivation? Do you think he's omitted any important motives?

• To what extent might the hierarchy reflect the culture and the historical time in which Maslow lived and wrote?

The early study of motivation

As with many other aspects of psychology, the study of motivation has its roots in philosophy (see Chapters 1 and 3). *Rationalists* saw human beings as free to choose between different courses of action. This makes the concept of motivation almost unnecessary: it's reason that determines behaviour. This idea of freedom and responsibility is a basic premise of both humanistic and cognitive approaches (see Chapter 49).

The seventeenth-century British philosopher Hobbes proposed the theory of *hedonism* (1651). This maintains that all behaviour is determined by the seeking of pleasure and the avoidance of pain. These are the 'real' motives (whatever we may believe), and this idea is central to Freud's psychoanalytic theory, captured in the concept of the *pleasure principle*. Similarly, the basic principles of *positive* and *negative reinforcement* can be seen as corresponding to the seeking of pleasure and avoidance of pain respectively, and these are central to Skinner's *operant conditioning*.

Box 9.1   Motives as instincts

The concept of instinct played a major role in early psychological approaches to motivation. Largely inspired by Darwin's (1859) theory of evolution (see Chapter 2), which argued that humans and animals differ only quantitatively, a number of psychologists identified human instincts that would explain human behaviour.

For example, McDougall (1908) originally proposed twelve, and by 1924 over 800 separate instincts had been identified. But to explain behaviour by labelling it is to explain nothing (e.g. 'We behave aggressively because of our aggressive instinct' is a circular statement). This, combined with the sheer proliferation of instincts, seriously undermined the whole approach. However, the concept of instinct – with certain important modifications – remains a central feature of the *ethological approach* to behaviour, in particular, non-human animal behaviour (see Chapter 2 and Gross *et al.*, 2000).

During the 1920s, the concept of instinct was largely replaced by the concept of *drive*. The term was first used by Woodworth (1918), who compared human behaviour with the operation of a machine: the mechanism of a machine is relatively passive and drive is the power applied to make it 'go'. The concept of drive has taken two major forms: *homeostatic drive theory* (Cannon, 1929), which is a physiological theory, and *drive reduction theory* (Hull, 1943), which is primarily a theory of learning.

Homeostatic drive theory

The term *homeostasis* is derived from the Greek *homos* (meaning 'same'), and *stasis*, (meaning 'stoppage'). It was coined by Cannon (1929) to refer to the process by which an organism maintains a fairly constant internal (bodily) environment, that is, how body temperature, blood sugar level, salt concentration in the blood, and so on are kept in a state of relative balance or equilibrium.

The principle underlying homeostasis is that when a state of imbalance arises (for example, through a substantial rise in body temperature), something must happen to correct the imbalance and restore equilibrium (here, sweating). In this case, the animal doesn't have to 'do' anything, because sweating is completely automatic and purely physiological. However, if the imbalance is caused by the body's need for food or drink (*tissue need*), the hungry or thirsty animal has to do something to procure food or water. This is where the concept of a homeostatic drive becomes important. Tissue need leads to internal imbalance, which leads to homeostatic drive, which leads to appropriate behaviour, which leads to restoration of internal balance, which leads to drive reduction.

The internal environment requires a regular supply of raw materials from the external world (Green, 1980). While oxygen intake, for example, is involuntary and continuous, eating and drinking are *voluntary* and *discontinuous* (or spaced). We talk about a hunger and thirst drive, but we don't talk about an 'oxygen drive'. Because of the voluntary nature of eating and drinking, hunger and thirst are the homeostatic drives that biopsychologists have been most interested in.

Hunger and eating

Does hunger cause eating?

If there is a commonsense theory of eating, it's that we eat because, and when, we're hungry. What could be simpler? If asked why we get hungry, most people would probably say that 'our bodies get hungry', that is, certain events take place in our bodies when we haven't eaten for a certain period of time, and these act as the 'signal' to eat. We experience that signal as hunger.

This fits very neatly with the outline of the hunger drive given above. If we place the experience of hunger in between 'internal imbalance' and 'homeostatic drive', we get a nice blend of the commonsense and drive reduction theories, with hunger towards the end of a chain of causation that results in eating.

But is hunger either a necessary or sufficient condition for eating to occur. Can eating occur in the absence of hunger, and is it possible that we might not eat despite being hungry? We've all been tempted by the look or the smell of food when not feeling hungry, and we're not usually still hungry by the time the dessert trolley comes along. In other words, we often eat simply because we enjoy it. This suggests that hunger isn't necessary for eating. Conversely, people who go on diets or hunger strike are avoiding eating (or eating less than they might otherwise do) despite being very hungry, suggesting that hunger isn't sufficient.

So, there seems to be no biological inevitability about the hunger–eating relationship. However, as Blundell & Hill (1995) point out, under many circumstances there's a close relationship between the pattern of food intake and the rhythmic fluctuation of hunger. For example, many experimental studies confirm the strong link between the intensity of experienced hunger sensations and the amount of food eaten. This fairly consistent finding has been interpreted as showing that there's a causal connection between hunger and the size of a following meal. But another interpretation is that certain physiological mechanisms are producing *both* the sensations of hunger *and* the eating behaviour.

Blundell and Hill propose an *appetite control system*, in which hunger, eating and physiological mechanisms are coupled together, but the coupling isn't perfect. There will be circumstances where uncoupling can occur, as in the hunger strike example, or in cases of eating disorders (such as obesity – see page 124 – and anorexia nervosa; see Chapter 44). So, what might some of these physiological mechanisms be? Assuming that, normally, these are 'coupled' (or correlated) with hunger, what happens when the 'body gets hungry'?

What prompts a meal?

As Carlson (1992) points out, the physiological signals that cause eating to begin aren't necessarily the ones that cause it to end. There's considerable delay between the act of eating (the *correctional mechanism*), and a change in the state of the body. So, while we may start eating because the level of nutrients has fallen below a certain point, we certainly don't stop because that level has been restored to normal. In fact, we usually stop eating long before this, since digestion takes several hours to complete. Therefore, the signals for hunger and for *satiety* (the state of no longer being hungry) are sure to be different. Probably the earliest formal theory of hunger was proposed by Cannon.

KEY STUDY 9.1

'Swallow a balloon if you're hungry' (Cannon & Washburn, 1912)

Cannon originally believed that the hunger drive is caused by stomach contractions ('hunger pangs') and that food reduces the drive by stopping the contractions.

Washburn swallowed an empty balloon tied to the end of a thin tube. Then Cannon pumped some air into the balloon and connected the end of the tube to a water-filled glass U-tube, so that Washburn's stomach contractions would cause an increase in the level of water at the other end of the U-tube (see Figure 9.2). He reported a 'pang' of hunger each time a large stomach contraction was recorded.

These results were soon confirmed by a case study (cited in Carlson, 1992) of a patient with a tube implanted through his stomach wall, just above the navel. He had accidentally swallowed some acid which caused the walls of his oesophagus (the muscular tube that carries food from the throat to the stomach) to fuse shut. The tube was a means of feeding himself and provided a window through which his stomach activities could be observed. When there was food in his stomach, small, rhythmic contractions (subsequently named peristaltic contractions/peristalsis) mixed the food and moved it along the digestive tract; when it was empty, the contractions were large and associated with the patient's reports of hunger.

However, patients who've had their stomachs removed (because of disease) and the oesophagus 'hooked up' directly to the duodenum or small intestine (the upper portion of the intestine through which most of the glucose and amino acids are absorbed into the bloodstream; see below) continue to report feeling hungry and satiated. Even though their stomachs are bypassed, they maintain normal body weights by eating more frequent, smaller meals (Pinel, 1993). Similarly, cutting the neural connections between the *gastrointestinal tract* (GIT) (comprising mainly the stomach and intestines) and the brain (i.e. cutting the vagus nerve) has little effect on food intake in experimental animals or human patients.

These findings suggest that Cannon exaggerated the importance of stomach contractions in causing hunger, but this doesn't mean that the stomach and the gastrointestinal tract play no part in hunger and satiety. If the vagus nerve is cut, signals arising from the gut can still be communicated to the brain via the circulatory system. Also, the presence of food in the stomach (*stomach loading*) is important in the regulation of feeding: if the exit from the stomach to the duodenum is blocked off, rats still eat normal-sized meals. It seems that information about the stretching of the stomach wall caused by the presence of food is passed to the brain (via the vagus nerve), allowing the brain's feeding centres to control meal size.

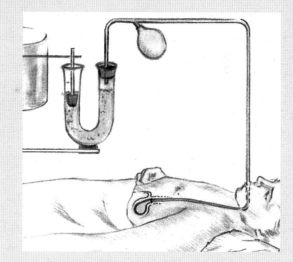

Figure 9.2 *The system developed by Cannon and Washburn in 1912 for measuring stomach contractions (from J. Pinel, 1993, Biopsychology, Boston, Allyn and Bacon)*

The information that's passed from the gut or gastrointestinal tract to the brain via the circulatory system, concerns the components of the food that's been absorbed. Some of the nutrients whose depletion acts as a signal to start eating are fats (lipids), carbohydrates (including glucose), vitamins/mineral salts, and proteins/amino acids. Fats and carbohydrates are burnt up in cellular reactions and provide the energy to fuel metabolic processes. *Metabolism* refers to all the chemical processes occurring in the body's cells and which are essential for the body's normal functioning. *Metabolic rate* refers to the amount of energy the body uses.

When we engage in vigorous physical activity, the muscles are fuelled by fats and carbohydrates, which are stored as energy reserves. The cells that store our fat reserves are called *adipocytes*, which clump together as *adipose tissue* (or simply 'fat'). Carbohydrates are stored as *glycogen*. Two major accounts of why we start eating are the *glucostatic* and *lipostatic theories*.

Glucostatic theory

According to glucostatic theory, the primary stimulus for hunger is a decrease in the level of blood glucose below a certain set-point. Glucose is the body's (especially the brain's) primary fuel. The glucostat was assumed to be a neuron (probably in the hypothalamus), which detects the level of blood glucose in much the same way as a thermostat measures temperature.

According to Pinel (1993), Mayer's (1955) version of the glucostatic theory was particularly influential, because it dealt with a serious problem associated with earlier versions. He proposed that it was glucose utilisation (the *rate* at which glucose is used), rather than absolute blood glucose level, that was regulated by feeding. While these are usually highly correlated, Mayer's version could account for those few occasions where high levels are associated with hyperphagia (overeating). For example, people with *diabetes mellitus* overeat, despite high blood glucose levels. This is because their pancreas fails to produce sufficient quantities of insulin (needed for glucose to enter most body cells and to be utilised by them).

Mayer's hypothesis was supported by experiments with mice (Mayer & Marshall, 1956), which appeared to identify the location of the glucoreceptors in the *ventromedial hypothalamus* (VMH). They concluded that the VMH is a satiety centre. However, although a fall in blood glucose may be the most important physiological signal for hunger, it's not the only one. If an animal eats a meal that's low in carbohydrate but high in fats or proteins, it still manages to eat a relatively constant amount of calories, even though its blood glucose is reduced slightly. If eating were controlled exclusively by blood glucose, we'd expect the animal to overeat and get fat (Carlson, 1992).

Lipostatic theory

According to Green (1994), lipostatic theory focuses on the end product of glucose metabolism, namely the storage of fats (lipids) in adipocytes. Body fat is normally maintained at a relatively constant level. Similarly, fluctuations in the amount of stored fats largely determine variations in body weight. According to Nisbett's (1972) version of the lipostatic theory, we all have a body weight set-point around which our weight fluctuates within quite narrow limits; this is determined by the level of fats in the adipocytes.

The most frequently cited evidence in support of the lipostatic theory is the failure of short-term dieting programmes to produce long-term weight loss: as soon as dieting stops, the person regains the weight that's been lost. Other evidence comes from animal experiments in which lesions are made in the hypothalamus. When the *lateral hypothalamus* (LH) is damaged, rats will stop eating, even when food is readily available, to the point of death from starvation. This failure to feed is called *aphagia*. It was originally taken to indicate that the LH normally functions to stimulate eating (and so represents another partial answer to the question 'why do we start eating?').

KEY STUDY 9.2

Lowering body weight before the lesion (Keesey & Powley, 1975)

Keesey and Powley deprived rats of food, so that their body weight was substantially lowered. When lesions were then made in their LHs, they started eating *more* food (not less). In a normal rat, the lesion lowers the body weight set-point, and the resulting failure to eat occurs because the animal is trying to adjust to this lower target weight. However, if the weight is reduced *before* the lesion is made to below the lesion-produced target, the rat now *increases* feeding (following the lesion) in order to reach the new (higher) set-point.

This means that damage to the LH affects feeding only indirectly (as Nisbett suggests), by altering the body weight set-point. Feeding is aimed at attaining this new target.

Set-point or settling point?

According to Pinel (1993), the two theories are complementary, rather than mutually exclusive. Glucostatic theory was meant to account for the initiation and termination of eating (relatively short-term processes), while lipostatic theory was proposed to explain long-term feeding habits and the regulation of body weight. They both assume that there are mechanisms within the CNS that are sensitive to deviations from one or more hypothetical set-points. This assumption is itself based on another, namely that homeostasis implies the existence of set-point mechanisms.

Many current biopsychological theories of eating reject these assumptions in favour of the view that body weight tends to drift around a natural *settling point*, that is, the level at which the various factors that influence it achieve balance or equilibrium. Pinel (1993) believes that earlier theorists were seduced by the analogy with the thermostat, which is a compelling set-point model. His analogy for a settling point theory is the leaky barrel model: the level of fat in the body, like the water level in a leaky barrel, is regulated around a natural settling point rather than a predetermined set-point.

Ask yourself ...

- What are your two or three favourite foods (or meals)?
- What exactly is it about them that you like so much?
- How much, if at all, do you consider social factors play a part in your eating behaviour?

Other factors that influence eating

A settling point theory is more compatible with research findings that point to factors other than internal energy deficits as causes of eating. As we noted earlier, hunger is neither a necessary nor a sufficient condition for eating to take place. For example, even if it were possible to explain hunger purely in terms of lowered levels of glucose and fat, we'd still need to identify other influences on eating. According to Pinel (1993):

'The modern era of feeding research has been characterised by an increasing awareness of the major role played by learning in determining when we eat, what we eat, how much we eat, and even how the food that we eat is digested and metabolised. The concept of the feeding system has changed from that of an immutable system that maintains glucose and fat levels at predetermined set-points, to that of a flexible system that operates within certain general guidelines but is "fine-tuned" by experience ...'.

Eating for pleasure

Both humans and other animals are *drawn* to eat (rather than driven to eat) by food's *incentive properties*, that is, its anticipated pleasure-producing effects or *palatability*. According to incentive theories, both internal and external factors influence eating in the same way, namely, by changing the incentive value of available foods. Signals from the taste receptors seem to produce an immediate decline in the incentive value of similar tasting food, and signals associated with increased energy supply from a meal produce a general decrease in the incentive properties of all foods.

Support for this view comes from the discovery of LH neurons that respond to the incentive properties of food, rather than food itself (Rolls & Rolls, 1982). When monkeys were repeatedly allowed to eat one palatable food, the response of LH neurons to it declined (a form of habituation?), although not to other palatable foods. Neurons that responded to the sight of food would begin to respond to a neutral stimulus that reliably predicted the presentation of food. These findings explain very neatly the common experience of our 'mouths watering' (salivating) at the mere mention of our favourite food, or even a picture of it.

KEY STUDY 9.3

Learning to salivate (Pavlov, 1927)

The smell of food, and the dinner bell, are *food-predicting cues* (or *classically conditioned stimuli*). They trigger digestive and metabolic events, such as salivation, insulin secretion and gastric secretions (*classically conditioned responses*). These digestive/metabolic events are also called cephalic phase responses. Pavlov (1927) was the first to demonstrate that a *cephalic phase response* can be conditioned: the sight or smell of milk produced abundant salivation in puppies raised on a milk diet, but not in those raised on a solid diet. Feeling hungry at those times of the day when we usually eat (whether or not we're experiencing an energy deficit) is another example of a classically conditioned response (see Chapter 11).

Knowing what to eat

If learning is involved in the way humans and other animals respond to foods that are already palatable, could learning be involved in what is found palatable in the first place?

■ We have innate preferences for tastes that are associated in nature with vital nutrients. For example, sweetness detectors on the tongue probably exist because they helped our ancestors to identify food that's safe to eat. Even when we're not particularly hungry, we tend to find a sweet taste pleasant, and eating something sweet tends to increase our appetite (Carlson, 1992).

■ Both humans and other animals also have the ability to learn the relationship between taste and the post-ingestion consequences of eating certain food. In *taste aversion studies*, rats learn to avoid novel tastes that are followed by illness (Garcia *et al.*, 1966: see Chapter 11). Rats are also able to learn to prefer tastes that are followed by the infusion of nutrients and flavours that they smell on the breath of other rats.

■ Rats and human beings have in common a metabolism that requires them to eat a variety of different foods: no single food provides all essential nutrients. We generally find a meal that consists of moderate amounts of several different foods more interesting than a huge plate of only one food, however palatable that food might be. If we have access to only one particular food, we soon become tired of it (*sensory-specific satiety*). This encourages the consumption of a varied diet.

■ It seems that cultural evolution helps the selection of balanced diets. For example, Mexicans increased the calcium in their diet by mixing small amounts of mineral lime into their tortillas. But in the industrialised societies of Europe and North America, we seem to prefer diets which are fundamentally detrimental to our health (see Chapter 12). Manufacturers tend to sell foods that are highly palatable and energy dense, but which often have little nutritional value. This encourages us to overeat and, as a result, to increase fat deposits and body weight. Blundell & Hill (1995) maintain that in *evolutionary terms*, overeating makes good sense:

> *'For human beings it can be supposed that during most of the tens of thousands of years of human evolution the biggest problem facing human-kind was the scarcity of food ... the existence of an abundance of food, highly palatable and easily available, is a very recent development in evolutionary terms. Accordingly, it's unlikely that evolutionary pressure has ever led to the development of mechanisms to prevent overconsumption ...'.*

What stops us eating?

According to Blundell & Hill (1995), *satiety* (feeling 'full up' or satisfied) is, by definition, not instantaneous but something that occurs over a considerable period of time. It's useful, therefore, to distinguish different phases of satiety associated with different mechanisms which, together, comprise the *satiety cascade*. Most important for understanding the suppression and subsequent control of hunger are:

■ *post-ingestive effects* which include gastric distension, the rate of gastric emptying, the release of hormones (such as CCK: see Box 9.2, page 124), and the stimulation of certain receptors along the GIT;

■ *post-absorptive effects* which are mechanisms arising from the action of glucose, fats, amino acids (and other metabolites) after absorption across the intestine into the bloodstream.

There's currently considerable research interest in whether protein, fat and carbohydrate differ in their satiating efficiency and their capacity to reduce hunger. One clear finding is that carbohydrates are efficient appetite suppressants. Also, the fat content of food influences its texture and palatability, but it has a disproportionately weak effect on satiety (Blundell & Hill, 1995).

Although the stomach may not be very important in causing hunger (see Key Study 9.1), it does seem to be important in satiety. For example, we noted that stomach loading and stretching of the stomach wall play a part in reducing hunger. The gastric branch of the vagus nerve carries emergency signals from the stretch receptors in the stomach wall, preventing us from overeating and damaging the stomach.

Box 9.2 Cholecystokinin (CCK)

After food reaches the stomach, the protein is broken down into its constituent amino acids. As digestion proceeds, food gradually passes into the *duodenum* (small intestine). This controls the rate of stomach emptying by secreting a peptide hormone (short chains of amino acids) called cholecystokinin (CCK). CCK is secreted in response to the presence of fats, detected by receptors in the walls of the duodenum. Many studies have found that injecting CCK into hungry rats causes them to eat smaller meals. Wolkowitz *et al.* (1990) gave people injections of a drug that blocks CCK receptors in the peripheral nervous system (but not in the brain): they reported feeling more hungry and less full after a meal than controls given a placebo.

(Based on Carlson, 1992)

The brain's control of eating

It's been known since the early 1800s that tumours of the hypothalamus can cause *hyperphagia* (excessive overeating) and obesity in humans (Pinel, 1993). But not until the advent of *stereotaxic surgery* in the late 1930s (see Chapter 4) were experimenters able to assess the effects of damage to particular areas of the hypothalamus on the eating behaviour of experimental animals.

KEY STUDY 9.4

Hyperphagia in rats (Hetherington & Ranson, 1942)

Figure 9.3 *A hyperphagic rat*

Hetherington and Ranson found that large, bilateral lesions in the lower, central portion of the hypothalamus (the *ventromedial nucleus/VMN*) cause *hyperphagia*: the rat will carry on eating until it becomes grotesquely fat, doubling or even trebling its normal body weight. Although several structures were damaged by such lesions, it was generally assumed that the *ventromedial hypothalamus* (VMH) was the crucial structure. The resulting hyperphagia was taken to indicate that the normal function of the VMH is to inhibit feeding when the animal is 'full'. Hence, the VMH became known as the *satiety centre*. It has been found in rats, cats, dogs, chickens and monkeys (Teitelbaum, 1967).

The VMH syndrome

Contrary to what you might expect, VMH-lesioned rats aren't 'hell-bent' on eating – they won't eat anything and everything. The taste of food seems to be especially important in hyperphagic rats. Most animals will eat even bad-tasting food ('you'll eat anything if you're hungry enough'). But hyperphagic rats are very fussy, and will refuse their regular food if quinine is added – even if this means that they become underweight (Teitelbaum, 1955).

What about people?

One possible explanation for the 'finicky' eating of VMH-lesioned rats is that they become less sensitive to internal cues of satiation (such as blood glucose level, and body fat content) and more responsive to external cues (such as taste). Schachter (1971) claims that this may also apply to overweight people. Schachter *et al.* (1968) found that normal-weight people responded to the internal cue of stomach distention ('feeling bloated') by refusing any more food. But obese people tended to go on eating. The latter seemed to be responding to the availability of food. However, they're less willing to make an effort to find food compared with normal-weight people, who'll search for food – but only if they're genuinely hungry (Schachter, 1971).

- Overweight people also tend to report that they feel hungry at prescribed eating times, even if they've eaten a short while before. Normal-weight people tend to eat only when they feel hungry, and this is relatively independent of clock time. However, this increased sensitivity to external cues isn't necessarily what causes some people to become obese – it could just as easily be an effect of obesity.
- Although people with hypothalamic tumours tend towards obesity, there's no evidence that the hypothalamus doesn't function properly in overweight people generally.

Differences in basal metabolic rate largely determine our body weight, and are probably hereditary. There's very little evidence to suggest that lack of impulse control, poor ability to delay gratification, or eating too quickly contribute to overweight (Carlson, 1992). However, the role of complex psychological variables has been studied much more extensively in relation to *anorexia nervosa* and *bulimia nervosa* (see Chapter 44).

The LH syndrome

If the VMH has traditionally been regarded as a 'brake' on eating, the *lateral hypothalamus* (LH) has been seen as the 'accelerator'. Bilateral lesions to the LH cause *aphagia*, a refusal to eat, even to the point of death from starvation (Anand & Brobeck, 1951; Teitelbaum & Stellar, 1954). Even rats made hyperphagic by VMH lesions will become aphagic by the addition of LH lesions. These findings suggest very strongly that the LH is a feeding centre. However, the LH syndrome also includes *adipsia* (the complete cessation of drinking). Both aphagia and adipsia are, in turn, part of a more general lack of responsiveness to sensory input. The LH itself is a relatively large, complex and ill-defined area, with many nuclei and several major nerve tracts running through it. While electrical stimulation of the LH produces eating in rats, it also triggers drinking, gnawing, temperature changes and sexual activity. Conversely, eating can also be elicited by stimulation of other areas of the hypothalamus, the amygdala, hippocampus, thalamus and frontal cortex. For all these reasons, Pinel (1993) believes that to call the LH a 'hunger centre' is a misnomer.

Ask yourself ...

- As with food, what is it exactly that you like about your favourite drinks, and might social factors play a greater role than with eating in your drinking behaviour (see Chapter 8)?

Thirst and drinking

What starts us drinking?

It was thought until recently that drinking is motivated by a deficit in the body's water resources, that is, by deviation from set-points, as part of a homeostatic drive mechanism. However, most drinking (like most eating) occurs in the absence of deficits. This suggests that the motivation to drink comes from anticipating its pleasurable effects (*positive incentive properties*). We tend to prefer drinks that have a pleasant taste (such as fruit juice), or pleasant pharmacological effects (such as alcohol, coffee and tea).

Positive incentive theory

Water deprivation increases the positive incentive value of almost all salt-free drinks. After 24 hours without a drink, people report that even plain water has a pleasant taste (Rolls *et al.*, 1980). If you add a little saccharine to the water of non-deprived rats, their water intake rockets. Like people, rats with unlimited access to water or other palatable fluids drink far more than they actually need. As with food, sensory-specific satiety has a major effect on drinking. As fond as rats are of saccharine, if saccharine solution is constantly available (on tap), they come to prefer it less than when it's available only periodically.

Dry-mouth theory

A dry mouth and throat are obvious cues to thirst (the counterpart of the stomach contraction cues to hunger: see Key Study 9.1). Although a dry mouth is one consequence of water deficiency, it's not the primary factor in thirst. For example, producing a chronic dry mouth by removal of the salivary glands doesn't substantially increase water intake, unless rats are fed dry food or kept in a very hot environment. Conversely, blocking the sensation of a dry mouth fails to decrease water intake. The most convincing evidence against the dry-mouth theory comes from *sham-drinking*, an experimental procedure in which water flows down the oesophagus and then out through a fistula before it can be absorbed. Despite the lack of a dry mouth, animals sham-drink continuously (Pinel, 1993).

What makes us stop drinking?

According to set-point theories, drinking brings about a return to an internal water resource set-point. When this has been achieved, drinking stops. However, like hunger, thirst and drinking seem to stop long before enough time has elapsed for the body to have absorbed the water from the stomach, and for the water–salt balance in the blood to have been restored.

Stomach distension probably contributes to satiety. Cold water is more thirst-quenching, because it moves out of the stomach much more slowly, and so provides a clearer stomach-distension signal to the brain. The *mouth-metering mechanism* also plays a part. This gauges the amount of water being ingested, and compares the amount needed to restore the water balance.

If set-point theories were correct, we'd expect that delivering water directly to where it's needed, would eliminate thirst and deprivation-induced drinking. However, if water is injected directly into a rat's stomach or bloodstream, drinking is reduced by only 30 per cent of the amount injected. Even total replenishment of an animal's water resources has only a modest inhibitory effect on deprivation-induced drinking (about 30 per cent). These findings pose difficulties for any set-point theory (Pinel, 1993).

Hull's drive-reduction theory

As we noted earlier, Hull's motivational theory must be considered in the context of his theory of learning. Drive reduction theory was intended to explain the fundamental principle of reinforcement, both *positive* (the reduction of a drive by the *presentation* of a stimulus) and *negative* (the reduction of a drive by the *removal* or *avoidance* of a stimulus).

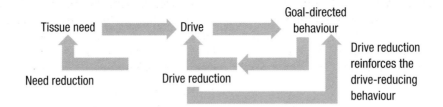

Figure 9.4 *Summary of drive-reduction theory*

Hull was interested in the primary (physiological), homeostatic needs and drives of hunger, thirst, air, avoiding injury, maintaining an optimum temperature, defecation and urination, rest, sleep, activity and propagation (reproduction). He believed that all behaviour (human and animal) originates in the satisfaction of these drives.

Needs vs drives

While the terms 'need' and 'drive' are often used interchangeably, they are fundamentally different:

■ Needs are *physiological* and can be defined objectively (for example, in terms of hours without food or blood sugar level).

■ Drives are *psychological* (behavioural), and are *hypothetical constructs*, that is, abstract concepts that refer to processes/events believed to be taking place inside the person/animal, but which cannot be directly observed or measured.

However, Hull operationalised drives as hours of deprivation. He proposed a number of equations, which were meant to be testable in laboratory experiments (Walker, 1984). Perhaps the most important of these was:

$$sEr = D \times V \times K \times sHr$$

where *sEr* stands for the intensity or likelihood of any learned behaviour. It can be calculated if four other factors are known, namely:

■ *D*: the drive or motivation, measured by some indicator of physical need, such as hours of deprivation;

■ *V*: the intensity of the signal for the behaviour;

■ *K*: the degree of incentive, measured by the size of the reward or some other measure of its desirability;

■ *SHr*: habit strength, measured as the amount of practice given, usually in terms of the number of reinforcements.

Evaluation of drive-reduction theory

Hull's basic premise is that animals (and, by implication, people) always and only learn through primary drive reduction. The relationship between primary drives and needs is very unclear, as we saw earlier when discussing the eating behaviour of obese people.

■ At its simplest, needs can arise without specific drives, as in learning what and how much to eat (see above). For example, we need vitamin C but we wouldn't normally talk of a 'vitamin C drive' (in the way that we talk about a general hunger drive).

■ Conversely, drives can occur in the absence of any obvious physiological need, an important example of a non-homeostatic drive in rats being *electrical self-stimulation of the brain* (ES-SB).

KEY STUDY 9.5

What a rat wouldn't do for a shock (Olds & Milner 1954)

Olds and Milner found that rats stimulated by an electrode implanted near the septum (part of the limbic system) would make between 3000 and 7500 lever-pressing responses (the response producing shock) in a 12-hour period. Olds (1956) reported that one rat stimulated itself more than 2000 times per hour for 24 consecutive hours, and in 1958 reported that rats which normally press a lever 25 times per hour for a food reward will press 100 times per minute for a reward of ES-SB (see Figure 9.5).

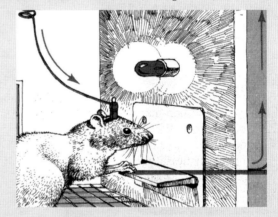

Figure 9.5 *Olds (1956) implanted electrodes in the hypothalami of rats. The rats could trigger an electrical stimulus by depressing a lever. Clearly, the region where the electrode was implanted constitutes some kind of pleasure centre (adapted from J. Olds ©1956 Pleasure centres in the brain. Scientific American, Inc. All rights reserved)*

Brain stimulation is such a powerful reinforcer that a male rat with an electrode in its LH will self-stimulate in preference to eating if hungry, drinking when thirsty, or mating if it has access to a sexually receptive female. This effect has been found in rats, cats, monkeys and pigeons (and humans, occasionally). The main reward site for ES-SB is the *median forebrain bundle* (MFB), a fibre tract which runs from the brainstem up to the forebrain through the LH (Beaumont, 1988; Carlson, 1992). The effect seems to depend on the presence of dopamine and noradrenaline. These reward centres are generally thought of as the neural substrate of 'pleasure', so that any behaviour defined as pleasurable involves their activation (see Chapter 8). ES-SB is seen as a 'short-cut' to pleasure, eliminating the need for natural drives and reinforcers.

- Tolman's *cognitive behaviourism* challenged Skinner's S–R psychology, because it showed that learning could take place in the absence of reinforcement (*latent learning*: see Chapter 11). By implication, Tolman showed that learning could take place in the absence of drive reduction.
- Hull's theory emphasised primary (homeostatic) drives to the exclusion of secondary (non-homeostatic) drives. Primary drives are based on primary (innate) needs, while much human (and, to a lesser extent, non-human) behaviour can only be understood in terms of secondary (acquired) drives. Several behaviourist psychologists, notably Miller (1948), Mowrer (1950) and Dollard & Miller (1950), modified Hull's theory to include acquired drives (in particular, anxiety) which led to a great deal of research on avoidance learning in the 1950s (see Chapters 11, 32, 44 and 45).
- In Maslow's terms, drive-reduction theory deals only with survival needs, completely ignoring the self-actualisation (or 'growth') needs which make human motivation distinctively different from that of non-humans

Just as ES-SB cannot be accommodated by drive reduction when considering only non-human motivation, so non-humans seem to have other non-homeostatic drives which they share, to some degree, with humans. The rest of this chapter will be devoted to these important, and pervasive, non-homeostatic needs and drives.

> ### Ask yourself ...
> - When we – and non-humans – aren't eating, drinking and doing all the other things we have to do to survive, what do we do? Why do we do it?
> - Are all our activities ultimately aimed at survival, or are even non-humans capable of doing things 'just for the sheer hell of it'?

Non-homeostatic needs and drives

Competence motives: motives without specific primary needs

According to White (1959), the 'master reinforcer' which keeps most of us motivated over long periods of time is the need to confirm our sense of personal competence: our capacity to deal effectively with the environment. It is *intrinsically* rewarding and satisfying to feel that we are capable human beings, to be able to understand, predict and control our world (which also happen to be the major aims of science: see Chapter 3).

Unlike hunger, which comes and goes, competence seems to be a continuous, ongoing motive. We can't satisfy it and then do without it until it next appears, because it's not rooted

in any specific physiological need. This is why it isn't very helpful to think of the competence motive as a drive which pushes us into seeking its reduction. While homeostatic drives involve an attempt to *reduce* something (tissue need), competence motives often involve the *search for stimulation*.

Seeking stimulation

If rats are allowed to become thoroughly familiar with a maze and then the maze is changed in some way, they'll spend more time exploring the altered maze. This occurs even in the absence of any obvious extrinsic reward, such as food. They're displaying a *curiosity drive* (Butler, 1954). Butler, and Harlow *et al.* (1950), gave monkeys mechanical puzzles to solve, such as undoing a chain, lifting a hook and opening a clasp. The monkeys did these puzzles over and over again, for hours at a time, with no other reward: they were displaying *their manipulative drive* (Harlow *et al.*, 1950).

Figure 9.6 *Research by Butler and Harlow has shown that animals are motivated to explore and manipulate their environments, quite unrelated to biological drives such as hunger and thirst. Monkeys will learn and work in order to open a door which allows them to view an electric train. They will also work diligently to open locks which lead to no tangible reward*

Play and motivation

Much of the behaviour normally described as play can be thought of in terms of the drives for curiosity, exploration and manipulation. The purpose of play from the child's point of view is simple enjoyment. The child doesn't consciously play in order to find out how things work, or to exercise its imagination, but simply because it's fun and intrinsically satisfying. Any learning which does result is quite incidental. However, for the young child there's no real distinction between 'work' and 'play' in an adult sense.

Piaget (1951) distinguishes between play, which is performed for its own sake, and 'intellectual activity' or learning, in which there's an external aim or purpose. This distinction is meant to apply to all three major types of play he describes:

mastery, symbolic/make-believe, and play with rules. (Piaget's theory is discussed in detail in Chapter 34). Nor is play confined to humans. The young of many species engage in activities, which seem to have little to do with homeostatic or survival needs. However, the higher up the evolutionary scale the species is, the more apparent and purposeful the play becomes, and the more the nature of play changes as the young animal develops (Fontana, 1981a).

Motivation and adaptation

Piaget saw play as essentially an adaptive activity. Throughout development, play helps to consolidate recently acquired abilities, as well as aiding the development of additional cognitive and social skills. In the same way, the competence motives of curiosity, exploration and manipulation undoubtedly have adaptive significance for an individual and, ultimately, for the species. Investigating and exploring the environment equips an animal with 'knowledge', which can be used in times of stress or danger (Bolles, 1967).

Optimal level (or arousal) theories

According to Berlyne (1960), investigation and exploration are based on an inbuilt tendency to seek a certain 'optimum' level of stimulation or activity. Exploring the unfamiliar increases arousal, but if it's too different from what we're used to, arousal will be too high (we feel anxious and tense). If it's not different enough, arousal is too low (we soon become bored).

Optimum level theories are supported by *sensory deprivation experiments*, involving mature animals, both human and nonhuman. Butler (1954) kept monkeys in small, barren cages where pressing a button brought a reward of opening a small observation window, through which they could see, for example, an electric train (see Figure 9.6). In the classic experiments on sensory deprivation carried out by Hebb and his colleagues at McGill University in the 1950s (Bexton *et al.*, 1954; Heron, 1957), participants were almost completely cut off from normal sensory stimulation, by wearing blindfolds, earmuffs, cardboard tubes on their arms and legs, and so on (see Figure 9.7). They soon began to experience extreme psychological discomfort, reported hallucinations, and couldn't usually tolerate their confinement for more than three days (see Figure 9.8, page 128).

Cohen & Taylor (1972) studied the psychological effects of long-term imprisonment, and found that sensory deprivation and monotony are experiences which prisoners share with explorers, space travellers and round-the-world sailors. Conversely, excessive stimulation ('sensory overload') is also debilitating, and may be responsible for some kinds of psychological disorders in our highly urbanised society (see Chapter 12's discussion of stress).

The need for control

Another major kind of competence motive is the need to be in control of our own destiny, and not at the mercy of external forces (Rubin & McNeil, 1983). This is closely linked to the need to be free from the controls and restrictions of others, to dictate our own actions and not be dictated to. According to Brehm (1966), when our freedom is threatened, we tend to react by reasserting our freedom (*psychological reactance*: see Chapter 49).

When people initially expect to have control over the outcomes of their actions, the first experience of not being so is likely to produce reactance. But further bad experiences are likely to result in *learned helplessness* (Seligman, 1975). Rotter's (1966) concept of *locus of control* refers to individual differences in people's beliefs about what controls events in their everyday lives (see Chapter 12).

Figure 9.7 *Sensory deprivation cubicle (Heron, 1957)*

versions are used for men and women, boys and girls. The participant is told that the TAT is a test of imagination and asked to make up a story that describes:

- what is happening and who the people are;
- what has led up to the situation;
- what is being thought and what is wanted and by whom;
- what will happen, what will be done.

The pictures are sufficiently ambiguous with regard to the events depicted and the emotions of the characters to allow a wide range of interpretations. How a person interprets them is assumed to reveal their unconscious motives. Hence, the TAT is a major *projective test* used in motivation and personality research (see Chapter 42). A person who scores high on nAch is concerned with standards of excellence, high levels of performance, recognition by others and the pursuit of long-term goals (they're *ambitious*).

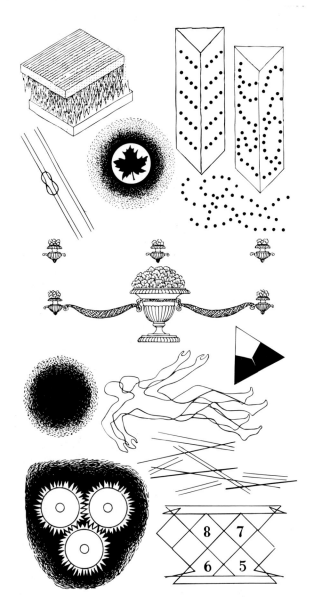

Figure 9.8 *Hallucinations of sensory-deprived participants*

Figure 9.9 *Sample TAT picture*

Cognitive motives

Consistency and achievement

One of the most researched cognitive motives is the need for *cognitive consistency*, which is discussed in Chapter 24 in relation to attitudes and attitude change. Another which has generated an enormous amount of research and theorising is *achievement motivation/need for achievement* (nAch). This was one of the 20 human motives identified by Murray in 1938. He drew a sharp distinction between 'psychogenic' (or psychological) needs, which are learned, and 'viscerogenic' (or physiological) needs, which are innate.

Murray agreed with Freud that people express their true motives more clearly in free association than in direct self-reports (or questionnaire-type personality tests: see Chapter 42). Based on this belief, Murray (together with Morgan, 1935) devised the thematic apperception test (TAT). It consists of a series of 20 pictures, presented one at a time, ten in each of two sessions separated by at least one day. Slightly different

Social motives

According to Geen (1995), social motivation refers to the activation of processes involved in the initiation, direction and energisation of individual behaviour '... by situations in which other people are in close contact with the individual ...'. It's usually assumed that these situations don't provide specific cues for individual behaviour (they're 'weak'). He contrasts them with 'strong' situations, such as those in which there is direct social influence (as in obedience experiments; see Chapter 27).

Geen gives three main examples of social motives:

- *social facilitation*: the enhancing effect on behaviour of the mere presence of others (see Chapter 31);
- *social presentation*: behaving in ways that attempt to present a desirable impression to others (see Chapter 22);
- *social loafing*: the tendency for individual effort to diminish in group task situations, partly as a result of diffusion of responsibility (again see Chapter 31).

Each of these may be thought of as a manifestation of the more general influence of *social anxiety*, a state created when a person who wishes to make a certain impression on others doubts that this impression can actually be made. But why should the fear of making a bad impression be such a powerful motive for individual behaviour?

One answer can be found at quite a low level of Maslow's hierarchy, namely the need for love and belongingness. This includes the need for affiliation, the company of other people, especially family, friends and work colleagues, the need to be accepted by, and included within, society. Certain kinds of conformity can be understood in terms of this basic need (a survival need in Maslow's terms: see Chapter 26). But does this need itself stem from some other, even more fundamental need?

According to Greenberg *et al.* (1986, cited in Geen, 1995), human culture, which society represents, provides a buffer against facing one's own vulnerability and mortality. Society provides a 'cultural drama' that gives meaning to life and without which the individual would experience a dread of being alive. We are, therefore, motivated to play an approved role in that drama: by meeting cultural standards, the individual achieves the approval and acceptance of others and avoids rejection and isolation. Ultimately this is satisfying safety needs, the second level of Maslow's hierarchy, and includes 'fear of the unknown'. The ultimate example of this is the fear of death (see Chapter 39). The general need for others (affiliation), and our attraction to particular others, are discussed in Chapter 28 on social relationships.

CHAPTER SUMMARY

- The study of motivation is the study of the causes of behaviour. While there is general agreement that motivated behaviour is purposeful, goal-directed behaviour, different theoretical approaches see the underlying causes in very different ways.

- Motives have been classified in various ways, but the most comprehensive classification is Maslow's **hierarchy of needs**, which distinguishes survival, deficiency or **D-motives** and, growth, being or **B-motives**.

- **Hedonism** can be seen as a central theme in both Freud's **psychoanalytic theory** and Skinner's **operant conditioning**.

- Influenced by Darwin's theory of evolution, many early psychologists tried to explain human behaviour in terms of large numbers of **instincts**. This approach was replaced by Woodworth's concept of **drive**.

- Two major forms of drive theory are Cannon's **homeostatic-drive theory** and Hull's **drive-reduction theory**.

- Hunger and thirst are the homeostatic drives that have been most researched by biopsychologists. The earliest formal theory of **hunger** was Cannon's theory of **stomach contractions**.

- According to the **glucostatic theory**, the primary stimulus for hunger is a decrease in the level of **blood glucose** below a certain **set-point**. The **glucostat** detects the level of blood glucose in the way a thermostat measures temperature.

- The other major set-point theory is the **lipostatic theory**, which focuses on the storage of **lipids** (fats) in the **adipose tissue**. It's supported by several observations, including the finding that damage to the LH affects feeding **indirectly** by altering the body weight set-point.

- The glucostatic theory was meant to account for the relatively **short-term processes** of eating initiation (and termination), while the lipostatic theory was meant to explain **long-term** feeding habits and regulation of body weight. They share the belief in predetermined set-points.

- Eating, in both humans and other animals, is partly determined by food's **palatability**. Food-predicting cues elicit **cephalic phase responses**, such as salivation, through **classical conditioning**.

- **Sensory-specific satiety** encourages the consumption of a varied diet. Although humans are capable of learning which diets best meet their biological needs, people in industrialised societies seem to prefer diets that are fundamentally harmful to health, with obesity becoming increasingly common.

- Lesions in the **VMH** of the rat's hypothalamus cause **hyperphagia** and the **VMH** became known as the '**satiety centre**'. However, the VMH syndrome also involves increased sensitivity to **external cues** of satiation. This also seems to be true of obese humans.

- Lesions to the **LH** cause **aphagia**, which suggests that it's a feeding centre. However, the effects of LH lesions are much more diffuse than originally thought.

- **Drinking** has traditionally been seen as motivated by deviation from set-points induced by water deprivation. Although there's some support for the **dry-mouth theory**, this isn't the primary factor in thirst.

- It's difficult for set-point theories to explain why drinking stops, whether this is water-deprived drinking or not. Both stomach distension and the **mouth-metering mechanism** play a part in satiety.

- Hull's **drive-reduction theory** was intended to explain the principle of **reinforcement**. However, needs can arise without specific drives and drives can occur in the absence of any obvious tissue need, as in **ES-SB**. Brain stimulation is a very powerful reinforcer, which can over-ride the primary drives of hunger, thirst and sex.

- **Latent learning** shows that learning can take place in the absence of reinforcement. Much behaviour can only be understood in terms of secondary (**non-homeostatic**) drives, such as anxiety and its avoidance.

- Humans and non-humans share certain non-homeostatic needs and drives, such as **curiosity**, **manipulation** and **play**. These are linked to the **search for stimulation** and the **need for competence**, important for **adaptation** to our environment.

- **Optimal level theories** can help explain why both **sensory deprivation** and **sensory overload** can be stressful and disturbing.

- **Cognitive consistency** and **need for achievement** (nAch) are two very important **cognitive motives**.

- Many kinds of social behaviour can be seen as a manifestation of **social anxiety**, which in turn may reflect the more fundamental need for safety and protection (ultimately) from our fear of death.

Self-assessment/revision questions

1 Discuss research studies into brain mechanisms involved in a motivational state such as hunger.
2 Describe and evaluate Hull's drive-reduction theory.
3 Discuss the concept of motivation in the light of **one** physiological and **one** psychological theory.

Web addresses

http://www.dana.org./dana/bwn_html/bwn_0698.htm/

http://www.medserv.dk/comp/1999/04/14/story04.htm

http://www.cc.emory.edu/WHSC/YERKES/NEWSROOM/kuharrls.htm

http://www.ndif.org/Translation/jstran_160.html

http://www.csun.edu/~vcpsy00h/students/explore.htm

http://www.tecfa.unige.ch/themes/sa2/act-app-dos2-fic-drive.htm

http://www.cho.fis.utoronto.ca/FIS/Courses/LIS1230/LIS1230sharma/motive6.htm

http://www.exnet.com:2000/resources/motivate.htm

http://sol.brunel.ac.uk/~jarvis/bola/motivation/masmodel.hm

Further reading

Carlson, N.R. (1992) *Foundations of Physiological Psychology* (2nd edition). Boston: Allyn and Bacon. A very thorough, well-illustrated textbook that covers all aspects of physiological psychology.

Pinel, J.P.L. (1993) *Biopsychology* (2nd edition). Boston: Allyn and Bacon. Like Carlson, a comprehensive text, but it has the advantage of being illustrated in colour, helping to make it even more user-friendly.

Chapter 10

Emotion

Introduction and overview

Mr Spock in *Star Trek* often points out to Captain Kirk how much energy human beings waste through reacting emotionally to things, when a more logical and rational approach would be more productive. But would we be human at all if we didn't react in this way? This isn't to advocate 'being emotional' in the sense of losing control of our feelings, or being unable to consider things in a calm and detached way. However, it is the richness of our emotions, and our capacity to have feelings as well as to think things through and to reason, which makes us unique as a species. Emotions set the tone of our experience and give life its vitality. They are internal factors which can energise, direct and sustain behaviour (Rubin & McNeill, 1983).

At the same time, we often respond emotionally to events and situations that we believe make demands on us that we can't meet – either because we don't have the necessary abilities or resources, or because they force us to make very difficult choices and decisions. We describe these negative kinds of events/situations as *stressful*, and our emotional responses to them as the experience of *stress* (see Chapter 12).

One of the key issues running through research into the nature of emotional experience is to what extent it is a *physiological* phenomenon. Related to this is the question of whether different subjective emotions (feeling angry, afraid, and so on) are also *physiologically distinct*. More recent theories have emphasised the role of *cognitive factors* in our experience of emotion, and are collectively referred to as *cognitive appraisal theories*.

What is emotion?

Wundt (1897), one of the founders of scientific psychology (see Chapters 1 and 3), believed that emotional experience can be described in terms of combinations of three dimensions – *pleasantness/unpleasantness*, *calm/excitement*, and *relaxation/tension* (based on introspection). Schlosberg (1941) also identified pleasantness/unpleasantness, together with *acceptance/rejection* and *sleep/tension* (based on photographs of posed facial expressions). Osgood (1966) too saw pleasantness as one dimension, plus activation and control, which correspond to the evaluative, activity and potency factors of the semantic differential (based on live emotional display): see Chapter 24.

Ekman *et al.* (1972) and Ekman & Friesen (1975) identified six primary emotions: surprise, fear, disgust, anger, happiness and sadness (based on photos of posed facial expressions: see Figure 10.1). These are taken to be *universal*, that is, they're expressed facially in the same way, and are recognised as such,

by members of a diversity of cultures. This suggests very strongly that they are *innate*.

Plutchik (1980) has proposed an emotion wheel (see Figure 10.2), in which eight basic/primary emotions (composed of four pairs of opposites) are shown inside the circle, with a further eight complex emotions on the outside. The primary emotions correspond to Ekman and Friesen's six, except that 'joy' and 'sorrow' are used for 'happiness' and 'sadness', respectively, plus acceptance and expectancy. Plutchik believes that the primary emotions are both biologically and subjectively distinct.

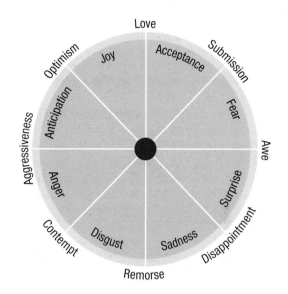

Figure 10.2 *The emotion wheel. Plutchik's model arranges eight basic emotions within a circle of opposites. Pairs of these adjacent primary emotions combine to form more complex emotions noted on the outside of the circle. Secondary emotions emerge from basic emotions more remotely associated on the wheel (from Zimbardo, 1992)*

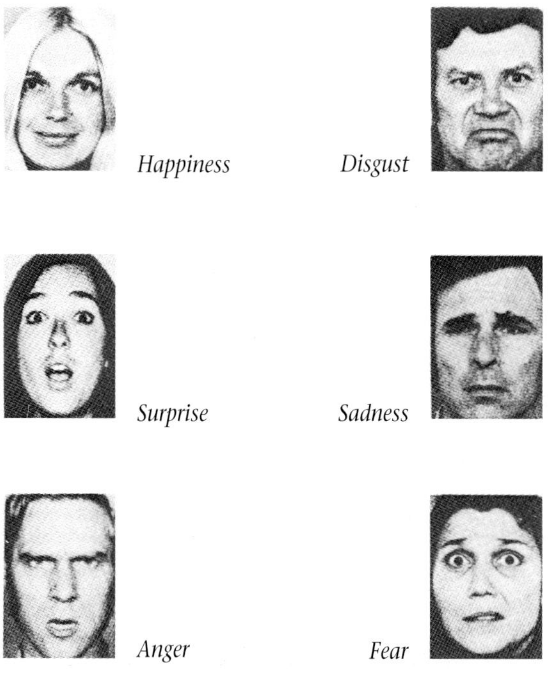

'Basic' or 'primary' emotions

For Ekman (1994), 'basic' is meant to emphasise the role that evolution has played in shaping both the unique and the common features that emotions display, as well as their current function. Emotions evolved for their adaptive value in dealing with fundamental life tasks: they helped species to survive. Three major characteristics of emotions follow from this adaptive function.

■ There will be certain common elements in the contexts in which emotions are found to occur, despite individual and cultural differences in social learning.
■ They're likely to be observable in other primates. While it's possible that there are certain emotions that are unique to humans, there's no convincing evidence that this is so.
■ They can be aroused so quickly that they start to happen before we're even aware of them:

> 'Quick onset is central to the adaptive value of emotions, mobilising us quickly to respond to important events'. (Ekman, 1994)

So, emotions can occur with very rapid onset, through automatic appraisal (see below), with little awareness, and with

Figure 10.1 *Six universal facial expressions*

Happiness

Disgust

Surprise

Sadness

Anger

Fear

involuntary changes in expression and physiology. Indeed, we often experience emotions as *happening to us*, rather than chosen by us.

We'll see below that there is recent evidence for distinctive patterns of ANS activity for various emotions. Ekman believes that these patterns are likely to have evolved because they support patterns of motor behaviour that were adaptive for each of these emotions, preparing the organism for quite different actions. For example, fighting might well have been the adaptive action in anger (which is consistent with the finding that blood flow increases to the hands when we're angry). There may also be unique patterns of CNS activity for each emotion, which isn't found in other mental activity.

Averill (1994) also recognises the influence that an evolutionary approach has had in the study of emotions, defining basic emotions as those '… that fulfil vital biological functions …' (vital to the survival of the species). Like Ekman, he believes that basic emotions should be universal, be seen (at least in rudimentary form) in non-human primates, and be heritable.

However, what's considered basic also varies between cultures and within the same culture over time. For example, in the Middle Ages, hope was classified as a basic emotion, while today it's regarded as secondary (if it's considered at all) by most emotion theorists (Averill, 1994). But most basic of all are emotions that are *psychologically* basic: when people are asked to recount emotional episodes that evoked their 'true feelings', they typically describe incidents that reinforce or transform or enhance their sense of self (Morgan & Averill, 1992).

Components of emotion

For each distinct emotion, there are three components:

- the *subjective experience* of happiness, sadness, anger, and so on;
- the *physiological changes* which occur, involving the autonomic nervous system (ANS) and the endocrine system, over which we have little, if any, conscious control. However, we may become aware of some of their effects (such as 'butterflies in the stomach', gooseflesh, and sweating: see Chapter 4);
- the *associated behaviour* such as smiling, crying, frowning, running away, and being 'frozen to the spot'.

The second and third are sometimes categorised together as 'bodily reactions', with the former being called *visceral* and the latter *skeletal*. This distinction relates to the ANS and central nervous systems (CNS) respectively. However, while running away is largely under voluntary (CNS) control, crying or sweating definitely are not, yet in all three cases we infer another person's emotional state from this observable behaviour.

Different theories of emotion can be distinguished by:

- how they see the relationship between these three components;
- the relative emphasis given to each component;
- how they see the relationship between the components and our *cognitive appraisal* or *interpretation* of the emotion-producing stimulus or situation.

Theories of emotion

Darwin's evolutionary theory

The publication of *The Expression of Emotions in Man and Animals* (1872) represents the first formal attempt, by any scientist, to study emotion. Based largely on anecdotal evidence, Darwin argued that particular emotional responses (such as facial expressions) tend to accompany the same emotional states in humans of all races and cultures, even those who are born blind. (This claim has, of course, been supported by the research of Ekman and Friesen: see above.) Like other human behaviours, the expression of human emotion is the product of evolution.

So, Darwin attempted to understand emotions by comparing them with similar behaviours in other species. Based on such comparisons, he proposed a theory of the evolution of emotional expression comprising three main ideas:

- Expressions of emotion evolve from behaviours that signal what an animal is likely to do next.
- If such behaviours benefit the animal that displays them, they'll evolve in ways that make them more effective as a form of communication, and their original function may be lost.

Figure 10.3 *The two woodcuts from Darwin's 1872 book* The Expression of Emotions in Man and Animals, *which he used to illustrate the principle of antithesis. The aggressive posture features ears forward, back up, hair up and tail up; the submissive posture features ears back, back down, hair down and tail down (from J. Pinel, 1993,* Biopsychology, *Boston, Allyn and Bacon)*

- Opposing messages are often signalled by opposing movements or postures (the *principle of antithesis*).

Taking *threat displays* as an example:

- Originally, facing one's enemies, rising up and exposing one's weapons, were just the early components of animal combat.
- Once the enemies began to recognise these behaviours as signals of imminent aggression, those aggressors that could communicate their aggressive intent most effectively and scare off their victims without actually fighting had a distinct advantage. As a result, elaborate threat displays evolved and actual combat declined.
- To be most effective, signals of aggression/submission must be clearly distinguishable, so that they tended to evolve in opposite directions. For example, primates signal aggression by staring at one another, and submission by averting their gaze (Pinel, 1993).

The James–Lange theory

If there is a commonsense theory of emotion, it is that something happens which produces in us a subjective emotional experience and, as a result of this, certain bodily and/or behavioural changes occur. James (originally in 1884 and then in 1890) and Lange (at first quite independently of James) turned this commonsense view on its head. They argued that our emotional experience is the *result*, not the cause, of perceived bodily changes.

To give an example used by James, the commonsense view says that we meet a bear, are frightened and run. The James–Lange theory maintains that we're frightened *because* we run! Similarly, 'We feel sorry because we cry, angry because we strike, afraid because we tremble …'. According to James (1890):

> '… the bodily changes follow directly the perception of the exciting fact, and …our feeling of the same changes as they occur is the emotion'.

The crucial factor in the James–Lange theory is feedback from the bodily changes (see Figure 10.4). We label our subjective state by inferring how we feel based on perception of our own bodily changes ('I'm trembling, so I must be afraid': see Chapter 18).

Ask yourself …

- Do you agree with James? Does the emotional experience always *precede* the associated behaviour (as commonsense would have it), or can the behaviour come first (as the James–Lange theory claims)?

You may be able to think of situations in which you've reacted in a fairly automatic way (for example, you've slipped coming down the stairs), and only after you've grabbed the banisters do you become aware of feeling frightened (and a little shaken). It's almost as if the sudden change in your behaviour has caused the fear, quite apart from why you grabbed the banisters in the first place!

Evaluating the James–Lange theory

The theory implies that by deliberately altering our behaviour, we can control our emotional experiences. Try smiling – do you feel any happier? A crucial test (which James admitted would be very difficult to perform) would be to examine the emotional experience of someone who is completely anaesthetised, but not intellectually or motor impaired.

In the examples that James himself gives of inferring emotion from bodily changes (such as running away from the bear), he clearly attaches much more importance to *skeletal* as opposed to *visceral* changes. In this respect, the James–Lange theory probably differs from other theories, which usually mean 'visceral' when they say 'physiological'. Given this emphasis on skeletal changes, there are two important studies which lend support to the James–Lange theory.

KEY STUDY 10.1

Listen to your heart and smile if you want to be happy (Valins, 1966; Laird, 1974)

Valins provided male participants with feedback of their heart rate while watching slides of semi-nude *Playboy* pin-ups. The heart rate was in fact pre-recorded and programmed to increase in response to presentation of half the slides: participants believed the feedback was an indication of their true responses. This is the *false feedback paradigm*. The slides associated with the apparent heart rate increase were judged to be more attractive than those associated with unchanged heart rate.

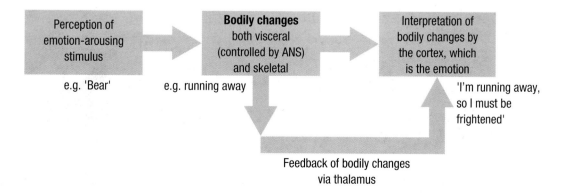

Figure 10.4 *The James–Lange theory of emotion*

Laird tested the *facial feedback hypothesis* by falsely informing 32 students that they were participating in an experiment to measure activity in facial muscles. Bogus electrodes were attached to their faces (as if to measure physiological response), and they were instructed to raise their eyebrows, contract the muscles in their foreheads, and make other facial expressions. They didn't realise the emotional significance of what they were being asked to do. While this was going on, cartoon slides were projected onto a screen. Regardless of their content, participants rated as funnier those slides they'd seen while 'smiling'. They also described themselves as happier when 'smiling', angrier when 'frowning', and so on.

What the Valins and Laird studies suggest is that overt behaviour may cause subjective feelings without there being any obvious physiological arousal taking place: visceral changes may not be necessary. But neither Valins nor Laird attempted to measure any accompanying visceral changes. What if smiling triggers certain physiological changes? Might these be the real cause of our feeling happy, rather than the change in our facial muscles? And if so, isn't this quite damaging to the James–Lange theory, which places so much stress on behavioural (skeletal) changes?

Levenson *et al.* (1990) asked participants to move particular facial muscles (to simulate the emotional expression of fear, anger, surprise, disgust, sadness and happiness). They also monitored several physiological responses controlled by the ANS while this was going on. They found that the simulated expressions *did* alter ANS activity. For example, anger increased heart rate and skin temperature, fear increased heart rate but decreased skin temperature, while happiness decreased heart rate without affecting skin temperature.

In the James–Lange theory, these bodily changes occur spontaneously, not consciously and deliberately. This makes it difficult to draw any firm conclusions from experiments like Valins' and Laird's. However, both studies strongly suggest that physiological arousal isn't sufficient to account for emotional experience. The fact that participants in the Valins study were prepared to infer emotion on the basis of (false) information about their reactions to stimuli suggests it may not even be necessary, and that cognitive factors may be sufficient (Parkinson, 1987). (We shall return to this issue below.)

Cannon's criticisms of the James–Lange theory

According to Cannon (1929), there are four major faults with the James–Lange theory:

■ It assumes that for each subjectively distinct emotion there is a corresponding set of physiological changes enabling us to label the emotion we are experiencing;

■ Even if this assumption were true, physiological arousal would still not be sufficient;

■ Physiological arousal may not even be necessary;

■ The speed with which we often experience emotions seems to exceed the speed of response of the viscera, so how could the physiological changes be the source of sudden emotion?

Cannon (1929) argued that: '... the same visceral changes occur in very different emotional states and in non-emotional

states'. In other words, the James–Lange theory was built on the assumption that different emotional stimuli induce different patterns of ANS activity, and that perception of these different patterns results in different emotional experiences. However, the Cannon–Bard theory (see page 138) claims that the ANS responds in the same way to all emotional stimuli: the sympathetic branch prepares the organism for flight or fight, through increased heart rate and blood pressure, pupil dilation, increased blood flow to the muscles, increased respiration and increased release of adrenaline and noradrenaline from the adrenal medulla (see Chapter 4). This means that there must be more to our emotional experience than simply physiological arousal, otherwise we wouldn't be able to tell one emotional state from another.

Evidence for physiological specificity

According to LeDoux (1994), this represents '... one of the most pesky problems in emotion research ...'. He points out that the emphasis of research has been on ANS activity, and this emphasis is partly due to Cannon's criticism of the James–Lange theory.

KEY STUDY 10.2

Be afraid: the Ax man's coming (Ax, 1953)

In a famous, but ethically highly dubious experiment, Ax measured various aspects of physiological activity, for instance *electrodermal* (skin conductance), *electromyographic* (muscle action potential), *cardiovascular*, and respiratory, in participants who were deliberately frightened and made angry. They were told that they were participating in a study of *hypertension* (high blood pressure), and were asked to lie quietly on a couch while physiological measures were being taken. As electrodes were being attached, it was casually mentioned that the regular technician (who usually operated the technical equipment in an adjacent room) was sick, and a man who'd recently been fired for incompetence and arrogance was filling in for him. A few minutes later (after baseline measures had been recorded), either the anger condition occurred, followed by the fear condition, or vice versa.

■ In the *fear condition*, a continuous mild shock was administered to one finger (without any warning or explanation). The intensity gradually increased, until the participant complained. Then sparks were made to fly.

■ In the *anger condition*, the technician (an actor) entered the room and spent five minutes checking the wiring. During this time, he jostled the participant, criticised the attending nurse, and blamed the participant for causing a fault in the equipment.

Of 14 different measures taken, Ax found that seven were significantly different between the two conditions. For example, fear was associated with increased heart rate, skin conduction level, muscle action potential frequency, and breathing rate (reflecting the effects of *adrenaline*). Anger was accompanied by increased diastolic blood pressure, frequency of spontaneous skin conduction responses and action potential size (reflecting the greater influence of *noradrenaline*).

While Ax's methods would be ethically unacceptable today, his findings have been confirmed by others (e.g. Frankenhaeuser, 1975). Schachter (1957) confirmed Ax's original findings that fear is influenced largely by adrenaline. But he also found that anger produces a mixed adrenaline–noradrenaline response, and pain produces a noradrenaline-like pattern. Schachter & Singer (1962) concluded that:

> 'Whether or not there are physiological distinctions among the various emotional states must be considered an open question. Any differences which do exist are at best rather subtle and the variety of emotion, mood and feeling states do not appear to be matched by an equal variety of visceral patterns'.

This conclusion is consistent with Schachter's *cognitive labelling theory* (1964). This sees physiological arousal as necessary for emotional experience, but the nature of the arousal as irrelevant (see pages 138–139).

Less extreme and controversial methods than Ax's include:

- the *directed facial action method*, in which participants are instructed to make the facial expressions characteristic of various emotions while ANS activity is recorded;
- the *relived emotion method*, in which participants are asked to think about previous emotional experiences while these measures are being made.

One of the leading researchers in the field is Levenson, who has carried out a series of experiments using both kinds of method. Levenson maintains that it is a 'myth' that every emotion is autonomically different. It seems far more likely that reliable differences will only be found between emotions for which there are different associated typical behaviours, and even among this smaller set, it's quite unlikely that they won't share some features.

Levenson *et al.* (1990) compared anger, disgust, fear, sadness (negative emotions), plus happiness (positive emotion) and surprise. They have identified a small number of fairly reliable differences in patterns of ANS activity, both between the negative emotions, and between the negative emotions as a group and happiness. For example, anger, fear and sadness all produce larger increases in heart rate than disgust, while anger produces a larger increase in finger temperature than fear. These differences have been found consistently across populations differing in occupation, age (from young people to 71–90-year-olds), culture (Americans and Minangkabau males living in Western Sumatra, Indonesia) and gender, as well as across the directed facial action and relived emotion methods.

As far as positive emotions are concerned, Levenson (1994) believes that they might not be associated with any particular pattern of behaviour or, if they are, it would be characterised by low activity, making little metabolic demand on the ANS:

> 'Instead of having distinctive autonomic signatures ... positive emotions might be associated with a state of physiological quiescence ... their primary function might be to 'undo' the autonomic activation produced by negative emotions ... to restore the organism to its prearousal state in a more efficient and rapid manner than would be the case if the negative emotions were allowed to run their natural course'.

What this implies is that, at least in our present state of knowledge, we cannot draw general conclusions about the specificity of the body's response to emotional stimuli – it depends partly on which emotion (positive or negative) we're talking about.

Must we choose between Cannon and James?

Pinel (1993) advocates a position falling between the extreme views represented by the Cannon–Bard and James–Lange theories. On the one hand, the Cannon–Bard view that the ANS responds in the same way to all emotional stimuli is clearly incorrect: several differences have been well documented. On the other hand, there's insufficient evidence to make a strong case for the James–Lange view that each emotion is characterised by a different pattern of ANS activity.

Ask yourself ...

- Given James's emphasis on skeletal, as opposed to visceral changes, could it be argued that Cannon's first criticism is not strictly relevant?
- Since we're almost completely unaware of visceral changes, could James have claimed that 'visceral feedback' is the emotion?

Even if there were identifiable patterns of physiological response associated with different subjective emotions, Cannon argued that such physiological changes themselves don't necessarily produce emotional states; in other words, physiological arousal isn't sufficient. This was demonstrated by Marañon (1924). However, the study by Hohmann (1966) suggests that, although physiological changes aren't sufficient for the experience of 'full-blooded' emotions, they may be necessary.

KEY STUDY 10.3

As if emotion were just adrenaline (Marañon, 1924)

Marañon injected 210 people with adrenaline. Seventy-one per cent said they experienced only physical symptoms, with no emotional overtones at all. Most of the rest reported 'as if' emotions. The few who experienced genuine emotion had to imagine – or remember – a highly emotional event.

KEY STUDY 10.4

Real emotions need an intact ANS (Hohmann, 1966)

Hohmann studied 25 adult males with spinal cord injuries, who suffered corresponding ANS damage. They reported significant changes in the nature and intensity of certain emotional experiences, especially anger, fear, and sexual feelings. Generally, the higher the lesion in the spinal cord, the greater the disruption of visceral responses, and the greater the disturbance of normal emotional experiences. Like Marañon's participants, they reported 'as if' emotions, a 'mental kind of anger', for example.

According to Schachter (1964), what Marañon's and Hohmann's participants reported is precisely what would be expected from his cognitive labelling theory, which sees emotional experience as a joint function of cognitive and physiological factors (see below).

The Cannon–Bard theory

Cannon (1927) removed the sympathetic nervous systems of cats and Sherrington (1900) severed the spinal cords and vagus nerves of dogs. In both cases, feedback from the viscera to the brain was prevented, but the animals showed apparently normal emotional reactions. Cannon took these findings to mean that physiological changes may not even be necessary for emotional experience. In addition, Dana (1921) studied a patient with a spinal cord lesion: despite having no sympathetic functioning and extremely limited muscular movement, the patient showed a range of emotions, including grief, joy, displeasure and affection. This seems to support Cannon's view.

> *Ask yourself ...*
> - Is it valid to generalise from the study of cats' and dogs' emotional reactions to human beings' emotional experience, as Cannon did?
> - Is it valid to generalise from a single case, as in Dana's study? (See Chapter 42.)

Cannon also argued that, as we often feel emotions quite rapidly, yet the viscera are quite slow to react, how could the physiological changes be the source of such sudden emotion (as required by the James–Lange theory)? However, although the viscera aren't sensitive to certain kinds of stimulation (such as burning and cutting), they provide much better feedback than Cannon suspected. Many visceral changes can occur sufficiently quickly that they could be the causes of feelings of emotion (Carlson, 1992).

So what is different about Cannon's theory (known as the Cannon–Bard theory)? As Figure 10.5 shows, the subjective emotion is quite *independent* of the physiological changes involved. The emotion-producing stimulus is processed by the thalamus. This sends impulses to the cortex, where the emotion is consciously experienced, and to the hypothalamus, which sets in motion certain autonomic physiological changes.

Schachter's cognitive labelling theory

According to Schachter (1964), Cannon was wrong in thinking that bodily changes and the experience of emotion are independent, and the James–Lange theory was mistaken in claiming that physiological changes cause the feeling of emotion. However, he shares the James–Lange belief that physiological changes precede the experience of emotion. However, we have to decide which particular emotion we're feeling, and the label we attach to our arousal depends on what we attribute that arousal to.

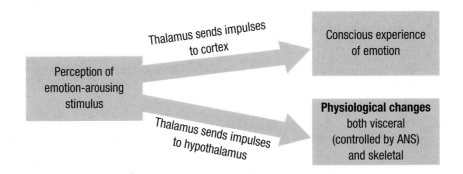

Figure 10.5 *The Cannon–Bard theory of emotion*

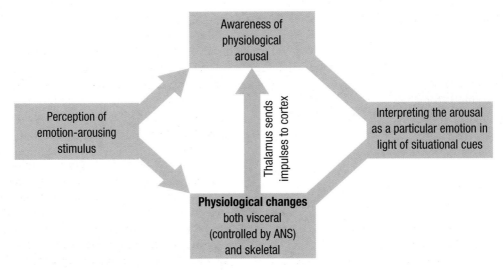

Figure 10.6 *Schachter's cognitive labelling theory (or two-factor theory)*

Schachter is saying that physiological arousal (factor 1) is necessary for the experience of emotion, but the nature of arousal is immaterial – what's important is how we interpret that arousal (factor 2). Hence, the theory is also known as the *two-factor theory of emotion*. The classic experiment which demonstrates this cognitive theory of emotion is Schachter & Singer's (1962) 'adrenaline experiment'.

KEY STUDY 10.5

Schachter & Singer's (1962) adrenaline experiment

Participants were given what they were told was a vitamin injection, to test its effect on vision. In fact, it was adrenaline, and they were tested under one of four conditions:

- Group A participants were given accurate information about the side-effects of the injection (palpitations, tightness in the throat, tremor, and sweating).
- Group B participants were given false information about its side-effects (itching and headache).
- Group C participants were given no information about side-effects (true or false).
- Group D participants (the control group) were given a saline injection (and otherwise treated like group C).

Before being given a 'vision test', each participant (one at a time) sat in a waiting room with another 'participant' (in fact, a stooge of the experimenters). For half the participants in each condition, the stooge acted in either a happy, frivolous way (making paper aeroplanes, laughing out loud, and playing with a hula-hoop: *euphoria condition*), or very angrily (eventually tearing up the questionnaire which he and every participant were asked to complete: *anger condition*). (In fact, the group B condition was run only with a euphoric stooge). Participants' emotional experience was assessed in two ways:

- observers' ratings of the degree to which they joined in with the stooge's behaviour;
- self-report scales.

As predicted:

- groups A and D were much less likely to join in with the stooge or to report feeling euphoric or angry;
- groups B and C were much more likely to assume the stooge's behaviour and emotional state.

Ask yourself ...

- Can you account for these findings in terms of Schachter's cognitive labelling/two-factor theory?

Schachter and Singer were testing three inter-related hypotheses regarding the interaction between physiological and cognitive factors in the experience of emotion:

1 If we experiences a state of physiological arousal for which we have no immediate explanation, we'll 'label' this state and describe it in terms of the cognitions available. So, precisely the same state of arousal could receive different labels (e.g. 'euphoria'/'anger' – groups B and C). (Physiological arousal *and* cognitive labelling are necessary.)

2 If we experience a state of physiological arousal for which we have a completely appropriate explanation (e.g. 'I've just been given an injection of adrenaline'), we'll 'label' this state accordingly (group A).

3 Given the same circumstances, we'll react emotionally or describe our feelings as emotions only to the extent that we experience a state of physiological arousal (all 3 groups). (Physiological arousal is necessary.)

Schachter & Wheeler (1962) confirmed these results by injecting participants either with adrenaline or chlorpromazine (which inhibits arousal); controls were injected with a placebo. While watching a slapstick comedy, the adrenaline participants laughed more, and the chlorpromazine participants less, than the controls. The participants attributed their physiological changes to the film.

KEY STUDY 10.6

Falling in love on a suspension bridge (Dutton & Aron, 1974)

The participants were unsuspecting males, aged 18–35, visiting the Capilano Canyon in British Columbia, Canada. An attractive female interviewer approached the men and asked them questions as part of a survey she was conducting on the effects of scenery on creativity. One of the things they were asked to do was to invent a short story about an ambiguous picture of a woman (a picture from the thematic apperception test/TAT: see Chapter 9). This was later scored for sexual content, taken to reflect the men's sexual attraction towards the interviewer.

Some men were interviewed on an extremely unstable suspension bridge, five feet wide, 450 feet long, composed of wooden boards attached to wire cables, running from one side of the canyon to the other. This bridge, 230 feet above the canyon, tends to sway, tilt and wobble, giving the impression that one is about to fall over the side, with only very low handrails of wire cable for support (the *high arousal condition*: see Figure 10.7).

Other men were interviewed on a solid wooden bridge upstream, a mere ten feet above a shallow rivulet, with high handrails and without any swaying or tilting (the *low arousal condition*).

As predicted, the stories of the men in the high arousal condition contained significantly more sexual imagery. The interviewer also invited the men to call her if they wanted more information about the research. Again in line with predictions, four times as many men from the high arousal condition called her compared with the low arousal condition.

To show that arousal was the independent variable, Dutton and Aron also arranged for another group of men to be interviewed ten or more minutes after crossing the suspension bridge. By this time, the symptoms of their physical arousal should have been declining. These non-aroused men didn't show the signs of sexual arousal shown by those in the high arousal condition.

The Capilano River bridge

Dutton and Aron's study confirms Schachter's claim that the autonomic arousal which accompanies all emotions is similar, and that it's our *interpretation* of that arousal that matters – even though this sometimes results in our misidentifying our emotions. Dutton and Aron's suspension bridge participants seemed to be *mislabelling* their fear as sexual attraction to the interviewer.

Ask yourself ...

- What do you think would have been the outcome if the interviewer had been male?

Evaluation of cognitive labelling theory

- The focus of Schachter's model is an atypical state of affairs, where the participant is unsure about the cause of arousal (groups B and C). But Schachter (1964) admitted that we usually *are* aware of a precipitating situation prior to the onset of arousal (which usually takes one to two seconds to reach consciousness). So, it's normally perfectly obvious to the person what aspects of the situation have provoked the emotion. However, even here the meaning of the emotion-inducing circumstances requires *some* cognitive analysis before the emotion can be labelled.

- Schachter claims that although the *quantitative* aspect of emotion can arise without cognitive mediation ('Am I in a state of emotional arousal?': see Valins' study), the *qualitative* aspect requires prior cognition ('What emotion is it I

am experiencing?': see Laird's study). Mandler (1984a) has called Schachter's theory the *'jukebox' theory* – arousal is like the coin which gets the machine going, and cognition is the button we push to select the emotional tune.

- According to Parkinson (1987), the view that affect (emotion) is post-cognitive is now probably the most popular attitude among emotion theorists. But even accepting the important role of cognitive factors, is our emotional experience really as malleable as Schachter claims? Are environmental cues really as easily accepted as the basis for inferences about our own feelings (Fiske & Taylor, 1991)?

- Using the original Schachter and Singer paradigm, several studies (Plutchik & Ax, 1967; Marshall & Zimbardo, 1979; Maslach, 1979) have concluded that when we look for an explanation of a state of arousal, we don't merely use others' behaviour as a guide to what we are feeling. We call on many other sources of information as well, particularly our own past history: we search for previous occasions on which we felt this arousal state to explain why it's occurring now. While other people's behaviour might suggest – or even dictate (through conformity) – how we should behave in that situation, it doesn't tell us how we're feeling. At the very least, others' behaviour must in some way be appropriate (Weiner, 1992).

- These later studies also found that people who don't have a ready-made explanation for their adrenaline-produced arousal are more likely to attach a *negative* emotional label to it (such as unease or nervousness, similar to 'free-floating anxiety'). This suggests that emotional malleability *isn't* as great as Schachter maintains: unexplained arousal has a negative, unpleasant quality about it.

The role of attribution

According to Schachter, group A participants in the adrenaline experiment could attribute their arousal to the injection (they had a ready-made explanation and so didn't need an emotional explanation). But for those in groups B and C, no such ready-made explanation was available, and so the confederate's behaviour was used as a cue for explaining their own state of arousal (as either euphoria or anger).

Taking one of James's original examples (running away from the bear), the original cause of the bodily reactions (the bear) is *irrelevant*. This is because our emotional experience is based on feedback from our bodily reactions (running away). But for Schachter, it's what we attribute our arousal to that determines the label we give to it. In the adrenaline experiment, the initially unexplained arousal is attributed to the (rather extreme) behaviour of the confederate, and so is labelled euphoria or anger accordingly.

Similarly, the men in Dutton and Aron's experiment who were tested on the swaying suspension bridge, were unaware of the 'real' cause of their arousal. They attributed it instead to the female interviewer. We know that arousal was the independent variable, and it's highly likely that had it not been for the intervention of the attractive interviewer, they would have labelled their arousal 'fear', because it would have been attributed to a frightening stimulus (the bridge).

What all these examples show is that the cognitive labelling theory is essentially based on *attributional principles* (see Chapter 23). This represents a major form of influence that

Schachter's theory has had on cognitive theories of emotion in general. For example, Abramson & Martin (1981) grafted attribution principles onto Seligman's (1975) *theory of learned helplessness* (see Chapter 12), in an attempt to explain clinical depression (see Chapter 44).

According to Weiner (1986, 1992), certain kinds of attribution produce specific emotions. For example, success produces a very general positive feeling (such as happiness), while failure produces a very general negative feeling (such as sadness). But if the outcome (either success or failure) is either very different from what's expected, or has very important consequences, we try to figure out the reasons (or causes) for the outcome. These reasons will take the form of *internal* or *external* attributions, which in turn can be broken down into *controllable* or *uncontrollable*. It's the combination of internal/external and controllable/uncontrollable attributions that will determine specific emotional responses (see Figure 10.7). (Weiner's attributional theory of emotion is also important for understanding helping behaviour: see Chapter 30.)

The misattribution effect

What the adrenaline and the Dutton and Aron experiments show is that people can make mistakes in how they attribute their arousal. This mislabelling of our feelings, and drawing mistaken conclusions about the causes of those feelings, is called the *misattribution effect* (Ross & Nisbett, 1991).

As part of their suspension bridge experiment, and in a later experiment, Dutton & Aron (1974, 1989) invited male students to participate in a learning experiment. After meeting an attractive female partner, half the students were frightened with the news that they'd be suffering some 'quite painful' electric shocks. Before the experiment was due to begin, they were given a short questionnaire 'to get some information on your present feelings and reactions, since these often influence people on the learning task'. Asked how much they'd like to date and kiss their partner, the aroused (frightened) men expressed more intense attraction than the non-frightened men.

By definition, the female partner was sexually attractive, and so it was far easier for the men to transfer their arousal to her, and so mislabel it as sexual arousal. In this way she represented a *salient* or *credible* source of arousal (Olson & Ross, 1988). Similarly, if female participants are shown slides of attractive male nudes, it may be easy to alter their preferences among the pictures based on false heart rate feedback, whereas it would be very difficult to achieve if the male nudes were replaced by slides of naked hippos! (The reference to naked hippos is a deliberately modified version of an example given by Taylor *et al.*, 1994.)

The misattribution effect is most likely to occur when the actual source of the arousal is unclear or ambiguous (Olson & Ross, 1988). For example, while we're unlikely to mistake what we're feeling in the presence of a coiled snake, we might well do so when bumping into a fellow student in the lunch queue (Taylor *et al.*, 1994).

Cognitive appraisal or affective primacy?

Perhaps the best known cognitive appraisal theory is that of Lazarus (1982), which is a development of Schachter's cognitive labelling theory. According to Lazarus, some degree of cognitive processing is an essential prerequisite for an affective reaction to a stimulus to occur, and is an integral feature of all emotional states.

KEY STUDY 10.7

Subincision in the Arunta (Speisman *et al.*, 1964)

Participants saw a film (*Subincision in the Arunta*), which shows aboriginal boys undergoing circumcision as part of a puberty rite. The boys are seen having their penises cut with a jagged flint knife. This usually causes high levels of stress in viewers of the film (and no doubt in the boys too!). In four different conditions, the sound track was manipulated, so that:

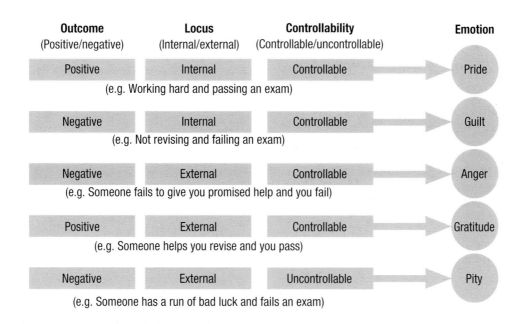

Figure 10.7 *Examples of how particular kinds of attribution can produce particular emotions (based on Weiner, 1986, 1992)*

- the pain, jaggedness of the knife and so on were emphasised (*trauma*);
- the boys' anticipation of entering manhood was stressed (*denial*);
- the emotional elements were ignored and the traditions of the aboriginal people were emphasised (*intellectualisation*);
- there was no commentary (*silent control*).

As predicted, arousal (measured by GSR and heart rate) was highest in the trauma condition, next highest in the control condition, and lowest in the other two. Clearly, what we tell ourselves about external situations (our cognitive appraisal of them) influences our level of arousal.

For Lazarus:

> '... emotion results from evaluative perception of a relationship (actual, imagined or anticipated) between a person (or animal) and the environment'.

He proposes that cognitive appraisal invariably *precedes* any affective reaction, although it doesn't have to involve any conscious processing. Zajonc (1984) argues that there is generally little direct evidence of either the existence or nature of such preconscious cognitive processing (although the study of *subliminal perception* suggests otherwise: see Chapter 15). Zajonc (1980a) argues that cognition and affect operate as independent systems, and an emotional response may precede cognitive processes under certain circumstances. For example, we may meet someone very briefly and form a positive or negative impression, despite not being able to remember any detailed information about them later (such as hair or eye colour: Eysenck & Keane, 1990).

Zajonc seems to overestimate the amount of cognitive processing which Lazarus and other cognitive appraisal theorists are claiming. For example, Lazarus simply argues that some minimal cognitive analysis at some level always precedes emotional experience. But this can be quite automatic, and so 'cognitive appraisal' is quite consistent with the sense of 'immediacy' which so much emotional experience has (and which Frijda (1994) sees as a characteristic of emotion).

So, what is an emotion?

Clore (1994) defines emotions as *mental states*. Neither physiological arousal nor feeling states provide the best way of trying to capture the nature of an emotion. Emotions are special kinds of feelings, namely those that we judge have an *emotional cause*. This is why feelings that are generated artificially by electrical stimulation or hormone injection or some other non-cognitive means, aren't emotions (see Marañon's study). For Clore, emotional terms seem to refer to something beyond feelings, to psychological states of which feelings are perhaps a necessary but not a sufficient condition.

Many of the examples Zajonc gives of emotion without cognition (*affective primacy* or 'preferences need no inferences') don't seem to be examples of emotional states at all. For example, when someone leaps out in front of you and shouts 'Boo!', your physiological and bodily response (including your facial expression) would be more accurately described as constituting a *startle reflex* than as the emotion of fear.

According to Scherer (1994), the classic debate between Lazarus and Zajonc, which had a major impact on the psychology of emotion during the 1980s, was mostly concerned with the level of processing involved, not whether *any* processing took place. This, in turn, revolved around the definition of 'cognition'.

"I know real men cry these days, Gerald, but not for getting soap in their eyes."

Reproduced with permission of www.CartoonStock.com

What is cognition?

If 'cognition' means or includes basic sensory processing, then most, if not all, emotions will have some cognitive component. However, LeDoux (1994) and Panksepp (1994), both biologists, suggest that the brain circuitry underlying emotion and cognition are different. Cognition is seen as depending on the neocortex and hippocampus (see Chapter 4). If 'cognition' is restricted to processes involving these brain areas, then emotion can occur without cognition, since non-humans with extensive lesions in these structures still display emotional responses.

Conclusions

According to Davidson & Ekman (1994), the older Lazarus–Zajonc debate has advanced considerably. Most theorists now acknowledge that emotion can be elicited in the absence of conscious cognitive mediation. If a broad view of cognition is taken, most would also agree that some cognitive processing is required for most emotion. Dalgleish (1998) maintains that the view that cognition is an integral part of emotion is predominant within the psychology of emotion. The challenge is to specify more precisely the types of cognitive processing that may be critical to the emotion generation process, and to identify the neural circuitries that underlie emotion and cognition respectively. We also need to study the interactions between emotion and cognition.

CHAPTER SUMMARY

- Ekman and Friesen identify six **primary**, universal emotions, which are probably innate. Plutchik's emotion wheel also incorporates primary emotions, but distinguishes these from complex emotions.

- An **evolutionary** approach to understanding primary or **basic** emotions includes considering their current function. But supposedly 'basic' emotions differ between cultures and over time within the same culture. They may be **psychologically** or **culturally basic** – not biologically.

- For each distinct emotion there is the **subjective experience**, **physiological changes**, **associated behaviour** and **cognitive appraisal** of the emotion-producing stimulus/situation.

- Darwin saw emotional behaviours (such as threat displays) as having evolved because they benefited those animals that used them effectively (they removed the need for actual combat).

- The **James–Lange theory** turns the commonsense theory of emotion on its head, by claiming that our emotional experience is the result of perceived bodily changes, in particular, skeletal changes.

- Studies by Valins (using the **false feedback paradigm**) and Laird (testing the **facial feedback hypothesis**) support the James–Lange theory, although they fail to take into account any visceral changes that may be taking place. They both suggest that physiological arousal isn't sufficient to account for emotional experience.

- Cannon criticised the James–Lange theory for assuming that different emotional states are associated with different patterns of ANS activity. The **Cannon–Bard theory** claims that the ANS responds in the same way to all emotional stimuli.

- Using the **directed facial action** and the **relived emotion methods**, Levenson reports physiological differences between anger, disgust, fear and sadness. The James–Lange and Cannon–Bard theories take too extreme a view regarding **physiological specificity**.

- Marañon's and Hohmann's studies support Cannon's claim that physiological arousal is not sufficient for emotional experience, although they indicate that it is necessary. However, Cannon's own study of cats, plus those of Sherrington and Dana, suggest that it might not even be necessary.

- According to Schachter's **cognitive labelling theory**, the experience of emotion depends both on **physiological changes** and **the interpretation** of those changes. Cannon was, therefore, mistaken in claiming that emotional experience and bodily changes are independent.

- Schachter and Singer's 'adrenaline experiment' demonstrates that while physiological arousal is necessary, the nature of the arousal is irrelevant. What's crucial is the **cognitive label** we give that arousal.

- Dutton and Aron's 'suspension bridge' experiment supports Schachter's theory, but also shows that our labelling of our arousal can be mistaken (the **misattribution effect**).

- Failure to replicate the adrenaline experiment suggests that emotional experience is much less malleable than Schachter claims, and that unexplained arousal is likely to be interpreted negatively.

- Cognitive labelling theory is essentially based on **attributional principles**. Several attributional theories of emotion have grown out of it, such as Abramson and Martin's theory of depression, and Weiner's theory.

- Lazarus's **cognitive appraisal theory** clams that some minimal cognitive analysis always precedes emotional experience, although this can be unconscious and automatic. Zajonc's **affective primacy theory** claims that emotional responses can occur without any cognition being involved.

- The basic disagreement between Lazarus and Zajonc seems to be about the **level of processing** involved, rather than whether or not any cognitive processing takes place. This, in turn, centres around the definition of 'cognition'.

Self-assessment questions

1. Describe and evaluate any **two** theories of emotion.
2. Discuss the claim that cognition is an integral part of emotion.
3. Assess the significance of physiological specificity in relation to **two or more** theories of emotion.

Web addresses

http://www.emotion.ccs.brabdeis.edu/emotion.html

http://www.erin.utoronto.ca/~w3psy398/answerkey2.html

http://serendip.brynmawr.edu/bb/

http://vassun.vassar.edu/~psych/FacultyPages/Spnotes2.html

http://www.britannica.com/bcomm/eb/article16/0,5716,33116+1,00.html

Further reading

Ekman, P. & Davidson, R.J. (Eds) (1994) *The Nature of Emotion: Fundamental Questions*. New York: Oxford University Press. A collection of original chapters by leading researchers in the field, covering all aspects of emotion.

Cox, T. (1978) *Stress*. London: Macmillan Education Ltd. An excellent source for theories of stress and research into the effects of stress on health, plus its management/alleviation. Also useful for emotion and the links between emotion and stress.

Lazarus, R.S. (1991) *Emotion and Adaptation*. Oxford: Oxford University Press. An excellent review of the topic, including his own ideas, by one of the key figures in modern emotion research.

Chapter 11

Learning and Conditioning

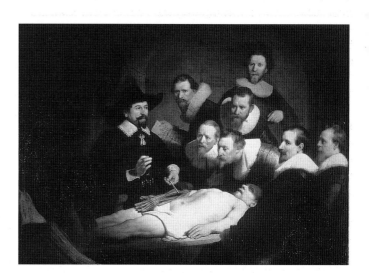

Introduction and overview

We've seen in earlier chapters how American psychology in particular was dominated by *behaviourism* for much of the first half of the twentieth century. Given the central role of learning in philosophical behaviourism, it's hardly surprising that the topic of learning itself should be central within psychology as a whole.

The concept of learning is a good example of the discrepancy between the everyday, common-sense use of a term, and its use in the scientific arena (see Chapter 1). When used in everyday conversation, the emphasis is usually on *what* is learned (the *end-product*), such as learning to drive a car, use the Internet, or speak French. But when psychologists use the term, their focus is on *how* the learning takes place (the learning process).

When the focus is on the end-product, we generally infer that the learning is *deliberate*. For example, we pay for driving lessons that will help us, eventually, to acquire a driving licence. But for psychologists, learning can take place without a 'teacher'. We can learn for example, by merely *observing* others, who may not even know they're being observed, let alone be trying to teach us anything. Learning can also happen without other people being involved at all, as when we observe recurring environmental events ('thunder always follows lightning').

So, the concept of learning as used by psychologists is very broad. Partly for this reason, psychologists disagree as to exactly what's involved in the learning process. Watson, the founder of behaviourism, was the first psychologist to apply Pavlov's concept of the *conditioned reflex/response* to human behaviour. A more active view of learning was taken by Thorndike, whose work formed the basis of Skinner's *operant conditioning*. Skinner's contribution, above all others, made behaviourism such a force within psychology as a whole (see Chapter 2).

What is learning?

Learning is a *hypothetical construct*: it can't be directly observed, but only *inferred* from observable behaviour. So, for example, if a person's performance on a task at Time 1 differs from performance on the task at Time 2, we might infer that learning has taken place. But if that change is observed just once, we may be much more hesitant about making such an inference. Learning, therefore, normally implies a fairly permanent change in a person's behavioural performance. Again, temporary fluctuations in behaviour can occur as a result of fatigue, drugs, temperature changes and so on, and this is another reason for taking permanence as a minimum requirement for saying that learning has taken place.

However, permanent changes in behaviour can also result from things that have nothing to do with learning, such as the effects of brain damage on behaviour, or the changes associated with puberty and other maturational processes. So, if a change in behaviour is to be counted as learning, the change must be linked to some kind of past experience (regardless of whether there was any attempt to bring about that change).

For these reasons, psychologists usually define learning as '... a relatively permanent change in behaviour due to past experience' (Coon, 1983), or '... the process by which relatively permanent changes occur in behavioural potential as a result of experience' (Anderson, 1995a).

Learning versus performance

Anderson's definition has one major advantage over Coon's, namely, it implies a distinction between *learning* (behavioural potential) and *performance* (actual behaviour).

Ask yourself ...

- What things have you learned to do/learned about, that you're not actually doing/thinking about right now?

If you can swim, you're almost certainly not doing so as you read this chapter – but you could readily do so if faced with a pool full of water! So what you could do (potential behaviour based on learning) and what you're actually doing (current performance) are two different things. But ultimately, of course, the only proof of learning is a particular kind of performance (such as exams). Performance can fluctuate due to fatigue, drugs, and emotional factors, and so is much more variable than learning, which is more permanent. (Exams come to mind again – many students have left an exam knowing what they couldn't demonstrate during the exam itself.)

Learning and other abilities

Howe (1980) defines learning as '... a biological device that functions to protect the human individual and to extend his capacities'. In this context, learning is neither independent of, nor entirely separate from, several other abilities, in particular memory and perception. Indeed, learning and memory may be regarded as two sides of the same coin (see Chapter 17).

According to Howe, learning is also cumulative: what we learn at any time is influenced by our previous learning. Developmental and learning processes are closely interlinked. Also, most instances of learning take the form of adaptive changes, whereby we increase our effectiveness in dealing with the environment. Similarly, Anderson (1995a) defines learning as '... the mechanism by which organisms can adapt to a changing and nonpredictable environment'.

Some basic questions about learning

While it's generally agreed by psychologists that learning is relatively permanent and due to past experience, there's much less agreement about exactly what changes when learning takes place, and what kinds of past experience are involved. Put another way, how do the changes occur and what mechanisms are involved? One important issue that divides psychologists is the extent to which they focus on the overt, behavioural changes as opposed to the covert, cognitive changes.

Behaviourist approaches

Skinner (1938) made the crucial distinction between *respondents* (or respondent behaviour), which are triggered automatically by particular environmental stimuli, and *operants* (or operant behaviour), which are essentially voluntary. A related distinction is that between classical or respondent (Pavlovian) conditioning, and operant or instrumental (Skinnerian) conditioning.

Classical conditioning: why do dogs drool over bells?

Ivan Pavlov was a physiologist interested in the process of digestion in dogs. He was awarded the Nobel Prize in 1904 (the year Skinner was born).

He developed a surgical technique for collecting a dog's salivary secretions. A tube was attached to the outside of its cheek, so the drops of saliva could be easily measured.

Pavlov (1927) noticed that the dogs would often start salivating *before* any food was given to them, as when they looked

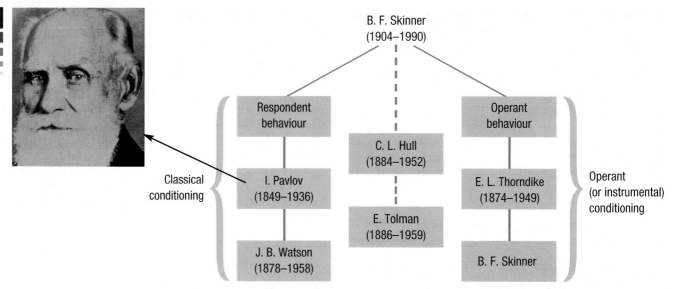

Figure 11.1 *Major figures in the behaviourist (learning theory) tradition*

at the food or saw the feeding bucket, or even when they heard the footsteps of the approaching laboratory assistant who was coming to feed them. These observations led to the study of what's now called classical (or Pavlovian) conditioning, whereby a stimulus (such as a bell), which wouldn't normally produce a particular response (such as salivation), eventually comes to do so by being paired with another stimulus (such as food) which *does* normally produce the response.

- *Before* conditioning, the taste of food will naturally and automatically make the dog salivate, but the sound of a bell won't. So, the food is referred to as an *unconditioned stimulus* (UCS), and the salivation is an *unconditioned response* (UCR): an automatic, reflex, biologically built-in response. The dog doesn't have to learn to salivate in response to food, because it does so naturally.
- During conditioning, the bell is paired with the food. Because the bell doesn't naturally produce salivation, it's

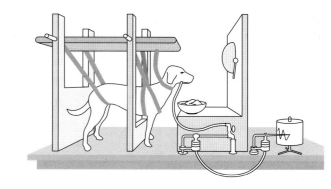

Figure 11.2 *The apparatus used by Pavlov in his experiments on conditioned reflexes*

called a *conditioned stimulus* (CS): it produces salivation only *on the condition* that it's paired with the UCS. It's also *neutral* with regard to salivation prior to conditioning.

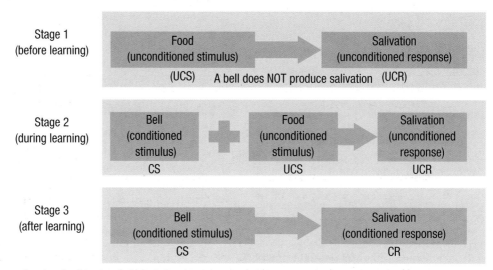

Figure 11.3 *The basic procedure involved in classical conditioning*

- If the bell and food are paired often enough, the dog starts to salivate as soon as it hears the bell and *before* the food is presented. When this occurs, conditioning has taken place. The salivation is now referred to as a *conditioned response* (CR), because it's produced by a conditioned stimulus (CS) – the bell.

This basic procedure can be used with a variety of conditioned stimuli, e.g. buzzers, metronomes, lights, geometric figures and so on. The exact relationship between the CS and the UCS can also be varied to give different kinds of conditioning. The procedure described above involves *delayed/forward* conditioning (see Table 11.1).

> ### Ask yourself ...
>
> - In the basic procedure described above, the CS is presented about half a second before the UCS. What do you think might happen if, instead, the CS is presented after the UCS?

Higher order conditioning

Pavlov demonstrated that a strong CS could be used instead of food, to produce salivation in response to a new stimulus which had never been paired with food. For example, a buzzer (previously paired with food) is paired with a black square. After ten pairings (using delayed conditioning), the dog will salivate a small but significant amount at the sight of the black square before the buzzer is sounded. Remember, the black square has never been associated with food directly but only indirectly, through association with the buzzer. It's as if the CS were functioning as a UCS.

The buzzer and food combination is referred to as *first order conditioning*, and the black square and buzzer pairing as *second order* conditioning. Pavlov found with dogs that learning couldn't go beyond third or fourth order conditioning. Even so, conditioning is beginning to look a rather more complex process.

Generalisation and discrimination

In *generalisation*, the CR transfers spontaneously to stimuli that are similar to, but different from, the original CS. For example, if a dog is trained using a bell of a particular pitch

and is then presented with a bell a little higher or lower in pitch, it will still salivate, although only one bell (the original CS) was actually paired with food. However, if the dog is continually presented with bells that are increasingly different from the original, the CR will gradually weaken and eventually stop altogether – the dog is showing *discrimination*.

CS_1 (The bell used in the original conditioning procedure) $\longrightarrow$ CR (salivation)

Bells CS_2, CS_3 and CS_4 are of increasingly lower pitch but still produce salivation through GENERALISATION
$\left.\begin{cases} CS_2 \longrightarrow CR \\ CS_3 \longrightarrow CR \\ CS_4 \longrightarrow CR \end{cases}\right\}$ Salivation is gradually becoming weaker as the pitch becomes lower compared with CS_1

Bells CS_5, CS_6 and CS_7 fail to produce salivation because they're sufficiently different from CS_1
$\left.\begin{cases} CS_5 \nrightarrow CR \\ CS_6 \nrightarrow CR \\ CS_7 \nrightarrow CR \end{cases}\right\}$ No salivation occurs

The dog is showing DISCRIMINATION

Figure 11.4 *An example of discrimination occurring spontaneously as a result of generalisation stopping*

Pavlov also trained dogs to discriminate in the original conditioning procedure. For example, if a high-pitched bell is paired with food but a low-pitched bell isn't, the dog will start salivating in response to the former, but not to the latter (*discrimination training*). An interesting phenomenon related to discrimination is what Pavlov called *experimental neurosis*.

> **Box 11.1** **Experimental neurosis: how to drive a dog mad**
>
> Pavlov (1927) trained dogs to salivate to a circle but not to an ellipse, and then gradually changed the shape of the ellipse until it became almost circular. As this happened, the dogs started behaving in 'neurotic' ways – whining, trembling, urinating and defecating, refusing to eat and so on. It was as if they didn't know how to respond: was the stimulus a circle (in which case, through generalisation, they 'ought' to salivate) or was it an ellipse (in which case, through discrimination, they 'shouldn't' salivate)?

Table 11.1 *Four types of classical conditioning based on different CS–UCS relationships*

1	Delayed or forward	The CS is presented *before* the UCS, and remains 'on' while the UCS is presented and until the UCR appears. Conditioning has occurred when the CR appears before the UCS is presented. A half-second interval produces the strongest learning. As the interval increases, learning becomes poorer. This type of conditioning is typically used in the laboratory, especially with non-humans.
2	Backward	The CS is presented *after* the UCS. Generally this produces very little, if any, learning in laboratory animals. However, much advertising uses backward conditioning (e.g. the idyllic tropical scene is set, and *then* the coconut bar is introduced).
3	Simultaneous	The CS and UCS are presented together. Conditioning has occurred when the CS on its own produces the CR. This type of conditioning often occurs in real-life situations (e.g. the sound of the dentist's drill accompanies the contact of the drill with your tooth).
4	Trace	The CS is presented and *removed* before the UCS is presented, so that only a 'memory trace' of the CS remains to be conditioned. The CR is usually weaker than in delayed or simultaneous conditioning.

Extinction and spontaneous recovery

If dogs have been conditioned to salivate to a bell, and the bell is repeatedly presented *without* food, the CR of salivation gradually becomes weaker and eventually stops altogether (*extinction*). However, if a dog that has undergone extinction is removed from the experimental situation, and then put back a couple of hours or so later, it will start salivating again. Although no further pairing of the bell and food has occurred, the CR of salivation reappears in response to the bell (*spontaneous recovery*). This shows that extinction doesn't involve an 'erasing' of the original learning, but rather a learning to *inhibit* or *suppress* the CR when the CS is continually presented without a UCS.

Classical conditioning and human behaviour

There have been many laboratory demonstrations involving human participants. It's relatively easy to classically condition and extinguish CRs, such as the eye-blink and galvanic skin response (GSR). But what relevance does this have for understanding human learning and memory, let alone thinking, reasoning or problem-solving (see Chapter 20)? In normal adults, the conditioning process can apparently be over-ridden by instructions: simply *telling* participants that the UCS won't occur causes *instant* loss of the CR, which would otherwise extinguish only slowly (Davey, 1983). Most participants in a conditioning experiment are aware of the experimenter's *contingencies* (the relationship between stimuli and responses), and in the absence of such awareness often fail to show evidence of conditioning (Brewer, 1974).

There are also important differences between very young children, or those with severe learning difficulties, and older children and adults, regarding their behaviour in a variety of *operant* conditioning and discrimination learning experiments. These seem largely attributable to language development (Dugdale & Lowe, 1990: see Chapter 19).

All this suggests that people have rather more efficient, language- (or rule-)based forms of learning at their disposal than just the laborious formation of associations between a CS and UCS. Even behaviour therapy, one of the apparently more successful applications of conditioning principles to human behaviour has given way to *cognitive–behaviour therapy* (Mackintosh, 1995: see Chapter 45).

Classical conditioning and phobias

Watson was the first psychologist to apply the principles of classical conditioning to human behaviour. He did this in what's considered to be one of the most ethically dubious psychology experiments ever conducted.

KEY STUDY 11.1

The case of Little Albert (Watson & Rayner, 1920)

Albert B.'s mother was a wet-nurse in a children's hospital. Albert was described as 'healthy from birth', and 'on the whole stolid and unemotional'. When he was about nine months old, his reactions to various stimuli were tested – a white rat, a rabbit, a dog, a monkey, masks with and without hair, cotton wool, burning newspapers, and a hammer striking a four-foot steel bar just behind his head. Only the last of these frightened him, so this was designated the UCS

(and fear the UCR). The other stimuli were neutral, because they *didn't* produce fear.

When Albert was just over eleven months old, the rat and the UCS were presented together: as Albert reached out to stroke the animal, Watson crept up behind the baby and brought the hammer crashing down on the steel bar! This occurred seven times in total over the next seven weeks. By this time, the rat (the CS) *on its own* frightened Albert, and the fear was now a CR. Watson and Rayner had succeeded in deliberately producing in a baby a phobia of rats.

The CR transferred spontaneously to the rabbit, the dog, a sealskin fur coat, cotton wool, Watson's hair, and a Santa Claus mask. But it didn't generalise to Albert's building blocks, or to the hair of two observers (so Albert was showing discrimination).

Five days after conditioning, the CR produced by the rat persisted. After ten days it was 'much less marked', but it was still evident a month later.

A very rare photograph of John Watson and Rosalie Rayner during the conditioning of Little Albert

---

Ask yourself ...

- Why do you think Watson and Rayner's experiment is considered to be so unsound ethically?

It's unclear whether Watson and Rayner intended to remove Albert's phobia. What is certain is that his mother removed him from the hospital before this could happen. They might have attempted to remove the phobia through the method of *direct unconditioning*, as used by Jones (1924: see Key Study 11.2). This is an early example of what Wolpe (1958) called *systematic desensitisation* (see Chapter 45).

KEY STUDY 11.2

The case of Little Peter (Jones, 1924)

Peter was a two-year-old living an a charitable institution. Jones was mainly interested in those children who cried and trembled when shown animals (such as frogs, rats or rabbits). Peter showed an extreme fear of rats, rabbits, feathers, cotton wool, fur coats, frogs and fish, although in other respects he was regarded as well adjusted. It wasn't known how these phobias had arisen.

Jones, supervised by Watson, put a rabbit in a wire cage in front of Peter while he ate his lunch. After 40 such sessions, Peter ate his lunch with one hand and stroked the rabbit (now on his lap) with the other hand. In a series of 17 steps, the rabbit (still in the cage) had been brought a little closer each day, then let free in the room, eventually sitting on Peter's lunch tray.

Behaviour therapists, such as Eysenck, regard the little Albert experiment as demonstrating how *all* phobias are acquired in everyday life.

B.F. Skinner

Ask yourself ...

- How could the basic classical conditioning procedure help to explain someone's fear of the dentist?

A fear of the dentist could be learnt in the following way:

- drill hitting a nerve (UCS) ⟶ pain/fear (UCR)
- sound of drill (CS) + drill hitting nerve (UCS) ⟶ pain/fear (UCR)
- sound of the drill (CS) ⟶ fear (CR).

If you're looking at the dentist peering into your mouth, you may become afraid of upside-down faces. If the dentist is wearing a mask, you may acquire a fear of masks too. Also, through generalisation, you can come to fear all drill-like noises or white coats worn by medical personnel or lab technicians (through generalisation).

Human phobias may be perpetuated through *avoiding* the object of our fears. In other words, we don't give the fear a chance to undergo extinction (see Chapter 43). This occurs in conjunction with *operant conditioning*, whereby the avoidance behaviour becomes strengthened through negative reinforcement.

Operant conditioning: why do rats press levers?

When Skinner drew the distinction between respondent and operant behaviour, he wasn't rejecting the discoveries of Pavlov and Watson. Rather, he was arguing that most animal and human behaviour isn't triggered or elicited by specific stimuli. He was interested in how animals *operate in their environments*, and how this operant behaviour is *instrumental* in bringing about certain consequences, which then determine the probability of that behaviour being repeated. Skinner saw the learner as much more active than did Pavlov or Watson (see Box 11.4).

Just as Watson's ideas were based on the earlier work of Pavlov, so Skinner's study of operant conditioning grew out of the earlier work of another American, Edward Thorndike.

Thorndike's law of effect

Thorndike (1898) built puzzle-boxes for use with cats, whose task was to operate a latch which would automatically cause

the door to spring open. Each time a cat managed to escape, there was a piece of fish, visible from inside the puzzle-box, waiting for it. The cats were deprived of food for a considerable time before the experiments began, and so were highly motivated. After eating the fish, the cats were put straight back in, and the whole process was repeated.

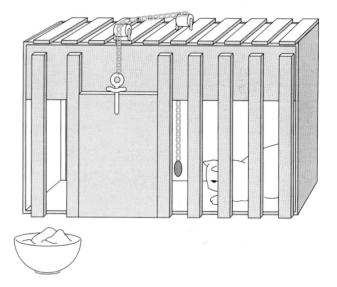

Figure 11.5 *Thorndike's puzzle-box*

At first the cats struggled to get out, behaving in a purely random way, and it was only by chance that the first escape was made. But each time they were returned to the puzzle-box, it took them less time to operate the latch and escape. For instance, with one of the boxes, the average time for the first escape was five minutes, but after 10–20 trials this was reduced to about five seconds.

Thorndike accounted for this by claiming that the learning was essentially random or *trial-and-error*. There was no sudden flash of insight into how the releasing mechanism worked, but rather a gradual reduction in the number of errors made and hence escape time (see Chapter 20). What was being learned was a connection between the stimulus (the manipulable components of the box) and the response (the behaviour which allowed the cat to escape). Further, the stimulus–response connection is 'stamped in when pleasure results from the act, and stamped out when it doesn't' (*law of effect*). This is crucially important as a way of distinguishing classical and operant conditioning, which Skinner did 40 years later.

Skinner's 'analysis of behaviour'

Skinner used a form of puzzle-box known as a *Skinner box*. This was designed for a rat or pigeon to do things in, rather than escape from. The box has a lever (in the case of rats), or illuminated discs (in the case of pigeons), under which is a food tray. The experimenter decides exactly what the relationship shall be between pressing the lever and the delivery of a food pellet, giving total *control* of the animal's environment. But it's the animal that has to do the work.

Skinner used the term *strengthen* in place of Thorndike's 'stamping in', and *weaken* in place of 'stamping out'. He regarded Thorndike's terms as too mentalistic, and his own as more objective and descriptive.

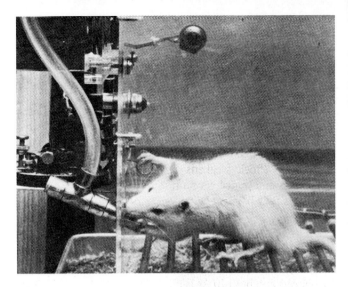

A rat in a Skinner box

Box 11.2	**Skinner's analysis of behaviour (or the ABC of operant conditioning)**

The *analysis of behaviour* requires an accurate but neutral representation of the relationship (or *contingencies*) between:

- **A**ntecedents (the stimulus conditions, such as the lever, the click of the food dispenser, a light that may go on when the lever is pressed);
- **B**ehaviours (or *operants*, such as pressing the lever);
- **C**onsequences (what happens as a result of the operant behaviour: reinforcement or punishment).

This is the ABC of operant conditioning.

According to Skinner's version of the law of effect, 'behaviour is shaped and maintained by its consequences'. The consequences of operants can be *positive reinforcement, negative reinforcement* or *punishment,* as shown in Figure 11.6.

While both positive and negative reinforcement *strengthen* behaviour (making it more probable), each works in a different way. *Positive reinforcement* involves presenting something pleasurable (such as food), while *negative reinforcement* involves the removal or avoidance of some 'aversive' (literally 'painful') state of affairs (such as electric shock). Punishment *weakens* behaviour (making it less probable), through the presentation of an aversive stimulus (as shown in Figure 11.7).

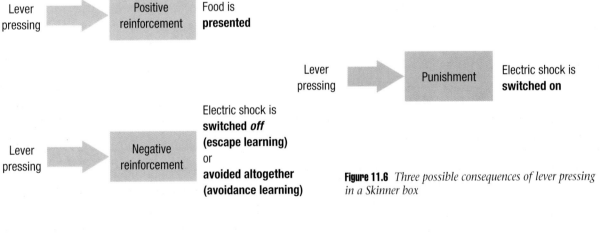

Figure 11.6 *Three possible consequences of lever pressing in a Skinner box*

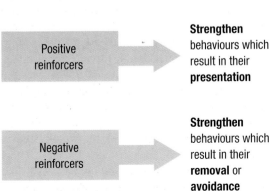

Figure 11.7 *The consequences of behaviour and their effects*

Reinforcers and reinforcement

Food itself is a reinforcer, electric shock a punisher. But the *process* whereby food is presented as a result of, say, lever-pressing is (positive) reinforcement, and when electric shock is presented instead it's called punishment. Skinner argues that deciding whether something is a reinforcer or a punisher can only be made *after* it's been made contingent on a specific behaviour on a number of occasions. So, if the behaviour is strengthened when followed by food, the food is a reinforcer, and if the shock weakens it, the shock is a punisher. Reinforcers and punishers cannot be defined *independently* of the effects they have on behaviour.

> ### Ask yourself ...
>
> * Do you consider this to be a valid way of defining reinforcers and punishers? Is it 'objective'?

Skinner's definition could be accused of circularity ('a reinforcer is whatever strengthens behaviour' and 'whatever strengthens behaviour is a reinforcer'). In practice, animals are starved for several hours before the experiments begin, to ensure they'll be motivated and find food reinforcing.

Skinner argues that his approach is more scientific, since the intended effect may not always coincide with the actual effect. For example, if a child who feels deprived of its parents' attention is smacked and shouted at when naughty, it's *more likely* to carry on being naughty. For a child who feels ignored, *any* attention is better than no attention at all. So, what is 'punishment' as far as the parents are concerned, may be a positive reinforcement for the child. Similarly, a positive reinforcement can only loosely be called a reward, since 'reward' implies that the rewarder *expects* to strengthen some behaviour, whereas 'positive reinforcement' refers to what has been shown to strengthen it.

Primary and secondary reinforcers

Primary reinforcers (such as food, water, sex) are *natural* reinforcers (reinforcing in themselves). *Secondary reinforcers* acquire their reinforcing properties through association with primary reinforcers, that is, we have to *learn* to find them reinforcing (through classical conditioning). Examples of human secondary (or conditioned) reinforcers are money, trading stamps, cheques and tokens (see Chapter 45).

In a Skinner box, if a click accompanies the presentation of each pellet of food, the rat will eventually come to find the click on its own reinforcing. The click can then be used as a reinforcer for getting the rat to learn some new response. Secondary reinforcers are important because they 'bridge the gap' between the response and the primary reinforcer, which may not be immediately forthcoming.

Schedules of reinforcement

Another important aspect of Skinner's work is concerned with the effects on behaviour of how frequently and how regularly (or predictably) reinforcements are presented. Ferster & Skinner (1957) identified five major schedules, each associated with a characteristic pattern of responding. This part of Skinner's research is largely counter-intuitive (Walker, 1984).

Rats and pigeons (and probably most mammals and birds) typically 'work harder' (press the lever/peck the disc at a faster rate) for scant reward: when reinforcements are relatively infrequent and irregular or unpredictable, they'll go on working long after the reinforcement has actually been withdrawn. So, each schedule can be analysed in terms of *pattern and rate of response* and *resistance to extinction* (see Table 11.2, page 152).

The rate of response can be represented by plotting responses cumulatively, as steps along a vertical axis, against the time when they're made along the horizontal axis. Skinner called this a *'cumulative record'*.

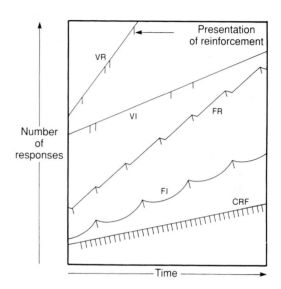

Figure 11.8 *Typical cumulative records for a response (such as lever pressing) reinforced using five schedules of reinforcement*

A continuous schedule is usually used only when some new response is being learned. Once emitted regularly and reliably, it can be maintained by using one of the four *partial* or *intermittent* schedules. But this change must be gradual. If the animal is switched from a continuous schedule to, say, a Variable Ratio (VR) 50, it'll soon stop responding. Skinner (1938) originally used an interval schedule, because a reinforcer is guaranteed, sooner or later, so long as one response is made during the interval.

Shaping: the reinforcement of successive approximations

Reinforcement can be used to build up relatively complex behaviour (not part of the animal's natural repertoire), by reinforcing closer and closer approximations to the desired behaviour (*shaping*). First, the behaviour must be broken down into a number of small steps, each of which is reinforced in sequence. Gradually, what the animal can do is much more like what the experimenter is trying to teach it. This is what animal trainers have been doing for hundreds of years, and is the method of reinforcement Skinner used to teach pigeons to play ping-pong or turn a full (anticlockwise) circle. Most human skills are learned in this step-by-step manner.

Shaping also provides an important foundation for *behaviour modification*, used to teach children and adults with

Table 11.2 *Common reinforcement schedules, and associated patterns of response and resistance to extinction*

Reinforcement schedule	Example	Pattern and rate of responding	Resistance to extinction	Example of human behaviour
Continuous reinforcement (CRF)	Every single response is reinforced	Response rate is low but steady	Very low – the quickest way to bring about extinction	1 Receiving a high grade for every assignment. 2 Receiving a tip for every customer served
Fixed interval (FI)	A reinforcement is given every 30 seconds (FI 30), provided the response occurs at least once during that time	Response rate speeds up as the next reinforcement becomes available; a pause after each reinforcement. Overall response rate fairly low	Fairly low – extinction occurs quite quickly	1 Being paid regularly (every week or month). 2 Giving yourself a 15-minute break for every hour's studying done
Variable interval (VI)	A reinforcement is given on average every 30 seconds (VI 30), but the interval varies from trial to trial. So, the interval on any one occasion is unpredictable	Response rate is very stable over long periods of time. Still some tendency to increase response rate as time elapses since the last reinforcement	Very high – extinction occurs very slowly and gradually	Many self-employed people receive payment irregularly (depending on when the customer pays for the product or service)
Fixed ratio (FR)	A reinforcement is given for a fixed number of responses, however long this may take, e.g. one reinforcement every ten responses (FR 10)	There's a pronounced pause after each reinforcement, and then a very high rate of responding leading up to the next reinforcement	As in FI	1 Piece work (the more work done, the more money earned. 2 Commission (extra money for so many goods made or sales completed)
Variable ratio (VR)	A reinforcement is given on average every ten responses (VR 10), but the number varies from trial to trial. So, the number of responses required on any one occasion is unpredictable	Very high response rate – and very steady	Very high – the most resistant of all the schedules	Gambling

learning difficulties to use the toilet, feed and dress themselves and other social skills. It's also been used to develop speech in autistic children and adult schizophrenics (see Chapter 45).

Negative reinforcement: escape and avoidance learning

Escape and avoidance learning are the two major ways in which negative reinforcement has been studied in the laboratory. *Escape learning* is relatively simple. For example, rats can learn to press a lever to turn off electric shock. *Avoidance learning* is more complex and more relevant to certain aspects of human behaviour (see Box 11.3).

Miller (1948) trained rats to run out of a white room, through a small door, into a black room by giving them shocks in the white room. After pretraining, the door was closed and could only be opened by the rat turning a wheel. Even though no further shocks were given, the residual 'aversiveness' of the white room (acquired through classical conditioning) was sufficient to motivate the rats to learn quickly to turn the wheel. This allowed them to run through into the 'safe' room, thus relieving their anxiety (negative reinforcement).

> **Box 11.3 Avoidance learning through negative reinforcement**
>
> Most laboratory studies use a shuttle box, a box divided into two compartments, sometimes with a barrier or door between them. Electric shocks can be delivered through the floor of either compartment independently of the other. Neither side is permanently safe, but only one is electrified at a time. The animal's task is to find which is the safe side on any one occasion. A *warning signal* (a light or buzzer) is given whenever the electrified side is to be changed, so the animal can always avoid being shocked if it switches sides when it hears (or sees) the signal.
>
> According to the two-factor theory (Mowrer, 1960) or the two-process theory (Gray, 1975):
>
> - the animal first learns to be afraid (the warning signal elicits an anticipatory emotional response of fear/anxiety through *classical conditioning*); and
> - it then learns a response to reduce the fear (jumping the barrier is *negatively reinforced* through avoiding the shock before it's switched on).

This illustrates an important difference between positive and negative reinforcement in relation to extinction. If we try to teach a rat a new response in order to get it into a black box which used to contain food, it will soon stop responding (it soon 'discovers' that the food is no longer available). But if a rat successfully escapes from a white room which used to be dangerous, it may go on escaping indefinitely (it doesn't stay around long enough to 'discover' that the shock no longer occurs).

So, responses motivated by conditioned fear/anxiety should take longer to extinguish than those motivated by positive incentives. Avoidance learning prevents the learner from testing reality, and this has been found in dogs and humans (Solomon & Wynne, 1953; Turner & Solomon, 1962). This can explain both the persistence of human phobias, and the use of methods to remove them based on the principle of *forced reality testing* (see Chapter 45).

Punishment

Skinner maintained that with both humans and non-humans, positive (and, to a lesser extent, negative) reinforcement is a much more potent influence on behaviour than punishment. This is largely because punishment can only make certain responses less likely: you cannot teach anything *new* by punishment alone.

However, Campbell & Church (1969) argue that punishments are, if anything, a *stronger* influence on behaviour than the incentive effects of reinforcements (at least as far as laboratory animals are concerned). The problem, however, is the unpleasant side-effects of stress, anxiety, withdrawal, aggression and so on.

Estes (1970) concluded that punishment merely *suppresses* lever pressing in the short term, but doesn't weaken it. Other experiments have shown that the strength and duration of the suppression effect depend on the intensity of the punishment and the degree of deprivation. However, the response is still suppressed rather than unlearned.

When alternative ways of obtaining reinforcers are available, punishment has a more powerful suppressive effect on the punished behaviour (Howe, 1980). For example, Azrin & Holz (1966) combined punishment and reinforcement, so that response A was punished while response B (incompatible with A) was positively reinforced. Skinner advocates this with human beings.

The antecedents of behaviour: stimulus control

In operant conditioning, the stimulus indicates the likely consequence of emitting a particular response: the operant behaviour is more likely to occur in the presence of some stimuli than others. If a rat has been reinforced for pressing the lever, it's more likely to go on emitting that response as the lever becomes associated both with reinforcement and the action of pressing (probably through classical conditioning). Technically, lever pressing has now come under the *stimulus control* of the lever. But there's still no inevitability about pressing it, only an *increased probability*. (This is why the term S–R psychology is sometimes used only to refer to classical conditioning.)

Similarly, drivers' behaviour is brought under the stimulus control of traffic signals, road signs, other vehicles, pedestrians and so on. Much of our everyday behaviour can be seen in this way. Sitting on chairs, answering the telephone, turning on the television, and so on, are all operants which are more likely to occur in the presence of those stimuli because of the past consequences of doing so.

A special case of stimulus control is a *discriminative stimulus*. If a rat in the Skinner box is reinforced for lever pressing only when a light is on, the light soon becomes a discriminative stimulus (the rat presses only when the light is on).

Box 11.4	Major similarities and differences between classical and operant conditioning

- They are both types of **associative learning**.
- **Generalisation**, **discrimination**, **extinction** and **spontaneous recovery** occur in both.
- In classical conditioning, the UCR or CR is **elicited** (triggered automatically) by the UCS or CS (it's essentially a reflex, involuntary response). In operant conditioning, behaviour is **emitted** by the organism and is essentially voluntary.
- In classical conditioning, the stimulus is guaranteed to produce the response, while the likelihood of a particular operant response being emitted is a function of the past consequences of such behaviour (it's more or less probable, but never certain).
- In classical conditioning, the UCS works in basically the same way regardless of whether it's pleasurable (such as food) or aversive (such as electric shock). In operant conditioning, responses that result in pleasurable outcomes are likely to be repeated, while those that result in aversive outcomes aren't.
- In classical conditioning, completely new stimulus–response connections are formed, while operant conditioning involves the strengthening or weakening of response tendencies already present in the animal's behavioural repertoire.
- In classical conditioning, the reinforcer (UCS) is presented regardless of what the animal does, and is presented **before** the response. In operant conditioning, the reinforcer is presented only if the animal emits some specified, pre-selected behaviour and is presented **after** the behaviour.
- In classical conditioning, the strength of conditioning is typically measured in terms of response magnitude (e.g. how many drops of saliva) and/or latency (how quickly a response is produced by a stimulus). In operant conditioning, strength is measured mainly as **response rate** (see Table 11.2, page 152).

Does conditioning work in the same way for all species?

The fact that many experiments involving a variety of species can all be described as classical conditioning doesn't in itself mean that there's only one mechanism involved, or only one explanation which applies, equally, to all species and all cases (Walker, 1984). Although *conditionability* seems to be an almost universal property of nervous systems (including those of sea snails, flatworms and fruit flies), many psychologists have argued that there can be no general laws of learning (Seligman, 1970).

If such laws exist, one of them is likely to be the *law of contiguity*: events (or stimuli) which occur close together in time and space are likely to become associated with each other. Most of the examples of conditioning we've considered so far would appear to 'obey' the law of contiguity.

KEY STUDY 11.3

Learning to feel as sick as a rat (Garcia & Koelling, 1966; Garcia *et al.*, 1966)

These represent an important exception to the 'law' of contiguity. In Garcia *et al.*'s study, rats were given a novel-tasting solution, such as saccharine-flavoured water (the CS), prior to a drug, *apomorphine* (the UCS), which has a delayed action, inducing severe intestinal illness (the UCR).

In two separate experiments, the precise time-lapse between tasting the solution and onset of the drug-induced nausea was either (a) 5, 6, 7, 8, 9, 10, 11, 12, 15, 16, 17, 18, 19, 20, 21, and 22 minutes, or (b) 30, 45, 75, 120 and 180 minutes. In (a), the rats received just four treatments (one every third day). In all cases, there was a conditioned aversive response to the solution: intestinal illness became a CR (a response to the solution alone). In some replications, just a single treatment has been required.

While rats can also be conditioned to novel smells, auditory, visual and tactile stimuli aren't so readily associated with internal illness. As for pigeons, it's impossible to deter them from water and, for other species, taste aversions are very difficult to establish, even if the animal is made very ill. In almost all species, aversions are learned more easily to new flavours than to familiar ones (saccharine solution is a novel taste for the rat).

Biological constraints on conditioning

It seems, then, that there are definite biological limitations on the ability of animals to develop a conditioned aversion. Similarly, rats typically learn very quickly to avoid shock in a shuttle box and to press a lever for food. However, they don't learn very readily to press a lever to avoid shock. Pigeons can be trained quickly to fly from one perch to another in order to avoid shock, but it's almost impossible to train them to peck a disc to avoid shock.

Findings like these have led Bolles (1980) and others to conclude that we cannot regard the basic principles of learning as applying equally to all species in all situations. We must take into account the evolutionary history of the species, as well as the individual organism's learning history. An important idea in this context is Seligman's (1970) concept of *preparedness*. Animals are biologically prepared to learn actions that are closely related to the survival of their species (such as learned water or food aversions), and these prepared behaviours are learned with very little training. Equally, *contraprepared* behaviours are contrary to an animal's natural tendencies, and so are learned with great difficulty, if at all. Seligman believes that most of the behaviour studied in the laboratory falls somewhere in between these two extremes.

As far as human behaviour is concerned, much of the relevant data relates to how easily certain conditioned fear responses can be induced in the laboratory or how common certain naturally occurring phobias are compared with others. For example, Ohman *et al.* (1975a,b) paired slides of snakes and spiders with a strong electric shock, and quickly established conditioned emotional responses to these slides – but *not* to slides of flowers, houses or berries.

Seligman (1972) observed that human phobias tend to fall into certain narrow categories, mostly animals or dangerous places. Most common of all were the fear of snakes, spiders, to dark, high places and closed-in places, and often there's no evidence for the fear actually having been previously conditioned (see Chapters 43 and 45). Also, classically conditioned responses extinguish faster in humans than animals. This is because the CRs are modulated by more complex human memories (Weiskrantz, 1982).

The role of cognition in conditioning

According to Mackintosh (1978), conditioning cannot be reduced to the strengthening of S–R associations by the automatic action of a process called reinforcement. It's more appropriate to think of it as a matter of detecting and learning about *relations between events*. Animals typically discover what signals or causes events that are important to them, such as food, water, danger or safety. Salivation or lever pressing are simply a convenient index of what the subject has learned, namely that certain relationships exist in its environment.

Classical conditioning

Pavlov himself described the CS as a 'signal' for the UCS, the relationship between CS and the UCS as one of 'stimulus substitution' and the CR as an 'anticipatory' response (or 'psychic secretions'), suggesting that his dogs were *expecting* the food to follow the bell. Consistent with this interpretation, Rescorla (1968) presented two groups of animals with the same number of CS–UCS pairings, but the second group also received additional presentations of the UCS on its own without the CS. The first group showed much stronger conditioning than the second, indicating that the most important factor (at least in classical conditioning) is how *predictably* the UCS follows the CS, *not* how often the CS and UCS are paired.

Blocking also supports a more cognitive interpretation (Kamin, 1969). For example, if an animal is shown a light, quickly followed by an electric shock, the light soon comes to elicit fear as a CR. If a noise is then added (noise + light + shock), then the noise should also soon become a CS, because it too is being paired with shock. However, this isn't what happens. If the noise is later presented alone, it fails to produce a CR. It seems that the noise has somehow been 'blocked' from becoming a CS because of the previous conditioning to the light. In cognitive terms, since the light already predicts shock, the noise is *irrelevant*. It provides no additional information – the animal already 'knows' that shock will follow the light.

Operant conditioning

Learned helplessness (Seligman, 1974, 1975)

Dogs were strapped into harnesses and given a series of shocks from which they couldn't escape. They were later required to jump a barrier in a shuttle box within ten seconds of a warning signal, or suffer 50 seconds of painful shock. While control dogs (which hadn't been subjected to the inescapable shocks) learned the avoidance response very quickly, about two-thirds of the experimental dogs seemed unable to do so. They seemed passively resigned to suffering the shock, and even if they did successfully avoid the shock on one trial, they were unlikely to do so on the next. Some dogs had to be pushed over the barrier 200 times or more before this learned helplessness wore off.

According to Seligman, the dogs learned that no behaviour on their part had any effect on the occurrence (or non-occurrence) of a particular event (the shock). This has been demonstrated using human participants by Miller & Norman (1979), and Maier & Seligman (1976) have tried to explain depression in humans in terms of learned helplessness (see Chapters 12 and 44).

Skinner's claim that reinforcements and punishments *automatically* strengthen and weaken behaviour has been challenged by Bandura (1977a). For Bandura:

> *'Reinforcements serve principally as an informative and motivational operation rather than as a mechanical response strengthener'.*

Reinforcement provides the learner with *information* about the likely consequences of certain behaviour under certain conditions; that is, it improves our prediction of whether a given action will lead to pleasant (reinforcement) or unpleasant (punishment) outcomes in the future. It also *motivates* us, by causing us to anticipate future outcomes. Our present behaviours are largely governed by the outcomes we *expect* them to have, and we're more likely to learn behaviour if we value its consequences.

This cognitive reinterpretation of reinforcement forms part of Bandura's *social learning theory* (SLT), which is discussed in more detail in relation to aggression (Chapter 29), and moral and gender development (Chapters 35 and 36). While not denying the role of both classical and operant conditioning, SL theorists focus on *observational learning* (or *modelling*), in which cognitive factors are crucial. This is reflected in Bandura's renaming (1986, 1989) of SLT as *social cognitive theory* (see Key Study 11.5).

Cognitive approaches

Tolman's cognitive behaviourism

Although working within the behaviourist tradition in the 1920s, 1930s and 1940s, Tolman would today be regarded as a cognitive psychologist. He explained the learning of rats in terms of inferred cognitive processes, in particular *cognitive* or *mental maps*.

Latent learning – who needs reinforcement?(Tolman & Honzik, 1930)

Group 1 rats were reinforced every time they found their way through a maze to the food box. Group 2 rats were never reinforced, and Group 3 rats received no reinforcement for the first ten days of the experiment but did so from day eleven.

Not surprisingly, Group 1 learned the maze quickly and made fewer and fewer mistakes, while Group 2 never reduced the time it took to find the food, and moved around aimlessly much of the time. Group 3, however, having apparently made no progress during the first ten days, showed a sudden decrease in the time it took to reach the goal box on day eleven, when they received their first reinforcement. They caught up almost immediately with Group 1.

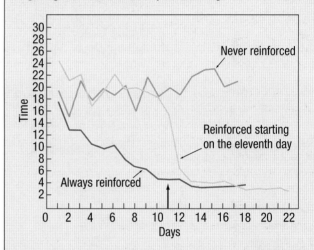

Figure 11.9 *The results of Tolman and Honzik's study of latent learning in rats*

Clearly, Group 3 rats had been learning their way through the maze during the first ten days, but that learning was *latent* (hidden or 'behaviourally silent'). In other words, it didn't show up in their actual behaviour until they received the incentive of the reinforcement on day eleven. Tolman and Honzik concluded that reinforcement may be important in relation to performance of learned behaviour, but that it's not necessary for the learning itself.

Tolman's (1948) *place learning* (or *sign learning*) theory maintains that rats learn *expectations* as to which part of the maze will be followed by which other part of the maze. Tolman called these expectations *cognitive maps*, a primitive kind of perceptual map of the maze, an understanding of its spatial relationships (much like the mental map you have of familiar streets leading to home or college).

Although a cognitive map can only be inferred from actual behaviour, it's difficult to know how else to explain the findings that rats will take short-cuts to the food box if the old path is blocked or how, if the maze were rotated, they could find the usual food location from several different starting points (Tolman *et al.*, 1946). Similarly, Restle (1957) flooded a maze immediately after a group of rats had learnt to run it, and they were able to swim to the goal-box with no more errors than when they'd walked. This clearly supports Tolman's interpretation that rats learn a cognitive map of the maze, not the individual movements of walking or running that take them to the food box.

Insight learning

Insight learning represents a view of learning as 'purely cognitive'. It stems from the Gestalt school of psychology, which is diametrically opposed to the S–R approach. The Gestalt psychologists are best known for their work on perception (see Chapter 15), and their view of learning is directly linked to their view of perception. Insight learning can be defined as a *perceptual restructuring* of the elements that constitute a problem situation: a previously missing 'ingredient' is supplied, and all the parts are seen in relation to each other, forming a meaningful whole. Some of the most famous studies of insight learning were conducted by Köhler, one of the founders of Gestalt psychology, with chimps. These, and other Gestalt studies of problem-solving, are discussed in Chapter 20.

Gagné's hierarchy of learning

Koestler (1970) believes that the debate between the S–R and cognitive theorists derives to a large extent from a refusal to take seriously the notion of *ripeness*. By this, he means a person's or animals' readiness to make a discovery or solve a problem, based on relevant knowledge, skills and past experience. Rats and cats have generally been presented with tasks for which they're biologically ill-fitted, and so the resulting learning was bound to appear gradual, piecemeal and at first quite random. But Köhler set chimps problems for which they were (almost) ripe, which gave the impression that all learning is based on insight.

Gagné (1970) has proposed a way of identifying the relationship between simple and complex forms of learning. Eight major varieties of learning are related hierarchically, with simpler abilities constituting prerequisites for more complex abilities (see Table 11.3).

Learning sets

According to Harlow (1949), S–R learning and insight learning are essentially two different phases of the same, continuous process. S–R learning predominates in the early stages, and insight develops out of prior S–R connections. Harlow suggests that the concept of a *learning set* (or 'learning to learn') represents an intervening process between S–R and insight learning. The greater the number of sets, the better equipped the learner is to adapt to a changing environment; a very large number of different sets 'may supply the raw material for human thinking'.

A learning set involves learning a general skill applicable to a whole new class of problems, a simple rule or code, based on

Table 11.3 *Gagné's hierarchy of learning*

1 Signal learning	Establishment of a simple connection, in which a stimulus takes on the properties of a signal (classical conditioning)
2 Stimulus–response (S–R) learning	Establishment of a connection between a stimulus and response, where the response is a voluntary movement and the connection is instrumental in satisfying a need/motive (operant conditioning)
1 and 2 are prerequisites for: **3 Chaining**	The connecting of a sequence of two/more previously learned S–R connections
4 Verbal association	The learning of chains that are specifically verbal, important for the acquisition/use of language. Enables several learned connections involving words to be emitted in a single sequence
3 and 4 are prerequisites for: **5 Discrimination learning**	Making different responses to similar stimuli. Involves more than simply making isolated S–R connections, because it's necessary to deal with the problem of interference between similar items
5 is a prerequisite for: **6 Concept learning**	Learning to make a common response to stimuli that form a class/category, but which differ in their physical characteristics. Requires representing information in memory, classifying events, and discriminating between them on the basis of abstract properties
6 is a prerequisite for: **7 Rule learning**	A rule is a chain of two/more concepts (e.g. 'if A then B')
7 is a prerequisite for: **8 Problem solving**	Involves recombining old rules into new ones, making it possible to answer questions and solve problems. Especially important for real-life human problem-solving situations

a *conceptual* (not a perceptual) relationship. In experiments with monkeys, Harlow demonstrated that insightful learning is itself (at least partially) learned and grows out of more random, trial-and-error learning.

Conclusions: Transfer of learning

Learning sets represent a special case of a more general phenomenon known as *transfer of learning* (or *training*). Essentially, transfer refers to the influence of earlier learning on later learning, which is an inherent feature of the learning process in general (Howe, 1980). Howe maintains that some kinds of transfer take the form of simple stimulus generalisation (equivalent to Gagné's signal learning), while in more complex learning situations transfer may depend on the acquisition of rules or principles that apply to a variety of different circumstances (Gagné's concept, rule learning and problem-solving). Learning sets can be viewed as intermediate between simple generalisation, and the more complex transfer phenomena involved in hierarchically organised skills.

CHAPTER SUMMARY

- **Learning** has played a major part in the development of psychology as a scientific discipline and is central to the **behaviourist** approach.
- Psychologists are interested in learning as a **process**. Theories of learning differ as to the nature of the process involved, especially the role played by **cognitive** factors.
- Learning involves a relatively permanent change in behaviour due to past experience. The distinction between **learning** and **performance** corresponds to **potential** and **actual behaviour** respectively.
- The distinction between **respondent** and **operant** behaviour corresponds to **classical** (**respondent** or **Pavlovian**) and **operant** (instrumental or **Skinnerian**) **conditioning** respectively.
- In **classical conditioning**, the pairing of a **conditioned** and an **unconditioned stimulus** results in the former eliciting a response that formerly was only produced by the latter.
- **Delayed/forward**, **backward**, **simultaneous** and **trace** conditioning differ according to the relationships between the conditioned and the unconditioned stimuli.
- **Generalisation**, **discrimination**, **extinction** and **spontaneous recovery** apply to both types of conditioning, making them more complex and versatile.
- Watson applied classical conditioning to human behaviour for the first time by inducing fear of a rat in Little Albert. Jones removed animal phobias from Little Peter using an early form of systematic desensitisation.
- Skinner's **operant conditioning** was based on Thorndike's **law of effect**. **Reinforcement** (both **positive** and **negative**) **strengthens** behaviour, while **punishment weakens** it.
- Different **schedules of reinforcement** can be analysed in terms of **pattern/rate of response** and **resistance to extinction**. **Variable** schedules involve high, steady rates of response and high resistance to extinction, compared with **fixed** and continuous schedules.

- **Escape** and **avoidance learning** are two forms of negative reinforcement. According to the **two-factor theory**, both classical and operant conditioning are involved. The persistence of human phobias can be understood in terms of avoidance learning.
- **Taste aversion** experiments contribute to the view that the basic principles of conditioning **don't** apply equally to all species in all situations.
- **Preparedness** helps to explain experimental findings which show that different species acquire certain conditioned responses more or less easily, and why certain human phobias are more common than others.
- Classical conditioning involves learning about **relations between environmental events**, rather than a simple strengthening of S–R associations.
- Tolman's studies of **latent learning** show that learning can take place in the absence of reinforcement. Rats learn **cognitive maps** of the maze, not the individual movements of walking or running leading to the food box.
- **Gestalt** psychologists saw **insight learning** as involving the **perceptual restructuring** of the elements that constitute a problem situation.
- Gagné's **hierarchy of learning** and Harlow's concept of **learning sets** show that insight and trial-and-error are related forms of learning. Learning set represents a special case of the more general **transfer of learning**.

Self-assessment questions

1 Describe and evaluate **either** classical **or** operant conditioning as an explanation of the behaviour of human **and/or** non-human behaviour.
2 Discuss the major similarities and differences between classical and operant conditioning.
3 Critically assess the role of cognitive factors in human **and/or** non-human learning.
4 Critically assess the claim that conditioning works in the same way for all species.

Web addresses

http://www.indiana.edu/~iuepsyc/Ch_8/C8E1.html

http://www.coedu.usf.edu/behavior/behavior.html

http://spsp.clarion.edu/topps/tptn5031.tm

http://www.coedu.usf.edu/behavior/listserv.html

Further reading

Walker, S. (1984) *Learning Theory and Behaviour Modification*. London: Methuen. A clear introduction to the basic concepts and issues, including the clinical applications of classical and operant conditioning.

Anderson, J.R. (1995) *Learning and Memory: An Integrated Approach*. New York: John Wiley & Sons. As the title suggests, an attempt to look at learning and memory as two sides of the same coin, so just as useful for Chapter 17 of this book as for the present one.

Chapter 12  *Application*

Health Psychology

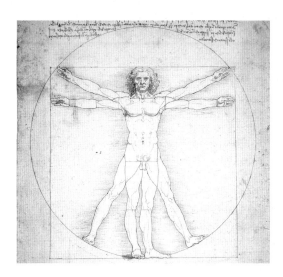

Introduction and overview

According to Ogden (2000), health psychology represents one of several challenges that were made during the twentieth century to the *biomedical model*. This model maintains that:

■ diseases come from either outside the body and invade it, causing internal physical changes, or originate as involuntary internal physical changes. Such diseases can be caused by chemical imbalances, bacteria, viruses, or genetic predisposition;

■ individuals aren't responsible for their illnesses, which arise from biological changes beyond their control. People who are ill are victims;

- treatment should consist of vaccination, surgery, chemotherapy, or radiotherapy, all of which aim to change the physical state of the body;
- responsibility for treatment rests with the medical profession;
- health and illness are qualitatively different: you're either healthy or ill, and there's no continuum between them;
- mind and body function independently of each other. The abstract mind relates to feelings and thoughts, and is incapable of influencing physical matter;
- illness may have psychological consequences, but not psychological causes.

In opposition to these ideas, health psychology maintains that human beings should be seen as complex systems. Illness is often caused by a combination of factors that can be biological (e.g. viruses), psychological (e.g. behaviours and beliefs), and social (e.g. employment). These assumptions reflect the *biopsychosocial model* of health and illness (Engel, 1977; 1980).

The shift to the biopsychosocial model reflects fundamental changes in the nature of illness, causes of death, and overall life expectancy, during the twentieth century. Average life expectancy in the USA has increased from 48 in 1900 to 76 in the year 2000. This is due mainly to the virtual elimination of death through infectious diseases, such as pneumonia, influenza, tuberculosis (TB), diphtheria, scarlet fever, measles, typhoid and polio. Although HIV and AIDS increased the percentage of infection-related deaths during the 1980s and early 1990s, at the beginning of the new millennium, the major killers are cardiovascular diseases (heart disease and strokes) and cancers, the former accounting for about 40 per cent of deaths in industrialised countries (Stroebe, 2000).

In fact, there's been a small but steady *decline* since the 1960s in deaths due to cardiovascular disease. This is due partly to improvements in medical treatment, but also to significant changes in lifestyle, specifically reduction in serum cholesterol levels and cigarette smoking. But at the same time, there's been an *increase* in deaths due to cancer in most industrialised countries, due almost entirely to increases in lung cancer. As Stroebe (2000) says, the influence of such non-medical factors is incompatible with the biomedical model. By conceptualising disease in purely biological terms, the model has little to offer in the way of *prevention* of chronic diseases through efforts to change people's health beliefs, attitudes and behaviour.

What is health psychology?

A brief history

Two of the other challenges to the biomedical model cited by Ogden (2000) are:

- *psychosomatic medicine*, developed in response to Freud's analysis of the relationship between mind and body (see Chapter 43); and
- *behavioural medicine*, which is concerned with health care, treatment, and prevention of physical diseases/physiological dysfunction, such as hypertension, addictive behaviours and obesity.

These are historical predecessors of health psychology (Penny, 1996). As we noted earlier, cardiovascular disease and cancer (and other chronic systemic disorders, such as diabetes) are the major killers in industrialised countries. The role of social and psychological factors is much more evident in the development and treatment of these diseases. The fact that they're chronic means that people may suffer them for many years, making psychological factors more relevant (Penny, 1996).

It was gradually recognised that psychologists could make a contribution to the health field, and health psychology formally began with the founding of the Division of Health Psychology within the American Psychological Association in 1978. The journal *Health Psychology* followed in 1982. In 1984, a Health Psychology Group was established within the British Psychological Society, which became the Health Psychology Section (1987), and finally the Special Group of Health Psychology (1992). There is also a European Health Psychology Society.

It became evident in the 1970s that national health spending in Western countries was getting out of control. Consequently, many countries began to explore disease *prevention*. The most powerful preventive strategy may be *health promotion*, and health psychology has made significant contributions in this area since the mid-1970s (Maes & van Elderen, 1998).

Definitions

Maes & van Elderen (1998) define health psychology as:

> '... a sub-discipline of psychology which addresses the relationship between psychological processes and behaviour on the one hand and health and illness on the other hand ... however ... health psychologists are more interested in "normal' everyday-life behaviour and "normal" psychological processes in relation to health and illness than in psycho-pathology or abnormal behaviour ...'.

From a health psychology perspective, they say, someone who avoids sex following a heart attack from fear of triggering another one is showing a normal, functional response to a dysfunctional situation, rather than an abnormal phobic response. However, Turpin & Slade (1998) maintain that within applied psychology there's a controversial debate regarding the boundaries between clinical and health psychology (see Chapter 1). They believe that health psychology is an *extension* of clinical psychology, focusing specifically on people with physical health problems and their associated psychological needs:

> '... we wish to stress the commonality of psychological approaches to mental and physical health. Indeed ... health and well-being should not be arbitrarily separated into "mental" and "physical". An approach that emphasises psychological, social and biological factors will be necessary for the understanding of all health problems ... it is essential to consider all three factors when seeking to account for experiences of health and illness'.

Turpin and Slade are advocating the biopsychosocial model that we saw earlier as the major alternative to the biomedical model of illness.

Defining health and illness

> *Ask yourself ...*
>
> - What do you understand by the terms 'health' and 'illness'? Are you healthy if you're not ill, or is health a more positive state than this?

Revisiting the biomedical model

According to the biomedical model, disease is a deviation from a measurable biological norm. This view, which still dominates medical thinking and practice, is based on several invalid assumptions. Most importantly, the *specificity assumption* maintains that understanding an illness is greater if it can be defined at a more specific biochemical level. This *reductionist* view (see Chapter 49) originated when infectious diseases were still the major causes of death (Maes & van Elderen, 1998: see above).

According to Maes & van Elderen, traditional medicine is more focused on disease than on health:

> *'It would be more appropriate to call our health care systems 'disease care systems', as the primary aim is to treat or cure people with various diseases rather than to promote health or prevent disease...'.*

By contrast with the biomedical model's *reactive* attitude towards *illness*, the biopsychosocial model underlying health psychology adopts a more *proactive* attitude towards *health*. Many definitions of health have been proposed since the 1940s, mostly in terms of the *absence* of disease, dysfunction, pain, suffering and discomfort.

Box 12.1 Defining health and illness

- According to the World Health Organisation (1948), *health* is:
  '... a complete state of physical, mental, and social well-being and not merely the absence of disease or infirmity'.
- *Disease* (which reflects the medical approach) is a:
  '... state of the body characterised by deviations from the norm or measurable biological or somatic variables...'. (Maes & van Elderen, 1998)
- *Illness* is:
  '... the state of being ill, implying that illness is a more psychological concept, which is closely related to one's own perception of a health problem (e.g. pain)...' (Maes & van Elderen 1998).

  Subjective psychological symptoms, such as anxiety, also play a substantial role in the construction of illness. Similarly, although illness is usually associated with evidence of medical abnormality:
  '... it also incorporates aspects of the individual's wider functioning, self-perceptions and behaviours, and requires consideration of social context and societal norms'. (Turpin & Slade, 1998)
- The concepts of health and illness incorporate physical, psychological and social aspects, reflecting the biopsychosocial model.

Revisiting the biopsychosocial model

In contrast with the biomedical model's reductionist view, the biopsychosocial model adopts a *holistic* approach, that is, the person as a whole needs to be taken into account. It maintains that both *'micro-level'* processes (small-scale causes, such as chemical imbalances) and *'macro-level'* processes (large-scale causes, such as the extent of available social support) interact to determine someone's health status.

Culture and health

Culture represents one of the 'macro-level' processes referred to above (see Chapter 47). *Cross-cultural health psychology* (Berry, 1994) involves two related domains:

- the earlier, more established study of how cultural factors influence various aspects of health;
- the more recent and very active study of the health of individuals and groups as they settle into and adapt to new cultural circumstances, through migration, and of their persistence over generations as ethnic groups.

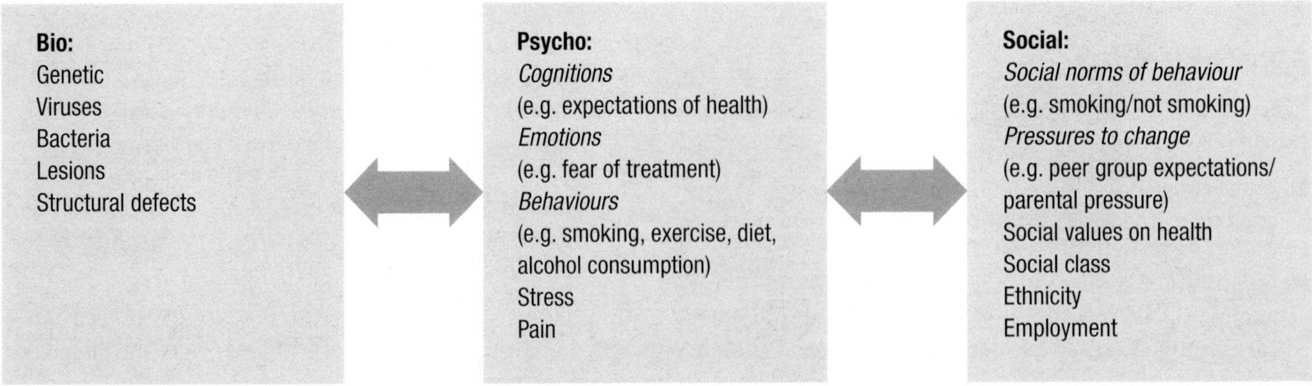

Bio:
Genetic
Viruses
Bacteria
Lesions
Structural defects
Psycho:
Cognitions
(e.g. expectations of health)
Emotions
(e.g. fear of treatment)
Behaviours
(e.g. smoking, exercise, diet, alcohol consumption)
Stress
Pain
Social:
Social norms of behaviour
(e.g. smoking/not smoking)
Pressures to change
(e.g. peer group expectations/ parental pressure)
Social values on health
Social class
Ethnicity
Employment

Figure 12.1 *The biopsychosocial model of health and illness (adapted from Ogden, Open University Press, 2000)*

Box 12.2   Health and disease as cultural concepts

Many studies have shown that the very concepts of health and disease are defined differently across cultures. While 'disease' may be rooted in pathological biological processes (common to all), 'illness' is now widely recognised as the culturally influenced subjective experience of suffering and discomfort (Berry, 1998: see Box 12.1).

Recognising certain conditions as either healthy or as disease is also linked to culture. For example, trance is seen as an important curing (health-seeking) mechanism in some cultures, but may be classified as a sign of psychiatric disorder in others. Similarly, how a condition is expressed is also linked to cultural norms, as in the tendency to express psychological problems *somatically* (in the form of bodily symptoms) in some cultures (e.g. Chinese) more than in other cultures (see Chapter 43).

Disease and disability are highly variable. Cultural factors (such as diet, substance abuse, and social relationships within the family) contribute to the prevalence of diseases including heart disease, cancer and schizophrenia (Berry, 1998).

Acculturation

Cross-cultural psychologists believe that there's a complex pattern of continuity and change in how people who've developed in one cultural context behave when they move to and live in a new cultural context. This process of adaptation to the new ('host') culture is called *acculturation*. With increasing acculturation (the longer immigrants live in the host country), health status tends to 'migrate' towards the national norm (Berry, 1998).

For example, coronary heart disease (CHD) among Polish immigrants to Canada increased, while for immigrants from Australia and New Zealand the reverse was true. Immigrants from 26 out of 29 countries shifted their rates towards those of the Canadian-born population. Similar patterns have been found for stomach and intestinal cancer among immigrants to the USA (Berry, 1998).

Ask yourself ...

• How could you explain such findings? What is it about living in a different cultural situation that can increase or decrease your chances of developing life-threatening diseases?

Was ET's near-fatal illness due to acculturation – or did he simply want to go home?

One possibility is exposure to widely shared risk factors in the physical environment (e.g. climate, pollution, pathogens), over which there's little choice. Alternatively, it could be due to choosing to pursue assimilation (or possible integration) as the way to acculturate. This may expose immigrants to *cultural* risk factors, such as diet, lifestyle, and substance abuse. This 'behavioural shift' interpretation would be supported if health status both improved *and* declined relative to national norms.

But the main evidence points to a *decline*, supporting the 'acculturative stress' (or even 'psychopathology') interpretation, that is, the very process of acculturation may involve risk factors that can reduce health status. This explanation is supported by evidence that stress can lower resistance to disease, such as hypertension and diabetes (Berry, 1998: see pages 175–177).

Other aspects of the biopsychosocial model include the beliefs that:

■ individuals aren't just passive victims, but are responsible for taking their medication, changing their beliefs and behaviour;

■ health and illness exist on a continuum: people aren't either healthy or ill, but move along the continuum – in both directions;

■ psychological factors contribute to the *aetiology* (causation) of illness – they're not just consequences of illness.

Ask yourself ...

• Can you think of examples of where being ill was (partly) caused by psychological factors, *and* where your illness affected you psychologically?

According to Ogden (2000), health psychology aims to:

■ *evaluate* the role of behaviour in the aetiology of illness, such as the link between smoking, CHD, cholesterol level, lack of exercise, high blood pressure (BP), and stress;

■ *predict* unhealthy behaviours. For example, smoking and the consumption of alcohol and high-fat diets are related to beliefs, and beliefs about health and illness can be used to predict behaviour;

■ *understand* the role of psychological factors in the experience of illness. For example, understanding the psychological consequences of illness could help to alleviate pain, nausea, vomiting, anxiety, and depression;

■ *evaluate* the role of psychological factors in the treatment of illness.

These aims are put into practice by:

■ *promoting* health behaviour, such as changing beliefs and behaviour;

■ *preventing* illness, for example, by training health professionals to improve communication skills and to carry out interventions that may help prevent illness.

Models of health behaviour

A fundamentally important question for health psychology is why people adopt – or don't adopt – particular health-related behaviours. Models of health behaviour try to answer this question, and most of those discussed below belong to the family of *expectancy-value models* (Stroebe, 2000). These assume that decisions between different courses of action are based on two types of cognition:

■ *subjective probabilities* that a given action will produce a set of expected outcomes;

■ *evaluation* of action outcomes.

Individuals will choose from among various alternative courses of action the one most likely to produce positive consequences and avoid negative ones. Different models differ in terms of the *types* of beliefs and attitudes which should be used in predicting a particular class of behaviour. They are rational reasoning models, which assume that individuals consciously deliberate about the likely consequences of behavioural alternatives available to them before engaging in action.

> ### Ask yourself ...
>
> • Do you agree with this view of people as rationally/consciously choosing health behaviours? How would you explain your own behaviours in relation to diet, smoking, alcohol, exercise and so on?

Health belief model (HBM)

This was originally developed by social psychologists working in the US Public Health Service (Becker, 1974; Janz & Becker, 1984). They wanted to understand why people failed to make use of disease prevention and screening tests for early detection of diseases not associated with clear-cut symptoms (at least in the early stages). It was later applied also to patients' responses to symptoms, and compliance with/adherence to prescribed medication among acutely and chronically ill patients. More recently, it's been used to predict a wide range of health-related behaviours (Ogden, 2000).

HBM assumes that the likelihood that people will engage in a particular health behaviour is a function of:

■ the extent to which they believe they're *susceptible* to the associated disease;

■ their perception of the *severity of the consequences* of getting the disease.

Together, these determine the *perceived threat* of the disease. Given the threat, people then consider whether/not the action will bring benefits that outweigh the costs associated with the action. In addition, *cues to action* increase the likelihood that the action will be adopted; these might include advice from others, a health problem, or mass media campaigns. Other important concepts include *general health motivation* (the individual's readiness to be concerned about health matters), and *perceived control* (for example, 'I'm confident I can give up smoking': Becker & Rosenstock, 1987).

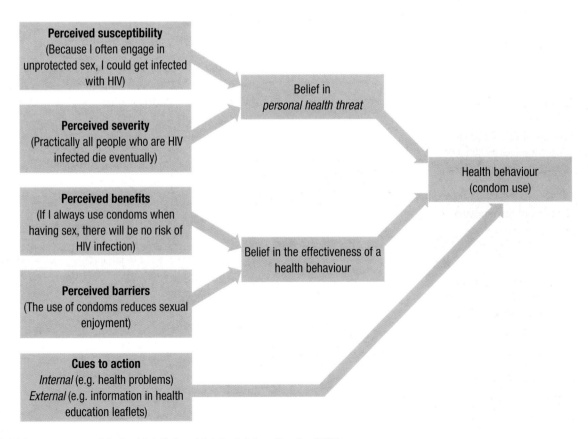

Figure 12.2 *Main components of the health belief model (adapted from Stroebe, 2000)*

Evaluation of HBM

There's considerable evidence supporting HBM's predictions, in relation to a wide range of behaviours. These include dietary compliance, practising safe sex, having vaccinations, having regular dental check-ups, and participation in regular exercise programmes. These are all related to people's perception of their susceptibility to the related health problem, their belief that the problem is severe, and their perception that the benefits of preventative action outweigh the costs (e.g. Becker, 1974; Becker *et al.*, 1977; Becker & Rosenstock, 1984).

However, there's also conflicting evidence. For example, Janz & Becker (1984) found that healthy behavioural intentions are related to *low* perceived seriousness (not high as the model predicts). Also, several studies have suggested an association between low perceived susceptibility (not high) and healthy behaviour (Ogden, 2000).

HBM has also been criticised for assuming that people's behaviour is governed by rational decision-making processes, overemphasising the individual, and ignoring emotional factors, such as fear and anxiety. There's also been a lack of standardisation of measures used to assess the model's various components, such as perceived susceptibility (Penny, 1996). A factor which may explain the persistence of unhealthy behaviours is people's inaccurate perceptions of risk and susceptibility.

Box 12.3 Are we unrealistic optimists?

Weinstein (1983, 1984) asked participants to examine a list of health problems and to answer the question 'Compared with other people of your age and sex, are your chances of getting [the problem] greater than, about the same, or less than theirs?'. Most believed they were *less* likely, displaying what Weinstein called *unrealistic optimism*: not everyone can be less likely! Weinstein identified four cognitive factors contributing to unrealistic optimism:

- lack of personal experience of the problem;
- belief that the problem is preventable by individual action;
- belief that if the problem hasn't yet appeared, it won't appear in the future;
- belief that the problem is uncommon.

These suggest that perception of one's own risk *isn't* a rational process. People show *selective focus*, ignoring their own risk-taking behaviour (for example, the times they've not used a condom) and concentrating primarily on their risk-reducing behaviour (the times they have). This is compounded by the tendency to ignore others' risk-reducing, and emphasise their risk-taking, behaviours. These tendencies produce unrealistic optimism.

Theory of reasoned action (TRA)

This theory has wider applications than just health psychology. It's been used extensively to examine predictions of behaviour and was central to the debate within social psychology regarding the relationship between attitudes and behaviour (see Chapter 24). TRA (Fishbein, 1967; Ajzen & Fishbein, 1970; Fishbein & Ajzen, 1975) assumes that behaviour is a function of the *intention* to perform that behaviour. A behavioural intention is determined by:

- a person's attitude to the behaviour, which is determined by (a) beliefs about the outcome of the behaviour, and (b) evaluation of the expected outcome;
- subjective norms: a person's beliefs about his/her social world. These are determined by normative beliefs, and motivation to comply.

Evaluation of TRA

TRA has successfully predicted a wide range of behaviours, including blood donation, smoking marijuana, dental hygiene, and family planning. However, attitudes and behaviour are only *weakly* related: people don't always do what they say they intend to (see Chapter 24). The model doesn't

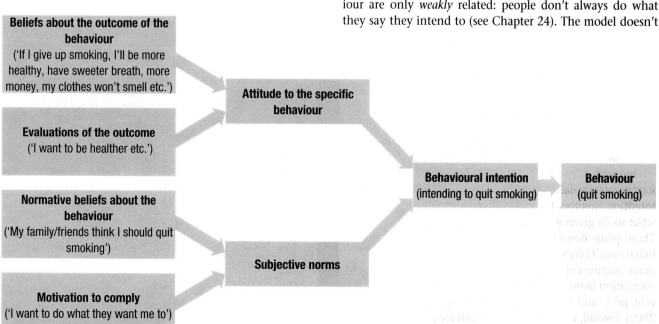

Figure 12.3 *Main components of the theory of reasoned action (adapted from Penny, 1996; Maes & van Elderen, 1998)*

consider people's past behaviour, despite evidence that this is a good predictor of future behaviour. Nor does it account for people's irrational decisions (Penny, 1996). Similarly, Maes & Elderen (1998) argue that:

> 'The assumption that behaviour is a function of intentions ... limits the applicability or heuristic value of the model to volitional behaviour, that is, to behaviours that are perceived to be under personal control...'.

Theory of planned behaviour (TPB)

This represents a modification of TRA. It reflects the influence of Bandura's (1977a, 1986) concept of *self-efficacy*, our belief that we can act effectively and exercise some control over events that influence our lives (see Chapter 35). Ajzen (1991) added the concept of self-efficacy to TRA, claiming that control beliefs are important determinants of the perception of behavioural control. This is crucial for understanding motivation: if you think you're unable to quit smoking, for example, you probably won't try. Perceived behavioural control can have a *direct* effect on behaviour, bypassing behavioural intentions.

Evaluation of TPB

TPB has been used to assess a variety of health-related behaviours. For example, Brubaker & Wickersham (1990) examined its different components in relation to testicular self-examination: attitude, subjective norm, and behavioural control (measured as self-efficacy) all correlated with the behavioural intention. Schifter & Ajzen (1985) found that weight loss was predicted by the model's components, especially perceived behavioural control.

TPB has the advantage over HBM (as does TRA) of including a degree of irrationality (in the form of evaluations), and it attempts to address the problem of social and environmental factors (normative beliefs). The extra 'ingredient' of perceived behavioural control provides a role for past behaviour. For example, if you've tried several times in the past to quit smoking, you're less likely to believe you can do so successfully in the future and, therefore, you're less likely to intend to try (Ogden, 2000; Penny, 1996).

An evaluation of models of health behaviour

As we've noted when discussing the models above, emotion is largely neglected, as are social and environmental factors. Another limitation shared by all the models is their failure to predict behavioural intentions consistently. Most seriously of all, they're unable to predict actual behaviour (*the intention–behaviour gap*).

One response to these criticisms has been the concept of *implementation intentions* (Gollwitzer, 1993). Carrying out an intention involves the development of specific plans about what to do given a specific set of environmental conditions. These plans describe the 'what' and 'when' of a particular behaviour. There's some evidence that encouraging people to make implementation intentions can actually increase the correlation between intentions and behaviour for taking vitamin pills, and performing breast self-examination (Ogden, 2000). Overall, though, current models are relatively poor predictors of actual behaviour (Turpin & Slade, 1998).

Lifestyles and health

Psychosocial determinants of sexual risk behaviour

Abstaining from penetrative sex is a rather unattractive option for most sexually active individuals. This is why research into strategies for reducing the risk of AIDS has focused mainly on psychosocial determinants of condom use, among both heterosexuals and gay men (Stroebe, 2000).

Heterosexuals

Sheeran *et al.* (1999) conducted a meta-analysis of factors influencing condom use, based on 121 studies. They found strong support for TRA and TPB (see above). Attitudes towards condom use, social norms, and intentions to use condoms were strongly related to condom use in both longitudinal and cross-sectional studies. There was also support for TPB's additional assumption that perceived behavioural control is likely to increase substantially the predictability of behaviour.

Sutton *et al.* (1999) failed to find a significant effect on behaviour of perceived behavioural control among a national sample of 946 young people in England. However, they did report a significant influence of attitudes and subjective norms. This may have been because all of the young people believed they had high control over condom use, regardless of the extent of their sexual experience (Stroebe, 2000).

> ### Ask yourself ...
>
> - How would HBM account for condom use? Would you expect it to be more/less successful than the other models?

Sheeran *et al.* found less support for HBM. Condom use should be determined by perceived threat of HIV infection (severity × vulnerability) and the perceived costs/benefits of condom use. But perceived threat seems to play a rather minor role. An even weaker association between vulnerability and condom use was reported in a meta-analysis of samples of heterosexuals and gay men (Gerrard *et al.*, 1996).

The original AIDS public health warning ad: AIDS as the scary iceberg. But perceived threat seems to play a rather minor role in condom use

Stroebe (2000) suggests that one factor which might have reduced the relationship between vulnerability and condom use is that the threat of HIV has now been known for many years, and individuals who were willing and able to adopt precautionary behaviour have already done so. This may also explain why knowledge of HIV and AIDS fails to influence condom use. While health education has to be continued to maintain the current level of knowledge, especially among the most vulnerable groups (adolescents), Stroebe observes that:

'... by now very few adult homosexual men are unaware of the health risks involved in unprotected anal intercourse. Thus the people who still engage in this high-risk activity do so knowing that it is dangerous'.

Sheeran *et al.* (1999) also found evidence of a strong association between (a) 'carrying a condom'/'condom availability' and (b) communication about condom use, with condom use. Neither of these two variables features in any of the models, although they could be seen as relevant to Gollwitzer's concept of *implementation intentions* (see above). Clearly, the availability of condoms is a precondition for their use, but carrying them reflects a strong intention to use them. Discussion between partners, about whether condoms should be used, was strongly associated with their actual use during sex.

Gay men

This last finding is consistent with results of intervention studies, which show that training in sexual negotiation skills increases safe sex among gay men (Stroebe, 2000). Overall, findings from studies involving gay samples based on TRA and TPB have been less consistent than those involving heterosexuals.

KEY STUDY 12.1

Partner relationship is the key to safe sex

Stroebe cites a study by de Wit *et al.* (in press), which found that the ability of TRA and TPB to predict safe sex (condom use and abstention from anal sex) depended very much on the relationship with the partner. With a steady partner, the intention to engage in safe sex was strongly related to attitudes, subjective norms, and perceived behavioural control. But with a casual partner, only perceived behavioural control proved to be a significant predictor of safe sex intentions. The same pattern emerged regarding the prediction of actual behaviour. TRA and TPB accounted for 64 per cent of the variance in safe sex behaviour with steady partners, but only 21 per cent with casual partners. Stroebe concludes that:

'... whether these homosexual men engaged in safe sex with their steady partner depended to a large extent on their intentions, but their safe sex behaviour with casual partners depended on their assertiveness and their social skills in persuading their casual partner to keep it safe'.

Another relevant study (de Vroome *et al.*, in press, cited in Stroebe) found that the better the relationship with their *steady partners*, the more likely gay men were to take protective measures with *casual partners*. But the quality of the relationship with the steady partner was *unrelated* to whether or not they had extra-relationship sex. These relational measures improved the prediction of behaviour, even when perceived behavioural control and intentions were controlled.

Implications for interventions

According to Stroebe (2000):

- interventions which rely on epidemiological information to emphasise the severity of AIDS, and the vulnerability of the target population, are likely to fail. These factors don't appear to be a major determinant of condom use. Instead, communications should aim at eroticising condom use;
- persuasive communications shouldn't only target beliefs, underlying attitudes, subjective norms, and perceived control, but also try to persuade people to be prepared, and to discuss condom use with their prospective partners;
- persuasive communications aimed at increasing condom use among gay men must differentiate clearly between condom use in steady as opposed to casual relationships. In the former, attitudes and subjective norms seem to be the crucial determinants of condom use, while in the latter it's perceived behavioural control. Persuasion and skills training respectively would probably be more effective.

Perceptions of invulnerability

According to Ogden (2000), one of the most consistent findings to emerge from the research is the perception of personal invulnerability to HIV, in both heterosexual and homosexual populations (see Box 12.3, page 163). For example, Woodcock *et al.* (1992) interviewed 125 16–25-year-olds about their sexual behaviour and examined how they evaluated their personal risk. Even though most acknowledged some degree of risk, some managed to dismiss it, by claiming 'it would show by now', 'it was in the past', 'AIDS wasn't around in those days [when I was most sexually active]', 'it's been blown out of proportion', and 'AIDS is a risk you take in living'. The themes of being run over by a bus, and 'it couldn't happen to me', were also quite common. These are classic examples of *rationalising* behaviour that conflicts with important aspects of self-concept as explained by Festinger's (1957) *cognitive dissonance theory* (see Chapter 24). Most commonly, people denied they'd ever put themselves at risk.

While most cognitive models, such as HBM, TRA and TPB emphasise people's rational decision-making, including their assessment of personal susceptibility to/being at risk from HIV:

'... many people do not appear to believe that they are themselves at risk, which is perhaps why they do not engage in self-protective behaviour, and even when some acknowledgement of risk is made, this is often dismissed and does not appear to relate to behaviour change'. (Ogden, 2000)

Exercise: doing what's good for you

Although most people, if asked, would agree that regular exercise is essential for improving health, such beliefs don't always translate into action. Even in the US, where health consciousness appears to be far higher than in Europe, only 15 per cent of the adult population exercise regularly and intensively enough in their leisure time to meet current guidelines for fitness (three times per week for at least 20 minutes at a time). This figure has changed very little during the 1990s, and we exercise less as we move from adolescence into adulthood (Stroebe, 2000).

> ### Ask yourself ...
>
> - What forms of exercise do you engage in on a fairly regular basis?
> - Why do you do it?
> - Why do you think people exercise less as they get older?
> - How do you think exercise benefits you?

The benefits of exercise

Physical benefits

Like high-fat, low-fibre diets, lack of exercise is correlated with an increased risk of CHD, and people who exercise regularly seem to accumulate less body fat (Carlson *et al.*, 2000). There is strong evidence that regular, vigorous, dynamic exercise decreases the risk of hypertension, cardiovascular disease, colon cancer, non-insulin-dependent diabetes mellitus, and death from all causes. It also appears to reduce symptoms of depression and anxiety, and improve mood.

Many researchers believe that such *aerobic* or endurance exercise, including jogging, cycling, and swimming, is superior to other forms of exercise for improving cardiovascular health. They involve expenditure of considerable amounts of energy, and increase blood flow and respiration, thereby stimulating and strengthening the heart and lungs, and increasing the body's efficiency in using oxygen.

> **Box 12.4 Do you have to sweat to benefit from exercise?**
>
> According to the American College of Sports Medicine (1979, in Stroebe, 2000), the most effective regime for developing and maintaining cardiovascular fitness is to exercise three to five times a week for 15–60 minutes per session, at more than 60 per cent of maximum heart rate.
>
> However, several short exercise sessions may be just as beneficial to men at risk of heart disease as a single lengthy burst of activity. Recent research conducted for the American Heart Association (in Henderson, 2000) examined the exercise habits and medical histories of over 7,300 men with an average age of 66. It found that physical activity needn't last longer than 15 minutes to reduce the risk of heart disease. The health benefits of a single lengthy exercise session were no greater than those that accrued from several short ones, provided the total amount of exercise was the same. Furthermore, men who participated in sport showed similar risks of heart disease as those who only walked or climbed stairs – provided the energy output was similar. However, the study also found that the *reduction in risk* of heart disease for men who jogged, swam, played tennis, or did aerobics (vigorous activities) was *greater* than for those who played golf or danced (moderate activities).

Psychological benefits

The effects of exercise on mood and cognition have been investigated by Sport and Exercise psychologists, both in the USA and the UK (see Chapter 31). But sports psychologists aren't interested only in 'professional' sportsmen and women. Exercise appears to be beneficial for mental health in several ways:

- many exercisers report feeling 'high' after exercise (the 'feel-good' effect: Carlson *et al.*, 2000);
- aerobic exercise reduces heart-rate response to psychological stress, making exercisers less vulnerable to the negative effects of stress (Carlson *et al.*, 2000: see pages 173–177);
- aerobic fitness programmes, such as jogging, dancing, and swimming are now frequently prescribed treatments for depression. There's evidence from both correlational and intervention studies that physical activity relieves the symptoms of depression and anxiety, and generally improves mood (Stroebe, 2000).

Psychological aspects of illness

The patient–practitioner relationship

Patient compliance: doing what you're told

Haynes *et al.* (1979) defined *compliance* as:

> '... the extent to which the patient's behaviour (in terms of taking medications, following diets or other lifestyle changes) coincides with medical or health advice'.

Damrosch (1995) prefers the term *adherence*, since this implies a more mutual relationship between the patient and the practitioner. 'Compliance' implies that the practitioner is an authority figure, while the patient is a fairly passive recipient (see Chapter 27).

> ### Ask yourself ...
>
> - Have you ever been non-compliant? For example, have you ever failed to complete a course of antibiotics?
> - Why didn't you comply?
> - Why do you think it's important to understand non-compliance?

This is an important area of research primarily because following health professionals' recommendations is considered essential to patient recovery. According to Damrosch (1995), poor adherence is almost epidemic. Reviews of adherence research have shown 20–80 per cent non-adherence, depending on the patient population and definitions used. Patients with chronic conditions (such as hypertension and diabetes) are less adherent than those with short-term problems. According to Ogden (2000), about half these patients are non-compliant.

But even with acute conditions, adherence is problematic. Patients are notorious for discontinuing antibiotics prematurely, even if prescribed for just a few days. Remarkably, patients who've undergone renal, liver, and heart transplants often fail to comply, despite good adherence prior to the transplant. Being informed that this can result in organ rejection and death, 34 per cent of renal patients still non-adhere. About 20 per cent of rejections and deaths in heart recipients are due to non-adherence (Damrosch, 1995). However, patients tend to overestimate their degree of compliance/adherence, because they wish to convey a socially desirable impression. Practitioners also tend to overestimate their patients' compliance. More objective methods of assessing compliance include pill counts, records of appointment keeping, physical testing, measures of cholesterol (to check on diet), and electronically monitored bottle caps (which record the date/time of every bottle-opening: Damrosch, 1995).

Box 12.5   What makes patients comply?

According to Damrosch (1995), there is theoretical agreement regarding the importance of five factors that make patients most likely to comply:

- they perceive the high severity of the disorder (*serious consequences*);
- they believe the probability of getting the disorder is also high (*personal susceptibility*);
- they have confidence in their ability to perform the behaviour prescribed to reduce the threat (*self-efficacy*);
- they're also confident the prescribed regimen will overcome the threat (*response-efficacy*);
- they have the intention to perform the behaviour (*behavioural intention*).

Damrosch refers to these five points as the 'double high/double efficacy/behavioural intention model'.

> *Ask yourself ...*
>
> - Which models of health behaviour do these five factors derive from?

Practitioner variables

Doctors' sensitivity to patients' non-verbal expression of feelings (such as tone of voice) is a good predictor of adherence. For example, Dimatteo *et al.* (1993) conducted a two-year longitudinal study of over 1800 patients with either diabetes, heart disease, or hypertension, and 186 doctors. The doctors' job satisfaction, willingness to answer questions, and practice of scheduling follow-up appointments, were all powerful predictors of adherence.

The way practitioners communicate their beliefs to patients also influences compliance. Misselbrook & Armstrong (2000) asked patients whether they'd accept treatment to prevent a stroke, and presented the effectiveness of this treatment in four different ways. Although the actual risk was the same in all four cases:

- 92 per cent said they'd accept the treatment if it reduced their chances of a stroke by 45 per cent (*relative risk*);
- 75 per cent if it reduced the risk from 1/400 to 1/700 (*absolute risk*);

- 71 per cent if a doctor had to treat 35 patients for 25 years to prevent one stroke (*number needed to treat*);
- 44 per cent if treatment had a three per cent chance of doing them good and a 97 per cent chance of doing no good/not being needed (*personal probability of benefit*).

According to Ogden (2000), these results indicate that:

'... not only do health professionals hold their own subjective views, but ... these views may be communicated to the patient in a way that may then influence the patient's choice of treatment'.

According to the traditional model of doctor–patient communication (the 'education model'), the doctor is an expert who communicates his/her knowledge to a naïve patient. The doctor is an authority figure, who instructs or directs the patient. Research has suggested that the communication process may be improved if a sharing, more interactive (two-way), patient-centred consulting style is used. This may produce greater patient commitment to any advice given, potentially higher levels of compliance, and greater patient satisfaction. However, a field experimental study by Savage & Armstrong (1990) of patients attending a group practice in an inner city area of London found a preference for the education model. Patients (aged 16–75, without serious illnesses) seemed to prefer an authority figure, who offered a formal diagnosis, to a sharing doctor who asked for their views.

Patient and regimen variables

In addition to what we said earlier about patients with certain disorders being more/less compliant, compliance is likely to decrease over time. It's also more problematic for conditions with no obvious symptoms, especially if treatment produces unpleasant side-effects, such as reduced sex drive. Also, the more complex the regimen, the lower the adherence. For example, home monitoring of blood sugar up to ten times per day, and multiple insulin injections, have been shown to reduce greatly or eliminate adherence. But this is a life-long practice, which is probably daunting to many patients (Damrosch, 1995).

According to Ley's (1981, 1989) *cognitive hypothesis model*, compliance can be predicted by a combination of:

- satisfaction with the process of consultation (see above);
- understanding of the information given;
- recall of this information.

Despite some supporting evidence, Ley's model is consistent with the education model of doctor–patient communication. Preferring a more interactive approach, Ogden and her colleagues have investigated (a) the level of agreement between patient and health professional, and (b) the impact of this agreement on patient outcome. It's important to understand the extent to which the two individuals 'speak the same language', share the same beliefs, and agree about the desired content and outcome of any consultation. This is especially relevant to general practice, where patient and health professional perspectives are most likely to coincide.

KEY STUDY 12.2

Not seeing eye-to-eye on depression and obesity

Ogden *et al.* explored GPs' and patients' models of depression. They agreed about the importance of mood-related symptoms, psychological causes, and non-medical treatments. But GPS had a more medical model.

Ogden *et al.* (2000, cited in Ogden, 2000) compared GPs' and patients' views on the causes of obesity. They agreed about most psychological, behavioural and social causes, but differed consistently regarding medical causes. In particular, patients rated glandular or hormonal problems, slow metabolism, and other medical causes more highly than the GPs did.

So, compared with their patients, GPs had a *more* medical model of depression, and a *less* medical model of obesity. It's possible that such disagreements may produce low compliance to medication and to recommended changes in behaviour, as well as low satisfaction with the consultation (Ogden, 2000).

Compliance and the placebo effect

Evidence suggests that simply adhering to medical recommendations to take pills may benefit patients recovering from a heart attack, *regardless* of whether the pills taken are active drugs or inert placebos (see Chapter 45). This has implications for understanding the mind–body relationship ('I believe I've taken my medication' is related to actually getting better: see Chapter 49), and the central role of beliefs and expectations in health and illness (Ogden, 2000).

Ogden cites data suggesting that the best predictor of mortality in men who'd survived a heart attack *wasn't* taking the lipid-lowering drug compared with a placebo, but adherence to taking *any drug at all* (active or placebo). Adherers had lower mortality after five years than non-adherers in both experimental and placebo groups. Ogden concludes by saying:

> '... *doing as the doctor suggests*' *appears to be beneficial to health, but not for the traditional reasons ("the drugs are good for you") but perhaps because by taking medication, the patient expects to get better...*'.

Pain

What is it?

> *Ask yourself ...*
>
> - Can you describe the experience of pain?
> - Are there different kinds of pain? If so, how do they differ?
> - Is pain a purely physical, bodily phenomenon?

According to the International Association for the Study of Pain (IASP), pain is:

> '... *an unpleasant sensory and emotional experience associated with actual or potential tissue damage, or described in terms of such damage*'.

This definition indicates that pain is a subjective, personal experience involving both sensory (e.g. shooting, burning, aching) and emotional (e.g. frightening, annoying, sickening) qualities. Fear/anxiety can increase the perception of pain, and depression often accompanies chronic pain, and is positively associated with the pain intensity ratings of chronic pain patients (Bradley, 1995).

Pain is basically a physiological phenomenon, whose biological function is to provoke special reactive patterns aimed at the removal/avoidance of the noxious stimulus. But this doesn't explain the pain *experience*, which includes both the pain sensation, and certain autonomic responses and 'associated feeling states' (Zborowski, 1952). For example, understanding the physiology of pain can't explain the tolerance of intense pain in torture, or the strong emotional reactions of certain individuals to the slight sting of a hypodermic needle. The IASP definition recognises that an individual needn't suffer actual tissue damage at a specific body site in order to perceive pain at that site, as in the 'phantom limb' phenomenon (see Chapter 4). In describing treatment of phantom limb pain, Ramachandran & Blakeslee (1998) maintain that:

> '... *pain is an opinion on the organism's state of health rather than a mere reflexive response to an injury. There is no direct hotline from pain receptors to 'pain centres' in the brain. On the contrary, there is so much interaction between different brain centres, like those concerned with vision and touch, that even the mere visual appearance of an opening fist can actually feed all the way back into the patient's motor and touch pathways, allowing him to feel the fist opening, thereby killing an illusory pain in a nonexistent hand*'.

According to Wall (in O'Connell, 2000), 'pure' pain is never detected as an isolated sensation. It's always accompanied by emotion and meaning, so that each pain is unique to the individual.

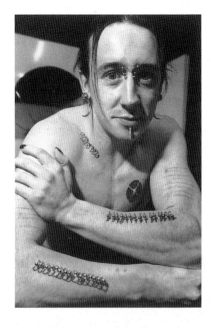

Body piercer Quille Desade after setting a new world record, with 75 separate insertions of foreign objects in his body

Pain and injury

Phantom limb pain is one of several examples of how it's possible to experience pain in the absence of any physical damage or injury. Others include *neuralgia* (nerve pain) and *caucalgia* (a burning pain that often follows a severe wound, such as stabbing), both of which develop *after* the wound/injury has healed. This represents the converse of phantom limb pain. People with *congenital analgesia* are incapable of feeling pain (a potentially life-threatening disorder), while those with *episodic analgesia* experience pain only minutes or even hours after the injury has occurred. This can sometimes be *life-saving*, as when soldiers suffer horrific injuries but suffer little or no pain while waiting for medical attention.

Pain as a cultural phenomenon

According to Rollman (1998), to say that pain is universal doesn't imply that it can be understood in only physiological or biochemical terms. The human pain experience comprises sensory, emotional and cognitive components. In both its expression and management, biological, psychological and social factors interact in complex ways. The influence of culture on the expression of pain almost certainly begins at birth, and extends throughout a person's lifetime.

In human society, pain acquires specific social and cultural significance. Members of different cultures may assume differing attitudes towards different types of pain. According to Zborowski (1952), two of these attitudes may be described as *pain expectancy* and *pain acceptance*.

- Pain expectancy refers to the anticipation of pain as being unavoidable in a given situation (such as childbirth, sport or battle).
- Pain acceptance is the willingness to experience pain, which is manifested mostly as the inevitable component of culturally accepted experiences (such as initiation rites and medical treatment).

So, labour pain is expected as part of childbirth. But in most Western cultures it's not accepted (and various steps are taken to keep it to a minimum), while in others (such as Poland) it's both expected and accepted (and little or nothing is done to relieve it).

Cognitive aspects of pain

Expectancy and acceptance are as much cognitive as emotional dimensions of pain. Trusting the doctor's ability to ease your suffering (whether this takes the form of a cure or merely the relief of pain and suffering) represents part of the *cognitive appraisal* aspect of pain, that is, the belief that the illness/symptoms are controllable. If we *attribute* our symptoms to something that is controllable, this should make us feel more optimistic (see Chapter 10). The *meaning* of our illness may be a crucial factor in how we react to it, which in turn may affect the illness itself.

Box 12.6 The meaning of illness

According to Brody (1995), the patient's health is most likely to change in a positive direction when the *meaning of the illness* has been changed for the patient in a positive way. For example, when Mr Smith goes to the doctor with an experience that means to him 'I might have cancer', and he leaves with an experience that means 'I have a bad case of bronchitis and it should be better in a few days if I take these antibiotics', there's a good chance that he will feel better and breathe more easily even before the antibiotics begin to take effect.

Although 'meaning' is hard to define, one component is giving patients an explanation (attribution) for their illness that is both understandable and as reassuring as is truthfully possible.

Treating pain

A number of methods and techniques used in the treatment of stress (see page 179) are also used for treating (mainly chronic) pain. Bradley (1995) groups these behavioural treatments into three major kinds: contingency management, biofeedback and self-management/cognitive–behaviour treatment.

Contingency management

This is a form of *behaviour modification* (see Chapters 11 and 45). Its goal is to achieve sufficient control over the patient's environment that reinforcement is withdrawn from 'pain' behaviours and made contingent on 'well' behaviours. Relatives are trained to positively reinforce the display of healthy behaviour at home, and to ignore the display of pain behaviour.

Biofeedback

This involves giving patients information (via monitors or buzzers) about certain autonomic functions (such as blood pressure, heart rate, muscle tension), enabling them to bring these functions under voluntary control. Bradley (1995) cites a study in which college students suffering from muscle contraction headaches were given seven 50-minute sessions, twice weekly, using feedback about muscle tension (electromyograph [EMG] biofeedback). They were also urged to practise their newly learned skills at home when free of headaches and at the first signs of a headache. Compared with a waiting-list control condition (no treatment until the study was over) and a placebo condition (which engaged in 'pseudomeditation'), the EMG biofeedback produced significant reductions in EMG and headache activity.

KEY STUDY 12.3

Giving birth the EMG way (Duchene, 1990)

Duchene used EMG biofeedback to reduce the acute pain associated with childbirth among 40 first-time mothers. They were randomly assigned to the experimental or control group, the former attending six weekly training sessions, and being loaned biofeedback machines for practice at home. The feedback was provided through both sound and a visual monitor, based on the tension of the abdominal muscles, which the women focused on relaxing when they felt a pain or contraction.

All the women were monitored for pain perception, starting at admission, and then at various points during labour, again at delivery and once more 24 hours after delivery (to recall the overall pain intensity). While 14 of the 20 control group women requested and had epidurals for pain relief, only eight of the experimental group did so (a significant difference). The experimental group's labours were also significantly shorter.

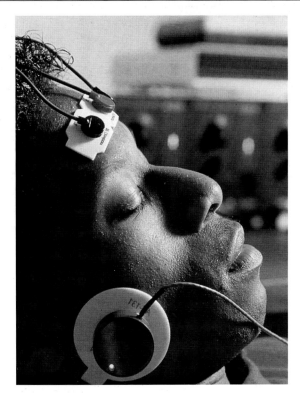

Figure 12.4 *Biofeedback*

Self-management/cognitive–behaviour treatment

This is based on the premise that patients' expectations influence their emotional and behavioural reactions to life events. This makes it critical that doctors help patients to believe that they can acquire the necessary skills for controlling pain and other forms of disability. Self-management interventions usually involve multiple treatments, such as learning coping skills, progressive muscle relaxation training, practice in communicating effectively with family members and health care providers, and providing positive reinforcement for displaying coping behaviour. Patients are encouraged to take responsibility for managing their pain, and to attribute their success to their own efforts. (See the discussion of cognitive–behaviour therapy for stress management, page 179.)

Stress

What is it?

Ask yourself ...

- What do you understand by the term 'stress'?
- Is the term used in different ways to refer to different things or processes?
- What makes you feel stressed, and how does it feel?

According to Bartlett (1998):

'... the notion that stress is bad for you and can make you ill has become a modern cultural truism. However, there is also a significant body of research evidence which lends support to this idea ... The study of stress must ... be central to ... health psychology which concerns, at its most basic level, the role of psychosocial processes in health and disease'.

Definitions of stress fall into three categories (Bartlett, 1998; Goetsch & Fuller 1995):

- stress as a *stimulus*;
- stress as a *response*;
- stress as *interaction* between an organism and its environment.

This classification corresponds very closely to three models of stress identified by Cox (1978):

- The *engineering model* sees external stresses giving rise to a stress reaction, or strain, in the individual. The stress is located in the stimulus characteristics of the environment: stress is what happens *to* a person (not what happens within a person).

The concept is derived from Hooke's law of elasticity in physics, which deals with how loads (stress) produce deformation in metals. Up to a point, stress is inevitable and can be tolerated, and moderate levels may even be beneficial (*eustress*: Selye, 1956). Complete *absence* of stress (as measured, say, by anxiety or physiological arousal) could be positively *detrimental* (for example, you could be so relaxed that you fail to notice the car speeding towards you as you're crossing the road). Stress helps to keep us alert, providing some of the energy required to maintain an interest in our environment, to explore it and adapt to it (see Chapter 9). However, when we're 'stretched beyond our limits of elasticity', it becomes positively harmful.

- The *physiological model* is primarily concerned with what happens *within* the person as a result of stress (the 'response' aspects of the engineering model), in particular the physiological changes.

The impetus for this view of stress was Selye's (1956) definition that 'Stress is the non-specific response of the body to any demand made upon it'. While a medical student, Selye noticed a general malaise or syndrome associated with 'being ill', regardless of the particular illness. The syndrome was characterised by:

- a loss of appetite;
- an associated loss of weight and strength;
- loss of ambition;
- a typical facial expression associated with illness.

Further examination of extreme cases revealed major physiological changes, (confirmed by Cox, 1978). This non-specific response to illness reflected a distinct phenomenon, which Selye called the *general adaptation syndrome* (GAS: see below, pages 173–175).

- The *transactional model* represents a blend of the first two models. It sees stress as arising from an interaction between people and their environment, in particular, when there's an imbalance between the person's perception of the demands being made of them by the situation, and their ability to meet the demands. Because it's the person's *perception* of this mismatch between demand and ability which causes stress, the model allows for important *individual differences* in what produces stress and how much stress is experienced. There are also wide differences in how people attempt to cope with stress, psychologically and behaviourally.

The engineering model is mainly concerned with the question 'What causes stress?', and the physiological model with the question 'What are the effects of stress?'. The transactional model is concerned with both these questions, plus 'How do we cope with stress?'.

What causes stress?

The causes of stress don't exist objectively, and individuals differ in what they see as a stressor in the first place (Lazarus, 1966). So, in this section we're really identifying *potential* stressors, the kinds of event or experience that most people are likely to find exceed their capacity to handle the demands that are involved.

Disruption of circadian rhythms

As we saw in Chapter 7, the word 'circadian' ('about one day') describes a particular periodicity or rhythm of a number of physiological and behavioural functions which can be seen in almost all living creatures. Many studies have shown that these rhythms persist if we suddenly reverse our activity pattern and sleep during the day and are active during the night. This indicates that these rhythms are internally controlled (*endogenous*).

However, our circadian rhythms are kept on their once-every-24-hours schedule by regular daily environmental (*exogenous*) cues called *Zeitgebers* (from the German meaning 'time givers'). The most important Zeitgeber is the daily cycle of light and dark. If we persist with our reversal of sleep and activity, the body's circadian rhythms will (after a period of acclimatisation) reverse and become synchronised to the new set of exogenous cues.

Individual differences and the effects of shift work

Some people take five to seven days to adjust, others take up to 14 days, and some may never achieve a complete reversal. But not all physiological functions reverse at the same time: body temperature usually reverses inside a week for most people, while the rhythms of adrenocortical hormone take much longer. During the changeover period, the body is in a state of *internal desynchronisation* (Aschoff 1979). This is very stressful, and shift-workers often report experiencing insomnia, digestive problems, irritability, fatigue, even depression, when changing work shifts. In shift-work, the Zeitgebers stay the same, but workers are forced to adjust their natural sleep–wake cycles in order to meet the demands of changing work schedules (Pinel, 1993).

> **KEY STUDY 12.4**
>
> **Night nurses aren't all the same (Hawkins & Armstrong-Esther, 1978)**
>
> Hawkins and Armstrong-Esther studied eleven nurses during the first seven nights of a period of night duty. They found that performance was significantly impaired on the first night, but improved progressively on successive nights. Body temperature hadn't fully adjusted to night-working after seven nights. There were significant differences between individual nurses, with some appearing relatively undisturbed by working nights, and others never really adjusting at all.

Jet lag

Other occupational groups affected by disruption to their circadian rhythms are airline pilots and cabin crews, who experience jet lag because they cross time zones during the course of the flight. If you've ever travelled across a time zone, you'll know what it's like to have your biological rhythms 'out of sync' with your surroundings. If you arrive in Washington DC at, say, 7 p.m. (after an eight-hour flight from London) you may be ready to start your evening's entertainment, but as far as your body is concerned, it's sleeping time (back in London it's 1 a.m., the middle of the night).

Most people suffer much less jet lag when travelling in an *East–West* direction than a West–East direction. When going West ('chasing the sun'), the day is temporarily lengthened. Because the natural circadian rhythm cycle is 25 hours (see Chapter 7), an increase in day length is much easier to deal with than a decrease. Secretion of *melatonin* reaches a peak during the night, helping to make us sleepy. After a long flight, the cyclical release of melatonin stays locked into the day–night pattern of the home country for some days. This could account for the fatigue felt during the day and the insomnia at night. If jet-lagged volunteers are given melatonin during the evening, far fewer report feeling jet-lagged than controls who receive only a placebo (Blakemore, 1988).

It has been found that cabin crews flying across time zones had significantly raised salivary *cortisol* (one of the *glucocorticoid* stress hormones) compared with when they flew short distances, and compared with ground crew. In a response-time test, the jet-lagged crew performed more poorly when there was a 25-second delay between presentation of the target symbol and having to recognise the symbol (but not when the delay was only one or five seconds (Cho *et al.*, 2000). De Quervain *et al.* (2000) found poorer recognition memory among non-flight crew participants given *cortisone* (another glucocorticoid). De Quervain *et al.* believe that raised glucocortocoid levels may cause impairments in memory retrieval in stressful situations such as taking exams, job interviews, combat, and giving courtroom testimony (see Chapter 17).

Life changes: the SRRS

Holmes & Rahe (1967) examined 5000 patient records, and made a list of 43 life events, of varying seriousness, which seemed to cluster in the months preceding the onset of their illnesses. Out of this grew the *Social Readjustment Rating Scale*

Rank	Life event	Mean value
1	Death of spouse	100
2	Divorce	73
3	Marital separation	65
4	Jail term	63
5	Death of close family member	63
6	Personal injury or illness	53
7	Marriage	50
8	Fired at work	47
9	Marital reconciliation	45
10	Retirement	45
11	Change in health of family member	44
12	Pregnancy	40
13	Sex difficulties	39
14	Gain of new family member	39
15	Business readjustment	39
16	Change in financial state	38
17	Death of close friend	37
18	Change to different line of work	36
19	Change in number of arguments with spouse	35
20	Mortgage over $10,000	31
21	Foreclosure of mortgage or loan	30
22	Change in responsibilities at work	29
23	Son or daughter leaving home	29
24	Trouble with in-laws	29
25	Outstanding personal achievement	28
26	Wife begins or stops work	26
27	Begin or end school	26
28	Change in living conditions	25
29	Revision of personal habits	24
30	Trouble with boss	23
31	Change in work hours or conditions	20
32	Change in residence	20
33	Change in schools	20
34	Change in recreation	19
35	Change in church activities	19
36	Change in social activities	18
37	Mortgage or loan less than $10,000	17
38	Change in sleeping habits	16
39	Change in number of family get-togethers	15
40	Change in eating habits	15
41	Vacation	13
42	Christmas	12
43	Minor violations of the law	11

Table 12.1 *Social Readjustment Rating Scale. The amount of life stress a person has experienced in a given period of time, say one year, is measured by the total number of life change units (LCUs). These units result from the addition of the values (shown in the right column) associated with events that the person has experienced during the target time period. The mean values (item weightings) were obtained empirically by telling 100 judges that 'marriage' had been assigned an arbitrary value of 500 and asking them to assign a number to each of the other events in terms of 'the intensity and length of time necessary to accommodate ... regardless of the desirability of the event relative to marriage'. The average of the numbers assigned each event was divided by 10 and the resulting values became the weighting of each life event (from Holmes & Rahe, 1967)*

(SRRS): see Table 12.1. Several studies have shown that people who experience many significant life changes (a score of 300 life-change units (LCUs) or over) are more susceptible to physical and mental illness than those with lower scores. The range of health problems include sudden death from cardiac arrest, non–fatal heart attacks, TB, diabetes, leukaemia, accidents and even athletics injuries.

Evaluation of studies using the SRRS

■ While many studies may have found statistically significant correlations between LCUs and subsequent illness, they are typically too low to be of any practical value (Lazarus, 1999)

■ The studies which claim to show that life change is responsible for illness are *correlational*. It's, therefore, possible that, instead of life events causing illness, some life events (e.g. being fired from work, sexual difficulties, trouble with in-laws, change in sleeping habits) are themselves early manifestations of an illness which is already developing (Brown, 1986; Penny, 1996).

■ Many of these studies are also *retrospective*. People are asked to *recall* both the illnesses and the stressful life events that occurred during the specified period, which is likely to produce unreliable data (see Chapter 17). For example, someone under stress (whatever the cause) may focus on minor physiological sensations and report these as 'symptoms of illness' (Davison & Neale, 1994).

Evaluation of the SRRS

■ The SRRS assumes that *any* change is, by definition, stressful, regardless of whether it's usually seen as positive (e.g. marriage) or negative (e.g. death of spouse). The available evidence seems to indicate that the undesirable aspects of events are at least as important as the fact that they change people's lives (Davison & Neale, 1994). A quick glance at Table 12.1 suggests that life changes have a largely negative feel about them, (especially those in the top ten which receive the highest LCU scores). So, the scale may be confusing 'change' and 'negativity'.

■ Some of the items are *ambiguous* (e.g. those that refer to 'changes in ...' could be positive or negative changes). Others (e.g. 6 and 12) refer to states of health, so the total LCU score is already 'contaminated' with an individual's current health status (Penny, 1996).

■ The list of life events is incomplete. For example, there's no death of a child, no reference to the problems of old age, and no mention of natural or 'man-made' disasters (Lazarus, 1999).

■ Life changes may be stressful only if they're unexpected and, in this sense, uncontrollable. In other words, it may not be change as such that's stressful, but change we cannot prevent or reverse. Studies have shown that when people are asked to classify the undesirable life events on the SRRS as either 'controllable' or 'uncontrollable', only the latter are significantly correlated with subsequent onset of illness.

The need for control

According to Parkes (1993), the *psychosocial transitions* that are most dangerous to health are those that are sudden and allow little time for preparation. The sudden death of a relative from a heart attack, in an accident or as a result of crime, are examples of the most stressful kind of life changes (see Chapter 39). Similarly, Brown (1986) suggests that it's *perceived uncontrollability* which makes life change stressful and, hence, dangerous to health.

Using Rotter's (1966) *locus of control scale*, and devising a new scale (the *life events scale*), Johnson & Sarason (1978) found that life-events stress was more closely related to psychiatric symptoms (in particular, depression and anxiety) among people rated as high on *external* locus of control than among those rated as high on internal locus of control. In other words, people who believe that they don't have control over what happens to them are more vulnerable to the harmful effects of change than those who believe they do. This is related to Seligman's (1975) concept of *learned helplessness* (see Chapter 11).

The hassles and uplifts of everyday life

By definition, most of the 43 changes included in the SRRS *aren't* everyday occurrences. Kanner *et al.* (1981) designed a *hassles scale* (comprising 117 items), and an *uplifts scale* (135 items). Kanner *et al.* define hassles as:

> '… the irritating, frustrating, distressing demands that to some degree characterise everyday transactions with the environment. They include annoying practical problems, such as losing things or traffic jams and fortuitous occurrences such as inclement weather, as well as arguments, disappointments, and financial and family concerns'.

Daily uplifts are:

> '… positive experiences such as the joy derived from manifestations of love, relief at hearing good news, the pleasure of a good night's rest, and so on'.

In a study of 100 men and women aged 45–64 over a twelve-month period, Kanner *et al.* confirmed the prediction that hassles were positively related to undesirable psychological symptoms. But the effect of uplifts was unclear, and research interest waned (Bartlett, 1998). They also found that hassles were a more powerful predictor of symptoms than life events (as measured by SRRS). 'Divorce', for example, may exert stress by any number of component hassles, such as having to tell people about it, handling money matters, and cooking for oneself. So, daily hassles may intervene between major life events and health. It's the cumulative impact of these day-to-day problems which may prove detrimental to health.

Evaluation of the hassles and uplifts scales

According to Lazarus (1999), life events (as measured by the SSRS) are *distal* (remote) causes of stress. We need to know the psychological meaning a person attaches to an environmental event, the personal significance of what's happening (the *proximal* cause). This is what makes Kanner *et al.*'s scales a more valid approach. According to Lazarus (1999):

> 'Although daily hassles are far less dramatic than major life changes … and what constitutes a hassle varies greatly from person to person, our research has suggested that, especially when they pile up or touch on special areas of vulnerability … they can be very stressful for some people and very important for their subjective well-being and physical health …'.

Bartlett (1998) claims that implicit in the concept of hassles is a stimulus-based definition of stress. This is inconsistent with the transactional approach which Lazarus advocates. This apparent contradiction stems from focusing on the hassles themselves, while simultaneously believing that it's their psychological meaning that causes stress.

Occupation-linked stressors

People working in the emergency services (police, fire, ambulance, emergency medical teams, and mountain rescue) routinely encounter death, tragedy, and horror. They're required to deal with people in pain and distress, and handle dead bodies. They may also face personal danger and injury.

McLeod (2000) studied over 800 fire-fighters, giving them a number of standard measures of stress and coping including the SRRS, Maslach & Jackson's (1981) *burnout scale*, and the *impact of event scale* (Horowitz *et al.*, 1979), a measure of post-traumatic stress disorder/PTSD (see Chapter 44). McLeod found that individuals in different roles experience varying patterns of stress, and cope in different ways. For example, the highest overall stress levels were found amongst the day-manning fire-fighters, who live close to the station and are frequently on call. But sub-officers are the most likely to experience PTSD: they're typically first on the scene of an incident and are most intensely exposed to the suffering of fire and road traffic accident victims.

Box 12.7	Caring for others is bad for your health: nurses and stress

In the case of nursing, intrinsic sources of stress (such as constantly having to deal with patients' pain, anxiety and death, as well as giving emotional support to patients' families) are made worse by the inadequate training received for handling such demands (Gaze, 1988). Those working in specialised areas or departments face additional demands. For example, nurses in ITU (intensive care) have to maintain high levels of concentration for long periods, are often emotionally drained by continuous close contact with distressed and frightened families, and the process of dying may not follow a natural course: technology (such as ventilators) and drugs may prolong it (Fromant, 1988).

Medical staff working in A & E are in the front line at times of major disasters, such as the 1989 Hillsborough disaster. However well prepared they may be practically, nothing can prepare them for the emotional demands. As David Smith, Charge Nurse at the Royal Hallamshire Hospital A & E Department in Sheffield which dealt with the Hillsborough casualties, put it: 'On the day, you deal with what happens. But it's the fall-out afterwards that's the problem' (in Owen, 1990).

What are the effects of stress?

The general adaptation syndrome (GAS)

According to Selye (1956), GAS represents the body's defence against stress. The body responds in the same way to any stressor, whether it's environmental or arises from within the body itself. He initially observed that injecting extracts of ovary tissue into rats produced enlargement of the adrenal glands, shrinkage of the thymus gland, and bleeding ulcers. When he used extracts of other organs (pituitary, kidney and spleen), as well as substances not derived from bodily tissue, the *same* responses were produced. He eventually found that this same 'triad' of 'non-specific' responses could be produced by such different stimuli as insulin, excessive cold or heat, X-rays, sleep and water deprivation and electric shock. Selye (1956) defined stress as:

> '... the individual's psychophysiological response, mediated largely by the autonomic nervous system and the endocrine system, to any demands made on the individual'.

GAS comprises three stages: the *alarm reaction, resistance* and *exhaustion*.

Alarm reaction

When a stimulus is perceived as a stressor, there's a brief, initial *shock phase*. Resistance to the stressor is lowered. But this is quickly followed by the *countershock phase*. The sympathetic branch of the ANS is activated, which, in turn, stimulates the *adrenal medulla* to secrete increased levels of adrenaline and noradrenaline (*catecholamines*). These are associated with sympathetic changes, collectively referred to as the *fight or flight syndrome* (see Chapter 4). The catecholamines mimic sympathetic arousal (and so are 'sympathomimetics'), and noradrenaline is the transmitter at the synapses of the sympathetic branch of the ANS. Consequently, noradrenaline from

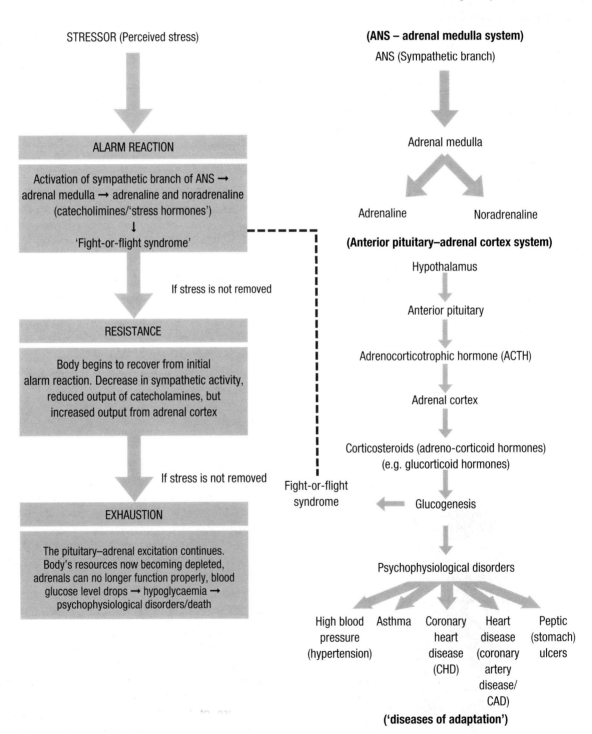

Figure 12.5 *Summary diagram of the three stages of the general adaptation syndrome (GAS) (Selye) and their relationship to the physiological changes associated with (i) the ANS – adrenal medulla and (ii) anterior pituitary – adrenal cortex systems (Cannon)*

the adrenals prolongs the action of noradrenaline released at synapses in the ANS. This prolongs sympathetic arousal after the stressor's removal. This is referred to as the *ANS–adrenal–medulla system* (or *sympatho–adrenomedullary axis*).

Resistance

If the stressor isn't removed, there's a decrease in sympathetic activity, but an increase in output from the other part of the adrenal gland, the adrenal cortex. This is controlled by the amount of adrenocorticotrophic hormone (ACTH) in the blood. ACTH is released from the anterior pituitary (the 'master' endocrine gland) upon instructions from the hypothalamus. The adrenal cortex is essential for the maintenance of life and its removal results in death.

The effect of ACTH is to stimulate the adrenal cortex to release corticosteroids (or adrenocorticoid hormones), one group of which are the glucocorticoid hormones (chiefly, corticosterone, cortisol and hydrocortisone). These control and conserve the amount of glucose in the blood (glucogenesis), which helps to resist stress of all kinds. The glucocorticoids convert protein into glucose, make fats available for energy, increase blood flow and generally stimulate behavioural responsiveness. In this way, the *anterior pituitary–adrenal cortex system* (or *hypothalamic–pituitary–adrenal axis*) contributes to the fight or flight syndrome.

Exhaustion

Once ACTH and corticosteroids are circulating in the bloodstream, they tend to inhibit the further release of ACTH from the pituitary. If the stressor is removed during the resistance stage, blood sugar levels will gradually return to normal. However, when the stress situation continues, the pituitary–adrenal excitation will continue. The body's resources are now becoming depleted, the adrenals can no longer function properly, blood glucose levels drop and, in extreme cases, hypoglycaemia could result in death.

It's at this stage that *psychophysiological disorders* develop, including high blood pressure (hypertension), heart disease (coronary artery disease, CAD), coronary heart disease (CHD), asthma and peptic (stomach) ulcers. Selye called these the *diseases of adaptation*.

An exhausted, stressed-out, junior hospital doctor

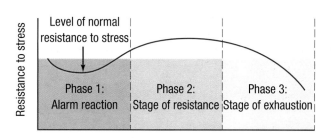

Figure 12.6 *Three stages of GAS*

Evaluation of GAS

Lazarus (1999) cites a study of patients dying from injury or disease. Post-mortem examination showed that those who remained unconscious had normal levels of corticosteroids, while the opposite was true for those who were conscious (and therefore presumably aware they were dying). Lazarus infers from this that:

'… some psychological awareness – akin to a conscious perception or appraisal – of the psychological significance of what is happening may be necessary to produce the adrenal cortical changes of the GAS'.

While Selye helped us understand how stressors affect the body, in order to understand what makes a psychological event stressful, we must put the person into the equation. In effect, says Lazarus:

'… it takes both the stressful stimulus conditions and a vulnerable person to generate a stress reaction …'.

How does stress make us ill?

An evolutionary perspective

The sympathetic branch of the ANS responds as a unit, causing a state of generalised, undifferentiated arousal. This was probably of crucial importance in our evolutionary past, when our ancestors were frequently confronted by life-threatening dangers. This is precisely what the *fight or flight syndrome* is for. While an increase in heart rate may be necessary to supply more blood to the muscles when facing a hungry-looking bear, it may be quite irrelevant to most of the stressors we face in modern life, which involve a far higher psychological element. Most commonly encountered stressors *don't* pose physical threat, but our nervous and endocrine systems have evolved in such a way that we typically react to stressors as if they did. What may have been adaptive responses for our ancestors have become maladaptive today. So, what happens to all that internal activity?

- In the case of heart rate and blood pressure (BP), chronic stress will involve repeated episodes of increases in heart rate and BP which, in turn, produce increases in plaque formation within the cardiovascular system.
- Stress also produces an increase in blood cholesterol levels, through the action of adrenaline and noradrenaline on the release of free fatty acids. This produces a clumping together of cholesterol particles, leading to clots in the blood and in the artery walls and occlusion of the arteries. In turn, raised heart rate is related to a more rapid build-up

of cholesterol on artery walls. High BP results in small lesions on the artery walls, and cholesterol tends to get trapped in these lesions (Holmes, 1994).

Stress and the immune system

The immune system is a collection of billions of cells which travel through the bloodstream and move in and out of tissues and organs, defending the body against invasion by foreign agents (e.g. bacteria, viruses, cancerous cells). These cells are produced mainly in the spleen, lymph nodes, thymus, and bone marrow (see Figure 12.7, below). The study of the effect of psychological factors on the immune system is called *psychoneuroimmunology* (PNI).

People often catch colds soon after a period of stress (such as final exams), because stress seems to reduce the immune system's ability to fight off cold viruses. Goetsch & Fuller (1995) refer to studies that show decreases in the activity of lymphocytes among medical students during their final exams. Lymphocytes ('natural killer cells') are a particular type of white blood cell, which normally fights off viruses and cancer cells. Lowe and Greenman (in Petit-Zeman, 2000) found that levels of immunoglobulin A (IgA) increase immediately after an oral exam, if it appeared to go well, but not after written exams. This suggests that with written exams, the stress is not relieved until much later, when the results come out.

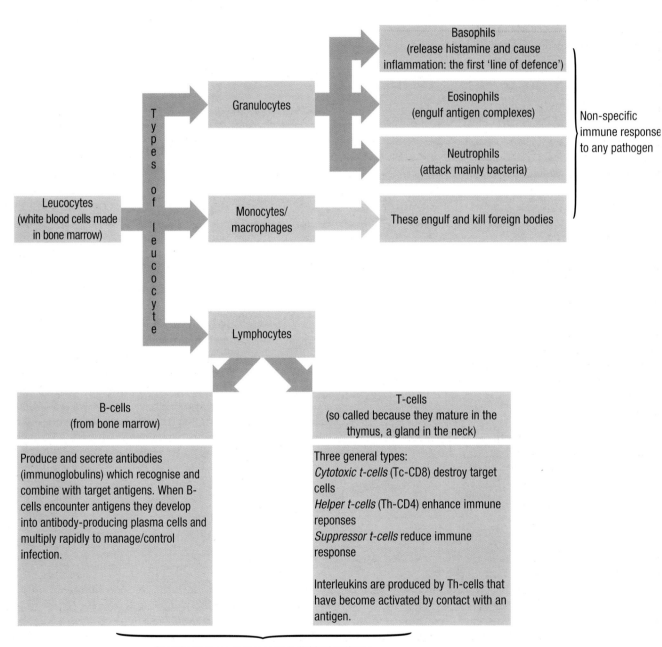

Figure 12.7 *The immune system (adapted from Hayward, 1998)*

KEY STUDY 12.5

Beating breast cancer (Greer *et al.*, 1979)

Greer *et al.* studied women who'd had mastectomies after being diagnosed with breast cancer. They found that those who reacted either by *denying* what had happened ('I'm being treated for a lump, but it's not serious'), or by showing a *'fighting spirit'* ('This is not going to get me'), were significantly more likely to be free of cancer five years later than women who stoically accepted it ('I feel an illness is God's will ...') or were described as 'giving up' ('Well, there's no hope with cancer, is there?'). A follow-up at 15 years (Greer *et al.*, 1990) confirmed the improved prognosis. According to Hegarty (2000):

'*Such research ... appears to give scientific support to the advice ...'to think positive' in the face of a diagnosis of cancer. It suggests the value of having psychological resources which will allow individuals to adapt to, rather than succumb to, a severe threat to their well-being. It might even be possible to teach such strategies to people who neither have nor use them'.*

More recently, Walker (in Norton, 2000a) reported that women with breast cancer, who visualise their white blood cells waging war against the cancer cells, are boosting their immune system in a way which could help them fight the disease. This guided imagery was combined with progressive muscle relaxation, as well as standard surgery, chemotherapy, and radiotherapy. Compared with women in a control group (given only the medical treatment), those who used the psychological techniques had higher numbers of mature T-cells, activated T-cells, and cells carrying T-cell receptors. These are important for attacking malignant cells. At the end of the nine-month study, these women also had higher levels of lymphokines (activated killer cells), which help prevent the disease from spreading. While it's too early to tell us whether these changes translate into a longer life expectancy, the women also reported a better quality of life, and fewer side-effects from medical treatments.

While the immune system is so vital, Sternberg & Gold (1997) warn that:

'*... its responses are so powerful that they require constant regulation to ensure that they are neither excessive nor indiscriminate and yet remain effective. When the immune system escapes regulation, autoimmune and inflammatory diseases or immune deficiency syndromes result'.*

As we've seen, GAS involves the release of cortisol (one of the major glucocorticoids) into the bloodstream. But the immune system, too, is capable of triggering this stream of biological events: it has a direct line to the hypothalamus. When the immune system is activated to fight an illness or infection, it sends a signal to the hypothalamus to produce its stress hormones (including cortisol). The flow of hormones, in turn, *shuts off* the immune response. This ingenious negative-feedback loop allows a short burst of immune activity, but prevents the immune system from getting carried away. In this way, a little stress is 'good for you'. But *chronic* stress produces such a constant flow of cortisol that the immune system is dampened too much. This helps explain how stress makes us ill (Sternberg, 2000).

Moderators and mediators of stress

Moderator variables are antecedent conditions (such as personality, ethnic background, and gender), that interact with exposure to stress to affect health outcome. *Mediator variables* intervene in the link between stress exposure and health outcome (for example, appraisal: Folkman & Lazarus, 1988b). If they reduce the impact of a stressful event, they're called 'protective' or 'buffering' variables (they soften or cushion the impact: Bartlett, 1998).

Personality

There's been an enormous amount of research into the type A behaviour pattern (TABP). This was originally called 'type A personality' (i.e. a stable personality trait: Friedman & Rosenman, 1974), but it's now conceptualised as a stereotypical set of behavioural responses. Typical responses are:

- *competitiveness* and *achievement orientation*;
- *aggressiveness* and *hostility*;
- *sense of time urgency*.

Many early studies showed that people who display TABP were at much greater risk of high BP and coronary heart disease (CHD) compared with 'type Bs'. However, these risks are only *relative*: the vast majority of type As doesn't develop CHD, and many type Bs *do* (Davison & Neale, 1994). Also, most studies have found that TAPB assessed immediately following a heart attack *doesn't* predict future attacks. This suggests that TAPB *isn't* a distinct risk for CHD in those already at risk of the disorder (Penny, 1996).

Recent research is increasingly pointing towards *hostility* as the best single predictor of CHD. In fact, hostility is a better predictor than the TAPB as a whole. Dembroski & Costa (1987) argue that 'potential for hostility' is a reasonably stable personality trait. In a review of the research, Furnham & Heaven (1999) conclude that:

'*... the type A behaviour pattern is a well-established individual difference factor that has been shown to be linked to health outcome, particularly CHD. There can be no doubt that the presence of type A characteristics ... is a significant predisposing factor for heart disease ...'.*

According to Temoshok (1987), *type C personalities* are cancer-prone. The type C personality has difficulty expressing emotion and tends to suppress or inhibit emotions, particularly negative ones such as anger. While there's no clear-cut evidence that these personality characteristics can actually cause cancer, it does seem likely that they influence the progression of cancer and, hence, the survival time of cancer patients (Weinman, 1995).

Greer & Morris (1975) found that women diagnosed with breast cancer showed significantly more emotional suppression than those with benign breast disease (especially among those under 50). This had been a characteristic for most of their lives. Cooper & Faragher (1993) reported that experiencing a major stressful event is a significant predictor of breast cancer. This was especially so in women who didn't express anger, but used denial as a form of coping (see Key Study 12.5).

Other personality variables can be *protective*. For example, Kobasa (1979) and Kobasa *et al.* (1982) describe *hardiness* as one such variable. Hardiness comprises the three Cs:

- *commitment*: a tendency to involve oneself in whatever one is doing, and to approach life with a sense of curiosity and meaningfulness;
- *control*: this relates to Rotter's *locus of control* (see above, page 173);
- *challenge*: a tendency to believe that change as opposed to stability is normal in life, and to anticipate change as an incentive to personal growth and development rather than a threat to security.

According to Funk (1992), hardiness seems to moderate the stress–illness relationship by reducing cognitive appraisals of threat, and reducing the use of regressive coping (see Table 12.2, page 178).

Cultural/ethnic background

Penny (1996) observes that Western culture seems to encourage and value the component responses of TABP. Competitiveness and striving for achievement are common goals in capitalist societies, but probably not in more traditional, communal ones. Similarly, the SRRS has been criticised for not taking account of cultural and ethnic differences in the kinds of potential stressors that people are exposed to.

For many years, it's been noted that both the physical and mental health of African Americans is worse than that of whites, due especially to the spread of AIDS and to hypertension. While this is partly caused by the direct negative effects of poverty, such as poor diet, low levels of education and poor medical care, there are many psychological and social stressors involved as well. Although these are extremely difficult to measure, especially across cultures:

> '... there is little dispute that blacks in North America and Europe face a unique kind of stress – racial discrimination'.
> (Cooper *et al.*, 1999)

Ask yourself ...

- Can you think of ways in which sexism might adversely affect women's health?
- Do women have access to protective factors that men don't?

How do we cope with stress?

Primary appraisal of an event as in some way harmful or threatening is really only the *beginning* of the stress process, not the end. In *secondary appraisal*, we consider what can be done about the stressful situation, by evaluating our *coping options* (Lazarus, 1999). Primary appraisal doesn't necessarily come first. The difference between them is *not* timing, but *content*. They are interdependent aspects of a common process. According to Lazarus (1999):

> 'The more confident we are of our capacity to overcome obstacles and dangers, the more likely we are to be challenged rather than threatened and vice versa, a sense of inadequacy promotes threat ...'.

Cohen & Lazarus (1979) have classified all the coping strategies that a person might use into five general categories:

- *direct action response*: the individual directly tries to change or manipulate his/her relationship to the stressful situation, such as escaping from it or removing it;
- *information seeking*: the individual tries to understand the situation better, and to predict future events that are related to the stressor;
- *inhibition of action*: doing nothing. This may be the best course of action if the situation is seen as short-term;
- *intrapsychic* or *palliative coping*: the individual reappraises the situation (for example, through the use of psychological defence mechanisms) or changes the 'internal environment' (through drugs, alcohol, relaxation or meditation);
- turning to others for help and emotional support.

These five categories of coping overlap with the distinction between problem-focused and emotion-focused coping.

Box 12.8 Problem-focused and emotion-focused coping (Lazarus & Folkman, 1984)

Problem-focused coping involves taking direct action in order to solve a problem, or seeking information that's relevant to a solution. *Emotion-focused coping* involves trying to reduce the negative emotions that are part of the experience of stress. Lazarus and Folkman argue that effective coping depends on the situation, and sometimes using *both* kinds might offer the 'best solution'.

In the transactional model (Cox, 1978), the 'stress response' refers to both psychological and physiological means of coping. In turn, the psychological response has two components, *cognitive defence* and *behavioural response*, and the consequences of both (perceived and actual) are being continuously appraised in relation to the stressful situation.

Ask yourself ...

- Which of the above best describes your typical response to stressful situations?
- How about your best friend or partner?
- Does the way you cope depend on the nature of the stressor?

Coping and defence mechanisms

Sometimes the term 'coping response' or mechanism is used in contrast to 'defence mechanism' (e.g. Grasha, 1983; Savickas, 1995). *Ego defence mechanisms* involve some degree of distortion of reality and self-deception (see Chapter 42). While desirable in the short term, they're unhealthy and undesirable (as long-term solutions to stress). *Coping mechanisms*, by contrast, are conscious ways of trying to adapt to stress and anxiety in a positive and constructive way. They use, for instance, thoughts and behaviours to search for information, problem-solving, seeking help from others, recognising our true feelings and establishing goals and objectives (see Table 12.2, page 179). According to Savickas (1995):

'In effect, coping improves fit [between the individual and the environment], whereas defence maintains misfit while reducing perceived stress'.

Stress management

Much of what we've said about coping with stress refers to what people do in a largely *spontaneous* way. In this informal sense, we all 'manage our stress' more or less effectively. But more formally, *stress management* refers to a range of psychological techniques used in a quite deliberate way, in a professional setting, to help people reduce their stress levels. These techniques may be used singly or in combination.

Table 12.2 *Some major coping mechanisms and their corresponding defence mechanisms (based on Grasha, 1983)*

Coping mechanism	Description mechanism	Corresponding defence
Objectivity	Separating one thought from another or our feelings from our thoughts. Allows us to obtain a better understanding of how we think/feel, and an objective evaluation of our actions	Isolation
Logical analysis	Systematically analysing our problems, in order to find explanations and make plans to solve them, based on the realities of the situation	Rationalisation
Concentration	Ability to set aside disturbing thoughts/ feelings, in order to concentrate on the task in hand	Denial
Playfulness	Ability to use past feelings/ ideas/behaviour appropriately to enrich the solution of problems/add enjoyment to life	Regression
Tolerance of ambiguity	Ability to function in situations where we/others can't make clear choices, because the situation's so complicated	
Suppression	Ability consciously to forget about/hold back thoughts/ feelings, until an appropriate time/place	Repression

Sublimation can be thought of as a coping mechanism *and* a defence mechanism. It involves channelling anxiety in socially desirable ways, and so is positive and constructive, as well as being a defence against anxiety.

- In the case of *biofeedback* (discussed above in relation to pain control: see pages 169–170), the focus is on treating the symptoms of stress rather than the stressor itself;
- The same is true for a number of procedures used to bring about a state of relaxation, in particular *progressive muscle relaxation*, meditation and hypnosis;
- *Cognitive restructuring* refers to a number of specific methods aimed at trying to change the way individuals think about their life situations and selves, in order to change their emotional responses and behaviour. This approach is based largely on the work of Beck (*the treatment of automatic thoughts*) and Ellis (*rational emotive therapy*), two major forms of *cognitive behaviour therapy* (see Chapter 45). This approach provides information to reduce uncertainty, and to enhance people's sense of control.

CHAPTER SUMMARY

- While traditional medicine is based on the **biomedical model** of disease, health psychology, psychosomatic medicine, and behavioural medicine all rest on the **biopsychosocial model**.
- **Health psychology** focuses on normal behaviour and psychological processes in relation to health and illness, although some psychologists see it as an extension of **clinical psychology**. It also attempts to **promote** health behaviour and **prevent** illness.
- **Health** is more than just the absence of **disease**, which is defined in **biological/somatic** terms. By contrast, **illness** is a more **psychological** concept.
- **Expectancy-value models** try to account for people's adoption/failure to adopt particular health behaviours. They are **rational reasoning models.**
- In the **health belief model** (HBM), belief in **susceptibility** to, and perception of **severity of the consequences** of, the disease, together determine the **perceived threat**.
- A factor which may explain the persistence of unhealthy behaviours is people's tendency towards **unrealistic optimism**. This suggests that perception of one's own risk **isn't** a rational process.
- The **theory of reasoned action** (TRA) assumes that behaviour is a function of behavioural **intention**, jointly determined by a person's **attitude** and **subjective norms**.
- The **theory of planned behaviour** (TPB) is a modification of TRA. The extra ingredient is perceived **behavioural control**, based on Bandura's concept of **self-efficacy**.
- All the models are poor predictors of actual behaviour (the **intention–behaviour gap**). One response to this criticism is the concept of **implementation intentions**.
- **Aerobic exercise** helps decrease the risk of several life-threatening diseases, as well as increasing positive mental health. Even short exercise sessions can be beneficial.
- Research indicates that **patient non-compliance/non-adherence** is very common, although this varies depending on the particular disorder. It applies to both chronic and acute conditions, and to organ transplant patients. The **double high/double efficacy/behavioural intention model** identifies the five factors that make compliance most likely.

- Compliance is affected by both **practitioner** and **patient/regimen variables**. The former include how doctors **communicate** their beliefs to patients, and the latter include patients' **satisfaction** with the consultation, and their **understanding** and **recall** of the information given.
- Although **pain** is basically physiological, the pain **experience** has both **emotional**, **cognitive** and **cultural** components. **Phantom limb pain** illustrates that people can feel pain in the absence of physical injury, and **congenital analgesia** illustrates the converse.
- **Treatment** of pain includes methods used to treat stress, such as **contingency management**, EMG **biofeedback**, and **self-management/cognitive behaviour treatment**.
- **Stress** can be conceptualised as a **stimulus** (corresponding to the **engineering model**), a **response** (corresponding to the **physiological model**), or as an **interaction** between organism and environment (corresponding to the **transactional model**).
- The **causes** of stress include **disruption of circadian rhythms**, **occupation-linked stressors**, especially for those working in the emergency services and health care professionals, **major life changes**, and **everyday hassles**.
- Selye's **general adaptation syndrome** (GAS) represents the body's defence against stress. It comprises the **alarm reaction**, **resistance**, and **exhaustion**.
- The alarm reaction involves the **fight or flight response**, in which the **ANS–adrenal–medulla system** is activated. In resistance, the **anterior pituitary–adrenal cortex system** is activated.
- While the fight or flight response may have been adaptive in our evolutionary past, it's inappropriate as a response to most 'modern' stressors. Stress can cause illness through maintaining a harmfully high level of physiological arousal.
- **Psychoneuroimmunology** studies the relationship between stress and health by assessing its effects on the **immune system**.
- **Moderators** of stress include **personality** and **ethnic background**. Considerable research has investigated the link between **type A behaviour pattern** (TABP) and coronary heart disease, and between **type C personalities** and cancer. Unlike these, **hardiness** is a **protective** factor against the harmful effects of stress.
- **Coping** with stress involves **primary** and **secondary appraisals**, **problem-focused** and **emotion-focused** coping, and **coping mechanisms** (as distinct from **defence mechanisms**). **Stress management** involves biofeedback, **progressive muscle relaxation**, and **cognitive restructuring**.

Self-assessment questions

1 **a** Explain the major similarities and differences between the biomedical and biopsychosocial models of illness.
  b Critically evaluate **one** of these models.
2 Describe and evaluate **two** models of health behaviour.
3 Discuss the role of psychological factors in illness.
4 Critically assess the relationship between stress and illness.

Web addresses

www.apa.org/divisions/div38/

www.ehps.net/

http://fisk.edu/vl/Stress

http://www.stressfree.com/

http://onhealth.com/

http://www.uiuc.edu/departments/mcinley/health-info/stress/stres.html

http://www.unl.edu.stress/

http://www.clas.ufl.edu/users/gthursby/stress/

http://amwa-doc.org/publications/WCHealthbook/stressamwa-ch09.html

http://future health.org/stresscn.html

http://stats.bls.gov/opub/ted/1999/Oct/wk4/art03.htm

http://www/workhealth.org/prevent/prred.html

Further reading

Bartlett, D. (1998) *Stress: Perspectives and Processes*. Buckingham: Open University Press. A fairly short but detailed review of all major aspects of the stress–health relationship.

Cox, T. (1978) *Stress*. London: Macmillan Education Ltd. Although a little dated, still an excellent resource for most aspects of stress. Also useful for the links between stress and emotion.

Lazarus, R.S. (1999) *Stress and Emotion: A New Synthesis*. London: Free Association Books. An extremely readable, wide-ranging review of the field by one of its most eminent researchers.

Ogden, J. (2000) *Health Psychology: A Textbook*. Buckingham: Open University Press. An excellent, thorough but readable, discussion of all the topics covered in this chapter – and many more.

Stroebe, W. (2000) *Social Psychology and Health*. Buckingham: Open University Press. As the title suggests, health psychology approached from a social psychological perspective. An excellent complement to Ogden's more general approach.

Three

Cognitive Psychology

Chapter 13

Attention and Performance

Introduction and overview

According to Titchener (1903), a student of Wundt:

'The doctrine of attention is the nerve of the whole psychological system'.

However, the Gestalt psychologists believed the concept of attention was unnecessary (they believed that a stimulus array's properties were sufficient to predict the perceptual response to it: see Chapter 15). The behaviourists argued that since 'attention' was unobservable, it wasn't worthy of experimental study (see Chapters 2 and 3).

Interest in the study of attention re-emerged following the publication of Broadbent's (1958) *Perception and Communication*, which also had a great impact on the development of cognitive psychology overall. Broadbent argued that the world is composed of many more sensations than can be handled by the perceptual and cognitive capabilities of the human observer. To cope with the flood of available information, humans must selectively attend to only some information, and somehow 'tune out' the rest. Attention, therefore, is the result of a limited-capacity information-processing system. Solso (1995) calls this a 'pipeline' theory. To understand our ability to selectively attend to things, researchers study *focused* (or *selective*) *attention*.

Central to the information processing approach is the *computer analogy*. This is arguably most evident in explanations of memory (see Chapter 17) and attention. Concepts such as buffer store, and limited-capacity processor, are drawn from information technology and built into the models of attention that we'll discuss in this chapter.

Almost all the early models of attention assumed *serial processing*, a step-by-step process in which each operation is carried out in turn. The first of these was Broadbent's (1958) *filter model*, followed by Treisman's (1964) *attenuation model*, and the *pertinence model* (Deutsch & Deutsch, 1963; Norman, 1969). These are all 'single-channel models' of selective attention. But early attempts to explain *divided attention*, such as Kahneman's (1973) *central capacity theory*, also assumed serial processing. In *parallel processing*, two or more operations are carried out at the same time. This is the view taken in Allport's (1980b) *multi-channel theory of divided attention* (doing more than one thing at a time).

Assumptions about serial or parallel processing reflect changes in the underlying computer analogy, which in turn reflect developments in computer technology. For much of the 1950s and 1960s, computers were only capable of serial processing. During the 1980s and 1990s, machines capable of massive parallel processing started to be built, and theorists have returned to an earlier belief that cognitive theories should be based more closely on the brain's neural networks (Eysenck & Keane, 1995; Jarvis, 1994; see chapter 20). The human brain is the parallel processing machine *par excellence* (see Chapter 4).

What is attention?

One famous definition of attention is that of William James (1890), according to whom:

'It is the taking possession by the mind, in clear and vivid form, of one out of what seem several simultaneously possible objects or trains of thought. Focalisation, concentration of consciousness are of its essence. It implies withdrawal from some things in order to deal effectively with others'.

Although we can't necessarily equate attention with consciousness (see below), James's definition underlines the selective nature of attention. This is echoed in Solso's (1995) definition: '... the concentration of mental effort on sensory or mental events'. However, this is only one of two major ways in which attention has been defined and investigated. A crucial distinction is made between:

1 the mechanisms by which certain information is registered and other information is rejected, whether or not the latter enters conscious awareness (*selective* or *focused attention*);
2 some upper limit to the amount of processing that can be performed on incoming information at any one time (*capacity* or *divided attention*).

As we saw in Chapters 7 and 9, the term 'attention' has also been used to refer to arousal level, vigilance and the ability to stay alert and concentrate.

Methods of studying attention

Selective attention

People are presented with two or more simultaneous 'messages', and are instructed to process and respond to only one of them. The most popular way of doing this is to use *shadowing*, in which one message is fed into the left ear and a different message into the right ear (through headphones). Participants have to repeat one of these messages aloud as they hear it.

The shadowing technique is really a particular form of *dichotic listening* (Broadbent, 1954). This is the simultaneous reception of two different stimulus inputs, one to each ear. Shadowing was first used by Cherry (1953), who wanted to study the *cocktail party phenomenon*, in which we manage to select one or two voices to listen to from the hubbub of conversations taking place at the same time and in the same room. The participant is asked to *select*, which can tell us something about the selection process and what happens to unattended stimuli. Most studies have looked at auditory attention.

Divided attention

In the *dual-task technique*, people are asked to attend and respond to both (or all) the messages. Whereas shadowing focuses attention on a particular message, the dual-task method deliberately divides people's attention. This provides useful information about a person's processing limitations, and also about attention mechanisms and their capacity.

Divided (or focused) auditory attention

Cherry's dichotic listening and shadowing research

In his initial experiments, Cherry's participants wore headphones through which pairs of spoken prose 'messages' were presented to both ears simultaneously (*binaural listening*). Cherry found that various physical differences affected a person's ability to select one of the messages to attend to, in particular voice intensity, the speaker's location and the speaker's sex. He also found that when these differences were controlled for in the two messages (so that each message was, say, spoken in an equally intense female voice), their meaning was extremely difficult to separate. In later experiments, he used dichotic listening and shadowing. While participants were able to shadow the specified message, little of the non-shadowed message was remembered.

Box 13.1 Other research findings using shadowing

Little of the non-shadowed message was remembered, even when the same word was presented 35 times to the non-shadowed ear (Moray, 1959). Also, participants didn't notice if the message was spoken in a foreign language or changed from English to a different language. While speech played backwards was reported as having 'something queer about it', most participants believed it to be normal speech. However, a pure tone of 400 cycles per second was nearly always noticed, as was a change of voice from male to female or female to male (Cherry & Taylor, 1954).

These data suggested that, while the physical properties of the message in the non-shadowed ear were 'heard', *semantic content* (its meaning) was completely lost. People quickly moved on from Cherry's original question about how we can attend to one conversation, and began asking why so little seemed to be remembered about the *other* conversations (Hampson & Morris, 1996).

Broadbent's split-span studies

Broadbent (1954) reported the results of a series of studies using the *split-span procedure*. In this, three digits (such as 8, 2 and 1) are presented via headphones to one ear at the rate of one every half a second. Simultaneously, three different digits (such as 7, 3 and 4) are presented to the other ear. The task is to listen to the two sets of numbers and then write down as much as can be remembered.

The digits can be recalled either:

1 according to the ear of presentation (*ear-by-ear recall*: the numbers above could be recalled as either 8, 2, 1, 7, 3, 4 or 7, 3, 4, 8, 2, 1), or
2 according to their chronological order of presentation (*pair-by-pair recall*). Since the digits have been presented in pairs, this would involve recalling the first pair (8, 7 or 7, 8), followed by the second pair (2, 3 or 3, 2) and finally the third pair (1, 4 or 4, 1).

When people are simply given a list of six digits at a rate of one every half a second, serial recall is typically 95 per cent accurate. However, Broadbent found that the split-span procedure produced accurate recall only 65 per cent of the time. Moreover, pair-by-pair recall was considerably poorer than ear-by-ear recall. If given a choice, people preferred ear-by-ear recall.

Single-channel theories of focused auditory attention

Single-channel theories propose that somewhere in information processing there's a 'bottleneck' or *filter* which allows some information to be passed on for further analysis, while the other information is either discarded or processed to only a limited degree. The three theories that have been proposed differ mainly over whether the filtering takes place early or late in information processing. This means that they differ in terms of the nature and extent of processing of the non-attended material.

Broadbent's early-selection filter theory

Broadbent's (1958) theory was the first systematic attempt to explain both Cherry's findings, and those of split-span experiments. Broadbent assumes that our ability to process information is *capacity limited*. Information from the senses passes 'in parallel' to a short-term store. This is a temporary 'buffer system', which holds information until it can be processed further and, effectively, extends the duration of a stimulus (see Chapter 17). The various types of information (such as two or more voices) are then passed, preserved in their original form, to a selective filter. This operates on the basis of the information's *physical characteristics*, selecting one source for further analysis and rejecting all others.

Information allowed through the filter reaches a limited-capacity channel (the filter is necessary precisely because the channel is capacity limited). This corresponds to the 'span of consciousness' (James, 1890) or what we experience as happening *now*. The information allowed through the filter is analysed in that it's recognised, possibly rehearsed, and then transferred to the motor effectors (muscles), producing an appropriate response (see Figure 13.1, page 186).

Broadbent considered the short-term store to be capable of holding information for a period of time before it decayed. So, two simultaneous stimuli can be processed provided the processor can get back to the store before the information in it has disappeared. Consequently, attending to one thing doesn't necessarily mean that everything else is lost. However, Broadbent maintained that processing two different pieces of information from two channels would always take longer, and be less efficient, than processing the same information from one channel. This is because switching attention between channels takes a substantial period of time.

Tests of Broadbent's theory

Broadbent's theory could explain Cherry's findings concerning the fate of the non-shadowed message, because the non-shadowed message isn't allowed to pass through the filter. It also explains the data from split-span experiments, by proposing that the input to the relevant ear is the physical property on which the information is selected.

However, the theory assumes that because the non-shadowed message is filtered out according to its physical characteristics, its meaning shouldn't be subject to any sort of higher-level analysis. But, when we're at a party, our attention sometimes switches from the person we're conversing with to another part of the room, if, for example, we hear our name mentioned. This was demonstrated experimentally by Moray (1959), who found that when the participant's name was presented to the non-attended (non-shadowed) ear, attention switched to that ear about one-third of the time.

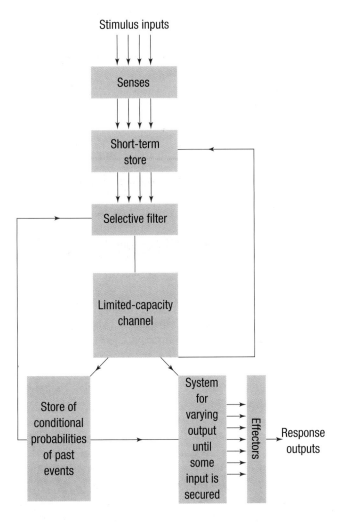

Figure 13.1 *Broadbent's theory of the flow of information between stimulus and response*

KEY STUDY 13.1

Why use one ear when two will do? (Gray & Wedderburn, 1960)

Gray & Wedderburn (1960) presented, to each ear alternately, the syllables composing a word, plus random digits. Thus, when one ear 'heard' a syllable, the other 'heard' a digit. For example, in one experiment, participants heard:

Left ear: OB 2 TIVE
Right ear: 6 JEC 9

In other experiments, phrases were used in place of words, such as 'Dear Aunt Jane', 'Mice eat cheese' and 'What the hell'.

> #### Ask yourself ...
>
> • What would Broadbent have predicted about participants' responses when asked to repeat what they'd heard in one ear (or channel)?

According to Broadbent, participants should have reported 'ob-two-tive', or 'six-jec-nine'. This, of course, is nonsense. But the filter model maintains that it's the *physical nature* of the auditory signal (which ear receives which input), and not *meaning* which determines what's attended to and, hence, what's recalled. What participants actually reported was 'objective' or 'Dear Aunt Jane' etc. In other words, they acted 'intelligently'. The ears *don't* always function as different information channels, and switching between channels is fairly easy to do.

The importance of meaning

■ Treisman (1960) found that if meaningful material presented to the attended ear was switched in mid-sentence to the non-attended ear, participants would occasionally change the focus of their attention to the non-attended ear, and shadow that material before changing back to the attended ear.

■ Treisman (1964) discovered that if a French translation of the shadowed material was presented as non-shadowed material, some bilingual participants realised that the shadowed and non-shadowed material had the same meaning.

■ Corteen & Wood (1972) conditioned participants to produce a *galvanic skin response* (GSR) whenever they heard a particular target word. A small electric shock was delivered immediately after the target word was heard. The target word produced a GSR when presented to the non-attended ear, as did synonyms. However, GSRs didn't occur every time the conditioned words were presented.

■ Mackay (1973) presented the word 'bank' in a sentence, and participants subsequently had to recognise the sentence they'd heard. Recognition was influenced by whether the word 'river' or 'money' had been presented to the non-attended ear.

What these studies, and that of Gray and Wedderburn (see Key Study 13.1) suggest, is that the meaning of the input to the non-attended ear is processed at least some of the time. Further, Underwood (1974) found that participants trained at shadowing can detect two-thirds of the material presented to the non-attended ear. This throws doubt on Broadbent's claim that the non-shadowed message is always rejected at an early stage of processing. Also, when material used is sufficiently different, such as one being auditory and the other visual, memory for the non-shadowed message is good. This indicates that it must have been processed at a higher level than proposed by Broadbent (Allport *et al.*, 1972).

Treisman's attenuation (or stimulus-analysis system) model

According to Treisman (1960, 1964), competing information is analysed for things other than its physical properties, including sounds, syllable patterns, grammatical structure and the information's meaning (Hampson & Morris, 1996). Treisman suggested that the non-shadowed message isn't filtered out early on, but that the selective filter *attenuates* it. So, a message that isn't selected on the basis of its physical properties wouldn't be rejected completely, but its 'volume' would be 'turned down'.

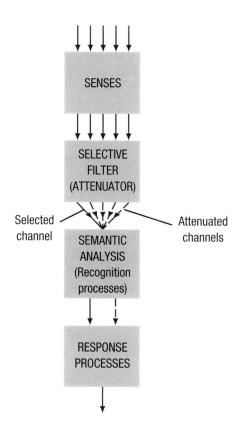

Figure 13.2 *Treisman's attenuation model*

Both non-attenuated and attenuated information undergo the further analyses mentioned above. These may result in an attenuated message being attended to, depending on its features. Treisman suggested that biologically relevant and emotionally important stimuli may be 'pre-sets' to which attention is switched, irrespective of the attenuated message's content. This accounts for our ability to switch attention to a different conversation when our name is mentioned. Since it's the features of a stimulus which determine whether or not it's attended to, the concept of *probabilistic filtering* is perhaps a better way of appreciating Treisman's theory than that of attenuation (Massaro, 1989).

The Deutsch–Norman late-selection filter model

Deutsch & Deutsch (1963) and Norman (1968, 1976) completely rejected Broadbent's claim that information is filtered out early on. According to the Deutsch–Norman model, filtering or selection only occurs after all inputs have been

analysed at a high level, for example after each word has been recognised by the memory system and analysed for meaning.

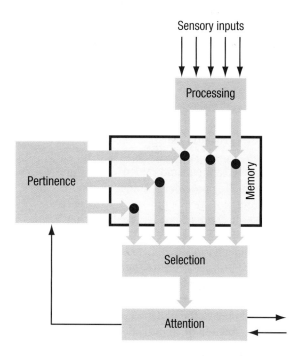

Figure 13.3 *The Deutsch–Norman theory of focused attention. All sensory inputs receive perceptual processing and are recognised in the sense that they excite their representations (the purple circles) in memory. The information selected is that which has the greatest pertinence (Norman, 1968)*

The filter is placed nearer the response end of the processing system; hence, it's a 'late' selection filter. Because processing will have already been undertaken on the information that's been presented, some information will have been established as pertinent (most relevant) and have activated particular memory representations. This is why it's sometimes called the *pertinence model*. When one memory representation is selected for further processing, attention becomes selective. The model implies that we perceive everything we encounter, but are only consciously aware of some of it (Hampson & Morris, 1996).

Tests of the Treisman and the Deutsch–Norman models

Both the Treisman and the Deutsch–Norman models can account for the processing of non-shadowed material (whereas Broadbent's theory cannot). If the Deutsch–Norman model is correct, then participants should be able to identify as many target words in the non-shadowed message as in the shadowed message, since both are allegedly completely analysed for meaning. Treisman & Geffen (1967), however, found that target words were much better detected in the shadowed message (87 per cent) than the non-shadowed message (eight per cent). This is consistent with Treisman's view that the non-shadowed message is attenuated.

However, Treisman and Geffen's findings assume that the shadowed and non-shadowed messages are equally important. Deutsch & Deutsch (1967) argued that this assumption wasn't met, because participants had to indicate when they heard a target word by tapping. In other words, they had to shadow *and* tap in one message, but only tap in the other.

This made the target words in the shadowed message more important than those in the non-shadowed message. Treisman & Riley (1969) overcame this problem by requiring participants to stop shadowing and to tap as soon as they detected a target word in either ear. Under such conditions, performance was still better for the shadowed message (76 per cent) than for the non-shadowed message (33 per cent).

This finding is consistent with Treisman's model, but inconsistent with the Deutsch–Norman claim that performance shouldn't differ, given that the targets were equally pertinent irrespective of the ear they were presented to. However, the detection rate for the non-attended ear in Treisman and Riley's study (33 per cent) was much higher than that in the Treisman and Geffen study (eight per cent), a finding which provides some support for the Deutsch–Norman model.

The Deutsch–Norman model predicts that participants asked immediately afterwards should be able to repeat back the words presented to the non-shadowed ear. However, the non-shadowed message gets into short-term memory for only a brief period and is then forgotten very quickly. Norman (1969) found that participants could remember the last couple of words presented to the non-attended ear if tested immediately, but not after a short continuation of the shadowing task. This finding was replicated by Glucksberg & Cowan (1970).

Ask yourself ...

- Can you think of examples of where you've remembered something later that you weren't aware of hearing at the time (such as something somebody said)?
- Which of the models discussed above best accounts for these incidents?

An evaluation of single-channel models

- Despite some support for the Deutsch–Norman model, Wilding (1982) believes that less is known about non-attended messages than it claims. However, more is known than can be explained by either Broadbent's or Treisman's models.
- The major criticism of single-channel theories is their lack of flexibility, and several more 'flexible' theories have been advanced. According to Johnston & Heinz (1978), attentional selectivity can occur at several different stages of processing, depending on the demands made by the experimental task. To minimise demands on capacity, selection is made as early as possible.
- Johnston & Heinz (1979) and Johnston & Wilson (1980) have presented findings consistent with their view that processing is more flexible than predicted by single-channel theories. For example, Johnston and Wilson showed that participants processed words presented to *both* ears, but only when they didn't know to which ear particular target words would be presented. These data suggest that non-target words are processed only to the extent necessary to perform a task.
- Many researchers question whether any single, general purpose, limited-capacity central processor can, in principle, account for the complexities of selective attention (Norman & Bobrow, 1975; Neisser, 1976; Allport, 1980b). Much of the relevant evidence comes from dual-task studies, which are more directly concerned with processing capacity, i.e. divided attention (see below).

Focused visual attention

According to Driver (1996):

'The cluttered scenes of everyday life present more objects than we can respond towards simultaneously, and often more than we can perceive fully at any one time. Accordingly, mechanisms of attention are required to select objects of interest for further processing. In the case of vision, one such mechanism is provided by eye movements, which allow us to fixate particular regions so that they benefit from the greater acuity of the fovea'.

The *fovea* (see Figure 5.2, page 69) provides maximum acuity for visual stimuli. So, when we fixate on an object, maximum visual processing is carried out on the object whose image is projected onto the fovea, while the resources given to the other parts of the visual field are 'attenuated' (Anderson, 1995b).

Posner *et al.* (1978, 1980) found that when people are told to fixate on one part of the visual field, it's still possible to attend to stimuli seven or so degrees either side of the fixation point. Also, attention can be shifted more quickly when a stimulus is presented in an 'expected' rather than an 'unexpected' location. Thus, visual attention isn't confined to the part of the visual field which is processed by the fovea, but can be shifted without corresponding changes in eye movements. Indeed, such shifts in attention frequently precede the corresponding eye movement (Anderson, 1995b). Posner (1980) calls this *covert attention*.

The internal mental spotlight and the zoom lens

Posner likened covert attention to an internal mental spotlight that 'illuminates' any stimulus in the attended region, so that it's perceived in greater detail. It essentially duplicates the functions of eye movements *internally*, by allowing a particular region of space to be perceptually enhanced (Driver, 1996).

LaBerge (1983) required participants to judge whether the middle letter of five letters (such as LACIE) came from the beginning or end of the alphabet (*directed attention condition*). But on some occasions, a stimulus such as –7– – – was presented, and the task was to determine whether the 7 was one of two letters (T or Z). LaBerge found that the speed of judgement was a function of the distance from the centre of attention. Thus, reaction times were fastest for items at the centre of the stimulus and slower for those at its periphery, even though all items were within the fovea's region.

LaBerge concluded that visual attention is most concentrated at the centre of the internal spotlight and least at its periphery. When information beyond its centre needs to be processed, the spotlight must be shifted to ensure maximal processing. Because this takes time, participants in Posner *et al.*'s experiments took longer to judge a stimulus when it appeared in an 'unexpected' location (Eriksen & Yeh, 1987).

LaBerge also found that when participants were required to attend to the whole five-letter word string (*global attention condition*), the 'width' of the spotlight's 'beam' increased, as indicated by the similarity of reaction times for items at the centre and periphery. These findings led Eriksen (1990) to propose the *zoom-lens model* of visual attention. This accepts the existence of an internal mental spotlight, but suggests that it has a beam which may be very narrow (in the case of LaBerge's letter task) or broad (in the case of LaBerge's word task). It's simply a variable-beam spotlight (Groome *et al.*, 1999).

Evaluating the spotlight model

Despite evidence that little or no processing occurs beyond the spotlight (Johnston & Dark, 1986), both the spotlight and zoom-lens models have been contradicted in several studies.

KEY STUDY 13.2

Neisser & Becklen's (1975) study of selective visual attention

Visual selective attention was studied by superimposing a film of three people playing a ball game on a film which showed two people's hands clapping (see Figure 13.4).

The task was to follow one of the films and press a key to indicate that a 'critical event', such as the ball being thrown, had occurred. While adults found it difficult to follow both films simultaneously, they were able to attend selectively to one or other of the films easily. This is difficult for the zoom-lens model to explain, since it proposes that the focus of attention is a given area in visual space, rather than objects within that area (Eysenck & Keane, 1995). Using Neisser and Becklen's methodology, it's been shown that infants as young as four months can selectively follow one of the two films and, as a result, that selective visual attention is innate rather than learned (Bahrick *et al.*, 1981: see Chapter 16).

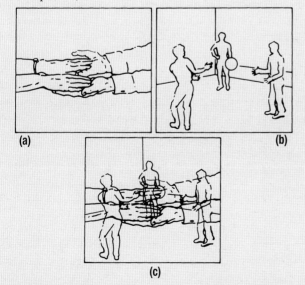

Figure 13.4 *A film of two people clapping hands (a), and three people playing a ball game (b), which have been superimposed (c)*

The fate of unattended visual stimuli

For Johnston & Dark (1986), stimuli beyond the focus of visual attention are subject to no, or virtually no, semantic processing. Any such processing is limited to mainly simple physical features. However, Driver (1996) disagrees. For example, when a picture is shown as the unattended stimulus on one trial, it slows the processing of an attended word with an identical or similar meaning on the next trial (*negative priming*). The fact that processing of the attended stimulus is reduced suggests that the meaning of the unattended stimulus must have been subject to some sort of processing (Tipper & Driver, 1988).

Treisman's feature-integration theory

Treisman's (1988) theory was developed on the basis of findings using the visual search procedure. Participants are presented with an array of visual material in which a target item is embedded on some trials but absent on others, and the 'distractor' items can be varied so that they're similar to the target letter, or different from it. The participant's task is to decide if the target is present or absent.

```
X P T L A B N T

A R H N J I F R

E W R N P A Z X

A H Y 5 Y T E S

A N H C E S T I

G D T K D Y U I
```

Figure 13.5 *A visual search array. The task is to find the number five in amongst the letters*

Neisser (1967) argued that when people perform a visual search task, they process many items simultaneously, without being fully 'aware' of the exact nature of the distractor items. Visual information processing might occur *pre-attentively*, depending on the nature of the stimuli (such as whether they have angular or curved features when the task is to detect a particular letter).

However, Treisman argues that attention must be focused on a stimulus before its features can be synthesised into a pattern. In one of Treisman & Gelade's (1980) experiments, participants were required to detect the presence of the letter T in amongst an array of Is and Ys. Because the horizontal bar at the top of a T distinguishes it from an I and a Y, this could be done fairly easily just by looking for the horizontal bar. Participants took around 800 milliseconds to detect the T, and the detection time wasn't affected by the size of the array (that is, the number of Is and Ys).

In another experiment, the T was embedded in an array of Is and Zs. Here, looking for a horizontal bar on its own doesn't aid detection, since the letter Z also has a horizontal bar on top of it. To detect a T, participants needed to look for the conjunction of a horizontal and vertical line. This took around 1200 milliseconds. Moreover, detection time was longer when the size of the array was increased. On the basis of these (and other) findings, Treisman proposed her feature-integration theory.

Box 13.2 Treisman's feature-integration theory

According to Treisman, it's possible to distinguish between *objects* (such as a strawberry) and their *features* (such as being red, possessing curves and being of a particular size). In the *first stage* of visual processing, we process the features of stimuli in the visual environment rapidly and in *parallel*, without attention being required. Next, the features are combined to form objects (such as a small, red curved object). This *second stage* of processing is a slow and *serial* process.

Focusing attention on an object's location provides the 'glue' which allows meaningless features to be formed into objects, although features can also be combined on the basis of knowledge stored in memory (such as the knowledge that strawberries are typically red). When relevant stored knowledge isn't available or focused attention is absent, feature combination occurs in a random way. This can produce *illusory conjunctions* (for example, a blue banana) or odd combinations of features.

(Based on Anderson, 1995b, and Eysenck & Keane, 1995)

An evaluation of Treisman's theory

■ Treisman has claimed evidence for the occurrence of illusory conjunctions in her visual search experiments. Treisman & Schmidt (1982), for example, required participants to identify two black digits flashed in one part of the visual field. In another part, letters in various colours were presented (such as a blue T or a red S). After reporting the digits, participants were asked what letters they'd seen and their colour. Most reported seeing illusory conjunctions (such as a blue S) almost as frequently as correct conjunctions. This supports the view that accurate perception only occurs when attention is focused on an object. When it's not, the features of objects are processed but not always combined accurately.

■ However, results from experiments in which moving items are intermingled with static items challenge Treisman's theory.

KEY STUDY 13.3

The moving target experiment (McLeod *et al.*, 1991)

Participants were asked to search for the presence or absence of a single moving X amongst static Xs and moving Os. The target is defined only by its specific conjunction of form and movement, since its shape is shared with the static Xs and its movement with the Os. Treisman's theory would predict that serial attention was necessary for each item when searching for the target, and hence that decision times would increase with an increasing number of distractors.

In fact, the target was found easily regardless of the display's size. This implies a parallel process, and in other experiments McLeod *et al.* showed that the parallel search arose because attention could be restricted to just the group of items with common motion to the exclusion of the static

---

items. Because the target has a unique shape, it can be detected in parallel.

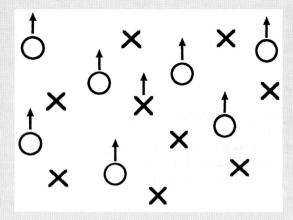

Figure 13.6 *A schematic representation of the display used by McLeod et al. (1991). The arrows indicate motion, and the task is to search for a single moving X among moving Os and intermingled static Xs*

Visual attention and brain damage

Many researchers are interested in the brain regions involved in attention (e.g. Muller & Maxwell, 1994; Halligan, 1995; Driver, 1996). People who've suffered a right-hemisphere stroke involving the *parietal lobe* may completely ignore stimuli occurring on the *left side* (see Chapter 4). For example, they may fail to eat food from the left side of their plate, and be unaware of their body on that side. The fascinating thing about this *unilateral visual neglect* is that these effects occur even though the pathways from the receptors to the central nervous system for the neglected information remain intact. According to Posner & Petersen (1990), the parietal lobe is responsible for disengaging attention from its present focus, and patients with damage to the *pulvinar nucleus* (part of the thalami) have difficulty in shifting attention to a new target (Rafal & Posner, 1987).

Figure 13.7 *Drawing of a parrot by a person with left-side neglect*

Interestingly, among four- to ten-year-old children, those who took less time to switch attention in a specially devised computer game were more likely to show awareness of traffic as they approached a busy road (Dunbar *et al.*, 1999).

Divided attention

> *Ask yourself ...*
> • What are you doing now, apart from reading this sentence?
> • What other examples can you give of being able to do more than one thing at a time?
> • How can you explain this ability?

Some demonstrations of dual-task performance

Allport *et al.* (1972) showed that skilled pianists were able to read music successfully while shadowing speech. Later, Shaffer (1975) reported the case of an expert typist who could type accurately from sight while shadowing speech. But perhaps the most striking example of dual-task performance comes from Spelke *et al.* (1976), who had two students spend five hours a week training at performing two tasks simultaneously.

Initially, the students were required to read short stories while writing down dictated words. At first they found this difficult, and both their comprehension and writing suffered. But after six weeks of training, they could read as quickly, and comprehend as much of what they read, when reading with dictation as when reading without it. Interestingly, though, they could remember very little of what they'd written down, even though thousands of words had been dictated to them over the course of the experiment.

At this point, the task was altered and the students had to write down the *category* a word belonged to (requiring more processing of the words), while simultaneously reading the short stories. Although the task was again difficult initially, the students eventually performed it without any reduction in their comprehension of the stories.

Factors affecting dual-task performance

According to Hampson (1989), factors which make one task easier also tend to make the other easier because:

'Anything which minimises interference between processes or keeps them "further apart" will allow them to be dealt with more readily either selectively or together'.

Eysenck & Keane (1995) identify three factors which affect our ability to perform two tasks at once. These are *difficulty*, *practice* and *similarity*.

> **Box 13.3 The effects of difficulty, practice and similarity on dual-task performance**
>
> **Difficulty**: Generally, the more difficult the task, the less successful dual-task performance is. However, it's hard to define task difficulty objectively, since a task that's difficult for one person might not be for another (and this relates to practice: see below). Also, the demands made by two tasks individually aren't necessarily the same as when they're performed concurrently. Thus, performing two tasks together may introduce fresh demands and the risk of interference.
>
> **Practice**: As we've seen, practice improves dual-task performance. This could be because people develop new strategies for performing each task, minimising interference between them. Another possibility is that practice reduces a task's attentional demands. Finally, practice may produce a more economical way of functioning that uses fewer resources (see pages 193–194).
>
> **Similarity**: Allport *et al.* (1972) showed that when people are required to shadow one message *and* learn pictorial information, both tasks can be performed successfully. This is presumably because they don't involve the same stimulus modality. Two tasks also disrupt performance when both rely on related memory codes (such as visual memory), make use of the same stages of processing (such as the input stage) or require similar responses to be made.
>
> (Based on Eysenck & Keane, 1995)

Theories of divided attention

As we noted earlier, models of selective attention assume the existence of a limited-capacity filter capable of dealing with one information channel at a time. As Hampson & Morris (1996) have observed, these theories:

'... imply a series of stages of processing, starting with superficial, physical analysis, and working "upwards" towards the "higher" cognitive analyses for meaning'.

In Hampson and Morris's view, these processes are better thought of as an *integrated mechanism*, with the high and low levels interacting and combining in the recognition of stimuli. Accordingly, it's better to look at the system's overall processing.

Limited-capacity theories
Kahneman's theory

According to Kahneman (1973), humans have a limited amount of processing capacity, and whether or not tasks can be performed successfully depends on how much demand they make on the limited-capacity processor. Some tasks require little processing capacity, leaving plenty available for performing another task simultaneously. Others require much more, leaving little 'spare'.

The process of determining how much capacity is available ('effort') is related to the allocation of that capacity. How much capacity a task requires depends on things like its difficulty and a person's experience of it. How capacity is allocated depends on *enduring dispositions*, *momentary intentions* and the *evaluation of the attentional demands* (see Figure 13.8, page 192). The central processor is responsible for the allocation policy, and constantly evaluates the level of demand. When demand is too high, the central processor must decide how available attention should be allocated.

Kahneman sees arousal as playing an important part in determining how much capacity is available. Generally, more attentional resources are available when we're aroused and alert than when we're tired and lethargic. Attention can be divided between tasks as long as the total available capacity isn't exceeded. This explains the findings of the dichotic listening tasks discussed earlier, in other words that shadowing requires almost all of the capacity available, leaving the non-shadowed message insufficient capacity. Kahneman's theory also predicts that as skill at carrying out a task increases, so less capacity is needed for it and more becomes available for other tasks. Thus, when people are trained at shadowing, they become able to shadow *and* to attend to the non-shadowed message (Underwood, 1974).

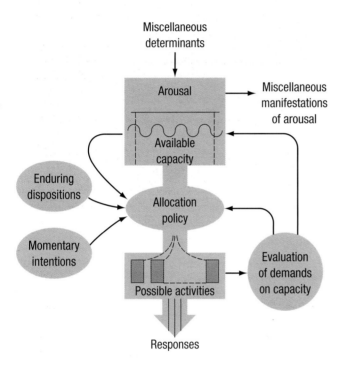

Figure 13.8 *Kahneman's theory of attention. Enduring dispositions are the rules for allocating capacity which are outside voluntary control. These include allocating capacity to novel stimuli and hearing one's own name used in a different conversation. Momentary intentions are voluntary shifts in attention such as listening to a message in a dichotic listening task. Evaluation of demands on capacity include rules for overload on the system, such as deciding to complete one task rather than failing to complete two*

Evaluation of Kahneman's theory

Kahneman's theory portrays attention as a much more flexible and dynamic system than do the models of focused attention. However, it doesn't address the issue of how decisions to channel attention are made, and the difficulty in defining the general limits of capacity has led some researchers to suggest that the concept of a limited capacity should be abandoned (Hampson & Morris, 1996).

Norman and Bobrow's theory

Following on from Kahneman, Norman & Bobrow (1975) have offered a *central capacity interference account* of attentional phenomena.

BOX 13.4 **Norman & Bobrow's (1975) central capacity interference theory**

This theory's central feature is its distinction between *resource-limited* and *data-limited* processes. On a complex task, performance is related to the amount of resources devoted to it. As more resources are allocated, so task performance improves *up to some point*. Performance is thus resource-limited. But on some tasks, applying more resources doesn't lead to improved performance because of external influences (as when participants are required to identify a quiet tone amongst loud, masking 'white' noise). This sort of task is data-limited, because performance can only be improved by altering the stimuli (such as by making the tone louder and/or the masking noise quieter).

Evaluation of Norman and Bobrow's theory

This distinction between resource- and data-limited processes can explain findings from both focused and divided attention research. For example, Treisman & Geffen (1967: see page 187) found that participants shadowing words in one ear had difficulty recognising target words presented simultaneously to the other ear. Lawson (1966), however, found that under similar conditions, participants could detect target tones presented in the non-attended ear. This finding can be explained by proposing that the tone-detection process becomes data-limited much sooner than the word-recognition process.

However, the theory's biggest weakness is its inability to predict beforehand the results an experiment is likely to produce. Because it allows for differential allocation of resources to tasks, an experimenter can never know the level of resources allocated to a particular task. Any results can therefore be interpreted in a way consistent with the theory, and no results can ever be taken as negative evidence.

Multi-channel theories

Supporters of limited-capacity models defend their approach by pointing out that the attentional system breaks down as more and more is demanded of it, and that if data from divided-attention studies are considered carefully it's *not* true that two tasks can be performed together with no disruption at all (Broadbent, 1982). Nevertheless, several researchers have rejected the concept of a general purpose, limited-capacity processor completely. For Allport (1980b, 1989, 1993), the concept of attention is often used synonymously with 'consciousness', with no specification of how it operates. This has done little to increase our understanding of the very problems it's meant to explain.

Modules and multiple resources

According to Allport, it's difficult to see how the neurology of the brain could produce a system of processing capacity that was completely open to any of the tasks that might be presented to it (Hampson & Morris, 1996). It's much more profitable to view the data in terms of tasks competing for the same specialised processing mechanisms or modules, each of which has a limited capacity but none of which is uniquely 'central'.

When two tasks are highly similar, they compete for the same modules, and this leads to performance impairments. However, because dissimilar tasks use different modules, both can be performed simultaneously. A virtually identical theoretical account has been proposed by Navon & Gopher (1979) and Wickens (1992) in their *multiple-resource theory*. Certainly, the findings of dual-task studies (e.g. Allport *et al.*, 1972) are consistent with the idea of different processing mechanisms handling the requirements of different tasks.

However, this approach is also non-falsifiable, since any pattern of data can be explained by proposing the existence of a particular pattern of modules (Navon, 1984). If multiple resources do operate in parallel, they must do so in a highly integrated way, since our behaviour is typically coherent (Eysenck & Keane, 1995).

Attempts at synthesising capacity and module accounts

According to Eysenck (1982, 1984, 1997a) and Baddeley (1986), a much better way of accommodating the data from divided-attention studies is to see capacity and module accounts as being complementary rather than competitive. *Synthesis models* propose the existence of a modality-free central capacity processor, which is involved in the coordination and control of behaviour, and specific processing systems. In Baddeley's (1986) *working memory model*, for example, there are two independently operating and specific systems, an *articulatory/phonological loop* and a *visuo-spatial scratch pad*. These systems can explain why overt repetition of an overlearned sequence of digits doesn't interfere with verbal reasoning, since the former uses an articulatory loop and the latter a central processor (see Chapter 17, pages 253–255).

Ask yourself ...

- Thinking of a skill you possess, such as driving a car or playing a musical instrument, how did demands on your attention and concentration change during the course of acquiring it?
- Can you now do things at the same time as performing these skills which you couldn't have done while learning them?

Automatic vs controlled processing

As we've seen, both laboratory evidence and everyday experience indicate that we can learn to perform two tasks simultaneously and highly efficiently. For some researchers, this is because many processes become *automatic*, i.e. they make no attentional demands, if they're used/practised often enough. Two important theoretical contributions are those of Schneider & Shiffrin (1977) and Norman & Shallice (1986).

Schneider and Shiffrin's automaticity model

Schneider & Shiffrin (1977; Shiffrin & Schneider, 1977) distinguish between controlled and automatic attentional processing:

- *controlled processing* makes heavy demands on attentional resources, is slow, capacity limited, and involves consciously directing attention towards a task;
- *automatic processing* makes no demands on attentional resources, is fast, unaffected by capacity limitations, unavoidable and difficult to modify (it always occurs in the

presence of an appropriate stimulus), and isn't subject to conscious awareness.

The results of several studies (e.g. Schneider & Fisk, 1982) are consistent with Schneider and Shiffrin's view. If people are given practice at a task, they can perform it quickly and accurately, but their performance is resistant to change. An example of apparent automaticity in real life occurs when we learn to drive a car. At first, focused attention is required for each component of driving, and any distraction can disrupt performance. Once we've learned to drive, and as we become more experienced, our ability to simultaneously attend to other things increases.

At first, learning to drive a car, like other psychomotor skills, requires focused attention. The experienced driver however displays automaticity

Logan (1988) suggests that automaticity develops through practice, because automatic responses involve an almost effortless retrieval of an appropriate and well-learned response from memory. This doesn't involve conscious memory, because no thought processes intervene between the presentation of a stimulus and the production of an appropriate response. In Logan's view, then, automaticity occurs when stored information about the sequence of responses necessary to perform a task can be accessed and retrieved rapidly.

An evaluation of Schneider and Shiffrin's model

Despite its intuitive appeal, it's unclear whether automaticity results from a *speeding up* of the processes involved in a task, or a change in the *nature* of the processes themselves. Also, the view that automatic processing makes no demands on attention has been challenged by findings indicating that allegedly automatic tasks *do* influence the performance of simultaneously performed tasks (e.g. Hampson, 1989). Additional problems occur with the Stroop effect.

KEY STUDY 13.4

The Stroop effect

Stroop (1935) showed that if a colour word (such as 'blue') is written in a conflicting colour (such as 'blue' being written in red), participants find it difficult to name the colour the word's been written in. Because reading is such a well-learned, unavoidable and automatic activity, the word interferes with the requirement to name the colour.

An analogue of the Stroop effect can be tried here. The task is to say as quickly as you can the number of characters in each of the rows below. Flowers *et al.* (1979) found that people have difficulty resisting saying the numbers that make up each row rather than counting the numbers, because number recognition is much more automatic compared with number counting. But automatic responses aren't always unavoidable (Eysenck, 1993).

5 5 5
1 1 1 1
2
3 3 3 3 3
4 4
5 5 5
4 4 4 4 4
5 5 5 5
3
4 4 4
2 2 2 2
3 3
4 4 4
1 1 1 1
3
2 2 2

Norman and Shallice's SAS model

To overcome what Eysenck (1993) calls the 'unavoidability criterion', Norman & Shallice (1986) proposed that processing involves two separate control systems: *contention scheduling* and the *supervisory attentional system* (SAS). Some behaviours involve fully automatic processing, which occurs with little conscious awareness of the processes involved, and is controlled by *schemas* (organised plans for behaviour: see below, and Chapter 17, page 259).

However, such processes are capable of disrupting behaviour, and so contention scheduling occurs as a way of resolving conflicts among schemas. This produces *partially automatic processing*, which generally involves more conscious awareness than fully automatic processing, but doesn't require deliberate direction or conscious control. *Deliberate control* involves the SAS and occurs in decision-making and trouble-shooting, allowing flexible responding to occur in novel situations. Baddeley (1997) claims that SAS is like the operation of free will, while contention scheduling leaves no place for free will (see Chapter 49).

An evaluation of Norman and Shallice's model

According to Eysenck & Keane (1995), Norman and Shallice's model is superior to Schneider and Shiffrin's because it:

'... provides a more natural explanation for the fact that some processes are fully automatic whereas others are only partially automatic'.

Although not worked out in the same degree of detail, nor empirically tested as extensively as Schneider and Shiffrin's automaticity model, Norman and Shallice's SAS model provides a very useful basis for conceptualising the *central executive* of Baddeley & Hitch's (1974) working-memory model (Baddeley, 1997: see Chapter 17, pages 253–255).

Action slips

These have been defined as the performance of unintended actions, or actions which deviate from the actor's intentions, and have been extensively researched by Reason (1979, 1992). Reason originally asked 36 participants to keep a diary record of the action slips they made over a four-week period. The participants recorded 433 action slips between them. Reason was able to place 94 per cent of these into one of five categories.

Box 13.5   Reason's five categories of action slips

Storage failures: These were the most common, accounting for 40 per cent of those recorded. They involve repeating an action that's already been completed. For example, pouring a second kettle of boiling water into a teapot of freshly made tea without any recognition of having made the tea already.

Test failures: These involve forgetting the goal of a particular sequence of actions and switching to a different goal. For example, intending to turn on the radio but walking past it and picking up the telephone instead. These accounted for 20 per cent of action slips recorded, and presumably occur because a planned sequence of actions isn't monitored sufficiently at some crucial point in the sequence.

Sub-routine failures: Accounting for 18 per cent of the action slips recorded, these involve either omitting or re-ordering the stages in a sequence of behaviour. For example, making a pot of tea but failing to put any tea bags in it.

Discrimination failures: These involve failing to discriminate between two objects involved in different actions. For example, mistaking toothpaste for shaving cream. These accounted for 11 per cent of the total recorded.

Programme assembly failures: This was the smallest category, accounting for five per cent of the total recorded. They involve incorrectly combining actions, as in unwrapping a sweet, putting the paper in your mouth and throwing the sweet in the waste-paper bin.

(Based on Reason, 1992 and Eysenck, 1997b)

Explaining action slips

Closed- and open-loop control

Paradoxically, action slips seem to occur with highly practised and over-learned actions (which should, therefore, be *least* subject to errors). Reason (1992) proposes that when we first learn to perform a behaviour, our actions are subject to closed-loop control (Adams, 1976). In this, a central processor or attentional system guides and controls a behaviour from start to finish. When we're skilled at a behaviour, it's under open-loop control, controlled by motor programmes or other automatic processes.

Closed-loop control is slow and effortful, whereas open-loop control is fast and allows attentional resources to be given over to other activities. However, closed-loop control is less prone to error and responds more flexibly to environmental demands than open-loop control. As a result, action slips occur because of an over-reliance on open-loop control when closed-loop control (selectively attending to the task) should be occurring.

As we saw in studies of focused attention, material not attended to is typically poorly remembered because it doesn't get stored in long-term memory. So, the most common type of action slip, storage failures, can be explained in terms of open-loop induced attentional failures leading to a failure to store (and hence recall) previous actions. As a result, an action may be repeated. Other slips also seem amenable to explanation in terms of open-loop control (Eysenck, 1997b).

Schema theory

An alternative theoretical account has been advanced by Norman (1981) and elaborated by Sellen & Norman (1992). Their theory is based on the concept of the *schema*, first proposed by Bartlett (1932). Briefly, a schema is an organised mental representation of everything we understand by a given object, concept or event, based on past experience (see Chapter 17, page 259 and Chapter 21, pages 309–312).

Box 13.6	Sellen & Norman's (1992) schema theory of action slips

Parent schemas are the highest-level schemas, corresponding to an overall intention or goal (such as going to a football match). At a lower level are *child schemas*, which correspond to the actions involved in accomplishing the overall intention or goal (such as driving the car to the football ground, buying a ticket and so on). Each schema has a particular *activation level*, and a behaviour occurs when the activation level is reached (which depends on the current situation and current intentions) and when appropriate 'triggering' conditions exist. If:

a there's an error in the formation of an intention;

b an incorrect schema is activated;

c activation of the correct schema is lost; or

d there's faulty triggering of an active schema,

e then an action slip occurs.

Reason & Mycielska (1982) believe that a thorough understanding of the nature of action slips is necessary to avoid potential disaster occurring in the real world. Eysenck (1995) maintains that action slips would be eliminated if we were to use closed-loop control for all behaviours, but this would be a waste of valuable attentional resources! The frequency of action slips reported by Reason's (1979) participants (an average of about one per day) suggests that people alternate between closed-loop and open-loop control as the circumstances dictate. For Eysenck (1995):

'The very occasional action slip is a price which is generally worth paying in order to free the attentional system from the task of constant monitoring of our habitual actions'.

Action slips represent the minor errors of an action system that typically functions very well indeed (Eysenck, 1997b). Similarly:

'Absent-minded errors demonstrate misapplied competence rather than incompetence'. (Reason, 1984)

Each type of action slip might require its own explanation. While the mechanisms underlying them may appear similar, they might actually be very different (Eysenck & Keane, 1995). Additionally, any theoretical account depends on the validity of the data it attempts to explain. The diary method used by Reason may supply weak data, because participants might not have detected some of their action slips or remembered to record them when they did (Eysenck, 1997b). As a result, the percentages reported by Reason may be inaccurate.

Box 13.7	Reason's (1992) 'oak–yolk effect' experiment

Participants are instructed to answer the following series of questions as quickly as possible:

Q What do we call the tree that grows from acorns?
A Oak
Q What do we call a funny story?
A Joke
Q What sound does a frog make?
A Croak
Q What is Pepsi's major competitor?
A Coke
Q What's another word for cape?
A Cloak
Q What do you call the white of an egg?
A Yolk

'Yolk' is, in fact, the wrong answer (correct answer = albumen). Reason found that 85 per cent of his participants made this error, compared with only five per cent of a control group given just the final question. However, are such trick-induced action slips comparable to those that occur spontaneously in everyday life? According to Sellen & Norman (1992), the laboratory environment is the least likely place to see truly spontaneous absent-minded errors.

Finally, in Eysenck & Keane's (1995) words:

'The number of occurrences of any particular kind of action slip is meaningful only when we know the number of occasions on which the slip might have occurred but did not. Thus, the small number of discrimination failures [reported by Reason] may reflect either good discrimination or a relative lack of situations requiring anything approaching a fine discrimination'.

Conclusions

It's sometimes possible to divide attention between two different tasks, although how this is achieved hasn't yet been satisfactorily explained. Two broad types of explanation are those which propose a general purpose limited-capacity processor, and those which identify modules, each with a limited capacity but none of which is central. The idea that many processes become automatic and make no demands on attention has some support, and helps explain why we sometimes perform behaviours we didn't intend. Action slips involve behaviours that are highly practised, and are the price we pay for not having to continuously monitor our actions.

CHAPTER SUMMARY

- According to Broadbent, who was trying to account for Cherry's **cocktail party phenomenon**, humans must **selectively attend** to some information and 'tune out' the rest.

- Using **binaural listening**, Cherry identified several physical differences affecting selective attention to one of two messages. He also used **dichotic listening**, in which participants had to **shadow** one of the messages. They could do this, but remembered little, if anything, of the non-shadowed message, whose meaning was completely lost.

- Three **single-channel models** share the belief in a 'bottleneck' or **filter** which allows some information to be passed on for further processing, either discarding the rest or processing it only to a limited degree. They differ mainly in terms of how early or late the filtering takes place.

- Broadbent's **early-selection filter model** accounts for Cherry's findings and his own **split-span** data. But people's ability to switch attention to the non-attended ear when their name is spoken, together with other research findings relating to the processing of **meaning**, are inconsistent with Broadbent's model.

- According to Treisman's **attenuation model**, competing information is analysed for its physical properties, **and** for sounds, syllable patterns, grammatical structures and meaning. The selective filter 'turns down' the non-shadowed message. If this includes biological 'pre-sets', our attention will switch to the non-shadowed message.

- The Deutsch–Norman **late-selection filter theory/pertinence model** sees selection as occurring only after all inputs have been analysed at a high level. The filter is nearer the response end of the processing system.

- Mechanisms involved in **focused visual attention** include eye movements that allow us to fixate specific regions of the visual field. But visual attention **isn't** confined to the part of the visual field processed by the fovea, as demonstrated by **covert attention**. This is like an **internal mental spotlight**.

- According to Eriksen's **zoom-lens model**, the internal spotlight has a beam which may be very narrow or very broad.

- According to Treisman's **feature-integration theory**, focusing attention on their location allows unitary **features** to be formed into their various **objects**. **Illusory conjunctions** can arise in the absence of relevant stored knowledge or focused attention.

- Researchers interested in **divided attention** typically measure **dual-task performance**. Three factors affecting dual-task performance are **task difficulty**, **practice** and **similarity**.

- According to Kahneman, humans have only a limited processing capacity. Different tasks require different amounts of processing capacity, leaving more or less available for performing other tasks.

- The **central processor** controls the allocation policy and constantly evaluates demand level. **Arousal** is important for determining the amount of available capacity, and the more skilled we are at a particular task, the less capacity is needed.

- Norman and Bobrow's **central capacity interference theory** distinguishes between **resource-limited** and **data-limited performance**.

- Several researchers have rejected the concept of a general purpose, limited-capacity processor. The most useful way of interpreting the data is in terms of tasks competing for the same **modules**, each of which has a limited capacity but none of which is uniquely 'central'.

- Two highly similar tasks compete for the same modules, leading to performance deficits, while dissimilar tasks use different modules and thus don't compete. This view is also taken by **multiple-resource theory**.

- **Synthesis models** propose the existence of a modality-free central capacity processor, plus specific independent processing systems, such as Baddeley's **articulatory/phonological loop** and **visuo-spatial scratch pad**.

- Schneider and Shiffrin distinguish between **controlled** and **automatic processing**. The '**Stroop effect**' shows that well-learned, unavoidable and automatic skills (such as reading) can interfere with other tasks (such as naming the colour of a written word).

- **Contention scheduling** is used to resolve conflicts among **schemas**, which control **fully automatic processing** and produces **partially automatic processing**. The **supervisory attentional system** (SAS) is involved in **deliberate control**, which allows flexible responses in novel situations.

- The most common type of **action slips** are **storage** failures. Other categories include **test**, **sub-routine**, **discrimination** and **programme assembly failures**.

- Action slips seem to involve actions that are highly practised or over-learned. Action slips reflect an over-reliance on **open-loop control** when **closed-loop control** (focused attention) is needed. Different types of action slip may require their own explanations.

Self-assessment questions

1 Describe and evaluate the contribution of psychological research to our understanding of focused (selective) attention.

2 Discuss **one** early-selection and **one** late-selection model of focused (selective) attention.

3 a Describe research into controlled and automatic processing.
  b Assess the extent to which such research helps us to identify the limits of divided attention.

4 Discuss research into slips associated with automatic processing.

Web addresses

http://www.bioscience.org/2000/v5/d/alain/fulltext.htm

http://www.diku.dk/~panic/eyegaze/node15.html

http://www.princeton.edu/~psych/psychsite/fac_treisman.html

http://www.multimedia.calpoly.edu

http://www.mb.jhu.edu

http://www.cc.gatetech.edu/~jimmyd/summaries/index.html

http://ear.berkeley.edu/auditory_lab/

http://www.wws.princeton.edu/faculty/kahneman.htm

Further reading

Eysenck, M.W. & Keane, M.T. (1995) *Cognitive Psychology – A Student's Handbook* (3rd edition). London: Lawrence Erlbaum Associates. A detailed, comprehensive, relatively non-threatening textbook. The chapter on attention discusses all the areas covered here.

Solso, R.L. (1995) *Cognitive Psychology* (4th edition). Boston: Allyn & Bacon. Another comprehensive, but fairly user-friendly text. The attention chapter includes sections on neuropsychology, and relates attention to consciousness.

Chapter 14

Pattern Recognition

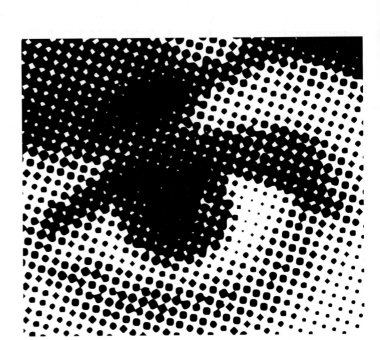

Introduction and overview

Pattern recognition is the process by which we assign meaning to visual input, by identifying the objects in the visual field (Eysenck, 1993). Although our ability to recognise, identify and categorise objects seems effortless, it actually comprises several remarkably complex achievements. While we're usually aware only of structured, coherent objects:

'Our visual systems have to 'decide' which edges, surfaces, corners and so on go together to form units or wholes'.

(Roth, 1995)

As Roth says, theories of pattern recognition must explain the complexity of a process which 'is so ingrained in our experience that we rarely even notice that we do it' (Houston *et al.*, 1991). A way of illustrating this challenge is to consider the ease with which we're able to recognise the letter T, whether it's printed on paper, handwritten or spoken.

T T T T T T T T T T T T T T T T T T T T T T T

A major contribution to our understanding of this process comes in the form of the Gestalt laws of perception, which are discussed in Chapter 15. Pattern (or object) recognition can be regarded as the central problem of perception and, indeed, the terms are almost synonymous. To this extent, all the theories of perception discussed in Chapter 15 can be thought of as trying to account for pattern recognition (PR).

However, the theories discussed here are usually referred to as theories of PR (rather than perceptual theories). *Face recognition* is a special case of PR.

Theories of PR

Template-matching hypothesis

According to the *template-matching hypothesis* (TMH), incoming sensory information is matched against miniature copies (or templates) of previously presented patterns or objects. These are stored in long-term memory. Template-matching is also used by computerised cash registers, which identify a product and its cost by matching a bar code with some stored representation of that code.

Figure 14.1 *The bar codes on the goods we buy identify them. When the bar code is read by a computerised cash register, the computer supplies the price, which is then entered on the cash register tape. The code is read by template-matching on the basis of the positions, widths and spacing of the lines*

The bar codes on the goods we buy identify them. When the bar code is read by a computerised cash register, the computer supplies the price, which is then entered on the cash register tape. The code is read by template matching on the basis of the positions, widths and spacing of the lines.

Given the complexity of the environment, we'd need an incredibly large number of templates, each corresponding to a specific visual input. Even if we were able to use a wheelbarrow to carry around the cerebrum needed for this, the time needed to search for a specific template would be inordinately long, and we'd never recognise unfamiliar patterns (Solso, 1995).

Ask yourself ...
- How would you describe (a) a cup; (b) a torch; (c) a penguin?
- What kinds of basic components could they be broken down into?

Biederman's geon theory

Biederman's (1987) *geon theory* of PR ('geon' stands for 'geometrical icon'), or *recognition-by-components model*, is intended to overcome TMH's limitations. Biederman's starting point is the everyday observation that if we're asked to describe an object, familiar or unfamiliar, we tend to use the same basic strategy. We almost certainly divide it into parts or components (parsing/segmentation), comprising various three-dimensional objects (volumetric concepts or geons) such as 'block', 'cylinder', 'funnel' and 'wedge'. The regions into which the object is divided are probably the regions of greatest concavity (parts which make sharp angles with other parts). According to geon theory, geons (simple geometric 'primitives') can be combined in various ways to produce more complex ones. In this way, a very large range of different objects can be described.

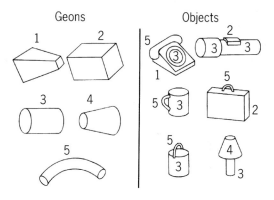

Figure 14.2 *Biederman's geons (left) and some of the objects they can combine to make (right)*

Component- or geon-based information extracted from the visual object is matched in parallel against stored representations of 36 geons that make up the basic set. The identification of any visual object is determined by whichever stored representation provides the best fit. But for a *complete* object to be recognised, there must also be a store of complete object descriptions, in which both the characteristic geon set and the *relationships within it* are specified (Roth, 1995).

An evaluation of geon theory

According to Roth (1995), Biederman's theory was designed to:

- provide an intuitively plausible account of how we recognise objects in terms of their obvious components;
- explain the fact that this recognition is both rapid and accurate, despite variations in angle of viewing and the often 'degraded' information available (due, for example, to poor lighting, one object obscuring another and so on).

One general prediction is that since an appropriate arrangement of geons provides a very powerful cue for object recognition, this recognition will occur even when an object's full complement of geons is absent.

Figure 14.4 *The middle column shows degraded but 'recognisable' versions; the right-hand column shows 'non-recognisable' versions*

Geons can be so degrading (Biederman, 1987)

Biederman produced line drawings of 36 common objects, differing in complexity (the number of basic geon components needed to draw them ranged from two to nine). For each drawing, there were 'partial' versions (one or more geons were missing), and each stimulus was presented for just 100 ms. Participants had to name the object aloud as quickly as possible.

Figure 14.3 *Complete and partial versions of objects used in Biederman's experiment*

Error rates for 'partial' objects were extremely low, with 90 per cent accuracy even for complex objects with two-thirds of their components missing. So, even the simplest line drawings can be readily and correctly identified, provided the relevant geons are present. These findings are consistent with geon theory. Also, response times were almost as fast for partial as for complete objects, although complex complete objects were slightly more quickly identified than simple ones. This too is consistent with the theory: if an object's geons are simultaneously matched with stored geon descriptions, then the greater the number of geons available, the faster the critical level needed for a 'match' will be reached.

A more stringent test is participants' ability to identify degraded versions of objects, in which the normal contours are disrupted. In a second experiment (using the same basic procedure as the first), Biederman presented stimulus objects like those shown in Figure 14.4.

The middle column shows degraded versions which are still recognisable, while those in the right-hand column are non-recognisable. In the latter, the contours have been deleted at regions of concavity. These stimuli were presented for 100, 200 or 750ms, with 25, 45 or 65 per cent of their contours removed. Once again, results supported the theory.

Roth (1995) believes that the idea of geons is intuitively appealing and also offers a relatively flexible and comprehensive system for describing objects. Geons include a range of different shapes that can be applied not only to artifacts such as chairs, tables and houses, but also to mammals and other animals. Although the theory makes clear predictions which can be tested experimentally (see Key Study 14.1), identification of the 36 geons and structural relationships is based more on intuition than empirical evidence. There have been *no* tests to determine whether it's *these* geons which are used in object recognition rather than other components.

Prototype theories of PR

Prototype theories propose that instead of storing templates, we store a smaller number of prototypes ('abstract forms representing the basic elements of a set of stimuli': Eysenck, 1993). Whereas TMH treats each stimulus as a separate entity, prototype theories maintain that similarities between related stimuli play an important part in PR. So, each stimulus is a member of a *category* of stimuli and shares basic properties with other members of the category.

The main weakness of this approach is its inability to explain how PR is affected by the context as well as by the stimulus itself (Eysenck, 1993). Knowing just what properties are shared by a category of stimuli is important, but isn't specified by the theories. What, for example, is an 'idealised' letter T, and what is the 'best representation of the pattern'? This question has been addressed by *feature-detection theories*.

Feature-detection theories

Feature-detection theories represent the most influential approach to PR, maintaining that every stimulus can be thought of as a configuration of elementary features. Gibson *et al.* (1968) argue that the letters of the alphabet, for example, are composed of combinations of twelve basic features (such as vertical lines, horizontal lines and closed curves).

In *visual scanning tasks*, participants search lists of letters as quickly as possible to find a randomly placed target letter. Since finding a target letter entails detecting its elementary features, the task should be more difficult when the target and non-target letters have more features in common. This is exactly what researchers have found (e.g. Rabbitt, 1967). Additional support comes from studies of eye movements and fixation. Presumably, the more a feature in a pattern is looked at, the more information is being extracted from it. The perception of features within complex patterns depends on higher cognitive processes (such as attention and purpose), as well as the nature of the physical stimuli being looked at.

It's also well established that the visual systems of some vertebrates contain both peripheral (retinal) and central (cortical) cells that respond only to particular features of visual stimuli. In their pioneering research, Hubel & Wiesel (1968) identified three kinds of cortical cell ('simple', 'complex' and 'hypercomplex', referring to the types of stimuli the cells respond to: see Box 5.9, pages 72–73). More recently, it's been claimed that there are face-specific cells in the infero-temporal cortex of the monkey (Ono *et al.*, 1993: see below, page 207).

In humans, Perrett (cited in Messer, 1995) has identified cells that respond to specific aspects of a face or to a set of features. There may also be cells which respond to many different views of a face, 'summing' inputs from a variety of sources.

An evaluation of feature-detection theories

Whether such cells constitute the feature-detectors proposed by feature-detection theories is unclear. These neurological detectors may be a necessary pre-condition for higher-level (or cognitive) pattern task analysis. However, feature-detection theories typically assume a *serial* form of processing, with feature extraction being followed by feature combination, which itself is then followed by PR (Eysenck, 1993). For example, Hubel and Wiesel saw the sequence of simple, complex and hypercomplex cells representing a serial flow of information, whereby only particular information is processed at any one time before being passed on to the next level upwards, and so on.

The alternative and widely held view is that considerable *parallel processing* takes place in the visual cortex, and that the relationship between different kinds of cortical cell is more complex than originally believed. An early example of a non-serial processing computer program is Selfridge's (1959) *Pandemonium model*.

KEY STUDY 14.2

Eye movements reflect what you're looking for (Yarbus, 1967)

Yarbus found that when participants were shown the scene in Figure 14.5, different patterns of eye movements were recorded depending on whether they were asked to:

- examine the picture at will;
- estimate the economic status of the people shown;
- judge their ages;
- query what they had been doing prior to the arrival of the visitor;
- remember their clothing;
- remember their positions (and objects in the room); or
- estimate how long since the visitor had last seen the family.

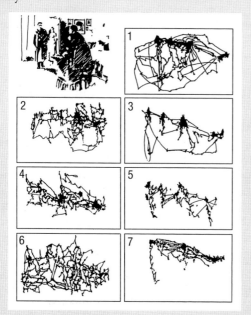

Figure 14.5 *Different patterns of eye movements corresponding to different instructions*

Box 14.1   Selfridge's (1959) Pandemonium model

Selfridge's computer program was designed to recognise Morse code and a small set of handwritten letters. The components of the model are known as *demons*, of which there are four kinds:

- *image demons* simply copy the pattern presented (and these are analogous to the retina);
- *feature demons* analyse the information from the image demons in terms of combinations of features;
- *cognitive demons* are specialised for particular letters and 'scream' according to how much the input from the feature demons matches their special letter; and finally,
- a *decision demon* chooses the 'loudest scream' and identifies the letter (see Figure 14.6, page 202).

Although Pandemonium was never intended as a model of human perception, Groome *et al.* (1999) ask what assumptions about human perception would need to be made if it were modelled. These could then be tested against human data. One such assumption is that context would have minimal effect on PR. Feature-detection theories in general have been criticised over their failure to take sufficient account of the role played by *context* and *perceiver characteristics* (such as

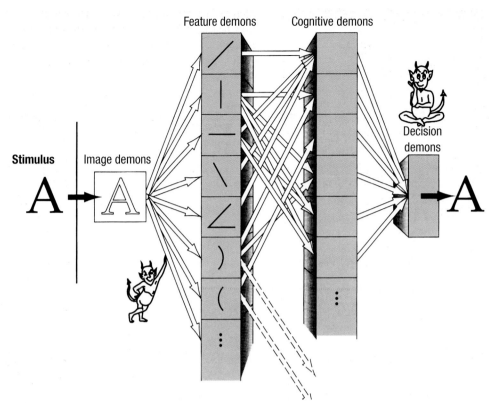

Figure 14.6 *A representation of Selfridge's Pandemonium model of pattern recognition (based on Ruch, 1984)*

expectations: see Box 15.4, page 221). An ambiguous feature can produce different patterns, and different features can produce the same pattern, depending on the context.

Context can tell us what patterns are likely to be present and hence what to expect. Sometimes, we may fail to notice the absence of something (such as a typing or printing error) because of its high predictability (i.e. we expect it to be there). The influence of context and expectation illustrates *top-down/conceptually-driven processing*, while most feature-detection theories involve *bottom-up/data-driven processing* (see theories of perception in Chapter 15). PR involves attending selectively to some aspects of the presented stimuli but not to others, aided by context. PR and selective attention are therefore closely related (Solso, 1995: see Chapter 13).

Face recognition

Just as we can identify different categories of dogs or chairs, so we can identify 'baby's face', 'man's face' or 'Japanese face'. We also have some ability to identify individual dogs or chairs, but in the case of human faces, the ability to identify individuals is of paramount importance (Bruce, 1995). Recognising faces is probably one of the most demanding tasks that we set our visual systems. Unlike most other cases of object identification, the task is to identify one specific instance of the class of objects known as faces (Groome *et al.*, 1999).

Strictly, *face recognition* (using the face to identify an individual) is part of the broader process of *face perception* (the whole range of activities whereby information is derived from the face, such as inferring emotional states from facial expressions).

According to Eysenck & Keane (1995), substantial recent research has provided greater knowledge about the processes involved in face recognition than about those involved in most other forms of PR.

> *Ask yourself ...*
>
> * Choose a familiar face (that of a friend, lecturer, film star) and describe it. What makes this face unique, i.e. what enables you to recognise it as that specific face?
> * What do all faces have in common?

Are faces more than the sum of their parts?

Based on theories of basic level PR (such as Biederman's geon theory), faces could be described as a set of parts (the features) and their spatial arrangement. When we're asked to describe a face, or speculate about how individual faces are represented in memory, we're likely to think in terms of separate features. This tendency is undoubtedly created partly by our language, which has discrete terms for the different functional parts of the face. But the visual system may not describe faces in this way. According to Bruce & Young (1998):

> '... there is a good deal of evidence that face patterns are treated more as wholes or as inter-relationships between different features, than simply as a list of their features ...'.

In other words, it seems more valid to describe faces in a more *configural* way (Bruce, 1995).

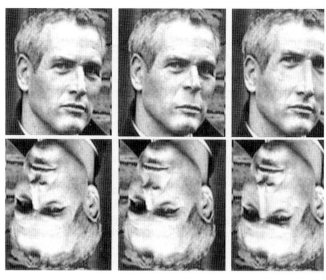

You should find it easy to detect which image shows the real Paul Newman, though the distortions are much easier to see in the upright than in the inverted images (from Bruce & Young 1998)

| Box 14.2 | The meanings of 'configural' |

According to Bruce (1995), although psychologists tend to agree that a face is greater than the sum of its parts, studies of face perception haven't always made explicit which sense of 'configural' is being investigated. She identifies three meanings:

- the spatial relationships between features are as important as the features themselves;
- facial features interact with one another (for example, perception of mouth shape is affected by the shape of the nose);
- faces are processed holistically (they aren't analysed into separable features at all).

However, early research into face recognition implicitly assumed that a part-based description might be appropriate, comprising a list of features each with different specific values. Many psychologists during the 1970s used artificially constructed faces, such as Bradshaw & Wallace's (1971) use of *Identikit* (see Figure 14.7). This is a set of varying line-drawn features used by the police to construct a criminal/suspect's face, based on a witness's description (see Chapter 21).

Bradshaw and Wallace presented pairs of faces to see how quickly participants decided that two faces in a pair were different, as a function of the number of features that differed. They found that the *more* differences between the two faces, the *faster* participants responded. They concluded that facial features are processed *independently* and *in sequence*. Sergent (1984) reviewed several other studies which reached similar conclusions.

However, Sergent also noted that faces which differed in several features also differed more in terms of overall configuration than those differing in only a few. If features really are processed independently, the number of feature differences shouldn't affect how quickly a 'difference' judgement is made (the judgement can be made as soon as any one feature difference is spotted). Accordingly, Sergent constructed eight slightly different faces from the same 'kit' of face features, but each had one of two different chins, eye colours and arrangements of

internal features (*internal space*). 'Different' pairs (one, two or three feature differences) were intermixed with pairs of identical faces, and participants were asked to decide whether the 'different' pairs were the same or different.

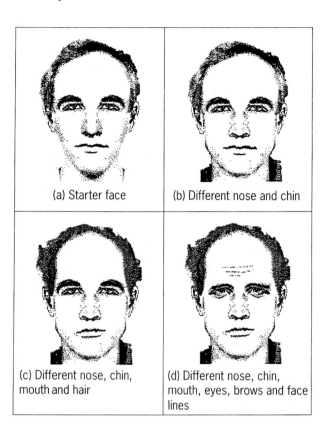

Figure 14.7 *Examples of Identikit faces used in Bradshaw & Wallace's (1971) experiment*

Sergent confirmed Bradshaw and Wallace's finding that the more features that differed, the faster a 'difference' decision was made. However, when only a single feature differed, 'difference' decisions were faster when this involved chins (and this was true for all participants). When something in addition to chins differed, the decisions were even faster. This latter finding suggests that there's *interactive processing* of different dimensions of facial appearance: a configuration emerges from a set of features that's more than the sum of its parts (see Box 14.2).

Are upright and inverted faces processed differently?

Ask yourself ...

- Before reading on, look at the photographs of Margaret Thatcher on page 204. Describe what you see.

An interesting additional finding of Sergent's study was that when she repeated the experiment using inverted face images, the results supported the view that the face is processed as a set of *independent* features. Several other studies have confirmed this finding.

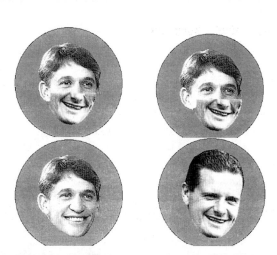

| Box 14.3 | Evidence relating to differential processing of upright and inverted faces |

- Tanaka & Farah (1993) found that facial features encountered in the context of an upright normal face were more likely to be identified correctly in the context of that face (as opposed to being tested in isolation). However, this advantage wasn't found for inverted faces. They concluded that the representation of whole faces is based on a holistic description, while inverted faces (as well as houses and scrambled faces: see Chapter 16) are represented as sets of independent components.

- According to Yin (1969), while upright faces are recognised more accurately than physical objects, the reverse is true for inverted faces. Somehow, the different features in inverted faces can't be integrated to give a coherent impression. This is one of the best established findings in the field of face recognition (Bruce, 1995).

- Young *et al.* (1987) took pictures of well-known faces and sliced them horizontally to form separate upper and lower face halves. They then paired the upper half with a 'wrong' lower half. Participants were asked to name the top halves of faces presented either in isolation or when paired with the 'wrong' lower halves. The top halves were much harder to name when combined with the wrong lower halves than when shown alone, or when the two correct halves were misaligned. Young *et al.*'s explanation was that combining the two halves produced a 'new' configuration (see 'Gazzaker' images above). Significantly, when composite faces were inverted, participants named them more accurately than when they were presented upright.

- In Thompson's (1980) *Thatcher illusion*, the eyes and mouth are cut out and inverted within the face. When viewed upright, this produces a grotesque appearance, but when inverted, it looks quite similar to the 'normal' version.

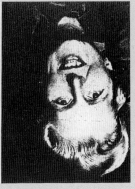

According to Bartlett & Searcy (1993), the most likely explanation of the Thatcher illusion is what they call the *configural processing hypothesis*. The relationship between the features is more difficult to perceive when the face is inverted (so the features are processed independently), and the strangeness of the grotesque face can't be seen (since it arises from the relationship between the features).

If Bartlett and Searcy are correct, does this necessarily mean that there's something special about face recognition? A study by Diamond & Carey (1986) of dog breeders and judges suggests that expertise may be the crucial variable. These dog experts were just as affected by the inversion of dog faces as non-experts were by the inversion of human faces. So, perhaps it is configural processing that enables experts to make fine discriminations within a particular category, all the members of which share the same overall structure. When it comes to human face recognition, we all appear to be experts.

Disorders of face processing

While we might all be experts at face recognition, there are rare but dramatic cases of people who are unable to recognise familiar faces, including those of their spouses, other relatives and friends. The most common such disorder is *prosopagnosia*.

Prosopagnosia

McNeil & Warrington (1993) report the case of W.J., a 51-year-old man who suffered a series of strokes, causing lesions in his left occipital, frontal and temporal lobes (see Chapter 4).

CASE STUDY 14.1

W.J. (McNeil & Warrington, 1993)

When W.J. was shown a set of three photographs (one famous and two unfamiliar faces), he couldn't select the famous one. However, if he was asked 'Which one is ...?', his performance improved significantly (showing *covert* or *unconscious recognition*). Following the onset of his prosopagnosia, he acquired a flock of sheep which he photographed. He knew them by number and could recognise at least eight of the 16 from their pictures. This represents remarkable evidence of an ability to learn to recognise individual sheep, while still being profoundly prosopagnosic for human faces (Groome *et al.*, 1999).

As the case of W.J. demonstrates, prosopagnosia appears to be a face-specific deficit. Several other case studies show that patients can still identify personal possessions (including non-human animals), and can recognise faces if tested indirectly (Groome *et al.*, 1999). Covert recognition suggests that prosopagnosia isn't a memory deficiency.

Some of these patients can derive particular kinds of *meaning* from faces (including emotional expression), despite being unable to recognise them. Conversely, some patients with a form of dementia find it difficult to recognise emotional expressions, being still able to classify famous faces according to occupation (which requires knowledge of personal identity: Kurucz & Feldmar, 1979). The task of recognising individual identity from a face, therefore, seems to be quite separate from that of recognising an emotional expression. While the former requires recognition of an individual regardless of the expression, the latter requires recognising emotion irrespective of other aspects of facial appearance. Experiments with normal adults have shown that identity seems to be ignored when identifying emotional expressions, and expressions are identified no more quickly from familiar than from unfamiliar faces.

Unilateral neglect

We saw in Chapter 13 that people who suffer strokes in the right parietal lobe display *left-sided neglect* (*unilateral neglect*). While this usually affects perception of a wide range of objects, in rare cases it may present as *face-specific* (as in the case of Keith: Young *et al.*, 1990). The parietal lobe is involved in attention, perception of the world's spatial layout, and especially in the visual abilities we need to control our actions (Milner & Goodale, 1996).

In evolutionary terms, the key task of vision is to construct a representation of the external environment, which will permit effective actions. Many parts of the visual system are tightly integrated with the mechanisms that control our movements (Bruce & Young, 1998). Unilateral neglect involves a deficit in a specific form of motor activity, namely eye movements (see Chapter 5). When people with left-sided neglect are shown a *chimeric*, comprising halves of two different photographs of faces joined at the midline, they often identify only the half-face falling to their *right*.

Robert (Walker *et al.*, 1996), who suffered a right-hemisphere stroke, was shown a photograph of Gorbachev, and the chimeric of Anna Ford and Terry Wogan (see below). The white squares represent the initial fixation position on the midline before the face was actually presented. Robert's saccades went from the midline to the right side of each image, but after that *only* the right side was explored. Despite being warned that the stimuli would be composed of two faces joined together, he still only identified Terry Wogan.

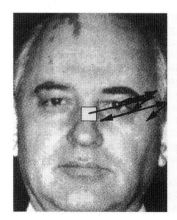

Neglect *doesn't* appear to be caused by an inability to scan the left side, but exactly what does cause it is still unclear. It most likely involves some kind of difficulty in forming an adequate representation of the face's left side, or an inability or disinclination to attend properly to it. Interestingly, neurologically normal people tend to overestimate the importance of information from the *left* side of the face (Bruce & Young, 1998).

Capgras delusion/syndrome

Once thought to be extremely rare, Capgras syndrome is one of the most extensively studied forms of delusional misidentification. It involves the belief that one or more close relatives have been replaced by near-identical impostors. Cases have been found in many cultures, and show a consistent pattern. Patients can be otherwise rational and lucid, and are able to appreciate that they're making an extraordinary claim (Bruce & Young, 1998).

CASE STUDY 14.2

Arthur (Ramachandran, 1998)

Arthur had been in a near-fatal car accident and lay in a coma for three weeks. When he finally awoke, he seemed restored to his former self, except for this one incredible delusion about his parents – they were impostors. Nothing could convince him otherwise.

Ramachandran asked him, 'Arthur, who brought you to the hospital?'

'That guy in the waiting room', Arthur replied. 'He's the old gentleman who's been taking care of me.'

'You mean your father?'

'No, no, doctor. That guy isn't my father. He just looks like him. But I don't think he means any harm.'

'Arthur, why do you think he's an impostor? What gives you that impression?'

'Maybe my real father employed him to take care of me, paid him some money so that he could pay my bills.'

Arthur's parents revealed that he didn't treat them as impostors when they spoke to him on the telephone, but only in face-to-face encounters. This implied that Arthur wasn't amnesic regarding his parents, and that he wasn't just 'crazy'.

Models of face recognition

According to Bruce (1995), the complete identification of a known face requires not just that we recognise the pattern of the face as a familiar one, but that we know the context in which we've encountered the person and can retrieve his/her name. Studies of both normal and brain-damaged people suggest that there's a sequence of distinct stages involved in retrieving someone's identity, with failures at each stage characterised by different problems of identification.

Hay & Young (1982) were the first to outline a stage model, which was supported by the pattern of errors reported by Young *et al.* (1985) in their diary study of everyday failures in person identification. On the basis of their data, Young *et al.* proposed a model of the functional components involved in person identification.

After representational processing, information about the face of the person encountered is processed by recognition units. These contain stored representations of known faces. If the currently viewed face matches one of these representations, information about the resemblance is signalled to *person identity nodes* (PINs). Basic information about personal identity is stored in the PINs, via which names and other details are accessed (from the additional information stores).

Decisions as to whether or not a particular face is familiar, or about the person's identity, are made as a result of communication between these levels and the cognitive system.

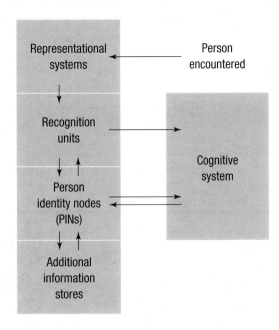

Figure 14.8 *Young* et al.*'s (1985) model of the functional components involved in person identification*

This model was revised by Bruce & Young (1986). The stages of person identification are now put into the broader context of their relationship with the other uses made of facial information. The model comprises several different processing 'modules' linked in sequence or in parallel.

Independent routes are drawn for the processing of emotional expressions, lip-reading ('facial speech') and identification, thus allowing the processing of information from both familiar and unfamiliar faces. Directed visual processing allows for certain kinds of operation to be performed on faces without accessing their identities (such as looking out for white-haired people when meeting your grandmother at the station). The route by which familiar faces are identified involves separate stages of representation of the face image (structural encodings), access of stored structural descriptions of known faces (face recognition units/FRUs), access of information about personal identity (via PINs), and finally, retrieval of proper names.

An evaluation of the Bruce & Young (1986) model

According to Groome *et al.* (1999), the dissociation between processing of emotional expression and person identification makes good sense. We need to be able to recognise a face irrespective of its expression and vice versa. Despite being broad, Bruce (1995) believes the model has the strength of being falsifiable.

Some relevant experimental evidence comes in the form of the *tip-of-the-tongue* (TOT) *phenomenon* involving people's names (see Key Study 17.9, page 261). Brennen *et al.* (1990) wanted to know if participants in a TOT state, after being asked to identify someone from a description, could be helped

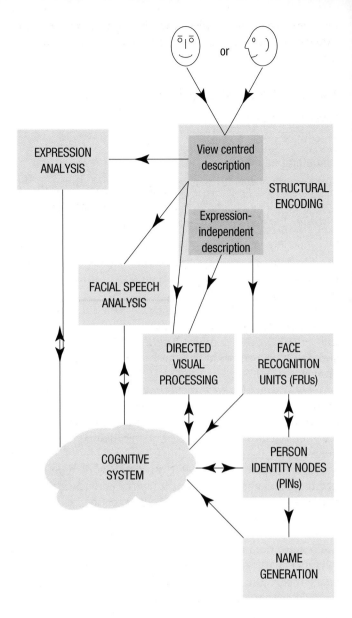

Figure 14.9 *Bruce & Young's (1986) functional model for face recognition*

to retrieve the name by viewing a picture of the person or by being given the initials of the missing name. Providing the initials allowed about half the missing names to be retrieved, but pictures produced just as little success as simply repeating the questions. These results are consistent with Bruce and Young's model. In a TOT state, participants must be at the stage of PINs, but are unable to reach the next stage of name retrieval. Seeing the face shouldn't help, since there's no direct link between faces and names. But the initials provide partial cues to help name retrieval.

However, evidence of covert recognition in prosopagnosic patients (see Case Study 14.1) are difficult for the model to explain. Familiarity judgements are supposedly made on the basis of activation levels at FRUs, forming an early stage in the sequence of establishing the person's full identity. If patients consistently fail to make familiarity judgements at better than chance levels, they should be unable to access information from later ('deeper') levels (stages) in the system. Yet this is exactly what covert recognition entails. Partly as an attempt to overcome these difficulties, the model was revised and extended by Burton *et al.* (1990) and Bruce (1992: see Bruce, 1995).

Face recognition and the brain

Given that face perception is such a demanding perceptual task, it's not surprising that brain damage can result in deficits in face processing, such as prosopagnosia (Groome *et al.*,1999). According to Young & Bruce (1998):

'Because faces are of such fundamental social importance to a creature that lives in a complex society, extensive areas of the brain are involved in their perception'.

The functions of these areas are being revealed in studies of the effects of different types of brain injury, and using modern neuro-imaging techniques to study face processing in the normal brain (see Chapter 4). The brain seems to 'farm out' different aspects of the task to different specialised areas. For example, some regions are more closely involved in determining an individual's identity from his/her facial appearance, and others in interpretation of facial expressions of emotion (Young *et al.*, 1993).

According to Ellis & Young (1990), when we look at the faces of people we know, we recognise who they are and parts of our brains set up preparatory emotional responses for the types of interaction that are likely to follow (the *orienting response*). Recognising *who* it is, and preparing for *what* is likely to happen (the orienting response) involve separate neurological pathways. If the pathway responsible for the orienting response is damaged, and the orienting response is impaired, faces that can still be recognised (and so look familiar) can somehow seem strange (because they don't elicit the usual reactions).

The temporal lobes contain regions that specialise in face and object recognition (the '*what pathway*'). Normally, these face recognition areas relay information to the *limbic system* (specifically, the *amygdala*), which then helps to generate emotional responses to particular faces. For example, our GSR increases when we see someone familiar (or just see their photograph), but we'd expect this *not* to happen in the case of Capgras patients. This was confirmed by Ramachandran (1998) in the case of Arthur (see Case Study 14.2). The discrepancy between recognition and the emotional response (there is none) produces a highly disturbing sense of strangeness. The belief that parents and so on are impostors (the delusion) might simply be a rationalisation of that disturbing experience (Bruce & Young, 1998).

Conclusions

Pattern recognition (PR) is closely related to perception. They both entail the identification and categorisation of objects, processes which seem effortless and automatic. But, in fact, they're extremely complex. Several theories of PR have been proposed, some of which have been much more influential than others. Biederman's geon theory, for example, is generally considered to be a significant improvement on TMH, but feature-detection theories have proved the most influential.

The chapter has also considered research into face recognition, which is really one aspect of face perception. Studies of brain-damaged patients whose face recognition abilities are impaired have figured prominently in this research area. Two models of face recognition have been discussed, showing the complexity of this fascinating aspect of PR.

CHAPTER SUMMARY

- **Pattern recognition** (PR) is the process of assigning meaning to visual input by identifying the objects in the visual field. Like perception, PR is more complex than it appears.

- According to the **template-matching hypothesis** (TMH), incoming sensory information is matched against miniature copies (or templates) of patterns/objects stored in long-term memory. However, TMH fails to account for our ability to recognise unfamiliar patterns.

- Biederman's **geon theory** (or **recognition-by-components model**) tries to overcome TMH's limitations. Descriptions of objects usually divide them into **volumetric concepts** or **geons**, and the regions used to divide them up are probably those of greatest **concavity**.

- Geon theory has been supported by experiments using 'partial' and 'degraded' objects. While geons are intuitively appealing, there's little empirical support for the specific geons which Biederman identifies.

- According to **prototype theories**, every stimulus belongs to a **category** of stimuli. This approach fails to take account of context.

- **Feature-detection theories** are the most influential approach to PR. Every stimulus can be regarded as a configuration of elementary features. Studies of **eye movements/fixations** show that the perception of features within complex patterns depends on attention and purpose.

- Hubel and Wiesel identified three kinds of cortical cell, which may or may not be the feature-detectors proposed by feature-detection theories. There may be face-specific cells in the monkey's cortex, and there also appear to be cells in the human cortex that respond to specific aspects of faces.

- While feature-detection theories typically assume a **serial** form of processing, it's widely believed that the visual cortex involves considerable **parallel** processing.

- Selfridge's **Pandemonium** computer program used parallel processing. Although not intended as a model of human perception, Pandemonium shares with other feature-detection theories the neglect of **context** and **perceiver characteristics** as influences on PR.

- **Face recognition** is part of face perception, which includes inferring emotional states and other information from the face.

- Although faces could be described in terms of basic components, it seems more valid to describe them in a more **configural** way. However, this can refer to different things, including the **interaction** between features and the **holistic** processing of the whole face.

- Early research often used **artificially constructed faces**, such as *Identikit* faces, and indicated that facial features are processed independently and in sequence. However, some features (such as chins) seemed to influence facial judgements more than others, and there was evidence of **interactive processing**.

■ According to the **configural processing hypothesis**, the relationship between the features is more difficult to perceive when the face is **inverted**. In a normal upright face, the configuration of the features is crucial.

■ Patients with **prosopagnosia** are unable to recognise familiar faces, despite an otherwise normal capacity for recognising individual objects or animals. However, they often display **covert** (unconscious) **recognition**.

■ Studies involving prosopagnosics, patients with other face-perception disorders, and normal adults also suggest that recognising individual identity is quite separate from recognising emotional expression.

■ In Bruce and Young's **model of face recognition**, several different processing 'modules' are linked in sequence or in parallel, including **face recognition units** (FRUs) and **person identity nodes** (PINs).

■ Studies of brain damage, and neuro-imaging studies of the normal brain, suggest that different areas of the brain are specialised for different aspects of face recognition. In **Capgras delusion**, the normal integration of face recognition and orienting response appears to be impaired.

Self-assessment questions

1 Discuss **two** theories of pattern recognition in relation to visual perception.

2 Describe and evaluate research into face recognition.

Web addresses

http://psych.st-and.ac.uk:8080/research/perception_lab/

http:///www.dbv.informatik.uni-bonn.de/

http://www.csrug.nl/~peterkr/FACE/face.html

http://www.stir.ac.uk/departments/humansciences/psychology/staff/vb1/

http://www.white.media.mit.edu/vismod/demos/facerec/

Further reading

Bruce, V. & Young, A. (1998) *In The Eye of the Beholder: The Science of Face Perception*. Oxford: Oxford University Press. A beautifully illustrated book, which is both an academic (but non-technical) text and a joy to look at – and to read. It was written to accompany an exhibition on 'The Science of the Face' at the Scottish National Portrait Gallery in 1998.

Bruce, V. (1995) 'Perceiving and recognising faces'. In I. Roth & V. Bruce *Perception and Representation: Current Issues* (2nd edition) Buckingham: Open University Press. A more difficult read than the first book, but full of relevant theory and research.

Roth, I. (1995) 'Object recognition'. In the same book as above. This covers material on PR in general, including theory and research relevant to Chapter 15 on perception.

Chapter 15

Perception: Processes and Theories

Introduction and overview

When we compare our experience of the world (in which objects remain stable and constant) with what our sense organs receive in the form of physical stimulation (a state of near-continuous flux), it's almost as if there are two entirely different 'worlds'. Psychologists call these *sensation* and *perception* respectively. Sensations are the experiences that physical stimuli elicit in the sense organs (see Chapter 5). Perception is the organisation and interpretation of incoming sensory information to form inner representations of the external world.

This chapter begins by looking at some basic visual perceptual phenomena, namely, *form* and *depth perception*, *perceptual constancy* and *visual illusions*. Many of the principles that govern human visual perception were first identified by the German 'school' of *Gestalt psychology*. As Dodwell (1995) has observed:

> 'To perceive seems effortless. To understand perception is nevertheless a great challenge'.

One response to this challenge claims that our perception of the world is the end result of a process which also involves making *inferences* about what things are like. Those who subscribe to this 'end result' view, such as Bruner (1957), Neisser (1967) and Gregory (1972, 1980), are called *top-down* (or *conceptually-driven*) *perceptual processing* theorists. Making inferences about what things are like means that we perceive them *indirectly*, drawing on our knowledge and expectations of the world. Others argue that our perception of the world is essentially determined by the information presented to the sensory receptors, so that things are perceived in a fairly *direct* way. The most influential of these *bottom-up* (or *data-driven*) *perceptual processing* theorists is Gibson (1966, 1979). Others still, notably Marr (1982), display elements of both approaches.

Gestalt psychology and perceptual organisation

Ehrenfels (1890) claimed that many groups of stimuli acquire a pattern quality which is greater than the sum of their parts. A square, for example, is more than a simple assembly of lines – it has 'squareness'. Ehrenfels called this 'emergent property' *Gestalt qualität* (or form quality). In the early 1900s, Gestalt psychologists (notably Wertheimer, Koffka and Köhler) attempted to discover the principles through which sensory information is interpreted. They argued that as well as creating a coherent perceptual experience that's more than the sum of its parts, the brain does this in regular and predictable ways, and that these organisational principles are largely innately determined. The claim about innateness is discussed in Chapter 16.

Form perception

In order to structure incoming sensory information, we must perceive objects as being separate from other stimuli and as having meaningful form.

Figure and ground

> #### Ask yourself ...
> - What do you see in the picture above?
> - Although it's visually quite simple, can you suggest how it might illustrate a basic principle of how we see things?

The first perceptual task when confronted with an object (or *figure*) is to recognise it (see Chapter 14). To do this, we must perceive the figure as being distinct from its surroundings (or *ground*). A figure's familiarity can help determine whether it's

Figure 15.1

perceived as figure or ground, but unfamiliar and even meaningless 'blobs' are also seen as figures. One of the strongest determinants of figure and ground is *surroundedness*. Areas enclosed by a contour are generally seen as figures, whereas the surrounding area is generally seen as ground. Size, orientation and symmetry also play a role in figure–ground separation.

Sometimes, though, there may not be enough information in a pattern to allow us to distinguish easily between figure and ground. A good example of this is shown in Figure 15.2 (see below), which illustrates the principle underlying camouflage.

Figure 15.2 *The dalmation dog (the figure) is difficult to distinguish from the ground because it has few visible contours of its own*

In *figure–ground reversal*, a figure may have clear contours, but is capable of being perceived in two very different ways: it's unclear which part of it is the figure and which the ground. A famous example is Figure 15.1, usually called Rubin's vase (Rubin, 1915). Here, the figure–ground relationship continually reverses, so that it's perceived as either a white vase with a black background, or two black profiles on a white background. However, the stimulus is always organised into a figure seen against a ground, and the reversal indicates that the same stimulus can trigger more than one perception.

The picture at the beginning of this chapter (page 209) shows how the artist Escher used figure–ground reversal.

> *Ask yourself ...*
> - Can you think of some 'everyday' examples of figure–ground (reversible or not)?
> - Can you think of some non-visual examples?

A map is another example. We normally see the land as figure and the sea as (back)ground, because we're more familiar with the shape of Africa, say, than with the shape of the Atlantic ocean. An auditory example is the *cocktail party phenomenon* (see Chapter 13). Here's another: try repeating 'over-run' out loud and you'll find the two words alternating as figure and ground.

Grouping

Once we've discriminated figure from ground, the figure can be organised into a meaningful form. Gestalt psychologists believed that objects are perceived as *Gestalten* ('organised wholes', 'configurations' or 'patterns') rather than combinations of isolated sensations. They identified several 'laws' of perceptual organisation or grouping, which illustrate their view that the perceived whole of an object is more than the sum of its parts.

These laws can be summarised under one heading, *the law of prägnanz* ('precision'), according to which:

> *'Psychological organisation will always be as good as the prevailing conditions allow. In this definition, "good" is undefined'.* (Koffka, 1935)

'Good' can be defined as possessing a high degree of internal redundancy, that is, the structure of an unseen part is highly predictable from the visible parts (Attneave, 1954). Similarly, according to Hochberg's (1978) *minimum principle*, if there's more than one way of organising a given visual stimulus, we're most likely to perceive the one requiring the least amount of information to perceive it.

In practice, the 'best' way of perceiving is to see things as symmetrical, uniform and stable, and this is achieved by following the laws of prägnanz.

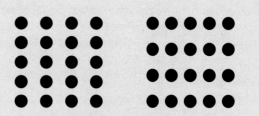

An auditory example would be the perception of a series of musical notes as a melody, because they occur soon after one another in time.

Similarity: Similar figures tend to be grouped together. So, the triangles and circles below are seen as columns of similar shapes rather than rows of dissimilar shapes.

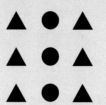

Hearing all the separate voices in a choir as an entity illustrates the principle of similarity.

Continuity: We tend to perceive smooth, continuous patterns rather than discontinuous ones. The pattern below could be seen as a series of alternating semi-circles, but tends to be perceived as a wavy line and a straight line.

Music and speech are perceived as continuous rather than a series of separate sounds.

Closure: Closed figures are perceived more easily than open/incomplete ones. So, we often supply missing information to close a figure and separate it from its background. By filling in the gaps, the illustrations below are seen as a triangle and a seashell.

Part–whole relationship: As well as illustrating continuity and proximity, the three figures below illustrate the principle that 'the whole is greater than the sum of its parts'. Despite the similarity of the parts (each pattern is composed of twelve crosses), the Gestalten are different.

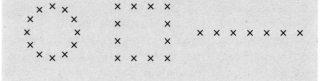

Box 15.1   Gestalt laws of perception

Proximity: Elements appearing close together in space or time tend to be perceived together, so that different spacings of dots produce four vertical lines or four horizontal lines:

The same melody can be recognised when hummed, whistled or played with different instruments and in different keys.

Common fate: Elements seen moving together are perceived as belonging together. This is why a group of people running in the same direction appear to be unified in their purpose.

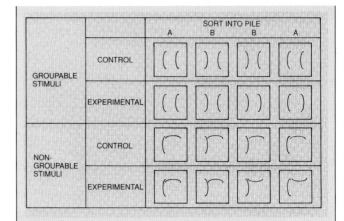

Figure 15.3 *Navon's (1977) experimental test of Gestalt laws*

An evaluation of the Gestalt contribution

A major philosophical influence on Gestalt psychology was *phenomenology*. This sees the world as we ordinarily experience it as being of central concern. Koffka, for example, believed that the most important question for perceptual psychologists was 'Why do things look as they do?', and for Köhler:

> *'There seems to be a single starting point for psychology, exactly as for all the other sciences: the world as we find it, naïvely and uncritically'.*

The most comprehensive account of perceptual grouping is still that provided by the Gestaltist psychologists (Roth, 1986), and in Gordon's (1989) view, Gestalt psychology's discoveries 'are now part of our permanent knowledge of perception'.

However, many contemporary researchers (e.g. Greene, 1990) have argued that, as originally expressed, the various Gestalt 'laws' are at best only descriptive and at worst extremely imprecise and difficult to measure. Several studies have attempted to address the various criticisms made of the Gestalt laws.

KEY STUDY 15.1

Trying to ignore what comes naturally (Pomerantz & Garner, 1973)

One objective measure of grouping is how quickly participants can sort/classify one element presented with others they must try to ignore. Pomerantz and Garner used a pile of cards, each with a pair of brackets printed on it. Participants had to sort the cards into two piles according to whether the *left-hand bracket* looked like '(' or ')', and were told to ignore the right-hand bracket completely.

In one condition, the pairs of brackets were identified as *groupable*, in the other condition, *non-groupable*. (As Figure 15.3 shows, there was an experimental and a control pack in each condition.) Pomerantz and Garner predicted that reaction times for the groupable cards would be longer than for the non-groupable, and this is what they found. Participants were having to select out one element of the pair, and this takes time.

Pomerantz & Schwaitzberg (1975) systematically manipulated proximity by using cards with brackets drawn further and further apart. Given a suitable distance between the brackets, grouping effects disappeared: there was no longer a difference in sorting times between the control and experimental packs of 'groupable' stimuli.

Navon (1977) tested the idea that the whole is perceived before the parts that make it up by presenting participants with various stimuli as shown in Figure 15.4 below.

Figure 15.4

Navon distinguished between the *global* (or 'whole-like' features of a stimulus) and the *local* (or more specific and 'part-like' features). Each stimulus consisted of a large (global) letter made up of many small (local) letters. In some cases, the global and local letters matched (as shown in the stimulus on the left), and in some cases they didn't (as shown on the right).

Participants had to identify either the large or the small letter as quickly as possible. Navon found that the time taken to identify the large letter was unaffected by whether the small letters matched or not. However, the time taken to identify the small letters was affected by whether the large letter matched or not, such that when the large letter was different, response times were longer. This suggests that it's difficult to avoid processing the whole, and that global processing necessarily occurs before any more detailed perceptual analysis.

Table 15.1 *Decision time for global and local letters under match or mismatch conditions (based on Navon, 1977)*

Time in msecs to respond to 'global' and 'local'

Condition	Match	Mismatch
Global	471	477
Local	581	664

Does the global always predominate?

While Navon's data support Gestalt laws, these are difficult to apply to the perception of solid (three-dimensional/3-D) objects (as opposed to two-dimensional/2-D drawings). Our eyes evolved to see 3-D objects, and when 3-D arrays have been studied, Gestalt laws haven't been consistently upheld (Eysenck, 1993). The world around us comprises 'whole' scenes, in which single objects are but 'parts' (Humphreys & Riddoch, 1987). As a result, many of the Gestalt displays, which involve single objects, have very low ecological validity, that is, they're not representative of 'the objects and events which organisms must deal with in order to survive' (Gordon, 1989).

Factors such as the sizes of the local and global features, the viewing conditions and the nature of the observer's task are all likely to play a part in determining the role played by individual features in pattern recognition (Eysenck & Keane, 1990). In everyday life, it's obviously easier sometimes to process 'forests' and sometimes easier to process 'trees' (Roth, 1986).

Some theorists (e.g. Palmer, 1975) have suggested that under most circumstances, the interpretation of parts and wholes takes place in top-down and bottom-up directions simultaneously, such as in the recognition of parts of a face with and without context. As shown in Figure 15.5, the features that can easily be recognised in context are somewhat ambiguous when seen alone (out of context). But they're recognisable when more detail is provided. (Compare Palmer's approach with that of Neisser's analysis-by-synthesis model: see page 224.)

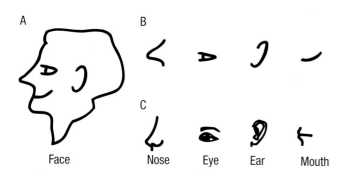

Figure 15.5 *The features that can easily be recognised in context (a) are rather ambiguous when seen alone – out of context (b), although recognisable when more detail is provided (c) (based on Palmer, 1975)*

Marr (1976) found the Gestalt principles useful in achieving accurate *segmentation*, that is, how visual information is used to decide which regions of a visual scene belong together and form coherent structures. He devised a computer program aimed at achieving segmentation (of a teddy bear, for example) using the Gestalt principles. He succeeded in obtaining appropriate segmentation of the teddy's outline, eyes and nose. But some scenes are ambiguous and require using knowledge about objects in order to achieve segmentation (such as two leaves overlapping substantially in a bowl of flowers: Marr, 1982).

Depth perception

From the 2-D images that fall on our retinas, we manage to organise 3-D perceptions. This ability is called *depth perception*, and it allows us to estimate an object's distance from us. Some of the cues used to transform 2-D retinal images into 3-D perceptions involve both eyes and rely on their working together. These are called *binocular cues*. *Monocular cues* are available to each eye separately.

> *Ask yourself …*
>
> - How do we judge the distance of objects from us?
> - Is it always done unconsciously, or do we sometimes try to 'work it out' consciously?

Non-pictorial (primary) cues

Most preyed-upon non-humans (such as rabbits) have their eyes on the side of the head, allowing them to see danger approaching over a wide area. Most predators (such as lions) have their eyes set close together on the front of the head, equipping them with binocular vision, which helps in hunting prey. Like non-human predators, humans have predatory vision, which influences the way we perceive the world. Four important non-pictorial cues are *retinal disparity*, *stereopsis*, *accommodation* and *convergence*. These are all binocular, except accommodation.

- Because our eyes are nearly three inches apart, each retina receives a slightly different image of the world. The amount of *retinal disparity* (the difference between the two images) detected by the brain provides an important cue to distance. For example, if you hold your finger directly in front of your nose, the difference between the two retinal images is large (and this can be shown by looking at your finger first with the left eye closed and then with the right eye closed). When the finger is held at arm's length, retinal disparity is much smaller.
- Ordinarily, we don't see double images, because the brain combines the two images in a process called *stereopsis* (literally, 'solid vision': Harris, 1998). This allows us to experience one 3-D sensation rather than two different images.
- In *accommodation*, which is a muscular cue, the lens of the eye changes shape when we focus on an object, thickening for nearby objects and flattening for distant objects (see Chapter 5, page 69).
- *Convergence*, another muscular cue to distance, is the process by which the eyes point more and more inward as an object gets closer. By noting the angle of convergence, the brain provides us with depth information over distances from about six to 20 feet (Hochberg, 1971).

Pictorial (secondary) cues

Except with relatively near objects, each eye receives a very similar retinal image when looking ahead. At greater distances, we depend on *pictorial* cues. These refer to features of the visual field itself (rather than to the eyes), and are all also monocular.

Table 15.2 *Some pictorial depth cues*

Depth cue	Description
Relative size	In an array of different sized objects, smaller ones are usually seen as more distant (especially if they're known to have a constant size).
Relative brightness	Brighter objects normally appear to be nearer.
Superimposition (or overlap)	An object which blocks the view of another is seen as being nearer.
Linear perspective	Parallel lines (e.g. railway tracks) appear to converge as they recede into the distance.
Aerial perspective	Objects at a great distance appear to have a different colour (e.g. the hazy, bluish, tint of distant mountains).
Height in the horizontal plane	When looking across a flat expanse (e.g. the sea), objects that are more distant seem *higher* (closer to the horizon) than nearer objects, which seem *lower* (closer to the ground).
Light and shadow	3-D objects produce variations in light and shade (for example, we normally assume that light comes from above).
Texture gradient	Textured surfaces (e.g. sand) look rougher close up than from a distance. A stretch of beach looks more smooth and uniform.
Motion parallax	This is the major *dynamic* depth cue (pictorial/non-pictorial). Objects nearer to us seem to move faster than more distant objects (e.g. telegraph poles seen from a (moving) train window flash by when close to the track).

Perceptual constancy

Having perceived an object as a coherent form and located it in space, we must next recognise the object without being 'fooled' by changes in its size, shape, location, brightness and colour. The ability to perceive an object as unchanging, despite changes in the sensory information that reaches our eyes, is called *perceptual constancy*.

Size constancy

As people move further away from us, the size of image they project on the retina decreases. However, rather than seeing people as 'growing smaller', we perceive them as being of a fixed height moving away from us. *Size constancy* occurs because the perceptual system takes into account an object's distance from the perceiver. So, perceived size is equal to retinal image size taking distance into account.

The perception of an *after-image* demonstrates how distance can be varied *without* changing the retinal image's size. If you stare at a bright light for a few seconds and then look away, you'll experience an after-image. This has a fixed size,

shape and position on the retina. But if you quickly look at a nearby object and then an object further away, the after-image seems to shrink and swell, appearing to be largest when you look at a more distant object. Real objects cast smaller images the further away they are, and to maintain perceptual constancy the brain 'scales up' the image (*constancy scaling*). The same constancy scaling is applied to an after-image, producing changes in its apparent size.

Shape constancy

We often view objects from angles at which their 'true' shapes aren't reflected in the retinal image they project. For example, rectangular doors often project trapezoid shapes and round cups often project elliptical-shaped images. Just as with size constancy, the perceptual system maintains constancy in terms of shape.

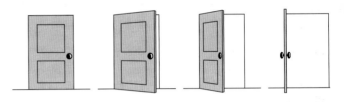

Figure 15.6 *No matter what angle a door is viewed from, it remains a door*

However, shape and size constancy don't always work. When we look down at people from the top of a very tall building, they do *look* more like ants to us, even though we know they're people.

Location constancy

Moving our heads around produces a constantly changing pattern of retinal images. However, we don't perceive the world as spinning around. This is because *kinaesthetic feedback* from the muscles and balance organs in the ear are integrated with the changing retinal stimulation in the brain to inhibit perception of movement. To keep the world from moving crazily every time we move our eyes, the brain subtracts the eye-movement commands from the resulting changes on the retina. This helps to keep objects in a constant location.

Brightness constancy

We see objects as having a more or less constant brightness, even though the amount of light they reflect changes according to the level of illumination. For example, white paper reflects 90 per cent of light falling on it, whereas black paper reflects only ten per cent. But in bright sunlight black paper still looks black even though it may reflect 100 times more light than does white paper indoors. Perceived brightness depends on how much light an object reflects relative to its surroundings (*relative luminance*). If sunlit black paper is viewed through a narrow tube such that nothing else is visible, it will appear greyish because in bright sunlight it reflects a fair amount of light. When viewed without the tube it appears black again, because it reflects much less light than the colourful objects around it.

Colour constancy

Familiar objects retain their colour (or, more correctly, their *hue*) under a variety of lighting conditions (including night light), provided there's sufficient contrast and shadow (see Chapter 5, page 75). However, when we don't already know an object's colour, colour constancy is less effective. If you've bought new clothes under fluorescent light without viewing them in ordinary lighting conditions, you'll probably agree.

Illusions

Although perception is usually reliable, our perceptions sometimes misrepresent the world. When our perception of an object doesn't match its true physical characteristics, we've experienced an illusion. Some illusions are due to the physical distortion of stimuli, whereas others are due to our misperception of stimuli (Coren & Girgus, 1978). An example of a *physical illusion* is the bent appearance of a stick when placed in water. Gregory (1983) identifies four types of *perceptual illusion*:

- distortions (or *geometric illusions*);
- ambiguous (or *reversible*) figures;
- paradoxical figures (or *impossible objects*);
- fictions.

Distortions

Figure 15.7 shows several examples of distortions. The Poggendorf illusion (Figure 15.7 (b)) is accentuated when the diagonal line is more steeply slanted and when the parallel bars are more separated. As the line is brought closer to the horizontal, the illusion disappears (MacKay & Newbigging, 1977). The horizontal–vertical illusion (Figure 15.7 (d)) illustrates our tendency to overestimate the size of vertical objects. This helps to explain why a small tree we've chopped down looks shorter than it did when it was standing (Coren & Girgus, 1978).

Ambiguous figures

In addition to Rubin's vase (see page 210), three other well-known reversible figures are shown in Figure 15.8 (a–c). In the Necker cube (Figure 15.8 (a)), the figure undergoes a *depth reversal*. The cube can be perceived with the crosses being drawn either on the back side of the cube or on the top side looking down. Although our perceptual system interprets this 2-D line drawing as a 3-D object, it seems unsure as to which of the two orientations should be perceived. Hence, the cube spontaneously reverses in depth orientation if looked at for about 30 seconds.

Figure 15.7 *Distortions (or geometric illusions). In the Ponzo illusion (a), the horizontal bar at the top is seen as being longer than the horizontal line at the bottom, even though they're both the same length. The Poggendorf illusion (b) suggests that the segments of the diagonal line are offset, even though they're not. The line with the outgoing fins in the Müller–Lyer illusion (c) appears to be longer than the line with the ingoing fins, but in fact they're the same length. In the horizontal–vertical illusion (d), the vertical line is seen as being longer, although it is the same as the horizontal line. In Titchener's circles (e), the central circle in the left-hand group is seen as being larger than the central circle of the right-hand group, but they're both the same size. Finally, in the twisted card illusion (f), the twisted cards appear to be a spiral pattern, but the circles are, in fact, concentric*

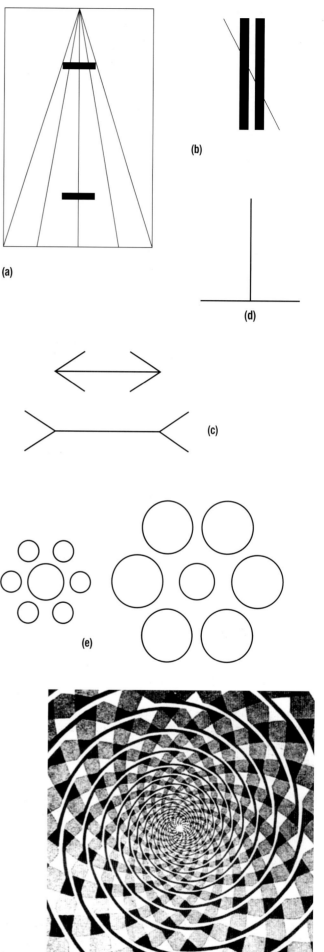

Figure 15.8 (b) shows Boring's 'Old/Young woman'. These two are examples of reversible figures in which the change in perception illustrates *object reversal*. The figure can be perceived as the profile of a young woman's face with the tip of her nose just visible, or the young woman's chin can be perceived as the (very large) nose of a much older woman (who also has a very long chin).

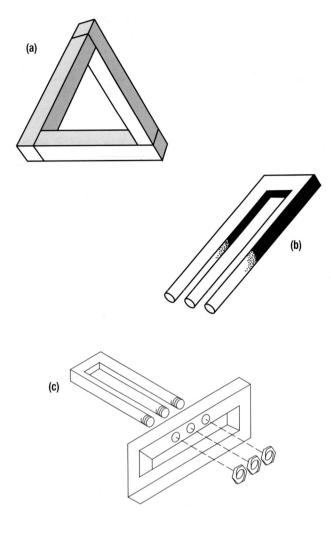

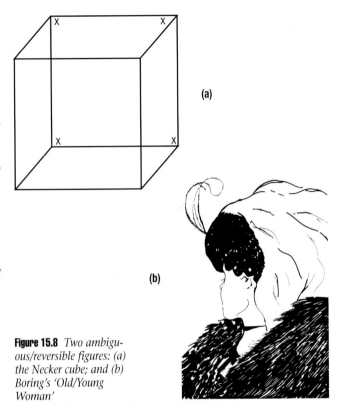

Figure 15.8 *Two ambiguous/reversible figures: (a) the Necker cube; and (b) Boring's 'Old/Young Woman'*

Paradoxical figures

While paradoxical figures look ordinary enough at first, on closer inspection we realise that they cannot exist in reality (hence 'paradoxical'). Figure 15.9 (a–d) illustrates four such paradoxical figures.

According to Hochberg (1970), it takes us a few seconds to realise that a figure is impossible. This is because we need time to examine it fully or scan it and organise its parts into a meaningful whole. When we look at a figure, our eyes move from place to place at the rate of about three changes per second (Yarbus, 1967: see Key Study 14.2, page 201). So, when we look at an impossible figure, it takes time for us to scan it and perceive its form, and only after this scanning can we appreciate its impossible nature.

Fictions

Fictions help explain how we perceive that objects possess specific shapes. The idea that shape is determined by the *physical contours* of an object (which cause edge-detectors in the cells of the visual system to fire: see Chapter 5) has been challenged by the existence of *subjective contours*. These are the boundaries of a shape perceived in the absence of physical contours (Kanizsa, 1976).

Figure 15.9 *Four paradoxical objects. (a) is the Penrose impossible triangle and (b) is variously known as 'Trident' and 'The Devil's Pitchfork'. In (c), Trident has been combined with another impossible object. (d) is M.C. Escher's* Relativity. *Although working in two dimensions, Escher has used perceptual cues in such a way as to encourage the viewer to perceive a three-dimensional figure*

In Figure 15.10 (a), although no white triangular contour is physically present, we perceive the shape of a white triangle which appears to be opaque and lighter than the background. There are some contours that are physically present (the overlap of the triangle and the disc), and these might cause enough edge-detector cells to fire. However, this explanation can't account for the fact that in Figure 15.10 (b), the partial and straight physical contours give rise to a curved triangle. Nor can it explain the subjective contour in Figure 15.10 (c), which is marked by lines in a totally different orientation (Krebs & Blackman, 1988).

It's the *relationship between its parts* that defines a shape, rather than its physical contours (Rock, 1984). Physical contours are, of course, usually indicative of the location of an object's parts. But the location of the parts can also be determined by subjective contours. As a result, the perception of shape must involve more than simply detecting the elements of a pattern (Krebs & Blackman, 1988).

Illusions of movement

We're surrounded by illusions in our everyday life. The use of perspective cues by artists leads us to infer depth and distance, that is, we *add* something to a picture which isn't physically present, just as we do to the images projected on our television screens. Television pictures also use the *illusion of movement*. Just as it's possible for changes in patterns of retinal stimulation not to be accompanied by the perception of movement, so it's possible to perceive movement without a successive pattern of retinal stimulation (Ramachandron & Anstis, 1986). This is called *apparent movement*.

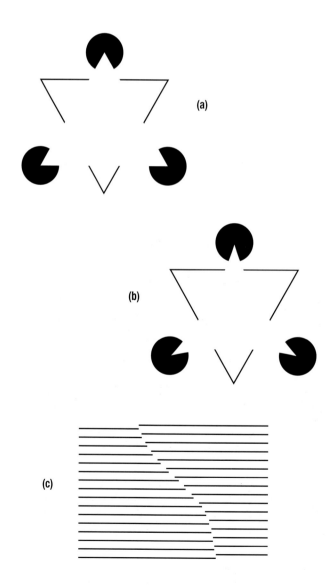

Figure 15.10 *Three fictions. In (a), the 'white triangle' is banded by a subjective contour, rather than a continuous physical one. In (b), the subjective contours are curved. In (c), lines of different orientation produce a subjective contour*

Box 15.2	**Some examples of apparent movement**

The autokinetic effect: If you look at a stationary spot of light in an otherwise completely dark room, the light will appear to move. According to Gregory (1973), this illusion is produced by small and uncontrollable eye movements. Another explanation suggests that it's caused by the absence of a stimulating background to provide a frame of reference for measuring movement. This is supported by the fact that the autokinetic effect disappears if other lights are introduced (see also Key Study 26.1, page 380).

Stroboscopic motion: The illusion of movement is created by the rapid succession of slightly different stationary images. If these are presented sufficiently quickly (around 16 to 22 frames per second), an illusory impression of continuous movement is produced. This is the mechanism by which moving pictures operate. With fewer than 16 frames per second, the moving picture looks jumpy and unnatural. Smooth *slow motion* is achieved by filming at a rate of 100 or more frames per second, and then playing back at about 20 frames per second.

The phi phenomenon: This is a simpler form of stroboscopic motion, in which a number of separate lights are turned on and off in quick succession. This gives the impression of a single light moving from one position to another. Both stroboscopic motion and the phi phenomenon can be explained by the *law of continuity* (see Box 15.1, page 211).

Induced movement: This occurs when we perceive an object to be moving, although in reality it's stationary and its *surroundings* are moving. Movie stars, for example, are often filmed in a stationary car with a projection of a moving background behind them. Similarly, when the moon is seen through a thin cover of moving clouds, we sometimes perceive it to be moving very quickly. Another example is the experience of sitting in a car at traffic lights and noticing that we are 'moving backwards', when in fact the car at our side is moving forwards.

Motion after-effects: People who work on inspection belts in factories experience movement after-effects when the belt suddenly stops but is then perceived as moving backwards. Similarly, if you stare at a waterfall and then switch your gaze to the ground surrounding it, the ground appears to be moving in the opposite direction.

Such after-effects are generally accepted as being due to the over-stimulation of particular movement-detector cells in the visual system. Because cells sensitive to, say, downward movement have been over-stimulated, they're momentarily insensitive when the stimulation ceases. However, the cells sensitive to, say, upward movement are relatively more active, resulting in a motion after-effect.

At least some examples of apparent movement can be termed *intelligent errors*, because they result from perceptual strategies that work most of the time (Rock, 1983). Motion after-effects, however, can be more easily explained in physiological terms.

Perception of real movement

The importance of eye movements

To perceive real (actual) movement, there must be changes in the retinal image. Indeed, it seems that the receptors only respond to changes in the environment. As we saw in Chapter 5, the eyes are constantly making minute, oscillatory movements which keep the receptors stimulated. A device for stabilising the retinal image (Cornsweet, 1970) shows that these movements are necessary for seeing things at all. A tiny slide projector, mounted on a contact lens, is attached to the cornea and a slide projected onto a screen. Since the lens and the projector move with the eye, the retinal image is stabilised. In other words, eye movements and the movement of the image on the screen 'cancel each other out' and so the retinal image stays in the same place. After initially seeing the picture with normal acuity, it begins to fade within a few seconds, and after a minute disappears altogether.

If you turn your head slowly around with your eyes open, or you scan a stationary scene, you'll create a succession of different retinal images, but you won't perceive movement (*location constancy* 'kicks in'). So, changes in the retinal image *cannot* be a sufficient basis for the perception of movement. Conversely, when an object moves across your visual field and you follow it with your eyes, the retinal image remains the same, but you do perceive movement.

Configurational change

Objects moving in the environment usually do so against a background of stationary (or differently moving) objects. Also, the nose and other anatomical borders to the visual field provide stationary reference points against which to judge movement. This causes a configuration change or change in the overall pattern and interrelationship between objects. However, although in practice this is often an important source of information, it may not be a necessary one. Gregory (1973) points out that if a lighted cigarette is moved about in a dark room it will be perceived as moving, even though there are no background cues or frames of reference. (This shouldn't be confused with the *autokinetic effect*: see Box 15.2.)

So how does the brain do it?

It seems that the brain is capable of distinguishing between eye movements which do signal movement of objects (real movement), and those (and head movements) which don't. Probably the *superior colliculus* plays an important role in making this distinction (see Chapter 5). Gregory (1973) describes two systems:

- the *image–retina system*, which responds to changes in the visual field which produce changes in the retinal image;
- the *eye–head system*, which responds to movements of the head and eyes.

The perception of movement is the product of an interplay between the two systems.

According to Braddick (1974), the human visual system seems to have two separate systems for measuring the speed and direction of individual features moving in the retinal image:

- a long-range, *feature-tracking* system seems to infer motion from one instant to the next, and this underpins our conscious impression of motion in films and television;
- a short-range, *motion-sensing* system seems to measure motion more directly by signalling changes in the image content over time.

Although neither system is fully understood, the basic requirements are in place even at the retina. *P-type* ganglion cells (see Chapter 5, pages 71–72) respond to abrupt *spatial* changes in the image, while *M-type* ganglion cells may respond to abrupt *temporal* (time-related) changes. Additionally, the temporal cortex contains many cells selective for different types of motion, and most visual cortical cells prefer moving to stationary stimuli (Harris, 1998).

Theories of visual perception

Classifying theories

As we noted at the beginning of the chapter, one way in which theories of perception differ is in terms of whether they regard perception as a *direct* (bottom-up/data-driven), or an *indirect* (top-down/conceptually-driven) process. Bruce & Green (1990) call these 'ecological' and 'traditional' respectively. The term 'ecological' was used by Gibson, the major bottom-up theorist, to imply that visual information from the whole physical environment is available for analysis by retinal receptor cells.

Another issue which divides theories relates to the *nature–nurture debate* (see Chapter 50). *Empiricists* regard perception as primarily the result of learning and experience, while *nativists* believe it's essentially an innate ability, requiring little, if any, learning. All the top-down theorists are also empiricists, and the major nativists are the Gestalt psychologists (see pages 210–212). Gibson was influenced by the Gestalt school, but he's generally regarded as an empiricist. Finally, Marr's theory has both top-down and bottom-up components, and he too was influenced by some of the Gestalt laws (see above, pages 210–212).

Table 15.3 *A classification of theories of perception*

	Direct (bottom-up/ecological)	Indirect (top-down/traditional)
Empiricist	Gibson (1966, 1979)	Gregory (1972, 1980) Bruner (1957)
	Neisser (1967) Marr (1982)	
Nativist	Gestalt	

Gregory's constructivist theory

According to Gregory (1966):

'Perception is not determined simply by stimulus patterns. Rather, it is a dynamic searching for the best interpretation of the available data … [which] involves going beyond the immediately given evidence of the senses'.

To avoid sensory overload, we need to select from all the sensory stimulation which surrounds us. Also, we often need to supplement sensory information, because the total information that we need might not be directly available to the senses. This is what Gregory means by 'going beyond the immediately given evidence of the senses', and it's why his theory is known as *constructivist*. For Gregory, we make inferences about the information the senses receive (based on Helmholtz's nineteenth-century view of perception as consisting of *unconscious inferences*).

Gregory's theory and perceptual constancies

Perceptual constancies (see pages 214–215) tell us that visual information from the retinal image is sketchy and incomplete, and that the visual system has to 'go beyond' the retinal image in order to test hypotheses which fill in the 'gaps' (Greene, 1990). To make sense of the various sensory inputs to the retina (*low-level information*), the visual system must draw on all kinds of evidence, including distance cues, information from other senses, and expectations based on past experience (*high-level knowledge*). For all these reasons, Gregory argues that perception must be an indirect process involving a construction based on physical sources of energy.

Gregory's theory and illusions

Gregory argues that when we experience a visual illusion (see pages 215–217), what we perceive may not be physically present in the stimulus (and hence not present in the retinal image). Essentially, an illusion can be explained in terms of a perceptual hypothesis which isn't confirmed by the data, so that our attempt to interpret the stimulus figure turns out to be inappropriate. In other words, an illusion occurs when we attempt unsuccessfully to construe the stimulus in keeping with how we normally construe the world.

Box 15.3 | **Explaining the Ponzo illusion**

In the Ponzo illusion (see Figure 15.7 (a), page 215), our system can either:

- accept the equal lengths of the two central bars as drawn on a flat 2-D surface (which would involve assuming that the bars are equidistant from us); *or*
- 'read' the whole figure as a railway track converging into the distance (so that the two horizontal bars represent sleepers, the top one of which would be further away from us but appears longer since it 'must' be longer in order to produce the same length image on the retina).

The second interpretation is clearly inappropriate, since the figure is drawn on a flat piece of paper and there are no actual distance differences. As a result, an illusion is experienced.

All illusions illustrate how the perceptual system normally operates by forming a 'best guess', which is then tested against sensory inputs. For Gregory (1966), illusions show that perception is an active process of using information to suggest and test hypotheses. What we perceive aren't the data, but an interpretation of them, so that:

'A perceived object is a hypothesis, suggested and tested by sensory data'.

As Gregory (1996) has noted, '… this makes the basis of knowledge indirect and inherently doubtful'.

Gregory argues that when we view a 3-D scene with many distance cues, the perceptual system can quickly select the hypothesis that best interprets the sensory data. However, reversible figures supply few distance cues to guide the system. For example, the spontaneous reversal of the Necker cube (see page 216) occurs because the perceptual system continually tests two equally plausible hypotheses about the nature of the object represented in the drawing.

One striking illusion is the *rotating hollow mask* (Gregory, 1970). There's sufficient information for us to see the mask as

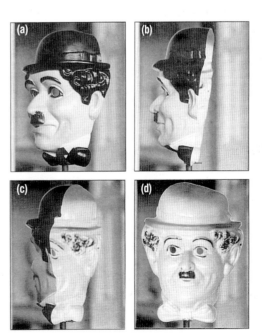

Figure 15.11 *The rotating hollow mask. (a) shows the normal face which is rotated to (d), which is a hollow face. However, (d) appears like a normal face rotating in the opposite direction*

hollow, but it's impossible not to see it as a normal face. The perceptual system dismisses the hypothesis that the mask is an inside-out face because it's so improbable. The hypothesis we select is strongly influenced by our past experiences of faces (Gregory, 1970).

With the impossible triangle (see Figure 15.9 (a)), our perceptual system makes reasonable, but actually incorrect, judgements about the distance of different parts of the triangle.

> **Ask yourself ...**
>
> - Knowing what you do about Gregory's theory, how do you think he might try to explain the Müller–Lyer illusion (see Figure 15.6 (c))? You may find Box 15.3 helpful.

Misapplied size constancy theory

According to Gregory, the Müller–Lyer illusion can be explained as follows:

- The arrow with the ingoing fins provides linear perspective cues, suggesting that it could be the outside corner of a building. Hence, the fins are seen as walls receding away from us, making the shaft look closer to us.
- In the arrow with the outgoing fins, the cues suggest that it could be the inside corner of a room, and the outgoing fins as walls coming towards us. This would make the shaft appear 'distant'.

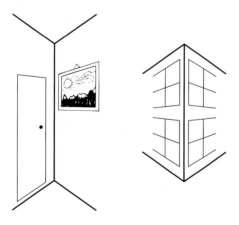

Figure 15.12 *A representation of the Müller–Lyer illusion as suggested by Gregory's misapplied size constancy theory*

However, the retinal images produced by the arrows are equal and, according to size constancy, if equally sized images are produced by two lines, one of which is further away from us than the other, then the line which is furthest from us must be longer! Because this interpretation is taking place unconsciously and quickly, we immediately perceive the illusion.

However, if the perspective cues are removed, the illusion remains, suggesting that the misapplied size constancy theory is itself misapplied (see Figure 15.13). Alternatively, the apparent distance of the arrow could be caused by the apparent size of the arrows rather than, as Gregory claims, the other way around (Robinson, 1972).

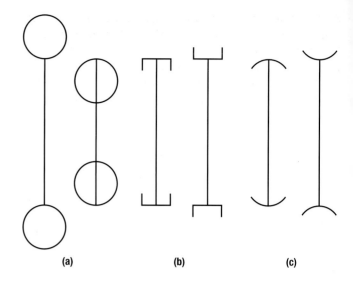

Figure 15.13 *The Müller–Lyer illusion with the depth cues removed (after Delboeuf, 1892)*

In a variation of the original Müller–Lyer illusion, Morgan (1969) placed a dot mid-way along the arrow (see Figure 15.14). The dot appears to be nearer the left-hand end, and the only way this can be explained by Gregory is to claim that the fins make the arrow appear to slope away from us, providing a rather odd perspective interpretation of the figure. According to Gregory (1972), such a slope can be demonstrated, although this claim has been disputed (Eysenck & Keane, 1995).

Figure 15.14 *Morgan's (1969) modified Müller–Lyer illusion*

In the Müller–Lyer illusion, we *know* the arrows are the same length, yet we still experience the illusion. Our knowledge should enable us to modify our hypotheses in an adaptive way. While some illusions can be explained in terms of the same unconscious processes occurring (an example being size constancy), not all illusions are amenable to explanation in the way Gregory proposes (Robinson, 1972).

Gregory's theory and perceptual set

Perceptual set is directly relevant to Gregory's view that perception is an active process involving selection, inference and interpretation. Allport (1955) describes perceptual set as:

> *'... a perceptual bias or predisposition or readiness to perceive particular features of a stimulus'.*

It refers to the tendency to perceive or notice some aspects of available sense data and ignore others. According to Vernon (1955), set acts as:

- a *selector*: the perceiver has certain expectations which help focus attention on particular aspects of the incoming sensory information; and
- an *interpreter*: the perceiver knows how to deal with the selected data, how to classify, understand and name them, and what inferences to draw from them.

Several factors can influence or induce set, most of them being *perceiver* (or *organismic*) *variables*, but some relate to the nature of the stimulus or the conditions under which it's perceived (*stimulus* or *situational variables*). Both types of variable influence perception indirectly, through directly influencing set which, as such, is a perceiver variable or characteristic.

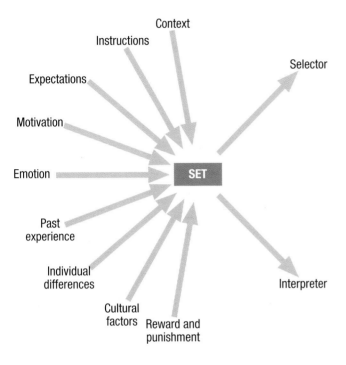

Figure 15.15 *The indirect influence of perceiver and stimulus variables on perception through their direct influence on set*

221

Context and expectations: The interaction between context and expectations was demonstrated by Bruner & Postman (1949) and Bruner *et al.* (1952). When participants are asked to copy a briefly presented stimulus such as:

PARIS	ONCE	A
IN THE	IN A	BIRD
THE SPRING	A LIFETIME	IN THE
		THE HAND

it's typically copied as PARIS IN THE SPRING/ONCE IN A LIFETIME/A BIRD IN THE HAND. One reason eyewitness testimony (see Chapter 21) is so unreliable is that our general expectation of people is that they'll be of 'average height and weight', and this is what almost all eyewitness accounts describe people as being (Loftus, 1980).

An evaluation of Gregory's theory of perception

Gregory's theory raises many important questions which have yet to be answered satisfactorily (Gordon, 1989). For example, if perception is essentially constructive, then we need to know how it gets started and why there's such common experience among different people, all of whom have had to construct their own idiosyncratic perceptual worlds. Also, given that perception is typically accurate (and our hypotheses are usually correct), it seems unlikely that our retinal images are really as ambiguous and lacking in detail as Gregory suggests.

Gregory has been much more successful in explaining at least some types of illusion than in explaining perception as a whole (Eysenck & Keane, 1995). His theory may be most relevant when stimuli are ambiguous or incomplete, presented very briefly, or their processing interrupted (Groome *et al.*, 1999). In Gordon's (1989) view, constructivist theories have underestimated the richness of sensory evidence in the real world. For Gordon:

'*It is possible that we perceive constructively only at certain times and in certain situations. Whenever we move under our own power on the surface of the natural world and in good light, the necessary perceptions of size, texture, distance, continuity, motion and so on, may all occur directly and reflexively'.*

Gibson's theory of direct perception

Constructivists use the retinal image as their starting point for explaining perception. According to Gibson (1966), this approach mistakenly describes the input for a perceiver in the same terms as that for a single photoreceptor, namely a stream of photons. For Gibson, it's better to begin by considering the input as a pattern of light extended over time and space (an *optic array* containing all the visual information from the environment striking the eye of a stationary perceiver). The optic array provides unambiguous, invariant information about the layout and relevant properties of objects in space, and this information takes three main forms: *optic flow patterns, texture gradient* and *affordances*. Perception essentially involves 'picking up' the rich information provided by the optic array in a direct way, which involves little or no (unconscious) information processing, computations or internal representations (Harris, 1998).

Optic flow patterns

During World War II, Gibson prepared training films describing the problems pilots experience when taking off and landing. He called the information available to pilots optic flow patterns (OFPs). As shown in Figure 15.16, the point to which a pilot moves appears motionless, with the rest of the visual environment apparently moving away from that point. Thus, all around the point there's an apparent radial expansion of textures flowing around the pilot's head.

The lack of apparent movement of the point towards which the pilot moves is an invariant, unchanging feature of the optic array. Such OFPs provide unambiguous information about direction, speed and altitude. OFPs in general refer to changes in the optic array as the perceiver moves about.

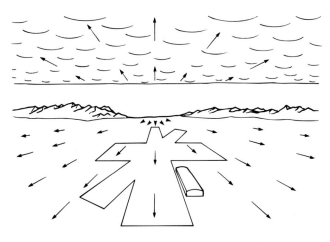

Figure 15.16 *The optic flow patterns as a pilot approaches the landing strip (from Gibson, 1950)*

Texture gradients

Textures expand as we approach them and contract as they pass beyond our heads. This happens whenever we move toward something, so that over and above the behaviour of each texture element, there's a 'higher-order' pattern or structure available as a source of information about the environment (and so the flow of the texture is invariant). Texture gradients (or *gradients of texture density*) are important depth cues perceived directly without the need for any inferences. The depth cues described in Table 15.2 are all examples of directly perceived, invariant, higher-order features of the optic array. For Gibson, then, the third dimension (depth) is available to the senses as directly as the other two dimensions, automatically processed by the sense receptors, and automatically producing the perceptual experience of depth.

Affordances

Affordances are directly perceivable, potential uses of objects (a ladder, for example, 'affords' climbing), and are closely linked with *ecological optics*. To understand an animal's perceptual system, we need to consider the environment in which it has evolved, particularly the patterns of light (the optic array) which reaches the eye (ecological optics). When an object moves further away from the eye, its image gets smaller (relative size), and most objects are bounded by texture

surfaces and texture gradient gets finer as an object recedes. In other words, objects aren't judged in complete isolation, and the optic array commonly contains far more information than that associated with a single stimulus array (often overlooked by the use of classical optics and laboratory experiments: Gordon, 1989).

An evaluation of Gibson's theory

Gibson was concerned with the problem of how we obtain constant perception in everyday life, based on continually changing sensations. According to Marr (1982), this indicated that he correctly regarded the problem of perception as that of recovering from sensory information 'valid properties of the external world'. However, as Marr points out, Gibson failed to recognise two equally critical things:

> *'First, the detection of physical invariants, like image surfaces, is exactly and precisely an information-processing problem ... Second, he vastly underrated the sheer difficulty of such detection'.*

An interesting study by Lee & Lishman (1975) tends to support Gibson's belief in the importance of movement in perception, and the artificiality of separating sensory and motor aspects of behaviour.

KEY STUDY 15.2

If the room sways, there may be an experiment going on (Lee & Lishman, 1975)

Lee and Lishman used a specially built swaying room (suspended above the floor), designed to bring texture flow under experimental control. As the room sways (so changing the texture flow), adults typically make slight unconscious adjustments, and children tend to fall over. Normally, the brain is very skilled at establishing correlations between changes in the optic flow, signals to the muscles, and staying upright.

Arguably, the most important reason for having a visual system is to be able to anticipate when contact with an approaching object is going to be made. Lee and Lishman believe that estimating 'time to contact' is crucial for actions such as avoidance of objects and grasping them, and thus represents extremely important ecological information. This can be expressed as a formula:

$$\text{Time to contact} = \frac{\text{Size of retinal image}}{\text{Rate of expansion of retinal image}}$$

This is a property shared by all objects, and so is another invariant, demonstrating the unambiguous nature of the retinal image. Measures of optic flow have also provided some understanding of how skilled long-jumpers control their approaches to the take-off position (Gordon, 1989).

Gibson's concept of affordances is part of his attempt to show that all the information needed to make sense of the visual environment is directly available in the visual input (a purely 'bottom-up' approach to perception). Bruce & Green (1990) argue that this concept is most powerful and useful in the context of *visually guided* behaviour, as in insects. Here, it makes sense to speak of an organism detecting information available in the light needed to organise its activities, and the idea of it needing a conceptual representation of its environment seems redundant.

However, humans act in a *cultural* as well as physical environment. It's inconceivable that we don't need any *knowledge* of writing or the postal system in order to detect that a pen affords writing or a postbox affords posting a letter, and that these are directly perceived invariants. People see objects and events as what they are in terms of a culturally given conceptual representation of the world, and Gibson's theory says much more about '*seeing*' than about '*seeing as*'.

'Seeing' and 'seeing as'

According to Fodor & Pylyshyn (1981):

> '*What you see when you see a thing depends upon what the thing you see is. But what you see the thing as depends upon what you know about what you are seeing*'.

This view of perception as 'seeing as' is the fundamental principle of *transactionalism*. Transactionalists (such as Ames, cited in Ittelson, 1952) argue that because sensory input is always ambiguous, the interpretation selected is the one most likely to be true given what's been perceived in the past.

In the Ames *distorted room* (see Figure 15.17), the perceiver has to choose between two different beliefs about the world built up through past experience. The first is that rooms are rectangular, consist of right angles, and so on. The second is that people are usually of 'average' height. Most observers choose the first and so judge the people to be an odd size. However, a woman who saw her husband in the room and judged the room to be odd, shows that particularly salient past experiences can override more generalised beliefs about the world.

The Ames room is another example of a visual illusion, and the inability of Gibson's theory to explain mistaken perception is perhaps its greatest single weakness. Gibson argues that most 'mistaken perceptions' occur in situations very different from those which prevail in the natural environment. However, to suggest that illusions are nothing but laboratory tricks designed to baffle ordinary people isn't true, since at least some produce effects similar to those found in normal perception. A striking example is the 'hollow mask' illusion (Bruce & Green, 1990: see Figure 15.11).

A possible synthesis of Gregory's and Gibson's theories

Despite the important differences between Gibson's and Gregory's theories, they also agree on certain points.

Similarities

- Visual perception is mediated by light reflected from surfaces and objects.
- Some kind of physiological system is needed to perceive.
- Perception is an active process. (In Gibson's, 1966, view, 'a perceiving organism is more like a map-reader than a camera'.)
- Perceptual experience can be influenced by learning.

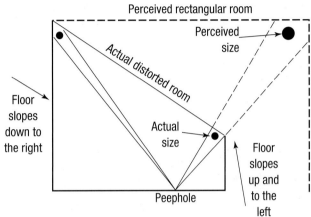

Figure 15.17 *The Ames room and a schematic representation of its 'secret'. The room is constructed in such a way that, when viewed with one eye through a peephole, a person at one end may appear very small and the person at the other end very tall. When they cross the room, they appear to change size. The room itself appears perfectly normal and regular to an observer*

Differences

- Gregory believes that meaningless sensory cues must be supplemented by memory, habit, experience and so on, in order to construct a meaningful world. Gibson argues that the environment (initially the optic array) provides us with all the information we need for living in the world. Perceptual learning consists not in 'gluing' together sensory 'atoms', but in coming to differentiate and discriminate between the features of the environment as presented in the optic array.
- To the extent that Gibson acknowledges the role of learning (albeit a different kind of learning from Gregory), he may be considered an *empiricist* (see above), together with his emphasis on what's provided by the physical world. In other respects, though, Gibson can be considered a *nativist*. As we noted earlier, he was very much influenced by the Gestalt psychologists, stressing the *organised quality* of perception. However, while for Gibson this organised quality is part of the physical structure of the light impinging on the observer's eye, for Gestaltists it's a function of how the brain is organised.

Eysenck & Keane (1995) argue that the relative importance of bottom-up and top-down processes is affected by several factors. When viewing conditions are good, bottom-up processing may be crucial. However, with brief and/or ambiguous stimuli, top-down processing becomes increasingly important. Gibson seems to have been more concerned with *optimal* viewing conditions, while Gregory and other constructivists have tended to concentrate on *sub-optimal* conditions (Eysenck, 1993). In most circumstances, both bottom-up and top-down processes are probably needed, as claimed by Neisser (1976).

Box 15.5 Neisser's (1976) analysis-by-synthesis model

Neisser assumes the existence of a *perceptual cycle* involving *schemata*, *perceptual exploration* and *stimulus environment*. Schemata contain collections of knowledge based on past experience (see Chapter 17), and these direct perceptual exploration towards relevant environmental stimulation. Such exploration often involves moving around the environment, leading the perceiver to actively sample the available stimulus information. If this fails to match the information in the relevant schema, then the hypothesis is modified accordingly.

An initial *analysis* of the sensory cues/features (a *bottom-up* process) might suggest the hypothesis that the object being viewed is, say, a chair. This initiates a search for the expected features (such as four legs and a back), which is based on our schema of a chair (and this *synthesis* is a *top-down* process). But if the environmental features disconfirm the original hypothesis (the 'chair' has only three legs and no back), then a new hypothesis must be generated and tested (it might be a stool), and the appropriate schema activated.

Neisser argues that perception never occurs in a vacuum, since our sampling of sensory features of the environment is always guided by our knowledge and past experience. Perception is an *interactive process*, involving both bottom-up feature analysis and top-down expectations.

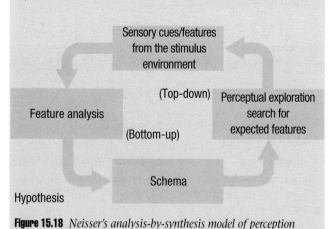

Figure 15.18 *Neisser's analysis-by-synthesis model of perception*

Marr's computational theory of vision

According to Marr (1982), the central 'problem' of perception is identifying the precise *mechanisms* and *computations* by which useful information about a scene is extracted from that scene ('useful information' being what will guide the thoughts or actions of the total system of which the visual system is part). Marr's theory begins by asking 'What is the visual system for?', because only by answering this can we understand how it works.

For Marr, there are three levels at which any process must be understood:

- *The computational theory level* is a theoretical analysis of the tasks performed by a system (in this case, the visual system), and the methods needed to perform them.
- *The algorithmic level* is concerned with identifying the actual operations by which perceptual tasks (processes and representations) are achieved.
- *The hardware or implementation level* is concerned with the mechanisms underlying the system's operation. In the case of a biological visual system, these are neuronal or nervous system structures.

Marr argues that vision's main 'job' is to derive a representation of the *shape* of objects from information contained in the retinal image. This happens via four successive stages, which constitute individual *modules*. Each stage or module takes as its input the information it receives from the previous stage/module, converting it into a more complex description/representation. By taking the image as the starting point, Marr's approach is strictly bottom-up (Roth, 1995). But as we'll see later, there are also top-down aspects.

Box 15.6 The four stages or modules of Marr's computational theory of vision

The image (or grey-level description): This represents the intensity of light at each point in the retinal image, so as to discover regions in the image and their boundaries. Regions and boundaries are parts of images, not parts of things in the world, so this represents the starting point of seeing.

The primal sketch: Useful attributes of a 3-D scene (such as object boundaries and shadows) can be recovered from the image by locating and describing the places where the image intensity changes relatively abruptly from place to place.

- The function of the *raw primal sketch* is to describe potentially significant regions, which may correspond in the real world to the boundaries between overlapping objects, their edges, and texture.
- The *full primal sketch* provides information about how these regions 'go together' to form structures (it provides a functional explanation of the Gestalt grouping principles: see Box 15.1). Grouping is necessary, since in complex scenes, the images of different objects may occlude (overlap) each other. Overall, it provides a more useful and less cluttered description of the image (hence 'sketch').

2½-D sketch: Its function is to make explicit the orientation and depth of visible surfaces, as if a 'picture' of the world is beginning to emerge. It's no longer an image, because it contains information about things in the world which provide the image. But it describes only the visible parts of the scene, and so isn't fully three-dimensional.

- Object recognition requires that the input representation of the object is mapped against a representation stored in memory, so that *non-visible* parts are taken into account (which is essentially what *perceptual constancy* involves: see pages 214–215).
- The sketch changes relative to the observer's perspective (it's *viewpoint-dependent*).

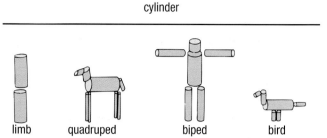

cylinder

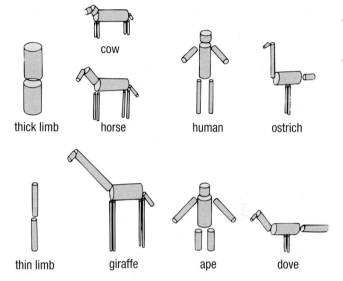

Figure 15.20 *Cylinders of various sizes can be combined to represent the shapes of various (parts of) objects (from Marr & Nishihara, 1978)*

3-D model representation and object recognition

Since the 3-D model representation involves top-down processes, Marr claimed that in many cases 3-D structures can be derived from the 2½-D sketch using only general principles of the kind used in the earlier stages. This view is based on the observation that stick-figure representations (especially of animals and plants) are easy to recognise (Garnham, 1991). The brain automatically transposes the contours derived from the 2½-D sketch onto axes of symmetry which resemble stick figures composed of pipe cleaners.

Marr & Nishihara (1978) argued that the parts of the body can be represented as jointed cylinders or generalised cylinders which change their size along their length (see Figure 15.20). They then showed that the cylinders which compose an object can be computed from the 2½-D sketch: the lines running down the centre of these cylinders (important in the recognition process) make up the stick figures. Once a generalised cylinder representation of objects in a scene has been computed, it can be compared with stored representations of objects in a catalogue of 3-D models, where objects are represented in 'standard' orientations (Garnham, 1991).

Evaluation of Marr's theory

According to Harris & Humphreys (1995), Marr was the first to popularise the computational approach, and his framework remains the widest-ranging computational account of visual object recognition. Marr's work is regarded by many as the most important development in perception theory in recent years (Gordon, 1989).

Marr & Hildreth (1980) have shown that Marr's model does, broadly speaking, what it claims to do. But this doesn't mean that biological vision systems necessarily work in the same

Figure 15.19 *The four basic stages or modules in Marr's model of the processing of a visual image (from I. Roth and V. Bruce (1995) Perception and Representation: Current Issues (2nd edition). Buckingham: Open University Press)*

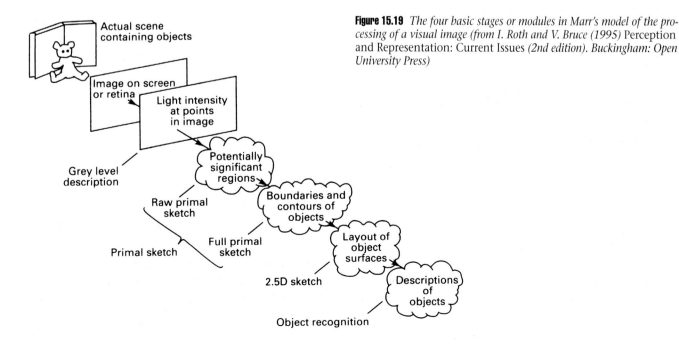

way (Roth, 1995). The main evidence supporting the relevance of Marr's model to biological vision comes from the neurophysiological studies of Hubel and Wiesel (see Chapter 5).

The general claim that the early stage of vision consists of a representation of simple components, such as edge segments, is generally accepted (Roth, 1995). But the least well supported stage is the 3-D model, since the early stages make only very general assumptions about the structure of the external world and don't require knowledge of specific objects. Although a bottom-up approach isn't an inevitable consequence of the computational approach, it has dominated recent research. This is partly because it's easier to derive computational theories from the early stages of perception, where the relationships between the stimulus and the world are much easier to specify (Harris & Humphreys, 1995).

Gardner (1985), too, has argued that most of Marr's theory focuses on the steps *prior* to recognition of real objects in the real world ('… the most central part of perception …'):

'… the procedures [Marr] outlined for object recognition may prove applicable chiefly to the perception of figures of a certain sort, for example, the mammalian body, which lends itself to decomposition in terms of generalised cylindrical forms'.

Researchers are beginning to reconsider whether top-down, domain-specific knowledge might be used. This trend has been encouraged by *connectionist models of visual perception* (see Chapter 20) and Biederman's (1987) *recognition-by-components theory* (see Chapter 14). Marr's general approach to perception, and his argument for computational theories, is, according to Harris & Humphreys (1995):

'… likely to remain as one of the most important contributions of research in artificial intelligence to psychological theory. Such theories are able to guide empirical and theoretical research, even if the detailed models specified at any one time later turn out to be wrong'.

Conclusions

This chapter has looked at some basic visual phenomena, namely form and depth perception, perceptual constancy and visual illusions. These are all concerned with perceptual organisation, and many of the principles governing perceptual organisation are commonly referred to as Gestalt laws.

The chapter has also considered various theories of visual perception, two major examples being Gregory's constructivist ('top-down') and Gibson's direct ('bottom-up') approaches.

While they may appear to contradict each other, it's possible to see them as complementary. According to Harris (1998):

'Perception is not just a single task but … contributes in many different ways to everyday life … Some of these … are obviously more difficult than others and it seems likely that some can be accomplished directly, as Gibson maintained, whilst others may require sophisticated internal knowledge and are thus better described by the indirect approach'.

CHAPTER SUMMARY

- **Sensation** involves physical stimulation of the sense organs, while **perception** is the **organisation** and **interpretation** of incoming sensory information.

- **Gestalt psychologists** identified innately determined principles through which sensory information is interpreted and organised. The most basic of these is **form perception**, which organises incoming sensory information into **figure and ground**.

- Laws for **grouping** stimuli together all rest on the belief that 'the whole is greater than the sum of its parts'. These laws can be summarised under Koffka's **law of prägnanz**. Major Gestalt laws of perception include **proximity**, **similarity**, **continuity**, **closure**, **part–whole relationship**, **simplicity** and **common fate**.

- The various 'laws' are merely descriptive and often imprecise and difficult to measure. Despite empirical support, Gestalt laws are difficult to apply to 3-D perception and to whole scenes (they lack **ecological validity**).

- **Depth perception** allows us to estimate the distance of objects from us. **Pictorial cues** refer to aspects of the visual field, and are monocular. **Non-pictorial cues** include **convergence** and **retinal disparity**, which are **binocular**.

- **Perceptual constancy** refers to the ability to recognise an object as unchanging despite changes in its **size**, **shape**, **location**, **brightness** and **colour**.

- Four main kinds of **perceptual illusion** are **distortions/geometric illusions**, **ambiguous/reversible figures**, **paradoxical figures**, and **fictions**. Other illusions include those involving **apparent movement**.

- According to **top-down** (**conceptually-driven**) perceptual processing theorists, perception is the end result of an **indirect** process that involves making **inferences** about the world, based on knowledge and expectations. **Bottom-up** (**data-driven**) theorists argue that perception is a **direct** process, determined by the information presented to the sensory receptors.

- According to **Gregory's constructivist theory**, we often supplement perception with **unconscious inferences**. His **misapplied size constancy theory** claims that we interpret the ingoing and outgoing fins of the arrows in the Müller–Lyer illusion as providing perspective cues to distance.

- **Perceptual set** acts as a **selector** and **interpreter**, and can be induced by **perceiver/organismic** and **stimulus/situational variables**. Perceiver variables include expectations, which often interact with context.

- According to **Gibson**, the **optic array** provides information about the layout and properties of objects in space requiring little or no (unconscious) information processing, computations or internal representations. **Optic flow patterns**, **texture gradients** and **affordances** are all **invariant**, unchanging and 'higher-order' features of the optic array.

- Gibson overlooked the role of culturally-determined knowledge in perception. He also failed to distinguish between **seeing** and **seeing as**, the latter forming the basic principle of **transactionalism**.

- Both Gibson and Gregory agree that perception is an active process, influenced by learning (making them **empiricists**), although they propose different kinds of learning. Gibson is also a **nativist** in certain respects and was influenced by the Gestalt psychologists.
- Bottom-up processing (Gibson) may be crucial under **optimal viewing conditions**, but under **sub-optimal** conditions, top-down processing (Gregory) becomes increasingly important.
- According to **Neisser's analysis-by-synthesis model**, perception is an **interactive** process, involving both bottom-up feature analysis and top-down expectations (appearing at different stages of a perceptual cycle).
- **Marr's computational theory** states that vision's main function is to derive a representation of object **shape** from information in the retinal image. This is achieved via a series of four increasingly complex stages/**modules**: the **image/grey-level description**, the **primal sketch**, the **2½-D sketch**, and the **3-D model representation/object recognition**.
- 3-D descriptions are often derived from the 2½-D sketch, using stick-figure representations composed of the lines running down the centre of jointed or generalised cylinders.
- It's easier to derive computational theories from the early (bottom-up) stages of perception, and the 3-D model representation (which involves top-down processes) is the least well supported.

Self-assessment questions

1 Discuss research into any **two** examples of perceptual organisation (e.g. constancies; illusions).
2 Describe and evaluate **one** constructivist and **one** direct theory of visual perception.

Further reading

Web addresses

http://www.illusionworks.com/

http://www.yorku.ca/research/vision/eye

http://aspen.uml.edu/~landigrad/ILLUSION.HTML

http://pantheon.yale.edu/~chunlab/chunlab_projects.html

Further reading

Classics by R.L. Gregory include:

Eye and Brain (1966). London: Weidenfeld and Nicolson.

The Intelligent Eye (1970). London: Weidenfeld and Nicolson.

Groome, D. *et al.* (1999) *Cognitive Psychology: Processes and Disorders*. London: Psychology Press. Very useful chapters on perception and attention, and disorders of perception and attention.

See also the *Further Reading* at the end of Chapter 14.

Chapter 16

The Development of Perceptual Abilities

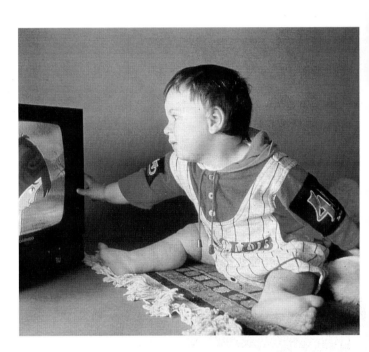

Introduction and overview

Chapters 5 and 15 showed that visual perception is a complex set of interconnected and overlapping abilities, including perception of depth, shape and movement. Whether these are present at birth or develop through experience has been one of psychology's most enduring debates. This chapter examines the evidence concerning the development of visual perception.

In Chapter 15, we distinguished between *nativists* and *empiricists*. While these terms originally denoted philosophical schools of thought (see Chapters 1 and 3), they're still used in the context of psychological debates regarding the origins of human abilities, such as language (see Chapter 19) and perception. Nativists are 'naturists', who believe that we're born with certain capacities to perceive the world in particular ways. These abilities may take time to appear, but they do so through the genetically-determined process of *maturation*, with little or no learning being involved (see Chapter 50). Empiricists, by contrast, are 'nurturists', maintaining that all our knowledge and abilities are acquired through experience; that is, they're *learned*. For Locke (1690), the mind at birth is a blank slate (or *tabula rasa*) on which experience 'writes'. Locke's belief was supported by James (1890), according to whom:

'The baby, assailed by eyes, ears, nose, skin and entrails at once, feels it all as one great booming, buzzing confusion'.

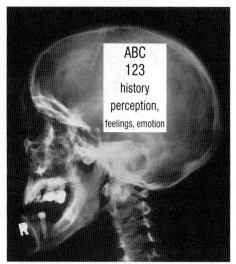

Nativist

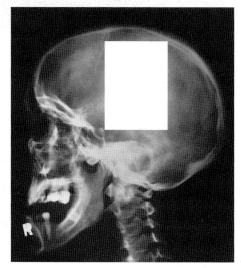

Empiricist

Most present-day psychologists wouldn't take such extreme views as described above. They'd probably consider themselves to be *interactionists*, believing that while we may be born with certain capacities, environmental influences are crucial for determining how – and even whether – these capacities actually develop. Although particular abilities may be more affected by genetic or environmental influences, *all* abilities are the product of an interaction between both sets of factors.

In a different sense, empiricists are also interactionists. Segall (1994) says that every perception is the result of an interaction between a stimulus and a perceiver, shaped by prior experience. This is essentially a 'top-down' view consistent with Gregory's theory (see Chapter 15). But it also helps to underline an important, but rarely acknowledged, similarity between those who favour the nativist or empiricist approaches: the perceiver isn't a passive responder to external stimuli, but in some way contributes to, and influences, the perceptual experience.

Overview of the research

> ### Ask yourself ...
>
> • What do you consider might be the main advantage and disadvantage of studying (a) newborns and (b) non-human animals in trying to understand the development of perceptual abilities?

Evaluating the research methods

Investigating the perceptual abilities of newborn babies (or *neonates*) represents the most direct way of investigating the nature–nurture issue. In general, the earlier a particular ability appears, the more likely it is to be under the influence of genetic factors. But the fact that it develops some time after birth doesn't necessarily mean it's been learnt: it could take time to mature. There are other special difficulties involved in studying speechless participants, as we'll see below.

Non-human animal experiments often involve depriving animals of normal sensory and perceptual stimulation, and recording the long-term effects on their sensory and perceptual abilities. Others study animals' brains to see how they control perceptual abilities. From a research point of view, the main advantage of studying animals is that we can manipulate their environments in ways which aren't permissible with humans. Deprivation studies can tell us how much and what kinds of early experience are necessary for normal perceptual development in those species being studied, but we must be very cautious about generalising these findings to humans. We must also be aware of the ethical objections to such research (see Chapter 48).

Studies of *human cataract patients* represent the human counterpart to non-human deprivation experiments. These patients have been deprived of normal visual experience through a physical defect, rather than through experimental manipulation/interference, and constitute a kind of 'natural experimental group'. Their vision is restored through surgical removal of the cataract, and the abilities that are evident immediately after removal of the bandages are normally taken to be unlearned. However, generalising from 'unusual' adults can be misleading.

In studies of *perceptual adaptation/readjustment*, human volunteers wear special goggles which distort the visual world in various ways. If they can adapt to such a distorted-looking world, then human 'perceptual habits' can't be as fixed or rigid as they would be if they were under genetic control. However, the adaptation involved may be motor, rather than perceptual, that is, learning to move about successfully in a very different-looking environment. If this is the case, then we can't conclude necessarily that our perceptual 'habits' are habits at all (learned in the first place), but only that we're good at changing our body movements to 'match' what we see.

Cross-cultural studies attempt to test whether or not the way that people in Western culture perceive things is universal, that is, perceived in the same way by people who live in cultures very different from our own. The most common method of testing is to present members of different cultural groups with the same stimulus material, usually visual illusions. Cross-cultural studies prevent us from generalising from a comparatively small sample of the earth's population (Price-Williams, 1966: see Chapter 47).

Consistent differences between different cultural groups are usually attributed to environmental factors of some kind. Such studies, therefore, enable us to discover the extent to which perceiving is structured by the nervous system (and so common to all human beings), and to what extent by experience. But as we'll see, psychologists can't agree as to the key features of such cultural experience.

What general conclusions can we draw?

As we noted at the beginning of the chapter, most psychologists are interactionists. However, some attempts have been made to test directly the merits of the nativist and empiricist positions, particularly in relation to neonates and infants. Most of the evidence supporting the nativist view derives from infant studies. We also noted above, that the earlier a particular ability appears, the less likely it is to have been learned, and so the more likely it is to be under genetic control.

Although the bulk of the evidence supports the interactionist position, there are grounds for concluding that relatively simple perceptual abilities are controlled more by genes and less susceptible to environmental influence. The reverse is true for more complex abilities. The most clear-cut demonstration of this comes from human cataract patients, and this is where we'll begin.

Ask yourself ...

- Looking back at Chapters 5 and 15, identify some examples of what you think may count as simple and complex visual abilities.
- What determined your choice; in other words, what makes them simple or complex?

Studies of human cataract patients

Most of the evidence comes from the work of von Senden (1932), a German doctor, who reported on 65 cases of people who'd undergone cataract-removal surgery between 1700 and 1928. A cataract is a film over the lens of the eye, which prevents normal (patterned) light from entering the eye. Cataracts can be present at birth or develop any time afterwards, and their removal 'restores' vision.

Hebb (1949) re-analysed von Senden's data in terms of:

- *figural unity*, the ability to detect the presence of a figure or stimulus; and
- *figural identity*, being able to name or in some other way identify the object, to 'say' what it is.

Initially, cataract patients are bewildered by an array of visual stimuli (rather like the 'booming, buzzing confusion' which James believed was the perceptual experience of newborn babies). However, they can distinguish *figure from ground* (see Chapter 15), *fixate* and *scan* objects, and follow moving objects with their eyes. But they can't identify by sight alone those objects already familiar through touch (including faces), distinguish between various geometrical shapes without counting the corners or tracing the outline with their fingers, or say which of two sticks is longer without feeling them (although they can tell there's a difference).

They also fail to show *perceptual constancy*. For example, even after recognising by sight alone a sugar lump held in someone's hand, patients may be unable to identify it correctly if it's suspended from a piece of string. This is contradicted by Bower's research with neonates suggesting that size and shape constancy are innate: see pages 238–239.

So, the more simple ability of figural unity is available very soon after cataract removal and doesn't seem to depend on prior visual experience, while the more complex figural identity seems to require learning. Hebb believes that this is how these two aspects of perception normally develop. Further evidence comes from the case of S.B.

CASE STUDY 16.1

S.B. (Gregory & Wallace, 1963)

S.B. was 52 when he received his sight after a corneal graft operation. His judgement of size and distance were good, provided he was familiar with the objects in question. Unlike most of the cases studied by Hebb, he could recognise objects visually if he was already familiar with them through touch (he displayed good *cross-modal transfer*). However, he seemed to have great difficulty in identifying objects visually if he wasn't already familiar with them in this way. A year after his operation, he still couldn't draw the front of a bus although the rest of the drawing was very well executed (see Figure 16.1).

As the months passed, it became clear that S.B. was in some ways like a newborn baby when it came to recognising objects and events by sight alone. For instance, he found it impossible to judge distances by sight alone. He knew what windows were, from touching them both from inside a room and from outside (while standing on the ground). But, of course, he'd never been able to look out from a top-floor window, and he thought 'he would be able to touch the ground below the window with his feet if he lowered himself by his hands'. The window in question was the one in his hospital room – 40 feet above the ground!

Figure 16.1 *This was drawn after S.B. had had some experience of sighted travel. Basically it shows the parts he knew by touch but clearly he had also, by this time, noticed the bright advertisement for Typhoo Tea on the side of the bus*

He never learnt to interpret facial expressions such as smiles and frowns, although he could infer a person's mood from the sound of their voice. He preferred to sit in the dark all evening, instead of putting on the light.

Evaluation of cataract patient studies

- Adult patients aren't the same as babies. While infants' sensory systems are all relatively immature (see pages 234–235), adults have other well-developed sensory modalities which tend to compensate for the lack of vision (especially touch and hearing). These other channels may actually hinder visual learning, because the patient may have to 'unlearn' previous experience. For example, S.B.'s continued preference for touch over vision may reflect a tendency to stick with what's familiar, rather than experiment with the unknown. This may be a safer conclusion to draw than Hebb's, which is that figural identity is (normally) learned.
- Traditionally, cataract patients haven't been adequately prepared for their 'new world of vision'. The resulting confusion and general emotional distress following the operation may make it difficult to be sure just what they can and cannot see. When blind, S.B. would cross the street on his own, but once he could see the traffic it frightened him so much that he refused to cross on his own. In fact, he died three years after his operation, at least partially from depression. Depression was also common amongst von Senden's cases.
- We don't know what physical deterioration of the visual system may have occurred during the years of blindness. Consequently, the absence of figural identity could be due some physical damage, rather than to lack of visual stimulation and learning (as Hebb maintains).
- The *reliability* of the case histories themselves is open to doubt. There's great variability in the ages of the patients, when they underwent surgery and when their cataracts first appeared, and hence in the amount of their previous visual experience.

Non-human animal experiments

Riesen (1947) deprived one group of chimps of light by raising them in darkness, except for several 45-second periods of exposure to light while they were being fed. This continued until they were 16 months old, when they were compared with a group of normally-reared chimps. The deprived group showed pupil constriction to light, and were startled by sudden, intense illumination. But they didn't blink in response to threatening movements made towards their faces, or show any interest in their toys unless they accidentally touched them.

Weiskrantz (1956) pointed out that the deprived group's visual deficiencies were probably due to failure of the retinas to develop properly, as a result of insufficient light stimulation. Riesen's experiment, therefore, may show only that a certain amount of light is physically necessary to maintain the visual system and allow it to mature normally.

In response to these objections, Riesen (1965) reared three chimps from birth to seven months of age, under three different conditions:

- Debi spent the whole time in darkness.
- Kova spent 1½ hours per day exposed to *diffuse* (or unpatterned) light by wearing translucent goggles. The rest of the time was spent in darkness.
- Lad was raised in normal lighting conditions.

As expected, only Debi suffered retinal damage. Lad was no different, perceptually, from any other normally reared chimp. It was Kova who was of special interest, because she was only exposed to unpatterned light but without suffering any retinal damage. Unpatterned light comprises patches of different colours and brightnesses – not distinguishable shapes or patterns. She was noticeably retarded as far as her perceptual development was concerned.

These, and similar experiments with monkeys, chimps and kittens, suggest that:

- light is necessary for normal physical development of the visual system (at least in chimps, some monkeys and kittens);
- *patterned light* is also necessary for the normal development of more complex visual abilities (in those species), such as following a moving object, differentiating between geometrical shapes, perceiving depth and distinguishing a moving from a stationary object.

Other animal experiments have also shown the impact of early experience on perceptual abilities.

KEY STUDY 16.1

Kitten carousel experiment (Held & Hein, 1963)

Held and Hein used a kitten carousel to study kittens' ability to guide their movements using vision (see Figure 16.2). For their first eight weeks, kittens were kept in darkness. They then spent three hours each day in the carousel, the rest of the time being spent in darkness. The 'active' kitten could move itself around (its legs were free), and its movements were transmitted to the 'passive' kitten via a series of pulleys. Every time the active kitten moved, the passive kitten moved the same distance, at the same speed. Since the visual environment was constant, both kittens had exactly the same visual experience.

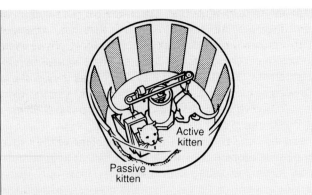

Figure 16.2 *The kitten carousel (from Held, 1965)*

When paw–eye co-ordination was tested several weeks later, the passive kittens were markedly inferior. For example, they showed no evidence of depth perception when placed onto the deep side of the visual cliff apparatus (see below and Figure 16.11). However, the passive kittens soon learned the normal avoidance responses on the deep side of the cliff when allowed to run around in a lighted environment. This suggests that what they'd failed to learn were the correct motor responses associated with depth perception (sensorimotor co-ordination), rather that depth perception as such (see perceptual readjustment studies below).

Blakemore & Cooper (1970) raised kittens from birth in darkness, except for a five-hour period each day when they were placed in a large round chamber. This had either vertical or horizontal stripes painted on the inside, and a glass floor which reflected the pattern of stripes. The kittens wore special collars which prevented them from seeing their own bodies, and the stripes were the only visual stimuli they encountered.

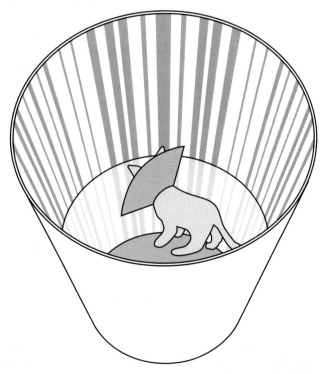

Figure 16.3 *The 'vertical' world used in Blakemore & Cooper's (1970) experiment*

At five months old, the kittens were tested for line recognition by being presented with a moving pointer, held either vertically or horizontally. Those reared in the 'vertical world' would reach out only to a vertical pointer, while those raised in the 'horizontal world' reached only for a horizontal pointer. Depending on their early visual experience, the kittens acted as if they were blind in the presence of the other kind of visual stimulus.

This 'behavioural blindness' mirrored 'physiological blindness'. By placing microelectrodes into individual cells in the visual cortex, Blakemore and Cooper found that the 'vertical' kittens didn't possess cells that were responsive to bars of light moved horizontally, and the reverse was true for the 'horizontal' kittens. The only receptive fields to have developed were those which reflected the kittens' early visual experience (see Chapter 5).

However, this *doesn't* show conclusively that responding to lines at different angles develops solely through environmental influence. It's possible that receptive fields for *all* angles are present at birth, but that where a kitten sees *only* vertical lines, those fields which would otherwise have responded to horizontal lines are 'taken over' by vertical fields. Nevertheless, these findings suggest very strongly that the environment is important in the development of at least certain kinds of perceptual ability in some species: in kittens, perception does seem to be at least partly learned.

Evaluation of non-human animal experiments

A general problem with non-human animal studies (as with studies of human infants) is that we can only *infer* their perceptual experiences through observing their behaviour or their physiological responses. They're unable to tell us more directly what they can or cannot see. We cannot be certain that animals deprived in particular ways don't perceive particular stimuli, only that they don't *behave* as if they do. It's possible that certain perceptual abilities have developed, but if they've not become linked to the animal's behaviour, we may have no way of knowing.

> *Ask yourself ...*
>
> - Do you consider the experiments by Riesen, Held and Hein, and Blakemore and Cooper to be ethically acceptable?
> - What kinds of scientific justification could be put forward in their defence?

Perceptual adaptation/readjustment studies

If it can be shown that people are capable of perceiving the world in a different way from normal, and adjusting to this altered perception, then perception is probably learned. The greater the degree of adaptation, the more significant the role of learning is taken to be. Neither salamanders (Sperry, 1943) nor chickens (Hess, 1956) show any evidence of being able to adapt to distorted perceptions, suggesting that genetic factors largely control their perceptual abilities.

One of the earliest recorded human studies was that of Stratton.

Turning the world upside down (Stratton, 1896)

Stratton fitted himself with a telescope on one eye which 'turned the world upside down'. The other eye was kept covered. He wore the telescope for a total of 87 hours over an eight-day period, wearing blindfolds at night and at other times when not wearing the inverting lens. As far as possible, he went about his normal routine. For the first three days, he was aware that part of his environment – the part not in his immediate field of vision but on the periphery – was in a different orientation. But by the fourth day he was beginning to imagine unseen parts as also being inverted, and by the fifth day he had to make a conscious effort to remember that he actually had the telescope on. He could walk round the house without bumping into furniture, and when he moved, his surroundings looked 'normal'. However, when he concentrated hard and remained still, things still appeared upside down. By the eighth day, everything seemed 'harmonious'; he began to 'feel' inverted, but this was quite normal and natural to him.

When Stratton removed the telescope, he immediately recognised the visual orientation as the one that existed before the experiment began. He found it surprisingly bewildering, although definitely *not* upside-down. This absence of an inverted after-image/after-effect means that Stratton hadn't actually learnt to see the world in an upside-down fashion. If he had, removal of the telescope would have caused the now normal (right-way-up) world to look upside-down again! Instead, it suggests that the adaptation took the form of learning the appropriate *motor responses* in an upside-down-looking world. (Compare this with the question of depth perception in Held and Hein's kittens: see Key Study 16.1.) But Stratton did experience an after-effect which caused things before him to 'swing and sweep' as he moved his eyes, showing that *location constancy* had been disrupted.

Figure 16.4 *One of Stratton's experiments in which goggles displaced the wearer's body image at right angles*

In another experiment, Stratton made goggles which visually displaced his body, so that he always appeared horizontally in front of himself (see Figure 16.4). Wherever he walked, he 'followed' his own body image, which was suspended at right angles to his actual body. When he lay down, his body would appear above him, vertically, again at right angles. After three days, he was able to go out for a walk on his own – and lived to tell the tale!

Gilling and Brightwell (1982) replicated Stratton's inverted goggles experiment.

Susannah Fienues (Gilling & Brightwell, 1982)

Susannah Fienues, a young art student, wore inverted goggles for a period of seven days. After first putting them on she reported:

> *'The cars are going upside down. They're going the wrong way. It's all going completely the wrong way to what you'd expect. It's really strange'.*

After one hour, she reported:

> *'In fact, looking at people in cars was quite normal, I didn't think they were upside down, and I just got adjusted to it, I think. But the difficult thing is just walking and being very disorientated, because how you feel is completely different to what you're doing … As for things being upside down, it just doesn't feel like that at all because I know very well that I'm sitting here and so I think my brain still knows that, so it's all right'.*

Like Stratton, she at first had great difficulty in pouring milk from a jug into a glass. By the fourth day, she could walk without difficulty, from the bedroom to the sitting room. And she could now pour the milk! She felt 'Just fine … I don't notice that things are upside down at all'. She could write her name normally, but only if she closed her eyes and didn't see her hand as she wrote it. With her eyes open, she could write it so that it appeared normal to her but inverted to anyone else!

By seven days her early problems seemed to have vanished – she could ride her bike, walk, run, climb stairs, turn corners, make coffee and put records on.

> *'The only thing that's still quite difficult is eating and using a knife and fork.'*

Again:

> *'It's become more and more difficult to imagine myself standing upright or sitting down normally. I almost want to sit upside down because I can't quite imagine myself sitting normally'.*

This account supports the view of vision as an active process, enabling us to deal with the world. When Susannah removed the goggles, she was annoyed that nothing seemed any different! She reverted to normal vision within a few minutes, very relieved that the experiment was over. Like Stratton, she learnt to match her vision with signals reported by the rest of her body. According to Gilling and Brightwell:

> 'She was not just seeing, but sampling the world as a whole with her senses, and organising them so that they told stories which could be sensibly related to each other. She saw with her whole body, the whole apparatus of her senses, as it were, and not just with her eyes ...'.

Snyder & Pronko (1952) made goggles which inverted *and* reversed the visual world. Their volunteers wore them continually for 30 days and adapted to the changes. Two years after the experiment, these participants coped just as well when refitted with the goggles as first-time participants at the end of the 30-day period, showing that motor adaptations are extremely resistant to forgetting.

Ask yourself ...

- What conclusions can we draw from adaptation studies?

Evaluation of adaptation studies

- When volunteers adapt to a distorted perceptual world, they're not, for the most part, actually learning to see 'normally', but are developing the appropriate *motor behaviour* which helps them to get around and function efficiently in their environment. What's learnt is not a new way of perceiving the world, but a new set of body movements.
- The visual system, at least in adults, is extremely *flexible*, and can adjust to distorted conditions. This strongly suggests that learning plays an important role in perceptual development, since a totally or largely innate system wouldn't allow such adaptation to occur.
- The volunteers are adults, who've already undergone a great deal of learning and in whom maturation has already taken place. This makes it difficult to generalise from these studies to how babies develop under normal circumstances.

Studying neonate and infant visual perception

Before looking at the perceptual world of the human neonate, we need to be familiar with some of the methods that have been used in this area.

Box 16.1	Some methods used to study neonate and infant perception

Spontaneous visual preference technique (or **preferential looking**): Two stimuli are presented simultaneously to the neonate. If more time is spent looking at one, it can reasonably be assumed that (a) the difference between the stimuli can be perceived, and (b) the stimulus which is looked at longer is preferred.

Sucking rate: A dummy (or pacifier) is used and the sucking rate in response to different stimuli is measured. First, a baseline sucking rate is established, and then a stimulus introduced. The stimulus may produce an increase or decrease in sucking rate but, eventually, habituation will occur, and the baby will stop responding. If the stimulus is changed and another increase or decrease in sucking rate occurs, it can be inferred that the baby has responded to the change as a novel stimulus, and hence can tell the difference between the two stimuli.

Habituation: This is used as a method in its own right. If an external stimulus and a baby's representation of it match, then the baby presumably knows the stimulus. This will be reflected by the baby ignoring it. Mismatches will maintain the baby's attention, so that a novel (and discriminable) stimulus presented after habituation to a familiar stimulus re-excites attention.

Conditioned head rotation: The infant is operantly conditioned (see Chapter 11) to turn its head in response to a stimulus. The stimulus can then be presented in, for example, a different orientation, and the presence or absence of the conditioned response noted. It has been used to test for shape constancy (see page 238) and in auditory perception (Bornstein, 1988).

Physiological measures: If a physiological change (such as heart rate and breathing rate) occurs when a new stimulus is presented, it can be inferred that the infant can discriminate between the old and new stimuli.

Measures of electrical activity in the brain: By using electrodes attached to the scalp, researchers can look for visually evoked potentials (VEPs) occurring in response to particular stimuli. If different stimuli produce different VEPs, the infant can presumably distinguish between those stimuli. A recent piece of equipment used for doing this is the 'geodesic hair-net' (see Chapter 4, page 50).

The perceptual equipment of babies

At birth, the whole nervous system is immature. The optic nerve is thinner and shorter than in adults, and myelin sheath won't be fully developed until about four months. As a result, visual information is transmitted less effectively to the immature cortex. Also, at birth a baby's eye is about half the size and weight of an adult's, and the eyeball is shorter. This reduces the distance between the retina and lens, making vision less efficient. So, although the new-born's eyeball is anatomically identical to an adult's, the relationship between the parts is different, and they don't develop at the same rate (see Chapter 5, pages 68–70).

Box 16.2	What can babies see?

Colour perception: The retina, rods and cones are reasonably well developed at birth. Using habituation, Bornstein (1976) found that in the absence of brightness cues, three-month-olds could discriminate blue-green from white, and yellow from green (tests which are typically failed by those who are red–green colour blind). Most babies possess largely normal colour vision at two months, and some as early as one month (Bornstein, 1988).

Brightness: The fovea is also reasonably well developed at birth. The developing foetus reacts to bright light, and the pupillary reflex is present even in premature babies, with the blink reflex present at birth. These findings suggest that a baby's sensitivity to brightness is reasonably similar to an adult's.

Movement: The optokinetic reflex (or optic nystagmus), which enables us to follow a moving object, is present within two days of birth. While less efficient than an adult's, it improves rapidly in the first three months. Horizontal movement is better tracked than vertical movement, but is still 'jerky'. This may be because convergence (essential for fixation and depth perception) is absent at birth, although fully developed by two to three months. Accommodation reaches adult standards by about four months, probably due to maturation (see Chapter 15, pages 214–215).

Visual acuity: The threshold of visual acuity (the ability to discriminate fine detail) is about 30 times poorer than in adults and, at birth, everything beyond 20 centimetres is seen as a blur (Gwiazda *et al.*, 1980). However, babies aged one to three months will learn to suck on a nipple connected to the focus on a projector to bring a blurred picture into focus (Kalnins & Bruner, 1973). Between six and 12 months, visual acuity comes within adult range (20/20 vision: Haith, 1990; Slater, 1994).

The perceptual abilities of babies

Pattern (or form) perception

Using the preferential looking technique, Fantz (1961) presented one- to 15-week-old babies with pairs of stimuli (see Figure 16.5). The stimuli were presented at weekly intervals, and Fantz measured how long the babies spent looking at each. There was a distinct preference for more complex stimuli; that is, stimuli which contain more information and in which there's more 'going on'. According to Fantz:

'The relative attractiveness of the two members of a pair depended on the presence of a pattern difference. There were strong preferences between stripes and bull's-eyes and between checkerboard and square. Neither the cross and circle nor the two triangles aroused a significant differential interest. The differential response to pattern was shown at all ages tested, indicating that it was not the result of a learning process'.

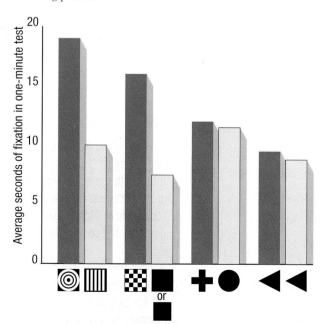

Figure 16.5 *Average time spent looking at various pairs of stimulus patterns in babies aged one to 15 weeks. (From Fantz, 1961)*

Fantz also found that preference for complexity is apparently a function of age. The babies tested at weekly intervals could discriminate between stimuli with progressively narrower stripes (cf. visual acuity in Box 16.2). Later, Fantz showed that two- to four-month-olds prefer patterns to colour or brightness, as shown in Figure 16.6.

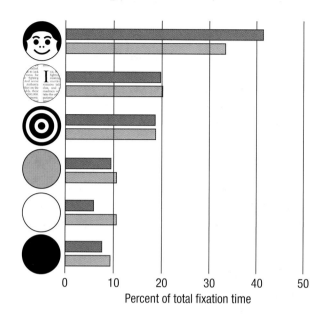

Percent of total fixation time

Figure 16.6 *Preference for complex stimuli over simple stimuli. The dark purple bars show the percentage of fixation time for two- to three-month-olds. The light purple bars show the percentage of fixation time for four-month-olds (from Fantz, 1961)*

The preference for increasing complexity suggests that the baby's capacity for differentiation steadily improves. Possibly, this is because its ability to scan becomes more efficient and thorough. Support for this comes from studies showing that very young infants confine their scanning to one corner of a triangle, suggesting a preference for areas of greatest contrast (Salapatek, 1975). Only later does the baby begin to explore all around the stimulus and inside it, and attend to the whole pattern and not just specific parts. Before two months of age, neonates probably discriminate between shapes on the basis of *lower-order variables*, such as orientation and contrast (Slater & Morison, 1985). After two months, however, 'true form perception' begins (Slater, 1989), and babies respond to *higher-order variables* (such as configurational invariance and form categories).

> *Ask yourself ...*
>
> • Can you think of any reasons why it would be 'a good idea' for babies to have an inborn knowledge of/preference for faces?
> • What is it about faces that babies are likely to find particularly attractive?

The perception of human faces

The human face is three-dimensional, contains high-contrast information (especially the eyes, mouth and hairline), constantly moves (the eyes, mouth and head), is a source of auditory information (the voice), and regulates its behaviour according to the baby's own activities. Thus, the human face combines complexity, pattern and movement (it's a *supernormal stimulus*: Rheingold, 1961), all of which babies appear innately to prefer. Whether this preference occurs because of this combination of factors, or whether there's an innate perceptual knowledge of a face *as a face*, was also addressed by Fantz (1961).

Fantz presented babies aged between four days and six months with all possible pairs of the three stimuli shown in Figure 16.7. The stimuli were coloured black, presented against a pink background, and of the approximate shape and size of an adult's head.

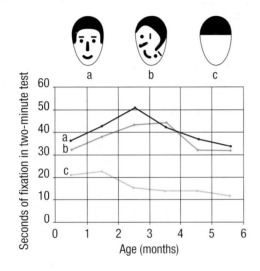

Figure 16.7 *Looking times for each of the stimulus used in Fantz's study of the perception of faces (from Fantz, 1961)*

Irrespective of age, the babies preferred to look at the schematic representation of a face (a) more than the 'scrambled' face (b). The control stimulus (c) was largely ignored. Even though the difference between (a) and (b) was small, Fantz concluded that 'there is an unlearned, primitive meaning in the form perception of infants', and that babies have an innate preference for 'facedness'.

But Hershenson *et al.* (1965) pointed out that (a) and (b) were more complex than (c), and this might account for Fantz's findings, rather than a preference for looking at human faces. They controlled for complexity, and presented neonates with all possible pairs of three equally complex stimuli:

- a real female face;
- a distorted picture which retained the outline of head and hair but altered the position of the other features;
- a scrambled face (stimulus (b) in Fantz's experiment).

They found no preference for any of the three stimuli, and concluded that a preference for real faces isn't innate, and doesn't appear until about four months of age.

KEY STUDY 16.3

Early evidence of face preference (Johnson *et al.*, 1991)

Lying on their backs, neonates (average age of 43 minutes) saw one of four patterned boards moved in an arc in front of their faces. Their eyes followed the most face-like pattern longer than the un-face-like patterns. Even the most face-like board was only a schematic representation, with only moderate realism. But it still contains intensity changes, which approximate (or even exaggerate) those of real faces, and for an innate mechanism, that's all that's needed (Bruce & Young, 1998).

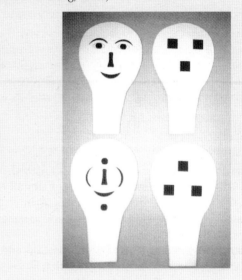

Figure 16.8 *Four face-like boards*

Meltzoff & Moore (1977) found that two- to three-week-olds can imitate facial expressions, including sticking out their tongues, opening their mouths, and protruding their lips. This suggests that infants must have some kind of inbuilt 'map' of their faces to indicate which of their own facial muscles correspond to those of another human face (Bruce & Young, 1998; Slater, 1994).

Baby imitating facial expressions

Babies as young as 12–36 hours old display a clear preference for their mother's face over a female stranger's, when variables such as overall brightness and hair colour are controlled for (Bushnell *et al.*, 1989; Walton *et al.*, 1992). So far, there's no evidence of a preference for their father's face over a male stranger's, even when he has spent more time with the baby than the mother has. There's no obvious explanation for this (Bee, 2000).

According to Slater (1994), the evidence indicates that:

'Some knowledge about faces is present at birth, suggesting that babies come into the world with some innate, genetically determined knowledge about faces'.

An inborn attraction to faces makes the baby seem interested in its caregivers, thereby encouraging them to provide the care it needs. Although the task of learning about the particular faces of parents and siblings is a lengthy process, it seems to happen very quickly in the case of mothers. This could be seen as evolutionarily determined attachment behaviour (see Chapter 32).

Depth perception

Perhaps the most famous way of investigating infants' depth perception is Gibson & Walk's (1960) *visual cliff apparatus* (see Figure 16.9). This consists of a central platform, on the *shallow* side of which is a sheet of plexiglass. Immediately below this is a black and white checkerboard pattern. On the *deep* side is another sheet of plexiglass, this time with the checkerboard pattern placed on the floor, at a distance of about four feet. This gives the appearance of a 'drop' or 'cliff'. The baby is placed on the central platform, and its mother calls and beckons to it, first from one side and then the other.

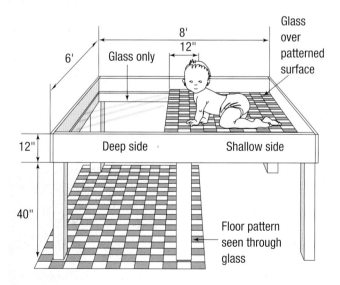

Figure 16.9 *The visual cliff (from Dworetzky, 1981)*

Gibson and Walk found that most babies aged between six and 14 months wouldn't crawl onto the 'deep' side when beckoned by their mothers. This was interpreted as indicating that neonates have the innate ability to perceive depth. Those babies who did venture onto the deep side did so 'accidentally', either by backing onto it or resting on it. It's likely that their poor motor control was responsible for this, rather than their inability to perceive depth.

The very nature of the visual cliff apparatus, however, required the researchers to use babies who could *crawl*, the youngest being six months old. An alternative explanation of Gibson and Walk's findings would be that the babies had learned to perceive depth during their first six months. Gibson and Walk subsequently tested a number of members of *precocial species* (capable of moving about independently at or shortly after birth): namely, chicks, goat kids, lambs, and rats with their sensitive whiskers removed. None would venture onto the deep side. If forcibly placed on the deep side, they invariably 'froze'.

KEY STUDY 16.4

Using heart rate to measure depth perception (Campos *et al.*, 1970)

In an ingenious way of assessing babies younger than six months, Campos *et al.* used heart rate as an index of depth perception. Babies of various ages had their heart rates monitored while they were on the visual cliff. Older babies (nine months) showed an increased heart rate, a response presumably indicating fear. The youngest (two months) showed a decreased heart rate when placed on the 'deep' side. They were less likely to cry, more attentive to what was underneath them, and clearly not frightened by what they saw. No such changes were observed when the infants were placed on the 'shallow' side. It seems that even two-month-olds can perceive depth, and that avoidance behaviour is probably learnt (perhaps after having a few experiences of falling).

Depth perception has also been studied by looking at how neonates react when an object approaches their faces from a distance. For example, if a large box is moved towards a 20-day-old neonate's face, it shows an *integrated avoidance response*, throwing back its head, shielding its face with its hands, and even crying (Bower *et al.*, 1970). This suggests that the baby understands that the box is getting closer and, because it's potentially harmful, some sort of protective reaction is needed. Interestingly, this response occurs even with one eye closed, but not when equivalent pictures are shown on a screen. This indicates that motion parallax (see Table 15.2, page 214) is the critical cue for distance.

The perception of 3-D objects

The integrated avoidance response suggests that as well as perceiving depth, neonates see boxes as solid, 3-D objects. To explore this, Bower (1979) devised a piece of apparatus that creates illusions of 3-D objects (see Figure 16.10, page 238). Babies aged 16 to 24 weeks were put in front of a screen. A plastic, translucent object was suspended between lights and the screen, casting a double shadow on the back. When the screen is viewed from the front and the baby wears polarising goggles, the double shadows merge to form the image of a solid 3-D object.

Bower found that none of the babies showed any surprise when they grasped a real and solid object. But when they reached for the apparent object, and discovered there was nothing solid to get hold of, they all expressed surprise and some were even distressed. This indicates that they expected to be able to touch what they could 'see', an ability Bower believes to be innate.

Figure 16.10 *Trying to grasp a 'virtual object' produces surprise in a four- to six-month-old baby*

Perceptual organisation: constancies and Gestalt principles

Size constancy

Despite a newborn's vision being much poorer than an adult's, its visual world is highly organised (Slater, 1994). According to *empiricists*, constancy is learned, and so neonates are likely to be 'tricked' by the appearance of things. For example, if something looks smaller (it projects a smaller retinal image), then it *is* smaller. *Nativists*, however, would argue that neonates are innately able to judge the size of an object regardless of retinal image.

KEY STUDY 16.5

'Peek-a-boo' and size constancy too (Bower, 1966)

To assess nativist and empirist claims, Bower initially conditioned two-month-olds to turn their heads whenever they saw a 30-centimetre cube at a distance of one metre (an adult popping up in front of the baby whenever it performed the desired behaviour served as a powerful reinforcer). Once the response was conditioned, the cube was replaced by one of three different cubes:

- a 30-centimetre cube presented at a distance of three metres (producing a retinal image one-third of the size of the original);
- a 90-centimetre cube presented at a distance of one metre (producing a retinal image three times the size of the original);
- a 90-centimetre cube presented at a distance of three metres (producing exactly the same-sized retinal image as the conditioned stimulus).

(See Figure 16.11.)

Bower recorded the number of times each stimulus produced the conditioned response (CR), and used this as a measure of how similar the neonate considered the stimulus to be to the original. The original stimulus produced a total of 98 CRs, while the first produced 58, the second 54, and the third 22. The finding that *most* CRs occurred in response to the first

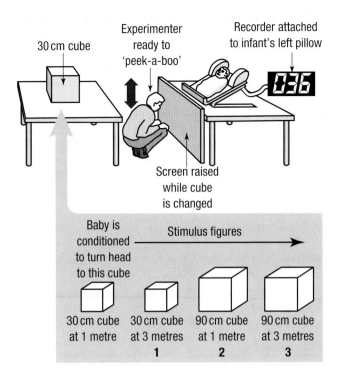

Figure 16.11 *The experimental set-up in Bower's study of size constancy*

stimulus indicates that the baby was responding to the *actual* size of the cube, irrespective of its distance. This suggests the presence of size constancy, and supports the nativist view that this constancy is inbuilt.

The nativist position is further strengthened by the finding that fewest CRs occurred in response to the third stimulus. If size constancy was absent, as predicted by empiricists, neonates would 'compare' retinal images and base their perception of similarity on these regardless of distance. Empiricists, then, would have expected the third stimulus to produce the most CRs. Bower's findings have been replicated with two-day-olds by Slater *et al.* (1990: cited in Slater, 1994). Although these findings demonstrate that size constancy is an organising feature of perception present at birth, learning still plays some part (Slater, 1994). For example, in the Slater *et al.* study, the procedure depends on infants learning the characteristics of the cubes in the early 'familiarisation trials'.

Shape constancy

According to Slater (1989), neonates can extract the constant real shape of an object that's rotated in the third dimension, that is, they're capable of recognising an object's form independently of (transformations in) its spatial orientation. For example, Bower (1966) found that if a two-month-old infant was conditioned to turn its head to look at a rectangle, it would continue to make the CR when the rectangle was turned slightly to produce a trapezoid retinal image. For Bornstein (1988), the evidence concerning shape constancy indicates that 'babies still only in their first year of life can perceive form *qua* form'.

Feature, identity and existence constancy

- *Feature constancy* is the ability to recognise the invariant features of a stimulus despite some detectable but irrelevant transformation. If a new-born has been *habituated* to a moving stimulus, it will display a *novelty preference* when shown the same stimulus paired with a novel shape, both of which are stationary. This indicates that the new-born perceives the familiar stationary stimulus as the same stimulus that was moving, and that feature constancy is present at birth.

■ Feature constancy is a prerequisite for *identity constancy* (the ability to recognise a particular object as being exactly the same object despite some transformation made to it). Distinguishing between feature and identity constancy is extremely difficult. In Bower's (1971) study, babies younger or older than 20 weeks were seated in front of mirrors which could produce several images of the mother. Babies younger than 20 weeks smiled, cooed and waved their arms to each of the 'multiple mothers', whereas older babies became upset. What this suggests is that only the older babies, who are aware that they have just one mother, possess identity constancy.

■ *Existence constancy* refers to the belief that objects continue to exist even when they're no longer available to the senses (what Piaget calls *object permanence*: see Chapter 34). Together, existence and identity constancy comprise the *object concept*, which typically appears around six months of age.

Gestalt principles

Bower has also looked at how neonate perception is organised in terms of certain Gestalt principles (see Chapter 15). Bower wanted to discover if *closure* (or *occlusion*) is, as Gestalt psychologists claim, an inborn characteristic.

KEY STUDY 16.6

Closure (Bower, 1977)

Two-month-olds were conditioned to respond to a black wire triangle with a black iron bar across it (Figure 16.12 top). Then, various stimuli (Figure 16.12 bottom) were presented. Bower found that the CR was generalised to the complete triangle (A), suggesting that the babies perceived an unbroken triangle to lie behind the black iron bar. Given that they were unlikely to have encountered many triangles, Bower concluded that closure is almost certainly an inborn feature of neonate perceptual ability.

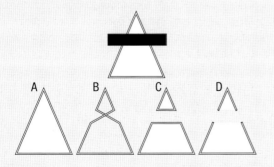

Figure 16.12 *The stimulus figures used in Bower's study of closure*

Bruce & Young (1998) sum up like this:

> *'These studies of infants allow us to glimpse the intricate interplay between the innate organisation of the brain and its astonishing capacity for perceptual-learning … the infant's brain is highly plastic – ready to be moulded by the experiences it encounters. But it also contains crafty mechanisms (such as attention-capturing properties for face-like stimuli) which keep the odds high that these experiences will be optimal for what the baby will need to learn'.*

Cross-cultural studies

Ask yourself ...

* We noted earlier that if we find consistent perceptual differences between different cultural groups, then we're likely to attribute them to environmental factors. In what ways do cultures differ that could suggest what these environmental factors might be?

Studies using visual illusions

There's a long history of cross-cultural research into perceptual development using visual illusions.

Box 16.3 Some early research into cross-cultural differences using visual illusions

* Rivers (1901) compared English adults and children with adult and child Murray Islanders (a group of islands between New Guinea and Australia) using the Müller–Lyer illusion and the horizontal–vertical illusion. The Murray Islanders were less susceptible to the Müller–Lyer illusion than their English counterparts, but more susceptible to the horizontal–vertical illusion.

* Allport & Pettigrew (1957) used the rotating trapezoid illusion. This is a trapezoid with horizontal and vertical bars attached to it to give the impression of a window.

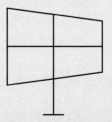

When attached to a motor and revolved in a circle, most Western observers report seeing a rectangle oscillating backwards and forwards, rather than a trapezoid rotating through 360° (which it actually is). Allport and Pettigrew reasoned that for people unfamiliar with windows (at least as people from Western cultures know them), the illusion wouldn't be perceived. When the trapezoid was viewed with both eyes and from a short distance, Zulus (who live in a rather 'circular environment') were less likely than either urban

Zulus or Europeans to perceive an oscillating rectangle, and more likely to perceive a rotating trapezoid.

- Segall *et al.* (1963) used the Müller–Lyer illusion with members of African and Filipino cultures. Compared with white South Africans and Americans, the Africans and Filipinos were much less susceptible to the illusion. But on the horizontal–vertical illusion, members of two African cultures (the Batoro and the Bayankole) were most susceptible. People of these cultures live in high, open country where vertical objects are important focal points used to estimate distances. For example, when a tree or pole falls away from you, it seems to grow shorter (foreshortening), but when it falls to the left or right across your field of vision its length does not appear to change (Price & Crapo, 1999). The Bete, who live in a dense jungle environment, were least likely of all groups tested to see the illusion. The white South Africans and Americans fell between the extremes of the three African cultures.
- Stewart (1973) used the Ames distorted room (see Figure 15.17, page 223) with rural and urban Tongan children. The rural children were less likely to see the illusion than those living in urban environments and European children. This was also true for other illusions, including the Müller–Lyer.

The carpentered world hypothesis

According to Segall *et al.*'s (1963) *carpentered world hypothesis*, people in Western cultures:

> '… *live in a culture in which straight lines abound and in which perhaps 90 per cent of the acute and obtuse angles formed on [the] retina by the straight lines of [the] visual field are realistically interpretable as right angles extended in space*'.

Segall *et al.*, therefore, believe that we tend to interpret illusions, which are 2-D drawings, in terms of our past experiences. In the 'carpentered world' of Western societies, we add a third dimension (depth), which isn't actually present in the drawing, and this leads to the illusion experience (cf. Gregory's account of visual illusions: see Chapter 15, pages 219–220).

Jahoda (1966) compared the Lobi and Dagomba tribes of Ghana, who live in open parkland in round huts, with the Ashanti, who live in dense forest in roughly rectangular huts. The prediction that the Lobi and Dagomba would be significantly more susceptible to the horizontal–vertical illusion, while the Ashanti would be significantly more susceptible to the Müller–Lyer, wasn't supported. Similarly, Gregor & McPherson (1965) found no significant differences between two groups of Australian aborigines on the two illusions, despite one group living in a relatively urbanised, carpentered environment and the other living primitively out of doors. However, both groups were significantly *less* prone to the Müller–Lyer than Europeans and *more* prone to the horizontal–vertical.

Despite some inconsistent evidence regarding illusion susceptibility and its interpretation, Segall *et al.* (1999) conclude their review by stating:

> '… *people perceive in ways that are shaped by the inferences they have learned to make in order to function most effectively in the particular ecological settings in which they live … we learn to perceive in the ways that we need to perceive. In that sense, environment and culture shape our perceptual habits*'.

Studies of other perceptual phenomena

In various African cultures, children and adults find it difficult to perceive depth in both pictorial material and under certain conditions, in the real world too.

CASE STUDY 16.3

Confusing your buffalo with your insects (Turnbull, 1961)

The BaMbuti pygmies live in the dense rainforests of the Congo, a closed-in world without open spaces. When a BaMbuti archer was taken to a vast plain and shown a herd of buffalo grazing in the distance, he claimed he'd never seen such insects before. When informed that the 'insects' were buffalo, the archer was offended. They then rode in a jeep towards the buffalo. The sight of the buffalo in the distance was so far removed from the archer's experience, that he was convinced Turnbull was using magic to deceive him. The archer lacked experience with distance cues, preventing him from relating distance to size (Price & Crapo, 1999).

'Reading' pictures

In Hudson's (1960) study, people from various African cultures were shown a series of pictures depicting hunting scenes (see Figure 16.13, page 241). Participants were first asked to name all the objects in the scene, then they were asked about the relationship between them, such as 'Which is closer to the man?' If the 'correct' interpretation was made, and depth cues were taken into account, respondents were classified as having 3-D vision. If such cues were ignored, they were classified as having 2-D vision. Hudson reported that both children and adults found it difficult to perceive depth in the pictorial material.

Deregowski (1972) refers to a description given of an African woman slowly discovering that a picture she was looking at portrayed a human head in profile:

> '*She discovered in turn the nose, the mouth, the eye, but where was the other eye? I tried turning my profile to explain why she could see only one eye, but she hopped round to my other side to point out that I possessed a second eye which the other lacked*'.

The woman treated the picture as an object rather than a 2-D representation of an object, that is, she didn't 'infer' depth in the picture. What she believed to be an 'object' turned out to have only two dimensions, and this is what the woman found bewildering. However, when familiar pictorial stimulus material is used, recognition tends to be better (Serpell, 1976). Thus, some (but not all) of the Me'en of Ethiopia found it much easier to recognise material when it was presented in the form of pictures painted on cloth (which is both familiar to them and free of distracting cues such as a border) than line drawings on paper (Deregowski, 1972).

Figure 16.13 *Hudson (1960) found that when shown the top picture and asked which animal the hunter is trying to spear, members of some cultures reply 'the elephant'. This shows that some cultures do not use cues to depth (such as overlap and known size of objects). The second picture shows the hunter, elephant and antelope in true size ratios when all are the same distance from the observer*

Ask yourself ...

- In Hudson's pictures (Figure 16.13), which depth cues are used (see Table 15.2, page 214)?
- Which cues aren't used, which you think could be important to people living in open terrain?

Are Hudson's pictures biased?

Hudson's pictures use *relative size* and *overlap/superimposition*, but *texture gradient*, *binocular disparity* and *motion parallax* are all missing. When the pictures were redrawn to show texture gradients (by, for example, adding grass to open terrain), more Zambian children gave 3-D answers than in Hudson's original study (Kingsley *et al.*, cited in Serpell, 1976). Research summarised by Berry *et al.* (1992) indicates that the absence of certain depth cues in pictorial material makes the perception of depth difficult for non-Western peoples (see Gross, 1999).

Conclusions: Nature, nurture or an interaction?

According to Bee (2000), as researchers have become increasingly ingenious in devising ways of testing infants' perceptual skills, they've found more and more skills already present in new-borns and very young infants. There's growing evidence to support Kagan's (1971) claim that:

> *'Nature has apparently equipped the newborn with an initial bias in the processing of experience. He does not ... have to learn what he should examine'.*

Slater (1994) is a little more cautious. Auditory perception and learning about the auditory world (not dealt with in this chapter) are well advanced even in very young babies, and a nativist view is closest to the truth. But in the case of vision, the truth lies somewhere in between a nativist and empiricist view. Evidence suggests that the new-born infant:

> *'... comes into the world with a remarkable range of visual abilities ... Some rudimentary knowledge and understanding of important stimuli such as objects and faces is present at birth, and experience builds on this genetically or evolutionarily provided range of abilities'.* (Slater, 1994)

Some of the strongest evidence in support of the role of nurture comes from cross-cultural studies, deprivation studies using non-humans, and studies of human cataract patients. However, nature and nurture are never entirely separable. For example, the neonate's ability to discriminate between the mother's face and that of a similar-looking female must be the result of experience, but the capacity to make the distinction must be built in. As Bee (2000) says, whenever there's a dispute between nativists and empiricists:

> *'Both sides are correct. Both nature and nurture are involved'.*

CHAPTER SUMMARY

- **Nativists** argue that we're born able to perceive the world in particular ways, with little or no learning necessary. **Empiricists** believe that our perceptual abilities develop through learning and experience. Most psychologists reject these extreme viewpoints in favour of an **interactionist** position.

- Studying neonates represents the most **direct** source of evidence, but we can only **infer** what their perceptual experience is.

- **Non-human animal experiments** usually involve **deprivation** of normal sensory experience, raising serious **ethical questions**. There's also the problem of generalising the results of such studies to humans.

- Studies of **human cataract patients** represent the human counterpart to non-human animal experiments. Problems in interpretation of the research findings include possible physical deterioration of the visual system and dubious reliability of the case histories.

- Studies of **perceptual adaptation/readjustment** demonstrate the flexibility of human perception, but caution is needed in deciding whether **perceptual** or **motor adaptation** is involved.

- **Cross-cultural studies** help to identify the influences on perceptual development, in particular the role of **learning** and **experience**. But psychologists disagree as to the key features of cultural learning.

- When analysing data from cataract patients, Hebb distinguished between **figural unity**, which he believed is largely **innate**, and **figural identity** which is largely **learnt**.

- Deprivation experiments suggest that light is necessary for normal physical development of the visual system, and that **patterned light** is necessary for the normal development of more complex abilities in chimps, cats and monkeys.

- Perceptual adaptation/readjustment studies illustrate the enormous adaptability of the human visual system, but this seems to involve learning appropriate **motor behaviour**.
- Methods used to study neonate perception include investigating **spontaneous visual preference/preferential looking**, **sucking rate**, **habituation**, **conditioned head rotation**, **physiological measures** and **measures of electrical brain activity**.
- Babies show a preference for **complexity**, which is a function of age. This is probably related to improvement in the ability to scan the whole pattern, rather than just areas of greatest contrast.
- One aspect of **form perception** that has been extensively investigated is '**facedness**'. Evidence that babies quickly learn to prefer their mothers' faces (and voices) is contributing to the view that the human face has **species-specific** significance from birth onwards.
- **Depth perception** has been studied using the **visual cliff apparatus**. Heart rate measures support Gibson and Walk's original claim (based on crawling) that depth perception is probably innate.
- Bower believes that babies have an inborn understanding of the **solidity** of 3-D objects, as well as **size** and **shape constancy** and the Gestalt principle of **closure**.
- **Cross-cultural studies** involve giving members of different cultural groups the same test materials, usually **visual illusions**, including the Müller–Lyer, horizontal–vertical and the rotating trapezoid.
- Segall *et al.* proposed the **carpentered world hypothesis** to explain why different cultural groups are more/less susceptible to different illusions. This stresses the role of the **physical environment** on perception.
- Evidence that contradicts the carpentered world hypothesis has led to the proposal that exposure to Western **cultural** variables may be more important, such as 2-D drawings and photographs.
- The generally accepted conclusion is that some perceptual abilities are present at birth, while others develop later. Perceptual development after birth involves a complex interaction between genetic/maturational and environmental/experiential influences.

Self-assessment questions

1 Discuss the claim that perception is a largely inborn ability.
2 a Describe how neonates have been used in the study of perceptual development.
  b Critically consider the contribution of such studies to our understanding of perceptual development.
3 Critically assess the methods used to study the development of perceptual abilities.

Web addresses

http://www.tue.nl/ipo/oldhome/html

http://mambo.ucsc.edu/

http://www.long.su.se/staff/hartmut/imito.htm

http://www.ecdgroup.com/archive/ecd06.html

http://www.uia.org/uiademo/h0665.htm

Further reading

Slater, A. & Bremner, G. (Eds) (1989) *Infant Development.* London: Lawrence Erlbaum Associates. A detailed, quite advanced textbook on most aspects of infant development. Especially relevant here are Chapter 2 (Slater: 'Visual memory and perception in early infancy,) and Chapter 4 (Bower: 'The perceptual world of the newborn child').

Bornstein, M.H. & Lamb, M.E. (Eds) (1988) *Perceptual, Cognitive and Linguistic Development: Part II of Developmental Psychology: An Advanced Textbook* (2nd edition) London: Lawrence Erlbaum Associates.

As the title says, this is also an advanced textbook but the chapter by Bornstein (Chapter 4: 'Perceptual development across the life-cycle') is very readable and very useful for discussion of the nature–nurture issue.

Berry, J.B., Poortinga, Y.H., Segall, M.H. & Dasen, P.R. (Eds) (1992) *Cross-cultural Psychology: Research and Applications.* New York: Cambridge University Press. Widely regarded as a 'classic' in this area of psychology. Chapter 6 is particularly useful here.

Chapter 17

Memory and Forgetting

Introduction and overview

As we noted in Chapter 11, learning and memory represent two sides of the same coin: learning depends on memory for its 'permanence', and memory would have no 'content' without learning. Hence, we could define memory as the *retention of learning and experience*. As Blakemore (1988) says:

'In the broadest sense, learning is the acquisition of knowledge and memory is the storage of an internal representation of that knowledge ...'.

Blakemore expresses the fundamental importance of memory like this:

> '... without the capacity to remember and to learn, it is difficult to imagine what life would be like, whether it could be called living at all. Without memory, we would be servants of the moment, with nothing but our innate reflexes to help us deal with the world. There could be no language, no art, no science, no culture. Civilisation itself is the distillation of human memory'.

Both learning and memory featured prominently in the early years of psychology as a science (see Chapters 1, 3 and 11). William James, one of the pioneers of psychology, was arguably the first to make a formal distinction between *primary* and *secondary memory*, which correspond to *short-term* and *long-term memory* respectively. This distinction is central to Atkinson & Shiffrin's (1968, 1971) very influential *multi-store model*.

As with other cognitive processes, memory remained a largely unacceptable area for psychological research until the cognitive revolution of the mid-1950s, reflecting the dominance of behaviourism up until this time. However, some behaviourists, especially in the USA, studied 'verbal behaviour' using paired–associate learning. This associationist approach was (and remains) most apparent in *interference theory*, an attempt to explain *forgetting*.

Several major accounts of memory have emerged from criticisms of the limitations of the multi-store model. These include Craik & Lockhart's *levels-of-processing approach*, Baddeley & Hitch's *working-memory model*, and attempts to identify different types of long-term memory (e.g. Tulving, 1972). Psychologists are increasingly interested in everyday memory, rather than studying it merely as a laboratory phenomenon. Theories of forgetting include *trace decay*, *displacement*, *cue-dependent forgetting*, and *repression*.

The meanings of 'memory'

Memory, like learning, is a hypothetical construct denoting three distinguishable but interrelated processes:

- *registration* (or *encoding*): the *transformation* of sensory input (such as a sound or visual imagery) into a form which allows it to be entered into (or registered in) memory. With a computer, for example, information can only be encoded if it's presented in a format the computer recognises;
- *storage*: the operation of *holding* or *retaining* information in memory. Computers store information by means of changes in the system's electrical circuitry. With people, the changes occurring in the brain allow information to be stored, though exactly what these changes involve is unclear.
- *retrieval*: the process by which stored information is extracted from memory.

Registration can be thought of as a necessary condition for storage to take place, but not everything which registers on the senses is stored. Similarly, storage is a necessary, but not sufficient, condition for retrieval: we can't recover information which hasn't been stored, but the fact that we know it is no guarantee that we'll remember it on any particular occasion. This is the crucial distinction between *availability* (whether or not the information has been stored) and *accessibility* (whether or not it can be retrieved), which is especially relevant to theories of forgetting (see pages 259–264).

Storage

Ask yourself ...

- Can saying 'I can't remember' mean different things?
- Do you consider yourself to have a 'good'/'poor' memory? What criteria do you apply in making that assessment?

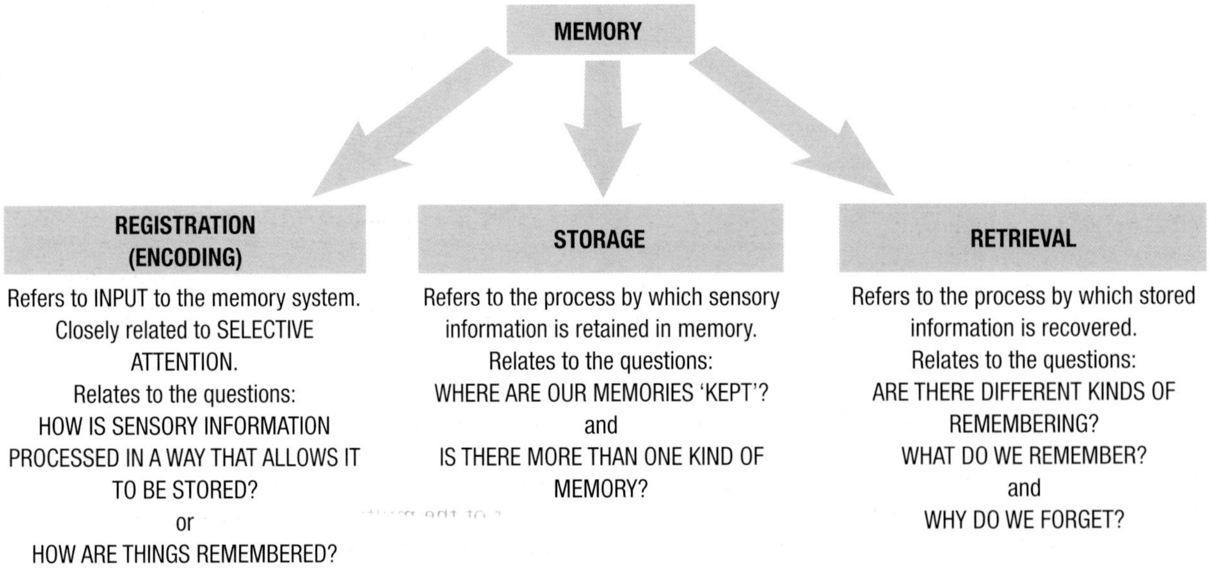

MEMORY		
REGISTRATION (ENCODING)	**STORAGE**	**RETRIEVAL**
Refers to INPUT to the memory system. Closely related to SELECTIVE ATTENTION. Relates to the questions: HOW IS SENSORY INFORMATION PROCESSED IN A WAY THAT ALLOWS IT TO BE STORED? or HOW ARE THINGS REMEMBERED?	Refers to the process by which sensory information is retained in memory. Relates to the questions: WHERE ARE OUR MEMORIES 'KEPT'? and IS THERE MORE THAN ONE KIND OF MEMORY?	Refers to the process by which stored information is recovered. Relates to the questions: ARE THERE DIFFERENT KINDS OF REMEMBERING? WHAT DO WE REMEMBER? and WHY DO WE FORGET?

Figure 17.1 *The three processes of memory*

In practice, storage is studied through testing people's ability to retrieve. This is equivalent to the distinction between learning and performance: learning corresponds to storage, while performance corresponds to retrieval (see Chapter 11). But there are several kinds of retrieval (see below, page 248). So, if we're tested by *recall* it may look as though we haven't learnt something, but a test of *recognition* may show that we have. For these reasons, it's useful to distinguish between memory as storage and memory as retrieval. When people complain about having a 'poor memory', they might mean storage or retrieval, but they're unlikely to make the distinction (they'd simply say 'I can't remember').

As we noted earlier, it was James who first distinguished between primary and secondary memory. Ebbinghaus (1885), the pioneer of memory research, would have accepted it. Many psychologists since James have also made the distinction, including Hebb (1949), Broadbent (1958), and Waugh & Norman (1965). In Atkinson & Shiffrin's (1968, 1971) multistore model, they're called short-term memory (STM) and long-term memory (LTM) respectively. Strictly, STM and LTM refer to experimental procedures for investigating short-term and long-term *storage* respectively.

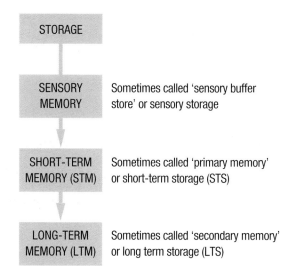

Figure 17.2 *The three forms of storage*

Sensory memory

Sensory memory gives us an accurate account of the environment as experienced by the sensory system. We retain a 'literal copy' of the stimulus long enough for us to decide whether it's worthy of further processing. Any information we don't attend to or process further is forgotten. It's probably more useful to think of sensory memory as an aspect of perception and as a necessary requirement for storage proper (i.e. STM).

The storage (such as it is) occurs within the sensory system that received the information (it's *modality-specific*). Additional information entering the same sensory channel immediately disrupts the storage. For example, if two visual stimuli are presented within quick successsion, memory of the first stimulus may be lost. But if the second stimulus is a sound or smell, it won't interfere with memory of the visual

stimulus. Although it's likely that a sensory memory exists for each of our sensory systems (see Chapter 5), most research has concentrated on:

- *iconic memory* (an icon is an image) stores visual images for about half a second;
- *echoic memory* stores sounds for up to two seconds.

We're usually unaware of sensory memory, but if you watch someone wave a lighted cigarette in a darkened room, you'll see a streak rather than a series of points (Woodworth, 1938). If we had no iconic memory, we'd perceive a film as a series of still images interspersed with blank intervals, rather than as a continuously moving scene. Without echoic memory, instead of hearing speech as such we'd hear a series of unrelated sounds (Baddeley, 1995).

> *Ask yourself ...*
>
> - Can you relate these examples to any of the Gestalt laws of perception discussed in Chapter 15?

KEY STUDY 17.1

Iconic memory (Sperling, 1960, 1963)

Sperling used a tachistoscope to flash visual displays for very brief intervals (50 milliseconds or 1/20 of a second). The display comprised three rows of four letters in a four by three matrix.

- In the **whole report condition** (or span of apprehension), participants were asked to recall as many as possible from the whole matrix. On average, they recalled 4.32 letters (out of 12), although they commonly reported having seen more than they could actually remember.
- In the **partial report condition,** participants were required to recall the top, middle or bottom row, depending on whether they heard a high-, medium- or low-pitched tone following the presentation. Although they couldn't know in advance which tone would be heard, they succeeded in recalling an average of 3.04 of the letters from each row. This meant that between nine and ten words were available immediately after presentation.

In the first condition, approximately five words must have been lost during the time it took to recall the whole array. This was supported by the finding that the advantage of partial reports was lost if the tone was delayed for a second or so.

Similar effects have been reported for the echoic store by Broadbent (1958) and Treisman (1964). Broadbent's filter model of selective attention was in many ways the main precursor of the multi-store approach to memory, and there's a definite resemblance between sensory memory (or storage) and Broadbent's sensory 'buffer' store (Eysenck & Keane, 1990: see Chapter 13).

Short-term memory (STM)

Probably less than one-hundredth of all the sensory information that impinges on the human senses every second reaches consciousness. Of this, only about five per cent is stored permanently (Lloyd *et al.*, 1984). Clearly, if we possessed only sensory memory, our capacity for retaining information about the world would be extremely limited. However, according to models of memory such as Atkinson and Shiffrin's multi-store model (1968, 1971), some information from sensory memory is successfully passed on to STM.

STM (and LTM) can be analysed in terms of:

■ *capacity*: how much information can be stored;
■ *duration*: how long the information can be held in storage;
■ *coding*: how sensory input is represented by the memory system.

Capacity

Ebbinghaus (1885) and Wundt (in the 1860s) were two of the first psychologists to maintain that STM is limited to six or seven bits of information. But the most famous account is given by Miller (1956) in his article 'The magical number seven, plus or minus two'. Miller showed how *chunking* can be used to expand the limited capacity of STM by using already established memory stores to categorise or encode new information.

If we think of STM's capacity as seven 'slots', with each slot being able to accommodate one bit or unit of information, then seven individual letters would each fill a slot and there'd be no 'room' left for any additional letters. But if the letters are chunked into a word, then the word would constitute one unit of information, leaving six free slots. In the example below, the 25 bits of information can be chunked into (or reduced to) six words, which could quite easily be reduced further to one 'bit' (or chunk) based on prior familiarity with the words:

```
S   A   V   A   O
R   E   E   E   G
U   R   S   Y   A
O   O   D   N   S
F   C   N   E   R
```

To be able to chunk, you have to know the 'rule' or the 'code', which in this case is: starting with F (bottom left-hand corner) read upwards until you get to S and then drop down to C and read upwards until you get to A, then go to N and read upwards and so on. This should give you 'four score and seven years ago'.

Chunking is involved whenever we reduce a larger to a smaller amount of information. This not only increases the capacity of STM, but also represents a form of encoding information by imposing a *meaning* on otherwise meaningless material. For example:

■ arranging letters into words, words into phrases, phrases into sentences;
■ converting 1066 (four bits of information) into a date (one chunk), so a string of 28 numbers could be reduced to seven dates;

■ using a rule to organise information: the series 149162536496481100121 (21 bits) is generated by the rule by which $1^2 = 1$, $2^2 = 4$, $3^2 = 9$ and so on. The rule represents a single chunk, and that's all that has to be remembered.

These examples demonstrate how chunking allows us to bypass the seven-bit 'bottleneck'. Although the amount of information contained in any one chunk may be unlimited (e.g. the rule above can generate an infinitely long set of digits), the number of chunks which can be held in STM is still limited to seven plus or minus two.

Duration

A way of studying 'pure' STM was devised by Brown (1958) and Peterson & Peterson (1959), and is called the *Brown–Peterson technique*. By repeating something that has to be remembered (maintenance rehearsal), information can be held in STM almost indefinitely. The Brown–Peterson technique overcomes this problem.

KEY STUDY 17.2

The Brown–Peterson technique (Peterson & Peterson, 1959)

In the Brown–Peterson technique, participants hear various trigrams (such as XPJ). Only one trigram is presented on each trial. Immediately afterwards, they're instructed to recall what they heard or to count backwards, in threes, out loud, from some specified number for 3, 6, 9, 12, 15 or 18 seconds (the retention interval). The function of this distractor task is to prevent rehearsal. At the end of the time period, participants try to recall the trigram.

Peterson and Peterson found that the average percentage of correctly recalled trigrams was high with short delays, but decreased as the delay interval increased. Nearly 70 per cent was forgotten after only a nine-second delay, and 90 per cent after 18 seconds. In the absence of rehearsal, then, STM's duration is very short, even with very small amounts of information. If a more difficult distractor task is used, it can be made even shorter.

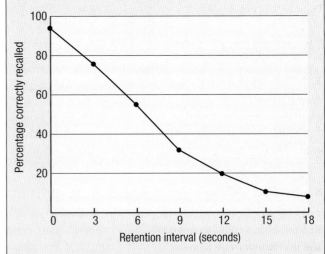

Figure 17.3 *The data reported by Peterson and Peterson in their experiment on the duration of STM*

Coding

Conrad (1964) presented participants with a list of six consonants (such as BKSJLR), each of which was seen for about three-quarters of a second. They were then instructed to *write down* the consonants. Mistakes tended to be related to a letter's *sound*. For example, there were 62 instances of B being mistaken for P, 83 instances of V being mistaken for P, but only two instances of S being mistaken for P. These *acoustic confusion errors* suggested to Conrad that STM must code information according to its sound. When information is presented visually, it must be somehow *transformed* into its acoustic code (see also Baddeley's, 1966, study below).

Other forms of coding in STM

Shulman (1970) showed participants lists of ten words. Recognition of the words was then tested using a visually presented 'probe word', which was either:

- a *homonym* of one of the words on the list (such as 'bawl' for 'ball'),
- a *synonym* (such as 'talk' for 'speak'), or
- identical to it.

> ### Ask yourself ...
> - Shulman found that homonym and synonym probes produced *similar* error rates. What does this tell us about the types of coding used in STM?

Shulman's results imply that some semantic coding (coding for *meaning*) had taken place in STM. If an error was made on a synonym probe, some matching for meaning *must* have taken place.

Visual images (such as abstract pictures, which would be difficult to store using an acoustic code) can also be maintained in STM, if only briefly.

Long-term memory (LTM)

Capacity and duration

It's generally accepted that LTM has unlimited capacity. It can be thought of as a vast storehouse of all the information, skills, abilities and so on, which aren't being currently used, but which are potentially retrievable. According to Bower (1975), some of the kinds of information contained in LTM include:

1. a spatial model of the world around us;
2. knowledge of the physical world, physical laws and properties of objects;
3. beliefs about people, ourselves, social norms, values and goals;
4. motor skills, problem-solving skills and plans for achieving various things;
5. perceptual skills in understanding language, interpreting music, and so on.

Many of these are included in what Tulving (1972) calls *semantic memory* (see below).

Information can be held for between a few minutes and several years (and may in fact span the individual's entire lifetime).

Coding

With verbal material, coding in LTM appears to be mainly *semantic*. For example, Baddeley (1966) presented participants with words which were either:

- *acoustically similar* (e.g. 'caught', 'short', 'taut', 'nought');
- *semantically similar* (e.g. 'huge', 'great', 'big', 'wide');
- *acoustically dissimilar* (e.g 'foul', 'old' and 'deep'); or
- *semantically dissimilar* (e.g. 'pen', 'day', 'ring').

When recall from STM was tested, acoustically similar words were recalled less well than acoustically dissimilar words. This supports the claim that acoustic coding occurs in STM . There was a small difference between the number of semantically similar and semantically dissimilar words recalled (64 and 71 per cent respectively). This suggests that while some semantic coding occurs in STM, it's not dominant. When an equivalent study was conducted on LTM, fewer semantically similar words were recalled, while acoustically similar words had no effect on LTM recall. This suggests that LTM's dominant code is semantic. Similarly, Baddeley (1966) found that immediate recall of the order of short lists of unrelated words was seriously impeded if the words were acoustically similar but not if they were semantically similar. After a delay, however, exactly the opposite effect occurred.

Does LTM use only semantic coding?

Findings such as Baddeley's don't imply that LTM uses only a semantic code (Baddeley, 1976). Our ability to picture a place we visited on holiday indicates that at least some information is stored or coded *visually*. Also, some types of information in LTM (such as songs) are coded *acoustically*. Smells and tastes are also stored in LTM, suggesting that it's a very flexible system, as well as being large and long-lasting.

Table 17.1 *Summary of main differences between STM and LTM*

	Capacity	Duration	Coding
STM	Seven bits of (unrelated) information. Can be increased through chunking	15–30 seconds (unaided). Can be increased by (maintenance) rehearsal	Mainly acoustic. Some semantic. Visual is also possible
LTM	Unlimited	From a few seconds to several years (perhaps permanently)	Semantic, visual, acoustic, and also olfactory (smells) and gustatory (tastes) Very flexible

Retrieval

There are many different ways of recovering or locating information which has been stored; that is, 'remembering' can take many different forms. Likewise, there are also different ways of measuring memory in the laboratory.

How is memory measured?

The systematic scientific investigation of memory began with Ebbinghaus (1885).

KEY STUDY 17.3

Pure memory (Ebbinghaus, 1885)

To study memory in its 'purest' form, Ebbinghaus invented three-letter nonsense syllables (a consonant followed by a vowel followed by another consonant, such as XUT and JEQ). Ebbinghaus spent several years using only himself as the subject of his research. He read lists of nonsense syllables out loud, and when he felt he'd recited a list sufficiently to retain it, he tested himself.

If Ebbinghaus could recite a list correctly twice in succession, he considered it to be learnt. After recording the time taken to learn a list, he then began another one. After specific periods of time, Ebbinghaus would return to a particular list and try to memorise it again. He calculated the number of attempts (or *trials*) it took him to *relearn* the list, as a percentage of the number of trials it had *originally* taken to learn it. He found that memory declines sharply at first, but then levels off. This finding has been subsequently replicated many times. Ebbinghaus carried out many experiments of this sort and showed that memory could be scientifically investigated under carefully controlled conditions.

Other techniques for measuring memory include:

- *Recognition*: This involves deciding whether or not a particular piece of information has been encountered before (as in a multiple-choice test, where the correct answer is presented along with incorrect ones).
- *Recall*: This involves participants actively searching their memory stores in order to retrieve particular information (as in timed essays). Retrieval cues are missing or very sparse. The material can be recalled either in the order in which it was presented (*serial recall*) or in any order at all (*free recall*).
- *Memory-span procedure*: This is a version of serial recall, in which a person is given a list of unrelated digits or letters, and then required to repeat them back immediately in the order in which they were heard. The number of items on the list is successively increased until an error is made. The maximum number of items that can be consistently recalled correctly is a measure of *immediate memory span*.
- *Paired-associates recall*: In this, participants are required to learn a list of paired items (such as 'chair' and 'elephant'). When one of the words (e.g. 'chair') is re-presented, the participant must recall the paired word ('elephant').

The multi-store model

Atkinson & Shiffrin's (1968, 1971) multi-store model (sometimes called the dual-memory model because of the emphasis on STM and LTM) was an attempt to explain how information flows from one storage system to another. The model sees sensory memory, STM and LTM as permanent *structural components* of the memory system; that is, built-in features of the human information-processing system. In addition to these structural components, the memory system comprises more transient control processes. *Rehearsal* is a key control process, serving two main functions:

- to act as a buffer between sensory memory and LTM by maintaining incoming information within STM;
- to transfer information to LTM.

Information from sensory memory is scanned and matched with information in LTM, and if a match (i.e. pattern recognition) occurs, then it might be fed into STM along with a verbal label from LTM.

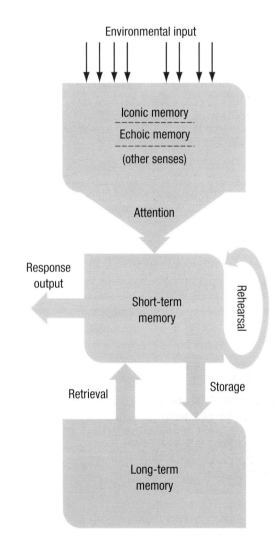

Figure 17.4 *The multi-store/dual-memory model of memory proposed by Atkinson and Shiffrin*

Evidence for the multi-store model

Three kinds of evidence are relevant here:

- experimental studies of STM and LTM (sometimes referred to as *two-component tasks*);
- studies of *coding*;
- studies of brain-damaged patients.

Experimental studies of STM and LTM

The serial position effect

Murdock (1962) presented participants with a list of words at a rate of about one per second. They were required to free-recall as many of these as they could. Murdock found that the probability of recalling any word depended on its position in the list (its *serial position*: hence the graph shown in Figure 17.5 is a serial position curve). Participants typically recalled those items from the end of the list first, and got more of these correct than earlier items (the *recency effect*). Items from the *beginning* of the list were recalled quite well relative to those in the middle (the *primacy effect*), but not as well as those at the end. Poorest recall is for items in the middle. The serial position effect holds regardless of the length of the list (Murdock, 1962).

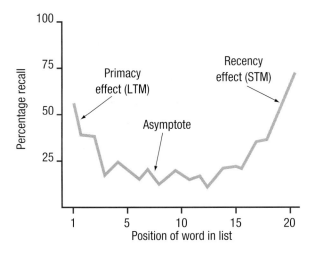

Figure 17.5 *A typical serial position curve (based on Glanzer & Cunitz, 1966)*

Ask yourself ...

- Using what you already know about STM, LTM and rehearsal, try to explain:

  a the primacy and recency effects;
  b why words in the middle of the list are the least well remembered.

The primacy effect occurs because the items at the beginning of the list have (presumably) been rehearsed and transferred to LTM, from where they're recalled. The recency effect presumably occurs because items currently in STM are recalled from there. Because STM's capacity is limited and can hold items for only a brief period of time, words in the middle are either lost from the system completely, or are otherwise unavailable for recall. The last items are only remembered if recalled first and tested immediately, as demonstrated by Glanzer & Cunitz (1966) in a variation of Murdock's study.

KEY STUDY 17.4

Removing the recency effect (Glanzer & Cunitz, 1966)

Glanzer and Cunitz presented two groups of participants with the same list of words. One group recalled the material immediately after presentation, while the other group recalled after 30 seconds. They had to count backwards in threes (the Brown–Peterson technique), which prevented rehearsal and caused the recency effect to disappear. The primacy effect was largely unaffected.

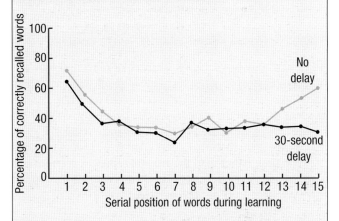

Figure 17.6 *Data from Glanzer and Cunitz's study showing serial position curves after no delay and after a delay of 30 seconds*

Ask yourself ...

- Try to account for Glanzer and Cunitz's findings.

It's likely that the earlier words had been transferred to LTM (from where they were recalled), while the most recent words were 'vulnerable' to the counting task (Eysenck, 1993).

Brown–Peterson technique and rehearsal

When discussing the characteristics of STM earlier (see pages 246–247), we noted the rapid loss of information from memory when rehearsal is prevented using the Brown–Peterson technique. This is usually taken as evidence for the existence of a STM with rapid forgetting (see below, page 260). But the concept of rehearsal itself has been criticised as both unnecessary and too general.

KEY STUDY 17.5

Maintenance vs elaborative rehearsal (Craik & Watkins, 1973)

Craik and Watkins asked participants to remember only certain 'critical' words (those beginning with a particular letter) from lists presented either rapidly or slowly. The position of the critical words relative to the others determined the amount of time a particular word spent in STM, and the number of potential rehearsals it could receive.

Craik and Watkins found that long-term remembering was unrelated to either how long a word had spent in STM or the number of explicit or implicit rehearsals it received.

Based on this and later findings, Craik and Watkins distinguished between:

- *maintenance rehearsal*, in which material is rehearsed in the form in which it was presented ('rote'), and
- *elaborative rehearsal* (or elaboration of encoding), which elaborates the material in some way (such as by giving it a meaning or linking it with pre-existing knowledge stored in LTM).

An earlier study by Glanzer & Meinzer (1967) found that participants required to repeat items aloud recalled fewer of them than those allowed an equal period of silent rehearsal. Perhaps in silent rehearsal the material isn't being merely repeated but recoded into a different form which enhances recall.

It seems, then, that what's important is the *kind* of rehearsal or processing, rather than the amount. This has been investigated in particular by Craik & Lockhart (1972), in the form of the levels-of-processing approach (see pages 255–256).

Elaborative rehearsal is much more like the rehearsal involved in a play than is maintenance rehearsal

Studies of coding

Table 17.1 (page 247) indicates that the major form of coding used in STM is acoustic, while LTM is much more flexible and varied in how it encodes information. It also suggests that semantic coding is used primarily by LTM. This is usually

taken to support the multi-store model. However, not everyone accepts this view.

Chunking, STM and LTM

When discussing the characteristics of STM (see page 246), we saw that chunking increases STM's capacity by imposing meaning on otherwise meaningless material. According to Miller (1956), chunking represents a linguistic recoding which seems to be the 'very lifeblood of the thought process'. But this can't occur until certain information in LTM is activated, and a match made between the incoming items and their representation in LTM.

Miller & Selfridge (1950) gave participants 'sentences' of varying lengths, which resembled (or approximated to) true English to different degrees, and asked them to recall the words in their correct order. The closer a 'sentence' approximated normal English, the better it was recalled. This suggests that knowledge of semantic and grammatical structure (presumably stored in LTM) is used to aid recall from STM.

In a similar study, Bower & Springston (1970) presented one group of American college students with letters that formed familiar acronyms (e.g. fbi, phd, twa, ibm). A second group was presented with the same letters, but in a way that didn't form those acronyms (e.g. fb, iph, dtw, aib, m). The first group recalled many more letters than the second group. The pause after 'fbi' and so on allowed the students to 'look up' the material in their mental dictionaries and so encode the letters in one chunk.

Clearly, an acoustic code isn't the only one used in STM. According to Wickelgren (1973), the kind of coding might reflect the processing which has occurred in a given context, rather than being a property of the memory store itself (see the discussion of levels of processing, pages 255–256).

The study of brain-damaged patients

Anterograde amnesia and the amnesic syndrome

If STM and LTM really are distinct, then there should be certain kinds of brain damage which impair one without affecting the other. One such form of brain damage is anterograde amnesia.

CASE STUDY 17.1

H.M. (Milner *et al.*, 1968)

H.M. had been suffering epileptic fits of devastating frequency since the age of 16. At 27 he underwent surgery to remove the hippocampus on both sides of his brain (see Chapter 4). While this completely cured his epilepsy, he was left with severe anterograde amnesia. He has near normal memory for anything learned before the surgery, but severe memory deficits for events which occurred afterwards.

His STM is generally normal. He can retain verbal information for about 15 seconds without rehearsal, and for much longer with rehearsal. But he cannot transfer information into LTM or, if he can, is unable to *retrieve* it. He seems entirely incapable of remembering any new fact or event. He has almost no knowledge of current affairs because he forgets all the news almost as soon as he's read about it. He has no idea what time of day it is unless he's just looked at the clock, he cannot remember that his father has died or that his family has moved house, and he rereads the same magazine without realising he's already read it.

People he met after the operation remain, in effect, total strangers to him and he has to 'get to know them' afresh each time they came into his house. Brenda Milner has known him for 25 years, yet she's a stranger to him each time they meet.

He's able to learn and remember perceptual and motor skills, although he has to be reminded each day just what skills he has. However:

> '... new events, faces, phone numbers, places, now settle in his mind for just a few seconds or minutes before they slip, like water through a sieve, and are lost from his consciousness'. (Blakemore, 1988)

An equally dramatic, but in many ways more tragic case is that of Clive Wearing.

CASE STUDY 17.2

Clive Wearing (based on Blakemore, 1988; Baddeley, 1990)

Clive Wearing was the chorus master of the London Sinfonietta and a world expert on Renaissance music, as well as a BBC radio producer. In March 1985 he suffered a rare brain infection caused by the cold sore virus (Herpes simplex). The virus attacked and dstroyed his hippocampus, along with parts of his cortex. Like H.M., he lives in a snapshot of time, constantly believing that he's just awoken from years of unconsciousness. For example, when his wife, Deborah, enters his hospital room for the third time in a single morning, he embraces her as if they'd been parted for years, saying, 'I'm conscious for the first time' and 'It's the first time I've seen anybody at all'.

At first his confusion was total and very frightening to him. Once he held a chocolate in the palm of one hand, covered it with the other for a few seconds till its image disappeared from his memory. When he uncovered it, he thought he'd performed a magic trick, conjuring it up from nowhere. He repeated it again and again, with total astonishment and growing fear each time.

Like H.M., he can still speak and walk, as well as read music, play the organ and conduct. In fact, his musical ability is remarkably well preserved. Also like H.M, he can learn new skills (e.g. mirror-reading). Over the course of a few days of testing, the speed of reading such words doubles, and it can be done just as well three months later. Yet for Clive it's new every time. But unlike H.M., his capacity for remembering his earlier life was extremely patchy. For example, when shown pictures of Cambridge (where he'd spent four years as an undergraduate and had often visited subsequently) he only recognised King's College Chapel – the most distinctive Cambridge building – but not his own

college. He couldn't remember who wrote *Romeo and Juliet*, and he thought the Queen and the Duke of Edinburgh were singers he'd known from a Catholic church.

According to Deborah, 'without consciousness he's in many senses dead'. In his own words, his life is 'Hell on earth – it's like being dead – all the bloody time'.

Ask yourself ...

- In what ways do the cases of H.M. and Clive Wearing support the multi-store model?
- In what ways do they challenge it?

Atkinson and Shiffrin regard the kind of memory deficits displayed by H.M. and Clive Wearing as 'perhaps the single most convincing demonstration of a dichotomy in the memory system'. According to Parkin (1987), the *amnesic syndrome* isn't a general deterioration of memory function, but a selective impairment in which some functions, (such as learning novel information) are severely impaired, while others (including memory span and language) remain intact. If amnesics do have intact STMs, they should show a similar recency effect (based on STM) but a poorer primacy effect (based on LTM) compared with normal controls. This is exactly what's found (e.g. Baddeley & Warrington, 1970). These results have led most psychologists to accept that in the amnesic syndrome, STM function is preserved but LTM function is impaired.

However, this difference in STM and LTM functioning could mean that:

- the problem for amnesics is one of *transfer* from STM to LTM, which is perfectly consistent with the multi-store model; or, alternatively,
- amnesics have difficulties in *retrieval* from LTM (Warrington & Weiskrantz, 1968, 1970). This interpretation is more consistent with Craik & Lockhart's (1972) levels-of-processing approach.

Another major implication of cases such as those of H.M. and Clive Wearing is that the multi-store model's 'unitary' LTM is a gross oversimplification (see next section).

Retrograde amnesia

In retrograde amnesia, a patient fails to remember what happens *before* the surgery or accident which causes it. It can be caused by head injuries, electroconvulsive therapy (ECT: see Chapter 45), carbon monoxide poisoning and extreme stress (see Chapter 12). As in anterograde amnesia, there's typically little or no disruption of STM, and the period of time for which the person has no memories may be minutes, days or even years. When retrograde amnesia is caused by brain damage, it's usually accompanied by anterograde amnesia. Similarly, patients with *Korsakoff's syndrome* (caused by severe, chronic alcoholism involving damage to the hippocampus: see Chapter 8) usually experience both kinds of amnesia.

Retrograde amnesia seems to involve a disruption of *consolidation* whereby, once new information has entered LTM, time is needed for it to become firmly established physically in the brain (see the discussion of forgetting, pages 259–264).

Alternatives to the multi-store model

Multiple forms of LTM
Episodic and semantic memory

Despite their brain damage, H.M. and Clive Wearing reatined many skills, both general and specific (such as talking, reading, walking, playing the organ). They were also capable of acquiring (and retaining) *new* skills – although they didn't know that they had them! This suggests very strongly that there are different kinds of LTM. But as far as the multi-store model is concerned, there's only 'LTM', i.e. LTM is unitary.

Box 17.1   Episodic and semantic memory (Tulving, 1972)

Episodic memory (EM) is an 'autobiographical' memory responsible for storing a record of our past experiences – the events, people, objects and so on which we've personally encountered. EM usually includes details about the particular time and place in which objects and events were experienced (they have a spatio-temporal context: e.g 'Where did you go on your holiday last year?' and 'What did you have for breakfast this morning?'). They have a subjective (self-focused) reality, but most could, in principle, be verified by others.

Semantic memory (SM) is our store of general, factual knowledge about the world, including concepts, rules and language, '... a mental thesaurus, organised knowledge a person possesses about words and other verbal symbols, their meanings and referents ...' (Tulving, 1972). SM can be used without reference to where and when that knowledge was originally acquired. For example, we don't remember 'learning to speak' – we just 'know English' (or whatever our native language happens to be). But SM can also store information about ourselves. For example, if we're asked how many brothers and sisters we have, or how much we like psychology, we don't have to remember specific past experiences in order to answer.

Our 'general' knowledge about, say, computers (part of our SM) is built up from past experiences with particular computers (part of EM), through abstraction and generalisation. This suggests that, instead of regarding EM and SM as two quite distinct systems within the brain (which is what Tulving originally intended), it might be more valid to see SM as made up from multiple EMs (Baddeley, 1995).

Autobiographical vs experimental EM

Tulving maintained that EM is synonymous with *autobiographical memory* (AM). For example, the forgetting of words in a free-recall task can be thought of as a failure in our EM since, clearly, we already know the words as part of our SM, but we've failed to remember that they appeared in that particular list just presented to us. However, Cohen (1993) argues that learning word lists isn't what most people understand by AM. Instead, AM is a special kind of EM, concerned with specific life events that have personal significance. Accordingly, she distinguishes between autobiographical EM and experimental EM; taking part in an experiment in which we're required to learn lists of words is an example of the latter.

Flashbulb memories

Flashbulb memories are a special kind of EM, in which we can give vivid and detailed recollections of where we were and what we were doing when we first heard about some major public national or international event (Brown & Kulik, 1977).

Ask yourself ...

- Where were you, and what were you doing, at the time of the total eclipse of the sun in the summer of 1999?

According to Brown & Kulik (1982), there's a neural mechanism that's triggered by events that are emotionally arousing, unexpected or extremely important, with the result that the whole scene becomes 'printed' on the memory. However, Neisser (1982) argued that the durability of flashbulb memories stems from their frequent rehearsal and reconsideration after the event. Also, the detail and vividness of people's memories aren't necessarily signs of their accuracy – we can be very confident about something and still be mistaken!

Procedural vs declarative memory

Procedural memory (PM) refers to information from LTM which can't be inspected consciously (Anderson, 1985; Tulving, 1985). For example, riding a bike is a complex skill which is even more difficult to describe. In the same way, native speakers of a language cannot usually describe the complex grammatical rules by which they speak correctly (perhaps because they weren't learnt consciously in the first place: see Chapter 19). By contrast, EM and SM are both amenable to being inspected consciously, and the content of both can be described to another person.

Cohen & Squire (1980) distinguish between PM and declarative memory, which corresponds to Ryle's (1949) distinction between *knowing how* and *knowing that* respectively (see Figure 17.7, page 253). Anderson (1983) argues that when we initially learn something, it's learned and encoded declaratively, but with practice it becomes compiled into a procedural form of knowledge. (This is similar to the distinction between controlled/automatic processing discussed in Chapter 13.)

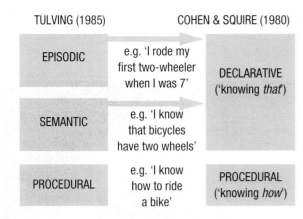

TULVING (1985)		COHEN & SQUIRE (1980)
EPISODIC	e.g. 'I rode my first two-wheeler when I was 7'	DECLARATIVE ('knowing *that*')
SEMANTIC	e.g. 'I know that bicycles have two wheels'	
PROCEDURAL	e.g. 'I know how to ride a bike'	PROCEDURAL ('knowing *how*')

Figure 17.7 *Distinctions between different kinds of LTM*

Ask yourself ...

• How do these different types of LTM help us understand the memory deficits of H.M. and Clive Wearing?

Most aspects of their PMs seemed to be intact (and they could both acquire new skills), but both their EM and SM were partially impaired. For instance, H.M. was given extensive training (by Gabrieli *et al.*, 1983) in the task of learning the meaning of unfamiliar words which had come into popular use since his operation. He made very little progress, despite extensive practice every day for ten days.

Most other amnesics similarly fail to update their SMs to take account of changes in the world since onset of their disfunction (Eysenck & Keane, 1990). For example, many don't know the name of the current Prime Minister or President, and have very poor recognition for faces of people who've become famous only quite recently (Baddeley, 1984).

When new learning does occur in amnesic patients (which may include psychomotor skills, problem-solving or cued verbal learning), they typically deny having encountered the task before despite simultaneously showing quite clear evidence of learning. These are all examples of PM, which involves more automatic processes, and allows patients to demonstrate learning without the need for conscious recollection of the learning process. But declarative learning/memory involves conscious recollection of the past. Damage to a number of cortical and subcortical areas (including the temporal lobes, hippocampus and mamillary bodies) seriously impairs declarative memory in amnesic patients. PM doesn't appear to be impaired by damage to these areas (Baddeley, 1995).

The working-memory (WM) model: rethinking STM

In their multi-store model, Atkinson and Shiffrin saw STM as a system for temporarily holding and manipulating information. However, Baddeley & Hitch (1974) criticised the model's concept of a unitary STM. While accepting that STM rehearses incoming information for transfer to LTM, they argued that it was much more complex and versatile than a mere 'stopping-off station' for information.

Ask yourself ...

• How does Miller & Selfridge's (1950) experiment (see page 250) demonstrate the two-way flow of information between STM and LTM?

Box 17.2	**The two-way flow of information between STM and LTM**

It's highly unlikely that STM contains only new information, and more likely that information is retrieved from LTM for use in STM. For example, the string of numbers 18561939 may appear to be unrelated. However, they can be 'chunked' into one unit according to the rule 'the years in which Sigmund Freud was born and died'. If we can impose meaning on a string of digits, we must have learned this meaning previously, the previously learned rule presumably being stored in LTM. Information has flowed not only from STM to LTM, but also in the opposite direction.

A vivid illustration of this comes from studies of people who are experts in some particular field. De Groot (1966), for example, showed that expert chess players had phenomenal STMs for the positions of chess pieces on a board, provided they were organised according to the rules of chess. When the pieces were arranged randomly, recall was no better than that of non-chess players. Chess experts use information about the rules of chess, stored in LTM, to aid recall from STM.

Other examples of how 'expertise' can increase STM capacity for information include the observation that avid football supporters can remember match scores more accurately than more casual fans (Morris *et al.*, 1985). Also, experienced burglars can remember details of houses seen in photographs a few moments before better than police officers or householders can (Logie *et al.*, 1992).

While some card games are largely a matter of chance, others require considerable expertise

These examples show that STM is an active store used to hold information which is being manipulated. According to Groome *et al.* (1999), working memory (WM) is like the computer screen, a kind of mental workspace where various operations are performed on current data. By contrast, LTM resembles the computer's memory ('storage memory'), which holds large amounts of information in a fairly passive state for possible future retrieval. WM is a cognitive function that:

■ helps us keep track of what we're doing or where we are from moment to moment;

■ holds information long enough to allow us to make a decision, dial a telephone number, or repeat a strange foreign word that we've just heard.

Instead of a single, simple STM, Baddeley & Hitch (1974) proposed a more complex, multi-component WM. This comprises a *central executive*, which is in overall charge, plus sub- or *slave systems*, whose activities are controlled by the central executive. These are the *articulatory* (or *phonological*) *loop* and the *visuospatial scratch* (or *sketch*) *pad*.

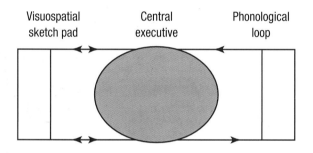

| Visuospatial sketch pad | Central executive | Phonological loop |

Figure 17.8 *A simplified representation of the working-memory model (from Baddeley, 1997)*

The central executive

This is thought to be involved in many higher mental processes, such as decision-making, problem-solving and making plans (see Chapter 20). More specifically, it may co-ordinate performance on two separate tasks, and attend selectively to one input while inhibiting others (Baddeley, 1996). Although capacity-limited, it's very flexible and can process information in any sense modality (it's modality-free). It resembles a pure attentional system (Baddeley, 1981: see Chapter 13).

The articulatory (or phonological) loop

This is probably the most extensively studied component of the model. It was intended to explain the extensive evidence for acoustic coding in STM (Baddeley, 1997). It can be thought of as a verbal rehearsal loop used when, for example, we try to remember a telephone number for a few seconds by saying it silently to ourselves. It's also used to hold words we're preparing to speak aloud. It uses an articulatory/phonological code, in which information is represented as it would be spoken. For this reason it's been called the *inner voice*.

Its name derives from the finding that its capacity isn't limited by the number of items it can hold, but by the length of time taken to recite them (Baddeley *et al.*, 1975). This is similar to the way that the faster you recite something into a microphone, the more words you can record on a short loop of recording tape (Groome *et al.*, 1999).

The articulatory loop has two components:

■ a phonological store capable of holding speech-based information; and

■ an articulatory control process based on inner speech.

While memory traces within the store fade after about two seconds, the control process feeds it back into the store (the process underlying silent rehearsal). The control process is also able to convert written material into a phonological code, which is then transferred to the phonological store (Baddeley, 1997).

The visuospatial scratch or sketch pad

This can also rehearse information, but deals with visual and/or spatial information as, for example, when we drive along a familiar road, approach a bend, and think about the road's spatial layout beyond the bend (Eysenck, 1986). It uses a visual code, representing information in the form of its visual features such as size, shape and colour. For this reason, it's been called the *inner eye*.

The scratch pad appears to contain separate visual and spatial components. The more active spatial component is involved in movement perception and control of physical actions, while the more passive visual component is involved in visual pattern recognition (Logie, 1995).

Ask yourself ...

• One way of understanding how WM operates can be gained from trying to calculate the number of windows in your house (Baddeley, 1995). Most of us do this by forming a visual image and then either 'looking' at the house from the outside, or taking a 'mental journey' through its various rooms. Complete the following sentences:

To set up and manipulate the image, we need the ____-____ ____ ____, and to sub-vocally count the number of windows we need the ____ ____. The whole operation is organised and run by the ____ ____.

(Answers can be found on page 265.)

Figure 17.9 *The visuospatial scratch pad is where we store information about familiar roads, so we know what's round the bend*

Research into WM has often used the *concurrent-* (*interference-* or *dual-*) task method, in which participants perform two tasks at the same time. Assuming that each slave system's capacity is limited:

- with two tasks making use of the *same* slave system(s), performance on one or both should be *worse* when they're performed together than when they're performed separately (Baddeley *et al.*, 1975);
- if two tasks require *different* slave systems, it should be possible to perform them as well together as separately.

Some researchers have used *articulatory suppression*, in which the participant rapidly repeats out loud something meaningless (such as 'hi-ya' or 'the').

Ask yourself ...

- Explain the reasoning behind the use of articulatory suppression. If this method produces poorer performance on another simultaneous task, what can we infer about the slave system involved in the first task?

Articulatory suppression uses up the articulatory loop's resources, so it can't be used for anything else. If articulatory suppression produces poorer performance on another simultaneous task, then we can infer that this task also uses the articulatory loop (Eysenck & Keane, 1995).

An evaluation of the WM model

- It's generally accepted that STM is better seen as a number of relatively independent processing mechanisms than as the multi-store model's single unitary store, and that attentional processes and STM are part of the same system (they're probably used together much of the time in everyday life).
- The idea that any one slave system (such as the phonological loop) may be involved in the performance of apparently very different tasks (such as memory span, mental arithmetic, verbal reasoning and reading) is a valuable insight.
- It has practical applications which extend beyond its theoretical importance (Gilhooly, 1996; Logie, 1999: see Box 17.3).
- One weakness of the WM model is that least is known about the most important component, namely the central executive (Hampson & Morris, 1996). It can apparently carry out an enormous variety of processing activities in different conditions. This makes it difficult to describe its precise function, and the idea of a single central executive might be as inappropriate as that of a unitary STM (Eysenck, 1986).

Box 17.3 Working memory and learning to read

One of the most striking features of children with specific problems in learning to read (despite normal intelligence and a supportive family) is their impaired memory span (Gathercole & Baddeley, 1990). They also tend to do rather poorly on tasks which don't test memory directly, such as judging whether words rhyme. These children show some form of phonological deficit that seems to prevent them from learning to read

(and which is detectable before they have started to learn). This deficit might be related to the phonological loop (see Chapter 40, page 585).

The levels of processing (LOP) model
Rehearsal and the multi-store model

As we noted above (see page 248), the multi-store model sees rehearsal as a key control process which helps to transfer information from STM to LTM. There's also only one type of rehearsal as far as the model is concerned, what Craik & Watkins (1973) call *maintenance* (as opposed to *elaborative*) rehearsal (see Key Study 17.5). This means that that what matters is how much rehearsal occurs. But maintenance rehearsal may not even be necessary for storage. Jenkins (1974) found that participants could remember material even though they weren't expecting to be tested – and so were unlikely to have rehearsed the material. This is called *incidental learning*.

According to Craik & Lockhart (1972), it's the kind of rehearsal or processing that's important. Craik and Lockhart also considered that the multi-store model's view of the relationship between structural components and control processes was, essentially, the wrong way round.

Ask yourself ...

- How does the multi-store model see the relationship between structural components and control processes?

The multi-store model sees the structural components (sensory memory, STM and LTM) as fixed, while control processes (such as rehearsal) are less permanent. Craik and Lockhart's levels-of-processing (LOP) model begins with the proposed control processes. The structural components (the memory system) are what results from the operation of these processes. In other words, memory is a *by-product of perceptual analysis*. This is controlled by the central processor, which can analyse a stimulus (such as a word) on various levels:

- at a superficial (or *shallow*) level, the surface features of a stimulus (such as whether the word is in small or capital letters) are processed;
- at an intermediate (*phonemic* or *phonetic*) level, the word is analysed for its sound;
- at a deep (or *semantic*) level, the word's meaning is analysed.

The level at which a stimulus is processed depends on both its nature and the processing time available. The more deeply information is processed, the more likely it is to be retained.

KEY STUDY 17.6

Does 'chicken' rhyme with 'wait' ? (Craik & Tulving, 1975)

Craik and Tulving presented participants with a list of words via a tachistoscope. Following each word, participants were asked one of four questions, to which they had to answer 'yes' or 'no'. The four questions were:

1 Is the word (e.g. TABLE/table) in capital letters? (This corresponds to shallow processing.)

2 Does the word (e.g. hate/chicken) rhyme with 'wait'? (This corresponds to phonemic processing.)

3 Is the word (e.g. cheese/steel) a type of food? (This corresponds to semantic processing.)

4 Would the word (e.g. ball/rain) fit in the sentence 'He kicked the ... into the tree'? (This also corresponds to semantic processing.)

Later, participants were unexpectedly given a recognition test, in which they had to identify the previously presented words which appeared amongst words they hadn't seen. There was significantly better recognition of words that had been processed at the deepest (semantic) level (questions 3 and 4). Also, recognition was superior when the answer was 'yes' rather than 'no'.

Elaboration vs distinctiveness

It's also been found that *elaboration* (the amount of processing of a particular kind at a particular level) is important in determining whether material is stored or not. For example, Craik & Tulving (1975) asked participants to decide if a particular (target) word would be appropriate in *simple* sentences (such as 'She cooked the ...') or *complex* sentences (such as 'The great bird swooped down and carried off the struggling ...'). When participants were later given a *cued recall test*, in which the original sentences were again presented but without the target words, recall was much better for those that fitted into the complex sentences.

More important than elaboration is *distinctiveness*, which relates to the *nature* of processing. For example, 'A mosquito is like a doctor because they both draw blood' is more distinctive than 'A mosquito is like a racoon because they both have hands, legs and jaws'. Although the former involves less elaboration, it was more likely to be remembered (Bransford *et al.*, 1979). However, because level of processing, elaboration and distinctiveness can occur together, it's often difficult to choose between them, and all three may contribute to remembering.

Evaluation of the LOP model

■ The model was proposed as a new way of intepreting existing data and to provide a conceptual framework for memory research. Prior to 1972, it was assumed that the same stimulus would typically be processed in a very similar way by all participants on all occasions. The LOP model proposed that perception, attention and memory are interrelated processes.

■ It's mainly descriptive rather than explanatory (Eysenck & Keane, 1995). In particular, it fails to explain why deeper processing leads to better recall.

■ It's difficult to define/measure depth *independently* of a person's actual retention score. So, if 'depth' is defined as 'the number of words remembered', and 'the number of words remembered' is taken as a measure of 'depth', this definition of depth is circular (what's being defined is part of the definition!). There's no generally accepted way of independently

assessing depth, which 'places major limits on the power of the levels-of-processing approach' (Baddeley, 1990).

■ Some studies have directly contradicted the model. For example, Morris *et al.* (1977) predicted that stored information (deep or shallow) would be remembered only to the extent that it was relevant to the memory test used. So, deep or semantic information would be of little use if the memory test involved learning a list of words and later selecting those that rhymed with the stored words, while shallow rhyme information would be very relevant. The prediction was supported.

■ According to Parkin (1993), different orienting tasks vary in the extent to which they require participants to treat the stimulus as a word (e.g. 'Is "tiger" a mammal?' compared with 'Does "tiger" have two syllables?'), yet retention tests always require participants to remember words. Since semantic tasks, by definition, always require attention to be paid to stimuli as words, the superior retention they produce could reflect the bias of the retention test towards the type of information being encoded. In other words, the orienting task and the retention test are both concerned with the same type of information, which isn't the case when other kinds of task are used.

Memory and the representation of knowledge

What psychologists have traditionally called knowledge is information that's represented mentally in a particular format and is structured or organised in some way (Eysenck & Keane, 1990). This leads to two interrelated questions about the nature of knowledge:

■ What format do mental representations take?

■ How are these mental representations organised?

This area was neglected until quite recently, when attempts to provide a knowledge base for computer systems stimulated an interest in how '... this enormously important but complex facility operates in people' (Baddeley, 1990).

The organised nature of memory

As we've seen, chunking is a way of increasing STM's limited capacity by imposing a meaning on unrelated items of information. We do this by organising it, giving it a structure that it doesn't otherwise have. As Baddeley (1995) says:

'The secret of a good memory, as of a good library, is that of organisation; good learning typically goes with the systematic encoding of incoming material, integrating and relating it to what is already known'.

Organisation can be either imposed by the experimenter (EO) or spontaneously by the participant ('subjective organisation' (SO): Tulving, 1962). Mandler (1967) found that instructions to organise will facilitate learning, even though the participant isn't trying to remember the material. A classic study of organisation is that of Bower *et al.* (1969).

MINERALS

METALS

STONES

RARE	COMMON	ALLOYS	PRECIOUS	MASONRY
Platinum	Aluminium	Bronze	Sapphire	Limestone
Silver	Copper	Steel	Emerald	Granite
Gold	Lead	Brass	Diamond	Marble
	Iron		Ruby	Slate

Figure 17.10 *An example of a conceptual hierarchy used in Bower* et al.*'s (1969) experiment*

KEY STUDY 17.7

Helpful hierarchies (Bower *et al.*, 1969)

Bower *et al.* gave participants the task of learning a list of 112 words arranged into conceptual hierarchies. For the experimental group, the words were presented as a hierarchy (28 on each of four trials: see Figure 17.10, page 257), while the control group was shown 28 words on each of four trials presented randomly. The former recalled an average of 73 words correctly, while the latter recalled an average of only 21. Clearly, organisation can facilitate retention.

Imagery as a form of organisation

According to Paivio (1969), probably the most powerful predictor of the ease with which words will be learned is their 'concreteness'; that is, how easily a word evokes a mental image. Richardson (1974) tested free recall of a series of 'concrete' and 'abstract' words. By varying the interval between presenting the stimulus and recalling it, he concluded that the 'effect of imageability lies in secondary memory'; in other words, 'concrete' words were recalled significantly more efficiently from LTM (compared with 'abstract' words), whereas there was no difference with recall from STM.

Bower (1972) showed that asking participants to form a mental image of pairs of unrelated nouns (e.g. 'dog' and 'bicycle'), where the two words were interacting in some way, resulted in significantly better recall than when they were instructed merely to memorise the words. Bower considers that the more bizarre the details of the image, the better (for example, a dog riding a bicycle).

Wollen *et al.* (1972) studied the relative contribution of these two dimensions by giving pictures to participants to help them learn paired associates, such as 'piano–cigar'. Figure 17.11 shows all four combinations of these two dimensions. Wollen *et al.* found a large effect of interaction, but not of bizarreness, which suggests that interaction promotes elaborative encoding that aids later recall. However, the study

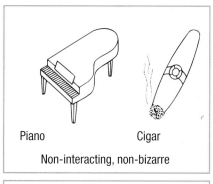
Piano — Cigar
Non-interacting, non-bizarre

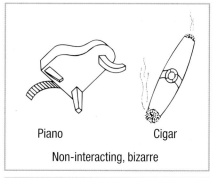
Piano — Cigar
Non-interacting, bizarre

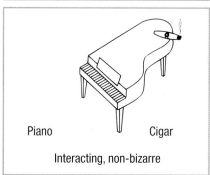
Piano — Cigar
Interacting, non-bizarre

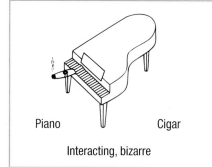
Piano — Cigar
Interacting, bizarre

Figure 17.11 *Examples of pictures used to associate piano and cigar in the Wollen* et al. *(1972) study of image bizarreness. From Wollen, K.A., Weber, A. & Lowry, D.H.,* Cognitive Psychology, *Volume 3. Copyright © 1972 Academic Press*

used an unrelated design, and when related designs are used, bizarre images stand out from the rest as the most distinctive, producing the best recall (Anderson, 1995a).

According to Paivio's (1986) *dual-coding hypothesis*, mental activity involves interaction between two interconnected but functionally independent subsystems:

- a *non-verbal imagery system*, which processes information about objects and events in the form of *imagens*; and
- a *verbal system*, specialised for handling speech and writing. Each known word is represented by a *logogen*.

The two systems are connected via *referential links*, which allow a word to be associated with its relevant image and vice versa. This can help explain the better learning of concrete words: they activate both verbal and non-verbal codes, while abstract words activate only a verbal code. Similarly, pictures are easier to memorise than words representing those pictures, because a picture is more likely to activate a verbal code as well as an imaginal one, while words are less likely to evoke a picture (especially if they're abstract) (Parkin, 1993).

A dramatic illustration of the role of imagery is the man with the exceptional memory documented by Luria (1968). Luria's 'S' can be seen as illustrating *eidetic imagery* (from the Greek *eidos* meaning 'that which is seen').

CASE STUDY 17.3

The mind of a mnemonist (Luria, 1968)

S. was a reporter for a Moscow newspaper in the early 1920s. His astounding ability to produce reports, rich in the minutest factual detail, without ever taking notes, so amazed the editor that he sent him to Luria for psychological evaluation. There seemed to be no limit either to his memory's capacity or durability. He could commit to memory, in a few minutes, long lists of numbers and recall them perfectly, hours, days or weeks later. Luria tested him 30 years after they first met, and S. could still remember perfectly the numbers of tables he'd previously learned!

He seemed to have spontaneously developed *mnemonic tricks*. For example, he would associate, in his mind's eye, lists of objects he wished to remember with familiar features of a

street or some other familiar place. He mentally placed each object at some point on the scene; all he had to do to remember the list was to recall the mental image of the scene and locate each object on display. He would imagine himself walking along a Moscow street looking in each hiding place for the object he'd put there (this is the *method of loci*). His recall was accompanied by extreme *synaesthesia*, in which sensory information from one modality evokes a sensation in another. For example, colours are associated with tastes. He once said to Luria, 'What a crumbly yellow voice you have'.

Knowledge and semantic memory
The hierarchical network model

The *hierarchical network model* of SM (Collins & Quillian, 1969, 1972) is concerned with our memory for words and their meanings. As shown in Figure 17.12, SM is portrayed as a network of concepts connected with other concepts by pointers. Each word or concept is represented by a particular node in the network. The meaning of a particular word is given by the configuration of pointers that connect that word with other words.

If we were asked whether the statement 'A canary can sing' is true, we'd need only to find the word 'canary' and retrieve the properties stored with that word. But to verify 'A canary can fly' we'd first have to find 'canary', and then move up one level to 'bird' before retrieving the property 'can fly'. Assuming that it takes time to move from one level to another, it should take longer to verify 'A canary can fly' than to verify 'A canary can sing', and it would take even longer to verify 'A canary has skin'. The model assumes that the various properties stored with each word are scanned simultaneously.

Collins and Quillian presented participants with various sentences, including the examples given above, which they had to judge as true or false by pressing an appropriate button as quickly as possible (reaction time was used as a measure of difficulty). The main finding was that the time taken to decide that a statement is true increased as a function of the number of levels that had to be worked through to verify it. So, as the model predicts, more time was needed to verify 'A canary is an animal' than 'A canary is a bird'.

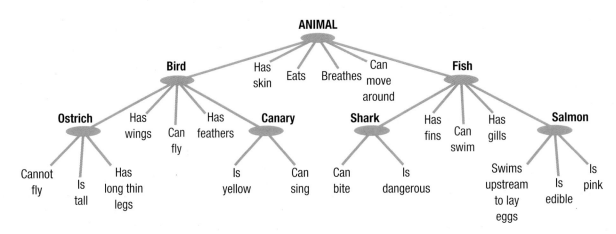

Figure 17.12 *Part of the semantic memory network for a three-level hierarchy (from Collins & Quillian, 1969)*

An evaluation of Collins and Quillian's model

- It takes longer to verify 'A canary is an animal' because there are more animals than birds. So Collins and Quillian's findings could be explained in terms of the relationship between category size and reaction time.
- Some members of a category are more typical than others. For example, 'canary' and 'ostrich' both belong to the category 'bird', but a 'canary' is judged to be a more typical bird than an 'ostrich'. Participants respond faster to typical instances ('A canary is a bird') than to atypical ones ('An ostrich is a bird'). That shouldn't happen according to the hierarchical model, since presumably the same distance has to be travelled in both cases (Baddeley, 1990).
- Rips *et al.* (1973) found that it took longer to verify 'A bear is a mammal' than 'A bear is an animal'. This is the opposite of what the hierarchical model predicts, since 'animal' is higher up in the hierarchy than 'mammal'.

> *Ask yourself ...*
>
> - Could the model be criticised in terms of the research into imagery (pages 257–258)?

- The findings could be explained in terms of how easy (or difficult) it is to imagine concepts at different levels. The higher up the hierarchy you go, the more abstract the category becomes, and the more difficult it becomes to form a mental image of it (it's easier to picture a canary than 'an animal').

The spreading-activation model

In the light of these criticisms, Collins & Loftus (1975) proposed a revised network model. The major changes include:

- The network is no longer hierarchically organised, making it more flexible.
- The new concept of *semantic distance* denotes that highly related concepts are located close together, and distance reflects how easily 'excitation' can flow from one node to the next.
- A range of different types of link is introduced, including *class membership associations* (or 'is a' links – 'A dog is a mammal', including some negative instances, such as 'A dolphin is not a fish'), 'has' links ('An animal has skin'), 'can' links ('A bird can fly'), and 'cannot' links ('An ostrich cannot fly').
- It no longer sees the memory network in terms of logical, hierarchical relationships. Human memory may simply not be as logical and systematic as originally proposed, and it allows for an individual's personal experience and the structure of the environment to act as at least partial influences on the relationship between concepts.
- The concept of *spreading activation* implies that when two concepts are stimulated, an activation from each spreads throughout the network until they're linked. This takes time, because semantically related concepts are closer together than semantically unrelated concepts.

An evaluation of the spreading-activation model

Johnson-Laird *et al.* (1984) believe that there are many examples where the interpretation offered by the network will tend, in actual discourse, to be overridden by the constraints of real-

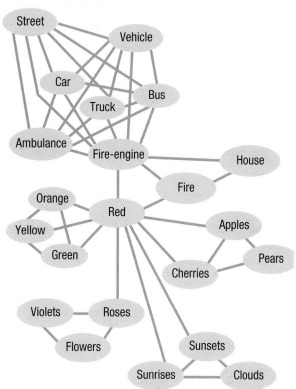

Figure 17.13 *An example of a spreading-activation model. The length of each line (or link) represents the degree of association between particular concepts (based on Collins & Loftus, 1975)*

world knowledge. Take, for instance, 'The ham sandwich was eaten by the soup'. This would appear to be nonsensical until you put it into the context of a restaurant, where waiters/waitresses sometimes label customers in terms of their orders. Johnson-Laird *et al.* call this failure to 'escape from the maze of symbols into the world' the *symbolic fallacy*: you have to know the relationship between symbols and what they refer to. (We shall return to this issue in Chapter 20 in the form of the controversy over whether computers can think.)

Schema theory and everyday memory

According to Baddeley (1990), it became increasingly obvious during the 1970s that SM must contain structures considerably larger than the simple concepts involved in network models such as those of Collins and Quillian, and Collins and Loftus. This 'larger unit' of SM is the schema, a concept first used by Bartlett (1932) in his theory of reconstructive memory. Because of the importance of reconstructive memory to eyewitness testimony, I shall postpone discussion of schema theory to Chapter 21.

Theories of forgetting

To understand why we forget, we must recall the distinction between availability (whether or not material has been stored), and accessibility (being able to retrieve what's been stored). In terms of the multi-store model, since information must be transferred from STM to LTM for permanent storage:

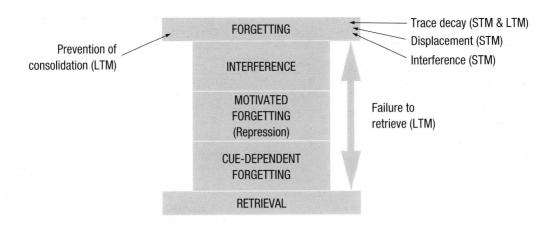

Figure 17.14 *Different theories of forgetting, including retrieval failure*

- availability mainly concerns STM and the transfer of information from STM into LTM;
- accessibility has to do mainly with LTM.

Forgetting can occur at the encoding, storage or retrieval stages.

So, one way of looking at forgetting is to ask what prevents information staying in STM long enough to be transferred to LTM (some answers are provided by *decay* and *displacement theories*). Some answers to the question about what prevents us from locating the information that's already in LTM include those offered by *interference theory, cue-dependent forgetting* and *motivated forgetting* (repression: this is discussed in Chapter 21).

Decay theory

Decay (or trace decay) theory tries to explain why forgetting increases with time. Clearly, memories must be stored somewhere, the most obvious place being the brain. Presumably, some sort of structural change (the *engram*) occurs when learning takes place. According to decay theory, metabolic processes occur over time which cause the engram to degrade/break down, unless it's maintained by repetition and rehearsal. This results in the memory contained within it becoming unavailable.

Hebb (1949) argued that while learning is taking place, the engram which will eventually be formed is very delicate and liable to disruption (the *active trace*). With learning, it grows stronger until a permanent engram is formed (the *structural trace*) through neurochemical and neuroanatomical changes.

Decay in STM and LTM

The active trace corresponds roughly to STM, and, according to decay theory, forgetting from STM is due to disruption of the active trace. Although Hebb didn't apply the idea of decay to LTM, other researchers have argued that it can explain LTM forgetting if it's assumed that decay occurs through disuse (hence, *decay-through-disuse theory*). So, if certain knowledge or skills aren't used or practised for long periods of time, the corresponding engram will eventually decay away (Loftus & Loftus, 1980).

> **Ask yourself ...**
>
> - Try to think of examples of skills/knowledge which, contrary to decay-through-disuse theory, *aren't* lost even after long periods of not being used/practised.

Is forgetting just a matter of time?

Peterson & Peterson's (1959) experiment (see Key Study 17.2) has been taken as evidence for the role of decay in STM forgetting. If decay did occur, then we'd expect poorer recall of information with the passage of time, which is exactly what the Petersons reported.

The difficulty with the Petersons' study in particular, and decay theory in general, is that other possible effects need to be excluded before a decay-based account can be accepted. The ideal way to study the role of decay in forgetting would be to have people receive information and then do nothing, physical or mental, for a period of time. If recall was poorer with the passage of time, it would be reasonable to suggest that decay had occurred. Such an experiment is, of course, impossible. However, Jenkins & Dallenbach (1924) were the first to attempt an approximation to it.

> **KEY STUDY 17.8**
>
> **Jenkins & Dallenbach (1924)**
>
> Participants learnt a list of ten nonsense syllables. Some then went to sleep immediately (approximating the ideal 'do nothing' state), while the others continued with their normal activities.
>
> As Figure 17.15 indicates, after intervals of one, two, four or eight hours, all participants were tested for their recall of the syllables. While there was a fairly steady increase in forgetting as the retention interval increased for the 'waking' participants, this *wasn't* true for the sleeping participants.
>
> If decay is a natural result of the passage of time alone, then we should have expected equal forgetting in both groups. The results suggest that it's what happens in between

learning and recall that determines forgetting, not time as such. This led Jenkins and Dallenbach to conclude that:

'Forgetting is not so much a matter of decay of old impressions and associations as it is a matter of interference, inhibition or obliteration of the old by the new'.

Interference theory is discussed in the text below.

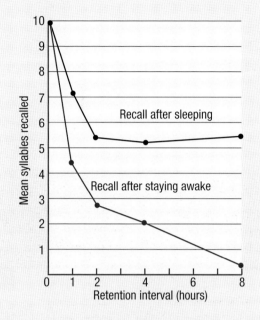

Figure 17.15 *Mean number of syllables recalled by participants in Jenkins and Dallenbach's experiment*

Although some data exist suggesting that neurological breakdown occurs with age and disease (such as Alzheimer's disease), there's no evidence that the major cause of forgetting from LTM is neurological decay (Solso, 1995).

Displacement theory

In a limited-capacity STM system, forgetting might occur through displacement. When the system is 'full', the oldest material in it would be displaced ('pushed out') by incoming new material. This possibility was explored by Waugh & Norman (1965) using the *serial probe task*. Participants were presented with 16 digits at the rate of either one or four per second. One of the digits (the 'probe') was then repeated, and participants had to say which digit followed the probe. Presumably:

- if the probe was one of the digits at the beginning of the list, the probability of recalling the digit that followed would be small, because later digits would have displaced earlier ones from the system;
- if the probe was presented towards the end of the list, the probability of recalling the digit that followed would be high, since the last digits to be presented would still be available in STM.

When the number of digits following the probe was small, recall was good, but when it was large, recall was poor. This is consistent with the idea that the earlier digits are replaced by later ones.

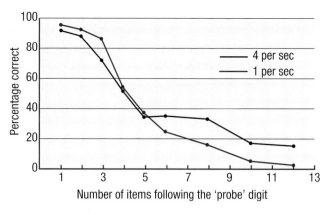

Figure 17.16 *Data from Waugh and Norman's serial probe experiment*

Ask yourself ...

- Waugh and Norman also found that recall was generally better with the faster (4 per second) presentation rate. How does this support decay theory?

Since less time had elapsed between presentation of the digits and the probe in the four-per-second condition, there would have been less opportunity for those digits to have decayed away. This makes it unclear whether displacement is a process distinct from decay.

Retrieval-failure theory and cue-dependent forgetting

According to retrieval-failure theory, memories can't be recalled because the correct retrieval cues aren't being used. The role of retrieval cues is demonstrated by the *tip-of-the-tongue phenomenon*, in which we know that we know something but can't retrieve it at that particular moment in time (Brown & McNeill, 1966).

KEY STUDY 17.9

It's on the tip of my tongue (Brown & McNeill, 1966)

Brown and McNeill gave participants dictionary definitions of unfamiliar words, and asked them to provide the words themselves. Most participants either knew the word or knew that they didn't know it.

Some, however, were sure they knew the word but couldn't recall it (it was on the tip of their tongue). About half could give the word's first letter and the number of syllables, and often offered words which sounded like the word or had a similar meaning. This suggests that the required words were in memory, but the absence of a correct retrieval cue prevented them from being recalled.

Examples of definitions used by Brown and McNeill:

1 A small boat used in the harbours and rivers of Japan and China, rowed with a scull from the stern, and often having a sail.

2 Favouritism, especially governmental patronage extended to relatives.

3 The common cavity into which the various ducts of the body open in certain fish, reptiles, birds and mammals.

Answers: sampan; nepotism; cloaca

Tulving & Pearlstone (1966) read participants lists of varying numbers of words (12, 24 or 48) consisting of categories (e.g. animals) of one, two, or four exemplars (e.g. dog) per list, plus the category name. Participants were instructed to try to remember only the exemplars. Half the participants (group 1) free-recalled the words and wrote them down on blank pieces of paper. The other half (group 2) was given the category names. Group 2 recalled significantly more words, especially on the 48-item list. However, when group 1 was given the category names, recall improved.

This illustrates very well the availability/accessibility distinction. The category name acted as a contextual cue, helping to make accessible what was available. Group 2 participants knew more than they could actually retrieve under the cue-less conditions.

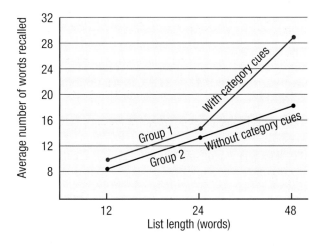

Figure 17.17 *Average number of words recalled with and without cues in Tulving & Pearlstone's (1966) experiment*

Tulving (1968) showed participants a list of words, and then asked them to write down as many as they could remember in any order. Later, and without being presented with the list again or seeing the words they'd written down previously, participants were asked to recall them. Later still, they were asked a third time to recall the words on the original list.

Ask yourself ...

- As Table 17.2 shows, the same words weren't recalled across the three trials. Why is this finding difficult for decay theory to explain?

Decay theory wouldn't predict the recall of a word on trial 3 if it wasn't recalled on trials 1 or 2. For it to be recalled on a later trial, it couldn't have decayed away on the earlier trials. But retrieval-failure theory can explain these findings by arguing that different retrieval cues were involved in the three trials.

Table 17.2 *Typical results from Tulving's experiment*

Trial 1	Trial 2	Trial 3
Table	Table	Table
Driver	Escalator	Driver
Escalator	Apple	Escalator
Apple	Railway	Apple
Railway	Pen	Pen
Pen		Fountain

According to Tulving's (1983) *encoding-specificity principle* (ESP), recall improves if the same cues are present during recall as during the original learning. In Tulving and Pearlstone's experiment, the category names were presented together with the exemplars for group 1, and so, presumably, were encoded at the time of learning. The ESP explains why recall is sometimes superior to recognition (even though recognition is generally considered to be easier than recall: see page 248).

Tulving (1974) used the term *cue-dependent forgetting* to refer jointly to *context-dependent* and *state-dependent* forgetting.

Table 17.3 *Cue-dependent forgetting*

Context-dependent forgetting	State-dependent forgetting
Occurs in absence of relevant environmental or contextual variables. These represent *external cues*.	Occurs in absence of relevant psychological or physiological variables. These represent *internal cues*.
Abernathy (1940): One group had to learn and then recall material in the same room, while a second group learned and recalled in different rooms. The first group's recall was superior.	Clark *et al.* (1987): Victims' inabilities to recall details of a violent crime may be due at least partly to the fact that recall occurs in a less emotionally aroused state. (See Chapter 21.)
Godden & Baddeley (1975): Divers learned lists of words *either* on land *or* 15 ft under water. Recall was then tested in the same or a different context. Those who learned and recalled in *different* contexts showed a 30% deficit compared with those who learned and recalled in the same context.	McCormick & Mayer (1991): The important link may be between mood and the sort of material being remembered. So, we're more likely to remember happy events when we're feeling happy rather than sad.

Interestingly, when Godden & Baddeley (1980) repeated their 'underwater' experiment using recognition as the measure of remembering, they found no effect of context. They concluded that context-dependent forgetting applies only to recall. According to Baddeley (1995), large effects of context on memory are found only when the contexts in which encoding and retrieval occur are very different. Although less marked changes can produce some effects, studies (other then Abernathy's) looking at the effects of context on examination performance have tended to show few effects. This may be because when we're learning, our surroundings aren't a particularly salient feature of the situation, unlike our internal state (such as our emotional state).

Interference theory

According to interference theory, forgetting is influenced more by what we do before or after learning than by the mere passage of time (see Key Study 17.8).

- In *retroactive interference/inhibition* (RI), *later* learning interferes with the recall of *earlier* learning. For example, if you originally learned to drive in a manual car, then learned to drive an automatic car, when returning to a manual, you might try to drive it as though it was an automatic.
- In *proactive interference/inhibition* (PI), *earlier* learning interferes with the recall of *later* learning. For example, say you learned to drive a car in which the indicator lights are turned on by using the stalk on the left of the steering wheel, and the windscreen wipers by the stalk on the right. After passing your driving test, you buy a car in which this arrangement is reversed. When you're about to turn left or right, you activate the windscreen wipers!

Interference theory has been extensively studied in the laboratory using paired-associate lists (see page 248). The usual procedure for studying interference effects is shown in Figure 17.18.

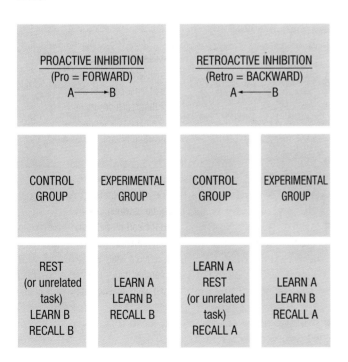

Figure 17.18 *Experimental procedure for investigating retroactive and proactive interference*

Usually, the first member of each pair in list A is the same as in list B, but the second member of each pair is different in the two lists.

- In RI, the learning of the second list interferes with recall of the first list (the interference works *backwards* in time).
- In PI, the learning of the first list interferes with recall of the second list (the interference works *forwards* in time).

Interference theory offers an alternative explanation of Peterson & Peterson's (1959) data (see Key Study 17.2). Keppel & Underwood (1962) noted that the Petersons gave two practice trials, and were interested in how these practice trials affected those in the actual experiment. While there was no evidence of forgetting on the first trial, there was some on the second and even more on the third.

Although forgetting can occur on the first trial (supporting decay theory), Keppel and Underwood's finding that performance didn't decline until the second trial suggests that PI was occurring in the Petersons' experiment (see Figure 17.19).

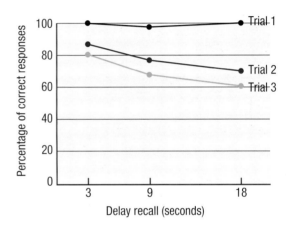

Figure 17.19 *Mean percentage of items correctly recalled on trials 1, 2 and 3 for various delay times (based on Keppel & Underwood, 1962)*

Like Keppel and Underwood, Wickens (1972) found that participants became increasingly poor at retaining information in STM on successive trials. However, when the category of information was changed, they performed as well as on the first list. So, performance with lists of numbers became poorer over trials, but if the task was changed to lists of letters, it improved. This is called *release from proactive inhibition*.

Limitations of laboratory studies of interference theory

The strongest support for interference theory comes from laboratory studies. However:

- Learning in such studies doesn't occur in the same way as it does in the real world, where learning of potentially interfering material is spaced out over time. In the laboratory, learning is artificially compressed in time, which maximises the likelihood that interference will occur (Baddeley, 1990). Such studies therefore lack ecological validity.
- Laboratory studies tend to use nonsense syllables as the stimulus material. When meaningful material is used, interference is more difficult to demonstrate (Solso, 1995).
- When people have to learn, say, the response 'bell' to the stimulus 'woj', the word 'bell' isn't actually learned in the

laboratory, since it's already part of SM. What's being learned (a specific response to a specific stimulus in a specific laboratory situation) is stored in EM (see above, page 252). SM is much more stable and structured than EM, and so is much more resistant to interference effects. No amount of new information will cause someone to forget the things they know that are stored in their SM (Solso, 1995).

However, in support of interference theory, it's generally agreed that if students have to study more than one subject in the same time frame, they should be as dissimilar as possible.

Ask yourself ...

• Think of examples of subjects that (a) should definitely not be studied together in the same time-frame, and (b) could be studied together without much risk of interference.

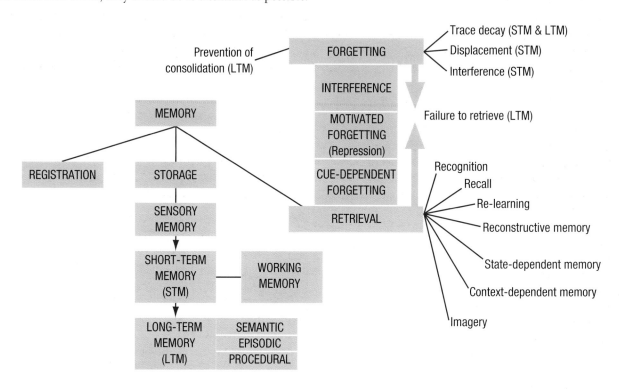

Figure 17.20 *A summary of the three components of memory and theories of forgetting*

CHAPTER SUMMARY

■ Memory can be defined as the **retention of learning** or **experience**. Learning and memory are **interdependent** processes.

■ Ebbinghaus began the systematic study of memory, using **nonsense syllables**. He showed that memory declined very rapidly at first, then levelled off.

■ Memory is now studied largely from an **information-processing approach**, which focuses on **registration/encoding**, **storage** and **retrieval**. Storage corresponds to **availability**, retrieval to **accessibility**.

■ Techniques for measuring memory include testing **recognition**, **recall** (serial or free), **paired associates** recall and the **memory-span procedure**.

■ James's distinction between **primary** and **secondary** memory corresponds to that between **short-term memory** (STM) and **long-term memory** (LTM).

■ **Sensory memory** is modality-specific and works in a similar way to the sensory buffer store in Broadbent's filter model of attention.

■ The limited capacity of STM can be increased by **chunking**, which draws on LTM to encode new information in a meaningful way. **Rehearsal** is a way of holding information in STM almost indefinitely, and the primary code used by STM is **acoustic**. But semantic and visual coding are also used.

■ LTM probably has an **unlimited capacity**, and information is stored in a relatively permanent way. Coding is mainly **semantic**, but information may also be coded visually, acoustically and in other ways.

■ Atkinson and Shiffrin's **multi-store/dual-memory model** sees sensory memory, STM and LTM as **permanent structural components** of the memory system. Rehearsal is a **control process**, which acts as a **buffer** between sensory memory and LTM, and helps the **transfer** of information to LTM.

■ The **primacy effect** reflects recall from LTM, while the **recency effect** reflects recall from STM. Together they comprise the **serial position effect**.

■ Studies of brain-damaged, amnesic patients appear to support the STM–LTM distinction. While STM continues to function fairly normally, LTM functioning is impaired.

- LTM isn't unitary, but comprises **semantic**, **episodic** and **procedural memory**. **Autobiographical memory** and **flashbulb memories** are two kinds of episodic memory. An overlapping distinction is that between **declarative** and **procedural memory/learning**.

- Baddeley and Hitch's **working-memory** (WM) **model** rejected the multi-store model's view of STM as unitary. Instead, STM is seen as comprising a **central executive**, which controls the activities of the **phonological loop** (inner voice), and **visuospatial scratch pad** (inner eye).

- Craik and Watkins' distinction between **maintenance** and **elaborative rehearsal** implies that it's not the amount but the kind of rehearsal or processing that matters.

- According to Craik and Lockhart's **levels-of-processing** (LOP) **model**, memory is a **by-product of perceptual analysis**, such that STM and LTM are the consequences of the operation of control processes.

- The more deeply information is processed, the more likely it is to be retained. **Semantic processing** represents the **deepest level**. **Distinctiveness** is probably more important than elaboration.

- Both chunking and **imagery** are forms of **organising** information, making it easier both to store and to retrieve.

- The **hierarchical network model** of SM sees the memory network in terms of logical, hierarchical relationships between words and concepts. This has been modified to include semantic distance and **spreading activation**, making it more flexible and realistic.

- **Decay/trace decay theory** attempts to explain why forgetting increases over time. STM forgetting is due to disruption of the **active trace**, and **decay through disuse** explains LTM forgetting.

- **Displacement theory** is supported by data from Waugh and Norman's **serial probe task**. However, displacement may not be distinct from decay.

- According to **retrieval-failure theory**, memories can't be recalled because the correct **retrieval cues** are missing. This is demonstrated by the **tip-of-the-tongue phenomenon** and the provision of **category names**. Unlike decay theory, retrieval-failure theory can explain our ability to recall different items on different occasions.

- **Cue-dependent forgetting** comprises **context-dependent** and **state-dependent forgetting**, which refer to **external** and **internal** cues respectively.

- According to **interference theory**, forgetting is influenced more by what we do before/after learning than by the mere passage of time. **Retroactive interference/inhibition** (RI) works **backwards** in time, while **proactive interference/inhibition** (PI) works **forwards** in time.

- Laboratory studies of interference lack **ecological validity**, and interference is more difficult to demonstrate when material other than nonsense syllables is used. Some types of LTM (such as episodic) are more vulnerable to interference effects than others (such as semantic).

Self-assessment questions

1 To what extent does psychological research support Atkinson and Shiffrin's multi-store model of memory?

2 Critically consider **one or more** alternatives to the multi-store model of memory.

3 'All forgetting can be explained in terms of the effects of later learning on earlier learning or vice versa.' To what extent does psychological research support the claims of interference theory?

4 Discuss the claim that forgetting is nothing more than a failure to retrieve.

Web addresses

http://www.brainresearch.com/

http://www.yorku.ca/faculty/academic/ecorcos/psy3390/eyem.htm

http://www.psy.jhu.edu/~nightfly/

http://www.memory.uva.nl/

http://www.wm.edu/PSYC/psy201efr/intro_70.htm

http://cogsci.umn.edu/millenium/home.html

http://members.xoom.com/tweety74/memory/index.html

http://www.exploratorium.edu/memory/index.html

http://www.usu.edu/~acaserv/center/pages/mnemonics.html

http://www.yorku.ca/dept/psych/classics/Miller

Further reading

Baddeley, A. (1997) *Human Memory: Theory and Practice* (revised edition). Hove: Psychology Press. An extremely broad, detailed but readable textbook by one of the leading figures in the field.

Baddeley, A. (1999) *Essentials of Human Memory*. Hove: Psychology Press. Equally broad, but a somewhat easier read than the above.

Parkin, A.J. (1993) *Memory: Phenomena, Experiment and Theory*. Oxford: Blackwell. A much briefer text than Baddeley's, with chapters on developmental aspects of memory.

Answers to questions on page 254

visuospatial scratchpad, articulatory loop, central executive

Chapter 18

Language, Thought and Culture

Introduction and overview

The relationship between language and thought is one of the most fascinating and complex issues within psychology, and it's been debated by philosophers for over 2000 years. Our thinking often takes the form of imagery, and our thoughts and feelings are often expressed (unconsciously) through gestures and facial expressions. Artists 'think' non-linguistically. Knowing what we want to say, but being unable to 'put it into words', is one of several examples of thought taking place without language (Weiskrantz, 1988).

However, the exact relationship between language and thought has been the subject of much debate amongst philosophers and psychologists. Views fall into four main categories.

- *Thought is dependent on/caused by, language.* This view is taken by people working in a variety of disciplines, including psychology, sociology, linguistics and anthropology. Sapir (a linguist and anthroplogist) and Whorf (a linguist) were both interested in comparing languages, which they saw as a major feature of a culture. Language is shared by all members of a culture, or sub-cultures within it, and this makes it a determining influence on how individuals think. Bernstein (a sociologist) focused on sub-cultural (social class) differences in language *codes*, which he saw as a major influence on intelligence and educational attainment. Social constructionists (e.g. Gergen) regard language as providing a basis for all our thought, a system of categories for dividing up experience and giving it meaning (see Chapter 2).
- *Language is dependent on, and reflects, thought.* Probably the most extreme version of this view is Piaget's, according to whom language reflects the individual's level of cognitive development. Piaget's theory is discussed in detail in Chapter 34.
- *Thought and language are initially quite separate activities,* which then come together and interact at a later point in development (about age two). This view is associated with the Russian psychologist, Vygotsky, whose developmental theory is also discussed in Chapter 34.
- *Language and thought are one and the same.* This rather extreme view is associated mainly with Watson, the founder of behaviourism.

The focus of this chapter are the various versions of the first of these viewpoints.

Language and thought are the same

Watson's 'peripheralist' approach

The earliest psychological theory of the relationship between language and thought was proposed by Watson (1913). In his view, thought processes are really no more than the sensations produced by tiny movements of the speech organs too small to produce audible sounds. Essentially, then, thought is talking to oneself very quietly. Part of Watson's rejection of 'mind' was his denial of mentalistic concepts such as 'thought', and hence his reduction of it to 'silent speech' (see Chapter 3, page 32).

Watson's theory is called *peripheralism*, because it sees 'thinking' occurring peripherally in the larynx, rather than centrally in the brain. Movements of the larynx do occur when 'thought' is taking place. But this indicates only that such movements may *accompany* thinking, not that the movements *are* thoughts or that they're necessary for thinking to occur.

Ask yourself ...

- Can you think of any ways in which you might test Watson's theory?

Smith (*et al.*, 1947) attempted to test Watson's theory by giving himself an injection of curare, a drug that causes total paralysis of the skeletal muscles without affecting consciousness. The muscles of the speech organs and the respiratory system are paralysed, and so Smith had to be kept breathing artificially. When the drug's effects had worn off, he was able to report on his thoughts and perceptions during the paralysis.

Additionally, Furth (1966) has shown that people born deaf and mute, and who don't learn sign language, can also think in much the same way as hearing and speaking people. For Watson, deaf and mute individuals should be incapable of thought, because of the absence of movement in the speech organs.

Thought is dependent on, or caused by, language

Bruner (1983) has argued that language is essential if thought and knowledge aren't to be limited to what can be learned through our actions (the *enactive mode of representation*) or images (the *iconic mode*). If the *symbolic mode* (going beyond the immediate context) is to develop, then language is crucial (see Chapter 34).

Social constructionists (e.g. Gergen, 1973) have argued that our ways of understanding the world derive from other people (past and present), rather than from objective reality. We're born into a world where the conceptual frameworks and categories used by people in our culture already exist. Indeed, these frameworks and categories are an essential part of our culture, since they provide meaning, a way of structuring experience of both ourselves and the world of other people. This view has much in common with the 'strong' version of the *linguistic relativity hypothesis*, the most extensively researched of the theories arguing that thought is dependent on, or caused by, language.

The linguistic relativity hypothesis

According to the philosopher Wittgenstein (1921), 'The limits of my language mean the limits of my world'. By this, he meant that people can only think about and understand the world through language, and that if a particular language doesn't possess certain ideas or concepts, these couldn't exist for its native speakers. The view that language determines *how* we think about objects and events, or even *what* we think (our ideas, thoughts and perceptions), can be traced to the writings of Sapir (1929) and Whorf (1956), a student of Sapir. Their perspective is often called the *Sapir–Whorf linguistic relativity hypothesis* (LRH), and is sometimes referred to as the *Whorfian hypothesis* in acknowledgement of the greater contribution made by Whorf. For Whorf (1956):

'We dissect nature along the lines laid down by our native languages. The categories and types that we isolate from the world of phenomena we do not find there because they stare every observer in the face; on the contrary, the world is presented in a kaleidoscopic flux of impressions that has to be organised by our minds – and this means largely by the linguistic systems in our minds. We cut nature up, organise it into concepts and ascribe significance as we do, largely

because we are parties to an agreement to organise it this way – an agreement that holds throughout our speech community and is codified in patterns of our language'.

According to Whorf's *linguistic determinism*, language determines our concepts, and we can think only through the use of concepts. So, acquiring a language involves acquiring a 'world view' (or *Weltanschauung*). People who speak different languages have different world views (hence linguistic 'relativity').

Ask yourself ...

- In a general sense, do you agree with the claims of linguistic determinism? Is language really that 'powerful'? Have another read of the *Introduction and overview*.
- If people who speak different (native) languages really do have different world views, what would that imply for communication between them?

What was Whorf's evidence?

Whorf compared standard average european (SAE) languages, such as English, French and Italian (Indo-European), with Native American languages, particularly Hopi (which Whorf studied for several years). While in English we have a single word for snow, the Inuit Eskimos have approximately 20 (including one for fluffy snow, one for drifting snow, another for packed snow, and so on). The Hopi Indians have only one word for 'insect', 'aeroplane' and 'pilot' and the Zuni Indians don't distinguish, verbally, between yellow and orange.

According to Whorf, the fact that Inuit Eskimos have 20 different words for snow means that they literally perceive more varieties of snow than native English speakers who have only one or two words

Whorf also saw a language's *grammar* as determining an individual's thought and perception. In the Hopi language, for example, no distinction is made between past, present and future which, compared with English, makes it a 'timeless language'. In European languages, 'time' is treated as an *objective* entity, with a clear demarcation between past, present and future. Although the Hopi language recognises duration, Hopis talk about time only as it appears *subjectively* to the

observer. For example, rather than saying 'I stayed for ten days', Hopis say 'I stayed until the tenth day' or 'I left on the tenth day'.

In English, nouns denote objects and events, and verbs denote actions. But in the Hopi language, 'lightning', 'wave', 'flame', 'meteor', 'puff of smoke' and 'pulsation' are all verbs, since events of necessarily brief duration must be verbs. As a result, a Hopi would say 'it lightninged', 'it smoked' and 'it flamed'.

Some questions (and question marks) about the Whorfian hypothesis

- Does the finding that Inuit Eskimos have 20 words for snow (if true) necessarily mean that native speakers of Inuit actually *perceive* more varieties of snow than speakers of English? Did Whorf show that the Hopi Indians can't discriminate between past, present and future in essentially the same way as SAE speakers?
- Greene (1975) asks us to imagine a Hopi linguist applying a Whorfian analysis to English. Would s/he think that we have 'primitive' beliefs that ships are really female or that mountains have feet or that 'driving a car', 'driving off in golf' and 'driving a hard bargain' all involve the same activity? Of course not. (See *Evaluation of the LRH*, pages 271–272.)

Testing the LRH

Miller & McNeill (1969) distinguish between three different versions of the LRH, all of which are consistent with it but vary in the *strength* of claim they make:

- the *strong* version claims that *language determines thought*;
- the *weak* version claims that *language affects perception*;
- the *weakest* version claims that *language influences memory*, such that information that's more easily described in a particular language will be better remembered than information that's more difficult to describe.

The questions and criticisms that we considered above relate mainly to the strong version, but almost all the research has focused on the weak and weakest versions. One of the few attempts to test the strong version was a study by Carroll & Casagrande (1958).

KEY STUDY 18.1

How Navaho children shape up on cognitive development (Carroll & Casagrande, 1958)

Carroll and Casagrande compared Navaho Indian children who either spoke only Navaho (Navaho–Navaho) or English and Navaho (English–Navaho) with American children of European descent who spoke only English. The children were tested on the development of *form* or *shape recognition*. The Navaho language stresses the importance of form, such that 'handling' verbs involve different words depending on what's being handled. For example, long and flexible objects (such as string) have one word form, whereas long and rigid objects (such as sticks) have another.

American children of European descent develop object recognition in the order: size, colour, and form or shape. If, as the strong version of the LRH claims, language influences cognitive development, then the developmental sequence of the Navaho children should differ from the English-only American children, and their form or shape recognition abilities should be superior. This is what Carroll and Casagrande found, thus supporting the strong version of the LRH. However, they also found that the English–Navaho group showed form recognition *later* than the English-only American children, which *doesn't* support the LRH strong version.

Carroll and Casagrande attributed the superior performance of the English-only children to the fact that they'd had a great deal of experience of shape classification at nursery school. This made them an atypical sample.

Ask yourself ...

- Would the Jalé or the Ibibio find tests of colour perception and memory more difficult, according to the the weak and weakest versions of the LRH?

According to the weaker versions of the LRH, tests of colour perception and memory should be more difficult for the Jalé than the Ibibio. Since the Ibibio word for green encompasses the English green, blue and yellow, the Ibibio should find colour perception and memory tasks more difficult than English speakers. Taking a previous example, since the Zuni language doesn't distinguish between yellow and orange, Zuni speakers should be unable to discriminate them (they should be 'blind' for these two colours).

Brown & Lenneberg (1954) found that Zuni Indians *did* make more mistakes than English speakers in recognising these colours. But Lenneberg & Roberts (1956) found that the number of errors made by *bilingual* Zuni–English speakers in distinguishing orange and yellow fell *midway* between that of monolingual Zuni and monolingual English speakers. This suggests that the two languages don't determine two different sets of conflicting perceptions, but rather two sets of *labels* for essentially the same colour perceptions. Language serves to draw attention to differences in the environment and acts as a label to help store these differences in memory. Sometimes

Attempts at testing the 'weak' and 'weakest' versions of the LRH have typically involved the perception and memory of *colour*. The Jalé (New Guinea) have terms only for black and white, while the Dani (New Guinea) use 'mola' for bright, warm hues, and 'mili' for dark, cold hues. The Shona people (Zimbabwe) have three colour words, and members of the Ibibio culture (Nigeria) have terms for black, white, red and green.

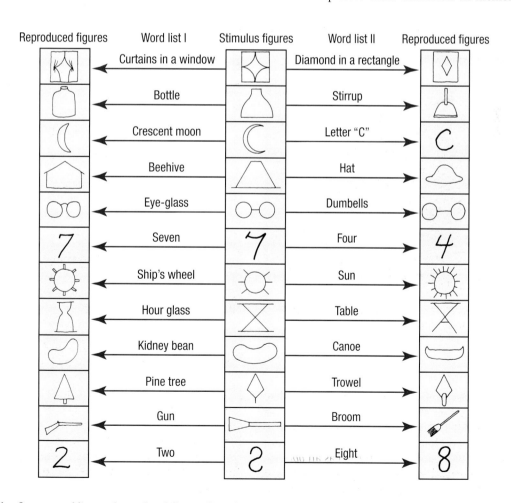

Figure 18.1 *Stimulus figures, word lists and reproduced figures (from the experiment by Carmichael et al., 1932)*

the label we apply to what we see may *distort* our recall of what was seen, since the label determines how we code our experiences into memory storage (see Chapter 17).

So, while there's very little direct evidence to support the strong form of the LRH, there's rather more support for the weaker versions. Language merely predisposes people to think or perceive in certain ways or about certain things (Brown, 1958). However, Brown & Lenneberg's (1954) results (and those of other researchers using a similar methodology) have been challenged in a way that throws doubt even on the weaker versions.

The 'Tower of Babel' by Breughel. From the Old Testament story of Babel, the word 'babble' is derived

Perceiving focal colours

Berlin & Kay (1969) used a chart with an array of 329 small coloured chips, comprising virtually all the hues that the human eye can discriminate. They asked native speakers of 20 languages (other than English) to (a) trace the boundaries of each of their native language's basic colour terms, and (b) to point to the chip which was the best example of each basic colour term. A basic or *focal* colour was defined by a list of linguistic criteria, including that:

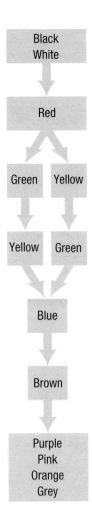

Figure 18.2 *The sequence in which focal colours emerge (Berlin & Kay, 1969)*

- a term should consist of only a single unit of meaning (e.g. 'red' as opposed to 'dark red'); and
- it should name only colours and not objects (e.g. 'purple' as opposed to 'wine').

As expected from anthropological research, there was considerable variation in the placement of boundaries. But the choice of best examples was surprisingly similar. The largest clusters were for black and white and red, for which all the 20 languages have colour terms, then 19 for green, 18 yellow, 16 blue, 15 brown and purple, 14 grey and eleven pink and orange. Berlin and Kay concluded that 'colour categorisation is not random and the foci of basic colour terms are similar in all languages'.

So, while cultures may differ in the number of basic colour terms they use, all cultures draw their focal terms from only eleven colours: black, white, red, green, yellow, blue, brown, purple, pink, orange and grey. Moreover, the colour terms emerge in a particular sequence in the history of languages.

For cultures with only two colours, these will always be black and white, whereas in cultures with three colours, these will always be black, white and red (Newstead, 1995). As Newstead has observed:

'This, then, gives a rather different perspective on the use of colour terms. It had been assumed that verbal labels were chosen more or less arbitrarily, and that those chosen influenced

the way in which colour was perceived. Berlin and Kay's findings suggest that there are certain focal colours which will always be labelled if colour terms are used at all. This suggests an alternative explanation for Brown and Lenneberg's findings: that the colours which participants in their study had found easier to learn were the focal colours and these were easy to remember not because they had verbal labels but because they were the most basic colours'.

A study which supports Berlin and Kay's findings was conducted by Heider & Oliver (1972).

KEY STUDY 18.3

Colour naming among the Dani (Heider & Oliver, 1972)

As we noted earlier, the Dani (a Stone-Age agricultural people of Indonesian New Guinea) have only two words for colours, whereas native English speakers have words for eleven basic colours. Heider and Oliver gave both Dani and English-speaking participants a coloured chip which they were allowed to look at for five seconds. After a 30-second delay, participants were asked to pick out a chip of the same colour among a set of 40 different coloured chips. On the weakest version of the LRH, the Dani's colour vocabulary should have influenced their memory for colours, and on the weak version they should have had difficulty discriminating similar colours of a slightly different hue that they'd labelled with the same name.

The results showed that, while the Dani-speaking and English-speaking participants made many mistakes, there were *no* significant differences between them in their rate of confusion of similar colours, despite the differences in their colour vocabularies. In other research, Heider showed that both Dani and English speakers were better at recognising focal colours than non-focal colours, and that the Dani found it much easier to learn labels for focal than non-focal colours.

Heider (1972) concluded that:

'Far from being a domain well suited to the study of the effects of language on thought, the colour-space would seem a prime example of the influence of underlying perceptual–cognitive factors on the formation and reference of linguistic categories'.

By this, Heider (sometimes referred to as Rosch – her married name) means that her data are better explained in terms of *physiological factors* underlying colour vision, rather than linguistic factors. Thus, people are sensitive to focal colours because the human visual system processes reality in a certain way (Lakoff, 1987). Indeed, evidence suggests that focal colours can be discriminated *before* any verbal labels for them have been learned. Bornstein (1988), for example, has argued that preverbal infants categorise the visible spectrum in a similar way to adults, namely, on the basis of the relatively discrete hues of blue, green, yellow and red (Box 16.2, page 234).

However, a study of another New Guinea people, the Berinmo, casts doubt on Heider's interpretation, and seems to support the weakest and weak versions of the LRH.

KEY STUDY 18.4

Colour naming among the Berinmo

Robertson *et al.* (cited in Hanlon, 1999b) studied the Berinmo people of New Guinea, who live a simple hunter–gatherer lifestyle in remote forests. They have five colour names: one for green, blue and purple, another for yellow, orange and brown, a third for all dark colours, a fourth for white and all light colours; and a fifth for all shades of red and pink. Using a procedure similar to Heider & Oliver's (1972), Robertson *et al.* found that the Berinmo could remember only those colours which matched their colour names, and that they were unable to discriminate between colours which their language didn't discriminate (for example, green and blue).

Although all the focal colours were 'represented' by the Berinmos' five colour names, the fact that green, blue and purple were lumped together, as were yellow, orange and brown, and also red and pink, seems inconsistent with the claim that colour terms emerge in a particular order in the history of languages (see Figure 18.2):

'While it has been assumed that a lot of low-level things like colour perception have taken place at a low, almost a genetic level, we found that even something as simple as colour is affected by culture'. (Robertson, cited in Hanlon, 1999b)

Evaluation of the LRH

- Berry *et al.* (1992) and Jackendoff (1993) have argued that Whorf's evidence was anecdotal rather than empirical, and that he exaggerated the differences between Hopi and other languages. Moreover, far from having 'over 20' words for 'snow', the Inuit Eskimos have relatively few such words (Newstead, 1995), and no more than do English speakers (Pinker, 1997a). According to Pagel (1995), Whorf simply got his facts wrong.

- There's an important difference between a language's grammar and our perceptual experience. The fact that Hopi can be translated into English (and vice versa) implies a universally shared knowledge of the world that's independent of the particular language in which it's expressed (Pagel, 1995).

- A crucial question that Whorf seems to have overlooked is *why* Eskimos have so many names for snow and SAE languages so few. One answer is that the more significant an experience or some feature of our environment is for us, the greater the number of ways of expressing it in the language. In other words, while Whorf argued that language structures the Eskimo's world, it could equally well be argued that the Eskimo's language develops *as a result of* his/her different perception of the world (Baddeley, 1999). According to Solso (1995):

  'The development of specific language codes ... is dependent on cultural needs; the learning of these codes by members of a language group also involves the learning of significant values of the culture, some of which must be related to survival ...'.

■ Solso's view is supported by the fact that English-speaking skiers learn to discriminate between varied snow conditions and invent a vocabulary to describe these differences. Such terms include 'sticky snow', 'powder', 'corn' and 'boilerplate' (or ice: Crooks & Stein, 1991). Similarly, the Hanunoo people of the Philippines have modified their language in response to environmental conditions. For example, women have developed a more complex vocabulary for shades of blue to distinguish the colours of dyed textiles that have been introduced into their society (Price & Crapo, 1999).

■ It's now widely accepted that Whorf overestimated the importance of language differences. As Berry *et al.* (1992) have observed:

> 'Language as an instrument for thinking has many cross-culturally variant properties. As humans, we may not all be sharing the same thoughts, but our respective languages do not seem to predestine us to different kinds of thinking'.

■ What language may do, though, is to affect the ease of information processing. Newstead (1995), for example, describes research conducted by Hunt & Agnoli (1991) which supports this view. The English word 'seven' has two syllables, whereas the equivalent French word ('sept') has only one. The English word 'eleven' has three syllables whereas the French word 'onze' has one. Hunt and Agnoli argue that when a name is shorter, information is processed more quickly, and so French speakers would have an advantage over English speakers when performing mental arithmetic involving these numbers, at least in processing terms.

■ According to Price & Crapo (1999), the study of semantic domains (such as colour naming) helps us to discover what's important in the daily lives of different cultural groups, as well as the changing cultural history of a society.

The LRH, social class and race
Social-class differences in language and thought

Stones (1971) gives examples of imaginary conversations on a bus between a mother and child:

1 Mother: Hold on tight.
  Child: Why?
  Mother: Hold on tight.
  Child: Why?
  Mother: You'll fall.
  Child: Why?
  Mother: I told you to hold on tight, didn't I?

2 Mother: Hold on tight, darling.
  Child: Why?
  Mother: If you don't you'll be thrown forward and you'll fall.
  Child: Why?
  Mother: Because if the bus suddenly stops, you'll jerk forward onto the seat in front.
  Child: Why?
  Mother: Now, darling, hold on tightly and don't make such a fuss.

Ask yourself ...

• How would you characterise the differences between these two conversations?

Restricted and elaborated codes

Bernstein (1961) was interested in language's role as a *social* (rather than individual) phenomenon, especially its relation to cultural deprivation. He showed that while there were generally no differences between the verbal and non-verbal intelligence test performance of boys from public schools, boys from lower-working-class homes often showed considerable differences, with non-verbal performance sometimes being as much as 26 points better than verbal performance. Bernstein argued that working- and middle-class children speak two different kinds (or codes) of language, which he called *restricted code* and *elaborated code* respectively.

Because Bernstein saw the relationship between potential and actual intelligence as being mediated through language, he argued that the lack of an elaborated code would prevent working-class children from developing their full intellectual potential. The different language codes underlie the whole pattern of relationships (to objects and people) experienced by members of different classes, as well as the patterns of learning which their children bring with them to school.

In support of Bernstein's views, Hess & Shipman (1965) found that social-class differences influence children's intellectual development. In particular, there was a lack of meaning in the mother–child communication system for low-status families. Language was used much less to convey *meaning* (to describe, explain, express and so on) and much more to give orders and commands to the child (see the two mother–child conversations above).

However, instead of seeing 'restricted' and 'elaborated' as distinct types of language code, they're better thought of as two ends of a continuum. Also, the terms 'restricted' and 'elaborated' imply a value judgement of middle-class speech as being superior to working-class speech (closer to 'standard' or 'the Queen's' English). The lack of objectivity makes this judgement difficult to defend.

Black English

A version of English spoken by segments of the African-American community is called 'Black English'. For example, when asked to repeat the sentence 'I asked him if he did it, and he said he didn't do it', one five-year-old girl repeated the sentence like this: 'I asks him if he did it, and he says he didn't did it, but I knows he did' (Labov, 1973). Bernstein argued that Black English is a restricted code, and that this makes the thinking of Black English speakers less logical than that of their white elaborated-code counterparts.

One major difference between Black and standard English relates to the use of verbs (Rebok, 1987). In particular, Black English speakers often omit the present tense copula (the verb 'to be'). So, 'he be gone' indicates standard English 'he's been gone for a long time' and 'he gone' signifies that 'he's just gone'. Black English is often termed *sub-standard* and regarded as illogical rather than *non-standard* (Bereiter & Engelman,

Table 18.1 *Characteristics of restricted and elaborated codes (Bernstein, 1961)*

Restricted code	Elaborated code
1 Grammatically crude, repetitive and rigid, limited use of adjectives and adverbs, greater use of pronouns than nouns. Sentences often short, grammatically simple and incomplete	1 Grammatically more complex and flexible. Uses a range of subordinate clauses, conjunctions, prepositions, adjectives and adverbs. Uses more nouns than pronouns. Sentences are longer and more complex
2 Context-bound: the meaning isn't made explicit but assumes the listener's familiarity with the situation being described, e.g. 'He gave me it'; listener can't be expected to know what 'he' or 'it' refers to	2 Context-independent: the meaning is made explicit, e.g. 'John gave me this book'
3 'I' very rarely used; much of the meaning conveyed non-verbally	3 'I' often used, making clear the speaker's intentions, as well as emphasising the precise description of experiences and feelings
4 Frequent use of uninformative but emotionally reinforcing phrases, such as 'you know', 'don't I'	4 Relatively little use of emotionally reinforcing phrases
5 Tends to stress the present, the here-and-now	5 Tends to stress the past and future
6 Doesn't allow expression of abstract/hypothetical thought	6 Allows expression of abstract/hypothetical thought

1966). According to Labov (1970), Black English is just one dialect of English, and speakers of both dialects are expressing the same ideas equally well.

While the grammatical rules of Black English differ from those of standard English, Black English possesses consistent rules which allow the expression of thoughts as complex as those permitted by standard English (Labov, 1973). Several other languages, such as Russian and Arabic, also omit the present-tense verb 'to be', and yet we don't call them 'illogical'. This suggests that black dialects are considered sub-standard as a matter of convention or prejudice, and not because they're poorer vehicles for expressing meaning and logical thinking. However, because the structure of Black English does differ in important ways from standard English, and since intelligence tests are written in standard English, Black English speakers are at a linguistic disadvantage (as, indeed, are white working-class children: see Chapters 41 and 47).

Labov also showed that the social situation can be a powerful determinant of verbal behaviour. A young boy called Leon was shown a toy by a white interviewer and asked to tell him everything he could about it. Leon said very little and was silent for much of the time, even when a black interviewer took over. However, when Leon sat on the floor and shared a packet of crisps with his best friend and with the same black interviewer introducing topics in a local black dialect, Leon became a lively conversationalist. Had he been assessed with the white or black interviewers on their own, Leon might have been labelled 'non-verbal' or 'linguistically retarded'.

Black children may actually be *bilingual*. In their home environments, the school playground and their neighbourhoods, they speak the accepted vernacular. In the classroom, however, and when talking to any one in authority, they must adopt standard English with which they're unfamiliar. This results in short sentences, simple grammar and strange intonation. But out of school, their natural language is easy, fluent, creative and often gifted. So, while Black English is certainly *non-standard*, it's another language with its own grammar which is certainly *not* sub-standard.

CRITICAL DISCUSSION 18.1

'Ebonics': an ongoing debate

Ebonics is a fusion of the words 'ebony' and 'phonics' and was coined in 1975 as an alternative to the term 'Black English'. In 1996, Ebonics (or African-American Vernacular English/AAVE) was officially recognised by the Oakland public school board in California, and schools were ordered to teach 28,000 black children in their own 'tongue'. The board claimed that Ebonics was a separate language, genetically rooted in the West-African and Niger–Congo language system, rather than a dialect of standard American English (Hiscock, 1996; Whittell, 1996).

In early 1997, the school board edited its statement so that the word 'genetically' referred to linguists' use of the word for the roots of a language rather than to a gene pool. They also indicated that it wasn't the intent to teach in Ebonics, but rather to have teachers use the vernacular to be able to understand their children (Zinberg, 1997). Both conservatives and liberals in America claim that the decision to require Ebonics to be taught would be 'political correctness run amok' (Cornwell, 1997). Educationalists such as Zinberg disagree. In her view, many students are:

> '… bewildered, then angered and finally alienated from the schools where their language and self-esteem are belittled by a seemingly insensitive system'.

Although regional dialects in the USA are diverging, there's no evidence of convergence between black and white vernaculars (Rickford, cited in Hawkes, 1998). By contrast, British blacks and whites still speak the same language, partly because there's no segregation in housing in Britain as there is in the USA (Labov, cited in Hawkes, 1998).

Social constructionism

Social constructionism can be thought of as a theoretical orientation which lies behind a number of recent alternative approaches to the study of human beings as social animals, including *critical psychology*, *discourse analysis* and *poststructuralism* (see Chapters 2 and 3).

One general characteristic of this approach is the belief that language is a precondition for thought. Our ways of understanding the world don't derive from objective reality, but from other people – past and present. We're born into a world where the conceptual frameworks and categories used by the people in our culture already exist. Indeed, these frameworks and categories are an essential part of our culture, since they provide meaning, a way of structuring our experience of both ourselves and the world of other people. These ideas are similar to the strong version of the LRH. The social constructionist view of language is very relevant to the understanding of prejudice and discrimination (see Chapter 25), gender (see Chapter 36) and personality (see Chapter 42).

> **Ask yourself ...**
>
> * What would you say are some of the fundamental categories that exist in contemporary Britain, taken-for-granted ways of thinking and perceiving, which we may/may not share with other Western cultures?

Language is dependent on, and reflects, thought

According to Piaget (1950), children begin life with some understanding of the world and try to find linguistic ways of expressing their knowledge. As language develops, it 'maps' onto previously acquired cognitive structures, and so language is dependent upon thought (Piaget & Inhelder, 1969). For example, a child should begin talking about objects that aren't present in its immediate surroundings only after *object permanence* has developed (see Box 19.4, page 282). Similarly, children who could *conserve* liquid quantity (see Chapter 34, page 492) understood the meaning of phrases and words such as 'as much as', 'bigger' and 'more'. However, children who couldn't conserve didn't improve their performance of the correct use of these words after receiving linguistic training (Sinclair-de-Zwart, 1969).

In Piaget's view, children can be taught words, but they won't *understand* them until they've mastered certain intellectual skills during the process of cognitive growth. So, language can exist without thought, but only in the sense that a parrot can 'speak'. Thought, then, is a necessary forerunner to language if language is to be used properly.

Contrary to Piaget's view that thought structures language, Luria & Yudovich (1971) suggest that language plays a central role in cognitive development.

C A S E   S T U D Y   18.1

The Russian twins (Luria & Yudovich, 1971)

Luria and Yudovich studied five-year-old twin boys whose home environment was unstimulating. They played almost exclusively together and had only a very primitive level of speech. The boys received little adult encouragement to speak, and made little progress towards the symbolic use of words. Essentially, their speech was *synpraxic*, a primitive form in which words can't be detached from the action or object they denote.

The twins hardly ever used speech to describe objects or events or to help them plan their actions. They couldn't understand other people's speech, and their own constituted a kind of signalling rather than symbolic system. Although they never played with other children, and played with each other in a primitive and repetitive way, they were otherwise normal.

After being separated, one twin was given special remedial treatment for his language deficiency, but the other wasn't. The former made rapid progress and, ten months later, was ahead of his brother. However, *both* made progress, and their synpraxic speech died away. For Luria and Yudovich:

> 'The whole structure of the mental life of both twins was simultaneously and sharply changed. Once they acquired an objective language system, [they] were able to formulate the aims of their activity verbally, and after only three months we observed the beginnings of meaningful play'.

Thought and language as initially separate activities

According to Vygotsky (1962), language and thought begin as separate and independent activities (see Chapter 34). Early on, thinking occurs without language (consisting primarily of images) and language occurs without thought (as when babies cry or make other sounds to express feelings, attract attention or fulfil some other social aim). But at about age two, *prelinguistic* thought and *pre-intellectual* language:

> '... meet and join to initiate a new kind of behaviour [in which] thought becomes verbal and speech rational'. (Vygotsky, 1962)

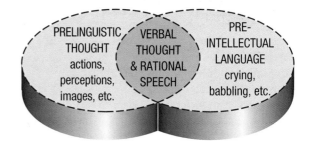

Figure 18.3 *A diagrammatic representation of Vygotsky's views on the relationship between language and thought*

Vygotsky believed that between ages two and seven, language performs two functions:

- an *internal* function, which enables internal thought to be monitored and directed;
- an *external* function, which enables the results of thinking to be communicated to others.

However, children cannot yet distinguish between the two functions and, as a result, their speech is *egocentric*. They talk out loud about their plans and actions, and can neither think privately nor communicate publicly to others. Instead, they're caught somewhere between the two, and cannot distinguish between 'speech for self' (what Piaget calls *autistic speech*) and 'speech for others' (*socialised speech*).

Vygotsky believed that around age seven (when children typically enter Piaget's *concrete operational stage* of intellectual development: see Chapter 34, page 495), overt language begins to be restricted to communication, while the thought function of language becomes internalised as internal speech or verbal thought. Piaget saw egocentric speech as a kind of 'running commentary' on the child's behaviour, and believed that around age seven it was replaced by socialised (or communicative) speech.

> **Box 18.1** **The function of egocentric speech**

Vygotsky (1962) showed that when six- or seven-year-olds are trying to solve a problem and a mishap occurs (such as a pencil breaking) which requires them to revise their thinking, they often revert to overt verbalisation. Adults sometimes do the same in similar situations, especially when they believe that no one can hear them. For example, we'll often re-trace our steps out loud (such as 'Now, I know I didn't have it when I went in the room, so what did I do before that?'). Vygotsky concluded that the function of egocentric speech was similar to that of inner speech. It doesn't merely accompany the child's activity but:

'... serves mental orientation, conscious understanding; it helps in overcoming difficulties, it is speech for oneself, intimately and usefully connected with the child's thinking. In the end it becomes inner speech' [see Figure 18.4].

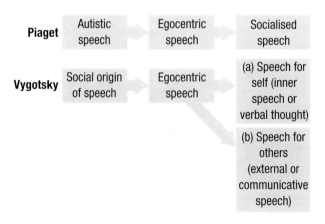

Figure 18.4 *The difference between Piaget and Vygotsky with respect to egocentric speech*

Eventually, Piaget accepted Vygotsky's view concerning the function and fate of inner speech. Both inner speech and egocentric speech differ from speech for others in that they don't have to satisfy grammatical conventions. Thus, both are abbreviated, incomplete and concerned more with the essential meaning rather than how it's expressed. For Vygotsky,

inner speech is a 'dynamic, shifting and unstable thing which "flutters" between word and thought' (see Figure 18.3).

Overt speech can sometimes resemble inner speech in its abbreviated nature, long after egocentric speech has been replaced. For example, people who know each other well may talk in an abbreviated form that wouldn't be used with strangers. Understanding occurs because the more familiar we are with others, and the more experiences we have in common, the less explicit our speech has to be. 'Coffee?', for example, asked with a rising inflection and in a particular context, would be interpreted as 'Would you like a cup of coffee?'. This is similar to how adults interpret the holophrastic speech of young children (see Box 19.2, page 280). In Bernstein's terms, we use restricted code when talking in familiar surroundings to familiar others, whose view of the world we assume is similar to our own.

Conclusions

While there are many examples indicating that thought can occur without language, the exact relationship between thought and language remains unclear. What is certain, however, is that no one account of this relationship is true and all others false; several theoretical perspectives can claim some support from the experimental literature. However, since language represents such a central feature of culture, both shaping it and being shaped by it, any theory which fails to take account of cultural factors is likely to be inadequate.

CHAPTER SUMMARY

- According to Watson's **peripheralism**, thought is no more than sensations produced by tiny movements of the larynx, too small to produce audible sounds. While these movements accompany thought, they're not necessary for thinking to occur. Thinking can occur despite complete paralysis, and people born deaf and mute are also capable of thinking.
- Bruner argues that language is essential for thought and knowledge to progress beyond the **enactive** and **iconic** modes of representation to the **symbolic mode**.
- **Social constructionists** claim that conceptual frameworks and categories provide meaning within a culture, a way of structuring our experience of ourselves and the world.
- According to the **Sapir–Whorf linguistic relativity hypothesis** (LRH), language determines how we think about objects and events, and even what we think. This is related to **linguistic determinism**.
- The 'weak' and 'weakest' versions of the LRH have typically been tested through perception and memory of **colour**. The fewer colour words there are in a language, the more difficult native speakers should find tests of colour perception and memory.
- Early studies seemed to support these two versions. But while cultures may differ in the number of basic colour terms they use, all cultures draw their colour terms from only eleven **focal colours**, which emerge in a particular sequence in the history of languages.

- Whorf's evidence was anecdotal rather than empirical, and he exaggerated the differences between Hopi and other languages. Also, he mistakenly equated language's grammar with perceptual experience. Translation between languages implies a universally shared knowledge of the world independent of any particular language.
- Bernstein claimed that working-class children speak a **restricted code** and middle class children an **elaborated code**. The relationship between actual and potential intelligence is mediated through language, so working-class children are prevented from developing their full intellectual potential.
- Differences between standard and Black English have resulted in the latter being called **sub-standard**, rather than **non-standard**. According to Labov, this is an expression of prejudice.
- Black children may be bilingual, using the accepted register fluently at home and with their peers, but adopting unfamiliar standard English in the classroom.
- According to Piaget, language 'maps' onto previously acquired cognitive structures, so that language is dependent on thought. Words can only be understood if certain intellectual skills (such as **object permanence** and **conservation**) have already been mastered.
- For Vygotsky, language and thought are initially separate and independent activities. At around age two, **pre-linguistic thought** and **pre-intellectual language** begin to interact to form verbal thought and rational speech.
- Between the ages of two and seven, language performs both **internal** and **external** functions. The child's failure to distinguish between them results in **egocentric speech**. For Vygotsky, this indicates the separation of the two functions.

Self-assessment questions

1 Critically consider research into the relationship between language and thought.
2 'The limits of my language mean the limits of my world.' (Wittgenstein, 1921)
Discuss ways in which social and/or cultural aspects of language use may influence thought.

Web addresses

http://www.cdipage.com/phonics.htm

http://www.june29.com/HLP

http://www.arts.uwa.edu.au/lingwww/LIN102-99/notes/whorf.html

http://www.lclarke.edu/~soan/context/htm

Further reading

Carroll, J.B. (1956) *Language, Thought and Reality: Selected Writings of Benjamin Lee Whorf*. Cambridge, MA: MIT Press. A good example of the need to read the original research to fully appreciate the issues.

Rosch, E. (1977) Human categorisation. In N. Warren (Ed.) *Studies in Cross-Cultural Psychology, Volume 1*. New York: Academic Press. A detailed but readable account of the colour perception research, within the broader context of 'By what principles do humans divide up the world in the way they do?', by one of the leading researchers in the field.

Chapter 19

Language Acquisition

Introduction and overview

Since our brains seem specially designed to enable us to use speech (see Chapter 4), it's hardly surprising that language is so crucial to most human activities. Many psychologists and philosophers have claimed that language is what makes us unique as a species.

Until quite recently, the study of language was largely the domain of linguistics, which is concerned primarily with the structure of language (its grammar). According to Durkin (1995), while developmental psychologists have always been interested in language, during the mid-twentieth century it became marginalised as an area of psychological research. As we noted Chapter 18, Piaget saw language as merely reflecting cognitive structures – a lens through which to inspect the child's thought. This seemed to reinforce the behaviourists' earlier rejection of anything 'mental' (such as grammar and meaning).

However, there's been a revival of interest in language since the 1960s, inspired largely by Chomsky's (1959) theory of an innate language acquisition device (LAD). This is probably the most extreme *nativist* theory in the whole of psychology (see Chapter 50). The 'marriage' between psychology and linguistics (Chomsky is a linguist) is called *psycholinguistics*, which studies the perception, understanding and production of language, together with their development.

According to *learning theory*, associated with Skinner and Bandura, language development can be attributed primarily to environmental input and learning. But Chomsky's nativist approach argues that, although the environment may supply the content of language, grammar is an inherent, biologically determined capacity of human beings. Hence, the process of language development is essentially one of *acquisition* (as distinct from *learning*). Attempts to teach language to non-humans have major implications for Chomsky's claim that language is a unique human ability.

What is language?

According to Brown (1965), language is a set of arbitrary symbols:

> '... which, taken together, make it possible for a creature with limited powers of discrimination and a limited memory to transmit and understand an infinite variety of messages and to do this in spite of noise and distraction'.

While other species are able to communicate with each other, they can do so only in limited ways, and it's perhaps the 'infinite variety of messages' part of Brown's definition that sets humans apart from non-humans. For example, wild chimpanzees use over 30 different vocalisations to convey a large number of meanings, and repeat sounds in order to intensify their meaning. However, they don't string these sounds together to make new 'words' (Calvin, 1994). The claim that chimpanzees are capable of using language is based largely, and until recently, on deliberate training (see below, pages 287–289). Human language is mastered spontaneously and quite easily within the first five years of life.

Brown (1973) pointed out that humans don't simply learn a repertoire of sentences but:

> '... acquire a rule system that makes it possible to generate a literally infinite variety of sentences, most of them never heard from anyone else'.

This rule system is called *grammar* (or *mental grammar*). However, for psycholinguists, grammar is much more than the parts of speech we learn about in school. It's concerned with the description of language, the rules which determine how a language 'works', and what governs patterns of speech (Jackendoff, 1993).

Graham Rawle's **LOST CONSONANTS**

MAGNIFICENT! I AM SURELY THE GREATEST ARCHITECT OF MY GENERATION

(672) **Nicholas had lots of ego to build things with**

A single missing letter can totally change a word's meaning – and with it, the meaning of the entire sentence

The major components of grammar

Grammar consists of *phonology*, *semantics* and *syntax* (see Figure 18.1, page 279).

Phonology

Phonologists are concerned with a language's sound system – what counts as a sound and what constitutes an acceptable sequence of sounds. Basic speech sounds are called *phones* or *phonetic segments*, and are represented by enclosing symbols inside square brackets. For example, [p] is the initial phone in the word 'pin'. Some languages have as few as 15 distinguishable sounds, and others as many as 85. The English language has some 46 phones (Solso, 1995).

Only those phones which affect the meaning of what's being said matter. For example, the difference between [p] and [d] matters because it can lead to two words with different meanings (such as 'pin' and 'din'). Because [p] and [d] can't be interchanged without altering a word's meaning, they belong to different functional classes of phones called *phonemes* (*phonological segments*). Languages differ in their numbers of phonemes. *Phonological rules* constrain the permitted sequence of phonemes, which are just sounds and correspond roughly to the vowels and consonants of a language's alphabet. However, languages (including English) can have more phonemes than letters in the alphabet (see above). This is because some letters, such as 'o', can be pronounced differently (as in 'hop' and 'hope').

The development of speech sounds continues for several years after birth, and most children recognise sounds in adult speech before they can produce them. So, in response to the instruction: 'I am going to say a word two times and you tell me which time I say it right and which time I say it wrong: rabbit, wabbit', a child might reply: 'Wabbit is wight and wabbit is wong', indicating that the 'r' sound can be recognised but not yet produced (Dale, 1976).

Semantics

Semantics is the study of the *meaning* of language, and can be analysed at the level of *morphemes* and *sentences*. Morphemes are a language's basic units of meaning and consist mainly of words. Other morphemes are *prefixes* (letters attached to the beginning of a word, such as 'pre' and 're') and *suffixes* (word-endings, such as 's' to make a plural). Some morphemes, such as the plural 's', are 'bound' (they only take on meaning when attached to other morphemes), but most morphemes are 'free' (they have meaning when they stand alone, as most words have). But single words have only a limited meaning and are usually combined into longer strings of phrases and sentences, the other level of semantic analysis.

Syntax

Syntax refers to the rules for combining words into phrases and sentences. One example of a syntactic rule is word order. This is crucial for understanding language development. Clearly, the sentences 'The dog bit the postman' and 'The postman bit the dog' have very different meanings!

'Then you should say what you mean', The March Hare went on. 'I do', Alice hastily replied; 'at least – at least I mean what I say – that's the same thing, you know'. 'Not the same thing a bit!' said the Hatter. 'Why, you might just as well say that 'I see what I eat' is the same thing as 'I eat what I see'!'

Another example of a syntactic rule occurs in the sentence 'The dog chased the ...'. In English, only a noun can complete this sentence. Some sentences may be syntactically correct but lack meaning. For example, 'The player scored a goal' and 'The goal post scored a banana' are both syntactically correct, but one has much more meaning than the other. While sentences have sounds and meanings, syntax refers to the structures which relate the two.

Stages in language development

For many psychologists, language development follows a universal timetable; that is, regardless of their language or culture, all children pass through the same sequence of

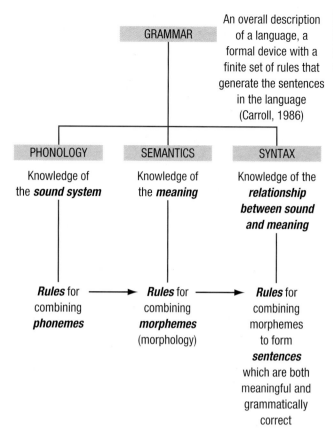

Figure 19.1 *The major components of grammar (adapted from Gross, 1996)*

stages at approximately the same ages (although children may vary with respect to their rate of development). While this belief implies the role of *maturation*, children can come to speak a language only if they're exposed to it. The claim that children are *programmed* to develop language if exposed to it is one of the competing theoretical views examined below (pages 284–286).

It's generally agreed that there are three major stages in language development. These are the *prelinguistic stage* (0–12 months), the *one-word stage* (12–18 months), and the stage of *two-word sentences*. This third stage is divided into two sub-stages: *stage 1 grammar* (18–30 months) and *stage 2 grammar* (30 months and beyond).

The prelinguistic stage (0–12 months)

In their first year, babies are essentially *prelinguistic*. They make various sounds with their vocal organs (including crying) long before they can talk. Crying tends to dominate in the first month, with parents gradually learning to discriminate between the various cries (Gustafson & Harris, 1990). By one month, babies are able to distinguish between phonemes (such as 'ba' and 'pa') and other sounds, even though these may be physically and acoustically almost identical (Aslin *et al.*, 1983). This perceptual ability (*categorical speech perception*) is probably innate (see Box 19.7, page 285).

At about six weeks, *cooing* begins. This is associated with pleasurable states and doesn't occur when babies are hungry, tired or in pain. Although vowel sounds may be produced at this age, they're different from those that will be made later and from which the first words will be formed. This is because the baby's oral cavity and nervous system aren't sufficiently mature to enable it to produce the sounds necessary for speech.

This is the major development in the first year of life, and usually begins between six and nine months. Phonemes are produced and take the form of combinations of consonants and vowels (such as *ma* and *da*). These may be repeated to produce *reduplicated monosyllables* (such as *mama* and *dada*). Although these are very different from the earlier cooing sounds, they have no meaning.

Babbling and pre-babbling vocalisations differ in two main ways:

- babies spend more time making noises, especially when alone in their cots (*spontaneous babbling*), and they seem to enjoy exercising their voices for the sake of it;
- babbling has *intonational patterns*, just like speech, with rising inflections and speech-like rhythms. By one year, syllables are often produced over and over again (as in *dadadada*), a phenomenon called *echolalia*.

Babbling occurs at around the same age in all babies regardless of culture, and even deaf babies of deaf–mute parents show a kind of 'sign-babbling' (Petitto, 1988). These findings suggest that the onset of babbling is based on maturation.

Babies initially produce only a few phonemes, but within a short period almost every available phoneme is produced, whether or not it belongs in what will become the baby's native language. The onset of this *phonemic expansion* is probably maturational. At around nine or ten months, *phonemic contraction* begins, and phoneme production is restricted to those used in the baby's native language. At this stage already, babies of different 'native tongues' can be distinguished by the sounds they produce. Additionally, deaf babies usually stop babbling at around nine or ten months, presumably because of the lack of feedback from their own voices. By two-and-a-half years, still only about 60 per cent of the phonemes used in English are mastered, and complete mastery won't be achieved until around age seven.

One-word stage

Ask yourself ...

- How do words differ from the baby's babbling?
- When people ask parents 'Is your baby talking yet?', what do they mean?

Typically, a child produces its first word at around one year, although there's considerable variability in this (Rice, 1989). Babies don't, of course, suddenly switch from babbling to the production of words, and non-words (*jargon*) continue to be produced for up to another six months. The baby's first words (or *articulate sounds*) are often invented, quite unlike 'adult words'. Scollon (1976) has defined a word as 'a systematic matching of form and meaning'. On this definition, 'da' is a word if it's consistently used to refer to a doll, since the same sound is being used to label the same thing or kind of thing, and there's a clear intention to communicate.

However, an infant's earliest words are usually *context-bound*, produced in only very limited and specific situations or contexts in which particular actions or events occur (Barrett, 1989). For example, one infant, at least initially, only produced the word 'duck' while hitting a toy duck off the edge of a bath. The word was never used in any other context. Barrett has argued that an infant's first words often don't serve a communicative purpose as such. Rather, because they typically occur as accompaniments to particular actions or events (as in the case above), they function as 'performatives'. Some words may be more like the performance of a ritualised action than the expression of a lexical meaning to another person. However, words seem to have either:

- an *expressive function*: they communicate internal states (such as pleasure and surprise) to others; or
- a *directive function*: the behaviour of others is directed (by, for example, requesting or obtaining and directing attention).

The one-word stage is also characterised by the use of *holophrases*. In holophrastic speech, a single word (such as 'milk') is used to convey a much more complex message (such as 'I want some more milk' or 'I have spilt my milk'). Because holophrases are accompanied by gestures and tone of voice to add full meaning to an individual word, they may be seen as precursors of later, more complex sentences (Greenfield & Smith, 1976). They represent 'two-word meanings' (word plus gesture) before two words are actually used together in speech (Bates *et al.*, 1987). But they depend on the recipient of the holophrase making the 'correct' interpretation.

Nelson (1973) identified six categories of words, and calculated the percentage of children's first 50 words (typically acquired by 19 to 20 months) that fell into each category (see Table 19.1, page 281).

Nelson argued that it's not just the amount of exposure to objects and words that's important in word acquisition. Rather, given that specific and general nominals and action words make up the vast majority of those produced (78 per cent), it's the child's *active involvement* with its environment that determines many of its first words.

Children understand more words than they can produce. For example, a child who uses 'bow-wow' to refer to all small animals will nonetheless pick a picture of a dog, rather than any other animal, when asked to select a 'bow-wow' (Gruendel, 1977). The child's *receptive vocabulary* (the words it can understand) is therefore much bigger than its *expressive vocabulary* (the words it uses in speech).

Even before age two, children begin acquiring words at the rate of about 20 per day (Miller, 1978). While some of these are context-bound, they gradually become *decontextualised* as the one-word stage progresses. Other words are used from the start in a decontextualised way (Barrett, 1989). As the one-

Table 19.1 *Nelson's six categories and the percentage of children's first 50 words falling into each of them*

1	**Specific nominals:**	names for unique objects, people or animals (14 per cent)
2	**General nominals:**	names for classes of objects, people or animals, e.g. 'ball', 'car', 'milk', 'doggie', 'girl', 'he', 'that' (51 per cent)
3	**Action words:**	describe or accompany actions or express or demand attention, e.g. 'bye-bye', 'up', 'look', 'hi' (13 per cent)
4	**Modifiers:**	refer to properties or qualities of things, e.g. 'big', 'red', 'pretty', 'hot', 'all gone', 'there', 'mine' (9 per cent)
5	**Personal–social words:**	say something about a child's feelings or social relationships, e.g. 'ouch', 'please', 'no', 'yes', 'want' (8 per cent)
6	**Function words:**	have only a grammatical function, e.g. 'what', 'is', 'to', 'for' (4 per cent)

word stage progresses, so the child becomes able to ask and answer questions, and provide comments on people and objects in the immediate environment. These abilities enable the child to participate in very simple conversations with other people.

Stage of two-word sentences

Like the one-word stage, this stage is universal (although individual differences become more marked) and, like the transition from babbling to the one-word stage, the transition to the two-word stage is also gradual (Slobin, 1979). As well as continued vocabulary development, the understanding of grammar grows, and Brown (1973) divides this stage into stage 1 and stage 2 grammar.

Stage 1 grammar (18–30 months)

Here, the child's speech is essentially *telegraphic* (Brown, 1973); that is, only those words which convey the most information (*contentives*) are used. Purely grammatical terms (*functors*), such as the verb 'to be', plurals and possessives, are left out. For example, children will say 'There cow' to convey the underlying message 'There is a cow'. It seems that irrespective of culture, children express basic facts about their environment (Brown, 1973).

Telegraphic speech has a *rigid word order*, which seems to preserve a sentence's meaning. For example, if asked 'Does John want some milk?', the child might reply 'John milk' (or, later on, 'John want milk'). Adult speech, by contrast, doesn't rely exclusively on word order to preserve meaning, as in the passive form of a sentence. So, 'John drank the milk' and 'The milk was drunk by John' both convey the same meaning, even though the word order is different.

Children's imitations of adult sentences are also simple and retain the original sentence's word order. For example, 'John is playing with the dog' is imitated as 'Play dog' (*imitation by reduction*: Brown, 1965). Complementary to this is *imitation with expansion*, in which the adult imitates the child's utter-

ances by inserting the 'missing' functors. The rigid order of the child's utterances makes it easier to interpret their meaning, but gestures and context still provide important clues (as with the one-word stage).

Ask yourself ...

- How would you adapt your speech when talking to a young child compared with how you talk to other adults?

Box 19.3 Motherese

Compared with talking to one another, adults talking to children tend to use much shorter sentences and simpler syntax, raise the pitch of their voices for emphasis, and repeat or paraphrase much of what the child says. This *motherese* (or infant-directed speech) helps to achieve a mutual understanding with children who haven't yet mastered the full complexity of language. Sensitivity to the child's vocabulary and its intellectual and social knowledge is an example of a *pragmatic rule* for ensuring a degree of shared understanding (Greene, 1990). It also supports a *social interaction* approach to language acquisition (see pages 286–287).

Children's two-word utterances aren't just random word combinations, but are based on rules. They focus on certain types of words, and put them together in particular orders. However, not all children seem to use exactly the same rules (Braine, 1976), and children convey many different *meanings* with exactly the same sentence forms.

For example, young children often use a sentence composed of two nouns, such as 'Mommy sock' or 'sweater chair' (Bloom, 1973). We might conclude from this that a 'two-noun' form is a basic grammatical characteristic of early language – but this would miss its complexity (Bee, 1989). For example, the child in Bloom's study said 'Mommy sock' when she picked up her mother's sock, and again when the Mother put the child's own sock on the child's foot. In the first case 'Mommy sock' seems to mean 'Mommy's sock' (a *possessive*

Table 19.2 *Some of the different meanings children appear to express in Stage 1 Grammar (Maratsos, 1983)*

Meaning	Examples
agent–action	Sarah eat; Daddy jump
action–object	eat cookie; read book
possessor–possessed object	Mommy sock; Timothy lunch
action–location	come here, play outside
located object–location	sweater chair; juice table
attribute–modified object	big book; red house
nomination	that cookie; it dog
recurrence	more juice; other book

relationship), while in the second instance, it conveys 'Mommy's putting the sock on me' (an *agent–object* relationship).

> #### Box 19.4 Cromer's (1974) cognition hypothesis
>
> Word order in two-word utterances seems to reflect the child's prelinguistic knowledge. According to Cromer's *cognition hypothesis*, language structures can be used correctly only when permitted by our cognitive structures. Children form schemata to understand the world and then talk about it. A good example is *object permanence*, which is a prerequisite for understanding that words can represent things. If a child didn't already understand the relationships between objects, people and events in the real world, its first words would be like random unconnected lists. These are important concepts in Piaget's developmental theory (see Chapter 34), and are consistent with his view of language development reflecting the child's stage of cognitive development (see Chapter 18, page 274).

Stage 2 grammar (from about 30 months)

This lasts until around age four or five, and while it may be different for different languages, the rule-governed nature of language development is universal. The child's vocabulary grows rapidly, and sentences become longer and more complex. *Mean length of utterance* (MLU) is the number of words in a sentence divided by the total number of sentences produced. So, a child who produced 100 sentences with 300 words would have a MLU of 3.00.

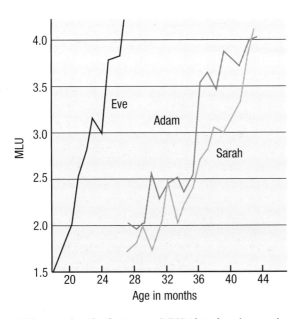

Figure 19.2 *Mean length of utterance (MLU) plotted against age in months for three children (based on Brown, 1973)*

The increase in MLU shown in Figure 19.2 is due largely to the inclusion of the functors that are omitted from the telegraphic speech of stage 1 grammar. For example, 'Daddy hat' may become 'Daddy wear hat' and finally 'Daddy is wearing a hat'. Sentences also become longer because conjunctions (such as 'and' and 'so') are used to form compound sentences

like 'You play with the doll and I play with the ball'. Stage 2 grammar, then, really begins with the first use of purely grammatical words. While most children up to 20 months still use one- or two-word sentences, by 24 months the longest sentences include four to five words. By 30 months, this has risen to between eight and ten. This is strongly linked to vocabulary development (Fenson *et al.*, 1994).

Brown (1973) has found a distinct regularity among English-speaking children in terms of the order in the addition of grammatical complexities. Similarly, de Villiers & de Villiers (1979) have found that, irrespective of culture, children acquire functional words in the same general order but at different rates. Each function word corresponds to a syntactic rule. Several studies show that when children begin to apply these rules (such as the rule for forming plurals), they're not just imitating other people.

KEY STUDY 19.1

Wugs rule OK (Berko, 1958)

Berko showed children a picture of a fictitious creature called a wug and told them 'This is a wug'.

This is a wug

They were then shown a second picture in which there were two of the creatures and told 'Now there is another one. There are two of them'.

Now there is another one.
There are two of them.
There are two ——

The children were asked to complete the sentence 'There are two ...'. Three- and four-year-olds answered 'wugs' despite never having seen a 'wug' before. Although the children couldn't have been imitating anybody else's speech, and hadn't been told about the rule for forming plurals, they were able to apply this rule. Significantly, they weren't consciously aware of having acquired the rule for forming a plural, and couldn't say what the rule was.

Ask yourself ...

• Can you think of any other examples of grammatical rules that children of this age display (including their speech errors)?

The rule-governed nature of language is also shown in children's grammatical mistakes. For example, while the rule 'add an "s" to a word to form a plural' usually works, there are exceptions to it (such as 'sheep' rather than 'sheeps' and 'geese' rather than 'gooses'). Similarly, the rule 'add "ed" to form the past tense' usually works, but not in the case of 'cost' and 'go'. The observation that children use words like 'costed' and 'goed', without ever having heard others use them, suggests that they're applying a rule rather than just imitating. But the rule is being *overgeneralised* or the language *over-regularised*.

By age four or five, basic grammatical rules have been acquired, but a typical five-year-old will have difficulty understanding passive sentences. There are also many irregular words still to be learned, and this aspect of grammatical development will take several more years.

By age 13, most English-speaking children have a vocabulary of 20,000 words, and by age 20, this will have risen to 50,000 or more (Aitchison, 1996). This vocabulary is acquired at an average rate of ten words per day (Pinker, 1994).

Theories of language development

Learning theory: operant conditioning

According to Skinner (1985):

> 'Verbal behaviour evidently came into existence when, through a critical step in the evolution of the human species, the vocal musculature became susceptible to operant conditioning'.

Ask yourself ...

- Given what you know about operant conditioning (see Chapter 11), how do you think Skinner might have tried to explain language development?

Skinner (1957) first applied operant conditioning principles to explain language development when he argued that:

> 'A child acquires verbal behaviour when relatively unplanned vocalisations, selectively reinforced, assume forms which produce appropriate consequences in a given verbal community'.

While Skinner accepted that prelinguistic vocalisations, such as cooing and babbling were probably inborn (see page x), he argued that adults *shape* the baby's sounds into words by *reinforcing* those which approximate the form of real words. Through selective reinforcement, words are shaped into sentences with correct grammar being reinforced and incorrect grammar ignored.

One form of positive reinforcement is the child getting what it asks for (*mands*). For example, 'May I have some water?' produces a drink that reinforces that form of words. Reinforcement may also be given by parents becoming excited and poking, touching, patting and feeding children when they vocalise. The mother's delight on hearing her child's first real word is exciting for the child, and so acquiring language becomes reinforcing in itself.

Skinner also believed that *imitation* (emitting *echoic responses*) plays an important role. When children imitate verbal labels

(*tacts*), they receive immediate reinforcement in the form of parental approval to the extent that the imitations resemble correct words. As children continue to learn new words and phrases through imitation, so their language becomes progressively more like that of adults (Moerk & Moerk, 1979).

Ask yourself ...

- How easily can operant conditioning explain the stages of language development described on pages 279–282?

An evaluation of Skinner's theory

- While imitation must be involved in the learning of accent and vocabulary, its role in complex aspects of language (syntax and semantics) is less obvious. As we saw earlier, when children do imitate adult sentences, they tend to convert them to their own currently operating grammar. So, between 18 and 30 months, the child's imitations are as telegraphic as its own spontaneous speech. However, a child is more likely to imitate a correct grammatical form after an adult has *recast* the child's own sentences than when the adult uses the same grammatical form spontaneously in normal conversation (Farrar, 1992; Nelson, 1977). Recasting, though, is relatively rare (or sometimes non-existent) in normal toddler–parent conversations, yet children still acquire a complex grammar (Bee, 2000). Furthermore, since at least some adult language is ungrammatical, imitation alone can't explain how children ever learn 'correct language'. Even if we don't always speak grammatically correctly ourselves, we still know the difference between good and bad grammar.

- In response to these criticisms, Bandura (1977a) has broadened the concept of imitation. Although the exact imitation of particular sentences plays a relatively minor role in language development, Bandura argues that children may imitate the *general form* of sentences, and fill in these general forms with various words. *Deferred imitations* are those word sequences and language structures stored in a child's memory for long periods before being used (often in the same situation in which they were first heard). *Expanded imitations* are repetitions of sentences or phrases not present in the original form (Snow, 1983). Children's language production sometimes exceeds their competence in that they imitate forms of language they don't understand. By storing examples of adult language in memory, children have a sort of 'delayed replay' facility that enables them to produce language forms after they've been acquired (see Chapter 35, pages 516–517).

- Operant conditioning can't explain the *creativity of language*, that is, native speakers' ability to produce and understand an infinitely large number of sentences never heard or produced before by anyone. As Chomsky (1968) states:

> 'The normal use of language is innovative, in the sense that much of what we say in the course of normal language use is entirely new [and] not a repetition of anything that we have heard before'.

- Operant conditioning cannot explain children's spontaneous use of grammatical rules which they've never heard or been taught. These rules are often overgeneralised and incorrectly used, and children are largely impervious to parental attempts to correct grammatical errors (see Box 19.5).

- Operant conditioning can't account for children's ability to understand sentence as opposed to word meaning. A sentence's meaning is not simply the sum of the meanings of the individual words. The structure of language is comparable to the structure of perception as described by the Gestalt psychologists (Neisser, 1967: see Chapter 15).
- Brodbeck & Irwin (1946) found that, compared with institutionalised children who received less attention, children whose parents reinforced their early attempts at meaningful sounds tended to vocalise more. Parents often reinforce children when they imitate adult language, and using *behaviour modification*, Lovaas (1987) has shown that selective reinforcement can be used successfully to teach language to emotionally disturbed or developmentally delayed children (see Chapter 45). However, Skinner's views have been challenged by a number of researchers.

Box 19.5 Does selective reinforcement have any influence on children's grammar?

- Mothers respond to the 'truth value', or presumed meaning of their children's language, rather than to its grammatical correctness or complexity. Mothers extract meaning from, and interpret, their children's incomplete and sometimes primitive sentences (Brown *et al.*, 1969).
- Tizard *et al.* (1972) argue that attempts to correct grammatical mistakes or teach grammar have very little effect. Indeed, vocabulary develops more slowly in children of mothers who systematically correct poor word pronunciation and reward good pronunciation (Nelson, 1973).
- Slobin (1975) found that children learn grammatical rules *despite* their parents, who usually pay little attention to the grammatical structure of their children's speech and often reinforce *incorrect* grammar. According to Slobin:

  'A mother is too engaged in interacting with her child to pay attention to the linguistic form of [its] utterances'.

These findings suggest that while parents usually respond to (or reinforce) true statements and criticise or correct false ones, they pay little regard to grammatical correctness. Even if they do, this has little effect on language development.

Noam Chomsky

Chomsky's LAD and the biological approach

Although language can't develop without some form of environmental input, Chomsky (1957, 1965, 1968), Lenneberg (1967) and McNeill (1970) believe that environmental factors could never explain language development adequately. Chomsky proposed the existence of an innate *language acquisition device* (LAD), whereby children are born already programmed to formulate and understand all types of sentences even though they've never heard them before.

Chomsky (1957) argued that language is much more complex and much less predictable than Skinner believed. Central to his theory of *transformational grammar* (TG) are *phrase-structure rules*, which specify what are acceptable/unacceptable utterances in a speaker's native language. When applied systematically, these rules generate sentences in English (or any other language).

Rule (1) An S (sentence) consists of (or can be broken down into) NP (noun phrase) and VP (verb phrase)

Rule (2)　NP ⟶ Article + (Adjective) + Noun

(The brackets denote 'optional')

Rule (3)　VP ⟶ Verb + NP

Rule (4)　Article ⟶ a(n), the ⎫ These are *lexical rewrite rules*.

Rule (5)　Adjective ⟶ big, small, red, etc. ⎬ The commas imply that only *one* word should be selected from the list

Rule (6)　Noun ⟶ boy, girl, stone, etc.

Rule (7)　Verb ⟶ hit, threw, helped, etc. ⎭

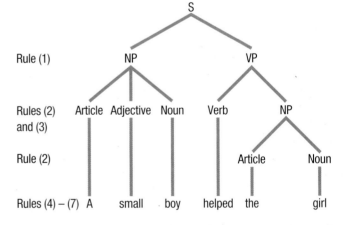

Figure 19.3 *Some of Chomsky's phrase-structure rules and an example of a sentence produced by using them*

While phrase-structure rules specify some important aspects of language, they don't specify them all (Chomsky, 1957).

Box 19.6 Deep and surface structure, and TG

A sentence's *surface structure* refers to the actual words or phrases used in the sentence (its *syntactical* structure), while its *deep structure* more or less corresponds to the *meaning*. Chomsky argued that when we hear a spoken sentence, we don't 'process' or retain its surface structure, but transform it into its deep structure. *Transformational grammar* (TG) is knowing how to transform a sentence's meaning into the words that make it up (and vice versa). This knowledge is an innate LAD, and is what enables us to produce an infinite number of meaningful sentences.

- A *single* surface structure may have *more than one* deep structure, as in the sentence 'The missionary was ready to eat'. This could be interpreted *either* as 'the missionary is ready to consume a meal' *or* 'the missionary has been prepared for consumption by others'.
- Conversely, *different* surface structures can have the *same* deep structure (as in the sentences 'A small boy helped the girl' and 'The girl was helped by a small boy').

Ask yourself ...

- Try a Chomsky-type analysis on the following:
  Cleaning ladies can be delightful;
  Shaving men can be dangerous.

For Chomsky, children are equipped with the ability to learn the rules for transforming deep structure into various surface structures. They do this by looking for certain kinds of linguistic features common to all languages, such as the use of consonants and vowels, syllables, modifiers and so on. Collectively, these linguistic features (*linguistic universals*) provide the deep structure. They must be universal, because all children can learn with equal ease any language to which they're exposed. So, a child born in England of English parents who went to live in China soon after its birth would learn Chinese, if brought up by a Chinese-speaking family, just as easily as a native-born Chinese child. Chomsky argues that only some kind of LAD can account for children's learning and knowledge of grammatical rules in view of the often ungrammatical and incomplete samples of speech they hear.

Chomsky didn't suggest that we go through the procedures of phrase structure and TG each time we prepare to speak a sentence (Hampson & Morris, 1996). A language's grammar is an idealised description of the *linguistic competence* of its native speakers. Any model of how this competence is applied in actual performance must acknowledge certain psychologically relevant factors such as memory, attention, the workings of the nervous system and so on (Lyons, 1970).

Box 19.7   Some evidence supporting Chomsky's theory

- The human vocal organs, breathing apparatus, auditory system and brain are all specialised for spoken communication.
- Babies as young as two days old can discriminate between 'ba' and 'pa' sounds (Eimas, 1975). According to Chomsky, these phonetic discriminations can be thought of as the first linguistic universals the baby discovers.
- All adult languages appear to have certain linguistic universals. TG is acquired in some form by all people (unless brain damaged or reared in isolation), irrespective of their culture and general intelli-

gence. For Lenneberg (1967), this shows that language acquisition must be controlled by genetic factors that are (at least partially) independent of those controlling general intelligence.

- Studies of congenitally deaf children have shown the emergence of 'gestural language', even though the children received no encouragement or training from their parents (Gerrard, 1997; Goldin-Meadow & Feldman, 1977). These languages have the characteristics of ordinary languages (such as verbs, nouns and syntax), supporting the view that knowledge of syntax is innate. These findings also demonstrate that language is very difficult to suppress even in adverse environmental circumstances. As Bee (2000) says:

  'The baby is somehow primed to learn 'language' in some form, be it spoken or gestural'.

Lenneberg has argued that the years leading to puberty constitute a *critical period* for language development, based on the still-developing brain's relative lack of specialisation. Children born brain-damaged or who lose their language abilities can relearn at least some of them because other, non-damaged, parts of the brain seem to take over. But adolescents or adults who experience an equivalent amount of damage are unable to regain abilities corresponding to the site of the injury, because the brain is now specialised (or 'committed') and no longer 'plastic' (see Chapter 4, page 58). But the first ten years or so may *not* necessarily be the critical period Lenneberg has argued for.

CASE STUDY 19.1

Genie (Curtiss, 1977)

Genie was an American child raised in conditions of extreme (de)privation until her discovery at the age of 13 years and seven months. Amongst other appalling treatment, Genie was beaten if she made any noise, and had learned to suppress almost all vocalisations except for a whimper. According to Curtiss, 'Genie was unsocialised, primitive, hardly human'.

Genie could understand a handful of words (including 'rattle', 'bunny' and 'red'), but always responded to them in the same way. Essentially, then, she had to learn language at the age of nearly 14. She never developed normal language skills, and by age 18 could produce only short sentences which lacked important aspects of grammar (such as the use of pronouns).

Her vocabulary expanded and she could hold a conversation, but her use of intonation was poor and only those who knew her well could understand much of what she said. Genie herself had great difficulty in understanding complex syntax. Nonetheless, the fact that she was capable of learning any language at all weakens Lenneberg's claim for a critical period. However, her obvious linguistic retardation is consistent with the existence of a *sensitive period* for language development.

An evaluation of Chomsky's theory

Aitchison (1983) agrees with Chomsky's claim that children are 'wired' with the knowledge that language is rule-governed, and that they make a succession of hypotheses about the rules underlying speech. However, she disputes the claim that the LAD also consists of TG (what she calls 'Content Cuthbert'). Aitchison prefers a *process* approach, in which children are seen as having inbuilt puzzle-solving equipment that enables them to process linguistic data along with other sorts of data ('Process Peggy').

By contrast, Chomsky (1979) argues that an innate language ability exists *independently* of other innate abilities, because the mind is constructed of 'mental organs' which are:

'... just as specialised and differentiated as those of the body ... and ... language is a system easy to isolate among the various mental faculties'.

According to Chapman (2000), belief in some kind of LAD has persisted despite evidence that language structure is acquired piecemeal, occurs over a period of many years, and that there are wide variations in how quickly children acquire language. Also, language input to young children is well-formed, responsive to the child's communicative attempts, well-adapted to the child's current focus of attention and understanding. This suggests that language development needs to be understood within the context of the child's social interactions, rather than by focusing almost exclusively on what the child possesses in the form of a LAD.

Some alternatives to learning theory and biological approaches

Recently, there has been a growing acceptance that neither operant conditioning nor nativist approaches offers a complete account of language development. Instead, an *integrated* view maintains that children can't acquire language until an appropriate maturational level has been reached, but that language development is more closely related to environmental input and cognitive development than Chomsky proposes. Maratsos (1983) has identified several assumptions made by integrative theorists.

> **Box 19.8 Some assumptions made by integrative theorists**
>
> - Children are highly motivated to communicate, and therefore are *active* language learners.
> - Children can learn the major aspects of grammar because they've already acquired important concepts on which grammar is based (namely that events involve agents, actions, objects of actions, and so on). For this reason, learning a grammar doesn't require much information-processing.
> - Other aspects of language can be explained by the language parents use to talk to children.
> - Those grammatical rules that don't fit in with children's natural cognitive processes, and aren't conveyed adequately through parental input, are unnatural and difficult for the child. They're also acquired very late (such as the passive voice in English).

> **Ask yourself ...**
>
> - What aspects of the interaction between a baby and its caregiver might be important for the baby's future language development? Think of this from the perspective of *both* partners.

The language and social-interaction approach

One alternative explanation to Chomsky's of the rule-bound nature of children's speech, is that it arises from the child's prelinguistic knowledge. During the 1970s, psychologists began to look at language development in the first 12 to 18 months of life, because the basic skills acquired then contribute substantially to the syntactic skills characteristic of adult language.

A purely syntactic analysis of language can't explain how children 'discover' their language; that is, how they learn that there's such a thing as language which can be used for communicating, categorising, problem-solving and so on. However, Smith *et al.*'s (1998) *language and social-interaction approach* sees language as being used to communicate needs and intentions, and as an enjoyable means of entering into a community.

Several studies have indicated how babies initially master a social world onto which they later 'map' language. Snow (1977), for example, notes that adults tend to attach meaning to a baby's sounds and utterances. As a result, burps, grunts, giggles and so on are interpreted as expressions of intent and feeling, as are non-verbal communications (such as smiling and eye contact). Snow sees this as a kind of primitive conversation (or *proto-conversation*). This has a rather one-sided quality, in that it requires a 'generous' adult attributing some kind of intended meaning to the baby's sounds and non-verbal behaviours. From this perspective, the infant is an inadequate conversational partner.

> **Box 19.9 Visual co-orientation and formats: two-way interaction**
>
> *Visual co-orientation* (or joint attention) and *formats* (Collis & Schaffer, 1975) are exchanges that are far more two-way. Visual co-orientation involves two individuals coming to focus on some common object. This puts an infant's environmental explorations into a social context, so that an infant–object situation is converted into an infant–object–mother situation (Schaffer, 1989). This entails joint attention, which provides opportunities for learning how to do things. So, as parents and children develop their mutual patterns of interaction and share attention to objects, some activities recur, as happens, for instance, in joint picture-book reading.
>
> Bruner (1975, 1978) uses Collis and Schaffer's term 'formats' to refer to rule-bound activity routines, in which the infant has many opportunities to relate language to familiar play (as when the mother inserts name labels into a game or activity), initially in *indicating* formats and later in *requesting* them. These ritualised exchanges stress the need for *turn-taking*, and so help the baby to discover the social

function of communication. As a result, the infant can learn about the structures and demands of social interaction, and prepare and rehearse the skills that will eventually become essential to successful interchanges such as conversation.

LASS: the active adult

According to Bruner (1983), formats comprise the *language acquisition support system* (LASS). He's concerned with the pragmatics and functions of language (what language is *for*). In Bruner's view:

'Entry into language is entry into discourse that requires both members of a dialogue pair to interpret a communication and its intent. Learning a language … consists of learning not only the grammar of a particular language, but also learning how to realise one's intentions by the appropriate use of that grammar'.

The emphasis on intent requires a far more active role on the adult's part in helping a child's language acquisition than just being a 'model', or providing the input for the child's LAD. According to Moerk (1989), 'the LAD was a lady', that is, the lady who does most of the talking to the child (namely its mother). Mothers simplify linguistic input and break it down into helpful, illustrative segments for the child to practise and build on. This view sees language development as a very sophisticated extension of the processes of meaningful interaction that the caregiver and child have constructed over several months (Durkin, 1995).

The active child

Another way of looking at the 'partnership' is to see the *infant* as being the more 'active' partner. The view of language as a *cause–effect analytic device* has been summarised by Gauker (1990), for whom:

'The fundamental function of words is to bring about changes in the speaker's environment … Linguistic understanding consists of a grasp of these causal relations'.

Box 19.10 The emergence of communicative intentionality

According to Gauker (1990), language comprises a set of symbols whose use results in a change of behaviour in the listener. The use of words as communicative tools is shown in the *emergence of communicative intentionality*. During the prelinguistic stage, children have no awareness that they can gain a desired effect indirectly by changing somebody else's behaviour. So, they may cry and reach for something, but not direct the cry towards the caregiver or look back at the caregiver. The cry merely expresses frustration, and isn't a communicative signal designed to affect the other's behaviour. This 'analysis' of means–ends relationships (what causes what) solely as a product of one's *own* actions, is called *first-order causality*.

The emergence of communicative intentionality involves *second-order causality*, the awareness that it's possible to bring about a desired goal by using *another person* as a tool. Pointing gestures and glances

now rapidly increase as a means of asking others to look at or act upon an object. According to Savage-Rumbaugh (1990), the child is beginning to understand in a general sense:

'… that it is possible to 'cause' others to engage in desired actions through the mechanism of communication about those actions'.

This use of animate tools (other people) parallels the use of inanimate tools (physical objects), which is an important feature of *sensorimotor intelligence* (Piaget, 1952: see Chapter 34). Some kind of *instrumental understanding* (what leads to what) seems to underlie both activities.

However, it's more difficult to analyse language *comprehension* than *language production* in terms of a cause–effect analysis: what do we cause to happen when we understand things that have been said to us? Based on her work with chimpanzees, Savage-Rumbaugh (1990) concludes that language comprehension is clearly the driving force underlying the language acquisition process, and that under normal circumstances, language production is just one outcome of the development of language comprehension (see below, pages 289–291).

Teaching language to non-human animals

As we've seen, Chomsky believes that language is unique to human beings. Similarly, Lenneberg claims that it represents a *species-specific behaviour*, common to all humans and found only in humans. But if non-humans can be taught to use language, then they must have the capacity for language. The obvious subjects for such language training are our closest evolutionary relatives, chimpanzees and gorillas (the non-human primates).

Criteria for language

We need to define language in a way that will enable us to evaluate the results of studies where humans have tried to teach it to speechless non-humans. Hockett (1960) proposed 13 'design features' of language (see Figure 19.4, page 288). Based on these, Aitchison (1983) proposed that ten criteria should be sufficient (not all of these are included in Hockett's list). These are shown in Table 19.3.

By analysing human and non-human animal language in terms of all ten criteria, Aitchison concludes that four are unique to humans. These are highlighted in Table 19.3 (page 288). It's in terms of these criteria that attempts to teach language to non-human primates have been evaluated.

Early studies

Early attempts to teach chimpanzees to speak were almost totally unsuccessful. Kellogg & Kellogg (1933) raised Gua with their own child and treated them exactly alike. Although she could understand a total of 70 words or commands, Gua failed to utter a single word. Hayes & Hayes (1951) used operant conditioning in what was the first deliberate attempt to teach human language to a non-human – Viki, a baby chimp.

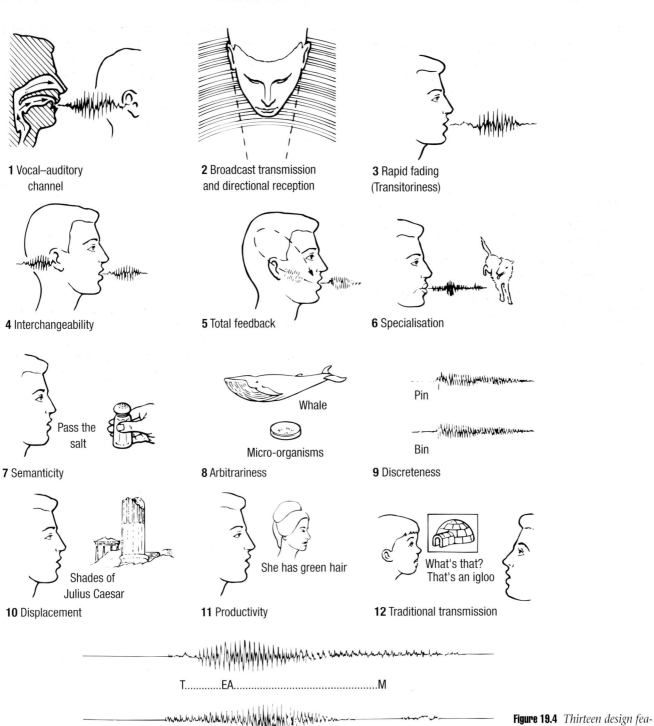

1 Vocal–auditory channel

2 Broadcast transmission and directional reception

3 Rapid fading (Transitoriness)

4 Interchangeability

5 Total feedback

6 Specialisation

7 Semanticity — Pass the salt

8 Arbitrariness — Whale / Micro-organisms

9 Discreteness — Pin / Bin

10 Displacement — Shades of Julius Caesar

11 Productivity — She has green hair

12 Traditional transmission — What's that? That's an igloo

13 Duality of patterning — T.........EA.........................M — M.................EA........................T

Figure 19.4 *Thirteen design features of language (Hockett, 1960)*

Table 19.3 *Ten criteria for language (Aitchison, 1983, based on Hockett, 1960)*

1	Use of the vocal–auditory channel	**6**	Turn-taking (conversation is a two-way process)
2	Arbitrariness (use of neutral symbols – words – to denote objects, actions etc.)	**7**	Duality (organisation into basic sounds plus combinations/sequences of sounds)
3	**Semanticity** (use of symbols to mean or refer to objects, actions etc).	**8**	Displacement (reference to things not present in time or space)
4	Cultural transmission (handing down the language from generation to generation)	**9**	**Structure dependence** (the patterned nature of language/use of 'structured chunks', e.g. word order)
5	Spontaneous usage (freely initiating speech)	**10**	**Creativity** (what Brown calls *productivity*: the ability to produce/understand an infinite number of novel utterances – see page 278).

N.B. Items in bold are criteria unique to humans

By age three, she could say 'up' and 'cup' and (less convincingly) 'mama' and 'papa'. It became obvious that the vocal apparatus of a chimp is unsuited to making English speech sounds. However, this doesn't rule out the possibility that chimps may still be capable of learning language in some non-spoken form. This is precisely what several psychologists have tried to demonstrate since the 1960s in what have come to be called *production-based training* (see Gross, 1999; Gross *et al.*, 2000).

> **Ask yourself ...**
>
> - Why do we need to know if non-human primates are capable of language?
> - Has this research any potential practical implications for the subjects?
> - Does it have implications for how we see ourselves as a species?

Evaluating production-based studies

One way of evaluating the studies summarized in Table 19.4 (*production–based training*) is to ask whether the language of children and chimps is qualitatively different. As far as *semanticity* is concerned, is the correct use of signs to refer to things a sufficient criterion? Savage-Rumbaugh *et al.* (1980) seriously doubt whether any of the apes (including their own, Lana) used the individual elements of their vocabularies as *words*. Terrace (1987) argues that the deceptively simple ability to use a symbol as a name required a cognitive advance in the evolution of human intelligence at least as significant as the advances that led to grammatical competence.

The function of much of a child's initial vocabulary of names is to inform another person (usually an adult) that it has noticed something (MacNamara, 1980). A child often refers to the object spontaneously, showing obvious delight from the sheer act of naming. This *hasn't* been observed in apes. MacNamara believes that no amount of training could produce an ape with such an ability, for the simple reason that the act of referring isn't learnt but is a 'primitive of cognitive psychology' (and is a necessary precursor of naming). Instead, a chimp usually tries to 'acquire' an object (approach it, explore it, eat it), and shows no sign of trying to communicate the fact that it has noticed an object as an end in itself (Terrace, 1987). Several critics have claimed that the linguistic abilities of chimps amount to a wholly 'instrumental use' of symbols. Referring to Savage-Rumbaugh's work with Kanzi (see below), Seidenberg & Petitto (1987) claim that Kanzi 'may not know what the symbols mean' but only 'how to produce behaviours that others can interpret'. However, Gauker (1990) argues that:

> '... we might do well to view 'knowing what symbols mean' as nothing other than an understanding of more or less sophisticated instrumental uses of symbols... even in human beings linguistic understanding consists in a grasp of the causal relations into which linguistic signs may enter ... '.

This relates to what we said earlier about the 'emergence of communicative intentionality' (see Box 19.10).

Helping chimps be more like children

Since the 1980s, Savage-Rumbaugh, at the Yerkes Primate Centre and Georgia State University, has been working with chimps in a way which is much more like how children acquire language (and in certain respects more like that of the pioneers in this field, the Kelloggs' and the Hayes'). Instead of putting the chimps through rote learning of symbols, gradually building up a vocabulary a symbol at a time, Savage-Rumbaugh aimed to use a large vocabulary of symbols

Table 19.4 *The major studies which have attempted to teach language to non-human primates*

Study	Subject	Method of language training
Gardner & Gardner (1969)	Washoe (female chimp)	American sign language (ASL or Ameslan). Based on a series of gestures, each corresponding to a word. Many gestures visually represent aspects of the word's meaning
Premack (1971)	Sarah (female chimp)	Small plastic symbols of various shapes and colours, each symbol standing for a word; they could be arranged on a special magnetised board. e.g. a mauve △ = 'apple'; a pale blue ◇ = 'insert'; a red ▢ = 'banana'
Rumbaugh *et al.* (1977)/Savage-Rumbaugh *et al.* (1980)	Lana (female chimp)	Special typewriter controlled by a computer. Machine had 50 keys each displaying a geometric pattern representing a word in a specially devised language ('Yerkish'). When Lana typed, the pattern appeared on the screen in front of her ◇ 'Lana' ◉ 'Eat'
Patterson (1978, 1980)	Koko (female gorilla)	American sign language
Terrace (1979)	Nim Chimpsky (male chimp)	American sign language

Operant conditioning is used in all these studies when signs, etc. are correctly used.

from the start, using them as language is used around human children. This represents a move away from an emphasis on grammatical structure (at least in the beginning) and towards *comprehension*:

> *'It seemed reasonable to me – obvious even – that comprehension was an important element of language, that language is first acquired through comprehension, and that production flows from that'.* (Savage-Rumbaugh, quoted in Lewin, 1991)

This new approach was applied on a limited scale with Austin and Sherman, two common chimps. But it really got going with some pygmy chimps (*bonobos*), which are slightly smaller than common chimps, and more vocal and communicative through facial expressions and gestures. In 1981, work began with Matata, who six months earlier had kidnapped a newborn infant, Kanzi, and kept him as her own. Instead of ASL, Savage-Rumbaugh used an extensive 'lexigram', a matrix of 256 geometrical shapes on a board (see the photograph in the *Introduction and overview*). Instructors touch the symbols, which represent verbs and nouns, to create simple requests or commands. At the same time, the sentence is spoken, with the aim of testing comprehension of spoken English. When the chimpanzee presses a symbol, a synthesised voice from the computer 'speaks' the word.

Although clearly intelligent in many ways, Matata was a poor learner and used only about six symbols. However, despite no attempt to teach Kanzi anything, he'd picked up the symbols Matata knew, as naturally as human children do. From that point onwards, an even greater effort was made to place language learning in a naturalistic context. Kanzi acquired a sister, Mulika, when he was 2½ years old and they grew up together.

of comprehension when he was nine years old, but not when he was younger than six. He also showed understanding of the syntactic rule that in two-word utterances, action precedes object and, significantly, he went from a random ordering initially to a clear, consistent preference.

Now 20, Kanzi's grammatical comprehension has been officially assessed as exceeding that of a 2½-year-old child, and he understands about 2000 words. His 15-year-old sister, Panbanisha, has a vocabulary of at least 3000 words, and Nyota, Panbanisha's son, is learning faster than her mother and uncle. It seems that the researchers' expectations were higher for those who came after Kanzi (Cohen, 2000).

According to Savage-Rumbaugh (1990), production-based language training can be said to disrupt the 'normal course' of language acquisition in the ape:

> *'When the environment is structured in a way that makes it possible for the chimpanzee to acquire language much as does the normal child, by coming to understand what is said to it before it elects to produce utterances, the perspective of language acquisition and function that emerges is very different from that seen by Sherman and Austin'.*

Kanzi was the first to demonstrate that *observational exposure* is sufficient for the acquisition of lexical and vocal symbols. Three other chimps (two pygmy and one common) have also learned symbols without training (so Kanzi's ability is neither unique to him nor his species). According to Savage-Rumbaugh (1990), chimps learn where one word ends and the next begins, that is, what the units are, through the learning of *routines* which emerge out of daily life that has been constructed for the chimpanzees.

CASE STUDY 19.2

Kanzi

By age ten (1991), Kanzi had a vocabulary of some 200 words, but it isn't the size of his vocabulary that's impressive but what the words apparently mean to him. He was given *spoken* requests to do things, in sentence form, by someone out of his sight. Savage-Rumbaugh's assistants in the same room with Kanzi wore earphones, so they couldn't hear the instructions and thereby cue Kanzi, even unconsciously. None of the sentences was practised and each one was different. 'Can you put the raisins in the bowl?' and 'Can you give the cereal to Karen?' posed no problems for Kanzi. Nor did 'Can you go to the colony room and get the telephone?' (there were four or five objects in the colony room, which weren't normally there).

More testing still was the instruction 'Go to the colony room and get the orange' when there was an orange in front of Kanzi. This caused him confusion about 90 per cent of the time. But if asked to 'Get the orange that's in the colony room', he did so without hesitation, suggesting that the syntactically more complex phrase is producing better comprehension than the simple one (Savage-Rumbaugh, cited in Lewin, 1991). Kanzi showed this level

Lana being taught language through a form of production-based training

Box 19.11 A day in the life of a chimp exposed to language

A typical day is like a field-based preschool for apes. Food can be found throughout a 50-acre forest. They have time off for social play with different companions, interesting places to visit, plus time devoted to structured testing, during which the chimps are asked to sit quietly and apply themselves as fully as possible.

Caretakers' only instructions are to communicate with them much as one would with very young children, except that they must accompany their speech with pointing to lexical symbols. They talk about things which are concrete and immediate (such as where they're going, and what just happened to them), and clarify their intent with gestures and actions. 'Conversations' move from topic to topic with the natural flow of the day and routines include nappy changing, getting ready to go outside, bathing, riding in the car, looking at a book, blowing bubbles, putting things in the backpack, visiting other apes, playing games of tickle and travelling down various forest trails.

At first, a symbol is only understood within an established routine; later it will be understood and used beyond the routine itself. The driving force that moves the ape from symbol comprehension to symbol production is the desire to exert some control over what happens next (Savage-Rumbaugh, 1990).

Ask yourself ...

- Is it ethically acceptable to use chimps and other apes for this kind of research?
- Is it right that they're treated as if they were human when they're not? (see Chapter 48)

Is language uniquely human?

According to Aitchison (1983), the apparent ease with which children acquire language, compared with apes, supports the suggestion that they're innately programmed to do so. Similarly, although these chimps have grasped some of the rudiments of human language, what they've learned and the speed at which they learn it, is *qualitatively* different from those of human beings (Carroll, 1986).

Aitchison and Carroll seem to be talking for a majority of psychologists. However, the criticisms of ape studies and the conclusions that have been drawn from them are based on the production-based studies (as summarised in Table 19.4). Savage-Rumbaugh believes that there's only a *quantitative* difference (one of degree) between ape and human language. Responding to criticisms by Terrace that Kanzi still uses his symbols only in order to get things done, to ask for things, rather than to share his perception of the world, Savage-Rumbaugh observes that so do young children. In fact, the predominant symbol use of normal children is 'requesting'.

Kanzi's capacity for comprehension far outstrips his capacity for producing language using the lexigram. This makes him extremely frustrated, at which times he often becomes very vocal, making high-pitched squeaks. Is he trying to speak? If Kanzi were to talk, maybe the first thing he'd say is that he's fed up with Terrace claiming that apes don't have language (Lewin, 1991).

Conclusions

This chapter has described the course of language development. Many psychologists believe that there's a biologically determined 'timetable' for language development, while others emphasise the role of conditioning. Although the evidence suggests that biologically based accounts are probably closer to the truth, it's unlikely that they offer a complete account of language development. According to Bee (2000):

'The fact that children learn complex and varied use of their native tongue within a few years remains both miraculous and largely mysterious'.

For Chapman (2000):

'The study of child language development is at an exciting moment, one in which new advances in research methods and multiple theoretical perspectives – psychological, linguistic, social, cognitive, anthropological, neurobiological – are converging on a new understanding of how children learn to talk. The older debates of the importance of nature vs nurture in explanations of language acquisition are giving way to interactionist perspectives ...'.

As for language being unique to human beings, opinions are still divided. But what's indisputable is that attempts to teach language to non-human primates have raised some fundamental *ethical* issues. Wise, an American lawyer, argues that bonobos and other chimps deserve basic legal rights. He rejects the idea of human superiority (Cohen, 2000).

CHAPTER SUMMARY

- Language involves the acquistion of a rule system (**grammar/mental grammar**), which consists of **phonology**, **semantics** and **syntax**.
- During the **prelinguistic stage**, babies make various non-speech sounds including crying and cooing. But **babbling** involves the production of **phonemes**. **Phonemic expansion** is replaced at around nine/ten months by **phonemic contraction**.
- The child's first **words** are often invented and **context-bound**, denoting specific actions, events or objects. They serve less of a communicative function and more of a performative function.
- The full meaning of **holophrases** is provided by accompanying gestures and tones of voice. They can be thought of as precursors of later, more complex sentences.
- Language in **stage 1 grammar** is **telegraphic**, consisting of **contentives** but no **functors**, and involving a **rigid word order**. The child's **imitation by reduction** is complemented by the adult's **imitation with expansion**.
- Word order seems to reflect the child's prelinguistic knowledge, as claimed by Cromer's **cognition hypothesis**. Similarly, Piaget believes that language development reflects the child's stage of cognitive development.
- In **stage 2 grammar**, sentences become longer and more complex, as measured by the **mean length of utterance** (MLU). MLU increase is due largely to the inclusion of

functors missing from stage 1 telegraphic speech.

■ Each functor corresponds to a **syntactic rule**. The rule-governed nature of language is also illustrated in children's grammatical mistakes, which often involve the **overgeneralised/over-regularised** application of a rule.

■ According to Skinner, verbal behaviour is acquired through **operant conditioning**. Cooing and babbling are **shaped** by adults into words, and selective reinforcement shapes words into grammatically correct sentences.

■ Operant conditioning cannot explain the culturally universal and invariant sequence in the stages of language development. It also fails to explain the **creativity of language**.

■ According to Chomsky, children are innately equipped with a **language acquisition device** (LAD), which consists essentially of **transformational grammar** (TG). TG enables us to transform **surface** into **deep structure** and vice versa.

■ LAD is used to look for **linguistic universals**, which collectively provide the deep structure. Children can learn any language they're exposed to with equal ease.

■ According to **integrative theorists**, children are **active** learners of language whose learning of grammar is based on important concepts already acquired. The **language and social-interaction approach** emphasises children's **prelinguistic knowledge**.

■ The **emergence of communicative intentionality** parallels the use of physical tools, an important feature of Piaget's **sensorimotor intelligence**.

■ Early attempts to teach chimps to speak failed because their vocal apparatus is unsuited to making speech sounds. **Production-based training** studies have found that, compared with children, chimps show little spontaneous naming of objects, and they seem to use symbols in a purely **instrumental** way.

■ Since the 1980s, Savage-Rumbaugh has been using a **comprehension-based approach**, with Kanzi and other bonobos. This structures the environment in a way that allows the chimp to acquire language through **observational learning**, much like a child, by exposing it to language in the course of daily life routines.

■ Data from studies involving Kanzi, other bonobos and common chimps, suggest that there's only a **quantitative** difference between ape and human language. Rejection of the claim that chimps are capable of language has arisen from the earlier, production-based studies.

Self-assessment questions

1 Discuss **one** environmental and **one** nativist theory of language acquisition.
2 Critically consider psychological research into the process of language acquisition.
3 Critically assess the claim that language is a human species-specific behaviour.

Web addresses

http://www.cogsci.ac.uk/~harnad/Papers/Psy104/pinker.langacq.html

http://carla.acad.umn.edu

http://williamcalvin.com/1990s/1994SciAmer.htm

http://ww2.med.jhu.edu/peds/neonatology/poi3.html

Further reading

Barrett, M. (1989) 'Early language development.' In A. Slater and G. Bremner (Eds) *Infant Development*. Hillsdale, NJ: Erlbaum. An excellent review of the emergence of early vocabulary and syntactic rules.

Jackendoff, R. (1993) *Patterns in the Mind: Language and Human Nature*. Hemel Hempstead: Harvester Wheatsheaf. An extremely readable, yet informative and challenging introduction to psycholinguistics, which examines what language and language acquisition can tell us about the human mind and human nature.

Chapter 20

Problem-solving, Decision-making and Artificial Intelligence

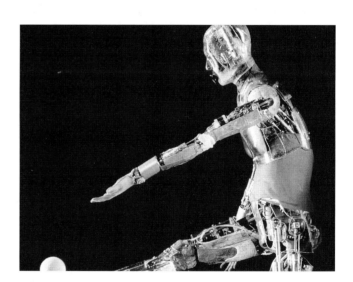

Introduction and overview

The basic cognitive processes we've considered in the previous chapters are all aspects of 'thought'. However, there's more to thinking than perception, attention and language. Two closely related aspects of thinking of interest to cognitive psychologists are *problem-solving* (PS) and *decision-making* (DM). DM is a special case of PS, in which we already know the possible solutions (or options). A problem can be defined as arising whenever a path to a desired goal is blocked.

In another sense, '... all thinking involves problem-solving, no matter how simple, immediate and effortless it may appear ...' (Boden, 1987a).

A good example of what Boden means is perception. As we noted in Chapter 15, the effortless and (usually) accurate nature of perception suggests that there's no problem-solving involved (no 'vision problem'). But that's not how psychologists – and other researchers – see it. For example, Marr (1982) considered that to understand vision, we must explain how useful information about a scene can be extracted from images of that scene. Specifically, we must define what computations must be performed.

Much of the work of computer simulation and artificial intelligence (AI) has been concerned with PS. If we can create computer programs that will solve 'human' problems, we might understand better how *we* solve them. This research is based on the argument that both computers and human problem-solvers are *information-processing machines* (Greene, 1987).

Although some research into human PS was being undertaken during the 1920s and 1930s, significantly, it was carried out in Germany and elsewhere in Europe, where the impact of American behaviourism was minimal. It wasn't until the mid-1950s that behaviourism's domination of American psychology gave way to cognitive psychology. The new information-processing approach to PS was quite different from early PS research, being largely inspired by computer scientists, including those working within AI.

The nature of problems

Stages in problem-solving (PS)

A problem is a situation in which there's a discrepancy between a present state and some goal state, with no obvious way of reducing it. PS is an attempt to reduce the discrepancy and achieve the goal state, and can be seen as progressing through a series of logical stages (Bourne *et al.*, 1979). These are:

- *defining or representing the problem*;
- *generating possible solutions*;
- *evaluating possible solutions*.

Some researchers have claimed that there's also an incubation stage (in which no attempt is made to solve the problem), which occurs between the generating and evaluating stages.

Classifying problems

Garnham (1988) distinguishes between two broad classes of problem, *adversary* and *non-adversary*.

Adversary problems

Adversary problems involve two or more people pitting their wits against each other, as in chess. Garnham says that game-playing is a special kind of PS, in which the problem is to find a winning strategy or the best current move. The focus of AI research here has been on two-player games, in which each player always has complete information about the state of play, and in which there's no element of chance. Apart from chess, games used include noughts and crosses (tic-tac-toe) and draughts (checkers).

Non-adversary problems

Most problems fall into the non-adversary category, in which another person is only involved as the problem setter. Some of the most commonly used include:

- **The eight-puzzle**: A three by three matrix containing the numbers one to eight, with one vacant square, must be moved until the numbers are in order.

5	4	8
7	2	6
3		1

Figure 20.1 *The eight-puzzle*

- **The missionaries and cannibals (or 'hobbits and orcs') problem**: The three missionaries and three cannibals must be transported across the river in a single boat, which can hold only two people but needs at least one to get it across the river. The cannibals must never outnumber the missionaries on either bank (or they'll be eaten).

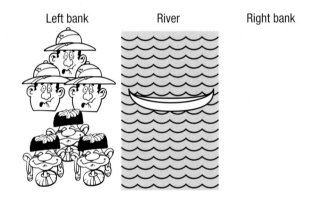

Left bank River Right bank

Figure 20.2 *The missionaries and cannibals problem*

- **The Tower of Hanoi problem**: There are three vertical pegs with four (or more) discs of increasing size stacked on one peg. The problem is to transfer the discs to the second peg, moving only one at a time and never placing a larger disc on top of a smaller one.

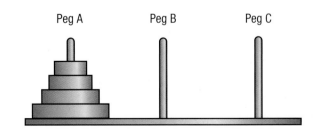

Peg A Peg B Peg C

Figure 20.3 *The Tower of Hanoi problem*

■ **Cryptarithmetic** (Bartlett, 1958): Given that D = 5 and each letter stands for a digit (0-9), find the digits which make the sum correct.

$$
\begin{array}{r}
\text{GERALD} \\
+ \text{DONALD} \\
\hline
\text{ROBERT}
\end{array}
$$

> *Ask yourself ...*
> • Have a go at solving these puzzles, trying to monitor the *strategies* you adopt as you do so.

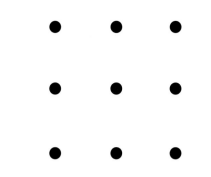

Figure 20.4 *Scheerer's nine-dot problem*

Explaining PS

Behaviourist accounts

According to behaviourists, PS is essentially a matter of *trial-and-error* and *accidental success* (Thorndike, 1911: see Chapter 11). Behaviourists argued that as acquired habits are learned, so PS (essentially a chain of stimulus–response associations) improves. While trial-and-error can be effective in solving some problems, the behaviourist approach was challenged by Gestalt psychologists. The Gestalt approach to PS looked at how we impose structure on problems by understanding how their elements are related to each another. Thus, rather than being 'senseless drill and arbitrary associations' (Katona's, 1940, criticism of the behaviourist approach), PS occurs through the perceptual restructuring of the problem, resulting in *insight* (see Chapter 15).

The Gestalt approach

Functional fixedness

Functional fixedness (or 'fixity') is a type of mental set (see below) in which we fail to see that an object may have functions (or uses) other than its normal ones. Duncker (1926, 1945) gave participants a candle and a box of drawing pins, and instructed them to attach the candle to a wall over a table so that it would stay upright and not drip onto the table underneath. Most tried to tack the candle directly to the wall, or glue it by melting it. Few thought of using the inside of the tack-box as a candle-holder and tacking that to the wall. Participants were 'fixated' on the box's normal function and they needed to reconceptualise it (to use *lateral thinking*: de Bono, 1967). Their past experience was leading them *away* from the solution. When people are shown an empty box and the drawing pins are scattered on a table, the box is much more likely to be used as a candle-holder (Glucksberg & Weisberg, 1966).

Similar is Scheerer's (1963) *nine-dot problem* (see Figure 20.4). The problem is to draw four continuous straight lines, connecting all the dots, without lifting the pencil from the paper. Most people fail, because they assume that the lines must stay within the square formed by the dots – they 'fixate' on the shape of the dots. (The solution can be found on page 307.)

Mental set

Mental (or problem-solving) set is a form of functional fixedness, in which we tend to continue using a previously successful strategy to solve new problems, even when more efficient strategies exist. Luchins (1942) and Luchins & Luchins (1959) asked people to imagine they had three different containers, each of a different size. The task was to use the containers to obtain a specific volume of liquid. Once this problem had been solved, the task was repeated, but participants had to imagine a different set of three containers.

Table 20.1 *The water container problems used by Luchins & Luchins (1959)*

Problem no.	Containers with capacity in fluid ounces			Obtain exactly these amounts of water
	Container A	Container B	Container C	
1	21	127	3	100
2	14	163	25	99
3	18	43	10	5
4	9	42	6	21
5	20	59	4	31
6	23	49	3	20
7	10	36	7	3

Problems 1–5 can be solved using the formula B–2C–A (that is, fill container B, pour its contents into container C twice, and then pour what remains in container B into container A to leave the desired amount in container B). While problem 6 can also be solved using this formula, there's a more direct solution, namely A–C. Problem 7 cannot be solved using the formula B–2C–A, but can be solved using the formula A–C.

Once people discovered a solution to the first problem, they continued to use it even when (in the case of problem 6) it was less efficient, or (in the case of problem 7) it didn't apply. In Gestalt terms, mental set produces *reproductive thinking*, when in fact a problem calls for *productive thinking* (Maier, 1931; Scheerer, 1963). In productive thinking, problems are solved by the principle of *reorganisation*, or solving a problem by perceiving new relationships among its elements.

Consider, for example, trying to arrange six matchsticks into four equilateral triangles with each side equal to one stick. If you try to arrange the matchsticks by pushing them around on a table, the problem can't be solved. Through reorganisation, though, and realisation that the matchsticks don't have to be arranged in two dimensions, the problem can be solved (as shown on page 307). The principle of reorganisation is similar to what Köhler (1925) called insight in his studies of PS in chimpanzees.

KEY STUDY 20.1

Sultan and the banana (Köhler, 1925)

Köhler suspended, out-of-reach, a bunch of bananas from the ceiling of the cage of a chimpanzee called Sultan. In the cage were several items that could be used to reach the bananas (such as sticks of different lengths), although none on its own was sufficient. Eventually, Sultan solved the problem by placing empty boxes beneath the bananas and climbing on the boxes.

Later, Köhler allowed Sultan to see a box being placed in the corridor leading to his cage. Sultan was then taken to his cage where, again, bananas were suspended from the ceiling. Sultan's first strategy was to remove a long bolt from the open cage's door. Quite suddenly, though, he stopped, ran down the corridor, and returned with the box which was again used to retrieve the bananas.

For Köhler, Sultan's behaviour was a result of sudden perceptual reorganisation or insight, which was different from trial-and-error learning. Other experiments showed that Sultan's perceptual reorganisation was maintained as a plan of action. So, when the bananas were placed outside the cage, Sultan still built several boxes. Experience can sometimes be an obstacle to PS!

An evaluation of the Gestalt approach

While Gestalt psychologists made a significant contribution to our understanding of the processes involved in solving certain types of problem, they didn't develop a theory that applies to all aspects of PS. Although the concepts of 'insight' and 'restructuring' are attractive because they're easily understood (especially when accompanied by perceptual demonstrations), they're extremely vague and ill-defined as theoretical constructs (Eysenck & Keane, 1995). Thus, it's very unclear under what conditions they occur and exactly what insight involves. However, in many ways, the spirit of Gestalt research, with its emphasis on the goal-directed and non-associationist nature of thinking, provides a basis for the information-processing approach. It also left a large body of experimental problems and evidence, which any later theory had to be able to account for; '... the legacy of the school was, therefore, substantial' (Eysenck & Keane, 1995).

The information-processing approach

Information-processing approaches analyse cognitive processes in terms of a series of separate stages. In the case of PS, the stages are those mentioned earlier; that is, representing the problem, generating possible solutions and evaluating those solutions.

Algorithms

An *algorithm* is a systematic exploration of every possible solution until the correct one is found. For example, to solve the anagram YABB, we could list all the possible combinations of letters, checking each time to see whether the result is a real word. So, we might generate BBAY (non-word), BYAB (non-word) and so on, until we eventually arrive at BABY. Algorithms guarantee a solution to a problem, and are effective when the number of possible solutions is small (as in the above example). But when the number of possible solutions is large, algorithms are time-consuming (unless we're fortunate enough to find the solution early).

Heuristics

Heuristics are 'rules of thumb':

> '... guidelines for selecting actions that are most likely to lead a solver towards a goal, but may not always do so'.
> (Greene, 1987)

So, while not guaranteeing a solution to a problem, heuristics can result in solutions being reached more quickly (Newell *et al.*, 1958). These 'fuzzy' procedures are based on intuition, past experience and any other relevant information. With solving anagrams, for example, a heuristic approach would involve looking for letter combinations that are and are not permitted in the English language. BB isn't a permitted combination of letters at the beginning of a word, and so this would immediately exclude BBAY as a solution to the example above. Although less likely with four-letter anagrams, heuristic devices applied to longer anagrams might not be successful, and we might miss a solution based on a lack of intuition, past experience and other relevant factors. Heuristic devices include *means–end analysis* (Newell & Simon, 1972).

Means–end analysis (MEA)

In MEA (or working backwards), the search for a solution begins at the goal (or end) and works backwards to the original state (the means being the steps that must be taken to get from the present state – the problem –to the goal of solving the problem).

However, it's often not possible to achieve the main goal all in one step. So, another important characteristic of MEA is to break down the main goal into subgoals (or a problem into subproblems), each of which has to be solved before the final (main) goal can be reached.

Ask yourself ...

- Give some examples of real-life/everyday problems which can be achieved only by being broken down into subgoals.

This form of MEA is called *problem-reduction representation* (a 'divide and conquer' approach: Garnham, 1991). As each of the sub-problems is solved, so the distance between the original state and the goal state decreases (Newell & Simon, 1972).

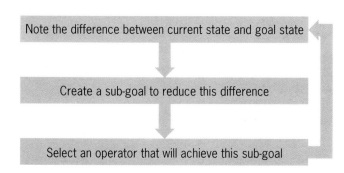

Figure 20.5 *Outline of major steps involved in subgoal MEA*

For example, in the Tower of Hanoi (see page 294), the overall goal is to move four discs from A to B, moving one disc at a time and never placing a larger disc on top of a smaller one. This overall goal can be subdivided into three subgoals:

1 transfer the three smaller discs from A to C;
2 transfer the largest disc from A to B;
3 transfer the three smaller discs from C to B.

(1) and (3) can be reduced further. (2) can be achieved directly, assuming that (1) has been achieved. Complete reduction analyses the problem into moves of single discs whose preconditions are met; they correspond to the rules (control strategies) about moving only one disc at a time and only smaller discs being placed on a larger one (not vice versa). But is it always this clear just what the subgoals are?

Box 20.1 Limitations of MEA

The missionaries and cannibals problem is a good example of how the final goal may be obvious enough, while the subgoals may be far less obvious. Indeed, many puzzles are chosen for experiments precisely

because the basis for selecting the shortest set of moves to reach the final goal is obscure. So how do you measure progress towards the final goal in such problems?

It cannot be measured simply by the total number of people transported from the left to the right, because if there are too many cannibals the missionaries will get eaten! While it's possible for a computer to work out a sequence of all possible moves and then to plot the quickest path of moves towards a solution, people cannot hold this type of structure in their limited-capacity working memories (see Chapter 17). The water-jug problem poses the same difficulties for human solvers. (If a computer program systematically checked every possible move until the goal were reached, it would be using a 'check-every-move' algorithm.)

A further problem with MEA as a heuristic for PS is that it's sometimes necessary to move *further away* from a goal in order to achieve a solution. One reason that the missionaries and cannibals problem is so difficult, is that at one point it becomes necessary to take a missionary and a cannibal back to the left bank from where they started. This apparently *increases* the distance from the final goal of getting them all over to the right bank (Greene, 1987).

Well-defined and ill-defined problems

Garnham (1988) believes that in everyday problems, and those requiring a high degree of creative thinking, one or more of: (i) the initial state; (ii) the goal state; or (iii) the operators are typically *ill-defined* (not made explicit). This makes it difficult to write AI programs designed to solve such problems. But in the missionaries and cannibals problem, Tower of Hanoi, and other puzzle problems, all three are clearly specified (they are *well-defined* problems) and AI programs are relatively successful in solving them. According to Greene (1987), there are two major differences between puzzle problems and real-life problems:

- Puzzle problems are unfamiliar problems about which the solver has little knowledge, whereas many everyday problems require considerable amounts of knowledge. The knowledge which is relevant in puzzle problems is called *general-purpose* or *domain-independent heuristic knowledge*. For example, MEA can be applied in a wide range of different situations (domains). By contrast, everyday problems require substantial *domain-specific knowledge*. Substantial domain-specific knowledge is also required in adversary problems, such as chess (see below).
- The knowledge required to solve puzzles is present in the statement of the problem, whereas much of the difficulty with everyday problems is finding the relevant information needed to solve them.

Solving adversary problems: the case of chess

According to Ginsberg (1998):

'The world watched with considerable amazement in May 1997 as IBM's chess computer, Deep Blue, beat Garry Kasparov, the world champion, in a six-game match. With a machine's victory in this most cerebral of games, it seemed

that a line had been crossed, that our measurements of ourselves might need tailoring'.

However, the contest was very close (two wins, one defeat, and three ties), and Kasparov clearly wasn't on top form. Although Deep Blue and other recent chess-playing programs generally play well, Ginsberg observes that:

'As an element of artificial intelligence, game-playing software highlights the key differences between the brute-force calculation of machines and the often intuitive, pattern-matching abilities of humans'.

The number of possible sequences of moves in a game of chess is frighteningly large (there are an estimated 10^{20} possible games of chess, compared with a mere 10^{12} microseconds per century: Garnham, 1988). Human players will consider tens (or perhaps hundreds) of positions when selecting a move, which represents a tiny fraction of the potential moves, and only rarely can they think through to a win, lose or stalemate situation. Chess-playing computer programs used to be like human players. They selected a small number of moves to follow up, then used the *minimax procedure* (*min*-imising the *maximum* loss that can be inflicted by the opponent) to analyse these in detail. Programs run on small computers still operate in this way.

But top programmers have access to the most powerful machines available, and they often revert to a more algorithmic method; for example, examining every possible position that can be reached in the next five moves by each player (which involves comparing hundreds of thousands of positions). While modern computers can perform many millions of operations per second (through 'brute-force' methods), this provides few insights for cognitive scientists, since it bears no relationship to the way that people solve difficult problems (Garnham, 1991).

- Considering the far superior computational capacity of computers, it might seem unlikely that humans could ever win. But although people look at a mere handful of successive positions, they tend to look at the *right* handful. They identify the best positions to consider through pattern matching (or PR: see Chapter 14). An expert chess player compares a given board position with the vast number of such positions that s/he has seen during his/her career, using lessons learned from analysing those other positions to identify good moves in the current game. For Deep Blue, however, there are no pre-exisiting lists of positions it can use to evaluate the current game. As Boden (1987b) puts it:

    'Master chess players develop global perceptual schemata in terms of which they can see threats and oppositions on the board much as a lesser mortal can see complex emotional response in a cartoon face ...'.

- Pattern matching is a *parallel process*, while the computer's capacity for searching through vast numbers of possibilities is a *serial process*. Since the brain is a massively parallel structure, it's far superior to computers at recognising patterns.

According to Boden (1987b):

'Like problem-solving in other ... domains ... chess playing needs more than quick thinking and a retentive memory: it requires an appreciation of the overall structure of the problem, so that intelligent action can be economically planned ...'.

De Groot (1965, 1966) compared the performance of five grand masters and five expert players on choosing a move from a particular board position. He asked participants to think aloud, and then determined the number and type of different moves they'd considered. Grand masters didn't consider more alternative moves or search any deeper than experts, and yet they took slightly less time to make a move. Independent raters judged the final moves of the masters to be superior to those of the experts.

De Groot's initial explanation for these differences was in terms of knowledge of different board positions stored in LTM. When participants were given a five-second presentation of board positions from actual games and asked to reconstruct them from memory, the masters were correct 91 per cent of the time compared with 41 per cent for the experts. Clearly, the masters could recognise and encode the various configurations of pieces using prior knowledge. When pieces were randomly arranged on the board, both groups did equally badly.

Chess experts are only better at remembering the position of chess pieces when they're positioned as they might be during a game. If the pieces are placed randomly, the experts are no better than non-experts at memorising their positions (de Groot, 1966)

Experts and domain-specific knowledge

According to Sternberg (1990):

'... intelligent systems rely to a great extent on stored problem patterns when they face a familiar task. Instead of creating solutions from scratch for every problem situation, they make use of previously stored information in such a way that it facilitates their coping with the current problem'.

Studies of experts and novices have revealed many important differences between them. These don't necessarily occur because experts are faster thinkers, have better memories or are cleverer than non-experts (Hampson & Morris, 1996). The gain from being an expert seems to be that it places *less strain on working memory* (see Chapter 17). Since PS strategies depend on knowledge which is already available, 'the more you know, the less you have to think' (Greene, 1987).

According to Greene (1987), what's missing from AI accounts of human PS are the different experiences people bring to different tasks. For example, MEA is meant to be typical of all PS by all problem-solvers. It was originally presented as a general characteristic of human thinking which can, in principle, be applied to any problem. However, the ability to implement a particular PS strategy depends on knowledge. Thinking mechanisms may be universal, but solvers are categorised as experts or novices in relation to different problem situations. Expertise is more far-reaching than simple knowledge of the rules which apply to a particular problem (otherwise we'd all be chess masters!).

Expert systems

Expert systems (ESs or intelligent knowledge-based systems) promise to be the first major application of AI research (Garnham, 1991). Basically, an ES is a computer program that embodies (some of) the knowledge of a human expert in a domain in which expertise comes with experience (Garnham, 1988).

In fields such as medicine, it's difficult to formulate explicitly an expert's knowledge – otherwise human experts would be easier to train. ESs are intended to do (some of) the work of human experts. Therefore, the first condition a problem must satisfy, if it's to be tackled by an ES, is that there should be recognised experts in solving it, and their performance should be demonstrably better than that of non-experts (e.g. a medical consultant compared with both the layperson and non-specialist GPs). The case of medical diagnosis illustrates certain other features a problem should have.

- There's no simple set of rules a medical expert can follow in diagnosing illness. If there were, diagnosis could be performed by non-intelligent programs (and there would probably be no experts). Instead, consultants draw on wide experience of the connection between manifestations of illnesses and underlying causes.
- A single manifestation (symptom, sign, test result) may indicate one of a number of different diseases, but it's unlikely to be associated with any one of them in every case. Further, some of the data that diagnosis is based on may be misleading, irrelevant or incorrect; in other words, reasoning about diagnosis is, in some sense, probabilistic.
- Diagnosis doesn't depend on general knowledge, but requires a large but manageable amount of domain-specific knowledge.

Apart from the primary goal of solving domain-specific problems (e.g. medical diagnosis), ESs should be able to explain how they reached a particular conclusion. They usually interact with people in solving problems, and those users often need to know how a decision has been reached.

How is ES knowledge obtained?

The process of encoding knowledge into the system is called *transfer of expertise*. However, experts can't always formulate explicitly the knowledge they use, nor can they say how they combine different items of information to make a judgement about a particular case. Lengthy interviews may need to be conducted, in which experts are asked to give their opinions on sample cases. These data may have to be supplemented by survey data, such as correlating patterns of medical symptoms and test results with eventual diagnosis. This makes the writing of ESs difficult and time-consuming.

Box 20.3   Some examples of ESs – MYCIN and GUESSING

MYCIN diagnoses bacterial infections requiring antibiotics, and is intended for use in situations where drugs must be prescribed before the micro-organism responsible for the infection has been properly identified (a laboratory culture may take up to two days to grow). A chronically sick patient needs earlier treatment, so drugs have to be prescribed on the basis of symptoms and the results of quick tests. MYCIN interacts with a medical expert, requesting information and suggesting treatments. It asks specific questions only related to the hypothesis it's currently considering.

While ESs have now been used in medicine for over 30 years, they've only fairly recently appeared in nursing. One example is the Glasgow University Expert Systems in Nursing Group (GUESSING), which has designed experiments to discover the cognitive skills of clinically excellent nurses in the area of pressure sore risk and preventative care planning. These were then formalised into a computer program, which can be used both as a decision support and a tutoring tool (Jones *et al.*, 1989, cited by Eaton, 1991).

An evaluation of ESs

According to Boden (1987a), ESs are much less flexible than their human counterparts and most in actual use are considerably less complex than MYCIN, which was one of the prototypes and took many work-years to create. In Boden's view:

'In almost every case, their 'explanations' are merely recapitulations of the previous firing of if – then rules … for they still have no higher-level representations of the knowledge domain, their own problem-solving activity, or the knowledge of their human user'.

Some researchers are trying to provide ESs with causal reasoning, so that they not only arrive at a conclusion but can also explain the reason to the user. Boden claims that ESs can't integrate knowledge from distinct domains, using concepts and patterns of inference from one domain to reason (by analogy) in another. Genuine expertise requires both high-level knowledge and *analogical thinking*.

Decision-making

Decision-making (DM) is a special case of PS, in which we already know the possible solutions (or choices). Some decisions we have to make are relatively trivial. Others are more important, such as deciding which university to study at, or deciding whether or not to have children. In DM, then, we're faced with various alternative choices from which one must be selected and the others rejected.

Compensatory and non-compensatory models of DM

Compensatory models

If we were completely logical in our DM, we'd evaluate how *all* the desirable potential outcomes of a particular decision might *compensate* for the undesirable potential outcomes. According to the *additive compensatory model*, we start the DM process by listing common features of various alternatives and assigning arbitrary weights that reflect their value to us. The weights are then added up to arrive at a separate score for each alternative. Provided that the criteria have been properly weighted and each criterion has been correctly rated, the alternative with the highest score is the most rational choice given the available information.

Another compensatory model is the *utility–probability model*, which proposes that important decisions are made by weighting the desirability of each potential outcome according to its utility (the value placed on potential positive or negative outcomes) and probability (the likelihood that the choice will actually produce the potential outcome).

Non-compensatory models

Evidence suggests that we actually use various, and less precise, non-compensatory models. In these, not all features of each alternative may be considered, and features *don't* compensate for each other. There are at least four such models.

Box 20.4   Some non-compensatory DM models

Elimination by aspects: When faced with complex decisions, we eliminate various options if they don't meet particular criteria, irrespective of their quality on other criteria (Tversky, 1972). This assumes that we begin with a maximum criterion and use it to test the various options. If, after applying this criterion, more than one alternative remains, the second most important criterion is used. The procedure continues until just one option remains. This is the chosen option.

Maximax strategy: After comparing the various options according to their best features, we then select the one with the strongest best feature.

Minimax strategy: After considering the weakest feature of each option, we select the option whose weakest feature is most highly rated.

Conjunctive strategy: This involves setting a 'minimum' acceptable value on each option. The next step is to discard any option which doesn't meet, or exceed, this value as the criteria are considered from most to least important. The chosen option is that which does meet or exceed the minimum acceptable value on each criterion.

Heuristics in DM

Clearly, important decisions should be approached rationally and systematically. But it's not always easy to make rational decisions, even in important matters, because of the absence of information about the various alternatives. Moreover, with all the decisions we have to make daily, there isn't time to engage in the rational processes described above. We also have only a limited capacity for reasoning according to formal logic and probability theory (Evans & Over, 1996). As a result, we often rely on heuristics. Two of these are the *availability heuristic* (or *bias*) and the *representativeness heuristic* (or *bias*: Tversky & Kahneman, 1973).

Availability heuristic (or bias)

Sometimes, decisions must be made on the basis of whatever information is most readily available in LTM. The availability heuristic is based on the assumption that an event's probability is directly related to the frequency with which it has occurred in the past, and that more frequent events are usually easier to remember than less frequent events.

Most people say the former. In fact, 'K' is three times more likely to appear as the third letter, but because words beginning with 'K' come to mind more easily, we assume they're more commonplace (Hastie & Park, 1986).

The availability heuristic also plays a role in our tendency to overestimate the chances of being the victim of a violent crime or a plane crash (Tyler & Cook, 1984). This is because the extensive media coverage of these statistically very rare events brings vivid examples of them to mind very readily.

Representativeness heuristic (or bias)

Tversky & Kahneman (1973) gave participants the following information about a person called 'Steve':

'Steve is very shy and withdrawn, invariably helpful, but with little interest in people, or in the world of reality. A meek and tidy soul, he has a need for order and structure, and a passion for detail'.

The participants were asked to guess Steve's occupation, from a number of options, including musician, pilot, physician, salesman and librarian. Most chose librarian, presumably because his personality characteristics matched certain *stereotypes* of librarians (see Chapter 22, pages 332–336). Whenever we judge the likelihood of something by intuitively comparing it with our preconceived ideas of a few characteristics that we believe represent a category, we're using the representativeness heuristic. It can also explain the *gambler's* fallacy (see Box 20.5, page 301) and the *base rate fallacy*.

Box 20.5　The gambler's fallacy

Ask yourself ...

- Consider the following possible outcomes of tossing a coin six times:

  HHHHHH, TTTHHH and HTTHTH.

  Which of these is the least, and which the most, likely?

Most people believe the *first* outcome to be the *least* likely of the three, and the *third* to be the *most* likely. In fact, the probability of the three sequences is *identical*. Our assumption that coin tossing produces a random sequence of heads and tails leads us to decide that the third is the most likely. Indeed, if people observe five consecutive heads and are asked to estimate the probability of the next toss being a head, they tend to suggest that a tail is the more likely outcome, even though the probability of either is actually 0.5. This tendency is called the *gambler's fallacy*.

In the *base rate fallacy*, we ignore important information about base rates (the relative frequency of different objects/events in the world). For example, Tversky & Kahneman (1973) asked participants to decide whether a student who could be described as 'neat and tidy', 'dull and mechanical' and 'a poor writer' was a computer-science student or a humanities student. Over 95 per cent decided the student studied computing. Even after they were told that over 80 per cent of students at their school were studying humanities, their estimates remained virtually unchanged. So, even when we know the relative frequency of two things, we tend to ignore this information and base a decision on how well something matches our stereotype; that is, how representative it is.

However, if prior odds are the only relevant information (base rates without the description of the student), then participants will estimate correctly. People may also be more inclined to take account of base rate information when it seems to be *causally* relevant (Tversky & Kahneman, 1980).

Box 20.6　Some other influences on DM

Belief perseverance: This is the tendency to cling to a belief even in the face of contrary evidence (Lord *et al.*, 1979). It can be overcome by *considering the opposite*. But some false beliefs, such as stereotypes, are difficult to remove even when information exists which clearly discredits them.

Entrapment: When we make costly investments in something that goes wrong (such as a relationship), we may come to feel we've no choice but to continue, because withdrawal cannot justify the costs already incurred (Brockner & Rubin, 1985). For example, industrial disputes often continue beyond the stage where either side can hope to achieve any gains (Baron, 1989).

Over-confidence: This is the tendency to overestimate the accuracy of our current knowledge, because it's generally easier for us to remember successful decisions or judgements than unsuccessful ones. So, using the availability heuristic, we overestimate our success at particular tasks. Over-confidence can be overcome by providing feedback about the accuracy of decisions and judgements.

Loss aversion and costs against losses: Typically, we tend to reject riskier, though potentially more rewarding, decisions in favour of a certain gain unless taking a risk is a way to avoid loss (Tversky & Kahneman, 1986). We also tend to see losses as being more acceptable if we label them as 'costs' rather than 'losses' (although the evaluation of a cost depends on the context: Kahneman & Tversky, 1984).

Expectations: Expectations can affect both our perception of the world (see Box 15.4, page 221) and what's done with the perceived information. For example, the shooting down of an ascending Iranian airliner by an American warship occurred as a result of initial, but later corrected, computer information that the plane was a descending F14 fighter jet. The expectation of an attack led the ship's captain to pay more attention to his crew's reports of an emergency than to the new computer information (Wade & Tavris, 1993).

Hindsight: Hindsight bias refers to our tendency, in retrospect, to overestimate the probability that something would have happened, as if we'd known this all along (Hawkins & Hastie, 1990).

Framing: When the same issue is presented (or framed) in two different but equivalent ways, we tend to make different judgements about it. For example, people respond more positively to minced beef if it's described as '75 per cent lean' rather than '25 per cent fat'. Also, medical treatments are seen as being more successful if framed as having a '50 per cent success rate' rather than a '50 per cent failure rate' (Levin & Gaeth, 1988: see Chapter 12 page 167).

Neville Chamberlain, the British Prime Minister, returned home in September 1938 from seeing Hitler in Munich with a pledge of non-aggression. He over-confidently declared 'I believe it is peace in our time'.

Gambling and risk-taking

Many laboratory studies have used gambling as a model of risk-taking behaviour, despite the fact that it isn't typical of the risks we take in everyday life (Jones, 1998). However, the heuristics discussed above (which are based largely on laboratory studies) can help explain an increasingly common case of real-life gambling, namely, playing the National Lottery. Although the odds against winning the jackpot are 14 million to one (far greater than any other form of average gambling return), 90 per cent of the population are estimated to have bought at least one ticket, and 65 per cent claim to play regularly (Hill & Williamson, 1998). Given these odds, it's likely that the ordinary 'social gambler' doesn't think about the actual probability of winning, but relies on heuristic strategies for handling the available information (Griffiths, 1997b).

The fact that there are so many heuristics and biases, and that several can be applied to any one particular situation, gives them little predictive value (Griffiths, 1997b; Wagenaar, 1988). However, the availability bias, illusory correlations and illusion of control can help explain the persistence of gambling (Griffiths, 1997b; Hill & Williamson, 1998). Uncovering the false beliefs underlying people's mistakes when becoming involved in a risk situation can help to reduce the irrational thinking of a potential gambler (Griffiths, 1990; Walker, 1992).

Ask yourself ...

- Try to relate these heuristics and biases to explanations of risky *health* behaviours (see Chapter 12, pages 164–165) and *addictive* behaviours (see Chapter 8, pages 113–114).

Artificial intelligence (AI)

Throughout the chapter so far, we've talked about computers as problem-solvers and have looked at some of the important differences between them and human problem-solvers. Also, we've mainly discussed puzzle problems. But what about the kind of 'problem' referred to in the *Introduction and overview*, such as vision and language understanding, which humans are 'designed' for? Can computers be programmed to mimic these basic human abilities and, if so, what can we learn about the way we use them?

Defining AI

According to Garnham (1988), AI is '... the science of thinking machines ...' and, again:

'... an approach to understanding behaviour based on the assumption that intelligence can best be analysed by trying

Table 20.2 *Heuristic strategies and biases that might be used by lottery players*

Heuristic	Application to lottery participation
Availability bias (see page 300)	Wide publicity concerning winners, and pleasant memories of an occasional small prize, make winning more salient than losing
Randomness bias: not expecting a random sequence to have any apparent biases and regularities (Teigen, 1994)	Despite the mechanical and random nature of the draw, many people seem to be trying to predict which numbers will be drawn (Haigh, 1995). So, there's difficulty in choosing six random numbers from 49
Representativeness bias: equating a 'random' sample with a 'representative' sample (Tversky & Kahneman, 1971; see also page 300)	A tendency to choose numbers that appear 'random' (irregular, no pattern), and avoid those which appear less random (adjacent numbers and repeating digits)
Gambler's fallacy: the belief that subsequent events will cancel out previous events to produce a representative sequence (Holtgraves & Skeel, 1992), and that the probability of winning will increase with the length of an ongoing run of losses (Wagenaar, 1988: see also Box 20.5, page 301)	Choosing numbers which have been least drawn (they're therefore 'due'), and overestimate the chances of winning
Illusory correlations: the use of superstitious behaviour when it's believed variables correlate when they don't (Wagenaar, 1988: see also Chapter 22, page 335)	Choosing 'lucky numbers' – birthdays, house numbers etc. – which causes players to discard statistical probabilities
Flexible attribution: tendency to attribute success to personal skill and failures to some external influence (Wagenaar, 1988: see Chapter 23, pages 346–347)	Preference for choosing own numbers rather than buying 'lucky dips', so that any win is due to player's own skill (game of luck), whereas losses are due to features of the game (game of chance)
Illusion of control: an expectancy of success which is greater than the objective probability warrants (Langer, 1975)	Being able to choose own numbers induces skill orientations, which cause players to feel inappropriately confident
Sunk cost bias: continuing an endeavour once an investment has been made (Arkes & Blumer, 1985)	Continuing to buy lottery tickets while experiencing losses. The more money that's spent, the more likely people are to continue 'investing', and to inflate their estimations of winning

(Based on Griffiths, 1997b, and Hill & Williamson, 1998)

to reproduce it. In practice, reproduction means simulation by computer. AI is, therefore, part of computer science ...'.

Garnham observes that most contemporary AI research is influenced more or less by consideration of how people behave. Very few researchers simply try to build clever machines disregarding the principles underlying its behaviour, and many still have the explicit goal of writing a program which works in the way people do (such as Marr's computational theory of vision: see Chapter 15). So, cognitive psychologists and workers in AI share an interest in the scientific understanding of cognitive abilities.

Abilities such as vision, language, PS and DM are all part of 'intelligence' in the broadest sense of that term, and intelligence has always been a central concern of psychologists (see Chapters 34 and 41). As we saw in Chapter 1, since the late 1970s cognitive psychology and AI have both become component disciplines of *cognitive science*. By the late 1970s, cognitive psychologists had more in common with AI researchers than with other psychologists, and AI researchers had more in common with cognitive psychologists than with other computer scientists (Garnham, 1988).

Boden (1987b) defines AI as '... the science of making machines do the sorts of things that are done by human minds ...'. The 'machines' in question are, typically, digital computers. But she's at pains to make clear that AI *isn't* the study of computers but the study of intelligence in thought and action. Computers are its *tools*, because its theories are expressed as computer programs which are tested by being run on a machine.

What is a computer?

The initial concept of the 'computer', and the first attempts to build the modern digital computer, were made by the Cambridge mathematician, Charles Babbage (1792–1871).

Box 20.7 Turing machines

Turing (1936) described an abstract computing device (a Turing machine), which performs its calculations with the help of a tape divided into squares, each with a symbol printed on it. Its basic operations comprise reading and writing symbols on the tape and shifting the tape to the left or right. It uses a finite vocabulary of symbols, but the tape is indefinitely long. A *universal Turing machine* can mimic the operation of any other Turing machine. To do this, it must be given a description of how that machine works, which can be written onto its tape in standard Turing machine format.

Every general-purpose digital computer is an *approximation* to the universal Turing machine (since no real machine has an indefinitely large memory). When it runs a program, it behaves as if it were a machine for performing just the task the program performs.

The basic active components of digital computers are normally in one or two stable states (on/off). This makes them essentially *binary* in nature; that is, they use only two symbols (e.g. 0/1) as in binary arithmetic. They can symbolise an indefinitely large number of things (as can the 26 letters of the alphabet), because they can be grouped together in indefinitely numerous ways. As described by Turing, they are machines which change according to the problem to be solved (based upon the particular instructions contained within the program). 'Digital' refers to the finger, and the fingers can be used as a kind of abacus, a simple form of computing machine. Computers are, in essence, autonomous abaci – working without continuous human intervention (Gregory, 1981).

Although originally designed as calculating machines ('compute' means to 'calculate'), computers aren't mere 'number crunchers' or supercalculating arithmetic machines. Digital computers are, in fact, *general-purpose symbol manipulating machines*. It's up to the programmer to decide what interpretations can sensibly (i.e. consistently) be made of the symbols of machine and programming languages, which, in themselves, are meaningless (Boden, 1987a).

Strong and weak AI and the computational theory of mind

> ### Ask yourself ...
>
> * Do you believe that computers literally think/behave intelligently (that is, are reproducing/ duplicating the equivalent human thinking/behaviour), or are they merely *simulating* (mimicking) human thought/intelligence?

This distinction corresponds to the one made by Searle (1980) between *strong* and *weak AI*, respectively:

> *'According to weak AI, the main value of the computer in the study of the mind is that it gives us a very powerful tool, e.g. it enables us to formulate and test hypotheses in a more rigorous and precise fashion than before. But according to strong AI the computer is not merely a tool; rather, the appropriately programmed computer really is a mind in the sense that computers given the right program can be literally said to understand and have other cognitive states. Further, because the programmed computer has cognitive states, the programs are not mere tools that enable us to test psychological explanations but the programs are themselves explanations ...'.*

Searle is very critical of strong AI, a view advocated by computer scientists such as Minsky (1975), who defines AI as '... the science of making machines do things that would require intelligence if done by men'. The implication of such a definition is that machines must be intelligent if they can do what humans can do (although this rather begs the question as to what it means to display intelligence). Underlying strong AI is the *computational theory of mind* (CTM), one supporter of whom is Boden (1987a):

> *'Intelligence may be defined as the ability creatively to manipulate symbols, or process information, given the requirements of the task in hand. If the task is mathematical, then numerical information may need to be processed. But if the task is non-numerical (or 'semantic') in nature ...*

then the information that is coded and processed must be semantic information, irrespective of the superficial form of the symbols used in the information code ...'.

Symbols have no inherent similarity to what they symbolise, and represent something in a purely formal way. Computer programs comprise formal systems, 'a set of basic elements or pieces and a set of rules for forming and transforming the elements or pieces' (Flanagan, 1984). In computer languages, symbols stand for whatever objects, relations or processes we wish. The computer manipulates the symbols, *not* their meaning. Programs consist of rules for manipulating symbols, and don't refer to anything in the world.

However, CTM defines all intelligent systems as symbol manipulators which, of course, include human minds. If symbols are meaningless to a computer, it follows that they're also meaningless to a human mind. But in that case, what's the 'meaning' which, according to Boden, the human programmer attaches to the meaningless symbols? Searle's attack on strong AI and CTM takes the form of a *Gedanken* experiment ('thought experiment') called the Chinese room.

Box 20.8 The Chinese room (Searle, 1980)

Suppose that I am locked in a room and am given a large batch of Chinese writing. Suppose that I know no Chinese, either written or spoken ... After this first batch of Chinese writing, I am given a second batch together with a set of rules for correlating the second batch with the first batch. The rules are in English and I understand them as well as any other English native speaker. They enable me to correlate one set of formal symbols with another set of formal symbols and all that 'formal' means here is that I can identify the symbols entirely by their shapes. I am then given a third batch of Chinese symbols together with some instructions, again in English, which enable me to correlate elements of this third batch with the first two batches and these rules instruct me how to give back certain Chinese symbols with certain sorts of shapes in response to certain sorts of shapes provided by the third batch. Unknown to me, the people giving me all these symbols call the first batch a 'script', the second batch a 'story', the third batch 'questions', the symbols I give back in response to the third batch, 'answers to the questions' and the set of English rules 'the program' ....

After a while I get so good at following the instructions for manipulating the Chinese symbols and the programmers get so good at writing the program that, from the point of view of somebody outside the room, my answers are indistinguishable from those of native Chinese speakers ... However ... I am manipulating uninterpreted formal symbols and in this respect I am simply behaving like a computer, i.e. performing computational operations on formally specified elements ... I am simply a realisation of the computer program.

The Chinese room and the Turing test

Searle believes the Chinese room demonstrates quite conclusively that there's more to intelligence and understanding than mere manipulation of symbols. In particular, he's trying to show that the Turing test (or *imitation game*) isn't the ultimate test of machine intelligence that supporters of strong AI have traditionally claimed it is.

Box 20.9 The Turing test (Turing, 1950)

Turing suggested that a suitable test for success in AI would be an 'imitation game', in which a human judge would hold a three-way conversation with a computer and another human and try to tell them apart. The judge would be free to turn the conversation to any topic, and the successful machine would be able to chat about it as convincingly as the human. This would require the machine participant to understand language and conversational conventions, and to have a general ability to reason. If the judge couldn't tell the difference after some reasonable amount of time, the machine would pass the test: it would seem human to a human.

'I believe that in about 50 years time it will be possible to program computers ... to make them play the imitation game so well that, on average, the interrogator will not have more than a 70 per cent chance of making the right identification after five minutes of questioning. When this occurs, there is no contradiction in the idea of thinking machines'. (Turing, 1950)

Computer participant   Human participant

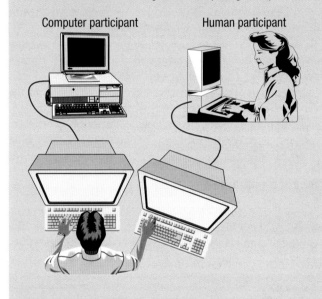

Figure 20.6 *The Turing test for artificial intelligence*

Both the Chinese room and the Turing test have been criticised. Gregory (1987b) argues that, because it's such a highly restricted and artificial environment:

'The Chinese room parable does not show that computer-based robots cannot be as intelligent as we are – because we wouldn't be intelligent from this school either'.

Boden (1993) contends that a functioning program is comparable to Searle-in-the-Chinese-room's understanding of *English* (not Chinese). A word in a language one understands is a mini-program, which causes certain processes to be run in one's mind. Clearly, this doesn't happen with the Chinese words, because Searle-in-the-Chinese-room doesn't understand Chinese.

The real aims of AI

According to Ford & Hayes (1998), the central defect of the Turing test is that it is *species-centred*. In other words, it assumes that human thought is the ultimate, highest form of thinking against which all others must be judged. Most contemporary AI researchers explicitly reject the goal of the Turing test. Instead, Ford and Hayes maintain that:

> *'The scientific aim of AI research is to understand intelligence as computation, and its engineering aim is to build machines that surpass or extend human mental abilities in some useful way. Trying to imitate a human conversation (however 'intellectual' it may be) contributes little to either ambition'.*

Ford and Hayes draw an analogy between AI and artificial flight. They argue that the traditional view of (strong) AI's goal – to create a machine that can successfully imitate human thought – is mistaken. The Turing test should be relegated to the history of science, in the same way that the aim of imitating a bird was eventually abandoned by the pioneers of flight. The development of aircraft succeeded only when people stopped trying to imitate birds:

> *'In some ways, aircraft may never match the elegant precision of birds. But in other ways, they outperform them dramatically. Aircraft do not land in trees, scoop fish from the ocean or use the natural breeze to hover motionless above the countryside. But no bird can fly at 45,000 feet or faster than sound'.*

Rather than limiting the scope of AI to the study of how to mimic (or reproduce) human behaviour:

> *'... the proper aim of AI is ... to create a computational science of intelligence itself, whether human, animal or machine ...'.*

This brings us back to the CTM.

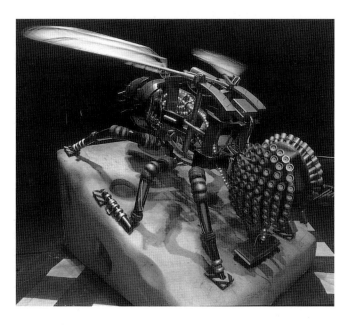

Giant robotic fly, designed to teach people about the structure and habits of this insect

Do we need brains to be brainy?

For supporters of strong AI, our bodies – including our brains – are in no way necessary to our intelligence. In Boden's terms 'You don't need brains to be brainy' (quoted in Rose, 1992); that is, what matters is the program (*software*), and the brain (*hardware*) is incidental. Strong AI claims that *any* physical system capable of carrying out the necessary computational processes can be described as intelligent, even if it's 'made of old beer cans' (in Searle's words). But many have argued that our brains *are* necessary:

- Flanagan (1984) finds it highly unlikely that our evolutionary history, genes, biochemistry, anatomy and neurophysiology have nothing essential to do with our defining features (even though it remains logically possible).
- Searle (1987) believes that mental states and processes are *real biological phenomena* in the world, as real as digestion, photosynthesis, lactation, and so on (they are 'caused by processes going on in the brain').
- Penrose (1987) agrees that there's more to understanding than just carrying out some appropriate program, and that the actual physical construction of the brain is also important. He argues that a computer designed to follow the logical operations of every detail of the workings of the human brain would itself *not* achieve 'understanding', even though the person whose brain is being considered would claim to understand.
- The earlier generations of computers were essentially *serial processors*. They could perform – although admittedly incredibly quickly – only one operation at a time in sequence (in a *linear* fashion). AI researchers became convinced that real (biological) brains *don't* not work like this at all, but instead carry out many operations *in parallel* and in a *distributed* manner. In other words, many parts of a network of cells are involved in any single function, and no single cell is uniquely involved in any. These considerations caused an explosion of interest in new computer designs based on *parallel distributed processing* (PDP) *principles*, promising new generations of machines.
- The central principle of this new brain-modelling approach is *connectionism*, which is based on the idea that the brain is composed of *neural networks* with multiple connections between them (see Chapter 4). If the aim of AI is to construct models which offer insights into human cognition, then it was necessary to look much more closely at the microstructure of the brain itself, to see if insights into the power of this natural information-processing engine might help develop a more realistic modelling system. Most PDP researchers were interested in how individual components (neurons) might operate *collectively* to produce the brain's information-processing capacity.

Can computers ever be like brains?

According to Rose (1992), the very concept of AI implies that intelligence is simply a property of the machine itself. However, the neuronal system of brains, unlike computers, is radically indeterminate:

> *'... brains and the organisms they inhabit, above all human brains and human beings, are not closed systems, like the molecules of a gas inside a sealed jar. Instead they are open*

systems, formed by their own past history and continually in interaction with the natural and social worlds outside, both changing them and being changed in their turn ...'.

This openness creates a further level of *indeterminacy* to the functioning of both brain and behaviour. Unlike computers, brains aren't error-free machines, and their mode of operation isn't simply reducible to a small number of hidden layers (as in connectionist models). Compared with digital computers, brains perform linear computations relatively slowly, yet they can make judgements with such apparent ease that computer modellers, both the rule-based and connectionist kinds, remain baffled (Rose, 1992). At least for the foreseeable future, it seems that brains will continue to outperform computers when doing the kinds of things that they were naturally designed to do.

One of these might be consciousness (see Chapters 4 and 7). Currently, we simply *don't know* what makes the brain conscious, and so we cannot design a conscious machine. Still, the brain is a physical entity and is conscious, so it must have some design features (presumably physical) which make it conscious (McGinn, 1987). This doesn't mean that a machine *couldn't* be conscious, only that it would have to be the same kind of machine the brain is. In support of Searle, Teichman (1988) states that, while we know that the computer hardware doesn't produce (initiate) the program, it's highly probable that the brain *does* help to produce mental states (see Chapter 49).

CHAPTER SUMMARY

- According to an **information-processing approach**, PS progresses through a series of logical stages: **defining/representing the problem, generating possible solutions** and **evaluating possible solutions**.
- The **behaviourist** view of PS as **trial-and-error** and **accidental success** was challenged by the **Gestalt** psychologists, who looked at how we impose **structure** on a problem.
- **Algorithms** and **heuristics** are two ways of generating possible solutions to a problem. Algorithms **guarantee** a solution, but can be time-consuming. Heuristics don't guarantee a solution, but can help produce solutions more quickly, as in **means–end analysis** (MEA).
- **Mental set/rigidity** and **functional fixedness/fixity** are ways in which past experience can hinder PS. Functional fixedness is a type of mental set, in which we fail to see that an object may have functions/uses other than its normal ones.
- Chess experts are only better at remembering board positions that could appear in an actual game, as opposed to random positions. Chess masters develop **global perceptual schemata** which allow them to see possible threats.
- **Expertise** reduces the strain on WM by enabling the expert to draw on already available, **domain-specific knowledge** stored in LTM.
- **Expert systems** (ESs) apply knowledge in specific areas (such as medical diagnosis), enabling a computer to function as effectively as a human expert. But human experts can't always say explicitly how they solve particular problems or make particular decisions.

- **Decision-making** (DM) is a special case of PS, in which we already know the possible solutions or choices. According to **compensatory models**, we evaluate how all desirable potential outcomes might compensate for undesirable ones.
- **Non-compensatory models** are less precise but more commonly used approaches, in which not all features of each alternative are considered, and features don't compensate for each other.
- Because of the absence of information and time, rational decisions can't always be made. So, we often resort to the **availability** and **representativeness heuristics**.
- Gambling is a form of **risk-taking** behaviour. Playing the National Lottery can be explained in terms of several heuristic strategies and biases, including the representativeness bias (which can explain the **gambler's fallacy**) and **availability bias, randomness bias, illusory correlation, flexible attribution, illusion of control**, and **sunk cost bias**.
- Every general-purpose digital computer is an approximation to a **universal Turing machine**. Although originally designed as powerful calculators, computers are **general-purpose, symbol-manipulating machines**.
- According to **weak AI**, computers merely **simulate/mimic** thought or intelligence, while according to **strong AI**, they're literally **reproducing/duplicating** thinking and intelligence.
- Underlying strong AI is the **computational theory of mind** (CTM), according to which intelligence is the ability to manipulate symbols. This is as true of a human mind as it is of a computer.
- Searle's **Chinese room thought experiment** is meant to show that the **Turing test** isn't the ultimate test of machine intelligence. But both have been criticised, and human intelligence shouldn't be regarded as the only or truest form of intelligence.
- According to CTM, the possession of a brain/the structure and mode of operation of the human brain are irrelevant. But many biologists, psychologists and others believe that there must be certain design features of the brain that have evolved to make it conscious.
- While digital computers process information in a **serial** fashion, brains operate in a **parallel** and also in a **distributed** manner. These considerations led to the development of **parallel distributed processing** (PDP).
- Brains and human beings are **open systems**, constantly interacting with the natural and social world. Brains may not be error-free machines, but they can perform certain tasks that are currently beyond the capability of any computer.

Self-assessment questions

1 Critically consider psychological research into problem-solving.
2 Discuss psychological research into risk-taking behaviour and/or errors in thinking about probability in relation to decision-making.
3 Describe and evaluate differences in the problem-solving strategies of humans and computers.
4 Critically assess the computational theory of mind.

Further reading

Le Voi, M. (1993) 'Parallel distributed processing and its application in models of memory,' in G. Cohen, G. Kiss and M. Le Voi (Eds) *Memory: Current Issues* (2nd edition) Buckingham: Open University Press. A very thorough but readable account of PDP, an extremely complex and technical topic for the non-computer-scientist.

Broadbent, D. (Ed.) (1993) *The Simulation of Human Intelligence.* Oxford: Blackwell. A collection of original chapters by several key figures, including Penrose, Newell, Boden and Broadbent, one of the 'founders' of cognitive psychology.

Solution to the nine-dot problem

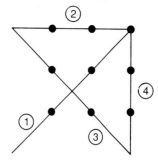

Solution to the matchsticks problem

Chapter 21 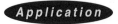 *Application*

Cognition and the Law

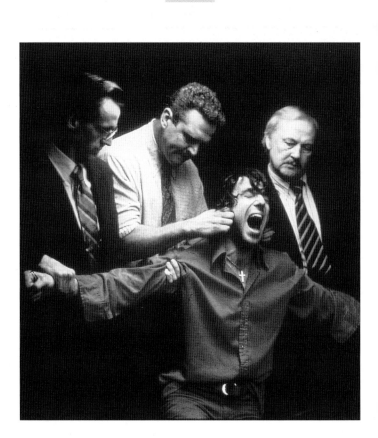

Introduction and overview

T his chapter is concerned mainly with *memory* and *forgetting*. But unlike Chapter 17, we'll be focusing on these crucially important cognitive processes from an *applied* perspective. Specifically, how has psychological research into memory and forgetting helped us understand and deal with certain situations that arise within our legal system, in particular, the issue of *eye-witness testimony* (EWT) and the controversy surrounding the recovery of repressed memories (sometimes referred to as the *false-memory debate*).

In 1973, the Devlin Committee was established to look at over 2000 legal cases in England and Wales that had involved identification parades (or line-ups). In 45 per cent of cases, suspects were picked out, and of those people prosecuted after being picked out, 82 per cent were subsequently convicted. Of the 347 cases in which prosecution occurred when EWT was the *only* evidence against the defendant, 74 per cent were convicted (Devlin, 1976). This indicates the overwhelming weight given to EWT (Baddeley, 1999).

Nevertheless, the *reconstructive* nature of memory has led some researchers to question the accuracy of EWT (e.g. Wells, 1993). The view of memory as reconstructive stems from the work of Bartlett (1932), and central to his theory is the concept of a schema. Bartlett has had an enormous impact on Loftus's research into EWT, as well as on theories of semantic memory (SM: see Chapter 17).

Since the early 1990s, considerable publicity has been given to court cases in the US, where parents are being sued for damages by their teenage or adult children, who accuse them of child sexual abuse (CSA). This has been remembered during the course of psychotherapy. It's assumed that these *recovered memories* had been repressed since the alleged CSA happened, and that the safety and support provided by the therapist allows them to become conscious many years later.

However, accused parents, and retractors (people who had recovered memories of CSA, accused their parents, then later withdrew the accusations) have also sued therapists and hospitals for implanting false memories in their children's minds. The False Memory Syndrome Foundation was set up in the US in 1992 and in 1993, the British False Memory Society was founded, with 1000 families currently on its books (Showalter, 1998). *Repression* is a theory of forgetting originally proposed by Freud, who's also regarded by many as at least partly responsible for the phenomenon of *false-memory syndrome*.

Schema theory and everyday memory

When discussing semantic memory (SM) in Chapter 17, we noted that it became increasingly obvious during the 1970s that SM must contain structures considerably larger than the simple concepts involved in Collins & Quillian's (1969) *hierarchical network model* and Collins & Loftus's (1975) *spreading-activation model*. This 'larger unit' of SM is the schema, a concept first used by Bartlett (1932) as part of his theory of reconstructive memory (see below, pages 311–312).

At the core of *schema theory* is the belief that what we remember is influenced by what we already know, and that our use of past experience to deal with new experience is a fundamental feature of the way the human mind works. Our knowledge is stored in memory as a set of schemas, simplified, generalised mental representations of everything we understand by a given type of object or event based on our past experience. They operate in a 'top-down' way to help us interpret the 'bottom-up' flood of information reaching our senses from the outside world. The term 'schema' was borrowed from the neurologist Henry Head, who used it to represent a person's concept of the location of limbs and body (see Penfield's *homunculus*, Chapter 4, page 53).

Two major modern schema theories are those of Rumelhart (1975) and Schank (1975) and Schank & Abelson (1977). There's a good deal of overlap between them, and the broad characteristics which they share are summarised by Rumelhart & Norman (1983, 1985):

- A schema is a packet of information comprising a *fixed/compulsory value* plus a *variable/optional value*. For example, a schema for buying something in a shop would have relatively fixed slots for the exchange of money and goods, while the variable values would be the amount of money and the nature of the goods. In particular cases, a slot may be left unspecified and can often be filled with a 'default' value (a best guess given the available information).
- *Schemas can be related together to form systems*. They aren't mutually exclusive packets of information, but can overlap. For example, a schema for a picnic may be part of a larger system of schemas including 'meals', 'outings' and 'parties'.
- *Schemas represent knowledge at all levels of abstraction*. They can relate to abstract ideologies, abstract concepts (e.g. justice), or concrete objects (e.g. the appearance of a face).
- *Schemas represent knowledge rather than definitions*. They embody knowledge and experience of the world, rather than abstract rules.
- *Schemas are active recognition devices*. This is very similar to Bartlett's 'effort after meaning', whereby we try to make sense of ambiguous and unfamiliar information in terms of our existing knowledge and understanding (see below).

According to Schank (1975) and Schank & Abelson (1977), schemas or *scripts* represent commonly experienced social events, such as catching a bus and going to a restaurant. These allow us to fill in much of the detail not specified in any text that we might read. For example:

> 'We had a tandoori chicken at the Taj Mahal last night. The service was slow and we almost missed the start of the play ...'

can only be interpreted by bringing in a great deal of additional information (Baddeley, 1990). We need schemas that predict what would happen next and fill in those aspects of the event which are left implicit in the text. Scripts are essential ways of summarizing common cultural assumptions, which not only help us to understand text and discourse but also predict future events and behave appropriately in given social situations. Scripts contain the sequences of actions we go through when taking part in familiar events, including the sorts of objects and actors we're likely to encounter.

Schank & Abelson (1977) built their scripts into a computer program (SAM), which they claim is capable of answering questions about restaurants and understanding stories about restaurants (see Chapter 20).

Ask yourself ...

- Try writing a script for going to a restaurant, i.e. what is the sequence of events that typically occurs when you go out for a meal, and who's involved at different times.

Table 21.1 *A simplified version of Schank & Abelson's (1977) schematic representation of activities involved in going to a restaurant (from Bower et al., 1979)*

Name:	Restaurant	Roles:	Customer
			Waiter
Props:	Tables		Cook
	Menu		Cashier
	Food		Owner
	Bill		
	Money		
	Tip		
Entry conditions:	Customer is hungry	**Results:**	Customer has less money
	Customer has money		Owner has more money
			Customer is not hungry
Scene 1:	Entering	**Scene 3:**	Eating
	Customer enters restaurant		Cook gives food to customer
	Customer looks for table		Customer eats food
	Customer decides where to sit		
	Customer goes to table		
	Customer sits down		
Scene 2:	Ordering	**Scene 3:**	Exiting
	Customer picks up menu		Waitress writes bill
	Customer looks at menu		Waitress goes over to customer
	Customer decides on food		Waitress gives bill to customer
	Customer signals to waitress		Customer gives tip to waitress
	Waitress comes to table		Customer goes to cashier
	Customer orders food		Customer gives money to cashier
	Waitress goes to cook		Customer leaves restaurant
	Waitress gives food order to cook		
	Cook prepares food		

Bower *et al.* (1979) asked people to list about 20 actions or events, in order, which commonly occur while eating at a restaurant, and found considerable agreement. For example, at least 73 per cent mentioned sitting down, looking at the menu, ordering, eating, paying the bill and leaving. Also, at least 48 per cent included entering, giving the reservation name, ordering drinks, discussing the menu, talking, eating salad or soup and ordering dessert, eating dessert and leaving a tip. So there were at least 15 events which formed part of many people's knowledge of what's involved in going to a restaurant. These findings broadly agreed with Schank and Abelson's restaurant script. When such events were incorporated into stories, people tended to recall falsely aspects of the passage which weren't explicitly included, but which were consistent with the script (that is, which could well have happened). The order of events was also changed to fit what would 'normally' happen. This is exactly what Bartlett would have predicted (see below).

An evaluation of schema theory

According to Cohen (1993):

- the whole idea of a schema is too vague to be useful;
- there's an overemphasis on the inaccuracies of memory, overlooking the fact that complex events are sometimes remembered very precisely and accurately (especially the unexpected, unusual aspects);

- it's unclear how schemas are acquired in the first place. There seems to be a kind of 'Catch-22' involved here, since without schemas we can't interpret new experiences, but we need new experiences to build up our schemas.

> *Ask yourself ...*
>
> - Can you apply this last criticism to Gregory's top-down theory of perception? (See Chapter 15.)

Schank's (1982) *dynamic-memory theory* attempts (as the name implies) to take account of the more dynamic aspects of memory, and is a more elaborate and flexible model. It tries to clarify the relationship between general knowledge schemas and memory for specific episodes, based on a more hierarchical arrangement of memory representations. *Memory organisation packets* (MOPs) are at the bottom of the hierarchy, storing specific details about particular events. At higher levels, the representations become more and more general and schema-like. MOPs aren't usually stored for very long, becoming absorbed into the event schemas which store those features that are common to repeated experience. However, details of unusual or atypical events are retained (Cohen, 1993).

Box 21.1   The War of the Ghosts

The title of this story is *The War of the Ghosts*. One night two young men from Egulac went down to the river to hunt seals and while they were there it became foggy and calm. Then they heard war-cries and they thought: 'Maybe this is a war party'. They escaped to the shore and hid behind a log. Now canoes came up and they heard the noise of paddles and saw one canoe coming up to them. There were five men in the canoe and they said: 'What do you think? We wish to take you along. We are going up the river to make war on the people'. One of the young men said 'I have no arrows'. 'Arrows are in the canoe', they said. 'I will not go along. I might be killed. My relatives do not know where I have gone. But you', he said, turning to the other, 'may go with them'. So one of the young men went but the other returned home. And the warriors went on up the river to a town on the other side of Kalama. The people came down to the water and they began to fight and many were killed. But presently the young man heard one of the warriors say: 'Quick, let us go home; that Indian has been hit'. Now he thought: 'Oh, they are ghosts'. He did not feel sick but they said he had been shot. So the canoes went back to Egulac and the young man went ashore to his house and made a fire. And he told everybody and said: 'Behold I accompanied the ghosts and we went to fight. Many of our fellows were killed and many of those who attacked us were killed. They said I was hit and I did not feel sick'. He told it all and then he became quiet. When the sun rose he fell down. Something black came out of his mouth. His face became contorted. The people jumped up and cried. He was dead.

Reconstructive memory

The Bartlett 'approach'

As we saw in Chapter 17, Ebbinghaus was the first to study memory systematically, using nonsense syllables. Although this 'tradition' is still popular with today's memory researchers, Bartlett (1932) argued that:

- Ebbinghaus's use of nonsense syllables excluded 'all that is most central to human memory';
- the study of 'repetition habits' had very little to do with memory in everyday life;
- research should examine people's *active search for meaning*, rather than their passive responses to meaningless stimuli presented by an experimenter.

Although meaningful material is more complex than meaningless material, Bartlett argued that it too could be studied experimentally. As we saw earlier, Bartlett's concept of a schema is central to theories which attempt to explain the structure and organisation of knowledge in SM (a major part of LTM). Because of the large amount of work on the organisational aspects of memory (see Chapter 17), and because of the growing recognition of the need to study meaningful material (as opposed to lists of unrelated words, numbers, and so on), there has been a 'rediscovery' of Bartlett's work.

Serial reproduction and *The War of the Ghosts*

One method Bartlett used was *serial reproduction*, in which one person reproduces some material, a second person has to reproduce the first reproduction, a third has to reproduce the second reproduction and so on, until six or seven reproductions have been made. The method is meant to duplicate, to some extent, the process by which gossip or rumours are spread or legends passed from generation to generation (and may be more familiar as 'Chinese whispers'). One of the most famous pieces of material Bartlett used was *The War of the Ghosts*, a North American folk tale.

When used with English participants, who were unfamiliar with its style and content, the story changed in certain characteristic ways as it was re-told:

- The story became noticeably *shorter*. Bartlett found that after six or seven reproductions, it shrank from 330 to 180 words.
- Despite becoming shorter, and details being omitted, the story became *more coherent*. No matter how distorted it became, it remained a story: the participants were interpreting the story as a whole, both listening to it and retelling it.
- It also became more *conventional*, retaining only those details which could be easily assimilated to the particpants' shared past experiences and cultural backgrounds.
- It became *more clichéd* – any peculiar or individual interpretations tended to be dropped.

Replications of Bartlett's findings

Hunter (1964) used *The War of the Ghosts* and the serial reproduction method. He found similar changes to those originally reported by Bartlett. But the use of this folk tale has been criticised, because it's written in an unusual style, making it difficult for Western participants to find connections between different parts of the story.

Another method used by Bartlett, *repeated reproduction*, involves the same participants recalling the story on different occasions. This produced similar results to those obtained with serial reproduction. Wynn & Logie (1998) used this alternative method, but instead of *The War of the Ghosts*, they used a real-life event, namely first-year undergraduates' recollections of details of their first week at university. They were asked to recall this information in November, January, March and May (the students being unaware that this would happen).

Contrary to Bartlett's findings, Wynn and Logie found that the accuracy of the descriptions was maintained across the different intervals and regardless of the number of repeated recalls. This suggests that memories for distinctive events can be relatively resistant to change over time, even when repeatedly reproduced.

CROSS-CULTURAL PERSPECTIVE 21.1

Remembering as a cultural activity

An important implication of Bartlett's work is that memory is a *social phenomenon* that cannot be studied as a 'pure' process. Because he emphasised the influence of previous knowledge and background experience, he found that remembering is integrally related to the social and cultural contexts in which it's practised. When members of Western and non-Western cultures are compared on tasks devised in psychology laboratories, such as free-recalling lists of unrelated words, the former do better; this seems to reflect the meaninglessness of such tasks for the latter (see Chapter 17).

According to Mistry & Rogoff (1994), culture and memory are enmeshed skills, and 'remembering' is an activity with goals whose function is determined by the social and cultural contexts in which it takes place. This helps to explain the phenomenal memory for lines of descent and history of Itamul elders in New Guinea, needed to resolve disputes over claims to property by conflicting clans. Bartlett himself described the prodigious ability of Swazi herdsmen to recall individual characteristics of their cattle. But since Swazi culture revolves around the possession and care of cattle, this ability isn't so surprising. What these examples show, is that remembering is a means of achieving a culturally important goal, rather than the goal itself (Mistry & Rogoff, 1994).

Schemas and reconstructive memory

Bartlett concluded from his findings that *interpretation* plays a major role in the remembering of stories and past events. Learning and remembering are both active processes involving 'effort after meaning'; that is, trying to make the past more logical, coherent and generally 'sensible'. This involves making inferences or deductions about what could or should have happened. We reconstruct the past by trying to fit it into our existing understanding of the world. Unlike a computer's memory, where the output exactly matches the input, human memory is an 'imaginative reconstruction' of experience.

Bartlett called this existing understanding of the world a *schema*. Schemas (or schemata):

- provide us with ready-made expectations which help to interpret the flow of information reaching the senses;
- help to make the world more predictable;
- allow us to 'fill in the gaps' when our memories are incomplete;

- can produce significant distortions in memory processes, because they have a powerful effect on the way in which memories for events are encoded. This happens when new information conflicts with existing schemata.

For example, Allport & Postman (1947) showed white participants a picture of two men evidently engaged in an argument.

Figure 21.1 *The stimulus material used by Allport & Postman (1947). The two men are engaged in an argument. The better-dressed man is black, and the white man has a cut-throat razor in his hand*

After looking briefly at the picture, participants were asked to describe the scene to someone who hadn't seen it. This person was then required to describe the scene to another person, and so on. As this happened, details changed. The most significant change was that the cut-throat razor was reported as being held by the black man.

Ask yourself ...

- What method was involved in Allport and Postman's experiment?
- What can you infer about the schema that the participants were using, which helps account for the distortion that took place?
- If the participants had been black, would you expect a similar distortion to have taken place?
- Are these results consistent with Bartlett's theory of reconstructive memory? Explain your answer.

Allport and Postman used serial reproduction, as Bartlett had done in his study using *The War of the Ghosts*. Presumably, the white participants used a schema which included the belief that black men are prone to violence. Black participants would be expected to have a rather different schema of black men, making them less likely to distort the details in the picture. Allport and Postman's findings are consistent with Bartlett's theory of reconstructive memory.

Eyewitness testimony

Loftus's research

Bartlett's view of memory as reconstructive is also taken by Loftus, who has investigated it mainly in relation to eyewitness testimony (EWT). Loftus argues that the evidence given by witnesses in court cases is highly unreliable, and this is explained largely by the kind of misleading questions that witnesses are asked. Lawyers are skilled in asking such questions deliberately, as are the police when interrogating suspects and witnesses to a crime or accident.

Loftus has tried to answer the following questions.

- Is EWT influenced by people's tendency to reconstruct their memories of events to fit their schemas?
- Can subtle differences in the wording of a question cause witnesses to remember events differently?
- Can witnesses be misled into remembering things that didn't actually occur?

How useful are identification parades?

The Devlin Committee (see *Introduction and overview*) recommended that the trial judge be required to instruct the jury that it isn't safe to convict on a single eyewitness's testimony alone, except in exceptional circumstances (such as where the witness is a close friend or relative of the accused, or where there's substantial corroborative evidence).

This recommendation is underlined by a famous case of misidentification involving an Australian psychologist. The psychologist in question had appeared in a TV discussion on EWT, and was later picked out in an identity parade by a very distraught woman who claimed that he'd raped her. The rape had in fact occurred while the victim was watching the psychologist on TV. She correctly recognised his face, but not the circumstances!

EWT, episodic memory (EM) and SM

According to Fiske & Taylor (1991), it's easy to see how a witness could confuse the mention of something in a question with its actual presence at the scene of the crime, if that something is commonly found in such situations. For example, a 'leading' question might refer to things that weren't actually present at the scene of the crime (stored in EM), but which might well have been (based on our schemas and stereotyped beliefs about the world stored in SM).

Similarly, a witness who examines a preliminary identification parade may later remember having seen one of the suspects before, but fail to distinguish between the identification parade and the scene of the crime – the innocent suspect may be misidentified as the criminal because he/she is *familiar*. This can be taken one stage further back. Several studies have shown that when witnesses view a line-up after having looked at mugshots, they're more likely to identify one of those depicted (regardless of whether that person actually committed the crime) than people who aren't shown the mugshot (Memon & Wright, 1999).

These (and the case of the Australian psychologist above) are examples of *source confusion* (or *source misattribution*: see page 317) – you recognise someone but are mistaken about where you know them from! This can have very serious consequences for the person who is misidentified!

Is a mistaken eyewitness better than none?

Using a fictitious case, Loftus (1974) asked students to judge the guilt or innocence of a man accused of robbing a grocer's and murdering the owner and his five-year-old grand-daughter. On the evidence presented, only nine of the 50 students considered the man to be guilty. Other students were presented with the same case, but were also told that one of the shop assistants had testified that the accused was the man who had committed the crimes. Thirty-six of these 50 students judged him to be guilty.

A third group of 50 students was presented with the original evidence and the assistant's EWT. However, they were also told that the defence lawyer had discredited the assistant: he was shortsighted, hadn't been wearing his glasses when the crime occurred, and so couldn't possibly have seen the accused's face from where he was standing at the time.

> ### Ask yourself ...
>
> - How many students in the third group do you think judged the accused to be guilty?
> - Explain your answer and say what this tells us about the importance of EWT.

In fact, 34 out of 50 thought he was guilty! So, a mistaken witness does seem to be 'better' than no witness. Moreover, *confident witnesses* are more likely to be seen as *credible* (i.e. accurate) compared with anxious witnesses, even though actual accuracy may not differ (Nolan & Markham, 1998).

Factors influencing EWT

- **Race**: Errors are more likely to occur when the suspect and witness are racially different (Brigham & Malpass, 1985). So, we're much better at recognising members of our own racial groups than members of other racial groups. This is reflected in the comment that 'They all look the same to me' when referring to members of different races (*the illusion of outgroup homogeneity*: see Chapter 25, page 375).
- **Clothing**: Witnesses pay more attention to a suspect's clothing than to more stable characteristics, such as height and facial features. It seems that criminals are aware of this, since they change what they wear prior to appearing in a line-up (Brigham & Malpass, 1985).
- **Social influence**: One source of social influence (see Chapter 26) is contact and exchange of information among witnesses. For example, Memon & Wright (1999) describe a study in which participants were asked in pairs whether they'd seen several cars in a previous phase of the study. When responding second, people were influenced by the first person's answers. If the first person said s/he did see the car previously, the second person was more likely to say the same, irrespective of whether the car really was previously seen.
- **Violence**: Does extreme emotion brand the experience indelibly on the victim's memory, or does it reduce the capacity for recollection, perhaps through repression (Baddeley, 1999: see below)? The usual method for investigating this is to expose participants to a film or a staged incident, in which some crucial violent event occurs (such as the apparent shooting of a child). Overall, the evidence

suggests that memory for violent events is *stronger* than for a neutral event, but that recollection of associated detail is *poorer*. For example, there appears to be a 'weapons focus', whereby victims may concentrate their attention on the weapon itself, rather than the attacker's appearance. So:

'... fear may put a crucial feature of a situation into sharp focus, but may reduce the reliability of the witness's account of peripheral features'. (Baddeley, 1999)

■ **Misleading questions and suggestibility**: It seems that both adults and children are subject to *reconstructive errors* in recall, particularly when presented with misleading information. In other words, a witness can be highly suggestible. Different types of misleading question include:

– *leading questions*, as illustrated by Loftus & Palmer's (1974) experiment (see Key Study 21.1);
– questions which introduce *after-the-fact information*, as illustrated by Loftus (1975: see Key Study 21.2).

Figure 21.2 *Assessments of speeds of crashing vehicles can be influenced by the verb used to describe the impact. While (a) represents 'two cars hitting', (b) represents 'two cars smashing'. Which word is used in a question can influence people's estimates of how fast the cars were travelling at the time of impact*

KEY STUDY 21.1

The effect of leading questions (Loftus & Palmer, 1974)

Loftus and Palmer tested the effect of changing single words in certain critical questions on the judgement of speed. Participants were shown a 30-second videotape of two cars colliding, and were then asked several questions about the collision.

One group was asked 'About how fast were the cars going when they *hit*?' For others, the word 'hit' was replaced by 'smashed', 'collided', 'bumped' or 'contacted'. These words have very different connotations regarding the speed and force of impact, and this was reflected in the judgements given.

Those who heard the word 'hit' produced an average speed estimate of 34.0 mph. For 'smashed', 'collided', 'bumped' and 'contacted', the average estimates were 40.8, 39.3, 38.1 and 31.8 mph respectively (see Figure 21.2).

What do leading questions actually do?

Loftus and Palmer wanted to know if memory for events actually *changes* as a result of misleading questions, or whether the existing memory is merely *supplemented*. *Memory as reconstruction* implies that memory itself is transformed at the point of retrieval, so that what was originally encoded changes when it's recalled.

To test this, Loftus & Palmer's (1974) study included a follow-up experiment. A week after the original experiment, those participants who'd heard the word 'smashed' or 'hit' were asked further questions, one of which was whether they remembered seeing any broken glass (even though there was none in the film). If 'smashed' really had influenced participants' memory of the accident as being more serious than it was, then they might also 'remember' details they didn't actually see, but which are consistent with an accident occurring at high speed (such as broken glass).

Of the 50 'smashed' participants, 16 (32 per cent) reported seeing broken glass. Only seven (14 per cent) of the 50 'hit' participants did so. These results appear to support the memory-as-reconstruction explanation.

KEY STUDY 21.2

The effect of 'after-the-event' information (Loftus, 1975)

Participants watched a short film of a car travelling through the countryside. They were all asked the same ten questions about the film, except for one critical question.

■ Group A was asked 'How fast was the white sports car going when it passed the 'Stop' sign while travelling along the country road?'. (There *was* a 'Stop' sign in the film.)
■ Group B was asked 'How fast was the white sports car going when it passed the barn while travelling along the country road?'. (There was *no* barn.)

'The' barn implies that there actually was a barn in the film, which is what makes it misleading.

A week later, all the participants were asked ten new questions about the film. The final question was 'Did you see a barn?'. Of Group A participants, only 2.7 per cent said 'yes', while 17.3 per cent of Group B participants said 'yes'.

Similarly, Loftus & Zanni (1975) showed participants a short film of a car accident, after which they answered questions about what they'd witnessed. Some were asked if they'd seen *a* broken headlight, while others were asked if they'd seen *the* broken headlight. Those asked about *the* headlight were far more likely to say 'yes' than those asked about *a* headlight.

As with leading questions, memory as reconstruction sees questions which provide misleading new information about an event becoming integrated with how the event is already represented in memory.

Suggestibility and source misattribution

As the Loftus studies show, witnesses may come to believe that they actually remember seeing items in an event that in fact have been (falsely) suggested to them. Currently, the most popular explanation for suggestibility effects is *source misattribution*. Witnesses are confusing information obtained outside of the context of the witnessed event (*post-event information*) with the witnessed event itself (Memon & Wright, 1999). Memories of details from various sources can be combined with memories of that event (*memory blending*).

An evaluation of Loftus's research

While the evidence described above suggests that eyewitnesses are unreliable, are they really as unreliable as Loftus believes?

- Bekerian & Bowers (1983) have argued that Loftus questions her witnesses in a rather unstructured way. If questions followed the order of events in strict sequence, then witnesses weren't influenced by the biasing effect of subsequent questions. Despite some failures to replicate these findings (e.g. McCloskey & Zaragoza, 1985), an important practical consequence of Bekerian and Bower's research is the *cognitive interview* (see Box 21.2).
- Contrary to the memory-as-reconstruction interpretation, Baddeley (1995) believes that '... the Loftus effect is not due to destruction of the memory trace but is due to interfering with its retrieval' (see Chapter 17).
- Stephenson (1988) points out that the bulk of the work on EWT has been carried out in laboratories and has concentrated on eyewitness identification of people seen under fairly non-threatening conditions, or even people seen on films. In sharp contrast were the participants of a study by Yuille & Cutshall (1986): see Case Study 21.1.
- Loftus herself acknowledges that when misleading information is 'blatantly incorrect', it has no effects on a witness's memory. For example, Loftus (1979) showed participants colour slides of a man stealing a red purse from a woman's bag. Ninety-eight per cent correctly identified the purse's colour, and when they read a description of the event which referred to a 'brown purse', just two per cent continued to remember it as red. This suggests that our memory for obviously important information accurately perceived at the time *isn't* easily distorted, as shown by Yuille & Cutshall's (1986) study.

According to Cohen (1993), people are more likely to be misled if:

- the false information they're given concerns insignificant details that aren't central to the main event;
- the false information is given after a delay (when the memory of the event has had time to fade);
- they have no reason to distrust it.

CASE STUDY 21.1

Eyewitness memory of a crime (Yuille & Cutshall, 1986)

The incident involved a shooting which occurred outside a gun shop in full view of several witnesses (in Vancouver, Canada). A thief had entered the gun shop, tied up the proprietor and stolen some money and a number of guns. The store-owner freed himself, picked up a revolver and went outside to take the thief's licence number. But the thief hadn't yet entered his car, and in a face-to-face encounter on the street, separated by six feet, the thief fired two shots at the store-owner. After a slight pause the store-owner discharged all six shots from his revolver. The thief was killed, but the store-owner recovered from serious injury. Witnesses viewed the incident from various vantage points along the street, from adjacent buildings or from passing automobiles.

Twenty-one of the witnesses were interviewed by the police shortly after the event, and 13 of them agreed to take part in a research interview four to five months later. In both sets of interviews (police and research), verbatim accounts of the incident were obtained and follow-up questions were asked in order to clarify points of detail. Also, the researchers asked two misleading questions based on Loftus's '*a* broken headlight'/'*the* broken headlight' technique.

The sheer volume of accurate detail produced in both sets of interviews is truly impressive. The researchers obtained much more detail than did the police, because they were concerned with memory for details which had no immediate forensic value. Witnesses who were central to the event gave more details than did peripheral witnesses, but there was no overall difference in accuracy between the two groups. Significantly, the wording of the misleading questions had no effect, and those who were most deeply distressed by the incident were the most accurate of the witnesses.

The cognitive interview

An increasing number of police forces are using the *cognitive interview* (CI). Traditionally, police officers and lawyers have used the standard interview procedure, which involves a period of free recall about the event, followed by specific questions about details that emerge from the free recall. The CI draws on Tulving's research concerning the relationship between encoding and retrieval cues (see Chapter 17, pages 261–263).

Box 21.2 The cognitive interview (Geiselman *et al.*, 1985)

- **Reinstating the context:** The interviewer and interviewee try to recreate the context in which the incident occurred (the surroundings, such as the temperature, smells, sounds, the witness's feelings) *before* any attempt is made to recall the events themselves.
- **Reporting the event:** The interviewee is asked to report absolutely everything, regardless of how unimportant/irrelevant it may seem.
- **Recalling the event in several orders:** This includes reporting the event in reverse order.

- **Reporting the event from multiple perspectives:** The interviewee is asked to recall the event from, say, the perspective of the cashier in the case of a bank robbery.

The first two 'stages' are based on the concept of *encoding specificity*, that is, trying to provide maximum overlap between the context in which the crime was committed and the context in which the recall attempt is made. The second two try to capitalise on the idea that material can be retrieved using a number of different routes that may produce information about rather different aspects of the original event (Baddeley, 1999).

The initial test of the CI (Geiselman *et al.*, 1985) used a police training film of a violent crime. Participants were interviewed 48 hours later, using either the new CI, or the standard Los Angeles police interview, or hypnosis prior to being asked to recall the incident using the standard procedure. Although the three methods didn't differ in the amount of false information they produced, the standard interview produced the least overall amount of information (an average of 29.4 items). The CI produced the most (41.2 items).

A second experiment introduced misleading information during the interview: 'Was the guy with the green backpack nervous?' (it wasn't green). Those tested with the CI were the *least likely* to be misled by this false information.

Fisher & Geiselman (1988) have continued to develop the CI, using hints obtained from watching 'good' and 'poor' interviewers. These include the greater use of open-ended questions, and attempts to fit the order of questioning to the witness's order of experience. This has increased accurate reporting from 40 to 60 per cent. Bekerian & Dennett (1993) reviewed 27 experiments comparing the effects of the CI with more standard techniques. The CI proved superior in all cases: on average, about 30 per cent more information is accurately reported, with false information being slightly less common.

Harrower (1998) maintains that the CI procedure may be particularly beneficial for those interviewing child witnesses, especially those who may have been the victims of physical or sexual abuse. However, the interviewer must be trained in assessing the linguistic and cognitive competence of each child interviewee, and to adapt the interview accordingly.

Recognising faces

While the face isn't the only route to person identification, it's probably the most reliable (Bruce & Young, 1998). Laboratory experiments have shown that people are remarkably accurate at remembering briefly viewed, previously unfamiliar faces, typically scoring over 90 per cent correct when asked to decide which of a large set of faces were previously presented. But this may seem to be at odds with our sometimes embarrassing failure to recognise or identify faces in everyday life (e.g. Young *et al.*'s 1985 diary study). Bruce and Young suggest two main reasons for this discrepancy.

■ Laboratory experiments tend to test memory for *identical pictures of faces*, thereby confounding *picture memory* with true *face memory*. But if memory for faces is tested with different pictures of the same target face, accuracy drops dramatically (to 60 per cent: Bruce, 1982).

■ Recognition can be affected by changes in *context* between where the face was originally encountered and where memory for it is subsequently tested. Context is broadly defined to include expectations (consistent with reconstructive memory; see also Chapter 15), clothing, head shape and hairstyle. Most criminals disguise themselves in some way when committing a crime, which suggests their implicit understanding of the importance of context for later recognition. With familiar people, head shape/hairstyle become less dominant, and internal facial features become more important for recognition.

> *Ask yourself ...*
>
> - How could you account for this difference between familiar and unfamiliar faces?

> *Ask yourself ...*
>
> - Without looking back at the photograph on page 311 of two men involved in a violent incident, try to answer the following questions:
>
>   **a** What are the two men doing?
>   **b** In which hand is one of the men holding a knife?
>   **c** Are both men clean-shaven?
>   **d** Is there anyone else in the picture?
>   **e** How would you describe the man who isn't holding the knife?
>
>   Now look back at the photograph and check your answers.

Figure 21.3 *Bill Clinton and Al Gore? Same face, different hair*

Helping people to remember faces

Two major techniques used to probe witnesses' memory for faces are *reconstruction* and *identification*. Reconstruction involves producing, from the witness's description, an image of the criminal for circulation to other police forces or for the general public. Typically, the witness, with or without a trained operator, tries to construct a target face using a 'kit' of isolated facial features. Identification involves looking through photographs in an album of 'mug-shots', or looking at a live 'line-up'/identity parade of potential offenders.

Reconstruction

Performance using *Photofit* (and other similar 'kits') is generally very poor (e.g. Ellis *et al.*, 1978). One problem is that kits assume that a face can be deconstructed into its component parts. But facial identity may be more *holistic* than this, and relationships between features are at least as important as the features themselves (see Chapter 14, pages 202–204). *Photofit* has only limited opportunities for the manipulation of such factors. There's a small number of 'cardinal' features, which people use regularly and reliably to describe and categorise faces, such as face shape, hair, and age, but these are difficult to manipulate directly using *Photofit* (Bruce & Young, 1998).

The rapid development of powerful computer graphics at relatively low cost has made it possible to develop more interactive systems. *E-fit*, for example, although still based around a basic 'kit' of photographic face parts, provides much greater opportunity for the blending and elaboration of these parts. This results in much more realistic images (Bruce & Young, 1998). Currently, as a witness gives a description of, say the eyes, the computer chooses the best set of eyes for you. The witness doesn't see the face until it's completed. But a modified 'jigsaw' *E-fit*, being pioneered by the UK Face Processing Research Group, allows the witness to watch the face as it's built up. But because it's important that the features are always seen as part of a face, a cartoon outline and features are used to replace those elements that haven't yet been described (Greenhaigh, 2000).

Identification

It's essential that the other members of a line-up/ID parade (the non-suspects or 'distractors') aren't obviously different from the suspect. For example, in one extreme case, the suspect was known to be Asian, and the line-up included only one Asian! (Baddeley, 1999). More subtle problems include:

- showing a photograph of the accused to a witness before the line-up. This could cause false identification based on *source confusion* (see above, page 313). This should be clearly avoided (Baddeley, 1999);
- there's often an assumption (usually implicit, but occasionally explicit) that the line-up actually includes the criminal. This reinforces a bias towards making a positive identification: witnesses are already highly motivated to do so and know the police don't go the trouble of arranging a line-up unless they have a suspect (Baddeley, 1999; Bruce & Young, 1998).

Video-witness testimony: a special case of EWT

Now that closed-circuit television (CCTV) is commonplace in shops, banks, and so on, there's an increased chance that an image of a criminal will be captured on videotape. This would seem to neatly side-step the problems with human face memory. Once a suspect has been apprehended (using some combination of eyewitness and other forensic evidence), the person's identity can be readily confirmed by comparison with the videotape. But things are rather more complicated than this (Bruce, 1998).

Cameras may be set to scan large public areas, so that images obtained of any individual may be of very poor resolution. Bruce cites the example of a prosecution case based entirely on the evidence of a CCTV image which showed a young black man robbing a building society. The defence used an expert witness, who helped get the evidence thrown out. Clearly, a CCTV image alone might prove very little about a suspect's precise identity.

Bruce has investigated face recognition and memory for over 25 years. She'd always assumed that people's difficulties in matching two different views, expressions or lightings were due to major changes along these dimensions. Evidence now suggests that rather subtle pictorial differences are difficult for human vision to deal with. Even the more successful computer systems for face recognition have the same difficulties.

The quality of CCTV images can vary considerably:

- camera and lighting angles may provide only a poorly lit, messy image of the top or back of someone's head;
- images may be blurred, and black-and-white images cast lots of shadows;
- even when the image quality is reasonably high, judging different images as being of the same individual may be remarkably prone to error;
- CCTV images may be most helpful in identifying criminals when the faces captured on tape are of someone known to a witness. People who are highly familiar are easily identified from CCTV images of a quality that would make identification of an unfamiliar face extremely difficult.

KEY STUDY 21.3

Make sure you know the offender (Burton *et al.*, 1999)

Bruce and her colleagues at Stirling and Glasgow Universities conducted two experiments, in which they manipulated familiarity.

- Male and female psychology lecturers were caught on security cameras at the entrance to the psychology department. This video footage was shown to both psychology and non-psychology students, and experienced police officers, who were then asked to indicate which of the people in a set of high-quality photographs they'd seen on tape. The psychology students made the most correct identifications, suggesting that previous familiarity with the target helps with recognition.
- The same video footage was used, but this time the head, body or gait was obscured. Participants performed quite poorly when the gait or body were obscured, but they did significantly worse when the head was obscured. Thus, the advantage of familiarity seems to be due to recognition of facial features, rather than body shape or how people walk. But unusual gait or body shape might produce different results.

Consistent with these findings are those of a study by Davies & Thasen (2000). When participants were asked to match unfamiliar faces seen on videotape to one of a series of 'mugshots', they found very low rates of correct identification, even when a close-up still of the target face was in constant view. Whether the video images were in colour or black and white made no difference.

Ask yourself ...

- According to Harrower (1998), research clearly shows that most people remember faces poorly and recall details not from memory, but in terms of what they believe criminals should look like. How can this finding be explained?

This is another example of how schemas are used to fill in the gaps in memory. It represents another demonstration of reconstructive memory.

Repression and the false-memory debate

Motivated-forgetting theory (repression)

According to Freud (1901), forgetting is motivated, rather than the result of a failure to learn or other processes. Memories which are likely to induce guilt, embarrassment, shame or anxiety are actively, but unconsciously, pushed out of consciousness as a form of *ego defence* (see Chapters 12 and 42):

> 'The essence of repression lies simply in turning something away, and keeping it at a distance, from the conscious …'. (Freud, 1915)

Unconscious or repressed memories are exceedingly difficult to retrieve (they're inaccessible) but remain available ('in storage': see Chapter 17). They continue to exert a great influence over us, even though we have no awareness of them.

Evidence for repression

Clinical evidence

As far as clinical evidence is concerned, it's widely accepted that repression plays a crucial role in different types of *psychogenic* (or *functional*) *amnesia* such as fugue and multiple personality disorder (see Gross *et al.*, 2000). These disorders involve a loss of memory associated with a traumatic experience (as opposed to brain injury or surgery). A relatively common form of psychogenic amnesia is *event-specific amnesia*: loss of memory for a fairly specific period of time. For instance, some violent criminals claim they cannot remember carrying out their crimes (see Chapter 46). Even when we have ruled out both malingering and the effects of intoxication at the time the crime was committed, there's still a substantial number of criminals whose memories of their crimes seem to have been repressed (Parkin, 1993). This is especially likely when murder victims are close relatives or lovers of the murderer killed in a crime of passion (Taylor & Kopelman, 1984).

Ian Brady (convicted along with Myra Hindley of the Moors Murders) repressed memories of his hideous crimes for many years before finally remembering where he'd buried his

victims (Parkin, 2000). However, in a study of children who'd seen a parent killed, none showed evidence of repression; on the contrary, the experience tended to be recalled all too frequently (Baddeley, 1999). This, and the observation that psychogenic amnesia can disappear as suddenly as it appeared, are difficult for motivated-forgetting theory to explain.

Parkin (1993) also cites evidence that repressive mechanisms may play a beneficial role in enabling people with *post-traumatic stress disorder* to adjust (see Chapters 12 and 44). For example, survivors of the Holocaust judged to be better adjusted were significantly *less* able to recall their dreams when woken from REM sleep (see Chapter 7) than less well-adjusted survivors (Kaminer & Lavie, 1991).

However, 'repression' doesn't necessarily imply a strictly Freudian interpretation. When the concept is considered more broadly than Freud intended, that is, in the general sense that our memory systems can in some way block particular forms of memory, it deserves to be taken seriously (Parkin, 2000). This is also the view taken by the British Psychological Survey on 'Recovered Memories' (BPS, 1995: see below, pages 319–321). Similarly, although traumatic experiences can undoubtedly produce memory disturbances, there's greater doubt as to whether Freud's explanation is the best one (Anderson, 1995a).

Experimental evidence

KEY STUDY 21.4

Testing Freud's repression hypothesis (Levinger & Clark, 1961)

Levinger and Clark looked at the retention of associations to negatively charged words (such as 'quarrel', 'angry', 'fear') compared with those for neutral words (such as 'window', 'cow', 'tree'). When participants were asked to give immediate free associations to the words (to say exactly what came into their minds), it took them longer to respond to the emotional words. These words also produced higher galvanic skin responses (GSR – a measure of emotional arousal).

Immediately after the word association tests had been completed, participants were given the cue words again and asked to try to recall their associations.

They had particular trouble remembering the associations to the emotionally charged words. This is exactly what Freud's repression hypothesis predicted, and for some years the study stood as the best experimental demonstration of repression (Parkin, 1993).

However, there are other studies which show that, while highly arousing words tend to be poorly recalled when tested immediately, the effect *reverses* after a delay (Eysenck & Wilson, 1973). If the words are being repressed, this shouldn't happen (they should stay repressed), suggesting that arousal was the crucial factor.

Ask yourself ...

* If you were to repeat the Levinger and Clark experiment, what change would you introduce in order to test the 'arousal hypothesis'?

Parkin *et al.* (1982) replicated the original study but added a delayed recall condition, in which participants were asked to recall their associations seven days after the original test. The results supported Eysenck and Wilson's interpretation – higher arousal levels inhibit immediate recall but increase longer-term recall.

In a later replication, Bradley & Baddeley (1990) used an immediate and a 28-day delayed condition. They found clear support for the arousal hypothesis. But later research hasn't always supported the arousal interpretation, and the question of emotional inhibition remains open (Parkin, 1993).

Recovered memories and the false-memory debate

As we noted in the *Introduction and overview*, the False Memory Syndrome Foundation (in the US) and the British False Memory Society (BFMS) were founded in the early 1990s, largely by parents accused by their grown-up children of having sexually abused them when they were children. The accusing children discovered repressed memories of child sexual abuse (CSA) during the course of psychotherapy; hence, from their and their therapists' perspectives, these are *recovered memories* (RMs).

However, from the perspective of the accused parents, these are *false memories* (FMs), implanted by therapists into the minds of their emotionally vulnerable patients/clients. These unethical, unscrupulous therapists are, in turn, accused by parents of practising *recovered-memory therapy*, which induces *false-memory syndrome* (FMS).

This brief account of the false-memory debate raises several, interrelated issues, spanning the psychology of memory and forgetting, the nature of psychotherapy (in particular, Freudian psychoanalysis), and the ethics of psychotherapy in general (see Chapter 48). When children sue their parents over alleged CSA, the family is inevitably torn apart and individual lives can be ruined. Hence, the need for support groups such as the BFMS. But the false memory debate has also caused division amongst psychologists, as well as between psychologists and psychiatrists. The key questions that we'll concentrate on in the remainder of this chapter are: do RMs exist, do FMs exist and, if so, how might they be created?

Do recovered memories exist?

The answer to this question depends very largely on how the concept of repression is understood. If these memories have been repressed, and are now retrieved from the unconscious during the course of therapy, then there must first be sound evidence for the existence of repression. This is the process which is supposed to keep recollections of the CSA hidden from the victim in the first place, until many years later, as an adult in therapy, the unconscious is 'unlocked'.

When discussing repression above, we saw that the strongest evidence is clinical, but that this is far from conclusive. We also need to take a closer look at Freud's view of memory.

Box 21.3 Freud and screen memories

According to Mollon (2000), it's sometimes asserted that Freud believed that the events of a person's life are all recorded accurately somewhere in the mind, like video-recordings. They're supposedly preserved in their original form, available but made inaccessible by repression.

However, in a paper on *Screen Memories* (1899), he argued that memories, especially of events of long ago, may be constructed like dreams (see Chapter 45). A 'screen memory' is one that's apparently emotionally insignificant, but is actually a substitute for a more troubling memory with which it's become associated. But he argued that the distinction between screen memories and other memories from childhood is unclear:

> 'It may indeed be questioned whether we have any memories at all from our childhood: memories relating to our childhood may be all that we possess. Our childhood memories show us our earliest years not as they were but as they appeared at the later periods when the memories were aroused. In these periods of arousal, the childhood memories did not, as people are accustomed to say, emerge; they were found at that time. And a number of motives, with no concern for historical accuracy, had a part in forming them, as well as in the selection of the memories themselves'.

Thus, Freud argued that memories of childhood may not be what they seem. The subjective sense of remembering doesn't mean that the memory is literally true. Memories are like dreams or works of fiction, constructed out of psychodynamic conflict, serving wish-fulfilment and self-deception. True memories of childhood may simply be unobtainable. Our apparent memories may be fabrications created later (Mollon, 2000).

If Freud is right, then RMs can no longer be memories of actual CSA, but phantasies of abuse. This reflects Freud's rejection of the *seduction theory* in favour of the *Oedipal theory* (see Chapter 35). Essentially, these correspond to actual abuse and phantasised abuse respectively as causes of adult neurosis. But, rightly or wrongly:

> '... that adult emotional disorders originate from repression of memories of experiences in early childhood which can be 'uncovered' by psychoanalysis ... [is] ... part and parcel of Freud's heritage. ... [it is an] essential element ... in the recovered memory therapist's armoury'. (Esterson, 2000: personal communication)

Freud appears to be in a no-win situation. Esterson is claiming that Freud's theory of repression and his therapeutic methods are the basic tools of RM therapists, which makes Freud the arch-enemy of accused parents and the BFMS. But if it's pointed out that RM therapists have misunderstood Freud's theory of repression and the nature of childhood memories, this also seems to play into the hands of Freud's accusers. In other words, if memories are essentially *constructed*, rather than 'discovered' or 'recovered' ('unearthed' to use an archaeological analogy which Freud himself used), it becomes easier to understand how FMS occurs: vulnerable patients can easily be 'persuaded' that a constructed memory (a phantasy that CSA took place) is, in fact, an objectively true, historically verifiable event (the CSA actually happened).

In defence of Freud, Ofshe (in Jaroff, 1993) contends that RM therapists have invented a mental mechanism ('robust' repression) that supposedly causes a child's awareness of sexual abuse to be driven entirely from consciousness. There's no limit to the number of traumatic events that can be repressed, or to the length of time over which the series of events can occur.

According to Loftus (in Jaroff, 1993):

'If repression is the avoidance in your conscious awareness of unpleasant experiences that come back to you, yes, I believe in repression. But if it is a blocking out of an endless stream of traumas that occur over and over that leave a person with absolutely no awareness that these things happen ... and re-emerge decades later in some reliable form, I don't see any evidence for it. It flies in the face of everything we know about memory'.

Many practising psychotherapists would agree with Loftus.

A report published in the *British Journal of Psychiatry* (Brandon *et al.*, 1998) distinguishes between (a) CSA that's reported in childhood or kept secret although unforgotten, and (b) RMs of CSA, previously completely forgotten, that emerge in adulthood during therapy, usually in women in their 30s or 40s. For some patients, RMs can escalate into FMS, in which a person's identity comes to centre around the:

'... memory of a traumatic experience which is objectively false but in which the person strongly believes ... The individual avoids confrontation with any evidence that might challenge the memory ...'.

Brandon *et al.* summarise the findings of studies which have compared these two kinds of CSA:

- Ninety per cent of RM patients are women, while in documented abuse cases the sex ratio is close to 50:50.
- While only three per cent of RM accusations are made against stepfathers, they are much more likely to be involved in documented childhood cases.
- While documented abuse usually involves older children or adolescents, RM cases recall abuse before the age of four, or even in infancy.

Ask yourself ...

- What conclusions can you draw from these reported differences about the validity of RMs?
- Do you find it plausible that we can recall events that occurred to us as infants?
- What's your earliest childhood memory?

Do false memories exist?

According to the 1995 British Psychological Society (BPS) report on RMs, CSA which is alleged to have occurred before four years of age and which doesn't continue beyond that age, might *not* be retrievable in adulthood in a narrative form, that is, *describable in words*. Very early memories are implicit rather than explicit, and are reflected in behaviour, outside conscious awareness. This means that we don't need the concept of repression in order to explain the 'forgetting' of childhood experiences, but it also implies that some RMs could be false (or at the very least inaccurate).

In a survey of 810 chartered psychologists, about 90 per cent believed that RMs are sometimes or usually 'essentially correct', a negligible number believed they're always correct, about 66 per cent believed they're possible, and over 14 per cent believed that one of their own clients has experienced FMs (BPS, 1995).

How might FMs be created?

According to Loftus (1997), false memories can be constructed by combining actual memories with the content of suggestions from others. This may result in source confusion (see above, page 313). Consistent with the role of suggestion is the fact that RMs began to be reported more frequently after the publication of *The Courage to Heal* (Bass & Davis, 1993) in the US. This book claimed that virtually every behavioural or emotional disorder is caused by CSA, and could be cured by recovering repressed memories of that abuse. It was largely responsible for the RM 'movement' in psychotherapy. Many therapists began to introduce 'memory work', which usually involved the use of hypnosis, under the false assumption that hypnosis can unlock forgotten memories (Parkin, 2000).

While there have been many experimental studies of FMs (see Loftus, 1997), their generalisability to the therapeutic setting may be limited (Lyddy, 1999). But the findings of a recent study by Loftus and her colleagues have serious implications for therapeutic practice. They simulated the kinds of activities that go on in psychotherapy, and examined how they affected a client's autobiographical memory.

KEY STUDY 21.5

Changing beliefs and memories through dream interpretation (Mazzoni *et al.*, 1999)

Participants were selected from a sample who completed a life events inventory (LEI) and reported not having experienced specific important childhood events (such as being bullied or lost in a crowd).

Two weeks following the initial LEI, those in the experimental group completed what they thought was an unrelated dream survey. In a 30-minute session, they received information about the content of their reported dreams that suggested they'd either been bullied or lost before age three. Their attitudes towards dream interpretation were also probed. Controls received no such suggestion, but completed unrelated filler tasks or participated in a non-suggestive dream session.

Two weeks later, participants completed another LEI. They were all fully debriefed, and a final sub-set of dream participants completed a questionnaire stating their post-experimental beliefs about their memories.

The mean LEI change showed that half of the experimental group participants was now confident that the critical event had occurred. Some also produced concrete specific memories of the events, and denied a link between the dream and childhood event sessions. In addition, a strong prior belief in the value of dream interpretation was associated with increased confidence in the target event. No such changes occurred in the controls.

Conclusions

The fact that FMs can be created doesn't mean that all RMs are false (Loftus, 1997). The BPS has published a draft set of new guidelines for psychologists working with clients in contexts in which issues related to RMs may arise. The preamble states that:

> '... there can be no doubt for psychologists of the existence of ... (CSA) as a serious social and individual problem with long-lasting effects. In addition, there can be little doubt that at least some recovered memories of CSA are recollections of historical events. However, there is a genuine cause for concern that some interventions may foster in clients false beliefs concerning CSA or can lead them to develop illusory memories'. (Frankland & Cohen, 1999)

CHAPTER SUMMARY

- **Schema theory** sees schemas as the 'units' of SM, rather than simple concepts. Our knowledge is stored in memory as simplified mental representations of objects and events, which we use to interpret new experiences. One influential form of schema theory is the notion of **scripts**.

- Bartlett introduced the concept of **schema** to help explain how we remember **meaningful material**, such as stories. Memory isn't a 'pure' process that can be studied outside the **social** and **cultural contexts** in which it takes place.

- Bartlett used **serial reproduction** to study **reconstructive memory**, which uses schemata to interpret new information. While schemata help to make the world more predictable, they can also distort our memories.

- Loftus has applied Bartlett's view of memory as reconstructive to the study of **eyewitness testimony** (EWT). The Devlin Committee recommended that convictions shouldn't be based on a single EWT alone (except in exceptional circumstances).

- **Source confusion/misattribution** can account for why suspects may be mistakenly selected from identification parades. EWT appears to be a persuasive source of evidence, even if the witness is discredited by the defence lawyer.

- **Misleading questions** can take the form of either **leading questions** or those which introduce **after-the-fact information**. Both types can induce **reconstructive errors**.

- Loftus believes that leading questions actually **change** the memory for events, rather than merely supplementing the existing memory. But the influence of misleading questions may be reduced if witnesses are interviewed in a structured way (as in the **cognitive interview**), and the 'Loftus effect' may relate to the **retrieval** of the original memory.

- Blatantly incorrect information has no effect on EWT. People are more likely to be misled if the false information is insignificant, presented after a delay, and believable.

- The use of CCTV hasn't removed the problem of misidentification of suspects. Both humans and computer systems have difficulty dealing with subtle pictorial differences, and the quality of CCTV images can vary considerably. Highly **familiar** faces are identified most reliably.

- According to Freud's **motivated-forgetting** theory, unacceptable memories are made inaccessible through **repression**. While cases of **psychogenic amnesia** are consistent with Freud's theory, a strictly Freudian interpretation may not be necessary, and experimental support for the repression hypothesis is inconclusive.

- There is currently great controversy over **recovered memories** (RMs) of CSA and **false-memory syndrome**. RM therapists are accused of implanting **false memories** of CSA into patients, while patients accuse their parents of the abuse.

- Most psychologists and psychiatrists seem to accept the **possibility** of FMs, but this doesn't mean that all RMs of CSA are false.

Self-assessment questions

1 'All remembering is reconstruction.'
  To what extent does psychological research support Bartlett's theory of reconstructive memory?
2 To what extent does psychological research into eyewitness testimony support the claim that eyewitness accounts are inherently unreliable?
3 Discuss Freud's theory of motivated forgetting.
4 Assess the contribution that psychological research into cognitive processes has made to legal issues.

Web addresses

http://www.brown.edu/Departments/Taubman_Center/Recovmem/Archive.html

http://www.rickross.com/reference/fsm19.html

http://faculty.washington.edu/eloftus

http://www.lgu.ac.uk/psychology/elander/Memory2.html

http://www.apa.org/pubinfo/mem.html

http://www.psychologicalscience.org/news_journal II.htm

http://weber.u.washington.edu/~eloftus/Articles/price.htm

Further reading

Loftus, E.F. (1997) Creating false memories. *Scientific American, 277* (3), 50–55, September. A very readable, short account of some experimental studies suggesting how FMs could be created.

Mollon, P. (2000) *Freud and False Memory Syndrome.* Cambridge: Icon Books. This is just 73 pages long, and is as useful for its coverage of Freud's theory as for his alleged role in FMS.

Four

Social Psychology

Chapter 22

Social Perception

Introduction and overview

S trictly, social (or person) perception refers to the perception of people (as opposed to physical objects: see Figure 22.1), but the focus of this chapter is on *interpersonal perception*. This refers to how we try to explain and predict other people's behaviour. It seems impossible to interact with other people without trying to make sense of their actions, and to anticipate how they're likely to act.

Probably in no other area of psychology is the unique nature of the discipline as a whole so apparent. Psychologists are, effectively, studying 'themselves': they're part of the subject matter. In order to study human behaviour, they must utilise the very same processes they try to explain, in this case, perception.

While social perception has deep roots in social psychology, it flourished during the 1950s, 1960s and 1970s, with considerable research into *forming impressions of other people*, and *attribution* (which is the focus of Chapter 23).

Much of the impression-formation research was conducted from the perspective of the *perceiver* and looked at *central vs peripheral traits*, the *primacy–recency effect*, *implicit personality theory*, and *stereotyping*. But we'll also discuss it from the *actor's* point of view (that is, the person being perceived), by considering some of the ways in which we try to influence others' impressions of us (*impression management/self-presentation*).

Since the 1980s, these traditional perspectives of person perception have been largely replaced by that of *social cognition*, which serves as a framework for the chapter. Social cognition is the study of how people understand their social world: people's cognition, their behaviour and the settings in which that behaviour occurs (Schneider, 1995). This differs from the earlier research more in terms of the overall approach than the phenomena being investigated.

While the study of impression formation was very 'cognitive', in that it was concerned with the *content* of our thoughts about others, social cognition reflected the *information-processing approach* that so dominated cognitive psychology in particular (see Chapters 13–21) and psychology in general. This is concerned less with the content, and more with the often unconscious, automatic *processes* that underlie our (usually) conscious impressions of others.

Perceiving objects and perceiving people

As Figure 22.1 shows, social (or person) perception comprises interpersonal perception (perception of others) and perception of self (see Chapter 33). Perceiving others involves:

■ *selection* (e.g. focusing on people's physical appearance or on just one particular aspect of their behaviour);
■ *organisation* (e.g. trying to form a complete, coherent impression of a person);

■ *inference* (e.g. attributing characteristics to someone for which there's no direct or immediate evidence, as in stereotyping).

Ask yourself ...

• In what ways does perceiving people differ from perceiving objects?

While selection, organisation and inference are common features of object and person perception, there are also some crucial differences:

■ People *behave* (but objects don't). It's often behaviour which provides the data for making inferences about what people are like.
■ People *interact* with other people (but they don't interact with objects or objects with each other). One person's behaviour can influence another's, so that behaviour is mutually influential.
■ People *perceive and experience* (but objects can't). One person's perception can influence the other's (especially his/her non-verbal behaviour), so that each person's perception of the other is at least partly a product of the other's perception of him/her.

Some psychologists, particularly the *phenomenological psychologists* (see Chapter 2), regard *experience* as the major source of 'data' (as opposed to behaviour) in social interaction. For example, Laing (1967) argued that the task of *social phenomenology* is to relate 'my experience of your behaviour to your experience of my behaviour'. In other words, it studies the relationship between experience and experience.

In his book *Knots* (1972), Laing dramatically (and often humorously) demonstrates the kinds of tangles that human relationships can get into. He does this in the form of short prose poems and diagrammatic poems. Here are two of the shorter and more straightforward examples:

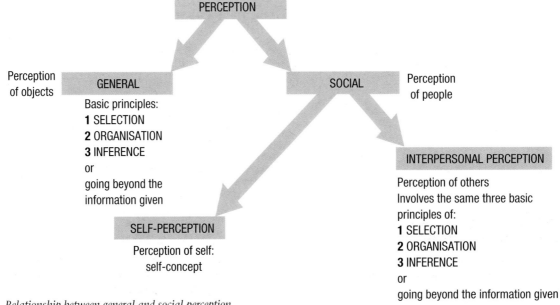

Figure 22.1 *Relationship between general and social perception*

a Jack frightens Jill that he will leave her because he is frightened she will leave him.

b Jack: 'You are a pain in the neck.
To stop you giving me a pain in the neck
I protect my neck by tightening my neck muscles,
Which gives me the pain in the neck you are.'

Jill: 'My head aches through trying to stop you giving me a headache.'

For Laing, 'knots' like these illustrate how 'my experience of another is a function of the other's experience of me' – and vice versa.

Are we all psychologists?

Ask yourself ...

- In what ways can we all be considered psychologists?

As we noted earlier, everyone tries to 'figure people out', explain, predict and, very often, control others' behaviour, as part of their everyday living in a social world. These also happen to be the three traditionally accepted aims of science, including psychology (see Chapter 3). Gahagan (1984) defines interpersonal perception as 'the study of how the layperson uses theory and data in understanding people'. She breaks this definition down further into three main components:

- The study of how people perceive others as *physical objects* and form impressions of their physical appearance, actions and the social categories to which they can be assigned. Often the first thing we're notice about other people is some aspect of their appearance (such as their clothes or hair: see Chapter 21), and to this extent we're treating them as no more than 'things'. This is usually the first step involved in stereotyping, since we usually categorise people on the basis of physical appearance.
- The study of how people perceive others as *psychological entities*. We form impressions of what kind of person they are, or we infer what their feelings, motives, personality traits, and so on might be (having already categorised them).
- The study of the lay person *as a psychologist*. According to Nisbett & Ross (1980), 'We are all psychologists. In attempting to understand other people and ourselves, we are informal scientists who construct our own intuitive theories of human behaviour. In doing so, we face the same basic tasks as the formal scientist ...'. 'Intuitive theories' is another way of referring to 'implicit personality theories' (see below, page 332).

Box 22.1 Some important differences between the psychologist and the lay person

The lay person uses his/her theories for *pragmatic* (or practical) and immediate purposes, as opposed to gaining knowledge for its own sake.

The lay person is rarely a disinterested observer of another's behaviour. We usually have a vested interest in what's going on, and are emotionally involved to some extent. The professional, as a scientist, has to be 'detached' and objective (although complete detachment is impossible: see Chapter 3).

The lay person may be completely unaware of the reasoning s/he has followed when making inferences about others, and this reasoning may change from one situation to another. So, the lay person's 'theories' aren't spelled out or articulated (hence 'implicit' personality theories) and may not be consistent. But psychologists must try to be consistent and make their reasoning explicit, so that other psychologists can examine it.

(Based on Gahagan, 1984, 1991)

The person as thinker

We've already noted that social psychology has always been strongly cognitive. People are thinking organisms (as opposed to emotional organisms or mindless automatons) who 'reside' between stimulus and response (a S–O–R model as opposed to a S–R model: see Chapters 2 and 11). We've also seen that social cognition represents a fairly recent way of looking at the thinking involved in our social interactions.

According to Fiske & Taylor (1991), there are four guises that the cognitive tradition has assumed. They see the thinker, respectively, as a:

- *Consistency seeker*. This refers to the principle of *cognitive consistency*, around which a number of theories of attitude change were built in the 1950s, the most influential being Festinger's cognitive dissonance theory (see Chapter 24). All the theories claimed that cognitive inconsistency produces a strong motivation to reduce the inconsistency.
- *Naïve scientist*. Attribution theories are central to the view that, by trying to infer unobservable causes from observable behaviour, we all operate as amateur scientists (see above). This view was first proposed by the 'father of attribution theory', Fritz Heider, in 1958, but most attribution theories were formulated between the mid-1960s and early 1970s. As we'll see in Chapter 23, these theories were *normative*; that is, they attempted to account for how people *ought* to attribute causes to behaviour under 'ideal' conditions. They also took the 'naïve scientist' model too far, by seeing ordinary people as completely logical and systematic in their thinking.
- *Cognitive miser*. Partly as a reaction against normative attribution theories, Nisbett & Ross (1980), Taylor (1981) and others introduced the term 'cognitive miser' to convey the idea that people are limited in their capacity to process information. They therefore take shortcuts whenever they can, adopting strategies that simplify complex problems. While this leads them to draw biased and hence inaccurate conclusions (relative to what the normative theories predict), seeing people as fallible thinkers represents a much more descriptively accurate account of how people actually think about behaviour. This is reflected in studies of error and bias in the attribution process (see Chapter 23)

but also, more generally, in *heuristics* (Tversky & Kahneman, 1974) or 'rules of thumb' (see Chapter 20). Some examples are given in Table 22.1.

■ *Motivated tactician.* This refers to a development of the cognitive miser view, 'putting back' the motivational and emotional variables that were removed from the original cognitive consistency model. The motivated tactician is a:

> '... *fully engaged thinker who has multiple cognitive strategies available and chooses among them based on goals, motives, and needs ...*' (Fiske & Taylor, 1991).

This corresponds to what Leyens & Codol (1988) call the 'cognitive–affective human being'.

Table 22.1 *Some examples of heuristics used in uncertain or ambiguous situations*

Availability: We judge the frequency/probability of an event according to the number of instances of it that can readily be brought to mind (remembered), and so which are cognitively available. For example, being able to think of several friends who are studying psychology in other colleges/universities leads you to believe that psychology is nationally one of the most popular subjects (which, in fact, it is!).

Representativeness: We decide whether a particular person/event is an example of a particular category. For example, if X has long hair, is wearing a skirt, has a high-pitched voice, and is called Jo, then there's a good chance X is female – but not necessarily! It's a safe bet, because there's a match between the person in front of you and your stereotyped belief (or prototype) of what females are like.

Simulation: Judging what's likely to be/have been the outcome of some event/incident, according to how easily different outcomes can be brought to mind. For example, we're often much more angry and upset by 'near misses' than when we 'missed it by a mile' – we can imagine '*If only* I'd ...', or '*If only* that man in front of me ...' much more easily in the former than in the latter.

Anchoring: When we have no information about a particular event, we may draw on information about a similar event as a reference point or 'anchor'. For example, if asked to estimate how many hours per week a fellow psychology student studies, in the absence of any specific knowledge you may base your answer on how many (or few!) hours you yourself put in.

Evaluation of social cognition: what's happened to the 'social'?

Critics of social cognition (e.g. Moscovici, 1982; Zajonc, 1989) have argued that it may have taken social psychology too far towards cognitive psychology, so that there may not be any 'social' in social cognition. Many of the cognitive processes and structures that have been proposed seem to be unaffected by social context: they seem to be taking place within an apparently isolated person who's thinking about social objects. But this isn't what's meant by 'social cognition'. Instead, we should be focusing on the link between people and the social object. This is truly social, because it's concerned with how cognition is socially constructed, shared and maintained by different members of a given social group, or

even a whole society. To study 'social' cognition by studying what's going on inside the head of individuals is *reductionist* (see Chapter 49).

Stereotypes illustrate the shared nature of cognition, but perhaps the best example of how cultural knowledge may be constructed and transmitted is Moscovici's (1961, 1981) theory of *social representations* (see Chapter 2, pages 23–24).

Social representations (SRs)

According to Moscovici (1981), social representations are:

> '... *a set of concepts, statements and explanations originating in daily life in the course of inter-individual communications. They are the equivalent, in our society, of the myths and belief systems in traditional societies; they might even be said to be the contemporary version of common sense*'.

Characteristics of SRs

■ Moscovici (1961) showed, for instance, that people have simplified (and often mistaken) ideas about Freud's psychoanalytic theory. Many people have heard of Freud, just as they've heard of Einstein or Stephen Hawking, but most will have only the vaguest knowledge of their respective ideas and theories. This illustrates the *personification* of new and complex ideas, that is, linking them with a person.

■ Complex ideas are also often converted into the form of visual images, as in a cartoon where the darker side of a person's nature is portrayed as a devil (in one balloon) and his/her conscience as an angel (in another). This kind of *figuration* is sometimes used to convey Freud's concepts of the id and superego respectively (with the person him/herself being the ego).

Figure 22.2 *A representation of Freud's concept of the id, ego, and superego, using figuration*

■ Both personification and figuration are examples of *objectification*, that is, the need to make the abstract concrete (Moscovici & Hewstone, 1983). For example, thinking of God as 'a father' gives some sort of reality to a supernatural concept. We also need to *anchor* new and unfamiliar ideas into some pre-existing system (see Table 22.1).

An example of anchoring is given in Jodelet's (1980) study of the re-housing of ex-psychiatric hospital patients in a French village. They were immediately labelled *bredins* (a local term for vagrants or 'half-wits'). Despite the term's almost total inaccuracy, it served to reduce something totally unknown and alien to something familiar.

The functions of SRs

- They facilitate communication between individuals and groups by establishing a shared 'social reality'.
- They also guide social action: individuals will interpret their own and others' behaviour in the light of this shared knowledge.
- Through socialisation, shared SRs are impressed on the child, infiltrating to the 'core of the personality', and imposing limits to perceptions and attitudes (Moscovici & Hewstone, 1983).
- In a way, the study of SRs is the study of the transformation from knowledge to common sense (Moscovici & Hewstone, 1983) or 'popular consciousness', and the theory of SRs 'explains how the strange and the unfamiliar become, in time, the familiar' (Farr & Moscovici, 1984). It's the study of how SRs evolve and are communicated between groups and individuals that makes this true social cognition.

SRs provide an evolving framework for making sense of the world, deriving from the mass media, scientific and religious movements, and intergroup relations (Moscovici, 1984). They also have important consequences for how we deal with one another, and how society responds to particular individuals and groups. For example, whether abnormal behaviour is conceptualised in moral, biological, religious, or social terms will determine how social policy-makers, the government, as well as the general public, will respond to it (see Chapter 43). When the Yorkshire Ripper was convicted for multiple rapes and murders, he was held to be criminally responsible (despite his schizophrenia). As Hogg & Abrams (2000) point out:

'Such distinctions are dependent more on society's current social representations of good and evil, sanity and insanity, than they are on objectively measurable criteria'.

Whenever people engage in conversation or debate controversial issues, such as 'what to do with paedophiles', whether homosexuals should be allowed to become foster/adoptive parents, whether cannabis should be legalised, or whether we should pay higher taxes to fund public services like the NHS, SRs become apparent.

SRs, prejudice and discrimination

According to Horton (1999), underlying much racist talk or discourse is a hidden core, which consists of:

'a social representation of human nature, including the belief in a hereditary factor in natural character. Biological, psychological and religious images and ideas make up this inner

core. Racialism corresponds to a social representation which gives replies to questions such as 'What is man?', 'What are his origins?' and 'Why are people different?'.*

Residents campaigning against the planned move of a convicted paedophile into their neighbourhood on his release from prison. The belief that they cannot help but reoffend is part of the Social Representation of paedophiles

Billig's (1978) participant observational study of the National Front (now the British National Party/BNP) revealed that underlying black stereotypes, and active hostility towards blacks, lay a complex set of ideas. These included the need for racial cleansing and belief in a Zionist conspiracy.

According to Horton (1999):

'By offering scapegoats instead of a rational analysis of the situation, the Nazis gave hope to the German people by attributing the crisis to a cause that was relatively easily controllable by elimination – the Jews'.

For Horton, SR theory, by providing a lay theory of causality:

'offers a social psychological explanation of 'prejudice' that takes into full account the phenomena of active hostility towards, and persecution and elimination of, outgroups, which experimental social psychology has not been able to offer'.

Scapegoating and other theories of prejudice and discrimination are discussed in Chapter 25.

According to Joffe (1996), the early representation of AIDS in the West, both by the scientific and lay communities, was in terms of outgroups, namely, homosexuals and/or Africans. This anchoring acts as a form of identity-protection, and has operated throughout the ages.

Joffe gives the example of syphilis as it swept through Europe in the fifteenth century. It became associated with foreigners and outgroups: the English called it the 'French pox', and for the Japanese it was the 'Chinese disease'. This applied also to typhus, leprosy, polio and cholera (the pandemic diseases).

'Blaming the foreigner' is necessary in order to punish the perceived cause of the crime and prevent its return. This *scapegoating* is vital for maintenance of the social order, and the greater the potential threat, the greater the need to exterminate the 'demons' (Poliakov, 1980, in Horton, 1999).

Forming global impressions of people

Central versus peripheral traits

Certain information we have about a person (certain traits we believe they possess) may be more important in determining our overall impression of that person than other information. This was demonstrated in Asch's (1946) classic study.

KEY STUDY 22.1

Building our impressions around something warm or cold (Asch, 1946)

Asch presented participants with a *stimulus list* of adjectives describing a fictitious person. For one group, the adjectives were: intelligent, skilful, industrious, warm, determined, practical and cautious. A second group had the same list, except that the word 'cold' replaced the word 'warm'.

Both groups were then presented with a *response list* of 18 different adjectives and were asked to underline those which described the target person. The two groups chose significantly and consistently different words from the response list. For example, the 'warm' group saw the character as generous, humorous, sociable and popular, while the 'cold' group saw him as having the opposite traits. There were also certain qualities attributed to him equally by both groups (reliable, good-looking, persistent, serious, restrained, strong and honest).

When 'polite' and 'blunt' were used instead of 'warm' and 'cold', participants underlined almost identical words in the response list. Asch concluded that 'warm–cold' represented a *central trait* or *dimension*, while 'polite–blunt' represented a *peripheral trait* or *dimension*. The central traits which seem to influence our global perception in this way are implicitly *evaluative*; that is, they're to do with whether the person is likeable or unlikeable, popular or unpopular, friendly or unfriendly, kind or cruel, and so on.

Kelley (1950) wanted to see whether the description of the target person as 'warm' or 'cold' would influence participants' behaviour towards a real (as opposed to hypothetical) person.

KEY STUDY 22.2

The 'warm–cold' variable in a naturalistic setting (Kelley, 1950)

Students were told that their regular teacher wouldn't be coming, that they'd be having Mr X instead, and that they'd be asked to assess him at the end of the session. Mr. X was a male member of staff not known to the students. Before he arrived, the students were given some biographical notes about Mr X. For half the students, these included the description 'rather warm' and for the other half 'rather cold'; otherwise the biographies were identical.

There then followed a 20-minute discussion between the teacher and the students, during which Kelley recorded how often each student attempted to interact with the teacher. After he left the room, students assessed him on 15 rating scales (e.g. 'knows his stuff–doesn't know his stuff', 'good-natured–irritable').

Those who'd read the 'warm' description consistently responded more favourably to him than those who'd read the 'cold' description. The two groups also responded differently when asked to write a free description. Moreover, 56 per cent of the 'warm' group participated in the discussion, compared with 32 per cent of the 'cold' group.

What makes central traits central?

For Asch, a set of traits produces an integrated impression or configuration (a *Gestalt*: see Chapter 15), in which the meaning of one trait has been influenced by the others. Central traits exert a major organising influence, and can generate inferences about additional traits not given in the set, while peripheral traits have little or no influence. But Bruner & Tagiuri (1954) argued that both general impressions and inferences about additional traits are due to people's *implicit personality theories* (IPTs: see below).

Wishner (1960) found that the impact of the traits 'warm' and 'cold' on inferences about other traits depends on their prior associations with those traits. So, 'warm' and 'cold' affect inferences of traits like 'generous' and 'popular', because they're all (already) associated in people's IPTs, but they *aren't* associated with other traits, such as 'reliable' and 'honest'. This suggests that central traits don't need to be incorporated into different Gestalten as Asch claimed. Indeed, Asch found only negligible differences in the traits inferred when 'warm' and 'cold' were presented alone, and when they were presented as described in Key Study 22.1.

However, the *meaning* of various traits may nevertheless be altered by the context in which they appear, as Asch originally suggested. For example, Zebrowitz (1990) cites studies in which, if someone is described as 'proud', this trait is rated as closer in meaning to 'confident' when it appears in the context of positive traits, but as closer to 'conceited' when presented in the context of negative traits.

Wishner also showed that whether or not a trait is central depends on what else is known about the person (it's *relative*). For example, in Asch's study, 'warm–cold' was central in relation to generous/humourous/sociable/popular, but peripheral (or at least neutral) in relation to reliable/good-looking/persistent/serious/restrained/strong/honest. This suggests that traits are neither central nor peripheral in themselves. Rather, it depends on the pattern of correlations with other traits in any particular study.

The primacy–recency effect

Ask yourself ...

- Do you believe that first impressions are more influential than later impressions? If so, why?
- Does it make a difference if the person is a potential sexual partner (i.e. does the element of potential sexual attraction affect the impact of initial impressions)?

The other major explanation of global perception concentrates on the *order* in which we learn things about a person: the *primacy effect* refers to the greater impact of what we learn first about someone ('first impressions count'); the *recency effect* refers to the greater impact of what we learn later on.

Initial support for a primacy effect came in another study by Asch (1946). He used two lists of adjectives describing a hypothetical person, one in the order: intelligent, industrious, impulsive, critical, stubborn and envious, and the other in the reverse order. Participants given the first list formed a favourable overall impression, while those given the second list formed an unfavourable overall impression.

Ask yourself ...

- How could you explain Asch's findings?

KEY STUDY 22.3

Forming an impression of Jim (Luchins, 1957)

Participants were allocated to one of four groups.

- Group 1 heard a description of an extrovert character called Jim.
- Group 2 heard an introvert description.
- Group 3 heard the first half of the extrovert description, followed by the second half of the introvert description.
- Group 4 heard the reverse of the list of group 3.
- Groups 1 and 2 were control groups used to establish that participants could accurately identify extroverts and introverts.

All the participants were then asked to rate Jim in terms of introversion–extroversion. Group 1 judged him to be the most extroverted and group 2 the most introverted (as you'd expect). Although the judgements of groups 3 and 4 were less extreme, group 3 rated Jim as being more extrovert than group 4.

Remember, groups 3 and 4 received the same information about Jim, only the *order* was different. Luchins concluded that the *earlier* elements of the description had a *greater* impact than the later elements.

Both the Luchins and Asch studies involved hypothetical people. In a study by Jones *et al.* (1968), participants watched a student (a stooge of the experimenters) trying to solve a series of difficult multiple-choice problems. They were then asked to assess his intelligence. The student always solved 15 out of 30 correctly, but one group saw him get most of the right answers towards the beginning, while another group saw him get most of the right answers towards the end.

Ask yourself...

- Which group do you think assessed him as more intelligent?
- According to common sense, which group would judge him to be more intelligent?

The common-sense prediction would be that when the student got most right towards the *end*, he'd be judged as *more* intelligent: he'd seem to be learning as he went along. When he got most right towards the *beginning*, his early successes could be attributed to guesswork or 'beginner's luck'. Jones *et al.* in fact made the common-sense prediction that there would be a *recency* effect. But what they found was a *primacy* effect. Significantly, when asked to recall how many problems the student had solved correctly, those who'd seen the 15 bunched at the beginning said 20.6 (on average), while those who'd seen them bunched at the end said 12.5 (on average). These memory distortions (over- and underestimations) also reflected the impact of the primacy effect.

Explaining the primacy effect

- Luchins says that when later information is discrepant with earlier information, people tend to regard the first information as revealing the 'real' person. The later information is discounted, because it contradicts what came first.
- Anderson (1974) maintains that people pay more attention to information presented when they're first trying to form an impression about someone. Having formed some initial impression, they pay less attention to any subsequent information.
- Asch's explanation is that the first bit of information affects the meaning of later information, which is made consistent with the former. For example, if you initially find out that someone is courageous and frank, and you later learn that he's also undecided, you may take that to mean 'open-minded' rather than 'wishy-washy' (Zebrowitz, 1990).

But does the primacy effect always prove more powerful than the recency effect? The answer seems to be yes, generally, but there are certain conditions.

- Luchins reasoned that if the primacy effect is due to decreased attention to later information, then it should be possible to prevent it by warning people against making snap judgements. He found this to be particularly effective if it was given between the presentation of the two inconsistent pieces of information about the same individual. Similarly, Hendrick & Constanini (1970) found that primacy seems to prevail unless participants are specifically instructed to attend closely to all the information.

- A negative first impression appears to be more resistant to change than a positive one. One explanation is that negative information carries more weight, because it's likely to reflect socially undesirable traits or behaviour and, therefore, the observer can be more confident in attributing the trait or behaviour to the person's 'real' nature. (This is relevant to Jones and Davis's attribution theory: see Chapter 23, pages 342–343.) It may be more adaptive for us to be aware of negative traits than positive ones, since the former are potentially harmful or dangerous.

- Luchins found that, although the primacy effect may be important in relation to strangers, as far as friends and other people whom we know well are concerned, the recency effect seems to be stronger. For example, we may discover something about a friend's childhood or something that happened to them before we knew them, which might change our whole perception of them. 'How well do we (or can we) know anybody?'

Inferring what people are like

The halo effect

Asch's original finding that the inclusion of 'warm' produces a more positive impression compared with the same list including 'cold' demonstrates the halo effect. If we're told a person is warm, then we tend to attribute them with other favourable characteristics (a *positive halo*). The reverse is true if we're told the person is 'cold' – we attribute them with a *negative halo*. The halo effect seems to illustrate very well two basic principles of perception (see Figure 22.1).

- We like to see people in as *consistent* (or organised) a way as possible. It's easier to regard someone as having either all good or all bad qualities than a mixture of good and bad. Two quite extreme examples of this are when lovers regard each other as perfect and faultless ('love is blind': see Chapter 28) and the 'mirror-image phenomenon', where enemies see each other as all bad (see Chapter 25).
- The halo effect is a very general form of IPT. These enable us to infer what people are like when we have only very limited information about them.

Implicit personality theories

As we saw earlier, we all have 'implicit' theories about what makes people 'tick'. One kind of implicit theory is to do with how personality is structured and what traits tend to go together or cluster. Zebrowitz (1990) refers to these as *'person type'* IPTs.

The importance of names

Our names are part of the central core of our *self-image* (see Chapter 33), and they can sometimes form the basis for others' expectations. Harari & McDavid (1973) pointed out that first names, like surnames, are often associated with particular characteristics, partly determined by the media (for example, in American movies the hero and heroine are often called Stephen and Elizabeth, and the villains and fall-guys Elmer and Bertha). They asked experienced teachers to evaluate a set of short essays written by 11-year-olds who were identified by

first name only. Some essays were randomly associated with four names stereotyped by other teachers as attractive and favourable (David, Michael, Karen and Lisa) and four stereotyped as unattractive and unfavourable (Elmer, Hubert, Bertha and Adelle). Although the same essays were associated with different names for different teachers, those written by 'attractive' names were graded a full letter grade higher than those by 'unattractive' names and, significantly, the effect was stronger with boys' names than with girls'.

KEY STUDY 22.4

Names and psychiatric diagnosis (Birmingham, in Adler, 2000)

Birmingham, a forensic psychiatrist at Southampton University, asked 464 British psychiatrists to provide a diagnosis based on a one-page description of a 24-year-old who'd assaulted a train conductor. When they were asked to assess 'Matthew', over 75 per cent gave him a sympathetic hearing, proposing that he was suffering from schizophrenia and in need of medical help. But when renamed 'Wayne', psychiatrists gave him a more sinister character: he was twice as likely as Matthew to be diagnosed as a malingerer, a drug abuser, or suffering from a personality disorder (see Chapter 43).

The importance of physical appearance

Another kind of IPT involves inferring what somebody is like psychologically from certain aspects of their physical appearance. Allport (1954) gave examples of widely held, but totally unfounded, beliefs that fat people are jolly, high foreheads are a sign of superior intelligence, eyes too close together are a sign of untrustworthiness, and redheads have fiery tempers.

A number of studies have demonstrated the 'attractiveness stereotype'; that is, the tendency to infer that physically attractive people also have more attractive personalities (see Chapter 28).

Stereotypes and stereotyping

Stereotypes can be thought of as a special kind of IPT that relates to an entire social group. The term was introduced into social science by Lippman (1922), who defined stereotypes as 'pictures in our heads'. Table 22.2 gives some other definitions.

Table 22.2 *Some definitions of stereotypes and stereotyping*

'… the general inclination to place a person in categories according to some easily and quickly identifiable characteristic such as age, sex, ethnic membership, nationality or occupation, and then to attribute to him qualities believed to be typical to members of that category …' (Tagiuri, 1969)

'… a shared conception of the character of a group …' (Brown, 1986)

'… the process of ascribing characteristics to people on the basis of their group memberships …' (Oakes *et al.*, 1994)

'… widely shared assumptions about the personalities, attitudes and behaviour of people based on group membership, for example ethnicity, nationality, sex, race and class …' (Hogg & Vaughan, 1995)

The process of stereotyping involves the following reasoning:

- we assign someone to a particular group (for example, on the basis of their physical appearance);
- we bring into play the belief that all members of the group share certain characteristics (the stereotype); and
- we infer that this particular individual must possess these characteristics.

The basic method of studying ethnic stereotypes is that used by Katz & Braly (1933) in one of the earliest studies of its kind. One-hundred undergraduates at Princeton University, USA, were presented with a list of ethnic groups (Americans, Jews, Negroes, Turks, Germans, Chinese, Irish, English, Italians and Japanese) and 84 words describing personality. They were asked to list, for each ethnic group, the five or six traits which were 'typical' of that group. The aim was to find out whether traditional social stereotypes (as typically portrayed in papers and magazines) were actually held by Princeton students. In fact, they showed considerable agreement, especially about negative traits. Rather disturbingly, most of the students had had no personal contact with any members of most of the ethnic groups they had to rate. Presumably, they'd absorbed the images of those groups prevalent in the media.

Table 22.3 *The five traits most frequently assigned to four ethnic groups by three generations of Princeton students (from Brown, 1986)*

Group	1933	1951	1967
Americans	industrious	materialistic	materialistic
	intelligent	intelligent	ambitious
	materialistic	industrious	pleasure-loving
	ambitious	pleasure-loving	industrious
	progressive	individualistic	conventional
Japanese	intelligent	imitative	industrious
	industrious	sly	ambitious
	progressive	extremely nationalistic	efficient
	shrewd	treacherous	intelligent
	sly		progressive
Jews	shrewd	shrewd	ambitious
	mercenary	intelligent	materialistic
	industrious	industrious	intelligent
	grasping	mercenary	industrious
	intelligent	ambitious	shrewd
Negroes	superstitious	superstitious	musical
	lazy	musical	happy-go-lucky
	happy-go-lucky	lazy	lazy
	ignorant	ignorant	pleasure-loving
	musical	pleasure-loving	ostentatious

Gilbert (1951) studied another sample of Princeton students, and this time found less uniformity of agreement (especially about unfavourable traits) than in the 1933 study. Many expressed great irritation at being asked to make generalisations at all. In 1967, Karlins *et al.* repeated the study (but reported their findings in 1969). Many students again objected to doing the task, but there was greater agreement compared with the 1951 study. There seemed to be a re-emergence of social stereotyping, but towards more favourable stereotypical images.

The traditional view of stereotypes: are they inherently bad?

For most of the time that psychologists have been studying stereotypes and stereotyping, they've condemned them for being both false and illogical, and dangerous, and people who use them have been seen as prejudiced and even pathological (see Chapter 25).

Lippman (1922), for example, described stereotypes as selective, self-fulfilling and ethnocentric, constituting a '… very partial and inadequate way of representing the world'. The research started by Katz & Braly (1933) was intended to trace the link between stereotypes and prejudice: stereotypes are public fictions arising from prejudicial influences 'with scarcely any factual basis'. So, should they be dismissed as completely unacceptable?

According to Allport (1954), most stereotypes do contain a 'kernel of truth', and Lippman had recognised the categorisation processes involved in stereotyping as an important aspect of general cognitive functioning. Allport built on these ideas, arguing that 'The human mind must think with the aid of categories …'. However, he also believed that prejudiced people tend to make extremely simple *dichotomous* (either/or) judgements compared with tolerant, non-prejudiced people.

Asch (1952) also rejected the view of stereotyping as 'faulty processing'. In a great many situations the behaviour of individuals (for example, members of audiences, committees, families, football teams, armies) is determined by their group membership. So, representing people in terms of these group memberships (i.e. stereotyping) could be seen as an important way of representing social reality. In keeping with his belief in Gestalt principles, Asch argued that groups have distinct psychological properties which cannot be reduced to the characteristics of the individual members (see Chapter 15).

Sherif (1967) also argued that stereotypes aren't in themselves deficient, but serve to reflect the reality of intergroup relations. Instead of asking if they are objectively true or accurate, stereotypes need to be understood in this intergroup context. To this extent, they are highly flexible, since changes in the relationship with other groups will result in changes to the stereotyped images of those groups (see Chapter 25).

The changing face of stereotypes: are they 'normal' after all?

All the researchers whose views of stereotyping have been discussed so far are American. According to Taylor & Porter (1994), there are compelling reasons why American psychologists should condemn stereotyping and wish to rid society of this evil. One of these is the political ideology, according to which everyone who lives in America is first and foremost 'American' regardless of the country they might have come from or their ethnic/cultural origins. This is the 'melting pot' idea, whereby differences are 'boiled away', leaving just one culture.

Rioting English soccer fans displaying stereotypical behaviour in Charleroi, Belgium, during Euro 2000

By contrast, European social psychologists, notably Tajfel, had been brought up in contexts where it was normal to categorise people into groups, where they expected society to be culturally diverse, and where people were proud of their cultural identities. From this personal experience, Tajfel and others mounted a challenge to the American view of stereotyping. Tajfel (1969), for example, reconceptualised stereotyping as the product of quite normal cognitive processes common to all (non-prejudiced) individuals. Specifically, it's a special case of categorisation, which involves an exaggeration of similarities within groups and of differences between groups (the *accentuation principle*). According to Oakes *et al.* (1994), Tajfel's contribution is widely seen as having been revolutionary. One effect of his ideas was to move researchers away from studying the content of stereotypes and towards the study of the process of stereotyping in its own right.

Stereotyping as a normal cognitive process

According to Brislin (1993):

> *'Stereotypes should not be viewed as a sign of abnormality. Rather, they reflect people's need to organise, remember, and retrieve information that might be useful to them as they attempt to achieve their goals and to meet life's demands …'.*

Stereotypes are 'categories about people' (Allport, 1954; Brislin, 1981), and categories in general, and stereotypes in particular, are shortcuts to thinking. From a purely cognitive point of view, there's nothing unique about stereotypes. They're universal and inevitable, '… an intrinsic, essential and primitive aspect of cognition …' (Brown, 1986).

Definitions claim that stereotypes are *exceptionless generalisations* (see Table 22.2). But clearly, the degree of generalisation involved is too great to make a stereotype factually true: no group is completely homogeneous and individual differences are the norm. Yet in Katz and Braly's study, the instruction to list the traits *typical of each ethnic/national group* was taken to mean 'true of all members of each group' (Brown, 1986). However, the early studies never actually found out what participants understood by 'typical'. McCauley & Stitt (1978) attempted to rectify this.

KEY STUDY 22.5

What does the 'typical' mean in 'stereotypical'? (McCauley & Stitt, 1978)

McCauley and Stitt chose Germans as the target group, plus three 'typical' traits (efficient/extremely nationalistic/scientifically minded), and two 'atypical' traits (pleasure-loving/superstitious). Junior college students were told they'd be asked a series of questions which they wouldn't be able to answer exactly (e.g. 'What percentage of American cars are Chevrolets?'). Intermixed with these were critical questions about Germans – 'What percentage of Germans are efficient/extremely nationalistic/scientifically minded/pleasure-loving/superstitious?' and, corresponding to these, 'What percentage of people in the world generally are efficient/extremely nationalistic/scientifically minded/pleasure-loving/superstitious?'.

The *diagnostic ratio* was calculated simply by dividing the percentage for Germans by the percentage for people in the world: anything over 1.00 represents a trait which belongs to the stereotype; anything below 1.00 represents a trait which doesn't. None of these values is even close to 100 per cent, so clearly 'typical' *doesn't* mean 'true of all'. 'Scientifically minded' isn't even attributed to a majority of Germans.

Table 22.4

Trait	% People in the world	% Germans	Diagnostic ratio
Efficient	49.8	63.4	1.27
Extremely nationalistic	35.4	56.3	1.59
Scientifically minded	32.6	43.1	1.32
Pleasure-loving	82.2	72.8	0.89
Superstitious	42.1	30.4	0.72

Ask yourself …

- What do McCauley & Stitt's results tell us about the meaning of 'typical'?

What 'typical' seems to mean, then, is *characteristic*, that is, true of a higher percentage of the group in question than of people in general (Brown, 1986). Stereotypes, then, seem to be *schemas* about what particular groups are like relative to 'people in general'. They are *not* exceptionless generalisations.

Stereotypes, ingroups and outgroups

Instead of seeing comments such as 'They're all the same' as simply bigoted and discriminatory, research has shown that such statements may stem from the *outgroup homogeneity effect* (Quattrone, 1986). People tend to perceive members of an outgroup as highly similar to each other (stereotype), whereas they tend to see all kinds of individual differences among members of their own groups (the *ingroup differentiation hypothesis*: Linville *et al.*, 1989). These are consequences of the act of categorisation, and could be seen as an extension of Tajfel's accentuation principle (see above).

This differential perception of ingroup and outgroup members isn't necessarily indicative of outgroup prejudice, but is the natural outcome of social interaction patterns. We tend to interact with members of our own groups and therefore perceive differences within them. We may have limited interaction with other social groups and this encourages a simplified social representation of these groups. In this context, it's both necessary and useful to see all outgroup members as similar. Ironically, study of the *processes* involved in stereotyping has suggested that it's the *content* that should – and can – be modified: the process itself may be 'hard-wired' as an element of human cognition, so that there's nothing we can do about it (Taylor & Porter, 1994).

Box 22.3 Stereotyping and the brain

Osterhout used EEG recordings to see what happens in people's brains when stereotypes are activated. He found that sentences in which gender stereotypes are violated (such as 'The surgeon prepared herself for the operation') provoke the same surge of electrical activity as sentences that don't make grammatical sense (such as 'The cat won't eating'). The telltale signal is a strong positive brainwave (the P600), which is often associated with surprise (see Chapter 7).

The brains of men and women showed this reaction, even if they consciously found the sentence completely acceptable. Their brains seemed to be 'saying' one thing, and their overt responses something quite different.

Other researchers have used MRI scans to measure the differing reactions in the amygdala of white participants to black and white faces. The amygdala (see Chapter 4) is thought to act like a spotlight, focusing attention on frightening or other emotionally charged events. There is greater amygdala activity in response to black faces or race-related words and images.

This dissociation between conscious beliefs and unconscious reactions supports the view that racial evaluations have a subtle influence on people's behaviour (Osterhout, based on Adler, 2000).

The *illusory correlation* (Chapman, 1967; Hamilton & Gifford, 1976) refers to the tendency to regard two variables that are unusual or distinct in some way, and which happen to become linked on one occasion, as always linked in that way (see Table 20.2, page 302). For example, if a member of a minority ethnic group is involved in a serious crime, majority group members are likely to associate the two, such that 'muggers are likely to be ...' becomes part of the negative stereotype of that group.

Stereotypes, expectations and memory

Buckhout (1974) gave participants a series of drawings in which some stereotypical pattern was violated. One drawing (based on Allport & Postman's, 1947, experiment: see Chapter 21, page 312) showed a casually dressed white man threatening a well-dressed black man on a subway train, with the white man holding a razor. After seeing the picture briefly, approximately half the (white) participants 'remembered' seeing a black man holding a razor.

Figure 22.3 *One of the drawings used by Buckhout (1974)*

Similarly, Rothbart *et al.* (1979) found that people often recall better those facts that support their stereotypes (*selective remembering*), and Howard & Rothbart (1980) found that people have better recall of facts which are critical of the minority group than facts which are favourable (*negative memory bias*).

Duncan (1976) showed white participants a video of a discussion between two males and told them it was a 'live' interaction over closed circuit television. At one point, the discussion became heated, and one actor gave the other a shove – the screen then went blank. Participants were asked to classify the shove as 'playing around', 'dramatising', 'aggressive behaviour' or 'violent behaviour'. Different participants saw different versions of the video, which differed only in the race of the two actors – two whites, two blacks, a white who shoved a black or a black who shoved a white.

Ask yourself ...

- How do you think participants classified the shove under different conditions?
- How could you explain the results?
- What relevance do all the above studies have for EWT (see Chapter 21)?

Duncan found that many more participants classified the black man's shove as violent behaviour, especially if he shoved a white man.

Stereotypes, expectations and behaviour

Our expectations of people's personalities or capabilities may influence the way we actually treat them, which in turn may influence their behaviour in such a way that confirms our expectation (the *self-fulfilling prophecy*). This illustrates how stereotypes can (unwittingly) influence our behaviour towards others, and not just our perception and memory of them (see, for example, page 332, and Chapter 33, page 487).

Stereotypes also affect our expectations of *ourselves*, which, in turn, can influence our behaviour. This may take place under naturalistic conditions and over a substantial period of time, as when members of minority groups *internalise* the negative stereotypes of them prevalent in the majority culture (see Chapter 25). But it can also happen under more artifical, experimental conditions in the short term.

KEY STUDY 22.6

How stereotypes can slow you down (Bargh *et al.*, 1996)

College students were asked to unscramble sentences scattered with negative age-related words. Students who'd sorted sentences containing negative words walked down the corridor at the end of the experiment significantly more slowly, and remembered less about the experiment, than students who'd sorted neutral words.

In an extension of Bargh *et al.*'s study, Dijksterhuis *et al.* (in Hogg & Abrams, 2000) asked participants to unscramble sentences containing words associated with negative stereotypes of the elderly. This *primed* the elderly stereotype, by making attributes of the elderly more accessible in participants' minds. Half were asked to make judgements about Princess Julianna (the 89-year-old Dutch Queen Mother). All the participants were then shown to the lifts, situated at the end of the corridor, and the time taken to reach them was recorded. Those who'd been primed with Princess Julianna walked significantly *faster*.

The studies described in Key Study 22.6 illustrate that when general stereotypes are activated, we may automatically adopt some of those characteristics ourselves. But when images of specific extreme individuals (exemplars) are activated, we automatically make a contrast between ourselves and the exemplar. This makes us react in the opposite way to how we think that person would react (Hogg & Abrams, 2000).

So, it's not stereotypes themselves which are dangerous or objectionable, but how they affect behaviour. While the experiments described above show that *anyone* can be affected by negative stereotypes, under normal circumstances it is the *elderly* who are affected by negative stereotypes of the elderly (see Chapter 39). The same applies, of course, to ethnic minority groups and race stereotypes, and to women and gender stereotypes (see Chapters 25 and 36).

Influencing how others see us

Impression management

Our impressions of others depend partly on their physical appearance and behaviour, both verbal and non-verbal, delib-

erate and unintentional. It's difficult to think of a social situation in which we're not trying (consciously or otherwise) to manipulate how others perceive us. This fundamental aspect of social interaction is referred to as *impression management* (or *self-presentation*), which Turner (1991) defines as '... the process of presenting a public image of the self to others ...'. Sometimes we may be trying to influence particular people on a particular occasion, such as in a job interview, or we may be trying to maintain an image of ourselves (as a caring or competent person, for example).

It's widely agreed that we usually try to influence others in a positive way; that is, we want them to have a favourable impression of us (Schlenker, 1980; Turner, 1991). This is relevant to *interpersonal attraction*: instead of simply sitting back and letting others be impressed (or not), we can take an active role in making ourselves likeable to others (Duck, 1988: see Chapter 28). According to Turner, several studies suggest that concerns with self-presentation may underlie a whole range of phenomena, including *bystander intervention* (see Chapter 30), *aggression and deindividuation* (see Chapter 29), *conformity* (see Chapter 26) and *cognitive dissonance* (see Chapter 24).

In books such as *The Presentation of Self in Everyday Life* (1971), Goffman, the Canadian sociologist, offers a '*dramaturgical*' analysis of social interaction. To create a successful impression requires the right setting, props (e.g. the way you're dressed), skills and a shared understanding of what counts as 'backstage'. The person who takes self-disclosure too far (see below), for instance, may be regarded as bringing onto stage what should be kept 'backstage' and so creates an unfavourable impression.

Woody Allen (with Diane Keaton in Manhattan*) typically plays a character who is unlucky in love. This is partly due to his inappropriate self-disclosure*

How is impression management carried out?

Impression management requires us to 'take the role of the other' (see Cooley and Mead's theories of self: Chapter 33). We must be able, psychologically, to step into someone else's shoes to see how we look from their viewpoint, and to adjust our behaviour accordingly. Fiske & Taylor (1991) identify five major components of impression management, or five ways of adjusting our behaviour to take into account other people's viewpoints.

Table 22.5 *Major components involved in impression management (based on Fiske & Taylor, 1991)*

In *behaviour matching*, we try to match the target person's behaviour. For example, if the other person is self-disclosing, we'll tend to do so to a comparable degree.

When we conform to situational norms, we use our knowledge of what's appropriate behaviour in a particular situation to adopt that behaviour ourselves. For every social setting, there's a pattern of social interaction which conveys the best identity for that setting (the 'situated identity'). High *self-monitors* (see text) are more likely to make a favourable impression.

Appreciating or flattering others (*ingratiation*) can sometimes produce a favourable response from the target person, especially if it's done sincerely. But if seen for what it is, flattery can backfire on the flatterer, who'll be seen as deliberately trying to achieve his/her own ends.

If we show *consistency* among our beliefs, or between our beliefs and behaviour, we're more likely to impress other people favourably. Inconsistency is usually seen as a sign of weakness.

Our *verbal* and *non-verbal behaviours* should match, which they usually do if we're sincere. But if we're flattering, or in some other way being dishonest, the non-verbal channel will often 'leak', giving away our true feelings. When people perceive an inconsistency between what someone says and what they're trying to convey with their body, the latter is usually taken as revealing the 'true' message (Argyle *et al.*, 1972; Mehrabian, 1972).

Are some positive impressions more positive than others?

Ask yourself ...
- Can you think of any exceptions to the rule that we always try to create favourable impressions in others? Or, do we sometimes go about creating negative impressions in a defensive, self-protective way?

■ We may feel constrained by the impressions others already have of us, and we act in order to 'muddy the waters'. For example, if you're continually being told how good a son or daughter you are, the responsibility this places on you might encourage you to behave in the opposite fashion, so that you 'free yourself' from the expectation that you'll go on behaving dutifully and respectfully.

■ You might protect yourself from anticipated failure by engaging in behaviours that will produce insurmountable obstacles to success, so that when the inevitable failure happens you have a ready-made excuse (*behavioural self-handicapping*). Alternatively, you may blame, in advance, things about yourself which could explain the failure (apart from your lack of competence). For example, lecturers at exam time get quite used to students telling them how badly they're going to do because of lack of sleep, not having been well, having been unable to revise, always getting anxious about exams and so on (*self-reported handicaps*).

One way of thinking about self-handicapping is to see it as an attempt to influence the kind of attribution that other people make about our behaviour. We want them to see our failures as caused by factors 'beyond our control' and that don't, therefore, threaten the positive impression they have of us (and that we have of ourselves). Making excuses for, as well as confessing, our socially undesirable behaviour after it's occurred can also be explained in attributional terms (Weiner, 1992: see Chapter 23).

Self-monitoring

While people in general are concerned with the impressions they make on others, people differ in the extent to which they can and do exercise intentional control over their self-presentation. *High self-monitors* are particularly talented in this way compared with *low self-monitors* (Snyder, 1995). Self-monitoring refers to the extent to which people normally attend to external, social situations as guides for their behaviour, as opposed to their own internal states.

High self-monitors are concerned with behaving in a socially appropriate manner, and so are more likely to monitor the situation (rather than themselves), looking for subtle cues as to 'how to behave'. They're more skilled in using facial expressions and their voices to convey particular emotions, and can interpret others' non-verbal communication more accurately compared with low self-monitors (Ickes & Barnes, 1977; Snyder, 1979). But carried to an extreme, their perceptiveness and social sensitivity can make them look like self-interested opportunists who change themselves and their opinions to suit the situation (Snyder, 1987). Their behaviour shows greater *cross-situational inconsistency* – they behave differently in different situations.

By contrast, low self-monitors remain 'themselves' regardless of the situation, rarely adapting to the norms of the social setting. They monitor their behaviour in relation to their own enduring needs and values. Carried to an extreme, they can be seen as insensitive, inflexible and uncompromising (Snyder, 1987). They show greater *cross-situational consistency*.

Snyder (1987) has developed a pencil and paper test (the self-monitoring scale), which comprises a number of statements with which the respondent has to agree or disagree. Some examples are given in Table 22.6.

Table 22.6 *Some sample items from the self-monitoring scale (Snyder, 1987, in Snyder, 1995)*

High scorers will tend to agree with the following:
- I would probably make a good actor.
- I'm not always the person I appear to be.
- In different situations and with different people, I often act like very different persons.

Low scorers will tend to agree with the following:
- I have trouble changing my behaviour to suit different people and different situations.
- I can only argue for ideas which I already believe.
- I would not change my opinions (or the way I do things) in order to please someone else or win their favour.

Self-disclosure

How accurately others perceive us is determined partly by how much we reveal to them about ourselves (self-disclosure). Wiemann & Giles (1988) define it as '... the voluntary making available of information about one's self that would not ordinarily be accessible to the other at that moment ...'.

According to Jourard (1971), we disclose ourselves through what we say and do (as well as what we omit to say and do). This means that we have greater control over some aspects of self-disclosure than others since, generally, we have greater control over verbal than non-verbal behaviour. However, Jourard believes that the decision to self-disclose (or to become 'transparent') is one taken freely, and the aim in disclosing ourselves is to 'be known, to be perceived by the other as the one I know myself to be'. Jourard believes that we can learn a great deal about ourselves through mutual self-disclosure and our intimacy with others can be enhanced. It's a way of both achieving and maintaining a healthy personality, but only if the self-disclosure meets the criterion of *authenticity* (or honesty).

Ask yourself ...

- Think of your various relationships. What determines the nature and extent of what you disclose to other people?

Factors influencing disclosure

- *Reciprocity*: The more personal the information we disclose to someone, the more personal the information they're likely to disclose to us. This relates to the *norm of reciprocity* (Gouldner, 1960), according to which our social behaviours 'demand' an equivalent response from our partners. We might sometimes feel the other person is giving too much away (or doing so too quickly), but we're still likely to reveal more about ourselves than we otherwise would.
- *Norms*: The situation we're in often determines how much (or what kind of) disclosure is appropriate. For instance, it's acceptable for someone we meet at a party to tell us about their job, but not to reveal details about medical problems or political beliefs.
- *Trust*: Generally, the more we trust someone, the more prepared we are to self-disclose to them.
- *Quality of relationships*: Altman & Taylor's (1973) *social penetration theory* maintains that the more intimate we are with somebody, the greater the range of topics we disclose to them and the more deeply we discuss any particular topic. Equally, a high degree of mutual self-disclosure can enhance the intimacy of the relationship, and is an excellent predictor of whether couples stay together over a four-year period (see Chapter 28).
- *Gender*: Women generally disclose more than men, and Jourard (1971) argues that men's limited self-disclosure prevents healthy self-expression and adds stress to their lives.

Conclusions

It would be quite appropriate to begin a textbook on psychology with a chapter on social perception. Since most of us are, by definition, neither psychologists nor any other kind of scientist in a literal sense, the person-as-psychologist is a *metaphor*. However, it combines two essential truths about human beings:

a science (including psychology) is conducted by people and, as far as we know is uniquely human;

b observing, explaining, predicting, and trying to control others' behaviour are activities shared by professional psychologists and all other human beings.

CHAPTER SUMMARY

- **Interpersonal perception** refers to how we all attempt to explain, predict and to some degree control the behaviour of other people. In these ways, we can all be thought of as psychologists.
- Although social psychology in general, and interpersonal perception in particular, has always been concerned with the content of people's thoughts about others, **social cognition** now emphasises the **information-processing approach**.
- Both object and person perception involve **selection**, **organisation** and **inference**. But only people behave, interact with each other, perceive and experience.
- **Social phenomenologists** regard **experience**, rather than behaviour, as the major source of 'data' in social interaction.
- Four views of people as thinking organisms have been identified, seeing us as **consistency seekers**, **naïve scientists**, **cognitive misers** and **motivated tacticians**.
- As cognitive misers, we use **heuristics** as shortcuts to thinking, including **availability**, **representativeness**, **simulation** and **anchoring**.
- **Social representations** refer to 'common sense', simplified, widely shared understanding of complex theories and ideas, and involve **personification** and **figuration**.
- **Central traits** exert a major organising influence on our overall impression of a person, while **peripheral traits** have little or no influence. An alternative, but not contradictory explanation, is that overall impressions and inferences about additional traits reflect our **implicit personality theories** (IPTs).
- While most of the evidence supports a **primacy effect** with regard to strangers, a **recency effect** may be more powerful with regard to people we know well.
- The **halo effect** is one kind of IPT, which enables us to infer what people are like when we have only limited information about them. IPTs may be based on people's names and their physical attractiveness.
- **Stereotypes** represent a special kind of IPT, and they characterise entire **groups**. Traditionally, American researchers studied stereotypes in relation to prejudice, and regarded them as false, illogical **overgeneralisations**.

- European psychologists saw the **categorisation** of people as normal and expected. From a cognitive point of view, stereotyping is a normal mental shortcut.
- The act of categorising people produces the **accentuation principle**, the **outgroup homogeneity effect** and the **ingroup differentiation hypothesis**. The **illusory correlation** can help explain the formation of negative stereotypes of minority groups.
- Stereotyping affects attention, perception and memory. Stereotypes may also influence people's **behaviour** towards members of outgroups, as well as the behaviour of outgroup members themselves through the **self-fulfilling prophecy**.
- We try actively to influence the impression that others form of us through **impression management/self-presentation**. This involves **behaviour matching**, **appreciating/flattering others**, showing **consistency** among our beliefs and matching our verbal and non-verbal behaviours.
- **High self-monitors** try to match their behaviour to the situation, while **low self-monitors** are more likely to 'be themselves'.
- Important factors that influence **self-disclosure** include **reciprocity**, **norms**, **trust**, **quality of relationship** and **gender**.

Self-assessment questions

1 Discuss research into the nature of social representations.
2 Discuss the process by which we form impressions of other people.
3 Critically evaluate psychological research into stereotypes and stereotyping.
4 Describe and evaluate psychological research into impression management/self-presentation.

Web addresses

http:www.csbs.utsa.edu/users/jreynolds/popcul.tx

http://www.psc-cftp.gc.ca/prcb/mono3-e.htm

http:www.msu.edu/user/amcconne/research/html

http://socpsych.jk.uni-linz.ac.at/SocReps/SRNet.html

http://lito.lse.ac.uk/socpsy/depthome.html

Further reading

Fiske, S.T. and Taylor, S.E. (1991) *Social Cognition* (2nd edition). New York: McGraw-Hill. Considered by many the 'classic' in this area of psychology, it's frequently cited by other writers.

Zebrowitz, L.A. (1990) *Social Perception*. Milton Keynes: Open University Press. Much shorter than the Fiske and Taylor but very thorough.

Oakes, P.J., Haslam, A. & Turner, J.C. (1994) *Stereotyping and Social Reality*. Oxford: Blackwell. In-depth coverage of all the issues raised in this chapter.

Chapter 23

Attribution

Introduction and overview

As we noted at the beginning of Chapter 22, attribution is an important aspect of social perception, theories of which flourished during the 1950s to the 1970s. Most of our impressions of others are based on their overt behaviour, and the setting in which it occurs. How we judge the causes of someone's behaviour will have a major influence on the impression we form about them. Was their behaviour something to do with them 'as a person', such as their motives, intentions or personality (an *internal cause*). Or was it something to do with the situation, including some other person or some physical feature of the environment (an *external cause*)?

Unless we can make this sort of judgement, we cannot really use the person's behaviour as a basis for forming an impression of them. Although we might mistakenly attribute the cause to the person instead of the situation, an attribution still has to be made.

Attribution theory deals with the general principles governing how we select and use information to arrive at causal explanations for behaviour. *Theories of attribution* draw on the principles of attribution theory, and predict how people will respond in particular situations (or *life domains*: Fiske & Taylor, 1991).

Rather than being a single body of ideas and research, attribution theory is a collection of diverse theoretical and empirical contributions sharing several common concerns (or mini-theories: Antaki, 1984). Six different traditions form the 'backbone' of attribution theory (Fiske & Taylor, 1991). These are: Heider's (1958) *'common-sense' psychology*, Jones & Davis's (1965) *correspondent inference theory*, Kelley's (1967, 1972, 1983) *covariation* and *configuration models*, Schachter's (1964) *cognitive labelling theory*, Bem's (1967, 1972) *self-perception theory*, and Weiner's (1986, 1995) *attributional theory of motivation*.

Schachter's cognitive labelling theory was discussd in Chapter 10 in relation to emotion, and Bem's self-perception theory is discussed in Chapter 24 in relation to attitude change. The models and theories of Heider, Jones and Davis, and Kelley see people as being logical and systematic in their explanations of behaviour. In practice, however, people tend to make attributions quickly, based often on very little information, and show clear tendencies to offer certain types of explanations for particular behaviours (Hewstone & Fincham, 1996). This chapter also examines some of the biases in the attribution process and why these biases occur.

Attribution and the naïve scientist

The process by which we make this judgement about internal/external causes is called the *attribution process*, which was first investigated by Heider (1958). In a famous study, Heider & Simmel (1944) demonstrated the strength of the human tendency to explain people's behaviour in terms of intentions, by showing that we sometimes attribute intentions to inanimate objects!

KEY STUDY 23.1

Even geometrical figures have intentions (Heider & Simmel, 1944)

Heider and Simmel showed animated cartoons of three geometrical figures (a large triangle, a smaller triangle and a disc) moving around, in and out of a large square. Participants tended to see them as having human characteristics and, in particular, as having intentions towards each other. A common perception was to see the two triangles as two men in rivalry for a girl (the disc), with the larger triangle being seen as aggressive and a bully, the smaller triangle as defiant and heroic, and the disc as timid. (Compare this with what Piaget calls *animism* in the child: see Chapter 34.)

In Chapter 22 we noted that there's a sense in which we're all psychologists. Perhaps this is most apparent in the case of attribution theory, which promises to:

> '... uncover the way in which we, as ordinary men and women, act as scientists in tracking down the causes of behaviour; it promises to treat ordinary people, in fact, as if they were psychologists ...'. (Antaki, 1984)

Heider's 'common-sense' psychology

Heider (1958) argued that the starting point for studying how we understand the social world is the 'ordinary' person. He asked 'How do people usually think about and infer meaning from what goes on around them?' and 'How do they make sense of their own and other people's behaviours?' These questions relate to what he called 'common-sense' psychology. In Heider's view, the 'ordinary' person is a naïve scientist who links observable behaviour to unobservable causes, and these *causes* (rather than the behaviour itself) provide the meaning of what people do.

What interested Heider was the fact that members of a culture share certain basic assumptions about behaviour. These assumptions belong to the belief system that forms part of the culture as a whole, and distinguishes one culture from another. As Bennett (1993) has observed:

> 'It is important that we do subscribe to a common psychology, since doing this provides an orienting context in which we can understand, and be understood by, others. Imagine a world in which your version of everyday psychology was fundamentally at odds with that of your friends – without a shared "code" for making sense of behaviour, social life would hardly be possible'.

Ask yourself ...

- Can you see any parallels between Heider's common-sense psychology and Moscovici's social representations? (See Chapter 22.)

As we noted in the *Introduction and overview*, we explain people's behaviour in terms of *dispositional* (or personal/internal) factors, such as ability or effort, and *situational* (or environmental/external) factors, such as circumstances or luck. When we observe somebody's behaviour, we're inclined to attribute its cause to one or other of these two general sources. This represents one of these culturally shared beliefs about behaviour that forms part of common-sense psychology.

Although Heider didn't formulate his own theory of attribution, he inspired other psychologists to pursue his original ideas. As well as his insight relating to personal and situational factors as causes of behaviour, three other ideas have been particularly influential (Ross & Fletcher, 1985):

- When we observe others, we tend to search for enduring, unchanging, and dispositional characteristics.
- We distinguish between intentional and unintentional behaviours.
- We're inclined to attribute behaviours to events (causes) that are present when the outcome is present, and absent when the outcome is absent.

Jones and Davis's correspondent inference theory

Correspondent inferences and intentionality

Very much influenced by Heider, Jones & Davis (1965) believe that the goal of the attribution process is to be able to make correspondent inferences. We need to be able to infer that both the behaviour and the intention that produced it correspond to some underlying, stable feature of the person (a *disposition*). An inference is 'correspondent' when the disposition attributed to an actor 'corresponds' to the behaviour from which the disposition is inferred. For instance, if someone gives up his seat on the bus to allow a pregnant woman to sit down, we'd probably infer that he's 'kind and unselfish'. This is a correspondent inference, because both the behaviour and the disposition can be labelled in a similar way ('kind and unselfish'). But if we attribute the behaviour to *compliance* with someone else's demands ('he' is a husband whose wife has told him to give up his seat), then we wouldn't be making a correspondent inference.

According to Jones and Davis, a precondition for a correspondent inference is the attribution of *intentionality*, and they specify two criteria or conditions for this. We have to be confident that the actor:

- is capable of having produced the observed effects; and
- knew the effects the behaviour would produce.

The analysis of uncommon effects

Having made these preliminary decisions, how do we then proceed to infer that the intended behaviour is related to some underlying disposition? One answer is the *analysis of uncommon effects*. When more than one course of action is open to a person, a way of understanding why s/he chose one course rather than another is to compare the consequences of the action that was taken with the consequences of those that weren't. In other words, what's distinctive (or uncommon) about the effects of the choice that's made?

For example, if you've a strong preference for one particular university, even though there are several that are similar with regard to size, reputation, type of course and so on, the fact that all the others require you to be in residence during your first year suggests that you've a strong preference for being independent and looking after yourself. Generally, the fewer the differences between the chosen and the unchosen alternatives, the more confidently we can infer dispositions. Also, the more *negative* elements involved in the chosen alternative, the more confident still we can be of the importance of the distinctive consequence. (If living out of residence means a lot of extra travelling, or is more expensive, then the desire to be self-sufficient assumes even greater significance.)

Other factors affecting dispositional attributions

Because the analysis of uncommon effects can lead to ambiguous conclusions, other cues must also be used:

- *Choice* is self-explanatory: is the actor's behaviour influenced by situational factors, or a result of free will?
- *Social desirability* relates to the *norms* associated with different situations. Because most of us conform most of the time,

the need to explain other people's behaviour doesn't often arise. We base our impressions of others more on behaviour which is in some way unusual, novel, bizarre or antisocial than on behaviour that's expected or conventional.

> ## Ask yourself ...
>
> - Do you agree? Give your reasons.

'Deviant' behaviour seems to provide more information about what the person is like, largely because when we behave unconventionally we're more likely to be ostracised, shunned or disapproved of.

For example, at a funeral we're expected to dress soberly, look sad and talk respectfully of the deceased. So, when we observe such behaviour, we can easily attribute it to the situation ('that's how one acts at funerals'). But if somebody arrives in brightly-coloured clothes, making jokes and saying what a lout the deceased was, they're 'breaking the rules'. His/her behaviour needs explaining, and we're likely to attribute it to personal/dispositional characteristics. This was demonstrated in an experiment by Jones *et al.* (1961).

> ### KEY STUDY 23.2
>
> #### If you want to be an astronaut, be a loner (Jones *et al.*, 1961)
>
> Participants heard a tape-recording of a job interview, where the applicant was, supposedly, applying to be an astronaut or a submariner. Prior to hearing the tape, participants were informed of the ideal qualities for the job: astronauts should be inner-directed and able to exist without social interaction, while submariners should be other-directed and gregarious. The participants believed the candidates also understood these ideal qualities.
>
> The tape presented the candidate as either displaying these qualities or behaving in the opposite way, and participants had to give their impressions of the candidate. When the candidate behaved in the *opposite* way, they more confidently rated him as actually being like that, compared with those who heard a 'conforming' candidate.

- *Roles* refer to another kind of conformity. When people in well-defined roles behave as they're expected to, this tells us relatively little about their underlying dispositions (they're 'just doing their job'). But when they display out-of-role behaviour, we can use their actions to infer 'what they're really like'. This is similar to the effects of social desirability, except that the norms are associated with particular social positions within an overall social context, rather than with the context or situation itself.
- *Prior expectations* are based on past experiences with the same actor. The better we know someone, the better placed we are to decide whether his/her behaviour on a particular occasion is 'typical'. If it's 'atypical', we're more likely to dismiss it, or play down its significance, or explain it in terms of situational factors.

An evaluation of Jones and Davis's theory

While there are data consistent with Jones and Davis's theory, several weaknesses have been identified. For example, Eiser (1983) has argued that intentions *aren't* a precondition for correspondent inferences. When someone is called 'clumsy', that dispositional attribution doesn't imply that the behaviour was intentional. In Eiser's view, behaviours which are unintended or accidental are beyond the scope of Jones and Davis's theory. Also, it isn't just behaviour which disconfirms expectations that's informative. 'Conforming' behaviour can also be informative, as when behaviour confirms a *stereotype* (Hewstone & Fincham, 1996: see Chapter 22, pages 332–336).

Although correspondent inference theory continues to attract interest, most of the studies supporting it didn't measure *causal* attributions (Gilbert, 1995). Inferring a disposition isn't the same as inferring a cause, and each appears to reflect different underlying processes (Hewstone & Fincham, 1996). Both of Kelley's models discussed next are concerned with the processes that determine whether an internal or external attribution is made for a behaviour's cause.

Kelley's covariation and configuration models

The covariation model

> ### Ask yourself ...
>
> - One of your fellow students (let's call her Sally) is late for psychology class one morning. How might you explain her late arrival? What kinds of information would you need in order to make a causal attribution?

Kelley's covariation model (1967) tries to explain how we make causal attributions where we have some knowledge of how the 'actor' usually behaves in a variety of situations, and how others usually behave in those situations. The *principle of covariation* states that:

> *'An effect is attributed to one of its possible causes with which, over time, it covaries'.*

In other words, if two events repeatedly occur together, we're more likely to infer that they're causally related than if they very rarely occur together. If the behaviour to be explained is thought of as an *effect*, the *cause* can be one of three kinds, and the extent to which the behaviour covaries with each of these three kinds of possible cause, is what we base our attribution on. To illustrate the three kinds of causal information, let's take the hypothetical example of Sally, who's late for her psychology class.

- *Consensus* refers to the extent to which other people behave in the same way. In this example, are other students late for psychology? If all (or most) other students are late, then consensus is *high* (she's in good company), but if only Sally is late, consensus is *low*.
- *Distinctiveness* refers to the extent to which Sally behaves in a similar way towards other, similar, 'stimuli' or 'entities'. Is she late for other subjects? If she is, then distinctiveness is *low* (there's nothing special or distinctive about psychology), but if she's only late for psychology, then distinctiveness is *high*.

- *Consistency* refers to how stable Sally's behaviour is over time. Is she regularly late for psychology? If she is, consistency is *high*, but if she's not (this is a 'one-off'), then consistency is *low*.

Kelley believes that a combination of *low consensus* (Sally is the only one late), *low distinctiveness* (she's late for all her subjects), and *high consistency* (she's regularly late) will lead us to make a *person* (*internal* or *dispositional*) attribution. In other words, the cause of Sally's behaviour is something to do with Sally, such as being a poor timekeeper.

However, any other combination would normally result in an external or situational attribution. For example, if Sally is generally punctual (*low consistency*), or if most students are late for psychology (*high consensus*), then the cause of Sally's lateness might be 'extenuating circumstances' in the first case or the subject and/or the teacher in the second.

Table 23.1 *Causal attributions based on three different combinations of causal information (based on Kelley, 1967)*

Consensus	Distinctiveness	Consistency	Causal attribution
Low	Low	High	Person (actor/internal)
Low	High	Low	Circumstances (external)
High	High	High	Stimulus/target (external)

Evaluation of Kelley's model

A number of empirical studies have found support for Kelley. McArthur (1972) presented participants with one-sentence descriptions of various behaviours relating to emotions, accomplishments, opinions and actions (for example, 'Sue is afraid of the dog', 'George translates the sentence incorrectly'). Each description was accompanied by high or low consensus information, high or low distinctiveness information, and high or low consistency information. The task was to attribute each behaviour to characteristics of the actor, the stimulus (target), circumstances or some combination of these. Predictions based on Kelley's model were strongly supported.

However, not all three types of causal information are used to the same extent in laboratory studies. For example, Major (1980) found that participants show a marked preference for consistency over the other two, with consensus being the least preferred. Similarly, Nisbett & Borgida (1975) found surprisingly weak effects of consensus information when they asked university students to explain the behaviour of a participant in a psychology experiment. This participant, like most others involved, had agreed to tolerate a high level of electric shock. But the students who were told that 16 of the 34 participants had tolerated the highest possible shock level, were *no more likely* to make situational attributions than those who had been given no consensus information at all. Nisbett and Borgida argued that people's judgements are less responsive to the dull and abstract base rates that constitute consensus information than to the more vivid information regarding the behaviour of one, concrete target person. However, consensus information can have more of an impact if it's made more salient (for example, if it's contrary to what we might expect most people to do: Wells & Harvey, 1977).

Consistent with Wells and Harvey's proposal is Hilton & Slugoski's (1986) *abnormal conditions focus model*. This can help explain why the three types of causal information aren't used to the same extent.

Box 23.1   The abnormal conditions focus model

According to Hilton and Slugoski, Kelley's three types of information are useful to the extent that the behaviour requiring explanation contrasts with the information given. So, with *low consensus information*, the *person* is abnormal, whereas with *low consistency* information the *circumstances* are abnormal. With *high distinctiveness* information, the *stimulus/target* is abnormal.

Another way of looking at 'abnormality' is, in Table 23.1, to read down the columns. Two 'values' are the same, and different from the third. For example, *high consensus* (the 'odd-one-out') corresponds to the *stimulus/target*, *low distinctiveness* corresponds to the *person/actor*, and *low consistency* corresponds to the *circumstances*. Here, then, 'abnormal' is taken to refer to the causal information, rather than the causal attribution. But the end result seems to be the same.

The model proposes that we attribute as a cause the necessary condition that's abnormal when compared with the background of the target event (Slugoski & Hilton, 2000).

Just because people make attributions *as if* they're using covariation 'rules', doesn't necessarily mean that they are (Hewstone & Fincham, 1996). Kelley seems to have overestimated people's ability to assess covariation. He originally compared the social perceiver to a naïve scientist (as did Heider), trying to draw inferences in much the same way as the formal scientist draws conclusions from data. More significantly, it's a *normative* model which states how, ideally, people should come to draw inferences about others' behaviour. However, the actual procedures that people use aren't as logical, rational and systematic as the model suggests.

The configuration model

Kelley recognised that in many situations (most notably when we don't know the actor), we might not have access to any or all of the covariation model's three types of information. Indeed, often the only information we have is a single occurrence of the behaviour of a particular individual. Yet we still feel able to explain the behaviour. The *configuration model* was Kelley's attempt to account for attributions about such *single occurrence* behaviours.

Causal schemata

When we make 'single event attributions' we do so using causal schemata (Kelley, 1972). These are general ideas (or ready-made beliefs, preconceptions, and even theories: Hewstone & Fincham, 1996) about 'how certain kinds of causes interact to produce a specific kind of effect' (Kelley, 1972). According to Fiske & Taylor (1991), causal schemata provide the social perceiver with a 'causal shorthand' for making complex inferences quickly and easily. They're based on our experience of cause–effect relationships, and what we've been taught by others about such relationships. They come

into play when causal information is otherwise ambiguous and incomplete.

The two major kinds of causal schemata are *multiple necessary schemata*, and *multiple sufficient schemata*.

Box 23.2   Multiple necessary and multiple necessary sufficient schemata

Multiple necessary causes: Experience tells us that to win a marathon, for example, you must not only be fit and highly motivated, but you must have trained hard for several months beforehand, you must wear the right kind of running shoes and so on. Even if all these conditions are met, there's no guarantee of success, but the *absence* of any one of them is likely to produce failure. So, in this sense, success is more informative than failure. Thus, there are many causes needed to produce certain behaviours – typically, those which are unusual or extreme.

Multiple sufficient causes: With some behaviours, any number of causes are sufficient to explain their occurrence. For example, a footballer who advertises shampoo may do so because he genuinely believes it's a good product, or because he's being paid a large sum of money to advertise it – either of these is a sufficient cause.

David Ginola, almost as famous for advertising shampoo as for playing football (here, for Tottenham Hotspur)

Ask yourself ...

- In this last example, do you think one of the proposed causes is more likely to be the real cause than the other? If so, which one? What do you base this attribution on?

Since it's reasonable to assume that it's the fee which accounts for the footballer's appearance in the commercial, we're likely to reject the other cause ('belief ' in the product) according to the *discounting principle* (Kelley, 1983). According to this:

> *'Given that different causes can produce the same effect, the role of a given cause is discounted if other plausible causes are present'.*

Multiple sufficient schemata are also associated with the *augmenting principle* (Kelley, 1983). This states that:

> *'The role of a given cause is augmented or increased if the effect occurs in the presence of an inhibitory factor'.*

So, we're more likely to make an internal attribution (to effort and ability) when a student passes an exam after (say) suffering the death of a relative, than would be the case for a student who'd passed without having suffered such a loss.

Weiner's attributional theory of emotion and motivation

As the name suggests, Weiner's (1986) theory is really an application of basic attributional principles to human emotion and motivation (see Chapters 9 and 10). According to Weiner, the attributions we make about our own and others' successes and failures produce specific kinds of *emotional response*, but these attributions are more complex than described by Heider, Jones and Davis or Kelley.

For Weiner, there are three dimensions of causality. These are:

- the *locus dimension*: causes can be internal/external (person/situation);
- the *stability dimension*: causes can be stable/transient (permanent/temporary);
- the *controllability dimension*: causes can be controllable or uncontrollable.

For example, we may blame failure in an exam on a really difficult paper (external, stable, uncontrollable), which is likely to make us feel *angry*. Or we may blame the really bad headache we awoke with on the morning of the exam (internal, unstable, uncontrollable), which may make us feel both *angry* and *disappointed*. But a third possibility is that we blame our failure on our basic lack of ability (internal, stable, uncontrollable), which is likely to make us feel quite *depressed* (see Figure 10.8, page 141).

What's important here is that not all internal or external causes are of the same kind. For Weiner, causes are *multidimensional*. This, together with the emotional responses associated with different attributions, has very important implications for a number of behaviours, including *impression management* (see Chapter 22), *self-esteem* (particularly in the context of gender differences in achievement motivation: see Chapters 9 and 36) and *helping behaviour* (see Chapter 30).

Error and bias in the attribution process

As we've already seen, people are far less logical and systematic (less 'scientific') than required by Kelley's covariation model. Research into sources of error and bias seems to provide a much more accurate account of how people actually make causal attributions. Zebrowitz (1990) defines sources of bias as:

> *'... the tendency to favour one cause over another when explaining some effect. Such favouritism may result in causal attributions that deviate from predictions derived from rational attributional principles, like covariation ...'.*

Even though almost all behaviour is the product of both the person and the situation, our causal explanations tend to emphasise one or the other. According to Jones & Nisbett (1971), we all want to see ourselves as competent interpreters of human behaviour, and so we naïvely assume that simple explanations are better than complex ones. To try to analyse the interactions between personal and situational factors would take time and energy, and we seldom have all the relevant information at our disposal.

The fundamental attribution error

The fundamental attribution error (FAE) refers to the general tendency to overestimate the importance of personal/dispositional factors relative to situational/environmental factors as causes of behaviour (Ross, 1977). This will tend to make the others' behaviour seem more predictable which, in turn, enhances our sense of control over the environment.

> ### Ask yourself ...
> - Can you relate the FAE to any of the Gestalt laws of perception (see Chapter 15)?

Heider (1958) believed that behaviour represents the 'figure' against the 'ground', comprising context, roles, situational pressures and so on. In other words, behaviour is conspicuous and situational factors are less easily perceived (see Chapter 15).

For Zebrowitz (1990):

> *'... the fundamental attribution error is best viewed as a bias towards attributing an actor's behaviour to dispositional causes rather than as an attribution error. This bias may be limited to adults in Western societies and it may be most pronounced when they are constrained to attribute behaviour to a single cause ...'.*

The FAE and the just world hypothesis

Related to the FAE, but not usually cited as an example of an attribution error, is the just world hypothesis (Lerner, 1965, 1980). According to this, 'I am a just person living in a just world, a world where people get what they deserve'. When 'bad' things happen to people, we believe it's because they're in some way 'bad' people, so that they have at least partly 'brought it on themselves'. This can help explain the phenomenon of 'blaming the victim'. In rape cases, for example, the woman is often accused of having 'led the man on' or giving him the sexual 'green light' before changing her mind.

Myers (1994) gives the example of a German civilian who, on being shown round the Bergen-Belsen concentration camp after the British liberation, commented 'What terrible criminals these prisoners must have been to receive such treatment'. What this person seems to have been saying is that s/he found it totally unbelievable that such horrors (as had obviously been perpetrated in that camp) could have happened to innocent people – if they happened to them, why couldn't they happen to me? Believing in a just world gives us a sense of being in control: so long as we're 'good', only 'good' things will happen to us.

In combination with the FAE, the just world hypothesis can help to explain certain aspects of prejudice (see Chapter 25) and helping behaviour (see Chapter 30).

Glenn Hoddle was sacked as England football manager in 1999 after allegedly claiming that disabled people were being punished for sins committed in a former life

The actor–observer effect

Related to the FAE is the tendency for actors and observers to make different attributions about the same event. This is called the actor–observer effect (AOE) (Jones & Nisbett, 1971; Nisbett *et al.*, 1973):

- Actors usually see their own behaviour as primarily a response to the *situation*, and therefore as quite *variable* from situation to situation (the cause is *external*).
- The observer typically attributes the same behaviour to the actor's *intentions* and *dispositions*, and therefore as quite *consistent* across situations (the cause is *internal*). The observer's attribution to internal causes is, of course, the FAE.

Nisbett *et al.* (1973) found that students:

- assumed that actors would behave in the future in ways similar to those they'd just witnessed;
- described their best friend's choices of girlfriend and college major in terms referring to dispositional qualities of their best friend (while more often describing their own similar choices in terms of properties of the girlfriend or major);
- attributed more personality traits to other people than to themselves.

One explanation for the AOE is that what's perceptually salient or vivid for the actor is different from what's perceptually salient or vivid for the observer (this is the figure–ground explanation which we noted when discussing the FAE). An important study by Storms (1973) supports this perceptual salience explanation of the AOE.

Videotape and the attribution process (Storms, 1973)

Two actor participants at a time engaged in a brief, unstructured conversation, while two observers looked on. Later, a questionnaire was used to measure the actors' attributions of their own behaviour in the conversation and the observers' attributions of the behaviour of one of the two actors to whom they'd been assigned. Visual orientation was manipulated by the use of videotapes of the conversation so that:

- the *no video* (control) group simply completed the questionnaire;
- the *same orientation* group simply saw a video of what they saw during the original conversation (before completing the questionnaire);
- the *new orientation* group saw a video which *reversed* the original orientation, with actors seeing themselves and observers seeing the other actor (again, before completing the questionnaire).

As predicted, in the first two groups the usual AOE was found. But, also as predicted, the AOE was reversed in the third group: actors made more *dispositional* attributions than did observers.

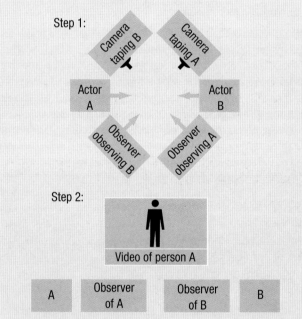

Figure 23.1 *Diagram depicting the arrangement in the Storms (1973) experiment*

The self-serving bias

Several studies have found that the AOE is most pronounced when judging *negative* behaviours, and may be absent or even reversed for positive ones.

Ask yourself ...

- Try to account for this finding.

Naturally, no one wants to admit to being incompetent, so we're more likely to 'blame' our failures on something external to ourselves. This is the *self-protecting bias*, which protects our self-esteem. However, we're quite happy to take the credit for our successes. This is the *self-enhancing bias*, which enhances our self-esteem. Together, they constitute the *self-serving bias* (SSB: Miller & Ross, 1975).

There's some evidence that positively valued outcomes (e.g. altruism) are more often attributed to people, and negatively valued outcomes (e.g. being late) to situational factors, *regardless* of who committed them. However, when either the self or someone closely associated with the self has committed the action, credit for positive events and denial of responsibility for negative ones are even stronger.

Attributional style and depression

An interesting exception to the SSB is the case of clinically depressed people. Abramson *et al.* (1978) found that they tend to explain their failures in terms of their own inadequacies, and their successes more in terms of external factors, such as luck and chance (see Chapter 10). Depressed people are displaying a different attributional style from non-depressed people.

There's also evidence that women are more likely than men to cope with stress by blaming themselves for their plights and to attribute their achievements to external factors (Davison & Neale, 1994: see Chapter 12). Differences in attributional style can also help to explain why married couples differ in their degrees of happiness (see Chapter 28).

The importance of the consequences

The more serious the consequences of the actor's behaviour, the more likely the FAE is to be made: the more serious the outcome, the more likely we are to judge the actor as responsible, regardless of his/her perceived intentions.

KEY STUDY 23.4

Consequences of behaviour and the FAE (Walster, 1966)

Walster gave participants an account of a car accident, in which a young man's car had been left at the top of a hill and then rolled down backwards.

- One group was told that very little damage was done to the car and no other vehicle was involved.
- A second group was told that it collided with another car, causing some damage.
- A third group was told that the car crashed into a shop, injuring the shopkeeper and a small child.

When participants had to assess how responsible the car owner was, the third group found him more 'guilty' or morally culpable than the second group, and the second group found him more guilty than the first.

If more serious consequences can result in greater blame and responsibility, can the reverse inference occur; that is, can belief that an act is intentional affect perception of the seriousness of the consequences? Darley & Huff (1990) found

that judgements of the damage caused by an action depended on whether participants believed it was done intentionally, through negligence or accidentally. Although the damage done was described in an identical way, those who read that the act was done intentionally inflated their estimation of the amount of damage done, compared with those who believed the damage was caused unintentionally (either through negligence or accident).

Another facet of the consequences of behaviour is how they affect us personally (*personal* or *hedonic relevance*): the more they affect us (the greater the hedonic relevance), the more likely we are to hold the actor responsible. Going one step further than hedonic relevance is *personalism*, which is the perceiver's belief that the actor *intended* to harm the perceiver. In terms of Jones and Davis's theory, this increases the chances of making a *correspondent inference*.

CHAPTER SUMMARY

- **Attribution theory** refers to psychologists' attempts to explain the **attribution process**. **Theories of attribution** draw on the principles of attribution theory to predict how people will respond in particular life domains.
- Heider's 'common-sense' psychology sees people as **naïve scientists**, inferring unobservable causes (or meaning) from observable behaviour. In Western culture, behaviour is explained in terms of both **personal** (dispositional/internal) and **situational** (environmental/external) factors.
- Jones and Davis were concerned with explaining why we make **correspondent inferences** about people's dispositions. One way of looking for dispositions that could have caused behaviour is through the **analysis of uncommon effects**.
- The likelihood of making dispositional attributions is influenced by **free choice**, **social desirability**, **roles** and **prior expectations**.
- Kelley's **covariation model** is concerned with the processes by which we make internal and external attributions for the causes of behaviour. The **principle of covariation** says that we're more likely to infer that two events are causally related if they repeatedly co-occur.
- Attributions about some effect/behaviour depend on the extent of its covariation with causal information regarding **consensus**, **consistency** and **distinctiveness**.
- Kelley's **configuration model** tries to account for 'single event attributions' in terms of **multiple necessary** and **multiple sufficient causal schemata**. The latter are associated with the **augmenting principle**, and we choose between two or more possible causes by using the **discounting principle**.
- Weiner's attribution theory identifies three dimensions of causality: **locus**, **stability** and **controllability**. It applies basic attributional principles to emotion and motivation.
- People are actually less rational and scientific than Kelley's **normative** model requires. A more accurate account of the attribution process involves looking at **systematic biases** in the attribution of cause.
- The **fundamental attribution error** (FAE) is the tendency to exaggerate the importance of internal/dispositional factors relative to external/situational

factors. The likelihood of making it depends on the serious-ness/importance of the **consequences** of behaviour, and **personal/hedonic relevance**.

■ In the **actor–observer effect** (AOE), actors see their behaviours as responses to **situational** factors, whereas observers explain the same behaviours in **dispositional** terms.

■ The AOE is most pronounced when one explains one's own negative behaviour (**self-protecting bias**). Personal successes tend to be explained in dispositional ways (**self-enhancing bias**). Together, they comprise the **self-serving bias** (SSB).

■ The SSB is **reversed** in clinically depressed people. This **attributional style** is also displayed by some non-depressed women.

Self-assessment questions

1 Discuss **two** theories of attribution.
2 Describe and evaluate research studies into any **two** errors or biases in the attribution process.

Web addresses

http://www.as.wvu.edu/~sbb/comm221/chapters/attrib.htm

explorer.scrtec.org/explorer/explorer-db/html/783751634-447DED81.htm

http://www.midcoast.com.au/~lars/Attribution_Bias

http://www.vcu.edu/hasweb/psy/faculty/fors/ratt1.html

http://www.psych.purdue.edu/~esmith/search.html

Further reading

Weiner, B. (1992) *Human Motivation: Metaphors, Theories, and Research*. Newbury Park, CA.: Sage. Chapter 6 is especially relevant, but other chapters cover other areas in social psychology where attributional principles have been applied (as indicated above). Excellent for motivation too (see Chapter 9 of this book).

Gross, R. (1999) *Key Studies in Psychology* (3rd edition). London: Hodder & Stoughton. Chapter 10 looks in detail at Nisbett *et al.*'s (1973) study of the AOE.

Chapter 24

Attitudes and Attitude Change

Introduction and overview

According to Gordon Allport (1935): 'The concept of attitudes is probably the most distinctive and indispensable concept in contemporary American social psychology ...'.

More than 50 years later, Hogg & Vaughan (1995) claim that: 'Attitudes continue to fascinate research workers and remain a key, if controversial, part of social psychology'.

However, the study of attitudes has undergone many important changes during that time, with different questions becoming the focus of theory and research. According to Stainton Rogers *et al.* (1995), psychologists have tried to answer four fundamental questions over the last 70 years:

1 Where do attitudes come from? How are they moulded and formed in the first place?
2 How can attitudes be measured?
3 How and why do attitudes change? What forces are involved and what intrapsychic mechanisms operate when people shift in their opinions about particular 'attitude objects'?
4 How do attitudes relate to behaviour? What is it that links the way people think and feel about an attitude object, and what they do about it?

In this chapter, we concentrate on some of the answers that have been offered to questions 3 and 4. This discussion is also relevant to prejudice, considered as an extreme attitude (see Chapter 25).

During the 1940s and 1950s, the focus of research was on attitude change, in particular *persuasive communication*. Much of the impetus for this came from the use of *propaganda* during World War II, as well as a more general concern over the growing influence of the mass media, especially in the US. The power of *advertising* was also beginning to interest psychologists and other social scientists. This period also saw the birth of a number of theories of attitude change, the most influential of these being Festinger's *cognitive dissonance theory*.

The 1960s and 1970s was a period of decline and pessimism in attitude research, at least partly due to the apparent failure to find any reliable relationship between measured attitudes and behaviour (Hogg & Vaughan, 1995). However, the 1980s saw a revival of interest, stimulated largely by the cognitive approach, so attitudes represent another important aspect of *social cognition* (see Chapter 22).

What are attitudes?

There's no single definition with which all psychologists would agree, and a sample of definitions is given in Table 24.1.

According to Rosenberg & Hovland (1960), attitudes are 'predispositions to respond to some class of stimuli with certain classes of response'. These classes of response are:

■ *affective*: what a person feels about the attitude object, how favourably or unfavourably it's evaluated;
■ *cognitive*: what a person believes the attitude object is like, objectively;
■ *behavioural* (sometimes called the '*conative*'): how a person actually responds, or intends to respond, to the attitude object.

This *three-component model*, which is much more a model of attitude structure than a simple definition (Stahlberg & Frey, 1988), is shown in Figure 24.1. It sees an attitude as an intervening/mediating variable between observable stimuli and responses, illustrating the influence that behaviourism was still having, even in social psychology, at the start of the 1960s. A major problem with this multi-component model is the assumption that the three components are highly correlated (see below, pages 353–355).

Table 24.1 *Some definitions of attitudes*

'An attitude is a mental and neural state of readiness, organised through experience, exerting a directive or dynamic influence upon the individual's response to all objects and situations with which it is related.' (Allport, 1935)

'A learned orientation, or disposition, toward an object or situation, which provides a tendency to respond favourably or unfavourably to the object or situation …' (Rokeach, 1968)

'… attitudes have social reference in their origins and development and in their objects, while at the same time they have psychological reference in that they inhere in the individual and are intimately enmeshed in his behaviour and his psychological make-up.' (Warren & Jahoda, 1973)

'The term *attitude* should be used to refer to a general, enduring positive or negative feeling about some person, object, or issue.' (Petty & Cacioppo, 1981)

'An *attitude* is an *evaluative disposition toward some object*. It's an evaluation of something or someone along a continuum of like-to-dislike or favourable-to-unfavourable ….' (Zimbardo & Leippe, 1991)

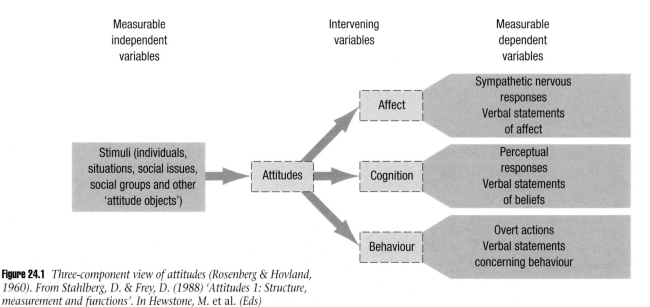

Figure 24.1 *Three-component view of attitudes (Rosenberg & Hovland, 1960). From Stahlberg, D. & Frey, D. (1988) 'Attitudes 1: Structure, measurement and functions'. In Hewstone, M.* et al. *(Eds)* Introduction to Social Psychology. *Oxford, Blackwell*

Attitudes, beliefs and values

An attitude can be thought of as a blend or integration of beliefs and values. Beliefs represent the knowledge or information we have about the world (although these may be inaccurate or incomplete) and, in themselves, are non-evaluative. According to Fishbein & Ajzen (1975), 'a belief links an object to some attribute' (e.g. 'America' and 'capitalist state'). To convert a belief into an attitude, a 'value' ingredient is needed. Values refer to an individual's sense of what is desirable, good, valuable, worthwhile and so on. While most adults will have many thousands of beliefs, they have only hundreds of attitudes and a few dozen values.

> **Ask yourself ...**
> - Try to identify some of your most cherished values (there should be a relatively small number of these). Then try to identify some related attitudes, which are less abstract than values.

What are attitudes for?

According to Hogg & Vaughan (1995):

> '... attitudes are basic and pervasive in human life ... Without the concept of attitude, we would have difficulty construing and reacting to events, trying to make decisions, and making sense of our relationships with people in everyday life ...'.

In other words, attitudes provide us with ready-made reactions to, and interpretations of events, just as other aspects of our cognitive 'equipment' do, such as schemas (see Chapter 21) and stereotypes (see Chapters 22 and 25). Attitudes save us energy, since we don't have to work out how we feel about objects or events each time we come into contact with them.

However, not all attitudes serve the same function. Katz (1960), influenced by Freud's psychoanalytic theory, believes that attitudes serve both conscious and unconscious motives. He identified four major functions of attitudes (see Table 24.2).

Katz's functional approach implies that some attitudes will be more resistant to efforts to change them than others, in particular those that serve an ego-defensive function. This is especially important when trying to account for prejudice and attempts to reduce it (see Chapter 25).

The measurement of attitudes

An attitude cannot be measured directly, because it's a *hypothetical construct*. Consequently, it's necessary to find adequate attitude indicators, and most methods of attitude measurement are based on the assumption that they can be measured by people's beliefs or opinions about the attitude object (Stahlberg & Frey, 1988). Most attitude scales rely on verbal reports, and usually take the form of standardised statements which clearly refer to the attitude being measured. Such scales make two further assumptions: (i) that the same statement has the *same meaning* for all respondents; and, more fundamentally, (ii) that subjective attitudes, when expressed verbally, can be *quantified* (represented by a numerical score).

Table 24.2 *Four major functions of attitudes (based on Katz, 1960)*

Knowledge function	We seek a degree of predictability, consistency and stability in our perception of the world. Attitudes give meaning and direction to experience, providing frames of reference for judging events, objects and people.
Adjustive (instrumental or utilitarian) function	We obtain favourable responses from others by displaying socially acceptable attitudes, so they become associated with important rewards (such as others' acceptance and approval). These attitudes may be publicly expressed, but not necessarily believed, as is the case with *compliance* (see Chapter 26).
Value-expressive function	We achieve self-expression through cherished values. The reward may not be gaining social approval, but confirmation of the more positive aspects of our self-concept, especially our sense of personal integrity.
Ego-defensive function	Attitudes help protect us from admitting personal deficiencies. For example, *prejudice* helps us to sustain our self-concept by maintaining a sense of superiority over others. Ego defence often means avoiding and denying self-knowledge. This function comes closest to being unconscious in a Freudian sense (see Chapters 2 and 42).

Thurstone's equal appearing intervals scale (1928)

Strictly, this is a technique for constructing an attitude scale. First, about 100 statements are collected, relevant to the attitude object. These statements must range from extreme positive to extreme negative, and should be short and unambiguous. Next, about 100 'judges' (representative of the population for whom the scale is intended) evaluate the statements on an eleven-point scale, assuming an equal interval scale. Any statements (items) which produce substantial disagreements are discarded, until 22 remain (two for each of the eleven points on the scale: eleven favourable, eleven unfavourable). The average numerical scale position of each statement is calculated.

Finally, the 22 statements are given, in random order, to participants who are asked to indicate every statement with which they agree. The final attitude score is the mean scale value for these statements. Though revolutionary in its time, the Thurstone scale is rarely used today, partly because it's so time-consuming, and partly because of the assumption that it's an interval (as opposed to an ordinal) scale.

> **Ask yourself...**
> - What's the difference between an ordinal and interval scale, and why do you think it's a problem in relation to attitude measurement?

Likert scale (1932)

This comprises a number of statements, for each of which participants indicate whether they strongly agree/agree/[are] undecided/disagree/strongly disagree. If possible, statements are selected so that for half 'agree' represents a positive attitude and for the other half a negative attitude. This controls for *acquiescence response set*, the tendency to agree or disagree with items consistently, or to tick the 'undecided' point on the scale.

It's one of the most popular standard attitude scales, partly because it's more statistically reliable than the Thurstone scale, and partly because it's easier to construct. It makes no assumptions about equal intervals.

LIKERT SCALE

'I believe that under no circumstances can animal experiments be justified'

5	4	3	2	1
Strongly agree	Agree	Undecided	Disagree	Strongly disagree

Sociometry (Moreno, 1953)

This represents a method for assessing interpersonal attitudes in 'natural' groups (at school, college, work); that is, it assesses who likes whom. Each group member is asked to name another who'd be his/her preferred partner for a specific activity or as a friend. The product of these choices is a *sociogram*, which charts the friendship patterns, revealing the popular and unpopular members, the 'isolates' and so on.

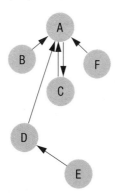

Each circle represents a group member, and the arrows indicate direction of preference.

> *Ask yourself ...*
>
> • Who's the most popular member of the group? Who's most isolated?

Guttman scalogram method

This is based on the assumption that a single, unidimensional trait can be measured by a set of statements that are ordered along a continuum of difficulty of acceptance. The statements range from those that are easy for most people to accept, to those that most people couldn't endorse. Such scale items are also *cumulative*, since accepting one item implies acceptance of all those 'below' it. It's constructed so that responses follow a step-like order (Hogg & Vaughan, 1995).

GUTTMAN SCALE
Attitude towards mixed-ethnic housing

How acceptable	Statement
Least	*Generally speaking, people should be able to live where they want.*
	Real estate agencies should not discriminate against minority groups.
	The local council should actively support the idea of open housing.
	There should be a local review board that would pass on cases of extreme discrimination of housing.
Most	*There should be laws to enforce mixed-ethnic housing.*

Semantic differential (Osgood *et al.*, 1957)

This assumes a hypothetical semantic space, in which the meaning or connotation of any word or concept can be represented somewhere on a seven-point scale. Unlike other scales, this allows different attitudes to be measured on the same scale. The attitude object is denoted by a single word (e.g. 'father'), and the scale comprises seven *bipolar* scales of adjectives (a value of seven usually being given to the positive end).

good_ _ _ _ _ _ _bad (illustrates the *evaluative factor*);

strong_ _ _ _ _ _ weak (illustrates the *potency factor*);

active _ _ _ _ _ _ _passive (illustrates the *activity factor*).

Some alternative methods of measuring attitudes

A problem with attitude scales (*self-report methods*) is that participants may be reluctant to reveal their true feelings. This can produce the effects of *social desirability*, in which participants give answers they think are expected or 'proper'. Incorporating a lie scale can help detect this tendency (see Chapter 42). Reassurance that their answers will remain anonymous, and stressing the importance of giving honest answers, can also help reduce the social desirability effect.

A very different kind of solution is to use cleverly planned inconspicuous observation, such as Milgram's (1965) *lost letter technique*. This was designed to measure people's political attitudes, and involves the distribution, throughout a city, of large numbers of letters, stamped but unposted and addressed to different political organisations (such as 'Friends of the Nazi Party' and 'Friends of the Communist Party'). Depending on the rate at which the letters were returned, Milgram could assess the popularity of each organisation and the corresponding ideological bias of particular parts of the city. Milgram (1992) stresses that the technique guarantees the anonymity of those who took part.

In the *bogus pipeline technique* (Jones & Sigall, 1971), participants are convinced that they can't hide their true attitudes. They're connected to a machine that resembles a lie detector and told that it can measure both the strength and direction of emotional responses, implying that there's no point in lying. Several studies have shown that participants are indeed convinced and are less likely to conceal socially undesirable attitudes (such as racial prejudice: Hogg & Vaughan, 1995).

The relationship between attitudes and behaviour

Once we've established people's attitudes, can we then accurately predict how they'll behave? Rosenberg & Hovland's (1960) three-components model (see page 350) implies that the behavioural component will be highly correlated with the cognitive and affective components.

An early study which shows the *inconsistency* of attitudes and behaviour is that of LaPiere (1934).

KEY STUDY 24.1

Some of my best friends are Chinese ... (LaPiere, 1934)

Beginning in 1930 and for the next two years, LaPiere travelled around the USA with a Chinese couple (a young student and his wife), expecting to encounter anti-Oriental attitudes which would make it difficult for them to find accommodation. But in the course of 10,000 miles of travel, they were discriminated against only once and there appeared to be no prejudice. They were given accommodation in 66 hotels, auto-camps and 'Tourist Homes' and refused at only one. They were also served in 184 restaurants and cafés and treated with '... more than ordinary consideration ...' in 72 of them.

However, when each of the 251 establishments visited was sent a letter six months later asking: 'Will you accept members of the Chinese race as guests in your establishment?', 91 per cent of the 128 which responded gave an emphatic 'No'. One establishment gave an unqualified 'Yes' and the rest said 'Undecided: depends upon circumstances'.

Influences on behaviour

It's generally agreed that attitudes form only one determinant of behaviour. They represent *predispositions* to behave in particualr ways, but how we actually act in a particular situation will depend on the immediate consequences of our behaviour, how we think others will evaluate our actions, and habitual ways of behaving in those kinds of situations. In addition, there may be specific *situational factors* influencing behaviour. For example, in the LaPiere study, the high quality of his Chinese friends' clothes and luggage and their politeness, together with the presence of LaPiere himself, may have made it more difficult to show overt prejudice. Thus, sometimes we experience a conflict of attitudes, and behaviour may represent a compromise between them.

Compatibility between attitudes and behaviour

The same attitude may be expressed in a variety of ways. For example, having a positive attitude towards the Labour Party doesn't necessarily mean that you actually become a member, or that you attend public meetings. But if you don't vote Labour in a general election, people may question your attitude. In other words, an attitude should predict behaviour to some extent, even if this is extremely limited and specific.

Indeed, Ajzen & Fishbein (1977) argue that attitudes can predict behaviour, provided that both are assessed at the same level of generality. There needs to be a high degree of *compatibility* (or *correspondence*) between them. They argue that much of the earlier research (LaPiere's study included) suffered from either trying to predict specific behaviours from general attitudes, or vice versa, and this accounts for the generally low correlations. A study by Davidson and Jaccard tried to overcome this limitation.

KEY STUDY 24.2

Attitudes can predict behaviour if you ask the right questions (Davidson & Jaccard, 1979)

Davidson and Jaccard analysed correlations between married women's attitudes *towards birth control* and their actual use of oral contraceptives during the two years following the study.

When 'attitude towards birth control' was used as the attitude measure, the correlation was 0.08. Clearly, the correspondence here was very low. But when 'attitudes towards oral contraceptives' were measured, the correlation rose to 0.32, and when 'attitudes towards *using* oral contraceptives' were measured, the correlation rose still further to 0.53. Finally, when 'attitudes towards using oral contraceptives during the next two years' was used, it rose still further, to 0.57. Clearly, in the last three cases, correspondence was much higher.

According to Ajzen and Fishbein, every single instance of behaviour involves four specific elements:

- a specific action
- performed with respect to a given target
- in a given context
- at a given point in time.

According to the *principle of compatibility*, measures of attitude and behaviour are compatible to the extent that the target, action, context and time element are assessed at identical levels of generality or specificity (Ajzen, 1988).

For example, a person's attitude towards a 'healthy lifestyle' only specifies the target, leaving the other three unspecified. A behavioural measure that would be compatible with this global attitude would have to aggregate a wide range of health behaviour across different contexts and times (Stroebe, 2000). Elaborating the psychological processes underlying the principle of compatibility, Ajzen (1996) suggested that to:

> '... the extent that the beliefs salient at the time of attitude assessment are also salient when plans are formulated or executed, strong attitude–behaviour correlations are expected'.

The reliability and consistency of behaviour

Many of the classic studies which failed to find an attitude–behaviour relationship assessed just *single instances of behaviour* (Stroebe, 2000). As we noted earlier when discussing the LaPiere study, behaviour depends on many factors in addition to the attitude. This makes a single instance of behaviour an unreliable indicator of an attitude (Jonas *et al.*, 1995). Only by sampling many instances of the behaviour will the influence of specific factors 'cancel out'. This *aggregation principle* (Fishbein & Ajzen, 1974) has been demonstrated in a number of studies.

According to Hogg & Vaughan (1995), what has emerged in the 1980s and 1990s is a view that attitudes and overt behaviour aren't related in a simple one-to-one fashion. In order to predict someone's behaviour, it must be possible to account for the *interaction* between attitudes, beliefs and behavioural intentions, as well as how all of these connect with the later action. One attempt to formalise these links is the *theory of reasoned action* (TRA) (Ajzen & Fishbein, 1970; Fishbein & Ajzen, 1975). This is discussed in relation to health behaviour in Chapter 12.

The strength of attitudes

Most modern theories agree that attitudes are represented in memory, and that an attitude's accessibility can exert a strong influence on behaviour (Fazio, 1986: see Chapter 17). By definition, strong attitudes exert more influence over behaviour, because they can be automatically activated. One factor that seems to be important is direct experience. For example, Fazio & Zanna (1978) found that measures of students' attitudes towards psychology experiments were better predictors of their future participation if they'd already taken part in several experiments than if they'd only read about them. This can be explained by the *mere exposure effect* (Zajonc, 1968), according to which the more contact we have with something or somebody, the more we like them (see Chapter 28).

A demonstration of attitude–behaviour consistency that amazed the world; a pro-democracy Chinese student stands up for his convictions and defies tanks sent in against fellow rebels in Tiananmen Square, Beijing, China. Some 2000 demonstrators died in the subsequent massacre and the student was tried and shot a few days later

So attitudes don't predict behaviour: what's the problem?

The so-called attitude–behaviour problem, that is, the failure to find a reliable relationship between attitudes and behaviour, threatened to undermine the entire study of attitudes. As we saw in the *Introduction and overview*, attitude research was a cornerstone of social psychology in general, and social cognition in particular, for much of their history (Stainton Rogers *et al.*, 1995).

But from the perspective of *discursive psychology*, there's no reason to expect such a correlation: inconsistency between attitudes and behaviour is what we'd expect to find. Traditional, mainstream, attitude research is based on the fallacy of *individualism* (see Chapter 3), according to which attitudes 'belong' to individuals. This implies something fairly constant, and which is expressed and reflected in behaviour. From a discursive perspective, attitudes are versions of the world that are *constructed* by people in the course of their interactions with others.

Discursive psychology is concerned with *action*, as distinct from cognition. In saying or writing things, people are performing actions, whose nature can be revealed through a detailed study of the discourse (e.g. recordings of everyday conversations, newspaper articles, TV programmes). Social psychologists have underestimated the centrality of *conflict* in social life; an analysis of *rhetoric* highlights the point that people's versions of events, and their own mental life, are part of ongoing arguments, debates and dialogues (Billig, 1987, 1992, in Potter, 1996).

Compared with traditional attitude research, discursive psychology tries to shift the focus away from single, isolated, individuals towards interactions between individuals and groups, a more *relational* or *distributed* focus (Potter, 1996).

Social influence and behaviour change

Persuasive communication

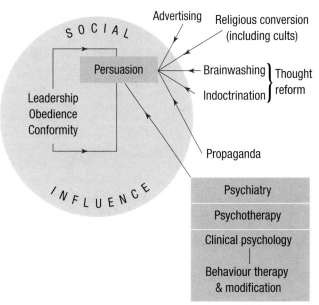

Figure 24.2 *Different kinds of attempt to change people's attitudes and behaviour. These range from professional help for emotional and behavioural problems, through inevitable features of social interaction/social influence, to deliberate attempts to manipulate and control others for the benefit of the manipulator*

According to Laswell (1948), in order to understand and predict the effectiveness of one person's attempt to change the attitude of another, we need to know 'Who says what in which channel to whom and with what effect'. Similarly, Hovland & Janis (1959) say that we need to study:

■ *the source* of the persuasive communication, that is, the communicator (Laswell's 'who');
■ *the message* itself (Laswell's 'what');
■ *the recipient* of the message or the audience (Laswell's 'whom'); and
■ the *situation or context*.

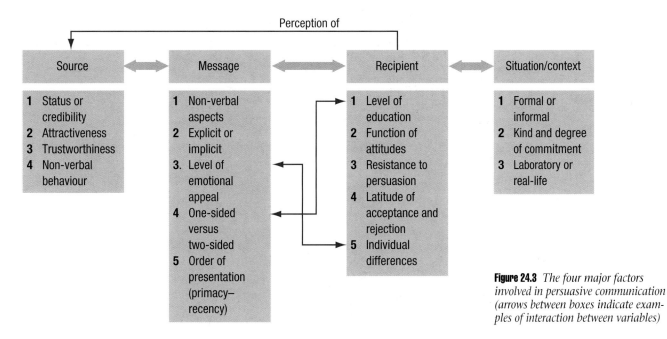

Figure 24.3 *The four major factors involved in persuasive communication (arrows between boxes indicate examples of interaction between variables)*

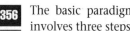

The basic paradigm in laboratory attitude-change research involves three steps or stages:

1 measure people's attitude towards the attitude object (*pre-test*);
2 expose them to a *persuasive communication* (manipulate a source, message or situational variable, or isolate a recipient-variable as the independent variable: see Figure 24.3, page 355);
3 measure their attitudes again (*post-test*).

If there's a difference between pre- and post-test measures, then the persuasive communication is judged to have 'worked'.

Theories of persuasion

The early research into persuasive communication was conducted for the US War Department's Information and Education Department. This largely pragmatic approach is known as the *Yale approach*, with Hovland being one of the leading figures involved. It told us a great deal regarding *when* attitude change is most likely to occur, and *how*, in practical terms, it can be produced. But it told us less about *why* people change their attitudes in response to persuasive messages.

Theories of systematic processing

According to *theories of systematic processing*, what's important is that the recipient processes the message content in a detailed way. This approach began with Hovland *et al.*'s (1953) proposal that the impact of persuasive messages can be understood in terms of a sequence of processes:

Attention to message ———> Comprehension of the content ———> Acceptance of its conclusions

If any of these fails to occur, persuasion is unlikely to be achieved.

McGuire (1969) proposed a longer chain of processes. We should ask if the recipient (i) attended to the message; (ii) comprehended it; (iii) yielded to it (i.e. accepted it); (iv) retained it; and (v) acted as a result. As with Hovland *et al.*'s theory, the failure of any one of these steps will cause the sequence to be broken.

Dual process/cognitive models

According to the the *dual-process* or *cognitive perspective* (e.g. Chaiken, 1987), the key questions are as follows.

■ What cognitive processes determine whether someone is actually persuaded?
■ What do people think about when exposed to persuasive appeals? and
■ How do their various cognitive processes determine whether and to what extent they experience attitude changes (Baron & Byrne, 1991)?

Chaiken's (1987) answer to these questions is in the form of his *heuristic model of persuasion*. Heuristics are rules of thumb or mental shortcuts, which we use in processing social or any other kind of information (see Chapters 20 and 22). When a situation is personally involving (for example, it involves attitudes which are salient for the individual concerned), careful, cognitive analysis of the input occurs. The degree of attitude change depends largely on the quality of the arguments presented.

However, when personal involvement is low, individuals rely on various heuristics to determine whether to change their attitudes. Much of the Yale approach, in fact, deals with the content of these heuristics. For example, experts are more believable than non-experts, and so we're more easily persuaded by the former, as we are by likeable sources (compared with non-likeable). Other examples of heuristics include being more persuaded by a greater number of arguments backed up by statistics than a smaller number, and 'if other people think something is right (or wrong), then I should too'. These are essentially peripheral, non-content issues.

An evaluation of heuristic models

It's assumed that attitudes formed or changed on the basis of heuristic processing will be less stable, less resistant to counter-arguments, and less predictive of subsequent behaviour than those based on systematic processing. Several studies show that attitude change accompanied by high levels of issue-relevant cognitive activity are more persistent than those accompanied by little such activity (Stroebe, 2000).

Attitude function and persuasion

The functions of attitudes also represent an important feature of the cognitive analysis of persuasion (see Table 24.2). Shavitt (1990) argues that persuasive messages which emphasise the appropriate (i.e. primary) attitude function of a given product should be more successful in changing attitudes than those which focus on other attitude functions. For example, a commercial which emphasises the practical function of air conditioners should be more successful than one which emphasises their social identity function (they project a particular kind of social image). The reverse would be true for a commercial advertising perfume.

Figure 24.4 *A First World War poster campaign, inducing people to invest in the war effort. Most people were sufficiently ego-involved that source credibility was irrelevant, nor was suspicion of the source's motives aroused since it was in everybody's best interest to invest in the war effort*

Fear and persuasion

A famous early attempt to induce attitude change through the manipulation of fear was made by Janis & Feshbach (1953).

KEY STUDY 24.3

Fear of the dentist as a means to healthier teeth (Janis & Feshbach, 1953)

Janis and Feshbach randomly assigned American high-school students to one of four groups (one control and three experimental). The message was concerned with dental hygiene, and degree of fear arousal was manipulated by the number and nature of consequences of improper care of teeth which were referred to (and shown in colour slides). Each message also contained factual information about the causes of tooth decay, and some advice about caring for teeth.

The *high fear condition* involved 71 references to unpleasant effects, including toothache, painful treatment and possible secondary diseases, including blindness and cancer. The *moderate fear condition* involved 49 references, and the *low fear condition* just 18. The control group heard a talk about the eye.

Before the experiment, participants' attitudes to dental health, and their dental habits, were assessed as part of a general health survey. The same questionnaire was given again immediately following the fear-inducing message, and one week later.

The results show that the stronger the appeal to fear, the greater their anxiety (an index of attitude change). But as far as actual changes in dental *behaviour* were concerned, the high fear condition proved to be the *least* effective. Eight per cent of the high fear group had adopted the recommendations (changes in toothbrushing and visiting the dentist in the weeks immediately following the experiment), compared with 22 per cent and 37 per cent in the moderate and low fear conditions respectively.

Similar results were reported by Janis & Terwillinger (1962), who presented a mild and strong fear message concerning the relationship between smoking and cancer.

These studies suggest that, in McGuire's terms, you can frighten people into attending to a message, comprehending it, yielding to it and retaining it, but not necessarily into acting upon it. Indeed, fear may be so great that action is *inhibited* rather than facilitated. However, if the audience is told how to avoid undesirable consequences and believes that the preventative action is realistic and will be effective, then even high levels of fear in the message can produce changes in behaviour. The more specific and precise the instructions, the greater the behaviour change (the *high availability factor*).

Ask yourself ...

• Can you relate the high availability factor to one of the principles we identified when discussing the measurement of attitude–behaviour correlations?

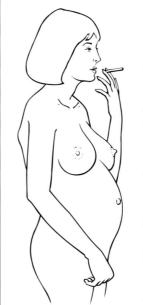

Is it fair to force your baby to smoke cigarettes?

This is what happens if you smoke when you're pregnant.

Every time you inhale you fill your lungs with nicotine and carbon monoxide.

Your blood carries these impurities through the umbilical into your baby's bloodstream.

Smoking can restrict your baby's normal growth inside the womb.
It can make him underdeveloped and underweight at birth.
It can even kill him.
Last year, in Britain alone, over 1,500 babies might not have died if their mothers had given up smoking when they were pregnant.

If you give up smoking when you're pregnant your baby will be as healthy as if you'd never smoked.

The Health Education Council

Figure 24.5 *Example of public health campaign poster in which an appeal to fear is combined with the high availability factor*

According to Stroebe (2000), mass media campaigns designed to change some specific health behaviour should use arguments aimed mainly at changing beliefs relating to that *specific* behaviour – rather than focusing on more general health concerns. This is another example of the compatibility principle. For example, to persuade people to lower their dietary cholesterol, it wouldn't be very effective merely to point out that coronary heart disease (CHD) is the major killer and/or that high levels of saturated fat are bad for one's heart. To influence diet, it would have to be argued that very specific dietary changes, such as less animal fats and red meat, would have a positive impact on blood cholesterol levels, which, in turn, should reduce the risk of developing CHD.

In situations of minimal or extreme fear, the message may fail to produce any attitude change, let alone any change in behaviour. According to McGuire (1968), there's an inverted U-shaped curve in the relationship between fear and attitude change (see Figure 24.6, page 358). In segment 1 of the curve, the participant isn't particularly interested in (aroused by) the message: it's hardly attended to and may not even register. In segment 2, attention and arousal increase as fear increases, but the fear remains within manageable proportions. In segment 3, attention will decrease again, but this time because defences are being used to deal with extreme fear: the message may be denied ('it couldn't happen to me') or repressed (see Chapter 12). Despite evidence of defensive processing, Stroebe (2000) maintains that:

'... the overwhelming majority of studies on fear appeals has found that higher levels of threat resulted in greater persuasion than did lower levels. However, the effectiveness of high-fear messages appeared to be somewhat reduced for respondents who feel highly vulnerable to the threat ...'.

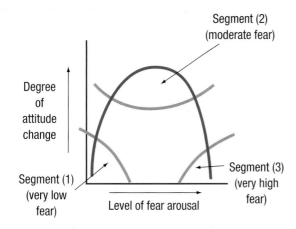

Figure 24.6 *Inverted U curve showing relationship between attitude change and fear arousal (based on McGuire, 1968)*

The importance of feeling vulnerable

In order to arouse fear, it isn't enough that a health risk has serious consequences, but the individual must also feel personally at risk (i.e. vulnerable). There's some evidence that unless individuals feel vulnerable to a threat, they're unlikely to form the intention to act on the recommendations in the message (Kuppens *et al.*, 1996). Fear appeals are also most likely to be effective for individuals who are unfamiliar with a given health risk. For example, when the dangers involved in unprotected anal intercourse among homosexuals became known in the early 1980s, the information appeared to produce an enormous reduction in such practices. But there was a hard-core of men who were unaffected by the information, illustrating that simply repeating the dangers of HIV infection doesn't achieve risk reduction with such individuals (Stroebe, 2000: see Chapter 12, pages 164–165).

Feeling vulnerable relates to what McGuire calls the *initial level of concern*. Clearly, someone who has a high level of initial concern will be more easily pushed into segment 3 of the curve than someone with a low level. The former may be overwhelmed by a high-fear message (in which case defences are used against it), while the latter may not become interested and aroused enough for the message to have an impact.

Propaganda and war

'Propaganda' comes from the Latin '*propagare*', which refers to the gardener's practice of pinning the fresh shoots of a plant into the earth in order to reproduce new plants which will later take on a life of their own. So, one implication of the term (as originally used in the seventeenth century) is the spread of ideas through their deliberate cultivation or artificial generation.

But in the twentieth century, propaganda implies something more sinister, a deliberate attempt to manipulate, often by concealed or underhand means, the minds of other people for ulterior ends (Brown, 1963). While this change can be dated from the official use of propaganda as a weapon in the total warfare of modern times, beginning with World War I, this was itself an effect of changes in the nature of communication within technically advanced societies. Pratkanis & Aronson (1991) define propaganda as:

'... mass suggestion or influence, through the manipulation of symbols and the psychology of the individual. Propaganda is the communication of a point of view with the ulterior goal of having the recipient of the appeal come to 'voluntarily' accept this position as if it were his or her own'.

The aims of propaganda

Regardless of the media used (such as pamphlets, leaflets, newspapers, posters, films and public speeches), and the particular war, the chief aims of wartime propaganda, according to Brown (1963) are to:

- mobilise and direct hatred against the enemy and undermine the enemy's morale;
- convince the home public of the rightness of the [Allied] cause and to increase and maintain fighting spirit;
- develop the friendship of neutrals and strengthen in their minds the belief that not only are the Allies in the right but they will be victorious in the end, and, if possible, to enlist their active support and co-operation;
- promote a picture of the enemy (as brutal, committing atrocities, wholly responsible for the war in the first place, and so on) that justifies the entry of a (usually) peaceable nation into war to '.... clear the conscience of the whole nation ...' (Brown, 1963);
- develop and strengthen the friendship of the Allies;
- build up strong ingroup attitudes and feelings and opposed feelings of hatred towards the enemy as a dangerous outgroup.

As Brown (1963) claims:

'There is nothing like a war for breaking down class and other barriers and creating feelings of friendship and co-operation within a country because all its previously inwardly-directed aggression and resentment comes to be directed against an external enemy, and it is only in the last stages of a losing effort or after a war has been won that disunity begins to show itself once more ...'.

Ask yourself ...

- How does Brown's quote relate to Tajfel's *social identity theory* as one explanation of prejudice and discrimination, and to Allport's advocacy of *equal status contact* and the *pursuit of common goals* as means of reducing them? (See Chapter 25.)

Propaganda tries to limit our choices deliberately, whether by avoiding arguments (the bald statement of one point of view to the exclusion of others), or by emotional, non-objective criticism of the other side and its opinions by use of caricature, stereotypes and other methods.

Box 24.1 Some specific techniques used in propaganda

The use of stereotypes: The Nazi portrayal of Jews (as shown below) is a good illustration of how a generalised belief about an entire group of people (see Chapter 22) is exaggerated in the form of a caricatured portrayal of that group – the negative characteristics are taken to an extreme form.

The substitution of names: Favourable or unfavourable names, with an emotional connotation, are substituted for neutral ones, for example, 'Red' (replaces Communist or Russian), 'Union bosses' (for the presidents of trade unions), 'Huns'/'Krauts' (Germans) and 'Yids' (Jews). Conversely, 'free enterprise' sounds better than 'capitalism'.

Selection: From a mass of complex facts, selection is made for propaganda purposes. *Censorship* is one way of achieving this and so is a form of propaganda.

Repetition: If a statement or slogan is repeated often enough, it will eventually come to be accepted by the audience, such as Hitler's 'Ein Volk, ein Reich, ein Fuhrer' ('One people, one empire, one leader'). During the First World War, there were demands for 'A War to End War' and to 'Make the World Safe for Democracy'.

Assertion: Instead of argument, bald assertions are used to support the propagandist's case, as in the presentation of only one side of the picture, the deliberate limitation of free thought and questioning.

Pinpointing the enemy: It's useful to present a message not only *for* something but also *against* some real or imagined enemy who's supposedly frustrating the audience's will. This is demonstrated by the Nazi campaign against the Jews (the scapegoats for Germany's humiliation and economic hardships following World War I – see Chapter 25), which pervaded every aspect of life in Germany in the 1930s. An example of this is the beer-mat with the inscription 'Whoever buys from a Jew is a traitor to his people'. (The caricatured face also illustrates the use of stereotypes – see above.)

Based on Brown (1963)

Propaganda versus education

Although public health campaigns (such as those for safe sex, and healthier eating: see above) fit Pratkanis and Aronson's definition of propaganda, these aren't usually what we have in mind when we use the term: such campaigns are aimed at *benefiting* the audience. Similarly, while education tries to encourage independence of judgement, individual responsibility and an open mind, as well as how to think, propaganda provides ready-made judgements for the un-thinking, promotes a closed mind and tells people what to think.

However, what about the vast majority of high-school textbooks in US history that virtually ignore the contributions of blacks and other minorities 'to the US scene' (Aronson, 1992)? Are such books merely imparting knowledge? This parallels the view that psychology discovers 'facts' about human behaviour, which exist objectively (see Chapters 3 and 47). A recent demonstration of 'history as doctrine' is described in Box 24.2.

Box 24.2   Changing the history of war

In 1997, a history professor in Japan won a 32-year fight to expose one of the darkest chapters in his country's wartime history. Saburo Ienaga won a Supreme Court ruling that censorship of references in his books to a germ warfare group (Unit 731) were 'unlawful'. Unit 731 conducted biological warfare experiments such as injecting prisoners with anthrax and cholera, exposing them to sub-zero temperatures, and manufacturing bubonic plague bombs (the latter killing thousands of Chinese civilians). None of the 3000 Chinese, Korean, Russian and Mongolian prisoners survived, many being dismembered alive to monitor the progress of the diseases through their bodies.

The Japanese government has never acknowledged these activities, let alone apologised for them. In August, 1997, the Supreme Court in Tokyo ruled that the Japanese education ministry acted illegally when it censored a proposed textbook by Mr Ienaga, but it upheld its right to continue screening all textbooks and removing anything it finds objectionable, including references to war crimes.

Source: *Daily Mail*, August 30, 1997

Advertising

An interesting link between psychology and advertising comes in the form of J.B. Watson, the founder of behaviourism (see Chapter 1). Following dismissal from his academic position at Johns Hopkins University, during which he devised health promotion films on venereal disease for the American military (propaganda?), Watson joined the J. Walter Thompson advertising agency, becoming one of the first and most successful applied psychologists (Banyard & Hayes, 1994).

Scott (1909, cited in Brown, 1963) wrote the first textbook published in Britain on advertising. In it, he identified a number of principles, the most fundamental being *association*. Not until the late 1930s did advertisers discover Freud – but little came of it until the late 1940s and early 1950s (Brown, 1963).

Ask yourself ...

- Taking some advertisements you're familiar with, try to identify the way that (a) association (as demonstrated by classical conditioning: see Chapter 11), and (b) aspects of Freud's psychoanalytic theory (see Chapter 42) are used. Are these 'techniques' more likely to influence:

   – developing a need (i.e. convincing people that they want or need the product);

- noticing the product;
- purchasing the product;
- behaviour after the purchase (encouraging repeat puchases)?

(Based on Banyard, 1996)

Subliminal advertising

This is by far the most controversial aspect of advertising. It originated with Jim Vicary, an American market researcher, who arranged with the owner of a New Jersey cinema to install a second special projector which, during a film, flashed on the screen phrases such as 'Hungry? Eat Popcorn' and 'Drink Coca-Cola'. These were either flashed so quickly or printed so faintly that they couldn't be consciously perceived ('subliminal perception' means recognition without awareness) superimposed on the actual film, even after a warning that they were about to appear.

Films treated in this way were alternated with untreated ones throughout the summer of 1956. In the former, sales of popcorn rose by about 50 per cent and soft drinks by about 18 per cent. Although Vicary himself believed it unlikely that a subliminal stimulus could produce any response at all unless prospective customers already intended buying the product, subliminal advertising caused a storm of protest in the American press, and, later on, in the UK too.

Seeking to scare, rather than sell, a movie producer used a similar technique to Vicary's to flash pictures of a skull and the word 'blood' at key points in pairs of horror movies (Packard, 1957). Despite subliminal messages being legally outlawed (even before it was established whether they really worked), they made a comeback in the mid-1970s. In *The Exorcist* (1974), for example, a death mask was flashed on to the screen subliminally and, more recently, in order to reduce theft, several department stores in America began mixing barely audible and rapidly repeated whispers (such as 'I am honest. I will not steal') with their piped music. Many stores reported dramatic decreases in shoplifting. Also, audio cassette tapes are readily available which supposedly cure stress with soothing sub-audible messages covered by mood music or the ambient sounds of nature (Zimbardo & Leippe, 1991).

More recently still, in 1990, the heavy-metal band Judas Priest went on trial for causing the suicide of two young fans through, allegedly, recording the subliminal message 'Do it' in one of their tracks. They won their case on the grounds that there's no scientific evidence that subliminal messages, even if perceived, could produce such extreme behaviour. It was this aspect of the trial which the media emphasised, rather than details of the troubled lives of the two young people concerned (Wadeley, 1996).

Box 24.3 Are subliminal messages effective?

To be effective, subliminal stimuli:

- must be able to influence judgements when superimposed on consciously attended-to material. Subliminals *can* have an impact even when presented simultaneously with something that dominates conscious attention (Greenwald *et al.*, 1989);

- must affect general reactions. So, in the popcorn/Coca-Cola example, Vicary didn't want the audience to like *the words* 'Hungry? Eat Popcorn' more than they did before, but to have an increased desire to *eat* popcorn that would lead to buying more. Subliminal priming studies (e.g. Bargh & Pietromonaco, 1982) show that evaluations of *other* stimuli are influenced by subliminal stimuli;

- need to be strong and persistent enough to affect the mental processes that lead to subsequent directed behaviour. There is little relevant evidence.

Subliminal *sounds* are less likely to be effective than visual messages, since they're apt to go *totally* unregistered if attention is given to other sounds. According to Pratkanis *et al.* (1990), subliminal 'self-help' tapes have little, if any, therapeutic effect (not even a potentially beneficial placebo effect: see Chapter 45).
According to Zimbardo & Leippe (1991):

'... so far none of the more fabulous claims for subliminals have been borne out by well-controlled and replicable studies. And while some of the touted subliminal techniques merit scientific study, others are simply not possible given what is known about the functioning of the human mind...'.

Based on Zimbardo & Leippe (1991)

Are subliminal messages ethically unacceptable?

Ask yourself ...

- Before reading on, try to identify some of the ethical objections to any form of subliminal advertising. How relevant is the evidence presented in Box 24.3 to the question of ethics?

As we noted earlier, subliminal advertising was banned in the 1950s both in the UK and the USA. The British Institute of Practitioners in Advertising published a booklet (*Subliminal Communication*, 1958, cited in Brown, 1963) and banned all its 243 affiliated agencies from using this type of advertising. It states:

'The free choice by the public to accept or reject is an integral part of all forms of professionally accepted advertising and does not appear to be available to recipients of subliminal communication'.

Whether subliminal messages are unethical depends on the ethics of social influence and persuasion in general (Zimbardo & Leippe, 1991). It's widely agreed that *any* technique used to influence others (excluding physical coercion) is unethical if it:

- *relies on deception*: subliminals are deceptive to the extent that their users keep their use a secret, but, conceivably, they might still be effective even when it's openly announced that they're present;
- *prohibits exposure to opposing messages* ('denial of the other side'): this doesn't apply to subliminals (but is relevant for evaluating attempts to indoctrinate people, as used by the Moonies, for example: see above);

- *unfairly prevents efforts to resist it*: it's here that subliminals can be viewed as unethical in the extreme. We cannot defend against something we don't know about and, by definition, we don't know about subliminals. Unlike other forms of influence, such as the image-processing of political candidates, or classical conditioning, we can't resist the influence of subliminals through being observant and mindful. It's only later on – at the time of behavioural decision – that we may ask ourselves why we feel a certain way. For Zimbardo & Leippe (1991):

> '... if subliminal influence should prove to work outside the laboratory in advertising contexts, it would seem highly unethical to use it – mainly because it deprives people of much of their opportunity to resist it'.

Theories of attitude change

The most influential theories of attitude change have concentrated on the principle of *cognitive consistency*. Human beings are seen as internally active information-processors who sort through and modify a large number of cognitive elements in order to achieve some kind of cognitive coherence. This need for cognitive consistency means that theories such as Heider's *balance theory* (1958), Osgood & Tannenbaum's *congruity theory* (1955), and Festinger's *cognitive dissonance theory* (1957) aren't just theories of attitude change, but are also theories of human motivation (see Chapter 9).

Cognitive dissonance theory

According to cognitive dissonance theory, whenever we simultaneously hold two cognitions which are psychologically inconsistent, we experience *dissonance*. This is a negative drive state, a state of 'psychological discomfort or tension', which motivates us to reduce it by achieving consonance. Attitude change is a major way of reducing dissonance. Cognitions are 'the things a person knows about himself, about his behaviour and about his surroundings' (Festinger, 1957) and any two cognitions can be consonant (A implies B), dissonant (A implies not-B) or irrelevant to each other.

For example, the cognition 'I smoke' is psychologically inconsistent with the cognition 'smoking causes cancer' (assuming that we don't wish to get cancer).

Ask yourself ...

- How might someone who smokes try to reduce dissonance?

Perhaps the most efficient (and certainly the healthiest!) way to reduce dissonance is to stop smoking, but many people will work on the other cognition; for example, they might:

- belittle the evidence about smoking and cancer (e.g. 'The human data is only correlational');
- associate with other smokers (e.g. 'If so-and-so smokes, then it can't be very dangerous');
- smoke low-tar cigarettes;

- convince themselves that smoking is an important and highly pleasurable activity.

These examples illustrate how dissonance theory regards human beings not as rational but *rationalising* creatures, attempting to *appear* rational, both to others and to oneself.

Dissonance following a decision

If we have to choose between two equally attractive objects or activities, then one way of reducing the resulting dissonance is to emphasise the undesirable features of the one we've rejected. This adds to the number of consonant cognitions and reduces the number of dissonant ones.

This was demonstrated in a study by Brehm (1956). Female participants had to rate the desirability of several household appliances on an eight-point scale. They then had to choose between two of the items (their reward for participating), which for half were ½ to 1½ points apart on the scale (high dissonance condition), while for the other half they were a full three points apart (low dissonance condition). When they were asked to re-evaluate the items they'd chosen and rejected, they showed increased liking for the chosen item and decreased liking for the rejected one.

Dissonance theory also predicts that there'll be *selective exposure* to consonant information; that is, seeking consistent information which isn't present at the time. However, selective perception also includes *selective attention* (looking at consistent information which is present) and *selective interpretation* (perceiving ambiguous information as being consistent with our other cognitions). According to Fiske & Taylor (1991), the evidence overall is stronger for selective attention and interpretation than for selective exposure.

Dissonance resulting from effort

KEY STUDY 24.4

Preferring things that turn out for the worst (Aronson & Mills, 1959)

Female college students volunteered for a discussion on the psychology of sex, with the understanding that the research was concerned with the dynamics of group discussion. Each student was interviewed individually, and asked if she could participate without embarrassment; all but one said yes.

If a student had been assigned to the *control condition*, she was simply accepted. But for acceptance to the *severe embarrassment condition*, she had to take an 'embarrassment test' (reading out loud to a male experimenter a list of obscene words and some explicit sexual passages from modern novels – remember the year was 1959!). For acceptance to the *mild embarrassment condition*, she had to read aloud words like 'prostitute' and 'virgin'. They then all heard a tape-recording of an actual discussion (by a group which they believed they'd later join) which was about sex in lower animals, and extremely dull. They then had to rate the discussion and the group members in terms of how interesting and intelligent they found them.

As predicted, the severe embarrassment group gave the most positive ratings, because they'd experienced the greatest dissonance!

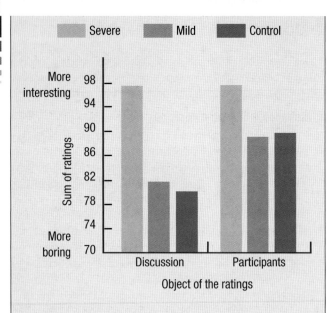

Figure 24.7 *Female students' ratings of how interesting a group discussion was in relation to degrees of embarrassment which they suffered in order to get accepted for the discussion (based on Aronson & Mills, 1959)*

When a voluntarily chosen experience turns out badly, the fact that we chose it motivates us to try to think that it actually turned out well. The greater the sacrifice or hardship associated with the choice, the greater the dissonance and, therefore, the greater the pressure towards attitude change (*the suffering-leads-to-liking effect*).

Engaging in counter-attitudinal behaviour

This aspect of cognitive dissonance theory is of most relevance to our earlier discussion of the relationship between attitudes and behaviour.

K E Y   S T U D Y   2 4 . 5

The 'one dollar/20 dollar' experiment (Festinger & Carlsmith, 1959)

College students were brought, one at a time, into a small room to work for 30 minutes on two extremely dull and repetitive tasks (stacking spools and turning pegs). Later, they were offered either one dollar or 20 dollars to enter a waiting room and to try to convince the next 'participant' (in fact, a female stooge) that the tasks were interesting and enjoyable.

Common sense would predict that the 20-dollar students would be more likely to change their attitudes in favour of the tasks (they had more reason to do so), and this is also what *reinforcement/incentive theory* (Janis *et al.*, 1965) would predict (the greater the reward/incentive, the greater the attitude change).

However, as predicted by dissonance theory, it was in fact the one-dollar group which showed the greater attitude change (the *less-leads-to-more effect*).

The large, 20-dollar incentive gave those participants ample justification for their counter-attitudinal behaviour and so they experienced very little dissonance. But the one-dollar group experienced considerable dissonance: they could hardly justify their counter-attitudinal behaviour in terms of the negligible reward, hence, the change of attitude to reduce the dissonance.

Festinger and Carlsmith's findings have been replicated by several studies, in which children are given either a mild or a severe threat not to play with an attractive toy (Aronson & Carlsmith, 1963: Freedman, 1965). If children obey a mild threat, they'll experience greater dissonance, because it's more difficult for them to justify their behaviour than for children given a severe threat. So, the mild threat condition produces greater reduction in liking of the toy.

However, dissonance only occurs when the behaviour is *volitional* (voluntary); that is, when we feel we acted of our own free will. If we believe we had no choice, there's no dissonance, and hence no attitude change. A study by Freedman (1963) shows that dissonance theory and reinforcement theory aren't mutually exclusive; instead, they seem to apply to voluntary and involuntary behaviour respectively.

Self-perception theory

According to Bem's self-perception theory (1965, 1967), the concept of dissonance is both unnecessary and unhelpful. Any self-report of an attitude is an *inference* from observation of one's own behaviour, and the situation in which it occurs. If the situation contains cues (e.g. offer of a large 20-dollar incentive) which imply that we might have behaved that way regardless of how we personally felt (we lie about the task being interesting even though it was boring), then we don't infer that the behaviour reflected our true attitudes. But in the absence of obvious situational pressures (one-dollar condition), we assume that our attitudes are what our behaviour suggests they are.

In attributional terms, the 20-dollar group can easily make a *situational attribution* ('I did it for the money'), whereas the one-dollar group had to make a *dispositional attribution* ('I did it because I really enjoyed it').

Eiser & van der Pligt (1988) believe that, conceptually, it's very difficult to distinguish between the two theories. Perhaps, as with dissonance and incentive theories, both processes operate but to different extents under different circumstances.

Fazio *et al.* (1977), for example, argue that dissonance may apply when people behave in a way which is contrary to their initial attitude (*counter-attitudinal behaviour*), while self-perception may apply better where their behaviour and initial attitude are broadly consistent (*attitude-congruent behaviour*).

An evaluation of dissonance and self-perception theory

■ Conflict or inconsistency often arises between two attitudes, rather than between an attitude and behaviour. Both situations can be explained by dissonance theory. But because self-perception theory is based on attribution principles, it requires some overt behaviour from which we then make an inference about our attitudes.

■ *Impression management theorists* (e.g. Tedeschi & Rosenfeld, 1981; Schlenker, 1982: see Chapter 22) argue that the effects of many dissonance experiments might not reflect genuine cases of 'private' attitude change (a drive to *be* consistent), but the need to *appear* consistent, and hence to avoid social anxiety and embarrassment, or to protect positive views of one's own identity. So, the one-dollar group's attitude change is genuine, but is motivated by *social* (rather than *cognitive*) factors.

■ Is there any independent evidence for the existence of dissonance? In a study by Zanna & Cooper (1974), participants wrote a counter-attitudinal essay under instructions which implied either high or low freedom of choice. Consistent with previous findings, the prediction that high-choice participants change their opinions more than low-choice participants was confirmed. The novel feature of the experiment was that participants were also given a placebo pill: they were either told it would make them feel tense or relaxed or told nothing about it at all.

> ### Ask yourself ...
>
> • The dissonance theory prediction was upheld when participants were given no information about the pill, and even more strongly when they were told it would relax them. But when they were told it would make them feel tense, no difference between the high- and low-choice conditions was found. How can you explain these findings?

If participants believe the pill will either relax them or have no effect, and they also believe they're acting of their own free will, they change their opinions, presumably because they experience an internal state of dissonance. But if told the pill will make them tense, they will (mis)attribute their tension to the pill, and so little attitude change will occur (as is also true of low-freedom-of-choice participants). This attribution explanation is consistent with Bem's self-perception theory and so the Zanna and Cooper experiment offers support for both Festinger *and* Bem.

Conclusions

Despite these and other challenges and reconceptualisations, Hogg & Vaughan (1995) maintain that:

> '... cognitive dissonance theory remains one of the most widely accepted explanations of attitude change and many other social behaviours. It has generated over one thousand research studies and will probably continue to be an integral part of social psychological theory for many years ...'.

CHAPTER SUMMARY

■ The **three-component model** of attitude structure sees **attitudes** as comprising **affective**, **cognitive** and **behavioural** components. Attitudes have much in common with beliefs and values, but they need to be distinguished.

■ Katz identifies the **knowledge**, **adjustive**, **value-expressive** and ego-defensive functions of attitudes.

■ Most methods of attitude measurement rely on verbal reports of people's opinions about the attitude object. They assume that attitudes can be **quantified**, and that the same statement has the same meaning for all respondents.

■ Thurstone's **equal appearing interval scale**, the **Likert scale**, the **Guttman scalogram method**, the **semantic differential** and **sociometry** are some of the major **self-report methods** used in attitude measurement.

■ Alternative methods attempt to get round problems such as **acquiescent response set** and the effects of **social desirability**. These include the **lost letter technique** and **bogus pipeline technique**. Whatever their methodological advantages, they pose very serious ethical questions.

■ Early research into the relationship between attitudes and behaviour showed that attitudes are very poor predictors of behaviour. But attitudes represent only one of several determinants of behaviour, including **situational factors**.

■ Attitudes can predict behaviour, provided there's a close correspondence between the way the two variables are defined and measured (the **principle of compatibility**). Also, measures of a representative sample of behaviours relevant to the attitude must be made (**the aggregation principle**).

■ According to **discursive psychologists**, attitudes are **constructed** in the course of social interaction, rather than possessed by isolated individuals.

■ **Persuasive communication** has traditionally been studied in terms of the influence of four interacting factors: the **source** of the persuasive message, the **message** itself, the **recipient** of the message and the **situation/context**.

■ **Theories of systematic processing** see the impact of persuasive messages as dependent on a sequence of processes, including **attending** to the message, **comprehending** it, **accepting** its conclusions, **retaining** it and **acting** as a result.

■ The more recent **cognitive perspective** focuses on **why** people change their attitudes, not merely **when** and **how** it's likely to happen. The **heuristic model of persuasion**, for example, explains why we're more likely to be persuaded when the situation isn't personally involving or if the arguments are convincing.

■ People can be frightened into attending to, comprehending, accepting and retaining a message, but the **high availability factor** is necessary for any behaviour change to take place.

■ People also need to feel personally **vulnerable** if fear appeals are to have any impact. There appears to be an inverted U-shaped curve in the relationship between fear and attitude change.

■ **Propaganda** tries to deliberately limit people's choices, either through **censorship**, or through use of **caricature**, **stereotypes**, **emotive names**, and **repetitive slogans**. By contrast, education encourages independent thinking, individual responsibility and an open mind.

■ **Subliminal messages** can influence judgements when superimposed on consciously attended-to material, producing general reactions (such as increasing the desire to eat popcorn). However, their influence on behaviour is much less certain.

■ The major theories of **attitude change** share the basic principle of **cognitive consistency**. The most influential of these is Festinger's **cognitive dissonance theory**.

■ Dissonance is most likely to occur after making a very difficult choice/decision, when putting ourselves through hardship or making a sacrifice only to find it was for nothing, or when engaging voluntarily in counter-attitudinal behaviour.

■ Bem's **self-perception theory** explains the results of dissonance experiments in terms of **attributional principles**. Dissonance theory may apply under conditions of 'true' counter-attitudinal behaviour, while self-perception theory applies to attitude-congruent behaviour.

■ **Impression management theory** stresses the **social** rather than the **cognitive** motivation underlying attitude change.

Self-assessment questions

1 Discuss attempts made by psychologists to measure attitudes.
2 Critically consider the relationship between attitudes and behaviour.
3 Critically assess attempts that are made to change people's attitudes **and/or** their behaviour.
4 Describe and evaluate **one or more** theory of attitude change.

Web addresses

www.mrs.umn.edu/~ratliff1/syllabus1.htm

www.buffalostate.edu/~zhang1/330/GD330n2.html

www.thomsonlearning.com/samples/psychology/1583160485ch14.pdf

www.princeton.edu/~psych/PsychSite/coopervita2.html

Further reading

Ajzen, I. (1988) *Attitudes, Personality and Behaviour*. Milton Keynes: Open University Press. Thorough discussion of most of the issues dealt with here by one of the leading researchers in the field. Part of a series of books on social psychology.

Zimbardo, P.G. & Leippe, M.R. (1991) *The Psychology of Attitude Change and Social Influence*. New York: McGraw-Hill. A very readable, but detailed text that, as the title implies, discusses attitude change in the broad context of social influence. Also part of an excellent series on social psychology.

Chapter 25

Prejudice and Discrimination

Introduction and overview

'... fifty years after the [Nazi] extermination and concentration camps were liberated, genocide continues unabated, neither punished nor prevented. In what used to be ... [Yugoslavia], torture, murder, rape, and starvation are everyday occurrences ...'.

(Hirsch, 1995)

While genocide – the systematic destruction of an entire cultural, ethnic or racial group – is the most extreme form of discrimination, the prejudice that underlies it is essentially the same as that which underlies less extreme behaviours. Prejudice is an *attitude* that can be expressed in many ways, or which may not be overtly or openly expressed at all. Like other attitudes, prejudice can be regarded as a *disposition* to behave in a prejudiced way (to practise discrimination), so the relationship between prejudice and discrimination is an example of the wider debate concerning the attitude–behaviour relationship. As we saw in Chapter 24, LaPiere's early study of this relationship was concerned with anti-Oriental prejudice and discrimination in the US in the 1930s.

Theories of prejudice and discrimination try to explain their origins: how do people come to be prejudiced and to act in discriminatory ways? Answers to these questions potentially answer the further question: how can they be reduced or even prevented altogether? This, of course, has much greater practical significance for people's lives, as the quote from Hirsch conveys.

Prejudice as an attitude

As an *extreme* attitude, prejudice comprises the components of all attitudes:

- the *cognitive* component is the *stereotype* (see Chapter 22);
- the *affective* component is a *strong feeling of hostility*;
- the *behavioural* component can take different forms. Allport (1954) proposed five stages of this component:
  1. *antilocution*: hostile talk, verbal denigration and insult, racial jokes;
  2. *avoidance*: keeping a distance but without actively inflicting harm;
  3. *discrimination*: exclusion from housing, civil rights, employment;
  4. *physical attack*: violence against the person and property;
  5. *extermination*: indiscriminate violence against an entire group (including genocide).

As we noted in the *Introduction and overview*, 'discrimination' is often used to denote the behavioural component, while 'prejudice' denotes the cognitive and affective components. But just as the cognitive and affective components may not necessarily be manifested behaviourally (as in LaPiere's study), so discrimination doesn't necessarily imply the presence of cognitive and affective components. People may discriminate if the prevailing social norms dictate that they do so, and if their wish to become or remain a member of the discriminating group is stronger than their wish to be fair and egalitarian (see below).

Definitions of prejudice

Although most definitions of prejudice stress the hostile, negative kind, prejudice can also be positive (just as stereotypes can be positive such as, 'all women are caring' – or neutral, such as 'all men are tall'). However, the research which tries to identify how prejudice arises, and how it might be reduced, focuses on hostile prejudice.

The definitions in Table 25.1 locate prejudice squarely *within the individual* – it's an attitude which represents one aspect of social cognition. However, Vivian & Brown (1995) prefer to see prejudice as a special case of *intergroup conflict*. Although conceptually distinct, they often coexist. For Vivian and Brown, intergroup conflict occurs when:

Table 25.1 *Some definitions of prejudice and discrimination*

'… an antipathy based on faulty and inflexible generalisation directed towards a group as a whole or towards an individual because he is a member of that group. It may be felt or expressed.' (Allport, 1954)

'Prejudice is an attitude (usually negative) toward the members of some group, based solely on their membership in that group …'. (Baron & Byrne, 1991)

'Prejudice is a learned attitude towards a target object that typically involves negative affect, dislike or fear, a set of negative beliefs that support the attitude and a behavioural intention to avoid, or to control or dominate, those in the target group … Stereotypes are prejudiced beliefs … when prejudice is acted out, when it becomes overt in various forms of behaviour, then discrimination is in practice …'. (Zimbardo & Leippe, 1991)

'… people think or behave antagonistically towards another group or its members in terms of their group membership and seem motivated by concerns relating to those groups'.

They also distinguish intergroup conflict and *interpersonal conflict*, a distinction we shall return to when discussing attempts to reduce prejudice (see pages 374–376).

Defining prejudice in terms of intergroup conflict 'lifts' it to the social plane. Consistent with this is Fernando's (1991) distinction between 'racial prejudice' and 'racism': the former denotes an attitude possessed by an individual, while the latter refers to a political and economic ideology, which is a characteristic of society. Similarly, Littlewood & Lipsedge (1989) argue that:

'Racist attitudes may be manifest as a highly articulated set of beliefs in the individual, but they are also found in less conscious presuppositions, located in society as a whole …'.

Strictly, then, it is societies (or institutions, such as the police or the armed forces) that are racist, and individuals who are racially prejudiced.

Ask yourself ...

- Apart from racism, what other 'isms' are there which meet these criteria for being *social*, rather than individual, phenomena?

Until quite recently, most of the theory and research into prejudice and discrimination was concerned with racism, '… the quite specific belief that cultural differences between ethnic groups are of biological origin and that groups should be ranked in worth' (Littlewood & Lipsedge, 1989). However, *gender* (as in *sexism*: see Chapters 36 and 47), *sexual orientation* or *preference* (as in *heterosexism*: see Chapters 43 and 47) and *age* (as in *ageism*: see Chapter 39) can all be targets for hostility and discrimination.

CRITICAL DISCUSSION 25.1

Prejudice and discrimination in health care

According to Rose & Platzer (1993), the attitudes of many nurses are grounded in their assumptions about people's heterosexual nature and their lack of knowledge about different lifestyles and how these affect people's health. Ignorance about how lesbians and gay men live can lead nurses to ask inappropriate questions during assessments, leading them to form mistaken judgements.

For example, one lesbian patient who was receiving a cervical smear test was asked if she was sexually active. After saying she was, she was asked what contraceptive she used and replied 'none'. She was then asked if she was trying to become pregnant, which she wasn't. She had to disclose her lesbianism in order to ensure that health professionals didn't make incorrect assumptions about her, which could have led to an incorrect diagnosis.

In another example, one patient's charts were labelled 'high risk'. These labels, which were clearly visible to other patients and members of staff, were there simply because he was gay and so was seen as being at risk of having HIV – the nurses simply assumed that gay men were likely to be HIV-positive and that heterosexual men weren't. Such assumptions are, of course, linked to stereotypes about what gay men do, rather than to a knowledge of sexual behaviours, which can differ widely regardless of sexual orientation.

One nurse in an accident and emergency department refused to give a male patient an analgesic suppository (a pain-relieving capsule inserted into the anus) 'in case he liked it'. Such examples suggest that homosexuality is seen only in terms of sexual behaviour and not lifestyle, and this interferes with nurses' ability to see patients as individuals with particular nursing needs. Another false but commonplace belief is that lesbians and gay men are less discriminating in their sexual habits than heterosexuals, and that they'd want to engage in sexual activity in any setting and regardless of personal preferences (Rose & Platzer, 1993: see Chapter 28).

Institutionalised prejudice and discrimination

Critical Discussion 25.1 illustrates that a great deal of prejudice and discrimination is unconscious, reflected in basic, stereotyped assumptions that we make about others. These assumptions influence our behaviour towards them, which may not be necessarily overtly hostile or 'anti'. It's this pervasive form of prejudice and discrimination that's perhaps the most difficult to break down, because we're unaware of it, and because it reflects *institutionalised* heterosexism, racism and so on.

Both Cochrane (1983) and Littlewood & Lipsedge (1989) show how ethnic minorities in England are more often hospitalised for mental illness than non-black English. This is interpreted as reflecting an implicit, unwitting, prejudice against minority groups which pervades the National Health Service *as an institution*. This definition of 'institutionalised racism' as 'unwitting' was included in the Government Report (1999) on the behaviour of the police in their investigation of the murder of the black London teenager, Stephen Lawrence (cited in Horton, 1999). Other social institutions include psychology, psychiatry and biology (see Chapters 43 and 47).

The concept of race

The classification of people into racial types based on physical appearance (mainly skin colour) has a long history in Western culture. Darwin's (1859) theory of evolution introduced a concept of 'race' which differed from its predecessors. By analogy with his description of numerous 'races' within each species of animals, the idea developed that, while human beings as a whole constitute 'a species' with fertile mating within it, individual (human) 'races' represent 'varieties' or 'subspecies', each being partially isolated reproductively from the others (Banton, 1987, cited in Fernando, 1991). The essential point here is that *individuals* differ much more from each other than do groups.

In his *Descent of Man* (1871), Darwin talked of the likely extinction of 'savage races', because of their inability to change habits when brought into contact with 'civilised races'. He then joined Galton in calling for the control of how different races breed (*eugenics*) in order to ensure the survival of the latter.

Twentieth-century genetics at first described different races in terms of *blood types*, but this proved unreliable. More recently, scientific advances have enabled geneticists to identify human genes that code for specific enzymes and other proteins. But the genetic differences between the classically described races (European, Indian, African, East Asian, New World, and Oceanian) are, on average, only slightly higher (ten per cent) than those which exist between nations within a racial group (six per cent), and the genetic differences between individual human beings within a population are far larger than either of these (84 per cent) (Fernando, 1991).

Despite this, the traditional view persists that people resembling each other in obvious physical ways, such as skin colour, belong to a 'race' that represents a genetically distinct human type. Anthropologists, biologists and medical people are all guilty of perpetuating the myth, despite the widely held belief that 'race' has ceased to have a scientific meaning. While geneticists occasionally use it as shorthand for something like 'large, long-isolated, inbreeding population or gene-pool', this *isn't* race as popularly understood. 'Race' is a *social*, not a biological category. As Richards (1996a) points out:

'Any theory that puts Colin Powell, Shirley Bassey, Maya Angelou, Frank Bruno and Snoop Doggy Dogg in the same 'isolated inbreeding population' cannot have much going for it. Humanity is a single gene-pool, parts of which were relatively (rarely completely) isolated for longer or shorter periods of time'.

Similarly, Wetherell (1996) argues that 'race' is a social as opposed to a natural phenomenon:

'... a process which gives significance to superficial physical differences, but where the construction of group divisions depends on ... economic, political and cultural processes ...'.

She points out that many writers prefer to put quotation marks around 'race' to indicate that we're dealing with one possible social classification of people and groups, rather than an established biological or genetic reality.

Sexism and psychology

The *sexist* nature of psychology is demonstrated in a variety of ways, including the biased nature of the study of sex differences (e.g. Unger, 1979: see Chapters 36 and 47) and discrimination against women within psychology itself. According to Paludi (1992), for example, the history of psychology is the history of the contributions of men, with women psychologists being kept largely invisible, despite their enormous contribution, both historically and currently. One manifestation of this is the devaluation (by men) of the areas of psychology in which women are traditionally more numerous and which they seem to prefer, compared with the traditionally 'male' areas. The former include person-oriented/service-oriented fields such as educational, developmental, clinical psychology and counselling, while the latter are the academic/experimental areas. These include learning and cognitive psychology, which are regarded (by men) as more scientifically rigorous and intellectually demanding (Paludi, 1992). Could it be that women are 'channelled' into certain fields of psychology, which then are defined as 'inferior' simply because they're populated mainly by women? Paludi sees certain individuals acting as *gatekeepers*, determining the career paths of others; in the case of psychology, the gatekeepers are usually men.

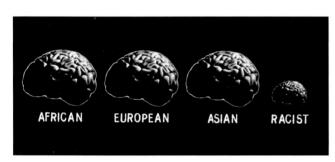

Poster used during the 1997 European Year against Racism

Reproduced by permission of The Commission for Racial Equality

---

CRITICAL DISCUSSION 25.2

Scientific racism

The attempt to present racist views as scientific 'fact' is revealed in the (not very subtle) form of 'scientific racism'. Chris Brand, a psychologist at the University of Edinburgh, had his book, *The g Factor: General intelligence and its implications*, withdrawn by the publisher (John Wiley) in April 1996 before its publication. He denies being a 'racist' while being 'perfectly proud to be a racist in the scientific sense', that is, a believer in the view that race and psychology have deep links (most likely genetic).

According to Brand (quoted in Richards, 1996a), 'You won't find any psychologist of repute who has said anything different [than that black people have lower intelligence] since the turn of the century'. However, according to Richards, dozens of psychologists of unimpeachable repute (including Bartlett, Freud, Piaget and Skinner) have either disagreed or, more commonly, not even been interested in the question. Some who've agreed turn out not to have been so reputable after all. For example, Cattell (see Chapter 42) was pro-Hitler in the 1930s, a ruthless racist eugenicist all his life, who even contemplated genocide ('genthenasia'). Brand is simply wrong!

Racism in psychiatry

Cartwright (1851), an American psychiatrist, proposed two diagnostic categories meant to apply exclusively to black people (at the time of slavery).

■ *Dysaesthesia Aethiopis* was a disease which afflicted all 'free negroes' without a white person to direct and take care of them, 'the natural offspring of negro liberty – the liberty to be idle ... wallow in filth ... indulge in improper food and drinks'. Symptoms included breaking, wasting and destroying everything they handled, tearing or burning their clothing, stealing from others to replace what they had destroyed, and apparent insensitivity to pain.

■ *Drapetomania* was, quite simply, the disease which caused slaves to run away (Fernando, 1991: see Chapter 43).

Theories of prejudice and discrimination

Attempts to explain prejudice and discrimination fall into three broad categories:

■ those which see prejudice as stemming from *personality variables* and other aspects of the psychological make-up of individuals;

■ those which emphasise the role of *environmental factors* (sometimes called the *conflict approach*);

■ those which focus on the effects of the mere fact of *group membership*.

Each approach may be important to a complete understanding of the causes of intergroup conflict and prejudice, and to their reduction (Vivian & Brown, 1995).

Prejudice and personality

The authoritarian personality

Adorno *et al.* (1950) proposed the concept of the *authoritarian personality* (in a book of the same name), someone who's prejudiced by virtue of specific personality traits which predispose them to be hostile towards ethnic, racial and other minority or outgroups.

Adorno *et al.* began by studying antisemitism in Nazi Germany in the 1940s, and drew on Freud's theories to help understand the relationship between 'collective ideologies' (such as fascism) and individual personality (Brown, 1985). After their emigration to the USA, studies began with over 2000 college students and other native-born, white, non-Jewish, middle-class Americans (including school teachers, nurses, prison inmates and psychiatric patients). These involved interviews concerning their political views and childhood experiences, and the use of *projective tests* (in particular, the thematic apperception test/TAT: see Chapter 9) designed to reveal unconscious attitudes towards minority groups.

A number of scales were developed in the course of their research (see Table 25.2, page 369).

■ *Antisemitism (AS) scale*: The 52 items were phrased so as to express a subtle hostility without seeming to offend the democratic values most respondents would feel bound to support, a kind of 'fair-minded and reasonable veneer' (Brown, 1965).

- *Ethnocentrism (E) scale*: The term 'ethnocentrism' was first defined by Sumner (1906) as: 'A view of things in which one's own group is the centre of everything, and all others are scaled and rated with reference to it ... each group ... boasts itself superior ... and looks with contempt on outsiders. Each group thinks its own folkways the only right one ...'. The scale comprised 34 items.
- *Political and economic conservatism (PEC) scale*: The central component of conservatism is attachment to things as they are, and a resistance to social change. This is the only scale to include items supporting both sides of the issues.
- *Potentiality for fascism (F) scale*: According to Brown (1965), Adorno *et al.* never referred to the F scale as the authoritarianism scale. But since it's supposed to identify the kind of personality the book is talking about, it's reasonable to suppose that the scale could also be correctly called the authoritarianism scale (as it has been in many subsequent research reports). The scale was revised several times during the course of the research, but the items never referred directly to minority groups or politico-economic issues. It was intended to measure implicit authoritarian and antidemocratic trends in personality, making someone with such a personality susceptible to explicit fascist propaganda. The 38 items were subclassified under nine general headings (six of which are included in Table 25.2).

Table 25.2 *Sample items from the various scales used by Adorno* et al. *(1950)*

Antisemitism (AS) scale	The trouble with letting Jews into a nice neighbourhood is that they gradually give it a typically Jewish atmosphere.
Ethnocentrism(E) scale	Negroes have their rights, but it's best to keep them in their own districts and schools and to prevent too much contact with whites.
Political and economic conservatism (PEC) scale	In general, full economic security is harmful; most men wouldn't work if they didn't need the money for eating and living.

Potentiality for fascism (F) scale

1 Conventionalism	Obedience and respect for authority are the most important virtues children should learn.
2 Authoritarian submission	Young people sometimes get rebellious ideas, but as they grow up they ought to get over them and settle down.
3 Authoritarian aggression	Sex crimes, such as rape and attacks on children, deserve more than mere imprisonment; such criminals ought to be publicly whipped or worse.
4 Power and toughness	People can be divided into two distinct classes: the weak and the strong.
5 Projectivity	Nowadays when so many different kinds of people move around and mix together so much, a person has to protect himself especially carefully against catching an infection or disease from them.
6 Sex	Homosexuals are hardly better than criminals and ought to be severely punished.

Table 25.3 shows the correlations between the different scales.

Table 25.3 *Correlations between scores on the different scales used by Adorno* et al. *(1950)*

	AS	E	PEC	F
AS		0.80	0.43	0.53
E			0.57	0.65
PEC				0.57
F (final version)	0.75			

Ask yourself ...

- What conclusions can you draw from the correlations in Table 25.3?

The pattern of intercorrelations suggests that:

- scores on the AS, E and F scales all correlate with each other much more strongly than any of them does with the PEC score; and, following from this,
- people who are antisemitic are also likely to be hostile towards 'Negroes', 'Japs' and any other minority group or 'foreigner' (all *outgroups*): the authoritarian personality is prejudiced in a very *generalised* way.

What's the authoritarian personality like?

Typically, the authoritarian personality is hostile to people of inferior status, servile to those of higher status and contemptuous of weakness. They are also rigid and inflexible, intolerant of ambiguity and uncertainty, unwilling to introspect feelings and an upholder of conventional values and ways of life (such as religion). This belief in convention and intolerance of ambiguity combine to make minorities 'them' and the authoritarian's membership group 'us'; 'they' are by definition 'bad' and 'we' are by definition 'good'.

How does the authoritarian personality become prejudiced?

Based on the interview and TAT data, Adorno *et al.* claimed that authoritarians have often experienced a harsh, punitive, disciplinarian upbringing, with little affection. While they consciously have very high opinions of their parents, they often reveal considerable latent (unconscious) hostility towards them, stemming from the extreme frustration they experienced as children.

Drawing on Freudian theory, Adorno *et al.* proposed that such unconscious hostility may be *displaced* onto minority groups, which become the targets for the authoritarian's hostility. Authoritarians also *project* onto these groups their own unacceptable, antisocial impulses (especially sexual and aggressive), so that they feel threatened by members of these groups. They have very little self-insight, and their prejudice serves a vital *ego-defensive function*, which protects them from the unacceptable parts of themselves (see Table 24.2, page 351).

Evaluation of the authoritarian personality theory

While some evidence is broadly consistent with the theory, there are a number of serious methodological and other problems which make it untenable.

- The items on the AS, E and F scales (all Likert-type questions: see Chapter 24) were worded in such a way that agreement with them always implies antisemitism, ethnocentrism and potential fascism respectively. Adorno *et al.* recognised the possibility that *acquiescent response set* (see Chapter 24) might be a problem.

- The interview and TAT data were intended partly to validate the F scale. But the clinical interviews were flawed, since the interviewer knew the interviewee's F score. This represents a serious source of *experimenter bias* (see Chapter 3).

- According to Brown (1988), if prejudice is to be explained in terms of *individual differences*, how can it then be manifested in a whole population or at least a vast majority of that population? In pre-war Nazi Germany, for example (and in many other places since), consistent racist attitudes and behaviour were shown by hundreds of thousands of people, who must have differed on most other psychological characteristics.

- Similarly, how can the theory account for the sudden rise and fall of prejudice in particular societies at specific historical periods? Antisemitism in Nazi Germany grew during a decade or so, which is much too short a time for a whole generation of German families to have adopted new forms of childrearing practices giving rise to authoritarian and prejudiced children (Brown, 1988). Even more dramatic was the anti-Japanese prejudice among Americans following the attack on Pearl Harbor. Brown believes that such examples:

  '... *strongly suggest that the attitudes held by members of different groups towards each other have more to do with the objective relations between the groups – relations of political conflict or alliance, economic interdependence and so on – than with the familial relation in which they grew up!*'

The open and closed mind

Another criticism of the authoritarian personality theory is that it assumed that authoritarianism is a characteristic of the political right, implying that there's no equivalent authoritarianism on the left. According to Rokeach (1960) 'ideological dogmatism' refers to a relatively rigid outlook on life and intolerance of those with opposing beliefs. High scores on the *dogmatism scale* reveal: (i) closedness of mind; (ii) lack of flexibility; and (iii) authoritarianism, regardless of particular social and political ideology.

Dogmatism is a *way of thinking*, rather than a set of beliefs (Brown, 1965). The dogmatic individual tends to accentuate differences between 'us and them' and displays *self-aggrandisement* (e.g. 'If I had to choose between happiness and greatness, I'd choose greatness'). S/he also has a *paranoid* outlook on life ('I often feel people are looking at me critically'), and is *uncompromising* in his/her beliefs and intolerant of others. These characteristics serve as defences against a sense of personal inadequacy.

Rokeach (1960) gave the F scale and the dogmatism scale to five English groups of different political persuasions, including a group of 13 communist students. While the communists scored low on the F scale, they had the highest dogmatism scores, which supported Rokeach's claim that the F scale measures only right-wing authoritarianism.

Scapegoating: the frustration–aggression hypothesis

According to the Dollard *et al.*'s (1939) *frustration–aggression hypothesis*, frustration always gives rise to aggression, and aggression is always caused by frustration (see Chapter 29). The source of frustration (whatever prevents us from achieving our goals) might often be seen as a fairly powerful threat (such as parents or employers) or may be difficult to identify. Drawing on Freudian theory, Dollard *et al.* claim that when we need to vent our frustration but are unable to do this directly, we do so *indirectly* by displacing it onto a substitute target (we find a *scapegoat*).

According to the frustration–aggression hypothesis, discrimination against outsiders (in this case eastern-European asylum seekers) is a form of displaced aggression

Ask yourself ...

- Can you see any parallels between the frustration–aggression hypothesis and certain parts of Adorno *et al.*'s theory?

The choice of scapegoat isn't usually random. In England during the 1930s and 1940s, it was predominantly the Jews, who were replaced by West Indians during the 1950s and 1960s, and during the 1970s, 1980s and 1990s by Asians from Pakistan. In the southern USA, lynchings of blacks from 1880 to 1930 were related to the price of cotton: as the price dropped, so the number of lynchings increased (Hovland & Sears, 1940). While this is consistent with the concept of displaced aggression, the fact that whites chose blacks as scapegoats rather than some other minority group suggests that there are usually socially approved (*legitimised*) targets for frustration-induced aggression.

Limitations of the personality approach

- Several writers (e.g. Billig, 1976; Brown, 1988; Hogg & Abrams, 1988) have argued that any account of prejudice and discrimination in terms of individuals *(interpersonal behaviour)* is *reductionist* (see Chapter 49). In other words, the *social* nature of prejudice and discrimination requires a *social* explanation (in terms of *intergroup behaviour*).

- Adorno *et al.* imply that racism is the product of the abnormal personality of a small minority of human beings, rather than a social and political ideology. This distinction is of great practical as well as theoretical importance, because what's considered to be the cause of prejudice has very real implications for its reduction. In fact, Adorno *et al.* recognised that, as important as personality dynamics are, it is *society* which provides the content of attitudes and prejudice and which defines the outgroups.

- According to Brown (1985), 'cultural or societal norms may be much more important than personality in accounting for ethnocentrism, outgroup rejection, prejudice and discrimination'.

The role of environmental factors

The impact of social norms: prejudice as conformity

Individual bigotry is only part of the explanation of racial discrimination. For example, even though overt discrimination has, traditionally, been greater in the southern USA, white southerners haven't scored higher than whites from the north on measures of authoritarianism (Pettigrew, 1959). So, clearly, *conformity to social norms* can prove more powerful as a determinant of behaviour than personality factors.

Minard (1952) found that black and white coalminers in West Virginia followed a pattern of almost complete integration below ground, but almost complete segregation above! This makes sense only when viewed in terms of conformity to the norms which operated in those different situations.

> *Ask yourself ...*
>
> - What do you think the two sets of norms may have been?

Pettigrew (1971) also found that Americans in the south are no more antisemitic or hostile towards *other* minority groups than those from the north (as the authoritarian personality explanation would require). In other words, prejudice isn't the generalised attitude which Adorno *et al.* claimed. According to Reich & Adcock (1976), the need to conform and not be seen as different may cause milder prejudices, but active discrimination against, and ill treatment of, minorities reflects a prejudice which already exists and which is maintained and legitimised by conformity.

Relative deprivation theory

According to the frustration–aggression hypothesis, people experience frustration when they feel deprived of something they believe they're entitled to. The discrepancy between our actual attainments (such as standard of living) and expectations (the standard of living we feel we deserve) is our relative

deprivation (Davis, 1959). When attainments suddenly fall short of rising expectations, *relative deprivation* is particularly acute, resulting in collective unrest. This is expressed as a J-curve (Davies, 1969).

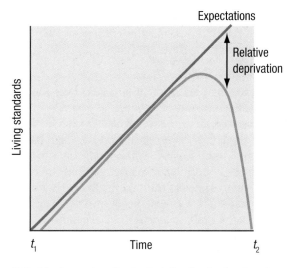

Figure 25.1 *The J-curve hypothesis of relative deprivation (based on Davies, 1969)*

A good example of such acute relative deprivation is the 1992 Los Angeles riots. The immediate cause was the acquittal, by an all-white jury, of four LA police officers accused of beating a black motorist, Rodney King. Against a background of rising unemployment and continuing disadvantage, the acquittal was seen by blacks as symbolic of their low esteem in the eyes of the white majority (Hogg & Vaughan, 1995). The great sense of injustice at the acquittal seemed to demonstrate in acute form the injustice which is an inherent feature of discrimination – and of relative deprivation.

The 1992 Los Angeles riots were triggered by an all-white jury's aquittal of four Los Angeles police officers accused of beating a black motorist, Rodney King

The LA riots illustrate *fraternalistic relative deprivation*, based on a comparison either with dissimilar others or with other groups (Runciman, 1966). This is contrasted with *egoistic relative deprivation*, which is based on comparison with other similar individuals. Vanneman & Pettigrew (1972) found that whites who expressed the most anti-black attitudes were those who felt most strongly that whites as a group were badly off relative to blacks. Objectively, they were actually better off, showing the subjective nature of relative deprivation. It has also been found that the most militant blacks seem to be those of higher socioeconomic and educational status. They probably have higher expectations, both for themselves and for their group, and consequently experience relative deprivation more acutely (Vivian & Brown, 1995).

Realistic conflict theory

According to Sherif's (1966) *realistic conflict theory*, intergroup conflict arises as a result of a conflict of interests. When two groups want to achieve the same goal but can't both have it, hostility is produced between them. Indeed, Sherif claims that conflict of interest (or *competition*) is a *sufficient* condition for the occurrence of hostility or conflict. He bases this claim on one of the most famous field experiments in social psychology, the Robber's Cave experiment, which Brown (1986) describes as the most successful field experiment ever conducted on intergroup conflict.

KEY STUDY 25.1

The Robber's Cave experiment (Sherif *et al.*, 1961)

The setting was Robber's Cave State Park in Oklahoma, where 22 white, middle-class, Protestant, well-adjusted boys, spent two weeks at a summer camp. They were randomly assigned to two groups of eleven, each occupying a separate cabin, out of sight of each other. None of the boys knew any of the others prior to their arrival at the camp.

- During the *first stage* of the experiment, each group co-operated on a number of activities (pitching tents, making meals, a treasure hunt), and soon a distinct set of norms emerged which defined the group's identity. One group called itself 'the Rattlers', and the other 'the Eagles'. Towards the end of the first week, they were allowed to become aware of the other's existence, and an 'us and them' language quickly developed.

- The *second stage* began with the announcement that there was to be a grand tournament between the two groups, comprising ten sporting events, plus points awarded for the state of their cabins and so on. A splendid trophy, medals and four-bladed knives for each of the group members would be awarded to the winning group.

Before the tournament began, the Rattlers' flag was burned, and the camp counsellors (the experimenters) had to break up a fight between the two groups. With some 'help' from the counsellors, the Eagles won and later the Rattlers stole their medals and knives.

There was a strong ingroup preference. Rattlers stereotyped all Rattlers as brave, tough and friendly, and (almost) all Eagles as sneaky, stinkers and smart alecks. The reverse was true for the Eagles.

Tyerman & Spencer (1983) challenged Sherif *et al.*'s conclusions that competition is a sufficient condition for intergroup conflict. They observed English boy scouts at their annual camp. The boys knew each other well before the start of camp, and much of what they did there was similar to what the Rattlers and Eagles did at Robber's Cave. They were divided into four 'patrols', competing in situations familiar to them from previous camps, but the friendship ties which existed prior to arrival at camp were maintained across the patrol groups. Competition remained friendly, and there was no increase of ingroup solidarity. The four groups continued to see themselves as part of the *whole* group, something that was deliberately encouraged by the leader.

Tyerman and Spencer concluded that Sherif *et al.*'s results reflect the transitory nature of their experimental group. The fact that the English boys knew each other beforehand, had established friendships, were familiar with camp life, and had a leader who encouraged co-operation, were all important *contextual/situational* influences on the boys' behaviour.

It seems, then, that 'competition' may not be a sufficient condition for intergroup conflict and hostility after all. If we accept this conclusion, the question arises whether it's even a necessary condition. In other words, can hostility arise in the absence of conflicting interests?

The influence of group membership

Minimal groups

According to Tajfel *et al.* (1971), the *mere perception* of another group's existence can produce discrimination. When people are arbitrarily and randomly divided into two groups, knowledge of the other group's existence is a sufficient condition for the development of pro-ingroup and anti-outgroup attitudes. These artificial groups are known as *minimal groups*.

Before any discrimination can occur, people must be categorised as members of an ingroup or an outgroup (making categorisation a *necessary* condition). More significantly, the very act of categorisation produces conflict and discrimination (making it also a *sufficient* condition). These conclusions are based on the creation of artificial groups among 14–15-year-old Bristol schoolboys. The criteria used to create the groups were arbitrary and superficial and differed from experiment to experiment. They included:

- chronic 'overestimations' or 'underestimations' on a task involving estimating the number of dots appearing on slide projections;
- preference for paintings by Klee or Kandinsky;
- the toss of a coin.

Box 25.1 The minimal group paradigm (Tajfel *et al.*, 1971)

Once these arbitrary groups had been formed, each boy worked alone in a cubicle on a task that required various matrices to be studied (see Figure 25.3). He had to decide how to allocate points to a member of his own group (but not himself) and a member of the other group. The boys were also told that the points could be converted to money after the study. The only information each boy had about another boy was whether he was a member of the same group or the other group; otherwise he was anonymous, unknown, unseen and identified only by a code number.

The top line in the figure represents the points that can be allocated to the boy's own group, and the bottom line the points to the other group. For example, if 18 points are allocated to the boy's own group, then five are allocated to the other group. If twelve are allocated to the boy's own group, eleven are allocated to the other group.

MATRIX 4

18	17	16	15	14	13	12	11	10	9	8	7	6	5
5	6	7	8	9	10	11	12	13	14	15	16	17	18

Figure 25.2 *One of the matrices used by Tajfel* et al. *(1971)*

In the Tajfel *et al.* experiments, the actual group assignments were always made randomly whatever the boys believed to be the basis for the categorisation. But Billig & Tajfel (1973) and Locksley *et al.* (1980) went even further, by actually *telling* the participants they were being randomly assigned, tossing the coin in front of them, and giving them obviously meaningless names (such as As and Bs, or Kappas and Phis). Even under these conditions, the groups still showed a strong *ingroup preference.*

An evaluation of minimal group experiments

- Brown (1988) points out that intergroup discrimination in this minimal group situation has proved to be a remarkably robust phenomenon. In more than two dozen independent studies in several different countries, using a wide range of experimental participants of both sexes (from young children to adults), essentially the same result has been found: the mere act of allocating people into arbitrary social categories is sufficient to elicit biased judgements and discriminatory behaviours.
- Wetherell (1982) maintains that intergroup conflict *isn't* inevitable. She studied white and Polynesian children in New Zealand, and found the latter to be much more generous towards the outgroup, reflecting cultural norms which emphasised co-operation.
- The *minimal group paradigm* has been criticised on several methodological and theoretical grounds, especially its artificiality (e.g. Schiffman & Wicklund, 1992; Gross, 1999).

Social identity theory (SIT)

Tajfel (1978) and Tajfel & Turner (1986) explain the minimal group effect in terms of *social identity theory* (SIT). According to SIT, an individual strives to achieve or maintain a positive self-image. This has two components: *personal identity* (the personal characteristics and attributes which make each person unique), and *social identity* (a sense of who we are, derived from the groups we belong to).

In fact, each of us has several social identities, corresponding to the different groups with which we identify. In each case, the more positive the image of the group, the more positive will be our own social identity, and hence our self-image. By emphasising the desirability of the ingroup(s) and focusing on those distinctions which enable our own group to come out on top, we help to create for ourselves a satisfactory social identity. This can be seen as lying at the heart of prejudice.

Box 25.2 Group status and self-esteem

Members of minimal groups in the laboratory (compared with controls who aren't assigned to a group) have been found to show higher self-esteem. For example, Lemyre & Smith (1985) claimed that it was the opportunity to display *intergroup discrimination* that increased self-esteem. Control participants who were categorised but could only distribute rewards between two ingroupers or two outgroupers, or couldn't distribute rewards at all, showed *lower* self-esteem than experimental participants able to make intergroup decisions.

Outside the laboratory, groups with lower social status in a particular society strive to improve their social identities, and thus members' self-esteem. If group members feel its inferior status is unfair or illegitimate, then the group can become very well organised and assertive in trying to change its objective status. Good examples are those working for the Welsh language revival, and the Basque Separatists in Spain. Dominant or high status groups typically react very negatively to threats to their privileged position, and this can take the form of extreme prejudices being expressed (Hogg & Abrams, 2000).

Some individuals may be more prone to prejudice because they have an intense need for acceptance by others. Their personal and social identities may be much more interconnected than for those with a lesser need for social acceptance. Prejudice can be seen as an adjustive mechanism which bolsters the self-concept of individuals who have feelings of personal inadequacy – but with potentially undesirable social implications.

Evaluation of SIT

- While there's considerable empirical support for the theory, much of this comes from minimal group experiments. Not only have they been criticised (see above), but SIT was originally proposed to explain the findings from those experiments. So, there's a *circularity* involved, making it necessary to test SIT's predictions in other ways.
- SIT has been criticised on the grounds that it presents racism (and other forms of prejudice) as 'natural', helping to justify it. Stemming from Allport's (1954) claims that stereotypes are 'categories about people' and that 'the human mind must think with the aid of categories' (see Chapter 22), Tajfel (1969; Tajfel *et al.*, 1971) saw the process of *categorisation* as a basic characteristic of human thought. If, as SIT implies, intergroup hostility is natural and built into our thought processes as a consequence of categorisation, then racism, conceived as a form of intergroup hostility (or ingroup favouritism), may also be construed as natural. In terms of the distribution of resources, racism is thus justified as the norm ('charity begins at home') (Howitt & Owusu-Bempah, 1994).
- Of course, Tajfel never intended SIT to be seen as a justification of racism; indeed, he was a life-long opponent of racism, having lost his family and community in the Holocaust. Taken out of context and elevated to the status of a universal human characteristic, SIT is easily *misrepresented* as an explanation and justification of racism (Milner, 1991, cited in Howitt & Owusu-Bempah, 1994).

- The evidence as it stands shows only a positive ingroup bias, and *not* derogatory attitudes or behaviour towards the outgroup, which is what we normally understand by 'prejudice'. In other words, although there's abundant evidence of intergroup discrimination, this appears to stem from raising the evaluation of the ingroup, rather than denigrating the outgroup (Vivian & Brown, 1995).

- Wetherell (1996) believes that SIT emphasises the 'ordinariness' of racism and its continuity with other forms of group behaviour. Intergroup conflict *isn't* seen as a psychopathology or the result of irrational prejudice, but as a form of behaviour involving complex psychological states which are also central to more positive group actions, such as developing a sense of solidarity with others, group loyalty, cohesiveness and national belonging. Racism is only inevitable given a particular social context, where 'racial' categories become significant and acquire meaning as group divisions. These categories aren't natural, but become powerful as a result of social history (see the earlier discussion of race, page 367).

Reducing prejudice and discrimination

Ask yourself ...

- What do the major theories we've discussed above imply about how prejudice and discrimination could be reduced – or prevented?

- The *authoritarian personality theory* implies that by changing the personality structure of the prejudiced individual, the need for an ego-defensive 'prop' such as prejudice is removed. By its nature, this is practically very difficult to achieve, even if it's theoretically possible. Equally difficult is the prevention of the kind of childrearing pattern which, according to Adorno *et al.*, determines the authoritarian personality in the first place.

- According to the *frustration–aggression hypothesis* and the *theory of relative deprivation*, preventing frustration, lowering people's expectations, and providing people with ways to vent their frustration in less antisocial ways than discrimination are all possible solutions. However, this would involve putting the historical clock back or changing social conditions in quite fundamental ways.

- *Realistic conflict theory* makes it very clear that removing competition and replacing it with superordinate goals and co-operation will remove or prevent hostility (this is discussed further below).

- *SIT* implies that if intergroup stereotypes can become less negative and automatic, and if boundaries between groups can be made more blurred or more flexible, then group memberships may become a less central part of the self-concept, making positive evaluation of the ingroup less inevitable. We shall return to this theme below.

The contact hypothesis

Probably the first formal proposal of a set of social–psychological principles for reducing prejudice was Allport's (1954) *contact hypothesis* (as it's come to be called), according to which:

'Prejudice (unless deeply rooted in the character structure of the individual) may be reduced by equal status contact between majority and minority groups in the pursuit of common goals. The effect is greatly enhanced if this contact is sanctioned by institutional supports (i.e. by law, custom or local atmosphere) and provided it is of a sort that leads to the perception of common interests and common humanity between members of the two groups'.

Most programmes aimed at promoting harmonious relations between groups that were previously in conflict have operated according to Allport's 'principles', in particular *equal status contact* and the *pursuit of common (superordinate) goals*.

Francois Pienaar, the South African rugby union captain, receiving the Rugby World Cup from Nelson Mandela in 1995

Equal status contact

When people are segregated, they're likely to experience *autistic hostility*, that is, ignorance of others, which results in a failure to understand the reasons for their actions. Lack of contact means there's no 'reality testing' against which to check our own interpretations of others' behaviour, and this in turn is likely to reinforce *negative stereotypes*. By the same token, ignorance of what 'makes them tick' will probably make 'them' seem more dissimilar from ourselves than they really are. Bringing people into contact with each other should make them seem more familiar, and at least offers the possibility that this negative cycle can be interrupted and even reversed.

Related to autistic hostility is the *mirror-image phenomenon* (Bronfenbrenner, 1960), whereby enemies come to see themselves as being in the right (with 'God on our side') and the other side as in the wrong. Both sides tend to attribute to each

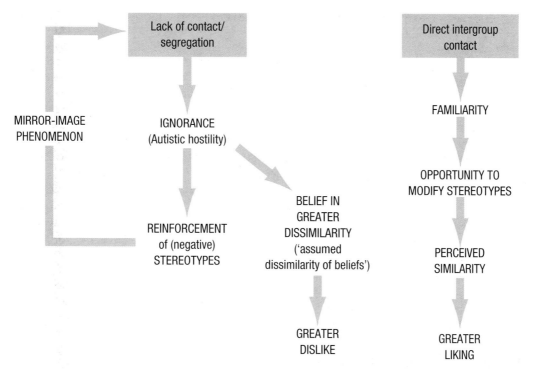

Figure 25.3 *Summary of how the negative cycle of lack of contact/segregation between racial/ethnic groups and reinforcement of negative stereotypes can be broken by direct contact (as advocated by Allport's contact hypothesis)*

other the same negative characteristics (the 'assumed dissimilarity of beliefs'). Increased contact provides the opportunity to disconfirm our stereotypes. The outgroup loses its strangeness, and group members are more likely to be seen as unique individuals, rather than an 'undifferentiated mass' (see Figure 25.3, above). This represents a reduction in the *illusion of outgroup homogeneity* (see Chapter 22).

How effective is equal status contact?

It's generally agreed that increased contact alone won't reduce prejudice. Despite evidence that we prefer people who are familiar (see Chapter 28), if this contact is between people who are consistently of unequal status, then 'familiarity may breed contempt'. Aronson (1980) points out that many whites (in the USA) have always had a great deal of contact with blacks – as dishwashers, toilet attendants, domestic servants and so on. Such contacts may simply reinforce the stereotypes held by whites of blacks as being inferior. Similarly, Amir (1994) argues that we need to ask 'Under what conditions does intergroup contact have an impact, for whom, and regarding what outcomes?'.

One early study of equal status contact was that of Deutsch & Collins (1951). They compared two kinds of housing project, one of which was thoroughly integrated (blacks and whites were assigned houses regardless of race), and the other segregated. Residents of both were intensively interviewed and it was found that both casual and neighbourly contact were greater in the integrated housing, with a corresponding decrease in prejudice among whites towards blacks.

As noted earlier, in Minard's study of miners in West Virginia, black and white miners were (equal status) colleagues in the mine, but the norms operating 'above ground' clearly didn't permit equality of status. Similarly, Stouffer *et al.* (1949) and Amir (1969) found that inter-racial attitudes

improved markedly when blacks and whites served together as soldiers in battle and on ships, but relationships weren't so good at base camp.

Stephan (1978) reviewed a number of studies of *desegregation* of American schools, and concluded that white prejudice towards blacks wasn't reduced, while black prejudice towards whites seemed to have increased. Several studies have found that, at first, interaction and friendship are totally governed by group attitudes and then slowly start to take account of personal qualities. But racial attitudes change very little. Aronson (2000) believes that the main reason for this failure was that very few of the studies reviewed by Stephan involved a school situation where all three of Allport's requisites – equal status contact, pursuit of common goals, and sanction by authority – were in place at the same time.

If intergroup contact does reduce prejudice, it's *not* because it encourages interpersonal friendship (as Deutsch and Collins would claim), but because of changes in *intergroup relationships*. If the contact between groups is *interpersonal* (people are seen as individuals and group memberships are largely insignificant), then any change of attitude may not generalise to other members of the respective groups. At the very least, individuals must be seen as typical members of their group if any generalisation is to occur (Brown & Turner, 1981; Hewstone & Brown, 1986). But what if 'typical' means, in practice, 'stereotypical' and the stereotype is negative? A study by Wilder (1984, cited in Vivian & Brown, 1995) suggests that at the very least the encounter with the 'typical' group member must be a pleasant experience.

Pursuit of common (superordinate) goals

In a *co-operative* situation, the attainment of one person's goal enhances the chances of attainment of the goals of other group members; this is the reverse of a competitive situation

(Brown, 1986). One of the few attempts to alter the classroom experience in order to realise equal status contact and mutual co-operation is Aronson *et al.*'s (1978) *jigsaw method*.

Box 25.4   The jigsaw method (Aronson *et al.*, 1978)

This is a highly structured method of interdependent learning, in which children are assigned to six-person, inter-racial learning groups. The day's lesson is divided into six parts, and each member is given material which represents one piece of the lesson to be learned. Each child must learn its part and then communicate it to the rest of the group and, at the end of the lesson, is tested on the whole lesson and is given an individual score. Each child is, therefore, dependent on the others in the group for parts of the lesson that can only be learned from them. Hence, there is complete mutual interdependence.

Evaluation of the jigsaw method

Ask yourself ...

- What do you think some of the benefits are of the jigsaw method compared with the conventional classroom?
- How might benefits contribute to a reduction in prejudice?

The aim of the research programme was to develop and evaluate a classroom atmosphere that could be sustained by the classroom teacher long after the researchers had left. Every student spends some time in the role of expert, and the most important, unique, aspect of this method is that each student has a special, vital gift for the other group members – a gift that's unattainable elsewhere (Aronson, 2000).

The experiment has been replicated in scores of classrooms with thousands of students. According to Aronson (1992, 2000), the jigsaw method consistently enhances students' self-esteem, improves academic performance, increases liking for classmates and improves some inter-racial perceptions, compared with children in traditional classrooms.

However, although the children of different racial/ethnic groups who'd actually worked together came to like each other better as individuals, their reduced prejudice *didn't* generalise to those ethnic groups as a whole. This may be partly accounted for by the fact that most experiments of this type are small-scale and relatively short-term interventions. The jigsaw method also works best with young children, before prejudiced attitudes have an opportunity to become deeply ingrained (Aronson, 1992).

K E Y   S T U D Y   2 5 . 2

Robber's Cave re-visited (Sherif *et al.*, 1961)

Sherif et al. introduced a *third stage* (see Key Study 25.1), in which seven equal status contact situations were created (including filling out questionnaires, seeing movies and having meals together). None of these, nor all of them in combination, did anything to reduce friction.

But it was also arranged that the camp's drinking water supply was cut off, and the only way of restoring it was by a co-operative effort by the Rattlers and Eagles. In order to afford to hire a movie, both groups had to chip in, and on a trip to Cedar Lake, one of the trucks got stuck and they all had to pull on a rope together to get it started again.

In the final few days, the group divisions disappeared and they actually suggested travelling home together in one bus. Sixty-five per cent of their friendship choices were now made from the other group, and their stereotypes of the other group became much more favourable.

Do common goals always work?

The imposition of superordinate goals may sometimes even increase antagonism towards the outgroup, if the co-operation fails to achieve its aims. Groups need distinctive and complementary roles to play, so that each group's contributions are clearly defined. When this doesn't happen, liking for the other group may actually *decrease*, perhaps because group members are concerned with the integrity of the ingroup (Brown, 1988).

But what if attempts are made to 'redraw the boundaries' between in- and outgroups? If the mere categorisation of oneself as a member of a particular group is sufficient to produce discrimination against other (out-) groups, it follows that *recategorisation* (people formerly viewed as 'them' come to be viewed as belonging to 'us') should reduce it (Baron & Byrne, 1991).

Conclusions: What to do with stereotypes?

If stereotyped beliefs form such a crucial part of our prejudices, then we must try to change people's stereotypes if we're to have any hope of reducing prejudice and discrimination. However, according to Brislin (1993):

'In many cultures, stereotypes of certain groups are so negative, so pervasive, and have existed for so many generations that they can be considered part of the culture into which children are socialised ...'.

As we've seen, stereotypes represent a way of simplifying the extraordinarily complex social world we inhabit by placing people into categories. This alone would explain why they're so resistant to change. But they also influence selective attention and selective remembering, processes that are to a large extent outside conscious control. For example, Devine (1989) found that both low- and high-prejudiced people are vulnerable to the automatic activation of the cultural stereotype of African Americans (see Chapter 22).

However, these automatic stereotyped reactions (like one I'm still 'guilty' of, namely inferring that 'doctor' denotes 'he') can be seen simply as habits that can be broken. Prejudice reduction is a *process* (rather than an all-or-none event), which involves learning to inhibit these automatic reactions and deciding that prejudice is an inappropriate way of relating to others (Devine & Zuwerink, 1994). But trying to suppress your stereotypes may actually strengthen their automaticity. Hogg & Abrams (2000) argue that:

'The knack would seem to be to get people to have insight into their stereotypes – to understand them and see through them rather than merely to suppress them'.

Relying on stereotypes to form impressions of strangers (*category-driven processing*) represents the cognitively easiest, least strenuous, route, while relying on their unique characteristics (*attribute-driven processing*) represents the most strenuous route (Fiske & Neuberg, 1990). While people are very skilled at preserving their stereotypes ('You're OK, it's the others'), the more often they come into contact with members of a particular group who don't fit the stereotype, the more likely it is to lose its credibility. Motivating individuals in some way to pay careful attention to others, and to focus on their unique attributes rather than their 'group' attributes, can be effective.

Finally, propaganda, education and the raising of consciousness can all contribute to the reduction and prevention of prejudice.

At the end of the experiment, Elliott debriefed the children. She told them its purpose was to provide them with an opportunity to experience the evils of prejudice and discrimination in a protected environment.

In a follow-up study of the students when they were 18, Elliott (1990) found that they reported themselves as being more tolerant of differences between groups and actively opposed to prejudice.

Elliott's experiment (described in her book *The Eye of the Storm*, and featured in the TV programme *A Class Divided*) demonstrates the potential impact of experiencing prejudice and discrimination first-hand. Prejudice is mindless. If we teach people, especially children, to be mindful of others, to think of them as complex, whole individuals, stereotypic reactions could be reduced (Hogg & Vaughan, 1995).

KEY STUDY 25.3

The blue eyes–brown eyes experiment (Elliott, in Aronson & Osherow, 1980)

Aronson and Osherow reported an experiment with third-graders (nine-year-olds) conducted by their teacher, Jane Elliott.

She told her class one day that brown-eyed people are more intelligent and 'better' people than those with blue eyes. Brown-eyed students, though in the minority, would be the 'ruling class' over the inferior blue-eyed children and be given extra privileges. The blue-eyed students were to be 'kept in their place' by being last in line, seated at the back of the class, and given less break-time. They also had to wear special collars as a sign of their low status.

Within a short time, the blue-eyed children began to do more poorly in their schoolwork, became depressed and angry, and described themselves more negatively. The brown-eyed group grew mean, oppressing the others and making derogatory comments about them.

Stills from the film of Elliot's classroom experiment, in which wearing collars as an overt sign of low status was part of the discrimination sanctioned by the teacher

The next day, Elliott announced that she'd made a mistake and that it was really blue-eyed people who are superior. The pattern of prejudice and discrimination quickly switched from the blue-eyed as victims to the brown-eyed.

CHAPTER SUMMARY

- As an extreme attitude, **prejudice** comprises **cognitive (stereotype)**, **affective (hostility)** and **behavioural components**. **Discrimination** usually refers to any kind of prejudiced behaviour.

- Most definitions of prejudice identify it as the characteristic of an individual, but it's often associated with **intergroup conflict**. Racism, sexism, heterosexism and ageism can all be regarded as **ideologies**, which are characteristics of society, not individuals.

- The most influential 'individual' theory of prejudice is Adorno *et al.*'s **authoritarian personality**. Adorno *et al.* concluded that the authoritarian personality is prejudiced in a very **generalised** way. This reflects a personality structure which divides the world rigidly into 'us' and 'them', and a punitive, unloving upbringing, from which considerable repressed hostility towards the parents is **displaced** and **projected** onto minority groups.

- Methodological problems with these data include **acquiescent response set** and **experimenter bias**. A major theoretical problem is how a theory of individual differences can account for the uniformity of prejudice as found in Nazi Germany.

- Rokeach's theory of **ideological dogmatism** identifies authoritarianism as an extreme way of thinking (the 'closed mind'), rather than a particular political persuasion.

- According to Dollard *et al.*'s **frustration–aggression hypothesis**, frustration-induced aggression is often displaced onto minority groups, which act as **scapegoats**.

- **Relative deprivation theory** claims that we experience frustration when attainments fall short of expectations. **Fraternalistic relative deprivation** will produce intergroup hostility, particularly if there's a sudden shortfall of attainments.

- According to Sherif's **realistic conflict theory**, **competition** between groups for scarce resources is a sufficient condition for inter-group hostility. This was demonstrated in the Robber's Cave field experiment.

- **Minimal group experiments** demonstrate that inter-group conflict can occur without competition, and that the mere **categorisation** of oneself as belonging to one group rather than another is sufficient for intergroup discrimination.

- The minimal group effect is explained in terms of Tajfel's **social identity theory**, according to which we try to increase self-esteem by accentuating the desirability of our ingroup(s). Prejudice can be seen as part of the attempt to boost self-image.

- An important framework for attempts to reduce prejudice is Allport's **contact hypothesis**, which stresses the need for **equal status contact** and the **pursuit of common (superordinate) goals** between members of different ethnic groups.

- Group segregation can produce **autistic hostility** and the related **mirror-image phenomenon**, with the likely reinforcement of negative stereotypes. Unequal status contact can also reinforce stereotypes.

- While interpersonal contact can increase liking for the individuals involved, it rarely generalises to the ethnic group as a whole. When this does happen, it's because of changes in **intergroup relationship**s.

- Co-operative learning in the classroom has been studied using the **jigsaw method**, which creates **mutual interdependence** between students. Despite its undoubted benefits for individuals and interpersonal relationships, it's unclear whether these generalise to intergroup attitudes.

- Stereotypes (**category-driven processing**) are very resistant to change, because they often form part of the culture. They can be activated automatically/unconsciously, but may be broken if people are encouraged to focus on the unique characteristics of individuals (**attribute-driven processing**).

Self-assessment questions

1 Describe and evaluate **two** theories of the origins of prejudice.
2 Discuss explanations **and** research studies relating to the reduction of prejudice and/or discrimination.
3 Critically assess the claim that if you removed prejudice from individuals, you would be removing prejudice from society as a whole.

Web addresses

http://www.socialpsychology.org/social.html#prejudice

http://www.noctrl.edu/~ajomuel/crow/topicprejudice.htm

http://www.colorado.edu/conflict/peace/problem/prejudisc.htm

Further reading

Allport, G.W. (1954) *The Nature of Prejudice*. Reading, MA: Addison-Wesley. The classic work, which still inspires theory and research in the field.

Brown, R. (1995) *Prejudice: Its Social Psychology*. Oxford: Blackwell. Hewstone describes this a '… wonderful, up-to-date alternative to Gordon Allport's (1954) classic …'.

Paludi, M.A. (1992) *The Psychology of Women*. Debuque, Iowa: W.C.B. Brown & Benchmark. An excellent text for readers interested in sexism, in all its forms, including within psychology itself.

Chapter 26

Conformity and Group Influence

Introduction and overview

I t's impossible to live amongst other people and not be influenced by them in some way. According to Allport (1968), social psychology as a discipline can be defined as:

'... an attempt to understand and explain how the thoughts, feelings and behaviours of individuals are influenced by the actual, imagined, or implied presence of others'.

Sometimes, other people's attempts to change our thoughts or behaviour are very obvious, as when, for example, a traffic warden tells us not to park our car in a particular place. If we do as we're told and move the car, we're demonstrating *obedience*, which implies that one person (in this example, the traffic warden, an authority figure) has more social power than others (motorists). Obedience is discussed in Chapter 27.

In common with obedience, other forms of *active social influence* involve deliberate attempts by one person to change another's thoughts or behaviour. These include impression management (see Chapter 22), persuasive communication, propaganda and advertising (see Chapter 24). However, on other occasions social influence is less direct and deliberate, and may not involve any explicit requests or demands at all. For example, sometimes the mere presence of other people can influence our behaviour. This can take the form of *inhibiting* our behaviour, as in bystander intervention (see Chapter 30) or social loafing, or *enhancing* it, as in social facilitation. Both social loafing and social facilitation are discussed in Chapter 31 in relation to the social psychology of sport.

Another form of indirect or passive social influence occurs when your choice of clothes or taste in music is affected by what your friends wear or listen to. This is *conformity*. Your peers (equals) exert pressure on you to behave (and think) in particular ways, a case of the majority influencing the individual (*majority influence*). But majorities can also be influenced by minorities (*minority influence*). Related to conformity are other group processes, such as the *risky shift* phenomenon and *group polarisation*.

Is there anything that these different forms of social influence have in common? According to Turner (1991):

> 'The key idea in understanding what researchers mean by social influence is the concept of a social norm. Influence relates to the processes whereby people agree or disagree about appropriate behaviour, form, maintain or change social norms, and the social conditions that give rise to, and the effects of such norms …'.

Turner defines a *social norm* as:

> '… a rule, value or standard shared by the members of a social group that prescribes appropriate, expected or desirable attitudes and conduct in matters relevant to the group …'.

Conformity

What is conformity?

Conformity has been defined in a number of ways. For Crutchfield (1955), it is 'yielding to group pressure'. Mann (1969) agrees with Crutchfield, but argues that it may take different forms and be based on motives other than group pressure. Zimbardo & Leippe (1991) define conformity as:

> '… a change in belief or behaviour in response to real or imagined group pressure when there is no direct request to comply with the group nor any reason to justify the behaviour change'.

Ask yourself …

- What do these definitions have in common?

Group pressure is the common denominator in definitions of conformity, although none of them specifies particular groups with particular beliefs or practices. Pressure is exerted by those groups that are important to the individual at a given time. Such groups may consist of 'significant others', such as family or peers (*membership groups*), or groups whose values a person admires or aspires to, but to which s/he doesn't actually belong (*reference groups*).

Conformity, then, doesn't imply adhering to any particular set of attitudes or values. Instead, it involves yielding to the real or imagined pressures of any group, whether it has majority or minority status (van Avermaet, 1996).

Experimental studies of conformity

A study by Jenness (1932) is sometimes cited as the very first experimental study of conformity, although it's usually discussed in the context of social facilitation (see Chapter 31). Jenness asked individual students to estimate the number of beans in a bottle, and then had them discuss it to arrive at a group estimate. When they were asked individually to make a second estimate, there was a distinct shift towards the group's estimate. Sherif (1935) used a similar procedure in one of the classic conformity experiments.

KEY STUDY 26.1

If the light appears to move, it must be the Sherif (Sherif, 1935)

Sherif used a visual illusion called the *autokinetic effect*, whereby a stationary spot of light seen in an otherwise dark room *appears* to move (see Chapter 15).

He told participants that he was going to move the light and that their task was to say how far they thought the light moved. They were tested individually at first, being asked to estimate the extent of movement several times. The estimates fluctuated to begin with, but then 'settled down' and became quite consistent. However, there were wide differences between participants. They then heard the estimates of two other participants, which constituted the group situation. Under these conditions, the estimates of different participants *converged* (they became more *similar*). Thus, a *group norm* developed, which represented the average of the individual estimates.

Just as different individuals produced different estimates, so did different groups. This happened both under the conditions already described, and also when participants were tested in small groups right from the start.

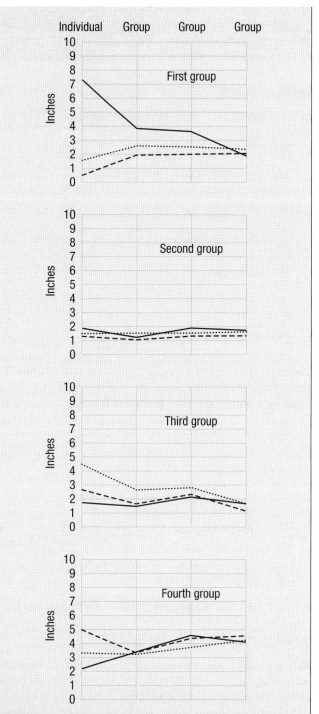

Figure 26.1 *Median judgements of the apparent movement of a stationary point of light given by participants in Sherif's (1935) experiment. In the data shown, participants first made their estimates alone ('individual'), and then in groups of three on three occasions ('group'). The figure shows the estimates given by four groups. Sherif also found that when the procedure was reversed, that is, participants made three estimates in groups followed by an estimate alone, the 'individual' estimates did not deviate from one another (from Sherif, 1936)*

According to Sherif, participants used others' estimates as a frame of reference in what was an ambiguous situation. Note that:

■ participants weren't in any way instructed to agree with the others in the group (unlike the Jenness study), despite initially wide differences between individuals;

■ when participants were tested again individually, their estimates closely resembled the group norm (rather than their original, individual, estimates).

Evaluating Sherif's experiment

According to Brown (1996), although Sherif's study is one of the classics of social psychology, it seems to raise questions rather than provide answers:

■ In what sense can Sherif's participants be described as a group?

■ Can we speak of group norms without any direct interaction taking place or participants seeing themselves as engaged in some kind of joint activity?

In post-experimental interviews, participants all denied being influenced by others' judgements. They also claimed that they struggled to arrive at the 'correct' answers on their own. In other words, they didn't consider themselves part of a group (although there's always doubt about taking participants' reports about the motivation for their behaviour at face value).

While Sherif believed he'd demonstrated conformity, others, notably Asch, disagreed. According to Asch, the fact that the task used by Sherif was *ambiguous* (there was no right or wrong answer) made it difficult to draw any definite conclusions about conformity. Conformity should be measured in terms of the individual's tendency to agree with other group members who unanimously give the *wrong answer* on a task where the solution is obvious or unambiguous. This is a much stricter test of conformity than where there's no correct or incorrect answer to begin with. Asch devised a simple perceptual task that involved participants deciding which of three comparison lines of different lengths matched a standard line.

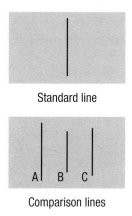

Standard line

Comparison lines

Figure 26.2 *Stimulus cards used in Asch's conformity experiments (1951, 1952, 1956)*

In a pilot study, Asch tested 36 participants individually on 20 slightly different versions of the task shown in Figure 26.2. They made a total of only three mistakes in the 720 trials (an error rate of 0.42 per cent).

> *Ask yourself ...*
>
> • What was the purpose of the pilot study? What conclusions do you think Asch drew from its results?

The purpose of the pilot study (which involved participants who weren't to take part in the actual experiment) was to establish that the task really was simple and the answers obvious and unambiguous. Asch concluded that they were. Because his procedure for studying conformity can be adapted to investigate the effects of different variables on conformity, it's known as the *Asch paradigm*.

Box 26.1 The Asch paradigm

Some of the participants who'd taken part in the pilot study were asked to act as 'stooges' (accomplices of the experimenter). The stooges were told they'd be doing the task again, but this time in a group. They were also told that the group would contain one person (a naïve participant) who was completely ignorant that they were stooges.

On certain critical trials, which Asch would indicate by means of a secret signal, all the stooges were required to say out loud the same wrong answer. In Asch's original experiment, the stooges (usually seven to nine of them) and the naïve participant were seated either in a straight line or round a table. The situation was rigged so that the naïve participant was always the last or last but one to say the answer out loud.

On the first two trials (neutral trials), all the stooges gave the correct answers. But the next trial was a critical trial (the stooges unanimously gave a wrong answer). This happened a further eleven times (making twelve critical trials in total), with four additional neutral trials (making six in total) between the critical trials.

The important measure in the Asch paradigm is whether the naïve participant conforms, and gives the same wrong answer as the unanimous stooges on the *critical* trials, or remains independent and gives the obviously correct answer. Asch found a *mean* conformity rate of 32 per cent; that is, participants agreed with the incorrect majority answer on about one-third of the critical trials.

A minority of one faces a unanimous majority. (Courtesy William Vandivert and Scientific American, November 1955)

As shown in Table 6.1, there were also wide individual differences in that:

- no one conformed on all the critical trials, and 13 of the 50 participants (26 per cent) never conformed;
- one person conformed on eleven of the twelve critical trials, and about three-quarters conformed at least once.

Table 26.1 *The findings from Asch's original experiment*

No of conforming responses made	No of people making those responses
0	13
1	4
2	5
3	6
4	3
5	4
6	1
7	2
8	5
9	3
10	3
11	1
12	0

Given that the task was simple and unambiguous, such findings indicate a high level of conformity. As van Avermaet (1996) has remarked:

'The results reveal the tremendous impact of an "obviously" incorrect but unanimous majority on the judgements of a lone individual'.

How did the naïve participants explain their behaviour?

When interviewed at length following the experiment, participants gave a number of specific reasons for conforming:

- Some wanted to act in accordance with the experimenter's wishes and convey a favourable impression of themselves by not 'upsetting the experiment' (which they believed they would have done by disagreeing with the majority); they thought some obscure 'mistake' had been made.
- A few, who had no reason to believe that there was anything wrong with their eyesight, genuinely doubted the validity of their own judgements by wondering if they were suffering from eye-strain or if their chairs had been moved so that they couldn't see the cards properly.
- Some denied being aware of having given incorrect answers – they'd unwittingly used the confederates as 'marker posts' (Smith, 1995).
- Others said they wanted to be like everyone else, didn't want to 'appear different', 'be made to look a fool', a 'social outcast' or 'inferior'. So, for these participants there was a discrepancy between the answer they gave in the group and what they *privately believed*: they knew the 'wrong' answer was wrong, but went along with it nonetheless.

Contrast this with Sherif's participants, for whom there was no conflict between the group's estimate and their own, individual estimates.

Factors affecting conformity

So far, we've described the original, basic experiment. Asch (1952, 1955) subsequently manipulated different variables in order to identify the crucial influences on conformity.

Size of the majority and unanimity

With one naïve participant and just one stooge, conformity was very low (about three per cent), ('it's my word against yours'). Where there were two stooges and one participant, conformity increased to 14 per cent, and with three stooges it reached the 32 per cent that Asch originally reported. But beyond three, conformity didn't continue to rise. This suggests that it's the *unanimity* of the majority which is important (the confederates all agree with each other), rather than the actual size of the majority (the number of confederates).

This was demonstrated when one of the stooges (a *dissenter*) agreed with the naïve participant. With one 'supporter', conformity dropped from 32 per cent to 5.5 per cent. Significantly, a dissenter who disagrees with *both* the naïve participant and the majority has almost as much effect on reducing conformity as one who gives the correct answer (that is, agrees with the naïve participant). In both cases, the majority is no longer unanimous. Thus, just *breaking the unanimity* of the majority is sufficient to reduce conformity (Allen & Levine, 1971). According to Asch (1951):

> '... a unanimous majority of three is, under the given conditions, far more effective than a majority of eight containing one dissenter ...'.

However, this reduction in conformity only seems to apply to unambiguous stimulus situations (like Asch's perceptual task), and not where opinions are being asked for (Allen & Levine, 1968).

Also, Gerard *et al.* (1968) and Latané & Wolf (1981) claim that adding more confederates *will* increase conformity, although the *rate of increase* falls with each extra majority member. Mann (1969) disagrees with Asch and these later studies by arguing for a *linear relationship* between group size and conformity: as group size increases, so conformity goes on increasing.

However, adding more members will produce more conformity only if the majority members are perceived as independent judges, and not as sheep following each other or as members of a group who've jointly reached a judgement. According to Hogg & Vaughan (1995), the most robust finding is that conformity reaches its full extent with a three-to-five-person majority, with additional members having little effect.

Fear of ridicule

In the original experiment, it seems that participants were justified in fearing that they'd be ridiculed by the rest of the group if they gave the answer they believed to be correct. When a group of 16 naïve participants and a single stooge were tested, the stooge's wrong answers on the critical trials were greeted with sarcasm, exclamations of disbelief and mocking laughter!

Task difficulty

When Asch made the comparison lines more similar in length, so that the task was more difficult, participants were more likely to yield to the incorrect majority answer. This was especially true when they felt confident that there was a right answer. When tasks are more ambiguous, in the sense that they involve expressing opinions or stating preferences (there's no objectively correct answer), conformity actually *decreases*.

Giving answers in private

Critics of Asch's experiment have pointed out that participants may conform because they're reluctant or too embarrassed to expose their private views in face-to-face situations (as many of them indicated in post-experimental inteviews). If so, the level of conformity should decrease if they're allowed to write their answers down, or where they remain anonymous in some other way. For example, Deutsch & Gerard (1955) used partitions which shielded participants from each other, with responses showing up on a light panel in front of them – the naïve participant had to press one of three buttons. Under these conditions, conformity was lower than in Asch's face-to-face situation. Indeed, when Asch himself allowed the naïve participant to answer in writing (while the confederates still gave their answers publicly), conformity dropped to 12.5 per cent.

Crutchfield (1954) also used a non-face-to-face procedure. He criticised Asch's experiments for being time-consuming and uneconomical, since only one participant could be tested at a time. So, he changed the experimental situation so that several (usually five) naïve participants could be tested at the same time. Altogether, he tested over 600.

Box 26.2 Testing conformity the Crutchfield way – private booths

Each participant sits in an open cubicle which has a panel with an array of lights and switches; neighbouring panels can't be seen. Questions, pictures and other kinds of stimuli are projected onto the wall, and participants are told that the lights on the display panel indicate the answers of other participants. In fact, everyone sees an identical display, and each believes that s/he is the last to respond. The answers are wrong on approximately half the trials.

Crutchfield presented a variety of tasks and conformity to the wrong answers differed according to the type of task involved.

- On the Asch-type perceptual judgement, he found 30 per cent conformity.
- When asked to complete a series of numbers (as in IQ tests), he also found 30 per cent conformity.
- When he presented a star which was obviously smaller in area than a circle (by about one-third), there was 46 per cent agreement that the *circle* was smaller than the star.
- Some of his participants were army officers attending a three-day assessment programme. Thirty-seven per cent of them agreed with the statement 'I doubt whether I would make a good leader' when it was presented in the booth, but significantly, none of them agreed with it when tested without reference to anyone else.

- A substantial proportion of college students agreed with statements which, under more 'normal' circumstances, they probably wouldn't have agreed with. For example: 'American males are, on average, taller than American females, by eight or nine inches'; 'the life expectancy of American males is only about 25 years'; 'Americans sleep four to five hours per night, on average, and eat six meals a day'; 'free speech being a privilege rather than a right, it is proper for a society to suspend free speech when it feels itself threatened'.

Replications of Asch's research

Were Asch's findings a reflection of the times?

The Asch studies have stimulated a great deal of research. Larsen (1974) found significantly lower conformity rates than Asch had found among groups of American students, and suggested that this was because of a changed climate of opinion in America in the 1970s towards independence and criticism and away from conformity. However, in a later (1979) study, Larsen *et al.* found results very similar to those of Asch. Perhaps the pendulum had begun to swing back again. Why might this have happened?

The early 1950s was the McCarthyism era in America. This is named after the US Senator Joseph McCarthy, who claimed to have unearthed an anti-American Communist plot. This resulted in a witch-hunt of alleged Communist sympathisers, which included academics and Hollywood stars. Under these social and political conditions, high conformity is to be expected (Spencer & Perrin, 1998). By the early 1970s, there was a more liberal climate, but this may have changed again by the late 1970s.

In Britain, Perrin & Spencer (1981) found very low rates of conformity among university students, during a period of self-expression and tolerance. As Spencer & Perrin (1998) say:

'The Asch findings are clearly an indicator of the prevailing culture'.

Ask yourself ...

- Perrin & Spencer (1981) tested young offenders on probation, with probation officers as stooges. How do you think conformity rates with these participants compared with those of Asch? Explain your answer.

We might expect the general social and political climate in Britain in the early 1980s to have had a different impact on university students than on young offenders. Additionally, the stooges were adult authority figures, which means that the group wasn't composed of peers (or equals). Not surprisingly, conformity rates were much higher than for the undergraduates and were similar to those reported by Asch.

It's also possible that experimenters exert an influence. As Brown (1985) has noted, experimenters may also have changed over time. Perhaps their expectations of the amount of conformity that will occur in an experiment are unwittingly conveyed to the participants, who respond accordingly (see Chapter 3, page 37).

Cross-cultural studies of conformity

As shown in Table 26.2, the vast majority of conformity studies using the Asch paradigm have been carried out in Britain and America. However, using a special statistical technique called *meta-analysis* (see Chapter 45), Bond & Smith (1996) were able to compare the British and American studies with the small number carried out in other parts of the world. After all relevant factors have been taken into account, the studies can be compared in terms of an *averaged effect size*, in this case, the conformity rate.

Table 26.2 *Asch conformity studies by national culture (based on Bond & Smith, 1996; taken from Smith & Bond, 1998)*

Nation	Number of studies	Averaged effect size
Asch's own US studies	18	1.16
Other US studies	79	0.90
Canada	1	1.37
UK	10	0.81
Belgium	4	0.91
France	2	0.56
Netherlands	1	0.74
Germany	1	0.92
Portugal	1	0.58
Japan	5	1.42
Brazil	3	1.60
Fiji	2	2.48
Hong Kong	1	1.93
Arab samples (Kuwait, Lebanon)	2	1.31
Africa (Zimbabwe, Republic of the Congo [Zaire], Ghana)	3	1.84

Ask yourself ...

- Are there any patterns in the conformity rates (averaged effect size) in Table 26.2? For example, are those countries with the highest and lowest conformity geographically and/or culturally related?

According to Smith & Bond (1998), the countries represented in Table 26.2 can be described as *individualist* (such as the US, the UK and other western European countries) or *collectivist* (such as Japan, Fiji and the African countries). In individualist cultures, one's identity is defined by personal choices and achievements, while in collectivist cultures it's defined in terms of the collective group one belongs to (such as the family or religious group). As might be expected, the tendency is for *more* conformity in *collectivist* cultures (see Box 26.4, page 388).

Majority or minority influence in Asch-type experiments?

Typically, the findings from experiments using the Asch paradigm have been interpreted as showing the impact of a (powerful) majority on the (vulnerable) individual (who's usually in a minority of one). While the stooges are, numerically, the majority, Asch himself was interested in the social and personal conditions that induce individuals to *resist* group pressure. (In 1950s' America, this group pressure took the form of McCarthyism: see page 384.)

Spencer & Perrin (1998) ask if reports of Asch's experiments have overstated the power of the majority to force minority individuals to agree with obviously mistaken judgements. Indeed, Moscovici & Faucheux (1972) argued that it's more useful to think of the naïve participant as the majority (s/he embodies the 'conventional', self-evident 'truth') and the stooges as the minority (they reflect an unorthodox, unconventional, eccentric and even outrageous viewpoint). In Asch's experiments, this minority influenced the majority 32 per cent of the time, and it's those participants remaining independent who are actually the conformists!

Is the majority always right?

Looked at from Moscovici and Faucheux's perspective, Asch-type experiments suggest how new ideas may come to be accepted (they explain *innovation*), rather than providing evidence about maintenance of the *status quo*. If groups always followed a majority decision rule ('the majority is always or probably right, so best go along with it'), or if social influence were about the inevitable conforming to the group, where would innovation come from? (Spencer & Perrin, 1998: see Box 26.3).

According to Moscovici (1976b), there's a *conformity bias* in this area of research, such that all social influence is seen as serving the need to adapt to the *status quo* for the sake of uniformity and stability. However, change is sometimes needed to adapt to changing circumstances, and this is very difficult to explain given the conformity bias. Without *active minorities*, social and scientific innovations would simply never happen (van Avermaet, 1996).

How do minorities exert an influence?

Moscovici (1976b) reanalysed the data from one of Asch's (1955) experiments, in which he varied the proportion of neutral to critical trials. In the original experiment this proportion was 1:2 (see Box 26.1). For example, when the proportion was 1:6, the conformity rate was 50 per cent, but when it was 4:1 it dropped to 26.2 per cent.

Moscovici interpreted these findings in terms of *consistency*. When there were more critical than neutral trials, the stooges (who embody the *minority* viewpoint) appear *more* consistent as a group, and this produces a *higher* conformity rate. They're more often agreeing with each other about something unconventional or novel, which makes it more likely that they'll change the views of the majority (as represented by the naïve participant). For example, Moscovici & Lage (1976) instructed a stooge minority of two to consistently describe a blue-green colour as green. The majority's views changed to that of the minority, and this effect persisted even when further colour judgements were asked for after the stooges left the experiment.

Although Moscovici's results haven't always been replicated, studies of minority influence show that it's achieved not so much by a particular style of behaviour in the group, but more by a combination of attributes and behaviour (Smith, 1995). Moscovici (1980) proposes that while majorities impose their views through directly requiring compliance (which often requires 'surveillance'), minorities use more *indirect* means to achieve a more lasting conversion, perhaps the most important behavioural style being consistency.

Box 26.3 **The importance of consistency and other factors in minority influence**

According to Hogg & Vaughan (1998), consistency has five main effects.

1 It disrupts the majority norm, producing uncertainty and doubt.
2 It draws attention to itself as an entity.
3 It conveys the existence of an alternative, coherent point of view.
4 It demonstrates certainty and an unshakeable commitment to a particular point of view.
5 It shows that the only solution to the current conflict is the minority viewpoint.

Minorities are more efficient if they:

- are seen to have made significant personal/material sacrifices (*investment*);
- are perceived as acting out of principle rather than ulterior motives (*autonomy*);
- display a balance between being 'dogmatic' (*rigid*) and 'inconsistent' (*flexible*);
- are seen as being *similar* to the majority in terms of age, gender and social category, particularly if they're categorised as part of the ingroup.

Why do people conform?

Different types of social influence

One very influential and widely accepted account of group influence is Deutsch & Gerard's (1955) distinction between *informational social influence* (ISI) and *normative social influence* (NSI).

Informational social influence (ISI)

Underlying ISI is the need to be right, to have an accurate perception of reality. So when we're uncertain or face an ambiguous situation, we look to others to help us perceive the stimulus situation accurately (or define the situation: see Chapter 30). This involves a *social comparison* with other group members in order to reduce the uncertainty.

As we saw earlier, Sherif's experiment involves an inherently *ambiguous* situation: there's no actual movement of the light, and so there can't be any right or wrong answers. Under these conditions, participants were only too willing to validate their own estimates by comparing them with those of others. The results were consistent with Sherif's *social reality hypothesis*, which states that:

'The less one can rely on one's own direct perception and behavioural contact with the physical world, the more susceptible one should be to influence from others ...'. (Turner, 1991)

According to Festinger's (1954) *social comparison theory*, people have a basic need to evaluate their ideas and attitudes and, in turn, to confirm that they're correct. This can provide a reassuring sense of control over one's world, and a satisfying sense of competence. In novel or ambiguous situations, social reality is defined by what others think and do. Significantly, Sherif's participants were relatively unaware of being influenced by the other judges (see page 381). As Turner (1991) observes:

'They appear to be largely unconsciously adjusting their judgement in the light of others' reports to arrive at a stable, agreed picture of a shared but initially unstructured world'.

Normative social influence (NSI)

Underlying NSI is the need to be accepted by other people and to make a favourable impression on them. We conform in order to gain social approval and avoid rejection – we agree with others because of their power to reward, punish, accept or reject us.

In Asch's experiment (and to a large extent in Crutchfield's too), most participants weren't unsure about the correct answer. Rather, they were faced with a *conflict* between two sources of information, which in unambiguous situations normally coincide, namely their own judgement and that of others. If they chose their own judgement, they risked rejection, ridicule and so on by the majority. Recall, though, that some participants were unaware of any conflict or of having given an incorrect response.

Internalisation and compliance

Related to ISI and NSI are two *kinds* of conformity:

■ *Internalisation* occurs when a private belief or opinion becomes consistent with a public belief or opinion. In other words, we say what we believe and believe what we say. Mann (1969) calls this *true conformity,* and it can be thought of as a *conversion* to other people's points of view, especially in *ambiguous* situations.

■ *Compliance* occurs when the answers given publicly aren't those that are privately believed (we say what we don't believe and what we believe we don't say). Compliance represents a compromise in situations where people face a *conflict* between what they privately believe and what others publicly say they believe.

Ask yourself ...

• Which kind of conformity was most common in Sherif's and Asch's experiments?
• How are internalisation and compliance related to NSI and ISI?

In Sherif's experiment, participants were *internalising* others' judgements and making them their own. Faced with an ambiguous situation, participants were guided by what others believed to reduce their uncertainty. So, internalisation is related to ISI.

By contrast, most of Asch's participants knew that the majority answers on the critical trials were wrong, but often agreed with them publicly. They were *complying* with the majority to avoid ridicule or rejection. So, compliance is related to NSI.

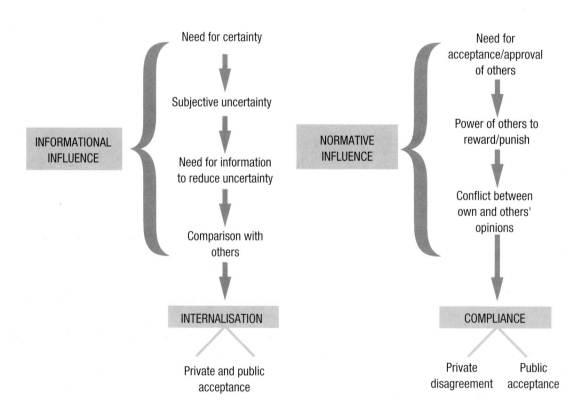

Figure 26.3 *The relationship between different kinds of influence and different kinds of conformity*

Do we have to choose between ISI and NSI?

While the ISI/NSI distinction has proved very influential, like all distinctions it faces the problem of false dichotomy: are they really separate, opposite forms of influence? A study by Insko *et al.* (1983) suggests that they can operate together.

KEY STUDY 26.2

The compatibility of ISI and NSI (Insko *et al.*, 1983)

Insko *et al.* had participants, in groups of six, judge whether a colour shown on a slide was more similar to another colour shown to the left or to one shown to the right.

On *critical* trials, four stooges who answered before the naïve participant, and another who answered last, gave answers which deviated from those given by most participants in a control condition who were tested alone.

There were two independent variables:

- participants answered either publicly or privately;
- the experimenter said that he either was or wasn't able to determine which response was more correct (in the 'determined' condition, he referred to an apparatus through which he could accurately measure which response was more correct; in the 'undetermined' condition, he said this was impossible).

Two hypotheses were tested:

- there will be greater conformity in the public than the private condition due to NSI;
- there will be greater conformity in the determined than the undetermined condition due to ISI.

Both hypotheses were confirmed. Also, the determined condition produced greater conformity in both private and public conditions, and all four conditions produced greater conformity than the control condition. Hence, even with 'objective stimuli', ISI can add to the effect of NSI (van Avermaet, 1996).

Remember that when Asch made the three comparison lines much more similar – and hence the task more difficult – conformity increased. Clearly, ISI was involved here. If we believe there's a correct answer and are uncertain what it is, it seems quite logical to expect that we'd be more influenced by a unanimous majority. This is why having a supporter or the presence of a dissenter has the effect of reducing conformity. By breaking the group consensus, the participant is shown both that disagreement is possible and that the group is fallible. As Turner (1991) puts it:

> '... the more consensual the group and the more isolated the individual (i.e. the less others agree with the deviant), the greater the power of the group to define reality, induce self-doubt in the deviant as to both her competence and social position, and threaten her with ridicule and rejection for being different'.

In other words, both informational and normative influence can operate in conjunction with each other, and shouldn't be seen as opposed processes of influence.

Scene from Twelve Angry Men, *starring Henry Fonda as the only dissenter in an (all-male) jury*

Conformity and group belongingness

The distinction between NSI and ISI has been called the *dual process dependency model* of social influence (e.g. Turner, 1991). But this model underestimates the role of group 'belongingness'. One important feature of conformity is that we're influenced by a group because, psychologically, we feel we belong to it. This is why a group's norms are relevant standards for our own attitudes and behaviour. The dual process dependency model emphasises the *interpersonal* aspects of conformity experiments, which could just as easily occur between individuals as group members.

The *self-categorisation approach* suggests that in Sherif's (1935) experiment, for example, participants assumed that the autokinetic effect was real, and expected to agree with each other. In support of this, it's been shown that when participants discover that the autokinetic effect is an illusion, mutual influence and convergence cease – the need to agree at all is removed (Sperling, 1946).

If, however, we believe that there's a correct answer, and we're uncertain what it is, then only those whom we categorise as belonging to 'our' group will influence our judgements. As Brown (1988) has remarked:

> 'There is more to conformity than simply "defining social reality": it all depends on who is doing the defining'.

KEY STUDY 26.3

Knowing what to think by knowing who you are (Abrams *et al.*, 1990)

Abrams *et al.* replicated Sherif's experiment with psychology students, but manipulated categorisation: stooges were introduced as students at a nearby university, but were either fellow psychology students or students of ancient history. Convergence only occurred when others were categorised as being equivalent to self, that is, a member of the ingroup (fellow psychology students). So self-categorisation may set limits on ISI.

It should also set limits on NSI, since individuals will presumably have a stronger desire to receive rewards, approval and acceptance from those categorised in the same way as themselves than from those categorised differently. Using the Asch paradigm but again manipulating categorisation, Abrams *et al.* found that conformity exceeded the usual level of 32 per cent in the ingroup condition, but was greatly below this level in the outgroup condition.

Abrams *et al.* (1990) argue that we only experience uncertainty when we disagree with those with whom we expect to agree. This is especially likely when we regard those others as members of the same category or group as ourselves with respect to judgements made in a shared stimulus situation. Social influence occurs, then, when we see ourselves as belonging to a group and possessing the same characteristics and reactions as other group members. Turner (1991) calls this kind of self-categorisation, in which group membership is relevant, *referent social influence*. What's important isn't the validation of physical reality or the avoidance of social disapproval, but the upholding of a group norm: people are the source of information about the appropriate ingroup norm.

Conformity: good or bad?

> *Ask yourself ...*
>
> - Is conformity always and necessarily desirable, and is failure to conform always and necessarily undesirable?

Sometimes, *dissent* is just an expression of disagreement, a refusal to 'go along with the crowd' (Maslach *et al.*, 1985). On other occasions, it's more creative or constructive, as when someone suggests a better solution to a problem. A refusal to 'go along with the crowd' may be an attempt to remain independent *as a matter of principle* (what Willis, 1963, calls *anticonformity*), and may betray a basic fear of a loss of personal identity.

According to Zimbardo & Leippe (1991), in most circumstances conformity serves a valuable social purpose in that it:

> '... lubricates the machinery of social interaction [and] enables us to structure our social behaviour and predict the reactions of others'.

For most people, though, the word 'conformity' has a *negative* connotation. As a result, it's been implicitly assumed that independence is 'good' and conformity is 'bad', a value judgement made explicit by Asch (1952). However, conformity can be highly functional, helping us to satisfy social and nonsocial needs, as well as being necessary (at least to a degree) for social life to proceed at all.

Since each of us has a limited (and often biased) store of information on which to make decisions, other people can often provide valuable additional information and expertise.

Conforming with others under these circumstances may be a *rational judgement*. However, while conformity can help preserve harmony:

> 'There are obvious dangers to conformity. Failure to speak our minds against dangerous trends or attitudes (for example, racism) can easily be interpreted as support'. (Krebs & Blackman, 1988)

Box 26.4 Japan: a strait-jacket society

The Japanese government is encouraging people to stop being so 'typically' Japanese. An advisory panel set up by the conservative prime minister, Keizo Obuchi, advocates that Japan must abandon its obsession with conformity and equality if it is to tackle its growing social problems, such as juvenile crime, suicide, bankruptcy and unemployment. This promotion of 'individual empowerment' represents a rejection of many of Japan's core values, but the country is desperate for spontaneity, innovation and ambition. In education, for example, the panel calls for action to curb 'the excessive degree of homogeneity and uniformity'. What the panel is recommending is a shift from collectivist to individualist values (see page 384).

Almost all Japanese school children aged up to 16 wear dark-blue sailor-style uniforms and follow the same rigid curriculum and textbooks (based on Watts, 2000)

The term conformity is often used to convey undesirable behaviour. In laboratory research, it has most often been studied in terms of the '... conspiratorial group ... [being] shown to limit, constrain, and distort the individual's response ...' (Milgram, 1965). However, in the context of his famous studies of obedience, Milgram showed that the presence of two defiant peers significantly reduced the obedience rate among naïve participants, and he wrote an article (1965) called 'Liberating effects of group pressure' (see Chapter 27).

Individual differences in conformity

Another way of trying to understand why people conform is to consider whether some people are more likely to conform than others and if so, why.

Crutchfield (1955) found that people who conform tend to be intellectually less effective, have less ego strength, less leadership ability, less mature social relationships and feelings of inferiority. They also tend to be authoritarian, more submissive, narrow-minded and inhibited, and have relatively little insight into their own personalities compared with those who tend not to conform. However, *consistency across situations* isn't high (McGuire, 1968), and the authoritarian personality (Adorno *et al.*, 1950: see Chapter 25) is perhaps as close to a 'conforming personality type' as can be found.

In general, men conform less than women. This is at least partly because men are traditionally more likely to see dissent or independence as a way of expressing their competence, while women tend to see co-operation and agreement with others as expressing competence (Zimbardo & Leippe, 1991: see Chapters 35 and 36). However, men with personal qualities and interests that are stereotypically 'feminine' conform as much as women with these same qualities and interests. Conversely, women and men with stereotypically 'masculine' qualities and interests conform less (Maslach *et al.*, 1987).

Other group processes

Risky shift

Based on the traditional interpretation of conformity studies as being concerned with majority influence and with how the *status quo* is maintained, the commonsense prediction is that groups, relative to individuals, will be more cautious and conservative. Convergence towards a group mean in Sherif's experiment is a clear demonstration of this prediction. However, Stoner (1961) found the opposite to be true. He presented participants with twelve *decision dilemmas* faced by hypothetical people, and their task was to advise the person about how much risk to take. Initially this was done individually, then in groups of about five.

To everyone's amazement, the group decisions were usually *riskier* than the individuals'. In other words, the group advised the hypothetical person to take a greater risk than the average of the individuals' advice (the *risky shift phenomenon*). Stoner sparked a wave of research into group decision-making, which initially found considerable support for risky shift, involving people of varying ages, occupations and from twelve different countries. However, it was eventually found that risky shift wasn't universal after all. It was possible to present decision dilemmas on which people became *more cautious* after discussion (Myers, 1994). So, is there a general principle that will predict how risky or cautious people's advice will be?

Group polarisation

In the context of decision dilemmas, there seems to be a strong tendency for discussion to accentuate individuals' initial leanings; that is, group discussion tends to enhance the individual's advice, whether this is risky or cautious. For this reason, risky shift came to be seen as part of a much wider phenomenon called *group polarisation* (Moscovici & Zavalloni, 1969). This is the tendency for groups to make decisions that are *more extreme* than the mean of individuals' initial positions, in the direction already favoured by that mean (Myers & Lamm, 1975; Wetherell, 1987). So, groups are likely to adopt more extreme views than individual members, but this can be in either a riskier or a more cautious direction. Why does it occur?

- According to Brown (1986), the mere exchange of information about which members made which decisions can produce polarisation. In discussion, group members may point out relevant information that others have missed and so may argue persuasively for its importance.
- Group members wish to define their identity more positively and distinctively, in contrast to members of other groups whom they might expect to adopt more average positions (Turner, 1991). This is supported by studies in which groups are told of the presumed decisions of other groups relevant to them (Smith, 1995).

Groupthink

Groupthink (Janis, 1971, 1982) is an example of how group decisions may become very extreme. Groupthink is defined as a mode of thinking, in which the desire to reach unanimous agreement over-rides the motivation to adopt proper, rational, decision-making procedures. Using archive material (people's retrospective accounts and content analysis), Janis analysed how the decisions were taken that led to certain major political/military fiascos, such as Pearl Harbor (1941), the Bay of Pigs invasion of Cuba (1961) which led to the Cuban Missile Crisis (1962), and the Vietnam War.

It's been suggested that groupthink is merely a specific instance of risky shift, in which a group that already tends towards making risky decisions polarises, through discussion, to an even riskier one (Myers & Lamm, 1975). Janis believes that groupthink stems from an excessively cohesive, closeknit group, the suppression of dissent in the interests of group harmony, and a directive leader who signals what decisions he or she favours.

Conclusions

Conformity represents a form of social influence in which our peers steer us, unwittingly, towards a particular way of thinking or behaving. Thinking like our peers, or merely acting like them, reflects different kinds of social influence and different kinds of conformity. While these aren't mutually exclusive, it's generally diffcult to remain 'completely independent of others' opinions, especially those whose opinions matter to us. However, majorities aren't necessarily all-powerful; indeed, minority influence is crucial for innovation and change.

CHAPTER SUMMARY

- **Social influence** can be **active** or **deliberate**, as in persuasive communication and obedience, or **passive** or **non-deliberate**, as in social facilitation and conformity. A common feature of all social influence is the concept of a **social norm**.
- Definitions of **conformity** commonly refer to **group pressure**, whether the group is a **membership** or a **reference group**.
- In Sherif's experiment using the **autokinetic effect**, individual estimates **converged** to form a **group norm**. Asch criticised Sherif's use of an ambiguous task, and in his own experiments used a comparison of lines task for which there was a correct answer.

- Asch found that the **unanimity/consensus of the majority** is crucial, not its size. The presence of a supporter or a dissenter both reduce conformity, because the majority is no longer unanimous.
- Conformity is increased when the task is made more difficult (more ambiguous), and reduced when participants give their answer anonymously. However, Crutchfield found that conformity rate still differs according to the type of task.
- Replications of Asch's experiment have produced higher or lower rates of conformity according to when and where they were conducted. Both **socio-historical** and **cultural factors** seem to play a part.
- Asch's findings are usually interpreted as showing the impact of **majority influence**. But Moscovici believes that the stooge majority should be thought of as embodying unconventional, minority beliefs, and that conformity experiments show how new ideas come to be accepted (**innovation**).
- One way in which **minority influence** works is by displaying **consistency**, together with **investment**, **autonomy** and a balance between **rigidity** and **flexibility**.
- Two major motives for conformity are the need to be right (**informational social influence**/ISI) and the need to be accepted by others (**normative social influence**/NSI).
- ISI is related to Sherif's **social reality hypothesis** and Festinger's **social comparison theory** and is demonstrated through **internalisation/true conformity**. NSI is linked to **compliance**.
- ISI and NSI aren't opposed forms of influence, but the **dual process dependency model** tends to emphasise the **interpersonal** aspects of conformity experiments. In contrast, **referent social influence** stresses the importance of **group membership** and **self-categorisation**.
- Despite evidence of **individual differences** in the tendency to conform, there's unlikely to be a 'conforming personality'.
- While **independence** is often seen as preferable to conformity, conformity also serves an important social function. Milgram has shown how it can have liberating effects in an obedience situation.
- Evidence for the **risky shift phenomenon** is mixed. It has come to be seen as part of **group polarisation**, in which group decisions tend to become more extreme than the mean of individuals' initial positions. One demonstration of group polarisation is **groupthink**, which stems from excessively cohesive groups with a directive leader.

Self-assessment questions

1 Discuss psychological research into why people conform.
2 'The majority opinion will always dominate the views of those who may initially hold alternative views.'
   To what extent does research into minority influence support this view?
3 Critically assess the claim that conformity is both inevitable and undesirable.

Web addresses

http://www.psych.upenn./edu/sacsec/text/about.htm

http://longman.awl.com/aronson/student/activities/aschconformityexperiment.asp

http://www.muskingum.edu/~psychology/psycweb/history/milgram.htm

http://www.cultsock.ndirect.co.uk/muhorne/cshtml/soc.inf/minority.html

Further reading

Milgram, S. (1992) *The Individual In A Social World: Essays and Experiments* (2nd edition.). New York: McGraw-Hill. While not exclusively devoted to social influence, this is a fascinating collection of reprinted journal articles and other papers revealing the creative mind of a very important researcher who died, prematurely, in 1984. Also relevant to Chapter 27.

Turner, J.C. (1991) *Social Influence.* Milton Keynes: Open University Press. A short but thorough discussion of all the main aspects of the topic, by one of the leading figures in the field.

Chapter 27

Obedience

Introduction and overview

As we saw at the beginning of Chapter 26, obedience is the result of an active or deliberate form of social influence, which involves someone in authority requiring us to behave in a particular way in a particular situation. If we obey, we are said to be *complying* with the authority figure's request or instruction. We also discussed *compliance* as a major kind of conformity, namely one in which overt behaviour doesn't reflect private beliefs.

Compliance also occurs whenever we do what someone else 'asks' us to do, that is, whenever people make direct requests, such as when a friend asks us for a 'favour' or a salesperson 'invites' us to try a product or service. Many researchers believe that attempts to gain compliance through direct requests is the most common form of social influence (Hogg & Vaughan, 1995).

Cialdini (1988) reviewed social influence strategies used by salespeople trying to sell a product. These include using:

- the *norm of reciprocity*: Giving away a free sample or a free estimate for a job may put the customer under a sense of obligation. This is based on the social norm that 'we should treat others the way they treat us'. This can apply to other relationships too, as in the belief that 'one good turn deserves another';
- the *'foot in the door' tactic*: Getting someone to agree to a small request makes them more likely to comply with a larger request at some later point, than if the larger request had been made initially. This can be explained partly in terms of people's need to appear consistent – both to themselves and others (see Chapter 24). According to Hogg & Vaughan (1995), this represents one of three multiple-request tactics, whereby an initial request functions as a set-up for a second (real) request. The other two are:
  - the *'door-in-the-face' tactic*, in which the initial request is large and unreasonable and is followed up with a second, much more reasonable request, which is more difficult to refuse; and
  - the *'low-ball'* tactic. For example, having induced a customer to commit him/herself to a purchase, the salesperson then reveals certain hidden costs that weren't previously mentioned. (The term comes from US baseball; in the UK, we might talk of 'moving the goal posts'.);
- *ingratiation*: Agreeing with others and in other ways showing how we're similar to them is an attempt to show what attractive and competent people we are. These are all designed to get them to like us, and ingratiation is often the first step in the influence process.

Like the demands of an authority figure, these tactics (some more subtle than others) are active and deliberate attempts to make us behave in particular ways. Unlike both obedience and conformity, there's no obvious 'penalty' to pay for not complying. And as we find in some obedience and conformity situations, the salesperson may be perceived as an expert with access to information (and goods/services) that we need. So, it's clear that the forms of social influence share many characteristics.

Distinguishing between conformity and obedience

According to Milgram (1992), both conformity and obedience involve the '... abdication of individual judgement in the face of some external social pressure ...'. However, there are three major *differences* between them.

- In conformity, there's no explicit requirement to act in a certain way, whereas in obedience we're being ordered or instructed to do something.
- In conformity, those who influence us are our *peers* (*equals*) and people's behaviour becomes more *alike* (*homogenisation of behaviour*). In obedience, there's a *difference in status* from the outset, with the authority figure influencing another person with inferior power or status: there's *no mutual influence*.
- Conformity has to do with the psychological 'need' for acceptance by others, and entails going along with one's peers in a group situation. Obedience has to do with the social power and status of an authority figure in a hierarchical situation. Although we typically deny that we conform (because it seems to detract from our sense of *individuality*), we usually deny *responsibility* for our behaviour in the case of obedience ('He made me do it', or 'I was only doing what I was told').

In addition, Brown (1986) says that conformity behaviour is affected by *example* (from peers or equals), while obedience is affected by *direction* (from somebody in higher authority).

Experimental studies of obedience

In the experiments of Sherif, Asch and Crutchfield (see Chapter 25), participants showed conformity by giving a verbal response of some kind, or pressing buttons representing answers on various tasks. In the most famous and controversial of all obedience experiments, Milgram's participants were required to 'kill' another human being.

Milgram's research

Milgram was attempting to test 'the "Germans are different" hypothesis'. This has been used by historians to explain the systematic destruction of millions of Jews, Poles and others by the Nazis during the 1930s and 1940s. It maintains that:

- Hitler couldn't have put his evil plans into operation without the co-operation of thousands of others; and
- the Germans have a basic character defect, namely a readiness to obey authority without question regardless of the acts demanded by the authority figure. It's this readiness to obey which provided Hitler with the co-operation he needed.

It's really the second part of the hypothesis which Milgram was trying to test. After piloting his research in America, he planned to continue it in Germany. But his results showed this was unnecessary.

The participants

The participants in the original (1963) experiment were 20–50-year-old men, from all walks of life. They answered advertisements that came by post or appeared in local newspapers, which asked for volunteers for a study of learning to be conducted at Yale University. It would take about one hour, and there'd be a payment of $4.50.

Public Announcement

WE WILL PAY YOU $4.00 FOR ONE HOUR OF YOUR TIME

Persons Needed for a Study of Memory

*We will pay five hundred New Haven men to help us complete a scientific study of memory and learning. The study is being done at Yale University.

*Each person who participates will be paid $4.00 (plus 50c carfare) for approximately 1 hour's time. We need you for only one hour: there are no further obligations. You may choose the time you would like to come (evenings, weekdays, or weekends).

*No special training, education, or experience is needed. We want:

Factory workers	Businessmen	Construction workers
City employees	Clerks	Salespeople
Laborers	Professional people	White-collar workers
Barbers	Telephone workers	Others

All persons must be between the ages of 20 and 50. High school and college students cannot be used.

*If you meet these qualifications, fill out the coupon below and mail it now to Professor Stanley Milgram, Department of Psychology, Yale University, New Haven. You will be notified later of the specific time and place of the study. We reserve the right to decline any application.

*You will be paid $4.00 (plus 50c carfare) as soon as you arrive at the laboratory.

— —

TO:
PROF. STANLEY MILGRAM, DEPARTMENT OF PSYCHOLOGY, YALE UNIVERSITY, NEW HAVEN, CONN. I want to take part in this study of memory and learning. I am between the ages of 20 and 50. I will be paid $4.00 (plus 50c carfare) if I participate.

NAME (Please Print). . . . .

ADDRESS . . . .

TELEPHONE NO. . . . . Best time to call you . . . .

AGE. . . . . . . OCCUPATION. . . . . SEX . . . . . .
CAN YOU COME:

WEEKDAYS . . . . EVENINGS . . . . . . WEEKENDS . . . .

Figure 27.1 *Announcement placed in a local newspaper to recruit participants (from Milgram, 1974)*

The basic procedure

Box 27.1 **The basic procedure used in Milgram's obedience experiment**

When participants arrived at Yale University psychology department, they were met by a young man in a grey laboratory coat, who introduced himself as Jack Williams, the experimenter. Also present was a Mr Wallace, introduced as another participant, in his late fifties, an accountant, a little overweight and generally a very mild and harmless-looking man. In fact, Mr Wallace was a stooge, and everything that happened after this was preplanned, staged and scripted: everything, that is, except the degree to which the real participant obeyed the experimenter's instructions.

The participant and Mr Wallace were told that the experiment was concerned with the effects of punishment on learning. One of them was to be the teacher and the other the learner. Their roles were determined by each drawing a piece of paper from a hat: both, in fact, had 'teacher' written on them. Mr Wallace drew first and called out 'learner', so, of course, the real participant was always the teacher.

They all went into an adjoining room, where Mr Wallace was strapped into a chair with his arms attached to electrodes, which would deliver a shock from the shock generator situated in an adjacent room. The teacher and experimenter then moved next door, where the genera-

tor was situated. The teacher was given a 45-volt shock to convince him that it was real, for he was to operate the generator during the experiment. However, that was the only real shock that either the teacher or the learner was to receive throughout the entire experiment.

The generator had a number of switches, each clearly marked with voltage levels and verbal descriptions, starting at 15 volts and going up to 450 in intervals of 15:

15–60	Slight shock
75–120	Moderate shock
135–180	Strong shock
195–240	Very strong shock
255–300	Intense shock
315–360	Intense to extreme shock
375–420	Danger: severe shock
435–450	XXX

The teacher had to read out a series of word pairs (e.g. 'blue–girl', 'nice–day', 'fat–neck'), and then the first of one pair (the stimulus word) followed by five words, of which one was the original paired response. The learner had to choose the correct response to the stimulus word by pressing one of four switches, which turned on a light on a panel in the generator room. Each time he made a mistake, the teacher had to deliver a shock, and each successive mistake was punished by a shock 15 volts higher than the one before.

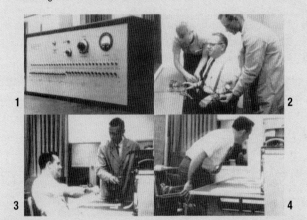

Figure 27.2 *1 Shock generator used in the experiments. Fifteen of the 30 switches have already been depressed. 2 Learner is strapped into chair and electrodes are attached to his wrist. Electrode paste is applied by the experimenter. 3 Subject receives sample shock from the generator. 4 Subject breaks off experiment. (Copyright 1965 by Stanley Milgram from the film Obedience, distributed by the Pennsylvania State University, Audio Visual Services.) (From Milgram, 1974)*

Milgram had asked 14 psychology students to predict what would happen for 100 participants in this situation. They thought that a few would break off early on, most would stop somewhere in the middle and a few would continue right up to 450 volts. He also asked 40 psychiatrists, who predicted that, on average, less than one per cent would administer the highest voltage.

These estimates were based on what Milgram called the *remote-victim condition*, which was the first of a series of 18 different experiments, all variations on the same basic theme. In this particular experiment, Mr Wallace was scripted to pound loudly on the wall at 300 volts and, after 315 volts, to stop pounding and *give no further answers*. In the second experiment (*voice feedback*), teachers heard a tape-recorded series of verbal responses, which they believed were the spontaneous reactions of Mr Wallace to the increasing shock levels:

At 75, 90 and 105 volts, he made a little grunt.

At 120 volts, he shouted to the experimenter that the shocks were becoming painful.

At 135 volts, he made pained groans.

At 150 volts, he cried out, 'Experimenter, get me out of here! I won't be in the experiment any more! I refuse to go on!' This continued with rising intensity until at 180 volts, he shouted, 'I can't stand the pain!'.

At 270 volts, he let out an agonised scream. (He continued to insist on being released.)

At 300 volts, he shouted desperately that he would no longer provide answers.

At 315 volts, he let out a violent scream, reaffirming vehemently that he was no longer participating.

After 330 volts, ominous silence!

The teacher was instructed to treat no response as if it were an incorrect response, so the shocks could continue beyond 300 volts. In addition, the experimenter had a script prepared for whenever the teacher refused to continue or showed any resistance or reluctance to do so:

■ 'Please continue' or 'Please go on';
■ 'The experiment requires that you continue';
■ 'It's absolutely essential that you continue';
■ 'You have no other choice, you must go on'.

There were also 'special prods' to reassure the participant that s/he wasn't doing the learner any permanent harm: 'Although the shocks may be painful there is no permanent tissue damage, so please go on'.

Ask yourself ...

• If you'd been one of Milgram's teacher–participants, how far up the voltage scale would you have continued to punish 'wrong answers'?

The results

In the first (remote-victim) experiment, every teacher shocked up to at least 300 volts, and *65 per cent* went all the way up to 450 volts. In the voice-feedback condition, *62.5 per cent* of participants went on giving shocks up to 450 volts.

Many displayed great anguish, attacked the experimenter verbally, twitched nervously or broke out into nervous laughter. Many were observed to:

> '... sweat, stutter, tremble, groan, bite their lips and dig their nails into their flesh. Full-blown, uncontrollable seizures were observed for three subjects'. (Milgram, 1974)

Indeed, one experiment had to be stopped because the participant had a violently convulsive seizure.

To determine *why* the obedience levels were so high, Milgram conducted several variations using the voice-feed-

back condition as his baseline measure. In all, a further 16 variations were performed.

KEY STUDY 27.1

Some variations on Milgram's basic procedure

Institutional context (variation 10): In interviews following the first experiment, many participants said they continued delivering shocks because the research was being conducted at Yale University, a highly prestigious institution. So, Milgram transferred the experiment to a run-down office in downtown Bridgeport.

Proximity and touch proximity (variations 3 and 4): In the original procedure, the teacher and learner were in adjacent rooms and couldn't see one another. But in variation 3 they were in the same room (about 1.5 ft/46 cm apart), and in variation 4 the teacher was required to force the learner's hand down onto the shock plate.

Remote authority (variation 7): The experimenter left the room (having first given the essential instructions), and gave subsequent instructions by telephone.

Two peers rebel (variation 17): The teacher was paired with two other (stooge) teachers. The stooge teachers read out the list of word-pairs, and informed the learner whether the response was correct. The naïve participant delivered the shocks. At 150 volts, the first stooge refused to continue and moved to another part of the room. At 210 volts, the second stooge did the same. The experimenter ordered the real teacher to continue.

A peer administers the shocks (variation 18): The teacher was paired with another (stooge) teacher and had only to read out the word-pairs (the shock being delivered by the stooge).

Ask yourself ...

• For each of the variations described in Key Study 27.1, estimate the rates of total obedience (those participants going all the way up to 450 volts), and try to explain why it might have been higher or lower than the 62.5 per cent in the voice-feedback condition.

■ In variation 10, the obedience rate was 47.5 per cent. This still very high figure suggests that the institutional context played some part, but wasn't a crucial factor.

■ In variation 3, the obedience rate dropped to 40 per cent, and in variation 4 it dropped further to 30 per cent. While it became much more uncomfortable for participants to see – as well as hear – the effects of their obedience, the figures are still very high.

■ In variation 7, obedience dropped to 20.5 per cent. Indeed, participants often pretended to deliver a shock or delivered one lower than they were asked to. This suggests that they were trying to compromise between their conscience and the experimenter's instructions. In his absence, it was easier to follow their conscience.

- In variation 17, there was only ten per cent obedience. Most stopped obeying when the first or second stooge refused to continue. According to Milgram (1965):

> 'The effects of peer rebellion are most impressive in undercutting the experimenter's authority'.

In other words, seeing other participants (our peers) disobey shows that it's *possible* to disobey, as well as *how* to disobey. Indeed, some participants said they didn't realise they *could*. This is a demonstration of the effects of *conformity*.

- In variation 18, obedience rose to 92.5 per cent. This shows that it's easier for participants to shift responsibility from themselves to the person who actually 'throws the switch'.

So why do people obey?

According to Milgram (1974):

> 'The most fundamental lesson of our study is that ordinary people simply doing their jobs, and without any particular hostility on their part, can become agents in a terrible destructive process'.

Unless there's reason to believe that people who go all the way up to 450 volts are especially sadistic and cruel, or are unusually obedient (which 'the "Germans are different" hypothesis' claimed about a whole nation), explanations of obedience must look 'outside' the individual participant. In this way, the emphasis is shifted away from personal characteristics to the characteristics of the *social situation:* most people facing that situation would probably act in a similar (obedient) way. What might some of these situational factors be?

Personal responsibility

Many participants raised the issue of responsibility for any harm to the learner. Although the experimenter didn't always discuss this, when he did say 'I'm responsible for what goes on here', participants showed visible relief. Indeed, when participants are told that *they* are responsible for what happens, obedience is sharply reduced (Hamilton, 1978).

Milgram saw this *diffusion of responsibility* as crucial to understanding the atrocities committed by the Nazis, and Eichmann's defence that he was 'just carrying out orders'. (Eichmann was in charge of the transportation of Jews and others to extermination camps, and was eventually tried in Jerusalem, in 1960). It can also explain the behaviour of William Calley, an American soldier who was court-martialed for the 1968 massacre by troops under his command of several hundred Vietnamese civilians at My Lai.

The perception of legitimate authority

As we mentioned earlier, many participants showed signs of distress and conflict, and so diffusion of responsibility can't tell the whole story. The conflict seems to be between two opposing sets of demands – the external authority of the experimenter who says 'Shock' and the internal authority of the conscience which says, 'Don't shock'. The point at which conscience triumphs is, of course, where the participant (finally) stops obeying the experimenter, who, in a sense, *ceases* to be a legitimate authority in the eyes of the participant. Thirty-five per cent in the original experiment

reached that point somewhere before 450 volts, and for many, the crucial 'prod' was when the experimenter said, 'You have no other choice, you *must* go on'. They were able to exercise the choice which, of course, they had from the start.

The most common mental adjustment in the obedient participant is to see him-/herself as an agent of external authority (the *agentic state*). This represents the opposite of an *autonomous state*, and is what makes it possible for us to function in a hierarchial social system. For a group to function as a whole, individuals must give up responsibility and defer to others of higher status in the social hierarchy. Legitimate authority thus replaces a person's own self-regulation (Turner, 1991). In Milgram's (1974) words:

> 'The essence of obedience consists in the fact that a person comes to view himself as the instrument for carrying out another person's wishes, and he, therefore, no longer regards himself as responsible for his actions. Once this critical shift of viewpoint has occurred in the person, all the essential features of obedience follow'.

> ### Ask yourself ...
>
> - What was it about Jack Williams, the experimenter, which conveyed to participants that he was 'in charge' in the experimental situation?

One of the many statues of Lenin brought crashing down in Eastern Europe after the collapse of Communism in 1989

Authority figures often possess highly visible symbols of their power or status that make it difficult to refuse their commands. In Milgram's experiments, the experimenter always wore a grey laboratory coat to indicate his position as an authority figure. The impact of such 'visible symbols' was demonstrated by Bickman (1974). When people were told by a stooge wearing a guard's uniform to pick up a paper bag or give a coin to a stranger, obedience was higher (80 per cent) than when the order was given by a stooge in civilian clothes (40 per cent). Similarly, a stooge wearing a firefighting uniform was obeyed more often than a stooge dressed as a civilian, even though the request (to give someone a dime) had nothing to do with the authority role in question (Bushman, 1984). For Milgram (1974):

> '*A substantial proportion of people do what they are told to do, irrespective of the content of the act and without limitations of conscience, so long as they perceive that the command comes from a legitimate authority*'.

Another major study which demonstrates the impact of uniforms and other symbols of authority is Zimbardo *et al.*'s (1973) 'prison simulation experiment', which is discussed on pages 398–399.

The 'foot in the door' and not knowing how to disobey

According to Gilbert (1981), Milgram's participants may have been 'sucked in' by the series of graduated demands. These began with the 'harmless' advertisement for volunteers for a study of learning and memory, and ended with the instruction to deliver what appeared to be potentially lethal electric shocks to another person. Having begun the experiment, participants may have found it difficult to remove themselves from it.

Ask yourself ...

- If the original advertisement had mentioned electric shocks, do you think there would have been many volunteers? In what ways might such volunteers have constituted a more biased sample than those who participated in the actual experiments?

Presumably, fewer volunteers would have come forward. Those who did may well have been more sadistic than Milgram's sample (assuming that they believed they'd be giving the electric shocks).

Socialisation

Despite our expressed ideal of independence, obedience is something we're socialised into from a very early age by significant others (including our parents and teachers). Obedience may be an *ingrained habit* that's difficult to resist (Brown, 1986).

An evaluation of Milgram's research

In evaluating Milgram's experiments, *ethical issues* are usually more prominent than scientific ones. These are discussed in detail in Chapter 48. However, Milgram asks whether the ethical criticisms are based as much on the nature of the (unexpected) results as on the procedure itself. Aronson (1988) asks if we'd question the ethics if none of the participants had gone beyond the 150-volt level, which is the point at which most people were expected to stop (according to Milgram's students and the 40 psychiatrists he consulted).

Aronson manipulated the results experimentally, and found that the higher the percentage going right up to 450 volts, the more harmful the effects of the experiment are judged to be.

Methodological issues

One criticism is that Milgram's sample was unrepresentative of the American population. However, a total of 636 participants were tested (in the 18 separate experiments as a whole), representing a cross-section of the population of New Haven, thought to be a fairly typical small American town. But Milgram admits that those who went on obeying up to 450 volts were more likely to see the learner as responsible for what happened to him, and not themselves! They seemed to have a stronger authoritarian character and a less advanced level of moral development. But as Rosenthal & Rosnow (1966) and others have found, people who volunteer for experiments are, on the whole, considerably *less authoritarian* than those who don't.

While only 40 women were included in Milgram's sample (Experiment 8), they showed a 65 per cent obedience rate, just like their male counterparts.

According to Orne & Holland (1968), Milgram's experiments lack *experimental realism*, that is, participants might not have believed the experimental set-up they found themselves in, and knew the learner wasn't really being given electric shocks. However, a study by Sheridan & King (1972) seems to exclude this possibility.

KEY STUDY 27.2

Obedience training for puppies (Sheridan & King, 1972)

Students trained a puppy to learn a discrimination task by punishing it with increasingly severe and real electric shocks whenever it made an error. Although the puppy actually received only a small shock, the participants could see it and hear its squeals.

After a time, an odourless anaesthetic was released into the puppy's cage, causing it to fall asleep. Although participants complained about the procedure (and some even cried), they were reminded that the puppy's failure to respond was a punishable error, and that they should continue to give shocks. Seventy-five per cent of participants delivered the maximum shock possible.

Orne & Holland (1968) also criticised Milgram's experiments for their lack of *mundane realism*, that is, the results don't extend beyond the particular laboratory setting in which they were collected. They base this claim on the further claim that cues in the experimental setting influenced the participants' perceptions of what was required of them. Obedience, then, might simply have been a response to the *demand characteristics* (see Chapter 3) of the highly unusual experimental setting. However, naturalistic studies of obedience dispute this.

KEY STUDY 27.3

A naturalistic study of nurses (Hofling *et al.*, 1966)

Twenty-two nurses working in various American hospitals received telephone calls from a stooge 'Dr Smith of the psychiatric department', instructing them to give Mr Jones (Dr Smith's patient) 20 mg of a drug called *Astrofen*. Dr Smith said that he was in a desperate hurry, and would sign the drug authorisation form when he came to see the patient in ten minutes' time.

The label on the box containing the *Astrofen* (which was actually a harmless sugar pill) clearly stated that the maximum daily dose was 10 mg. So, if the nurse obeyed Dr Smith's instructions she would be exceeding the maximum daily dose. Also, she would be breaking the rules requiring written authorisation before any drug is given and that a nurse be absolutely sure that 'Dr Smith' is a genuine doctor.

Ask yourself ...

• What do you think you'd have done if you'd been one of the nurses?

In interviews, 22 graduate nurses who hadn't participated in the actual experiment were presented with the same situation as an issue to discuss; 21 said they wouldn't have given the drug without written authorisation, especially as it exceeded the maximum daily dose.

A real doctor was posted nearby, unseen by the nurse, and observed what the nurse did following the telephone call. Twenty-one out of the 22 nurses complied without hesitation, and eleven later said they hadn't noticed the dosage discrepancy!

But could the unfamiliarity of *Astrofen* (a dummy drug, invented for the purposes of the experiment) have influenced the nurses' responses? Also, Hofling *et al.* failed to report what proportion of nurses actually tried to check the instruction with fellow nurses or superiors – they reported only the number of those who (eventually) complied.

Rank & Jacobson (1977) repeated the experiment, but with two important changes:

■ they recorded any checking that nurses did;
■ they changed the prescription to 30 mg of *Valium*, with which they were familiar.

Under these conditions, only two out of 18 nurses were prepared to administer the drug without any checking; ten prepared the drug but then tried to recontact the doctor, pharmacy, or a supervisor; and six tried to check the order before preparing the drug. The limitations of Hofling *et al.*'s experiment, therefore, offer only modest support to Milgram.

A further methodological criticism concerns the *cross-cultural replicability* of Milgram's findings (see Table 27.1).

Unfortunately, it's very difficult to compare these studies because of methodological discrepancies between them (Smith & Bond, 1998). For example, different types of stooges were used (e.g. a 'long-haired student' in Kilham and Mann's

study), some of whom may have been perceived as more vulnerable – or more deserving of shocks – than others. In the Meeus and Raajimakers study, the task involved participants having to harass and criticise someone who was completing an important job application.

Table 27.1 *Cross-cultural replications of Milgram's obedience experiment (adapted from Smith & Bond, 1998)*

Study	Country	Participants	Percentage obedient
Ancona & Pareyson (1968)	Italy	Students	85
Kilham & Mann (1974)	Australia	Male students	40
		Female students	16
Burley & McGuiness (1977)	UK	Male students	50
Shanab & Yahya (1978)	Jordan	Students	62
Miranda *et al.* (1981)	Spain	Students	over 90
Schurz (1985)	Austria	General population	80
Meeus & Raajimakers (1986)	The Netherlands	General population	92

While Milgram found no gender differences (as noted above), the Australian female students were asked to shock another *female* (but the learner was always *male* in Milgram's experiments). Also, with the exception of Jordan (Shanab & Yahya, 1978), all the countries studied have been Western industrialised nations, so we should be cautious when concluding that a universal aspect of social behaviour has been identified. But Smith and Bond (1998) observe that:

> *'In none of the countries studied is obedience to authority the kind of blind process that some interpreters of Milgram's work have implied. Levels of obedience can and do vary greatly, depending on the social contexts that define the meaning of the orders given'.*

Issues of generalisation

As we noted earlier, Orne & Holland (1968), along with several other researchers, have argued that Milgram's experiments lack mundane realism (or *external* or *ecological validity*). But Milgram (1974) maintains that the process of complying with the demands of an authority figure is essentially the same whether the setting is the artificial one of the psychological laboratory, or a naturally occurring one in the outside world. While there are, of course, differences between laboratory studies of obedience and the obedience observed in Nazi Germany:

> *'Differences in scale, numbers and political context may turn out to be relatively unimportant as long as certain essential features are retained'.*

The 'essential features' that Milgram refers to is the *agentic state* (see page 395).

What do Milgram's studies tell us about ourselves?

Perhaps one of the reasons Milgram's research has been so heavily criticised is that it paints an unacceptable picture of human beings. Thus, it's far easier for us to believe that a war criminal like Eichmann was an inhuman monster than that 'ordinary people' can be destructively obedient (what Arendt, 1965, called the *banality of evil*).

Yet atrocities, such as those committed in Rwanda, Kosovo and East Timor, continue to occur. According to Hirsch (1995), many of the greatest crimes against humanity are committed in the name of obedience.

Box 27.2   Genocide

Hirsch (1995) maintains that genocide, a term first used in 1944, tends to occur under conditions created by three social processes:

- *authorisation* relates to the 'agentic state'; that is, obeying orders because of where they come from;
- *routinisation* refers to massacre becoming a matter of routine, or a mechanical and highly programmed operation;
- *dehumanisation* involves the victims being reduced to something less than human, allowing the perpetrators to suspend their usual moral prohibition on killing.

The ingredients of genocide were personified by Eichmann who, at his trial in 1960, denied ever killing anybody. However, he took great pride in the way he transported millions to their deaths 'with great zeal and meticulous care' (Arendt, 1965).

The power of social situations

Social roles provide models of power and powerlessness, as in the parent–child, teacher–student, and employer–employee relationships. Rather than asking what makes some people more obedient than others, or how we'd have reacted if we'd been one of Milgram's participants, we could instead ask how we would behave if put into a position of authority ourselves. How easily could we assume the role and use the power that goes with it?

Zimbardo's research

Almost as famous – and controversial – as Milgram's obedience studies is the *prison simulation experiment* (Zimbardo *et al.*, 1973). We mentioned earlier (page 396) that this experiment illustrates the impact of uniforms and other visible symbols of authority, and for this reason it's usually discussed in relation to obedience. However, it's also relevant to certain aspects of *conformity*, as well as demonstrating the *power of social situations* on people's behaviour.

KEY STUDY 27.4

The prison simulation experiment (Zimbardo *et al.*, 1973)

Zimbardo *et al.* recruited male participants through newspaper advertisements asking for student volunteers for a two-week study of prison life. From 75 volunteers, 24 were selected. They were judged to be emotionally stable, physically healthy, and 'normal to average' (based on personality tests). They also had no history of psychiatric problems and had never been in trouble with the police.

Participants were told they'd be randomly assigned to the role of either 'prisoner' or 'prison guard'. At the beginning of the experiment, then, there were no differences between those selected to be prisoners and guards. They constituted a relatively homogeneous group of white, middle-class college students from all over America.

The basement of the Stanford University psychology department was converted into a 'mock prison'. Zimbardo *et al.* wished to create a prison-like environment which was as *psychologically real* as possible. The aim was to study how prison life impacts upon both prisoners and guards.

The experiment began one Sunday morning, when those allocated to the prisoner role were unexpectedly arrested by the local police. They were charged with a felony, read their rights, searched, handcuffed, and taken to the police station to be 'booked'. After being fingerprinted, each prisoner was taken blindfold to the basement prison.

Upon arrival, the prisoners were stripped naked, skin-searched, deloused, and issued with uniforms and bedding. Each prisoner wore a loose-fitting smock with his identification number on the front and back, plus a chain bolted around one ankle. He also wore a nylon stocking to cover his hair (rather than having his head shaved). They were referred to by number only and accommodated in 6 × 9 ft 'cells', three to a cell.

The guards wore military-style khaki uniforms, silver reflector sunglasses (making eye contact with them impossible) and carried clubs, whistles, handcuffs and keys to the cells and main gate. The guards were on duty 24 hours a day, each working eight-hour shifts. They had complete control over the prisoners, who were kept in their cells around the clock, except for meals, toilet privileges, head counts and work.

Figure 27.3 a *A prisoner in one of the three-bedded cells*
      b *A prison guard asserting his authority over a prisoner*

After an initial 'rebellion' had been crushed, the prisoners began to react passively as the guards stepped up their aggression each day (by, for example, having a head count in the middle of the night simply to disrupt the prisoners' sleep). This made the prisoners feel helpless, and no longer in control of their lives.

Social power became the major dimension on which everyone and everything was defined. Every guard at some time or another behaved in an abusive, authoritarian way. Many seemed to positively enjoy the newfound power and the almost total control over the prisoners which went with the uniform:

- Guard A said: 'I was surprised at myself – I made them call each other names and clean the toilets out with their bare hands. I practically considered the prisoners cattle and I kept thinking I have to watch out for them in case they try something'.
- Guard B (preparing for the visitors' first night): 'I made sure I was one of the guards on the yard, because this was my first chance for the type of manipulative power that I really like – being a very noticed figure with complete control over what is said or not'.
- Guard C: 'Acting authoritatively can be fun. Power can be a great pleasure'.

After less than 36 hours, one prisoner had to be released because of uncontrolled crying, fits of rage, disorganised thinking and severe depression. Three others developed the same symptoms, and had to be released on successive days. Another prisoner developed a rash over his whole body, which was triggered when his 'parole' request was rejected. Prisoners became demoralised and apathetic, and even began to refer to themselves and others by their numbers. The whole experiment, planned to run for two weeks, was abandoned after six days because of the pathological reactions of the prisoners.

What conclusions can be drawn from the prison experiment?

An outside observer, who had a long history of imprisonment, believed that the mock prison, and both the guards' and prisoners' behaviours, were strikingly similar to real prison life. This supports Zimbardo et al.'s major conclusion that what make prisons such evil places are prisons themselves – *not* prisoners or guards. As Zimbardo (1973) says:

'Not that anyone ever doubted the horrors of prison, but rather it had been assumed that it was the predispositions of the guards ('sadistic') and prisoners ('sociopathic') that made prisons such evil places. Our study holds constant and positive the dispositional alternative and reveals the power of social, institutional forces to make good men engage in evil deeds'.

Ask yourself ...

- What does Zimbardo mean by 'Our study holds constant and positive the dispositional alternative'?

Volunteers were selected for their emotional stability, 'normality' and so on, and then randomly allocated to the prisoner/guard roles. Therefore, their different behaviours and reactions *couldn't* be attributed to their personal characteristics (or dispositions). Rather, the differences could be explained only in terms of the different roles they played in the context of the mock prison.

But according to Banuazizi & Mohavedi (1975), the behaviour of both guards and prisoners may have arisen from the *stereotyped expectations* of their respective roles. The participants were 'merely' role-playing (based on their prior expectations about how guards and prisoners 'ought' to behave). However, one reply to this criticism is to ask at what point 'mere' role-playing becomes a 'real' experience. As Zimbardo (1971, quoted in Aronson, 1992) says:

'It was no longer apparent to us or most of the subjects where they ended and their roles began. The majority had indeed become "prisoners" or "guards", no longer able to clearly differentiate between role-playing and self'.

This strongly suggests that their experiences were very real, and that even if they were 'merely' role-playing at the beginning, they were soon taking their roles very seriously indeed! This was 'aided and abetted' by the environmental conditions. A brutalising atmosphere, like the 'mock' prison, produces brutality. Had the roles been reversed, those who suffered as the prisoners may just as easily have inflicted suffering on those who were randomly chosen as guards.

Conclusions: How can we resist obedience?

In 1992, an East German judge sentenced a former East German border-guard for having shot a man trying (three years earlier) to escape to the West. The judge's comments echo the spirit of the Nuremberg Accords which followed the Nazi war crimes trials:

'Not everything that is legal is right ... At the end of the twentieth century, no one has the right to turn off his conscience when it comes to killing people on the orders of authorities'. (Cited in Berkowitz, 1993)

As we've seen, it's difficult to disobey authority. But we're most likely to rebel when we feel that social pressure is so strong that our freedom is under threat.

Milgram himself felt that obedience would be reduced by:

- educating people about the dangers of blind obedience;
- encouraging them to question authority;
- exposing them to the actions of disobedient models.

According to Brehm (1966), we need to believe that we have freedom of choice. When we believe that this isn't the case and when we believe we're entitled to freedom, we experience *reactance*, an unpleasant emotional state. To reduce it, and restore the sense of freedom, we disobey (see Chapter 49).

CHAPTER SUMMARY

- **Compliance** is a factor in different kinds of social influence, including conformity, obedience and our responses to other people's direct requests.

- While both conformity and obedience involve the **abdication of personal responsibility**, obedience involves orders from someone in higher authority, with influence being in one direction only.

- Milgram's series of 18 obedience experiments involve a basic procedure (**remote victim/voice feedback**) and variations on this, involving the manipulation of critical variables.

- Increasing the proximity to the victim, reducing the proximity of the experimenter and having the social support of 'rebel' fellow teachers all reduced obedience, while having someone else actually deliver the shock increased it.

- Two related variables that are crucial for understanding obedience are **acceptance/denial of responsibility** and the '**agentic state**'. The wearing of uniform and other such symbols of authority are also important.

- Milgram's experiments have caused great ethical controversy but have also been criticised on scientific grounds. The results have been replicated **cross-culturally**, but identical procedures haven't always been used, making it difficult to draw comparisons. But blind obedience hasn't been found anywhere, and social context influences obedience levels.

- The **mundane realism** of the procedure is supported by Hofling *et al.*'s naturalistic experiment involving nurses, and Milgram believes that obedience is essentially the same process regardless of the particular context.

- Many of the greatest crimes against humanity are committed in the name of obedience. **Genocide** tends to occur under conditions of **authorisation**, **routinisation** and **dehumanisation**.

- Zimbardo's **prison simulation experiment**, like Milgram's obedience studies, demonstrates the **power of social situations** to make people act in uncharacteristic ways. A brutalising atmosphere, like a prison, can induce brutality in people who aren't usually brutal.

- Participants were selected for their emotional stability and general 'normality', and then randomly allocated to the roles of prisoner or prison guard. Therefore, their pathological reactions couldn't be attributed to their personal characteristics.

- While they may have been merely **role-playing** at the beginning of the experiment, they soon 'became' prisoners or guards.

Self-assessment questions

1 'While there are obvious differences between obedience observed in laboratory studies and in Nazi Germany, they may turn out to be relatively unimportant as long as certain essential features are retained.'
To what extent does Milgram's research help us to understand why people obey?

2 'Anyone acting as a participant in an obedience experiment is likely to behave as Milgram's or Zimbardo *et al.*'s participants did.'
To what extent does psychological research support the view that obedience is the product of situational factors, rather than people's personal characteristics?

Web addresses

http://www.cba.uri.edu/Faculty/dellabitta/mr415s98/EthicEtcLinks/Milgram.htm

http://www.elvers.stjoe.udayton.edu/history/people/Milgram.html

http://www.stolaf.edu/people/huff/classes/headbook/Milgram.html

http://muskingum.edu/~psychology/psychweb/history/milgram.htm

http://www.sonoma.edu/people/g/goodman/zimbardo.htm

http://www.prisonexp.org/

http://www.stanford.edu/dept/news/relaged/970108/prisonexp.html

Further reading

Milgram, S. (1974) *Obedience to Authority*. New York: Harper & Row. An extremely readable account of all his major obedience research.

Gross, R. (1999) *Key Studies in Psychology* (3rd edition). London: Hodder & Stoughton. Chapters 6 and 7 cover Milgram's and Zimbardo *et al.*'s research respectively in considerable detail.

Chapter 28

Interpersonal Relationships

Introduction and overview

According to popular belief, it's love that makes the world go round. But according to Rubin & NcNeil (1983), liking perhaps more than loving is what keeps it spinning. How are liking and loving related? Are there different kinds of love, and can this help us understand how romantic relationships develop over time and why some break down? How do we get into relationships in the first place?

The importance of relationships, both sexual and non-sexual, is 'obvious'. According to Duck (1999):

> '... We need merely to reflect for a moment on the sources of our greatest pleasure and pain to appreciate that nothing else arouses the extremes of emotion that are experienced in the course of personal relationships with other human beings ...'.

Relationships make life meaningful, whether they're good or bad. When asked 'What's necessary for your happiness?', most people say, before anything else, satisfying close relationships with friends, family and romantic partners (Berscheid, 1985).

Most relationship research has focused on 'voluntary' relationships. When describing relationships breaking up (or down), we often use language that implies a degree of choice ('Why don't you get out of that relationship?', or 'I wish I'd never got involved in the first place'). One way of trying to understand the *dissolution* of relationships is to see it as the process of relationship *formation* in reverse.

Traditionally, social psychologists have been interested in *interpersonal attraction* (really an aspect of interpersonal perception: see Chapter 22), which relates to the question 'How do relationships start?'. But during the last 20 years or so, the emphasis has shifted to relationships as *processes* (Duck, 1999), reflected in two further questions: 'What makes people stay in relationships (*maintenance* and *progression*)?' and 'Why and how do relationships go wrong (*breakdown* or *dissolution*)?'

Affiliation: The need for other people

Affiliation is the basic human need for the company of other human beings. The need to belong and to be accepted by others is one of Maslow's basic survival needs (see Chapter 9), and is also a major motive underling conformity (see Chapter 26). We also saw in Chapter 26 that conformity can be explained in terms of the need to evaluate our beliefs and opinions by comparing them with those of other people, especially in ambiguous or unstructured situations. This is the central idea behind Festinger's (1954) *social comparison theory*.

According to Duck (1988), we're more 'affiliative' and inclined to seek others' company under certain conditions than others, for example, when we're anxious, when we've just left a close relationship (the 'rebound' situation), and when we've moved to a new neighbourhood. One of the most powerful factors influencing affiliation is *anxiety*.

KEY STUDY 28.1

'Anxiety loves anxious company' (Schachter, 1959)

Female psychology students were led to believe they'd be receiving electric shocks. One group was told the shocks would be painful (*the high-anxiety condition*), while another group was told they wouldn't be at all painful (*the low-anxiety condition*). They were then told that there would be a delay while the equipment was set up, and they were given the option of either waiting alone or with another participant (this was the dependent variable and no actual shock

was given). As predicted, the high-anxiety group showed a greater preference for company (20 out of 32) than the low-anxiety group (ten out of 30).

In a separate, related experiment, all the participants were told the shocks would be painful, but for half the choice was between waiting alone and waiting with another participant in the same experiment, and for the other half it was between waiting alone and waiting with another student who was waiting to see her tutor. For the first group, there was a strong preference for waiting with another high-anxiety participant, while the second group preferred to wait alone.

Ask yourself ...

- What do these results tell you about the students' motives for affiliation?

Schachter's results strongly suggest that *social comparison* was the motive for affiliation (rather than distraction) – if we have something to worry about, we prefer to be with other worriers.

Kulik & Mahler (1989) studied patients about to undergo coronary bypass surgery. Most preferred to share a room with someone who'd already undergone coronary surgery, rather than another patient waiting for the same operation. The main motive for this preference seemed to be the need for information about the stress-inducing situation.

Liking, love and intimacy

Ask yourself ...

- How does liking differ from loving?
- Is love just an intense form of liking?
- Are there different types of love?

Liking and loving

Rubin (1973) defines liking as positively evaluating another. Loving is *qualitatively* different from liking and comprises three main components:

- *attachment*: the need for the physical presence and emotional support of the loved one (on the *love scale*, 'If I could never be with _____ I would feel miserable');
- *caring*: a feeling of concern and responsibility for the loved one ('If _____ were feeling badly my first duty would be to cheer him/her up');
- *intimacy*: the desire for close and confidential contact and communication, wanting to share certain thoughts and feelings with the loved one more fully than with anyone else ('I feel that I can confide in _____ about practically everything').

The *love scale* can also be applied to same-sex friends, and Rubin found that females reported loving their friends more than men did. But there was no difference between males and females on the *liking scale*. Other studies suggest that women's friendships tend to be more intimate than men's, engaging in more spontaneous joint activities and more exchange of confidences. Rubin & McNeil (1983) suggest that loving for men may be channelled into single, sexual relationships, while women may be better able to experience attachment, caring and intimacy in a wider range and variety of relationships.

Although love is a label that we learn to attach to our own state of physiological arousal (see Chapter 10), most of the time love doesn't involve intense physical symptoms. Love, therefore, is more usefully thought of as a particular sort of *attitude* that one person has towards another (Rubin & McNeil, 1983).

Different types of love

Berscheid & Walster (1978) distinguish between *companionate love* ('true love' or 'conjugal love'), 'the affection we feel for those with whom our lives are deeply entwined', including very close friends and marriage partners, and *passionate love* (romantic love, obsessive love, infatuation, 'love sick' or 'being in love'). Romantic love is 'A state of intense absorption in another … A state of intense physiological arousal'. These are qualitatively different, but companionate love is only a more extreme form of liking ('the affection we feel for casual acquaintances') and corresponds to Rubin's 'love'.

Similarly, Sternberg (1988b) has proposed a 'triangular' model of love, in which three basic components (intimacy, passion and decision/commitment) can be combined to produce *consummate love*. When only two are combined, the resulting love is either *romantic*, *companionate* or *fatuous* respectively (see Figure 28.1).

Berscheid and Walster's, and Sternberg's models are *multidimensional*, in contrast with Rubin's, according to which love is a single, underlying dimension on which individuals can be ranked in terms of the strength of feelings for their partners. These distinctions are important for understanding how intimate relationships change over time.

Is romantic love unique to Western culture?

The popular ('Hollywood') view is that people fall in love and then commit themselves to each other through marriage. However, in cultures where 'arranged marriages' occur, the relationship between love and marriage is the other way around, and marriage is seen as the basis on which to explore a loving relationship (Bellur, 1995: see below). As Bellur notes, the cultural background in which people have learned about love is important in shaping their ideas of it.

When Kephart (1967) asked Americans 'If someone had all the other qualities you desire in a marriage partner, would you marry this person if you were not in love?', well over twice as many men replied 'no' as did women. When Simpson *et al.* (1986) repeated the study, more than 80 per cent of both men and women said 'no'. This can be explained at least partly by the fact that, twenty years on, financial independence had allowed women to choose marriage partners for reasons other than material necessity. But this doesn't explain why romantic love has become so central for both American men and women (Moghaddam, 1998).

Box 28.1	Exporting love from Hollywood to the rest of the world

According to Moghaddam (1998), romantic love isn't exclusive to Western societies. The notion of people falling in love is found in one form or another in most human societies, even where marriages are traditionally arranged by families or friends. For example, an analysis of songs and folklore in 166 societies indicates that 'Western' romantic love is recognised in more than 85 per cent of them (Jankowaik & Fischer, 1992). However, Moghaddam (1998) believes that:

'What is unique about romantic love in late twentieth-century Western societies is its pervasiveness: the idea that everyone should marry only when they are in love. Such an idea is fairly new historically and is still limited to Western societies'.

Perhaps no other feature of Western culture is being exported or internationalised more than romantic love 'Hollywood style'. Over the last century, there's been an increasing acceptance in Western societies of the idea that one should marry for love, and that it's right to end the relationship when love dies. As societies become industrialised and more individualistic, the percentage of people who believe that love must precede marriage increases.

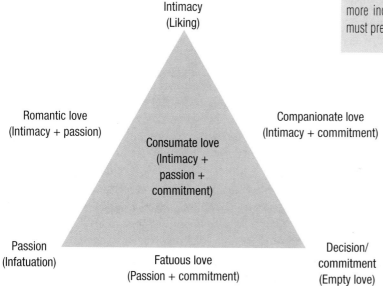

Figure 28.1 *Robert Sternberg's (1988b) model of different kinds of love as combinations of three basic components of love (from Myers, D.G. (1994),* Exploring Social Psychology. *New York, McGraw-Hill)*

Cultural differences still exist. For example, Levine *et al.* (1995) studied young people in Australia, Brazil, England, Hong Kong, India, Japan, Mexico, Pakistan, the Philippines, Thailand, and the USA. When given the question previously asked by Kephart and Simpson *et al.* (see above), participants from India, Thailand and Pakistan gave the highest proportion of 'yes' replies, while those from England and the USA gave the lowest. These are collectivist and individualist cultures, respectively.

Based on studies conducted in Canada, the Caribbean, Senegal, Uganda, the USA, and South Africa, Smith & Bond (1998) conclude that:

> 'There are relatively universal ways in which people speak about their attachment to others. However, the more detail we add to the measures, explicating exactly what attitudes and behaviours are entailed within the generalised notion of love or romance, the more differences we start to find'.

There are also important differences *within* culturally diverse societies, such as Britain, America and Canada. For example, first generation Indian immigrants to Canada (those born abroad who subsequently emigrated to Canada) tend to endorse the idea that marriage precedes love more than second generation Indian Canadians (whose parents came from abroad but who were themselves born in Canada: Vaidyanathan & Naidoo, 1991). Similarly, Dion & Dion (1993) found that Asian Canadians tend to interpret love as more friendship- and caring-based than something 'mysterious', compared with European Canadians. Both these findings are consistent with the distinction between collectivist and individualist cultural beliefs and practices, such as arranged marriages (see below).

Cultural differences in relationships

Although different types of relationships are found in many cultures, their importance varies considerably between them. For example, while Western cultures place great emphasis on the desirability of romantic love in dyads (two-person groupings), most non-Western cultures attach greater importance to family ties and responsibilities (Segall *et al.*, 1990). A related, more general, difference is that interpersonal relationships in Western cultures tend to be *individualistic*, *voluntary* and *temporary*, whereas those in non-Western cultures are more *collectivist*, *involuntary* and *permanent* (Moghaddam *et al.*, 1993: see Box 47.5, page 703). According to Moghaddam *et al.* (1993):

> 'The cultural values and environmental conditions in North America have led North American social psychologists to be primarily concerned with first-time acquaintances, friendships and intimate relationships, primarily because these appear to be the relationships most relevant to the North American urban cultural experience'.

In other words, there's a tendency for Western psychologists to equate 'relationships' with 'Western relationships', which is a form of *ethnocentrism* (specifically, Anglo- or Eurocentrism: see Chapter 47). However, wide and important cultural variations are found even when the 'same' relationship (such as marriage) is being considered.

Culture and marriage

Westerners think of *monogamy* (marriage to one spouse at any one time) as the normal, even moral, form of marriage (Price & Crapo, 1999: see Chapter 38). Indeed, this belief is enshrined in the law (bigamy is a criminal offence), and reflects basic Judeo-Christian doctrine. However, cultures differ in their marital arrangements. In addition to the monogamous pattern, there are several other patterns. *Polygamy* (having two or more spouses at once) can take the form of *polygyny* (one man having two or more wives) or, less commonly, *polyandry* (one woman with two or more husbands). Another arrangement is *mandatory marriage to specific relatives*, as when a son marries the daughter of his father's brother (his first cousin: Triandis, 1994).

Monogamy is 'natural' from a Western perspective, and probably fewer than 0.5 per cent of human societies have practised polyandry as a common or preferred form of marriage (Price & Crapo, 1999). However, throughout Tibet and the neighbouring Himalayan areas of India, Nepal and Bhutan, polyandry has been common for generations. In this region, it usually takes the form of a woman marrying two or more brothers (*fraternal polyandry*), which minimises population growth in order to cope with scarce resources (Tibet is a land of scarce resources and relatively little productive land). It keeps brothers together and slows the growth of the family, since several brothers will produce only the number of children their one wife can bear. In this way, land doesn't need to be divided up (as would happen if each brother married monogamously), and a single family is preserved as an economic unit (Westermarck, 1894; Goldstein, 1979).

Arranged marriages

Ask yourself ...

- Do you consider that arranged marriages are necessarily wrong, or undesirable?
- Do you come from a cultural background in which this is the norm?
- Is there a sense in which all marriages are 'arranged'?

The meanings of 'arranged'

As we saw earlier, a large percentage of American men and women say they wouldn't marry if they weren't in love, and the idea of an arranged marriage is quite alien to them. Yet, almost 50 per cent of Americans marry for reasons *other than* love (Collins & Coltrane, 1995), examples including security, money, family pressure, and to have children. Furthermore, Kerckhoff & Davis's (1962) *filter model* implies that most relationships are 'arranged', in the sense that we mostly marry within our own *demographic* groups (religious, ethnic, educational and so on). As Duck (1999) says:

> 'Many of us would perhaps not recognise – or accept – that marriages are actually 'arranged' by religion, social position, wealth, class, opportunity and other things over which we have little control, even within our own culture ...'.

Conversely, parentally arranged marriages in some cultures are gladly entered into, and are considered to be perfectly normal, natural relationships that are anticipated with pleasure (Duck, 1999). Indeed, evidence suggests that these marriages may produce more long-term happiness than 'love' marriages.

For example, Gupta & Singh (1982) found that couples in India who married for love reported *diminished* feelings of love if they'd been married for more than five years. By contrast, those who'd undertaken arranged marriages reported *more* love if they weren't newly-weds. These findings reveal that passionate love 'cools' over time, and that there's scope for love to flourish within an arranged marriage. In the case of those cultures in which arranged marriages occur, then, courtship is accepted to a certain degree, but love is left to be defined and discovered after marriage (Bellur, 1995).

Arranged marriages are far more common in collectivist cultures, where the whole extended family 'marries' the other extended family. This is distinct from individualist cultures, in which the individuals marry one another (Triandis, 1994). In one modern collectivist culture, Japan, almost a quarter of marriages are arranged (Iwao, 1993).

In general, divorce rates among those who marry according to parents' wishes are much *lower* than among those who marry for love. This is one argument in favour of arranged marriages. As Triandis (1994) argues:

> *'Marriage, when seen as a fifty-year relationship, is more likely to be a good one if people enter it after careful, rational analysis, which is more likely to be provided by older adults than by sexually aroused young people ...'.*

However, divorce rates among couples who entered arranged marriages are rising, an indication that personal freedom is gaining importance, and that traditional structures which define set roles for family members are becoming less viable (Bellur, 1995). Among the more liberal-minded Asians living in the West, arranged marriages operate more like a dating facility ('arranged meetings' rather than 'arranged marriages'). The transition from meeting to marrying occurs when both parties formally agree to the commitment, with love being left to be developed after marriage (Bellur, 1995).

Stage theories of relationships

Our own experience tells us that intimate relationships change and develop over time. Indeed, those that stagnate ('we're not going anywhere'), especially sexual/romantic relationships, may well be doomed to failure (Duck, 1988). A number of theories have been proposed charting the course of both sexual and non-sexual relationships.

The filter model

Kerckhoff & Davis (1962) compared 'short-term couples' (together for less than 18 months) with 'long-term couples' (18 months or more) over a seven-month period. According to their *filter model*, it is *similarity of sociological* (or *demographic*) *variables* that determine the likelihood of individuals meeting in the first place. To some extent, our choice of friends and partners is made for us. Social circumstances reduce the '*field of availables*' (Kerckhoff, 1974), that is, the range of people that are *realistically* available for us to meet (as opposed to those who are theoretically available). There's considerable *preselection* of the types of people we come into contact with, namely those from our own ethnic, racial, religious, social-class and educational groups. These are the types of people we tend to find most attractive initially, since similarity makes communication easier and we've something immediately in common with them, as a group. At this point, attraction has little to do with other people's individual characteristics.

The next 'filter' involves the psychological characteristics of individuals, specifically *agreement on basic values*. This was found to be the best predictor of the relationship becoming more stable and permanent. Those who'd been together for less than 18 months tended to have stronger relationships when the partners' values coincided. But with the long-term couples, similarity wasn't the most important factor. The best predictor of a longer term commitment was *complementarity of emotional needs*. This constitutes the third filter.

Stimulus–value–role theory

According to Murstein's (1976, 1986, 1987) *stimulus–value–role* (*SVR*) *theory*, intimate relationships proceed from a *stimulus stage*, in which attraction is based on external attributes (such as physical appearance), through a *value stage*, in which similarity of values and beliefs becomes much more important, and finally to a *role stage*, which involves a commitment based on successful performance of relationship roles, such as husband and wife. Although all three factors have some influence throughout a relationship, each one assumes greatest significance during one particular stage.

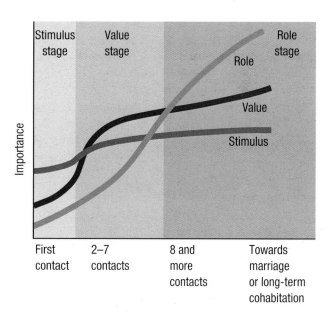

Figure 28.2 *States of courtship in SVR theory (Murstein, 1987, based on Brehm, 1992)*

An evaluation of stage theories

Brehm (1992) points out that many studies have provided only weak evidence for a fixed sequence of stages in intimate relationships. 'Stages' are probably best regarded as 'phases' that take place at different times for different couples.

However, the claim that relationships change and develop isn't in dispute, and it's useful to think of this as involving a beginning, a middle and an end, corresponding to the three questions that were posed at the beginning of the chapter (see *Introduction and overview*).

Interpersonal attraction: How relationships get started

A general theoretical framework for explaining initial attraction is that we are attracted to individuals whose presence is *rewarding* for us (e.g. Clore & Byrne, 1974; Lott & Lott, 1974). The more rewards someone provides for us, the more we should be attracted to that individual. A number of factors have been found to influence initial attraction through their reward value, including *proximity*, *exposure* and *familiarity*, *physical attractiveness*, and *similarity*.

Proximity, exposure and familiarity

Proximity

Proximity (physical or geographical closeness) represents a minimum requirement for attraction, because the further apart two people live, the lower the probability that they'll ever meet, let alone become friends or marry each other. Festinger *et al.* (1950) studied friendship patterns in a university campus housing complex for married students. People were more friendly with those who lived next door, next most friendly with those living two doors away, and least friendly with those who lived at the end of the corridor. Families separated by four flats hardly ever became friends, and in two-storey blocks of flats the residents tended to interact mainly with others living on the same floor. On all floors, people who lived near stairways had more friends than those living at the end of corridors.

Personal space

> *Ask yourself ...*
>
> • If you're sitting in an otherwise empty row of seats in a train, and someone comes and sits right next to you, how do you think you'd react, and why?

In a series of studies by Sommer, the experimenter deliberately sat close to unsuspecting people when there was plenty of available space elsewhere, in order to see how likely they were to react to this invasion of their personal space.

KEY STUDY 28.2

Beware of space invaders in the library (Felipe & Sommer, 1966)

The unsuspecting participants were female students studying at a large table with six chairs on either side of the table, with at least two empty chairs on either side of each student and one opposite. There were a number of experimental conditions in which, for example, the experimenter:

- sat next to her and moved his chair nearer to hers;
- sat two seats away from her (leaving one chair between them);
- sat three seats away;
- sat immediately opposite her.

The students were more likely to leave, move away, adjust the chair or erect barriers (such as putting a bag on the table between themselves and the 'intruder') when he sat next to them.

Similar results were found for psychiatric patients (Felipe & Sommer, 1966) and for people sitting on park benches (Sommer, 1969). In the last study, the experimenter sat six inches away from someone on an otherwise empty bench and these participants were much more likely to move away – and sooner – than control participants who weren't joined by the over-friendly stranger.

The term 'personal space' was first used by Hall (1959, 1966) to describe the human version of the 'individual distance' of zoo animals (the distance which two individuals of the same species try to keep between each other: Hediger, 1951).

Box 28.2 Personal space

Personal space is a sort of invisible bubble that surrounds us. According to Hall, we learn *proxemic rules*, which prescribe:

- the amount of physical distance that's appropriate in daily relationships; and
- the kinds of situations in which closeness or distance is proper.

Hall identifies four main regions or zones of personal space.

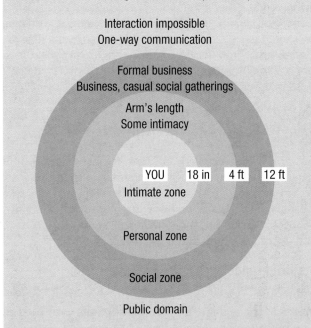

Figure 28.3 *Hall's four zones of personal space (from Nicholson, 1977)*

There are important *cultural differences* regarding proxemic rules. Each zone of personal space allows the use of different cues of touch, smell, hearing and seeing, which are more important in some cultures than others.

Watson & Graves (1966) observed discussion groups of Americans and those from Arab countries; in the latter, there was more direct face-to-face orientation, greater closeness and touching. South Americans and Arabs have been called '*contact cultures*', while the Scots and Swedes have been called '*non-contact cultures*'. The *caste system* in India represents a highly formalised, institutionalised set of proxemic rules.

A similar concept to personal space is the *body-buffer zone*, the point at which a person begins to feel uncomfortable when approached by another. Criminals convicted of violent crimes compared with non-criminals, and schizophrenics compared with other kinds of psychiatric patients, tend to have larger body-buffer zones; that is, they more easily begin to feel uneasy when others walk towards them (Nicholson, 1977).

Our feelings for others may depend on whether proxemic rules are followed, and these rules are themselves influenced by the nature of the relationship. For instance, relatives and intimate friends are allowed much closer proximity – and bodily contact – than mere acquaintances or strangers. As far as bodily contact is concerned, there are different rules for different relatives depending on gender and age, and this applies to friends too (see Figure 28.4).

Proximity is just one of several kinds of *social act* which make up the degree of intimacy which exists between two people. According to Argyle & Dean (1965), we all have dual tendencies, to approach others and seek their company on the one hand, and to avoid them and remain separate and independent on the other. The balance between these two opposing tendencies is 'negotiated', non-verbally, in each social situation, so that we try to find a level of intimacy we feel comfortable with.

Successful friendships may require an initial establishment of *boundary understandings*. In Hall's terms, strangers must be 'invited' into our intimate zone and not 'trespass' from an initial casual personal distance. In terms of Argyle and Dean's equilibrium model of intimacy, strangers (like the experimenter in Sommer's studies) who make a situation uncomfortably intimate too soon are unlikely to become friends.

> ## Ask yourself ...
>
> - Do you think it's ethically acceptable to conduct research like Sommer's 'library study'?

Exposure and familiarity

Proximity increases the opportunity for interaction (*exposure*), which, in turn, increases *familiarity*. There's considerable evidence that, far from breeding contempt, familiarity breeds fondness, which Zajonc (1968) calls the *mere exposure effect*. For example, the more times university students saw photographs of men's faces, the more they liked them (see Figure 28.5, page 408).

According to Argyle (1981), the more two people interact, the more *polarised* their attitudes towards each other become, usually in the direction of greater liking. This, in turn, increases the likelihood of further interaction, but only if the interaction is on an equal footing.

The impact of familiarity on attraction was demonstrated by Newcomb (1961). He found that while similarity of beliefs, attitudes and values was important in determining liking (see below), the key factor was familiarity. So, even when students were paired according to the similarity or dissimilarity of their beliefs, attitudes and values, room-mates

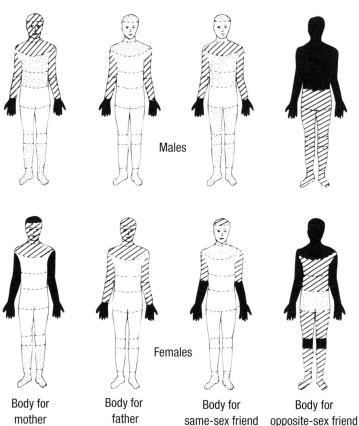

	%
☐	0–25
▨	26–50
▧	51–75
■	76–100

Males

Females

| Body for mother | Body for father | Body for same-sex friend | Body for opposite-sex friend |

Figure 28.4 *Male and female 'bodies for others', as experienced through the amount of touching received from others (Jourard, 1966)*

became friends far more often than would be expected on the basis of their characteristics.

This preference for what is familiar extends to our own facial appearance. Mita *et al.* (1977) photographed women students and later showed each student her actual picture together with a mirror-image of it. Most students preferred the latter – this is how we're used to seeing ourselves – while their friends preferred the latter – this is how others are used to seeing us! So, we tend to like what we know and what we're familiar with, perhaps because it's predictable.

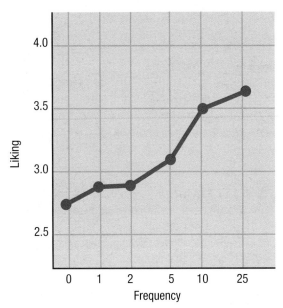

Figure 28.5 *The relationship between frequency of exposure and liking. Participants were shown photographs of different faces and the number of times each face was shown was varied. The more they saw a particular face, the more they said they liked the person shown (based on Zajonc, 1968)*

Similarity

> ### Ask yourself ...
>
> - Do you consider your friends to be similar to you? If so, in what ways?
> - Does this also apply to sexual partners?

Evidence suggests that 'birds of a feather flock together', and that the critical similarities are those concerning *beliefs, attitudes* and *values*. For example, Newcomb (1943) studied students at an American college with a liberal tradition among teaching staff and senior students. Many students coming from conservative backgrounds adopted liberal attitudes (presumably) in order to gain the liking and acceptance of their classmates. Griffitt & Veitch (1974) paid 13 males to spend ten days in a fall-out shelter. Those with similar attitudes and opinions liked each other most by the end of the study, particularly if they agreed on highly salient issues.

Rubin (1973) suggests that similarity is rewarding because:

- agreement may provide a basis for engaging in joint activities;
- a person who agrees with us helps to increase our confidence in our own opinions, which enhances our

self-esteem. According to Duck (1992), the validation that friends give us is experienced as evidence of the accuracy of our *personal constructs* (see Chapter 42);

- most people are vain enough to believe that anyone who shares their views must be a sensitive and praiseworthy individual;
- people who agree about things that matter to them generally find it easier to communicate;
- we may assume that people with similar attitudes to ourselves will like us, and so we like them in turn (*reciprocal liking*).

While it often takes time to find out about other people's attitudes and values, their physical attractiveness is immediately apparent. Physical attractiveness has been studied as an influence on attraction in its own right, as well as one aspect of similarity.

Physical attractiveness

The attractiveness stereotype

As we saw in Chapter 22, we tend to perceive attractive-looking people as also having more attractive personalities (the *attractiveness stereotype*). Dion *et al.* (1972) found that photographs of attractive people, compared with unattractive people, were consistently credited with more desirable qualities – sexually warm and responsive, kind, strong, outgoing, nurturant, sensitive, interesting, poised, sociable, exciting dates, better character, happily married, socially and professionally successful and enjoying more fulfilling lives.

However, Dermer & Thiel (1975) found that extremely attractive women were judged (by female participants) to be egotistic, vain, materialistic, snobbish and less likely to be successfully married. This suggests that it's not always to our advantage to be seen as highly attractive, and one situation where this may apply is where a criminal's good looks played a part in the crime (see Chapter 46).

Dion & Dion (1995) observe that stereotyping based on facial attractiveness appears at least as early as six years old. They also suggest that this might be linked to the *just world hypothesis*, such that there's a positive bias towards 'winners', equivalent to 'blaming the victim' (see Chapter 23).

What makes someone attractive?

Different cultures have different criteria concerning physical beauty. For example, chipped teeth, body scars, artificially elongated heads and bound feet have all been regarded as beautiful, and in Western culture, definitions of beauty change over time, as in the 'ideal' figure for women (see Chapter 44.) Traditionally, facial beauty has been generally regarded as more important in women than men, while men's stature, particularly height, plus a muscular body and (currently) firm, rounded buttocks influence how attractive they're judged to be (by women, anyway!).

According to Brehm (1992), in the context of personal ads and commercial dating services, the primary 'resource' (or reward) offered by females seeking a male partner is still physical attractiveness, which matches what men are actually seeking from a female partner. But this appears to be an almost universal male preference, not one confined to Western culture (Buss, 1989: see Critical Discussion 28.1, page 413).

Defining facial attractiveness

The idea that beauty is in the eye of the beholder stems from the philosopher, Hume (1757). This maxim implies, of course, that beauty cannot be defined objectively. However, although any two individuals can vary widely in what they consider facially attractive, these differences actually vary around an underlying norm, which is surprisingly consistent across cultures (Langlois & Roggman, 1990). Langlois *et al.* (1987) found that when babies under one year are shown faces that adults consider attractive or unattractive, they spend longer looking at the former (implying that they prefer them: see Box 16.1, page 234). Clearly, they're too young to have learned cultural standards of beauty.

Langlois & Roggmann (1990) took photographs of faces with standard pose, expression and lighting, and then scanned them into a computer. Each image was then divided into a very large number of tiny squares (or *pixels*), and the brightnesses of corresponding pixels in different same-sex faces were *averaged* to produce *computer-composite images*. When people were asked to judge the attractiveness of these composite faces (made from four, eight, 16, or 32 faces), they rated them as increasingly attractive the more faces that went into each image. This applied to both male and female faces.

The greater the number of faces making up a composite image, the more the peculiarities of particular faces become ironed out. Hence, as Bruce & Young (1998) observe:

'It seems that moving a facial image closer to the average ... increases its perceived attractiveness ...'.

If this is a genuine phenomenon, how can we explain it? Bruce and Young suggest two possible explanations.

■ Although we've not seen composite faces before, *averaged* faces (close to the average of faces we *have* seen before) are preferred because they seem *familiar* (see above, pages 407–408);

■ Individuals whose characteristics are close to the average of the population might be preferred, because they're less likely to carry harmful genetic mutations (Langlois & Roggman, 1990).

But is attractiveness really no more than averageness? This seems unlikely. For example, if we describe someone as 'average looking', we usually mean that s/he is neither 'good-looking' nor 'ugly', and movie stars and sex symbols obviously *aren't* average (otherwise most of us would be sex symbols!).

According to Perret *et al.* (1994), the average derived from highly attractive faces is consistently preferred to the average of the entire set of photographs they were taken from. This wouldn't happen if 'attractive' equalled 'average'. When the difference between the average shape of attractive faces and the average shape of the entire set was increased, perceived attractiveness of the former also increased. But the effect of this was to make the resulting faces *more different* from the

Computer-composite faces. The columns show composite sets created from female faces (left) or from male faces (right). From top to bottom, rows show composites created by averaging across 4, 8, 16 and 32 faces (from Bruce & Young, 1998)

average. Perret *et al.* found exactly the same pattern of results for European and Japanese faces, regardless of whether they were judged by European or Japanese people.

We also seem to prefer more *symmetrical* faces. While most faces (to varying degrees) are, in fact, asymmetrical around the vertical midline, even those with only slight asymmetry can be made more attractive by improving symmetry (Bruce & Young, 1998).

From a *sociobiological* perspective (see Chapter 2), attractive facial features may signal sexual maturity or fertility. This is also consistent with the tendency to equate beauty with youthfulness (but see Chapters 22 and 39, and Box 28.3, page 410).

Box 28.3 The sociobiology of beauty

According to Singh (in Charter, 1995), anyone whose waist size exceeds their hip measurement (i.e. whose *waist–hip ratio* – WHR –is greater than one) is at higher risk of heart disease and diabetes. Furthermore, he claims to have shown that women with a waist–hip ratio of 0.7 have universal appeal as potential partners, because their body shape transmits signals about health, sexual maturity, and fertility. For males the ideal is more like 0.85–0.9.

This fits in perfectly with Darwinian theories of human mate selection, which claims that both men and women select partners who should enable them to enhance reproductive success, thus ensuring the survival of their genes into the next generation (see Chapter 2 and Gross *et al.*, 2000).

In her hey-day Twiggy's WHR was a surprising 0.73 (her vital statistics were 31–24–33), and although *Playboy* centerfolds have shown a 20 per cent decline in plumpness over the years (see Chapter 44), they've shown a consistent WHR of 0.7.

Singh has been criticised on several grounds. The diseases he claims are correlated with high WHRs affect mainly older (post-menopausal) women, and so aren't relevant to mating, and they're historically quite recent.

According to Pond (in Charter, 1995), the ideal WHR identified by Singh signalled proto-human female's erect posture and her ability to give birth to large-brained, upright-walking offspring.

The matching hypothesis

According to *social exchange theory* (e.g. Thibaut & Kelley, 1959: see below, pages 411–412), people are more likely to become romantically involved if they're fairly closely matched in their ability to reward one another. Ideally, we'd all have the 'perfect partner' because, the theory says, we're all selfish. But since this is impossible, we try to find a compromise solution. The best general bargain that can be struck is a *value-match*, a subjective belief that our partner is the most rewarding we could realistically hope to find.

Several studies have tested the *matching hypothesis* (Walster *et al.*, 1966; Dion & Berscheid, 1974; Berscheid *et al.*, 1971; Silverman, 1971; Murstein, 1972; Berscheid & Walster, 1974). These studies generally show that people rated as being of high, low or average attractiveness tend to choose partners of a corresponding level of attractiveness. Indeed, according to Price & Vandenberg (1979):

> 'The matching phenomenon [of physical attraction between marriage partners] is stable within and across generations'.

The findings from the various matching hypothesis studies imply that the kind of partner we'd be satisfied with is one we feel won't reject us, rather than one we positively desire. Brown (1986), however, maintains that the matching phenomenon results from a well-learned sense of what's 'fitting', rather than a fear of being rebuffed. For Brown, we learn to adjust our expectations of rewards in line with what we believe we have to offer others.

An evaluation of attraction research

According to Duck (1999), the 'magnetic metaphor' of attraction implies that people are unwittingly, and almost against their will, pulled towards one another's inherent, pre-existing characteristics. It's a view of relationships as:

> '... *implicitly independent of interaction, co-construction, mutually responsive behaviour, or shared understandings derived from active conversation ... In short, it leaves out most of the other things that humans do in everyday life, and so it serves to caricature social and personal relationships as the unthinking domain of reactive magnetism ...*'.

More recent research has considered the *dynamics* of relationships (how they develop and unfold over time), and how relationships are actually conducted in real life. One feature of 'real' relationships is their inherent tensions, such as the need to balance our desire for disclosure and openness, connectedness and interdependence on the one hand, and the desire for autonomy and independence, privacy and the right to retain secrets on the other.

Not surprisingly, this shift has involved fewer controlled laboratory studies, and more exploration of life as it's lived 'out there' (Duck, 1999). This now includes such diverse research areas as *homosexual*, and *electronic* (online or cyberspace) *relationships*.

Homosexual relationships

According to Kitzinger & Coyle (1995), since the mid-1970s psychological research on homosexuality has moved away from a 'pathology' model (see Chapter 43) towards one comprising four overlapping themes:

- belief in a basic, underlying similarity between homosexual and heterosexual people;
- rejection of the concept of homosexuality as a central organising principle of the personality in favour of recognising the diversity and variety of homosexuals as individuals;
- an assertion that homosexuality is as natural, normal and healthy as heterosexuality;
- denial of the notion that homosexuals pose any threat to children, the nuclear family or the future of society as we know it.

Bee (1994) argues that homosexual partnerships are far more like heterosexual relationships than they are different. However, Kitzinger and Coyle argue that certain factors are found to be omitted or distorted when homosexual relationships are assessed in terms derived from heterosexual relationships. These include the observations that:

- cohabitation is much less common for homosexuals than heterosexuals. The reasons for this are unclear, but probably include concern amongst 'closet' homosexuals about the increased visibility entailed in openly living with a person of the same sex, plus a concern not to duplicate the conditions of heterosexual marriage;
- compared with married heterosexuals, *sexual exclusivity* (having only one sexual partner at a time) is less common in lesbian relationships and *much less* common in gay relationships (Peplau, 1982). However, the ideal of sexual exclusivity is based on an assumed heterosexual norm or 'blueprint' (Yip, 1999), which many gays and lesbians reject. Sexual non-exclusivity may lead to relationship breakdown in heterosexuals, largely because it's likely to be

'secretive'. In homosexual couples, those who have sex outside their relationships:

'... tend to do so after negotiation of relationship rules and sexual activity guidelines, in the context of an open relationship ... and are consequently less likely to experience their own, or their partners' sexual affairs as signalling the end of the couple relationship' (Kitzinger & Coyle, 1995);

■ most gays and lesbians actively reject traditional husband–wife or masculine–feminine *sex roles* (as clearly exist in heterosexual relationships) as a model for enduring relationships (Peplau, 1991). On the whole, gay and lesbian couples seem to embrace 'the ethic of equality and reciprocity', deliberately rejecting the 'heterosexist model' which is characterised by power inequality. This is particularly true for lesbians who've previously been in 'unequal' heterosexual relationships (Yip, 1999).

Online relationships

Probably one of the most unexpected uses of the Internet is the development of online relationships (or *cyberaffairs*: Griffiths, 2000). In the UK, one newspaper reported that there have been over 1000 weddings resulting from Internet meetings. Cyberspace is now becoming another 'singles bar', as there are now many sites aimed at those who are looking for romance or a sexual liaison. Some are directed at singles, while others appear to encourage or facilitate virtual adultery.

Online relationships can proceed through chat-rooms, interactive games or newsgroups. What may begin as a simple e-mail exchange or innocent chat-room encounter can escalate into an intense and passionate cyberaffair, and eventually into face-to-face sexual encounters. Griffiths (2000) claims that:

'It could perhaps be argued that electronic communication is the easiest, most disinhibiting and most accessible way to meet potential new partners'.

Ask yourself ...

- Have you had an online relationship?
- What do you think their potential benefits and dangers might be?

Griffiths (1999) identifies three basic types of online relationship:

■ *purely virtual*: while these are usually sexually very explicit, the 'correspondents' never meet, just want sexual kicks, and don't consider they're being unfaithful to their actual partners;

■ increasingly sexually intense *online contact* may eventually lead to the exchange of photographs, secret telephone calls, letters, and meetings. Once they've met and if practically possible, actual time spent together will largely replace online contact;

■ an initial meeting *offline* will be maintained largely by an online relationship. This usually involves people living in different countries.

Box 28.4 Some concerns about online relationships | 411

- The disinhibiting, anonymous nature of the Internet can make online relationships seductive and potentially addictive (see Chapter 8). As Griffiths (2000) points out:

  'What might take months or years in an offline relationship may only take days or weeks on line ... the perception of trust, intimacy, and acceptance has the potential to encourage online users to see these relationships as a primary source of companionship and comfort'.

- The sociologist, Laurie Taylor (in Williams, 2000) argues that:

  'Face-to-face relationships are steadily declining. Fewer and fewer people take part in civic activities such as ... political party involvement or trade unions as the mass movement towards faceless electronic liaisons continues to increase. In the long run we will become incapable of relating to each other in person at all'.

Given the emphasis placed on physical attractiveness in such an image-conscious society as ours, the disembodied, anonymous nature of online relationships may help individuals' focus on the content of the message: '... there's no such thing as a bad hair day on the Internet ...' (Joinson, in Williams, 2000). For the normally inhibited, this aspect of the Internet is probably a Godsend, as it is for those who wish to finish a romantic relationship but are too cowardly to do it in person (Williams, 2000).

What keeps people together?

Ask yourself ...

- What do all the important relationships in your life have in common?

You may say something to the effect that they provide you with security, happiness, contentment, fun and so on, and (if you're honest) that they can also be complex, demanding and, at times, even painful. If all relationships involve both positive and negative, desirable and undesirable aspects, what determines our continued involvement in them?

Social exchange theory

Social exchange theory provides a general framework for analysing all kinds of relationship, both intimate and non-intimate, and is really an extension of *reward theory* (see page 406).

According to Homans (1974), we view our feelings for others in terms of profits (the amount of reward obtained from a relationship minus the cost). The greater the reward and lower the cost, the greater the profit and hence the attraction. Blau (1964) argues that interactions are 'expensive': they take time, energy and commitment, and may involve unpleasant emotions and experiences. Because of this, what we get out of a relationship must be more than what we put in.

Similarly, Berscheid & Walster (1978) argue that in any social interaction there's an exchange of rewards (such as affection, information and status), and that the degree of attraction or liking will reflect how people evaluate the rewards they receive relative to those they give.

> **Ask yourself ...**
>
> - Is it appropriate to think of relationships in this economic, even capitalist, way?

Are relationships really like this?

Social exchange theory sees people as fundamentally selfish and human relationships as based primarily on self-interest. But this is a *metaphor* for human relationships, and it shouldn't be taken too literally. However, although we like to believe that the joy of giving is as important as the desire to receive, we have to admit that our attitudes towards other people are determined to a large extent by our assessments of the rewards they hold for us (Rubin, 1973).

Equally, though, Rubin believes that social exchange theory doesn't provide an adequate, complete account:

> *'Human beings are sometimes altruistic in the fullest sense of the word. They make sacrifices for the sake of others without any consideration of the rewards they will obtain from them in return'.*

Altruism is most often and most clearly seen in close interpersonal relationships (see Chapter 30).

Indeed, some psychologists make the distinction between 'true' love and friendship, which are altruistic, and less admirable forms which are based on considerations of exchange (Brown, 1986). Fromm (1962) defines true love as giving, as opposed to the false love of the 'marketing character' which depends upon expecting to have the favours returned. Support for this distinction comes from a study by Mills & Clark (1980), who identified two kinds of intimate relationship:

- the *communal couple*, in which each partner gives out of concern for the other;
- the *exchange couple*, in which each keeps mental records of who's 'ahead' and who's 'behind'.

Equity theory

Social exchange theory is really a special case of a more general account of human relationships called *equity theory*. The extra component in equity theory that's added to reward, cost and profit is *investment*. For Brown (1986):

> *'A person's investments are not just financial; they are anything at all that is believed to entitle him to his rewards, costs, and profits. An investment is any factor to be weighed in determining fair profits or losses'.*

Equity *doesn't* mean equality, but a *constant ratio* of rewards to costs or profit to investment. So, equity theory involves a concern with *fairness*, and it's *changes* in the ratio of what you put in and what you get out of a relationship which are likely to cause changes in how you feel about it, rather than the initial ratio. You may believe it's fair and just that you give more

than you get, but if you start giving very much more than you did and receiving proportionately less, then you're likely to become dissatisfied.

Some versions of social exchange theory do actually take account of factors other than the simple and crude profit motives of social interactors. One of these was introduced by Thibaut & Kelley (1959).

Box 28.5	The concepts of comparison level and comparison level for alternatives (Thibaut & Kelley, 1959)

- *Comparison level* (CL) is essentially the average level of rewards and costs you're used to in relationships, and is the basic level you expect in any future relationship. So, if your current reward–cost ratio falls below your CL, the relationship will be unsatisfying. If it's above your CL, you'll be satisfied with the relationship.
- *Comparison level for alternatives* (CL alt.) is essentially your expectation about the reward–cost ratio which *could* be obtained in other relationships. If your current ratio in a relationship exceeds the CL alt., then you're doing better in it than you could do elsewhere. As a result, the relationship should be satisfying and likely to continue. But if the CL alt. exceeds your current reward–cost ratio, then you're doing worse than you could do elsewhere. As a result, the relationship should be unsatisfying and unlikely to continue.

The concept of CL alt. implies that the endurance of a relationship (as far as one partner is concerned) could be due to the qualities of the other partner and the relationship, or to the negative and unattractive features of the perceived alternatives, or to the perceived costs of leaving (Duck, 1988). This, however, still portrays people as being fundamentally selfish, and many researchers (e.g. Walster *et al.*, 1978; Duck, 1988) prefer to see relationships as being maintained by an equitable distribution of rewards and costs for both partners. In this approach, people are seen as being concerned with the equity of outcomes both for themselves and their partners.

Murstein *et al.* (1977) argue that concern with either exchange or equity is negatively correlated with marital adjustment. People in close relationships don't think in terms of rewards and costs at all – until they start to feel dissatisfied (Argyle, 1987). Murstein & MacDonald (1983) have argued that although the principles of exchange and equity play a significant role in intimate relationships, a conscious concern with 'getting a fair deal', especially in the short term, makes *compatibility* (see below) very hard to achieve. This is true both in friendship and, especially, marriage. This corresponds to Mills and Clark's *exchange couple* (see above).

Complementarity

According to Kerckhoff & Davis's (1962) filter model (see above, page 405), *complementarity of needs* becomes increasingly important as relationships become long-term. According to Winch (1958), happy marriages are often based on each partner's ability to fulfil the needs of the other. For example, a domineering person could more easily satisfy a partner who needs to be dominated than one who's equally domineering, and Winch found some empirical support for this view.

However, although some complementarity may evolve as a relationship develops, people seem, if anything, slightly more likely to marry those whose needs and personalities are *similar* (the *matching phenomenon*) (e.g. Berscheid & Walster, 1978). According to Buss (1985, cited in Myers, 1994), 'The tendency of opposites to marry, or mate ... has never been reliably demonstrated, with the single exception of sex'.

Complementarity of resources

Instead of complementary needs, what about complementarity in resources (Brehm, 1992)? As we noted earlier, men seem to give a universally higher priority to 'good looks' in their female partners than do women in their male partners, while the situation is reversed when it comes to 'good financial prospect' and 'good earning capacity'. Based on a study of 37 cultures (including Nigeria, South Africa, Japan, Estonia, Zambia, Columbia, Poland, Germany, Spain, France, China, Palestinian Arabs, Italy and The Netherlands) involving over 10,000 people, Buss (1989) concluded that these sex differences '... appear to be deeply rooted in the evolutionary history of our species ...'.

CRITICAL DISCUSSION 28.1

Do our genes dictate what we want in a mate?

According to Buss (1988, 1989), the chances of reproductive success should be increased for men who mate with younger, healthy adult females, as opposed to older, unhealthy ones. Fertility is a function of the mother's age and health, which also affects pregnancy and her ability to care for her child. Men often have to rely on a woman's physical appearance in order to estimate her age and health, with younger, healthier women being perceived as more attractive (see Box 28.2). For women, mate selection depends on their need for a provider to take care of them during pregnancy and nursing: men seen as powerful and controlling resources that contribute to the mother and child's welfare will be seen as especially attractive.

Whatever the virtues of this sociobiological argument, it seems to take male–female relationships out of any cultural or historical context (as captured in the use of the term 'mate selection'). Perhaps women have been forced to obtain desirable resources through men, because they've been denied direct access to political and economic power. Traditionally, a woman has been regarded as the man's property, whereby her beauty increases his status and respect in others' eyes (Sigall & Landy, 1973).

What Buss conveniently seems to overlook is that in his (1989) cross-cultural study, 'kind' and 'intelligent' were universally ranked as *more important* than 'physically attractive' or 'good earning power' by both men and women! And how can Buss's argument account for homosexual relationships, which clearly don't contribute to the survival of the species, despite being subject to many of the same sociopsychological influences involved in heterosexual relationships (Brehm, 1992: see pages 410–411)?

Compatibility

The importance of similarity

Complementarity, as far as it exists, can be seen as a component of *compatibility*, but *similarity* plays a much larger part in keeping couples together. For example, individuals with similar needs (Meyer & Pepper, 1977), attitudes, likes and dislikes (Newcomb, 1978), and who are similar in attractiveness (White, 1980), are more likely to remain in a relationship than dissimilar individuals.

Princess Diana and Prince Charles pictured before their marriage. They seemed the perfect couple, but compatibility is complex and appearances can be deceptive

Hill *et al.* (1976) studied 231 steadily dating couples over a two-year period, at the end of which 103 couples had broken up (45 per cent). The surviving couples tended to be more alike in terms of age, intelligence, educational and career plans, as well as physical attractiveness, while those who split up often mentioned differences in interests, background, sexual attitudes and ideas about marriage. About 80 per cent of the couples who described themselves as being 'in love' at the start stayed together, compared with 56 per cent of those who didn't. Of couples in which both members initially reported being equally involved in the relationship, only 23 per cent broke up, but where one member was much more involved than the other, 54 per cent did so. The latter is a highly unstable couple, in which the one who's more involved (putting more in but getting less in return) may feel dependent and exploited, while the one who's less involved (putting less in but getting more in return) may feel restless and guilty (which implies some sense of fairness).

Marital satisfaction

This is another way of looking at compatibility. In a review of studies looking at marital satisfaction and communication, Duck (1992) found that happy couples give more positive and consistent non-verbal cues than unhappy couples, express more agreement and approval of the other's ideas and suggestions, talk more about their relationships, and are more willing to compromise on difficult decisions.

Lauer & Lauer (1985) asked several hundred couples married for at least 15 years why they thought their marriages had lasted. They stressed *friendship* (e.g. 'My spouse is my best friend'), *commitment* ('Marriage is a long-term commitment'), *similarity* ('We agree on how and how often to show affection'), and *positive affect* ('We laugh together') as the basic elements in an enduring relationship. These findings could be seen as implying a successful transition from passionate to companionate love.

Relationship breakdown and dissolution

Marital unhappiness and divorce

Duck (1988, 1992) has identified several factors that make it more likely that the marriage will be unhappy and/or end in divorce:

- Marriages in which the partners are *younger than average* tend to be more unstable. This can be understood by reference to Erikson's concept of *intimacy* (see Chapter 38). Such marriages often involve early parenthood; the young couple has little time to adjust to the new responsibilities of marriage before financial and housing problems are added with the arrival of a baby (Kellmer Pringle, 1986).
- Marriages between couples from *lower socioeconomic groups* and *educational levels* tend to be more unstable. These are also the couples which tend to have their children very early in marriage.
- Marriages between partners from *different demographic backgrounds* (race, religion, and so on) also tend to be more unstable. This can be related to Kerckhoff and Davis's filter model.
- Marriages between people who've experienced *parental divorce* as children, or who've had a *greater number of sexual partners* than average before marriage tend to be more unstable.

While these factors are important, only a proportion of marriages involving young, lower-class individuals or those from different cultural backgrounds and so on actually end in divorce. Conversely, many divorces will involve couples who don't fit any of these descriptions. So what other factors may be involved?

According to Brehm (1992), there are two broad types of cause: *structural* (specifically, gender, duration of the relationship, the presence of children and role strain created by competing demands of work and family), and *conflict resolution*.

Gender differences

Men and women seem to differ in their perception of problems in a relationship. In general, women report more problems, and there's some evidence that the degree of female dissatisfaction is a better predictor than male unhappiness of whether the relationship will end. This could be because women are more sensitive to relationship problems than men. Alternatively, men and women may come into relationships with different expectations and hopes, with men's generally being fulfiled to a greater extent than women's.

Consistent with this possibility is evidence of gender differences in the specific type of problems that are reported. For example, although divorcing men and women are equally likely to cite communication problems as a cause of their splitting up, women stress basic unhappiness and incompatibility more than men do. Also, men seem particularly upset by 'sexual withholding' by a female partner, while women are distressed by a male partner's sexual aggression.

Duration of relationships and the passage of time

The longer partners have known each other before marriage, the more likely they are to be satisfied in the marriage, and the less likely they are to divorce. However, couples who've cohabited before marriage report fewer barriers to ending the marriage, and the longer a relationship lasts, the more people blame their partners for negative events.

Two major views of changes in marital satisfaction over time are Pineo's (1961) *linear model* and Burr's (1970) *curvilinear model*. According to the linear model (see Figure 28.6), there's an inevitable fading of the romantic 'high' of courtship before marriage. Also, people marry because they've achieved a 'good fit' with their partners; any changes that occur in either partner will reduce their compatibility. For example, if one partner becomes more self-confident (ironically, through the support gained from the relationship), there may be increased conflict between two 'equals' competing for superiority.

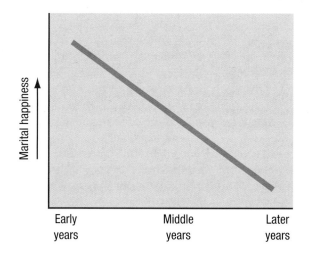

Figure 28.6 *A linear life-cycle (based on Brehm, 1992)*

The curvilinear model (see Figure 28.7, page 415) proposes that marital happiness is greatest in the earliest years. Marital satisfaction declines as children are born and grow up, then increases again as they mature and leave home.

While it's generally agreed that there's a decline in satisfaction during the early years, whether there's an actual increase or just a levelling off after that remains a matter of debate. Gilford & Bengtson (1979) argue that it's an oversimplification to talk about 'marital satisfaction'. Instead, we should look at two life cycles: the *pattern of positive rewards*, and the *pattern of negative costs*. The early years are associated with very high rewards and very high costs, while in the middle years there's a decline in both. In the later years, costs continue to decline, but there's an increase in rewards.

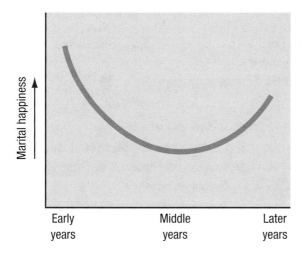

Figure 28.7 *A curvilinear life cycle (based on Brehm, 1992)*

Marriage, divorce, and parenthood are discussed further in Chapter 37.

Conflict resolution

According to Duck (1988), some kind and degree of conflict is inevitable in all relationships. But the process of resolving conflicts can often be positive, promoting growth of the relationship (Wood & Duck, 1995). The important question, therefore, isn't whether there's conflict, but *how* it's handled. However, recurring conflicts may indicate an inability to resolve the underlying source; the partners may come to doubt each other as reasonable persons, leading to a 'digging in of the heels', a disaffection with each other and, ultimately, a 'strong falling out' (Berry & Willingham, 1997).

According to Bradbury & Fincham (1990), happy and unhappy couples resolve conflict in typically different ways, which can be understood as involving different *attributional patterns* (see Chapter 23). Happy couples use a *relationship-enhancing pattern*, while unhappy couples use a *distress-maintaining pattern* (see Figure 28.8 below).

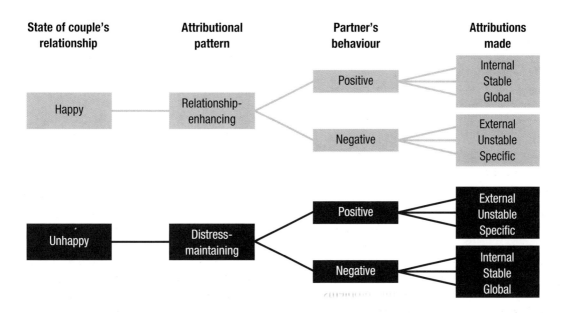

Figure 28.8 *Attributions made by happy and unhappy couples according to Bradbury and Fincham (1990) (from Brehm S.S. (1992)* Intimate Relationships *(2nd edition). New York, McGraw-Hill)*

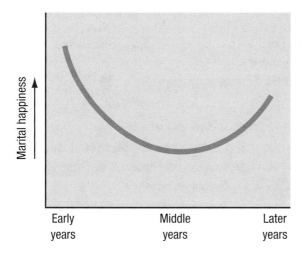

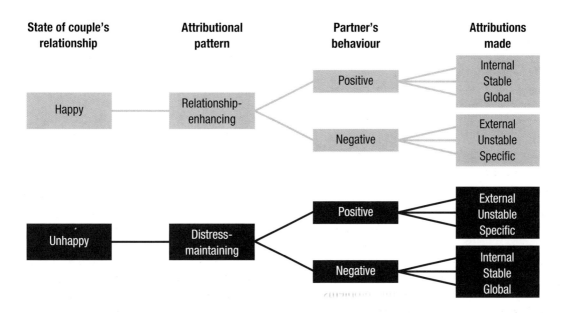

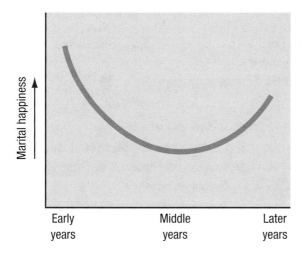

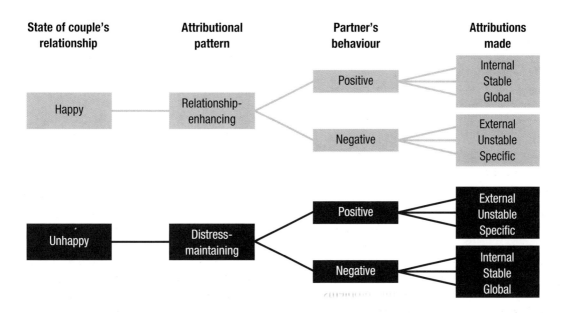

Rule-breaking and deception

> *Ask yourself ...*
> • What's the worse thing that a friend or partner could do as far as your relationship is concerned? Is there anything which *in principle* you wouldn't tolerate?

Argyle & Henderson (1984) and Argyle *et al.* (1985) identified a number of rules thought to apply to all or most relationships, such as 'Should respect the other's privacy', 'Should not discuss what is said in confidence', 'Should be emotionally supportive'. There are additional rules for particular types of relationship. Relationships fall into clusters, with similar rules applying within a cluster. For example, one cluster includes spouse, siblings and close friends, and another includes doctor, teacher and boss.

The role regarding *deception* probably represents the most important rule that shouldn't be broken. Although what counts as deception will depend on the nature of the relationship, if you can't trust your friend or partner, the relationship is almost certainly doomed.

Relationship dissolution as a process

Relationships are highly complex, and this applies to their break-up as much as it does to their formation and maintenance. It applies to the break-up of friendships and sexual relationships, and not just marriages, particularly if the relationship is a long-term one that has embraced many parts of the person's emotional, communicative, leisure and everyday life (Duck, 1988).

As we noted earlier, not all marriages involving young partners will break up while they're still young, so research needs to focus on the *processes* by which the lasting/non-lasting relationships may be distinguished (Gottman, 1994; Aldous, 1996). As Duck (1999) says:

Michael Douglas and Kathleen Turner in a scene from War of the Roses

'*In accounting for break-up, therefore, we need to consider it as a long-term process in the lives of the partners and their associates ...*'.

Also, people sometimes think about and plan their break-ups, or maybe about how to prevent them: they don't always come at people 'out of the blue'. Recent research has begun to look more closely at the specific characteristics of those relationships that do break apart. What is it about the partners and their behaviour towards each other that accounts for their problems? For example, do troubled couples have particular ways of communicating and relating (Duck, 1999)?

Researchers have also begun to look at the break-up of friendships, and the actions, strategies, and persuasive techniques people deliberately take to cause break-up. As Duck (1999) observes:

'*Break-up is not just the waning of intimacy or reduction in feelings towards the partner ... the dissolution of relationships highlights the operation of relationship processes, such as interpersonal judgements, assessments of social exchange, and interactions that are present throughout a relationship but go unnoticed in routine interaction*'.

Lee's model

Lee (1984) proposed five stages of premarital romantic break-ups. *Dissatisfaction* (D) is discovered, then it's *exposed* (E). There's some *negotiation* (N) about it, attempts are made to *resolve* (R) the problem, and finally the relationship is *terminated* (T).

Lee surveyed 112 such break-ups. (E) and (N) tend to be experienced as the most intense, dramatic, exhausting and negative aspects of the whole experience. Those who skipped these stages (by just walking out) felt less intimate with their ex-partners, even while the relationship had been going satisfactorily. Where the whole passage from (D) to (T) is particularly prolonged, people reported feeling more attracted to their ex-partners, and experienced greatest loneliness and fear during the break-up.

Table 28.1 *A sketch of the main phases of dissolving personal relationships (based on Duck, 1982, from Duck, 1988)*

Breakdown–dissatisfaction with relationship

Threshold: '*I can't stand this any more*'

INTRAPSYCHIC PHASE

- Personal focus on partner's behaviour
- Assess adequacy of partner's role performance
- Depict and evaluate negative aspects of being in the relationship
- Consider costs of withdrawal
- Assess positive aspects of alternative relationships
- Face 'express/repress dilemma'

Threshold: '*I'd be justified in withdrawing*'

DYADIC PHASE

- Face 'confrontation/avoidance dilemma'
- Confront partner
- Negotiate in 'our relationship talks'
- Attempt repair and reconciliation?
- Assess joint costs of withdrawal or reduced intimacy

Threshold: '*I mean it*'

SOCIAL PHASE

- Negotiate post-dissolution state with partner
- Initiate gossip/discussion in social network
- Create publicly negotiable face-saving/blame-placing stories and accounts
- Consider and face up to implied social network effect, if any
- Call in intervention team

Threshold: '*It's now inevitable*'

GRAVE-DRESSING PHASE

- 'Getting over' activity
- Retrospective; reformative post-mortem attribution
- Public distribution of own version of break-up story

Duck's model

Duck's (1982) model comprises four phases, each of which is initiated when a threshold is broken. (See Table 28.1.)

Each person needs to emerge with an intact reputation for relationship reliability. 'Dressing the grave' involves 'erecting a tablet' which provides a credible, socially acceptable account of the life and death of the relationship. While helping to save face, it also serves to keep alive some memories and to 'justify' the original commitment to the ex-partner. As Duck (1988) puts it:

'Such stories are an integral and important part of the psychology of ending relationships … By helping the person to get over the break-up they are immensely significant in preparing the person for future relationships as well as helping them out of old ones'.

Conclusions: What happens after divorce?

One growing area of research interest is 'postmarital' and 'remarital relationships', and family reorganisation after divorce. The increasing incidence of divorce is making blended families the norm. Indeed, there's a shift in ideology, from viewing divorce as pathology to viewing it as an institution (Duck, 1999).

Once divorce is seen as a common transition, rather than as pathological, researchers can reasonably begin to attend to a much wider range of issues, such as 'getting over' and prevention. Moreover, they can focus on the processes of entering *new* relationships as well as to those to do with leaving the old ones (Masheter, 1997: see Chapter 38).

CHAPTER SUMMARY

- Intimate relationships with relatives and romantic partners represent crucial factors in determining people's general happiness.
- The **need for affiliation** represents a precondition for attraction, and can be related to the need for social comparison. Both are enhanced under conditions of increased anxiety.
- Loving is **qualitatively** different from liking, and involves attachment, caring and intimacy. There are also different kinds of love.
- Interpersonal relationships in Western cultures tend to be **individualistic**, **voluntary** and **temporary**, whereas those in non-Western cultures tend to be more **collectivist**, **involuntary** and **permanent.**
- Westerners think of **monogamy** as the normal, even moral form of marriage. But cultures differ in their marital arrangements. **Polygamy** can take the form of **polygyny** or **polyandry.** Another arrangement is **mandatory marriage to specific relatives**.
- The notion of people falling in love is found in one form or another in most human societies, even where marriages are traditionally arranged by families or friends.
- Kerckhoff and Davis's '**filter model**', and other 'stage' theories, aren't strongly supported by empirical evidence. But it's generally agreed that relationships change and develop.

- A general theoretical framework for explaining initial attraction is that the presence of others must be **rewarding**.
- **Proximity** provides increased opportunity for interaction, which increases **familiarity** through the **mere exposure effect.** But people can become too familiar by invading our **personal space**.
- **Similarity** of attitudes and values is a powerful influence on attraction, but this usually only emerges as the relationship develops. However, **physical attractiveness** has an immediate effect.
- There are important **cultural differences** in what counts as physical beauty, but there's a universal tendency for men to regard physical attractiveness in their partners as more important than women do in theirs.
- Certain factors are found to be omitted or distorted when **homosexual relationships** are assessed in terms derived from heterosexual relationships. These include **cohabitation**, **sexual exclusivity**, and **sex role**.
- The anonymous and disinhibiting nature of **online relationships** has both benefits and dangers. They reduce the importance of physical attractiveness, but they may make face-to-face interaction less common and are potentially addictive.
- **Social exchange theory** is a major explanation of all kinds of relationships, both intimate and non-intimate. It sees people as fundamentally **selfish**, but humans are capable of **altruism** as well as selfishness.
- Central to **equity theory** is the concept of **fairness.** Changes in **reward–cost ratio** are likely to cause dissatisfaction with the relationship.
- While there's little evidence for the **complementarity of psychological needs**, there's more support for complementarity in **resources.** But sociobiologists' claim that the universal male preference for physical attractiveness and female preference for financial security are genetically determined ignores cultural and historical factors.
- **Conflict** is an inherent part of all relationships, and what's crucial is how constructively it's resolved. Happy couples tend to deal with conflict in a **relationship-enhancing way**, while unhappy couples use a **distress-maintaining pattern** of conflict resolution.
- **Rule-breaking** is a major cause of relationship breakdown, especially **deception.**
- Relationship breakdown is a **process**, involving a number of stages or phases. Research is increasingly concerned with the **aftermath** of relationship break-down, especially divorce, and not just the breakdown itself.

Self-assessment questions

1 Critically consider research into interpersonal attraction.
2 Describe and evaluate research relating to the maintenance **or** dissolution of relationships.
3 Discuss psychological insights into differences in relationships between Western and non-Western cultures.
4 Describe and evaluate research into homosexual **or** 'online' relationships.

Web addresses

http://www.octrl.edu/~ajomuel/crow/topicattraction.htm

http://www.socialpsychology.org/social.htm#romance

miavx1.muohio.edu/~psybersite/attraction/

http://faculty.edu.umuc.edu/~motsowit/psyc334.htm/

http://www.socialpsychology.org/social.htm#cultural

http://www.socialpsychology.org/social.htm#family

http://www.socialpsychology.org/social.htm#divorce

http://www.erlbaum.com/html/500.htm

http://www.socialpsychology.org/social.htm#cultural

http://www.socialpsychology.org/social.htm#sexuality

http://www.socialpsychology.org/social.htm#lesbigay

Further reading

Brehm, S.S. (1992) *Intimate Relationships* (2nd edition). New York: McGraw-Hill. An excellent source of research and theory, written by one of the authorities in the field.

Duck, S. (1999) *Relating to Others* (2nd edition). Buckingham: Open University Press. Covers all the issues discussed in this chapter, in a challenging yet entertaining way.

Kitzinger, C. & Coyle, A. (1995) Lesbian and gay couples: Speaking of difference. *The Psychologist, 8 (2)*, 64–9. An extremely interesting article, which compares and contrasts straight and gay relationships and contains much useful material about the more traditional, heterosexual research.

Chapter 29

Aggression and Antisocial Behaviour

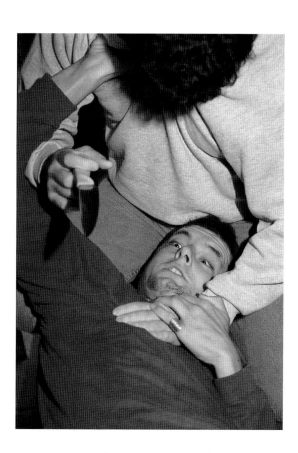

Introduction and overview

Philosophers and psychologists have been interested in human aggression for a long time. According to Hobbes (1651), people are naturally competitive and hostile, interested only in their own power and gaining advantage over others. Hobbes argued that to prevent conflict and mutual destruction, people need government.

This pessimistic view of human nature was shared by Freud and Lorenz, albeit for different theoretical reasons. Like McDougall, Freud and Lorenz saw aggression as an instinct (see Chapter 9). In Freud's *psychoanalytic theory*, aggression is inherently self-destructive, but in practice is directed outwards mainly at other people, as demonstrated all too clearly in the carnage of war. According to Lorenz's *ethological theory*, human beings have lost the means of controlling their aggression that other species possess, and in addition have invented weapons that allow aggression to take place from a distance.

Other explanations of aggression have combined elements of instinct theories with those of learning theory, such as Dollard *et al.*'s *frustration–aggression hypothesis*, and Berkowitz's *aggressive-cue theory*. Bandura's study of *observational learning*'s role in aggression stimulated research into the effects of violence in the media, in particular television, and, more recently, so-called 'video nasties'. Perhaps the 'purest' *social psychological* account of aggression is the theory of *individuation*.

Baron & Richardson (1994) define antisocial behaviours as those 'which show a lack of feeling and concern for the welfare of others'. While aggression represents just one such lack of feeling and concern, it's the one that psychologists have focused on. But aggression itself can take different forms, and can be linked to motives other than wishing to harm or injure another person.

Defining aggression

> ## Ask yourself ...
>
> - What do you understand by 'aggression'?
> - Are there different kinds of aggression?
> - Is aggression the same as violence?

We all seem to recognise aggression when we witness or encounter it, but defining it often proves much more difficult. When used as a *noun*, aggression usually conveys some behaviour which is intended to harm another (or at least which has that effect). Yet even this definition is too broad: self-defence and unprovoked attack may both involve similar 'acts' and degrees of aggression, but only the latter would normally be considered 'antisocial' (and the law also recognises this distinction). When used as an *adjective*, 'aggressive' can convey that an action is carried out with energy and persistence (Lloyd *et al.*, 1984), something which may even be regarded as socially desirable.

Moyer (1976) and Berkowitz (1993) see aggression as always involving behaviour, either physical or symbolic, performed with the intention of harming someone. They reserve the word *violence* to describe an extreme form of aggression in which a deliberate attempt is made to inflict serious physical injury on another person or damage property.

Other important distinctions include:

- *hostile aggression*, which is aimed solely at hurting another (gratuitous aggression or 'aggression for aggression's sake'), which would exclude self-defence;
- *instrumental aggression*, which is a means to an end (and so would include self-defence: Buss, 1961; Feshbach, 1964).

- *natural* or *positive aggression*, which is aimed largely at self-defence or combating prejudice and other social injustice; and
- *pathological aggression* or violence, which results when our inner nature has become twisted or frustrated (e.g. Maslow, 1968).

Theories of aggression

Instinct theories

Lorenz's ethological approach

Ethologists consider aggression to be instinctive in all species and important in the evolutionary development of the species, allowing individuals to adapt to their environments, survive in them and successfully reproduce (see Chapter 2 and Gross *et al.*, 2000). When space or food are scarce, many species limit their reproduction and survive by marking off living space which they defend against 'trespassers' (*territoriality*). Aggressiveness is clearly important in competing successfully for limited resources, in defending territory and for basic survival.

According to Lorenz (1966), it's legitimate to make direct comparisons between different species, although his theory of human aggression is based on the study of non-primates and mainly non-mammals, in particular fish and insects. He defines aggression as:

> '... the fighting instinct in beast and man which is directed against members of the same species'.

Differences between non-human and human aggression

According to Lorenz, in non-humans, aggression is basically constructive, but in humans it's become distorted:

- *Ritualisation* refers to a way of discharging aggression in a fixed, stereotyped pattern, whereby fights between members of the same species result in relatively little physical harm to either victor or vanquished, but at the same time allow a victor to emerge. For example, the fighting that takes place between stags is highly ritualised, and the triumphant one is the male who 'makes his point' rather than the one who kills or incapacitates his opponent. Similarly, wolves will end their fight with the loser exposing its jugular vein – but this is sufficient and no blood is spilled.

■ Sometimes, antagonists may approach each other in a threatening manner but not actually engage in combat. One will show *appeasement rituals* (or *gestures*), which prevent the other from engaging in actual conflict. For example, in one species of jackdaw, the nape section at the bottom of the head is clearly marked off from the rest of the body by its plumage and colouring, and when one bird 'offers' its nape to an aggressor, the latter will never attack, even if on the verge of doing so.

Although human appeasement responses (such as smiling, cowering, cringing or begging for mercy) are normally very effective, we've developed a *technology* of aggression. However naturally aggressive we are as a species compared with other species, our superior brains have enabled us to construct weapons which remove combat from the eye-to-eye, face-to-face situation. This inevitably reduces the overall role – and effectiveness – of appeasement rituals. Indeed, the deadliest weapons (as measured by the number of victims who can be killed or injured at one time) are precisely those which can be used at the greatest distance from the intended victims (e.g. bombs and intercontinental nuclear missiles). According to Lea (1984):

'We have developed a technology which enables our intentions to override our instincts'.

A passenger train destroyed in a NATO missile attack in Serbia in April, 1999, during the Kosovo conflict. At least ten people were killed and 16 others injured

An evaluation of Lorenz's theory

■ In keeping with his belief that humans are naturally highly aggressive, Lorenz maintains that their 'natural condition' is that of 'warrior'. However, it's generally agreed that early human beings *weren't* warriors but 'hunter–gatherers' (such as the present-day Inuit Eskimos, Pygmies of the Ituri forest, Aborigines, Kalahari Bushmen, the Punan of Borneo and so on), who live in small clans which hardly ever come into contact with other groups of people (Siann, 1985).

■ Even without the most primitive weapons, other primates, including chimps, can and do kill each other. Goodall (1978) describes warfare between two colonies of chimps which ended in the killing of every male in one of the groups, and infanticide is one of the more common kinds of unrestrained aggression among non-human species. For example, male lions that succeed in taking over a 'pride' of females (so displacing other adult males) will often attack and kill any cubs that are present (which then makes the females available for mating). According to Lea (1984), Lorenz's claim that non-human aggression always stops before an animal is killed is basically a myth.

■ Lorenz totally ignored the role of *learning* and *cultural influences*, which are far more important determinants of human aggression than biological factors. Whatever potential for aggression we may have inherited as a species, it's culturally over-ridden and repackaged into forms which fit current circumstances. Cultures differ in the degrees and kinds of aggression which are permissible, including gender-related aggression (see Chapter 36).

■ Lorenz claims that aggression (like hunger, sexuality and flight, which collectively he calls the 'big four') isn't a response to environmental stimuli, but occurs *spontaneously*, when instinctive aggressive energy builds up and demands discharge (*the hydraulic model of instinct*). The evidence for this energy model is very sparse indeed (Siann, 1985), and many modern biologists and ethologists, believe that aggression in animals is reactive and modifiable by a variety of internal and external conditions (Hinde, 1974).

Freud's psychoanalytic approach

As we saw in Chapter 9, Freud's theory is normally regarded as an *instinct theory*. It wasn't until late in his life that Freud recognised aggression as an instinct distinct from sexuality (libido). This change in his thinking occurred in response to the horrific carnage of the First World War. In *Beyond the Pleasure Principle* (1920) and *The Ego and the Id* (1923), he distinguished between the *life instinct* (or *Eros*), including sexuality, and the *death instinct* (*Thanatos*).

Thanatos represents an inborn destructiveness, directed primarily against *the self*. The aim (as with all instincts in Freud's view) is to reduce tension or excitation to a minimum and, ultimately, to eliminate it completely. This was the idyllic state we enjoyed in the womb, where our needs were met as soon as they arose, and, for a while, at our mother's breast. But after this, the only way of achieving such a *Nirvana* is through death.

Self-directed aggression, however, conflicts with the life instinct, especially the self-preservative component. But because the impulse to self-destruction is so strong, Freud believed that we must destroy some other thing or person if we're not to destroy ourselves. Conflict with the life instinct results in our aggression being *displaced* onto others. More positively, aggression can be *sublimated* into sport, physical occupations and domination and mastery of nature and the world in general. Like Freud, Lorenz also argued that we need to acknowledge our aggressiveness and to control it through sport (e.g. the Olympics), expeditions, explorations and so on, especially if international co-operation is involved (Lorenz called these 'displacement' activities). Freud shared Lorenz's view that aggressive energy builds up until eventually it has to be discharged in some way.

KEY STUDY 29.1

The overcontrolled violent criminal (Megargee, 1966)

Megargee reported that brutally aggressive crimes are often committed by *overcontrolled individuals*. They repress their anger, and over a period of time the pressure to be aggressive builds up. Often it's an objectively trivial incident which provokes the destructive outburst, with the aggressor then returning to his previously passive state, once more seeming incapable of violence.

The extremely violent offender often proves to be a rather passive person, with no previous history of aggression. In Phoenix, an eleven-year-old boy who stabbed his brother 34 times with a steak knife was described by all who knew him as being extremely polite and softly spoken with no history of violent behaviour. In New York, an 18-year-old youth who confessed he'd assaulted and strangled a seven-year-old girl in a church, and later tried to burn her body in the furnace, was described in the press as an unemotional person who planned to be a minister. A 21-year-old man from Colorado who was accused of the rape and murder of two little girls had never been a discipline problem and, in fact, his stepfather reported, 'When he was in school the other kids would run all over him and he'd never fight back. There is just no violence in him'.

In these cases, the homicide wasn't just one more aggressive offence in a person who'd always displayed inadequate controls. Rather, it was a completely uncharacteristic act in a person who'd always displayed extraordinarily high levels of control. According to Megargee & Mendelsohn (1962):

'... the extremely assaultive person is often a fairly mild-mannered, long-suffering individual who buries his resentment under rigid but brittle controls. Under certain circumstances he may lash out and release all his aggression in one, often disastrous, act. Afterwards he reverts to his usual overcontrolled defences. Thus he may be more of a menace than the verbally aggressive 'chip-on-the-shoulder' type who releases his aggression in small doses'.

An evaluation of Freud's theory

Despite supportive evidence such as Megargee's, Freud's ideas on aggression made little impact either on the public imagination or on other psychologists (including other psychoanalysts) until Dollard *et al.* (1939) proposed their *frustration–aggression hypothesis* (see below). Fromm's *The Anatomy of Human Destructiveness* (1977) was influenced by Freud's ideas, as was Storr's *Human Aggression* (1968). Storr (like Fromm, a psychoanalyst) dedicated his book to Lorenz, and in the introduction he says:

'That man is an aggressive creature will hardly be disputed. With the exception of certain rodents, no other vertebrate habitually destroys members of his own species... the extremes of 'brutal' behaviour are confined to man; and there is no parallel in nature to our savage treatment of each other... we are the cruellest and most ruthless species that has ever walked the earth; and that, although we may recoil in horror when we read in newspaper or history book of the atrocities committed by man upon man, we know in our hearts that each one of us harbours within himself those same savage impulses which lead to murder, to torture and to war'.

Storr identifies four forms of psychopathology attributable to the inadequate resolution of the aggressive drive, namely depression, schizoid behaviour, paranoia (see Chapter 44) and psychopathy (see Chapter 46).

The frustration–aggression hypothesis

Dollard *et al.*'s (1939) *frustration–aggression hypothesis* was intended partly to 'translate' some of Freud's psychoanalytic concepts into learning theory terms. It claims that:

'... aggression is always a consequence of frustration and, contrariwise ... the existence of frustration always leads to some form of aggression'.

While agreeing with Freud that aggression is an innate response, Dollard *et al.* argued that it would be triggered only by frustrating situations and events. Some support for this view comes from the displacement of aggression, as demonstrated in the *scapegoating* account of racial discrimination (see Chapter 25).

Ask yourself ...

- Can you think of any exceptions to the claims made by the frustration–aggression hypothesis? Do we necessarily become aggressive when we're frustrated?

Some criticisms of the original frustration–aggression hypothesis

It soon became apparent that the frustration–aggression hypothesis, in its original form, was an overstatement:

- Miller (1941) argued that frustration is an *instigator* of aggression, but situational factors (such as *learned inhibition* and *fear of retaliation*) may prevent actual aggressive behaviour from occurring. So, although frustration may make aggression more likely, it's far from being a sufficient cause of aggression.
- Frustration can produce a variety of responses (of which aggression is one), including *regression* (see Chapter 42), depression and lethargy (Seligman, 1975: see Chapter 12).
- Bandura (1973) argued that frustration might be a source of *arousal*, but frustration-induced arousal (like other types of arousal) could have a variety of outcomes, of which aggression is only one. Whether it actually occurs is more the result of learned patterns of behaviour triggered by environmental cues.
- Frustration may also produce different responses in different people in different situations. According to Miell (1990), for example, experiments seem to suggest that frustration is

most likely to produce aggression if (a) the person is close to achieving his/her goal, or (b) the frustrating event seems arbitrary. Berkowitz (1993) says that if a frustration is either arbitrary or illegitimate it's seen as unfair.

KEY STUDY 29.2

Don't frustrate me without a good reason (Kulik & Brown, 1979)

Kulik and Brown found that frustration was more likely to produce aggression if it wasn't anticipated, and if participants believed that the person responsible for frustrating them did so deliberately and without good reason. This shows the importance of *cognitive factors* as cues for aggressive behaviour.

Participants were told they could earn money by telephoning people and persuading them to make a pledge to charity. Some expected that about two-thirds of those contacted would agree to make a pledge, while others expected a very low response rate. All the people telephoned were stooges, none of whom agreed to pledge.

The first group of participants showed more aggression by slamming down the phone, speaking more aggressively, and so on. Also, those given reasonable excuses (such as 'I can't afford it') showed less aggression than those given less reasonable excuses (such as 'Charities are a waste of time and a rip-off').

The attributional perspective

One of the important cognitive factors identified by Kulik and Brown is the *attribution of intention*. According to Berkowitz (1993), we aren't usually bothered by a failure to reach our goals unless we believe that the frustrater intentionally or improperly tried to interfere with our efforts. In other words, the attribution must involve a cause that's seen as *internal*, *controllable* and *improper* (in violation of generally accepted rules of conduct). This is consistent with Weiner's (1986) attributional theory of emotion and motivation (see Chapter 23).

This attributional perspective is consistent with the definition of aggression as the (perceived) intention to harm another person (see above). If there are *mitigating circumstances*, the cause may now be seen as *external* and *uncontrollable*, (although still improper). Apologising or confessing can have similar effects (Weiner, 1992), and represent important aspects of *impression management* (see Chapter 22).

Children who display chronic aggression appear to have a particular type of *attributional style*. They display a strong attributional bias towards seeing others as acting against them with hostile intent, especially in ambiguous situations. Such biased attributions often lead to retaliatory aggression (Taylor *et al.*, 1994).

Aggressive-cue theory

Berkowitz (1966) argued that frustration produces *anger* rather than aggression. Frustration is psychologically painful, and anything which is psychologically (or physically) painful can lead to aggression. According to *aggressive-cue* (or *cue–arousal*)

theory, for anger/psychological pain to be converted into actual aggression, certain *cues* are needed. These are environmental stimuli associated either with aggressive behaviour or with the frustrating object or person.

Aggressive or violent behaviour is, at least partly, a reaction to specific features of the surrounding situation which 'pull out' responses that heighten the strength of the behaviour. This happens either when the environmental cues are associated in the aggressor's mind with aggression, and/or when they somehow remind the aggressor of decidedly unpleasant experiences.

Box 29.1 Berkowitz's paradigm for investigating cue-related aggression

When participants arrive, they're told they'll be paired with another person (a stooge) in a study concerned with the physiological reactions to stress. To do this, they'll be asked to offer a written solution to a problem. Stress will be introduced by their solution being evaluated by their partner, who will deliver between one and ten electric shocks to them (according to his/her evaluation of the solution). After completing their solutions, half the participants receive a single shock, while the rest receive seven (all fairly mild), the lower number of shocks indicating a very favourable evaluation.

Following this first stage, participants take their turn in evaluating the stooge's solution, *either* after seeing a violent film (*Champion*, depicting a brutal prize fight and starring Kirk Douglas), or a non-violent film (showing highlights of an exciting track race), *or* in the presence of objects that are/aren't associated with violence. Aggression is measured as the number of shocks the participant delivers.

Experimental tests of aggressive-cue theory

Berkowitz & Geen (1966) introduced the stooge to the real participant either as Bob Anderson or Kirk Anderson. As expected, the largest number of shocks were delivered by participants who were angry (had received seven shocks from the confederate), had witnessed the violent film, and believed the confederate's name was Kirk (his name was linked to the witnessed aggression through Kirk Douglas).

In a parallel experiment, the stooge was introduced either as Bob Kelly, Bob Dunne or Bob Riley; Dunne was the name of the victorious character in *Champion*, and Kelly (played by Kirk Douglas) was the loser. As predicted, the stooge received more shocks from participants who'd seen the violent film, but most importantly, he received most shocks when he was called Kelly.

Ask yourself ...

- Try to account for these findings.

In both cases (the stooge called 'Kirk' or 'Kelly' receiving the most shocks), participants encountered someone who reminded them of the victim in the witnessed aggression. He was associated with an instance of successful (i.e. rewarded) aggression, which made it more likely that anger would be converted into aggression (Berkowitz, 1993).

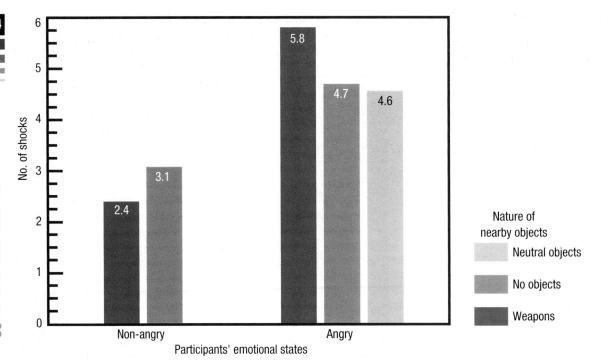

Figure 29.1 *Mean number of shocks given as a function of presence of weapons (adapted from Berkowitz & LePage, 1967). Copyright 1967 by the American Psychological Association. Adapted by permission)*

Berkowitz & Le Page's (1967) participants were taken to a 'control room' and shown the shock apparatus. For some, there was a shotgun and a revolver on a table next to the shock apparatus, while for others there were badminton rackets and some shuttlecocks. For each participant, these objects were pushed aside by the experimenter, who said that 'they must have been left there by another experimenter'. There was a third group for whom there were no 'planted' objects. As predicted, angry participants delivered more shocks to the stooge if a shotgun and revolver were nearby (objects that, for most people, are associated with violence) than when badminton rackets were present. This is known as the *weapons effect* (see Figure 29.1 above).

An evaluation of aggressive-cue theory

These and several other similar studies seem to suggest that people's actions towards others are sometimes influenced in a relatively thoughtless, automatic way by particular details of the immediate situation. The mere physical presence of weapons, even when not used in the performance of aggressive actions, may still increase the occurrence of such behaviour. As Berkowitz (1968) put it:

'Guns not only permit violence, they can stimulate it as well. The finger pulls the trigger, but the trigger may also be pulling the finger'.

Apart from some failures to replicate these findings, critics have argued that participants disregarded the explanation of what the weapons and other 'props' were doing there, and realised that the experimenter expected them to be aggressive. In other words, they were responding to the *demand characteristics* of the experimental situation (see Chapter 3).

But Berkowitz (1993) cites a study in which the more that participants believed the experimenter was interested in their aggressive responses, the *less* punitive they were towards the stooge. So, it could be that in the original Berkowitz and LePage

study, the increased aggression produced by exposure to weapons occurred *despite* participants' suspicions, *not* because of their beliefs about what the experimenter expected to happen.

Berkowitz (1995) points to a number of successful replications, including studies carried out in Belgium, Canada, Croatia, Italy and Sweden. In the Swedish study (Frodi, 1975), the weapons effect was shown by high-school boys even when they hadn't been 'angered' (i.e. shocked). According to Baron (1977):

'It is clear that Berkowitz's more general proposal that aggression is 'pulled' or elicited from without by external stimuli rather than merely 'pushed' from within has attained widespread acceptance ... his views in this regard have been highly influential in causing social psychologists to shift their search for the determinants of aggression largely from internal conflict and motives to external environmental factors ...'.

Zillman's excitation-transfer theory

According to Zillman (1982), arousal from one source can be transferred to, and energise, some other response. This is because arousal takes time to dissipate. When we're aroused, aggression may be heightened provided that the aroused person has some disposition to react aggressively, and that the arousal is incorrectly attributed to the aggression-provoking event rather than to the correct source.

In one test of this, Zillman & Bryant (1974) created states of arousal in participants by requiring them to ride bicycles. In some, high levels of arousal were induced, while in others low levels were induced. Then, participants played a game during which they were verbally insulted by a stooge. When participants were later given the opportunity to deliver a harsh noise in headphones worn by the stooge, significantly more noise was delivered by highly aroused participants.

Excitation-transfer theory sees the relationship between arousal and aggression as a sequence, in which arousal is generated and then, depending on its perceived causes, labelled, producing a specific emotion such as anger (Mummendey, 1996). Berkowitz (1990), however, disputes the existence of 'unspecific' or 'neutral' arousal. According to his *cognitive–neoassociationistic approach*, anger and aggression are *parallel* rather than sequential processes, because aversive events automatically lead to the instigation of aggression, depending on what situational cues are present (Mummendey, 1996).

The social learning theory approach and media violence

Social learning theory

According to *social learning theory* (SLT), aggressive behaviours are learned through reinforcement and the imitation of aggressive 'models' (Bandura, 1965, 1973, 1994: see Chapters 35 and 42).

Imitation is the reproduction of learning through observation (*observational learning*), and involves observing other people who serve as models for behaviour. Bandura *et al.* (1961, 1963) demonstrated how a child's aggressive tendencies can be strengthened through *vicarious reinforcement* (seeing others being rewarded for behaving aggressively).

SLT and the effects of the media

SLT has contributed to our understanding of the role played by the media in both pro- (see Chapter 30) and antisocial behaviour. According to Baron (1977), the Bobo doll experiments constitute the 'first generation' (or 'phase one') of scientific research into the effects of media violence: almost all involved filmed (symbolic) models. The basic finding was that young children can acquire new aggressive responses not previously in their behavioural repertoire, merely through exposure to a filmed or televised model. It was reasoned that if children could learn new ways of harming others through such experience, then mass-media portrayals of violence might be contributing, in some degree, to increased levels of violence in society (Baron, 1977).

However, Bandura himself (1965) warned against such an interpretation in the light of his distinction between learning and performance. Nevertheless, the mere *possibility* of such effects was sufficient to focus considerable public attention on his research.

There was also a number of methodological problems with the Bobo doll research, which made it very difficult to generalise from it to 'real world' media influence. This helped to promote 'phase two' of the study of the effects of media violence, with Berkowitz being one of the leading figures.

How much violence is there on television?

The basic method of quantifying the amount of violence shown on TV involves simple counting techniques. Researchers define violence objectively, and then code samples of TV programmes for incidents matching those definitions.

Gerbner and his colleagues (Gerbner *et al.*, 1972, 1980, 1986; Gerbner & Gross, 1976) monitored samples of all major network prime-time and weekend daytime programmes since 1967. They defined violence as:

'... the overt expression of physical force (with or without a weapon) against self or other, compelling action against one's will on pain of being hurt or killed, or actually hurting or killing'.

Since 1967, the percentage of TV programmes containing violent episodes has remained fairly constant, but the number of violent incidents per programme has gradually increased. In 1986, there was an average of five violent acts per hour on prime-time TV. This figure rose to 20 on children's weekend programmes (mainly cartoons).

Gerbner's analysis provided the framework for British research initiated by Halloran & Croll (1972) and the BBC's Audience Research Department. Both studies found that violence was a common feature of programming, although it wasn't as prevalent on British as on American TV. Cumberbatch (1987), commissioned by the BBC, analysed all programmes broadcast on the (then) four terrestrial channels in four separate weeks between May and September 1986.

KEY STUDY 29.3

How much violence is there on British TV? (Cumberbatch, 1987)

Cumberbatch found that 30 per cent of programmes contained some violence, the overall frequency being 1.14 violent acts per programme and 1.68 violent acts per hour. Each act lasted around 25 seconds, so violence occupied just over one per cent of total TV time. These figures were lower if boxing and wrestling were excluded, but higher (at 1.96 violent acts per hour) if verbal threats were included.

Death resulted from violent acts in 26 per cent of cases, but in 61 per cent of acts no injuries were shown, and the victim was portrayed as being in pain or stunned. In 83 per cent of cases, no blood was shown as a result of a violent act, and considerable blood and gore occurred in only 0.2 per cent of cases. Perpetrators of violent acts were much more likely to be portrayed as 'baddies' than 'goodies', and violence occurred twice as frequently in law-breaking than in law-upholding contexts.

Cumberbatch argued that while violence, and concerns about it, had increased in society in the decade up to 1987, this wasn't reflected by a proportional increase on TV, even in news broadcasts. He concluded that:

'While broadcasters may take some comfort from our data on trends in television violence, they must expect to be continually reminded of their responsibilities in this area and be obliged to acknowledge that a significant minority of people will remain concerned about what's on the box'.

More recently, the BBC and ITV commissioned Gunter & Harrison (1998) to look at the frequency of violence on terrestrial and satellite channels.

KEY STUDY 29.4

Violence on British TV (Gunter & Harrison, 1998)

Gunter and Harrison monitored 2084 programmes on eight channels over four weeks in October 1994 and January/February 1995. The findings include that:

- on BBC 1 and 2, ITV and Channel 4, 28 per cent of programmes contained violent acts, compared with 52 per cent on Sky One, UK Gold, Sky Movies and the Movie Channel;
- violence occupied 0.61 per cent of time on the terrestrial channels and 1.53 per cent on the satellite stations;
- the greatest proportion of violent acts (70 per cent) occurred in dramas and films; 19 per cent occurred in children's programmes;

- most violent acts occurred in contemporary settings in inner-city locations. The majority of perpetrators were young, white males;
- one per cent of programmes contained 19 per cent of all violent acts. *Double Impact*, shown on the Movie Channel, for example, contained 105 violent acts, as against an average of 9.7;
- the US was the most common location for violence (47 per cent), followed by the UK (twelve per cent). The third most likely location was a cartoon setting (seven per cent), and then science fiction locations (four per cent).

Based on the finding that violent acts account for one per cent of programme content on terrestrial channels and less than two per cent on some satellite stations, and the fact that one per cent of programmes contained 19 per cent of all violent acts, Gunter and Harrison concluded that:

'The picture that emerges is not one of a television system permeated by violence, but rather one in which violence represents only a tiny part of the output and where it tends to be concentrated principally in a relatively small number of programmes'. (Cited in Frean, 1995)

An almost identical conclusion was reached by the American Academy of Paediatrics (Murray & Whitworth, 1999).

As well as TV, violent behaviour can also be seen at the cinema or on video (and what's shown may or may not be subsequently screened on TV). Evidence indicates that a large percentage of nine- to eleven-year-olds have watched 18-rated videos, including the particularly violent *Nightmare on Elm Street*, *The Silence of the Lambs*, and *Pulp Fiction* (Ball & Nuki, 1996; Wark & Ball, 1996).

How much TV do people watch?

American research conducted since 1965 suggests that the time spent in a typical household in front of the TV has, in general, been steadily increasing (Burger, 1982; Liebert & Sprafkin, 1988). However, these data are typically derived from paper-and-pen surveys concerning viewing habits and may not be reliable.

Anderson *et al.* (1986) installed automated time-lapse video-recording equipment in the homes of 99 families consisting of 462 people aged between one and 62. The recordings began when the TV was switched on and stopped when it was switched off. One camera used a wide-angled lens to record people's behaviour in the room where the TV was, while a second focused on the TV screen itself. Two of their main findings were that no one actually watches the TV for more than 75 per cent of the time it's on, and that the number of hours spent looking at TV increases up to the age of ten, after which it decreases, levels off at about age 17, and continues around the same level (ten hours per week) into adulthood.

How do viewers perceive violence?

According to Gunter & McAleer (1997), viewers can be highly discriminating when it comes to portrayals of violence, and don't invariably read into TV content the same meanings researchers do. Thus, merely knowing how often certain pre-defined incidents occur in programmes doesn't tell us how significant these features are for viewers.

Viewers' perceptions of how violent TV content is, then, may not agree with objective counts of violence in programmes. According to Gunter (2000), the potential for emotional upset is increased:

- by violent portrayals in *realistic settings*: real-life incidents in news and documentary programmes are generally rated as being more violent than those in fictional settings;
- when the violence is depicted as justified or rewarded;
- when viewers strongly identify with the characters;
- when the victim's pain and suffering are shown graphically.

Very young children are frightened by monsters they can see on the screen (such as *The Incredible Hulk*), while older children (nine- to twelve-year-olds) are scared by hidden evils in disguise or that lurk unseen off-camera (as in *Poltergeist*, where much of the 'horror' is covert and depends on a more sophisticated reading of story events: Gunter, 2000).

Programmes which are extremely violent according to 'objective' counts of violent acts can be seen by children as 'containing hardly any violence', and this is especially true of cartoons. *Subjective assessment* of violence should, therefore, be incorporated into assessments of the amount of violence shown on TV (Gunter & McAleer, 1997).

Tex Avery: The Shooting of Dan McGoo. *Evidence suggests that children see such cartoons as less violent than more realistic portrayals*

Methods used to study TV violence

Correlational studies

Typically, these involve asking people which programmes they like best and which they watch most often. These data are then correlated with measures of aggression given by parents, teachers, self-reports, peers, and so on. Evidence from such studies has generally been inconsistent, but one finding is that the overall amount of viewing is related to self-reports of aggressive behaviour. Of course, it's possible that those who watch violent TV are different in some way from those who

don't, and the impossibility of inferring cause and effect from correlational studies weakens this methodology.

Laboratory studies

These are designed to enable the causal link between watching violent TV and behaving aggressively to be established (if it exists). Liebert & Baron (1972) randomly assigned children to two groups. One watched *The Untouchables*, a violent TV programme, while the other watched an equally engaging and arousing, but non-violent, sports competition. Afterwards, the children were allowed to play. Those who'd watched the violent programme behaved more aggressively than the others.

The problem with laboratory studies is that most use small and unrepresentative samples which are exposed to the independent variable under highly contrived and unnatural viewing conditions. The measures of TV viewing and aggression tend to be so far removed from normal everyday behaviour, that it's doubtful whether such studies have any relevance to the real world (Gunter & McAleer, 1997).

Field experiments

These are much more ecologically valid, and involve children or teenagers being assigned to view violent or non-violent programmes for periods of a few days or weeks. Measures of aggressive behaviour, fantasy, attitude and so on are taken before, during and after the periods of controlled viewing. To ensure control over actual viewing, children in group or institutional settings are studied, mostly from nursery schools, residential schools, or institutions for adolescent boys. In general, the results show that children who watch violent TV are more aggressive than those who don't (Parke *et al.*, 1977).

KEY STUDY 29.5

Creating violence – a cottage industry? (Parke *et al.*, 1977)

Parke *et al.* studied Belgian and American male juvenile delinquents living in small-group cottages in low-security institutions. Their normal rates of aggressive behaviour were assessed (using several measures of physical and verbal aggression). Then the boys in one cottage were exposed to five commercial films involving violence over a period of one week, while boys in another cottage saw five non-violent films during the same period. The former showed significant increases in aggressive behaviour for some of the categories, but increases in other measures of aggression were confined to boys who were naturally high in aggression (and who saw the violent film).

Ask yourself ...

- What do you consider to be the major *disadvantage* of field experiments compared with laboratory experiments
- What particular limitations did the Parke *et al.* study have?

In field experiments the setting cannot be controlled as well as in laboratory experiments. Consequently, we cannot be certain that the only difference between the children is the watching of either violent or non-violent TV, especially when participants aren't assigned randomly to conditions. In Parke *et al.*'s study, for example, 'cottages' (or pre-existing groups), rather than individuals, were assigned to the viewing conditions. Also, their participants (juvenile delinquent males) aren't representative of children or adolescents in general.

Natural experiments

Here, the researcher doesn't manipulate an independent variable, but takes advantage of fortuitous and naturally occurring events. Williams (1986) studied a community in Canada ('Notel') where TV had been only recently introduced. This community was compared with one in which there was a single TV channel and another with several channels. Verbal and physical aggression in both male and female six- to eleven-year-olds increased over a two-year period following the introduction of TV to 'Notel', but no such increase occurred in the communities that already had TV.

KEY STUDY 29.6

A natural experiment on the island of St Helena

In July 1994, a study began to look at the effects of the introduction of TV to St Helena. This remote island in the south-east Atlantic has fewer than 6000 inhabitants, none of whom had ever seen live TV. Of its nine- to twelve-year-olds, only 3.4 per cent had behavioural problems, compared with 14 per cent of children in London. Of the three- to-four-year-olds, less than seven per cent had behavioural problems, compared with twelve per cent in London. The figure of 3.4 per cent for the nine- to twelve-year-olds is the lowest ever recorded for any age-range anywhere in the world.

Prior to the introduction of several 24-hour channels (including BBC World Television, MNET [a South African commercial service] and the American satellite channel, CNN), the only access the islanders had to news was on short-wave radio from the BBC World Service. While the island has three video libraries, it doesn't have a cinema.

The study's leader, Tony Charlton, looked at the effects of the introduction of TV on 59 pre-school children, who will be monitored until they're 13, and all 800 children on the island who are of first- and middle-school age. According to Charlton:

'The children on the island represent a unique control group – it is extraordinarily difficult to find a group that doesn't have television'.

Before the study began, Charlton noted that:

'It could be that excessive viewing interferes with the development of social skills and mental capacities which children need to acquire. But there could be enormous educational benefits'.

In the fourth year of the seven-year study, *prosocial behaviour* (defined as helping others and playing amicably: see

Chapter 30) hadn't only been maintained, but actually improved slightly.

(Based on Cooper, 1994; McIlroy, 1994; Frean, 1994; Lee, 1996, and Midgley, 1998)

Longitudinal panel studies

Like experiments, but unlike correlational studies, longitudinal panel studies can say something about cause and effect, and normally use representative samples. In this case, their aim is to discover relationships that may exist or develop over time between TV viewing and behaviour. These studies, then, look at TV's *cumulative* influence and whether or not attitudes and behaviour are linked with watching it.

American (e.g. Lefkowitz *et al.*, 1972; Eron & Huesmann, 1985; Phillips, 1986) and British research (e.g. Sims & Gray, 1993; Bailey, 1993) shows that such a link exists. Sims and Gray, for example, reviewed an extensive body of literature linking heavy exposure to media violence and subsequent aggressive behaviour. Similarly, Bailey's study of 40 adolescent murderers and 200 young sex offenders showed repeated viewing of violent and pornographic videos to be 'a significant causal factor'. This was particularly important in adolescents who carried out abusive behaviour while they were babysitting, where videos provided 'a potential source of immediate arousal for the subsequent act', including imitating violent images.

However, at least some studies have failed to find such a link. Milavsky *et al.* (1982) found only small associations between exposure to violent programmes and verbal and physical aggression amongst 3200 elementary school children and adolescents. Variables such as family background, social environment, and school performance were actually much better predictors of aggressiveness, if not of actual crime (Ford, 1998).

How does television exert its effects?

Four specific effects of TV violence have been investigated. These are arousal, disinhibition, imitation and desensitisation.

■ *Arousal* is a non-specific, physiological response, whose 'meaning' is defined by the viewer in terms of the type of programme being watched (Zillman, 1978). It's been claimed that watching TV violence increases a viewer's overall level of emotional arousal and excitement (Berkowitz, 1993). However, there doesn't seem to be any strong overall relationship between perceiving a programme as violent and verbal or physiological reports of emotional arousal (Gadow & Sprafkin, 1993, Bryant & Zillman, 1994). But the more realistic the violence is perceived to be, the greater the reported arousal and involvement (see above, page 427).

■ *Disinhibition* is the reduction of inhibitions about behaving aggressively oneself, or coming to believe that aggression is a permitted or legitimate way of solving problems or attaining goals. Berkowitz's aggressive-cue theory, which we discussed earlier, is relevant here.

- *Imitation* is perhaps the most direct link between watching TV and the viewer's own behaviour, and relates to Bandura's studies of imitative aggression (see pages 516–518). However, social learning theorists acknowledge the role of cognitive factors as mediating between stimulus and response (Bandura, 1994). How TV violence is perceived and interpreted, and the issue of realism, are clearly important *intervening variables* for both children and adults (see Box 35.8, page 157).

- *Desensitisation* is the reduction in emotional response to TV violence (and an increased acceptance of violence in real life) as a result of repeatedly viewing it. As with drug tolerance (see Chapter 8), increasingly violent programmes may be required to produce an emotional response (Gadow & Sprafkin, 1989). A study by Drabman & Thomas (1974) supports the desensitisation hypothesis. Eight-year-olds saw either a violent or a non-violent programme before witnessing a 'real' (staged) fight between two other children in a playroom. The former were less likely to tell an adult what was happening than the latter.

Reconsidering media violence

The debate about the relationship between media violence and aggression is far from being resolved (Harrower, 1998). In Britain, the link between the two was brought back into the spotlight following two-year-old James Bulger's murder by two teenage boys in February, 1993. At their trial, Mr Justice Moreland said:

'It is not for me to pass judgement on their upbringing, but I suspect that exposure to violent video films may, in part, be an explanation'. (Cited in Cumberbatch, 1997)

The call for legislation controlling the supply of videos to children was supported by many psychologists, including Newson (1994), whose report (*Video Violence and the Protection of Children*) was also endorsed by many psychiatrists and paediatricians.

Cumberbatch (1997), however, has questioned the validity of the evidence on which Newson's report was based. While it might be true that the father of one of the murderers of James Bulger had rented the video *Child's Play 3* some weeks before the murder occurred (as one British tabloid claimed), his son wasn't living with him at the time, disliked horror films, and was upset by violence in videos. Similarly, it was claimed that the massacre of 16 people in Hungerford in 1987 was inspired by the murderer seeing the character 'Rambo' in the film *First Blood*. In fact, there's no evidence to support this claim (Cumberbatch, 1997).

More recently, two fourteen-year-old British schoolboys were convicted of attempted murder, apparently as a result of watching the film *Scream*. In the film, college students became victims of fatal knife attacks by two of their classmates. At their trial, though, the schoolboys denied that the film had influenced their behaviour (Stokes, 1999).

Cumberbatch has also criticised Comstock & Paik's (1991) conclusion that, based on Huesmann & Eron's (1986) cross-national survey in six countries (Holland, Australia, USA, Israel, Poland and Finland), viewing TV violence at an early age is a predictor of later aggression.

Box 29.4 Criticisms of the claim that viewing TV violence at an early age is a predictor of later aggression

- The Dutch researchers concluded that their results showed no effects of TV, and refused to allow their findings to be included in Huesmann and Eron's edited book of the research study.
- The Australian research showed *no* significant correlations between early TV violence viewing and later aggression.
- The American study found that when initial aggression was controlled for, the correlation between early TV viewing and later aggression was significant only in girls.
- Israeli researchers found significant effects in their city samples, but not in their kibbutz samples.
- In Poland, the researchers agreed that a greater preference for violent viewing was predictive of later aggression, but that 'the effects are not large and must be treated cautiously'.
- The Finnish researchers appeared to misunderstand their own data. Rather than showing a positive correlation between viewing violent TV and aggressive behaviour, the correlation was actually *negative*, indicating that the more TV is watched, the *less aggressive* children were later.

(Adapted from Cumberbatch, 1997)

Cumberbatch cites several other studies, which also cast doubt on claims about the connection between media violence and aggression in children.

According to Taylor *et al.* (1994):

'... media violence is not a sufficient condition to produce aggressive behaviour, nor is it a necessary one. Aggressive behaviour is multiply determined and media violence in and of itself is unlikely to provoke such behaviour ... However ... media violence can be a contributing factor to some aggressive acts in some individuals ...'.

Putting the discussion into a wider social and political context, Taylor *et al.* argue that TV and movies contribute only a small incentive effect to crime and violence over and above the contribution of social factors such as unemployment, racial prejudice and the widespread availability of drugs and guns.

Deindividuation

Ask yourself ...

- Do you think people are more likely to behave in anti-social ways in a group or crowd than when they're alone? If so, why?

The concept of *deindividuation* has been used to try to explain why people in groups may behave in an uncharacteristically aggressive way (and in other antisocial ways), compared with their individual behaviour. When an individual's identity is lost in a mass of people, and when the markers of personality are reduced, the individual is said to be *deindividuated* (Gergen & Gergen, 1981).

Festinger *et al.* (1952) first introduced the concept of deindividuation, based on Le Bon's (1895) study of the aggressive behaviour sometimes associated with *crowds*. They defined deindividuation as a state of affairs in a group where members don't pay attention to other individuals as individuals and, correspondingly, the members don't feel they're being singled out by others. Belonging to a group not only provides people with a sense of identity and *belongingness* (see Maslow's hierarchy of needs – Chapter 9), but allows individuals to *merge* with the group, to forego individuality, and to become *anonymous*.

Empirical studies of deindividuation

While most relevant studies have been laboratory experiments, Diener *et al.* (1976) observed 1300 trick-or-treating children on Halloween night. When they wore costumes which prevented them from being recognised and went from house to house in large groups, they were more likely to steal money and candy.

Zimbardo (1969) regarded *anonymity* as a major source of deindividuation, and was the first to operationalise anonymity by having participants wear hoods and masks.

KEY STUDY 29.7

Anonymity can be bad for your health (Zimbardo, 1969)

Female students had to deliver electric shocks to another student 'as an aid to learning'. Half wore bulky lab-coats and hoods that hid their faces, were spoken to in groups of four, and were never referred to by name. The other half wore their normal clothes, were given large name-tabs to wear, were introduced to each other by name, and could see each other dimly while giving the shock. The student who received the shock was seen through a one-way mirror and pretended to be in extreme discomfort – writhing, twisting, grimacing and finally tearing her hand away from the strap. The hooded, deindividuated participants gave twice as much shock as the individuated group. If they were told that the student receiving the shock was honest, sincere and warm, she didn't receive any less shock than those believed to be conceited or critical. By contrast, the individuated participants *did* adjust the shock they delivered according to the victim's character.

An evaluation of deindividuation research

Manipulating anonymity hasn't always proved very easy (Brown, 1985). The participants in Zimbardo's (1969) study wore clothing resembling that worn by the Ku Klux Klan (see page 365). This uniform may have acted as a *demand characteristic* (see Chapter 3), such that the participants believed they *should behave* in a more extreme way (Johnson & Downing, 1979). In support of this, Johnson and Downing found that when participants wore surgical masks and gowns, they delivered significantly *less* electric shock than those participants whose names and identities were emphasised. This suggests that the participants' clothing and related behavioural expectations, rather than deindividuation, may have influenced their behaviour.

Similarly, in another of Zimbardo's (1969) studies, the participants were Belgian soldiers. When these soldiers wore hoods, they *didn't* behave more aggressively. Instead, they became self-conscious, suspicious and anxious. Their apparently individuated counterparts, who wore army-issue uniform, retained their 'normal' level of deindividuation resulting from their status as uniformed soldiers. One of the functions of uniforms in the 'real world' is to reduce individuality and hence, at least indirectly, to increase deindividuation (Brown, 1985).

Indeed, dispossessing people of their 'civilian' clothes is a major technique of *depersonalising* them in 'total institutions' such as prisons and psychiatric hospitals (Goffman, 1968, 1971). As Brown (1985) observes, the victims of aggression are often dehumanised by having their heads shaved and being dressed in ill-fitting clothes, making them appear less human. This, in turn, makes it easier for people to humiliate and abuse them (see Zimbardo *et al.*'s *prison simulation experiment* in Chapter 27).

While it may be true that the deindividuation produced by wearing military or police uniform increases the likelihood of brutality, the anonymity of massed ranks of police or soldiers may make them appear less human thus making them a more obvious target for a rioting crowd's violence.

Riot police using tear-gas and batons in the protests against the World Trade Organisation in Seattle, Washington, 1999

The positive side of deindividuation

Brown (1988) refers to the US urban riots of the 1960s, where looting and violence *weren't* completely random but showed signs of selectivity. Similarly, the St Paul's riots in Bristol in 1984 were violent, but also relatively controlled. Violence was aimed at specific targets (avoiding local shops and houses), and was geographically confined to a small area in the heart of the community. Far from losing their identities, the rioters seemed quite unanimous in a new sense of pride in their community produced by their activities (Brown, 1988).

Finally, deindividuation doesn't necessarily produce antisocial behaviour. In Gergen *et al.*'s, (1973) 'black room experiment', participants spent an hour together, either in a completely dark room or in a normally lit room. In the dark room, they chatted and explored the physical space to begin with, and then began to discuss serious matters. Conversation then faded and was replaced by physical contact; 90 per cent of participants deliberately touched each other. Almost 50 per cent hugged, and 80 per cent admitted to being sexually aroused. By comparison, controls talked politely in the light, for the whole hour.

It seems that we can become uninhibited in the dark, where the usual norms of intimacy no longer prevail. We feel less accountable for our behaviour in such situations, but this state of deindividuation can be to the mutual benefit of all participants (Gergen & Gergen, 1981).

The social constructionist approach

Mummendey (1996) has proposed that whether or not a behaviour is considered aggressive depends on a judgement made by either an observer or by the performer. In Mummendey's view, the *appraisal* of a behaviour as aggressive involves going beyond a description to an evaluation of it. For Mummendey:

'When asking about the causes of aggression, more is of interest than simply the conditions for the occurrence of that behaviour. Of even greater importance are the conditions for judging the individual behaviour as "aggressive"'.

Mummendey's own research (Mummendey & Otten, 1989) and that of others (e.g. Mikula, 1994) suggests that the intention to harm, actual harm, and norm violation are the main criteria people use to label behaviour as aggressive. In looking for the cause of aggressive behaviour, then:

'We should not concentrate on the conditions that energise individual drives or reduce the rational control of behaviour. Rather, we should look for the conditions (at least from the actor's point of view) which make intentionally harming another person seem both situationally appropriate and justified'. (Mummendey, 1996)

The case of soccer hooliganism

Ask yourself ...

- How might the theories of aggression discussed above explain soccer hooliganism?
- How easily can they account for the fact that most people at soccer matches *don't* behave in this way?

Marsh *et al.* (1978) used an *ethogenic* and *phenomenological* approach in their study of football hooliganism ('*The Rules of Disorder*'). This involved mainly participant observation and interviews, (both formal and informal) to gather self-reports of behaviour, in an attempt to uncover the *rules* to which football hooligans attribute their behaviour.

Marsh *et al.* were less concerned with aggression or violence as such, and more concerned with trying to interpret the social lives of particular segments of contemporary young people. They argued that all human beings need to achieve personal dignity, a sense of self-worth and personal identity,

and certain sections of young people in contemporary British society are deprived of the means of achieving these within the conventional worlds of school and work. So, they're forced to turn to the worlds of their own sub-cultures, which provide 'a sense of belonging and prestige'.

For urban *young men* in particular, it's the football terraces that allow for the emergence of sub-cultural rituals. The ritual 'warfare' between rival groups of supporters allows the construction of alternative social hierarchies, within which those who are destined to fail in conventional terms (school, work etc.) may succeed. Confrontation between rival supporters is usually symbolic and consequently non-violent, as in the parading of gear (scarves, boots, denim jackets), the yelling of chants and the chorusing of football songs. Rival fans who follow their group's rules quite carefully can avoid real physical harm to themselves or others. For example, chasing the opposition after a match ('seeing the others off') doesn't inevitably end in violence, since part of the agreed code is not to actually catch anyone.

Although people do get injured (and occasionally killed), *all* such confrontation is governed by rules. Far from being lawless, random behaviour indicating a mob's loss of control, rules exist to ensure that aggression is kept within certain bounds. Soccer hooliganism is a kind of staged production. Much of what *appears* to be aggression is simply part of an identity-enhancing symbolic display, a cultural drama. While aggression may be a taken-for-granted human predisposition, what society defines as antisocial behaviour may well be a set of functional activities dressed up as a cultural drama. According to Stainton-Rogers *et al.* (1995):

'If we look for the explanation of aggression within the individual actor, rather than addressing the complexity of the cultural drama, we fail to recognise the social, political and economic factors which are involved in such social activity'.

Marsh *et al.*'s research demonstrates one of the ways in which aggression is *socially constructed*: there are no objective 'facts' about aggression (or anything else), only accounts, interpretations, ways of talking about it and attempts to represent it.

Conclusions

Taking the example of soccer hooliganism, violence and aggression need to be explained at several different *levels*. Most of the theories we've discussed are *individualistic*. Stemming from Le Bon's original study of rioting crowds, even deindividuation theory stresses how crowds release the primitive, uncivilised/unsocialised tendencies within the psyche of every *individual*.

What's needed is an analysis which integrates many levels of explanation. While the largely symbolic and ritualistic nature of much supporter behaviour can be explained in terms of the 'rules' identified by Marsh *et al.*:

'... individual or group frustrations coupled with the highly emotional atmosphere of a match may occasionally tip the balance towards real aggression. In the mix, there may also be individuals who are simply aggressive, and who find the ferment of a match an ideal context in which to indulge in overt aggression'. (Hogg & Abrams, 2000)

- Lorenz argues that aggression between members of non-human species is characterised by **ritualisation** and **appeasement rituals/gestures**, which prevent conflict resulting in serious injury or death. In humans, these have been over-ridden by destructive technology.

- Lorenz's account seriously underestimated the extent to which members of other species kill each other, together with the role of **cultural evolution**.

- According to Freud, our self-destructive **death instinct** is 'diverted' into outwardly directed aggression. Both Freud and Lorenz believed that aggression builds up spontaneously and needs regular release. Some support for this view comes from studies of **overcontrolled violent criminals**.

- The **frustration–aggression hypothesis** represented an attempt to integrate some of Freud's ideas with those of learning theory. Several modifications were made to the original theory, concerning the conditions under which frustration is likely to produce aggression.

- According to Berkowitz's **aggressive-cue theory**, environmental stimuli which have an aggressive meaning are necessary for anger to be converted into aggressive behaviour. One demonstration of this is the **weapons effect**.

- **Excitation-transfer theory** sees the arousal–aggression relationship as a sequence. However, the existence of 'neutral' arousal has been questioned. The cognitive approach sees anger and aggression as **parallel** processes.

- Bandura's Bobo doll experiments were carried out in the context of his **social learning theory**, which gives central place to **observational learning/modelling**. They represent the first phase of scientific research into the effects of media violence.

- Perception of the level of TV violence is **subjective** and may not correspond with objective counts of violent incidents. Real-life incidents in news and documentaries are generally rated as more violent than those in fictional settings or cartoons.

- Several different methodologies have been used to study the effects of media violence. These include **correlational studies**, **laboratory experiments**, **field experiments**, **longitudinal panel studies**, and **natural experiments**.

- The four specific effects of TV that have been investigated are **arousal**, **disinhibition**, **imitation** and **desensitisation**. These have all been shown to increase following exposure to media violence.

- **Deindividuation** explains aggression in terms of the reduction of inhibition against antisocial behaviour when individuals are part of a group. In this setting, there is a **loss of individuality** and an increase in **anonymity**.

- Anonymity has been operationalised by wearing hoods and masks, which make it more likely that individuals will give more punitive electric shocks to an innocent person.

- However, group/crowd behaviour isn't always random, antisocial and uncontrolled. Anonymity can reduce inhibitions to produce positive effects.

- **Social constructionists** see behaviour as being aggressive or non-aggressive if that's how it's **evaluated**. Soccer hooliganism may only **appear** to be violent if judged externally, and without understanding the 'rules' and rituals governing it.

Self-assessment questions

1 Describe and evaluate research relating to any **two** psychological theories of aggression.
2 Critically assess the influence of both individual **and** social factors on aggressive behaviour.
3 Critically consider research into media influences on antisocial behaviour.

Web addresses

http://www.socialpsychology.org/social.htm#violence

http://www.socialpsychology.org/social.htm#generalviolence

http://www.noctrl.edu/~ajomuel/crow/topic.aggression.htm

http://www.apa.org/pubinfo/violence.html

http://www.cdc.gov/od/oc/media/fact/violence.htm

http://www.dukeedu/~cars/vmedia.html

http://www.medialit.org/Violence/indexviol.htm

Further reading

Berkowitz, L. (1993) *Aggression: Its Causes, Consequences and Control.* New York: McGraw-Hill. A thorough review of the whole field by one of the leading figures.

Chapter 30

Altruism and Prosocial Behaviour

Introduction and overview

What do human kidney donors and rabbits that drum their feet on the ground have in common? At first sight, very little. But on closer inspection, they both seem to be doing things that benefit others (another person or other rabbits, respectively). In the case of the kidney donor, this is self-evident. In the case of the rabbit, drumming its feet serves as a warning to other rabbits of some threat or danger.

These are both examples of *helping behaviour*, a major form of *prosocial behaviour*. They're also often cited as cases of *altruism*, that is, help performed for the benefit of others with no expectation of personal gain. But are people – let alone rabbits – capable of acting in a purely unselfish way? Is our helping always motivated by the prospect of some benefit for ourselves – however subtle? According to Batson (2000):

> *'We want to know whether anyone ever, in any degree, transcends the bounds of self-interest and helps out of genuine concern for the welfare of another. We want to know whether altruism – motivation with the ultimate goal of increasing another's welfare – exists'.*

According to the theory of *universal egoism*, people are fundamentally selfish and altruism is an impossibility (Dovidio, 1995). This has been, and still is, the dominant ethos in social science, including psychology. Similarly, *sociobiologists* consider acts of *apparent* altruism to be acts of selfishness in disguise (see Gross *et al.*, 2000).

Philosophers have debated for centuries whether people are by nature selfless or selfish. McDougall (1908) proposed that 'sympathetic instincts' are responsible for altruistic acts (see Chapter 10). Only about 20 psychological studies of helping were published before 1962, but the murder of Kitty Genovese in 1964 (see below) opened up the floodgates of research into *bystander intervention and altruism* (Schroeder *et al.*, 1995). Latané and Darley were the pioneers of this research.

Helping and bystander intervention

CASE STUDY 30.1

Kitty Genovese (Adapted from *New York Times*, March, 1964)

37 Who Saw Murder Didn't Call the Police
Apathy at Stabbing of Queens Woman Shocks Inspector
By Martin Gansberg

For more than half an hour 38 respectable, law-abiding citizens in Queens watched a killer stalk and stab a woman in three separate attacks ....

Twice the sound of their voices and the sudden glow of their bedroom lights interrupted him and frightened him off. Each time he returned, sought her out and stabbed her again. Not one person telephoned the police during the assault; one witness called after the woman was dead.

'He Stabbed Me!'
She got as far as a street light in front of a bookstore before the man grabbed her. She screamed. Lights went on in the ten-storey apartment house ... which faces the bookstore. Windows slid open and voices punctured the early-morning stillness.

Miss Genovese screamed: 'Oh, my God, he stabbed me! Please help me! Please help me!'.

From one of the upper windows in the apartment house, a man called down: 'Let that girl alone!'.

The assailant looked up at him, shrugged and walked ... toward a white sedan parked a short distance away. Miss Genovese struggled to her feet.

Lights went out. The killer returned to Miss Genovese, now trying to make her way around the side of the building ... to her apartment. The assailant grabbed her again.

'I'm dying!' she shrieked.

'I'm dying!'

A City Bus Passed
Windows were opened again, and lights went on in many apartments. The assailant got into his car and drove away. Miss Genovese staggered to her feet. It was 3.35 a.m.

The assailant returned. By then, Miss Genovese had crawled to the back of the building ... he saw her slumped on the floor at the foot of the stairs. He stabbed her a third time – fatally.

It was 3.50 by the time the police received their first call, from a man who was a neighbour of Miss Genovese ...The man explained that he had called the police after much deliberation. He had phoned a friend ... for advice and then he had crossed the roof of the elderly woman to get her to make the call.

'I didn't want to get involved', he sheepishly told the police.

Suspect is Arrested
Today witnesses from the neighbourhood ... find it difficult to explain why they didn't call the police.

The police said most persons had told them they had been afraid to call, but had given meaningless answers when asked what they had feared.

'We can understand the reticence of people to become involved in an area of violence', Lieutenant Jacobs said, 'but where they are in their homes, near phones, why should they be afraid to call the police?'

... A housewife ... said, 'We thought it was a lovers' quarrel'. A husband and wife both said, 'Frankly, we were afraid'. They seemed aware of the fact that events might have been different. A distraught woman ... said, 'I didn't want my husband to get involved'.

One couple, now willing to talk about that night, said they heard the first screams ...'We went to the window to see what was happening', he said, 'but the light from our bedroom made it difficult to see the street'. The wife, still apprehensive, added: 'I put out the light and we were able to see better'.

Asked why they hadn't called the police, she shrugged and replied, 'I don't know'.

Ask yourself ...

- What do you think you'd have done if you'd been one of Kitty's neighbours?

The Kitty Genovese murder, together with findings from their laboratory studies, led Latané and Darley to introduce the concept of the *unresponsive bystander* (or *bystander apathy*) to denote people's typically uncaring attitude towards others in need of their help.

While the American media thought it remarkable that out of 38 witnesses not a single one did anything to help, Latané and Darley believed that it was precisely *because* there were so many that Kitty Genovese wasn't helped. So, how does the presence of others determine whether any particular individual will intervene in an emergency, and what other influences are involved?

The decision model of bystander intervention

According to Latané & Darley's (1970) *decision model*, before someone helps another, that person must:

- notice that something is wrong;
- define it as a situation requiring help;
- decide whether to take personal responsibility;
- decide what kind of help to give;
- implement the decision to intervene.

This represents a logical sequence of steps, such that a negative response at any one step means that the bystander won't intervene, and the victim won't receive help (at least not from that bystander: see Figure 30.1).

Defining the situation as an emergency

In one of the first bystander experiments (Latané & Darley, 1968), participants were shown into a room in order to complete some questionnaires. In one condition they were alone, while in another condition there were two others present. After a time, steam (resembling smoke) began to pour through a vent in the wall. Seventy-five per cent of those working alone reported the smoke, half of them within two minutes, while 62 per cent of those in the three-person groups carried on working for the full six minutes (by which time it was difficult to see the questionnaires and the experiment was terminated).

Latané & Rodin (1969) obtained similar results when participants heard the female experimenter in an adjoining room fall, cry out and moan. They were much faster to react when alone than when others were present. In a variation of Latané and Rodin's experiment, 70 per cent of participants on their own responded within 65 seconds, and two friends together responded within a similar time. Two strangers together were less likely to react at all (but more slowly if they did), and if someone was paired with a stooge who'd been instructed not to intervene at all, that person showed the least and slowest reaction of all.

Pluralistic ignorance

In post-experimental interviews, each participant reported feeling very hesitant about showing anxiety, so they looked to others for signs of anxiety. But since everyone was trying to appear calm, these signs weren't found and each person defined the situation as 'safe'. This is called *pluralistic ignorance*.

Ask yourself ...

- Can pluralistic ignorance account for the inaction of the witnesses to Kitty Genovese's murder?

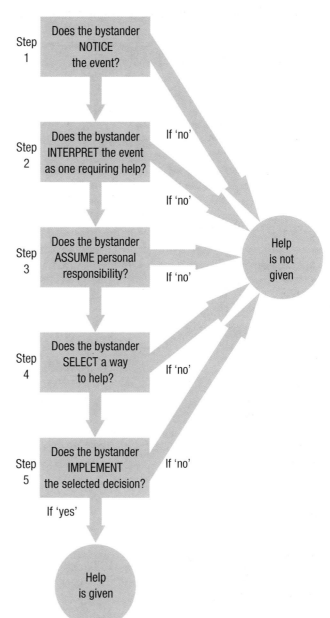

Figure 30.1 *Latané and Darley's five-step decision model of bystander intervention and non-intervention (based on Schroeder et al., 1995)*

There seems little doubt that the witnesses realised at the time what was going on. Although one woman claimed she thought it was a 'lover's quarrel', most claimed they were afraid to intervene (they didn't deny that help was needed), and Kitty's second lot of screams (if not the first) must have made the nature of the situation quite unambiguous.

Genuine ambiguity may sometimes account for lack of intervention, as in situations of domestic violence. According to Shotland & Straw (1976), we'd be much more likely to help a victim if we believed s/he didn't know the attacker than if we believed a relationship existed between the two. Male participants were shown a staged fight between a man and a woman. In one condition the woman screamed 'I don't even know you', while in another, she screamed 'I don't even know why I married you!' Three times as many men intervened in the first condition as in the second condition.

Chapter 30 Altruism and prosocial behaviour

KEY STUDY 30.1

The stresses of urban living (Darley & Latané, 1968)

College students were recruited to discuss the problems of living in a high-pressure urban environment. Instead of face-to-face discussion, they communicated via an intercom system ('so as to avoid any embarrassment'). Each participant would talk for two minutes, then each would comment on what the others had said. The other 'participants' were, in fact, tape recordings. Early in the discussion, the victim (a stooge) casually mentioned that he had epilepsy and that the anxiety and stress of urban living made him prone to seizures. Later, he became increasingly loud and incoherent, choking, gasping and crying out before lapsing into silence.

Darley and Latané were interested in the percentage of participants who responded within five minutes (by coming out of the small room to look for the victim). Of those who believed they were the only other participant, 85 per cent intervened. Of those who believed there were two others (three altogether), 62 per cent intervened, and of those who believed there were five others (six altogether), only 31 per cent intervened. The most responsive group was also the fastest to respond. These findings were confirmed by Latané *et al.* (1981).

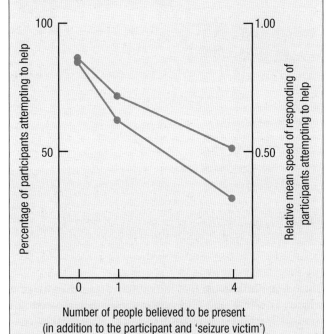

Number of people believed to be present
(in addition to the participant and 'seizure victim')

Figure 30.2 *Percentage of participants attempting to help (by leaving their room to look for the 'victim' within five minutes) as a function of the number of others believed to be present, and the relative mean speed of responding of participants attempting to help (adapted from Darley & Latané, 1968)*

While pluralistic ignorance may make it less likely that we'll define a situation as an emergency in the first place, this cannot apply in Darley and Latané's study. The best explanation is *diffusion of responsibility*, that is, the denial of personal responsibility and the belief that someone else will probably do what's necessary. The more bystanders that are present (or believed to be present), the lower the probability that any one of them will accept responsibility. This is more likely to happen when the victim is remote (can only be 'heard' from some other room in the building).

Kitty Genovese could be both heard and seen (by those who made the effort to look out of their windows), and the second lot of screams must have made it obvious that no one had gone for help!

Piliavin *et al.* (1981) use the term *dissolution of responsibility* to describe what happens when the behaviour of other witnesses cannot be observed and the participant 'rationalises' that someone else must have already intervened (as in the 'seizure' experiment). Diffusion occurs when *all* the witnesses accept responsibility. Regardless of which term is used, it's consistently found that the presence of others *inhibits* an individual from intervening (Pilivian *et al.*, 1981).

However, there are limits to diffusion of responsibility. Piliavin *et al.* (1969) found that help was offered on crowded subways in New York as frequently as on relatively empty ones (see Key Study 30.3). As Brown (1985) suggests, perhaps it's more difficult not to help in a face-to-face situation and in an enclosed space.

Choosing a way to help: the role of competence

Related to diffusion of responsibility, and something which may interact with it, is a bystander's competence to intervene and offer appropriate help. In the presence of others, one or more of whom you believe is better equipped to offer help, diffusion of responsibility will be increased. However, if you believe you're best equipped to help, the presence of others will have relatively little effect on your behaviour. For example, if a swimmer is in trouble, we'll usually let the lifeguard go to the rescue, and even if we were the only other person at the pool, we'd be extremely unlikely to dive in if we couldn't swim ourselves! But if we are an excellent swimmer and are trained in life-saving skills, we'd be much more likely to help even if others were present (Baron & Byrne, 1991).

According to Schroeder *et al.* (1995), we shouldn't take the inhibiting effects of other people as necessarily indicating bystander apathy, as Latané and Darley did. People may be truly concerned about the victim's welfare but sincerely believe that someone else is more likely – or better qualified in some way – to help. For example, Bickman (1971) replicated the 'seizure' experiment, but manipulated the participants' belief about proximity to the victim. Those who believed the other person was as close to the victim as they were (in the same building) and equally capable of helping, were less likely to help than those who believed they were alone (diffusion of responsibility). But when they believed the other person was in another building and so unable to help, they helped as much as those who believed they were alone.

Evaluation of the decision model

Schroeder *et al.* (1995) believe that Latané and Darley's model provides a valuable framework for understanding bystander intervention. Although originally designed to explain helping in emergency situations, aspects of the model have been successfully applied to many other situations, ranging from preventing someone from drinking and driving, to deciding to donate a kidney to a relative.

However, it doesn't provide a complete picture. For example, it doesn't tell us very much about why 'no' decisions are taken at any of the five steps, particularly after the situation has been defined as an emergency and personal responsibility has been accepted: a great deal takes place between steps 3 and 5. Also, as Dovidio (1995) points out, the model focuses on why people *don't* help others – we also need to ask why they *do*.

The arousal–cost–reward model

The *arousal–cost–reward* model (Piliavin *et al.*, 1969, 1981; Dovidio *et al.*, 1991) is a major alternative to the decision model and represents a kind of 'fine-tuning' of some of the processes outlined in the decision model. It identifies a number of critical *situational* and *bystander variables*, which can help predict how likely it is that intervention will take place under any particular set of circumstances. The model was first introduced by Piliavin *et al.* (1969) as a 'heuristic device' in attempting to account for the results of the New York subway experiment (see Key Study 30.3). It was subsequently revised and expanded to cover both emergency and non-emergency helping (Piliavin *et al.*, 1981).

The model identifies two conceptually distinct but functionally interdependent influences on helping:

- *Arousal* in response to the need or distress of others is an emotional response. This is the basic *motivational construct*. When attributed to the distress of the victim, arousal is experienced as unpleasant, and the bystander is motivated to reduce it.
- The *cost–reward* component involves cognitive processes by which bystanders assess and weigh up the anticipated costs and rewards associated with both helping and not helping. (This corresponds to the exchange theory explanation of intimate relationships that we discussed in Chapter 28; the arousal component is what distinguishes the arousal–cost–reward model from exchange theory.)

According to Dovidio *et al.* (1991):

'People are aroused by the distress of others and exhibit emotionally empathic reactions to the problems and crises of others … also … the severity and clarity of another person's emergency and the relationship to the victim systematically influence arousal …'.

While arousal and helping are often only correlated, the model sees arousal as *causing* the helping. There is considerable empirical support for this claim (Dovidio *et al.*, 1991). The model proposes that bystanders will choose the response that most rapidly and completely reduces the arousal, incurring as few costs as possible. So, the emotional component provides the *motivation* to do something, while the cognitive component determines what the *most efficient or effective response* will be.

Ask yourself …

- Try to remember a situation in which you helped someone who was clearly upset or distressed.
- How did you reach the decision to help?
- What were your motives for helping – at the time and in retrospect?

Former nursery nurse Lisa Potts, shows off her George Medal for bravery, after protecting primary school children from a man wielding a machete

The cost–reward analysis

Research has concentrated on this part of the model and, specifically, on the relative costs of helping and not helping.

- The *costs of helping* include lost time, effort, possible physical danger, embarrassment, disruption of ongoing activities and psychological aversion (as in the case of a victim who's bleeding, or drunk).
- The *rewards of helping* include fame, gratitude from the victim and relatives, the intrinsic pleasure and self-satisfaction derived from the act of helping, the avoidance of guilt (for not helping) and even money.
- The *costs of not helping* include guilt, blame from others and cognitive and/or emotional discomfort associated with knowing that another person is suffering.

What's high cost for one person may be low cost for another (and vice versa). Cost may also differ for the same person from one situation to another, and even from one occasion to another (depending on mood, for example).

Table 30.1 (see page 438) is based largely on the model as it had been proposed prior to 1981. Piliavin *et al.* (1981) and Dovidio *et al.* (1991) elaborated the model by considering the influence of a new range of variables, such as bystander personality and mood, the clarity of the emergency, victim characteristics, the relationship between the victim and potential helpers, and attributions made by potential helpers of the victim's deservingness. Many of these variables interact and contribute to (a) how aroused the bystander is, and (b) the perceived costs and rewards for direct intervention.

Different kinds of costs

Two kinds of costs associated with not helping are *personal costs* (e.g. self-blame, public disapproval) and *empathy costs* (e.g. knowing that the victim continues to suffer). According to Dovidio *et al.* (1991):

'In general … costs for not helping affect intervention primarily when the costs for helping are low'.

Table 30.1 *Costs of helping/not helping in emergencies/non-emergencies, and the likelihood/type of intervention, as predicted by the arousal–cost–reward model (based on Piliavin et al., 1969)*

Costs of helping/not helping and likely outcome	Examples
• Costs of helping are *low* • Costs of not helping are *high* Likelihood of intervention **very high – and direct**	You're unlikely to be injured yourself; the victim is only shocked. You'd feel guilty; other people would blame you.
• Costs of helping are *high* • Costs of not helping are *high* Likelihood of intervention **fairly high – but indirect** Or **redefine the situation** (see text)	You don't like the sight of blood; you're unsure what to do. It's an emergency – the victim could die. Call for ambulance/police, or ask another bystander to assist. Ignore the victim and/or leave the scene.
• Costs of helping are *high* • Costs of not helping are *low* Likelihood of intervention **very low**	'This drunk could turn violent or throw up over me' 'Who'd blame me for not helping?' Bystander may well turn away, change seats, walk away etc.
• Costs of helping are *low* • Costs of not helping are *low* Likelihood of intervention **fairly high**	'It wouldn't hurt to help this blind man across the road' 'He seems capable of looking after himself; there's very little traffic on the road' Bystanders will vary, according to individual differences and how they perceive the norms operating in the particular situation

Although *indirect helping* becomes more likely as the costs for helping increase (as in serious emergencies), it's relatively infrequent, possibly because it's difficult for bystanders to pull themselves away from such involving situations in order to seek other people to assist (Schroeder *et al.*, 1995). The most common (and positively effective) way of resolving the *high-cost-for-helping/high-cost-for-not-helping dilemma* (see section 2 of Table 30.1) is *cognitive reinterpretation*. This can take one of three forms:

■ redefining the situation as one not requiring help;
■ diffusing responsibility;
■ denigrating (blaming) the victim. (This is another application of the 'just world' hypothesis: see Chapter 23.)

Each of these has the effect of reducing the perceived costs of not helping. (They could also be seen as rationalisations which reduce the bystander's cognitive dissonance: see Chapter 24). Schroeder *et al.* (1995) stress that cognitive reinterpretation doesn't mean that bystanders are uncaring (or 'apathetic'). On the contrary, it's the fact that they care that creates the dilemma in the first place.

The cost of time

The importance of loss of time as a motive for not helping was shown in a content analysis of answers given in response to five written traffic accident scenarios (Bierhoff *et al.*, 1987, in Bierhoff & Klein, 1988). We're often in a hurry in many real-life situations, and waiting can be very frustrating. This is why the willingness to sacrifice time for a person in need can be seen as generous (time is money: Bierhoff & Klein, 1988). The most frequently mentioned motives for helping were enhancement of self-esteem and moral obligation.

KEY STUDY 30.2

If you need help, avoid a late Samaritan (Darley & Batson, 1973)

Darley and Batson's participants were students at a theological seminary, who were instructed to present a talk in a nearby building. Half the students were to give a talk on the Good Samaritan, while for the other half it was about jobs most enjoyed by seminary students. Each student was then told:

a he was ahead of schedule and had plenty of time (to get to the other building); or
b he was right on schedule; or
c he was late.

On the way to give their talk, all the students passed a man (a stooge) slumped in a doorway, coughing and groaning . Although the topic given for the talk had little effect on helping, time pressures did: the percentages offering help were 63, 45 and ten for conditions a, b and c, respectively.

Ironically, on several occasions the 'late' students who were on their way to talk about the Good Samaritan literally stepped over the victim!

This experiment shows that seemingly trivial variables can exert a profound effect on altruistic responses (Bierhoff & Klein, 1988). By contrast, Bierhoff (1983) asked students to volunteer for a psychology experiment. If they participated without payment, the money would be sent to children in need. They could choose up to twelve half-hour sessions and, on average, students volunteered for 3.71 sessions. These findings indicate that the general level of helpfulness is higher than some pessimists might have assumed.

Different types of helping

Certain kinds of *casual helping* (McGuire, 1994) or *low-cost altruism* (Brown, 1986) seem to be fairly common, such as giving a stranger directions or telling them the time. Latané & Darley (1970) had psychology students approach a total of 1500 passers-by in New York to ask them such routine, low-cost favours. Depending on the nature of the favour, between 34 and 85 per cent of New Yorkers proved to be 'low-cost altruists'. However, most people refused to tell the student their names.

Generally, as the type of intervention that's required changes from casual helping through 'substantial personal helping' (e.g. helping someone move house) and 'emotional helping' (e.g. listening to a friend's personal problems) to 'emergency helping' (which is what's involved in most of the studies discussed so far), the costs of intervention increase. But so do the costs of *not* helping.

Helping different kinds of victim

> ### Ask yourself ...
>
> - Would you be more likely to go the aid of a stranger who collapses apparently due to the effects of alcohol or for some other (medical) reason?
> - If the victim were bleeding, would you be less likely to offer help?

KEY STUDY 30.3

Good Samaritanism – an underground phenomenon? (Piliavin *et al.*, 1969)

Student experimenters pretended to collapse in subway train compartments – they fell to the floor and waited to see if they'd be helped. Sometimes they were carrying a cane (the 'lame' condition); sometimes they were wearing a jacket which smelled very strongly of alcohol and carried a bottle in a brown paperbag (the 'drunk' condition). As predicted, help was offered much less often in the 'drunk' than in the 'lame' condition (20 per cent compared with 90 per cent, within 70 seconds).

In a second study, the person who 'collapsed' bit off a capsule of bloodlike dye, which trickled down his chin. The helping rate dropped from 90 per cent to 60 per cent. People were much more likely to get someone else to help, especially someone they thought would be more competent in an emergency (Piliavin & Piliavin, 1972).

Similarly, Piliavin *et al.* (1975) found that when the victim had an ugly facial birthmark, the rate of helping dropped to 61 per cent. Other studies have reported that a smartly dressed and well-groomed stranded motorist is far more likely to receive help from passing motorists than one who's casually dressed or looks untidy.

The importance of difference

The greater the victims' distress, injury or disfigurement, or the more we disapprove of them or blame their plight on their undesirable behaviour, the more likely we are to perceive

them as being different from ourselves. This, in turn, makes it less likely that we'll offer them help. The psychological costs of helping someone perceived as being different from ourselves seem to be greater than the same help offered to someone perceived as being similar.

On this basis, we'd expect help to be offered less often to someone of a different racial group from the bystander. But the evidence isn't so clearcut. For example, in the New York subway experiment, there was no evidence of greater same-race helping when the victim was apparently ill. However, when he appeared drunk, blacks were much more likely to help a black drunk and whites a white drunk.

Foreign beggars on the streets of London. Are they less likely to be given money because they are foreigners – or more likey because they have children?

This can be explained by *aversive racism*, a moderate, subtle form of racist bias (e.g. Gaertner & Dovidio, 1986: see Chapter 25). Many whites who may truly believe they're not prejudiced still harbour unconscious negative feelings. As a result of possessing both conscious, non-prejudiced convictions and unconscious, prejudiced feelings, aversive racists discriminate in certain situations but not others. Where the social norms for appropriate behaviour are clear and unambiguous (e.g. people who are ill should be helped), aversive racists won't discriminate. If they did behave in a discriminatory way, their self-concept (as non-racists) would be threatened, and this would mean that significant costs were incurred by not helping a victim on the grounds of race/ethnic group. However, when social norms are weak or ambiguous, or where aversive racists can justify a negative response based on some factor other than race/ethnic group (e.g. 'drunks can turn nasty, so leave them alone'), then discrimination will occur.

KEY STUDY 30.4

Diffusion of responsibility as a 'cover' for racism (Gaertner & Dovidio, 1977)

Gaertner and Dovidio used the cubicle and intercom procedure, as in the Darley & Latané (1968) 'seizure' experiment (see Key Study 30.1). White bystanders, who believed they were the only witness to an emergency and when appropriate behaviour was clearly defined, didn't discriminate against a black victim. In fact, they were slightly more likely to help a black than a white victim (94 per cent compared with 81 per cent). But when they believed there were other bystanders, they helped a black victim about half as often as a white victim (38 and 75 per cent respectively).

The opportunity to diffuse responsibility offered a non-race-related excuse to treat blacks differently, thereby allowing them to avoid recognising racial bias as a factor (Schroeder *et al.*, 1995).

Personality differences

People who are characteristically more sensitive to the needs of others might experience greater arousal in response to another's plight, or experience this arousal more negatively or perceive greater costs for not helping. Helpers are generally more 'other-oriented' than non-helpers. One particularly interesting study (Oliner & Oliner, 1988) compared 231 non-Jews who helped save Jews in Nazi Europe with 126 non-savers; the former had stronger beliefs in equality and showed greater empathy.

As Table 30.1 shows, individual differences will have their main impact when the costs for helping and not helping are both low, and when the situation is ambiguous and 'psychologically weak' or less 'evocative'. But the more emergency-like the situation (and, hence, the more compelling and evocative it is), the less relevant person variables will be. Indeed, several studies have failed to find personality differences in helping in emergency situations (Dovidio *et al.*, 1991).

Gender differences

Women may experience greater empathy for others' feelings than men and are more attentive to others' needs, which would predict greater helping by women. On the other hand, Eagly & Crowley (1986) reviewed 172 studies and found that men turn out to be significantly more helpful than women. How can we reconcile these two things? One answer relates to traditional gender roles and the kind of helping required in most experimental studies of bystander intervention. According to Eagly (1987), the female gender role involves caring for others, providing friends with personal favours, emotional support, counselling about personal problems, and so on (*communal helping*). By contrast, the male gender role requires heroism and chivalry: men are more likely to help another when there's an audience present to witness the helping act, and/or where there's an element of risk involved in helping (*agentic helping*). Most studies of bystander intervention (at least those involving emergencies) seem to require agentic helping.

'We-ness'

According to Piliavin *et al.* (1981), this:

> '... connotes a sense of connectedness or the categorisation of another person as a member of one's own group ...'.

The closer the relationship to the person in need, the greater the initial arousal and costs for not helping, and the lower the costs for helping.

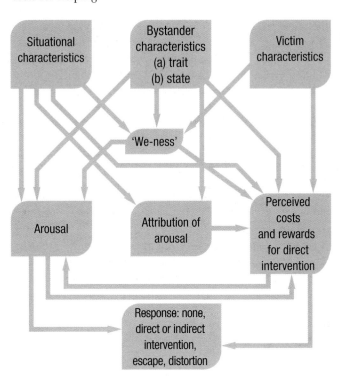

Figure 30.3 *Summary diagram of influences on bystander behaviour*

Evaluation of the arousal–cost–reward model

As we noted in the *Introduction and overview*, the crucial question as far as altruism is concerned is why we help other people.

> *Ask yourself ...*
> * Is helping ever motivated by a genuine wish to benefit someone else, or are we always motivated by self-interest?

Universal egoism and empathy–altruism

Underlying the arousal–cost–reward model (like exchange theory on which it's partly based) is an *economic* view of human behaviour: people are motivated to maximise rewards and minimise costs (Dovidio *et al.*, 1991). Faced with a potential helping situation, we weigh the probable costs and rewards of alternative courses of action, then arrive at a decision that produces the best outcome – *for ourselves*. This is one form of *universal egoism*: everything we do, no matter how noble and beneficial to others, is really directed towards the ultimate goal of self-benefit.

Those who advocate the *empathy–altruism hypothesis* don't deny that much of what we do (including much that we do for others) is egoistic. But they claim that there's more than

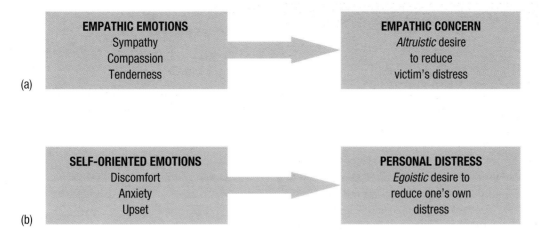

Figure 30.4 *Summary of (a) the empathy–altruism hypothesis, and (b) the universal egoism account of helping behaviour*

just egoism: under certain circumstances, we're capable of a qualitatively different form of motivation, whose ultimate goal is to benefit another person. The egoism–altruism debate has been a central focus in helping behaviour research during the past ten years or so (Dovidio, 1995).

Empathic emotions include sympathy, compassion, tenderness and so on, and are associated with *empathic concern*. These empathic emotions can and should be distinguished from the more *self-oriented emotions* of discomfort, anxiety and upset, which are associated with *personal distress*. (This corresponds to the distinction between personal and empathic costs for not helping: see above, page 437.) While personal distress produces an egoistic desire to reduce one's own distress, empathic concern produces an altruistic desire to reduce the other's distress. These are qualitatively different responses.

According to Darley (1991):

> 'In the United States and perhaps in all advanced capitalist societies, it is generally accepted that the true and basic motive for human action is self-interest. It is the primary motivation, and is the one from which other motives derive. Thus it is the only 'real' motivation, a fact that some celebrate and some bemoan but most accept … To suggest that human actions could arise for other purposes is to court accusations of naïveté or insufficiently deep or realistic analysis'.

Testing the empathy–altruism hypothesis

If helping benefits the person in need *and* the helper (as it often does), how are we to know the ultimate goal? If ultimate goals are reached by the *same* behaviour, how are we ever to know which goal or goals are ultimate? According to Batson (2000), this puzzle has led many scientists to give up on the question of the existence of altruism – it can't be answered empirically. But Batson disagrees.

Over the past 20 years, Batson and others have conducted a series of laboratory experiments, in which people are given an unexpected opportunity to help someone in need. Some are induced to feel empathy, others not. In addition, circumstances have been systematically varied in order to disentangle the altruistic ultimate goal (benefiting others) and one or more possible egoistic ultimate goals (benefiting self).

One way of teasing these goals apart is to vary the situation, so that sometimes the arousal can be reduced in a less costly way than by helping. If the ultimate goal is to reduce one's own arousal, then aroused individuals should help less when they believe they'll no longer be exposed to the person in need of help. But if the ultimate goal is to reduce the other's distress, this variation should have no effect. Several experiments using this logic have supported the empathy–altruism hypothesis (Batson, 2000).

These and other experiments have led to what Piliavin & Charng (1990) call a 'paradigm shift' away from universal egoism, according to which behaviour that *appears* altruistic always turns out to be self-interest in disguise. This paradigm shift indicates that the dominant view of human motivation – and indeed of human nature – is wrong. As Batson (2000) says:

> '… it is not true that everything we do is directed towards the ultimate goal of benefiting ourselves. It seems that we are capable of being altruistic as well as egoistic'.

Universal egoism and sociobiology

If, according to universal egoists, all human acts of apparent altruism are really driven by self-interest, we might not be surprised to find a similar interpretation of the equivalent behaviours in non-human animals. There are many examples of apparently altruistic behaviour in non-humans, including the feet-drumming rabbits that we mentioned at the beginning of the chapter. This is referred to as the *paradox of altruism*.

Box 30.1 **The paradox of altruism**

From a Darwinian perspective, altruistic behaviour isn't adaptive. This is because it reduces the likelihood that an individual who raises an alarm will survive: the predator is likely to be attracted to that individual. According to sociobiologists, this '*paradox of altruism*' can be resolved if apparently altruistic behaviour is viewed as selfish behaviour 'in disguise' (see Chapter 2).

Sociobiologists argue that an individual animal should be seen as a set of genes rather than a separate 'bounded organism', and that these 'selfish genes' (Dawkins, 1976) aim to secure their own survival. For a detailed account of how this can be achieved see Gross *et al.* (2000).

Theories that explain the apparently altruistic behaviour of non-humans can, at least for sociobiologists, be applied to humans (Wilson, 1978: see Chapter 2 and Clamp, 2001).

Biological and psychological altruism

The sociobiological explanation of altruism fails to make the fundamental distinction between *biological* (or *evolutionary*) and psychological (or *vernacular*) altruism (Sober, 1992). Biological altruism is the kind displayed by birds, bees, ants, rabbits and so on. We wouldn't normally attribute the rabbit which warns its fellow rabbits with altruistic motives or intentions: it's simply part of its biologically determined repertoire. Psychological altruism is displayed by higher mammals, in particular primates and especially human beings.

Are humans capable of biological altruism?

According to Brown (1986), the closeness of kinship is construed very differently from one society to another, so there is no simple correspondence between perceived and actual (genetic) kinship. If altruistic behaviour directly reflected actual kinship, rather than learned conceptions of kinship, it would be impossible for adoptive parents to give their adopted children the quality of care they do.

As a species, much of our behaviour is altruistic, and as Brown says:

> 'Human altruism goes beyond the confines of Darwinism because human evolution is not only biological in nature but also cultural, and, indeed, in recent times primarily cultural'.

Biological altruism and impulsive helping

However, biological altruism may be triggered under very specific conditions, such as a highly arousing emergency situation. People often display a rapid, almost unthinking, reflexive type of helping (impulsive helping) in extreme situations such as natural – and other kinds of – disasters.

Biological altruism in action when Hurricane Hortense hit Puerto Rico in 1996

Piliavin *et al.* (1981) found considerable evidence of this impulsive helping in a review of a large number of experiments involving apparently real emergencies. It's generally unaffected by social context (such as diffusion of responsibility) or the potential costs of intervention. They proposed that clear, realistic situations, especially if they involve friends or acquaintances, produce high levels of arousal and focus attention on the victim's plight. As a result, the bystander is most concerned with:

> '... the costs for the victim receiving no help. Personal costs of helping (to the bystander) become peripheral and are not attended to. Therefore, the impulsive helping behaviour that may appear irrational to an uninvolved observer ... may be a quite 'rational' response for a bystander attending primarily to the costs for the victim receiving no help'. (Piliavin *et al.*, 1981)

This description comes very close to Sober's definition of evolutionary altruism (Schroeder *et al.*, 1995). Where very close friends or loved ones are the (potential) victims, impulsive helping is even more likely to occur, because of increased arousal and sensitivity to the other's distress (Clark *et al.*, 1989).

So, both sophisticated reasoning (as in psychological altruism) and more primitive, non-cognitive, biological mechanisms may permit humans to perform a range of altruistic behaviours well beyond those of other species. According to Schroeder *et al.* (1995):

> 'We may well indeed be a uniquely compassionate and altruistic beast ... altruism may be both a behaviour that has evolved because it is vital to the survival of humanity and a behaviour that is learned and reinforced by most societies because it is vital to the survival of their culture'.

The media and prosocial behaviour

Television and prosocial behaviour

If TV can have harmful effects as a result of watching antisocial behaviour (see Chapter 29) then, presumably, it can have beneficial effects by promoting prosocial behaviour. According to Gunter & McAleer (1997):

> 'Concern about the possible antisocial influences of television far outweighs the consideration given to any other area of children's involvement with television ... Television programmes contain many examples of good behaviour, of people acting kindly and with generosity. It is equally logical to assume that these portrayals provide models for children to copy'.

> **Box 30.2 Evidence for the prosocial effects of TV**
>
> - **Laboratory studies with specially produced instructional film or video materials:** Specially prepared materials have been shown to influence courage, the delay of gratification, adherence to rules, charitable behaviour, friendliness, and affectionate behaviour.
> - **Laboratory studies with educational broadcasts specially produced for social skills teaching purposes:** TV productions designed to enhance the social maturity and responsibility of young viewers include *Sesame Street* and *Mister Rogers' Neighborhood*. Children who watch these programmes are able to identify and remember the co-operative and helping behaviours

emphasised in certain segments of them. Some programmes are better at encouraging prosocial behaviour in children than others, but the reasons for this are unclear.

- **Laboratory studies with episodes from popular TV series:** Specially manufactured TV programmes or film clips influence children's prosocial tendencies, at least when the prosocial behaviour portrayed is very similar to that requested of the child. But only some evidence indicates that ordinary broadcast material can enhance a wide range of helping behaviours.

- **Field studies relating amount of viewing of prosocial TV content to strength of prosocial behaviour tendencies:** Children who watch little TV, but watch a lot of programmes with high levels of prosocial content, are more likely than others to behave prosocially. But the correlations between viewing habits and prosocial behaviour are lower than those between viewing habits and antisocial behaviour.

In part, this may be because prosocial behaviours are verbally mediated and often subtle, whereas antisocial behaviours are blatant and physical. Children learn better from simple, direct and active presentation, and so aggressive behaviours may be more readily learned. Also, the characters who display prosocial behaviour (typically female and non-white) and antisocial behaviour (typically male and white) may confound the relative influence of prosocial and antisocial behaviours with the types of character that portray them.

(From Gunter & McAleer, 1997, and Gunter, 1998)

Television violence and catharsis

Ask yourself ...

How might Freud's and Lorenz's theories of aggression explain the benefits of watching TV violence (see Chapter 29)?

One positive effect of TV might be that witnessing others behaving aggressively helps viewers to get their aggressive feelings 'out of their systems', and hence be less likely to behave aggressively. The claim that TV can act as a form of *vicarious catharsis* is based partly on Freud's and Lorenz's theories of aggression (see Chapter 29).

However, the evidence doesn't support the view that TV is cathartic for everybody. If a discharge of hostile feelings occurs at all, it's probably restricted to people of a particular personality type, or those who score high on cognitive measures of fantasy, daydreaming and imagination (Singer, 1989). Only for some people does TV violence have positive effects and provide a means of reducing aggressive feelings (Gunter & McAleer, 1990).

Computer games: good or bad?

Antisocial behaviour

According to Griffiths (1998), little is known about the long-term effects of playing violent computer games. However, great concern has been voiced that such games may have a more adverse effect on children than TV, because of the child's active involvement (Keegan, 1999). Griffiths's review of research indicates that the effects of long-term exposure to computer games on subsequent aggressive behaviour 'are at best speculative'.

However, recent research by Colwell (in Leake, 2000) claims that violent computer games are strongly linked with aggression in teenage boys, and that they are increasingly becoming substitutes for friendship. Colwell's study of 204 12–14-year-olds in London claims to have shown that there is a causal link between playing violent games and aggressive behaviour.

Prosocial behaviour

As far as prosocial behaviour is concerned, computer games:

- give children access to 'state of the art' technology, a sense of confidence, and equip them with computer-related skills for the future (Surrey, 1982);
- may also promote *social interaction*. In a study on the impact of computers on family life, Mitchell (1983, cited in Griffiths, 1993) found that families generally viewed computer games as promoting interaction in a beneficial way through co-operation and competition;
- may be cathartic in that they allow players to release their stress and aggression in a non-destructive way, and relax them (Kestenbaum & Weinstein, 1985). Other benefits include enhancing cognitive skills, a sense of mastery, control and accomplishment, and a reduction in other youth problems due to 'addictive interest'(!) in video games (Anderson & Ford, 1986: see Chapter 8).

According to Griffiths (1997a), there appear to be some genuine applied aspects of computer game-playing, although he notes that many of the assertions made above were subjectively formulated and not based on empirical research findings.

Conclusions

In March, 1984, the Catherine (Kitty) Genovese Memorial Conference on Bad Samaritanism was held. Experts shared what they had learned in the 20 years since her murder. The *New York Times* again reported on the conference:

'It's held the imagination because looking at those 38 people, we were really looking at ourselves. We might not have done anything either. That's the ugly side of human nature'. [O'Connor, law professor]

'The case touched on a fundamental issue of the human condition, our primordial nightmare. If we need help, will those around us stand around and let us be destroyed or will they come to our aid? Are those other creatures out there to help us sustain our life and values or are we individual flecks of dust just floating around in a vacuum?' [Milgram, psychology professor]

- **Helping** as a form of **prosocial behaviour** has been studied largely in the form of **bystander intervention**. The murder of Kitty Genovese, together with early laboratory experiments, led Latané and Darley to introduce the concept of the **unresponsive bystander/bystander apathy**.

- According to Latané and Darley's **decision model**, a bystander will pass through a logical series of steps before actually offering any help. A negative decision at any step leads to non-intervention.

- The more potential helpers there are (believed to be) present, the more likely it is that **diffusion** (or '**dissolution**') **of responsibility** will take place.

- How **competent** we feel to offer appropriate help will influence diffusion of responsibility. This suggests that diffusion of responsibility **doesn't** imply apathy about what happens to the victim.

- The decision model emphasises only why people don't help, rather than why they do. The **arousal–cost–reward model** is an extension of the decision model, identifying a number of critical **situational** and **bystander variables**, which help predict the likelihood of helping under particular circumstances.

- **Arousal** constitutes the **motivational** part of the model, while **cost–reward** involves the **cognitive** weighing-up of anticipated costs and rewards for both helping and not helping.

- The most common solutions to the **high-cost-for-helping/high-cost-for-not-helping dilemma** are **redefining the situation**, **diffusing responsibility** and **blaming the victim**. These are all forms of **cognitive reinterpretation**.

- The costs of helping and not helping differ according to the **type of help required**, **victim characteristics** (including perceived similarity to the bystander), **personality** and **gender** of the bystander, and the **bystander–victim relationship**.

- Helping can be called **altruism** only if the motive is to benefit the victim (**empathic concern**). According to the **empathy–altruism hypothesis**, human beings are capable of altruistic acts, but according to the theory of **universal egoism**, helping is always motivated by **personal distress**.

- While non-humans are incapable of **psychological altruism**, humans are capable of **biological altruism** (**impulsive helping**), triggered by highly arousing emergency situations, especially where friends or relatives are involved.

- **Field studies** indicate that the amount of prosocial TV content viewed is related to the strength of prosocial behaviour. But this relationship is weaker than that between viewing habits and antisocial behaviour. This may be because antisocial behaviours are learnt more easily than verbal and subtle prosocial behaviours.

- Little is known about the long-term effects of playing **violent computer games**, but the child's active involvement makes them potentially more harmful than TV. The **benefits** of computer games could include providing an opportunity for **releasing stress** and aggression in a non-destructive way.

Self-assessment questions

1 Discuss psychological research into bystander intervention.
2 Critically assess the claim that human beings are incapable of altruism.
3 Discuss research studies relating to media influences on prosocial behaviour.

Web addresses

http://www.ios.org/pubs/Article16.asp

http://www.socialpsychology.org/social.htm#prosocial

http://www.noctrl.edu/~ajomuel/crow/topic.altruism.htm

http://fccjvm.fccj.cc.h.vs/~jwisner/social.html/

Further reading

Schroeder, D.A., Penner, L.A., Dovidio, J.F. & Piliavin, J.A. (1995) *The Psychology of Helping and Altruism: Problems and Puzzles*. New York: McGraw-Hill. A very thorough, very readable, up-to-date review by some of the leading researchers in the field.

Gross, R. (1999) *Key Studies in Psychology* (3rd edition) London: Hodder & Stoughton. Chapter 8 discusses Piliavin *et al.*'s (1969) New York subway field experiment in detail, together with many related issues.

Chapter 31 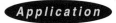 *Application*

The Social Psychology of Sport

Introduction and overview

As we saw in Chapter 30, sociobiologists believe that an individual animal should be seen as a *set of genes*, and that these *selfish genes* (Dawkins. 1976) aim to secure their own survival. This view of evolution implies that there's no such thing as society: sociobiologists have ridiculed the idea that *groups* of organisms might gain a survival advantage over other groups because they shared some beneficial trait.

However, biologists are starting to understand that evolution takes place on a variety of levels (Dicks, 2000). Natural selection may favour certain genes, but it can also favour particular societies. Provided a group of individuals can co-operate without any cheats trying to sneak an unfair advantage, then it may evolve as a single unit. Indeed, Darwin's solution to the *paradox of altruism* was to suggest that natural selection operates among *groups* of organisms. As Dicks puts it:

> 'A group of people who are kind and helpful to each other may not do so well individually, but as a team they may do better than other groups of people, and so the tendency to work as a team spreads through the population'.

While not all sport is team sport, of course, applications of social psychology to sport tend to focus on *group processes* (see Chapter 26), such as *social facilitation*, factors affecting group performance (such as *social loafing*), and *group cohesion*.

What is sport psychology?

Walley & Westbury (1996) define sport psychology as the:

> '... *scientific study of human behaviour and experience in sport (where ... "sport" is used to cover various levels of recreational activities, competitive sports, and health-oriented exercise programmes)*'.

Triplett's (1898) study of social facilitation (see below) is often cited as the first experiment in social psychology, but on closer inspection it had stronger links with psychophysiology and sport psychology (Hogg & Vaughan, 1998). Indeed, sport psychology is generally seen as having started with Triplett's study (Hardy, 1989). But it first became recognised as an academic discipline in the UK in the late 1960s, going from strength to strength since the early 1980s, with the psychology content of sports science degrees gradually increasing. However, it wasn't until 1992 that the British Psychological Society acknowledged sport psychology by forming an interest group. A fully fledged Sport and Exercise Psychology Section was established in 1993.

The British Association of Sports Sciences has set up a register of sport psychologists. To become registered, sport psychologists are normally expected to have a first degree in sports science and a higher degree in psychology – or vice versa. Many sports-governing bodies require trainee coaches to attend short courses and workshops aimed at increasing awareness of the importance of sport psychology. These courses are co-ordinated by the National Coaching Foundation.

Ask yourself ...

• What do you think sport psychologists do?

The scope of sport psychology

According to Walley & Westbury (1996):

> 'The image that many people have of a sport psychologist is someone who comes in to "psych up" players before a game,

the purpose being to make them more competitive or even aggressive ...'.

They believe this image is very misleading.

Box 31.1 | **Different areas of work involving sport psychologists**

Clinical sport psychology: Trained clinical psychologists (see Chapter 1) deal with performers' emotional and behavioural problems. Several Olympic-standard US and British performers have been successfully treated for a range of problems, including acute anxiety, eating disorders, depression, and obsessive–compulsive behaviour.

Research sport psychology: This is a largely *applied* area of research, concerned with real-life problems confronting coaches and players. Researchers also try to ensure that their findings are made available not just to the academic community, but also to coaches, athletes, and teachers. Some of the issues addressed are how stress affects performance, what factors affect performers' decision to drop out of sport, and how complex skills are learned and controlled.

Education sport psychology: This aims to teach participants in sport *mental skills* which will enhance both their performance in, and enjoyment of, sport. Sport psychologists may be consulted on:

- how to manage performance-related stress and anxiety;
- how to increase and maintain self-confidence;
- how to use mental rehearsal to facilitate learning of skills;
- team-building;
- coach education.

British sport psychology reflects international trends. Some additional research areas include:

■ identification of factors which determine peak performance, such as stress (see Chapter 12), motivation (see Chapter 9), and mental preparation. The role of stress in athletic performance grew out of the early interest in social facilitation (see below). According to Hardy (1989):

> 'Competitive athletes ... may represent an invaluable microcosm within which we may test and refine our understanding of human adaptation. The athlete must learn to cope with a wide range of stressors – performance standards, the experience of failure, ageing and so on. In evaluating our theories and developing new treatment techniques, the athlete may, therefore, be an able and willing ally ...';

■ skill development (including in children and performers with special needs);
■ psychological effects of participation in sport, and exercise and sport as a means of promoting health (see Chapter 12);
■ identification of personality factors underlying elite performance and attraction to different sports (very popular in the late 1960s and early 1970s: see Chapter 42).

Zuckerman's (1979) *sensation-seeking scale* has attracted quite a lot of attention and has been successful in predicting leisure preferences and participation. The high sensation-seeker displays a need for varied, novel sensations, and appears willing to take physical and social risks to gain these experiences (Furnham & Heaven, 1999). As predicted by Zuckerman's scale, white-water canoeists and kayak paddlers showed higher than average scores (especially on the thrill and adventure-seeking sub-scales: Campbell *et al.*, 1993). Also, athletes scored higher than non-athletes, contact sports athletes scored higher that non-contact sports athletes, and male athletes scored higher than female athletes (Schroth, 1995).

Box 31.2 T types and the adrenaline rush

Type T (for 'thrill') personalities thrive on taking risks (Farley, in Schueller, 2000b). The most visible members of the type T group today are the *extreme athletes*, such as the hand-gliders, bunjee jumpers, and those who jump off tall buildings. For example, Kristen Ulmer considers herself to be a full-time 'adrenaline sports' athlete. As well as being voted the craziest skier in North America, she rock climbs, paraglides, and dabbles in ice climbing and mountain biking.

But Farley believes that you can get an adrenaline rush without jumping off a building or hand-gliding. It can come from sex or gambling (see Chapter 8), and those who push the frontiers of the mind rather than the body are also thrill-seekers. Adrenaline surges have been recorded during chess tournaments, and Farley cites Einstein as a mental T type. Type Ts need to push their abilities –physical or intellectual – to the limits.

What makes a type T may be at least partly due to 'thrill-seeking' genes, which affect dopamine receptors in the brain (see Chapter 4). One study has found that people with certain addictive and impulsive personality traits have fewer dopamine receptors to record sensations of pleasure and satisfaction (see Chapter 8). This drives them to overindulge in substances or activities that stimulate their existing receptors.

Farley believes that human progress demands risk-taking. There's a very simple motive underlying creativity, risk-taking, exploring and adventure; namely, thrill.

(Based on Schueller, 2000)

According to Moran (2000), the traditional role of the sport psychologist as expert is giving way to a new model for the delivery of sport psychological services:

> '... this model identifies the coach rather than the athlete as the primary target for psychological education. Accordingly, the role of the sport psychologist changes from that of a medical expert to that of a management consultant – somebody who works as part of a team with the coach/manager and the support staff ...'.

Of course, this model doesn't eliminate the need for individual consultation; there'll always be situations which warrant one-to-one interactions between athletes and sport psychologists. But for Moran:

> '... what *does* change in this new approach is the expectation that sport psychologists are "mind-benders" who provide some arcane expertise to athletes who are beyond the help of their coaches ...'.

It's only when such myths are dispelled that either theoretical or practical progress in sport psychology is possible.

Social facilitation

Triplett's research

As we noted earlier, Triplett (1898) carried out what's widely considered to be the first social psychology experiment (and the first study of social motivation: see Chapter 9). But it seems to be at least as relevant to sport psychology.

Cycling had increased enormously in popularity in the last decade of the nineteenth century, both as a pastime and a sport, and Triplett's interest was stimulated by the common observation that racing cyclists go faster when racing or being paced, than when riding alone (Hogg & Vaughan, 1998).

Ask yourself ...

- Why do you think this effect might occur?

Triplett identified various possible explanations for this superior performance:

- The pacer in front produces a suction to pull the rider behind along, helping to conserve energy and providing shelter from the wind.
- A 'brain-worry' theory, popular at the time, predicted that solitary cyclists did poorly because they worried about whether they were going fast enough. This exhausted their brain muscles!
- Friends usually rode as pacers and probably encouraged the cyclists to keep up their spirits.
- In a race, a follower might be hypnotised by the wheels in front, thus riding automatically and leaving more energy for a later, controlled burst.
- A *dynamogenic theory* (favoured by Triplett) proposed that racing another person aroused a 'competitive instinct', which released 'nervous energy' (similar to arousal). The sight of movement in another rider suggested a higher speed and inspired greater effort. The energy of a movement was

proportional to the idea of that movement. (It was believed at the time that to perform an action or movement, there first had to be an 'idea' of that action/movement; the idea 'suggested' the action/movement to be performed).

KEY STUDY 31.1

Is this a wind-up, or a social psychology experiment? (Triplett, 1898)

In his most famous experiment, 40 boys and girls aged 8–17 were tested under two conditions, working alone and working in pairs, each child competing against the other member of the pair. The apparatus consisted of two fishing reels which turned silk bands around a drum (a 'competition machine'). Each reel was connected by a loop of cord to a pulley two metres away, and a small flag was attached to each cord. To complete one trial, a flag sewn to the silk band had to travel four times around the wheel.

Some of the children were slower when competing against another child, most were faster, and others little affected. The faster children showed the effects of both 'the arousal of their competitive instincts and the idea of a faster movement'. The slower ones were overstimulated or 'going to pieces'.

In expanding on the dynamogenic theory, Triplett emphasised the ideo-motor responses; that is, the effects of one child's bodily movements acting as a cue for another child. These are essentially *non-social*. According to Hogg & Vaughan (1998), 'What is clear is that Triplett himself cannot be considered a social psychologist ...'. So, while Triplett's experiment is often cited as a (very early) study of social facilitation, it's not strictly a social psychological study at all.

Allport's research

According to Floyd Allport (1924), Triplett's narrow view of the role of competition could be broadened to include a more general principle: an improvement in performance can be produced by the *mere presence of conspecifics* (i.e. members of the same species). This is a form of influence he called *social facilitation*.

Allport instructed his participants *not* to try to compete against one another (and also prevented any collaboration) while engaging on a variety of tasks. These included crossing out all the vowels in a newspaper article, multiplication, and finding logical flaws in arguments. He found they performed better when they could see others working than when they worked alone, and he called this form of social facilitation the *co-action effect*.

Social facilitation also occurs when someone performs a task in front of an audience, that is, other people who aren't doing what s/he is doing. This is the *audience effect*. Other studies have shown that social facilitation can occur by simply *telling* participants that others are performing the same task elsewhere (Dashiell, 1935).

For the sportsperson, the fact that the presence of others may improve or impair performance is of considerable interest. Although most of the research has taken place in non-sports settings, it still has a direct bearing on sports situations (Woods, 1998).

Ask yourself ...

- In your own experience, do you 'perform' better when there are other people around?
- Does it matter that they're engaged in the same task as you?
- Might an 'audience' inhibit you?
- How is all of this affected by the particular task you're engaged in?

Explaining social facilitation

Zajonc's drive theory

The considerable research interest in social facilitation (much of it involving a range of species and a range of behaviours, from eating to copulation) died down at the end of the 1930s. But it was revived by Zajonc's (1965) *drive theory*, according to which social facilitation depends on the nature of the task, in particular, how simple and well learned it is. According to Zajonc:

> '... an audience impairs the acquisition of new responses and facilitates the emission of well-learned responses'.

In other words, things a person already knows how to do (e.g. cancelling numbers and letters, and simple multiplication) are done *better* when others are present, but things which are complex or which participants are required to learn are done *less well* when others are present. These findings have been confirmed by others. But why?

Because people are relatively unpredictable, there's a clear advantage to the species for their presence to induce in us a state of alertness or readiness. So, an instinctive response to the presence of others (in whatever capacity) is an increase in drive level (or level of arousal). This, in turn, energises (causes us to enact) our *dominant* responses, that is, our best learned or habitual responses in that situation. On subjectively simple tasks (those considered to be simple by the performer), those dominant responses are likely to be correct. Hence, the presence of others will facilitate performance on simple tasks (*task enhancement*).

However, when the task is complex, the effect of increased arousal is to make it more likely that incorrect or irrelevant responses will be performed and, hence, more errors are made (*task impairment*). The arousal produced by the presence of others, together with that produced by the task itself, produce a level beyond the optimum for ideal performance (Zajonc's explanation is based on Hull's learning theory: see Chapter 9).

An evaluation of Zajonc's drive theory

Some critics have argued that even on well-learned tasks, a skilled athlete may perform poorly in front of others. This can be better explained by the *inverted U theory* (based on the Yerkes–Dodson law: see Figure 31.1, page 449 and the discussion of fear arousal and attitude change in Chapter 24).

Oxendine (1970) found an inverted U relationship in several sports, but the amount of arousal necessary for optimal performance depended on the *nature of the skill* involved.

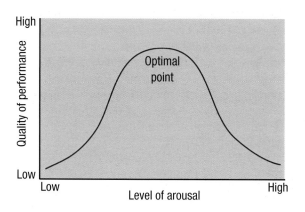

Figure 31.1 *Graph showing the inverted U relationship between arousal and performance*

More complex skills (putting in golf) need a *lower* level of arousal, because arousal interferes with fine muscle movement and co-ordination, and cognitive activities such as concentration. But *high* arousal is useful in less complex skills that require strength, endurance and speed (like tackling in football).

Many skills involve *both* strength and complexity, which are difficult to separate out (Jones & Hardy, 1990). For example, preparing to putt requires low muscle activity in the forearms, but high cognitive activity, while performing a maximum bench press in gym requires high muscle activity in the forearms and lower cognitive activity.

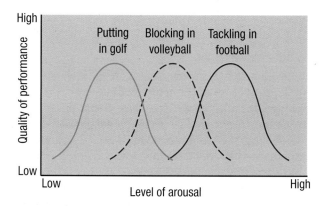

Figure 31.2 *Graph showing the relationship between level of arousal and level of performance in three skills*

Open and closed skills

According to Woods (1998), arousal can be more detrimental to performance of open than closed skills.

- Open skills are performed in an unpredictable environment, so they make more cognitive demands on the performer. The environment is constantly changing and players don't know what will happen; they have to make rapid decisions about what to do and when to do it.

An example is that of a basketball player who has to be able to control the ball while noting the movement of team-mates and opposing players, as well as making tactical decisions. Dribbling a basketball is best learned by practising under a variety of conditions, so that it can be performed effectively whatever the circumstances.

- Closed skills are performed in a constant, predictable environment, so the performer knows in advance what to do and when to do it. Learning involves refining the skill until it's as perfect as possible, and then repeating it until it can be performed automatically (it becomes *habitual*).

A gymnast starting a routine is performing a closed skill, which is *self-paced*. But closed skills may also occur in an 'open' situation. For example, a netball player taking a penalty shot is performing a closed skill, but she must take account of environmental factors, such as the position of other players and likely rebounds. So, the penalty shot cannot be purely habitual and has some characteristics of an open skill (Woods, 1998).

Level of expertise

To perform well, someone just learning a sport should experience only very low levels of arousal. But the experienced performer will need much higher levels in order to achieve optimum performance. Because the learner's skills aren't yet automatic, s/he uses cognitive abilities to direct, monitor and control them. Any additional arousal may interfere with concentration, reducing the ability to control the skill successfully.

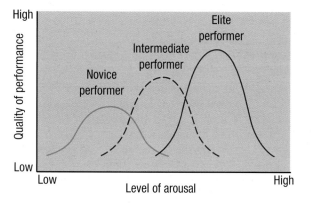

Figure 31.3 *Graph showing the relationship between level of arousal and level of expertise*

Personality

Performers with low *impulsivity* (that is, low *extroversion*/E and low *neuroticism*/N: see Chapter 42) tend to be more highly aroused during the early part of the day. By contrast, those high on impulsivity are more highly aroused later in the day. This has implications for performance. For example, athletes rated high on impulsivity will need to use more relaxation and stress-reduction strategies when running in an evening compared with a morning race (Woods, 1998).

Cottrell's evaluation apprehension model

Cottrell *et al.* (1968) found no social facilitation effect on three well-learned tasks when the two-person audience was inattentive (blindfolded) or merely present (only incidentally present, while supposedly waiting to participate in a different experiment). However, a non-blindfolded audience that carefully attended to the participant's performance, and had expressed an interest in watching, did produce a social facilitation (audience) effect.

According to Cottrell's (1968) *evaluation apprehension model*, it's not the *presence* of other people that increases arousal (as Zajonc's drive theory claims), but *apprehension* about being *evaluated* by them. We quickly learn that the social rewards and punishments (such as approval and disapproval) are dependent on others' evaluations of us, so the presence of others triggers an *acquired arousal drive* based on evaluation apprehension (a form of *social anxiety*: see Chapter 44).

An evaluation of Cottrell's model

If we're confident about our ability, then the awareness of being watched makes us perform well, but if we're not confident, then we're constantly worrying about how others are evaluating us. Cottrell *et al.* also showed that the more expert the audience, the more performance was impaired (the greater the evaluation apprehension).

> ### Ask yourself ...
>
> - Have you had personal experience of this (not necessarily in an athletic context)? (Consult the answers you gave to the previous *Ask yourself* box.)

Markus (1978) found support for Cottrell on an easy task (dressing in one's own clothes, having first undressed), but support for drive theory on a more difficult task (dressing in a laboratory coat and special shoes). Schmitt *et al.* (1986) found that mere presence appears to be a sufficient cause of social facilitation effects, and evaluation apprehension not to be necessary.

Zajonc (1980b) elaborated his earlier model by proposing that *socially generated drive* may be the product of *uncertainty*. The presence of others implies the possibility of action on their part, and the individual must always be alert to possible changes in the environment caused by others' behaviour. Uncertainty may be caused by the inability to anticipate how they'll act (Geen, 1995).

Baron's distraction–conflict theory

The amount of information we can attend to at the same time is limited (see Chapter 13). Little attention is needed to perform an easy task, but more is needed for a complex one. According to Baron's (1986) *distraction–conflict theory*, while distraction alone can impair task performance, attentional conflict can also induce a drive that facilitates dominant responses. Together, these processes improve performance of easy tasks, but impair performance of difficult ones. The presence of other people makes demands on our attention, which can either impair or enhance performance, depending on the nature of the task.

Attention-overload causes people to narrow their attention and focus on a small number of central cues. Complex tasks require attention to a large number of cues, so attention narrowing is likely to impair performance. On simple tasks (which involve few central cues), attention narrowing eliminates distraction and is likely to improve performance. This corresponds to Manstead & Semin's (1980) distinction between *controlled* and *automatic task performance*.

An evaluation of distraction–conflict theory

Sanders *et al.* (1978) had participants perform easy and difficult tasks, either alone or co-acting with someone performing either the same or a different task. The reasoning is that someone performing a *different* task wouldn't be a relevant source of social comparison, and so distraction should be minimal. But another person performing the *same* task would be highly distracting. As predicted, participants in the same-task (distraction) condition made more mistakes on the difficult task and did better on the simple task, compared with the other conditions.

Research shows that *any* form of stimulation (such as noise, movement, flashing lights) – not only the presence of other people – can produce the same facilitation or distraction effects (Hogg & Vaughan, 1998). An implication of this theory is that one way of preventing 'overload' is to cut out awareness of others and focus on the task in hand (Woods, 1998).

Non-drive explanations

The theories discussed above differ as to whether the drive is considered to be an innate response to the mere presence of other people, or a learned response based on evaluation apprehension or the product of attentional conflict. Although these are the best established and most extensively researched explanations, they aren't the only ones.

According to *self-awareness theory* (Carver & Scheier, 1981; Duval & Wicklund, 1972; Wicklund, 1975), we compare our actual selves (actual task performance) and ideal selves (how we'd like to perform: see Chapters 33 and 42). The discrepancy between them motivates us to close the gap. So, on easy tasks there's improved performance, but on difficult tasks the discrepancy may be too great and people give up trying, resulting in poorer performance. Self-awareness can be produced by co-actors, audience, or simply looking in a mirror.

An evaluation of explanations of social facilitation

There are many different accounts of what might originally have seemed a rather basic, straightforward social phenomenon. Some have fared better than others, and many questions remain unanswered. Nevertheless, the study of audience effects remains an important topic for social psychology (Hogg & Vaughan, 1998). However, in a meta-analysis of social facilitation experiments involving over 24,000 participants, Bond & Titus (1983) concluded that the mere presence of other people accounted for no more than 0.3–3.0 per cent of the variation in performance.

Social facilitation in a sports setting

Most of the research described above has involved passive, and unbiased, audiences. But in a sports context, the 'audience' is usually far from unbiased. Rather, it is composed of active, often passionate, supporters.

Patriotic pro-Tim Henman fans at Wimbledon

While research involving 'real' audiences is rare, one relevant area of research has looked at 'home advantage'.

| Box 31.3 | Does playing 'at home' improve or impair performance? |

- For the major sports in the US, teams win more home than away matches. This is true even when the visitors' 'away disadvantage' (such as the effects of travel and lack of familiarity with the ground) has been taken into account.
- Home advantage may be more important in the early rounds of a competition.
- When defending champions play at home, there's more chance of the home team cracking under the pressure.
- Home advantage is greater in sports such as basketball, where supporters are closer to the players. It's the intimacy with the crowd – not its size – which has most effect.

(Based on Woods, 1998)

Ask yourself ...
- If you support a football or rugby team, for example, check their results for last season. Did they perform better at home or away? (The chances are that unless they either won the championship or got relegated – in which case they probably performed consistently well or badly home and away – they did better at home.)
- How might the theories of social facilitation discussed above account for the various findings reported in Box 31.3?

Using social facilitation in coaching

According to Woods (1998):

■ athletes who train alongside others are likely to put more effort into routine tasks, such as warm-ups;

■ when learning a new skill, it's preferable to keep observers away;

■ athletes should be encouraged to learn techniques that minimise the effect of distractors (other people, noise, heat and so on). Some techniques which help in the management of arousal include relaxation, imagery and self-talk.

Influences on group performance

Social inhibition

The Ringelmann effect

Can the presence of others have an inhibiting effect on performance, as well as a facilitating effect? Several years after Triplett's experiments, Ringelmann, a French professor of engineering, reported a series of studies in which the presence of others seemed to produce a loss in motivation. (The studies had actually been conducted prior to Triplett's research, so strictly speaking these are the very first experiments in social psychology: Geen, 1995; Smith, 1995). Ringelmann found that the more members there were in a tug-of-war team, the less hard each member pulled; that is, as the size of the group increased, so the amount of force exerted per person decreased (the *Ringelmann effect*). He explained this largely in terms of a loss of physical co-ordination, but he conceded that loss of motivation could also be involved.

Social loafing

Latané *et al.* (1979) revived the Ringelmann effect under the name of *social loafing*. Early demonstrations involved simple physical acts, such as shouting and hand-clapping, individually or in groups, with the general result that the intensity of output per person declined as additional members were added. For example, when participants were asked to cheer and clap as loudly as possible, the amount of noise produced per person (compared with individual performance) dropped by 29 per cent in a pair, 49 per cent in a four-person group, and 60 per cent in a six-person group.

Social loafing can be defined as the tendency for individuals to work less hard (to loaf) on a task when they believe that others are also working on the task, and that one's own effort will be pooled with that of the other group members, compared with either working alone or co-actively (where others are doing the same task but independently of each other). According to Geen (1995), the data are consistent with one of the major claims of *social impact theory* (Latané & Nida, 1980). This states that when a person is a member of a group subjected to social forces, the impact of those forces on each person in the group is diminished in inverse proportion to the number of people in the group – the larger the group, the smaller the impact.

Later studies have shown the effect to be very reliable and general, occurring in both physical and cognitive tasks, in laboratory and naturalistic settings, in both genders and in several cultures. However, a review by Karau & Williams (1995) concluded that gender and culture appear to moderate people's tendency to loaf. Although men and women in different cultures are susceptible to loafing, the effect is smaller for women than men, and for people living in Eastern cultures. Both women and people living in Eastern cultures tend to be more group- or collectively oriented in their thinking and behaviour (see Chapters 35 and 47).

Explanations of social loafing

Geen (1995) identifies four main explanations: 'free-riding', equalisation of perceived output, evaluation apprehension and matching to standard.

■ *Free-riding* (Kerr, 1983) occurs when each member of a group perceives that there's a high probability that some other group members will solve the problem at hand, and that the benefits from this person's performance will go to all members. Each individual concludes that his/her contribution is dispensable, and so puts little effort into the group task. As a result, the importance of individual effort decreases as the size of the group increases (rather like diffusion of responsibility in bystander intervention: see Chapter 30).

■ Related to this is the *sucker effect*: if people expect their fellow group members to become free-riders ('goof off'), they may respond by loafing in an effort to bring equality to an inequitable situation ('Why should I make more effort than the others?' or 'I'm no sucker'). This is sometimes called the *output equity hypothesis* (McIlveen, 1995). Men seem to dislike the sucker role more than women.

■ *Evaluation apprehension*, as we saw earlier when discussing social facilitation, refers to anxiety about how others will judge us. If, as has been claimed, the tasks commonly used in social loafing studies are boring and meaningless, people will try to avoid doing them. If the efforts of group members are pooled, individuals can remain anonymous ('hide in the crowd', which is very similar to free-riding). It follows that making each person's contribution identifiable should eliminate social loafing.

Williams *et al.* (1981) simply informed participants that their shouting responses would be identifiable to the experimenter, and, as predicted, they shouted as loudly in groups as when alone. This suggests that participants become apprehensive about being evaluated by the experimenter. This is especially likely when participants believe that their performance is being *compared* with that of their co-actors performing the same task. They are, effectively, in competition. The higher the level of evaluation apprehension, the lower the level of social loafing (Harkins & Jackson, 1985).

In group-oriented (collectivist) cultures, such as China and Japan, making the tasks more realistic and relevant to everyday life not only eliminates social loafing but reverses it. The presence of others enhances performance on the same tasks which, in more individualist, Western cultures produce social loafing (Smith & Bond, 1993).

■ *Matching to standard* assumes that apprehension over the possibility of being evaluated by the experimenter causes the participant to match a standard for performance set by the experimenter (and that this matching is avoided under conditions that allow social loafing). According to Szymanski & Harkins (1987), the explicit statement of a standard relevant to the activity is sufficient to reduce social loafing.

Implications of social loafing for sports coaches

Ask yourself ...

• Based on the social loafing research discussed above, what advice would you give sports coaches?

According to Woods (1998), social loafing is essentially the result of a decrease in motivation. While 'There's no "I" in "team"' is a well-worn sporting cliché, she believes that research on social loafing shows that coaches ignore the 'I' at their peril. For Woods:

'Group goals are achieved by individuals, so it is important to identify individual behaviours which help group performance and try to encourage those behaviours. Monitoring and feedback on performance (to both individuals and the group) are better than feedback only on group performance ...'.

Group cohesion

Ask yourself ...

• How would you define a 'team'? Is it more than just the sum of the individual members (as with any group)?
• Apart from their skill levels, how do teams differ from each other?

According to Hogg & Vaughan (1998), *group cohesion* (or *cohesiveness*) is one of the most basic properties of a group, and is otherwise known as solidarity, *esprit de corps*, team spirit or morale. For Hogg and Vaughan, a cohesive group or team is:

'... the way it "hangs together" as a tightly knit, self-contained entity characterised by uniformity of conduct and mutual support among members ...'.

Cohesion can vary between groups, contexts, and across time. Groups with extremely low levels of cohesion hardly appear to be groups at all, and so the term may capture the very essence of being a group: the psychological process that transforms a collection of individuals into a group.

Festinger (1950) defined cohesiveness as a field of forces acting on the individual deriving from the attraction of the group and its members, and the degree to which the group satisfies individual goals. Cohesiveness is responsible for the continuity of group membership and adherence to group norms/standards.

According to Hogg (1992), most research defines cohesiveness in terms of attraction to the group and interpersonal attraction. Factors which increase interpersonal attraction (such as similarity, co-operation, interpersonal acceptance and shared threat: see Chapter 28) generally increase cohesiveness. This, in turn, causes, or is associated with, *conformity* to group norms, accentuated similarity, improved ingroup communication, and increased liking.

England's 1966 World Cup-winning team at Wembley Stadium

Personal vs social attraction

Hogg (1992, 1993) proposed a distinction between *personal attraction* (true interpersonal attraction based on close relationships) and *social attraction* (inter-individual liking based on common group membership). As Hogg & Vaughan (1998) say:

> *'Personal attraction is nothing to do with groups, while social attraction is the "liking" component of group membership ...'.*

Ask yourself ...

- How might social attraction be understood in terms of self-identity theory (SIT: see Chapter 25)?
- In what other ways might SIT be relevant to understanding group cohesiveness?

Attraction is merely one of a large number of effects produced by *self-categorisation*, as specified in self-identity theory (SIT). Others include stereotyping (see Chapter 22), conformity (see Chapter 26), intergroup differentiation, ethnocentrism, and ingroup solidarity (see Chapter 25).

One advantage of this distinction between personal and social attraction is that group cohesiveness isn't *reduced* to interpersonal attraction (see Chapter 49), and it also applies equally to small interactive groups and to large-scale social categories (such as 'ethnic group' and 'nation').

Hogg & Hardie (1991) gave questionnaires to a football team in Australia. Perceptions of team *prototypicality* (the typical/ideal defining features of team members) and *norms* were significantly related to measures of group-based social attraction, but *not* to measures of interpersonal attraction. This differential effect was strongest among members who themselves identified most strongly with the team. Similar findings were obtained with netball teams (Hogg & Hains, 1996).

Task vs social cohesion

Athletes often report that team cohesion is a source of satisfaction in their lives. Yet there is conflicting evidence as to whether the most cohesive teams are always the most successful. This is related to whether teams have been analysed in terms of:

- *task cohesion*: the degree to which group members work together and are committed to achieve common goals, such as winning a match; or
- *social cohesion*: the degree to which group members like each other and get on well, trust, and support each other.

These two aspects/dimensions are independent of each other. You might be very committed to achieving your team's goals, but not be particularly attached to the other team members. A team in which members get on well and are very committed to achieving common goals are at the *performing* stage of group development (Tuckman, 1965). This team *may* be successful. But equally, a team in which there are major disputes (and which is at the *storming* stage: Tuckman, 1965) *could* do well if there's a high degree of commitment to the common goal (Woods, 1998).

Factors associated with group cohesion

Type of sport

In *interactive* sports, such as football, the cohesive team (where members rely on each other to perform successfully) tends to be more successful. But in *co-active* sports, such as swimming (in which individual performance doesn't depend on others' performance), degree of cohesion seems to have little effect.

Ask yourself ...

- Can you relate this finding to Aronson's *jigsaw method* used to reduce racial prejudice and discrimination (see Chapter 25)?
- Analyse other sports in terms of the interactive/co-active distinction. Do some sports combine elements of both?
- Can a similar distinction be made with respect to *opponents*?

Box 31.4 Other factors associated with group cohesion

- **Stability:** Greater stability in group membership allows time for relationships between members to develop.
- **Group size:** The smaller the group, the greater the cohesion. This may be because there's more opportunity for members to interact, and less chance that faulty group processes will occur.
- **Similarity:** The more similar the members (in terms of status and characteristics, such as age and skill level), the greater the cohesion.
- **Success:** The more successful the team, the greater the cohesion.
- **External threats:** These may increase group cohesion by forcing members to ignore internal divisions and conflicts.

(Based on Woods, 1998)

Ask yourself ...

- Can you relate external threats to *common/superordinate goals* that we discussed in Chapter 25?

Factors affecting group performance

A good team is more than a group of skilled players. Members need to work together effectively in order to be successful. According to Steiner (1972), this can be expressed as:

Actual productivity = Potential productivity – Losses due to faulty group processes

In other words, to improve team performance, coaches need to increase the skills and performance of individuals (potential productivity), while reducing *faulty group processes*. The latter includes coping with excess arousal, and dealing with *social loafing* (both discussed above), *competitiveness*, and *poor co-ordination*.

Competition and co-operation

Although competitiveness is an essential part of sporting activity, co-operation is also essential, especially in team sports. In a review of the research, Johnson & Johnson (1985) concluded that co-operation produced higher standards in many more situations than competitiveness (including individual situations). But most of these studies weren't conducted in sports settings, in which competitiveness can produce exceptional effort, as well as damaging consequences. The latter may be most evident with younger or novice players, whose experience of failure in a highly competitive setting may even cause them to quit the sport. Increasingly, coaches are trying to strike a balance between these twin aspects of sport (Woods, 1998).

Co-ordination factors

These refer to the degree to which each player's skills are meshed together as tightly as possible, and are a central feature of interactive sports (such as football, rugby and volleyball). Training time should include practice in passing, timing and the pattern of players' movements. For example, co-ordination between the three players involved in taking a penalty corner in hockey is crucial:

'One notices time and time again that technically superior teams ... (can be beaten because of) ... lack of concentration, careless positioning and too much improvisation in execution ... the penalty corner is grossly neglected in training, especially by club teams'. (Wein, 1985, in Woods, 1998)

Co-active sports (such as swimming and golf), where individual performance doesn't depend on others, suffer much less from co-ordination factors (Woods, 1998).

CHAPTER SUMMARY

- **Sport psychology** is the scientific study of human behaviour and experience in sport. This includes recreational activities and exercise, as well as competitive sport.
- While their roles overlap, it's possible to distinguish **clinical**, **research** and **education sport psychologists**. Many of the issues they address draw on areas of research in mainstream and applied psychology, such as treatment of mental disorders, stress management, skill learning, and the role of personality factors.
- Zuckerman's **sensation-seeking scale** has successfully predicted attraction to sporting activities that involve high levels of risk and thrill.
- **Extreme athletes** have been described as **T types**, who may have fewer dopamine receptors in their brains. But **adrenaline surges** have also been recorded during more mental activities, such as chess.
- Triplett proposed a number of **non-social explanations** for why racing cyclists go faster when racing or being paced, compared with riding alone.
- Allport coined the term **social facilitation** to refer to improved performance caused by the **mere presence of conspecifics**. Two forms of social facilitation are the **co-action** and **audience effects**.
- Several explanations of social facilitation have been proposed, including Zajonc's **drive theory**, Cottrell's **evaluation apprehension model**, Baron's **distraction–conflict theory**, and **self-awareness theory**.
- There is evidence for an **inverted U relationship** between performance and arousal. This depends on the **nature of the skill** involved (such as **open/closed**), **level of expertise**, and **personality**.
- The '**Ringelmann effect**' describes one way in which the presence of others can **inhibit** performance. This idea was later revived and renamed **social loafing**.
- Major explanations of social loafing include '**free-riding**', the **sucker effect/output equity hypothesis**, **evaluation apprehension** and **matching to standard**.
- **Group cohesion/cohesiveness** is a basic property of a group. Most research defines cohesiveness in terms of attraction, but fails to distinguish between **personal** and **social attraction**. Only social attraction is relevant to group membership as such.
- Factors affecting group cohesion include the **type of sport** (interactive or co-active), **stability**, **group size**, **similarity**, and **external threats**.
- Factors affecting **group performance** include **arousal**, **social loafing**, **competitiveness**, **co-operation** and **co-ordination**.

Self-assessment questions

1 Critically assess research into social facilitation **and/or** social loafing in relation to sports-related performance.

2 Describe and evaluate psychological explanations of social facilitation.

3 Discuss factors affecting group cohesion.

Web addresses

http://www.sportspsychology.co.uk

spot.colorado.edu/~collins1/

spot.colorado.edu/~aaasp/sportpsy.html

www.psyc.unt.edu/apadiv47

Further reading

Woods, B. (1998) *Applying Psychology to Sport.* London: Hodder & Stoughton. A clearly written and thorough account of all major aspects of sport psychology, both social and non-social.

Kremer, J. & Scully, D. (1994) *Psychology in Sport.* Taylor & Francis. A fairly accessible British text (most are American).

Cox, R.H. (1994) *Sports Psychology: Concepts and Applications* (3rd edition). Dubuque, IA: (W.C. Brown & Benchmark). A fairly high level text, covering arousal, motivation, causal attribution, aggression, audience effects, teams, leadership and much more.

Five

Developmental Psychology

Chapter 32

Early Experience and Social Development

Introduction and overview

The study of attachments and their loss or disruption represents an important way of trying to understand how early experience can affect later development. Although it was a central tenet of Freud's psychoanalytic theory that experience during the first five years of life largely determines the kind of adults we become, it's really only since the 1950s that developmental psychologists have systematically studied the nature and importance of the child's tie to its mother.

This began with the English psychiatrist John Bowlby. He was commissioned by the World Health Organisation (WHO) to investigate the effects on children's development of being raised in institutions (in the aftermath of World War II). The central concept discussed in his report (*Maternal Care and Mental Health*, 1951) was *maternal deprivation*, which has become almost synonymous with the harmful effects of not growing up within a family.

However, Bowlby has been criticised for exaggerating the importance of the *mother–child relationship*. There's much more to attachment than attachment to the mother. *Fathers* are attachment figures in their own right, as are *siblings*. As social development continues, so the child's network of relationships increases to include teachers, classmates, neighbours and so on, and it begins to form its first *friendships*.

There's now a considerable body of research into attachments beyond infancy and childhood, especially between adult sexual partners, and many psychologists have questioned the deterministic nature of the early years.

The development and variety of attachments

What is sociability?

Sociability refers to one of three dimensions of *temperament* (the others being *emotionality* and *activity*), which are taken to be present at birth and inherited (Buss & Plomin, 1984). Specifically, sociability is:

■ seeking and being especially satisfied by rewards from social interaction;
■ preferring to be with others;
■ sharing activities with others;
■ being responsive to and seeking responsiveness from others.

While babies differ in their degree of sociability, it's a general human tendency to want and seek the company of others (c.f. the *need for affiliation*: see Chapter 28). As such, sociability can be regarded as a prerequisite for attachment development: the attraction to people in general is necessary for attraction to *particular* individuals (attachment figures). It corresponds to the *pre-attachment* and *indiscriminate attachment* phases of the attachment process (see below).

What is attachment?

According to Kagan *et al.* (1978), an attachment is:

'*... an intense emotional relationship that is specific to two people, that endures over time, and in which prolonged separation from the partner is accompanied by stress and sorrow*'.

While this definition applies to attachment formation at any point in the life cycle, our first attachment acts as a *prototype* (or model) for all later relationships. Similarly, although the definition applies to any attachment, the crucial first attachment is usually taken to be with the mother.

Phases in the development of attachments

The attachment process can be divided into several phases (Schaffer, 1996a):

1 The *pre-attachment phase* lasts until about three months of age. From about six weeks, babies develop an attraction to other human beings in preference to physical aspects of the environment. This is shown through behaviours such as nestling, gurgling and smiling, (*the social smile*) which are directed to just about anyone.

2 At about three months, infants begin to discriminate between familiar and unfamiliar people, smiling much more at the former (the social smile has now disappeared). However, they'll allow strangers to handle and look after them without becoming noticeably distressed, provided they're cared for adequately. This i*ndiscriminate attachment phase* lasts until around seven months.

3 From about seven or eight months, infants begin to develop specific attachments. This is demonstrated through actively trying to stay close to certain people (particularly the mother) and becoming distressed when separated from them (*separation anxiety*). This *discriminate attachment phase* occurs when an infant can tell consistently the difference between its mother and other people, and has developed *object permanence* (the awareness that things – in this case, the mother – continue to exist even when they cannot be seen: see Chapter 34).

   Also at this time, infants avoid closeness with unfamiliar people and some, though not all, display the *fear-of-strangers response*, which includes crying and/or trying to move away. This response will usually be triggered only when a stranger tries to make direct contact with the baby (rather than when the stranger is just 'there').

4 In the *multiple attachment phase* (from about nine months onwards), strong additional ties are formed with other major caregivers (such as the father, grandparents and siblings) and with non-caregivers (such as other children). Although the fear-of-strangers response typically weakens, the strongest attachment continues to be with the mother.

Theories of the attachment process

'Cupboard love' theories

According to *psychoanalytic* accounts, the infant becomes attached to its caregiver (usually the mother) because of his/her ability to satisfy its instinctual needs. For Freud (1926):

'*The reason why the infant in arms wants to perceive the presence of its mother is only because it already knows that she satisfies all its needs without delay*'.

Freud believed that healthy attachments are formed when feeding practices satisfy the infant's needs for food, security and oral sexual gratification (see Chapter 42). Unhealthy attachments occur when infants are *deprived* of food and oral pleasure, or are *overindulged*. Thus, psychoanalytic accounts stress the importance of feeding, especially breast-feeding, and of the maternal figure.

The *behaviourist* view of attachment also sees infants as becoming attached to those who satisfy their physiological needs. Infants associate their caregivers (who act as *conditioned* or *secondary reinforcers*) with gratification/satisfaction (food being an *unconditioned* or *primary reinforcer*), and they learn to approach them to have their needs met. This eventually generalises into a feeling of security whenever the caregiver is present (see Chapter 11).

An evaluation of 'cupboard love' theories

Both behaviourist and psychoanalytic accounts of attachment as 'cupboard love' were challenged by Harlow's studies involving rhesus monkeys (e.g. Harlow, 1959; Harlow & Zimmerman, 1959). In the course of studying learning, Harlow separated new-born monkeys from their mothers and raised them in individual cages. Each cage contained a 'baby blanket', to which the monkey became intensely attached, showing great distress when it was removed for any reason. This apparent attachment to its blanket, and the display of behaviour comparable to that of an infant monkey actually separated from its mother, seemed to contradict the view that attachment comes from an association with nourishment.

By fitting only the wire mother with a bottle, Harlow was trying to *separate* the two variables (the need for food and the need for something soft and cuddly), so as to assess their relative importance. If the cloth mother had been fitted with a bottle, it would have been impossible to interpret the infants' clinging behaviour: was it due to the food or to her being soft and cuddly?

Rhesus monkey displaying contact comfort

The cloth surrogate also served as a 'secure base' from which the infant could explore its environment. When novel stimuli were placed in the cage, the infant would gradually move away from the 'mother' for initial exploration, often returning to 'her' before exploring further. When 'fear stimuli' (such as an oversized wooden insect or a toy bear loudly beating a drum) were placed in the cage, the infant would cling to the cloth mother for security before exploring the stimuli. But when it was alone or with the wire surrogate, it would either 'freeze' and cower in fear or run aimlessly around the cage.

Infant monkeys frightened by a novel stimulus (in this case a toy teddy bear banging a drum) retreat to the terry cloth-covered 'mother' rather than to the wire 'mother'

Is there more to attachment than contact comfort?

Later research showed that when the cloth 'mother' had other qualities, such as rocking, providing warmth and food, the attachment was even stronger (Harlow & Suomi, 1970). This is similar to what happens when human infants have contact with parents who rock, cuddle and feed them.

Although attachment clearly doesn't depend on feeding alone, the rhesus monkeys reared exclusively with their cloth 'mothers' failed to develop normally. They became extremely aggressive adults, rarely interacted with other monkeys, made inappropriate sexual responses, and were difficult (if not impossible) to breed. So, in monkeys at least, normal development seems to depend on factors other than having something soft and cuddly to provide comfort. Harlow and Suomi's research indicates that one of these is *interaction with other members of the species* during the first six months of life. Research on attachment in humans also casts doubt on 'cupboard love' theories.

KEY STUDY 32.2

Feeding isn't everything for Scottish infants (Schaffer & Emerson, 1964)

Sixty infants were followed up at four-weekly intervals throughout their first year, and then again at 18 months. Mothers reported on their infants' behaviour in seven everyday situations involving separations, such as being left alone in a room, with a babysitter, and put to bed at night. For each situation, information was obtained regarding whether the infant protested or not, how much and how regularly it protested, and whose departure elicited it.

Infants were clearly attached to people who didn't perform caretaking activities (notably the father). Also, in 39 per cent of cases, the person who usually fed, bathed and changed the infant (typically the mother) wasn't the infant's primary attachment figure.

Schaffer & Emerson (1964) concluded that the two features of a person's behaviour which best predicted whether s/he would become an attachment figure for the infant were:

■ *responsiveness* to the infant's behaviour;
■ the *total amount of stimulation* s/he provided (e.g. talking, touching and playing).

For Schaffer (1971), 'cupboard love' theories of attachment put things the wrong way round. Instead of infants being passive recipients of nutrition (they 'live to eat'), he prefers to see them as *active seekers of stimulation* (they 'eat to live').

Ethological theories

The term 'attachment' was actually introduced to psychology by *ethologists*. Lorenz (1935) showed that some non-humans form strong bonds with the first moving objects they encounter (usually, but not always, the mother). In *precocial species* (in which the new-born is able to move around and possesses well-developed sense organs), the mobile young animal needs to learn rapidly to recognise its caregivers and to stay close to them. Lorenz called this *imprinting*. Since imprinting occurs simply through perceiving the caregiver without any feeding taking place, it too makes a 'cupboard love' account of attachment seem less valid, at least in goslings.

Box 32.1   Some characteristics of imprinting

- The response of following a moving individual/object indicates that a bond has been formed between the infant and the individual/object on which it's been imprinted.
- Ethologists see imprinting as an example of a *fixed-action pattern*, which occurs in the presence of a species-specific releasing stimulus (or *sign stimulus*).
- Lorenz saw imprinting as unique, because he believed it occurred only during a brief critical period of life and, once it had occurred, was irreversible. This is supported by the finding that when animals imprinted on members of other species reach sexual maturity, they may show a sexual preference for members of that species.

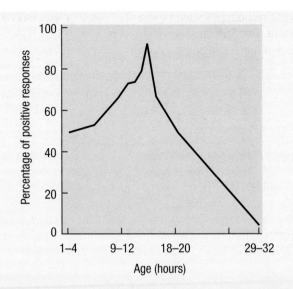

Figure 32.1 *The graph represents the relationship between imprinting and the age (hours after hatching) at which a duckling was exposed to a moving model of a male duck*

Lorenz being followed by goslings which had imprinted on him soon after hatching

A *critical period* is a restricted time period during which certain events must take place if normal development is to occur (Bornstein, 1989). Lorenz saw imprinting as being genetically 'switched on' and then 'switched off' again at the end of the critical period. However, studies have shown that the critical period can be extended by changing the environment in certain ways. This has led some researchers (e.g. Sluckin, 1965) to propose instead the existence of a *sensitive period*: learning is *most likely* to happen at this time, and will occur most easily, but it *may still* occur at other times. Also, imprinting is reversible (at least in the laboratory: see Gross *et al.*, 2000).

Ask yourself ...

- How relevant are Harlow's and Lorenz's findings with rhesus monkeys and goslings respectively to understanding human attachments?

Most psychologists would agree that the only way to be sure about a particular species is to study that species. To generalise the findings from rhesus monkeys and goslings to human infants is dangerous (although less so in the case of rhesus monkeys). However, Harlow's and Lorenz's findings can suggest how attachments might be formed in humans. Indeed, Bowlby was greatly influenced by ethological theory, especially by Lorenz's concept of imprinting.

Bowlby's theory

This represents the most comprehensive theory of human attachment formation. Bowlby (1969, 1973) argued that because new-born human infants are entirely helpless, they're *genetically programmed* to behave towards their mothers in ways that ensure their survival.

Box 32.2	Species-specific behaviours used by infants to shape and control their caregivers' behaviour

Sucking: While sucking is important for nourishment, not all sucking is nutritive. Non-nutritive sucking, also seen in non-humans, seems to be an innate tendency which inhibits a new-born's distress. In Western societies, babies are often given 'dummies' (or 'pacifiers') to calm them when they're upset.

Cuddling: Human infants adjust their postures to mould themselves to the contours of the parent's body. The reflexive response that encourages front-to-front contact with the mother plays an important part in reinforcing the caregiver's behaviour (see Box 32.1).

Looking: When parents don't respond to an infant's eye contact, the infant usually shows signs of distress. An infant's looking behaviour, therefore, acts as an invitation to its mother to respond. If she fails to do so, the infant becomes upset and avoids further visual contact. By contrast, mutual gazing is rewarding for an infant.

Smiling: This seems to be an innate behaviour, since babies can produce smiles shortly after birth. Although the first 'social smile' doesn't usually occur before six weeks (see page 460), adults view the smiling infant as a 'real person', which they find very rewarding.

Crying: Young infants usually cry only when hungry, cold, or in pain, and crying is most effectively ended by picking up and cuddling them. Caregivers who respond quickly during the first three months tend to have babies that cry less during the last four months of their first year than infants with unresponsive caregivers (Bell & Ainsworth, 1972).

The mother also inherits a genetic blueprint which programmes her to respond to the baby. There's a critical period during which the *synchrony* of action between mother and infant produces an attachment. In Bowlby's (1951) view, mothering is useless for all children if delayed until after two-and-a-half to three years, and for most children if delayed until after twelve months.

Strictly speaking, it's only the child who's *attached* to the mother, while she is *bonded* to her baby. The child's attachment to its mother helps to regulate how far away from the mother the child will move, and the amount of fear it will show towards strangers. Generally, attachment behaviours

(see Box 32.2) are more evident when the child is distressed, unwell, afraid, in unfamiliar surroundings and so on.

Bowlby believed that infants display a strong innate tendency to become attached to one particular adult female (not necessarily the natural mother), a tendency he called *monotropy*. This attachment to the mother-figure is *qualitatively* different (different in kind) from any later attachments. For Bowlby (1951):

> *'Mother love in infancy is as important for mental health as are vitamins and proteins for physical health'.*

Ask yourself ...

- Do you agree with Bowlby that the infant's relationship with its mother is unique, or are men just as capable as women of providing adequate parenting and becoming attachment figures for their young children?

An evaluation of Bowlby's theory

Bowlby's views on monotropy have been criticised. For example, infants and young children display a whole range of attachment behaviours towards a variety of attachment figures other than their mothers. In other words, the mother isn't special in the way the infant shows its attachment to her (Rutter, 1981). Although Bowlby didn't deny that children form multiple attachments, he saw attachment to the mother as being unique: it's the first to develop and is the strongest of all. However, Schaffer & Emerson's (1964) study (see Key Study 32.2, page 462) showed that multiple attachments seem to be the rule rather than the exception:

- At about seven months, 29 per cent of infants had already formed several attachments simultaneously (ten per cent had formed five or more).
- At 10 months, 59 per cent had developed more than one attachment.
- By 18 months, 87 per cent had done so (one-third had formed five or more).

Although there was usually one particularly strong attachment, most infants showed multiple attachments of varying intensity:

- Only half of the 18-month-olds were most strongly attached to their mothers.
- Almost one-third were most strongly attached to their fathers.
- About 17 per cent were equally attached to both parents.

What about fathers?

For Bowlby, the father is of no direct emotional significance to the young infant, but only of indirect value as an emotional and economic support for the mother. *Evolutionary psychologists* (see Chapter 2) see mothers as having a greater *parental investment* in their offspring, and hence are better prepared for child-rearing and attachment (Kenrick, 1994: see Gross *et al.*, 2000). However, Bowlby's views on fathers as attachment figures are disputed by findings such as those of Schaffer & Emerson (1964).

According to Parke (1981):

'Both mother and father are important attachment objects for their infants, but the circumstances that lead to selecting mum or dad may differ'.

Rather than being poor substitutes for mothers, fathers make their own unique contribution to the care and development of infants and young children (at least in two-parent families).

Individual and cultural variations in attachment

A pioneering study of individual differences in children's attachment to their mothers was conducted by Ainsworth (1967) in Uganda.

CROSS-CULTURAL STUDY 32.1

Ainsworth's (1967) Ganda project

Ainsworth studied 28 unweaned babies from several villages near Kampala, Uganda. At the beginning of the study, the babies ranged from 15 weeks to two years of age and they were observed every two weeks, for two hours at a time, over a nine-month period. Visits took place in the family living-room, where Ugandan women generally entertain in the afternoon. The mothers were interviewed (with the help of an interpreter), and naturalistic observations were made of the occurrence of specific attachment-related behaviours.

Ainsworth was particularly interested in *individual differences* between mother–child pairs regarding the quality of their attachment relationships. To tap into these differences, she devised various rating scales. The most important of these in terms of her future research was a scale for evaluating *maternal sensitivity* to the baby's signals.

Individual differences among babies were assessed by classifying them into three groups: securely attached, insecurely attached, and the not-yet-attached. These infant classifications were significantly correlated with ratings of the mothers' sensitivity (based purely on interview data) and the amount of holding by the mother (based on observation).

Ainsworth replicated her Ugandan study in Baltimore, USA (Ainsworth *et al.*, 1971, 1978). Van Ijzendoorn & Schuengel (1999) describe the Baltimore study as the most important study in the history of attachment research. Like the earlier study, both interviews and naturalistic observation were used, but the latter now played a much greater role.

Also like the Ganda project, the Baltimore study was *longitudinal*: 26 mother–infant pairs were visited at home every three to four weeks, each visit lasting three to four hours, for the first year of the baby's life. In order to make sense of the enormous amount of data collected for each pair (72 hours' worth), there needed to be an external criterion measure (some standard against which to compare the observations). The criterion chosen was the *Strange Situation* (see Figure 32.2, page 465, and Table 32.1 below).

Table 32.1 *The eight episodes of the 'Strange Situation'*

Episode	Persons present	Duration	Brief description
1	Mother, baby, observer	30 seconds	Observer introduces mother and baby to experimental room, then leaves
2	Mother, baby	3 minutes	Mother is non-participant while baby explores; if necessary, play is stimulated after two minutes
3	Stranger, mother, baby	3 minutes	Stranger enters. First minute: stranger silent. Second minute: stranger converses with mother. Third minute: stranger approaches baby. After three minutes, mother leaves unobtrusively
4	Stranger, baby	3 minutes or less*	First separation episode. Stranger's behaviour is geared to the baby's
5	Mother, baby	3 minutes or more**	First reunion episode. Stranger leaves. Mother greets and/or comforts baby, then tries to settle baby again in play. Mother then leaves, saying 'bye-bye'
6	Baby	3 minutes or less*	Second separation episode
7	Stranger, baby	3 minutes or less*	Continuation of second separation. Stranger enters and gears her behaviour to baby's
8	Mother, baby	3 minutes	Second reunion episode. Mother enters, greets baby, then picks up baby. Meanwhile, stranger leaves unobtrusively

*Episode is ended early if baby is unduly distressed.

** Episode is prolonged if more time is required for baby to become reinvolved in play.

(Based on Ainsworth *et al.*, 1978; Krebs & Blackman, 1988)

Table 32.2 *Behaviour associated with three types of attachment in one-year-olds using the 'Strange Situation'.*

Category	Name	Sample (%)
Type A	Anxious–avoidant	15

Typical behaviour: Baby largely ignores mother, because of *indifference* towards her. Play is little affected by whether she's present or absent. No or few signs of distress when mother leaves, and actively ignores or avoids her on her return. *Distress is caused by being alone*, rather than being left by the mother. Can be comforted as easily by the stranger as by the mother. In fact, *both adults are treated in a very similar way.*

Category	Name	Sample (%)
Type B	Securely attached	70

Typical behaviour: Baby plays happily while the mother is present, whether the stranger is present or not. Mother is largely 'ignored', because she can be trusted to be there if needed. Clearly distressed when the mother leaves, and play is considerably reduced. Seeks immediate contact with mother on her return, quickly calms down in her arms, and resumes play. The *distress is caused by the mother's absence*, not by being alone. Although the stranger can provide some comfort, *she and the mother are treated very differently.*

Category	Name	Sample (%)
Type C	Anxious–resistant	15

Typical behaviour: Baby is fussy and wary while the mother is present. Cries a lot more than types A and B, and *has difficulty using mother as a safe base*. Very distressed when she leaves, seeks contact with her on her return, but simultaneously shows anger and resists contact (may approach her and reach out to be picked up, then struggles to get down again). This demonstrates the baby's *ambivalence* towards her. Doesn't return to play readily. *Actively resists stranger's efforts to make contact.*

Mother   Stranger

Figure 32.2 *One of the eight episodes in the 'Strange Situation'*

The Strange Situation had been devised earlier by Ainsworth & Wittig (1969). They wanted to study how the baby's tendencies towards attachment and exploration interact under conditions of low and high stress. They believed that the balance between these two systems could be observed more easily in an unfamiliar environment. In the Baltimore study, the Strange Situation was modified to enable infant and maternal behaviour patterns to be classified.

Group data confirmed that babies explored the playroom and toys more vigorously in the mothers' presence than after the stranger entered or while the mothers were absent. However, Ainsworth was particularly fascinated by the unexpected variety of infants' reactions to the mothers' return (*reunion behaviours*: see Table 32.2).

In the Strange Situation technique, although every aspect of the participants' reactions is observed and videotaped, what's most carefully attended to is the child's response to the mother's return. This provides a clearer picture of the state of attachment than even the response to separation itself (Marrone, 1998).

The role of maternal sensitivity

The crucial feature determining the quality of attachment is the mother's sensitivity. The sensitive mother sees things from her baby's perspective, correctly interprets its signals, responds to its needs, and is accepting, co-operative and accessible. By contrast, the insensitive mother interacts almost exclusively in terms of her own wishes, moods and activities. According to Ainsworth *et al.*, sensitive mothers tend to have babies who are *securely attached*, whereas insensitive mothers have *insecurely attached* babies (either *anxious–avoidant/detached* or *anxious–resistant/ambivalent*).

Although both the Uganda and Baltimore studies provided support for the idea that parental sensitivity is the key factor in attachment development, both used rather small samples and so could only be considered promising explorations into the roots of early differences in attachment. During the past 20 years or so, however, several studies with larger samples have tested, and supported, the original claim that parental sensitivity actually causes attachment security (van Ijzendoorn & Schuengel, 1999).

Evaluation of the Strange Situation

According to Goldberg (2000) the Strange Situation:

> '... represents a unique combination of experimental and clinical methods, as the procedure itself is well standardised but allows controlled opportunities for natural interactions ...'.

The observer focuses on the infant, with the mother's caregiving behaviour regarded primarily as the *context* for the infant's behaviour. The advantage of this is that while the mother may try to please the experimenter and show herself to be a 'good mother', infant behaviour is free of such biases and is more transparent.

When the family's living conditions don't change, the children's attachment patterns also remain fairly constant, both in the short-term (six months: Waters, 1978) and the long-term (up to five years: Main *et al.*, 1985). This is commonly interpreted as reflecting a *fixed characteristic of the child*, such as temperament (see page 460). However:

Vaughn *et al.* (1980) showed that attachment type may change depending on variations in the family's circumstances. Children of single parents living in poverty were studied at twelve and 18 months. Significantly, 38 per cent were classified differently on the two occasions, reflecting changes in the families' circumstances, particularly changes in accommodation and the mothers' degree of stress. This suggests that attachment types aren't necessarily permanent characteristics;

Patterns of attachment to mothers and fathers are *independent*, so the same child might be securely attached to its mother, but insecurely attached to its father (Main & Weston, 1981). This shows that attachment patterns derived from the Strange Situation reflect *qualities of distinct relationships*, rather than characteristics of the child. If temperament, for example, were the main cause of attachment classification, the same child should develop the same kind of attachment pattern to both parents (van Ijzendoorn & De Wolff, 1997);

According to Main (1991), there's a fourth attachment type, namely *insecure–disorganised/disoriented* (type D). This describes a baby that acts as if afraid of the attachment figure (as well as the environment). Fear usually increases attachment behaviour, which includes seeking closer proximity to the attachment figure. But since the attachment figure is itself a source of fear, the infant faces a conflict between seeking and avoiding closeness to the attachment figure.

CROSS-CULTURAL STUDY 32.2

Cross-cultural studies of attachment using the Strange Situation

Cross-cultural studies have also revealed important differences, both within and between cultures. Van Ijzendoorn & Kroonenberg (1988) carried out a major review of 32 worldwide studies involving eight countries and over 2000 infants, and reached three main conclusions:

1 There are marked differences within cultures in the distribution of types A, B and C. For example, in one of two Japanese studies, there was a complete absence of type A but a high proportion of type C, while the other study was much more consistent with Ainsworth *et al.*'s findings.

2 The overall worldwide pattern, and that for the USA, was similar to the Ainsworth *et al.* 'standard' pattern. But within the USA there was considerable variation between samples.

3 There seems to be a pattern of cross-cultural differences, such that while type B is the most common, type A is relatively more common in Western European countries and type C is relatively more common in Israel and Japan.

How can we account for these differences? As far as point 3 is concerned, Japanese children are rarely separated from their mothers, so that the departure of the mother is the most upsetting episode in the Strange Situation. For children raised

on Israeli kibbutzim (small, close-knit groups), the entrance of a stranger was the main source of distress. Valid interpretations of the Strange Situation in cross-cultural settings require intimate knowledge of child-rearing customs and goals (Goldberg, 2000).

While the Strange Situation is the most widely used method for assessing infant attachment to a caregiver (Melhuish, 1993), Lamb *et al.* (1985) have criticised it for:

being highly artificial;
being extremely limited in terms of the amount of information that is actually gathered;
failing to take account of the mother's behaviour.

Ask yourself ...

• How could the Strange Situation be criticised on ethical grounds?

As we noted earlier, the Strange Situation is designed to see how young children react to stress, with the stranger becoming more intrusive over the course of the eight episodes. According to Marrone (1998), although the Strange Situation has been criticised for being stressful, it's modelled on common, everyday experiences: mothers do leave their children for brief periods of time in different settings, and often with strangers, such as baby-sitters. However, *deliberately* exposing children to stress as part of a psychological study is very different from what happens in the course of normal, everyday life (see Chapter 48).

Deprivation and privation

Bowlby's maternal-deprivation hypothesis

As noted earlier, Bowlby argued for the existence of a critical period in attachment formation. This, along with his theory of monotropy (see page 463), led him to claim that the mother–infant attachment couldn't be broken in the first few years of life without serious and permanent damage to social, emotional and intellectual development. For Bowlby (1951):

'An infant and young child should experience a warm, intimate and continuous relationship with his mother (or permanent mother figure) in which both find satisfaction and enjoyment'.

Bowlby's *maternal-deprivation hypothesis* was based largely on studies conducted in the 1930s and 1940s of children brought up in residential nurseries and other large institutions (such as orphanages).

KEY STUDY 32.3

Some early research findings on the effects of institutionalisation

Goldfarb (1943): Fifteen children raised in institutions from about six months until three-and-a-half years of age were matched with 15 children who'd gone straight from their mothers to foster homes. The institutionalised children lived in almost complete social isolation during their first year. The matching was based on genetic factors and natural mothers' education and occupational status.

At age three, the institutionalised group was behind the fostered group on measures of abstract thinking, social maturity, rule-following and sociability. Between ten and 14, the institutionalised group continued to perform more poorly on the various tests, and their average IQs (intelligence quotients) were 72 and 95 respectively.

Ask yourself ...

- Note that the children weren't assigned randomly to the two 'conditions' (as would happen in a true experiment). So, how was the decision made? Try to identify characteristics of the children which might have determined whether they were fostered or kept in the institution, and how this might have accounted for the results.

Those who appeared to be brighter or more easygoing, more sociable and healthy, were more likely to have been fostered. In this case, the differences in development of the two groups might have been due to these initial characteristics. However, Goldfarb concluded that *all* the institutionalised children's poorer abilities were due to the time spent in the institutions.

Spitz (1945, 1946) and Spitz & Wolf (1946): Spitz found that in some very poor South American orphanages, overworked and untrained staff rarely talked to the infants, hardly ever picked them up even for feeding, gave them no affection and provided no toys. The orphans displayed *anaclitic depression* (a reaction to the loss of a love object). This involves symptoms such as apprehension, sadness, weepiness, withdrawal, loss of appetite, refusal to eat, loss of weight, inability to sleep, and developmental retardation. It's similar to *hospitalism*.

After three months of unbroken deprivation, recovery was rarely, if ever, complete. In their study of 91 orphanage infants in the USA and Canada, Spitz and Wolf found that over one-third died before their first birthdays, despite good nutrition and medical care.

Interpreting the findings from studies of institutions

Bowlby, Goldfarb, Spitz and Wolf explained the harmful effects of growing up in an institution in terms of what Bowlby called maternal deprivation. In doing so, they failed to:

- recognise that the understimulating nature of the institutional environment, as well as (or instead of) the absence of maternal care, could be responsible for the effects they observed;
- disentangle the different types of deprivation and the different kinds of retardation produced (Rutter, 1981);
- distinguish between the effects of deprivation and privation. Strictly, *deprivation* ('de-privation') refers to the loss, through separation, of the maternal attachment figure

(which assumes that an attachment has already developed). *Privation* refers to the absence of an attachment figure (there's been no opportunity to form an attachment in the first place: Rutter, 1981).

Poor, unstimulating environments are generally associated with learning difficulties and retarded language development. Language development is crucial for overall intellectual development. Hence, a crucial variable in intellectual development is the amount of *intellectual stimulation* a child receives, *not* the amount of mothering.

The studies described in Key Study 32.5 (on which Bowlby originally based his maternal deprivation hypothesis) are most accurately thought of as demonstrating the effects of *privation*. However, Bowlby's own theory and research were mainly concerned with *deprivation*. By only using the one term (deprivation), he confused two very different types of early experience, which have very different types of effect (both short- and long-term).

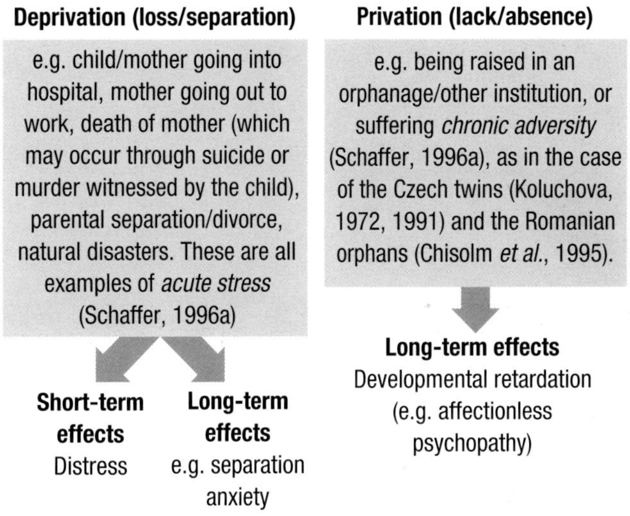

Deprivation (loss/separation)	Privation (lack/absence)
e.g. child/mother going into hospital, mother going out to work, death of mother (which may occur through suicide or murder witnessed by the child), parental separation/divorce, natural disasters. These are all examples of *acute stress* (Schaffer, 1996a)	e.g. being raised in an orphanage/other institution, or suffering *chronic adversity* (Schaffer, 1996a), as in the case of the Czech twins (Koluchova, 1972, 1991) and the Romanian orphans (Chisolm *et al.*, 1995).

Short-term effects
Distress

Long-term effects
e.g. separation anxiety

Long-term effects
Developmental retardation (e.g. affectionless psychopathy)

Figure 32.3 *Examples of the difference between deprivation and privation, including their effects*

Deprivation (separation or loss)

Short-term deprivation and its effects

One example of short-term deprivation (days or weeks, rather than months or years) is that of a child going into a nursery while its mother goes into hospital. Another is that of the child itself going into hospital. Bowlby showed that when young children go into hospital, they display *distress*, which typically involves three components or stages.

Box 32.3   The components or stages of distress

Protest: The initial, immediate reaction takes the form of crying, screaming, kicking and generally struggling to escape, or clinging to the mother to prevent her from leaving. This is an outward and direct expression of the child's anger, fear, bitterness, bewilderment and so on.

Despair: The struggling and protest eventually give way to calmer behaviour. The child may appear apathetic, but internally still feels all the anger and fear previously displayed. It keeps such feelings 'locked up' and wants nothing to do with other people. The child may no longer anticipate the mother's return, and barely reacts to others' offers of comfort, preferring to comfort itself by rocking, thumb-sucking and so on.

Detachment: If the separation continues, the child begins to respond to people again, but tends to treat everyone alike and rather superficially. However, if reunited with the mother at this stage, the child may well have to 'relearn' its relationship with her and may even 'reject' her (as she 'rejected' her child).

Factors influencing distress

Evidence suggests that not all children go through the stages of distress, and that they differ in how much distress they experience. Separation is likely to be most distressing:

- between the ages of seven or eight months (when attachments are just beginning to develop: see page 460) and three years, with a peak at 12–18 months (Maccoby, 1980). This is related to the child's inability to retain a mental image of the absent mother and its limited understanding of language. For example, because young children cannot understand phrases like 'in a few days' time' or 'next week', it's difficult to explain to them that the separation is only temporary. They might believe that they've been abandoned totally and that they're in some way to blame for what's happened ('Mummy's going away because I've been naughty');
- for boys (although there are also wide differences *within* each gender);
- if there have been any behaviour problems, such as aggression, that existed before the separation. Such problems are likely to be accentuated if separation occurs;
- if the mother and child have an extremely close and protective relationship, in which they're rarely apart and the child is unused to meeting new people. Children appear to cope best if their relationships with their mothers are stable and relaxed, but not too close, and if they have other attachment figures (such as their fathers) who can provide love and care. Many institutions used to be run in a way which made the development of substitute attachments very difficult. High staff turnover, a large number of children competing for the attention of a small number of carers, and the sometimes deliberate policies preventing special relationships, could all have worked against the provision of high-quality substitute attachments (Tizard & Rees, 1974).

One *long-term* effect of short-term separation is separation anxiety. This is also associated with long-term deprivation and is discussed below.

Long-term deprivation and its effects

Long-term deprivation includes the permanent separation resulting from parental death, and the increasingly common separation caused by divorce. Perhaps the most common effect of long-term deprivation is what Bowlby called *separation anxiety* (the fear that separation will occur again in the future).

John (17 months) experienced extreme distress while spending nine days in a residential nursery when his mother was in hospital having a second baby. According to Bowlby, he was grieving for the absent mother. Robertson & Robertson (1969) (who made a series of films called Young Children in Brief Separation*) found that the extreme distress was caused by a combination of factors: loss of the mother, strange environment and routines, multiple caretakers and lack of a mother substitute*

Separation anxiety

Separation anxiety may manifest itself in:

- increased aggressive behaviour and greater demands towards the mother;
- clinging behaviour: the child is unable to let the mother out of its sight. This may generalise to other relationships, so that a man who experienced 'bad' childhood separations may be very dependent on, and demanding of, his wife;
- detachment: the child becomes apparently self-sufficient, because it cannot afford to be let down again;
- some vacillation between clinging and detachment;
- psychosomatic (*psychophysiological*) reactions (physical symptoms associated with/caused by stress, anxiety or other psychological factors see Chapter 12, pages 174–177).

The effects of divorce

According to Schaffer (1996a), nearly all children (especially boys), regardless of their age, are adversely affected by parental divorce, at least in the short term. However, despite the stresses involved, most children are resilient enough to adapt to their parents' divorce eventually (Hetherington & Stanley-Hagan, 1999). The nature, severity and duration of the effects vary greatly between children. These are influenced by many factors, including:

- continuity of contact with the non-custodial parent;
- the financial status/lifestyle of the single-parent family;
- whether the custodial parent remarries and the nature of the resulting step-family.

Box 32.4	**Some of the major effects on children of parental divorce**

Compared with children of similar social backgrounds whose parents remain married, those whose parents divorce show small but consistent differences throughout childhood. They also have different life courses as they move into adulthood. The differences include:

- lower levels of academic achievement and self-esteem;
- a higher incidence of antisocial and delinquent behaviour, and other problems of psychological adjustment during childhood and adolescence (see Chapter 46);
- earlier social maturity, with certain transitions to adulthood (such as leaving home, beginning sexual relationships, cohabiting or getting married, and becoming pregnant) typically occurring younger (see Chapters 28 and 38);
- a tendency in young adulthood to more frequent changes of job, lower socioeconomic status, and indications of a greater frequency of depression and lower scores on measures of psychological well-being (see Chapter 44);
- more distant relationships in adulthood with parents and other relatives.

(Based on Hetherington & Stanley-Hagan, 1999; Richards, 1995)

These findings are *correlational*, so we cannot be sure that it's divorce (or divorce alone) that's responsible for the differences that have been reported. For example, *divorce-prone couples* (those most likely to divorce) might have particular child-rearing styles which account for the differences. This possibility is supported by the finding that some of the effects associated with divorce can be seen *before* couples separate (Elliott & Richards, 1991). But this hypothesis cannot account for all the effects seen later (Booth & Amato, 1994).

According to Schaffer (1996a), *inter-parental conflict* before, during and after the separation/formal divorce, is the single most damaging factor. Amato (1993), for example, showed that conflict between parents who live together is associated with low self-esteem in children. In turn, low self-esteem may lead to other problems, including lower school achievement and difficulties in forming relationships.

However, Hetherington & Stanley-Hagan (1999) argue that we cannot just assume (as is often done) that conflict declines following divorce. In fact, conflict often *increases* in the first few years after divorce, over financial settlements, access arrangements, co-parenting, parents' rights and responsibilities and so on. Under these conditions, it's better for children to remain in an unhappy two-parent household than to suffer the effects of divorce. If there's a shift to a more harmonious household, then a divorce is advantageous to both boys and girls. But even in low-conflict divorced families, boys (but not girls) are worse off than those in low-conflict non-divorced families (Hetherington & Stanley-Hagan, 1999).

The effects of day care

This is regarded by some as another form of long-term deprivation. According to Scarr (1998), day care includes all varieties of non-maternal care of children who reside with their parent(s) or close relatives, and so excludes foster care and institutional (residential) care.

A deep-seated and widely held assumption is that childcare provided by anyone other than the child's mother deserves

special attention, because it's *non-normative* (it's not how most children are cared for). This partly reflects the continuing influence of Bowlby's theory of attachment. However, shared childcare is actually a normative experience for contemporary American (and British) children, the vast majority of whose mothers are employed. More than half the mothers of infants under twelve months of age, and three-quarters of those of school-age children, are in the labour force. According to Scarr (1998), non-maternal shared care is normative, both historically and culturally (and so is universal).

In industrialised societies, such as Britain and the USA, mothers' employment outside the home has made non-maternal care of various kinds necessary. The demand for childcare is driven entirely by the economic need for women in the labour force. In 1997, women comprised 49.5 per cent of those in paid employment in the UK, and in 2000 they outnumbered men (although with a far higher percentage in part-time work: Kremer, 1998).

Despite these changing patterns of female employment, the belief that women are born and reared to be, first and foremost, mothers (the *motherhood mystique/mandate*) remains an influence on our attitudes about working mothers (Kremer, 1998: see Chapter 38).

Ask yourself ...

- What would Bowlby's theory predict about the effects of working mothers on their child's attachment development?

According to Bowlby, a child whose mother goes out to work experiences maternal deprivation. If this happens during the child's first year (before an attachment has formed), an attachment may not develop at all (strictly, this is *privation*). If it happens after an attachment has developed, the child will be distressed, may experience separation anxiety and so on (see above, page 468).

The results have tended to show that there's no weakening of the attachment to the mother resulting from the daily separations involved in day care. Provided certain conditions are met, especially the *stability* and *quality* of the care, children *don't* suffer any ill effects and will benefit from them in certain respects (Schaffer, 1996a).

However, Belsky & Rovine (1988) concluded that infants in day care were more likely to develop insecure attachments if they'd been receiving day care for at least four months before their first birthday and for more than 20 hours per week. Although many children 'at risk' develop secure attachments, they are also more likely to develop insecure attachments than children who stay at home (see Table 32.2).

However, Belsky and Rovine's findings were obtained exclusively from one method of assessing attachment, namely the Strange Situation (see Table 32.1). Clarke-Stewart (1989) argues that this is an inappropriate technique for children in day care. As we saw earlier, the Strange Situation is based on the assumption that repeated separations from the mother put children under stress, and so highlights their attempts at security-seeking. But day care children are used to such separations and so may not experience stress. When they respond to the mother's return in the Strange Situation with (what looks like) indifference, they may be showing *independence* and *self-reliance*, not the 'avoidance' or 'resistance' that are used to classify children as insecurely attached. According to Schaffer (1996a):

'It is possible that the Strange Situation procedure is not psychologically equivalent for children of working and of non-working mothers. If that is so, it becomes even more important to ensure that any conclusions are based on a variety of assessment techniques'.

Ask yourself ...

- If day care were harmful to young children's attachments, what kind of distribution of secure and insecure attachments would you expect among those whose mothers work compared with those who don't (e.g. what percentage of type A and type C attachments)?

- The observed distribution of insecure infants of working mothers in the USA (22 per cent type A; 14 per cent type C) is virtually identical to the overall distribution for studies around the world (21 per cent and 14 per cent, respectively, based on almost 2000 children of mainly non-working mothers: van Ijzendoorn & Kroonenberg, 1988).

- In theory, an attachment is a relationship, not a global personality trait (see page 466). If the children of working mothers are more insecure with them, this doesn't necessarily mean that they're emotionally insecure in general. We need to assess their emotional health in a range of situations, with a variety of attachment figures. Several studies have shown that children who were in day care as infants do as well as those who weren't, using measures of security, anxiety, self-confidence and emotional adjustment (Clarke-Stewart, 1989).

(For a discussion of the effects of day care on children's *cognitive development*, see Gross *et al.*, 2000.)

CRITICAL DISCUSSION 32.1

To work or not to work?

As Horwood & Fergusson (1999) point out, much of the research into the effects of day care has been carried out in the USA. The conclusions from these studies may not apply to other societies and cultures where patterns of maternal, and paternal, participation in the labour force and at home may differ from those in the USA.

In a review of 40 years' research, Mooney and Munton (cited in Judd, 1997) conclude that there's no evidence that working mothers stunt their children's emotional or social development. Even poor quality childcare may make no difference to a child from a stable family, while good quality care may provide positive benefits. Instead of debating

the rights and wrongs of working mothers, we should focus on how to provide enough good childcare.

British families have changed fundamentally in the past 25 years. In more than 70 per cent of two-parent families with dependent children, both parents work, and the proportion of children living in single-parent families has risen from eight to 21 per cent (see Chapter 38). What's needed is a national strategy for childcare which ensures that all employees are properly trained and paid. Similarly (in relation to the American scene), Clarke-Stewart (1989) states that:

'Maternal employment is a reality. The issue today, therefore, is not whether infants should be in day care but how to make their experiences there and at home supportive of their development and of their parents' peace of mind'.

Privation

As we noted earlier, privation is the failure to develop an attachment to any individual. Given the importance of the child's first relationship as a model or prototype of relationships in general, failure to develop an attachment of any kind is likely to affect all subsequent relationships adversely.

Harlow's research (see page 461) showed that monkeys brought up with only surrogate mothers were very disturbed in their later sexual behaviour. For example, females had to be artificially inseminated because they wouldn't mate naturally. The unmothered females also became very inadequate mothers, rejecting their infants whenever they tried to cling to their bellies and, literally, walking all over them.

Affectionless psychopathy

According to Bowlby, maternal deprivation in early childhood causes affectionless psychopathy. This is the inability to care and have deep feelings for other people and the consequent lack of meaningful interpersonal relationships, together with the inability to experience guilt.

KEY STUDY 32.4

Growing up with TB (Bowlby *et al.*, 1956)

Bowlby *et al.* studied 60 children aged seven to 13, who'd spent between five months and two years in a tuberculosis (TB) sanatorium (which provided no substitute mothering) at various ages up to four. About half had been separated from their parents before they were two years old. When compared with a group of non-separated 'control' children from the same school classes, the overall picture was that the two groups were more similar than different. The separated children were more prone to 'daydreaming', showed less initiative, were more over-excited, rougher in play, concentrated less well and were less competitive. But they weren't more likely to show affectionless psychopathy, regardless of when their separation had occurred (before or after two).

Bowlby *et al.* admitted that 'part of the emotional disturbance can be attributed to factors other than separation', such as the common occurrence of illness and death in the sanatorium children's families. So, there was very little evidence for the link between affectionless psychopathy and *separation* (or bond disruption). However, Bowlby may have provided evidence for an association with privation instead (a failure to form bonds in early life). According to Rutter (1981), privation is likely to lead to:

- an initial phase of clinging, dependent behaviour;
- attention-seeking, and uninhibited, indiscriminate friendliness;
- a personality characterised by lack of guilt, an inability to keep rules and an inability to form lasting relationships.

Are the effects of privation reversible?

Suomi & Harlow (1972) found that the effects on rhesus monkeys of being reared in isolation from other monkeys (their mothers or siblings) *could* be reversed, or at least moderated. This was achieved by allowing them to have extensive contact with 'monkey therapists' (young, normally-reared, monkeys). In humans, there are (at least) three kinds of study which demonstrate that it's possible to undo the effects of early privation:

1 *Case studies* of children who've endured *extreme* early privation, often in near complete isolation. Examples include the Czech twins studied by Koluchova (1972, 1991: see Case Study 32.1) and the concentration camp survivors (Freud & Dann, 1951: see Case Study 32.2).
2 Studies of *late adoption*: children raised in institutions are adopted after Bowlby's critical period for attachment development (twelve months for most children, up to two-and-a-half/three years for the rest). Studies include those of Tizard and her colleagues (e.g. Hodges & Tizard, 1989: see Key Study 32.7, pages 473–474), and Chisolm *et al.* (1995: see Key Study 32.6).
3 Studies of *developmental pathways* (see page 473).

Studies of extreme privation

This represents the toughest test of the hypothesis that early experience, important at the time, will have long-term effects only if similar experiences occur subsequently (Clarke & Clarke, 2000). What happens to children who suffer extreme early privation but are then 'rescued' and enjoy much improved conditions?

CASE STUDY 32.1

The case of PM and JM (Koluchova, 1972, 1991)

Identical twin boys, born in 1960 in the former Czechoslovakia, lost their mother shortly after birth and were cared for by a social agency for a year, and then fostered by a maternal aunt for a further six months. They then went to live with their father who'd remarried, but his new wife proved to be excessively cruel to the twins, banishing them to the cellar for the next five-and-a-half years. During this time they also received harsh beatings.

When discovered in 1967, they were very short in stature, had rickets, no spontaneous speech (communicating largely by gestures), and were terrified of many aspects of their new environment.

Legally removed from their parents, they first underwent a programme of physical rehabilitation and entered a school for children with severe learning difficulties. They were subsequently adopted legally by two exceptionally dedicated women. Academically, they caught up with their peers and achieved emotional and intellectual normality. At follow-up in 1974 (at age 14), they showed no signs of psychological abnormality or unusual behaviour. They'd gone on to technical school, training as typewriter mechanics, but later went on to further education, specialising in electronics.

They both had very good relationships with their adoptive mothers, their adopted sisters, and the women's relatives. Both were drafted for national service, and later married and had children. At the age of 29, they were said to be entirely stable, lacking abnormalities and enjoying warm relationships. One had become a computer technician and the other a technical training instructor (Koluchova, 1991).

Clearly, the twins' experience of prolonged privation didn't predestine them to a permanent condition of severe handicap (Clarke & Clarke, 2000).

CASE STUDY 32.2

Childhood survivors of the Holocaust (Freud & Dann, 1951)

Anna Freud and Sophie Dann studied six German-Jewish orphans rescued from a concentration camp at the end of the Second World War. They'd all been orphaned when a few months old, after which they were kept together as a group in a deportation camp. They were cared for by camp inmates, who were successively deported to Auschwitz. One of the inmates who survived later said, 'We looked after the bodily welfare of the children as much as possible ... but it was not possible to attend to their other needs' (Moskovitz, 1985).

During their time in the camp, they'd been subjected to many terrifying experiences, including witnessing camp hangings. On release, at age three, all were severely malnourished, normal speech had hardly developed, and they'd developed the same kind of intense attachment to each other that children normally have for their parents – but there was none of the jealousy and rivalry usually found among siblings. They refused to be separated even for a moment, and were extremely considerate and generous to each other. But they showed cold indifference or fearful hostility towards adults. After the camp was liberated, they were flown to Bulldog's Bank in England.

They obviously cared greatly – and only – for each other. But gradually they began to form attachments to specific adult caretakers, and they showed a spurt in social and language development. In a one-year follow-up, it was clear that they were hypersensitive, aggressive, and difficult to follow. But, as Clarke & Clarke (2000) observe:

> '... they were neither deficient, delinquent nor psychotic. They ... had mastered some of their anxieties, and developed social attitudes. That they were able to acquire a new language in the midst of their upheavals, bears witness to a basically unharmed contact with their environment'.

Within the next two years, all but one of the children were adopted.

All six were traced and interviewed by Moskovitz during 1979 and 1980 (Moskovitz, 1983, 1985). While it had previously been thought that they'd been irreparably damaged:

> 'What now became apparent ... was the wide range of adaptation when there was theoretically no reason to see anything positive ... Many made adaptations that are not only impressive but inspiring.' (Clarke & Clarke, 2000)

Like the study of the Czech twins, the fate of the Holocaust survivors seems to highlight the fundamental importance of having *somebody* (not necessarily a mother-figure) with whom to form an emotional bond. According to Tizard (1986), Freud and Dann's study:

> '... provides ... evidence of the protective function of attachments in development, even when they are not directed to the mother, or indeed to an adult'.

In other words, it's *attachment formation* as such that's important for the development of social and emotional relationships in later childhood and adulthood, rather than with whom the bond is formed.

Studies of late adoption

Tizard (1977) and Hodges & Tizard (1989) studied children who, on leaving care between the ages of two and seven, were either adopted or returned to their own families. The institutions they grew up in provided good physical care and appeared to provide adequate intellectual stimulation. However, staff turnover was high, and they operated a policy against allowing strong attachments to develop between the staff and children.

Consequently, the children had little opportunity to form close, continuous relationships with adults. Indeed, by age two, they'd been looked after for at least a week by an average of 24 different caregivers. By age four, this had risen to 50. The children's attachment behaviour was very unusual and, in general, the first opportunity to form long-term attachments came when they left the institutions and were placed in families.

By age eight, the majority of the adopted children had formed close attachments to their adoptive parents (who very much wanted a child), despite the lack of early attachments in the institutions (Tizard & Hodges, 1978). But only some of those children returned to their own families had formed close attachments. The biological parents often had mixed feelings about having the child back, with other children competing for their attention (as well as material hardship).

As reported by their parents, the ex-institutional children as a whole didn't display more problems than a comparison group that had never been in care. But their teachers described them as displaying attention-seeking behaviour, restlessness, disobedience and poor peer relationships.

KEY STUDY 32.5

Ex-institution children at age 16 (Hodges & Tizard, 1989)

At age 16, the family relationships of most of the adopted children seemed satisfactory, both for them and their parents. They differed little from a non-adopted comparison group who'd never been in care. Hence, early institutional care hadn't necessarily led to a later inability to form a close attachment to parents (contrary to Bowlby's predictions). By contrast, those children returned to their families still suffered difficulties and poor family relationships. These included mutual difficulty in showing affection, and the parents reported feeling closer to the children's siblings than to the returned children.

Outside the family, however, *both* the adopted and returned children showed similar relationships with peers and adults. Compared with a control group, they were:

- still more likely to seek adult affection and approval;
- still more likely to have difficulties in their relationships with peers;
- less likely to have a special friend or to see peers as sources of emotional support;
- more likely to be friendly to any peer rather than choosing their friends.

These findings *are* consistent with Bowlby's maternal-deprivation hypothesis.

Hodges and Tizard's research indicates that children who fail to enjoy close and lasting relationships with adults in the first years of life *can* make such attachments later on. But these don't arise automatically, simply by being placed in a family. Rather, they depend on the adults concerned and how they nurture such attachments. Also, if these children experience difficulties in their relationships outside the family, they may have difficulties in future adult relationships and with their own children.

These ex-institution children have now been followed up into adulthood (average age 31 years). This took the form of postal questionnaires (Hodges *et al.*, in preparation; Jewett, 1998), and interviews using the adult attachment interview (see below) with a subsample of the ex-institution group (Williams, 1999).

There were very few significant differences between the ex-institution group and the comparison group, including evidence of psychiatric disorder. However, the former consistently reported difficulties in relationships with friends, partners and children, and significantly greater difficulties in relationships with their families of upbringing. They also reported a tendency to be over-aggressive in their interpersonal relationships, and to be independent and self-reliant.

But they also reported *more rewarding* intimate friendships, with higher levels of companionship, and higher self-esteem than the comparison group (these differences *weren't* statistically significant). While acknowledging the small sample size (22 ex-institution, 23 comparisons), Hodges (personal communication, 2000) states that:

'... the evidence seems to support both the view that the effects of earlier adversity fade given the right later circumstances, and the view that there are some enduring effects producing continuities in personal characteristics'.

KEY STUDY 32.6

Late adoption of Romanian orphans (Chisolm *et al.*, 1995)

Romanian orphans, reared in extremely poor conditions in large-scale institutions, were adopted by Canadian families between the ages of eight months and five-and-a-half years (Chisolm *et al.*, 1995). It seems that some negative impact on the children's relationships with adoptive parents can result from their institutional experiences. For example, their behaviour was often described as *ambivalent* (they simultaneously wanted contact and resisted it: see Table 32.2). Also, they weren't easily comforted when distressed.

Follow-up is needed to see if life in a loving family can eventually overcome this impairment. However, based on their intellectual recovery, there are good reasons for being optimistic (Schaffer, 1998).

Developmental pathways

Quinton & Rutter (1988) wanted to find out whether children deprived of parental care become depriving parents themselves. They observed one group of women, brought up in care, interacting with their own children, and compared them with a second group of non-institutionalised mothers. The women brought up in care were, as a whole, less sensitive, supportive and warm towards their children. This difference could be explained in terms of both:

- various subsequent experiences the women had as a result of their early upbringings (such as teenage pregnancy, marrying unsupportive spouses and marital breakdown);
- their actual deprived childhoods.

However, there was also considerable variability *within* the group brought up in care, with some women displaying good parenting skills. This could be explained in terms of *developmental pathways*. For example, some of the women had more positive school experiences than others. This made them three times more likely as adolescents or young adults to make proper career and marriage partner choices (Rutter, 1989). Such positive experience represents an escape route from the early hardships associated with being brought up in care. Similar adverse childhood experiences can have *multiple* outcomes (Schaffer, 1996b). *Starting off* at a disadvantage doesn't necessarily mean having to *finish up* at a disadvantage.

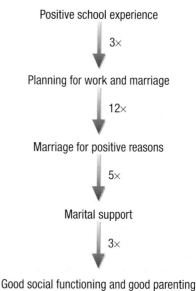

Figure 32.4 *A simplified adaptive chain of circumstances in institution-raised women (based on Quinton & Rutter, 1988; Rutter, 1989)*

Continuity between early and later attachment patterns

The effects of early attachments on later adult relationships

Although until recently attachment was studied almost exclusively within parent–child relationships, Bowlby (1977) maintained that 'attachment behaviour is held to characterise human beings from the cradle to the grave'. According to Hazan & Shaver (1987), attachment theory, as developed by Bowlby and Ainsworth in particular, offers a valuable perspective on adult romantic love, helping to explain both *positive emotions* (caring, intimacy and trust) and *negative emotions* (fear of intimacy, jealousy, and emotional 'ups and downs').

Hazan and Shaver were the first to apply Ainsworth *et al.*'s three basic attachment styles to adult–adult sexual/romantic relationships. Their study tried to answer the question: how are *adults'* attachment patterns (in their adult relationships) related to their *childhood* attachments to their parents?

KEY STUDY 32.7

Romantic love conceptualised as an attachment process (Hazan & Shaver, 1987)

Ainsworth *et al.*'s three attachment styles were 'translated' in a way that would make them suitable for the study of adult attachments. As part of a 'love quiz' in a local newspaper, respondents were asked to indicate which of three descriptions best applied to their feelings about romantic relationships:

Table 32.3 *Responses to the question 'Which of the following best describes your feelings?'*

Classification	Response	% of respondents
Secure	I find it easy to get close to others and am comfortable depending on them and having them depend on me. I don't worry about being abandoned or about someone getting too close to me	56
Anxious–avoidant	I am somewhat uncomfortable being close to others. I find it difficult to trust them completely, difficult to allow myself to depend on them. I am nervous when anyone gets too close, and often, love partners want me to be more intimate than I feel comfortable being	24
Anxious–ambivalent	I find that others are reluctant to get as close as I would like. I often worry that my partner doesn't really love me or won't want to stay with me. I want to merge completely with another person, and this desire sometimes scares people away	20

They were also asked to complete a simple adjective checklist describing their childhood relationships with their parents (their recollections of the kind of parenting they received). This was then correlated with their chosen attachment style.

Table 32.4 *Correlation between attachment style and type of parenting in adult respondents*

Attachment style	Type of parenting
Secure	Readily available, attentive, responsive
Anxious–avoidant	Unresponsive, rejecting, inattentive
Anxious–ambivalent	Anxious, fussy, out of step with child's needs; only available/responsive some of the time.

The correlation shown in Table 32.4 closely mirrors Ainsworth *et al*.'s findings with 12–18-month olds. Although these results provided encouraging support for an attachment perspective on romantic love, Hazan and Shaver warned against drawing any firm conclusions about the continuity between early childhood and adult experience. It would be excessively pessimistic, at least from the point of view of the insecurely attached person, if continuity were the rule, rather than the exception. They suggest that as we go further into adulthood, continuity with our childhood experiences decreases. The average person participates in several important friendships and love relationships, which provide opportunities for revising our *mental models* (or what Bowlby, 1973, called *internal working models*) of self and others (see below).

Rap singer Enimem's lyrics sometimes tell of a very disturbed relationship with his mother. How might this influence his relationship with his own children?

Intergenerational continuity

Another way of looking at the continuity between early and later attachment patterns is to ask how *parents'* attachment styles are related to their *children's* attachment styles. In other words, do people parent their children as they themselves were parented? This is the issue of *intergenerational continuity*.

A commonly used measure of how parents are/were attached to their own parents is the *adult attachment interview* (AAI). Apart from the Strange Situation, the AAI is probably the most widely used and best-developed measure of attachment (Goldberg, 2000). It's based on the assumption that what's crucial for predicting parenting behaviour isn't so much the objective facts about our early attachments, but rather how we *construe* these facts, that is, the nature of our *internal working models*.

Box 32.5 **The adult attachment interview (AAI) (Main *et al.*, 1985)**

The AAI is a structured interview, comprising 15 questions designed to tap an individual's experience of attachment relationships in childhood, and how s/he considers those experiences to have influenced later development and present functioning.

More specifically, for each parent, the person is asked to choose five adjectives which best describe that relationship during childhood. The person then has to illustrate each of these choices by drawing on childhood memories. Later, the person is asked how they reacted when upset, to which parent they felt closest and why, whether they ever felt rejected or threatened, why parents may have acted as they did, how these relationships may have changed, and how these earlier experiences (including major loss up to the present time) may have affected their adult functioning and personality.

Each interview (which lasts about 90 minutes) is classified as a whole, giving an overall 'state of mind' regarding attachment. Four *attachment styles* are possible:

- **Secure/autonomous (F):** People with this style discuss childhood experiences openly, coherently and consistently, acknowledging both positive and negative events and emotions. This is the most common style among parents of *secure* infants.
- **Dismissing (D):** These individuals seem cut off from the emotional nature of their childhood, denying especially their negative experiences and dismissing their significance. The importance of attachment experiences is minimised. They appear co-operative, but contradictions make them seem dishonest. This is the most common style among parents of *anxious–avoidant* infants.
- **Preoccupied/entangled (E):** Such people are overinvolved with what they recollect, appearing so overwhelmed that they become incoherent, confused, even angry. They're still actively trying to please their parents. This is the most common style among *anxious–resistant* infants.
- **Unresolved/disorganised (U):** This style describes mainly those who've experienced a trauma (which may include physical or sexual abuse), or the early death of an attachment figure, and who haven't come to terms with it or worked through the grieving process (see Chapter 39). This is the most common style among parents of *disorganised* infants.

(Based on Goldberg, 2000; Heard & Lake, 1997; Main *et al.*, 1985; Schaffer, 1996a)

So, the AAI may predict how the mother's child will be attached to her as determined by the Strange Situation (Heard & Lake, 1997; Main, 1995). However, it's possible that these findings are affected by the mother's *selective recall*: how she remembers her childhood might be influenced by her *current* experiences with her own child.

Ask yourself ...

- How could you try to control this potential confounding variable?

Fonagy *et al.* (1991) tried to rule out this possibility by giving the AAI to 96 women *before* the birth of their children (i.e. during pregnancy), then classifying the children (using the

Strange Situation) when they were twelve and 18 months old. As shown in Table 32.5, Main *et al.*'s (1985) results (see Box 32.5) were largely replicated (with the exception of the preoccupied mothers). The correlation was especially strong for the autonomous mother–secure child pairing.

Table 32.5 *Mother's prenatal AAI classification and children's Strange Situation classification (based on Fonagy* et al.*, 1991)*

Classification of the children	Classification of the mother		
	Dismissing	Autonomous	Preoccupied
Anxious–avoidant	15	8	7
Secure	5	45	5
Anxious–resistant	2	6	3

These results have been replicated in later studies by Fonagy and his colleagues (Fonagy *et al.*, 1994; Steele *et al.*, 1995). Overall, mothers' perceptions of their own childhood attachments predicted their childrens' attachments to them 75 per cent of the time. While acknowledging the need to explain the 25 per cent 'failure' rate (Clarke & Clarke, 2000), how can we explain this evidence for intergenerational continuity?

Inner working models

According to Bowlby (1973), expectations about the availability and responsiveness of attachment figures are built into our inner working models of attachment. These reflect memories and beliefs stemming from our early experiences of caregiving, which are carried forward into new relationships, both during childhood and beyond. They play an active role in guiding perceptions and behaviour.

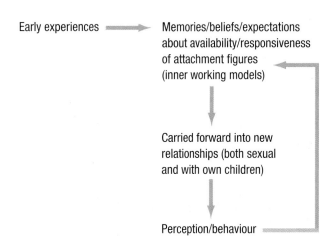

Figure 32.5 *How inner working models link early caregiving experiences and later relationships*

Bowlby (1973) argued that, at least under normal circumstances, our inner working models are resistant to change:

'Because ... children tend unwittingly to identify with parents and therefore to adopt, when they become parents, the same patterns of behaviour towards children that they have themselves experienced during their own childhood, patterns of interaction are transmitted, more or less faithfully, from one generation to another'.

However, inner working models usually can be updated or modified, as new interactions develop. While for young children such change must be based on actual physical events, such direct interaction isn't necessary in older children and adults. Main *et al.* (1985), for example, found that some adults, who reported being insecure in their relationships with their own parents, managed to produce children who were securely attached, at both twelve months and six years. They'd mentally worked through their unpleasant experiences with their parents, and their inner working models were now more typical of secure types (Hazan & Shaver, 1987).

Van Ijzendoorn & Bakermans-Kranenburg (1996) reviewed 33 studies involving the AAI. Similar proportions of mothers, fathers, and older adolescents fell into the four attachment categories, but people from lower socioeconomic groups were slightly more likely to be classified as dismissing. The largest difference is for people having treatment for mental disorder, who are very unlikely to score as autonomous.

Some mothers who'd had very negative early experiences seemed to have come to terms with them, explaining them in rational terms (such as marital stress, overwork). They were more likely to have secure infants, perhaps because they'd successfully updated their own internal working models. In fact, Bowlby (1988) recognised that attachment behaviour and internal working models *cannot* be regarded as fixed in infancy and unchanging throughout life.

Other attachments

Relationships with siblings

Ask yourself ...

- What is it about your relationships with brothers and/or sisters that makes them special?
- Are you closer to one sibling than the others? If so, why?
- If you're an only child, do you feel you've 'missed out'?
- If you're the younger/older of two, how might this have affected your development?

According to Dunn (2000):

'... our relationships with our siblings are the longest-lasting we'll probably have – longer than those with our parents or partners, or with our children. Indeed, towards the end of the lifespan, relationships between siblings take on particular importance for many people as sources of support ...'.

Like friendships (see below), sibling relationships are *horizontal* (Hartup, 1989), that is, reciprocal and egalitarian, while relationships with parents (and other adults) are *vertical* (see Chapter 38). Children need to experience *both* types of relationship (Bee, 2000). While relationships with friends and

parents seem to be more important for most school-age children than those with their siblings, there's enormous variation.

Box 32.6   Patterns/styles of sibling relationships

Based on direct studies of young children, as well as retrospective reports by young adults about their sibling relationships when they were of school age, several patterns/styles have emerged:

- **Caregiver:** One sibling serves as a kind of quasi-parent for the other. This style is most commonly found between an older sister and younger brother.
- **Buddy:** Both siblings try to be like one another and take pleasure in being together. This is rather more common among pairs of sisters.
- **Critical/conflictual:** One sibling tries to dominate the other, teasing and quarrelling.
- **Rival:** Similar to the critical relationship, but also lacking friendliness or support. This seems to be most common in boy/boy pairs.
- **Casual/uninvolved:** The siblings have relatively little to do with each other.

(Based on Bee, 2000)

Sibling relationships are intense and intimate, and this, together with the significance of *sharing parents*, means that the relationships have considerable potential for affecting children's well-being. For Dunn:

'The nature of the sibling relationship – with its uninhibited, no-holds barred expression of negative emotions in many families, and the processes of comparison between siblings – suggests it may well be important in fostering aggression, and in feelings of inadequacy and low self-esteem'.

Self-esteem is discussed in Chapter 33. The other side of the coin is that many siblings are extremely affectionate, supportive and companionable. But whatever its emotional colour, the sibling relationship offers children unique opportunities for learning about others and themselves.

Venus and Serena Williams holding the Women's Double at Wimbledon

Attachment to parents and to siblings

Some studies have found that children who are securely attached to their parents have friendly sibling relationships. But others report findings more consistent with a 'compensatory model', that is, intensely supportive sibling relationships are found in families where the parents are distant and uninvolved with their children. This latter finding is more likely, however, where the family is experiencing extreme stress and relationship difficulties (Dunn, 2000).

Siblings and the development of understanding

The study of siblings has contributed materially to our understanding of children's discovery of the mind (Dunn, 1999: see Chapter 40), including *individual differences*. Children who've engaged frequently in shared pretend play (see Chapter 34) with a sibling, and talked about mental states, are especially successful on tasks that assess understanding of emotion and mental states. Although the data are only correlational:

> '… social processes are likely to play a significant role in shaping the remarkable individual differences in what children understand about others. These differences are linked to moral sensibility and adjustment to school, as well as to relationships with others'. (Dunn, 2000)

Friendships and peer relationships

Attachment and peer relationships

According to Goldberg (2000), the most impressive data on the link between attachment and peer relationships come from the Minnesota longitudinal study (Troy & Sroufe, 1987). Attachment was assessed at twelve and 18 months using the Strange Situation, then again at age four, in middle childhood and at ages 13 and 15.

At age four, *securely attached* children were ranked highest in social competence, were the least isolated and the most popular. They were also the most likely to respond empathetically to another child's distress (see Chapter 35), and least likely to be bullies or bullied. *Bullies* were most likely to be classified as *anxious–avoidant*, while victims were most often *anxious–resistant*.

In middle childhood, securely attached children were twice as likely to form friendships, spend time with a special friend, and become involved in group activites as insecure children. As adolescents, the securely attached were rated higher on couple relationships and relationships with mixed-sex groups, more self-confident and showing more leadership qualities.

Pre-school friendships

More than 50 per cent of three- and four-year-olds have at least one mutual friend, and most of these friendships last for at least six months (Dunn, 1993; Howes, 1996). Although not nearly as deep or intimate as among school-age or adolescent pairs, these early friendships show more mutual liking and reciprocity, more extended interactions, more positive and less negative behaviour, more forgiveness, and more supportiveness in novel situations than is true of non-friend pairs of the same age. They're also more likely to 'make up' after a quarrel (Dunn, 1993; Hartup *et al.*, 1988). These early friendships are more likely among same-sex pairs.

School-age friendships

Peers become more important at school-age. Among seven- to ten-year-olds, playing with friends (along with watching TV) takes up almost all the time they're not in school, eating and sleeping. They centre around shared play interests and activities (rather than shared values or attitudes), and this 'concreteness' is entirely consistent with their self-concept at this age (see Chapter 33) and with their level of cognitive development (see Chapter 34) (Bee, 2000).

Peer-group interests are highly *gender-segregated*, which appears to be a universal pattern. In the case of girls, this may be because they're 'put off' by boys' typical rough-and-tumble style of play and strong emphasis on competition and dominance, and they also find it difficult to influence boys (Maccoby, 1990). But, if anything, boys' same-gender preferences are *stronger* than girls' (Bee, 2000).

Sex differences in friendship quality

According to Waldrop & Halverson (1975), boys' relationships are *extensive*, while girls' are *intensive*. Boys' friendship groups are larger and more accepting of newcomers than girls', and boys play more outdoors. Girls are more likely to play indoors and in smaller groups or pairs, and are less accepting of newcomers (Bee, 2000). The level of competition between pairs of male friends is *higher* than it is between strangers – the *opposite* of girls. Girls' friendships also involve more agreement, compliance and self-disclosure.

However, collaborative and co-operative exchanges are the most common forms of communication in *both* boys' and girls' friendships. These differences may well have enduring implications for patterns of friendship over the entire lifespan (Bee, 2000). (Adolescent peer relationships and friendships are discussed in Chapter 37.)

Conclusions

According to Clarke & Clarke (1998):

> 'The evidence is firm; while there is a range of outcomes, early social experience by itself does not predestine the future'.

Similarly:

> '… the life path is not predetermined by the experiences of the early years alone, but results from the longer-term cumulative development of genetic and environmental interactions and transactions …'. (Clarke & Clarke, 2000)

Schaffer (1998) believes that psychological development is far more flexible than was previously thought. Our personalities are not fixed once and for all by events in the early years. Given the right circumstances, the effects of even quite severe and prolonged deprivation can be reversed. As Clarke & Clarke (2000) conclude:

> '… there is no suggestion that what happens in the early years is unimportant. For most children, however, the effects of such experiences represent no more than a first step in an ongoing life path … There is little indication that any one point of development is more critical than another; all are important …'.

- **Sociability** is necessary for the development of **attachments**, which are intense, enduring emotional ties to specific people. The **mother–child relationship** is usually taken as a model for all later relationships.
- The attachment process can be divided into **pre-attachment**, **indiscriminate**, **discriminate**, and **multiple attachment phases**.
- The development of specific attachments is shown through **separation anxiety**. Some babies also display the **fear-of-strangers response**.
- According to **'cupboard love' theories**, attachments are learned through satisfaction of the baby's need for food. However, Schaffer and Emerson found that not only were infants attached to people who didn't perform caretaking activities, but those who did weren't always their primary attachment figures.
- According to Bowlby, new-born humans are **genetically programmed** to behave towards their mothers in ways that ensure their survival. There's a **critical period** for attachment development, and attachment to the mother-figure is based on **monotropy**.
- The **Strange Situation** is used to classify the baby's basic attachment to the mother into three main types: **anxious–avoidant**, **securely attached** and **anxious–resistant**. The crucial feature determining the quality of attachment is the mother's **sensitivity**.
- Patterns of attachment to mothers and fathers are **independent**. Attachment type may change depending on variations in the family's circumstances, and there are also **cultural variations** in the distribution of attachment types.
- Bowlby's **maternal-deprivation hypothesis** was used to explain the harmful effects of growing up in institutions. But this fails to recognise the understimulating nature of the institutional environment, and to disentangle the different kinds of retardation produced by different types of **privation**.
- According to Bowlby's theory, **short-term deprivation** produces **distress**. **Privation** produces long-term **developmental retardation** (such as **affectionless psychopathy**).
- Parental death and divorce are examples of **long-term deprivation**, and are associated with long-term effects, particularly **separation anxiety**.
- Children whose parents **divorce** are inevitably adversely affected, both in the short- and long-term. But most children eventually adapt. **Inter-parental conflict** is the single most damaging factor and may actually **increase** following divorce.
- Provided the **stability** and **quality** of **day care** are satisfactory, a child's attachment to its mother shouldn't be weakened. Since children in day care experience regular separations, the Strange Situation may be an inappropriate method for assessing their attachments.
- Case studies of children who've endured **extreme privation**, studies of **late adoption**, and Quinton and Rutter's study of **developmental pathways**, all indicate that the effects of early privation are **reversible**.

- There appears to be nothing special about early experiences, and our personalities are **not determined** once and for all by early events. The 'same' early experience may have many alternative outcomes.
- **Sibling relationships** are among the most important – and longest-lasting – we experience. They can affect many aspects of development, including aggressiveness, self-esteem, and the understanding of emotion and mental states.
- Securely attached infants are more likely to be socially competent and popular with their peers throughout childhood and adolescence. They're also more self-confident and show more leadership qualities.
- **Friendships** become quite common at ages three and four, becoming more important amongst school-age children. Despite some important **gender differences** in **friendship quality**, collaboration and co-operation are the most common forms of communication in both boys' and girls' friendships.

Self-assessment questions

1 'Mother love in infancy is as important for mental health as are vitamins and proteins for physical health.' (Bowlby, 1951)
   To what extent has research supported Bowlby's claim that the child's attachment to the mother is unique?
2 Critically consider the use of the Strange Situation as a method for studying young children's attachments.
3 'Early experiences ... do not necessarily produce irreversible effects just because they are early ....' (Schaffer, 1996a)
   Critically consider the impact of early experience on later development.
4 Discuss the influence of early attachments on later relationships.

Web addresses

http://galton.psych.nwu/greatideas/attachment.html

http://samiam.colorado.edu/~mcclella/expersim/introimprint.html

http://www.bereavement.org.uk

http://www.geocities.com/Athens/Acropolis/3041/ARChrome.html

http://www.psychematters.com/

http://www./theamgroup.com/child/htm

http://blue.census.gov/population/www/socdemo/childcare.html

http://www.acf.dhhs.gov/programs/ccb/

http://www.psychology.sunysb.edu/ewaters/

http://www.johnbowlby.com

Further reading

Clarke, Ann & Clarke, Alan (2000) *Early Experience and the Life Path*. London: Jessica Kingsley Publishers. A compact, but very detailed and challenging review of recent research.

Goldberg, S. (2000) *Attachment in Development*. London: Arnold. An extremely thorough and comprehensive, but very readable review of all aspects of attachment theory and research.

Chapter 33

Development of the Self-Concept

Introduction and overview

According to Hampson (1995), the human capacity for self-awareness permits us to try to see ourselves as others see us. When personality psychologists study personality via self-reports, such as questionnaires (see Chapter 42), they're assessing people's perceptions of themselves. Social psychologists also study people's self-perceptions through their study of the *self-concept*.

Self-perception changes in fairly predictable ways from infancy onwards, with adolescence being a crucial period for its development. A major account of how the self-concept changes in adolescence is Erikson's *psychosocial theory*, which is discussed in Chapter 37.

Discussion of the self-concept brings together theory and research from the schools of both developmental and social psychology. But even when tracing how self-perception changes in the individual, we'll see that this is *inherently social*, as reflected in the early theories of James, Cooley, and Mead, as well as the more recent extensions of these which see the self as *constructed in language* (e.g. Harré).

Consciousness and self-consciousness

Ask yourself ...

- What do you think is the difference between consciousness and self-consciousness?

When you look in the mirror at your face, you're both the person who's looking and that which is looked at. Similarly, when you think about the kind of person you are or something you've done, you're both the person doing the thinking and what's being thought about. In other words, you're both *subject* (the thinker or looker) and *object* (what's being looked at or thought about). We use the personal pronoun 'I' to refer to ourselves as subject and 'me' to refer to ourselves as object, and this represents a rather special relationship we have with ourselves, namely *self-consciousness/self-awareness*.

While other species possess consciousness (they have sensations of cold, heat, hunger, thirst and can feel pleasure, pain, fear, sexual arousal, and so on: see Chapter 48), only humans possess self-consciousness. We often use the term 'self-conscious' to describe our response to situations where we're made to feel object-like or exposed in some way (for example, we get on the bus in the morning to discover our sweater's on back-to-front). But this is a secondary meaning: the *primary* meaning refers to this unique relationship in which the same person, the same self, is both subject and object.

What is the self?

'*Self*' and '*self-concept*' are used interchangeably to refer to an individual's overall self-awareness. According to Murphy (1947), 'the self is the individual as known to the individual', and Burns (1980) defines it as 'the set of attitudes a person holds towards himself'.

Components of the self-concept

The self-concept is a general term that normally refers to three major components: *self-image*, *self-esteem*, and *ideal self*.

Self-image

Ask yourself ...

- Give 20 different answers to the question: 'Who are you?'

Self-image refers to the way we describe ourselves, what we think we're like. One way of investigating self-image is to ask people the question 'Who are you?' 20 times (Kuhn & McPartland, 1954). This typically produces two main categories of answers – social roles and personality traits. *Social roles* are usually objective aspects of the self-image (e.g. son, daughter, brother, sister, student). They are 'facts' that can be verified by others. *Personality traits* are more a matter of opinion and judgement, and what we think we're like may be different from how others see us. But how others behave towards us has an important influence on our self-perception (see below).

As well as social roles and personality traits, people's answers to the 'Who are you?' question often refer to their *physical characteristics* (such as tall, short, fat, thin, blue-eyed, brown-haired). These are part of our *body image/bodily self*, the 'bodily me' which also includes bodily sensations, such as pain, cold, and hunger. A more permanent feature of our body image relates to what we count as part of our body (and hence belonging to us), and what we don't.

Allport (1955) gives two rather dramatic examples of how intimate our bodily sense is, and just where we draw the boundaries between 'me' and 'not me':

- Imagine swallowing your saliva – or actually do it! Now imagine spitting it into a cup and drinking it! Clearly, once we've spat out our saliva, we've disowned it – it no longer belongs to us!
- Imagine sucking blood from a cut on your finger (something we do quite automatically). Now imagine sucking the blood from a plaster on your finger! Again, once it's soaked into the plaster it has ceased to be part of ourselves!

Ask yourself ...

- Can you think of any exceptions to this 'rule'?

We might feel we've lost part of ourselves when we have very long hair cut off, and lovers often keep locks of each other's hair as constant (and tangible) reminders that the other exists. Whenever our body changes in some way, so our body image changes. In extreme cases (such as losing a limb, being scarred, or having cosmetic surgery), we'd expect a correspondingly dramatic change in body image.

Box 33.1 **Developmental changes in body image**

Throughout our lives, as part of the normal process of maturation and ageing, we all experience growth spurts, changes in height, weight and the general appearance and 'feel' of our body. With each change, we have to make an adjustment to our body image.

- The bodily changes involved in *puberty* affect the adolescent's body image, which, in turn, affects the self-concept as a whole (see Chapter 37).
- Another fundamental aspect of body image is that of *biological sex*. Gender is the social equivalent or social interpretation of sex, and our *gender/gender identity* is another part of the central core of our self-image (see Chapter 36).

Self-esteem

While the self-image is essentially descriptive, self-esteem (or *self-regard*) is essentially evaluative. It refers to how much we like and approve of ourselves, how worthy a person we think we are. Coopersmith (1967) defined it as 'a personal judgement of worthiness, that is expressed in the attitudes the individual holds towards himself'.

How much we like or value ourselves can be an overall judgement, or it can relate to specific areas of our lives. For example, we can have a generally high opinion of ourselves and yet not like certain of our characteristics or attributes (such as our curly hair when we want it straight, or our lack of assertiveness when we want to be more assertive). Conversely, it may be very difficult to have high overall esteem if we're very badly disfigured, or are desperately shy.

Our self-esteem can be regarded as how we evaluate our self-image, that is, how much we like the kind of person we think we are. Clearly, certain characteristics or abilities have a greater value in society generally, and so are likely to influence our self-esteem accordingly (for example, being physically attractive as opposed to unattractive: see Chapter 28). The value attached to particular characteristics will also depend on culture, gender, age, social background and so on.

Jocelyne Wildenstein (the 'Cat Woman') has had several plastic surgery procedures to make herself look like a cat

Ideal self

Self-esteem is also partly determined by how much the self-image differs from the ideal self. If our self-image is the kind of person we think we are, then our ideal self (*ego-ideal* or *idealised self-image*) is the kind of person we'd *like to be*. This can vary in extent and degree. We may want to be different in certain aspects, or we may want to be a totally different person. (We may even wish we were someone else!) Generally, the greater the gap between our self-image and our ideal self, the lower our self-esteem (see Rogers' *self theory*: Chapter 42).

Self-schemata

Just as we represent and store information about other people, so we represent and store information about ourselves (see Chapter 17), but in a more complex and varied way. This information about the self constitutes the self-concept. We tend to have very clear conceptions of ourselves (self-schemata) on some dimensions (such as those that are very important to us), but not others. For example, if you think of yourself as athletic, as definitely not unathletic, and being athletic is important to you, then you are *self-schematic* on that dimension (it is part of your self-concept: Hogg & Vaughan, 1995).

> ### Ask yourself ...
>
> • What are you self-schematic on?

Most people have a complex self-concept with a relatively large number of self-schemata. These include an array of *possible* selves, *future-oriented* schemata of what we'd like to become (ideal self) (Markus & Nurius, 1986). Visions of future possible selves may influence how we make important life decisions, such as career choice.

The idea of *multiple selves* raises the question of whether there's any one self that's more real or authentic than the others. For example, perhaps we feel most real (most 'ourselves') when with someone we believe sees us as we wish to be seen. Personality theorists tend to assume that the person has a single, unitary self. This is implied by the fact that typical instructions at the top of a personality questionnaire don't specify which self the respondent should describe (Hampson, 1995). By contrast, social psychologists recognise the possibility that the self refers to a complex set of perceptions, composed of a number of schemata relating both to what we're like and how we *could be*.

Theories of self

Symbolic interactionism

A major theoretical approach to the self is *symbolic interactionism*, which is mainly associated with Mead (1934). Mead was influenced by the earlier theories of James (1890) and Cooley (1902). According to symbolic interactionism, human beings act towards things in terms of their *meanings*. People exist in a *symbolic* as well as a physical environment, such that the importance of a social interaction is derived from the meaning it holds for the participants. The 'interaction' refers specifically to the fact that people communicate with each other, which provides the opportunity for meanings to be learned. Because we share a common language and have the ability for symbolic thought, we can (at least in principle) look at the world from the point of view of other perceivers; that is, take the role of the other. According to Mead, this is essentially the process by which the self develops.

James's theory

It was James (1890) who first made the distinction between *self-as-subject* or *knower* ('I') and *self-as-object* or *known* ('me'). The 'I' represents the principal form of the self, lying at the centre of our state (or 'stream') of consciousness. We have as many selves as we have social relationships: the self is *multi-faceted*. This is consistent with the widely shared view that we modify our behaviour to some extent depending on whom we're with: different others bring out different aspects of our personality (Hampson, 1995). It's also consistent with Goffman's (e.g. 1971) account of *self-presentation*, which he defined as the creation and maintenance of a public self. By analogy with the theatre, each participant in a social interaction is engaged in a performance designed as much for its effect on the audience as it is for honest and open expression of the self (see Chapter 22). Indeed, according to this *dramaturgical approach*, personality is equated with the various roles the person plays in life. But James's idea of multiple selves goes much further than this, by suggesting that different personalities are *constructed* in the context of every relationship one has (Hampson, 1995).

> ### Ask yourself ...
>
> • Do you agree with James or Goffman, or do you believe there is just one 'self', that remains constant regardless of who we're interacting with or the context of the interaction?

Cooley's theory

Cooley's theory of the *looking-glass self* maintains that the self is reflected in the reactions of other people, who are the 'looking-glass' for oneself. That is, in order to understand what we're like, we need to see how others see us, and this is how children gradually build up impressions of what they're like. We receive reflections of judgements and evaluations of our behaviour and appearance, which produce some form of *self-feeling* (such as pride or shame). Consistent with the notion of multiple selves, Cooley claims that the looking-glass isn't a 'mere mechanical reflection', because it will differ depending on whose view we take. The individual and society are opposite sides of the same coin (Denzin, 1995).

Mead's theory

Mead turned James and Cooley on their heads. The self *isn't* mentalistic (something privately going on inside the individual) but, like mind, is a *cognitive process* lodged in the ongoing social world. However, like Cooley, he saw self and society as two terms in a reciprocal process of interaction (Denzin, 1995). Knowledge of self and others develops *simultaneously*, both being dependent on social interaction: self and society represent a common whole and neither can exist without the other.

According to Mead, the human being is an organism with a self. This converts him into a special kind of actor, transforms his relation to the world, and gives his actions a unique character. The human being is an object to himself, that is, he can perceive himself, have conceptions about himself, communicate with himself and so on. In sum, he can *interact* with himself, and this self-interaction is a great influence upon his transactions with the world in general and with other people in particular.

Buddhist monk in meditation

Self-interaction is a *reflexive* process, which is Mead's way of making the 'I'/'me' distinction. The experiencing 'I' cannot be an object, it cannot itself be experienced, since it's the very *act of experiencing*. What we experience and interact with is our 'me'.

As we saw earlier, symbolic interactionism regards language as an important feature of interaction and represents a fundamental means by which we come to represent ourselves to ourselves. But the *key process* by which we develop a concept of self is *role-taking*. By placing ourselves in the position of others, we can look back on ourselves. The idea of self can only develop if the individual can 'get outside himself (experientially) in such a way as to become an object to himself' (Mead, 1934); that is, to see ourselves from the standpoint of others.

> **Box 33.2** **Mead's developmental theory of the self**
>
> • Initially, the child thinks about his conduct as 'good or bad only as he reacts to his own acts in the remembered words of his parents'. 'Me' at this stage is a combination of the child's memory of his own actions and the kind of reaction they received.
>
> • In the next stage, the child's pretend play, in particular 'playing at mummies and daddies' or 'doctors or nurses', helps the child to understand and incorporate adult attitudes and behaviour. Here, the child isn't merely imitating but also 'calls out in himself the same response as he calls out in the other'. So he's being, say, the child and the parent and, as the parent, is responding to himself as the child. So, in playing with a doll, the child 'responds in tone of voice and in attitudes as his parents respond to his cries and chortles'.
>
> • Play is distinguished from games, which involve rules: 'The child must not only take the role of the other, as he does in the play, but he must assume the various roles of all the participants in the game, and govern his action accordingly...'. Games are a later development than play.

- In this way, the child acquires a variety of social viewpoints or 'perspectives' (mother, father, nurse, doctor), which are then used to accompany, direct and evaluate its own behaviour. This is how the *socialised part of the self* (Mead's 'me') expands and develops.
- At first, these viewpoints or perspectives are based upon specific adults but, in time, the child comes to react to itself and its behaviour from the viewpoint of a 'typical mother', a 'typical nurse' or 'people in general' (the *generalised other*). The incorporation of the generalised other marks the final, qualitative change in the 'me'. 'It is this generalised other in his experience which provides him with a self.'

Grammatically, our 'me' is third person (like 'she' or 'he'), and it's an image of self seen from the perspective of a judgemental, non-participant observer. By its very nature, 'me' is social, because it grows out of this role playing, whereby the child is being the other person.

(Based on Mead, 1934)

Social constructionist approaches

Influenced by Mead, many sociologists and social psychologists see the role of language as fundamental to the *construction* and maintenance of the self. What we say about ourselves often depends on who's listening. In selecting what to say and not to say, we're actively constructing a self in relation to another person: we're constantly 'making a self'. The self is not a static, internal entity but a constantly changing *process* (Petkova, 1995).

According to Harré (1985, 1989), our understanding and experiences of ourselves as human beings, our subjective experiences of selfhood, are laid down by the beliefs about being a person that are implicit in our language. The structure of our language implies certain assumptions/beliefs about human nature, which we live out in our daily interactions with others. For example, the words 'I' and 'me' mislead us into believing that each of us is represented by a coherent, unified self which operates mechanisms and processes (the subject matter of psychology) that are responsible for our actions. But 'self', 'ego', 'mind' and so on *don't* refer to anything that exists objectively in the world: they're *hypothetical constructs* which perform the very important function of helping us to organise and structure our world (Burr, 1995).

Similarly, Potter & Wetherell (1987) argue that the very experience of being a person, the kind of mental life one can have, perhaps even how we experience sensory information, are dependent on the particular *representations of selfhood*, the particular ways of accounting for/talking about ourselves, that are available in our culture. These 'stories' or accounts, whose meaning is shared by members of a culture, are called *discourses*. Since these differ from culture to culture, it follows that members of different cultures will experience being human ('selves') in different ways.

The self-concept as a cultural phenomenon

In Maori culture, the person is invested with a particular kind of power (*mana*), given by the gods in accordance with the person's family status and birth circumstances. This is what enables the person to be effective, whether in battle or everyday dealings with others. But this power isn't a stable resource and can be increased or decreased by the person's day-to-day conduct. For example, it could be reduced by forgetting a ritual observance, or committing some misdemeanour. People's social standing and successes and failures are seen as dependent on external forces, not internal states (such as personality or level of motivation). In fact, mana is only one of these external forces which inhabit the individual.

People living in such a culture would necessarily experience themselves quite differently from what people in Western culture are used to. Instead of representing themselves as the centre and origin of their actions, which is crucial to the Western concept of the self:

> 'The individual Maori does not own experiences such as the emotions of fear, anger, love, grief; rather they are visitations governed by the unseen world of powers and forces...'. (Potter & Wetherell, 1987)

According to Moscovici (1985), 'the individual' is the greatest invention of modern times. Only recently has the idea of the autonomous, self-regulating, free-standing individual become dominant, and this has fundamental implications for the debate about free will and determinism (see Chapter 49). Smith & Bond (1998) argue that we need to distinguish between *independent* and the *interdependent selves*: the former is what is stressed in Western, *individualist* cultures, and the latter by non-Western, *collectivist* cultures (see Chapter 47).

Factors influencing the development of the self-concept

Much of the research into factors that influence the self-concept can be understood in relation to the symbolic interactionist position. But the importance of these factors extends beyond childhood – our self-concept is constantly being revised. But the most significant 'change' is probably the time when it's first being formed.

Argyle (1983) identifies four major influences:

1 the reaction of others;
2 comparison with others;
3 social roles;
4 identification (see Chapters 35 and 36).

Reaction of others

We've already seen in the theories of Cooley and Mead how central the reactions of others are in the formulation of our self-concept. Any attempt to explain how we come to be what we are, and how we change, involves us in the question of what kind of evidence we use. Kelly (1955), like Cooley and Mead, believes that we derive our pictures of ourselves through what we learn of other people's pictures of us (see Chapter 42). So, the central evidence is the reaction of others to us, both what they say of us and the implications of their behaviour towards us. We filter others' views of us through our views of them. We build up continuous and changing pictures of ourselves out of our interaction with others.

Guthrie (1938) tells the famous story of a dull and unattractive female student. Some of her classmates decided to play a trick on her by pretending she was the most desirable girl in the college, and drawing lots to decide who would take her out first, second and so on. By the fifth or sixth date, she was no longer regarded as dull and unattractive.

Ask yourself ...

- Try to explain this change in the student.

By being treated as attractive she had, in a sense, *become* attractive (perhaps by wearing different clothes and smiling more), and her self-image had clearly changed. For the boys who dated her later, it was no longer a chore! 'Before the year was over, she had developed an easy manner and a confident assumption that she was popular' (Guthrie, 1938).

Preschool children are extremely concerned with how adults view them, and few things are more relevant than the reactions to them of *significant others* (parents, older siblings and other people whose opinions the child values). Strictly speaking, it's the child's perception of others' reactions that makes such an important contribution to how the child comes to perceive itself. After all, the child has no frame of reference for evaluating parental reactions: parents are all-powerful figures, and what they say is 'fact'. If a child is consistently told how beautiful she is, she'll come to believe it (it will become part of her self-image). Similarly, if a child is repeatedly told how stupid or clumsy he is, this too will become accepted as the 'truth', and the child will tend to act accordingly.

The first child is likely to develop high self-esteem and the second low self-esteem. Argyle explains this in terms of *introjection* (a process very similar to identification), whereby we come to incorporate into our own personality the perceptions, attitudes and reactions to ourselves of our parents. It's through others' reactions that the child learns its *conditions of worth*, that is, which behaviours will produce *positive regard* and which will not (Rogers, 1959: see Chapter 42).

When the child starts school, the number and variety of significant others increase to include teachers and peers. At the same time, the child's self-image is becoming more *differentiated*, and significant others then become important in relation to different parts of the self-image. For example, the teacher is important as far as the child's academic ability is concerned, parents as far as how loveable the child is, and so on.

How others' reactions influence self-esteem

KEY STUDY 33.1

The development of self-esteem (Coopersmith, 1967)

From an original sample of hundreds of nine- and ten-year-old white, middle-class boys, Coopersmith selected five groups (17 per group), including those who scored high, and those who scored low, on each of three measures of self-esteem:

- his self-esteem inventory;
- teachers' evaluations of the boys' reactions to failure, self-confidence in new situations, and so on;
- scores on the thematic apperception test (TAT) (see Chapter 9, page 129).

The *high-esteem* boys were confident about their own perceptions and judgements, expected to succeed at new tasks and to influence others, and readily expressed their opinions. They were also doing better in school and were more often chosen as friends by other children than the low-esteem boys. They had a realistic view of themselves and their abilities, weren't unduly worried by criticism, and enjoyed participating in things.

By contrast, the *low-esteem* boys were a 'sad little group', isolated, fearful, reluctant to join in, self-conscious, over-sensitive to criticism, consistently under-rating themselves, tending to underachieve in class, and preoccupied with their own problems.

But there were *no* significant differences in intelligence or physical attractiveness between the two groups, who were all white, middle-class, and free from any obvious emotional disturbance.

Based on a questionnaire and in-depth interviews with the mothers, plus interviews with the boys about their parents' childrearing methods, Coopersmith found significant differences between the two sets of parents. The optimum conditions for the development of high self-esteem seem to involve a combination of firm enforcement of limits on the child's behaviour, plus a good deal of acceptance of the child's autonomy and freedom within those limits. Firm management helps the child to develop firm inner controls: a predictable and structured social environment helps the child to deal effectively with the environment, and hence to feel 'in control' of the world (rather than controlled by it).

Coopersmith followed the boys through into adulthood, and found that the high-esteem boys consistently outperformed the low-esteem boys and proved more successful – educationally and vocationally.

Ask yourself ...

- Can you think of any limitations of Coopersmith's study, which would make it difficult to generalise the results?

Coopersmith's data are only *correlational*, so we cannot be sure that how the boys were raised was actually responsible for their level of self-esteem. Remember, too, that the boys were white middle-class and therefore not representative of the American population as a whole – what about working-class, black and female children?

Generally, girls have lower self-esteem than boys. For example, when paired with boys in problem-solving tasks, they sometimes artificially depress their performance so as not to outshine their male partners (boys very rarely do this!). Some girls seem to feel uncomfortable in the superior role, as if this is inconsistent with their 'true' position in life. They also tend to rate themselves less highly than boys on written tests of self-esteem, set themselves lower goals in life, and are more inclined to underestimate their abilities than boys, even in primary school, where in reading and language skills they often tend to surpass boys (see Chapter 36).

An interesting contrast with the parents of high-esteem boys in Coopersmith's study is the study of interaction between parents and their schizophrenic children. These parents tend to deny communicative support to the child, and often fail to respond to the child's statements and demands for recognition of its opinions. When the parents do communicate with the child, it's often in the form of an interruption or an intrusion, rather than a response to the child. In fact, they respond selectively to those of the child's utterances which they themselves have initiated, rather than those initiated by the child. Laing (1971) suggests that these kinds of communication patterns within the family make the development of *ego boundaries* in the child very difficult; that is, there's a confusion between self and not-self (me and not-me). This impaired autonomy of the self and appreciation of external reality are often found to be fundamental characteristics of schizophrenic adolescents and adults (see Chapter 44).

Comparison with others

According to Bannister & Agnew (1976), the personal construct of 'self' is intrinsically *bipolar*, that is, having a concept of self implies a concept of not-self. (This is similar to Cooley and Mead's view that self and society are really two sides of a coin.) So, one way in which we come to form pictures of what we're like is to see how we compare with others. Indeed, certain components of self-image are only meaningful through comparison with others. For example, 'tall' and 'fat' aren't absolute characteristics (like, say, 'blue-eyed'), and we're only tall or fat in *relation to* others who are shorter or thinner than us. This is true of many other characteristics, including intelligence (see Chapter 41).

Parents and other adults often react to children by comparing them with other children (such as siblings: see Chapter 32). If a child is told repeatedly that she's 'less clever than [her] big sister', she'll come to incorporate this into her self-image, and will probably have lower self-esteem as a result. This could adversely affect her academic performance, so that she doesn't achieve in line with her true ability. A child of above average intelligence who's grown up in the shadow of a brilliant brother or sister may be less successful academically than an average or even below average child who's not had to face these unfavourable comparisons.

Social roles

As we noted earlier, social roles are what people commonly regard as part of 'who they are'. Kuhn (1960) asked seven-year-olds and undergraduate students to give 20 different answers to the question, 'Who are you?'. The seven-year-olds gave an average of five answers relating to roles, while the undergraduates gave an average of ten. As we get older, we incorporate more and more roles into our self-image, reflecting the increasing number and variety of roles we actually take on. The preschooler is a son or daughter, perhaps a brother or sister, has other familial roles and may also be a friend to another child. But the number and range of roles are limited compared with those of the older child or adult.

Developmental changes in the self-concept

How do we get to know ourselves?

Achieving identity, in the sense of acquiring a set of beliefs about the self (a *self-schema*), is one of the central developmental tasks of a social being (Lewis, 1990). It progresses through several levels of complexity and continues to develop through the lifespan (see Chapters 38 and 39).

During the first few months, the baby gradually distinguishes itself from its environment and from other people, and develops a sense of *continuity through time* (the *existential self*). But at this stage, the infant's self-knowledge is comparable to that of other species (e.g. monkeys). What makes human self-knowledge distinctive is becoming aware that we have it – we're conscious of our existence and uniqueness (Buss, 1992).

According to Maccoby (1980), babies are able to distinguish between themselves and others on two counts:

- Their own fingers hurt when bitten (but they don't have any such sensations when they're biting their rattle or their mother's fingers).
- Probably quite early in life, they begin to associate feelings from their own body movements with the sight of their own limbs and the sounds of their own cries. These sense impressions are bound together into a cluster that defines the bodily self, so this is probably the first aspect of the self-concept to develop.

Other aspects of the self-concept develop by degrees, but there seem to be fairly clearly defined stages of development. Young children may know their own names, and understand the limits of their own bodies, and yet be unable to think about themselves as coherent entities. So, self-awareness/self-consciousness develops very gradually.

According to Piaget, an awareness of self comes through the gradual process of *adaptation to the environment* (see Chapter 34). As the child explores objects and accommodates to them (thus developing new *sensorimotor schemas*), it simultaneously discovers aspects of its self. For example, trying to put a large block into its mouth and finding that it won't fit is a lesson in selfhood as well as a lesson about the world of objects.

Self-recognition

One way in which the development of bodily self has been studied is through self-recognition, and this involves more than just a simple discrimination of bodily features. To determine that the person in a photograph or a film or reflected in a mirror is oneself, certain knowledge seems to be necessary:

- at least a rudimentary knowledge of oneself as continuous through time (necessary for recognising ourselves in photographs or movies) and space (necessary for recognising ourselves in mirrors); and
- knowledge of particular features (what we look like).

Although other kinds of self-recognition are possible (e.g. one's voice or feelings), only *visual* self-recognition has been studied extensively, both in humans and non-humans.

Many non-human animals (including fish, birds, chickens, and elephants) react to their mirror-images as if they were other animals, that is, they don't seem to recognise them as their own reflections at all. But self-recognition has been observed in the higher primates – chimpanzees and other great apes.

Chimpanzees learn to use mirrors to explore parts of their bodies they cannot usually see

---

KEY STUDY 33.2

Mirror, mirror ... (Gallup, 1977)

Gallup, working with preadolescent, wild-born chimps, placed a full-length mirror on the wall of each animal's cage. At first, they reacted as if other chimps had appeared – they threatened, vocalised or made conciliatory gestures. But this quickly faded out, and by the end of three days had almost disappeared. They then used their images to explore themselves. For example, they'd pick up food and place it on their faces, which could not be seen without the mirrors (see photographs opposite).

After ten days exposure, each chimp was anaesthetised and a bright red spot was painted on the uppermost part of one eyebrow ridge and a second spot on the top of the opposite ear, using an odourless, non-irritating dye. When the chimp had recovered from the anaesthetic, it was returned to its cage, from which the mirror had been removed, and it was observed to see how often it touched the marked parts of its body. The mirror was then replaced, and each chimp began to explore the marked spots around 25 times more often than it had done before.

The procedure was repeated with chimps that had never seen themselves in the mirror, and they reacted to the mirror-image as if it were other chimps (they didn't touch the spots). So, the first group had apparently learned to recognise themselves. Lower primates (monkeys, gibbons and baboons) are unable to learn to recognise their mirror-images.

A number of researchers (e.g. Lewis & Brooks-Gunn, 1979) have used modified forms of Gallup's technique with 6–24-month-old children. The mother applies a dot of rouge to the child's nose (while pretending to wipe its face), and the child is observed to see how often it touches its nose. It's then placed in front of a mirror, and again the number of times it touches its nose is recorded. At about 18 months, there's a significant change. While touching the dot was never seen before 15 months, between 15 and 18 months, five to 25 per cent of infants touched it, and 75 per cent of the 18–20-month-olds did.

In order to use the mirror-image to touch the dot on its nose, the baby must also have built up a schema of how its face *should* look in the mirror before it will notice the discrepancy created by the dot. This doesn't develop before about 18 months. This is also about the time when, according to Piaget, *object permanence* is completed, so object permanence would seem to be a necessary condition for the development of self-recognition (see Chapter 34).

Interpreting Gallup's findings

It's generally agreed that passing the mirror test is strong evidence that a chimp has a self-concept, and that only chimps, orangutans and humans consistently pass it. However, Gallup (1998) infers much more than this. He claims that:

'*... not only are some animals aware of themselves but ... such self-awareness enables these animals to infer the mental states of others. In other words, species that pass the mirror test are also able to sympathise, empathise and attribute intent and emotions in others – abilities that some might consider the exclusive domain of humans*'.

He believes that self-awareness or self-consciousness is the expression of some underlying process that allows organisms to use their experience as a means of modelling the experience of others. He considers that the best support for this *mind-reading hypothesis* comes from mirror studies involving human infants and young children (see above). His research also points to the *right prefrontal cortex* (see Chapter 4) as the brain area that mediates self-awareness and mental states (such as deception and gratitude) – and this is the brain region that grows most rapidly between 18 and 34 months.

As additional support for his mind-reading hypothesis, Gallup cites studies by Povinelli and his colleagues involving chimps (see Gross *et al.*, 2000). These studies are often taken to show that chimps have a 'theory of mind' (see Chapter 40).

Ironically, Povinelli (1998) himself disgrees with Gallup's mind-reading hypothesis. While agreeing that passing the mirror test indicates that chimps possess a self-concept, he disagrees that this means that they also possess the deep psychological understanding of behaviour that seems so characteristic of humans.

If chimps *don't* genuinely reason about mental states, what can we say about their understanding of self based on the mirror test? Povinelli has tried to answer this by shifting his attention from chimps to two-, three-, and four-year-old children.

KEY STUDY 33.3

Stickers, lies and videotape (Povinelli, 1998)

In a series of experiments, children were videotaped while they played an unusual game. The experimenter placed a large, brightly coloured sticker secretly on top of the child's head. Three minutes later they were shown *either* a live video image of themselves *or* a recording made several minutes earlier, which clearly depicted the experimenter placing the sticker on the child's head.

Two- and three-year-olds responded very differently, depending on which video they saw. With the live image (equivalent to seeing themselves in a mirror), most reached up and removed the stickers from their heads. But with the recording, only about one third did so. However, this wasn't because they failed to notice the stickers (when the experimenter drew their attention to them and asked 'What is that?', most gave the correct answer).

They also 'recognised' themselves in the recording – they all confidently responded with 'Me' and stated their name when asked 'Who is that?'. But this reaction didn't seem to go beyond a recognition of facial and bodily features. When asked 'Where is that sticker?', they often referred to the 'other' child (e.g. 'It's on her/his head'), as if they were trying to say 'Yes, that looks like me, but that's not *me* – she's not doing what I'm doing right now'. One three-year-old said 'It's Jennifer' (her name), then hurriedly added 'but why is she wearing my shirt?'

By about four, a significant majority of the children began to pass the delayed self-recognition test. Most four- and five-year-olds confidently reached up to remove the stickers after watching the delayed video images of themselves. They no longer referred to 'him/her' or their proper names.

According to Povinelli, these results are consistent with the view that genuine *autobiographical memory* (AM) appears to emerge in children between three-and-a-half and four-and-a-half (not the two-year mark favoured by Gallup). AM implies understanding that memories constitute a genuine 'past' – a history of the self leading up to the here-and-now (see Chapter 17).

It also suggests that self-recognition in chimps – and human toddlers – is based on recognition of the self's behaviour, not the self's psychological states. When chimps and orangutans see themselves in a mirror, Povinelli (1998) believe they:

'... form an equivalence relation between the actions they see in the mirror and their own behaviour. Every time they move, the mirror image moves with them. They conclude that everything that is true for the mirror image is also true for their own bodies, and vice versa. Thus, these apes can pass the mirror test by correlating coloured marks on the mirror images with marks on their own bodies. But the ape does not conclude, "That's me!". Rather the animal concludes, "That's the same as me!"'.

In short, chimps possess explicit mental representations of the positions and movements of their own bodies, which Povinelli calls the *kinaesthetic self-concept* (see Chapter 5).

Self-definition

Piaget, Mead and many others have pointed to the importance of language in consolidating the early development of self-awareness, by providing labels which permit distinctions between self and not-self ('I', 'you', 'me', 'it' and so on). These labels can, of course, then be used by the toddler to communicate notions of selfhood to others. One important kind of label is the child's name.

Names aren't usually chosen arbitrarily – either the parents particularly like the name or they want to name the child after a relative or famous person. Names aren't neutral labels in terms of how people respond to them and what they associate with them. Indeed, they can be used as the basis for stereotyping (see Chapter 22). Jahoda (1954) described the naming practices of the Ashanti tribe of West Africa. Children born on different days of the week are given names accordingly, because of the belief that they have different personalities. Police records showed that among juvenile delinquents, there was a very low percentage of boys born on Monday (believed to have quiet and calm personalities), but a very high rate of Wednesday-born boys (thought to be naturally aggressive).

Ask yourself ...

- How might the boys' names have contributed to these statistics?

This demonstrates the *self-fulfilling prophecy*. It's reasonable to believe that these Ashanti boys were treated in a way consistent with the name given to them, and that, as a result, they 'became' what their name indicated they were 'really' like. In English-speaking countries, days of the week (e.g. Tuesday) and months of the year (April, May and June) are used as names, and they have associations which may influence others' reactions (for example, 'Monday's child is fair of face, Tuesday's child is full of grace ...').

When children refer to themselves as 'I' (or 'me') and others as 'you', they're having to *reverse* the labels that are normally used to refer to them by others ('you', 'he', 'she'). Also, of course, they hear others refer to themselves as 'I' and not as 'you', 'he', or 'she'. This is a problem of *shifting reference*. Despite this, most children don't invert 'I' and 'you'. However, two interesting exceptions are autistic and blind children, who often use 'I' for others and 'you' for self (see

Chapter 40). This may be associated with the abnormal inter-actions and relationships these children experience which, in turn, would further support Cooley and Mead.

The psychological self

Maccoby (1980) asks what children mean when they refer to themselves as 'I' or 'me'. Are they referring to anything more than a physical entity enclosed by an envelope of skin?

KEY STUDY 33.4

There's more to children than meets the eye (Flavell *et al.*, 1978)

Flavell *et al.* (1978) investigated development of the *psychological self* in two-and-a-half to five-year-olds. In one study, a doll was placed on the table in front of the child, and it was explained that dolls are like people in some ways – they have arms, legs, hands and so on (which were pointed to). Then the child was asked how dolls are different from people, whether they know their names and think about things, and so on. Most children said a doll doesn't know its name and cannot think about things, but people can.

They were then asked, 'Where is the part of you that knows your name and thinks about things?' and 'Where do you do your thinking and knowing?' Fourteen out of 22 children gave fairly clear localisation for the thinking self, namely 'in their heads', while others found it very difficult. The experimenter then looked directly into the child's eyes and asked, 'Can I see you thinking in there?'. Most children thought not.

These answers suggest that by three-and-a-half to four years, a child has a rudimentary concept of a private, thinking self that's not visible even to someone looking directly into its eyes. The child can distinguish this from the bodily self, which it knows is visible to others. In other words, by about age four, children begin to develop a *theory of mind*, the aware-ness that they – and other people – have mental processes (e.g. Leekam, 1993; Shatz, 1994; Wellman, 1990). However, one group failing to develop a theory of mind is that of autis-tic children (see Chapter 40).

The categorical self

Age and *gender* are both parts of the central core of the self-image. They represent two of the categories regarding the self which are also used to perceive and interpret the behaviour of others.

Age is probably the first social category to be acquired by the child (and is so even before a concept of number devel-ops). Lewis & Brooks-Gunn (1979) found that six- to twelve-month-olds can distinguish between photographs, slides and papier-mâché heads of adults and babies. By twelve months, they prefer interacting with unfamiliar babies to unfamiliar adults. Also, as soon as they've acquired labels like 'mummy' and 'daddy' and 'baby', they almost never make age-related mistakes.

Before age seven, children tend to define the self in *physical terms* – hair colour, height, favourite activities and posses-sions. Inner, psychological experiences and characteristics aren't described as being distinct from overt behaviour and external, physical characteristics. During middle childhood through to adolescence, self-descriptions now include many more references to internal, psychological characteristics, such as competencies, knowledge, emotions, values and per-sonality traits (Damon & Hart, 1988). However, Damon and Hart also report important cultural differences in how the self-concept develops (see Critical Discussion 33.1, page 484).

School highlights others' expectations about how the self should develop. It also provides a social context in which new goals are set and comparisons with others (peers) are prompted. This makes evaluation of the self all the more important (Durkin, 1995). This comparison becomes more important still during adolescence (see Chapter 37).

CHAPTER SUMMARY

■ An important distinction is that between **consciousness** and **self-consciousness/awareness**. Self-awareness allows us to see ourselves as others see us.

■ Our **self-concept** refers to our perception of our personal-ity, and comprises the **self-image** (which includes **body image/bodily self**), **self-esteem** and **ideal self**. It can also be defined in terms of a complex set of **self-schemata**, which themselves include an array of possible selves.

■ A major theoretical approach to the self is **symbolic interactionism**, associated mainly with Mead, who was influenced by James's **'I'/'me' distinction** and by Cooley's theory of the **looking-glass self**.

■ Mead denied that the self is mentalistic, seeing it as a **process of social interaction**. It develops through **role-taking**, in particular, taking the perspective of the **'generalised other'** in the context of the child's play.

■ Based on Mead, many sociologists and social psychologists see language as fundamental to how the self is **con-structed**. Our language provides stories or accounts of what being a person is like ('**discourses**'), which differ between cultures. The view of people as independent, self-contained individuals is a relatively recent invention of Western, individualist cultures.

■ Two major influences on the development of the self-con-cept are the **reaction of others** and **comparison with others**. Much of the relevant research is consistent with the theories of James, Cooley and Mead.

■ The self-concept develops in fairly regular, predictable ways. During the first few months, the **existential self** emerges, but the **bodily self** is probably the first aspect of the self-concept to develop.

■ The bodily self has been studied through (mainly visual) **self-recognition** in **mirrors**. Self-recognition appears at about 18 months in children, and is also found in chimps. While it's generally agreed that passing the mirror test implies a self-concept, this may be no more than a **kinaes-thetic** self-concept, which doesn't involve understanding of psychological states.

■ **Self-definition** is related to the use of language, includ-ing the use of labels, such as **names**. By three-and-a-half to four, children seem to have a basic understanding of a **psy-chological self** (or **'theory of mind'**).

- **Age** and **gender** are two basic features of the **categorical self**. The categorical self changes from being described in physical to more psychological terms during middle childhood through to adolescence.

Self-assessment questions

1 Describe and evaluate **two or more** theories of the self.
2 Discuss psychological research into the development of the self-concept.

Web addresses

teach.valdosta.edu/whuitt/col/regsys/self.html

novaonline.nv.cc.va.us/eli/spd110td/interper/self/self.htlm

members.truepath.com/Counselme/Self-con.htm

Recommended reading

Durkin, K. (1995) *Developmental Social Psychology: From Infancy to Old Age*. Oxford: Blackwell. An extremely lucid and often witty, as well as thorough, textbook that brings together social and developmental psychology, from the lifespan perspective. Chapters 9, 15 and 16 are especially relevant here.

Gallup, G. (1998) Can animals empathise? Yes. *Scientific American Presents, 9(4)*, 66, 68–71.

Povinelli, D.J. (1998) … Maybe not. *Scientific American Presents, 9(4)*, 67, 72–75.

Both researchers present their sometimes conflicting viewpoints in the same issue in an engaging, lively manner.

Chapter 34

Cognitive Development

Introduction and overview

According to Meadows (1993, 1995), cognitive development is concerned with the study of 'the child as thinker'. However, different theoretical accounts of how the child's thinking develops rest on very different images of what the child is like:

- Piaget sees the child as an organism *adapting to its environment*, as well as a scientist constructing its own understanding of the world.

- Information-processing theorists see children, like adults, as *symbol manipulators*.
- Vygotsky, in contrast with both of these two approaches, sees the child as a participant in an *interactive process*, by which socially and culturally determined knowledge and understanding gradually become *individualised*.
- Bruner, like Vygotsky, emphasises the *social* aspects of the child's cognitive development.

Some years ago, Piaget's theory was regarded as the major framework or paradigm within child development. But despite remaining a vital source of influence and inspiration, both in psychology and education, today there are hardly any 'orthodox' Piagetians left (Dasen, 1994). Many fundamental aspects of Piaget's theory have been challenged, and fewer and fewer developmental psychologists now subscribe to his or other 'hard' *stage theories* (Durkin, 1995).

Piaget's theory

Rather than trying to explain individual differences (why some children are more intelligent than others: see Chapter 41), Piaget was interested in how intelligence itself changes as children grow. He called this *genetic epistemology*.

According to Piaget, cognitive development occurs through the interaction of innate capacities with environmental events, and progresses through a series of *hierarchical, qualitatively different, stages*. All children pass through the stages in the same sequence without skipping any or, except in the case of brain damage, regressing to earlier ones (they're *invariant*). The stages are also the same for everyone irrespective of culture (they're *universal*). Underlying the changes are certain *functional invariants*, fundamental aspects of the developmental process which remain the same and work in the same way through the various stages. The most important of these are *assimilation, accommodation* and *equilibration*. The principal cognitive structure that changes is the *schema* (plural *schemas* or *schemata*).

Schemas (or schemata)

A schema (or scheme) is the basic building block or unit of intelligent behaviour. Piaget saw schemas as mental structures which organise past experiences and provide a way of understanding future experiences. For Bee (2000), they're not so much categories as the *action of categorising* in some particular way. Life begins with simple schemas, which are largely confined to inbuilt reflexes (such as sucking and grasping). These

operate independently of other reflexes, and are activated only when certain objects are present. As we grow, so our schemas become increasingly complex.

Assimilation, accommodation and equilibration

Assimilation is the process by which we incorporate new information into existing schemas. For example, babies will reflexively suck a nipple and other objects, such as a finger. To learn to suck from a bottle or drink from a cup, the initial sucking reflex must be modified through *accommodation*.

When a child can deal with most, if not all, new experiences by assimilating them, it's in a state of *equilibrium*. This is brought about by *equilibration*, the process of seeking 'mental balance'. But if existing schemas are inadequate to cope with new situations, *cognitive disequilibrium* occurs. To restore equilibrium, the existing schema must be 'stretched' in order to take in (or 'accommodate') new information. The necessary and complementary processes of assimilation and accommodation constitute the fundamental process of *adaptation* (see Figure 34.1).

Stages of cognitive development

Each of Piaget's four stages represents a stage in the development of intelligence (hence *sensorimotor intelligence, pre-operational intelligence* and so on), and is a way of summarising the various schemas a child has at a particular time. The ages shown in Table 34.1 are approximate, because children move through the stages at different rates due to differences in both the environment and their biological maturation. Children also pass through transitional periods, in which their thinking is a mixture of two stages.

Table 34.1 *Piaget's four stages of cognitive development*

Stage	Approximate age
Sensorimotor	0-2 years
Pre-operational	2-7 years
Concrete operational	7-11 years
Formal operational	11 years onwards

The concept of developmental 'stages' is often taken to mean that development is *discontinuous*. But for Piaget, development is a gradual and continuous process of change, although later stages build on earlier ones (which is why the sequence is

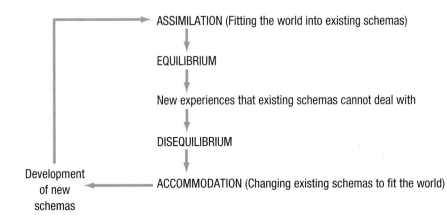

Figure 34.1 *Relationship between assimilation, equilibrium, disequilibrium and accommodation in the development of schemas*

invariant). The passage from one stage to the next occurs through cognitive disequilibrium. To achieve equilibrium, the child is 'forced' to higher levels of intellectual understanding (Krebs & Blackman, 1988).

The sensorimotor stage

This lasts for approximately the first two years of life. Infants learn about the world primarily through their senses ('sensori-'), and by doing ('motor'). Based on observations of his own children, Piaget (1952) divided the sensorimotor stage into six substages.

Box 34.1 **The six substages of the sensorimotor stage**

- **Exercising reflexes (birth to 1 month):** Reflexes are practised until they function smoothly. Infants have no intentionality, and no understanding of an object.
- **Primary circular reactions (1 to 4 months):** Reflexes are extended to new objects, and infants co-ordinate simple schemas (such as grasping and looking). Behaviours causing specific events are repeated. Infants look briefly at where a disappearing object was last seen.
- **Secondary circular reactions (4 to 10 months):** All the senses become co-ordinated, and the infant can anticipate events and results of actions. A partially hidden object can be found.
- **The co-ordination of secondary circular reactions (10 to 12 months):** Infants represent objects in their minds, and demonstrate the beginning of symbolic behaviour and memory. A goal can be decided and then acted on. A completely hidden object can be found.
- **Tertiary circular reactions (12 to 18 months):** Infants search for environmental novelty and use several interchangeable schemas to achieve goals. Experiments are conducted to see what will happen. An object hidden under one of several covers can be found.
- **Invention of new means through mental combinations (18 to 24 months):** Infants think about a problem before acting, and thoughts begin to dominate actions. Objects can be manipulated mentally to reach goals. An object placed in a container and then hidden can be found.

(Based on Tomlinson-Keasey, 1985)

Object permanence

Frequent interaction with objects ultimately leads to the development of *object permanence*. As Box 34.1 shows, in the second substage, an infant will look where an object disappears for a few moments, but won't search for it. If the object doesn't reappear, the infant apparently loses interest. Piaget called this *passive exploration*, because the infant expects the object to reappear but doesn't actively search for it ('out of sight' is 'out of mind').

In the third substage, an infant will reach for a partially hidden object, suggesting that it realises that the rest of it is attached to the visible part. But if the object is completely hidden, infants make no attempt to retrieve it.

In the fourth substage, a hidden object will be searched for ('out of sight' is no longer 'out of mind'), but the infant will persist in looking for it where it was *last* hidden, even when it's hidden somewhere else (see Figure 34.2).

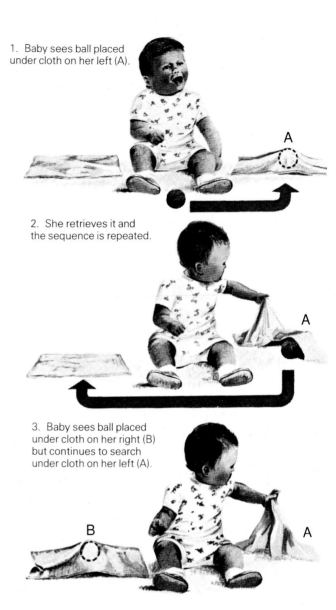

1. Baby sees ball placed under cloth on her left (A).

2. She retrieves it and the sequence is repeated.

3. Baby sees ball placed under cloth on her right (B) but continues to search under cloth on her left (A).

Figure 34.2 *Piaget's demonstration of the limited object permanence of babies beteen eight and twelve months. They can retrieve a hidden object only from its original hiding place, not where it was last hidden. Not until about twelve months will they search under the cushion where they last saw the object hidden; they can do this even when three or four cushions are used. (Others have suggested that this ability appears as early as nine months.) (from Barnes-Gutteridge, 1974)*

CASE STUDY 34.1

An illustration of lack of object permanence (Piaget, 1963)

At 0,7 (28) [7 months, 28 days] Jacqueline tries to grasp a celluloid duck on top of her quilt. She almost catches it, shakes herself and the duck slides down beside her. It falls very close to her hand but behind a fold in the sheet. Jacqueline's eyes have followed the movement, she has even followed it with her outstretched hand. But as soon as the duck has disappeared – nothing more! It does not occur to her to search behind the fold of the sheet, which would be very easy to do (she twists it mechanically without searching at all) ... I try showing it to her a few times. Each time she tries to grasp it, but when she is about to touch it I replace it very obviously under the sheet. Jacqueline immediately withdraws her hand and gives up... Everything occurs as though the child believed that the object is alternately made and unmade ... .

While this no longer occurs after twelve months, object permanence isn't yet fully developed. Suppose an infant sees an object placed in a matchbox, which is then put under a pillow. When it's not looking, the object is removed from the matchbox and left under the pillow. If the matchbox is given to the infant, it will open it expecting to find the object. On not finding it, the infant *won't* look under the pillow. This is because it cannot take into account the possibility that something it's not actually seen might have happened (*failure to infer invisible displacements*). Once the infant can infer invisible displacements (after 18 months), the development of object permanence is complete.

Box 34.2 The general symbolic function

Other cognitive structures that have developed by the end of the sensorimotor stage include *self-recognition* (see Chapter 33), and symbolic thought, such as language.

Two other manifestations of the *general symbolic function* are *deferred imitation* and *representational* (or *make-believe*) *play*. Deferred imitation is the ability to imitate or reproduce something that's been perceived but is no longer present (Meltzoff & Moore, 1983). Representational play involves using one object as though it were another. Like deferred imitation, this ability depends on the infant's growing ability to form mental images of things and people in their absence (to remember).

The pre-operational stage

Probably the main difference between this and the sensorimotor stage is the continued development and use of internal images (or 'interiorised' schemas), symbols and language, especially important for the child's developing sense of self-awareness (see Chapter 33). However, the child tends to be influenced by how things *look*, rather than by logical principles or operations (hence the term 'pre-operational').

Piaget subdivided the stage into the *pre-conceptual* (age two to four) and the *intuitive substages* (age four to seven). The absolute nature of the pre-conceptual child's thinking makes relative terms such as 'bigger' or 'stronger' difficult to understand (things tend to be 'biggest' or just 'big'). The intuitive child can use relative terms, but its ability to think logically is still limited.

Seriation and artificialism

In *seriation*, the pre-conceptual child has difficulty arranging objects on the basis of a particular dimension, such as increasing height (Piaget & Szeminska, 1952). *Artificialism* is the belief that natural features have been designed and constructed by people. For example, the question 'Why is the sky blue?' might produce the answer 'Somebody painted it'.

Syncretic thought, transductive reasoning and animism

Syncretic thought is the tendency to link together any neighbouring objects or events on the basis of what individual instances have in common. For example, if a three-year-old is given a box of wooden shapes of different colours and asked to pick out four that are alike, the child might pick the shapes shown in Figure 34.3. Here, the characteristic the child focuses on changes with each second shape that's chosen: a red square is followed by a red circle, which is followed by a blue circle, which is followed by a blue triangle. There's no one characteristic that all four have in common. A five-year-old would be able to select four of the same shape, or four of the same colour, and say what they have in common.

Transductive reasoning involves drawing an inference about the relationship between two things based on a single shared attribute. If both cats and dogs have four legs, then cats must be dogs. This sort of reasoning can lead to *animism*, the belief that inanimate objects are alive.

Box 34.3 Examples of children's animism during the pre-operational stage (from Piaget, 1973)

Cli (three years nine months) speaking of a motor in a garage: 'The motor's gone to bye-byes. It doesn't go out because of the rain ...'.

Nel (two years nine months) seeing a hollow chestnut tree: 'Didn't it cry when the hole was made?'. To a stone: 'Don't touch my garden! ... My garden would cry'. Nel, after throwing a stone on to a sloping bank, watching the stone rolling down said: 'Look at the stone. It's afraid of the grass'.

Nel scratched herself against a wall. Looking at her hand: 'Who made that mark? – It hurts where the wall hit me'.

Dar (one year eight months/two years five months) bringing his toy motor to the window: 'Motor see the snow'. Dar stood up in bed, crying and calling out: 'The mummies (the ladies) all on the ground, hurt!'. Dar was watching the grey clouds. He was told that it was going to rain. 'Oh, look at the wind! Naughty wind, smack wind'. ... On a morning in winter when the sun shone into the room: 'Oh, good! The sun's come to make the radiator warm'.

Ask yourself ...

• Can you think of any examples of adults displaying animistic thinking? Do you ever think this way yourself?

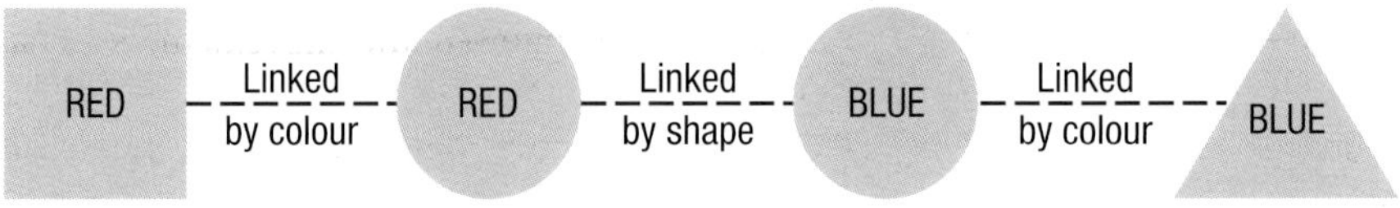

RED — Linked by colour — RED — Linked by shape — BLUE — Linked by colour — BLUE

Figure 34.3 *Simple example of syncretic thought*

Centration

This involves focusing on only a single perceptual quality at a time. A pre-conceptual child asked to divide apples into those that are 'big and red' and those that are 'small and green' will either put all the red (or green) apples together irrespective of their size, or all the big (or small) apples together irrespective of their colour. Until the child can *decentre*, it will be unable to classify things logically or systematically. Centration is also associated with the *inability to conserve* (see below).

> ### Ask yourself ...
> * How is centration illustrated by syncretic thought (see above)?

Egocentrism

According to Piaget, pre-operational children are egocentric, that is, they see the world from their own standpoints and cannot appreciate that other people might see things differently. They cannot put themselves 'in other people's shoes' to realise that other people don't know or perceive everything they themselves do. Consider the following example (Phillips, 1969) of a conversation between an experimenter and a four-year-old boy:

Experimenter:	'Do you have a brother?'
Child:	'Yes.'
Experimenter:	'What's his name?'
Child:	'Jim.'
Experimenter:	'Does Jim have a brother?'
Child:	'No.'

KEY STUDY 34.1

The 'Swiss mountain scene' test of egocentrism (Piaget & Inhelder, 1956)

The three papier-mâché model mountains in Figure 34.4 below are of different colours. One has snow on the top, one a house, and one a red cross. The child walks round and explores the model, and then sits on one side while a doll is placed at some different location. The child is shown ten pictures of different views of the model and asked to choose the one that represents how the doll sees it.

Four-year-olds were completely unaware of perspectives other than their own, and always chose a picture which matched *their* views of the model. Six-year-olds showed some awareness, but often chose the wrong picture. Only seven- and eight-year-olds consistently chose the picture that represented *the doll's* view. According to Piaget, children below the age of seven are bound by the *egocentric illusion*. They fail to understand that what they see is *relative to their own positions*, and instead take it to represent 'the world as it really is'.

Conservation

Conservation is the understanding that any quantity (such as number, liquid quantity, length and substance) remains the same despite physical changes in the arrangement of objects. Piaget believed that pre-operational children cannot conserve because their thinking is dominated by the perceptual nature of objects (their 'appearance').

The inability to conserve is another example of centration. With liquid quantity, for example, the child centres on just one dimension of the beaker, usually its height, and fails to take width into account. (See Figure 34.5, page 495.)

Only in the concrete operational stage do children understand that 'getting taller' and 'getting narrower' tend to cancel each other out (*compensation*). If the contents of the taller beaker are poured back into the shorter one, the child will again say that the two shorter beakers contain the same amount. But it cannot perform this operation mentally and so lacks *reversibility* (understanding that what can be done can be undone *without any gain or loss*). These same limitations apply to other forms of conservation, such as number, and substance/quantity. (See Figures 34.6 and 34.7, page 495.)

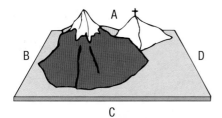
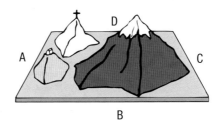
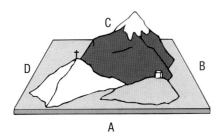
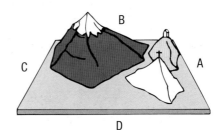

Figure 34.4 *Piaget and inhelder's three-mountain scene, seen from four different sides (from Smith & Cowie, 1988)*

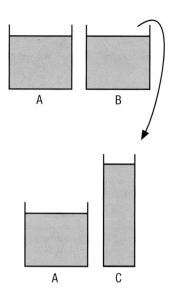

Figure 34.5 *The conservation of liquid quantity. Although the child agrees that there's the same amount of liquid in A and B, when the contents of B are poured into C, the appearance of C sways the child's judgement so that C is now judged to contain more liquid than A ('it looks more' or 'it's taller'). Although the child has seen the liquid poured from B into C and agrees that none has been spilled or added in the process (what Piaget calls 'identity'), the appearance of the higher level of liquid in the taller, thinner beaker C is compelling*

Box 34.4   Horizontal and vertical décalage

Some types of conservation are mastered before others, and their order tends to be invariant. *Liquid quantity* is mastered by age six to seven, *substance/quantity* and *length* by seven to eight, *weight* by eight to ten, and *volume* by eleven to twelve. This step-by-step acquisition of new operations is called *décalage* (displacement or 'slips in level of performance').

In conservation, décalage is *horizontal* because there are inconsistencies *within* the same kind of ability or operation (a seven-year-old child can conserve number but not weight, for example). *Vertical* décalage refers to inconsistencies *between* different abilities or operations (a child may have mastered all kinds of classification, but not all kinds of conservation).

The concrete operational stage

The child is now capable of performing logical operations, but only in the presence of actual objects. S/he can conserve, and shows reversibility and more logical classification.

Further examples of the child's ability to decentre include its appreciation that objects can belong to more than one class (as in the case of Andrew being Bob's brother *and* Charlie's best friend). There's also a significant decline in egocentrism (and the growing *relativism* of the child's viewpoint), and the onset of seriation and reciprocity of relationships (such as knowing that adding one to three produces the same amount as taking one from five).

One remaining problem for the concrete operational child is *transitivity tasks*. For example, if told that 'Alan is taller than Bob, and Bob is taller than Charlie' and asked whether Alan or Charlie is taller, children under eleven cannot solve this problem entirely in their heads. They can usually only solve it using real (or concrete) objects (such as dolls).

The formal operational stage

While the concrete operational child is still concerned with manipulating things (even if this is done mentally), the formal operational thinker can manipulate *ideas* or *propositions* and can reason solely on the basis of verbal statements ('first order' and 'second order' operations respectively). 'Formal' refers to the ability to follow the form of an argument without reference to its particular content. In transitivity problems, for example, 'If A is taller than B, and B is taller than C, then A is taller than C', is a form of argument whose conclusion is logically true, regardless of what A, B and C might refer to.

Formal operational thinkers can also think *hypothetically*, that is, they can think about what *could* be as well as what actually is. For example, asked what it would be like if people had tails, they might say 'Dogs would know when you were happy' or 'Lovers could hold their tails in secret under the table'. Concrete operational thinkers might tell you 'not to be so silly', or say where on the body the tail might be, showing their dependence on what they've actually seen (Dworetzky, 1981).

The ability to imagine and discuss things that have never been encountered is evidence of the continued decentration that occurs beyond concrete operations: formal operational thinkers display *hypothetico-deductive reasoning*.

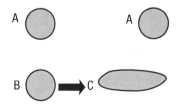

Figure 34.7 *Substance or quantity conservation using plasticine. Two equal-sized balls of plasticine are used. B is rolled into a sausage shape (C); the pre-operational child typically thinks there's more plasticine in C than A, having originally agreed that A and B have the same amount*

Figure 34.6 *Number conservation using counters. Two rows of counters are put in a one-to-one correspondence and then one row is pushed together. The pre-operational child usually thinks there are more counters in A than in C because A is 'longer', despite being able to count correctly and agreeing that A and B have equal numbers*

KEY STUDY 34.2

A demonstration of formal operational thinking (Inhelder & Piaget, 1958)

Inhelder and Piaget gave adolescents five containers filled with clear liquid. Four were 'test chemicals' and one an 'indicator'. When the correct combination of one or more test chemicals was added to the indicator, it turned yellow. The problem was to find this combination.

Pre-operational children simply mixed the chemicals randomly, and concrete operational children, although more systematic, generally failed to test all possible combinations. Only formal operational thinkers considered all alternatives and systematically varied one factor at a time. Also, they often wrote down all the results and tried to draw general conclusions about each chemical.

An evaluation of Piaget's theory

As we noted in the *Introduction and overview*, Piaget's theory has had an enormous impact on our understanding of cognitive development. However, as Flavell (1982) has remarked:

'Like all theories of great reach and significance ... it has problems that gradually come to light as years and years of thinking and research get done on it. Thus, some of us now think that the theory may in varying degrees be unclear, incorrect and incomplete'.

Object permanence

Piaget's claims about the sensorimotor stage have been criticised in both general and specific terms. Bower & Wishart (1972), for example, found that how an object is made to disappear influences the infant's response. If the infant is looking at an object and reaching for it and the lights are turned off, it will continue to search for up to one-and-a-half minutes (using infrared cameras). This suggests that it *does* remember the object is there (so, 'out of sight' *isn't* 'out of mind'). Baillargeon (1987) has shown that object permanence can occur as early as three-and-a-half months, and that it isn't necessary for a baby younger than six months to see the whole object in order to respond to it.

Centration

One way to study centration (and classification) is through *class inclusion tasks*. If a pre-operational child is presented with several wooden beads, mostly brown but a few white, and asked 'Are they all wooden?', the child will respond correctly. If asked 'Are there more brown or more white beads?', the child will again respond correctly. But if asked 'Are there more brown beads or more beads?', the child will say there are more brown beads.

Ask yourself ...

- Why do you think they say there are more brown beads?

The brown beads are more numerous than the white, and can be perceived in a more immediate and direct way than the wooden beads as a whole (despite the first question being answered correctly). For Piaget, the child fails to understand the relationship between the whole (the *superordinate* class of wooden beads) and the parts (the *subordinate* classes of brown and white beads). This was another example of the inability to decentre. However, Donaldson (1978) has asked if the difficulty the child experiences is to do with what is expected of it and how the task is presented.

KEY STUDY 34.3

Alternatives to Piaget's class-inclusion task

Donaldson describes a study with six-year-olds using four toy cows, three black and one white. The cows were laid on their sides and the children told they were 'sleeping'. Of those asked 'Are there more black cows or more cows?', 25 per cent answered correctly. However, of those asked 'Are there more black cows or more sleeping cows?', 48 per cent answered correctly.

Similarly, the word 'more' has a different meaning for children and adults (Gelman, 1978). Adults use 'more' to mean 'containing a greater number'. But for children 'more' refers to the general concept of larger, longer, occupying more space and so on.

Egocentrism

Gelman (1979) has shown that four-year-olds adjust their explanations of things to make them clearer to a blindfold listener. This isn't what we'd expect if, as Piaget claims, children of this age are egocentric. Nor would we expect four-year-olds to use simpler forms of speech when talking to two-year-olds (Gelman, 1979) or choose appropriate birthday presents for their mothers (Marvin, 1975, in Morris, 1988).

Critics of the 'Swiss mountain scene' test (see Key Study 34.1) see it as an unusually difficult way of presenting a problem to a young child. Borke (1975) and Hughes (cited in Donaldson, 1978) have shown that when the task is presented in a meaningful context (making what Donaldson calls 'human sense'), even three-and-a-half-year-olds can appreciate the world as another person sees it. These are all examples of perspective-taking.

Box 34.5 Perspective-taking, false beliefs and theory of mind

According to Flavell *et al.* (1990), there are two levels of perspective-taking ability:

- level 1 (two- to three-year-olds): the child knows that some other person experiences something differently;
- level 2 (four- to five-year-olds): the child develops a whole series of complex rules for figuring out precisely what the other person sees or experiences.

In a study of children's ability to distinguish between appearance and reality, Flavell (1986) showed children a sponge painted to look like a rock. They were asked what it looked like and what it 'really' was. Three-year-olds said either that it looked like a sponge and was a sponge, or that it looked like a rock and was a rock. However, four- and five-year-olds could say that it looked like a rock but was in fact a sponge.

Gopnik & Astington (1988) allowed children to feel the sponge before asking them the questions used in Flavell's study. They were then told: 'Your friend John hasn't touched this, he hasn't squeezed it. If John just sees it over here like this, what will he think it is? Will he think it's a rock or a sponge?'. Typically, three-year-olds said that John would think it was a sponge (which it is), while four- and five-year-olds said he'd think it was a rock (because he hadn't had the opportunity of touching/squeezing it). In other words, the older children were attributing John with a *false belief*, which they could only do by taking John's perspective.

Evidence like this has led several theorists (e.g. Gopnik & Wellman, 1994) to propose that four-to five-year-olds have developed a quite sophisticated *theory of mind* (Premack & Woodruff, 1978). This refers to the understanding that people (and not objects) have desires, beliefs and other mental states, some of which (such as beliefs) can be false. The older children in Gopnick and Astington's study understood that John wouldn't know something which they did (see Chapters 33 and 40).

Conservation

The ability to conserve also seems to occur earlier than Piaget believed. Rose & Blank (1974) showed that when the *pre-transformation question* (the question asked before one row of counters, say, is rearranged) was dropped, six-year-olds often succeeded on the number conservation task. Importantly, they made fewer errors on the standard version of the task when tested a week later.

These findings were replicated by Samuel & Bryant (1984) using conservation of number, liquid quantity and substance. The standard version of the task unwittingly 'forces' children to produce the wrong answer against their better judgement by the mere fact that the same question is asked twice, before *and* after the transformation (Donaldson, 1978). Hence, children believe they're expected to give a different answer on the second question. On this explanation, *contextual cues* may override purely linguistic ones.

According to Piaget, it shouldn't matter *who*, in the case of number conservation, rearranges the counters/Smarties or how this happens. Yet when 'Naughty Teddy', a glove puppet, causes the transformation 'accidentally', pre-operational children can conserve number and length (McGarrigle & Donaldson, 1974; Light *et al.*, 1979). This also applies when the transformation is made by a person other than the experimenter (Hargreaves *et al.*, 1982; Light, 1986).

While Piaget's original procedure might convey the implicit message 'take note of the transformation because it's relevant', studies using *accidental* transformations might convey the message 'ignore the transformation, it makes no difference'. It follows that if some change actually takes place, the implicit message to ignore the transformation would make children give an incorrect answer. The standard Piagetian task involves an *irrelevant perceptual change* (nothing is added or taken away), but where some *actual change* occurs, children tested under the accidental/incidental transformation condition should do *worse* than those tested in the standard way. This prediction has been supported in several studies (Light & Gilmour, 1983; Moore & Frye, 1986).

Cross-cultural tests of the stages

CRITICAL DISCUSSION 34.1

Cultural influences on cognitive development

Dasen (1994) cites studies he conducted in remote parts of the central Australian desert with eight- to 14-year-old Aborigines. He gave them *conservation*-of-liquid, weight and volume tasks, plus a task that tested understanding of *spatial relationships*. This involved either:

- two landscape models, one of which could be turned round through 180°. The participants had to locate an object (doll or sheep) on one model and then find the same location on the second model; or
- a bottle was half-filled with water, then tilted into various positions, with a screen hiding the water level. Participants were shown outline drawings of the bottle and they had to draw in the water level.

On *conservation* tasks, the same shift from pre-operational to concrete operational thought was found as with Swiss children – but it took place between ten and 13 (instead of five and seven). A fairly large proportion of adolescents and adults also gave non-conservation answers. On the *spatial tasks*, again there was the same shift from pre- to concrete operational thought as for Swiss children, but they found the spatial task easier than the conservation tasks. In other words, operational thinking develops *earlier* in the spatial domain, the *reverse* of what's found for Swiss children.

According to Dasen, this makes good sense in terms of Aboriginal culture, where things *aren't quantified*. Water is vital for survival, but the exact quantity matters little. Counting things is unusual, and number words only go up to five (after which everything is 'many'). By contrast, finding one's way around is crucial: water-holes must be found at the end of each journey and family members meet up at the end of the day after having split up in order to search for water. The acquisition of a vast array of spatial knowledge is helped by the mythology, such as the 'dream time' stories that attribute a meaning to each feature of the landscape and to routes travelled by ancestral spirits.

The few cross-cultural studies of the sensorimotor stage have shown the substages to be universal. Overall, it seems that ecological or cultural factors *don't* influence the sequence of stages, but *do* affect the *rate* at which they're attained (Segall *et al.*, 1999). For Dasen (1994):

'The deep structures, the basic cognitive processes, are indeed universal, while at the surface level, the way these basic processes are brought to bear on specific contents, in specific contexts, is influenced by culture. Universality and cultural diversity are not opposites, but are complementary aspects of all human behaviour and development'.

Dasen has argued that only one-third of adolescents and adults actually attains formal operations, and that in some cultures it's not the typical mode of thought. However, Shea (1985) argues that it would be premature to conclude that formal operations don't 'exist' in certain societies based on the results of a few Piagetian tasks. Highly abstract thinking of some kind can often be found in traditional court cases (Jahoda, 1980), and land disputes (Hutchins, 1980) – even if they're not strictly 'formal'. According to Segall *et al.* (1999), it might be more accurate to argue that formal operational thinking '… in effect, scientific reasoning – is not what is valued in all cultures …'.

The role of social factors in cognitive development

Meadows (1995) maintains that Piaget implicitly saw children as largely independent and isolated in their construction of knowledge and understanding of the physical world (children as scientists). This excluded the contribution of other people to children's cognitive development. The social nature of knowledge and thought is a basic propostion of Vygotsky's theory (see below).

Despite all these (and other) criticisms, Bee (2000) believes that:

'… his [Piaget's] theory sets the agenda for most research in this area for the past thirty years and still serves as a kind of scaffolding for much of our thinking about thinking'.

Applying Piaget's theory to education

Piaget didn't actually advocate a 'theory of instruction' (Ginsberg, 1981). However, his theory has three main implications for education (Brainerd, 1983). These are the concept of *readiness*, the *curriculum* (what should be taught), and *teaching methods* (how the curriculum should be taught).

Readiness relates to limits set on learning by a child's current stage of development (see Box 34.6). Regarding the curriculum, appropriate content would include logic (such as transitive inference), maths (numbers), science (conservation) and space (Euclidean geometry). Teaching materials should consist of concrete objects that children can easily manipulate.

However, Ginsberg (1981) has argued that attempting to base a curriculum on the teaching of Piagetian stages is a misapplication of his theory. It would be more useful to modify the curriculum in line with what's known about the various Piagetian stages, without allowing them to limit teaching methods. Piaget's theory seems to suggest that there are definite sequences in which concepts should be taught. For example, different types of conservation appear at different times (see Box 34.4). But many traditional schools don't base their teaching on this or other developmental sequences (Elkind, 1976).

Central to a Piagetian perspective is the view that childen learn from actions rather than from passive observation (*active self-discovery/discovery learning*). Regarding teaching methods, teachers must recognise that each child needs to construct knowledge for itself, and that deeper understanding is the product of active learning (Smith *et al.*, 1998).

Box 34.6 | **The role of the teacher in the Piagetian classroom**

- It's essential for teachers to assess very carefully each individual child's current stage of cognitive development (this relates to the concept of readiness). The child can then be set tasks tailored to its needs which become *intrinsically motivating*.
- Teachers must provide children with learning opportunities that enable them to advance to the next developmental step. This is achieved by creating *disequilibrium* (see page 491). Rather than providing the appropriate materials and allowing children to 'get on with it', teachers should create a proper balance between actively guiding and directing children's thinking patterns, and providing opportunities for them to explore by themselves (Thomas, 1985).
- Teachers should be concerned with the learning process rather than its end product. This involves encouraging children to ask questions, experiment and explore. Teachers should look for the reasoning behind children's answers, particularly when they make mistakes.
- Teachers should encourage children to learn from each other. Hearing other (and often conflicting) views can help to break down egocentrism. Peer interaction has both a *cognitive* and a *social value*. As a result, small-group activity is as important as individual work.
- Teachers are the guides in children's process of discovery, and the curriculum should be adapted to each child's individual needs and intellectual level (Smith *et al.*, 1998).

Vygotsky's theory

Vygotsky outlined a major alternative to Piaget's theory, which was published in the former Soviet Union in the 1920s and 30s, but not translated into English until the early 1960s (Vygotsky, 1962).

Internalisation and the social nature of thinking

As we noted in the *Introduction and overview*, Vygotsky believed that a child's cognitive development doesn't occur in a social vacuum. The ability to think and reason by and for ourselves (*inner speech* or *verbal thought*: see Chapter 18) is the result of a fundamentally *social* process. At birth, we're social beings capable of interacting with others, but able to do little either practically or intellectually, by or for ourselves. Gradually, however, we move towards self-sufficiency and independence, and by participating in social activities, our abilities become transformed. For Vygotsky, cognitive development involves an active *internalisation* of problem-solving processes that takes place as a result of *mutual interaction* between children and those with whom they have regular social contact (initially the parents, but later friends and classmates).

This is the reverse of how Piaget (at least initially) saw things. Piaget's idea of 'the child as a *scientist*' is replaced by the idea of 'the child as an *apprentice*', who acquires the culture's knowledge and skills through graded collaboration with those who already possess them (Rogoff, 1990). According to Vygotsky (1981):

'Any function in the child's cultural development appears twice, or on two planes. First it appears on the social plane, and then on the psychological plane'.

Scaffolding and the zone of proximal development

Scaffolding refers to the role played by parents, teachers and others by which children acquire their knowledge and skills (Wood *et al.*, 1976). As a task becomes more familiar to the child and more within its competence, so those who provide the scaffold leave more and more for the child to do until it can perform the task successfully. In this way, the developing thinker doesn't have to create cognition 'from scratch': there are others available who've already 'served' their own apprenticeship.

The internalised cognitive skills remain social in two senses. First, as mature learners we can 'scaffold' ourselves through difficult tasks (self-instruction), as others once scaffolded our earlier attempts. Second, the only skills practised to a high level of competence for most people are those offered by their culture: cognitive potential may be universal, but cognitive expertise is culturally determined (Meadows, 1995).

Since the 1980s, research has stressed the role of social interaction in language development, especially the facilitating effects of the use of child-contingent language by adults talking with children (Meadows, 1995: see Chapter 19). This 'fit' between adult and child language closely resembles the concept of 'scaffolding'.

KEY STUDY 34.4

Scaffolding (or individual abilities are built on social support) (Wood *et al.*, 1976)

Wood *et al.* found that on a construction task with four- and five-year-olds, different mothers used instructional strategies of varying levels of specificity. These ranged from general verbal encouragement to direct demonstration of a relevant action. No single strategy guaranteed learning, but the most efficient maternal instructors were those who combined general and specific interventions according to the child's progress.

The most useful help is that which adapts itself to the learner's successes and failures (Bruner, 1983). An example would be using a general instruction initially until the child runs into difficulties. At this point, a more specific instruction or demonstration is given. This style allows the child considerable autonomy, but also provides carefully planned guidance at the boundaries of its abilities (Vygotsky's *zone of proximal development* or ZPD).

As would be predicted from Vygotsky's theory, there's also evidence of scaffolding processes in everyday, naturalistic contexts. These are often linked to the transmission across generations of culturally valued skills, such as weaving among the Zinacauteco Mexicans and American mothers' involvement in their preschoolers' development of number (Durkin, 1995).

The zone of proximal development defines those functions that haven't yet matured but are in the process of maturing (Vygotsky, 1978). These could be called the 'buds' or 'flowers' rather than the 'fruits' of development. The actual developmental level characterises mental development *retrospectively*, while the ZPD characterises mental development *prospectively*.

An evaluation of Vygotsky's theory

Vygotsky's theory clearly 'compensates' for one of the central limitations of Piaget's theory. As Segall *et al.* (1999) put it:

'Piaget produced a theory of the development of an "epistemic subject", an idealised, non-existent individual, completely divorced from the social environment.'

For Vygotsky, culture (and especially language) plays a key role in cognitive development: the development of the individual cannot be understood – and indeed cannot happen – outside the context of social interaction.

While Vygotsky's theory hasn't been tested cross-culturally as Piaget's has, it has influenced cross-cultural psychology through the development of *cultural psychology* (e.g. Cole, 1990: see Chapter 47) and related approaches, such as 'socially shared cognition' (Resnick *et al.*, 1991) and 'distributed cognition' (Salomon, 1993). According to all these approaches:

> '... cognitive processes are not seen as exclusively individual central processors, but ... are situation specific ... therefore cognition is not necessarily situated "within the head" but is shared among people and settings ...'. (Segall *et al.*, 1999)

Applying Vygotsky's theory to education

Vygotsky defines intelligence as the capacity to learn from instruction. Rather than teachers playing an enabling role, Vygotsky believes they should guide pupils in paying attention, concentrating and learning effectively (a *didactic* role: Sutherland, 1992). By doing this, teachers scaffold children to competence.

The introduction of the National Curriculum and national testing at various ages has returned Britain to the 'teacher-centred' or 'traditional' approach to young children's education. While this approach was dominant up to the 1960s, it was 'revolutionised' by the Piagetian-influenced 'child-centred' or 'progressive' approach. However, Sutherland (1992) insists that Vygotsky didn't:

> '... advocate mechanical formal teaching where children go through the motions of sitting at desks and passing exams that are meaningless to them ... On the contrary, Vygotsky stressed intellectual development rather than procedural learning'.

Vygotsky rejected any approach advocating that teachers have rigid control over children's learning. Rather, as with Piaget, teachers' control over children's activities is what counts. Teachers extend and challenge children to go beyond where they would otherwise have been.

Box 34.8 Applying the concept of the ZPD to education

Suppose a child is currently functioning at level 'x' in terms of attainment. Through innate/environmental means, the child has the potential to reach level 'x + 1'.

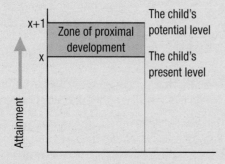

Figure 34.8 *Vygotsky's zone of proximal development*

The area between 'x' and 'x + 1' is the child's ZPD. The ZPD may be different for individual children, and children with large ZPDs will have a greater capacity to be helped than those with small ZPDs. Irrespective of the ZPD's size, Vygotsky saw the teacher as being responsible for giving children the cues they need or taking them through a series of steps towards the solution of a problem.

(Based on Sutherland, 1992)

Vygotsky also believed in *collaborative learning*. As well as being helped by teachers, more advanced children are important in helping less advanced children. Educators now believe that group learning and peer tutoring can offer an effective environment for guiding a child through its ZPD. This may be because these settings encourage children to use language, provide explanations, and work co-operatively or competitively, all of which help produce cognitive change (Pine, 1999).

Bruner's theory

Similarities and differences between Bruner, Piaget and Vygotsky

Bruner has helped to extend Vygotsky's ideas, and to apply them in the context of education (for example, the concept of scaffolding). Bruner has also been influenced by Piaget, and they share certain basic beliefs, in particular that:

- children's underlying cognitive structures mature over time, so that they can think about and organise their world in an increasingly complex way;
- children are actively curious and explorative, capable of adapting to their environment through interacting with it. Abstract thinking grows out of action: competence in any area of knowledge is rooted in active experience and concrete mental operations.

However, there are also some basic areas of disagreement between Bruner and Piaget, stemming from Vygotsky's influence. In particular, Bruner stresses the role of language and interpersonal communication, and the need for active involvement by expert adults (or more knowledgeable peers) in helping the child to develop as a thinker and problem-solver. Language plays a crucial part in the scaffolding process. He also sees instruction as an essential part of the learning process, both in naturalistic and educational settings.

Modes of representation

Unlike Piaget, Bruner (1966) doesn't identify stages of development as such. Instead, he describes three modes of representing the world, different forms that our knowledge and understanding can take. He isn't, therefore, concerned exclusively with cognitive growth but also with knowledge in general. The three modes are the *enactive*, *iconic* and *symbolic*, which develop in that order.

The enactive mode

At first, babies represent the world through *actions*. Any knowledge they have is based upon what they've experienced through their own behaviour (this corresponds to Piaget's *sensorimotor stage*). Past events are represented through appropriate motor responses. Many of our motor schemas, such as 'bicycle riding, tying knots, aspects of driving, get represented in our muscles, so to speak', and even when we have the use of language, it's often extremely difficult to describe in words how we do certain things.

Ask yourself ...
- Try describing how to tie a shoelace.

Through recurrent events and environmental conditions, we build up virtually automatic patterns of motor activity which we 'run off' as units in the appropriate situation. Like Piaget, Bruner sees the onset of *object permanence* as a major *qualitative* change in the young child's cognitive development.

The iconic mode

An icon is an *image*, so this form of representation involves building up mental images of things we've experienced. Such images are normally composite, that is, made up of a number of past encounters with similar objects or situations.

Ask yourself ...
- To which stage(s) of Piaget's theory does the iconic mode correspond?

This mode corresponds to the last six months of the sensorimotor stage (where schemas become interiorised) and the whole of the *pre-operational stage*, where the child is at the mercy of what it perceives in drawing intuitive conclusions about the nature of reality: things are as they *look*.

The symbolic mode

Bruner's main interest was in the transition from the iconic to the symbolic mode. He and Piaget agree that a very important cognitive change occurs at around six to seven years. For Piaget, this is the start of *logical operations* (albeit tied to concrete reality), while Bruner sees it as the appearance of the *symbolic mode*. Language comes into its own as an influence on thought. The child is now freed from the immediate context and is beginning to be able to 'go beyond the information given' (Bruner, 1957: see Chapter 15).

KEY STUDY 34.5

The transition from iconic to symbolic modes (Bruner & Kenney, 1966)

Bruner and Kenney arranged nine plastic glasses in a three by three matrix (as shown in Figure 34.9, page 502). Three- to seven-year-olds were familiarised with the matrix. The glasses were then scrambled, and the children were asked to put them back as they were before (the *reproduction task*). In the *transposition task*, the glasses were removed from the matrix, and the glass which had been in the bottom right-hand square was placed in the bottom left-hand square; the child had to rebuild the matrix in this transposed manner.

Ask yourself ...
- Which task would you expect children to find easier – and why?

Children generally could reproduce it earlier than they could transpose it. The reproduction task involves the iconic mode (60 per cent of the five-year-olds could do this, 72 per cent of the six-year-olds, and 80 per cent of the seven-year-olds). But the transposition task involves the symbolic mode (the results were nil, 27 per cent and 79 per cent, respectively). Clearly, the five-year-olds were dominated by the visual image of the original matrix, while the six-to-seven-year-olds translated their visual information into the symbolic mode. They relied upon verbal rules to guide them, such as, 'It gets fatter going one way and taller going the other'. So, a child using images but not symbols can reproduce but not restructure.

Applying Bruner's theory to education

The 'spiral curriculum'

Bruner's modes of representation lie at the heart of the 'spiral curriculum', according to which the principles of a subject come to be understood at increasingly more complex levels of difficulty. Like Vygotsky, Bruner was unhappy with Piaget's concept of 'readiness', and proposed a much more active policy of intervention, based on the belief that 'any subject can be taught effectively in some intellectually honest form to any child at any stage of development' (1966).

Educators need to provide learners with the means of grasping the structure of a discipline, that is, the underlying principles and concepts (rather than just mastering factual information). This enables learners to go beyond the information given, and develop ideas of their own. Teachers also need to encourage learners to make links, and to understand the relationships within and between subjects (Smith *et al.*, 1998).

Information-processing theories

According to Bee (2000), it's more accurate to talk of the information-processing (IP) *approach* than a distinct IP theory of cognitive development. This approach grew out of, and in some ways represents a reaction to, Piaget's theory (Pine, 1999). Like Piaget, IP theorists believe there are psychological structures in people's minds that explain their behaviour, and which are essentially independent of the individual's social relationships, social practices and cultural environment (Meadows, 1995).

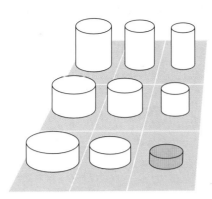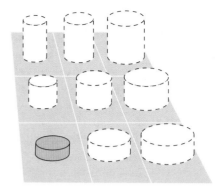

Figure 34.9 *The two arrangements of glasses used by Bruner & Kenney (1966)*

Box 34.9 How different are Piaget's and the IP approaches?

IP theorists can explain cognitive development (the child makes better and more efficient use of basic cognitive processes) *without* having to assume any global reorganisation of the cognitive system (*qualitatively different stages*) as proposed by Piaget. For example, based on research using Piagetian-type tasks, Siegler (1976) claims that what changes as children develop is their acquisition of increasingly complex rules for problem-solving.

Consistent with Piaget's theory, Siegler's research suggests that there's a sequence in children's acquisition of new strategies, but this is still very different from identifying developmental stages. Nevertheless, we shouldn't assume that a child either has or doesn't have a particular strategy in its repertoire at any time. When learning a new strategy in maths, for example, a child may forget to use it all the time, or fail to see that it can be applied to new problems. One important developmental change is knowing where and when to use new strategies (Siegler, 1989). This is related to *metacognition* (see text below).

According to Bee (2000), some of the changes Piaget attributed to new mental structures can be more simply explained in terms of increased experience with tasks and problems, and faster and more efficient processing of information (all *quantitative changes*). At the same time:

'There also seems to be a real qualitative change in the complexity, generalisability, and flexibility of strategies used by the child'.

Box 34.10 Task analysis

To understand why children cannot solve problems that adults can, we need to understand a particular task's component steps (Oakhill, 1984). For example, five elements are necessary to solve the following problem: 'If Ann is not as bad as Betty, and Betty is not as bad as Carole, who is the best?':

1 The child must perceive and encode the important statements (premisses) contained in the question, which involves attending to it (see Chapter 13).
2 The premisses must be stored in working memory (WM: see Chapter 17).
3 They must be combined in memory to form an integrated representation.
4 The question must be encoded.
5 The representation of the premisses must be scanned to answer the question or formulate a conclusion about it.

Underlying the IP approach is the *computer analogy* (see Chapters 2, 17 and 20). This examines more closely than Piaget's theory how major cognitive processes, such as memory and attention, come into play when children deal with particular tasks and problems (Pine, 1999). To understand cognitive development, we need to discover whether the basic capacity of the system, or the programs, change in any systematic way with age (Bee, 2000). One key assumption is that as children grow, they develop better strategies for remembering and organising knowledge, and for encoding more aspects of a problem. To study the claim that children become better information-processors as they develop, IP theorists use *task analysis*.

IP theorists argue that children fail to solve such problems correctly because of errors in encoding the problem, being unable to hold information in memory for long enough, or because holding it in memory may interfere with other task performance (Trabasso, 1977).

Keeney *et al.* (1967) gave children of different ages a series of pictures to remember. Before being tested on recall, most eight- to ten-year-olds could be seen mouthing the picture series (*rehearsal*), while the five-year-olds didn't do this. Although the younger children recalled far fewer items than the older children, they could be taught the rehearsal strategy and then performed as well as the older children. So, their memory was just as good, but they didn't use it as efficiently as the older children.

A large amount of research has found that as children grow they acquire more and more powerful strategies for remembering, use them more efficiently and flexibly, and apply them to an increasing variety of problems. Also, school-age children are capable of applying a wider range of different strategies to the *same* problem, so that if the first attempt fails, a back-up or alternative strategy can be used (Bee, 2000; Pine, 1999).

Metacognition

One form of new strategy (new 'software') is the child's increasing awareness of its own mental processes (*metacognition*). This is part of a larger category of *executive processes* (planning what to do and considering alternative strategies). It may be precisely such metacognitive/executive skills that gradually emerge with age. Performance on a whole range of tasks will be better if the child can monitor its own performance, and recognise when a particular strategy is required or not. This self-monitoring improves fairly rapidly, beginning at school age (Bee, 2000).

According to Pascual-Leone (1980) and Case (1985), children don't use just one cognitive strategy in solving Piagetian tasks (as Piaget believed), but several, the number required being correlated with a problem's difficulty. Like Oakhill (1984), Pascual-Leone and Case also see WM as storing the information necessary to solve problems. The amount of memory space necessary is also correlated with the problem's complexity and, as the child develops, so available memory space increases. Pascual-Leone and Case also believe that certain strategies become automatic with practice, and so require less space in memory (see Chapter 17). An adult, for example, would instantly 'see' that (10 + 6) – (10 + 6) equals zero. A child, however, would require time to solve this problem, since each component must be stored in memory before a solution can be reached.

Applying IP theories to education

One strength of the IP approach is its emphasis on memory, and young children's limited capacity to process information. As well as memory's importance in the child's ability to operate effectively, knowledge also has a considerable influence on learning, and the more children know about a situation, the more successfully they'll deal with it. As Sutherland (1992) has noted:

> *'One of the teacher's main roles is to help children find strategies for reducing their memory load – for instance to write down a list of the facts they need to solve a maths problem'.*

While young children can add numbers together when two digits are involved (e.g. 22 + 56), they make errors when three digits are used (Van Lehn, 1983). For example, faced with the problem:

231 +
42

young children tend to either ignore the third column and arrive at 73 as the answer, or muddle up the hundreds and tens columns to produce 673. Van Lehn uses the term *repair* to refer to the process by which addition involving three digits can be successfully achieved. This process implies a teacher-led approach to teaching mathematics. However, IP theories also see metacognition (see above) as playing a vital role. In the case of learning to read, the child needs to be aware of which words it knows and doesn't know, which sentences it understands and doesn't understand, and how to get the information it needs. A variety of research shows that younger and poorer readers are less skilled at all these metacognitive tasks compared with older and better readers (Flavell *et al.*, 1993: see Chapter 40).

Conclusions

Piaget's theory revolutionised the way that cognitive development has been investigated and understood. Both Vygotsky's theory and the information-processing approach disagree with some of Piaget's basic assumptions, but they adopt radically different views from each other as to what cognitive development involves. While Vygotsky emphasises the social nature of cognitive change, both Piaget and the information-processing approach see development as occurring quite *independently* of social interaction. Bruner's theory reflects the influence of both Piaget and Vygotsky. All four theories have contributed to our understanding of the education of young children.

CHAPTER SUMMARY

- Piaget sees intelligence as **adaptation to the environment**, and he was interested in how intelligence changes as children grow (**genetic epistemology**). Younger children's intelligence is **qualitatively different** from that of older children.

- Cognitive development occurs through the interaction between innate capacities and environmental events. It progresses through a series of **hierarchical**, **invariant** and **universal stages**: the **sensorimotor**, **pre-operational**, **concrete operational** and **formal operational** stages.

- Underlying cognitive changes are **functional invariants**, the most important being **assimilation**, **accommodation** (which together constitute **adaptation**) and **equilibration**. The major cognitive structures that change are **schemas/schemata**.

- During the **sensorimotor stage**, frequent interaction with objects ultimately leads to **object permanence**, which is fully developed when the child can **infer invisible displacements**.

- By the end of the sensorimotor stage, schemas are now '**interiorised**'. **Representational/make-believe play**, like **deferred imitation**, reflects the **general symbolic function**.

- **Pre-operational children** have difficulty in **seriation tasks** and also display **syncretic thought**, **transductive reasoning** and **animism**. **Centration** is illustrated by the **inability to conserve**. Pre-operational children are also **egocentric**.

- During the **concrete operational stage**, logical operations can be performed only in the presence of actual or observable objects. Some types of conservation appear before others (**horizontal décalage**), and a child who's mastered all kinds of classification but not all kinds of conservation displays **vertical décalage**.

- **Formal operational thinkers** can manipulate **ideas** and **propositions** ('second order' operations) and think **hypothetically**.

- Four- and five-year-olds are capable of **perspective-taking**, enabling them to attribute **false beliefs** to other people. This is a crucial feature of the child's **theory of mind**.

■ While basic cognitive processes may be **universal**, how these are brought to bear on specific contents is influenced by culture.

■ Central to Piagetian views of the educational process is **active self-discovery/discovery learning**. Teachers assess each individual child's current stage of cognitive development to set intrinsically motivating tasks, and provide learning opportunities that create disequilibrium.

■ According to Vygotsky, the initially helpless baby actively **internalises** problem-solving processes through **interaction with parents**. Vygotsky's **child apprentice** acquires cultural knowledge and skills through **graded collaboration** with those who already possess them (**scaffolding**).

■ The most useful assistance a mother can give her child with task performance is to use general instruction initially until the child experiences difficulties, then give more specific instruction. This relates to Vygotsky's **zone of proximal development** (ZPD).

■ For Vygotsky, intelligence is the capacity to learn from instruction. Teachers occupy a **didactic role**, guiding pupils in paying attention, concentrating and learning effectively. In this way, children are scaffolded.

■ Bruner shared Piaget's belief that abstract thinking grows out of **action**. He was also influenced by Vygotsky's ideas and stressed the role of language in the scaffolding process, and the need for the active involvement of more expert others.

■ Bruner identifies three **modes of representation**, the **enactive**, **iconic** and **symbolic**. He stressed the transition from iconic to symbolic at ages six to seven, seeing logical thought as dependent on language. This implies that language training can speed up cognitive development.

■ **Information-processing** (IP) **theories** are based on the **computer analogy**. **Task analysis** is used to study the development of children's 'mental programs' and strategies for processing information.

■ While children appear to acquire new strategies in a particular sequence, this is not equivalent to a Piagetian stage.

Nevertheless, children can be inconsistent when using new strategies. Improvement with age is related to improved monitoring of performance (part of **metacognition**).

■ Emphasis on **memory** and young children's **limited IP capacity** can explain why they're poorer at tasks involving memorising and reading. Storing knowledge linguistically is a vital prerequisite of successful IP performance. Teachers have a crucial role to play in helping children to find strategies for reducing memory load.

Self-assessment questions

1 a Describe Piaget's theory of cognitive development.
   b Assess the extent to which this theory is supported by research evidence.
2 Critically consider practical applications of **two** theories of cognitive development.
3 Discuss the role of social **and/or** cultural influences on cognitive development.

Web addresses

http://129.7160.115/inst5931/piagetl.html

http://www.funderstanding.com/learningtheoryhow3.html

http://gwu.edu/~yip/piaget.html

http://www.uiademo.hum/h0146.htm

http://nces.ed.gov

Further reading

Meadows, S. (1993) *The Child as Thinker*. London: Routledge. An extremely thorough review of theory and research, including physical and social influences on children's cognition, individual differences and applied areas, such as reading and writing.

Piaget, J. (1973) *The Child's Conception of the World*. London: Paladin. This provides a good insight into Piaget's whole approach to the study of cognitive development, including the clinical method as an investigative tool.

Chapter 35

Moral Development

Introduction and overview

At birth, we're *amoral*, lacking any system of personal values and judgements about right and wrong. By adulthood, though, most of us possess morality. Psychologists aren't interested in morality as such, but in the *process* by which it's acquired. The nature of that process is seen very differently by different psychological theories, which attempt to answer quite different questions.

According to Haste *et al.* (1998), historically four main questions have been asked about moral development.

■ How do conscience and guilt develop, acting as sanctions on our misdeeds? This relates to Freud's *psychoanalytic theory*.

■ How do we come to understand the basis of rules and moral principles, so that we can make judgements about our own and others' behaviour? This relates to the *cognitive–developmental theories* of Piaget, Kohlberg, and Eisenberg.

■ How do we learn the appropriate patterns of behaviour required by our culture? This relates to learning theories, including Bandura's *social learning theory*.

■ How do we develop the moral emotions that motivate our concern for others? Eisenberg's theory is also relevant here.

The relationship between morality and human nature has been debated by philosophers for thousands of years. According to Rousseau (1762), humans are 'naturally' good, but this natural goodness may be constrained and distorted by external factors. Only *sociobiologists* (such as Wilson, 1975: see Chapter 2) among modern-day scientists agree with this view of morality as innate. While we may like to believe that our actions are governed by higher moral principles, the reality is that 'The genes hold culture on a leash' (Wilson: see Chapter 30).

In contradiction of Wilson's claims, all the major theories to be discussed in this chapter share the assumption that the acquisition of morality is part of the wider process of *socialisation*. In other words, morality develops according to the same principles which govern the development of other aspects of socialised behaviour (see Chapter 2).

Freud's psychoanalytic theory

Freud's account of moral development is closely related to other aspects of his psychoanalytic theory, in particular the *structure of the personality* and the *stages of psychosexual development*.

The psychic apparatus

Freud believed that the personality (or psychic apparatus) comprises three parts, the id, ego and superego (see Figure 35.1). The *id*:

> '… contains everything that is inherited, that is present at birth, that is laid down in the constitution – above all, therefore, the instincts'. (Freud, 1923)

The wishes and impulses arising from the body's needs build up a pressure or tension (*excitation*), which demands immediate release or satisfaction. Since the id's sole aim is to reduce excitation to a minimum, it's said to be governed by the *pleasure principle*. It is – and remains – the infantile, presocialised part of the personality. The two major id instincts are sexuality and aggression (see Chapter 29).

The *ego* is:

> '… that part of the id which has been modified by the direct influence of the external world'. (Freud, 1923)

It can be thought of as the 'executive' of the personality, the planning, decision-making, rational and logical part of us. It enables us to distinguish between a wish and reality (which the id cannot do), and is governed by the *reality principle*. While the id demands immediate gratification of our needs and impulses, the ego will postpone satisfaction until the appropriate time and place (*deferred gratification*):

> 'The ego seeks to bring the influence of the external world to bear upon the id and its tendencies … For the ego, perception plays the part which in the id falls to instinct. The ego represents … reason and common sense, in contrast to the id, which contains the passions'. (Freud, 1923)

Not until the *superego* has developed can we be described as moral beings. It represents the *internalisation* of parental and social moral values:

> 'It observes the ego, gives it orders, judges it and threatens it with punishment, exactly like the parents whose place it has taken'. (Freud, 1933)

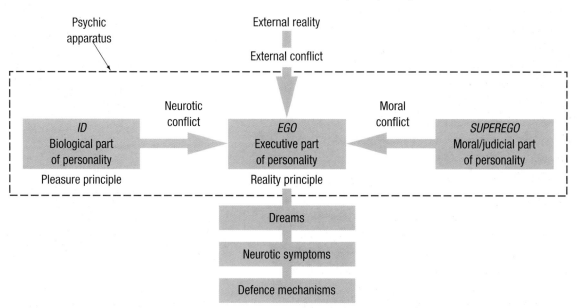

Figure 35.1 *The psychic apparatus, showing sources of conflict and ways of resolving it*

It is in fact the *conscience* which threatens the ego with punishment (in the form of guilt) for bad behaviour, while the *ego-ideal* promises the ego rewards (in the form of pride and high self-esteem) for good behaviour. These correspond to the *punishing* and *rewarding* parents respectively.

Psychosexual development

Although the id, ego and superego develop within the individual in that order, this isn't strictly part of Freud's developmental theory. According to his theory of *infantile sexuality*, sexuality isn't confined to physically mature adults, but is evident from the moment of birth. So, babies and young children have sexual experiences and are capable of sexual pleasure, which is derived from the rhythmical stroking or stimulation of any part of the body. However, different parts of the body (the *erogenous zones*) are particularly sensitive at different times during infancy and childhood, and become the focus of sexual pleasure (and frustration).

While the sequence of these *psychosexual stages* is determined by *maturation* (it's biologically programmed), what's crucial is how a child is treated by others, especially the parents. Either excessive gratification or extreme frustration can result in an individual getting emotionally 'stuck' (*fixated*) at the particular stage at which this occurs, producing associated *adult personality traits*. For example, an *anal expulsive* trait is orderliness (a preoccupation with punctuality, routine, and everything being in its proper place), while *anal retentive* traits include parsimony (miserliness) and obstinacy. In this way, Freud was able to explain how individual differences arise from common developmental patterns (see Chapter 42).

Box 35.1 Freud's stages of psychosexual development

- **Oral stage (0–1 year):** The nerve-endings in the mouth and lips are highly sensitive, and the baby derives pleasure from sucking for its own sake (*non-nutritive sucking*). In the earlier *incorporative substage*, the major oral activities are sucking, swallowing and mouthing. In the later *biting/aggressive substage*, hardening gums and erupting teeth make biting and chewing sources of pleasure.
- **Anal stage (1–3 years):** The anal cavity and sphincter muscles of the bowel are now the main sources of pleasure. In the earlier *expulsion substage*, the child undergoes potty-training and so has its first encounter with external restrictions on its wish to defecate where and when it pleases. Parental love is no longer unconditional, but now depends on what the child does. In the later *retention substage*, parents come to be seen for the first time as authority figures:

  'By producing them [the contents of the bowels] ... [the infant] can express his active compliance with his environment, and by withholding them, his disobedience'. (Freud, 1905)

- **Phallic stage (3-5/6 years):** Sensitivity is now concentrated in the genitals, and masturbation (in both sexes) becomes a new source of pleasure. The child becomes aware of anatomical sex differences (*'phallic'* comes from the Greek word *phallus* meaning penis), which marks the beginning of the *Oedipus complex*. The name derives from the classical Greek tragedy *Oedipus Rex*, in which Oedipus kills his father and marries his mother. Both boys and girls experience conflicting emotions in relation to their same-

and opposite-sex parents, and how successfully these conflicts are resolved is crucial for future personality development. It's through the resolution of the Oedipus complex that a child's superego and sex role are acquired.

- **Latency period (5/6 to puberty):** The sexual preoccupations of the earlier years are repressed, which allows the child's energies to be channelled into developing new skills and acquiring new knowledge. In relative terms, the balance between the id, ego and superego is greater than at any other time in the child's life.
- **Genital stage (puberty–maturity):** Latency represents the calm before the storm of puberty, which marks the beginning of adolescence. The relative harmony within the child's personality is disrupted by the id's powerful new demands in the form of heterosexual desires (see Chapter 37).

The Oedipus complex, identification and the superego

A boy, like a girl, takes his mother as his first love-object (see Chapter 32). Starting at about three, a boy's love for his mother becomes increasingly passionate, and he doesn't wish to share her with anyone. The boy is also jealous of his father, who already 'possesses' her, and wants him out of the way ('dead'), so that he can have his mother all to himself. However, his father is bigger and more powerful than he is, and he eventually becomes afraid that his father will punish him by cutting off his penis (*fear of castration/castration anxiety*). He reaches this conclusion partly as a result of previous punishments for masturbation, and partly based on his observation that females don't have a penis.

To resolve the dilemma, the boy *represses* (makes unconscious) his desire for his mother and his hostile feelings for his father, and *identifies* with his father (he comes to act, think and feel as if he were his father). Through this *identification with the aggressor*, a boy acquires the superego and the male sex role (see Chapter 36).

Norman Bates (Anthony Perkins), the main character in Hitchcock's Psycho, *identifies very strongly with his dead mother. He attempts, unconsciously, to 'keep her alive' by, for example, dressing up in her clothes*

As for the girl, her Oedipus complex (sometimes referred to as the *Electra complex*) begins with the belief that she's already been castrated. She blames her mother for her lack of a penis, and experiences *penis envy* (she wants what males have). But she eventually realises that this is unrealistic, and substitutes the wish for a penis with the wish for a baby. This causes her to turn to her father as a love-object, in the hope that he'll provide her with a (preferably male) baby.

In order to identify with the mother, the girl must give up her father as a love-object and move back to her mother (while boys only have to make one 'move', from the mother to the father). However, Freud was much less sure about *why* the girl identifies with the mother than he was about the boy's motive for identifying with the father. The stronger the motive, the stronger (or more complete) the identification, which in turn makes for a stronger superego. So, boys' fear of castration is associated with a strong identification with the father (the 'aggressor') and a strong superego. As Freud (1924) says:

'The fear of castration being thus excluded in a little girl, a powerful motive also drops out for the setting up of a superego'.

One suggestion Freud made was that the girl may fear loss of the mother's love. To keep the mother 'alive' inside her, she internalises her, becoming the 'good' child that her mother would want her to be (*anaclitic identification*). But what he was quite sure about was that identification with the mother is less complete. The girl's love for her father doesn't have to be as thoroughly abandoned as the boy's for his mother, and her Oedipus complex doesn't have to be so completely shattered (Mitchell, 1974). Consequently, females a have weaker superego and their identity as separate, independent persons is also less well developed.

Ask yourself ...

• Do you agree with Freud regarding females' moral inferiority?

CRITICAL DISCUSSION 35.1

Are females morally and sexually inferior to males?
Because her identification with the mother is less complete, the girl relies more on external authority figures throughout her childhood, and has to be more compliant, and less 'naughty' (there's no equivalent of 'boys will be boys'). It's through his strong identification with the father that the boy achieves independence, which the girl will have to try to achieve in adolescence. According to Mitchell (1974):

'Many women, though nominally they leave home, understandably, never make it'.

But there's little evidence to support this view. For example, Hoffman (1975) reviewed several studies in which children were left alone and tempted to violate a prohibition (such as looking round to see a toy placed on a table behind them). There were usually no overall gender differences, but, if anything, girls were *better* able to resist temptation than boys were.

As we noted earlier, Freud saw women as having to make do with babies as penis-substitutes, a view that has aroused fierce criticism, particularly from feminist psychologists (see Chapter 47). For example, Horney (1924) and Thompson (1943), both eminent psychoanalysts, argued that what girls (and women) envy isn't the penis as such, but males' superior social status (the penis is a *symbol* for male privilege). Moreover, it's men, not women, who equate lack of a penis with inferiority!

An evaluation of the Oedipus complex

Critical Discussion 35.1 has considered some of the criticisms of Freud's account of sex differences in morality which follows from his theory of the Oedipus complex ('the central phenomenon of the sexual period of early childhood': Freud, 1924). Another criticism concerns its potential *cultural bias*. Freud assumed that the Oedipus complex was a universal phenomenon, but even if true for Western cultures, the Oedipus complex may not apply to every culture or to all historical periods (Segall *et al.*, 1990).

CROSS-CULTURAL STUDY 35.1

Trobriand Island boys and their fathers (Malinowski, 1929)
Among the Trobriand Islanders of Papua, New Guinea, boys were traditionally disciplined by their maternal uncle (their mother's brother), rather than by their own biological father. It was an uncle's role to guide his nephew through to adulthood. Such societies are described as *avuncular*. However, the father remained the mother's lover. Hence, the two roles (disciplinarian and mother's lover) were adopted by *different* men, whereas in Viennese society at the time that Freud was proposing his theories, the boy's father played *both* roles.

As Segall *et al.* (1990) point out, by explaining the boy's hostility towards the father wholly in terms of sexual jealousy, Freud overlooked the possibility that he resented his father's power over him. What Malinowski found was that a Trobriand Island boy's relationship with his father was very good, free of the love–hate ambivalence which is central to Freud's Oedipal theory. By comparison, the relationship with the uncle *wasn't* usually so good.

However, this doesn't necessarily mean that Malinowski was right and Freud was wrong (Price & Crapo, 1999). Segall *et al.* (1990) suggest that more societies need to be examined, including both Western and avuncular.

Freud (1909) cited his case study of 'Little Hans' as supporting his Oedipal theory. This five-year-old developed a phobia of being bitten by a horse, which Freud interpreted as a fear of castration (see Chapter 44). A common criticism made of Freud's developmental theory as a whole is that it was based largely on the study of his adult patients. This makes the case of Little Hans especially important, because he was Freud's only child patient.

Freud saw Hans as a 'little Oedipus', having formulated his theory four years earlier (in *Three Essays on the Theory of Sexuality*, 1905). Hence, the case study is biased and provides no *independent* evidence to support Freud. In addition, Hans's therapy was conducted mainly by his own father, a supporter of Freud's ideas! Even more seriously, perhaps, other psychoanalytic theorists have provided alternative explanations of Hans's fear of horses, including Bowlby (1973) who reinterpreted the case in terms of attachment theory (see Chapter 32, and Gross, 1999).

Ask yourself ...

- What kind of independent evidence might be considered valid?
- Why is it a problem that Hans's therapy was conducted by his own father?
- How do you think Bowlby might have reinterpreted Hans's fear of horses?

Bee (2000) maintains that attachment research provides a good deal of support for the basic psychoanalytic hypothesis that the quality of the child's earliest relationships affects the whole course of later development. Both Bowlby (1973) and Erikson (1963: see Chapter 37) regard early relationships as *prototypes* of later relationships. Despite the considerable evidence showing that all types of early privation are reversible (see Chapter 32), and accepting all the criticisms of the Oedipal theory, belief in the impact of early experience is a lasting legacy of Freud's developmental theory.

Cognitive–developmental theories

According to Haste *et al.* (1998), the question regarding moral rules, principles and judgements (see *Introduction and overview*) has dominated research on moral development for 30 years, through work within the cognitive–developmental theoretical framework. While Kohlberg's theory has been the focus of research during this time, Piaget (1932) pioneered this approach to moral development. Cognitive–developmental theories maintain that it's the reasons *underlying* behaviour, rather than the behaviour itself, which make it right or wrong.

Piaget's theory

Piaget argued that morality develops gradually during childhood and adolescence. While these changes are usually referred to as qualitatively different stages of moral development, Piaget explicitly *didn't* use the concept of developmental stages in relation to moral development. Rather, he differentiated two *types of moral orientation*, namely *heteronomous* and *autonomous* (see Box 35.3, page 510). Instead of seeing morality as a form of cognition, Piaget discussed morality in the context of affects and feelings (Eckensberger, 1999).

Understanding rules

To discover how moral knowledge and understanding change with age, Piaget began by looking at children's ideas about the rules of the game of marbles. He believed that the essence of morality lies in rules, and that marbles is a game

in which children create and enforce their own rules free from adult influence. Piaget felt that in this way he could discover how children's moral knowledge in general develops. As he noted:

> 'Children's games constitute the most admirable social institutions. The game of marbles, for instance, as played by boys, contains an extremely complex system of rules ... that is to say, a code of laws, a jurisprudence of its own ... All morality consists in a system of rules'.

Pretending he didn't know the rules, Piaget asked children to explain them to him and, during the course of a game, to tell him who made the rules, where they came from, and whether they could be changed. He found that children aged between five and nine or ten tended to believe that the rules had always existed in their present form, and that they'd been created by older children, adults or even God. The rules were sacred, and couldn't be changed in any way (an *external law*). Nevertheless, children unashamedly broke them to suit themselves, and saw nothing contradictory in the idea of both players winning the game.

Children aged ten and above understood that the rules were invented by children themselves and could be changed, but only if all players agreed. The function of rules was to prevent quarrelling and ensure fair play. They adhered rigidly to the rules, and discussed the finer points and implications of any changes. Piaget called this moral orientation towards co-operation with peers *mutual respect*, which he distinguished from the *unilateral respect* shown by younger children towards adult authority.

According to Piaget, the rules of marbles could be used to study morality, since all morality consists of a system of rules

Moral judgement and punishment

Piaget also told children pairs of stories about (hypothetical) children who'd told lies, stolen or broken something.

Box 35.2   Examples of pairs of stories used by Piaget

Example 1a: A little boy called John was in his room. He was called to dinner and went into the dining room. Behind the door there was a chair and on the chair there was a tray with 15 cups on it. John couldn't have known that the chair was behind the door, and as he entered the dining room, the door knocked against the tray and the tray fell on the floor, breaking all of the cups.

Example 1b: One day, a little boy called Henry tried to get some jam out of a cupboard when his mother was out. He climbed onto a chair and stretched out his arm. The jam was too high up, and he couldn't reach it. But while he was trying to get it, he knocked over a cup. The cup fell down and broke.

Example 2a: A little girl called Marie wanted to give her mother a nice surprise and so she cut out a piece of sewing for her. But she didn't know how to use the scissors properly and she cut a big hole in her dress.

Example 2b: A little girl called Margaret went and took her mother's scissors one day when her mother was out. She played with them for a bit and then, as she didn't know how to use them properly, she made a hole in her dress.

Ask yourself ...

- Who do you think five- to nine- or ten-year-olds and children over ten judged to be the naughtier? Why?

Piaget asked children who they believed was the naughtier and should therefore be punished more. He was more interested in the *reasons* the children gave for their answers than the answers themselves. While five- to nine- or ten-year-olds could distinguish an intentional act from an unintentional one, they tended to base their judgements on the *severity of the outcome* or the sheer amount of damage done. So, John and Marie were typically judged to be naughtier (*objective* or *external responsibility*).

By contrast, children aged ten or above judged Henry and Margaret to be naughtier, because they were both doing something they shouldn't have been. Although the damage they caused was accidental, older children saw the motive or intention behind the act as being important in determining naughtiness (*internal responsibility*).

Regarding punishment, younger children believed that naughty people should pay for their crimes. In general, the greater the suffering the better, even though the form of punishment might be quite arbitrary. Such *expiatory* ('paying the penalty for') punishment is seen as decreed by authority and accepted as just because of its source (*moral realism*). Thus, when a child in a class doesn't admit to a misdeed and the rest of the class doesn't identify the offender, young children see *collective punishment* (i.e. the whole class is punished) as being acceptable.

Younger children often construed a misfortune which happens to someone who's behaved naughtily and 'got away with it' as a punishment for the misdeed (*immanent justice*). For example, a child who lied but wasn't found out and later fell and broke his arm was being punished for the lie. God (or an equivalent force) is in league with those in authority to ensure that 'the guilty will always be caught in the end'.

By contrast, older children saw punishment as bringing home to the offender the nature of the offence, and as a deterrent to behaving wrongly in the future. They also believed that collective punishment was wrong, and that 'the punishment should fit the crime'. So, if one child stole another's sweets, the offender must give his/her own sweets to the victim (based on the *principle of reciprocity*) or be punished in some other appropriate way. Older children no longer saw justice as being tied to authority (*moral relativism*), and there was less belief in immanent justice.

David Beckham being sent off in the World Cup finals in France, 1998. Was the whole England team being punished for his moment of impulsiveness?

Box 35.3 Heteronomous and autonomous morality

Piaget called the morality of young children *heteronomous* ('subject to another's laws or rules'). Older children possess *autonomous morality* ('subject to one's own laws or rules'), and see rules as the product of social agreements rather than sacred and unchangeable laws (the *morality of co-operation*).

Piaget believed that the change from heteronomous to autonomous morality occurred because of the shift at about seven from egocentric to operational thought (see Chapter 34). This suggests that cognitive development is necessary for moral development, but since the latter lags at least two years behind the former, it cannot be sufficient. Another important factor is the change from *unilateral respect* (the child's unconditional obedience of parents and other adults) to *mutual respect* within the peer group (where disagreements between equals have to be negotiated and resolved).

An evaluation of Piaget's theory

Piaget believed that popular girls' games (such as hop-scotch) were too simple compared with boys' most popular game (marbles) to be worthy of investigation. While girls eventually achieve similar moral levels to boys, they're less concerned with legal elaborations. This apparent gender bias is also evident in Kohlberg's theory (see below).

Challenges to Piaget's claims regarding intention

Children's understanding of intention is much more complex than Piaget believed, and children are able to bring this understanding to bear on moral decision-making. The pre-school child *isn't* amoral (Durkin, 1995):

- Piaget's stories make the *consequences* of behaviour explicit rather than the intentions behind it (Nelson, 1980). When three-year-olds see people bringing about negative consequences, they assume that their intentions are also negative. But when information about intentions is made explicit, even three-year-olds can make judgements about them, *regardless* of the consequences. This suggests that three-year-olds are only less proficient than older children at discriminating intentions from consequences, and in using these separate pieces of information to make moral judgements.

- Armsby (1971) found that 60 per cent of six-year-olds (compared with 90 per cent of ten-year-olds) judged the deliberate breaking of a cup as more deserving of punishment than accidental damage to a TV set. This suggests that at least some six-year-olds are capable of understanding intention in the sense of 'deliberate naughtiness', and that a small amount of deliberate damage is naughtier than a large amount of accidental damage.

- According to some information-processing theorists (e.g. Gelman & Baillargeon, 1983: see Chapter 34), aspects of development which Piaget attributed to the increasing complexity and quality of thought, are actually the result of an increasing capacity for the storage and retrieval of information (see Chapter 17). Most five-year-olds say that John is naughtier because he broke more cups than Henry. This is because they can remember who broke more cups, but they cannot remember all the other details of the stories. When efforts are made to rectify this, five-year-olds often take intention into account, as well as the amount of damage.

Cross-cultural validity

Although evidence regarding the *process* of moral development is mixed, many of the age *trends* (not necessarily the actual ages) Piaget described are supported by later research. This includes *cross-cultural data*, mainly from Africa (Eckensberger & Zimba, 1997).

However, based on his idea of a balance between the individual and society, Piaget didn't assume that the developmental changes he observed in his Swiss sample would necessarily be found in other cultures. On the contrary, he claimed that the essential issue was whether the cultural context would allow certain developmental changes to occur (contrast this with his theory of general cognitive development: see Chapter 34). This general orientation towards *contextualisation* is evident in current cross-cultural research (Eckensberger, 1999), and an interesting example is a study of lying and truth-telling by Lee *et al.* (1997).

Lee *et al.*'s results suggest a close link between sociocultural practices and moral judgement in relation to lying and truth-telling. China is a communist–collectivist society, which values the community over the individual and promotes personal sacrifice for the social good (see Chapter 47). Admitting a good deed is viewed as a violation of both traditional Chinese cultural norms and communist–collectivist doctrine.

By contrast, in Western culture 'white lies' and deceptions to avoid embarrassment are tolerated, and concealing positive behaviour is not explicitly encouraged (especially in the early school years). Taking credit for good deeds is an accepted part of individualistic self-promotion in the West, while in China it's seen as a character flaw. Although cognitive development plays an undeniable role (as argued by Kohlberg: see below), cultural and social factors are also key determinants in children's moral development (Lee *et al.*, 1997).

Kohlberg's theory

As we noted earlier, Kohlberg's theory has dominated research in the field of moral reasoning for 30 years. Like Piaget, by whom he was greatly influenced, Kohlberg believed that morality develops gradually during childhood and adolescence. Also like Piaget, he was more interested in people's *reasons* for their moral judgements, than the judgements themselves. For example, our reasons for upholding the law, as well as our views about whether there are circumstances in which breaking the law can be justified, might change as we develop.

Kohlberg assessed people's moral reasoning through the use of *moral dilemmas*. Typically, these involved a choice between two alternatives, both of which would be considered socially unacceptable. One of the most famous of these dilemmas concerns 'Heinz'.

Ask yourself ...

- Read Box 35.4 and try answering the questions about Heinz.

Box 35.4 An example of a moral dilemma

In Europe, a woman was near death from a special kind of cancer. There was one drug that the doctors thought might save her. It was a form of radium that a druggist in the same town had recently discovered. The drug was expensive to make, but the druggist was charging ten times what the drug cost him to make. He paid $400 for the radium and charged $4000 for a small dose of the drug. The sick woman's husband, Heinz, went to everyone he knew to borrow the money, but he could only get together about $2000, which was half of what the drug cost. He told the druggist that his wife was dying and asked him to sell it cheaper or let him pay later. But the druggist said, 'No, I discovered the drug and I'm going to make money from it'. So Heinz got desperate and considered breaking into the man's store to steal the drug for his wife.

1 Should Heinz steal the drug? (Why or why not?)
2 If Heinz doesn't love his wife, should he steal the drug for her? (Why or why not?)
3 Suppose the person dying isn't his wife but a stranger. Should Heinz steal the drug for the stranger? (Why or why not?)
4 (If you favour stealing the drug for a stranger.) Suppose it's a pet animal he loves. Should Heinz steal to save the pet animal? (Why or why not?)
5 Is it important for people to do everything they can to save another's life? (Why or why not?)
6 Is it against the law for Heinz to steal? Does that make it morally wrong? (Why or why not?)
7 Should people try to do everything they can to obey the law? (Why or why not?)
8 How does this apply to what Heinz should do?

(From Kohlberg, 1984)

The original study (beginning in 1956) involved 72 Chicago boys (ten to 16 years), 58 of whom were followed up at three-yearly intervals for 20 years (Kohlberg, 1984; Colby *et al.*, 1983; Colby & Kohlberg, 1987). Based on the answers given by this sample to the Heinz and other dilemmas, Kohlberg identified six qualitatively different *stages* of moral development, differing in complexity, with more complex types being used by older individuals. The six stages span three *levels* of moral reasoning.

At the *preconventional level*, we don't have a personal code of morality. Instead, it's shaped by the standards of adults and the consequences of following or breaking their rules. At the *conventional level*, we begin to internalise the moral standards of valued adult role models. At the *postconventional level*, society's values (such as individual rights), the need for democratically

determined rules, and *reciprocity* (or *mutual action*) are affirmed (stage 5). In stage 6, individuals are guided by *universal ethical principles*, in which they do what their conscience dictates, even if this conflicts with society's rules.

Box 35.5 Kohlberg's three levels and six stages of moral development and their application to the Heinz dilemma

Level 1: Preconventional morality

Stage 1 (punishment and obedience orientation): What's right and wrong is determined by what is and isn't punishable. If stealing is wrong, it's because authority figures say so and will punish such behaviour. Moral behaviour is essentially the avoidance of punishment.

- Heinz should steal the drug. If he lets his wife die, he'd get into trouble.
- Heinz shouldn't steal the drug. He'd get caught and sent to prison.

Stage 2 (instrumental relativist orientation): What's right and wrong is determined by what brings rewards and what people want. Other people's needs and wants are important, but only in a reciprocal sense ('If you scratch my back, I'll scratch yours').

- Heinz *should* steal the drug. His wife needs it to live and he needs her companionship.
- Heinz *shouldn't* steal the drug. He might get caught and his wife would probably die before he got out of prison, so it wouldn't do much good.

Level 2: Conventional morality

Stage 3 (interpersonal concordance or 'good boy–nice girl' orientation): Moral behaviour is whatever pleases and helps others and doing what they approve of. Being moral is 'being a good person in your own eyes and the eyes of others'. What the majority thinks is right by definition.

- Heinz *should* steal the drug. Society expects a loving husband to help his wife regardless of the consequences.
- Heinz *shouldn't* steal the drug. He'll bring dishonour on his family and they'll be ashamed of him.

Stage 4 (maintaining the social order orientation): Being good means doing one's duty – showing respect for authority and maintaining the social order for its own sake. Concern for the common good goes beyond the stage 3 concern for one's family: society protects the rights of individuals, so society must be protected by the individual. Laws are unquestionably accepted and obeyed.

- Heinz *should* steal the drug. If people like the druggist are allowed to get away with being greedy and selfish, society would eventually break down.
- Heinz *shouldn't* steal the drug. If people are allowed to take the law into their own hands, regardless of how justified an act might be, the social order would soon break down.

Level 3: Postconventional morality

Stage 5 (social contract–legalistic orientation): Since laws are established by mutual agreement, they can be changed by the same democratic process. Although laws and rules should be respected, since they protect individual rights as well as those of society as a whole, individual rights can sometimes supersede these laws if they become destructive or restrictive. Life is more 'sacred' than any legal principle, and so the law shouldn't be obeyed at all costs.

- Heinz *should* steal the drug. The law isn't set up to deal with circumstances in which obeying it would cost a human life.
- Heinz *shouldn't* steal the drug. Although he couldn't be blamed if he did steal it, even such extreme circumstances don't justify a person taking the law into his own hands. The ends don't always justify the means.

Stage 6 (universal ethical principles orientation): The ultimate judge of what's moral is a person's own conscience operating in accordance with certain universal principles. Society's rules are arbitrary and may be broken when they conflict with universal moral principles.

- Heinz *should* steal the drug. When a choice must be made between disobeying a law and saving a life, one must act in accordance with the higher principle of preserving and respecting life.
- Heinz *shouldn't* steal the drug. He must consider other people who need it just as much as his wife. By stealing the drug, he'd be acting in accordance with his own particular feelings with utter disregard for the values of all the lives involved.

(Based on Rest, 1983; Crooks & Stein, 1991)

Both Piaget and Kohlberg saw cognitive development as necessary for, and setting a limit on, the maturity of moral reasoning, with the latter usually lagging behind the former. So, for example, formal operational thought (see Chapter 34) is needed to achieve stages 5 and 6, but it cannot *guarantee* it. Because formal operational thought is achieved by a relatively small proportion of people, it's hardly surprising that the percentage of those attaining stages 5 and 6 is only about 15 per cent (Colby *et al.*, 1983 see Table 35.1).

An evaluation of Kohlberg's theory

Findings from his longitudinal study showed that those who were initially at low stages had advanced to higher stages, suggesting 'moral progression' (Colby *et al.*, 1983). Based on these findings, Kohlberg argued that the first five stages are *universal*, and that they occur in an *invariant sequence*. Similarly, Rest's (1983) 20-year longitudinal study of men from adolescence to their mid-thirties showed that the developmental stages seem to occur in the order described by Kohlberg.

Is it culturally biased?

According to Snarey's (1987) review of 45 studies conducted in 27 different cultures, the data 'provide striking support for the universality of Kohlberg's first four stages'. However, Kohlberg & Nisan (1987) studied Turkish youngsters, both from a rural village and a city, over a twelve-year period. Their scores overall were lower than Americans', and rural youngsters scored lower than the urban dwellers. Snarey *et al.* (1985) reported that Israeli youngsters (aged 12 to 24) educated in kibbutzim scored *higher* than Americans at all ages.

These findings suggest that cultural factors play a significant part in moral reasoning. According to the *sociocultural approach*, what 'develops' is the individual's skill in managing the moral expectations of one's culture, expressed through linguistic and symbolic practices. This contrasts sharply with Kohlberg's cognitive–developmental model, which concentrates on individual processes 'inside the head' (Haste *et al.*, 1998).

CROSS-CULTURAL STUDY 35.3

Cultural bias in Kohlberg's theory

As we've seen, stage-6 reasoning is based on supposedly 'universal' ethical principles, such as justice (which is central to Kohlberg's theory), equality, integrity and reverence for life. However, these *aren't* universally held (Shweder, 1991; Eckensberger, 1994).

For example, South East Asian culture places family loyalty at the centre of its ethical system. Shweder *et al.* (1987) gave the Heinz dilemma to people living in Indian Hindu villages. One very morally sophisticated reasoner reached very different conclusions, supported by very different arguments, from that expected in Western culture. He was clearly using a high stage of reasoning, but it was impossible to score him on the Kohlberg measure, because his arguments were too far removed from the Western position (Shweder, 1990).

Iwasa (1992) compared Americans and Japanese using the Heinz dilemma. There was no difference in the overall level of moral development, but there were qualitative differences in *why* human life was valued, reflecting cultural norms. While Americans were concerned to prolong length of life, the Japanese were concerned to make it purer and cleaner. Hence, most Americans thought Heinz should steal, while most Japanese thought he shouldn't.

Table 35.1 *The relationship between Kohlberg's stages and Piaget's types of moral development, and Piaget's stages of cognitive development*

Kohlberg's levels of moral development	Age group included within Kohlberg's developmental levels	Corresponding type of morality (Piaget)	Corresponding stage of cognitive development (Piaget)
Preconventional (stages 1 and 2)	Most 9-year-olds and below. Some over nine	Heteronomous (5–9/10)	Pre-operational (2–7)
Conventional (stages 3 and 4)	Most adolescents and adults	Heteronomous (e.g. respect for the law/authority figures) *plus* autonomous (e.g. taking intentions into account)	Concrete operational (7–11)
Postconventional (stages 5 and 6)	10–15% of adults, not before mid-30s	Autonomous (10 and above)	Formal operational (11 and above)

Eckensberger (1999) maintains that Kohlberg's theory isn't as 'Western based' as some critics have claimed. For example, the highest stages can be found in India, Taiwan and Israel. It appears to be the degree of 'complexity' (industrialisation) – and not 'Westernisation' – that assists the development to higher stages.

Nevertheless, cultural psychologists believe that instead of looking for universal moral stages, we should be trying to understand moral *diversity*. A focus on justice may be very far from some cultures' primary ethical concerns:

> *'If the researchers try to measure justice reasoning, rather than eliciting people's usual moral framework, stage scores may be misleading, but more importantly, the results would fail to give a true picture of people's moral lives'.* (Haste *et al.*, 1998)

Is it gender biased?

This criticism of Kohlberg's theory as being biased towards Western cultural ideals (*Eurocentrism*) mirrors a second major criticism, namely that it's biased in favour of males (*androcentrism*: see Chapter 47). Gilligan (1982, 1993) has argued that because Kohlberg's theory was based on an all-male sample, the stages reflect a male definition of morality.

While men's morality is based on abstract principles of law and justice, women's is based on principles of compassion and care. In turn, the different 'moral orientations' of men and women rest on a deeper issue, namely how we think about *selfhood*. An ethic of justice (male) is a natural outcome of thinking of people as *separate* beings, in continual conflict with each other, who make rules and contracts as a way of handling that conflict. A 'female' ethic of caring/responsibility follows from regarding selves as being in connection with one another.

However, the claim that women 'think differently' about moral issues has been challenged. According to Johnston (1988), each sex is competent in each mode, but there are gender-linked preferences. While boys tended to use a justice orientation, if pressed they'd also use the care orientation. Similarly, girls preferred a care orientation, but also switched easily. According to Haste *et al.* (1998), these findings support Gilligan's argument that there's more than one moral 'voice', but *not* her claim that the 'caring' voice was more apparent amongst women. Several studies show that sex differences in moral orientations are less important than the kind of dilemmas being considered.

KEY STUDY 35.1

Are males and females morally different? (Walker, 1989)

Walker studied a large sample of males and females, aged five to 63. Participants were scored for both moral stage and orientation on both hypothetical and personally generated, real-life dilemmas. The only evidence of sex differences was for adults on real-life dilemmas.

When asked to produce real-life dilemmas, females reported more *relational/personal* ones and males reported more non-relational/impersonal dilemmas (Walker *et al.*, 1987). A relational/personal conflict involves someone with whom the participant has a significant and continu-

ing relationship (e.g. whether or not to tell a friend her husband is having an affair). A non-relational/impersonal conflict involves acquaintances or strangers (e.g. whether or not to correct a shop assistant's error in giving too much change). Regardless of gender, personal/relational dilemmas produced a higher level of response than impersonal/non-relational dilemmas. This is the *opposite* of what Gilligan claimed, namely that Kohlberg's stages are biased against an ethic of care (Walker, 1996).

Both males and females tended to use the ethic of care mostly in personal dilemmas, and most people used both orientations to a significant degree, with no clear focus or preference. According to Walker (1996), the nature of the dilemma is a better predictor of moral orientation than is gender.

Walker (1984, 1995) also refuted Gilligan's claim that Kohlberg's scoring system was biased against females, making them more likely to be rated at the conventional level, and men at the postconventional level. He reviewed all the available research evidence relating to sex differences (80 studies, 152 distinct samples, and over 10,000 participants) and found that, regardless of age category, the typical pattern was one of non-significant differences. Once any educational or occupational differences favouring men were controlled for, there was no evidence of a systematic sex difference in moral-stage scores.

Kohlberg has also been criticised for his emphasis on moral thinking based on quite unusual hypothetical dilemmas. Moral reasoning and behaviour aren't necessarily correlated (Gibbs & Schnell, 1985). While moral reasoning may determine moral talk, 'talk is cheap' (Blasi, 1980), and what we say and what we do when faced with a moral dilemma often differ, particularly under strong social pressure (see Chapters 26 and 27). Moral development research should really look at what people do, rather than what they say they'd do (Mischel & Mischel, 1976).

The higher stages in Kohlberg's theory are associated with education and verbal ability (Shweder *et al.*, 1987). While 'college-educated' people give higher-level and more mature *explanations* of moral decisions, this doesn't make them more moral than the non-college-educated. The former might simply be more sophisticated verbally. Nor is postconventional morality necessarily superior to conventional morality (Shweder, 1991), and even Kohlberg (1978) acknowledges that there may not be a separate sixth stage.

Eisenberg's theory of prosocial moral reasoning

Kohlberg's concept of moral reasoning is *prohibition-oriented*. In the case of Heinz, for example, one prohibition (stealing) is pitted against another (allowing his wife to die). But not all 'moral conflicts' are like this. Eisenberg (1982, 1986; Eisenberg *et al.*, 1991) argues that if we want to understand developmental changes in helping or altruism (see Chapter 30), we need to examine children's reasoning when faced with a conflict between their own needs and those of others, in a context where the role of laws, rules, and the dictates of authority are minimal. This describes *prosocial moral reasoning*.

In a series of studies during the 1980s, Eisenberg presented children of different ages (sometimes followed up to early adulthood) with illustrated hypothetical stories, in which the character can help another person, but at a personal cost.

Based on children's responses to this and other similar dilemmas, Eisenberg identified six stages of prosocial moral reasoning (see Table 35.2).

An evaluation of Eisenberg's theory

In a review of her research, Eisenberg (1996) points out that, as predicted, children almost never said they'd help in order to avoid punishment or because of blind obedience to authority, such as adults. This would be expected, given that children are seldom punished for not acting in a prosocial way (but *are* often punished for wrongdoing). This differs greatly from what's been found for prohibition-oriented moral reasoning.

While for Kohlberg other-oriented reasoning emerges relatively late, Eisenberg expected to find it by the pre-school years. Even four- to five-year-olds appeared frequently to orient to others' needs showing what seemed to be primitive empathy. Also, references to empathy-related processes (such as taking the other's perspective and sympathising) are particularly common in prosocial moral reasoning.

Contrary to Kohlberg's claims, even individuals who typically used higher-level reasoning occasionally reverted to lower-level reasoning (such as egotistic, hedonistic reasoning). This was especially likely when they chose *not* to help, suggesting the influence of *situational variables*. These are also implicated by some cross-cultural studies. For example, children raised on Israeli kibbutzim are especially likely to emphasise reciprocity between people, whereas city children (Israeli and from the USA) are more likely to be concerned with personal costs for helping others. If individuals' moral reasoning can vary across situations, then there's likely to be only a modest relationship between their typical level of moral reasoning and their actual prosocial behaviour. This is supported by Eisenberg's research.

One additional factor that's been implicated is emotion, in particular, *empathy*. Whether or not children help others depends on the *type* of emotional response that others' distress induces in them (rather than *whether or not* they respond emotionally). People who respond *sympathetically/empathically* (associated with, for instance, lowered heart rate) are more likely to help than those who experience *personal distress* (associated with accelerated heart rate).

Table 35.2 *Stages of prosocial moral reasoning (based on Eisenberg, 1982, 1986)*

Level 1 (hedonistic, self-focused orientation): The individual is concerned with selfish, pragmatic consequences, rather than moral considerations. For example, 'She shouldn't help, because she might miss the party'. What's 'right' is whatever is instrumental in achieving the actor's own ends/desires. Reasons for helping/not helping include direct gain for the self, expectations of future reciprocity, and concern for others whom the individual needs and/or likes.

[This is the predominant mode for preschoolers and younger primary-schoolers.]

Level 2 (needs of others orientation): The individual expresses concern for the physical, material and psychological needs of others, even though these conflict with his/her own needs. For example, 'She should help, because the girl's leg is bleeding and she needs to go to the doctor'. This concern is expressed in the simplest terms, without clear evidence of self-reflective role-taking, verbal expressions of sympathy, or reference to internalised affect, such as guilt.

[This is the predominant mode for many preschoolers and primary-schoolers.]

Level 3 (approval and interpersonal orientation and/or stereotyped orientation): Stereotyped images of good and bad persons and behaviours and/or considerations of others' approval/acceptance are used in justifying prosocial or non-helping behaviours. For example, 'It's nice to help' or 'Her family would think she did the right thing'.

[This is the predominant mode for some primary-schoolers and secondary-school students.]

Level 4a (self-reflective empathic orientation): The individual's judgements include evidence of self-reflective sympathetic responding, role-taking, concern with others' humanness, and/or guilt or positive affect related to the consequences of one's actions. For example, 'She cares about people', and 'She'd feel bad if she didn't help because she'd be in pain'.

[This is the predominant mode for a few older primary-schoolers and many secondary-school students].

Level 4b (transitional level): The individual's justifications for helping/not helping involve internalised values, norms, duties or responsibilities, or refer to the need to protect the rights and dignity of others. But these aren't clearly or strongly stated. For example, 'It's just something she's learnt and feels'.

[This is the predominant mode for a minority of people of secondary-school age and older.]

Level 5 (strongly internalised stage): As for 4b, but internalised values, norms etc., are much more strongly stated. Additional justifications for helping include the desire to honour individual and societal contractual obligations, improve the conditions of society, and belief in the dignity, rights and equality of all human beings. It's also characterised by the wish to maintain self-respect for living up to one's own values and accepted norms. For example, 'She'd feel bad if she didn't help because she'd know she didn't live up to her values'.

[This is the predominant mode for a very small minority of secondary-school students and no primary-schoolers.]

Ask yourself ...

• How are these findings related to the *empathy–altruism hypothesis* and *universal egoism* discussed in Chapter 30?

According to Eckensberger (1999), emotions (especially positive emotions) are increasingly being seen as the basis for moral development. This represents a move away from Kohlberg's theory and a return to Piaget's, in which feelings of mutual respect and empathy were seen as central.

Social learning theory

Social learning theories (SLTs), such as those of Bandura (1977a) and Mischel (1973), originated in the USA in the 1940s and 1950s. They were an attempt to reinterpret certain aspects of Freud's psychoanalytic theory in terms of *conditioning theory* (classical and operant conditioning: see Chapter 11). In the 1960s and 1970s, Bandura and his colleagues tried to make Freud's concept of identification more objective by studying it experimentally in the form of *imitation*.

More specifically, many of these experiments were concerned with *aggression* (see Key Study 35.2 and Chapter 29), but SLT has been applied to many aspects of development, such as gender (see Chapter 36) and morality. This focus on *human social behaviour* is one feature that sets SLT apart from conditioning (or orthodox learning) theory.

Some important similarities and differences between SLT and orthodox learning theory

■ While SL theorists agree that all behaviour is learned according to the same learning principles, they're interested specifically in *human* learning.

■ Although SL theorists agree that we should observe what's observable, they also believe that there are important *cognitive* or *mediating variables* which intervene between stimulus and response, without which we cannot adequately explain human behaviour (see Box 35.7, page 517).

■ SL theorists emphasise *observational learning* or *modelling* (learning through watching the behaviour of others, called *models*). This occurs spontaneously, with no deliberate effort by the learner, or any intention by the model to teach anything.

Observational learning takes place without any reinforcement – mere exposure to the model is sufficient for learning to occur (Bandura, 1965). However, whether the model's behaviour is imitated depends partly on the *consequences* of the behaviour, both for the model and the learner. Reinforcement is important only in so far as it affects *performance* (not the learning itself).

KEY STUDY 35.2

Learning versus performance (Bandura, 1965)

Bandura (1965) showed three groups of children a film of an adult behaving aggressively towards a *bobo doll*.

■ **Group A (control)** saw the adult kicking, pummelling and punching the bobo doll.

■ **Group B (model-rewarded)** saw what group A saw, but a second adult appeared near the end of the film and commended the model's aggressive behaviour. Sweets and lemonade were offered to the model.

■ **Group C (model-punished)** also saw the same filmed aggression, but this time a second adult scolded the model and warned against further aggression.

So, the only difference between the three groups was the *consequences for the model* of his/her aggression.

After the film, all the children (individually) went into a playroom, which contained a large number of toys, including a bobo doll and a mallet. They were observed for ten minutes, and the number of acts of *imitiative aggression* was recorded for each child. While group C children showed *significantly fewer* aggressive acts than groups A and B, there was no difference between these two groups. This suggests that *vicarious punishment* is more powerful than *vicarious reinforcement*.

More importantly, all the children were later asked to reproduce as much of the model's behaviour as they could, and were directly rewarded for each act of imitative aggression. Under these conditions, all three groups showed the same high levels of imitative aggression.

Ask yourself ...

• What do these findings tell us about what children in the different groups learned when originally observing the model?

This shows that group C children must have attended to and remembered the model's behaviour (i.e. *learned* from the model) to the same extent as those in groups A and B. But this learning hadn't been apparent in their *performance* when they were first observed, but only after receiving direct reinforcement. Hence, reinforcement (either vicarious or direct) wasn't needed for learning (acquisition), but it was for imitation (performance).

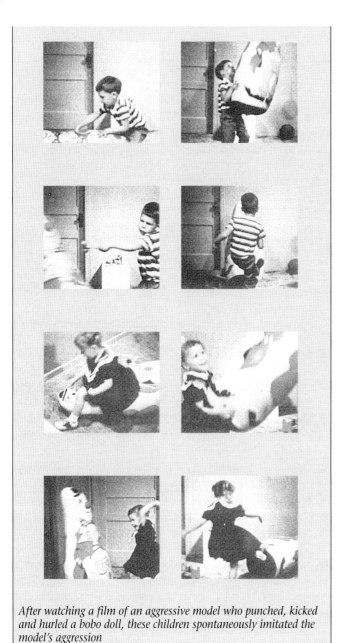

After watching a film of an aggressive model who punched, kicked and hurled a bobo doll, these children spontaneously imitated the model's aggression

The role of cognitive factors in observational learning

The learning process is much more complex for Bandura than it is for Skinner, for whom 'the mind' had no part to play in a scientific psychology (see Chapter 2). In Bandura's (1974) view:

'Contrary to mechanistic metaphors, outcomes change behaviour in humans through the intervening influence of thought'.

Box 35.7	**Five cognitive/mediating variables influencing the likelihood of learning and/or performance**

- The learner must *pay attention* to the relevant clues and ignore those aspects of the model and the environment that are incidental and irrelevant (see Chapter 13). Attention can be influenced by the model's distinctiveness, attractiveness or power (whether or not the model's behaviour has *functional value* for the learner), the learner's level of arousal, and expectations about the model.
- A visual *image or semantic code* for the modelled behaviour is recorded in memory. Without an adequate coding system, the learner will fail to store what's been seen or heard (see Chapter 17). Whereas infants are largely confined to immediate imitation, older children can defer imitation because of their superior use of symbols (see Chapter 34).
- *Memory permanence* derives from the use of devices such as rehearsal and organisation, and employing multiple codes to help retain the stored information over long periods (again see Chapter 17).
- *Reproducing the observed motor activities* accurately usually requires several trials to get the muscular 'feel' of the behaviour. Older children enjoy greater muscular strength and control.
- *Motivation* refers to the role of reinforcement, which can be *direct* (as when the child is praised by an adult), or *vicarious* (as when a child sees another child being praised: see Key Study 35.2) *Self-reinforcement* is also possible (as when the child praises itself/feels pleased with itself).

Reinforcement as information about the future

Bandura (1977a) challenged Skinner's claim that reinforcements and punishments *automatically* strengthen and weaken behaviour (see Chapter 11). For Bandura:

'Reinforcement serves principally as an informative and motivational operation rather than as a mechanical response strengthener'.

Reinforcement provides the learner with *information* about the likely consequences of certain behaviour under certain conditions; that is, it improves our prediction of whether a given action will lead to pleasant (reinforcement) or unpleasant (punishment) outcomes in the *future*. It also *motivates* us by causing us to anticipate future outcomes. Our present behaviours are largely governed by the outcomes we *expect* them to have, and we're more likely to try to learn the modelled behaviour if we value its consequences.

An evaluation of Bandura's SLT

Is SLT a developmental theory?

As noted in Box 35.7, changes take place in cognitive or mediating processes as children get older. However, these processes essentially apply at any age, which means that the theory isn't a true theory of development (Durkin, 1995). Bandura resists the notion of a general structural reorganisation of the kind proposed by Piaget (see Chapter 34), and so he fails to take account of cognitive *development* (Grusec, 1992). As Bee (2000) points out, SLT can say how a child might acquire a particular behaviour pattern, but it doesn't take into account the underlying developmental changes that are occurring. For example, do three-year-olds and ten-year-olds typically learn the same amount or in the same way from modelling? As Bee (2000) notes:

'Given Bandura's emphasis on cognitive aspects of the modelling process, a genuinely developmental social learning theory could be proposed, although no such theory now exists'.

Indeed, the importance of cognitive factors is reflected in Bandura's (1986, 1989) re-naming of SLT as *social cognitive theory*. Other important cognitive processes are those relating to the self.

Box 35.8 Self-concept, self-monitoring and self-efficacy

According to Bandura, children learn both overt behaviour/concrete skills and information, and also abstract skills and information through modelling. Indeed, *abstract modelling* is part of his 'social cognitive theory' (1986, 1989). For example, the 'rule' underlying a model's behaviour can be extracted from observing the behaviour, without the rule being made explicit or articulated. In this way, the child can acquire attitudes, values, expectancies, ways of solving problems, and standards of self-evaluation.

By incorporating (or internalising) societal standards into its self, the child can monitor its own behaviours in terms of these standards. This *self-monitoring* ensures that behaviour is regulated even in the absence of reinforcement. Indeed, according to Bandura (1971), 'There is no more devastating punishment than self-contempt'; that is, we are our own harshest critics. This mirrors Freud's view of the young child's superego, which is often more punitive than the parents it has replaced (see page 506).

Another internalised standard or expectancy is *self-efficacy*. This refers to our belief that we can act effectively and exercise some control over events that influence our lives (Bandura, 1977a, 1986). This is crucially important for motivation, since how we judge our own capabilities is likely to affect our expectations about future behaviour. For example, if we feel that a model's actions are within our capabilities, then we may attempt to imitate them, but a low sense of self-efficacy regarding the modelled skill is likely to inhibit us (Durkin, 1995).

One of the strengths of Bandura's SLT (and other versions, such as that of Mischel, 1973) is that behaviour can be understood only by taking the actor's self-concept, self-monitoring, self-efficacy and other mediating variables into account. However, these internal processes don't constitute 'personality', a concept which most SL theorists tend to dismiss (Durkin, 1995: see Chapter 42). Nevertheless, they make the theory far less mechanistic than Skinner's, for example, which focuses entirely on external events. For Bandura (1973):

'The environment is only a potentiality, not a fixed property that inevitably impinges upon individuals and to which their behaviour eventually adapts. Behaviour partly creates the environment and the resultant environment, in turn, influences the behaviour'.

This view is called *reciprocal determinism* (Bandura, 1977a, 1986). People are both products and producers of their environments (see Chapters 49 and 50).

Conclusions

As we noted in the *Introduction and overview*, different psychological theories attempt to answer quite different questions about moral development. To the extent that all these questions are relevant to understanding the full complexity of moral development, psychoanalytic theory, cognitive developmental theories, and social learning theory all make significant contribution to our understanding of this critically important aspect of socialisation.

CHAPTER SUMMARY

- According to Freud, the **psychic apparatus** consists of the **id**, **ego** and **superego**. The id and the ego are governed by the **pleasure principle** and **reality principle** respectively. The superego comprises the **conscience** and **ego-ideal**, representing the **punishing** and **rewarding** parent respectively.

- A boy's **Oedipus complex** ends when he identifies with his father (**identification with the aggressor**), motivated by **his fear of castration/castration anxiety**. Since a girl's Oedipus complex begins with her belief that she's already been castrated, Freud found it difficult to explain her identification with her mother. One suggestion was **anaclitic identification**.

- There's no evidence to support Freud's claim that females have weaker superegos than males, and **penis envy** has been reinterpreted as envy of men's superior social status.

- **Cognitive–developmental theories** are concerned with the **reasons** underlying moral judgements, rather than the judgements themselves.

- According to Piaget, the change from **heteronomous** to **autonomous morality** occurs due to the shifts from egocentric to operational thought, and from **unilateral respect** and adult constraint to **mutual respect** within the peer group.

- Although children's understanding of **intention** is much more complex than Piaget believed, many of the **age trends** he described have been supported by cross-cultural studies, mainly from Africa.

- Kohlberg identified six qualitatively different **stages** in moral development, spanning three basic **levels** of moral reasoning: **preconventional**, **conventional** and **postconventional morality**.

- Despite extensive empirical support for the sequence and universality of the (first four) stages, the **sociocultural approach** maintains that cultural factors play a significant part in moral reasoning. For Kohlberg, the focus is on what takes place within the individual's head.

- Kohlberg's theory has been criticised for its bias towards **Western** cultures, and for being based on a **male** definition of morality. However, several studies show that sex differences in morality are less important than the **kind of dilemmas** being considered.

- Kohlberg has also been criticised for overemphasising moral **thinking** (rather than behaviour), and those who attain the highest stages may simply be more sophisticated verbally. A separate stage 6 may not even exist.

- While Kohlberg's theory is **prohibition-oriented**, Eisenberg concentrates on the development of **prosocial moral reasoning**. Many of the predictions derived from her theory have been supported, and her research has also indicated that **situational variables** influence moral reasoning.
- **Empathy**, and other positive emotions, are becoming increasingly important in explanations of moral development.
- Bandura's **social learning theory** (SLT) investigated Freud's concept of identification, largely through laboratory experiments of **imitative aggression**.
- Bandura emphasised **observational learning/modelling**, distinguished between **learning** and **performance**, and identified several cognitive variables which **mediate** between observation of a model's behaviour and its imitation.
- **Reinforcement** is a source of both **information** and **motivation**. While not necessary for **learning**, reinforcement (direct, vicarious, or self-administered) may be needed for **performance**.
- Self-reinforcement is related to **self-monitoring**, the SLT equivalent of Freud's superego. This represents an internalised societal standard or expectancy, another example being **self-efficacy**.

Self-assessment questions

1 Describe and evaluate **one** theory of the development of moral understanding.
2 Critically consider the influence of gender **and/or** cultural variations in the development of moral understanding.
3 Critically assess the claim that no single theory provides a complete account of moral development.

Web addresses

http://www.stg.brown.edu/projects/hypertext/landow/HTatBrown/Freud/Psychosexual_Development.html

http://www.uia.org/uiademo/hum/h1543.htm

http://www.uia.org/uiademo/hum/h0285.htm

http://www.wynja.com/personality/theorists.html

http://www.awa.com/w2/erotic_computing/Kohlberg.stages.html

http://www.uk.edulnucci/MoralEd/overview.html

http://www.cortland.edu/www/c4n5rs/home.htm

http://www.unikonstanz.de/SIG-MDE/

http://www.nd-edu/~rbarger/Kohlberg.html

Further reading

Gilligan, C. (1993) *In A Different Voice: Psychological Theory and Women's Development*. Cambridge, MA: Harvard University Press. This is about much more than moral development. A feminist critique of male-centred psychology.

Haste, H., Diomedes, M. & Helkama, K. (1998) 'Morality, wisdom and the life-span'. In A. Demetriou, W. Doise & C. van Lieshout, (Eds) *Lifespan Developmental Psychology*. New York: Wiley. An authoritative, but readable up-to-date account.

Chapter 36

Gender Development

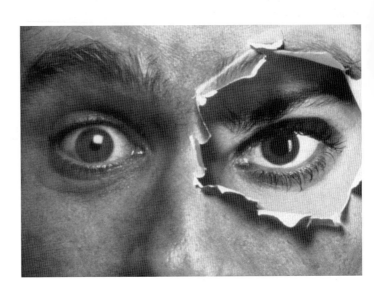

Introduction and overview

Often the first thing we notice about other people is whether they're male or female. The importance of *sexual identity* to our self-concept and our interactions with others (see Chapter 33) is a reflection of the fact that every known culture distinguishes between male and female. In turn, this distinction is accompanied by widely and deeply held beliefs (*stereotypes*: see Chapter 22) about the psychological make-up and behaviours belonging to each sex. The study of *psychological sex differences* is really an attempt to see how accurate these stereotypes are.

At the beginning of the twentieth century (especially in the US), many of the first generation of scientifically trained women psychologists channelled their research efforts into the extent and nature of sex differences. But psychology's interest in this research area waned with the rise of behaviourism (Crawford & Unger, 1995). Interest was revived in the 1970s, driven largely by *feminist psychologists*. Feminist interpretations of sex differences share the belief that social, political, economic and cultural factors determine *gender*, our awareness and understanding of the differences that distinguish males from females. This view is directly opposed to those of *sociobiologists* and *evolutionary psychologists*, who argue that sex differences are 'natural', having evolved as a part of the more general adaptation of the human species to its environment (see Chapter 2 and Clamp, 2001).

Feminist psychology and sociobiology fall at the two extremes of the continuum of the *nature–nurture* or *heredity–environment debate* (see Chapter 50). Several other theoretical accounts of gender and gender differences have been advanced, including biological approaches, biosocial theory, psychoanalytic theory, social learning theory, cognitive–developmental theory and gender schema theory. All of these, with the exception of biological approaches, stress the *interaction* between biological and environmental influences, albeit in quite different ways.

Renée Richards, formerly known as Richard Raskin, one of the world's best known transsexuals. Born male, Richard had his sex reassigned through surgery and continued her tennis career as a woman

The 'vocabulary' of sex and gender

Ask yourself ...

• What's the difference between sex and gender?

Feminist psychologists (e.g. Unger, 1979) distinguish between *sex* and *gender*. Sex refers to the biological facts about us, such as genetic make-up, reproductive anatomy and functioning, and is usually referred to by the terms 'male' and 'female'. Gender, by contrast, is what culture makes out of the 'raw material' of biological sex. It is, therefore, the social equivalent or social interpretation of sex.

Sexual identity is an alternative way of referring to our biological status as male or female. Corresponding to gender is *gender identity*, our classification of ourselves (and others) as male or female, boy or girl, and so on. Sexual and gender identities correspond for most people, but not in *transsexualism*. While being anatomically male or female, transexuals firmly believe that they belong to the opposite sex. As a result, their biological sexual identity is fundamentally inconsistent with their gender identity.

Gender role (or *sex role*) refers to the behaviours, attitudes, values, beliefs and so on which a particular society either expects from, or considers appropriate to, males and females on the basis of their biological sex. To be *masculine* or *feminine*, then, requires males or females to conform to their respective gender roles.

All societies have carefully defined gender roles, although their precise details differ between societies. *Gender* (or *sex*) *stereotypes* are widely held beliefs about psychological differences between males and females which often reflect gender roles (see pages 524–525).

Sex typing is our acquisition of a sex or gender identity and learning the appropriate behaviours (adopting an appropriate sex role). Sex typing begins early in Western culture, with parents often dressing their new-born baby boy or girl in blue or pink. Even in the earliest days of infancy, our gender influences how people react to us (Condry & Ross, 1985). Indeed, usually the first question asked by friends and relatives of parents with a new-born baby is 'Boy or girl?'. By age three or four, most children have some knowledge about their own genders. They know, for example, that boys become men and girls become women, and that some games are played by boys and others by girls. A permanent gender identity is usually acquired by age five (see Box 36.3, page 528).

Biology and sexual identity

Biologically, sex *isn't* a unidimensional variable, and attempts to identify the biological factors influencing gender identity have produced at least five categories.

Box 36.1 Five categories of biological sex

Chromosomal sex: Normal females inherit two X chromosomes, one from each parent (XX). Normal males inherit one X chromosome from the mother and one Y chromosome from the father (XY). Two chromosomes are needed for the complete development of both internal and external female structures, and the Y chromosome must be present for the complete development of male internal and external structures (Page *et al.*, 1987). For many years it was believed that if the Y chromosome were absent, female external genitals would develop. However, a *female-determining gene* has been located on the X chromosome (Unger & Crawford, 1996). Female embryos begin synthesising large quantities of oestrogen, which is thought to play a key role in the development of the female reproductive system. A gene on the Y chromosome called TDF (*testis-determining factor*) appears to be responsible for testis formation and male development (Hodgkin, 1988).

Gonadal sex: This refers to the sexual or reproductive organs (ovaries in females and testes in males). *H-Y antigen*, controlled by genes on the Y chromosome, causes embryonic gonads to be transformed into testes. If H-Y antigen isn't present, gonadal tissue develops into ovaries (Amice *et al.*, 1989).

Hormonal sex: When the gonads are transformed into testes or ovaries, genetic influences cease and biological sex determination is controlled by *sex hormones*. The male sex hormones are called *androgens*, the most important being *testosterone* (secreted by the testes). The ovaries secrete two distinct types of female hormone, *oestrogen* and *progesterone*. Although males usually produce more androgens, and females more oestrogens, both males and females produce androgens and oestrogens. So, strictly, there are no exclusively 'male' or 'female' hormones (Muldoon & Reilly, 1998).

Sex of the internal reproductive structures: The Wolffian ducts in males and the Müllerian ducts in females are the embryonic forerunners of the internal reproductive structures. In males, these are the prostate gland, sperm ducts, seminal vesicles and testes. In females, they are the Fallopian tubes, womb and ovaries.

Sex of the external genitals: In males, the external genitalia are the penis and scrotum. In females, they are the outer lips of the vagina (*labia majora*). In the absence of testosterone (which influences both the internal and external structures of chromosomal males), female structures develop (see text and Figure 36.1).

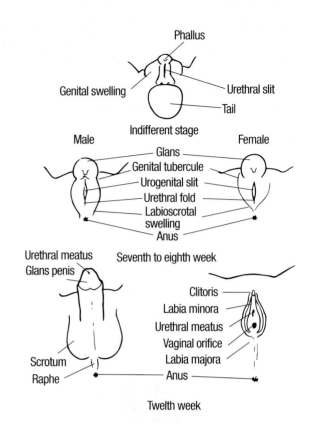

Figure 36.1 *Prenatal differentiation of male and female genitalia. From a relatively undifferentiated state, development proceeds by means of the relative enlargement of structures that have analogues in members of the other sex (from Unger, R.K. (1979)* Female and Male, *New York: Harper & Row)*

Hermaphroditism

The categories identified in Box 36.1 are usually highly correlated, so that a person tends to be male (or female) in all respects. The categories also tend to be correlated with non-biological aspects of sex, including the sex the baby is assigned to at birth, how it's brought up, gender identity, gender-role identity and so on. Either pre- or postnatally, however, disorders can occur leading to an inconsistency or low correlation between the categories. These disorders can tell us a great deal about the development of gender identity, gender role and gender-role identity.

People with such disorders are called hermaphrodites. *True hermaphrodites* (from the mythical Greek god/goddess *Hermaphrodite*, who had attributes of both sexes) have either simultaneously or sequentially functioning organs of both sexes. They are very rare, and their external organs are often a mixture of male and female structures.

> ### CASE STUDY 36.1
>
> #### Mr Blackwell: hermaphrodite (Goldwyn, 1979)
>
> In an article called 'The Fight to be Male', Goldwyn cites the case of Mr Blackwell, only the 303rd true hermaphrodite in all of medical history . He's described as a handsome and rather shy 18-year-old Bantu. Although he had a small vaginal opening as well as a penis, he was taken to be a boy and brought up as such. But when he was 14 he developed breasts and was sent to hospital to discover why this had happened. It was found that he had an active ovary on one side of his body and an active testicle on the other. He expressed the wish to remain male, and so his female parts were removed.
>
> Goldwyn points out that if his internal ducts had been differently connected, Mr Blackwell could have actually fertilised himself without being able to control it.

Pseudohermaphrodites are more common. Although they too possess ambiguous internal and external reproductive structures, they are born with gonads that match their chromosomal sex (unlike true hermaphrodites).

■ In *androgen insensitivity syndrome* (AIS) (or *testicular feminising syndrome*), pre-natal development in a chromosomally normal (XY) male is feminised. The internal reproductive structures of either sex fail to develop, and the external genitals fail to differentiate into a penis and scrotum. Normal-looking female external genitals and a shallow vagina are present at birth. At puberty, breast development occurs, but the individual fails to menstruate. Because of the presence of a very shallow (or 'blind') vagina, little or no surgery is needed for the adoption of a female appearance.

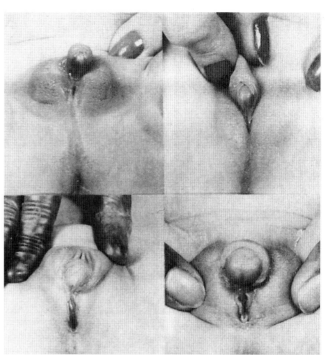

Ambiguous appearance at birth of the genitalia of individuals with the adrenogenital syndrome (XX, but with excessive androgen during pre-natal differentiation) (from Money & Ehrhardt, 1972)

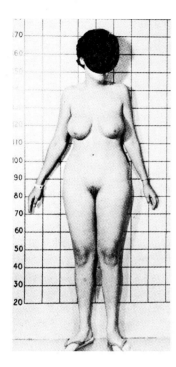

Adult with testicular feminisation (XY but with an insensitivity to androgen). These individuals are usually taller than the average female and tend to have an attractive 'female' physique (from Money & Ehrhardt, 1972, reprinted with permission)

- In *adrenogenital syndrome* (AGS), a chromosomally normal (XX) female is exposed to an excessive level of androgens during the critical period of prenatal sexual differentiation. While the internal reproductive structures are unaffected, the external structures resemble those of a male infant. For example, an enlarged clitoris appears to be a penis. These individuals are usually raised as females. (See photographs opposite.)
- In *DHT-deficient males* (or 5-alpha-reductase deficiency), a genetic disorder prevents the normal prenatal conversion of testosterone into *dihydrotestosterone* (DHT). This hormone is necessary for the normal development of male external genitals. These males are usually incorrectly identified as females and raised as girls (but see Case Study 36.2).
- In *chromosome abnormalities* there's a discrepancy between chromosomal sex and external appearance, including the genitalia. The most common examples are Turner's syndrome (where a female individual has a single sex chromosome: XO) and Klinefelter's syndrome (where a male individual has an extra X chromosome: XXY).

Supporters of a biological approach argue that males and females are biologically programmed for certain kinds of activities compatible with male and female roles.

CASE STUDY 36.2

The Batista family: an overnight sex change? (Imperato-McGinley *et al.*, 1974)

Imperato-McGinley *et al.* studied a remarkable family who live in Santo Domingo in the Dominican Republic (in the Caribbean). Of the ten children in the Batista family, four of the sons have changed from being born and growing up as girls into muscular men: they were born with normal female genitalia and body shape but when they were twelve, their vaginas healed over, two testicles descended and they grew full-size penises.

The Batistas are just one of 23 affected families in their village in which 37 children have undergone this change. All these families had a common ancestor, Attagracia Carrasco, who lived in the mid-eighteenth century. She passed on a mutant gene which shows only when carried by both parents.

In the Batista boys, the change that occurs at puberty is due to the flood of testosterone which, in turn, produces enough dihydrotestosterone to give the normal male appearance (which would normally happen ten to twelve years earlier). Their ability to adopt a male gender identity and gender role suggests that their testosterone had preprogrammed masculinity into their brains.

Several researchers have argued that male and female brains are structurally different. For example, destruction of small parts of rats' hypothalami resulted in new-born males behaving as though they were female (Dorner, 1976). But evidence from human studies tends not to support this claim. For example, Daphne Went, although chromosomally male, has a female external appearance, is married, and leads an active and successful life as a woman (Goldwyn, 1979).

However, there's some evidence of sex differences in *hemispheric specialisation* (see Chapter 4). For example, when males perform spatial tasks, there's greater electrical activity in the right hemisphere (Bryden & Saxby, 1985). In women, both hemispheres are activated. According to McGlone (1980), the right hemisphere is generally the dominant one in men, while the left is generally dominant in women (see Box 36.2).

Despite evidence that the corpus callosum is larger overall in women and longer towards the back of the brain (an example of a 'dimorphic' characteristic), Kimura (1993) has warned against accepting this evidence uncritically. It hasn't been clearly established that the number of fibres is the crucial male–female difference (as has been assumed), and sex differences in cognitive functioning have yet to be related to the size of the corpus callosum (see Chapter 4).

Gender stereotypes and gender differences

Ask yourself ...

- What do you consider to be 'typical' feminine and masculine characteristics?
- Are these *merely* stereotypes, or do you think there are real, actual differences between males and females?
- If there are real differences, how do they arise?

There appears to be a high degree of agreement across 30 countries regarding the characteristics associated with each gender group (Williams & Best, 1994). For example, male-associated terms included 'aggressive', 'determined' and 'sharp-witted', while female-associated terms included 'cautious', 'emotional' and 'warm'. However, as far as actual differences are concerned, many stereotypes about males and females have little empirical support.

Box 36.2 Some findings relating to gender differences

Aggression: According to Maccoby & Jacklin (1974) and Weisfeld (1994), boys are more aggressive verbally and physically than girls, a difference which appears as soon as social play begins (around two-and-a-half years). While both sexes become less aggressive with age, boys and men remain more aggressive throughout development (see Chapter 29). However, some studies have shown that women score higher for certain kinds of indirect non-physical aggression (Durkin, 1995), while others have found *no* sex differences at all (e.g. Campbell & Muncer, 1994, see Chapter 46).

Verbal ability: From preschool to adolescence, the sexes are very similar with respect to verbal ability. But at age eleven females become superior, and this increases during adolescence and possibly beyond

(Maccoby & Jacklin, 1974). Again, though, evidence suggests that any such differences are so small as to be negligible (Hyde & Linn, 1988).
Spatial ability: Males' ability to perceive figures or objects in space and their relationship to each other is consistently better than females', in adolescence and adulthood (Maccoby & Jacklin, 1974). But while there's male superiority on some spatial tasks, *within-sex* variability is large. Moreover, when between-sex differences are found, they're usually small (Durkin, 1995).
Mathematical ability: Mathematical skills increase faster in boys, beginning around age twelve or 13 (Maccoby & Jacklin, 1974). But while there are significant sex differences, these are in the *reverse* direction to the stereotype (Hyde *et al.*, 1990).

(Adapted from Durkin, 1995)

Durkin (1995) suggests that:

'The overwhelming conclusion to be drawn from the literature on sex differences is that it is highly controversial'.

A statistically significant difference doesn't imply a large behavioural difference. Rather, what determines a significant result is the *consistency* of the differences between groups, such that if, for example, all the girls in a school scored 0.5 per cent higher than all the boys on the same test, a small but highly significant result would be produced (Edley & Wetherell, 1995).

Eagly (1983), however, has argued that in at least some cases a significant difference *does* reflect a substantial sex difference. By combining the results of different but comparable studies (*meta-analysis*), substantial sex differences emerge on some measures. According to Eagly, research has actually tended to *conceal* rather than *reveal* sex differences. However, the differences *within* each gender are, as noted earlier, at least as great as the differences between them (Maccoby, 1980).

CRITICAL DISCUSSION 36.1

The politics of sex difference research

According to Edley & Wetherell (1995), debates in the nineteenth century about which sex is more intelligent were clearly more than just academic. Early attempts to prove that men's brains are larger and more powerful were just as much about justifying men's dominant social position as about trying to discover the 'natural' order of things. Similarly, the argument over inherent or natural sex differences is often part and parcel of a more general political debate about how society should be organised. For example, the claim that women are naturally more subjective, empathic and emotional leads very neatly to the decision that they are best suited to childcare and other domestic tasks which are devalued, by men, precisely because they're typically performed by women.

More specifically, within psychology as a whole but perhaps in the study of gender in particular, there's a strong bias towards publishing studies that have produced 'positive' results, i.e. where statistically significant sex differences have been found. When sex differences aren't found, the findings tend to remain unreported: the far more convincing evidence for 'sex similarity', therefore, is ignored, creating the very powerful impression that differences between men and women are real, widespread and 'the rule'. Indeed, the very term 'sex similarities' sounds very odd (Jackson, 1992; Tavris, 1993; Unger, 1979). According to Denmark *et al.* (1988), ignoring studies which fail to produce non-significant sex differences represents a form of *sexism* or gender bias in psychological research (see Chapters 47 and 48).

Theories of gender development

Biosocial theory

According to Edley & Wetherell (1995), to ask 'What is the biological basis of masculinity (or femininity)?' is to pose a false question. In their view:

'It requires us to separate what cannot be separated: men [and women] are the product of a complex system of factors and forces which combine in a variety of ways to produce a whole range of different masculinities [and femininities]'.

Biosocial theory takes social factors into account in relation to biological ones. It sees the *interaction* between biological and social factors as important, rather than biology's direct influence. Adults prefer to spend time with babies who respond to them in 'rewarding' ways, and 'demanding' babies tend to receive more attention than 'passive' babies.

As far as other people are concerned, the baby's sex is just as important as its temperament. For example, the 'baby X' experiments (Smith & Lloyd, 1978) involved dressing babies in unisex snowsuits and giving them names which were sometimes in line with their true genders and sometimes not. When adults played with them, they treated the babies according to the genders they believed them to be. This indicates that a person's (perceived) biological make-up becomes part of his/her social environment through others' reactions to it.

According to Money & Ehrhardt (1972), 'anatomy is destiny': how an infant is labelled sexually determines how it's raised or socialised. In turn, this determines the child's gender identity, and from this follow its gender role, gender-role identity and sexual orientation. Psychologically, sexuality is *undifferentiated* at birth: it becomes differentiated as masculine or feminine in the course of the various experiences of growing up.

KEY STUDY 36.1

Pseudohermaphrodites and gender identity (Money & Ehrhardt, 1972)

Money and Ehrhardt studied girls with AGS (see above, page 523) who were initially raised as boys. When the mistake was discovered, their genitals were surgically corrected, and they were reassigned and raised as girls. Money and Ehrhardt claim that it's possible to change the sex of rearing without any undue psychological harm being done, provided this occurs within a 'critical' or 'sensitive period' of about two-and-a-half to three years. But after this, reassignment to the opposite sex can cause extreme psychological disturbance.

Money and Ehrhardt also studied ten people with testicular feminising syndrome. These people showed a strong preference for the female role, which also supports the view that sex of rearing is more important than biological sex. The case of Daphne Went (see text above) also tends to support this view.

Evaluation of biosocial theory

Just because some people appear to be flexible in their psychosexual identities doesn't in itself disprove that 'built-in biases' still have to be overcome (Diamond, 1978). Money and Ehrhardt's participants form an atypical sample, and there's no evidence that people *in general* are as flexible in their psychosexual orientation and identity.

CASE STUDY 36.3

The case of the penectomised twin (Money, 1972)

Money reported a case in which, as a result of an accident during circumcision, one of a pair of identical twins lost his penis (*penectomised*). At 22 months, 'he' was surgically castrated, oestrogen was given, and a vaginal canal constructed. He was subsequently raised as Joan. At age four, Joan preferred dresses to trousers, took pride in her long hair, and was cleaner than her brother, Kevin. At age nine, although Joan had been the dominant twin since birth, she expressed this by being a 'fussy little mother' to Kevin. Money took these findings to support the view that gender identity (and gender role) is *learned*.

The reversal of original sexual assignment is possible if it takes place early enough and is consistent in all respects, which includes the external genitalia conforming well enough to the new sex. But castration and the use of oestrogen clearly contributed to the ease of reassignment, and probably also account for Joan being shorter.

In *Man and Woman, Boy and Girl* (1972), Money and Erhardt referred to Joan's 'tomboyish traits' in passing, but focused on the ways she conformed to the stereotypes of female behaviour. No mention was made of the rejection and teasing she'd encountered in school. Significantly, when Joan had reached her teens she was an unhappy adolescent, with few friends, uncertain about her gender, and maintaining that boys 'had a better life'.

When Joan was twelve, she (reluctantly) began taking oestrogen, and soon breast development and fat around the hips and waist began to appear. But she resisted any further (vaginal) surgery. By age 14, the female hormones were now in competition with her male hormonal system. She decided to stop living as a girl, changed her name back to John, and underwent sex change surgery just before his sixteenth birthday. A rudimentary penis was constructed, but this neither resembled nor performed like the real thing. His popularity with girls caused him terrible distress and unhappiness, and at 18 he tried to commit suicide on two separate occasions. At 21, he had a second operation on his penis, which produced a significant improvement. Two years later, he met and fell in love with a single mother of three children – they married in 1990 (Colapinto, 2000).

Colapinto (2000) met him in 1997 (he was then 31 years old):

'The strongest impression I was left with was of John's intense, unequivocal masculinity. His gestures, walk, attitudes, vocabulary – none of them betrayed the least hint that he had been raised as a girl ... when conversation turns to his childhood ... his voice ... takes on a tone of aggrievement and anger, and he tends to drop the pronoun "I" from his speech, replacing it with the distancing "you" – almost as if he were speaking about someone else altogether. Which, in a sense, he is'.

Ask yourself ...

- What conclusions could you draw from the case of Joan/John?

These findings indicate that biology had ultimately proven irrepressible: gender identity is 'hardwired' into the brain virtually from conception (Diamond, 1982; Diamond & Sigmundson, 1997). Agreeing with Diamond, Reiner (cited in Fletcher, 1997) argues that:

'The organ that appears to be critical to psychosexual development and adaptation is not the genitalia but the brain'.

Sociobiological theory

Sociobiologists (evolutionary theorists: see Chapter 2) argue that gender has gradually evolved over the course of human development as part of our broader adaptation to the environment (Lumsden & Wilson, 1983). Males and females have developed different roles as a function of their respective contributions to reproduction and domestic labour (Wilson, 1978; Hoyenga & Hoyenga, 1979). The relatively greater physical strength, lung capacity and so on of males make them better suited to hunting and defending territory and family. Females' child-bearing and milk-producing capacities make them ideally suited to childcare and other nurturant roles.

According to *parental investment theory* (Kenrick, 1994), females invest considerably more in reproduction than do males. Society came to be organised in sexually exclusive domestic partnerships as a way of meeting the female's needs for protection, and the male's need for preventing his mate from mating with other males. The consequence of this was the evolution of different courtship displays and roles (such as 'playing hard to get'), which are still evident in many cultures,

including Western. According to Buss (1994), what females universally find attractive in males are the characteristics associated with the provision of resources. Men, by contrast, see physical beauty as being of greatest importance (see Chapter 28).

Evaluation of the sociobiological approach

CRITICAL DISCUSSION 36.2

Evolutionary psychology, sexual dimorphism and rape

Like other *evolutionary psychologists*, Cosmides & Tooby (in Horgan, 1995) see the mind as comprising a number of specialised mechanisms or modules, designed by natural selection to solve problems that faced our hunter–gatherer ancestors, such as acquiring mates, raising children and dealing with rivals. The solutions often involve emotions such as lust, fear, affection, jealousy and anger. Evolutionary psychology is mainly concerned with universal features of the mind, but individual differences are seen as the expression of the same universal human nature as it encounters different environments.

The crucial exception to this rule is *gender*: natural selection has constructed the mental modules of men and women very differently as a result of their divergent reproductive roles. Buss (1994) claims that there's a distinct gender gap in 'mate choice', and Thornhill & Wilmsen-Thornhill (1992) argue that human sexual psychology is *dimorphic* (i.e. the respective adaptations differ in men and women). The sexes differ in their feelings about whether, when and how often it's in their interests to mate.

Because women are more selective about their mates and more interested in evaluating them and delaying intercourse, men, to get sexual access, must often break through female resistance. According to Thornhill and Wilmsen-Thornhill's *'rape adaptation hypothesis'*, during human evolutionary history there was enough directional selection on males in favour of traits that solved the problem of forcing sex on a reluctant partner to produce a psychological tendency specifically towards rape.

In other words, not only does this hypothesis recast an oppressive form of behaviour in a much more positive light (it's 'adaptive'), but it also represents it as a natural characteristic of men ('they can't help it'). Not surprisingly, it has been condemned as not simply trying to explain men's sexual coercion, but justifying it (Edley & Wetherell, 1995).

The sociobiological approach has been criticised on several grounds (see Chapter 2). For example, dominance patterns are not, as sociobiological approaches assume, equated with greater aggression. In humans, at least, dominance often relates to status seeking, which implies the role of culturally determined values (Sayers, 1982). Sociobiological approaches to sex differences are also difficult to test: we have only incomplete knowledge about the ways in which our ancestors adapted to their environments. So, our hunches about which characteristics were adaptive and why differences between the sexes evolved are 'educated guesses' at best (see Chapter 2).

Freud's psychoanalytic theory

Freud's account of gender development is related to his explanation of moral development which, in turn, is part of his theory of psychosexual development (as we saw in Chapter 35). Up until the resolution of the Oedipus complex, gender identity is assumed to be flexible. Resolution of the Oedipus complex occurs through identification with the same-sex parent, and results in the acquisition of both a superego and gender identity. Like the development of conscience, Freud also saw the development of gender identity as being weaker in girls than boys.

Evaluation of the psychoanalytic approach

There are at least three reasons for doubting a Freudian interpretation of gender identity's development.

- Children of a particular age don't appear to acquire gender identity in 'one fell swoop' (Krebs & Blackman, 1988).
- Children who grow up in 'atypical' families (e.g. single-parent or lesbian couples) aren't necessarily adversely affected in terms of their gender identities (Golombok *et al.*, 1983). Indeed, children reared in fatherless families (whether lesbian or heterosexual) appear to have *more secure* attachments (Golombok *et al.*, 1997: see Chapter 32).
- While identification might promote gender identity, children are aware of gender roles well before the age at which Freud believed their Oedipus complex is resolved. For example, boys prefer stereotypically masculine toys (such as trucks) and girls stereotypically feminine toys (such as dolls) in *infancy* (O'Brien *et al.*, 1983).

Social learning theory

Ask yourself ...

- How do you think SLT tries to explain gender development? (See Chapter 35.)

According to *social learning theory* (SLT), one reason girls and boys learn to behave differently is that they're *treated differently* by their parents and others. As the 'baby X' study shows (see page 525), when informed of a child's biological sex, parents and others often react to it according to their gender-role expectations. Thus, girls and boys are often given different toys, have their rooms decorated differently, and are even spoken about in different terms (Rubin *et al.*, 1974).

However, Karraker *et al.* (1995) found that this strong sex-typing of infants at birth has declined, and that there were no differences between mothers and fathers in this respect. A consistent and persistent finding is that fathers treat their children in a more gendered way than mothers (Maccoby, 1990). Typically, fathers interact in a more instrumental and achievement-oriented way, and give more attention to their sons, while mothers attend equally to sons and daughters (Quiery, 1998).

SLT also emphasises the roles of *observational learning* and *reinforcement*. By observing others behaving in particular ways and then imitating that behaviour, children receive reinforcement from 'significant others' for behaviours considered to be *sex-appropriate* (Bandura, 1977b: see Chapter 35). Boys tend to be positively reinforced more for behaviours reflecting independence, self-reliance and emotional control. But girls tend to be reinforced for, dependence, nurturance, empathy and emotional expression (Block, 1979). Fathers tend to reinforce these sex-typed behaviours more than mothers do (Kerig *et al.*, 1993: see above).

Playing with dolls and displaying nurturant behaviour, and playing with guns and displaying assertive, even aggressive, behaviour, conform to female and male gender role expectations/stereotypes respectively. According to social learning theory, children receive parental reinforcement for displaying such gender-appropriate behaviours

Evaluation of SLT
Findings supporting SLT

- Sears *et al.* (1957) found that parents allowed sons to be more aggressive in their relationships with other children, and towards their parents, than daughters. For some mothers, 'being a boy' meant being aggressive, and boys were often encouraged to fight back. Although parents believe they respond in the same way to aggressive acts committed by boys and girls, they actually intervene much more frequently and quickly when girls behave aggressively (Huston, 1983).
- Boys were more likely to imitate aggressive male models than were girls (Bandura *et al.*, 1961, 1963). Children are

also more likely to imitate a same-sex model than an opposite-sex model, even if the behaviour is 'sex-inappropriate' (see Chapter 35).

- Although parents are important models, SL theorists are also interested in media portrayals of males and females. A large body of evidence suggests that gender-role stereotypes are portrayed by the media, as well as by parents and teachers (Wober *et al.*, 1987). Moreover, children categorised as 'heavy' viewers of TV hold stronger stereotyped beliefs than 'lighter' viewers (Gunter, 1986: see Chapter 29).

Findings not supporting SLT

- According to Maccoby & Jacklin (1974), there are no consistent differences in the extent to which boys and girls are reinforced for aggressiveness or autonomy. Rather, there appears to be remarkable uniformity in the sexes' socialisation. This is supported by Lytton & Romney (1991), who found very few sex differences in terms of parental warmth, overall amount of interaction, encouragement of achievement or dependency, restrictiveness and discipline, or clarity of communication.

- Although Bandura *et al.*'s research is often cited, the evidence concerning imitation and modelling is actually inconclusive, and some studies have failed to find that children are more likely to imitate same-sex models than opposite-sex models. Indeed, children have been shown to prefer imitating behaviour that's 'appropriate' to their own sex regardless of the model's (Maccoby & Jacklin, 1974).

- The view that TV can impact upon a passively receptive child audience with messages about sex-role stereotyping, and mould young children's conceptions of gender is over-simplistic (see Chapter 29). For Gunter & McAleer (1997), children respond selectively to particular characters and events, and their perceptions, memories and understanding of what they've seen may often be mediated by the dispositions they bring with them to the viewing situation. While 'heavy' TV viewers might hold stronger stereotyped beliefs than other children, no precise measures were taken of the programmes they actually watched.

- While modelling plays an important role in children's socialisation, there's no consistent preference for the same-sex parent's behaviour (Hetherington, 1967). Instead, children prefer to model the behaviour of those with whom they have most contact (usually the mother). Also, there's no significant correlation between the extent to which parents engage in sex-typed behaviours and the strength of sex-typing in their children (Smith & Daglish, 1977). However, fathers' adoption of either traditional (sex-typed) or egalitarian attitudes has been found to correlate with four-year-olds' perceptions of sex roles (Quiery, 1998).

Cognitive–developmental theory

The cognitive–developmental approach (Kohlberg, 1969; Kohlberg & Ullian, 1974) emphasises the child's participation in developing both an understanding of gender and gender-appropriate behaviour (see Chapter 35). Children's discovery that they're male or female *causes* them to identify with members of their own sex (*not* the other way round, as psychoanalytic and SL theories suggest). While rewards and punishments influence children's choices of toys and activi-

ties, these don't mechanically strengthen stimulus–response connections, but provide children with information about when they're behaving in ways that other people deem appropriate (see Chapter 35).

According to cognitive–developmental theorists, young children acquire an understanding of the concepts *male* and *female* in three stages.

Box 36.3   Stages in the development of gender identity

Stage 1 (Gender labelling or basic gender identity): This occurs somewhere around age three (Ruble, 1984) and refers to the child's recognition that it's male or female. According to Kohlberg, knowing one's gender is an achievement that allows us to understand and categorise the world. But this knowledge is fragile, and children don't yet realise that boys invariably become men and girls always become women.

Stage 2 (Gender stability): By age four or five, most children recognise that people retain their genders for a lifetime. But children still rely on superficial signs (such as the length of a person's hair) to determine their gender (Marcus & Overton, 1978).

Stage 3 (Gender constancy or consistency): At around age six or seven, children realise that gender is *immutable*. So, even if a woman has her hair cut very short, her gender remains constant. Gender constancy represents a kind of *conservation* (see Chapter 34) and, significantly, appears shortly after the child has mastered the conservation of quantity (Marcus & Overton, 1978).

Once children acquire gender constancy, they come to value the behaviours and attitudes associated with their sex. Only at this point do they identify with the adult figures who possess the qualities they see as being most central to their concepts of themselves as male or female (Perry & Bussey, 1979).

Evaluation of cognitive–developmental theory

Evidence suggests that the concepts of gender identity, stability and constancy do occur in that order across many cultures (Munroe *et al.*, 1984). Slaby & Frey (1975) divided two- to five-year-olds into 'high' and 'low' gender constancy. The children were then shown a silent film of adults simultaneously performing a series of simple activities. The screen was 'split', with males performing activities on one side and females on the other. Children rated as 'high' in gender constancy showed a marked same-sex bias, as measured by the amount of visual attention they gave to each side of the screen. This supports Kohlberg's belief that gender constancy is a *cause* of the imitation of same-sex models rather than an effect. Children actively *construct* their gender-role knowledge through purposeful monitoring of the social environment. They engage in *self-socialisation*, rather than passively receiving information (Whyte, 1998).

Ask yourself ...

- According to the theory, what will be the relationship between gender constancy and the child's gender-appropriate behaviour?

A major problem for cognitive–developmental theory is that it predicts there should be *little or no* gender-appropriate behaviour *before* gender constancy is achieved. But even in infancy, both sexes show a marked preference for stereotypical male and female toys (Huston, 1983: see pages 527–528). While such children might have developed a sense of gender identity, they are, as far as cognitive–developmental theory is concerned, some years away from achieving gender stability and constancy (Fagot, 1985).

Gender-schematic processing theory

This addresses the possibility that gender identity *alone* can provide children with sufficient motivation to assume sex-typed behaviour patterns (e.g. Bem, 1985; Martin, 1991). Like SLT, this approach suggests that children learn 'appropriate' patterns of behaviour by observation. However, consistent with cognitive–developmental theory, children's active cognitive processing of information also contributes to their sex-typing.

Children learn that strength is linked to the male sex-role stereotype and weakness to the female stereotype, and that some dimensions (including strength–weakness) are more relevant to one gender (males) than the other (Rathus, 1990). So, a boy learns that the strength he displays in wrestling (say) affects others' perceptions of him. Unless competing in some sporting activity, most girls don't see this dimension as being important. But while boys are expected to compete in sports, girls aren't, and so a girl is likely to find that her gentleness and neatness are more important in the eyes of others than her strength (Rathus, 1990).

According to gender-schematic processing theory, then, children learn to judge themselves according to the traits considered to be relevant to their genders. Consequently, the self-concept becomes mixed with the gender schemas of a particular culture which provides standards for comparison (see Chapter 33). The theory sees gender identity as being sufficient to produce 'sex-appropriate' behaviour. The labels 'boy' and 'girl', once understood, give children the basis for mixing their self-concepts with their society's gender schemas. Children with gender identity will actively seek information about gender schemas, and their self-esteem will soon become influenced by how they 'measure up' to their gender schema (Rathus, 1990).

Cultural relativism

This really represents the most direct challenge to the biological approach. If gender differences do reflect biological differences, then we'd expect to find the same differences occurring in different cultures. Any differences that exist between cultures with regard to gender roles (*cultural relativism*) support the view that gender role is *culturally determined*.

Margaret Mead (1935) claimed that the traits we call masculine and feminine are completely unrelated to biological sex. Just as the clothing, manner and head-dress considered to be appropriate in a particular society, at a particular time, aren't determined by sex, so temperament and gender role aren't biologically but culturally determined. She studied three New Guinea tribes, who lived quite separately from each other within about a 100-mile radius:

Figure 36.2 *Jane Couch (the 'Fleetwood Assassin'), women's world welter-weight boxing champion, after winning her sex discrimination case in 1998 against the British Boxing Board of Control over its refusal to grant her a license to box professionally*

- The *Arapesh*, who lived on hillsides, were gentle, loving and co-operative. Boys and girls were reared in order to develop these qualities, which in Western society are stereotypically feminine. Both parents were said to 'bear a child', and men took to bed while the child was born.
- The *Mundugumor* were riverside dwellers and ex-cannibals. Both males and females were self-assertive, arrogant, fierce and continually quarrelling, and they both detested the whole business of pregnancy and child-rearing. Sleeping babies were hung in rough-textured baskets in a dark place against the wall and when they cried, someone would scratch gratingly on the outside of the basket.
- The *Tchambuli*, who lived on the lakeside, represented the reversal of traditional Western gender roles. Girls were encouraged to take an interest in the tribe's economic affairs, and the women took care of trading and food gathering. Men, on the other hand, were considered sentimental, emotional and incapable of making serious decisions, spending much of the day sitting around in groups, gossiping and 'preening' themselves.

However, by 1949, after she'd studied four other cultures (Samoa, Manus, Iatmul and Bali), Mead had rather dramatically changed her views about gender roles. From a rather extreme 'cultural determinism', she now concluded that women were 'naturally' more nurturing than men, expressing their creativity through childbearing and childbirth, and are superior in intellectual abilities requiring intuition. While motherhood is a 'biological inclination', fatherhood is a 'social invention': by implication, societies which encourage a gender role division other than that in which dominant, sexually energetic men live with passive, nurturant women are 'going against nature'. Significantly, by this time she'd given birth to a child of her own! (Booth, 1975).

Are there cultural universals?

A finding which may seem to support Mead in her search for 'natural' differences is that there's no known society in which the female does the fighting in warfare (including the Tchambuli and Arapesh: Fortune, 1939). However, there's more to aggression than warfare (see Chapter 29). Malinowski (1929), studying the Trobriand Islanders, reported that, in order to foster their tribe's reputation for virility, groups of women would catch a man from another tribe, arouse him to erection and rape him! This 'gang rape' was carried out in a brutal manner and the women often boasted about their achievement.

Ask yourself ...

- Even if men are, universally, the hunters and war-makers, does this necessarily mean that males are naturally more aggressive than females?

According to Wade & Tavris (1994), because early researchers *assumed* that men are naturally aggressive (and women are naturally nurturant), they often defined nurturing in a way that excluded the altruistic, caring activities of men. For example, men can nurture the family by providing food for mother and child and sometimes by going off to fight in faraway places, sacrificing their lives if necessary, in order to provide a safe haven for their people.

While most cultures distinguish between 'men's' and 'women's work' and while biological factors undoubtedly play some part in the sexual division of labour, the *content* of this work varies enormously between cultures. As Hargreaves (1986) observes, in some cultures:

> '... *men weave and women make pots, whereas in others these roles are reversed; in some parts of the world women are the major agricultural producers, and in others they are prohibited from agricultural activity*'.

Western culture has no formally recognised and accepted equivalent of the berdache. However, in recent times, as the economic lives of men and women have become more similar (see Chapter 38), we have at least informally developed some acceptance of berdache-like alternatives. For example, the concept of *androgyny* (Bem, 1974: see Gross, 1999) refers to people who've developed both the 'masculine' and 'feminine' sides of themselves more fully than most. Similarly, the concept of *sexual orientation* implies an awareness that relationships aren't simply an expression of a single inborn norm (Price & Crapo, 1999).

Box 36.4 Are there more than two genders?

Among the Sakalavas in Madagascar, boys who are thought to be pretty are raised as girls and readily adopt the female gender role. Similarly, the Alentian Islanders in Alaska raise handsome boys as girls; their beards are plucked at puberty and they are later married to rich men. They too seem to adapt quite readily to their assigned gender role.

Studies of certain Native American peoples reveal the possibility of more than two basic gender roles. For example, the 'berdache', a biological male of the Crow tribe, simply chooses not to follow the ideal role of warrior. Instead, he might become the 'wife' of a warrior but he's never scorned or ridiculed by his fellow Crows. (Little Horse in the film *Little Big Man*, starring Dustin Hoffman, was a 'berdache'.)

The Mohave Indians recognised four distinct gender roles: (i) traditional male; (ii) traditional female; (iii) 'alyha'; and (iv) 'hwame'. The 'alyha' was a male who chose to live as a woman (to the extent of mimicking menstruation by cutting his upper thigh and undergoing a ritualistic pregnancy) and the 'hwame' was a female who chose to become a man.

Conclusions

While every known culture distinguishes between male and female, the evidence for the truth of sex stereotypes is inconclusive. Although anatomical sex is universal and unchangeable, *gender*, which refers to all the duties, rights and behaviours a culture considers appropriate for males and females, is a *social invention*. It's gender that gives us a sense of personal identity as male or female (Wade & Tavris, 1994). An even stronger argument for the social construction of gender comes from studies of societies in which gender reversal is relatively commonplace or, more importantly, where there are more than two genders. All the perspectives discussed in this chapter have contributed to our understanding of that process, and they should be seen as complementary explanations (Whyte, 1998).

CHAPTER SUMMARY

- Feminist psychologists distinguish between **sex/sexual identity** and **gender/gender identity**.

- There's little empirical support for actual gender differences in terms of either **aggression** or **verbal**, **spatial** or **mathematical abilities**.

- Biologically, sex refers to **chromosomal sex**, **gonadal sex**, **hormonal sex**, sex of the **internal reproductive structures** and sex of the **external genitalia**. While these are usually highly correlated with each other, in **hermaphroditism/pseudohermaphroditism**, pre- and postnatal disorders produce an inconsistency between these categories.

- Major types of pseudohermaphroditism are **androgen insensitivity syndrome** (AIS)/**testicular feminising syndrome**, **adrenogenital syndrome** (AGS) and **dihydrotestosterone** (DHT)-**deficiency/5-alpha-reductase deficiency**.

- According to the **biological approach**, males and females are biologically programmed for certain activities compatible with gender roles.

- While studies of **hemispheric specialisation** are consistent with some of the claimed male–female differences in cognitive abilities, evidence that the corpus callosum is sexually dimorphic is inconclusive.

- **Biosocial theory** stresses the **interaction** of social and biological factors. A person's (perceived) biological make-up (such as sex) becomes part of his or her social environment through others' reactions to it.

■ Money and Ehrhardt claim that there's a 'critical' or 'sensitive' period for the development of gender identity. But cases of penectomised boys raised as girls tend to support the claim that gender identity and role are **biologically determined**.

■ According to **sociobiologists**, gender has evolved as part of human beings' broader adaptation to the environment. **Parental investment theory** claims that sexually exclusive domestic partnerships meet the female's need for protection and the male's need for preventing his mate from mating with other males.

■ **Psychoanalytic theory** sees gender identity as being related to moral and overall psychosexual development. But gender identity develops much more gradually than Freud claimed, and studies of children who grow up in 'atypical' families show that their gender identity isn't adversely affected.

■ According to **social learning theory** (SLT), girls and boys learn to behave differently through being **treated differently** by parents and others. SLT also stresses the role of **observational learning** and **reinforcement** for imitating sex-appropriate behaviours.

■ Evidence is inconclusive regarding the importance for imitation of the **sex-appropriateness** of a model's behaviour and the model's sex. There's no consistent preference for the same-sex parent's behaviour, but rather for the parent the child spends most time with.

■ According to the **cognitive–developmental approach**, children's discovery that they're male or female **causes** them to identify with and imitate same-sex models. Three stages in the development of gender identity are **gender labelling/basic gender identity**, **gender stability** and **gender constancy/consistency**.

■ **Gender-schematic processing theory** maintains that gender identity alone can provide a child with sufficient motivation to assume sex-typed behaviour. Children learn to judge themselves according to the traits seen as relevant to their genders, resulting in self-concepts that are mixed with the **gender schemas** of a particular culture.

■ According to **cultural relativism**, any differences in gender roles between cultures are likely to be **culturally determined**.

■ The enormous cultural diversity of the content of men's and women's work, and the existence of more than two genders in some Native American peoples strongly suggests that gender is **socially constructed**.

Self-assessment questions

1 Describe and evaluate psychological insights into the development of gender identity and gender roles.
2 a Describe **one** theory of the development of gender.
  b Assess the extent to which this theory is supported by research evidence.
3 Discuss the influence of biological **and** social psychological factors on the development of gender.

Web addresses

http://www.upm.edu.my/llsgend.html

http://www.hfni.gsehd.gwu.edu/~tip/theories.html

http://www.apa.org/journals/cntlcntl44131.html

http://www.garysturt.free-online.co.uk/gender.htm

Further reading

Unger, R.K. (1979) *Female and Male: Psychological Perspectives.* New York: Harper & Row. An excellent review of the study of psychological sex differences by a leading feminist psychologist.

Edley, N. & Wetherell, M. (1995) *Men in Perspective: Practice, Power and Identity.* Hemel Hempstead: Prentice Hall/Harvester Wheatsheaf. A critical review of a wide range of contemporary theoretical perspectives on the nature of masculinity.

Trew, K. & Kremer, J. (1998, Eds) *Gender and Psychology.* London: Arnold. An excellent collection of original chapters discussing gender in relation to a wide variety of issues.

Chapter 37

Adolescence

Introduction and overview

The word 'adolescence' comes from the Latin *ado-lescere* meaning 'to grow into maturity'. As well as being a time of enormous physiological change, adolescence is also marked by changes in behaviour, expectations, and relationships with both parents and peers. In Western, industrialised societies, there's generally no single initiation rite signalling the passage into adulthood.

The lack of such initiations into adulthood makes this a more difficult transition than it appears to be in more traditional, non-industrialised societies. Relationships with parents

1950s films such as Rebel Without A Cause, *starring James Dean, have been seen as helping to create the concept of the 'rebellious teenager'*

in particular, and adults in general, must be renegotiated in a way that allows the adolescent to achieve greater independence. This process is aided by changing relationships with peers.

Historically, adolescence has been seen as a period of transition between childhood and adulthood. But writers today are more likely to describe it as one of *multiple transitions*, involving education, training, employment and unemployment, as well as transitions from one set of living circumstances to another (Coleman & Roker, 1998).

This change in perspective in many ways reflects changes in the adolescent experience compared with those of previous generations: it starts five years earlier, marriage takes place six or seven years later than it did, and cohabitation, perhaps as a prelude to marriage, is rapidly increasing (Coleman & Hendry, 1999). Passage into adulthood may also be deferred by the delay in acquiring an income: not only has there been an extension in compulsory education but pressure on the workforce to become more highly skilled places a premium on continuing education (Hendry, 1999).

Coupled with these 'adulthood-postponing' changes, in recent years adolescents have enjoyed greater self-determination at steadily younger ages. Yet this greater freedom carries with it more risks and greater costs when errors of judgement are made. As Hendry (1999) says:

'... "dropping out" of school, being out of work, teenage pregnancy, sexually transmitted diseases, being homeless, drug addiction and suicide, are powerful examples of the price that some young people pay for their extended freedom'.

Normative and non-normative shifts

Ask yourself ...
- What kinds of transitions do adolescents in Western societies experience?
- Are they necessarily the same for all adolescents?

One way of categorising the various transitions involved in adolescence is in terms of normative and non-normative shifts (Hendry & Kloep, 1999; Kloep & Hendry, 1999).

- *Normative, maturational shifts* include the growth spurt (both sexes), menarche (first menstruation), first nocturnal emissions ('wet dreams'), voice breaking (boys), changes in sexual organs, beginning of sexual arousal, changed romantic relationships, gender-role identity, changed relationships with adults, increasing autonomy and responsibility.
- *Normative, society-dependent shifts* include the change from primary to secondary school, leaving school, getting started in an occupation, acquiring legal rights for voting, sex, purchasing alcohol, driving licence, military service, and cohabitation.
- *Non-normative shifts* include parental divorce, family bereavement, illness, natural disasters, war, incest, emigration, disruption of peer network, risk-taking behaviours, 'disadvantage' (because of gender, class, regional or ethnic discrimination), physical and/or mental handicap.

According to Kloep & Hendry (1999):

'Although all adolescents have to cope with the psychosocial challenges associated with their maturing body, new relationships with parents and peers, with school and the transitions toward employment, a growing number encounter additional problems like family disruption, economic deprivation or social or cultural changes ...' .

A normative shift may become non-normative, if, say, there are other circumstances that cause a normal developmental 'task' to become more difficult, for example, if the onset of puberty occurs unusually early or late.

Puberty: The social and psychological meaning of biological changes

Puberty and body image

Adjusting to puberty is one of the most important adjustments that adolescents have to make (Coleman & Hendry, 1999). Even as a purely *biological* phenomenon, puberty is far from being a simple, straightforward process. While all adolescents experience the same bodily changes (see Box 37.1 and Figure 37.1, page 534), the sequence of changes may vary within individuals (*intraindividual asynchronies*: Alsaker, 1996). For example, for some girls menstruation may occur very early on in puberty, while for others it may occur after most other changes (e.g. growth spurt, breast development) have taken place.

Major changes in puberty

Physiologically, puberty begins when the seminal vesicles and prostate gland enlarge in the male, and the ovaries enlarge in the female. Both males and females experience the *adolescent growth spurt*. Male *secondary sex characteristics* include growth of pubic and then chest and facial hair, and sperm production. In females, breast size increases, pubic hair grows, and menstruation begins.

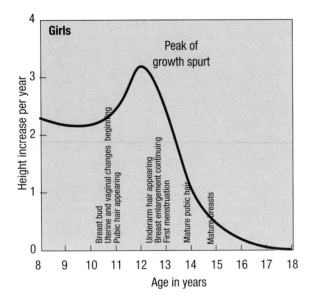

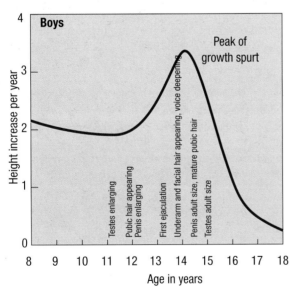

Figure 37.1 *The development of secondary sex characteristics. The curved lines represent the average increase in height from eight to 18 years of age. The characteristics shown may occur earlier or later in a person's development, but usually occur in the order shown (based on Tanner, 1978, and Tanner & Whitehouse, 1976)*

Box 37.1 | **Adolescents' brains**

According to some neuroscientists, the brain undergoes some fundamental restructuring during adolescence, just as it does during the earliest years of childhood. While the *plasticity* of the infant's and young child's brain is widely accepted (see Chapter 4), this has traditionally been seen as stopping at puberty.

However, two MRI studies, one *longitudinal* (which followed up the same set of youngsters over several years: Giedd *et al.*, 1999), the other *cross-sectional* (which compared a group of 14-year-olds with a group in their mid-twenties: Sowell *et al.*, 1999) suggest otherwise.

Areas of the cortex that deal with more basic functions, such as sensory and motor processing, do indeed stabilise in early childhood. But the parietal and frontal lobes, which are specialised for visuospatial and 'executive functions' (e.g. planning and self-control) respectively, show a growth surge between the ages of ten and twelve. This sudden 'bulking up' is then followed by an equally dramatic *reduction* in size, which continues right through the teenage years and into the early twenties. It only stops when these areas have reached their adult proportions.

This late shrinkage is taken to be a sign of maturation. As McCone (2000) puts it:

'... *brains are believed to develop mainly by a pruning of their neural thickets to form orderly processing paths*'.

(Based on McCone, 2000)

According to Davies & Furnham (1986), the average adolescent isn't only sensitive to, but also critical of, his or her changing physical self. Because of gender and sexual development, young people are inevitably confronted, perhaps for the first time, by cultural standards of beauty in evaluating their own body images (via the media and the reactions of others). This may produce a non-normative shift in the form of dieting practices, leading to eating disorders (see Chapter 44). Young people may be especially vulnerable to teasing and exclusion if they're perceived by their peers as over- or underweight (Kloep & Hendry, 1999).

Gender differences

While puberty may be a normative, maturational shift, it may be a more difficult transition for girls than boys. This is because of the *subjective meaning* of bodily change (what it means for the individual), which mirrors the *sociocultural significance* of puberty (its significance for society). According to the *cultural ideal hypothesis* (Simmons & Blyth, 1987), puberty will bring boys *closer* to their physical ideal (an increase in muscle distribution and lung capacity produces greater stamina, strength and athletic capacities), while girls move further *away from* theirs.

For girls, who begin puberty on average two years ahead of boys, it's normal to experience an increase in body fat and rapid weight gain, thus making their bodies less like the Western cultural ideal of the thin, sylph-like supermodel. In addition, they have to deal with menstruation, which is negatively associated with blood and physical discomfort (Crawford & Unger, 1995).

The importance of timing

If the cultural ideal hypothesis is valid, it follows that *early-maturing boys* will be at an *advantage* relative to their 'on-time' and late-maturing peers (they'll be moving faster towards the male ideal). By the same token, *early-maturing girls* will be at a *disadvantage* (they'll be moving faster away from the female ideal). Indeed, according to Alsaker (1996):

> '... pubertal timing is generally regarded as a more crucial aspect of pubertal development than pubertal maturation itself'.

In other words, it's not the *fact* of puberty that matters as much as *when* it occurs, and it matters mainly in relation to body image and self-esteem.

Box 37.2   The falling age of puberty onset

One in six girls reaches puberty by the age of eight, compared with one in 100 a generation ago. Also, one in 14 eight-year-old boys has pubic hair (an early indicator of puberty), compared with one in 150 of their fathers' generation.

Bristol University's Institute of Child Health tracked the development of 1150 children from birth. It's the first study of puberty in Britain since the 1960s (see Figure 37.1). Not only are children starting puberty earlier, but it's lasting longer. The reasons are unclear, but likely causes are higher oestrogen levels in mothers, diet, lifestyle and pollution. There could also be a genetic link, since the mothers of girls who begin puberty earlier also matured earlier.

Separate research has found that the average age of menarche has fallen below 13 in Britain for the first time. It's now twelve years ten-months, compared with 13 years six months in 1969.

These findings mean that children could be developing sexually before they have the emotional maturity to deal with the possible consequences.

(Based on Peek, 2000)

Ask yourself ...

- A common finding is that early-maturing girls and late-maturing boys suffer lower self-esteem. Why do you think this might be?

Box 37.3   Why do early-maturing girls and late-maturing boys feel less good about themselves?

One popular explanation is the *deviancy hypothesis*, according to which those who are 'off-time' in physical maturation are socially deviant compared with peers of the same age and sex (Wichstrom, 1998). Since girls begin puberty on average two years before boys, early-maturing girls are the first to enter this deviant position, followed by late-maturing boys.

An alternative explanation is the *developmental readiness hypothesis* (Simmons & Blyth, 1987). In the case of early or sudden puberty, too little time will have been spent on ego development during latency, with early-maturing girls once more being most affected. (This explanation is similar to Coleman's *focal theory*, which is discussed below: see page 541.)

As far as the *cultural ideal hypothesis* is concerned, Wichstrom (1998) maintains that the suggestion that the pubertal girl moves further away from the Western stereotyped female ideal may *not* be true. *Both* boys and girls move closer to their ideals, provided they don't put on excessive weight (Wichstrom, 1998).

According to Wichstrom, the cultural ideal hypothesis is sensitive to changes in time and context. For example, in Norway there may be less emphasis on sterotypical male stature compared with the USA and UK. Perhaps also the embarrassment and negative affect experienced by American girls when starting their periods and becoming sexually responsive is less prevalent among Norwegian girls, due to relatively greater openness about adolescent sexuality (Wichstrom, 1998).

Theories of adolescence

Hall's theory: adolescence as storm and stress

This is probably the earliest formal theory of adolescence. Influenced by Darwin's evolutionary theory (see Gross *et al.*, 2000), Hall (1904) argued that each person's psychological development *recapitulates* (or recaptures) both the biological and cultural evolution of the human species. He saw adolescence as a time of 'storm and stress' (or *Sturm und Drang*), which mirrors the volatile history of the human race over the last 2000 years.

Some evidence suggests that emotional reactions are more *intense* and *volatile* during adolescence compared with other periods of life, such as the study by Csikszentmihalyi & Larson (1984: see Key Study 37.1). However, more important indicators of storm and stress are (a) mental disorder, and (b) delinquent behaviour.

KEY STUDY 37.1

Volatile adolescents (Csikszentmihalyi & Larson, 1984)

Seventy-five Chicago-area high-school students from diverse social and racial backgrounds were asked to wear electronic pagers for a week. Every two hours, the pager signalled to the students that they were to write a description of what they were doing and how they felt about it. After a week, they filled out questionnaires about both their general moods and their specific mood during particular activities. About 40 per cent of waking time was spent pursuing leisure activities, the other 60 per cent being more-or-less equally divided between 'maintenence activities' (such as commuting and eating) and 'productive activities' (such as studying and working).

Particularly revealing were the adolescents' extreme mood swings, from extreme happiness to deep sadness (and vice versa) in less than an hour. Adults usually require several hours to reach the same emotional peaks and troughs.

Studies of mental disorder

Several studies have found that *early-maturing girls* score higher on measures of depressive feelings and sadness (e.g. Alsaker, 1992; Stattin & Magnusson, 1990), although this was only true when the measures were taken before or simultaneously with changing schools (Petersen *et al.*, 1991). They've also been reported to have more psychosomatic (psychophysiological) symptoms (e.g. Stattin & Magnusson, 1990), to display greater concerns about eating (e.g. Brooks-Gunn *et al.*, 1989), and to score higher on Offer's psychopathology scale (e.g. Brooks-Gunn & Warren, 1985).

As far as *early-maturing boys* are concerned, the evidence is much more mixed (Alsaker, 1996). While early maturation is usually found to be advantageous, it's also been found to be associated with *more* psychopathology (e.g. Petersen & Crockett, 1985), depressive tendencies and anxiety (e.g. Alsaker, 1992).

KEY STUDY 37.2

The 'Isle of Wight' study (Rutter *et al.*, 1976)

This involved a large, representative sample of 14–15-year-olds (more than 2000), whose parents and teachers completed a behaviour questionnaire about them. More detailed data were obtained from two subsamples: (i) 200 randomly selected from the total popualtion; (ii) 304 with extreme scores on the teacher/parent questionnaires (suggesting 'deviant' behaviour).

Those in both subsamples were given questionnaires and tests and interviewed by psychiatrists. The major findings regarding rates of psychiatric disorder among the adolescents, compared with a sample of ten-year-olds and the adolescents' parents, are shown in Table 37.1.

Table 37.1 *Percentage of ten-year-olds, 14–15-year-olds, and the latter's parents, displaying psychiatric disorder*

	Ten-year-olds	14–15-year-olds	Adults (parents)
Males	12.7	13.2	7.6
Females	10.9	12.5	11.9

According to Rutter *et al.* (1976):

- there's a rather modest peak in psychiatric disorders in adolescence;
- although severe clinical depression is rare, some degree of inner turmoil may characterise a sizeable minority of adolescents. While it's not a myth, neither should it be exaggerated;
- a substantial proportion of those adolescents with psychiatric problems had had them since childhood. Also, when problems did first appear during adolescence, they were mainly associated with stressful situations (such as parents' marital discord):

  '... adolescent turmoil is fact, not fiction, but its psychiatric importance has probably been overestimated in the past'. (Rutter *et al.*, 1976)

In Western societies, while some adolescents may display affective disturbances or disorders, it's a relatively small minority who'll show clinical depression or report 'inner turmoil' (Compas *et al.*, 1995). Instead, the majority worry about everyday issues, such as school and examination performance, finding work, family and social relationships, self-image, conflicts with authority and the future generally (Gallagher *et al.*, 1992).

Studies of delinquent behaviour

Caspi *et al.* (1993) studied all the children born in Dunedin, New Zealand between April 1972 and March 1973, following

Figure 37.2 *Pre-teens are growing up faster than ever before, and early-maturing girls are most at risk of mental disorder and delinquency*

them up every two years from ages three to 15. Compared with on-time (menarche 12.5–13.5 years) and late maturers (after 13.5), early-maturing girls were more at risk for:

- *early deliquency* (breaking windows, getting drunk, making prank phone calls, stealing from other pupils at school);
- *familiarity with delinquent peers* (having friends or knowing others who engaged in these activities); and
- *delinquency* (shoplifting, car theft, smoking marijuana, using weapons).

However, the risk for early delinquency was greater only in mixed-sex schools, and (as with a sample of Swedish girls studied by Magnusson *et al.*, 1985) early maturers were likely to mix with older peers. As for boys, *off-time* (early and late) maturation has been shown to be related to alcohol consumption, with late maturers also being at risk for *later* alcohol problems (Anderson & Magnusson, 1990).

Erikson's theory: identity crisis

Erikson (1963) believed that it's human nature to pass through a genetically determined sequence of *psychosocial stages*, spanning the whole lifespan. Each stage involves a struggle between two conflicting personality outcomes, one of which is positive (or *adaptive*), while the other is negative (or *maladaptive*). Healthy development involves the adaptive outweighing the maladaptive.

The major challenge of adolescence is to establish a strong sense of personal identity. The dramatic onset of puberty (combined with more sophisticated intellectual abilities: see Chapter 34) makes adolescents particularly concerned with finding their own personal place in adult society.

In Western societies adolescence is a *moratorium*, an authorised delay of adulthood, which frees adolescents from most responsibilities and helps them make the difficult transition from childhood to adulthood. Although this is meant to make the transition easier, it can also have the opposite effect. Most of the societies studied by cultural anthropologists have important public ceremonies to mark the transition from childhood to adulthood. This is in stark contrast to Western, industrialised nations, which leave children to their own devices in finding their identity. Without a clearly defined procedure to follow, this process can be difficult – both for adolescents and their parents (see *Generation gap* below).

Does society create identity crisis?

> *Ask yourself ...*
>
> - Can you think of any inconsistencies or contradictions that adolescents face between different aspects of their development?
> - How do they perceive their social status?

As well as the perceived absence of 'rites of passage' in Western society, a problem for both adolescents and their parents at the end of the twentieth century is the related lack of consensus as to where adolescence begins and ends, and precisely what adolescent rights, privileges and responsibilities are. For example, the question 'When do I become an adult?' elicits a response from a teacher which is different from that of a doctor, parent or police officer (Coleman, 1995).

The 'maturity gap' refers to the incongruity of achieving biological maturity at adolescence without simultaneously being awarded adult status (Curry, 1998). According to Hendry & Kloep (1999):

> '... young people, as they grow up, find themselves in the trap of having to respond more and more to society's demands in a 'responsible' adult way while being treated as immature and not capable of holding sound opinions on a wide range of social matters'.

One possible escape route from this trap is *risk-taking behaviour* (see Critical Discussion 37.1, below). As well as having to deal with the question 'Who am I?', the adolescent must also ask 'Who will I be?'. Erikson saw the creation of an adult personality as achieved mainly through choosing and developing a commitment to an occupation or role in life. The development of *ego identity* (a firm sense of who one is and what one stands for) is positive, and can carry people through difficult times.

Two child soldiers on a NPFL militia vehicle ride through the streets of Moravia

When working with psychiatrically disturbed soldiers in World War II, Erikson coined the term *identity crisis* to describe the loss of personal identity which the stress of combat seemed to have caused. Some years later, he extended the use of the term to include:

> *'severely conflicted young people whose sense of confusion is due ... to a war within themselves'.*

Role confusion

Failure to integrate perceptions of the self into a coherent whole results in *role confusion*, which, according to Erikson, can affect several areas of life:

- *Intimacy*: Here, a fear of commitment to, or involvement in, close relationships, arises from a fear of losing one's own identity. This may result in stereotyped and formalised relationships, or isolation.
- *Time perspective*: The adolescent is unable to plan for the future or retain any sense of time. It's associated with anxieties about change and becoming an adult.
- *Industry*: Here, difficulty is experienced in channelling resources in a realistic way into work or study, both of which require commitment. As a defence, the adolescent may find it impossible to concentrate, or become frenetically engaged in a single activity to the exclusion of all others.
- *Negative identity*: Engaging in abnormal or delinquent behaviour (such as drug-taking, or even suicide) is an attempt to resolve the identity crisis. This extreme position, which sets such adolescents apart from the crowd, is preferable to the loneliness and isolation that come with failing to achieve a distinct and more functional role in life ('a negative identity is better than no identity').

Related to Erikson's claims about negative identity is risk-taking behaviour. Hendry (1999) asks if risk-taking is:

> '... part of the psychological make-up of youth – a thrill-seeking stage in a developmental transition – a necessary rite of passage en route to the acquisition of adult skills and self-esteem? ...'.

Many teenagers seek out excitement, thrills and risks as earnestly as in childhood, perhaps to escape a drab existence or to exert some control over their own lives and to achieve *something*.

CRITICAL DISCUSSION 37.1

Sex and drugs

Traditionally, what parents of teenagers have most feared is that their children will engage in (particularly unprotected) sex and (especially hard) drugs. Recent research suggests that they may have good reason to fear the former, but can feel a little less fearful about the latter.

Figures for 1998 showed that the rate of teenage pregnancies was at its highest for almost a decade (47 per 1000 girls under 18 – 101,500 – compared with 45.6 per 1000 in 1991), with Britain having the highest rate in Europe. Pregnant teenagers are also increasingly likely to opt for abortion. Research conducted in Scotland in 1996/1997 found that young people who have sex before the age of 15 often regret it. The researchers concluded that young people need more help to feel in control of their sexual activities, such as being helped to develop relationship and negotiation skills (see Chapter 12).

By contrast, a recent survey of 2600 15–16-year-old boys and girls, shows that use of illegal drugs among British youngsters has dropped for the first time since the 1960s. An exception is girls in Northern Island. Figures for 1999 show a 'startling' turnaround since 1995, when UK teenagers had the highest rates of drug use in the world. Certain drugs, such as ecstasy, have acquired a bad name and have gone out of fashion. Nevertheless, drug use is widespread, and heroin use has actually increased (although it remains a minority choice: see Chapter 8).

(Based on Boseley, 2000; Norton, 2000b; Vasagar, 2000)

For some, delinquency may be the solution: it could actually be *adaptive* as a way of facilitating self-definition and expressing autonomy (Compas *et al.*, 1995).

Such conflict seem to be largely absent in societies where the complete transition to adulthood is officially approved and celebrated at a specific age, often through a particular ceremony. These enable both the individual and society to adjust to change and enjoy a sense of continuity (Price & Crapo, 1999).

CROSS-CULTURAL STUDY 37.1

Initiation into adulthood in non-Western cultures

Cohen (1964) looked at 45 non-industrialised societies which held adulthood ceremonies. In societies where adult skills were hard and dangerous, or where father–son relationships were weak but men had to co-operate in hard work, male initiation rituals were dramatic and painful. They allowed the boy to prove his manhood to the community – and to himself.

Sometimes they're designed to *give boys strength*, often by associating them with animals or plants. For example, in the Merina of Madagascar, the boy is associated with the banana tree, which bears much fruit resembling the erect penis (an ideal symbol of virility and fertility). The to-be-initiated boy is removed from his mother's home (a symbol of his attachment to her), before being circumcised in the company of men.

Brown (1963) described 'rites of passage' for girls in 43 societies from all major regions of the world. They most commonly occur where young girls continue to live and work in their mothers' home after marriage, but they also sometimes occur even when young women permanently leave home, and here they involve genital operations or extensive tattooing. These dramatically help the girl understand that she must make the transition from dependent child to a woman, who'll have to fend for herself in a male-dominated environment (Price & Crapo, 1999).

In recent years, *infibulation*, the most extreme form of female circumcision, has become a global human rights issue. Its purpose is to preserve the virginity of young girls before marriage, and to tame the disturbing power of women. In many traditional Islamic countries, especially Sudan, Ethiopia, and Somalia, millions of young girls continue to undergo painful and risky genital operations.

Although the act of infibulation may, from a Western perspective, deindividualise and depersonalise women:

'... *it acts as a transition or a rite of passage to a greater female adult collective; one where women hold relatively few advantages in a male-dominated world. It may in fact be one of the few positive status markers for women in traditional Islamic societies ...'*. (Price & Crapo, 1999)

Segall *et al.* (1999) maintain that tension and some antisocial behaviour are only to be expected in Western societies, due to the much longer adolescent and youth period:

'... *without a clear marking by ritual, no or little productive role or community participation, no child-rearing duties, and distance from observing adult activities'.*

According to Coleman & Roker (1998), an important trend in adolescence research is an increasing focus on identity development among ethnically diverse populations, such as young black women (e.g. Robinson, 1997) and mixed-race young people (Tizard & Phoenix, 1997). Coleman and Roker believe that notions of identity and identity formation are likely to become more central to the study of adolescence as this life stage becomes longer and more fragmented, and entry into adulthood becomes more problematic.

Studies of self-esteem

Tests of Erikson's theory have typically used measures of self-concept (especially *self-esteem*) as indicators of crisis. Girls' dissatisfaction with their appearance begins during puberty, along with a decline in self-esteem (Crawford & Unger, 1995). Comparisons between *early- and late-maturing girls* indicate that dissatisfaction with looks is associated with the rapid and normal weight gain that's part of growing up (Attie & Brooks-Gunn, 1989; Blyth *et al.*, 1981).

Early maturers have a less positive body image, despite the fact that they date more and earlier. Also, sexual activity is more problematic for adolescent girls (as it is for females in general): there are persisting double standards regarding sex (as reflected in the terms 'slag' and 'stud' for sexually active females and males respectively), together with differential responsibility for contraception and pregnancy (see Critical Discussion 37.1).

However, Offer *et al.* (1988) deny that there's any increase in disturbance of the self-image during early adolescence. For Coleman & Hendry (1999), although such disturbance *is* more likely in early than late adolescence, only a very small proportion of the total adolescent population is likely to have a negative self-image or very low self-esteem.

By contrast, *early-maturing boys* feel more attractive (Tobin-Richards *et al.*, 1983) and tend to be more satisfied with their bodies, looks and muscle development (Blyth *et al.*, 1981; Simmons & Blyth, 1987). However, Alsaker (1996) refers to two studies, which have found a correlation between pubertal boys' *dissatisfaction* with their bodies and the development of pubic and body hair. She asks if this reflects some contemporary images of men in advertisements, and a new trend for men to shave their bodies and be *less* hairy.

Most of these (and other similar) studies have been conducted in the USA, UK and other English-speaking countries. But a recent study of a very large, nationally representative Norwegian sample found that the global self-esteem of both late-maturing boys and girls suffered, while early- and on-time maturers (of both sexes) enjoy equally high self-esteem (Wichstrom, 1998).

Marcia's theory: identity statuses

In an extension of Erikson's work, Marcia (1980) proposed four *statuses* of adolescent identity formation, which characterise the search for identity. A mature identity can be achieved only if an individual experiences several *crises* in exploring and choosing between life's alternatives, finally arriving at a *commitment* or investment of the self in those choices (see Box 37.4).

Although identity moratorium is a prerequisite for identity achievement, Marcia *doesn't* see the four statuses as Erikson-type stages. However, evidence suggests that, amongst twelve-to 24-year-old men, they're broadly age-related. For example, Meilman (1979) reported that younger men (twelve to 18) were more likely to experience diffusion or foreclosure, whereas older men were increasingly likely to be identity achievers. Irrespective of age, relatively few men were achieving moratorium, which casts doubt on the validity of the theory.

Several *longitudinal* studies have indicated clear patterns of movement from foreclosure and diffusion to moratorium and achievement (Kroger, 1996). However, when applied to females, even Marcia (1980) accepts that his statuses work 'only more or less'. This is an example of *androcentrism*, that is, taking the male experience as the standard and applying it to both men and women. Erikson's theory has been criticised in a similar way (Gilligan, 1982: see Chapters 38 and 47).

Sociological approaches: generation gap

Sociologists see *role change* as an integral aspect of adolescent development (Coleman, 1995). Changing school or college, leaving home and beginning a job, all involve new sets of relationships, producing different and often greater expectations. These expectations themselves demand a substantial reassessment of the self-concept and *speed up* the socialisation process. Some adolescents find this problematic because of the wide variety of competing socialising agencies (such as the family, mass media and peer group), which often present *conflicting* values and demands (see discussion above of the identity crisis).

Sociologists also see socialisation as being more dependent on the adolescent's *own generation* than on the family or other social institutions (*auto-socialisation*: Marsland, 1987). As Marsland says:

'The crucial meaning of youth is withdrawal from adult control and influence compared with childhood ...'.

Young people withdraw into their peer groups, and this withdrawal is (within limits) accepted by adults. What Marsland is describing here is the *generation gap*.

Box 37.4 The four identity statuses proposed by Marcia (1980)

Table 37.2 *Four identity statuses as defined by high/low commitment and high/low crisis*

		Degree of crisis	
		High	**Low**
Degree of commitment to particular role/values	**High**	Identity achievement	Foreclosure
	Low	Moratorium	Diffusion (or confusion)

Diffusion/confusion: The individual hasn't really started thinking about the issues seriously, let alone formulated any goals or made any commitment. (This represents the *least mature* status.)

Foreclosure: The individual has avoided the uncertainties and anxieties of crisis by quickly and prematurely committing to safe and conventional (parental) goals and beliefs. Alternatives haven't been seriously considered.

Moratorium: This is the height of the crisis as described by Erikson. Decisions about identity are postponed while the individual tries out alternative identities, without committing to any particular one.

Identity achievement: The individual has experienced a crisis but has emerged successfully with firm commitments, goals and ideology. (This represents the *most mature* status.)

> **Ask yourself ...**
>
> - While adolescents and their parents are, by definition, different generations, does this necessarily and inevitably mean that there's a generation gap; that is, that there'll be conflict between them because they occupy 'different worlds'?

Parent–adolescent relationships

According to Hendry (1999).

'Adolescence as a transition from childhood to adulthood requires changes from child–parent relationships to young-adult–parent relationships ...'

Failure to negotiate new relationships with parents, or having highly critical or rejecting parents, is likely to make adolescents adopt a negative identity (Curry, 1998). Also, parents who rated their own adolescence as stormy and stressful reported more conflict in their relationships with adolescent children and were less satisfied with their family (Scheer & Unger, 1995). Parents of adolescents in general are often going through a time of transition themselves, reappraising their life goals, career and family ambitions, and assessing whether they've fulfilled their expectations as parents (see the discussion of the 'mid-life crisis' in Chapter 38).

Kevin (Harry Enfield) and Perry (Kathy Burke): every parent's worst nightmare?

However, for most adolescents relationships with parents become more equal and reciprocal, and parental authority comes to be seen as open to discussion and negotiation (e.g. Coleman & Hendry, 1999; Hendry *et al.*, 1993). The study by Hendry *et al.* (1993) also suggests that relationships with mothers and fathers don't necessarily change in the same ways and to the same extent.

KEY STUDY 37.3

Adolescent–parent relationships (Hendry *et al.*, 1993)

In a longitudinal Scottish study, Hendry *et al.* (1993) found that parents were chosen in preference to friends when discussing progress and problems at school, and careers, but not necessarily more personal matters. Mothers were preferred over fathers as confidantes in all areas except careers and sex (boys) and problems with mothers (both sexes). Most girls and nearly half the boys chose to confide in their mothers over problems with friends, and nearly half the girls and a third of the boys conveyed doubts about their own abilities to her.

These figures suggest a *disengagement* by fathers. Girls tend to be very uncomfortable discussing pubertal issues with their fathers and learn almost nothing from him about puberty. The mother's role in enforcing family rules brings her into conflict with the children more readily, but she's still seen as being supportive and caring, not 'distanced' like the father.

Studies conducted in several countries have found that young people get along well with their parents (e.g. Hendry *et al.*, 1993; Kloep & Tarifa, 1993), adopt their views and values, and perceive family members as the most important 'significant others' in their lives (McGlone *et al.*, 1996). Furthermore, most adolescents who had conflicts with their parents already had poor relationships with them before puberty (Stattin & Klackenberg, 1992).

Disagreements between young people and their parents are similar everywhere in Europe: Greece (Besevegis & Giannitas, 1996), Italy (Jackson *et al.*, 1996), Scotland (Hendry *et al.*, 1993), Germany (Fischer *et al.*, 1985), Albania and Sweden (Kloep & Tarifa, 1993). Teenagers have daily quarrels about how long or often they may stay out, how much they should help at home, tidiness of their bedrooms, volume of music and school achievement.

According to Jackson *et al.* (1996) disagreements can arise because:

■ parents expect greater independence of action from their teenagers;
■ parents don't wish to grant as much autonomy as the adolescent demands (with young women having more conflict than young men over independence);
■ parents and adolescents have different personal tastes and preferences.

Despite this potential for conflict, evidence suggests that competence as an independent adult can best be achieved within the context of a secure family environment, where exploration of alternative ideas, identities and behaviour is allowed and actively encouraged (Barber & Buehler, 1996). So, while detachment and separation from the family are necessary and desirable, young people *don't* have to reject their parents in order to become adults in their own right (Ryan & Lynch, 1989; Hill, 1993: see Chapter 32).

Peer relationships

Adolescent friendship groups (established around mutual interests) are normally embedded within the wider network of peer groups (which set 'norms', provide comparisons and pressures to conform to 'expected' behaviours). Friendship groups reaffirm self-image, and enable the young person to experience a new form of intimacy and learn social skills (such as discussing and solving conflicts, sharing and self-assertion). They also offer the opportunity to expand knowledge, develop a new identity, and experiment away from the watchful eyes of adults and family (Coleman & Hendry, 1999).

Generally, peers become more important as providers of advice, support, feedback and companionship, as models for behaviour and as sources of comparison with respect to personal qualities and skills. But while peer groups and friendship groups become important points of reference in social development and provide social contexts for shaping day-to-day values, they often *support* traditional parental attitudes and beliefs. Hence, peer and friendship groups can work in concert with, rather than in opposition to, adult goals and achievements (Hendry, 1999).

Coleman's focal theory: managing one change at a time

According to Coleman & Hendry (1990), most theories of adolescence help us to understand young people with serious problems and those belonging to minority or deviant groups. However, what's needed is a theory of *normality*. The picture that emerges from the research as a whole is that while adolescence is a difficult time for some, for the majority it appears to be a period of relative stability. Coleman's (1980) *focal theory* is an attempt to explain how this is achieved.

The theory is based on a study of 800 six-, eleven-, 13-, 15- and 17-year-old boys and girls. Attitudes towards self-image, being alone, heterosexual and parental relationships, friendships and large-group situations all changed as a function of age. More importantly, concerns about different issues reached a peak at different ages for both sexes.

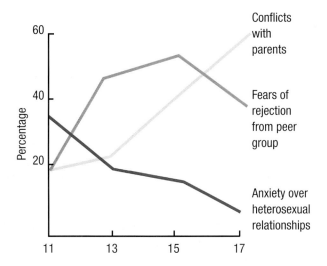

Figure 37.3 *Peak ages of the expression of different themes. These data are for boys only (from Coleman & Hendry, 1990)*

Particular sorts of relationship patterns come into *focus* (are most prominent) at different ages, although no pattern is specific to one age. The patterns overlap and there are wide individual differences.

Coleman believes that adolescents are able to cope with the potentially stressful changes as well as they do by dealing with one issue at a time. They spread the process of adaptation over a span of years, attempting to resolve one issue first before addressing the next. Because different problems and relationships come into focus and are dealt with at different points during the adolescent years, the stresses resulting from the need to adapt don't all have to be dealt with together.

According to Coleman & Hendry (1999), it's those adolescents who, for whatever reason, must deal with *more than one issue* (or normative shift) at a time, who are most likely to experience difficulties. If normative shifts coincide with non-normative ones, the situation is even more problematic (Hendry & Kloep, 1999).

Coleman's original findings have been successfully replicated by Kroger (1985) with large North American and New Zealand samples. Others have successfully tested hypotheses

derived from the theory. For example, Simmons & Blyth (1987) predicted that, if change (such as puberty):

- occurred at too young an age (causing the individual to be developmentally 'off-time');
- was marked by sharp discontinuity (i.e. sudden change); or
- involved accumulation of significant and temporally close issues (important shifts occurred together),

then adjustment would be more difficult. Their results strongly supported their predictions.

Conclusions

Adolescence involves a number of important transitions from childhood to adulthood, including puberty. The potential for *storm and stress* in Western societies is increased by the lack of clear definitions regarding when adulthood is reached. This makes the task of attaining an adult identity, as well as relationships with parents, more difficult compared with non-industrialised societies.

However, adolescence in Western societies *isn't* as problem-ridden as the popular stereotype would have it. If any serious problems do arise, they're directly linked to *rapid social change* (Dasen, 1999), with the associated extension of adolescence and youth. Young people aren't given a productive role to play when entering adult society (Segall *et al.*, 1999).

While most of the major theories of adolescence paint a picture of adolescence as an *inherently* difficult developmental stage, the evidence suggests that this isn't necessarily so. Certain groups may be more vulnerable than others (such as early-maturing girls), but the majority seem to cope well. According to Coleman's theory, it *isn't* adolescence itself that's stressful, but the timing and combination of the transitions faced by young people.

CHAPTER SUMMARY

- Adolescence involves **multiple transitions**. Compared with previous generations, it begins sooner and ends later. Various 'adulthood-postponing' changes have coincided with increased freedom at earlier ages.
- These transitions or **shifts** can be categorised as **normative maturational**, **normative society-dependent** and **non-normative**. Normative shifts can become non-normative, as when puberty begins unusually early or late.
- **Puberty** involves the **adolescent growth spurt** and the development of **secondary sex characteristics** (both sexes). While girls typically enter puberty two years before boys, there are important individual differences within each sex (such as **intraindividual asynchronies**).
- Adolescents evaluate their changing body images in terms of cultural standards of beauty, especially as these relate to weight. According to the **cultural ideal hypothesis**, girls move further away from their physical ideal and **early-maturing girls** will face a double disadvantage. **Early-maturing boys** will move fastest towards their physical ideal.
- Hall's **recapitulation theory** saw adolescence as a time of **storm and stress**. While mood swings are more common

during adolescence, rates of mental disorder (and delinquency rates) are only higher in early-maturing girls and adolescents with problems prior to puberty. The evidence for **off-time** maturation in boys is more mixed.

■ According to Erikson, adolescence involves a conflict between **ego identity** and **role confusion**. In Western societies, adolescence is a **moratorium**, intended to help ease the transition to adulthood. However, the lack of clear definitions of adulthood may contribute to the adolescent **identity crisis**.

■ Role confusion can take the form of **negative identity**, related to which is **risk-taking behaviour**. These problems are largely absent in societies which mark the transition to adulthood by **initiation ceremonies**.

■ While **self-esteem** may decline in early adolescence, especially in girls, this affects only a very small proportion of all adolescents. But research findings from English-speaking countries may not generalise to other cultures.

■ Marcia's four **identity statuses** are defined by high/low **commitment** and **crisis**. Although these aren't meant to be Erikson-type stages, the evidence suggests otherwise, but only for men.

■ **Sociological approaches** stress **role change**, the **conflicting** values and demands of different socialising agencies, and **auto-socialisation**, which produces the **generation gap**.

■ Renegotiating relationships with parents is necessary, and while there are inevitable disagreements, adult status is probably best achieved within the context of a **secure family environment**.

■ **Friendship groups** (as 'sub-groups' of the wider **peer group**) assume much greater significance during adolescence, such as helping to shape basic values. But these values are often **consistent** with parents' values, goals and achievements.

■ According to Coleman's **focal theory**, most adolescents cope as well as they do by spreading the process of adaptation over several years, dealing with **one issue at a time**.

Having to deal with more than one issue at a time is stressful, especially if changes occur too early or suddenly.

Self-assessment questions

1 Discuss psychological insights into the development of identity in adolescence.
2 Describe and evaluate research into social relationships in adolescence.
3 Critically assess the claim that adolescence inevitably involves storm and stress, identity crisis, and generation gap.

Web addresses

http://education.indiana.edu/cas/adol/adol.html

http://www.stanford.edu/group/adolescent.ctr/

http://www.hec.ohio-state.edu/famlife/adolescence/adolmain.html

http://csbsnt.csbs.unit.edu/dept/csa

www.independent.co.uk/links/

www.ich.bris.ac.uk

Further reading

Coleman, J.C. & Hendry, L.B. (1999) *The Nature of Adolescence* (2nd edition). London: Routledge. One of the 'modern classics' of adolescence.

Hendry, L.B. (1999) 'Adolescents in society.' In D. Messer & F. Jones (Eds) *Psychology and Social Care*. London: Jessica Kinsley. A very useful review of adolescence research in a more applied context.

Coleman, J.C. & Roker, D. (1998) Adolescence. *The Psychologist*, *11(12)*, 593–596. An article in the 'State of the Art' series.

Chapter 38

Adulthood

Introduction and overview

Assuming that we enjoy a normal lifespan, the longest phase of the life cycle will be spent in adulthood. Until recently, however, personality changes in adulthood attracted little psychological research interest. Indeed, as Levinson *et al.* (1978) have observed, adulthood is:

> '... one of the best-kept secrets in our society and probably in human history generally'.

This chapter attempts to reveal some of these secrets by examining what theory and research have told us about personality change in adulthood, including the occurrence of crises and transitions.

Many theorists believe that adult concerns and involvements are patterned in such a way that we can speak about *stages* of adult development. However, evidence concerning the *predictability* of changes in adult life (or what Levinson, 1986, calls *psychobiosocial transitions*) is conflicting. Three kinds of influence can affect the way we develop in adulthood (Hetherington & Baltes, 1988):

■ *Normative age-graded influences* are biological (such as the menopause) and social changes (such as marriage and parenting) that normally occur at fairly predictable ages.
■ *Normative history-graded influences* are historical events that affect whole generations or cohorts at about the same time (examples include wars, recessions and epidemics).
■ *Non-normative influences* are idiosyncratic transitions, such as divorce, unemployment and illness.

Levinson's (1986) term *marker events* refers to age-graded and non-normative influences. Others prefer the term *critical life events* to describe such influences, although it's probably more accurate to describe them as *processes*. Some critical life events, such as divorce, unemployment and bereavement, can occur at any time during adulthood (bereavement is discussed in Chapter 39). Others occur late in adulthood, such as retirement (also discussed in Chapter 39). Yet others tend to happen early in adulthood, such as marriage (or partnering) and parenting.

Erikson's theory

Ask yourself ...

- What do you understand by the term adulthood?
- What does it mean to be an adult?

As we saw in Chapter 37, Erikson believes that human development occurs through a sequence of *psychosocial stages*. As far as early and middle adulthood are concerned, Erikson described two primary developmental crises (the sixth and seventh of his psychosocial stages: see Table 38.1, page 545).

The first is the establishment of *intimacy*, which is a criterion of having attained the psychosocial state of adulthood. By intimacy, Erikson means the ability to form close, meaningful relationships with others without 'the fear of losing oneself in the process' (Elkind, 1970). Erikson believed that a prerequisite for intimacy was the attainment of identity (the reconciliation of all our various roles into one enduring and stable personality: see Chapter 37, pages 536–539). Identity is necessary, because we cannot know what it means to love someone and seek to share our life with them until we know who we are, and what we want to do with our lives. Thus, genuine intimacy requires us to give up some of our sense of separateness, and we must each have a firm identity to do this.

Intimacy needn't involve sexuality. Since intimacy refers to the essential ability to relate our deepest hopes and fears to another person, and in turn to accept another's need for intimacy, it describes the relationship between friends just as much as that between sexual partners (Dacey, 1982). By sharing ourselves with others, our personal identity becomes fully

realised and consolidated. Erikson believed that if a sense of identity isn't established with friends or a partner, then *isolation* (a sense of being alone without anyone to share with or care for) would result. We normally achieve intimacy in young adulthood (our 20s and 30s), after which we enter middle age (our 40s and 50s). This involves the attainment of *generativity*, the second developmental crisis.

Box 38.1 Generativity

The central task of the middle years of adulthood is to determine life's purpose or goal, and to focus on achieving aims and contributing to the well-being of others (particularly children). *Generativity* means being concerned with others beyond the immediate family, such as future generations and the nature of the society and world in which those future generations will live. As well as being displayed by parents, generativity is shown by anyone actively concerned with the welfare of young people and in making the world a better place for them to live and work.

People who successfully resolve this developmental crisis establish clear guidelines for their lives, and are generally productive and happy within this directive framework. Failure to attain generativity leads to *stagnation*, in which people become preoccupied with their personal needs and comforts. They indulge themselves as if they were their own (or another's) only child.

Evaluation of Erikson's theory

The sequence from identity to intimacy may not accurately reflect present-day realities. In recent years, the trend has been for adults to live together before marrying, so they tend to marry later in life than people did in the past (see below, page 550). Many people struggle with identity issues (such as career choice) at the same time as dealing with intimacy issues.

Additionally, some evidence suggests that females achieve intimacy *before* 'occupational identity'. The typical life course of women involves passing directly into a stage of intimacy without having achieved personal identity. Sangiuliano (1978) argues that most women submerge their identities into those of their partners, and only in mid-life do they emerge from this and search for separate identities and full independence. There's also a possible interaction between gender and *social class*. For example, working-class men see early marriage as a 'good' life pattern: early adulthood is a time for 'settling down', having a family and maintaining a steady job. By contrast, middle-class men and women see early adulthood as a time for exploration, in which different occupations are tried. Marriage tends to occur after this, and 'settling down' doesn't usually take place before 30 (Neugarten, 1975). There's also evidence of an interaction between gender, *race* and *culture* (see Cross-Cultural Study 38.1, page 545).

Another example of how Erikson's stages may not apply to everyone is the case of 'baby fathers', the name given to young black men who have children with a number of women and wear this as a 'badge of honour' (Alibhai-Brown, 2000).

Table 38.1 *Comparison between Erikson's and Freud's stages of development (based on Thomas, 1985; Erikson, 1950)*

No. of stage	Name of stage (psychosocial crisis)	Psychosocial modalities (dominant modes of being and acting)	Radius of significant relationships	Human virtues (qualities of strength)	Freud's psychosexual stages	Approx. ages
1	Basic trust vs basic mistrust	To get. To give in return	Mother or mother-figure	Hope	Oral	0–1
2	Autonomy vs shame and doubt	To hold on. To let go	Parents	Willpower	Anal	1–3
3	Initiative vs guilt	To make (going after). To 'make like' (playing)	Basic family	Purpose	Phallic	3–6
4	Industry vs inferiority	To make things (completing). To make things together	Neighbourhood and school	Competence	Latency	6–12
5	Identity vs role confusion	To be oneself (or not to be). To share being oneself	Peer groups and outgroups. Models of leadership	Fidelity	Genital	12–18
6	Intimacy vs isolation	To lose and find oneself in another	Partners in friendship, sex, competition, co-operation	Love		20s
7	Generativity vs stagnation	To make be. To take care of	Divided labour and shared household	Care		Late 20s–50s
8	Ego integrity vs despair	To be, through having been. To face not being	'Humankind', 'my kind'	Wisdom		50s and beyond

---

CROSS-CULTURAL STUDY 38.1

Intimacy and identity (Ochse & Plug, 1986)

Ochse and Plug studied over 1800 South African black and white men and women. Their findings raise questions about both the timing of particular stages and the exact *sequence* of the developmental tasks involved. For example, amongst whites, 25–39-year-old women appeared to develop a sense of identity *before* men. This may be because developing a true sense of intimacy must *precede* a sense of identity (not vice versa, as Erikson claimed). According to Price & Crapo (1999):

'It is quite feasible that by sharing and risking themselves in close relationships, people may learn to know themselves, to reconcile their conception of themselves with the community recognition of them, and to develop a sense of mutuality with their community'.

Not until this process is complete can a sense of identity be achieved. Due to prevailing social conditions in South Africa (including minority status, high poverty rates, and fragmented living conditions), black women had a difficult time achieving a sense of intimacy and hence of identity. Black men also didn't achieve a sense of identity until late in life. In turn, this adversely affected black women, who still experienced a lack of self-definition, intimacy and well-being far into middle age:

'It appears that the experience of the 'adult years' was one thing for whites and something quite different for blacks. As social conditions change in South Africa, whole groups of blacks may expect to experience a completely different psychological development than they would have under apartheid'. (Price & Crapo, 1999)

Erikson's psychosocial stages were meant to be *universal*, applying to both genders in all cultures. However, he acknowledged that the sequence of stages is different for a woman, who suspends her identity as she prepares to attract the man who will marry her. Men achieve identity before achieving intimacy with sexual partners, whereas for women, Erikson's developmental crises appear to be fused (see Chapter 47). As Gilligan (1982) has observed:

'The female comes to know herself as she is known, through relationships with others'.

All the above evidence suggests that it's almost certainly impossible to describe universal stages for adults. Moreover, as we saw in Chapter 37, there's evidence of a growing prolongation of adolescence.

Box 38.2	**Perpetual adolescence**

According to Sheehy (1996), while childhood is ending earlier, adults are prolonging adolescence into their 30s. Indeed, many people aren't acknowledging maturity until they reach 40. Sheehy suggests that:

'Adolescence is now prolonged for the middle classes until the end of their twenties, and for blue-collar men and women until their mid-twenties, as more young adults live at home longer. True adulthood does not begin until 30. Most Baby Boomers, born after World War II, do not feel fully 'grown up' until they are in their forties, and even then they resist'.

Beaumont (1996) argues that we've evolved into a generation of 'Peter Pans', stuck in adolescence:

'You see them in Hyde Park – thirty- and forty-somethings on rollerblades and skateboards, hanging out at Glastonbury or discussing the merits of Oasis versus Blur at dinner parties'.

The fictional models of this 'new generation' are Gary and Tony from the BBC TV programme *Men Behaving Badly*, and Patsie and Eddy from *Absolutely Fabulous*. Real-life examples of 'Peter Pans' include Mick Jagger, Cliff Richard and Richard Branson.

According to Orbach (cited in Beaumont, 1996), one problem created by adults who refuse to grow up is their own parenting. Unable to look up to figures of authority themselves, they feel a sense of loss and look to their own children for emotional sustenance in a curious role reversal (see Chapter 32).

Levinson *et al.*'s 'seasons of a man's life'

Perhaps the most systematic study of personality and life changes in adulthood began in 1969, when Levinson *et al.* interviewed 40 men aged 35 to 45. Transcripts were made of the five to ten tape-recorded interviews that each participant gave over several months. Levinson *et al.* looked at how adulthood is actually experienced.

In *The Seasons of a Man's Life*, Levinson *et al.* (1978) advanced a *life-structure theory*, defining life structure as the underlying pattern or design of a person's life at any given time. Life structure allows us to 'see how the self is in the world and how the world is in the self', and evolves through a series of *phases* or *periods* which give overall shape to the course of adult development. Adult development comprises a sequence of eras which overlap in the form of *cross-era transitions*. These last about five years, terminating the outgoing era and initiating the incoming one. The four eras are pre-adulthood (age 0–22), early adulthood (17–45), middle adulthood (40–65) and late adulthood (60 onwards).

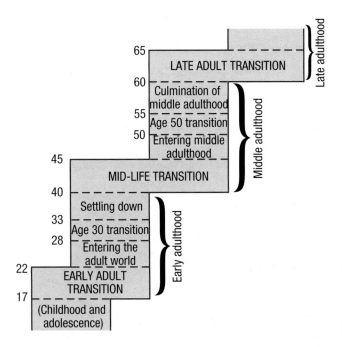

Figure 38.1 *Levinson* et al.*'s theory of adult development. The life cycle is divided into four major eras that overlap in the form of cross-era transitions*

The phases or periods alternate between those that are *stable* (or *structure-building*) and *transitional* (or *structure-changing*). Although each phase involves biological, psychological and social adjustments, family and work roles are seen as central to the life structure at any time, and individual development is interwoven with changes in these roles.

The era of early adulthood

Early adult transition (17–22) is a developmental 'bridge' between adolescence and adulthood.

Box 38.3 Separation and attachment

Two key themes of the early adult transition are *separation* and the formation of *attachments* to the adult world. *External* separation involves moving out of the family home, increasing financial independence, and entering more independent and responsible roles and living arrangements. *Internal* separation involves greater psychological distance from the family, less emotional dependence on the parents, and greater differentiation between the self and family. Although we separate from our parents, Levinson *et al.* argue that we never complete the process, which continues throughout life. Attachment involves exploring the world's possibilities, imagining ourselves as part of it, and identifying and establishing changes for living in the world before we become 'full members' of it.

Between ages 22 and 28, we *enter the adult world*. This is the first *structure-building* (rather than *structure-changing*) phase, and hence is referred to as the *entry life structure for early adulthood*. In it, we try to fashion:

> '… a provisional structure that provides a workable link between the valued self and adult society'.

In the *novice phase*, we try to define ourselves as adults and live with the initial choices we make concerning jobs, relationships, lifestyles and values. However, we need to create a balance between 'keeping our options open' (which allows us to explore possibilities without being committed to a given course) and 'putting down roots' (or creating stable life structures).

Our decisions are made in the context of our *dreams*: the 'vague sense' we have of ourselves in the adult world and what we want to do with our lives. We must overcome disappointments and setbacks, and learn to accept and profit from successes, so that the dream's 'thread' doesn't get lost in the course of 'moving up the ladder' and revising the life structure. To help us in our efforts at self-definition, we look to *mentors*, older and more experienced others, for guidance and direction. Mentors can take a *formal* role in guiding, teaching and helping novices to define their dreams. Alternatively, a mentor's role may be *informal*, providing an advisory and emotionally supportive function (as a parent does).

The *age-30 transition* (28–33) provides an opportunity to work on the flaws and limitations of the first life structure, and to create the basis for a more satisfactory structure that will complete the era of young adulthood. Most of Levinson *et al.*'s participants experienced age-30 crises which involved stress, self-doubt, feelings that life was losing its 'provisional quality' and becoming more serious, and time pressure. Thus, the participants saw this as being the time for change, if change was needed. However, for a minority the age-30 transition was crisis-free.

Box 38.4 Settling down

The *settling down* (or *culminating life structure for early adulthood*: 33–40) phase represents consolidation of the second life structure. This involves a shift away from tentative choices regarding family and career towards a strong sense of commitment to a personal, familial and occupational future. Paths for success in work and husband and father roles are mapped out and, instead of just beginning to find out what's important and what our opinions are, we see ourselves as responsible adults.

The settling down phase comprises two sub-stages: *early settling down* (33–36) and *becoming one's own* man or *BOOM* (36–40). In the latter, men strive to advance and succeed in building better lives, improve and use our skills, be creative, and in general contribute to society. A man wants recognition and affirmation from society, but he also wants to be self-sufficient and free of social pressure and control. Although a 'boy–man' conflict may be produced, this can represent a step forward. This sub-stage may also see him assume a mentor role for someone younger (see above).

The era of middle adulthood

The *mid-life transition* (40–45) involves terminating one life structure, initiating another, and continuing the process of individuation started during the BOOM sub-stage. This is a time of soul-searching, questioning and assessing the real meaning of the life structure's achievement. It's sometimes referred to as the *mid-life crisis*, although Levinson *et al.* didn't actually use this term. For some people, the change is gradual and fairly painless. But for others, it's full of uncertainties.

The crisis stems from unconscious tensions between attachment and separation, the resurfacing of the need to be creative (which is often repressed in order to achieve a career), and retrospective comparisons between dreams and life's reality.

Most participants in Levinson *et al.*'s study hadn't reached age 45. Following interviews two years after the main study was concluded, some were chosen for more extensive study. But the evidence for the remaining phases is much less detailed than for the earlier ones.

In *entering middle adulthood* (or *early life structure for middle adulthood*: 45–50), we've resolved (more-or-less satisfactorily) whether what we've committed ourselves to really is worthwhile. It's again necessary to make choices regarding a new life structure. Sometimes, these choices are defined by *marker events* such as divorce, illness, occupational change, or the death of a loved one. However, the choices may also be influenced by less obvious but significant changes, such as shifts in the enthusiasm for work or in the quality of marriage. As before, the resulting life structure varies in how satisfying it is and how connected it is to the self. It may not be intrinsically happy and fulfilling. The restructuring consists of many steps, and there may be setbacks in which options have to be abandoned ('back to the drawing board').

The validity of the 'mid-life crisis'

Just as the 'identity crisis' is part of the popular stereotype of adolescence (see Chapter 37), Levinson *et al.* have helped to make the 'mid-life crisis' part of the common-sense understanding of adult development. Like Erikson, Levinson *et al.* see crisis as *inevitable*. As they note:

> 'It is not possible to get through middle adulthood without having at least a moderate crisis in either the mid-life transition or the age-50 transition'.

They also see crisis as *necessary*. If we don't engage in soul searching, we'll:

> '... pay the price in a later developmental crisis or in a progressive withering of the self and a life structure minimally connected to the self'.

The view that crisis is both inevitable and necessary (or *normative*, to use Erikson's term) is controversial. People of all ages suffer occasional depression, self-doubt, sexual uncertainty and concerns about the future. Indeed, there appears to be an increasingly wide age range and a growing number of people who decide to make radical changes in their life-style, both earlier and later than predicted by Levinson *et al.*'s theory.

'Downshifting'

According to Tredre (1996), the concept of a mid-life crisis is too narrow in that traditionally, or stereotypically, it refers to someone in his/her late forties, with grown-up children, who gives up a secure and well-paid 'respectable' career, and moves to a small market town or village in order to enjoy a less stressful, more peaceful and generally better quality of life. We need to spread the net wider nowadays, and think in terms of early-, mid- and late-life crises: people of all age groups and walks of life are 'feeling the itch'.

Downshifting refers to voluntarily opting out of a pressurised career and interminably long hours in the office, and often involves giving up an exceptionally well-paid job in a high-profile industry in the pursuit of a more fulfilling way of life. Tredre identifies a number of possible reasons for downshifting, including anti-urbanism (fuelled by concerns over urban pollution), crime, violence, and increasing job insecurity.

Box 38.5 Identity crisis and the life cycle

Marcia (1998) also believes that the concept of a mid-life crisis is misleading and too narrow. He argues that 'adolescing' (making decisions about one's identity) occurs *throughout* the lifespan, whenever we review or reorganise our lives. At the very least, we might expect identity crises to accompany (in Erikson's terms) intimacy–isolation, generativity–stagnation, and integrity–despair (see Chapter 39).

Just as puberty and other changes in early adolescence disrupt the partial identities of childhood, so the demands of intimacy require a reformulation of the initial identity achieved at late adolescence. Similarly, the generative, care-giving requirements of middle age differ from those of being with an intimate partner. The virtues of fidelity, love and care (see Table 38.1), which derive from positive resolution of young and middle adulthood, don't emerge without a struggle. According to Marcia (1998):

> 'Periods of adolescing are normal, expectable components of life cycle growth'.

However, while crises aren't limited to specific times in our lives, those associated with middle (and old) age are especially difficult.

Kevin Spacey as a man experiencing a mid-life crisis in American Beauty. *This becomes focused (literally) on his daughter's friend, played by Mena Suvari*

Ask yourself ...

- Who's 'more right', Levinson *et al.* or Marcia?

Durkin (1995) notes that a large proportion of middle-aged people actually feel *more* positive about this phase of life than earlier ones, with only ten per cent reporting feeling as though they'd experienced a crisis. For Durkin, the mid-life crisis isn't as universal as Levinson *et al.* suggest, and the time and extent to which we experience uncomfortable self-assessments vary as a function of several factors (such as personality). Although the evidence is sparse, it appears that going through middle age in a relatively peaceful and untroubled way is actually a *favourable* indicator of future development, that is, a lack of emotional disturbance predicts *better* rather than poorer functioning in later life (Rutter & Rutter, 1992).

Two other components of the mid-life crisis are much less contentious. The first is a wide range of adaptations in the life pattern. Some of these stem from role changes that produce fairly drastic consequences, such as divorce, remarriage, a major occupational change, redundancy or serious illness. Others are more subtle, and include the ageing and likely death of parents, the new role of grandparent, and the sense of loss which sometimes occurs when children have all moved away from the family home (*empty-nest distress*).

The second non-controversial component is significant change in the *internal* aspects of life structures, which occurs regardless of external events. This involves reappraising achievements and remaining ambitions, especially those to do with work and relationships with our sexual partners. A fundamental development at this time is the realisation that the final authority for life rests with us. (This is similar to Gould's, 1978, 1980, theory: see below.)

CRITICAL DISCUSSION 38.1

Is there a male menopause?

A recent World Health Organisation conference on the ageing male concluded that there's definitely a male biological andropause, and that men also suffer from osteoporosis (as do women). There's also an increased risk of heart attack from declining testosterone levels.

The critical measure, though, is 'bio-available' testosterone. As testosterone declines, sex hormone binding globulin (SHBG) increases. SHBG traps much of the testosterone that's still circulating and prevents it from affecting the body's tissues. What's left over ('bioavailable') does the beneficial work, but this is what radically declines from about the age of 45. Hence, the case for testosterone (male hormone) replacement therapy.

But even more critical may be a second hormone, DHEA (a steroid produced by the adrenals), levels of which decline dramatically in the early thirties. DHEA elevates mood, cognition, immune response, promotes lean body mass, increases sexual drive, reduces fatigue, and prevents hardening of the arteries. Above all, it appears to improve brain function and repair memory loss.

(Based on Hodson, 2000)

The seasons of a woman's life

Levinson et al.'s research was carried out on an all-male sample. Similar research investigating women has produced similar findings. However, men and women have been shown to differ in terms of their dreams.

Box 38.6 Women's dreams and 'gender-splitting'

Levinson (1986) argues that a 'gender-splitting' phenomenon occurs in adult development. Men have fairly unified visions of their futures, which tend to be focused on their careers. But women have 'dreams' which are more likely to be split between a career and marriage. This was certainly true of academics and business-women, although the former were less ambitious and more likely to forego a career, whereas the latter wanted to maintain their careers but at a reduced level. Only the *homemakers* had unified dreams (to be full-time wives and mothers, as their own mothers had been).

Roberts & Newton (1987) saw the family as playing a 'supportive' role for men. Women's dreams were constructed around their relationships with their husbands and families, which subordinated their personal needs. So, part of *her* dream is *his* success. For Durkin (1995), this difference in women's and men's priorities may put women at greater risk:

'... of disappointment and developmental tension as their investment in others' goals conflict with their personal needs'.

Women who give marriage and motherhood top priority in their 20s tend to develop more individualistic goals for their 30s. However, those who are career-oriented early on in adulthood tend to focus on marriage and family concerns later. Generally, the transitory instability of the early 30s lasts longer for women than for men, and 'settling down' is much less clear-cut. Trying to integrate career and marriage/family responsibilities is very difficult for most women, who experience greater conflicts than their husbands are likely to.

Gender-splitting is relevant to discussion of marriage/partnering and parenthood. The changing roles of women in paid employment and of men in the home are discussed later in the chapter (see pages 554–556).

The validity of stage theories of adult development

Erikson's and Levinson et al.'s theories of adult development emphasise a 'ladder-like' progression through an inevitable and universal series of stages/phases. But this view of adult development as 'stage-like' has been criticised on the grounds that it underestimates the degree of *individual variability* (Rutter & Rutter, 1992). Many members of the mainstream working-class population don't grow or change in systematic ways. Instead, they show many rapid fluctuations, depending on things like relationships, work demands and other life stresses that are taking place (Craig, 1992).

Stage theories also imply a *discontinuity* of development. But many psychologists believe there's also considerable *continuity* of personality during adult life. The popular stereotype sees middle adulthood as the time when a person is responsible, settled, contented and at the peak of achievement.

Current views of adult development stress the transitions and milestones that mark adult life, rather than a rigid developmental sequence (Baltes, 1983, Schlossberg, 1984). This is commonly referred to as the *life-events approach*. Yet, despite the growing unpredictability of changes in adult life, most people still unconsciously evaluate their transitions according to a social clock, which determines whether they're 'on time' with respect to particular life events (such as getting married: Schlossberg et al., 1978). If they're 'off time', either early or late, we're age-deviant. Like other types of deviancy, this can result in social penalties, such as amusement, pity or rejection.

While all cultures have social clocks that define the 'right' time to marry, begin work, have children and so on, these clocks vary greatly between cultures (Wade & Tavris, 1999). Craig (1992) sees changes in adult thought, behaviour and personality as being less a result of chronological age or specific biological changes, and more a result of personal, social and cultural events or forces. Because of the sheer diversity of experiences in an adult's life, Craig doesn't believe it's possible to describe major 'milestones' that will apply to nearly everyone.

Gould's theory of the evolution of adult consciousness

Whereas Levinson et al. discussed adult development in terms of evolving life structures, Gould (1978, 1980) prefers to talk about the evolution of *adult consciousness* which occurs when:

'... we release ourselves from the constraints and ties of childhood consciousness'.

Gould sees the thrust of adult development as being towards the realisation and acceptance of ourselves as creators of our own lives, and away from the assumption that the rules and standards of childhood determine our destinies. His theory is an extension of the Freudian idea of separation anxiety (see Chapter 32). According to Gould, we have to free ourselves of the *illusion of absolute safety*, an illusion which dominated childhood. This involves transformations, giving up the security of the past to form our own ideas. We have to replace the concept of parental dependency with a sense of autonomy, or owning ourselves. But this is difficult, because dependency on parents is a normal feature of childhood. Indeed, without it, childhood would be very difficult. As well as shedding childhood consciousness, Gould believes that our sense of time also changes.

Box 38.7 Our changing sense of time

Up until age 18 or so, we feel both protected and constrained by our parents, and never quite believe that we'll escape the 'family world'. This is like being in a timeless capsule in which 'the future is a fantasy space that may possibly not exist'. But we begin to glimpse an endless future and see an infinite amount of time ahead of us.

In our 20s, we become confident about being separated from the family. However, we haven't yet formed early-adult life structures. Gould (1980) puts it like this:

'*Because of all the new decisions and novel experiences that come with setting up new adult enterprises, our time sense, when we're being successful, is one of movement along a chosen path that leads linearly to some obscure prize decades in the future. There is plenty of time, but we're still in a hurry once we've developed a clearer, often stereotyped, picture of where we want to be by then*'.

At the end of our 20s, our sense of time incorporates our adult past as well as future. The future is neither infinite nor linear, and we must choose between different options because there isn't time to take them all. From our mid-30s to mid-40s, we develop a sense of urgency and that time is running out. We also become aware of our own mortality which, once attained, is never far from our consciousness. How we spend our time becomes a matter of great importance. Additionally, we begin to question whether our 'prize' (freedom from restrictions by those who have formed us – our parents) either exists or, if it does, whether it's been worth it (cf. Levinson *et al.*'s 'dream').

Marriage

Ask yourself ...

• Identify some arguments for and against marriage, as compared with 'living together' (cohabitation).

Since over 90 per cent of adults in Western countries marry at least once, marriage is an example of a *normative age-graded influence* (see *Introduction and overview*). Marriage is an important transition for young adults, because it involves a lasting personal commitment to another person (and, so is a means of achieving Erikson's *intimacy*), financial responsibilities and, perhaps, family responsibilities. But it cannot be the same type of transition for everyone. In some cultures, for example, people have little choice as to who their partners will be (as is the case in arranged marriages: see Chapter 28).

Marriage and preparation for marriage can be very stressful. Davies (1956) identified mental disorders occurring for the first time in those who were engaged to be married. Typically, these were anxiety and depression, which usually began in connection with an event that hinged on the wedding date (such as booking the reception). Since the disorders improved when the engagement was broken off or the wedding took place, Davies concluded that it was the *decision* to make the commitment that was important, rather than the act of getting married itself.

Cohabitation

Couples who live together (or *cohabit*) before marriage are *more* likely to divorce later, and be less satisfied with their marriages, than those who marry without having cohabited. Also, about 40 per cent of couples who cohabit don't marry. While this suggests that cohabitation may prevent some divorces, cohabitees who do marry are more likely to divorce.

Ask yourself ...

• Why do you think cohabitees who marry are more likely to divorce?

According to Bee (1994), this is because people who choose to cohabit are *different* from those who choose not to. As a group, cohabitees seem to be more willing to flout tradition in many ways (such as being less religious and disagreeing that one should stay with a marriage partner no matter what). Those who don't cohabit include a large proportion of 'more traditional' people.

The benefits of marriage

It's long been recognised that mortality is affected by marital status. Married people tend to live longer than unmarried people, are happier, healthier and have lower rates of various mental disorders than the single, widowed or divorced (see Chapter 28). The greater mortality of the unmarried relative to the married has generally been increasing over the past two to three decades, and it seems that divorced (and widowed) people in their 20s and 30s have particularly high risks of dying compared with other people of the same age (Cramer, 1995: see Chapter 40).

Ask yourself ...

- Why – or how – might marriage produce these beneficial effects? Look back at your answers to the previous Ask yourself box. Did any of the arguments for marriage include its psychological/emotional benefits?
- Are there any reasons for believing that either men or women derive greater benefits?

Measures of marital adjustment indicate that agreement between partners on various issues (a measure of marital compatability) is positively correlated with other components of relationship adjustment, such as satisfaction, affection and doing various activities together (Eysenck & Wakefield, 1981: again see Chapter 28).

CRITICAL DISCUSSION 38.2

Do men get more from marriage than women?

Bee (1994) argues that the greatest beneficiaries of marriage are men, partly because they're less likely than women to have close confidants outside marriage, and partly because wives provide more emotional warmth and support for husbands than husbands do for wives. Marriage is less obviously psychologically protective for women, not because a confiding and harmonious relationship is any less important for them (indeed, if anything it's more important), but because:

■ many marriages don't provide such relationships; and
■ other consequences of marriage differ between the sexes.

(The 'advantage' of marriage for men is reflected in the higher rates of men's re-marriage following divorce: see text below.)

Although our attitudes towards education and women's careers have changed, Rutter & Rutter (1992), echoing Levinson's concept of 'gender-splitting' (see above), have proposed that:

'The potential benefits of a harmonious relationship may, for a woman, be counterbalanced by the stresses involved in giving up a job or in being handicapped in a career progression or promotion through having to combine a career and parenthood'.

This is discussed further on pages 554–556.

homes, but this is usually only temporary, since 65 per cent of women, and over 75 per cent of men remarry. Rates of cohabitation are high in those who don't remarry. Divorce rates are even higher in remarriages than first marriages. This means that children exposed to multiple marital transitions experience the most adverse consequences in adjustment (Hetherington & Stanley-Hagan, 1999).

So, in recent decades, the structure and stability of families in Western societies have undergone considerable changes. An increasing number of adults live in subsequent cohabiting or remarried relationships and, in turn, these changes have led to a marked rise in the number of children living in stepfamily situations (Nicholson *et al.*, 1999: see pages 556–557).

National statistics conceal important racial and ethnic differences. For example, compared with non-Hispanic Whites, African-Americans wait longer before marrying and are less likely to marry, but are also more likely to separate and divorce and to remain separated without a legal divorce. They're also less likely to remarry (Hetherington & Stanley-Hagan, 1999).

The stress of divorce

Divorce is a stressor for both men and women (see Chapter 12), since it involves the loss of one's major attachment figure and source of emotional support. But men appear to experience *more* stress than women, which is perhaps not altogether surprising given the greater benefits to men of marriage (see above). Also, divorce can have serious effects on the psychological adjustment of children whose parents are separating (see Chapter 32).

The potential benefits of divorce

According to Woollett & Fuller (cited in Cooper, 1996), mothers who've been through a divorce often report experiencing a sense of achievement in their day-to-day activities and a feeling of 'a job well done'. This is because they use their experiences of divorce in a positive way to 'galvanise' them into taking charge of their lives. According to Woollett:

'When the marriage breaks down, the mother is thrown into all sorts of things that are unfamiliar. There are new areas, new decisions, and she is forced to cope'.

However, Lewis (cited in Cooper, 1996) warns that:

'We must be careful about thinking about the positive changes [divorced women report] because we are always comparing a positive change against the negative feeling that went before. The positive is only relative'.

Divorce

Although divorce rates in the US have shown a modest decline since 1979, over 45 per cent of marriages still end in divorce (Simons, 1996). Divorce rates are highest during the first five years of marriage and then peak again after couples have been married for 15–25 years (Turnbull, 1995).

In 1996, there were about 1,150,000 divorces in the US, involving over one million children. Following divorce, 84 per cent of children reside with their mothers in single-parent

Parenthood

For most people, parenthood and child-rearing represent key transitions. According to Bee (1994), 90 per cent of adults will become parents, mostly in their 20s and 30s. But parenthood varies in meaning and impact more than any other life transition. It may occur at any time from adolescence to middle age, and for some men, may even occur in late adulthood! Parenthood may also be planned or unplanned, wanted or unwanted, and there are many motives for having children.

Traditionally, parenthood is the domain of the married couple. However, it may involve a single woman, a homosexual couple (see page 557), a cohabiting couple or couples who adopt or foster children. Since the 1950s, sexuality among young people has become more acceptable, and this has been accompanied by a marked rise in the number of teenage pregnancies (see Critical Discussion 37.1, page 537).

Equally, though, the increasing importance of work careers for women has also led to more and more couples postponing starting a family so that the woman can become better established in her career (see Critical Discussion 38.3, page 553). Consequently, there's a new class of middle-aged parents with young children (Turnbull, 1995).

> ### Ask yourself ...
>
> • Assuming that they're planned, why do people have children? What are their motives ?
> • Is it 'natural' (at least for women) to want children?

Parenthood brings with it several psychological adaptations. For example, many women worry that that their baby may be abnormal, and about the changes in their body and how well they'll cope with motherhood. Another concern is how the relationship with their husbands or partners will be affected. While pregnancy brings many couples closer together, most men take longer than women to become emotionally involved in it – and some feel left out. This feeling of exclusion may continue after the baby is born, as the mother becomes preoccupied with it.

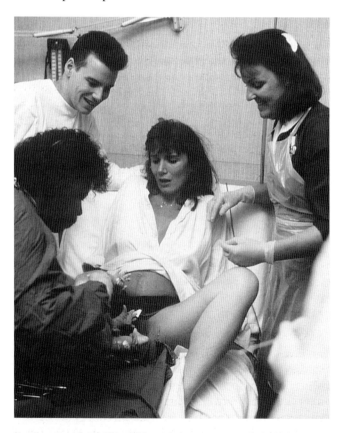

Being at the birth of his child can help counteract a father's feelings of being excluded during the pregnancy – and afterwards. It can also help him to form an emotional bond with the baby

Marital satisfaction tends to be highest before children arrive. It then drops and remains relatively low as long as there are dependent children in the home. Finally, it rises again during the 'post-parental' and retirement stages (see Chapter 28). For new parents, the roles of parent and spouse are at least partially incompatible. New parents report having less time for each other, whether it be conversing, having sex, being affectionate or carrying out routine chores that used to be done together (Bee, 1994).

Parents are, of course, attachment figures for their dependent children. Unlike the relationship with a partner, the relationship with a child is *asymmetrical* (the child *isn't* an attachment figure for its parents: see Chapter 32). This new form of responsibility can be very stressful, and has implications for how parents adapt to these new role demands, and the quality of their interactions with the child (Durkin, 1995). An unhappy couple may stay together not just 'for the kids' sake', but because the parental role has sufficient meaning and value for each partner to outweigh the dissatisfaction with their marriage (Levinson *et al.*, 1978).

> ### Box 38.8 Empty nest or crowded nest: which is more distressing?
>
> Regarding *empty-nest distress*, most parents don't find their children's departure from home to be a distressing time (Durkin, 1995). Indeed, many report that the end of child-rearing responsibilities is a 'liberating experience', and they welcome new opportunities for closer relationships with their partners, personal fulfilment through work, a return to education and so on. The extent to which women report empty-nest distress may be *cohort-related*, that is, it may be more typical of women who reached maturity during historical periods when traditional roles were stressed (Durkin, 1995).
>
> The *crowded nest* (Datan *et al.*, 1987) can, however, be a source of stress. This occurs when grown-up children opt not to leave home, which defies the demands of the 'social clock' established by preceding generations. As we saw in Chapter 37, the extension of the period of adolescence makes this an increasingly common problem for parents, who find it difficult to adjust to 'adult children' living at home (see Figure 38.2, page 553).

Womanhood and motherhood

According to Kremer (1998), in the post-industrial/post-modern world of the twenty-first century we're still influenced by beliefs and attitudes regarding work and the sexes (or 'gendered employment profiles') inherited from an earlier time. For example, the *motherhood mystique/mandate* refers to the belief that women are born and reared to be, first and foremost, mothers (while the 'fatherhood mandate' is hardly, if ever, mentioned: see Chapter 32). Another example is the stereotype of men as inherently more committed to work than women, whose attitudes towards it are less positive than men's.

The motherhood mandate has at least three important implications. The first is that motherhood is 'natural'. Berryman (in Lacey, 1998) maintains that motherhood is still seen as synonymous with womanhood:

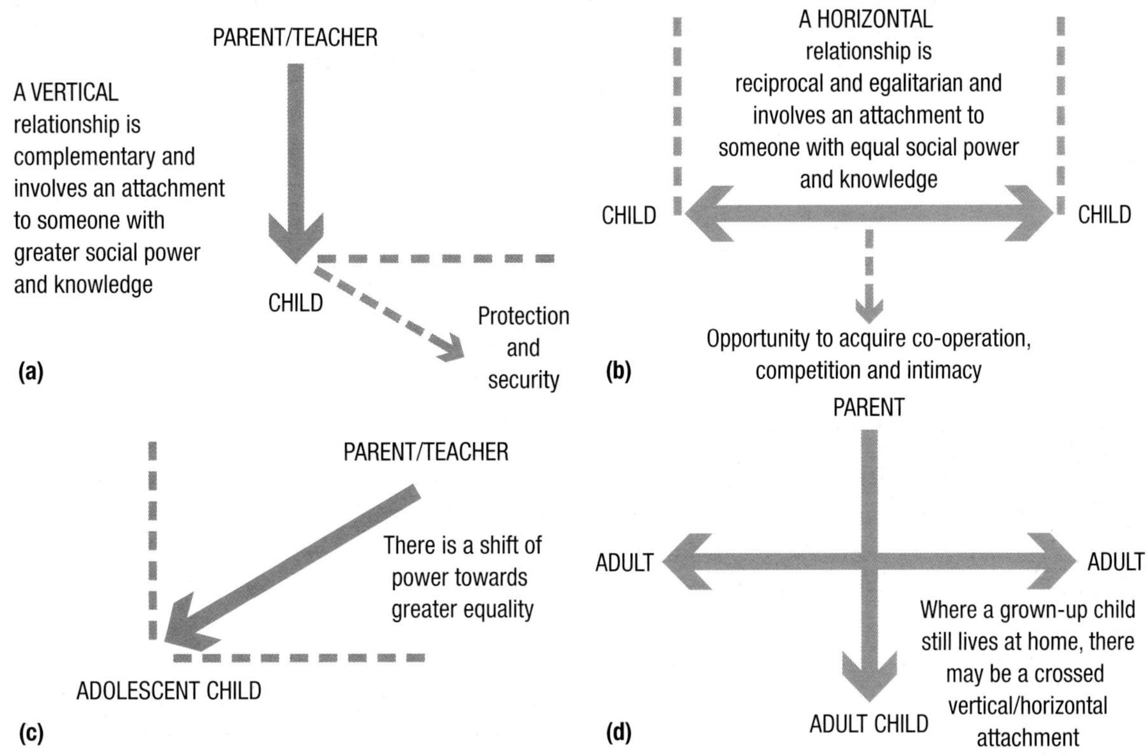

Figure 38.2 *Different kinds of relationships based on Hartup's (1989) distinction between vertical and horizontal relationships. While (a) and (b) are clear-cut in terms of this distinction, (c) involves a change from vertical to horizontal, while (d) involves both dimensions simultaneously. Both (c) and (d) may involve conflict – but for different reasons*

'Parenthood is seen as a central, key role in women's lives in a way that it isn't for men. Women who don't become mothers are seen as psychologically inadequate – wanting in some way. But there is plenty of evidence that motherhood doesn't come naturally to all women; it is a skill that many women have to learn'.

For example, Berryman maintains that, because smaller families and fewer siblings are now the norm, many women today have little experience of children when they start their own families – and the reality can come as a shock. This belief that mothering comes 'naturally' is so deep-rooted that women who don't bond immediately with their babies feel inadequate or guilty, or perhaps both (see Bowlby's theory of attachment in Chapter 32). However, there are indications that attitudes towards having children are changing.

CRITICAL DISCUSSION 38.3

Do people still want to become parents?

According to Jones (1995), 20 per cent of women in the UK born between 1960 and 1990 are unlikely ever to become mothers. They're likely to be well-educated, middle-class women, not necessarily pursuing a career, but realising that 'it's OK to go through life without having children' (Root Cartwright, in charge of the British Organisation of Non-Parents (BON)).

Norton (1999) cites a market research survey conducted by Mintel (the *Pre-Family Lifestyles Report*, 1999), involving almost 700 20–34-year-olds without children. It found that more women than men thought it important to be financially secure and established in their careers before starting a family. More significantly, a quarter of women, compared with less than one-fifth of men, saw their work as a career rather than a job.

Married men and women were more likely than co-habiting couples to say they didn't want children, with those living alone being keenest on starting a family (85 per cent). Overall, one in ten women said she was undecided about children. One-quarter of the sample didn't want to assume the responsibility of parenthood, and only three per cent thought that having children early in adulthood outweighed the financial and career advantages.

A second implication of the motherhood mandate is that most people would probably consider it to be 'unnatural' (or 'wicked') for a mother to leave her children, even if they're left in the care of their father whom she believes will look after them better than she could herself. However, the number of absent mothers targeted by the Child Support Agency trebled between 1995 and 1998, with over 37,000 being approached to pay child maintenance. One in 20 absent parents is a woman (Lacey, 1998). Either there are a lot more 'unnatural' or 'wicked' women out there than was previously thought, or the motherhood mandate needs serious revision!

A third implication is that it's 'unnatural' or simply 'wrong' for a mother of young children to go out to work (see Chapter 32). Related to this is the stereotype concerning women's attitudes towards paid employment. Is there any foundation for this stereotype?

The changing role of women in the work force

Traditionally, men have been seen as dominating the primary employment sector, with their employment histories remaining unbroken from school to retirement. In contrast, women predominate in the secondary employment sector, which is typically unstable, offering poor career prospects and working conditions. There's also a dip or gap in paid employment associated with child-rearing during the mid-twenties to early thirties (Kremer, 1998).

However, at the end of the 1990s employment profiles for both genders were changing rapidly. Women comprised about half the workforce (although a far higher proportion were part-time than men) and mothers were less likely to leave work to care for young children. Yet women were still more likely than men to interrupt their careers, at least temporarily, to take care of children, while men rarely did (Craig, 1992; Nicholson, 1993). (This relates to the 'gender-splitting' phenomenon identified by Levinson (1986) and will be discussed further below.)

Cherie Blair: mother and barrister first, Prime minister's wife second

Women's attitudes to paid employment

Kremer (1998) cites several surveys (conducted in the 1980s and 90s) showing that, despite poorer working conditions, the overwhelming majority of working women prefer to be in paid employment. Additionally, most of those not in work

(especially those under 50) would prefer to be. When asked to rate the importance of various factors at work, the differences between men and women are few, and usually only involve clashes between work commitments and domestic responsibilities. Men and0 women also tend to agree about the motivation for working, such as money, stimulation and feeling useful, and, ironically (given their poorer working conditions), women consistently express *higher* job satisfaction (especially part-time workers and those working from home).

Box 38.9 **Women, work and evolution**

According to Hrdy (1999), these findings should come as no surprise. Arguing from an evolutionary perspective, Hrdy claims that being ambitious is just as natural for a mother as breastfeeding. It's a fallacy to believe that mothers who go out to work are in conflict with their natural instincts. She argues that there's nothing new about working mothers: for most of human existence, and for millions of years before that, primate mothers have combined productive lives with reproduction. This combination of work and motherhood has always entailed trade-offs.

What's new for modern mothers is the *compartmentalisation* of their productive and reproductive lives. The factories, laboratories and offices where women in post-industrial societies go to 'forage' are even less compatible with childcare than jaguar-infested forests and distant groves of mongongo nuts. Hrdy is especially interested in the Pleistocene period, which extends from about 1.6 million years ago (when humans emerged from apes) to the invention of agriculture (about 10,000 years ago). It was during this period that many human instincts – including mothering – evolved through natural selection. Pleistocene woman would have striven for status and 'local clout' among her female peers. Ambition was just as much the driving force for women as for men, serving the Darwinian purpose of producing offspring who survived to adulthood (see Chapter 2 and Gross *et al.*, 2000).

However, a recent survey in the UK (conducted by *Top Santé* magazine and BUPA) paints a rather different picture (Brown, 1999). Involving 5000 women, average age 36, the majority in managerial and professional jobs, the survey found that 77 per cent would give up work tomorrow if they could. At an age when most would have expected to be at the pinnacle of their professions, nearly half were dreaming of a life of leisure and almost a third wanted to be homemakers. 'Superwoman' may exist, but it seems she feels overworked and disillusioned from juggling the demands of career and family. Contrary to the equation of womanhood with motherhood, many feel under pressure to go out to work and raise families, as they feel that society doesn't value mothers who stay at home (Brown, 1999).

Ask yourself ...

- If women are having to juggle career and family, what does this tell us about the contribution of their husbands or partners? Does 'New Man' exist?

Fathers' involvement in childcare, though on the increase, is still not seen as 'men's work', but is more of a bonus – for child and father alike. Nor does it seem to reduce any of the mother's burden of responsibility

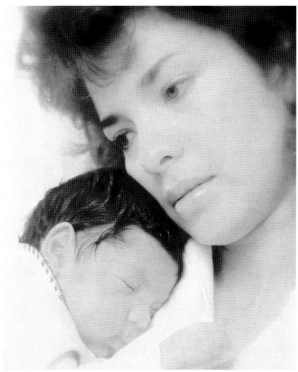

While childcare is still regarded as predominantly 'woman's work', mothers are increasingly likely to have a 'second career' outside of the home. Whether her paid employment is full- or part-time, this is likely to be additional to her domestic duties

Does 'New Man' exist?

The phenomenon of 'dual-earner couples/marriages' (where the husband works full-time and the wife works at least 20 hours per week) has become quite common, both in the US (Craig, 1992) and the UK (Nicholson, 1993). Compared with more 'traditional' couples, these husbands report more marital dissatisfaction and conflicts over family and work responsibilities, and the wives similarly report higher levels of conflict, as well as a very realistic work overload.

Despite some evidence that domestic tasks (especially childcare) are more evenly shared in some dual-earner families, it's nearly always the woman who's still primarily responsible for both housework and childcare, regardless of the age of the children and whether she works full- or part-time. Based on studies in eastern and western Europe, and North and South America, it seems that when there are no children, working wives do the bulk of the shopping and so on. But when there are children, the husband's contribution to running the home actually declines (in relative terms) with each child: the wife's increases by five to ten per cent with each child (Nicholson, 1993). While there are no apparent social class differences in men's contributions to the domestic division of labour, there are cultural ones, with Swedish men doing much more than their North American counterparts (Durkin, 1995).

A survey in the UK (Montgomery, 1993) found that 82 per cent of husbands had never ironed, 73 per cent had never washed clothes, and 24 per cent had never cooked. Kremer (1998) concludes that:

'There is little evidence to suggest that domestic responsibilities have been lifted from the shoulders of women. Instead, women's dual roles (home carer and worker) persist. Indeed, even in situations where both partners are not in paid employment, or where the woman is the primary wage earner, then this pattern often still endures'.

Similarly, Quiery (1998) maintains that while there have been some changes in fathers' behaviour over the last 15–20 years, they're not dramatic and the burden of child-rearing and home-making still falls on mothers. However, evidence from America suggests a rather more significant change is taking place.

KEY STUDY 38.1

Are American men participating more in their children's activities? (Pleck, 1999)

Pleck compared eleven studies dating from the mid-1960s to the early 1980s with 13 studies conducted between the mid-1980s and early 1990s. As shown in Figure 38.3, fathers' *engagement* with their children (as a percentage of the mothers' engagement) *increased* over that period from 34.3 per cent to 43.5 per cent. Engagement refers to interaction with one's children, such as playing with them, reading to them, and helping them with their homework.

In that same period, fathers' *availability* also increased (again, as a percentage of the mothers') from 51.8 per cent to 65.6 per cent (see Figure 38.4). Availability is a measure of how much time fathers spend near their children, either interacting with them or not (such as working on the computer while the children play video games).

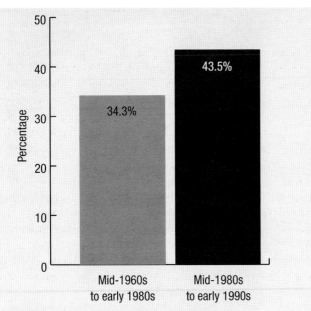

Figure 38.3 *Amount of time fathers interact with their children as percentage of mothers' engagement (from Pleck, 1999)]*

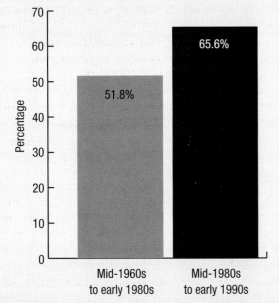

Figure 38.4 *Amount of time fathers are near their children, either interacting or not, as percentage of mothers' availability (from Pleck, 1999)*

Pleck (1999) concludes that although men still perform less childcare than women, men's participation in family activities is increasing. However, most of the relevant data come from studies of *married* fathers, which excludes a substantial proportion of the adult male population. When these other groups are taken into account, the *opposite* picture emerges. For example, the increase in divorce rates since the 1950s has weakened many men's family ties. Most divorced fathers' contact with their children drops off rapidly after divorce. Almost half of all divorced fathers haven't seen their children in the past year, and high proportions of them don't pay child maintenance. In addition, the recent increase in the proportion of men who never marry also indicates decreasing family involvement. Most unmarried fathers – teen and adult – refuse to accept any responsibility for their children.

Thus, it seems that American family life (and probably in the UK and other Western countries also) is changing in two *contradictory directions*. In two-parent families, fathers' involvement with children and overall gender equality are increasing. However, two-parent families have become a smaller proportion of all families, and families headed by single mothers have become more common. The overall effect of this is that more children don't have resident fathers (Pleck, 1999).

Pleck also challenges the popular view among social scientists (including psychologists, such as Levinson) that family is more central than work for women's identity, while the reverse is true for men. He cites evidence (from both his own and others' research) showing that family is far more central psychologically to men than work, just as it is for women. For example, fathers and mothers experience similar levels of anxiety over separation from their children during the first two years of parenthood. This suggests that 'gender-splitting' may not be such a clearly defined phenomenon as Levinson proposed. However, men are more likely to take workplace emotions home with them than are mothers, who keep these separate from their family experience.

Step-parenthood

In the early 1960s, almost 90 per cent of children spent their childhood and adolescence in homes with two biological, married parents. Now that's true of about 40 per cent of children in the US and about 50 per cent in the UK (Hetherington & Stanley-Hagan, 1999). This is attributed to increases in divorce, out-of-wedlock childbearing, and dramatically escalating rates of cohabitation.

Although 38 per cent of white American children experience parental divorce before their sixteenth birthdays, the figure for African-American children is almost 74 per cent. Thus, compared with white children, more African-American children experience their parents' marital dissolutions and spend longer in single-parent households, which often include cohabiting partners and relatives.

KEY STUDY 38.2

The effects of living in a step-family (Nicholson *et al.*, 1999)

Nicholson *et al.* examined the effects of living in a step-family during childhood and adolescence on a range of psychosocial outcomes. Data were collected for over 900 children in New Zealand as part of the Christchurch Health and Development Study. They'd all lived in step-families (for the first time) from ages six to 16, and were assessed at age 18 in terms of mental health, antisocial behaviour, substance use, restricted life opportunities, and sexual risk-taking.

Compared with a control group (children who hadn't been exposed to step-families for the first time between six and 16), they were more likely to become juvenile offenders, nicotine dependent, to abuse or become dependent on illegal substances, leave school without qualifications, engage in early sexual activity, and have multiple sexual partners. However, when factors such as family socioeconomic status, family history of instability, adversity and conflict, gender and pre-existing child-behaviour and attentional problems were controlled for, the differences became non-significant:

> 'Although young people exposed to living in a step-family had increased risks of poor psychosocial outcomes, much of this association appeared to be spurious and arose from confounding social, contextual and individual factors that were present prior to the formation of the step-family'. (Nicholson et al., 1999)

Lesbian and gay parenting

In the context of advocating that psychologists should study homosexual relationships in their own terms (and not by comparison with heterosexual ones), Kitzinger & Coyle (1995) suggest that we might want to ask how the children of lesbian/gay couples understand and talk about their parents' relationships, and how they can develop positive views about homosexuality in a heterosexual culture. Homosexual couples have always been involved in parenting through partners' previous heterosexual relationships. The recent increase in fostering/adoption of children by gay men, and the ongoing 'lesbian baby boom', mean that many more homosexual couples are parents than used to be the case (see Chapter 28).

According to Kitzinger et al. (1998), research into lesbian/gay parenting was initially concerned with whether or how far the children of lesbians and (to a lesser extent) gay men could be distinguished psychologically from those of heterosexuals. On balance, this research suggested that these children were no more 'at risk' than children raised in heterosexual families (see discussion of Freud's theory in Chapter 35).

For example, Taylor (1993) found no evidence that children reared in gay/lesbian families were more disturbed or had greater gender identity confusion than those reared in heterosexual families. Barrett & Robinson (1994) reviewed the impact of gay fathering on children. They stress the need to take into account that these children are likely to have experienced parental divorce and to show the psychological distress that often accompanies it (see Chapter 32). Although these children may be isolated, angry and in need of help sorting out their feelings about homosexuality in general, they're in little danger of being sexually abused, and adjust well to their family situations. While the relationships with their fathers may be stormy at first, they also have the potential for considerable honesty and openness.

Increasingly, psychologists are researching areas directly rooted in the concerns of lesbian/gay parents themselves, including coming out to one's children, and managing different co-parenting arrangements (such as a lesbian mother with her female lover, her ex-husband, a gay male sperm donor, or a gay male co-parent: Kitzinger et al., 1998).

Conclusions

Although some of the most influential and popular explanations of personality change in early and middle adulthood have adopted *stage approaches*, critics argue that adult development doesn't occur in predictable and ordered ways. An alternative, yet complementary, approach is to assess the impact of *critical life events*. These include two major *normative age-graded* influences, marriage/partnering and parenthood, and one *non-normative* influence, divorce.

In the case of parenthood, the changing roles of men and women have been shown to be crucial, especially women's participation in the labour market. This means that to appreciate the impact of various life events, they must be examined in the broader context of social norms, which, at least in Western countries, are constantly shifting. The chapter has also illustrated the mutual influence of different life events involving family and relationships.

CHAPTER SUMMARY

- In Erikson's **psychosocial theory**, the task of **young adulthood** is to achieve **intimacy** and to avoid **isolation**. The central tasks of **middle adulthood** are the attainment of **generativity** and to avoid **stagnation.**

- Many people struggle with issues of identity and intimacy **at the same time**, and women tend to achieve intimacy **before** 'occupational identity', submerging their identity into those of their partners. There are also important social class, racial and cultural differences in the timing of marriage and 'settling down'.

- Levinson et al. were concerned with how adulthood is actually **experienced**. Their **life-structure theory** identifies **phases/periods** which are either **stable** (**structure-building**) or **transitional** (**structure-changing**). A sequence of **eras** overlaps in the form of **cross-era transitions**.

- **Early adult transition** is a developmental bridge between adolescence and adulthood, and **entry life structure for early adulthood** is the first **structure-building** phase.

- Levinson et al. see crisis as both inevitable and necessary (**normative**). But people of all ages suffer crises ('**adolescing**'), and a growing number of people are deciding to make radical changes in their life-styles (**downshifting**), both earlier and later than 'mid-life'.

- While men have fairly unified, career-focused visions of the future, women's **dreams** are split between career and marriage/family responsibilities (**gender-splitting**).

- The **age-30 transition** generally lasts longer for women than for men, and '**settling down**' is much less clear-cut. Trying to integrate career and marriage and family responsibilities is very difficult for most women.

- The view that adult development is 'stage-like' has been criticised on the grounds that it underestimates **individual variability**. Stage theories also imply a **discontinuity** of development.

- According to Gould, the thrust of adult development is towards **adult consciousness** and freeing ourselves of the **illusion of absolute safety**. Adult development also involves a change in the **sense of time**.

- Marriage and parenting are **normative**, **age-graded influences**, while divorce is a **non-normative influence**. These are also called **marker events** or **critical life events**.
- Couples who **cohabit** before marriage are more likely to divorce later, or be less satisified with their marriages, than those who don't cohabit.
- **Married people** tend to live longer, and are happier, healthier and have lower rates of mental disorder than unmarried people. Men benefit most from marriage, and the potential benefits of marriage for women may be counterbalanced by gender-splitting.
- **Parenthood** has greater variability in meaning and impact than any other life transition. While pregnancy can bring couples closer together, men can feel excluded, especially after their babies are born.
- There's little evidence for **empty-nest distress**, and marital satisfaction usually increases once children have left home. The **crowded nest** is more likely to be distressing.
- The **motherhood mystique/mandate** can make women who don't bond immediately with their babies feel inadequate. But women are increasingly **postponing** having children or deciding not to have children at all.
- The motherhood mandate also implies that it's unnatural for mothers to leave their children, and that it's wrong for a mother of young children to go out to work.
- Despite evidence that domestic duties are more evenly shared in some **dual-earner families**, it's invariably the woman who's still primarily responsible for both housework and childcare.
- Although **married fathers** are **engaging** more with their children, most **divorced** fathers have little contact with their children, and an increasing number of men remain unmarried, and deny responsibility for their children. The overall effect is that more and more children are living without resident fathers.

- Many more **lesbian/gay** couples are parents than used to be the case. Early research examined whether the children of such parents were more 'at risk' than those raised in heterosexual families, but more recently the emphasis has shifted to issues such as co-parenting arrangements.

Self-assessment questions

1 Describe and critically evaluate any **one** theory of development in early and middle adulthood.
2 Critically consider the evidence for the existence of crises and transitions in early and middle adulthood.
3 Discuss psychological research into the effects of marriage (or partnering) **and** parenthood.
4 Critically consider the role of gender **and/or** cultural differences in marriage (or partnering) **and/or** divorce.

Web addresses

http://www.personal.psu.edu/faculty/n/x/nxd10/family3.htm

http://www.ben2ucla.edu/~jeffwood/

http://www.hec.ohio-state.edu/famlife/family/famlinks.htm

http://www.cleveland.cc.nc.us/staff/bolich/psyche/oage4g5.html

http://midmac.med.harvard.edu/research.html

http://www.hope.edu/academic/psychology/335/webrep2/crisis.html

http://www.mhhe.com/socscience/devel/common/middleadulthood.htm

Further reading

Schaie, K.W. & Willis, S.L. (1999) *Adult Development and Ageing* (5th edition) New York: Harper Collins. A good, up-to-date, American text. Also relevant for Chapter 39.

Sheehy, G. (1996) *New Passages*. London: HarperCollins (revised, UK edition) An account of changing adult roles. Can be read like a novel – but is essentially serious social–developmental research.

Chapter 39

Old Age

Introduction and overview

While 'growing up' is normally seen as desirable, 'growing old' usually has far more negative connotations. The negative view of ageing is based on the *decrement model*, which sees ageing as a process of decay or decline in physical and mental health, intellectual abilities and social relationships.

An alternative to the decrement model is the *personal growth model*, which stresses the potential advantages of late adulthood (or 'old age'), such as increased leisure time, reduced responsibilities, and the ability to concentrate only on matters of high priority (Kalish, 1982). This much more positive view is how ageing has been studied within the *lifespan approach*. In this chapter we consider some of the theories and research concerned with *adjustment to late adulthood*. It begins by looking at what's meant by the term 'old', which turns out to be more compex than it might seem. Stereotyped beliefs about what elderly people are like are an inherent part of prejudiced attitudes towards them. Research into some of the cognitive and social changes that occur in late adulthood bring these stereotypes and prejudice into sharp focus. The chapter also discusses the impact of two major life events, *retirement* (a *normative, age-graded influence*, often taken to mark the 'official' start of old age) and *bereavement* (a *non-normative influence*, although death of one's spouse becomes increasingly likely as we attain late adulthood).

The meaning of 'old'

Ask yourself ...

- How old is old?
- Is 'old' simply a matter of chronological age?

People today are living longer and retaining their health better than any previous generation (Baltes & Baltes, 1993). The proportion of older people in the British population has increased dramatically in recent years. In 1961, two per cent of the population (one million people) were aged 80 or over. By 1991, this figure had risen to four per cent (two million people). The number of centenarians has risen from 271 (in 1951), to 1185 (1971), to 4400 (1991). In 1997, the number stood at 8000 with projections of 12,000 (2001) and 30,000 (2030) (McCrystal, 1997). Figures for the USA show that the number of centenarians doubled between 1990 and 2000, and may increase more than eleven-fold by 2050 (Brown, 2000).

The oldest person who ever lived: Jeanne Calment died in 1997 at the age of 122

Because of this *demographic imperative* (Swensen, 1983), developmental psychologists have become increasingly interested in our later years. But what do we mean by 'old'? Kastenbaum's (1979) *'The ages of me'* questionnaire assesses how people see themselves at the present moment in relation to their ages.

Ask yourself ...

- How old are you according to Kastenbaum's questionnaire?

Box 39.1 Kastenbaum's 'The ages of me' questionnaire

Figure 39.1 *While (c) might depict someone's chronological age, (a) might correspond to his biological age and (b) might represent his subjective age*

- My **chronological age** is my actual or official age, dated from my time of birth. My chronological age is ...
- My **biological age** refers to the state of my face and body. In other people's eyes, I look as though I am about ... years of age. In my own eyes, I look like someone of about ... years of age.
- My **subjective age** is indicated by how I feel. Deep down inside, I really feel like a person of about ... years of age.
- My **functional age**, which is closely related to my **social age**, refers to the kind of life I lead, what I am able to do, the status I believe I have, whether I work, have dependent children and live in my own home. My thoughts and interests are like those of a person of about ... years of age, and my position in society is like that of a person of about ... years of age.

(Adapted from Kastenbaum, 1979)

Few people, irrespective of their chronological ages, describe themselves *consistently* (that is, they tend to give *different* responses to the different questionnaire items). For example, people over 20 (including those in their 70s and 80s) usually describe themselves as feeling younger than their chronological ages. We also generally consider ourselves to be *too old*.

Ageism

It seems, then, that knowing a person's chronological age tells us little about the sort of life that person leads or what s/he is like. However, one of the dangerous aspects of *ageism* is that chronological age is assumed to be an accurate indicator of all the other ages. According to Comfort (1977), ageism is:

'... the notion that people cease to be people, cease to be the same people or become people of a distinct and inferior kind by virtue of having lived a specified number of years ... Like racism, which it resembles, it is based on fear'.

Similarly, Bromley (1977) argues that most people react adversely to the elderly because they seem to deviate from our concept of 'normal' human beings. As part of the 'welfarist approach' to understanding the problems of an ageing society (Fennell et al., 1988), 'they' (i.e. the elderly) are designated as different, occupying another world from 'us' – a process that for all perceived minorities tends to be dehumanising and sets lower or different standards of social value or individual worth (Manthorpe, 1994: see Chapter 25).

The effects of stereotyping

Box 39.2 Can stereotypes make you ill?

In April 2000, the charity Age Concern highlighted the plight of Jill Baker, a cancer patient in her 60s. She was shocked to discover that, despite still being in a generally good state of health, a junior doctor she'd never met had put 'not for resuscitation' on her records.

According to Ebrahim (in Payne, 2000):

'Medical students still rejoice in their stereotypes of "geriatric crumbly" and "GOMER" (get out of my emergency room) patients'.

Ebrahim cites US evidence showing that 'do not resuscitate' orders are commonly used for people with HIV, blacks, alcohol misusers and non-English speakers, suggesting that doctors have stereotypes of who isn't worth saving (see Chapter 25).

In the UK, one in 20 people aged over 65 had been refused treatment by the NHS, with one in ten over-50s believing they were treated differently (i.e. worse) because of their age (based on an Age Concern survey).

Adler (2000) cites American research by Levy and her colleagues showing that stereotypes can affect how the elderly think about themselves in ways that can be detrimental to their mental and physical health. In one study, elderly participants spent a few minutes concentrating on a computer-based reaction-time test. Age-related words were subliminally presented on the screen (too quickly to be consciously registered), and were either negative (e.g. 'senile, 'forgetful', diseased'), or positive (e.g. 'wise', 'astute', 'accomplished').

The participants were subsequently asked if they'd request an expensive but potentially life-saving medical treatment, without which they'd die within a month. Most of those who'd 'seen' the positive words (evoking a positive stereotype) chose the life-saving treatment, but most of those who were exposed to negative words declined.

In another study, participants were challenged with a series of maths problems following ten minutes' exposure to positive or negative words. The latter showed signs of stress – heart rate, blood pressure and skin conductance all increased, and stayed high for over 30 minutes. In contrast, those exposed to positive words sailed through the challenge stress free.

Since many studies have linked chronic stress to disease (see Chapter 12), Levy suspects that repeated triggering of negative stereotypes over a period of several years may be making elderly people ill (Adler, 2000). (Levy's research is discussed further in Key Study 39.1, page 563.)

Stereotypes of the elderly are more deeply entrenched than (mis)conceptions of gender differences. It's therefore not surprising that people are overwhelmingly unenthusiastic about becoming 'old' (Stuart-Hamilton, 1997). According to Jones (1993), everyone over retirement age is seen as forming a strange homogeneous mass, with limited abilities, few needs and few rights:

'What other section of the population that spans more than 30 years in biological time is grouped together in such an illogical manner? ... As a consequence, older people suffer a great deal ... As for experience and wisdom, these qualities are no longer valued in this fast-moving high-technology world. They are devalued by the community, as well as by their owners'. (Jones, 1993)

Box 39.3 A decade-by-decade description of 'the elderly'

The young old (60–69): This period marks a major transition. Most adults must adapt to new role structures in an effort to cope with the losses and gains of the decade. Income is reduced due to retirement. Friends and colleagues start to disappear. Although physical strength wanes somewhat, a great many young old have surplus energy and seek out new and different activities.

The middle-aged old (70–79): This is often marked by loss or illness. Friends and family may die. The middle-aged old must also cope with reduced participation in formal organisations, which can produce restlessness and irritability. Their own health problems become more severe. The major developmental task is to maintain the personality reintegration achieved in the previous decade.

The old old (80–89): The old old show increased difficulty in adapting to and interacting with their surroundings. They need help in maintaining social and cultural contacts.

The very old old (90–99): Although health problems become more acute, the very old old can successfully alter their activities to make the most of what they have. The major advantage of old age is freedom from responsibilities. If previous crises have been resolved satisfactorily, this decade may be joyful, serene and fulfilling.

(Based on Burnside *et al.*, 1979, and Craig, 1992)

As Box 39.3 suggests, the aged aren't one cohesive group (Craig, 1992). Rather, they're a collection of subgroups, each with its unique problems and capabilities, but all sharing to some degree the age-related difficulties of reduced income, failing health and the loss of loved ones. For Craig, however:

'Having a problem is not the same as being a problem, and the all-too-popular view of those over age 65 as needy, non-productive, and unhappy needs revision'.

Similarly, Dietch (1995) has commented that:

'Life's final stage is surrounded by more myths, stereotypes and misinformation than any other developmental phase'.

Cognitive changes in old age

Consistent with the *decrement model* (see *Introduction and overview*), it's commonly believed that old age is associated with a decrease in cognitive abilities. Until recently, it was thought that intellectual capacity peaked in the late teens or early 20s, levelled off, and then began to decline fairly steadily during middle age and more rapidly in old age.

The evidence on which this claim was based came from *cross-sectional studies* (studying different age groups at the same time).

Ask yourself ...

- Why can't we generalise from cross-sectional studies?

However, we cannot draw firm conclusions from such studies, because the age groups compared represent different generations with different experiences (the *cohort effect*). Unless we know how 60-year-olds, say, performed when they were 40 and 20, it's impossible to say whether or not intelligence declines with age.

An alternative methodology is the *longitudinal study*, in which the same people are tested and retested at various times during their lives. Several such studies have produced data contradicting the results of cross-sectional studies, indicating that at least some people retain their intellect well into middle age and beyond (Holahan & Sears, 1995). However, the evidence suggests that there are some age-related changes in different *kinds* of intelligence and *aspects* of memory.

Changes in intelligence

Although psychologists have always disagreed about the definition of intelligence, there's general acceptance that it is *multi-dimensional* (composed of several different abilities). *Crystallised intelligence* results from accumulated knowledge, including a knowledge of how to reason, language skills and an understanding of technology. This type of intelligence is linked to education, experience and cultural background, and is measured by tests of general information.

By contrast, *fluid intelligence* is the ability to solve novel and unusual problems (those not experienced before). It allows us to perceive and draw inferences about relationships among patterns of stimuli and to conceptualise abstract information, which aids problem-solving. Fluid intelligence is measured by tests using novel and unusual problems not based on specific knowledge or particular previous learning.

Crystallised intelligence *increases* with age, and people tend to continue improving their performance until near the end of their lives (Horn, 1982). Using the *cross-longitudinal* method (in which *different* age groups are *retested* over a long period of time), Schaie & Hertzog (1983) reported that fluid intelligence declines for all age groups over time, peaking between 20 and 30 (see Chapter 41). The tendency to continue adding to our knowledge as we grow older could account for the constancy of crystallised intelligence. Alternatively, regular use of our crystallised abilities may help to maintain them (Denney & Palmer, 1981). The decline in fluid intelligence may be an inevitable part of the ageing process related to the reduced efficiency of neurological functioning. However, we may also be less often challenged to use our fluid abilities in old age (Cavanaugh, 1995).

Changes in memory

Some aspects of memory appear to decline with age, possibly because we become less effective at processing information (which may underlie cognitive changes in general: Stuart-Hamilton, 1994). On recall tests, older adults *generally* perform more poorly than younger adults. But the *reverse* is sometimes true, as shown by Maylor's (1994) study of the performance of older contestants on *Mastermind*. On recognition tests, the differences between younger and older people are less apparent and may even disappear (see Chapter 17). As far as everyday memory is concerned, the evidence indicates that the elderly do have trouble recalling events from their youth and early lives (Miller & Morris, 1993).

Alzheimer's disease

Significant memory deficits are one feature of *dementia*, the most common form of which is Alzheimer's disease. However, over 90 per cent of people over 65 show little deterioration (Diamond, 1978), and even very late in life cortical neurons seem capable of responding to enriched conditions by forming new functional connections with other neurons. This is supported by the finding that those who keep mentally active are those who maintain their cognitive abilities (Rogers *et al.*, 1990).

However, there are those who claim that Alzheimer's disease is an accelerated form of normal changes in the ageing brain, so that we'd all get the disease if we lived long enough. The opposing view is that cognitive decline *isn't* an inevitable part of ageing, but rather it reflects a disease process which is more likely to affect us as we get older (Smith, 1998). Work by the Oxford Project to Investigate Memory and Ageing (OPTIMA) has used *X-ray computerised tomography* (CT: see Chapter 4) to examine the medial temporal lobe (again see Chapter 4). While this tiny area comprises only two per cent of the volume of the whole cerebral cortex, it includes the *hippocampus*, a structure known to be crucial for memory (see Chapter 17). Also, the neurons of the medial temporal lobe connect with almost all other parts of the cortex, so any damage to this part of the brain is likely to have consequences for the functioning of the rest of the cortex.

X-ray CT images show that the medial temporal lobe is markedly smaller in people with dementia who eventually die of Alzheimer's disease than in age-matched controls without cognitive deficit. Repeated CT scans over periods of several years have found that shrinkage is slow in control participants (about 1–1.5 per cent per year), compared with an alarming rate of some 15 per cent per year in Alzheimer's patients (Smith, 1998).

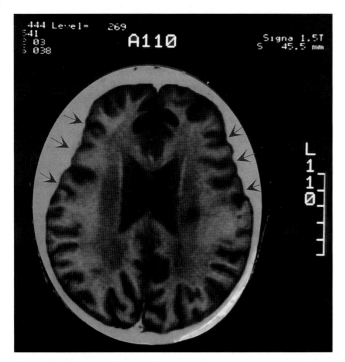

A CT scan of a patient with Alzheimer's disease. The arrows indicate widespread destruction of brain tissue

These, and other supportive data, led the OPTIMA researchers to conclude that Alzheimer's disease is *distinct* from normal ageing, and that it cannot be simply an acceleration of normal ageing. Although cognitive decline does appear to increase with age for the population as a whole, if we rigorously exclude those with pathological changes (such as early Alzheimer's), then a majority may not show any significant decline. According to Smith (1998):

'We must abandon the fatalistic view that mental decline is an inevitable accompaniment of ageing'.

Consistent with this conclusion is the belief that negative cultural stereotypes of ageing actually cause memory decline in the elderly.

KEY STUDY 39.1

The influence of stereotypes on memory (Levy & Langer, 1994)

Levy and Langer investigated the memory capabilities of hearing Americans, members of the American deaf community and people from mainland China. It was assumed that members of the deaf community were less likely to have been exposed to negative cultural stereotypes. People from mainland China were chosen because of the high esteem in which Chinese society holds its aged members. The older American deaf participants and the Chinese participants performed much better on memory tasks than the older American hearing participants.

Also, younger hearing Americans held less positive views of ageing than any of the other groups. Amongst the older participants, attitudes towards ageing and memory performance were positively correlated. Levy and Langer believe

that negative stereotypes about ageing may become *self-fulfilling prophecies*, so that low expectations mean that people are less likely to engage in activities that will help them maintain their memory abilities.

The subliminal (below conscious awareness) presentation of negative self-stereotypes (e.g. 'Because of my age I am forgetful') tended to worsen memory performance, while positive self-stereotypes (e.g. 'Because of my age I have acquired wisdom') tended to improve it (Levy, 1996). Levy found no such effect with young participants, for whom stereotypes of ageing are obviously less salient (see text above, page 561).

Social changes in old age

Social disengagement theory

According to Manthorpe (1994), Cumming & Henry's (1961) *social disengagement theory* represented the first major attempt to produce a theory about individuals' relationships with society. Based on a five-year study of 275 50–90-year-olds in Kansas City, USA, Cumming and Henry claimed that:

'Many of the relationships between a person and other members of society are severed and those remaining are altered in quality'.

This social disengagement involves the *mutual withdrawal* of society from the individual (through compulsory retirement, children growing up and leaving home, the death of a spouse and so on) and of the individual from society (Cumming, 1975). As people grow older, they become more solitary, retreat into the inner world of their memories, become emotionally quiescent, and engage in pensive self-reflection.

Cumming sees disengagement as having three components:

- *shrinkage of life space* refers to the tendency to interact with fewer other people as we grow older, and to occupy fewer roles;
- *increased individuality* means that in the roles that remain, older people are much less governed by strict rules and expectations;
- *acceptance* (even embrace) *of these changes*, so that withdrawal is a voluntary, natural and inevitable process, and represents the most appropriate and successful way of growing old.

As far as society is concerned, the individual's withdrawal is part of an inevitable move towards death – the ultimate disengagement (Manthorpe, 1994). By replacing older individuals with younger people, society renews itself and the elderly are free to die (Bromley, 1988).

An evaluation of social disengagement theory

Bee (1994) sees the first two components as difficult to dispute. However, the third is more controversial because of its view of disengagement as a natural, voluntary and inevitable process, rather than an imposed one. Bromley (1988) argues that such a view of ageing has detrimental practical consequences for the elderly, such as encouraging a policy of segregation, even indifference, and the very destructive belief that old age has no value (see page 561). For Bromley, an even more serious criticism concerns whether everyone actually does disengage.

Social disengagement theory focuses on *quantitative* changes, such as the reduced number of relationships and roles in old age. But for Carstensen (1996), it's the *qualitative* changes that are crucial:

> '*Although age is associated with many losses, including loss of power, social partners, physical health, cognitive efficiency, and, eventually, life itself – and although this list of losses encompasses the very things that younger people typically equate with happiness – research suggests that older people are at least as satisfied with their lives as their younger counterparts*'.

The importance of friendships

Although many of these losses are beyond the older person's control (Rosnow, 1985), such as retirement (see below), *friendships* are voluntary, non-institutionalised and relatively enduring relationships which offer comfort and stability. *Informal* support from friends (and other primary relationships) also reduces dependency on social security agencies, the helping professions and other formal organisations (Duck, 1991; Rainey, 1998). It's the choice element that differentiates friendships from other types of relationships (Baltes & Baltes, 1986), providing older people with control over at least one life domain (Rainey, 1998).

Maintaining close relationships with others is often a significant factor in determining whether older people feel a sense of belonging to the social system. This may become more important with age, because society withdraws from

older adults both *behaviourally* (compulsory retirement) and *attitudinally* (attributing diminishing powers, abilities and qualities to the elderly). Both relatives and friends are crucial for determining how life is experienced by the elderly. Overall, individual adaptation to old age on all levels has been shown to be highly dependent on personal tolerance of stress and life events, and on the availability of informal social support networks (Duck, 1991). These findings regarding the role of friendships and other relationships are consistent with *socioemotional selectivity theory* (see pages 565–566).

Activity (or re-engagement) theory

The major alternative to disengagement theory is *activity* (or *re-engagement*) theory (Havighurst, 1964; Maddox, 1964). Except for inevitable biological and health changes, older people are essentially the same as middle-aged people, with the same psychological and social needs. Decreased social interaction in old age is the result of the withdrawal of an inherently ageist society from the ageing person, and happens against the wishes of most elderly people. The withdrawal *isn't* mutual.

Optimal ageing involves staying active and managing to resist the 'shrinkage' of the social world. This can be achieved by maintaining the activities of middle age for as long as possible, and then finding substitutes for work or retirement (such as leisure or hobbies) and for spouses and friends upon their death (such as grandchildren). It's important for older adults to maintain their role counts, to ensure they always have several different roles to play.

Activity theory personified

An evaluation of activity theory

According to Bond *et al.* (1993), activity theory can be criticised for being:

> '... unrealistic because the economic, political and social structure of society prevents the older worker from maintaining a major activity of middle age, namely, "productive" employment'.

The implication seems to be that there really is *no* substitute for paid employment (at least for men: see above). According to Dex & Phillipson (1986), society appears to measure people's worth by their ability to undertake paid labour, and the more autonomous people are in their working practices, the more respect they seem to deserve. When someone retires, they not only lose their autonomy and right to work for money, but they also lose their identity: they cease to be a participant in society and their status is reduced to 'pensioner/senior citizen' or simply 'old person'.

As noted in Key Study 39.2, some elderly people seem satisfied with disengagement, suggesting that activity theory alone cannot explain successful ageing. Nevertheless, activity or re-engagement prevents the consequences of disengagement from going too far in the direction of isolation, apathy and inaction.

Just as disengagement may be involuntary (as in the case of poor health), so we may face involuntarily high levels of activity (as in looking after grandchildren). Both disengagement and activity may, therefore, be equally maladaptive. Quite possibly, disengagement theory actually *under*estimates, and activity theory *over*estimates, the degree of control people have over the 'reconstruction' of their lives.

Additionally, both theories see ageing as essentially the same for everyone. They both refer to a legitimate process through which some people come to terms with the many changes that accompany ageing (they represent *options*: Hayslip & Panek, 1989). However, people will select styles of ageing best suited to their personalities and past experiences or lifestyles, and there's no single 'best way' to age (Neugarten & Neugarten, 1987). For Turner & Helms (1989), personality is the key factor and neither theory can adequately explain successful ageing.

Increasingly, theorists are emphasising the *continuity* between earlier and later phases of life (see Chapter 38). Satisfaction, morale and adaptations in later life seem to be closely related to a person's life-long personality style and response to stress and change. According to Reedy (1983):

> 'In this sense, the past is the prologue to the future. While the personality changes somewhat in response to various life events and changes, it generally remains stable throughout all of adult life'.

Social exchange theory

According to Dyson (1980), both disengagement and activity theories fail to take sufficient account of the physical, social and economic factors which might limit people's choices about how they age. Age robs people of the capacity to engage in the reciprocal give-and-take that is the hallmark of social relationships, and thus weakens their attachment to others. In addition, Dowd (1975) argues that:

> 'Unlike the aged in traditional societies, older people in industrialised societies have precious few power resources to exchange in daily social interaction'.

The elderly couple above seem to fit the stereotype of the withdrawn, isolated, 'disengaged' person, while the couple below illustrate an alternative, but less common, stereotype, of the person who remains as active in old age as when s/he was middle-aged

This inequality of power results in dependence on others and compliance with others' wishes. But for both Dyson and Dowd there's a more positive aspect to this loss of power. Adjusting to old age in general, and retirement in particular, involves a sort of *contract* between the individual and society. The elderly give up their roles as economically active members of society, but in *exchange* they receive increased leisure time, take on fewer responsibilities and so on. Although the contract is largely unwritten and not enforceable, most people will probably conform to the expectations about being old which are built into social institutions and stereotypes (see Key Study 39.1).

Socioemotional selectivity theory

According to *socioemotional selectivity theory* (SST: Carstensen, 1992, 1993; Carstensen & Turk-Charles, 1994), social contact is motivated by various goals, including basic survival, information-seeking, development of self-concept and the regulation of emotion. While they all operate throughout life, the importance of specific goals varies, depending on one's place in the life cycle. For example, when *emotional regulation* is the major goal, people are highly selective in their choice of social partners, preferring familiar others. This selectivity is at its peak in infancy (see Chapter 32) and old age: the elderly turn increasingly to friends and adult children for emotional support (see above).

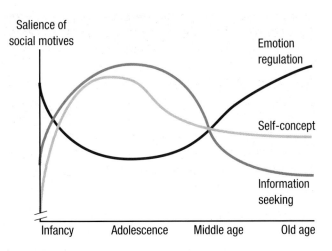

Figure 39.2 *Idealised illustration of the lifespan trajectory (from Carstensen, 1996)*

According to SST, a major factor contributing to these changes in social motives is *construal of the future*, which is indicated by chronological age. When the future is perceived as largely open-ended, long-term goals assume great significance. But when the future is perceived as limited (see Gould's theory, pages 549–550), attention shifts to the present. Immediate needs, such as emotional states, become more salient. So, contrary to disengagement theory (which sees reduced social contact as being caused by emotional states becoming diluted and dampened down), SST predicts that emotional concerns will become *more* important in old age.

If SST is correct, it would follow that when younger people hold expectations about the future which are similar to those of the elderly, they should make the same kinds of social choices as those typically made by older people.

KEY STUDY 39.3

How a limited future can influence current concerns (Carstensen, 1996)

Carstensen describes a study involving a group of healthy gay men, a group of HIV-positive, asymptomatic gay men, and a group of HIV-positive, symptomatic gay men. A group of young, middle-aged and old men representing the general population served as a control group.

The social preferences of the healthy gay men were similar to those of the young men from the control group. Those of the asymptomatic group mimicked those of the middle-aged controls, while those of the symptomatic group were strikingly similar to those of the oldest control participants. In other words:

'The closer the men were to the end of their lives, the greater weight they placed on affective qualities of prospective social partners ... changes in social preferences appear to be altered in much the same way when futures are limited by age as when futures are limited by disease'. (Carstensen, 1996)

According to Carstensen (1996), the findings relevant to SST taken together paint quite an optimistic picture. Age-related reduction in social contact appears to be highly selective (rather than reflecting a reduced capacity), such that interaction is limited to those people who are most familiar and can provide the greatest emotional security and comfort. This is an excellent strategy when time and social energy need to be invested wisely.

Psychosocial theory

Another alternative to disengagement and activity theories is Erikson's *psychosocial theory* (see Chapter 38). A more valid and useful way of looking at what all elderly people have in common might be to examine the importance of old age as a stage of development, albeit the last (which is where its importance lies).

Erikson's theory suggests that in old age, there's a conflict between *ego-integrity* (the positive force) and *despair* (the negative force). As with the other psychosocial stages, we cannot avoid the conflict altogether, which occurs as a result of biological, psychological and social forces. The task is to end this stage, and hence life, with greater ego-integrity than despair, and this requires us to take stock of our life, reflect on it, and assess how worthwhile and fulfilling it has been.

The characteristics of ego-integrity

- We believe that life does have a purpose and makes sense.
- We accept that, within the context of our lives as a whole, what happened was somehow inevitable and could only have happened when and how it did.
- We believe that all life's experiences offer something of value, and that we can learn from everything that happens to us. Looking back, we can see how we have grown psychologically as a result of life's ups and downs, triumphs and failures, calms and crises.
- We see our parents in a new light and understand them better, because we've lived through our own adulthood and have probably raised children of our own.
- We realise that we share with all other human beings, past, present and future, the inevitable cycle of birth and death. Whatever the historical, cultural and other differences, we all have this much in common. In the light of this, death 'loses its sting'.

Fear of death is the most conspicuous symptom of despair. In despair, we express the belief that it's too late to undo the past and turn the clock back in order to right wrongs or do what hasn't been done. Life isn't a 'rehearsal'; this is the only chance we get.

Retirement

Retirement has figured prominently in the discussion above of theories of social adjustment in old age. As a normative, age-graded influence, it's an inevitable and anticipated loss of work, which many people experience without undue psychological upheaval (Raphael, 1984). However, it may be unacceptable to those who, for example, see themselves as 'too young' to stop work.

Ask yourself ...

- What do you imagine some of the major benefits and negative aspects of retirement might be?

One consequence of retirement is the loss of everyday, ritualised patterns of activity, which contribute to the very fabric of our lives. While the early weeks of not working may be celebrated, emptiness may be experienced for a time following retirement. As the months pass, frustration and a sense of 'uselessness' can set in, and this may produce an angry and irritable response to the world.

Victor Meldrew (star of BBC TV's One Foot in the Grave*) seems to personify the sense of frustration and uselessness that often sets in, especially for men, after the 'honeymoon period' of retirement*

Retirement is a *process* and *social role* which unfolds through a series of six phases, each of which requires an adjustment to be made (Atchley, 1982, 1985). The phases don't correspond with any particular chronological ages, occur in no fixed order, and not all of them are necessarily experienced by everyone.

Box 39.4 The six phases in the process of retirement

Pre-retirement phase: (i) In the *remote* subphase, retirement is seen as being in a reasonably distant future; (ii) the *near* subphase may be initiated by the retirement of older friends and colleagues, and there may be much anxiety about lifestyle changes, especially financial ones.
Honeymoon phase (immediate post-retirement): This typically involves euphoria, partly due to newfound freedom, and is often a busy period.
Disenchantment phase: This involves a slowing down after the honeymoon phase, with feelings of being let down and even depression. The degree of disenchantment is related to declining health and finances. Eagerly anticipated postretirement activities (e.g. travel) may lose their original appeal. Disenchantment may be produced by unrealistic pre-retirement fantasies, or inadequate preparation for retirement.
Reorientation phase: This is a time to develop a more realistic view of life alternatives, and may involve exploring new avenues of involvement,

sometimes with the help of community groups (e.g. special voluntary or paid jobs for the retired). This helps to decrease feelings of role loss and is a means of achieving self-actualisation (see Chapter 9).
Stability phase: This involves the establishment of criteria for making choices, allowing people to deal with life in a fairly comfortable and orderly way. They know what's expected of them, what their strengths and weaknesses are, allowing mastery of the retirement role.
Termination phase: Illness and disability usually make housework and self-care difficult or impossible, leading to the assumption of a sick or disabled (as opposed to retired) role.

(Based on Atchley, 1982, and Atchley & Robinson, 1982)

People who retire *voluntarily* seem to have very little or no difficulty in adjusting. But those who retire because they've reached a compulsory age tend to be dissatisfied at first, although they eventually adapt. The least satisfied are those whose health is poor when they retire (which may have caused their retirement), although health often improves following retirement.

Bromley (1988) believes that it's the *transition* between employment and retirement that causes adjustment problems. Those who are most satisfied in retirement tend to be scientists, writers and other academics, who simply carry on working with little loss of continuity from very satisfying jobs. Those who discover satisfying leisure activities, with at least some of the characteristics of work, also adjust well. Conversely, some people decide to take early retirement (for reasons other than ill-health). This means that retirement isn't necessarily a sudden and enforced dislocation of a working life, inevitably causing feelings of rejection and producing psychological problems.

Retirement and gender

Ask yourself ...

- What particular problems would you expect retiring women to experience?

As we saw in Chapter 38, women are increasingly entering the labour market and remaining in it, and so more and more women are having to adjust to their own retirement. At the same time, 'gender-splitting' will mean that home and family still occupy a major part of a working woman's time, and retirement will involve *less* of a lifestyle change than it will for her husband.

According to Rainey (1998), the increase in numbers of working women aged 45–64 is particularly significant. They're the very age-group that, traditionally, contributes the most time to voluntary organisations and provides informal support for the elderly. There's no evidence that these women are abandoning their caring roles. In fact, these 'women in the middle' appear to be assuming multiple roles: caring for their own families (which includes helping their husbands adjust to retirement), for aged parents, possibly parents-in-law, as well as working. They're caught in the 'caring trap' (Rainey, 1998).

Retirement and unemployment

While retirement is an anticipated loss of work, unemployment is sudden and generally unanticipated. According to Campbell (1981), retirement is also an accepted and 'honourable' social status (it's 'achieved'), whereas unemployment isn't. Moreover, retirement is seen as a proper reward for a lifetime of hard work, while for many people unemployment implies failure, being unwanted (or incompetent), and a 'scrounger' who's 'living off the state'. There's a stigma attached to unemployment which can make it a disturbing and degrading experience, while most men see retirement as a rather benign condition of life.

Bereavement

Although the loss, through death, of loved ones can occur at any stage of the life cycle, it becomes more likely as we get older that we'll suffer *bereavement*. The psychological and bodily reactions that occur in people who suffer bereavement are called *grief*. The 'observable expression of grief' (Parkes & Weiss, 1983) is called *mourning*, although this term is often used to refer to the social conventions surrounding death (such as funerals and wearing black clothes).

Approaches to the understanding of grief

According to Archer (1999), grief has been variously depicted as (a) a natural human reaction; (b) a psychiatric disorder; and (c) a disease process. All three approaches contain an element of truth. As far as (a) is concerned, grief is a univeral feature of human existence, found in all cultures. But its form and the intensity of its expression varies considerably (see pages 569–570). As far as (b) is concerned, although grief itself has never been classified as a mental disorder (see Chapter 43):

> *'The psychiatric framework emphasises the human suffering grief involves, and therefore provides a useful balance to viewing it simply as a natural reaction'.* (Archer, 1999)

Regarding (c), although there may be increased rates of *morbidity* (health deterioration) or *mortality* (death) amongst bereaved people, these aren't necessarily *directly* caused by the grief process. For example, the effects of change in lifestyle (such as altered nutrition or drug intake), or increased attention to physical illness which predated the bereavement, might be mistaken for the effects of grief itself. However, there's substantial evidence that bereaved spouses are more at risk of dying themselves compared with matched non-bereaved controls. This is true mainly for widowers (Stroebe & Stroebe, 1993), and especially for younger widowers experiencing an unexpected bereavement (Smith & Zick, 1996).

Stage or phase accounts of grief

According to Archer (1999), a widely held assumption is that grief proceeds through an orderly series of stages or phases, with distinct features. While different accounts vary in the details of particular stages, the two most commonly cited are those of Bowlby (1980) and Kübler-Ross (1969).

According to Bowlby (1980), adult grief is an extension of a general distress response to separation commonly observed in young children (see Chapter 32). Adult grief is a form of *separation anxiety* in response to the disruption of an attachment bond.

Phase of numbing: Numbness and disbelief, which can last from a few hours up to a week, may be punctuated by outbursts of extremely intense distress and/or anger.
Yearning and searching: These are accompanied by anxiety and intermittent periods of anger, and can last for months or even years.
Disorganisation and despair: Feelings of depression and apathy occur when old patterns have been discarded.
Reorganisation: There's a greater/lesser degree of recovery from bereavement and acceptance of what's occurred.

Kübler-Ross's stage theory: anticipatory grief

Kübler-Ross's (1969) stage view was based on her pioneering work with over 200 terminally ill patients. She was interested in how they prepared for their own imminent deaths (*anticipatory grief*), and so her stages describe the process of dying. But she was inspired by an earlier version of Bowlby's theory (Parkes, 1995) and her stages were later applied (by other researchers) to *grief for others*. Her theory remains very influential in nursing and counselling, both with dying patients and the bereaved (Archer, 1999).

Box 39.6 Kübler-Ross's stages of dying

Denial ('No, not me'): This prevents the patient from being overwhelmed by the initial shock. It may take the form of seeking a second opinion, or holding contradictory beliefs.
Anger ('It's not fair – why me?'): This may be directed at medical staff and other healthy people who'll go on living.
Bargaining ('Please God let me ...'): This is an attempt to postpone death by 'doing a deal' with God (or fate, or the hospital), much as a child might bargain with its parents in order to get its own way.
Depression ('How can I leave all this behind?'): This is likely to arise when the patient realises that no bargain can be struck, and that death is inevitable. S/he grieves for all the losses that death represents.
Acceptance ('Leave me be, I am ready to die'): Almost devoid of feelings, the patient seems to have given up the struggle for life, sleeps more and withdraws from other people, as if preparing for 'the long journey'.

Almost all the patients she interviewed initially denied they had life-threatening illnesses, although only three remained in a constant state of denial (the rest drifted in and out). Denial was more common when someone had been given the diagnosis in an abrupt or insensitive way, or if they were surrounded by family and/or staff who were also in denial. Searching for a second opinion was a very common initial reaction, representing a desperate attempt to change the unpredictable world they'd just been catapulted into, back to the world they knew and understood (March & Doherty, 1999).

Depression is a common reaction in the dying. For example, Hinton (1975) reported that 18 per cent of those who committed suicide suffered from serious physical illnesses, with four per cent having illnesses that probably would have killed them within six months (see Chapter 44). Terminally ill patients suffer from what Kübler-Ross called *preparatory depression* (as opposed to *reactive*).

Elderly people who've lived full lives have relatively little to grieve for – they've gained much and lost few opportunities. But people who perceive lives full of mistakes and missed opportunities may, paradoxically, have *more* to grieve for as they begin to realise that these opportunities are now lost forever. This resembles Erikson's despair (see page 566), as does *resignation*, which Kübler-Ross distinguished from acceptance. The detachment and stillness of those who've achieved acceptance comes from calmness, while in those who've become resigned it comes from despair. The latter cannot accept death, nor can they deny its existence any longer (March & Doherty, 1999).

An evaluation of stage theories of grief

Generally, stage models haven't been well supported by subsequent research. Both Bowlby's and Kübler-Ross's accounts were proposed before any prolonged, detailed follow-up studies of bereaved people had been undertaken (Archer, 1999). According to March & Doherty (1999), they represent generalisations from the experience of some individuals and lack the flexibility necessary to describe the range of individual reactions. Grief *isn't* a simple, universal process we all go through (Stroebe *et al.*, 1993).

Some researchers prefer to talk about the components of grief. Ramsay & de Groot (1977), for example, have identified nine such components, some of which occur early and others late in the grieving process.

Box 39.7	**Ramsay and de Groot's nine components of grief**

Shock: This is usually the first response, most often described as a feeling of 'numbness', which can also include pain, calm, apathy, depersonalisation and derealisation. It's as if the feelings are so strong that they're 'turned off'. This can last from a few seconds to several weeks.

Disorganisation: This can be the inability to do the simplest thing, or, alternatively, organising the entire funeral and then collapsing.

Denial: Behaving as if the deceased were still alive is a defence against feeling too much pain. It's usually an early feature of grief, but one that can recur at any time. A common form of denial is searching behaviour (e.g. waiting for the deceased to come home, or having hallucinations of them).

Depression: This emerges as the denial breaks down but can occur, usually less frequently and intensely, at any point during the grieving process. It can consist of either 'desolate pining' (a yearning and longing, an emptiness interspersed with waves of intense psychic pain') or 'despair' (feelings of helplessness, the blackness of the realisation of powerlessness to bring back the dead).

Guilt: This can be both real and imagined, for actual neglect of the deceased when they were alive, or for angry thoughts and feelings.

Anxiety: This can involve fear of losing control of one's feelings, of going mad, or more general apprehension about the future (changed roles, increased responsibilities, financial worries, and so on).

Aggression: This can take the form of irritability towards family and friends, outbursts of anger towards God or fate, doctors and nurses, the clergy or even the person who's died.

Resolution: This is an emerging acceptance of the death, a 'taking leave of the dead and acceptance that life must go on'.

Reintegration: This involves putting acceptance into practice by reorganising one's life in which the deceased has no place. However, pining and despair may reappear on anniversaries, birthdays, and so on.

However, many stage theorists have explicitly *denied* that the stages are meant to apply equally and rigidly to everyone. For example, Bowlby (1980) himself said that:

> 'These phases are not clear-cut, and any one individual may oscillate for a time back and forth between any two of them'.

Yet stages provide us with a framework or guidelines for understanding the experiences of bereaved and dying individuals, while at the same recognising that there's a huge variability in the ways individuals react. Stages don't prescribe where an individual 'ought' to be in the grieving process (March & Doherty, 1999).

Cultural influences on reactions to bereavement

Because of the huge individual variability, trying to distinguish 'normal' from 'abnormal' grief seems quite arbitrary (Schuchter & Zisook, 1993). According to Middleton *et al.* (1993), the validity of the concept of pathological grief must be considered in terms of *cultural norms*. Although grief is a universal response to major loss, its meaning, duration and how it's expressed are all culturally prescribed.

Inter- and intra-cultural differences

Cultures differ in how they define death and what's an appropriate expression of grief. According to Rosenblatt (1993):

> 'Culture is such a crucial part of the context of bereavement that it is often impossible to separate an individual's grief from culturally required mourning'.

For example, in cultures that believe 'do not grieve because grief will cause the ghost of the deceased to take you away' or 'do not grieve because the deceased has gone to a better life', it's difficult to assesss accurately what appears to be muted or restrained grief. Similarly, when the 'rules' say 'cry', and people cry, how do we know the grief is genuine, deeply felt and likely to occur in the absence of the cultural demands for crying (what kind of attribution should we make?: see Chapter 23).

The Jewish rites of mourning are believed to be of therapeutic benefit, enabling the expression, rather than the repression, of grief. For the first few days following a burial, mourners are expected to be distressed and their despair is recognised and supported by relatives and friends who come to pay their respects.

By contrast, the Hindu, Sikh, Muslim and Buddhist religions all discourage too much weeping (Firth, 1993). The

Hindus believe that weeping makes a river which the soul of the deceased has to cross, and Sikhs believe the deceased has gone to God. However, the expression of grief is less inhibited in villages on the Indian sub-continent compared with Sikhs and Hindus living in Britain. Similarly, wailing is still very common among Muslims in Muslim countries (Firth, 1993).

Compared with Western women, Japanese women accept their husbands' death with composure and resignation. They believe strongly in an afterlife, and that their ancestors are always with them. Their beliefs mitigate feelings of complete loss and, to this extent, they have less to grieve about. The long-lasting grief and depression observed among the bereaved in the UK is partly a result of the lack of rituals and beliefs, as well as the lack of an externally based end to the grieving process (March & Doherty, 1999).

Box 39.8 Culture and the length of the grieving process

- In traditional Navajo Indian culture, the expression of grief lasts for four days following the death (March & Doherty, 1999).
- For Hindus in India, the mourning period lasts 10–16 days.
- For orthodox Jews, there are five graduated periods of mourning: (i) between death and the burial (which occurs as soon as can be arranged); (ii) immediate postburial; (iii) seven days following the burial (the *shiva* week); (iv) thirty days from the burial (marking the official end of mourning, unless it's a parent who's died, in which case it continues for a whole year); finally (v) between 30 days and one year, when the memorial stone is erected (Katz, 1993).

According to Firth (1993), all the major religions of the world teach that there's some sort of continuity or survival after death. They also comfort and reassure the bereaved by helping to make sense of death and personal loss, providing shape and meaning to the grieving process. As Box 39.8 shows, mourning lasts for a clearly defined period in different cultures, providing 'milestones'. These allow the bereaved a gradual time to let go of the deceased and adjust to the psychological and social changes in their lives.

As well as differences between cultures, there are also important differences *within* culturally diverse countries, such as the USA and the UK. For example, WASP (white Anglo-Saxon Protestant) Americans tend to 'psychologise' their emotional pain (e.g. depression), while people in many ethnic minority groups tend to 'somatise' theirs (e.g. bodily symptoms: Kleinman & Kleinman, 1985).

Conclusions

The different meanings of 'old' suggest that chronological age is a poor indicator of what a particular elderly individual is like, both psychologically and socially. However, major theories of social adjustment to old age, such as social disengagement and activity theories, tend to regard the elderly as basically all the same. This implies that there's a particular way of ageing successfully, a view not shared by other theories and not supported by research evidence.

Similarly, the view that ageing inevitably involves rapid and generalised cognitive decline is also not supported by

research evidence. Both intelligence and memory have many facets, which tend to decline at very different rates.

Retirement is a socially imposed loss of work, which has both social and psychological effects, as does bereavement. Attempts to identify stages of grief that apply equally to everyone have proved largely unsuccessful, partly because of individual variability and partly because of both inter- and intra-cultural differences in how death and grief are understood and managed.

CHAPTER SUMMARY

- While 'growing up' has positive connotations, 'growing old' has negative ones, reflecting the **decrement model**. An alternative, more positive view, is the **personal growth model**.
- One feature of **ageism** is the assumption that **chronological age** is an accurate indicator of **biological**, **subjective**, **functional** and **social** age. **Stereotypes** of the elderly are deeply rooted in rapidly changing Western societies, where their experience and wisdom are no longer valued.
- The aged are a collection of **subgroups**, each with its own problems and capabilities. We need to change our stereotypes of the elderly as being needy, non-productive and unhappy.
- The claim that intelligence declines fairly rapidly in old age is based on **cross-sectional studies**, which suffer from the problem of the **cohort effect**. **Longitudinal studies** indicate that while **crystallised intelligence** increases with age, **fluid intelligence** declines for all age groups over time.
- Some aspects of memory decline with age, perhaps due to less effective **information-processing**. Older adults generally perform more poorly than younger adults on recall tests, but the differences are much smaller when recognition tests are used.
- Evidence from the **OPTIMA project** suggests that **dementia** isn't an accelerated form of normal ageing. Rather, it appears to reflect a disease process which is more likely to affect us as we get older.
- **Negative cultural stereotypes** of ageing actually cause memory decline in the elderly, and may become **self-fulfilling prophecies**.
- The most controversial claim made by **social disengagement theory** is that the elderly accept and even welcome disengagement, and that this is a natural and inevitable process.
- Social disengagement theory emphasises the **quantitative** changes to the exclusion of the **qualitative** changes, which may become more important with age. The latter include **friendships**, which are under the older person's control and provide essential informal support.
- **Activity or re-engagement theory** claims that older people are psychologically and socially essentially the same as middle-aged people. The withdrawal of society and the individual isn't mutual, and optimal ageing involves maintaining the activities of middle age for as long as possible.
- According to **social exchange theory**, older people in industrialised societies have few power resources to

exchange in everyday social interaction, making them dependent on others. But the elderly relinquish their roles as economically active members of society in exchange for increased leisure time and fewer responsibilities.

- **Socioemotional selectivity theory** maintains that for the elderly, **emotional regulation** assumes major importance, making them highly selective as regards social partners. This change in social motives is largely determined by **construal of the future**.
- According to Erikson's **psychosocial theory**, old age involves a conflict between **ego-integrity** and **despair**. The task of ageing is to assess and evaluate life's value and meaning. Despair is characterised by a fear of death.
- **Retirement** is an inevitable, anticipated loss of work. People who retire **voluntarily** have little or no difficulty in adjusting, compared with those who are forced to retire. It's the **transition** between employment and retirement that causes adjustment problems.
- Compared with unemployment, **retirement** has an **accepted** and **honourable** social status and is, a proper reward for a hard life's work.
- **Grief** has been portrayed as a **natural**, **universal human reaction to bereavement**, a **psychiatric disorder** and a **disease process**.
- **Stage theories** have been criticised on the grounds that grief isn't a simple, universal process which is the same for everyone. However, stages provide a **framework** for understanding bereaved people's experiences, which display a huge **variability**.
- Although grief is a universal response to major loss, its meaning, duration and expression are all **culturally prescribed**. Cultures differ in how they define death, and it's often impossible to separate an individual's grief from cuturally required mourning.

- All the world's major religions teach that there's some kind of **after-life**. They also comfort the bereaved by helping to make sense of death and by providing '**milestones**', which allow a gradual time to adjust to life without the deceased.

Self-assessment questions

1 Discuss psychological research into the effects of retirement **and/or** bereavement in late adulthood.
2 a Describe **one** theory of how people adjust to old age.
   b Evaluate this theory by reference to alternative theories **and/or** research studies.

Web addresses

http://www.aoa.dhhs.gov/
http://www.iog.wayne.edu.apadiv20/newslet.htm
http://www.iog.wayne.edu/APADIV20/lowdiv20.htm
http://www.psy.flinders.edu.au/labs/cogsci3.htm
www.beeson.org/Livingto100/

Further reading

Scientific American Presents (2000) The quest to beat ageing. *Scientific American, 11(2)*. A collection of original articles, mainly concerned with the physical aspects of ageing (including Alzheimer's and Parkinson's diseases). Good for theories of (biological) ageing not covered in this chapter.

Also see Chapter 38's *Further Reading*.

Chapter 40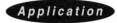

Exceptional Development

Introduction and overview

Sufiah Yusof began a maths degree at Oxford University in 1997 at the age of 13, becoming one of the youngest ever undergraduates in the UK. A few years earlier, Ruth Lawrence graduated with a first class degree from Oxford – she was also 13. At 14, Alexander Faludy became one of the youngest ever people to win a place at Cambridge University. With an IQ of 178 (see Chapter 41), he can deliver verbal dissertations of enormous range and complexity, but he can write only two (illegible) words a minute: he's dyslexic (Martin, 2000).

The drawing above of the Royal Opera House, Covent Garden, was done by Stephen Wiltshire, who, as well as having extraordinary artistic skill, is autistic. Recent UK research suggests that a certain proportion of children with Down's syndrome may also be autistic.

What do all these cases have in common? They are all *exceptional*, in the sense of *atypical* (see Chapter 43). The average age for becoming an undergraduate is 18, most undergraduates don't have IQs anywhere close to 178, most people aren't dyslexic, or autistic, nor do they have the artistic (or other exceptional) abilities demonstrated by Stephen Wiltshire and other *idiots savants*. Down's syndrome occurs in about 100 per 100,000 live births (Carpenter, 1997).

'Exceptional' usually implies 'exceptionally bright' or 'unusually gifted', but these various examples illustrate the more accurate sense of 'exceptionally different'. However:

> *'It is very easy, when dealing with an atypical child, to be overwhelmed by the sense of differentness. But as Sroufe and Rutter and all the other developmental psychopathologists are beginning to say so persuasively, the same basic processes are involved'*. (Bee, 2000)

To emphasise the differences implies that 'ordinary' and 'exceptional' are *qualitatively different*, while to look for common processes implies that the differences are merely *quantitative*. The examples also illustrate that different types of exceptional abilities (e.g. very high IQ and dyslexia) can be found together *in the same individual*.

Giftedness

What do we mean by 'gifted'?

According to Smith *et al*. (1998):

> *'A child may be described as 'gifted' who is outstanding in either a general domain (such as exceptional performance on an intelligence test) or a specific area of ability, such as music, or sport …'*.

However, the borderline between gifted children and others isn't clearly defined, and different researchers have used different criteria. In Winner's (1998) view, gifted children and child *prodigies* (who are just extreme versions of gifted children) differ from average and bright children in three ways:

- They're *precocious*: they master subjects earlier and learn more quickly.
- They 'march to their own drummers': they make discoveries on their own and can often solve problems intuitively, without going through a series of logical, linear steps.
- They're driven by 'a rage to master': they have an intense interest in the area or domain in which they excel, and can readily focus so intently on work in this domain that they lose sense of the outside world.

They also seem to have unusually good *metacognitive skills*: they know what they do and don't know, and spend *more* time than average-IQ children planning how to go about solving a problem (Bee, 2000: see Chapter 34). They seem to teach themselves to read as toddlers, breeze through college maths in middle school, and draw more skilfully at age seven than most adults:

> *'Their fortunate combination of obsessive interest and an ability to learn easily can lead to high achievement in their chosen domain. But gifted children are more susceptible to interfering social and emotional factors than once was thought'*. (Winner, 1998)

KEY STUDY 40.1

Gifted Termites (Terman, 1925; Terman & Ogden, 1959; Holahan, 1988)

The most famous study of giftedness is Terman's Stanford *longitudinal* study, which began in 1921. Having defined giftedness as an IQ score of around 140 (on the Stanford–Binet test: see Chapter 41), 643 Californian ten-year-olds (the 'Termites') were first nominated by their teachers and then their intelligence was assessed. Their mean score was 151, with a range of 130–190 (only 22 scored below 140). They were followed up at various points for much of their lives.

Their physical health and growth were superior from birth onwards, they walked and talked early, and excelled in reading (which they learnt to do before starting school), language and general knowledge. Their parents described them as insatiably curious and having superb memories.

By 1947 (average age 35), their initial level of intelligence had been maintained. Sixty-eight per cent had graduated from college, and many were already enjoying outstanding careers. By 1959, this occupational achievement continued. For example, 70 had been listed in the *American Men of Science*, and three were members of the highly prestigious National Academy of Science. In addition, 31 were listed in the *Who's Who in America*, and ten appeared in the *Directory of American Scholars*.

(Based on Smith *et al*., 1998; Sternberg, 1990; Winner, 1998)

Charlotte Church singing at the Inauguration of President Bush

An evaluation of Terman's study

Terman's study showed that gifted children are, perhaps not surprisingly, highly likely to become successful adults. However, the sample of children was biased in at least two important ways (Winner, 1998):

■ Working class and ethnic minority children were under-represented. Almost one-third of the children came from middle-class, professional families, so that at least some of their success may have been due to social-class factors as to their high IQs.

■ Children only participated in the study if nominated by their teachers, who probably overlooked those gifted children who were misfits, loners, or difficult to teach. It was these same admiring teachers who gave such glowing evaluations of their social adjustment and personality.

Terman described the children as superior not just intellectually, but also in terms of their health, social adjustment and moral attitude. According to Winner, this helped create the myth that gifted children are happy, well-adjusted by nature, requiring little special attention and easy-to-teach. The myth persists despite more recent evidence to the contrary.

Some disadvantages of giftedness

Children with exceptionally high abilities in any area (including the visual arts, music and athletics) are out of step socially with their peers. They tend to be highly driven, independent in their thinking, and introverted. They spend an unusual amount of time alone, and, although deriving pleasure and energy from their solitary mental lives, they also report feeling lonely. The more extreme the level of giftedness, the more isolated they feel (Winner, 1998).

It's been estimated that 20–25 per cent of profoundly gifted children have social and emotional problems (about twice the normal rate), while the moderately gifted show the average rate. By mid-childhood, they often try to hide their abilities in the hope of becoming more popular. One group particularly at risk for such underachievement is that of academically gifted girls, who report more depression, lower self-esteem, and more psychosomatic symptoms than academically gifted boys.

Ask yourself ...

• Why do you think this sex difference might occur?

CASE STUDY 40.1

Sufiah Yusof

As mentioned in the *Introduction and overview*, Sufiah Yusof became an Oxford University maths undergraduate at the age of 13. She made the headlines in the summer of 2000, when she disappeared shortly after completing her final exams. After the police found her, they took the unusual step of revealing that Sufiah had requested that her whereabouts should remain secret – even (especially) from her parents. Earlier in the week that she was found, she sent her family an e-mail, in which she declared:

'I've finally had enough of 15 years of physical and emotional abuse ...'.

She vowed never to return to the 'living hell' of home. She accused her father of ruining his five children's lives by brainwashing and *hothousing* them (in her father's words: 'The goals were to prove that you can accelerate children's learning process ... one can nurture and accelerate learning programmes').

At eleven, she had twice attempted suicide.

(Based on Hattenstone & Brockes, 2000)

While Sufia's case may not be typical, it's not unique. There are some striking parallels between Sufia's case and that of Ruth Lawrence (see *Introduction and overview*).

Gross (1993) describes the case of Ian. At age five, he hated school, was uncontrollable in class, aggressive towards other children, and was referred to a special school for behaviourally disturbed children. He was found to have an IQ of over 170 (on the Stanford–Binet) and a reading age of twelve. At age nine, his IQ was 200, but his school insisted that he follow the curriculum designed for nine-year-olds. This raises crucial questions regarding how gifted children in general should be educated (see Box 40.1, page 577).

Other researchers (e.g. Gottfried *et al.*, 1994), however, maintain that gifted children have about the same risk of social and emotional problems as normal-IQ children, so that most are well adjusted and socially adept. But the *profoundly gifted* (e.g. IQs over 180) are *so* different from their peers, that they're likely to be seen as strange and disturbing. They have difficulty finding others who can play at their level (Bee, 2000).

The unevenness of giftedness

Certain gifted children can leap years ahead of their peers in one area, yet fall behind in another. These *unevenly gifted* children sometimes seem hopelessly out of sync. Terman promoted the view that gifted children were *globally* gifted, that is, evenly talented in all academic areas. Indeed, some children do fit this stereotype of the all-round high-achiever. However, many display giftedness in one area but are unremarkable, or even disabled, in others. These may be creative children who are difficult in school, and not immediately recognised as gifted.

This unevenness is quite common. Winner (1998) cites a survey of over 1000 highly academically gifted adolescents, which found that over 95 per cent had a strong disparity between mathematical and verbal abilities. Extraordinarily strong mathematical and spatial abilities often accompany average or even deficient verbal skills. A good example is Albert Einstein, who was sacked from two teaching jobs for terrible spelling, and once said: 'If I can't picture it, I can't understand it'. Similarly, Thomas Edison, inventor of the light bulb and phonograph, had spelling, grammar and learning problems ('I almost decided I must be a dunce', he once admitted). Even Leonardo da Vinci had erratic spelling, and scribbled notes backwards (Martin, 2000).

Savants

Many children who struggle with language may have strong spatial skills, and the association between verbal deficits and spatial gifts seems especially strong among visual artists. The most unevenly gifted of all are the *savants*, such as Stephen Wiltshire (see his drawing of Canary Wharf above).

The term 'idiots savants' was first used by Langdon Down (1887) to describe the coexistence in some individuals of low general cognitive functioning and above-average specific ability. They appear to be able to use processing strategies within a particular domain that seems independent of their general level of intelligence. While recognised for almost 200 years, savants were reported mainly in the form of descriptive case histories.

In 1983, O'Connor & Hermelin began a series of systematic, controlled experimental studies with groups of musical, calendar-calculating and artistic savants. Their main aim was to find out why there was a marked frequency of individuals with autism in the savant population.

In discussing Stephen Wiltshire, Sacks (1995) asked whether one could speak of a 'distinctive autistic art'. He points to the concreteness, detailed perceptual accuracy, and the 'thisness' of Stephen's drawings of cars and buildings, with which he's preoccupied. At art school, he displayed an exceptional ability to depict space and distance in perspective (Pring & Hermelin, 1997). Such a remarkable focusing on perceptual details of a display, and on their accurate reproduction, are reminiscent of some of the characteristics considered to be typical of autism (Hermelin *et al.*, 1999: see pages 577–582). However, Hermelin *et al.*'s study of several autistic artists strongly suggests that there's *no* stereotyped 'autistic art'; that is, their art reflects true artistic talent rather than being a manifestation of their autism.

> 'It relieves an individual from direct precise visual input and by necessity gives him the freedom to impose his own distorted image, thus generating his own representation of reality'.

Stephen Wiltshire also has an outstanding visual memory (Pring & Hermelin, 1997). Such domain-specific memory is also found in gifted musicians (e.g. Sloboda *et al.*, 1985) and calendar-calculators (Heavey *et al.*, 1999).

A biological explanation of savants

Left-hemisphere deficits (e.g. language and logical abilities) may be offset by strengths in the right hemisphere (visuo spatial abilities). It's been observed that many savants were premature babies. Late in pregnancy, the foetal brain undergoes *pruning*, where a large number of excess neurons die off (see Chapter 4, and discussion of the adolescent brain in Chapter 37). But premature babies' brains may not have been pruned yet. If their left hemisphere experiences trauma (e.g. lack of oxygen during birth, or too much afterwards), many uncommitted neurons elsewhere in the brain remain to compensate for the loss, perhaps resulting in strong right-hemisphere ability. Excess oxygen can cause blindness, and many musical savants display the pattern of prematurity, blindness and strong right-hemisphere skills (Winner, 1998).

CASE STUDY 40.3

Hikari Kenzaburo

Hikari was born in 1963 with a growth on his brain that made him look as if he had two heads. He was severely autistic, had constant seizures, and poor vision. He could fly into rages and needed constant attention, patience and reassurance. He never cried and didn't seem ever to dream.

Yet even as a toddler, he'd listen, enthralled, to music, and to bird-song. His parents encouraged this sign of imagination, feeling that music could perhaps reach and touch him as nothing else could. In fact, Hikari could also express himself and reach others through music. While words are blunt and hopeless tools, he can compose musical works for violin and piano, which his father describes as a 'wailing soul', embodying a 'core of sorrow'.

(Based on Gerrard, 1996)

CASE STUDY 40.2

Richard (Hermelin *et al.*, 1999)

Richard (born 1952) is autistic, mentally handicapped, and suffers from a severe congenital visual impairment: he's extremely myopic and has glaucoma (increased pressure in the eye) which is well controlled by medication. His verbal IQ is 47, and his non-verbal IQ is 55. He began to draw at the age of four, and now uses exclusively oil-based coloured crayons on paper.

He doesn't look at other artists' work, but goes to the local library and studies landscape photographs and brochures in the travel agency. Days, weeks, or even months later he'll reproduce one of these pictures from memory. Sometimes he'll draw a natural setting he's looked at through binoculars. He's had many exhibitions all over the world, and he earns a living as a professional artist.

Based on a comparison between his drawings and the photographs they're often based on, an art expert judges him to display true artistic talent. Moreover, like Cezanne and Monet, who were both myopic, Richard's visual impairment may have worked to his advantage. Hermelin *et al.* suggest that:

Accounting for giftedness

Brain development and organisation

Non-savant gifted children most likely have atypical brain organisation to some extent too (Winner, 1998). Individuals with pronounced right-hemisphere abilities (maths, music and art) are disproportionately *non*-right-handed (they're either left-handed or ambidextrous). They also have higher than average rates of left-hemisphere deficits (such as delayed speech onset, stuttering or dyslexia).

Geschwind and Galaburda (in Winner, 1998) hypothesised that this association of gift and disorder ('the pathology of superiority') results from the effects of testosterone on the developing foetal brain. Raised levels can delay development of the left hemisphere ('testosterone poisoning'), which might in turn produce compensatory right-hemisphere growth. This might also account for the larger number of males than females who display mathematical and spatial gifts, non-right-handedness, and language disorders.

Although this hypothesis is controversial, and there's only scant evidence to support the theory of damage and compensation in savants, Winner (1998) believes that:

'... it seems certain that gifts are hardwired in the infant brain, as savants and gifted children exhibit extremely high abilities from a very young age before they have spent much time working at their gift'.

Ask yourself ...

- Does describing someone as talented help explain his/her exceptional ability?
- If so, where do you think this talent comes from?

The 'talent account': geniuses are born

The quote from Winner above can be seen as partially defining the 'talent account' of giftedness, that is, the widely held belief that the likelihood of becoming exceptionally competent depends on the presence or absence of inborn attributes ('talents', 'gifts', 'natural aptitudes': Howe *et al.*, 1998). The judgement that someone is talented is believed to help *explain* (not merely describe) that person's success. According to Howe *et al.*, certain assumptions are made about innate talent:

■ It originates in *genetically transmitted* structures, and so is at least partly *innate*.

■ Its full effects may not be evident at an early age, but there will be some advance indications that allow trained people to spot its presence before exceptional levels of mature performance have been shown.

■ These early indications of talent provide the basis for predicting who's likely to excel.

■ Only a minority is talented; if all children were, we couldn't predict or explain differential success.

■ Talents are relatively domain-specific.

For Gardner (1993), talent is a sign of precocious biopsychological potential in a particular domain, such as dance, chess or maths (see his theory of *multiple intelligences*: Chapter 41). Similarly, Winner (1996) sees talents as unlearned, domain-specific traits that may develop or 'come to fruition' in favourable circumstances – but they cannot be manufactured. Another way of expressing this is to say that talents develop through *maturation* (see Chapter 50).

Is the talent account valid?

According to Howe (1999), although it's widely accepted that innate talents can explain how genetic differences between people impact on their capabilities,

'... there are good reasons for thinking that such talents are mythical rather than real'.

Genetic contributions to human activities are complex and indirect (see Chapters 41 and 50). Also, it tends to be assumed that if there are qualities that make some people more capable than others and that have an inherited component, these will be closely related to a person's *cognitive* attributes (such as cleverness or creativity). But according to Howe (1999):

'... it is just as likely that those – conceivably largely inherited – human qualities that make the larger contributions towards setting geniuses apart from other people are ones of temperament and personality rather than being narrowly intellectual ones ...'.

Indeed, the qualities that contemporaries of geniuses such as Newton and Mozart most often remarked on were broadly temperamental; doggedness, persistence, capacity for fierce and sustained concentration, and intense curiosity. Several geniuses, including Darwin and Einstein, denied having any superior inherent intelligence (see above, page 574), but none has ever denied either possessing or relying on a capacity for diligence and healthy curiosity (Howe, 1999).

People fear that geniuses will be diminished if we remove the mystery or magic surrounding them by denying that they're a breed apart. On the contrary:

'... it is not until we understand that they are made from the same flesh and blood as the rest of us that we start to appreciate just how wonderfully remarkable these men and women really are. They show us what humankind is capable of ...'. (Howe, 1999).

Portrait of Wolfgang Amadeus Mozart, aged 14 (Blanchet)

Howe *et al.* (1998) reviewed the arguments on both sides. They found no evidence of innate attributes operating in the predictable and specific way they felt 'talent' implies, and concluded that differences in early experiences, preferences, opportunities, habits, training and practice are the real determinants of excellence. One of the challenges to the talent account has focused on musical genius (e.g. Sloboda *et al.*,

1994a, b). For example, top violinists by the time they're 20 have practised more than 10,000 hours in total (and less successful ones only 5,000). This began as early as ages four to six for international performers – about four concentrated hours per day.

According to Sloboda (in Aldersey-Williams, 1999):

'Early ability is not evidence of talent unless it emerges in the absence of special opportunity to learn'.

Even that prodigy of prodigies, Mozart, had a composer–father who was also famously ambitious for his son and bullied him towards musical greatness. Demonstrations of exceptional musical skill tend to *follow* rather than precede attempts to encourage it.

Similarly, Ericsson & Charness (1994) note that the winning time of the first Olympic marathon is comparable to the qualifying time achieved by thousands of runners in the modern Boston marathon.

Ask yourself ...

- Try to explain these dramatic changes in runners' capacity.

Greater knowledge about running, better nutrition and medical care, better training techniques and so on can adequately explain these changes, without having to bring genetic factors into it. Similarly, differences between world-class athletes (as with violinists) reflect differences in training and practice from an early age – *not* genetic differences.

Ask yourself ...

- Howe *et al.* acknowledge that theirs is an *extreme environmentalist* position, which many would reject. Try to identify some counter-arguments.

Howe *et al.* conclude their review by saying that, if excelling is a consequence of possessing innate gifts, there's no point trying to nurture them in children without them:

'... categorising some children as innately talented is discriminatory. The evidence suggests that such categorisation is unfair and wasteful, preventing young people from pursuing a goal because of the unjustified conviction of teachers or parents that certain children would not benefit from the superior opportunities given to those who are deemed to be talented'.

Box 40.1   How should gifted children be educated?

Generally, schools focus whatever resources they have on the moderately academically gifted: bright students with strong but not extraordinary abilities, who don't face the problems of precocity and isolation to the same degree as the profoundly gifted. The moderately gifted comprise the majority of the current 'pull-out' programs in American schools (i.e. removal from regular classes), but they (and indeed most children) would be better served by schools teaching a more demanding standard curriculum.

The use of IQ as a filter for gifted programmes tends to tip them towards the moderately gifted, at the expense of the profoundly but unevenly gifted children. Many of the latter do poorly on IQ tests, because their talent lies in either maths *or* language – but not both. Those whose talent is musical, artistic or athletic are also regularly omitted. It makes more sense to identify the gifted by examining past achievements in specific areas, rather than relying on 'plain-vanilla IQ tests' (Winner, 1998). Schools should then place the profoundly gifted in advanced courses only in their areas of giftedness – other subjects can continue to be taught in regular classes.

Social development seems to be as favourable for gifted children who've been accelerated through school as for those who've been kept with their age-mates but provided with 'enrichment' programmes. But many gifted children are so bored by school that they become disengaged, even dropping out, often because their school districts don't allow grade acceleration or have no special programmes. According to Bee (2000):

'Given ... that grade skipping does not seem to be linked to social maladjustment (and is linked to better achievement among the gifted), it seems to make good sense to encourage accelerated schooling, if only to ward off terminal boredom for the gifted child'.

Autism

Definitions and diagnosis

Autism was first identified by Kanner in the USA (1943) and Asperger in Austria (1944), quite independently of each other. Kanner used the term 'early infantile autism' (*'autos'* is Greek for 'self') to describe individuals who had an 'aloneness', which involved the ignoring and shutting out of the world and living in an isolated, essentially asocial state. They were limited in language and obsessive about the need for sameness in particular aspects of their environment. Kanner speculated (incorrectly) that they fall within the average range of intelligence, and that any poor learning performance resulted from their difficulties with the social aspects of learning.

Asperger worked with an older age-group, but his observations overlapped with Kanner's. He also used the term 'autistic', and there's an ongoing debate as to whether autism and what's now called Asperger's syndrome are distinct disorders, expressions of the same disorder, or both part of an autistic spectrum (with those displaying Asperger's constituting a high-IQ subgroup). According to Powell (1999), they aren't mutually exclusive – Asperger's individuals have a particular form of autism.

Later, ritualistic and compulsive dimensions were identified as crucial, resulting in the *triad of impairments* (social relationships, language and rigidity of thought: Wing, 1988). Also, Wing & Gould (1979) found that learning disabilities (IQ below 70: see Table 40.1, page 583) were clearly associated with the triad. Ninety per cent of those having 'full', typical autism had an IQ between 20 and 69. As a result of their findings, it became clear that there's a wide spectrum of autistic disorders, of which 'Kanner's autism' is only a part. They estimated that

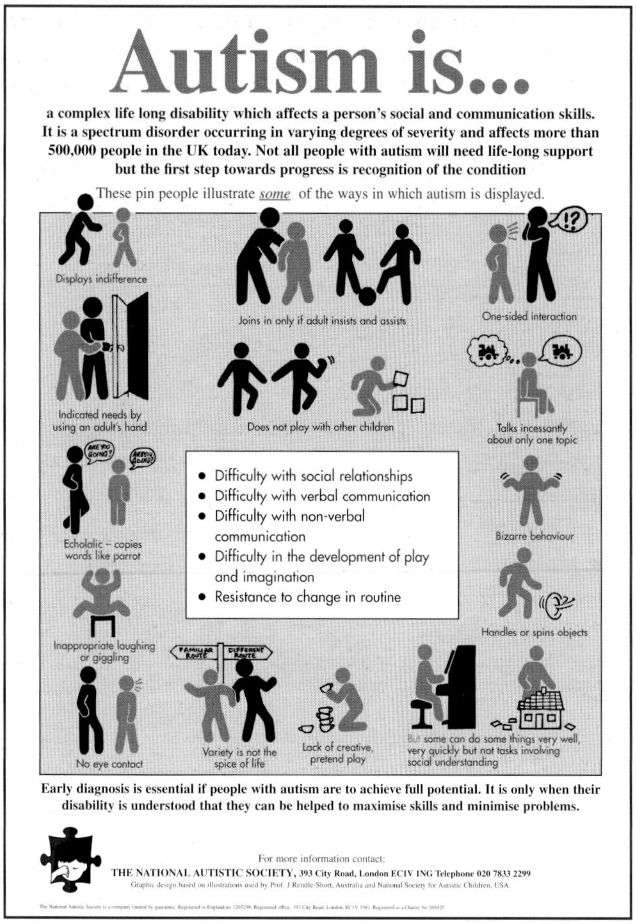

Figure 40.1 *National Autistic Society leaflet*

(reproduced by permission of the National Autistic Society)

20 children per 10,000 have autistic spectrum disorders and mental retardation (learning disabilities), a figure that was revised by Wing (1997) to nine per 1000. Does this reflect changes in diagnostic criteria or an increasing prevalence? (Powell, 1999).

According to Mitchell (1997), the incidence of autism is one to two per 1000 live births, with boys outnumbering girls by four or five to one, at least for those with Asperger's or mild autism. In the more seriously affected, boys still outnumber girls by two to one.

The current edition of the *Diagnostic and Statistical Manual of Mental Disorders* (DSM-IV, 1994), published by the American Psychiatric Association, stresses three fundamental impairments. These relate to (a) *reciprocal and social interaction*, (b) *communication*, and (c) *restricted repetitive and stereotyped behaviours, interests and activities*.

Box 40.2	**Criteria for diagnosing autism (based on DSM-IV)**

- **Qualitative impairments in social interaction:** impaired non-verbal behaviours (especially eye-contact), failure to engage in genuinely social games (such as turn-taking), no attempt to share interests through *joint-attentional behaviours*, and a failure to

develop any friendship beyond the most superficial acquaintance. A lack of empathy is often seen as the central feature of the social deficit (Baron-Cohen, 1988; Kanner, 1943).

- **Qualitative impairments in communication:** failure to develop language and communication in the normal way (such as delayed and restricted language development, stereotyped and repetitive or idiosyncratic use of language), and failure to use gesture properly. Also, a lack of varied, spontaneous make-believe/symbolic play (Leslie, 1987), and engaging in play which is often lacking in creativity and imagination (Baron-Cohen, 1987).

- **Repetitive and stereotyped patterns of behaviour:** an inflexible adherence to specific routines, becoming distressed if prevented from performing repetitive rituals, stereotyped and repetitive motor mannerisms, and persistent preoccupation with parts of objects.

Autism is often described as the most severe of all child psychiatric disorders, because, unlike other disorders, people with autism seem to be virtually cut off from other people ('in a world of their own'). This is why it's sometimes categorised as a *psychosis*, implying that it's unlike anything in the normal range of experience (Baron-Cohen, 1995a: see Chapter 43).

Autism and Down's syndrome

Mitchell (1997) identifies some similarities and differences between autism and *Down's syndrome*.

- Both conditions are present from birth. But whereas Down's is usually evident from the baby's facial appearance (and will often have been detected prenatally, especially with older mothers), autistic babies look perfectly normal and the diagnosis isn't made until the child is aged four or over. If the diagnosis is made later, this doesn't mean they've 'acquired' it at an older age. Rather, a new label has been applied to existing behaviour patterns.

- Down's is classified as a chromosome abnormality (the child inherits an extra twenty-first chromosome) and is the most commonly occurring such abnormality (see Chapter 36). Diagnosis is based on the detection of this extra chromosome, while autism is diagnosed on the basis of characteristic behaviours (see Box 40.2). Little is known about its physiological basis (see Box 40.5, page 581).

- Neither condition can be 'cured', although adaptation and development can and do occur (see page 582). For example, 50 years ago life expectancy among people with Down's was considerably lower than that of the general population. But the gap has narrowed significantly, mainly because of antibiotics and general improvements in diet, care and living conditions (Moddia, 1996).

- Learning difficulties are characteristic of Down's and common in autism (see above). But some autistic individuals have normal IQs, and some (five to 30 per cent) may have above-average IQs. With increasing IQ, autism becomes more difficult to diagnose – and may escape diagnosis altogether.

- As we saw when discussing giftedness, many autistic individuals display outstanding musical or artistic abilities (*savants*). This doesn't occur in individuals with Down's syndrome.

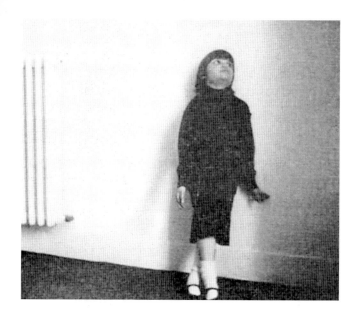

The self-absorption displayed by this autistic girl prevents her from developing a normal 'theory of mind'

Interestingly, recent research has suggested that about seven per cent of children with Down's syndrome also have some level of autistic disorder (Kent *et al.*, 1999). Children with Down's who appear different from their peers need a full assessment of social, language and communication skills, and health professionals need to distance themselves from the stereotypical idea of the Down's syndrome personality.

Theories of autism

According to Smith *et al.* (1998):

> 'The challenge for any researcher investigating autism is trying to explain how one syndrome can lead to the specific combination of impairments which typify a person with autism (lack of socialisation, communication and imagination); how different people with autism can be affected in markedly different ways; and how it is that people with autism can sometimes have better than average abilities in one or two areas (the 'islets of ability')'.

'Refrigerator parenting' hypothesis

Kanner had originally suggested that autism was partly the result of 'cold', unemotional parenting, specifically the mother. However, the prevailing current view is that parents' behaviour doesn't initiate or in any way provoke autism. Indeed, any difference in parents' behaviour towards their autistic child is more likely to be caused *by* the autism than vice versa (Powell, 1999).

Also, autism seems to strike indiscriminately. It's no respector of social class or family environment: it can affect a child with extremely warm and loving parents and where there are no autistic siblings (Mitchell, 1997).

Genetic theories

Kanner originally suggested that autism has a genetic component. According to Rutter *et al.* (1999), findings from several independent studies provide compelling evidence for a strong genetic component underlying autism.

■ The rate of autism in siblings of children with autism (two to six per cent) is consistently found to be many times the rate in the general population (ranging from one to sixteen per 10,000). Rutter *et al.* maintain that:

> 'Whatever the precise figure, it is clear that there is a very substantial degree of familial clustering of autism. Although this could reflect shared environmental factors, a loading as high as this points to the likelihood of a genetic component'.

■ The *concordance rate for monozygotic* (identical) *twins* (MZs) is 60–90 per cent, compared with less than five per cent for *dizygotic* (non-identical or fraternal) *twins* (DZs: see Chapter 41). In other words, if one member of a twin pair is autistic, the probability that the other will also be autistic depends to a significant degree on whether they share all their genes (MZs) or only half their genes (DZs: the same as ordinary siblings). Rutter *et al.* believe that several different genes are involved, working in combination, and they argue that the twin data indicate that autism is the most strongly genetically influenced of all multifactorial child psychiatric disorders.

However, the statistics are difficult to analyse because autism is still rare, as are MZs, and so the prospects of finding autism in a member of an MZ pair is very remote. Hence, adding just one MZ pair either with or without concordance can radically shift the overall concordance rate (Mitchell, 1997). If autism isn't caused solely by genetic factors, then there must be an environmental component. For example, Piven & Folstein (1994) found that about 30 per cent of parents with an autistic child show at least some autistic mannerisms, such as deficient turn-taking in conversation, misinterpreting or not noticing implied meanings of their conversational partner's utterances. Parents of Down's syndrome children, as controls, showed no such difficulties.

Ask yourself ...

- Why was it necessary to have a control group at all?
- Why do parents of Down's children make a suitable control group?

Box 40.3 Where might autistic genes be found?

Not only have there been reports of an association between autism and anomalies on almost all autosomal chromosomes (i.e. the non-sex chromosomes), but these are usually based on individual cases. This makes the validity and meaning of the association highly dubious. More encouraging is the finding that the portion of chromosome 15 that seems to be implicated in autism is also where the genes for Prader-Willi and Angelman syndromes are located.

Probably most interest has focused on claims of a strong association between *fragile X syndrom*e and autism. Boys have only one X chromosome, so, unlike girls, any defects on it aren't 'cancelled out' by normal genes on the other. Defective genes carried on the X chromosome are the second most common genetic cause of learning difficulties (after Down's syndrome). Affected individuals tend to have prominent jaws and large ears. The original claim was that fragile X occurred in at least 16 per cent of autistic individuals, although the accurate figure is almost certainly below five per cent. Given the strong male preponderance in autism, it's reasonable to consider that one of the genes that predisposes individuals to autism might be located on the X chromosome. Although the International Molecular Genetic Study of Autism Consortium (1998) failed to find any supporting evidence, it did find evidence suggesting the roles of chromosomes 7 and 10, something which hasn't been previously reported.

(Based on Lauritsen *et al.*, 1999; Mitchell, 1997; Rutter *et al.*, 1999)

Theory of mind and mind-blindness

The currently most influential theory of autism maintains that what all autistic people have in common (the core deficit) is *mind-blindness* (Baron-Cohen, 1990), a severe impairment in their understanding of mental states and in their appreciation of how mental states govern behaviour (e.g. Baron-Cohen, 1993, 1995a,b). They, therefore, lack a '*theory of mind*' (ToM), a term originally coined by Premack & Woodruff (1978) based on their work with chimps (see Gross *et al.*, 2000).

When the ability to 'read minds' is in any way impaired, enormous difficulties arise. Autistic individuals fail to develop the ability to attribute mental states to other people, and this has fundamental implications for communication, where making sense of others' intentions enables the listener to understand what's being said (Baron-Cohen, 1995).

Ask yourself ...

- Try to think of examples of 'mind-reading', either from real-life interactions with others, or from TV programmes, films, or literature.
- How vital is it that we take into account the fact that not everyone has access to the same information about a situation?

Testing the ToM hypothesis

Wimmer & Perner (1983) devised a *false belief* task, with four-, six-, and eight-year-olds, involving two small dolls (Maxi and his mother), who enact a story in which the mother moves Maxi's chocolate from a green drawer (put there by Maxi) to a blue drawer (while Maxi's outside playing). Children are asked *where Maxi would look for the chocolate* when he returned. A *correct answer* ('green drawer') involves attributing to Maxi a *false belief*: the children *know* the chocolate's in the blue drawer, but they also know that Maxi *doesn't* have this knowledge (so he thinks it's still in the green drawer). An *incorrect answer* ('blue drawer') indicates that children cannot distingush between what they themselves know and what Maxi knows. A correct answer reflects a ToM.

Has Sally lost her marbles? (Baron-Cohen *et al.*, 1985)

This was a replication of the Wimmer and Perner 'Maxi' study, retaining the vital elements but adapted to make it shorter and simpler and more appropriate in content for older children (Mitchell, 1997). Sally and Anne replace Maxi and his mother, and the story involves transfer of a marble from a basket to a box.

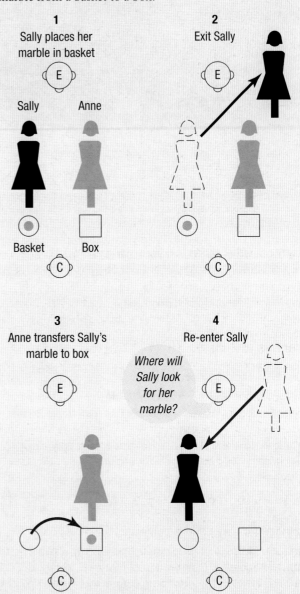

Figure 40.2 *The experimental scenario used in Baron-Cohen* et al.*'s (1985) study*

A crucial difference between Baron-Cohen *et al.*'s and the Wimmer and Perner study is that the latter involved only normal children. Baron-Cohen *et al.* tested:

- 20 autistic children, chronological age (CA) 6–16 (mean 11.11), mean verbal mental age (vMA) 5.5;
- 14 Down's syndrome children, CA 6–17 (mean 10.11), mean vMA 2.11;
- 27 normal children, CA 3–5 (mean 4.5), assumed to have vMAs equivalent to their CAs.

The *dependent variable* was success or failure on the Sally–Anne test, specifically, on the question: 'Where will Sally look for her marble?' (*belief question*).

The results for Down's Syndrome and normal children were strikingly similar: 23 out of 27 normal children, and 12 out of 14 Down's Syndrome children *passed* the belief question. By contrast, 16 of the 20 autistic children (80 per cent) *failed*. This difference between the groups was highly significant.

It was as if the autistic chidren had been asked: 'Where is Sally's marble?' They performed much like clinically normal young children do (i.e. below four), but their average CA was just below twelve (Mitchell, 1997). They also performed far worse than the Down's children, despite having a higher mean verbal MA.

Baron-Cohen (1995a) proposed the existence of four modules involved in 'mindreading': the *intentionality detector* (ID), *eye-direction detector* (EDD), *shared-attention mechanism* (SAM), and the *theory of mind mechanism* (ToMM). ToMM is innately determined and begins to mature from about twelve to 18 months to four years. It processes information in the form of *metarepresentations*: it's specialised for representing *mental* representations ('beliefs about beliefs') (Leslie, 1987, 1994; Leslie & Roth, 1993).

An evaluation of the ToM hypothesis

Since Baron-Cohen *et al.*'s (1985) study, researchers from all over the world have replicated and extended the basic findings (see Happé, 1994a). Despite the ToM hypothesis being both convincing and powerful, a substantial amount of evidence is accumulating which undermines it (Mitchell, 1997).

One of the criticisms made of ToM is that it's an incomplete explanation of autism, that is, it doesn't account for *all* the deficits/difficulties associated with autism, such as a restricted range of interest, the obsessive need for sameness, and preoccupation with parts rather than the whole. Equally, it fails to address some of the apparent strengths of at least some autistic individuals, such as their excellent rote memories and the exceptional abilities (the 'islets of ability'), as demonstrated by Stephen Wiltshire and other savants (Frith, 1996; Mitchell, 1997; Powell, 1999).

Weak central coherence

Frith (1989; Frith & Happé, 1994a, b) attempted to resolve some of these problems by proposing that the deficits and strengths stem from the same cognitive source involving how information is integrated. Specifically, they claimed that autism is, at least partly, the result of a '*weak drive for central coherence*'.

Box 40.4 Central coherence

While we normally process information at a *global* (holistic or 'top-down') level, autistic individuals tend to do this as a local (*segmental* or 'bottom-up') level. This corresponds to 'the whole' and 'the parts' respectively (see Chapter 15). The former allows us to *disambiguate* ambiguous words (homographs) within the context of a sentence, something which autistic children couldn't do even if they *did* succeed at ToM tasks (Frith & Snowling, 1983; Happé, 1994b).

These same children also tend to have difficulties in real-life situations where ToM is required, since they cannot extract information from its context:

'*Knowing the theory of how other minds work is simply not enough if that knowledge does not take account of context and in the social world context is all important, ever-changing and often implicit'.* (Powell, 1999)

Weak central coherence may help to explain at least some of the exceptional abilities shown by savants, where attention to detail is paramount. For example, Stephen Wiltshire's drawings seem to be built up from detail to the whole (not vice versa: Powell, 1999), but this interpretation wouldn't apply to the artist Richard described by Hermelin *et al.* (1999: see Case Study 40.2, page 575).

The tendency to process at a local level will benefit when tasks require an analytical approach, and where global processing can be distracting (as in finding embedded figures: Shah & Frith, 1983). This may also account for the everyday observation that autistic individuals may locate fine detail or identify slight changes to familiar objects or layouts that go unnoticed by others (Powell, 1999). However, this style of thinking may not be unique to people with autism.

Impaired executive functioning

Executive functions refer to the ability to 'maintain an appropriate problem-solving set for the attainment of a future goal' (Ozonoff *et al.*, 1991) and include planning, impulse control, and working memory (WM: see Chapter 17). Autistic individuals may become distressed by changes in their immediate environment which interfere with their ritualised behaviours, they don't plan ahead well, and they often seem unable to anticipate the consequences of their actions.

Box 40.5 Executive functioning and the brain

Executive functioning is believed to depend on intact frontal lobes (see Chapter 4). There's increasing evidence for poor performance on many 'frontal' tasks in autism (Frith, 1996). Rigidity and *perseveration* (ritualistic repetition of certain behaviours) are found both in patients with frontal lobe damage and individuals with autism, implying that autism may involve frontal lobe impairments. But patients with frontal lobe damage are strikingly *not* autistic (Frith, 1996).

One possible explanation for these apparently inconsistent findings is that brain damage from birth and in later life produce very different behavioural pictures – even if the same brain area is involved. The later damage would be expected to have more *specific* consequences.

While executive functioning impairments don't replace ToM as an explanation of autism, they can potentially explain several features not tackled by ToM (Frith, 1996). Frith concludes by saying:

'It seems unlikely that one single cognitive abnormality can be identified that would explain all the abnormalities present in autism. The existence of multiple deficits … might help us understand why autism can exist in many different forms ranging from mild to severe. The explanation of autism at the cognitive level needs to be complemented by the explanation at the biological level …'.

Treating autism

As a result of their research, Baron-Cohen *et al.* (1992) have been able to improve the early diagnosis of autism. In one study, they were able to predict which of a group of 'at risk' 18-month-olds would be diagnosed as autistic by age three. Treatment approaches include *biological*, *behavioural* and more *cognitively based* therapies.

Biological approaches

These include the neuroleptic drug *haloperidol* and serotonin-reducing drugs such as *fenfluramine* (see Chapter 45). However, results have been disappointing and as with all powerful psychoactive drugs, are associated with side-effects (again, see Chapter 45).

Other biological approaches derive from the observation that certain allergies produce behaviours similar to those seen in autism, such as headbanging and screaming. Consequently, *orthomolecular therapy*, in which autistic children are placed on low-carbohydrate diets, and *megavitamin therapy*, in which large daily doses of vitamin B6 are given, have been tried.

Behavioural approaches

These include *behaviour modification*, which has been used to eliminate some aspects of autism such as self-mutilative behaviour. These behaviours, as with screaming, aren't unique to autism, and are actually more common in those with severe learning difficulties (see below and Chapter 45). Typically, these approaches use positive reinforcement or extinction, although these can be time-consuming (Harris *et al.*, 1991).

For example, Simmons & Lovaas (1969) found that it took 1800 head bangs over an eight-day period before that behaviour was extinguished – by the withdrawal of social attention. Controversially, punishment (in the form of electric shock) has been used with autistic children, mainly for removing self-harming behaviour, and appears to be highly effective. As Lovaas (1977) states:

'Seemingly independently of how badly the child is mutilating himself or how long he has been doing so, we can essentially remove the self-destructive behaviour within the first minute'.

Ask yourself ...

- Formulate some arguments for and against the use of electric shock for self-mutilative behaviour in autistic (or other) children.

Autistic children are clearly not transformed into 'normal' children by behavioural methods, and the behavioural changes that may be achieved in the therapeutic setting may not generalise to other settings (see Chapter 45). However, they may provide autistic children with enough adaptive behaviours to cope more effectively with the world. Perhaps even more importantly, such methods may make the children more socially acceptable and more 'rewarding' for other people. This, in turn, will provide the children themselves with more rewarding experiences and exchanges with others.

Cognitively based approaches

More cognitively based therapies involve *structural therapy*, in which the environment is arranged so that the child will receive spontaneous physical and verbal stimulation in the form of play and games. By increasing the amount of stimulation, the therapy aims to make them more aware of themselves and their environment, and relate more to it.

Other approaches aim to include the parents of autistic children in the treatment programmes (which recognises their role as potential agents of change), and teaching children sign language. This takes advantage of their sensitivity to touch and movement, and gets round the quite common problem of their failure to respond to spoken language (Webster *et al.*, 1973). Music may represent an alternative form of communication – and self-expression – as illustrated by the case of Hikari Kenzaburo (see Case Study 40.3, page 575).

Learning difficulties

Learning difficulties and disabilities, and mental impairment

'Learning difficulty' is defined by the Education Act (1993) as:

'A condition that exists if a child has significantly greater difficulty in learning than the majority of children of his age, or a disability which either prevents or hinders him from making use of educational facilities of a kind generally provided for children of his age in schools within the area of the local education authority'.

While the term 'learning disability' isn't used in any relevant legislation (Lyon, 1995), it's the generally accepted term in service provision in the UK (e.g. by social workers). But education authorities, and the Code of Practice for Special Educational Needs use the legally defined term 'learning difficulties' to refer to preschool and school-age children who, as adults, would be identified as having 'learning disabilities' (Dockrell *et al.*, 1999).

Learning difficulties (children)/learning disabilities (adults) cover what have variously been called 'mental handicap', 'mental subnormality', and 'mental retardation'. The last term is still commonly used in the US, is used by the two major systems for classifying mental disorders, DSM–IV

(1994) and ICD-10 (1992: see Chapter 43), and is the internationally used term (Carpenter, 1997; Gelder *et al.*, 1999).

Another legally defined term is '*mental impairment*'. According to the Mental Health Act (1983), mental impairment is:

'*A state of arrested or incomplete development of mind which includes significant impairment of intelligence and social functioning*'.

Diagnosing learning difficulties

People diagnosed with learning difficulties (LDs) don't all experience the same type or degree of problem. They come from all social-class and ethnic backgrounds, but black people with LDs experience two sorts of oppression at the same time (see Chapter 25). Assessment measures may be biased, either in terms of the materials used or the assessment situation itself. Many standard test procedures and equipment are based on white, middle-class values and experiences, producing an underestimation of an individual's level of competence (Chaudhury, 1988).

IQ is still the main criterion used to diagnose LDs. However, the extent of impairment in children's ability to adapt to the demands of society is crucial for considering the likelihood of their successful integration into mainstream school (Dockrell *et al.*, 1999). Also, a diagnosis of LD (or mental retardation) is made only if the individual is under 18 (Carpenter, 1997). A distinction is commonly made between LDs which have known *organic* (genetic or brain-related) causes, and those which don't, and this distinction is associated with different degrees of difficulty (see below).

Prevalence has changed little since the 1930s, because people with LDs are living longer. However, the *incidence* (the number of new cases) of severe mental retardation has fallen by one-third. Fifty per cent of that fall is attributable to improved antenatal and neonatal care (Gelder *et al.*, 1999).

The causes of LDs

According to Carpenter (1997):

'*... because of the multiple stages in producing 'disability', it is usually a gross simplification to speak of one cause for the aetiology of a person's learning difficulty. Similarly, it is very difficult to predict accurately the degree of learning difficulty that will be produced by a specific organic cause*'.

People with *mild* LDs don't usually have clear aetiological diagnoses, that is, there's seldom an obvious, single cause. Most have family histories of low IQ, but it's unclear if this reflects a genetic influence, the effects of the environment, or the effects of undocumented specific causes. For example, it was traditionally assumed that mild LDs were caused by genetic and sociocultural factors. The discovery of *fragile X syndrome* (see Box 40.3, page 579) and *foetal alcohol syndrome* (FAS: see Box 40.6, page 584) has suggested that (other) more specific causes will be discovered in time. However, it's rare for a child from a high socio-economic background to have either mild or severe LDs without some medical cause being apparent (Carpenter, 1997).

As Dockrell *et al.* (1999) say:

'*The mild level of learning difficulty is viewed primarily as an academic dysfunction, or as a deficiency in learning*

Table 40 1 *Different categories of mental retardation*

Name	IQ range	Prevalence (proportion of the whole population which is retarded)	Description
Mild	50–70	3% (80% of all cases)	Adults can be expected to acquire some independence in most self-care/domestic activities, and earn money from unskilled work. Main difficulties will be in reading, writing, monetary skills, emotional and social immaturity, and inability to adapt readily to social expectations and external stressors.
Moderate	36–49	0.3% (12% of all cases)	Adults frequently have additional disabilities, such as epilepsy, and physical and sensory disabilities. Most need supervision with self-care.
Severe	20–35	0.04% (7% of all cases)	As above
Profound	Below 20	0.05% (1% of all cases)	Adults usually need close supervision and care their whole life. Many can feed themselves with a spoon, most can understand and make simple statements and requests. Most have multiple disabilities.

(Based on Carpenter, 1997; Gelder *et al.*, 1999)

ability with aetiology unknown, while severe learning difficulty (IQ below 50) is often viewed as physiologically caused handicap'.

People with severe or profound LDs are more likely to have an identifiable *primary* cause, usually genetic. The most common known autosomal chromosomal abnormality responsible for intellectual impairment is Down's syndrome (see above, page 578). This occurs in one-third of people with an IQ below 50 (Carpenter, 1997). The most common well-documented single-gene recessive defect is *phenylketonuria* (PKU), which affects 12 in 1,000,000 people. This is routinely tested for at birth in the UK, and a special diet can prevent LDs from developing. But an appreciable minority still isn't put on the special diet within three weeks of birth (Carpenter, 1997: see Chapter 50).

Secondary causes include:

■ *hypothyroidism*: in its severe form, this used to be called 'cretinism'. One cause is cerebral palsy (see below), and early detection and administering thyroxine within the first three months of life will prevent intellectual impairments.

But many affected children will also be deaf, which can impair intellectual development;

■ *cerebral palsy*: this can be congenital (present at birth), as in congenital *rubella* (German measles) but may also result from postnatal events. About one-third of full-term infants with cerebral palsy have severe LDs, and it's much more common in low-birthweight (premature) babies (but only 20 per cent of the latter have severe LDs);

■ *neural tube abnormalities*: spina bifida is one example, affecting 70–150 per 100,000 live births. Up to ten per cent will have LDs, and almost all of these will be multiply handicapped;

■ *foetal alcohol syndrome* (FAS).

Box 40.6 Foetal alcohol syndrome (FAS)

Children with FAS (first identified by Jones *et al.*, 1973) are typically smaller than normal and suffer from *microcephaly* (unusually small heads and brains). Such children often have heart defects, short noses, and low nasal bridges. The eyes, too, have a distinctive appearance. FAS children are generally mildly retarded, though some may be moderately retarded and others of average intelligence. But in those of average intelligence, there are significant academic and attentional difficulties (Sue *et al.*, 1994).

The syndrome is a consequence of the mother's excessive alcohol consumption during pregnancy. While there doesn't seem to be an agreed 'safe' level of maternal drinking during pregnancy, there appears to be a *linear relationship* between the amount of alcohol consumed and the risk of FAS. Binge drinking may be as dangerous as regular drinking.

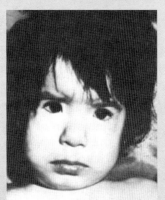

A child with FAS (from Bee, 1992)

Specific learning difficulties: dyslexia

What is dyslexia?

Ask yourself ...

- What do you understand by the term?
- How do you think the term is commonly understood?

The terms 'specific learning difficulty' and *dyslexia* (literally 'non-reading') are often used interchangeably. People with dyslexia are of average intelligence, and have no visual or auditory impairments. *Acquired* dyslexia occurs in previously literate people following brain injury, while *developmental* dyslexia occurs in children as they get older. Most psychological theory and research is concerned with the latter.

Dyslexia (or 'congenital word blindness') became categorised as a learning difficulty in the 1981 Education Act, but it was first described in 1896 (in the *British Medical Journal*: Snowling, 1998). The case described 14-year-old Percy, who displayed many common characteristics, including:

■ *dysphonetic spelling errors* (e.g. 'carefully' becomes 'calfuly');
■ *substitutions of phonemes* (e.g. 'peg' becomes 'pag');
■ *transpositions of letters* (e.g. 'Percy' becomes 'Precy').

Percy seemed to have *phonological dyslexia*, which affects letter–sound conversion. The individual cannot convert written words to their sounds directly or pronounce written words s/he hasn't seen before. For example, if asked to pick two words which rhyme from a list of 'rite', 'rit', and 'knight', the individual is more likely to select the first two – because they're *visually similar*.

Surface dyslexia affects whole word recognition. So, the individual can only recognise a word by sounding it out, rather than reading it by sight. Words which break standard pronunciation rules, such as 'broad', cannot be read correctly, and their pronunciation may be *regularised* ('brode'). *Deep dyslexia* affects reading for meaning. The individual is unable to pronounce aloud non-words, has difficulty with function words (sometimes substituting one for another), and often responds to real words with words of similar meaning (Coltheart *et al.*, 1983).

Diagnosing dyslexia

Children with dyslexia are usually contrasted with those who have reading difficulties in the context of more general learning problems (*reading backwardness*) (Rutter & Yule, 1975; Silva *et al.*, 1985). Many children are poor readers, but their underachievement can usually be attributed to below-average ability, emotional/behavioural disorders (such as attention-deficit hyperactivity disorder/ADHD), or environmental factors (such as school absence or sociocultural deprivation). Conversely, the reading and writing attainments of children with dyslexia is *significantly below* the level predicted based on their levels of general intelligence – *despite* normal functioning and adequate educational opportunity (Egan, 1998). It's on this discrepancy (between expected and actual reading attainment) that diagnosis of dyslexia is based (Snowling, 1998).

The incidence of dyslexia

It has been reported in most countries with universal education, and in both European and non-European languages. It's often familial and occurs in all ability ranges and social-class groups. Allowing for differences in diagnostic criteria, it's estimated that about four per cent of school-age children are dyslexic (Egan, 1998). Snowling (1998) puts the figure at between four and seven per cent. Early studies typically reported an excess of boys (four to one), but more recently the reported ratios have been much closer (Snowling, 1998).

Explaining dyslexia

According to Egan (1998), since reading isn't a 'natural' skill (unlike speech), it's unlikely to have its own specialised brain area controlling it. Models of word-recognition suggest that reading involves two letter–brain routes: visual and phonemic (see Chapter 19).

Visual perceptual deficits

The visual route is used to match letter sequences to particular words stored in memory. Some fairly common visual errors include:

- reading words/letters in a back-to-front way (e.g. 'saw'/'was'; 'b'/'d');
- contracting words (e.g. 'tenable'/'table');
- reading sentences in the wrong order (e.g. 'he was going out'/'he was out going').

Dyslexics make these visual errors only on perceptual tasks involving *symbolic* material (i.e. word-related), and their visual errors are also similar to those made by young children learning to read. These data suggest that dyslexics' visual errors are *caused* by their reading disability – not vice versa. However, the case of A.S. casts some doubt on this conclusion.

CASE STUDY 40.4

A.S. (Wydell & Butterworth, in Uhlig, 1996)

A.S. is a 17-year-old boy living in Japan with his English mother and Australian father. His first language is English, which is used exclusively at home. But at age six, he went to a Japanese-speaking school. A.S. has no difficulty with Japanese, and can use university textbooks. His English, though, is behind his classmates', and at age 13 it was confirmed that he was dyslexic in English but not in Japanese.

Japanese has two written forms – *kanji* and *kana*. Kanji symbols have meaning but no phonetic values. If A.S.'s dyslexia were the result of a visual processing problem, he should have more difficulties with kanji than English – but he clearly doesn't. He appears to suffer from a form of dyslexia that could be unique to English. The many pronunciation and spelling irregularities in English apparently confuse the method by which A.S. assigns sounds to letters.

Phonological deficits

The phonemic route is used to match letters and combinations of letters with the spoken form of words. Although skilled readers rarely use this route, it's important in learning to read. Young children first learn to associate particular patterns of letters with pictures or spoken words ('whole word' reading), but this doesn't allow them to 'decode' new words. So, they need to identify the individual sounds (phomenes) in words and blend them to produce words (e.g. 'k-ah-tuh'…'k-ahtuh'…'kat'…'cat': Egan, 1998).

Dyslexics have extreme difficulty with this process. Words appear to be *indivisible* and they seem to be 'arrested' at the 'whole word' reading stage (Frith, 1985). For example, when M.B. (a twelve-year-old, with an IQ of 116 but a reading age of eight years two months) was presented with unfamiliar words, he replaced them either with real words that *looked* like the target (e.g. 'smoulder'/'soldier') or with nonsense words (e.g. 'saucer'/'shaller') (Egan, 1998).

The ability to segment, 'sound out' or blend words are all functions of *phonological awareness*: the ability to reflect on or mentally process the sound structure of spoken words. According to the *core phonological deficit* (CPD) *model* of dyslexia (Stanovich, 1986; Stanovich & Siegel, 1994), dyslexia essentially involves very limited phonological awareness.

Box 40.7 Dyslexia and the brain

Some people with developmental dyslexia show atypical asymmetry in the *plenum temporale* (in Wernicke's area: see Chapter 4). This is evidently directly associated with phonological coding deficits. However, these neurological problems are also found in children who are generally poor readers.

Studies using imaging techniques (such as PET: see Chapter 4) have found reduced activity in the *insula* of dyslexic participants compared with non-dyslexic controls on phonological tasks (but not on visual-processing tasks). The insula is located between Wernicke's and Broca's areas, and is known to be involved in the transmission of language. It may play a role in translating between spoken inputs and speech production (Snowling, 1998).

Is dyslexia really a distinct reading difficulty?

Just as some of the brain abnormalities implicated in dyslexia may not be unique to dyslexics, so the underlying phonological deficits also occur in 'plain' poor readers (age-matched controls whose poor reading ages can be accounted for by their lower IQs). In other words, phonological deficits cannot differentiate dyslexics from other poor readers. This and other evidence makes it increasingly difficult to justify studying and treating developmental dyslexia as if it were entirely distinct from the poor reading shown by children disadvantaged by low general intelligence, inadequate home preparation, or poor teaching (Coltheart & Jackson, 1998; Snowling, 1998).

Does dyslexia involve a mainly phonological deficit?

Further, there's evidence to suggest that the primary cause of reading difficulties in developmental dyslexia has nothing to do with phonology at all. For example, Castles & Coltheart (1993) found that some children's difficulties were *orthographic*, that is, they failed to develop an adequately large *sight vocabulary* (while their ability to map from letters to sounds was normal). This is *surface* dyslexia. Where this second ability is also impaired, the impairment is called *phonological* dyslexia. These represent two distinct patterns of developmental reading difficulty (Coltheart & Jackson, 1998).

Other researchers (e.g. Stein & Fowler, 1985) believe that in at least some children with developmental dyslexia the central difficulty is *oculomotor*, that is, the reading difficulty is caused by poor control of eye movements.

Some concluding comments about dyslexia

According to Coltheart & Jackson (1998), the *same proximal cause* (some abnormality in the information-processing system the child is using, such as weak phonological awareness), can itself be the product of *different distal causes* (the reason for this system being abnormal, e.g. congenital, environmental, educational). Coltheart and Jackson believe that effective *treatment interventions* will be defined largely (although not exclusively) by the *proximal* causes. This approach treats children as individuals, producing individual profiles which are then compared with age-related norms. When such an approach is adopted:

'The term 'dyslexia' has no role to play …'.

CHAPTER SUMMARY

- **Gifted children** tend to be **precocious**, make discoveries on their own, have an obsessive interest in their domain of giftedness, and have unusually good **metacognitive skills**.

- Cases like those of Sufiah Yusof and Ruth Lawrence illustrate the kinds of social and emotional problems gifted children are prone to.

- Terman's study of giftedness also created the myth that these children are **globally** gifted. In fact, the **unevenness** of gifted children's abilities is quite common and **savants** such as Stephen Wiltshire illustrate the unevenness of abilities in an extreme form.

- Both savants and non-savant gifted children appear to have atypical brain organisation. This may account for the **'pathology of superiority'** and may be caused by **'testosterone poisoning'**.

- The belief that giftedness is hardwired in the infant brain is consistent with the **'talent account'**. But critics argue that talents are mythical, that temperamental and personality qualities, rather than cognitive ones, are what set geniuses apart from the rest of us, and that practice from an early age is the crucial environmental influence.

- **Autism** has been defined in terms of the **triad of impairments: social relationships**, **language** and **rigidity of thought**. There's a wide spectrum of autistic disorders, which includes learning difficulties and Asperger's syndrome.

- An early, unsuccessful, attempt to explain autism was the **'refrigerator parenting'** hypothesis. Many researchers believe that there's compelling evidence for a strong **genetic** component underlying autism, based on studies of siblings of autistic individuals and of identical/non-identical twins.

- The strongest evidence for autistic childrens' lack of a **theory of mind** (ToM) and **mind-blindedness** is their consistent failure on **false belief tasks**. By comparison, Down's syndrome and normal children reliably pass them.

- However, ToM cannot explain all aspects of autism. Two alternative, complementary, **cognitive** explanations are **weak central coherence** and **impaired executive functioning**.

- Autism is treated by **drugs** and other **biological approaches**, **behaviour modification**, and more **cognitively based approaches**, such as **structural therapy**.

- **Learning difficulty** is a legally defined term, which is synonymous with **learning disability**, and the internationally used term **mental retardation**. **Mental impairment** is another legally defined term that overlaps with learning difficulty.

- Learning difficulties are defined primarily in terms of IQ, but the ability to adapt to society's demands (children) and to be self-sufficient (adults) are also taken into account. **Mental retardation** is usually subdivided into **mild**, **moderate**, **severe** and **profound**.

- **Primary** (**organic**: genetic or brain-related) causes, such as Down's and fragile X syndromes, are usually associated with severe and profound learning difficulties. **Secondary** (non-genetic) causes include FAS and sociocultural and other **environmental** factors.

- **Dyslexia** (or **specific learning difficulty**) may be **developmental** or **acquired**, **surface** or **deep**. It's distinguished from **reading backwardness**, in which low reading attainment is predicted from more general learning problems.

- The most influential account of dyslexia has been the **core phonological defect** (CPD) **model**, according to which dyslexics have very limited **phonological awareness**.

- However, this deficit (and related brain abnormalities) may not be unique to dyslexia. Also, the core deficit may sometimes be **orthographic** or **oculomotor**. It's important to distinguish between **proximal** and **distal causes** of dyslexia.

Self-assessment questions

1 Critically evaluate the 'talent account' of giftedness.
2 Describe and evaluate **two** theories of autism.
3 Discuss research into the nature and causes of learning difficulties.
4 Critically assess the claim that dyslexia is just a form of reading backwardness.

Web addresses

www.rmplc.co.uk/orgs/nagc/index.htmlm

www.users.dircon.co.uk/~tutorcom/chl

www.gifted.uconn.edu/hogerenz.html

members.aol.com/discanner/asynch.htm

www.socsci.kun.nl/psy/cbo/engels.htm

www.autism-society.org/

www.autism.org/contents.html

www.bda-dyslexia.org.uk/

www.interdys.org/

Further reading

Happé, F. (1999) Why success is more interesting than failure. *The Psychologist, 12 (11)*, 540–545. An excellent review article, which emphasises the positive side of autism.

Mitchell, P. (1997) *Introduction To Theory Of Mind: Children, Autism and Apes.* London: Arnold. There are three chapters specifically on autism, but this is set in the context of ToM research as a whole. An excellent read.

Howe, M.J.A. (1999) *Genius Explained.* Cambridge: Cambridge University Press. A critique of the talent account of giftedness which looks at the lives of Darwin, Einstein and other assorted outstanding achievers.

Six

Individual Differences

Chapter 41

Intelligence

Introduction and overview

The concept of intelligence is one of the most elusive in the whole of psychology. Perhaps nowhere else in psychology does so much of the research and theory attempt to define the concept under investigation.

But intelligence isn't just of academic interest. The intelligence test (in one form or another) has impinged on the lives of most of us, whether in the context of educational or occupational selection, or even selection for Mensa, the high-IQ society.

How intelligence is conceptualised varies enormously. *Biological definitions* see intelligence as related to *adaptation to the environment* (see Chapter 34). For Piaget (1950), intelligence is:

> '… essentially a system of living and acting operations, i.e. a state of balance or equilibrium achieved by the person when he is able to deal adequately with the data before him. But it is not a static state, it is dynamic in that it continually adapts itself to new environmental stimuli'.

Piaget is interested in the *qualitative* aspects of intelligence, that is, the nature of intelligence itself.

By contrast, the *psychometric* ('mental measurement') approach is concerned with measuring *individual differences* in intelligence, through the use of intelligence (IQ) tests, and so emphasises the *quantitative* aspects of intelligence. It is this approach, associated with psychologists such as Spearman, Burt, Vernon, Thurstone and Guilford, that has predominated until fairly recently. Important alternatives to the psychometric approach are Sternberg's *information-processing approach* and Gardner's *theory of multiple intelligences*.

The near-obsession of Western society with measuring and categorising people is emotionally charged and politically sensitive, especially in relation to the 'race and IQ' debate. This is an example of the nature–nurture/heredity–environment issue, which has become associated with extremes of political viewpoints. It highlights the impossibility of completely divorcing the social from the scientific functions of psychology (see Chapters 3 and 48).

Defining intelligence

Ask yourself ...

- How would you define intelligence?

Most definitions reflect the *psychometric approach*. As we saw in the *Introduction and overview*, this is concerned with the measurement of intelligence in order to compare 'how much' of it different individuals possess (see Table 41.1).

Ask yourself ...

- What similarites and differences are there between the different definitions in Table 41.1?

The definitions of Terman, Burt and Vernon all stress the purely cognitive/intellectual aspects of the concept, while those of Binet and Wechsler are much broader and perhaps closer to commonsense understanding. But Heim objects to the use of intelligence as a noun, because it smacks of an 'insoluble entity or thing'. This is contrary to her belief that intelligence should be regarded as part of *personality as a whole*. Consequently, she prefers to talk about 'intelligent activity' rather than 'intelligence'.

Table 41.1 *Some definitions of intelligence*

'It seems to us that in intelligence there is a fundamental faculty, the impairment of which is of the utmost importance for practical life. This faculty is called judgement, otherwise called good sense, practical sense, initiative, the faculty of adapting one's self to circumstances. To judge well, to comprehend well, to reason well …' (Binet, 1905)

'An individual is intelligent in proportion as he is able to carry on abstract thinking.' (Terman, 1921)

'… innate, general, cognitive ability' (Burt, 1955)

'… the aggregate of the global capacity to act purposefully, think rationally, to deal effectively with the environment' (Wechsler, 1944)

'… the effective all-round cognitive abilities to comprehend, to grasp relations and reason' (Vernon, 1969)

'Intelligent activity consists in grasping the essentials in a situation and responding appropriately to them.' (Heim, 1970)

'… the ability to deal with cognitive complexity' (Gottfredson, 1998)

Other definitions

An *operational definition* defines intelligence in terms of tests designed to measure it, that is, 'Intelligence is what intelligence tests measure' (Boring, 1923). But this begs the question as to what intelligence tests measure and is *circular* (the concept being defined is part of the definition itself). Miles (1967) argues that if we substitute the names of particular tests, then we can break into the circle, but Heim points out that this merely decreases the circumference of the circle!

Like Heim, Ryle (1949) believes that 'intelligence' doesn't denote an entity or an engine inside us causing us to act in particular ways. Rather, any action can be performed more or less intelligently, so it should be used as an adjective and not as a noun.

Theories of intelligence

Psychometric (factor analytic) theories

Psychometric theories are based upon analysis of scores of large numbers of individuals on various intelligence tests using a statistical technique called *factor analysis* (FA) (see Chapter 42).

Box 41.1 Factor analysis (FA)

This involves correlating the scores of a large sample of participants to determine whether scores on certain tests are related to scores on certain other tests (whether some, or any, of the tests have something in common). The basic assumption is that the more similar the scores on two or more tests (the higher the correlation), the more likely it is that these tests are tapping the same basic ability (or factor).

For example, if we find that people's scores on tests A, B, C, D and E are highly correlated (if they score highly on one they tend to score highly on the others), then it could be inferred that all five tests are measuring the same ability and individuals differ according to how much or how little of that particular ability they have. But if there's very little relationship between scores on the five tests, then each test may be measuring a distinct ability, and when comparing individuals we'd have to look at each ability separately.

The two hypothetical outcomes in Box 41.1 correspond roughly to two theories of intelligence: (a) the 'London line' is associated with Spearman (1904, 1967), Burt (1949, 1955) and Vernon (1950); (b) the mainly American approach of Thurstone (1938) and Guilford (1959).

Spearman's two-factor theory

Spearman factor-analysed the results of children's performance on various tests, and found that many tests were moderately positively correlated. He concluded that every intellectual activity involves both a general factor (g or general intelligence) and a specific factor (s), and differences between individuals are largely attributable to differences in their g. (g is, in fact, an abbreviation for neogenesis, the ability to 'educe relations', as in a common kind of test item which asks 'A is to Y as B is to ?'). g accounts for why people who perform well using one mental ability also tend to perform well in others, and is entirely innate.

Spearman himself believed that he'd discovered the elusive entity, the innate essence of intelligence, that would make psychology a true science. As Gould (1981) puts it:

'Spearman's g would be the philosopher's stone of psychology, its hard, quantifiable 'thing' – a fundamental particle that would pave the way for an exact science as firm and as basic as physics'.

Although this proved to be a rather exaggerated claim, Guilford (1936, quoted in Gould, 1981) believed that:

'No single event in the history of mental testing has proved to be of such momentous importance as Spearman's proposal of his famous two-factor theory'.

Burt and Vernon's hierarchical model

Burt (who was a student of Spearman) agreed that there's a g factor common to all tests, but also thought that the two-factor model was too simple. He and Vernon elaborated and extended Spearman's model by identifying a series of *group factors* (major and minor) in between g and s factors (see Figure 41.1). g is what *all* tests measure, the *major group factors* (v:ed and k:m) are what *some* tests measure (some to a greater extent than others), the *minor group factors* are what *particular tests* measure whenever they're given, while *specific factors* are what particular tests measure on *specific occasions* (Vernon, 1971).

An important *educational* implication of this model is that, given the dominance of g in the hierarchy, each child can be ranked on a single scale of (innate) intelligence. g can be measured early in life, and children sorted according to their intellectual promise. (This is the thinking behind the eleven-plus examination: see Box 41.3, pages 596–597.)

Thurstone's primary mental abilities

Using 14-year-olds and college students as his participants, Thurstone (1935, 1938, 1947) found that not all mental tests correlate equally. Rather, they appear to form seven distinct factors or groupings, which he called *primary mental abilities* (PMAs), namely:

- *spatial* (S): the ability to recognise spatial relationships;
- *perceptual speed* (P): the quick and accurate detection of visual detail;
- *numerical reasoning* (N): the ability to perform arithmetical operations quickly and accurately;
- *verbal meaning* (V): understanding the meaning of words and verbal concepts;
- *word fluency* (W): speed in recognising single and isolated words;
- *memory* (M): the ability to recall a list of words, numbers or other material;
- *inductive reasoning* (I): the ability to generate a rule or relationship that describes a set of observations.

Thurstone sometimes referred to these mental abilities as 'mental faculties' or 'the vectors of mind' (the title of his 1935 book). He saw g as a grand average of positive correlations for

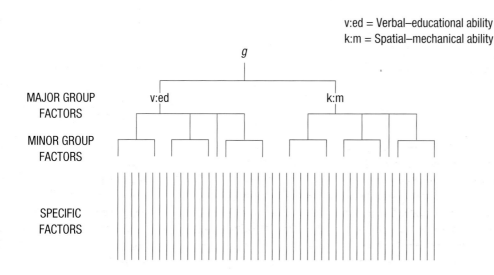

v:ed = Verbal–educational ability
k:m = Spatial–mechanical ability

Figure 41.1 *The hierarchical model of intelligence (after Vernon, 1950)*

a particular battery of tests. This means that *g* can change according to the particular battery of tests used and, so it:

'... has no fundamental psychological significance beyond the arbitrary collection of tests that anyone happens to put together... We cannot be interested in a general factor which is only the average of any random collection of tests'.
(Thurstone, 1940, quoted in Gould, 1981)

So the PMAs are independent and uncorrelated. They correspond to the group factors in the hierarchical model, but there's no general factor to which they're all related. As there's no general ability, the overall ranking of pupils is inappropriate: some children will be good at some things, others at other things. He advocated the use of *individual profiles* of all PMAs. However, Thurstone later (1947) admitted that *g* does seem to be involved in all PMAs (having carried out a 'second-order' factor analysis on the results of the first: see Chapter 42).

Jensen (1980), a major advocate of the view that intelligence differences are largely genetic, believes that this change of mind by Thurstone proves that Spearman and Burt were right all along. Jensen is a 'pure Spearman-ian' (Gould, 1981), who claims that:

'To the extent that a test orders individuals on g, it can be said to be a test of intelligence'.

However, Gould (1981) argues that *g* was still of secondary importance to the PMAs. Even after admitting a second-order *g*, Thurstone continued to contrast himself with the 'London line'.

Guilford's 'structure of intellect' model

This represents the most extreme alternative to Spearman's two-factor theory, and totally rejects the notion of a general intelligence factor. Guilford first classified a cognitive task along three major dimensions:

■ *content* (what must the participant think about?);
■ *operations* (what kind of thinking is the participant being asked to perform?);
■ *products* (what kind of answer is required?).

He identified five kinds of content, five kinds of operation and six kinds of product which, multiplied together, yields a total of 150 distinct mental abilities (see Figure 41.2). Guilford set out to construct tests to measure each of the 150 abilities, and tests have been devised to assess more than 70 (Shaffer, 1985). However, people's scores are often correlated, suggesting that the number of basic mental abilities is much smaller than Guilford assumed (Brody & Brody, 1976).

An evaluation of factor-analytic models

According to Vernon (1950, 1971), intelligence is neither a single general mental ability nor a number of more specific, independent abilities, but *both*. General intelligence plays a part in all mental activities, but more specific abilities are also involved in producing performance. Sternberg (1995) believes that this combined, hierarchical approach is probably the most widely accepted factorial description of intelligence. However:

■ There's more than one way of factor-analysing a set of data, and there's no 'best' way. Thurstone originally used a form of FA which gives a 'simple structure' solution in

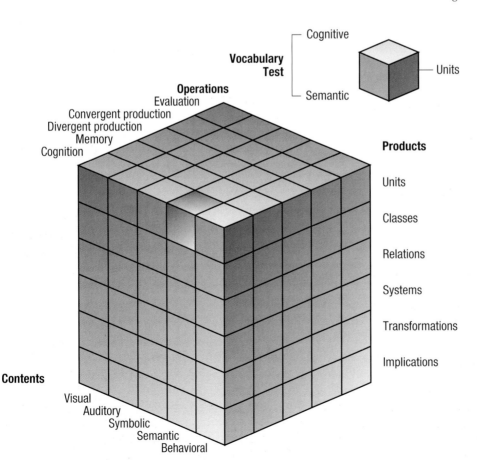

Figure 41.2 *Guilford's (1967, 1982) structure of intellect model. (From Zimbardo P.G, (1992)* Psychology and Life, *13th ed. New York, Harper Collins Publishers. (Originally, Guilford identified 120 abilities, but he later distinguished between visual and auditory content (previously included under 'figural') giving 5 × 5 × 6 = 150)*

contrast to the 'principal component' solutions resulting from Spearman's and Burt's analyses. Shackleton & Fletcher (1984) say that these two alternatives are mathematically equivalent, and the same data from the same sample can produce a number of different patterns of factors depending on which alternative is used.

■ Thurstone and Guilford used mainly college students, while Spearman, Burt and Vernon used mainly schoolchildren.

Ask yourself ...

- In what ways do these groups differ in terms of their intellectual abilities?
- How might these differences affect the resulting picture of how abilities are related?

Compared with schoolchildren, college students are much more *homogeneous* in terms of their all-round intelligence (as well as being a much more *self-selected* group). So, differences between college students are likely to reflect differences in certain, relatively independent, abilities, while differences between schoolchildren are likely to reflect more global, all-round ability.

■ FA produces a cluster of intercorrelations between different tests and sub-tests – it's then up to the researcher to scan these patterns of intercorrelations and to label them. As Radford (1980) says, factors don't come 'ready-labelled' and the labels that are attached to the factors are only 'best guesses' about the psychological meaning of the factors – they may or may not reflect 'psychological reality'. In other words, clusters of intercorrelations are meaningless until they're given an interpretation by a psychologist.

■ Once a factor has been labelled (e.g. 'verbal ability'), there's the danger of believing that it exists in some objective way (this is called *reification*). But in reality, a factor is merely a statistic (or 'mathematical abstraction': Gould, 1981). As Gillham (1978) puts it:

'Factors, like human beings, are born with no name although there is usually one waiting for them, which may not fit their character very well. But as with their human counterparts they soon become assimilated to their name … .

Human beings, however, have the advantage over factors in that their meaning does not reside just in their name. Factors, like correlation coefficients, have no intrinsic psychological significance: meaning is ascribed to them by a psychologist with his preferences and presuppositions …'.

Fluid and crystallised intelligence

Working within the FA approach, Cattell (1963) and Horn & Cattell (1967, 1982) have proposed a model which can to some degree reconcile the different models discussed above. They argue that *g* can be subdivided into two major dimensions – fluid and crystallised intelligence.

■ *Fluid intelligence* ('*gf*') is the ability to solve abstract relational problems of the sort that aren't taught, and which are relatively free of cultural influences. It increases gradually throughout childhood and adolescence as the nervous system matures, then levels off during young adulthood and after that begins a steady decline.

■ *Crystallised intelligence* ('*gc*') increases throughout the lifespan, and is primarily a reflection of one's cumulative learning experience. It involves understanding relations or solving problems which depend on knowledge acquired as a result of schooling and other life experiences (e.g. general knowledge, word comprehension and numerical abilities: see Chapter 39).

The information-processing approach

According to Fishbein (1984), the *information-processing approach* sees intelligence as the steps or processes people go through in solving problems. One person may be more intelligent than another, because s/he moves through the same steps more quickly or efficiently, or is more familiar with the required problem-solving steps (see Chapter 34).

Advocates of this view (e.g. Sternberg, 1979) focus on: (i) how information is internally represented; (ii) the kinds of strategies people use in processing that information; (iii) the nature of the components (e.g. memory, inference, comparison) used in carrying out those strategies; and (iv) how decisions are made as to which strategies to use. Regarding (iii), Sternberg (1987) identifies five major kinds of components:

■ *metacomponents*: higher-order control processes used in planning how a problem should be solved, in making decisions regarding alternative courses of action during problem-solving, and in monitoring one's progress during the course of problem solution;

■ *performance components*: processes used in the actual execution of a problem-solving strategy;

■ *acquisition components*: processes used in learning (acquisition of knowledge);

■ *retention components*: processes used in remembering (retrieval of previously acquired information);

■ *transfer components*: processes used in generalising (transfer of knowledge from one task or task context to another).

Ask yourself ...

- How might these five kinds of components be applied in the solution to the problem presented in Box 41.2?

Box 41.2

Mrs Smith decided to impress Mrs Jones. She went to a costume jewellery shop and bought three imitation diamonds of equal value. She received £4 in change from the £10 note she gave the assistant. (But as Mrs Smith was receiving her change, Mrs Jones walked into the shop!) How much did each imitation diamond cost?

Metacomponents would be used in setting up the equations for solving the problem (e.g. in deciding that the problem can be solved by subtracting £4 from £10 and dividing the difference by three). They must also decide what information is relevant and what isn't. *Performance components* would be used in the actual solution of these equations to obtain first £6 as the price of the imitation diamonds and, then, £2 as the price of each item. *Acquisition components* were used in the problem-solver's past to learn how to set up the equation, how to subtract, divide and so on. *Retention components* are used to retrieve this information from memory when it's needed, and *transfer components* are used to draw an analogy between this problem and previous problems of a similar kind.

According to Sternberg, the *g* factor results from the operations of components, which are general across the range of tasks represented on IQ tests and are mainly metacomponents. Burt and Vernon's major group factors and Thurstone's PMAs are the result of the operation of the other four kinds of component.

While the components involved in the solution of the 'same' problem would overlap regardless of the particular culture, the kinds of problems needing solution will differ widely from one culture to another. As Sternberg (1987) says:

'... the kinds of persons who are considered intelligent may vary widely from one culture to another, as a function of the components that are important for adaptation to the requirements of living in the various cultures'.

The cultural nature of intelligence is discussed further later in the chapter (see pages 599–600).

Information-processing theories are intended (like Piaget's) to be *universal*, and at the same time (like factor-analytic theories) to explain *individual differences*. As Fishbein (1984) puts it, they see intelligence as neither an 'it' (for example *g*) nor a 'them' (for example, primary mental abilities) but as everything the mind does in processing information.

Sternberg's triarchic theory

Sternberg's (1985, 1988a) *triarchic theory* incorporates the components involved in information-processing but is far broader. It comprises three *subtheories* which attempt to explain, in an integrative way, the relationship between:

- intelligence and the individual's *internal* world; that is, the mental mechanisms which underlie intelligent behaviour (the *componential subtheory*);
- intelligence and the individual's *external* world; that is, how these mechanisms are used in everyday life to attain an intelligent fit with the environment (the *contextual sub-theory*);
- intelligence and experience; that is, '... the mediating role of one's passage through life between the internal and external worlds of the individual ...' (Sternberg, 1990) (the *experiential subtheory*).

Componential subtheory

One of the most interesting classes of performance components are those found in *inductive reasoning*, the kind of thinking required in series completion tasks and analogies (e.g. 'A is to B as Y is to ?'). Sternberg (1990) believes that identifying these performance components can provide insight into the nature of *g*. However:

'... there is more to intelligence than a set of information-processing components. One could scarcely understand all of what it is that makes one person more intelligent than another by understanding the components of processing on, say, an intelligence test ...'.

Contextual subtheory

Intelligent thought isn't aimless or random mental activity, but is directed towards one or more of three behavioural goals: *adaptation* to an environment, *shaping* of an environment and *selection* of an environment. Regarding adaptation, Sternberg (1990) argues that what is intelligent in one culture may be considered unintelligent in another:

'To understand intelligence, one must understand it ... in terms of how thought is intellectually translated into action in a variety of different contextual settings ...'.

Shaping may represent the essence of intelligent thought and behaviour:

'Perhaps it is this skill that has enabled human kind to reach its current level of scientific, technological, and cultural advancement... In science, the greatest scientists are those who set the paradigms (shaping), rather than those who merely follow them (adaptation) ...'.

Experiential subtheory

Intelligence is best measured at those regions of the experiential continuum that involve tasks or situations that are either relatively novel, on the one hand, or in the process of becoming automatised, on the other. To test how far children's understanding extends, you might give them problems which are just at the limits of their current understanding (this is similar to Vygotsky's *zone of proximal development*: see Chapter 34). Several sources of evidence suggest that the ability to deal with relative novelty is a good way of measuring intelligence (and is a characteristic of gifted children: see Chapter 40).

Ask yourself ...

- In terms of *attention* theory and research (see Chapter 13), why is the ability to automatise so important?

The ability to *automatise* information-processing (e.g. as shown by a skilled reader: again, see Chapter 40) makes more resources available for dealing with novelty.

According to Bee (1989), standard IQ tests have omitted many of the kinds of abilities included under the contextual and experiential subtheories. In the world outside school, these may be required at least as much as those included under the componential subtheory. Clearly, traditional IQ tests don't measure all significant aspects of intellectual skill (see below, pages 597–600).

Gardner's theory of multiple intelligences

Gardner's (1983) *theory of multiple intelligences* (MI theory) is based on three fundamental principles:

- Intelligence isn't a single, unitary thing but a collection of multiple intelligences, each one a system in its own right (as opposed to merely separate aspects of a larger system, i.e. 'intelligence').

- Each intelligence is independent of all the others.
- The intelligences interact, otherwise nothing could be achieved.

MI theory also makes two strong claims:

- All humans possess all these intelligences, and collectively, they can be considered a cognitive definition of *homo sapiens*.
- Just as we all look different and have unique personalities and temperaments, so we also have different profiles of intelligences. No two individuals, not even identical twins, have exactly the same mix of intelligences, with the same strengths and weaknesses (see Chapter 42).

Gardner (1998) defines an intelligence as:

'… a psychobiological potential to solve problems or fashion products that are valued in at least one cultural context'.

Entire cultures may encourage the development of one or other intelligence. For example, the seafaring Puluwat of the Caroline Islands (in the South Pacific) cultivate spatial intelligence and excel at navigation. The Manus children of New Guinea learn the canoeing and swimming skills that elude the vast majority of Western children (Gardner, 1998).

Gardner (1983) originally identified seven intelligences, and added an eighth, *naturalistic* (or 'the naturalist'), in 1995. Darwin is a good example. Gardner is currently considering the possibility of a ninth – *existential* intelligence, which captures the human tendency to raise and ponder fundamental questions about existence, life, death and so on (e.g. the existential philosopher, Kierkegaard) (Gardner, 1998).

Table 41.2 *Gardner's eight intelligences*

Linguistic: Includes skills involved in reading, writing, listening and talking

Logical–mathematical: Involved in numerical computation, deriving proofs, solving logical puzzles, and most scientific thinking

Spatial: Used in marine navigation, piloting a plane, driving a car, working out how to get from A to B, figuring out one's orientation in space. Also important in the visual arts, playing chess, and recognising faces and scenes

Musical: Includes singing, playing an instrument, conducting, composing and, to some extent, musical appreciation

Bodily–kinaesthetic: Involves the use of one's whole body or parts of it, to solve problems, construct products and displays. Used in dance, athletics, acting and surgery

Interpersonal: Includes understanding and acting upon one's understanding of others – noticing differences between people, reading their moods, temperaments, intentions, and so on. Especially important in politics, sales, psychotherapy and teaching

Intrapersonal: Self-understanding – symbolised in the world of dreams

Naturalistic: Permits the recognition and categorisation of natural objects (as in biology, zoology etc.)

Gardner identifies eight different criteria for distinguishing an independent intelligence, including:

- *potential isolation by brain damage*: each intelligence resides in a separate region of the brain, so that a given intelligence should be isolable by studying brain-damaged patients. For example, *naturalistic* intelligence is based on evidence that certain parts of the temporal lobe are dedicated to naming and the recognition of natural things, while others are attuned to human-made objects. Braindamaged people sometimes lose the capacity to identify living things, but can still name inanimate objects (Gardner, 1998: see Chapter 4);
- an identifiable *core operation* or *set of operations*;
- support from *psychometric findings* (patterns of intercorrelations, based on FA: see Box 41.1, page 590);
- the existence of *idiots savants*, *prodigies* and other *exceptional individuals* (see Chapter 40).

Ask yourself …

- Explain how savant abilities suggest the existence of separate intelligences.

According to Gardner (1998), critics of MI theory are nervous about moving away from standardised tests and adopting a set of criteria that is less quantifiable. Many prefer to talk about musical or bodily–kinaesthetic *talents* rather than intelligences:

'Such a narrow definition, however, devalues these capacities, so that orchestra conductors and dancers are talented but not smart. In my view, it would be all right to call those abilities talents, so long as logical reasoning and linguistic facility are then also termed talents'.

Intelligence testing

A brief history of intelligence tests

The Stanford–Binet test

In 1904, Binet and Simon were commissioned by the French government to devise a test which would identify those children who wouldn't benefit from ordinary schooling because of their inferior intelligence. The result was the Simon–Binet test (1905), generally accepted as the first intelligence test. The sample of children used for the development of the test (the *standardisation sample*) was very small, and it was subsequently revised in 1908 and 1911, using much larger samples.

In 1910, Terman, at Stanford University in California, began adapting the Simon–Binet test for use in the USA. The test became known as the *Stanford–Binet* test, and is still referred to in this way. The first revision was published in 1916, followed by the Terman–Merrill revision (1937), which comprised two equivalent forms (L and M). In 1960, the most useful questions from the 1937 revision were combined into a single form (L–M) and an improved scoring system was used. Prior to 1960, the Stanford–Binet test was designed for individuals up to age 16 (starting at two-and-a-half to three), but this was extended to 18 in the 1960 revision. A further revision was published in 1973, and the most recent in 1986, which is designed for people from age two years up to 23 years eleven months. Subtests assess verbal reasoning, quantitative (mathematical) reasoning, abstract and visual reasoning, and memory. The testee is given a vocabulary test that serves as a routing test to determine the starting level for all the other scales (Sparrow & Davis, 2000).

In the 1986 revision, items are grouped into four broad areas of intellectual ability: (i) verbal reasoning; (ii) abstract/visual reasoning; (iii) quantitative reasoning; and (iv) short-term memory. A separate score is obtained for each area (whereas previously a single overall IQ score was given).

The Wechsler tests

Wechsler developed the most widely used test of adult intelligence, the Wechsler *adult* intelligence scale (WAIS, 1944), revised in 1958 and again in 1981 (WAIS-R). WAIS-III (1997) is designed for use with adults 16–89. Like WAIS-R, WAIS-III is constructed much like the Wechsler intelligence scale for children (WISC). This was first published in 1949 and revised in 1974 (WISC-R), and again in 1991 (WISC-III), and is designed for children between five and 15 years. Finally, the Wechsler preschool primary scale of intelligence (WPPSI, 1963; WPPSI-R, 1989) is designed for four- to six-and-a-half year-olds.

The Wechsler tests produces *three* IQ scores: *verbal*, *performance*, and *full* (combined or general) IQs. Although there's much debate about the *atheoretical* nature of all the Wechsler tests, they're by far the most widely used cognitive assessment instruments today, both in the US and around the world, having been translated into French, Greek, Japanese and Chinese (Sparrow & Davis, 2000).

Army alpha and beta tests

While the Stanford–Binet and Wechsler tests are *individual* tests (i.e. given to one person at a time), *group* tests are administered to several people at once (as in written exams.) A major impetus to the development of group testing was America's involvement in World War I. A quick and easy method of selecting over one million recruits was needed, and the result was the *army alpha* and *beta* tests (see Gould, 1981; Gross, 1999).

The British ability scales (BAS)

The *British ability scales* (Elliot *et al.*, 1979) was designed for use with two-and-a-half to 17-year-olds. Five major 'mental processes' are assessed, including retrieval and application of knowledge and speed of *information-processing*. The latter is meant to underlie performance on all the other subscales, and is one of the novel features of the test, reflecting the influence of the information-processing approach (see Chapter 34).

Like the Wechsler scales, the BAS gives three IQ scores – verbal, visual and overall (general) IQs. In keeping with Thurstone's PMA model, the aim was to construct an intelligence scale which would provide a profile of special abilities rather than merely produce an overall IQ figure (Richardson, 1991).

The original British test was revised and standardised in the US as the *differential abilities scale* (Elliott, 1990), although it's used mainly in the UK. Its British revision (BASII, 1996) was based on a new standardisation sample of 1700 British children, and the upper age limit is now 17 years eleven months. Scales are now clearly divided into *early years* (two years, six months to five years, eleven months) and *school age* (six years to 17 years, eleven months).

Box 41.3	Some differences between individual and group tests

- *Individual tests* are used primarily as *diagnostic tests* in a clinical setting (for example, to assess the ability of a child with learning difficulties (see Chapter 40). *Group tests* are used primarily for

Table 41.3 *Some items from the Stanford–Binet (1973) and the two scales of the WAIS-R (1981)*

Stanford–Binet	Wechsler adult intelligence scale (WAIS-R)
Children of three should be able to: Point to objects that serve various functions (e.g. 'goes on your feet') Repeat a list of two words or digits (e.g. 'can', 'dog')	**Verbal scale** (none of the subtests is timed): • **Information:** general knowledge • **Comprehension:** ability to use knowledge in practical settings (e.g. 'What would you do if you were lost in a large, strange town?')
Children of four should be able to: Discriminate visual forms (e.g. squares, circles, triangles) Define words (e.g. 'ball', 'bat') Repeat 10-word sentences, count up to four objects, solve problems (e.g. 'In daytime it is light, at night it is …')	• **Arithmetic** • **Similarities:** conceptual and analogical reasoning (e.g. 'In what ways are a book and TV alike?') • **Digit span:** STM (e.g. repeating a string of digits in the same/reverse order) • **Vocabulary:** word meaning
Children of nine should be able to: Solve verbal problems (e.g. 'Tell me a number that rhymes with tree') Solve simple arithmetic problems and repeat four digits in reverse order	**Performance scale** (all subtests are timed): • **Picture completion:** assessment of visual efficiency and memory by spotting missing items in drawings • **Picture arrangement:** assessment of sequential understanding by arranging a series of pictures to tell a story
Children of twelve should be able to: Define words (e.g. 'skill', 'muzzle') Repeat five digits in reverse order Solve verbal absurdities (e.g. 'One day we saw several icebergs that had been entirely melted by the warmth of the Gulf Stream. What's foolish about that?')	• **Block design:** ability to perceive/analyse patterns by copying pictures using multicoloured blocks • **Object assembly:** jigsaw puzzles • **Digit symbol:** ability to memorise and order abstract visual patterns

purposes of *selection* and *research*. For example, until the mid-1960s the eleven-plus examination determined the kind of secondary schooling that every child in England and Wales would receive. It consisted largely of an intelligence test, designed largely to assess *g*.

- *Individual tests* usually involve some *performance items* (as in the Wechsler *performance scale*: see Table 41.3). *Group tests* are 'pencil-and-paper' tests, and in this way are much like other written exams.

> ### Ask yourself ...
>
> - Can you think of some advantages and disadvantages of individual and group tests?

- *Individual tests* are much more time-consuming than group tests, and can be administered only by specially trained testers – usually educational or clinical psychologists (see Chapter 1). There's some degree of flexibility as to how the test is conducted (such as how long the child is allowed to relax before the test proper begins), and some room for interpreting the child's answers.
- *Group tests*, which are timed, can be administered by teachers, researchers, and other non-trained personnel. Marking is usually done using a special marking key or by computer. In this respect, group tests are more *objective*.

What do intelligence tests measure?

IQ tests represent one kind of *ability* test, designed to measure underlying constructs that aren't a direct result of training (Coolican *et al.*, 1996). This contrasts with *attainment* (or *achievement*) tests (such as tests of reading and comprehension, spelling and numeracy) designed to assess *specific* school learning. *Aptitude* tests are aimed at measuring *potential* performance (such as a logic test aimed at predicting how good someone would be at computer programming). Gottfredson (1998) describes IQ tests as tests of 'mental aptitude rather than accumulated knowledge' or 'pure *g*'.

The relationship between intelligence and IQ

> ### Ask yourself ...
>
> - Try to formulate some arguments for and against the claim that IQ is a valid measure of intelligence.

From the *psychometric* perspective, an individual's score on an intelligence test (his/her *intelligence quotient* or IQ) is an accurate measure of his/her *intelligence*. Effectively, and implicitly, an operational definition of intelligence is made (see above, page 590). But this begs many fundamental questions, relating to the *meaning* of the IQ (first introduced by Stern in 1912).

Ratio and deviation IQs

Before 1960, the Stanford–Binet test calculated IQ by expressing *mental age* (MA) as a ratio of *chronological age* (CA) and

multiplying by 100 (so as to produce a whole number). Hence, the first IQ was a *ratio IQ*. The Wechsler tests have instead always used a *deviation IQ*. This expresses the test result as a *standard score*, that is, it tells the tester how many standard deviations (SDs) above or below the mean of the testee's age group the score lies. Although all tests are designed in such a way as to produce a normal curve (a symmetrical distribution of IQ scores with a mean of 100), the SD (or dispersal of the scores around the mean) can still differ from test to test.

Box 41.4	Demonstrating the difference between intelligence and IQ

Imagine two tests, A and B. Test A has a SD of 10, and test B has a SD of 20. In both cases, 68 per cent (approximately) of children would be expected to have scores one SD below or above the mean (i.e. between 90 and 110 in test A, and between 80 and 120 in test B).

So, a particular child might have a score of 110 on test A and 120 on test B, and yet the scores would be telling us the same thing.

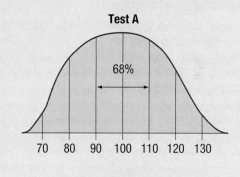

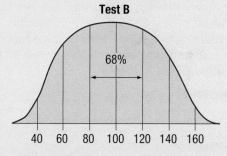

Figure 41.3 *Normal curves of two hypothetical IQ tests, each with a different standard deviation*

Based on Fontana (1981b)

This suggests that while intelligence is a *psychological* concept, IQ is a purely *statistical* concept. If it's possible for the same characteristic (intelligence) to be assigned different values according to which test is used to measure it, then instead of asking 'How intelligent is this individual?', we should ask 'How intelligent is this individual as measured by this particular test?'. Since the IQ score of the same individual can vary according to the SD of the particular test being used, we cannot equate 'IQ' with 'intelligence'.

While an operational definition of, say, someone's height is uncontroversial, in the case of intelligence there's a genuine debate concerning what it *is* – and unless we know what it is, we cannot be sure we're measuring it properly. This is why IQ is an unwarranted 'reduction' of intelligence (something very diverse and complex) to a single number (see Chapter 49). In agreeing with Heim that to name the particular test used is merely to reduce the circumference of the circle represented by an operational definition (see page 590), we could take this a step further by saying that for each separate test there exists a separate circle!

According to Ryan (1972), IQ creates the impression that we know in some absolute way what an individual's intellectual ability is (in the same way that metres and centimetres tell us about someone's height). However, IQ is measured on an *ordinal scale*, which tells us only whether one person is more or less intelligent than another (it's a *relative* measurement). In contrast, height is measured on an *interval scale*: we can measure one person's height accurately *without* knowing anyone else's. The BAS *claims* to give 'direct estimates of ability' (that is, it claims to use interval scaling), as if by a dipstick or linear rule, but Richardson (1991) doubts that this claim is valid.

Are IQ tests properly standardised?

Standardisation requires testing a large, representative sample of the population for whom the test is intended, otherwise the resulting *norms* cannot be used legitimately for certain groups of individuals. In the 1960 revision of the Stanford–Binet test, Terman and Merrill took only the population included in the census as their reference group, which excluded many migrant and unemployed workers. More seriously, both tests were standardised on whites only, and yet they were to be used with both black and white children. As Ryan (1972) says, these tests are therefore tests of white abilities. This means that any comparison between black and white children is really an assessment of 'how blacks do on tests of white intelligence'. The 1973 revision of the Stanford–Binet *did* include black children in the 2100-strong standardisation sample.

Are IQ tests valid?

> ## Ask yourself ...
>
> - What do you understand by the validity of a psychological test?
> - What does it mean in the context of intelligence?

A test is valid if it measures what it claims to measure. In relation to intelligence tests, the question is 'Do they measure intelligence?'. There are different kinds of validity and ways of measuring it (see Coolican, 1999), but probably the most commonly used in relation to psychological tests in general, and IQ tests in particular, is *predictive validity* (or *efficiency*). This refers to the correlation of a test with some future criterion measure, and the most common and powerful external criterion is educability or educational success. Also important is occupational success.

Before 1937, the mean score of women on the Stanford–Binet was ten points lower than that of men, and it was decided to eliminate this discrepancy by modifying the items so that average scores for men and women were the same. Heather (1976) asks why this hasn't been done with blacks. The answer lies in the test's *predictive validity*. Changing a test in order to eliminate racial differences, while not also changing social inequalities, would make the test a less efficient predictive tool. Removing the male–female bias did, in fact, make the test less efficient as a predictor of gender differences in educational and occupational success (Heather, 1976).

Do IQ tests predict educational success?

According to Gottfredson (1998):

> *'Intelligence as measured by IQ tests is the single most effective predictor known of individual performance at school and on the job. It also predicts many other aspects of well-being, including a person's chances of divorcing, dropping out of high school, being unemployed or having illegitimate children'.*

Typically, conventional IQ tests will correlate 0.4–0.6 with school grades. However, a test that predicts performance with a correlation of, say, 0.5, still accounts for only 25 per cent of the variation between the performance of different individuals (variation is calculated as the correlation squared = 0.5 squared = 0.25). This leaves 75 per cent of the variation unexplained, so there must be more to school performance than IQ! (Sternberg, 1998).

The predictive validity of tests declines when they're used to forecast outcomes in later life, such as job performance, salary, or obtaining the job in the first place. Generally, the correlations are just over 0.3, meaning that the tests account for roughly ten per cent of the variation in people's performance. Also, the content of IQ tests has changed little from what it was at the beginning of the twentieth century (Sternberg, 1998).

> | Box 41.5 | What the predictive validity of IQ tests really means |
> |---|---|
>
> - All the variables (including cognitive ability) that contribute to school success also contribute to performance on IQ tests. So, we'd expect a high correlation for this reason alone.
> - Heather (1976) argues that 'general intelligence' can be called 'school intelligence', the ability to do well at school. Similarly, Richardson (1991) asks whether the correlation with school performance makes IQ tests valid tests of *educational prediction* rather than valid tests of intelligence.
> - Ryan (1972) maintains that to the extent that tests measure educability, they're measuring something which is influenced to a considerable extent by various social and motivational factors. This conflicts with the test's purpose, namely, to measure only cognitive ability or potential.

Can IQ tests measure potential?

As we noted at the beginning of this section, IQ tests are designed as tests of mental aptitude or potential (basic capacity or underlying *competence*), rather than as tests of attainment/achievement (*performance*). But according to Ryan (1972), it's logically impossible to measure potential separately from some actual behaviour. In other words, some of the skills that individuals have developed during their lifetime must be used when they do intelligence tests:

> 'There is nothing extra "behind" the behaviour corresponding to potential that could be observed independently of the behaviour itself'.

She concludes that the notion of 'innate potential' itself makes no sense.

Each of us presumably has some upper limit of ability (what we could do under ideal conditions, when we're maximally motivated, well and rested). But everyday conditions are rarely ideal, and we typically perform *below* this hypothetical ability. Bee (1994) agrees with Ryan that it's *not possible* to measure competence, and so we're *always* measuring 'today's' performance. As Bee says:

> 'All IQ tests are really achievement tests to some degree. The difference between tests called IQ tests and those called achievement tests is really a matter of degree'.

Are IQ tests culturally biased?

Ask yourself ...

- What do you understand by the terms '*culture-fair*' and '*culture-free*'?
- How do you think they might apply to IQ tests?

If the potential/achievement distinction is untenable in principle, it assumes even greater significance in the context of the debate concerning *culture-fair* and *culture-free* tests. According to Frijda & Jahoda (1966), a *culture-free* test would actually measure some inherent quality or capacity equally well in all cultures. There's no such test. A *culture-fair* test:

- could be a set of items which are equally unfamiliar to all possible persons in all possible cultures, so that everyone has an equal chance of passing (or failing) them (this is often called a *culture-free* test); or
- could comprise multiple sets of items, modified for use in each culture to ensure that each version would contain the same degree of familiarity. This would give members of each culture about the same chance of being successful with their respective versions.

The first option is virtually impossible. According to Segall *et al.* (1999), the second option is a theoretical possibility, but in practice it's very difficult to construct. Since the emphasis on language has been one of the more obvious sources of bias in traditional IQ tests, tests claiming to be culture-fair are often non-verbal. A well-known example is *Raven's progressive matrices* (see Figure 41.4).

Even without any written instructions, you can probably infer what you have to do. However, the very nature of the task is something which is likely to reflect particular cultural experiences. Owen & Stoneman (1972) believe that because the influence of language is so pervasive, any attempt to devise a culture-fair test by removing 'overt language structures' is doomed to failure. Vernon (1969) rejects the idea of a culture-fair test.

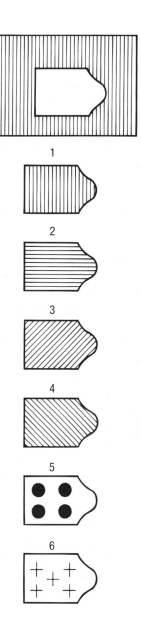

Figure 41.4 *A sample item from Raven's progressive matrices test*

CRITICAL DISCUSSION 41.1

Intelligence as a cultural phenomenon

A major reason that the construction of culture-fair tests has proved so problematical could be that the very notion of intelligence is itself culturally defined. For example, Bruner (in Gillham, 1975) maintains that:

> 'The culture-free test is the intelligence-free test, for intelligence is a cultural concept'.

Similarly, Gillham (1975) argues that any attempts to 'define' intelligence which don't involve identifying 'specially valued cultural attainments' must fail. The concept of intelligence derives its meaning only within a particular cultural and social context (see Sternberg's *contextual subtheory*: page 594).

Something which can never be 'built-in' to a test's construction (or translation) is the meaning of the experience of taking an intelligence test. Taking tests of various kinds is a familiar experience for members of Western culture (both within and outside education), but what about cultures in which there's no generally available schooling?

The very nature or form of the tasks involved in an IQ test (as distinct from the content) is something that has a cultural meaning. For example, Glick (1975, cited in Rogoff & Morelli, 1989) asked members of the Kpelle people to sort 20 familiar objects into groups. They did this by using *functional groupings* (such as knife with orange, potato with hoe), rather than taxonomic groups, which the researcher thought more appropriate. When their way of classifying the objects was challenged, they often explained that this was how a wise man would do it. When the exasperated researcher finally asked 'How would a fool do it?', the objects were immediately arranged into four neat piles of foods, tools, clothing and utensils (i.e. taxonomic groups!). The Kpelle participants and the American researcher differed in their beliefs about the intelligent way of doing things.

Different cultures may also promote the development of different abilities. For example, Serpell (1979) predicted that Zambian children would perform better than English children on a task in which they were required to copy objects using bits of wire. This was based on the observation that children all over central and southern Africa are very skilled at constructing wire cars from scraps of wire as a popular form of play. He also predicted that the English children would perform better when asked to draw the objects. Both predictions were supported, demonstrating that the abstract psychological function of pattern reproduction can be manifested in different ways according to the demands of the ecocultural niche to which participants' behaviour is adapted (Serpell, 1994).

We need to take culture into account when considering both the nature and the assessment of intelligence (Sternberg, 1995).

Explaining individual differences: Heredity and environment

According to Sternberg & Grigorenko (1997), virtually all researchers accept that:

- both heredity and environment contribute to intelligence;
- heredity and environment interact in various ways;
- extremely poor, as well as highly enriched, environments can interfere with the realisation of a person's intelligence, regardless of his/her heredity.

Genetic influences

Studies of IQ stability

Since people's genetic inheritance is a constant, then if measured intelligence (an IQ test score) is largely determined by genetic factors, there should be a high degree of continuity in IQ throughout a person's lifespan (McGurk, 1975). IQ isn't normally used as a measure of intelligence below age two.

Instead, a *developmental quotient* (DQ) is used. This assesses a child's developmental rate compared with an 'average' child of the same age (Bayley, 1969). The younger a child is when given a developmental test, the lower the correlation between its DQ and later IQ. Once IQ is measurable, it becomes a better predictor of adult IQ.

Although the stability coefficients reported by some researchers (e.g. Honzik et al., 1948) are impressive, they're based on large numbers of people and tend to obscure individual differences. Others have reported unimpressive stability coefficients. For example, McCall et al. (1973) found that in 140 middle-class children, the average IQ change between the ages of two-and-a-half and 17 was 28 points. The most 'stable' children changed an average of ten points, while 15 per cent shifted 50 points or more in either direction. One child's IQ increased by 74 points!

Even in studies where the correlation between IQ at different ages is statistically significant, the stability coefficients are low and suggest greater fluctuation in scores than a simple genetic theory predicts. So, there's a large amount of convincing evidence that a person's intelligence level can alter, sometimes substantially (Howe, 1997).

Family resemblance studies

These examine the correlation in intelligence test scores among people who vary in genetic similarity. If genetic factors influence IQ, then the closer the genetic relationship between two people, the greater should be the correspondence (or *concordance*) between their IQs.

Monozygotic (MZ) or identical twins are unique in having exactly the same genetic inheritance, since they develop from the same single fertilised egg. *Dizygotic* (DZ) or non-identical twins, by contrast, develop from two fertilised eggs, and are no more alike than ordinary siblings (they share about 50 per cent of their genes). If genes have any influence on the development of measured intelligence, then MZs should show the greatest correspondence in terms of their intelligence test performance. Any difference between them would have to be attributed to environmental or experiential influences. Many studies (e.g. Erlenmeyer-Kimling & Jarvik, 1963; Bouchard & McGue, 1981) have shown that the closer people's genetic similarity, the more strongly correlated are their IQs. Table 41.4 (page 601) presents a summary of Bouchard and McGue's world-wide review of 111 studies reporting IQ correlations between people of varying genetic similarity.

> ### Ask yourself ...
>
> - What conclusions can you draw from Table 41.4 regarding the influence of genetic factors?

Table 41.4 shows that the closer the genetic relationship between two individuals, the stronger the correlation between their IQ scores. So, the correlation between cousins (who share roughly 12.5 per cent of their genes) is weaker than that for parents and their offspring (who share roughly 50 per cent of theirs). The strongest correlation of all is for MZs. At first sight, these data suggest that heredity is a major influence on IQ test performance. However, as the genetic similarity

Table 41.4 *Familial correlations for IQ. The vertical bar on each distribution indicates the median correlation. The arrow indicates the correlation predicted by a simple polygenic model (that is, the view that many pairs of genes are involved in the inheritance of intelligence) (based on Bouchard & McGue, 1981)*

	No. of correlations	No. of pairings	Median correlation	Weighted average
Monozygotic twins reared together	34	4672	0.85	0.86
Monozygotic twins reared apart	3	65	0.67	0.72
Midparent–midoffspring reared together	3	410	0.73	0.72
Midparent–offspring reared together	8	992	0.475	0.50
Dizygotic twins reared together	41	5546	0.58	0.60
Siblings reared together	69	26 473	0.45	0.47
Siblings reared apart	2	203	0.24	0.24
Single parent–offspring reared together	32	8433	0.385	0.42
Single parent–offspring reared apart	4	814	0.22	0.22
Half-siblings	2	200	0.35	0.31
Cousins	4	1176	0.145	0.15
Non-biological sibling pairs (adopted/natural pairings)	5	345	0.29	0.29
Non-biological sibling pairs (adopted/adopted pairings)	6	369	0.31	0.34
Adopting midparent–offspring	6	758	0.19	0.24
Adopting parent–offspring	6	1397	0.18	0.19
Assortative mating	16	3817	0.365	0.33

between people increases, so does the similarity of their environments: parents and offspring usually live in the same households, whereas unrelated people don't.

Studies of separated twins

One way of overcoming this problem is to compare the IQs of MZs reared together in the same environments with those raised separately in different environments. As Table 41.4 shows, MZs reared together show a greater similarity in IQ scores than those reared separately. However, the fact that MZs reared separately are still more similar than same-sex DZs reared together suggests a strong genetic influence (Bouchard *et al.*, 1990).

Some problems with twin studies

■ 'Separated' twins often turn out not to have been reared separately at all. In Shields's (1962) and Juel-Nielsen's (1965) studies, some of the twins were raised in related branches of the parents' families, attended the same schools and/or played together (Farber, 1981; Horgan, 1993). When these are excluded from analysis in Shields's study, for example, the correlation decreases from 0.77 to 0.51. Moreover, even if the twins are separated at birth, they've shared the same environment of the mother's womb for nine months. Their identical *prenatal* experiences may account for the observed similarities in IQ (Howe, 1997).

■ When twins have to be separated, the agencies responsible for placing them generally try to match the respective families as closely as possible. When the environments are substantially different, there are marked IQ differences between the twins (Newman *et al.*, 1937).

■ In Newman *et al.*'s and Shields's studies, the experimenters knew which twins were identical and which had been separated. Participants in Bouchard *et al.*'s (1990) study were recruited by means of media appeals and 'self-referrals'. Kaprio (cited in Horgan, 1993) claims that Bouchard *et al.*'s study has tended to attract people who enjoy publicity, and therefore constitute an atypical sample.

■ Different studies have used different IQ tests, making comparisons between them difficult. Moreover, some of the tests used were inappropriate and/or not standardised on certain groups (see above, page 598).

■ The most widely cited and best-known studies of MZs are those reported by Burt (e.g. 1966), who found high correlations between the IQs of 53 pairs of twins supposedly reared in very different environments. After noticing several peculiarities in Burt's procedures and data, Kamin (1974) and Gillie (1976) questioned the genuineness of Burt's research. Even Burt's most loyal supporters have conceded that at least some of his data were fabricated (e.g. Hearnshaw, 1979).

While these, (and other) problems undoubtedly led to an overestimation of genetic influences. methodological improvements have produced correlations that are still impressive and which, for Plomin & DeFries (1980):

'… implicate genes as the major systematic force influencing the development of individual differences in IQ'.

A major ongoing study is that directed by Bouchard at the University of Minnesota. Separated and non-separated twins are given comprehensive psychological and medical tests, and answer some 15,000 questions! For some abilities (such as verbal ability), the correlations between MZs reared apart are very high, suggesting a strong genetic influence. But for others (such as memory), the correlations are low or, as with spatial ability, inconsistent (Thompson *et al.*, 1991).

Barbara Herbert and Daphne Goodship, one of the pairs of (English) separated identical twins reunited through their participation in the Minnesota twin study

Adoption studies

Adopted children share half their genes but nothing of their environment with their biological parents, and they share at least some of their environment but none of their genes with their adoptive parents. One research methodology involves comparing the IQs of children adopted in infancy with those of their adoptive and biological parents. Support for the influence of genetic factors would be obtained if the correlation between the adopted children's IQ scores and those of their biological parents was stronger than that between the adopted children and their adoptive parents.

This is exactly what some studies have shown. Munsinger (1975) found that the average correlation between adopted children and their biological parents was 0.48, compared with 0.19 for adopted children and their adoptive parents. Also, by the end of adolescence, adopted children's IQs are correlated only weakly with their adoptive siblings, who share the same environments but are biologically unrelated (Plomin, 1988).

Some problems with adoption studies

One problem with adoption studies is the difficulty in assessing the amount of similarity between the biological and adoptive parents' environments. When the environments are very different (as when the children of poor, under-educated parents are adopted into families of high socio-economic status), substantial increases in IQ scores are observed.

KEY STUDY 41.1

Adoption studies involving very different natural and adoptive parental environments (Capron & Duyme, 1989; Scarr & Weinberg, 1976; Schiff et al., 1978)

Scarr and Weinberg's 'transracial' study involved 101 white families, above average in intelligence, income and social class, who adopted black children. If genetics were the only factor influencing the development of measured intelligence, then the average IQ of the adopted children

should have been more or less what it was before they were adopted. In fact, their average IQ was 106 following adoption, compared with an average of 90 before adoption.

This finding has been replicated in other studies. For example, Schiff *et al.* (1978) studied a group of economically deprived French mothers who'd given up one baby for adoption while retaining at least one other child. The average IQ of the children adopted into middle class homes was 110, while that of the siblings who remained with the biological mother was 95. Similarly, French adoptees raised by parents of high socio-economic status were around 12 IQ points higher than adoptees raised by parents of low socio-economic status – irrespective of the socio-economic status of their biological parents (Capron & Duyme, 1989).

Scarr & Weinberg's (1976) data also indicated that children adopted early in life (within their first year) have higher IQs than those adopted later. So, when adoptive homes provide a superior intellectual climate, they can have a substantial effect on the development of measured intelligence. But when the economic status of the biological and adoptive parents is roughly equal, the IQs of adopted children tend to be much more similar to those of the biological parents than the adoptive parents (Scarr & Weinberg, 1978).

Plomin & DeFries's Colorado Adoption Project (begun in 1975) is an ongoing study involving over 200 adopted children. By middle childhood, natural (birth) mothers and their children who were adopted were just as similar as control parents and their children on measures of both verbal and spatial ability. In contrast, the adoptees' scores don't resemble their adoptive parents' at all.

According to Plomin & DeFries (1998), these results are consistent with a growing body of evidence suggesting that the shared family environment doesn't contribute to similarities between family members:

> *'Rather, family resemblance on such measures [verbal and spatial ability] seems to be controlled almost entirely by genetics, and environmental factors often end up making family members different, not the same'.*

(See Chapter 50 for a more detailed discussion of shared and non-shared environments.)

Environmental influences

While not denying the role of genetic factors, those who believe that the environment influences IQ identify a whole range of (pre- and postnatal) environmental factors.

Prenatal environmental influences

Prenatal non-genetic factors account for the largest proportion of biologically caused learning difficulties and lowered IQ. Known prenatal *teratogens* include certain infections (e.g. maternal rubella), toxic chemicals in the mother's body (e.g. drugs like heroin, cocaine and alcohol: see Box 40.6, page 584), radiation and pollutants. Other toxins are produced by the mother's own faulty metabolism, or as a result of incompatibility between the rhesus factors in the mother's blood and that of her developing foetus (Frude, 1998).

Anxiety has also been found to lead to low birth-weight babies (due to impaired blood flow to the uterus: Teixeira, 1999). In turn, low birth-weight is associated with neurological impairment, lower IQ and greater problems in school (e.g. Hack *et al*., 1994).

Postnatal environmental influences

Other studies, however, suggest that periodic or chronic subnutrition can adversely affect cognitive development in its own right. For example, when children in developing countries are given high-quality nutritional supplements in infancy and early childhood, their later IQ and vocabulary scores are higher than those of non-supplemented children (Pollitt & Gorman, 1994). (See also Chapter 40, pages 583–584.)

Environmental enrichment studies

Skeels (1966) followed up a group of children removed from orphanages into more stimulating environments 20 years earlier (Skeels & Dye, 1939). Most of those raised by foster mothers showed significant improvements in their IQs, whereas those raised in the orphanage had dropped out of high school, or were still institutionalised or not self-supporting. Other studies of children raised in orphanages have also shown that environmental enrichment can have beneficial effects. The Rutter *et al*. (1998) study of Romanian orphans is a striking example.

Hunt (1961) and Bloom (1964) argued that intelligence isn't a fixed attribute but depends on, and can be increased by, experience. This led to President Johnson, as part of his 'war against poverty', initiating a number of *intervention programmes*, based on the assumption that intelligence could be increased through special training. The first of these was *Operation Headstart* (1965).

Operation Headstart was an ambitious compensatory programme designed to give culturally disadvantaged preschool children enriched opportunities in early life. Operation

Headstart started as an eight-week summer programme, and shortly afterwards became a full year's preschool project. In 1967, two additional *Follow Through* programmes were initiated, in an attempt to involve parents and members of the wider community. Early findings indicated that there were significant short-term gains for the children, and this generated much optimism. But when IQ gains did occur, they disappeared within a couple of years, and the children's educational improvement was minimal.

An evaluation of early intervention studies

Given that the Milwaukee project was one of the most ambitious preschool programmes ever attempted, it raises the fundamental question of whether there can be any lasting benefits unless early intervention radically alters the whole context of family and other social and school relationships. Once the programme ended, all the adversities associated with poor social conditions and poor schooling provided an antidote to the earlier intervention (Clarke & Clarke, 2000).

Hunt (1969) argued that Headstart was inappropriate to the children's needs, and didn't provide them with the skills they'd failed to develop at home during their first four years (and which are developed by most middle-class children). Also, it emphasised IQ changes as an outcome measure in

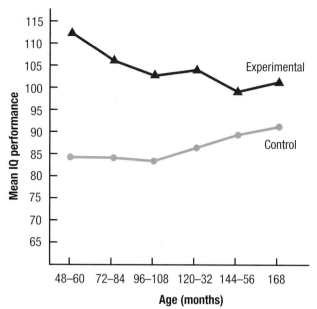

Figure 41.5 *IQ performance with increasing age of severely disadvantaged children participating in a broad-ranging intensive intervention programme in the preschool years (data from Garber, 1988 and taken from Rutter & Rutter, 1992)*

evaluating its effectiveness. Critics have argued that measures which reflect social competence, adaptability and emotional health are much better criteria of success (Weinberg, 1989). According to Bee (2000), because children aren't randomly allocated to Headstart or non-Headstart, interpreting the differences becomes very difficult.

However, the criticisms were apparently premature, and several reviews looking at Headstart's long-term effects have concluded that the programme has brought about lasting changes in children's cognitive abilities, with the greatest gains being shown by children with the lowest initial IQs. There's also a *sleeper effect* at work; that is, the impact of intervention programmes is *cumulative* (Collins, 1983).

Box 41.6 | **The longer-term effects of Headstart and other intervention programmes**

Compared with non-participants, children enrolled in intervention programmes:

- will usually show gains of about ten IQ points. These gains occur while the programme's running, but then fade and disappear within the early years of elementary (primary) school (Zigler & Styfco, 1993);
- are less likely to be placed in special education/remedial classes, are slightly less likely to repeat a grade and slightly more likely to graduate from high school (Darlington, 1991; Haskins, 1989);
- tend to score higher on tests of reading, language and maths, with this 'achievement gap' widening between the ages of six and 14 (Collins, 1983);
- show better school adjustment than their peers (Zigler & Styfco, 1993);
- are more likely to want to succeed academically (Collins, 1983).

According to Bee (2000), although enrolled children don't necessarily test much higher than non-enrolled children, they function better in school. When some kind of supportive

intervention continues into the early years of elementary school, and when the school is of a reasonable quality, the beneficial effects on school peformance are even more evident (e.g. as in the *Abcedarian Project*: Ramey & Ramey, 1992).

Howe (1997, 1998) believes that it would be inconceivable if the improvements in IQ produced by intervention programmes *didn't* fade. In the case of Headstart schemes, for example, the urban environments where they've been set up have often involved squalor, addiction, violence, unemployment, poor housing and inadequate parenting. Together, these negative influences work to restrict a child's opportunities to practise and maintain recently acquired mental skills. This makes it highly likely that they'll fade (see Key Study 41.2).

For Howe, evidence of fading simply confirms that intelligence is changeable. Similarly, even if the vast majority of intervention studies had failed to raise children's IQs at all, this wouldn't be conclusive evidence that intelligence was fixed. Before 1972, the total amount of time a child would have spent in a Headstart programme was 180 hours. This rose to 720 hours after 1972. But when compared with real-life exposure to language of children from different social class backgrounds, 720 hours represents a rather modest intervention:

> '*Regarded in that light, the finding that educational intervention programmes … have nevertheless yielded large … IQ gains would appear to provide rather conclusive evidence that IQ scores are highly changeable'*. (Howe, 1998)

Computers have great educational value, especially perhaps for the highly inquisitive pre-schooler

Hothousing

Ask yourself …

- Do you think it's possible or, indeed, desirable to speed up children's development deliberately?

Some psychologists believe that, while accelerated progress can occur in some areas, other skills (such as language) are essentially preprogrammed and not much affected by early experience (Howe, 1995; see Chapter 19).

Parents determined to make their child into a genius or prodigy can pressurise it with their high expectations, and by sending it to an organisation established to serve 'gifted children'. Moreover, there's no convincing evidence that such organisations are actually effective (Llewellyn-Smith, 1996). Also, children who experience intensive hothousing regimes may miss other experiences which, while not necessarily 'educational', are important for healthy development (Howe, 1995). A child who successfully completes a mathematics degree before the age of 14 has clearly developed a useful skill. But s/he might not have developed important social skills (such as the ability to make friends), because of an inability to join in 'normal' children's conversations (see Chapter 40).

Box 41.7   Dimensions of family interaction affecting cognitive development

According to Bee (2000), how infants and young children are treated can make a real difference to their cognitive development, regardless of whether they come from poor working-class or middle-class families. These differences in early experience have been the focus of most of the research into environmental effects on IQ.

Bee identifies several dimensions of family interaction or stimulation which seem to make a difference. Parents of higher-IQ children, or whose IQs show an increase over time, tend to:

- provide interesting and complex physical environments, including play materials that are appropriate for the children's ages and developmental levels;
- be emotionally responsive and involved with the children: smiling when the children smile, answering their questions, and generally responding to their cues;
- talk to the children often, using language that's diverse, descriptively rich and accurate;
- operate within the children's *zone of proximal development* (ZPD: see Chapter 34, page 499) during play and interaction;
- avoid excessive restrictiveness, punitiveness or control, providing opportunities for the children to ask questions, as opposed to giving commands;
- expect their children to do well and develop rapidly, especially academically.

A study which is relevant to Bee's second dimension was conducted by Crandell & Hobson (1999), involving 36 middle-class mothers and their three-year-olds. Children of securely attached mothers (based on a version of Main *et al.*'s, 1985, *adult attachment interview:* see Chapter 32) scored 19 points higher on the Stanford–Binet intelligence scale compared with children of insecure mothers. In turn, a mother's attachment type was related to how well synchronised her behaviour was with her child's: the higher-IQ children tended to enjoy more synchronised interactions with their mothers.

The interaction between genetic and environmental factors

Clearly, both genetic and environmental factors can influence IQ. This relates to the first of Sternberg & Grigorenko's (1997)

points (see above, page 600). The second point acknowledges that measured intelligence can be attributed to an *interaction* between genetic and environmental factors. As Weinberg (1989) has noted:

'Genes do not fix behaviour. Rather, they establish a range of possible reactions to the range of possible experiences that environments can provide. Environments can also affect whether the full range of gene reactivity is expressed. Thus, how people behave, or what their measured IQs turn out to be or how quickly they learn, depends on the nature of their environments and on their genetic endowments bestowed at conception'.

How much does each contribute?

To acknowledge that both genetic and environmental factors influence intelligence raises the question: how much does each contribute? Researchers have attempted to determine the *relative* contributions made by genetic and environmental factors. The term *heritability* is used by behaviour geneticists to refer to the mathematical estimate of how much variability in a particular trait is a result of genetic variability (Carlson, 1988). Eye colour, for example, is affected almost entirely by heredity and little, if at all, by environmental factors. As a result, the heritability of eye colour is close to 100 per cent.

Early *heritability estimates* for IQ of 80 per cent (Jensen, 1969) have been revised more recently down to around 50 to 60 per cent (Bouchard & Segal, 1988). However, to say that the heritability of measured intelligence is 50 to 60 per cent *doesn't* mean that 50 to 60 per cent of measured intelligence is determined by genetic factors. This is because heritability estimates apply only to a particular *population* or group of people at a particular time, and *not* to a single individual. So, of the variation in intelligence test scores within a group of people, about 50 to 60 per cent (if Bouchard and Segal's estimate is correct) can be attributed to genetic factors.

However, heritability describes what *is* rather than what *could be* (Pike & Plomin, 1999). If environmental factors within a population change (e.g. educational opportunities), then the relative impact of genes and environment will change. Even for a highly heritable trait such as height, environmental changes could make a large difference. Indeed, the huge increase in height during the twentieth century is almost certainly the result of improved diet (Pike & Plomin, 1999). As far as intelligence is concerned, heritability of 50 per cent means that environmental factors account for as much variance as genes do (Plomin & DeFries, 1998: see Chapter 50).

Box 41.8   Why between-group differences cannot be inferred from within-group differences

Lewontin (1976) asks us to consider ten tomato plants grown in poor soil (see Figure 41.6 below). Their different heights are the result of *genetic* factors. If the same ten plants were grown in fertile soil, differences in height would again be due to genetic factors.

But the difference in the average height of the plants grown in poor and fertile soil is due to the *environmental* differences of the soils. So, even when the heritability of a trait is high within a particular group, differences in that trait *between* groups may have environmental causes (Myers, 1990).

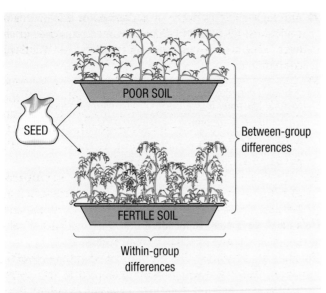

Figure 41.6 *Although we can account for within-group differences in terms of genetic factors, between-group differences may be caused by environmental factors (i.e. poor/fertile soil)*

How do heredity and environment contribute?

If we accept that genetic and environmental factors *interact*, then the focus shifts from how much they contribute to *how* they exert their influence. An example of how this might occur is *cumulative deficit*. Dozens of studies show that children from poor families, or families where the parents are relatively uneducated, have lower IQ scores than those from middle-class families (Bee, 2000). This could reflect either genetic or environmental factors, or both.

However, these social-class differences aren't found before the age of two-and-a-half to three, after which they widen steadily. This suggests that the longer a child lives in poverty, the more negative become the effects on IQ test scores and other measures of cognitive functioning (Duncan, 1993; Smith *et al.*, 1997). Hence, the effects of any genetic differences that may be involved to begin with are *accentuated* by environmental factors, especially poverty. Poverty has a significant effect on children's IQ scores *over and above* what the parents' own genes may have contributed (Bee, 2000). Other examples of *gene–environment interaction* are discussed in Chapter 50.

The race and IQ debate

The false assumption that *between-group differences* can be inferred from *within-group differences* (see Box 41.8) forms a major part of the *hereditarian fallacy* (Gould, 1981). In turn, the fallacy is central to the claim that certain racial groups are genetically inferior to others.

Jensen (1969) published an article called 'How much can we boost IQ and scholastic achievement?', in which he reviewed all the literature which compared black and white IQ scores. The basic finding, that 'On average, Negroes test about one standard deviation (15 IQ points) below the average of the white population in IQ' is not itself a matter of dispute. What's controversial is Jensen's explanation of these findings:

> 'Genetic factors are strongly implicated in the average Negro–white intelligence differences. The preponderance of the evidence is, in my opinion, less consistent with a strictly environmental hypothesis than with a genetic hypothesis ...'. (Jensen, 1969)

Others, including Eysenck (1971) and Herrnstein (1971), agree with Jensen.

Some of the evidence on which Jensen based his genetic theory was the apparent failure of compensatory preschool programmes such as Headstart (see above). Perhaps the most fundamental criticism of Jensen is that he bases his view of black–white differences (between-group differences) on the heritability estimate (of 80:20) derived from studies of the white population (and so is based on within-group differences).

> **Ask yourself ...**
>
> • If we apply the argument in Box 41.8 to Jensen's (1969) claim that 80 per cent of the differences between blacks and whites on IQ tests are due to blacks' 'genetic inferiority', then his claim must be rejected. How else could you explain black–white differences?

Explaining race differences

Environmental factors which could account for such differences include bias in the tests used to measure intelligence. According to Segall *et al.* (1999), IQ tests are biased against those (such as blacks and other minorities) whose cultural backgrounds differ from that of the test's normative sample (whites). This relates to the earlier discussion of *culture-fair/culture-free tests* (see pages 599–600), and to the *emic–etic distinction* (see Chapter 47, and Gross, 1999).

So, it's perfectly possible that individual differences in IQ (within-group differences) are heavily influenced by genetic factors, while group differences (between-group differences) are largely or entirely the result of environmental factors. Jensen's response to this is to appeal to studies in which environmental factors are controlled.

For example, Shuey (1966) compared middle- and working-class blacks and whites and found the same average 15-point difference. But isn't there more to 'environment' than social class (measured largely in terms of occupation and income)? Given their history of slavery and continuing prejudice and discrimination, surely the *experiences* of working-class and middle-class blacks can't be considered equivalent to that of their white counterparts. According to Bodmer (1972):

> 'Measuring the environment only by standard socioeconomic parameters is ... like trying to assess the character of an individual by his height, weight and eye colour'.

Conclusions

By the late 1980s, the size of the black–white IQ gap had significantly narrowed – by about half to seven or eight points (Williams & Ceci. 1997) – although this trend doesn't appear to have continued into the 1990s. Closure of the gap seems to reflect increases in educational spending throughout the twentieth century, increased educational attainment by black parents, and reduction in the size of black families (Price & Crapo, 1999).

As important as these socio-economic factors are, both genetic and environmental factors can influence the development of IQ. These factors are intertwined, not separate. According to Segall *et al.* (1999):

'... *no behaviour is determined solely by culture or solely by biology. The two major classes of behavioural determinants always operate in such an interactive manner that they are difficult to separate. For intelligence, as for any other human characteristic, biological factors provide a broad range of potential and the outer limits or constraints of that potential, but experience has much room to operate within those limits*'.

CHAPTER SUMMARY

■ Piaget's **biological** definition of intelligence sees it as related to **adaptation to the environment**. In contrast with his emphasis on the **qualitative** aspects of intelligence, the **psychometric approach** is concerned with **individual differences** in measured intelligence (**quantitative** aspects).

■ According to Spearman's **two-factor theory**, every intellectual activity involves both a general factor (*g*) and a specific factor (*s*). Burt and Vernon's **hierarchical model** extended this by identifying **major** and **minor group factors**.

■ Thurstone identified seven distinct **primary mental abilities** (PMAs). Instead of ranking individuals in terms of general intelligence, individuals should be profiled on all PMAs. Guilford's '**structure of intellect**' model also totally rejects the idea of *g*.

■ Differences between British and American models reflect different forms of **factor analysis** (FA). Factors have to be given a **psychological interpretation**, which isn't an objective process and involves **reification** of factors once they've been labelled.

■ According to the **information-processing approach**, people differ according to how quickly or efficiently they move through the steps involved in solving problems.

■ Sternberg's information-processing model comprises one part of his **triarchic theory**, namely the **componential subtheory**. The others are the **contextual** and **experiential subtheories**.

■ According to Gardner's **theory of multiple intelligences**, intelligence is a collection of separate, independent but interacting systems. Criteria for distinguishing an independent intelligence include potential isolation by **brain damage**, an identifiable **core operation**, and the existence of **idiots savants** and other exceptional individuals.

■ **Individual tests** of intelligence are used mainly as **diagnostic** tests in clinical settings, while group tests are used mainly for educational **selection** and **research**.

■ Although all tests now use a **deviation IQ**, standard deviations (SDs) can still differ between tests. While intelligence is a **psychological** concept, IQ is a **statistical** concept.

■ Both the **Stanford–Binet** and **Wechsler** scales were originally **standardised** on whites only, and the restandardisation of the former so as to equalise the mean scores of women and men reveals the **ideological significance** of IQ. This adjustment changes the test's **predictive validity** (or **efficiency**).

■ A strictly **culture-free** test is impossible, while a **culture-fair** test is possible but very difficult to construct in practice. The very concept of intelligence is cultural, and no test can assess the meaning that the experience of taking an intelligence test has for the testee.

■ Although several studies show high **stability coefficients** for IQ, these obscure sometimes very large individual differences, and there are many short-term fluctuations.

■ As people's genetic similarity increases, generally so does the similarity of their environments. This can be overcome by comparing the IQs of MZs reared together with those raised separately.

■ MZs reared separately are still more similar than same-sex DZs reared together, suggesting a strong genetic influence. However, studies of separated MZs have been criticised on several important grounds.

■ Further support for the influence of genetic factors comes from **adoption studies**. However, when children from disadvantaged parents are adopted into high socio-economic families, substantial gains in IQ can occur.

■ **Intervention programmes** started with Operation Headstart. Early findings indicated significant short-term IQ gains, but these were short-lived and the educational improvements were minimal. Similar results were reported for the Milwaukee Project.

■ Studies of the longer-term effects have concluded that Headstart has lasting cognitive benefits, especially for those whose IQ scores were initially the lowest. There's also a **sleeper effect**.

■ **Heritability** refers to how much of the variability in a particular trait is due to genetic variability **within** a particular group/population. Even when a trait's heritability is high within a particular group, differences in that trait **between** groups may have environmental causes.

■ One assumption involved in the **hereditarian fallacy** is that heritability estimates based on within-group differences (such as are found in twin studies) can be applied to between-group differences (such as between blacks and whites).

■ Trying to equate the environments of blacks and whites in terms of social class is invalid, and IQ tests are racially biased.

Self-assessment questions

1 Critically assess the claim that intelligence (IQ) tests are a valid method of measuring intelligence.

2 Describe and discuss **two/more** theories of intelligence.

3 Critically consider the role of genetic **and/or** cultural influences on IQ test performance.

Web addresses

http://www.cycad.com/cgi-bin/Upstream/Issues/psychology/IQ/index.html

http://www.netlink.co.uk/users/vess/mensal.html

http://www.apa.org/monitor/may97/twinstud.html

http://www.abacon.com/bee/links/html

http://www.queendom.com.tests.html

Further reading

Howe, M.J.A. (1997) *IQ in Question: The Truth about Intelligence*. London: Sage. An examination of some of the crucial, largely mythical, beliefs regarding IQ and intelligence.

Sternberg, R.J. (1990) *Metaphors of Mind: Conceptions of the Nature of Intelligence*. Cambridge: Cambridge University Press. An extremely wide-ranging discussion of intelligence from a variety of psychological perspectives, as well as anthropology and sociology.

Sternberg, R.J. & Grigorenko, E. (Eds) (1997) *Intelligence, Heredity and Environment*. New York: Cambridge University Press. A collection of academically quite demanding, but rewarding, original articles covering all aspects of the topic.

Chapter 42

Personality

Introduction and overview

However different they may be in other respects, most personality theories share the basic assumption that personality is something that 'belongs' to the individual: 'the appropriate unit of analysis for personality psychology is the person' (Hampson, 1995).

To the extent that each of us 'has' a personality that's stable and relatively permanent, our behaviour will be consistent from one situation to another. An alternative view is that behaviour is largely determined by situational factors and that it will vary considerably across situations. This is referred to as the *trait versus situation* debate or the *consistency controversy*.

Personality theorists differ with respect to whether they're trying to compare individuals in terms of a specified number of traits or dimensions common to everyone (the *nomothetic approach*), or trying to identify individuals' unique characteristics and qualities (the *idiographic approach*).

According to the *constructionist approach* (Hampson, 1995), personality is constructed, in the course of social interaction, from three elements: a person's *self-presentation* (the actor: see Chapter 22), the *perception of this presentation* by an audience (the observer: see Chapter 22), and *self-awareness* (the self-observer: see Chapter 33). To this extent, personality isn't merely an abstraction which helps to explain people's behaviour (it's not something people 'have'), but it's to do with how we relate to other people and deal with the world in general.

Classifying theories of personality

> ### Ask yourself ...
>
> - Try to define 'personality'.

If we wish to identify some of the dimensions along which various theories differ, then a useful definition of personality would be:

> '... *those relatively stable and enduring aspects of individuals which distinguish them from other people, making them unique, but which at the same time allow people to be compared with each other*'.

This definition brings into focus two key questions:

- Does personality consist of *permanent traits* or characteristics?
- Is the study of personality the study of *unique individuals*, or is it aimed at comparing individuals and discovering the factors which constitute personality *in general*?

Psychologists who answer 'yes' to the first question, and who are interested in personality in general, belong to the *psychometric tradition* (*type* and *trait theorists*). The major figures are

Eysenck and Cattell. They use personality questionnaires and the results from these are analysed using *factor analysis* (FA): see Chapter 41. In trying to establish factors in terms of which everyone can be compared, they adopt a *nomothetic approach*.

Psychologists who believe in the uniqueness of every individual adopt the *idiographic approach*, but beyond this it's difficult to say what else they have in common. For example, they may or may not see personality as permanent, or may differ as to how much or what kinds of change in personality are possible. But they are concerned with the whole person, whereas psychometric theorists want to rank or order individuals with respect to particular aspects of personality. Idiographic theorists include Allport, Kelly (whose *personal construct theory* isn't so much a theory of personality as a total psychology), and the *humanistic* psychologists Maslow (whose hierarchy of needs was discussed in Chapter 5) and Rogers. Humanistic theories share a concern for the characteristics which make us distinctively human, including our experience of ourselves as people (see Chapter 2).

The *psychodynamic* theories of Freud and Jung are clearly idiographic: they're based on case studies of patients in the clinical context of psychotherapy and aren't concerned with measuring personality. However, they're also concerned with the *nature* of personality and try to account for individual differences. For example, Jung was the first to distinguish between introverts and extroverts, which Eysenck later measured in his personality questionnaires. These theorists all allow for the possibility of personality change, primarily through psychotherapy.

Nomothetic versus idiographic approaches

> ### Ask yourself ...
>
> - Do you believe that every person is unique, or are we all basically the same, differing only in the degree to which we display certain tendencies or characteristics?

Table 42.1 *A classification of personality theories*

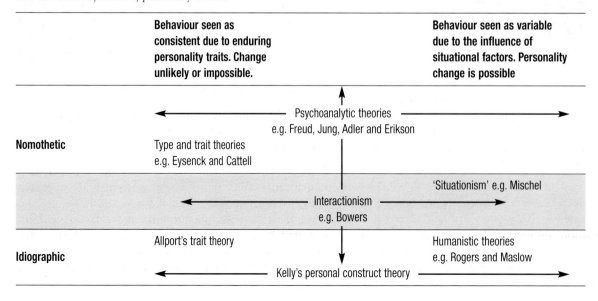

According to Kluckhohn & Murray (1953):

> 'Every man is in certain respects like all other men, like some other men and like no other men'.

What we have in common with *all* other human beings is the subject of experimental or 'general' psychology, which includes the study of cognitive and physiological processes and learning. Much of developmental and social psychology too are concerned with discovering 'universal norms' which apply equally to all individuals.

What we have in common with *some* other human beings is examined through the study of *individual differences*. Personality differences represent one kind of *group norm*, others being age, gender, ethnic and cultural background and intelligence. It's the study of 'how and how much a particular individual is similar to or differs from others' (Shackleton & Fletcher, 1984) which constitutes the factor-analytic/psychometric approach. As we've seen, this is also a nomothetic approach.

Finally, what we have in common with *no* other human being are the qualities that make us unique. This is the idiographic approach, which attempts to discover *individual/idiosyncratic norms*.

Allport's trait theory

Allport (1961) defined personality as:

> 'The dynamic organisation within the individual of those psychophysical systems that determine his characteristic behaviour and thoughts'.

Gordon W. Allport (1897–1967) (UPI/Bettmann Archive)

Allport & Odbert (1936) found over 18,000 terms describing personal characteristics and, even after omitting evaluative terms and transient states, there remained 4–5,000. Allport believed that this large number of 'trait words' could be divided into just two basic kinds:

- *common traits:* basic modes of adjustment applicable to all members of a particular cultural, ethnic or linguistic background. For example, since we must all interact in a competitive world, we must each develop our own most suitable level of aggression. Each of us can be placed somewhere along a scale of aggressiveness. Common traits are the subject matter of the nomothetic approach.

- *Individual traits:* a unique set of personal dispositions and ways of organising the world, based on life experiences. They're not dimensions which can be applied to all people. They cannot be measured by a standardised test, and can be discovered only by the careful and detailed study of individuals. Individual traits are the subject matter of the idiographic approach. Individual traits can take one of three forms: *cardinal, central* or *secondary*.

Box 42.1   **Three kinds of individual traits**

- **Cardinal traits:** These are so all-pervading that they dictate and direct almost all of an individual's behaviour, such as someone who's consumed by greed, ambition or lust. However, such traits are quite rare, and most people don't have one predominant trait.
- **Central traits:** These are the basic building blocks which make up the core of personality and which constitute the individual's characteristic ways of dealing with the world (e.g. honest, loving, happy-go-lucky). A surprisingly small number of these is usually sufficient to capture the essence of a person.
- **Secondary traits:** These are less consistent and influential than central traits, and refer to tastes, preferences, political persuasions, reactions to particular situations and so on.

Individual traits are peculiar (idiosyncratic) to each person in at least three senses:

- A trait that's central for one person may only be secondary for another person, and irrelevant for a third. What makes a trait central or secondary is determined not by what it is, but by how often and how strongly it influences the person's behaviour (Carver & Scheier, 1992).
- Some traits are possessed by only one person. Indeed, there may be as many separate traits as there are people.
- Even if two different people are given, for convenience, the same descriptive label (such as 'helpful'), it may not be used in the same way to describe both individuals and, to that extent, it's *not* the same trait. For Allport (1961), since personality dispositions reflect the subtle variations that distinguish a particular individual from all others, they must often be described at length e.g. 'Little Susan has a peculiar anxious helpfulness all her own', instead of by a single label (helpful).

This makes it very difficult to compare people:

> '[Any given individual] is a unique creation of the forces of nature. There was never a person just like him and there never will be again ...'.

Comparing people in terms of a specified number of traits or dimensions is precisely what the nomothetic approach involves: traits have the same psychological meaning for everyone, so that people only differ in the extent to which each trait is present. For example, Eysenck maintains that everyone will score somewhere on the extroversion (E) scale, and the difference between individuals is one of degree only (i.e. a *quantitative difference*).

For Allport (1961), people can only be compared in terms of common traits, which at best only provide a rough approximation to any particular personality. The nomothetic approach can only portray human personality in an oversimplified way: even the traits that people apparently share with one another will always differ from individual to individual.

Does the wholly unique individual exist?

Holt (1967) argues that the idiographic–nomothetic issue is based on a *false dichotomy*. All description involves some degree of generalisation, so that to imagine we can describe an individual in terms which make no reference to any other individual is a fallacy. To describe an individual, we must already have a concept of a person (a *schema* about people in general). As Kirby & Radford (1976) argue, a 'truly unique individual would be incomprehensible, in fact not recognisable as an individual'.

Disagreement between Allport and nomothetic theorists isn't so much to do with whether or not they believe in the idea of uniqueness, but rather how uniqueness is defined. Eysenck, for example, sees uniqueness as reflecting a particular combination of levels on trait dimensions, with the dimensions themselves being the same for all:

> 'To the scientist, the unique individual is simply the point of intersection between a number of quantitative variables'. (Eysenck, 1953, quoted in Carver & Scheier, 1992)

For Allport, this is a definition of uniqueness based on *common traits* and is a contradiction in terms: only *individual traits* capture people's individuality.

According to Krahé (1992), the idiographic claim that there are unique traits that apply to only one individual is undoubtedly false, if taken literally. Traits are defined as differential constructs that refer to a person's position on a trait dimension relative to that of other people. But Krahé also believes that, at the opposite extreme, the nomothetic view of traits as explanatory constructs which apply to everyone is equally misguided.

Rather like Eysenck, Kline (1981b) believes that the existence of personality scales or questionnaires is compatible with the notion of uniqueness. In any particular sample, individuals will have very different profiles across a range of scales, but this doesn't mean they don't share certain characteristics with other members of the sample.

Is a science of unique individuals possible?

> *Ask yourself ...*
>
> - Is either the idiographic or nomothetic approach more compatible with the aims of science in general, and psychology in particular (as discussed in Chapter 3)?

Increasingly, psychologists are coming to believe that the idiographic and nomothetic approaches, far from being opposed and mutually exclusive, are complementary and interdependent (Krahé, 1992). Even Allport didn't reject the nomothetic approach completely. For example, when discussing the nature of psychology as a science, Allport (1960) says that:

> 'Science aims to achieve powers of understanding, prediction and control above the level of unaided common sense. From this point of view it becomes apparent that only by taking adequate account of the individual's total pattern of life can we achieve the aims of science. Knowledge of general laws ... quantitative assessments and correlational procedures are all helpful: but with this conceptual (nomothetic) knowledge must be blended a shrewd diagnosis of trends within an individual ... Unless such idiographic (particular) knowledge is fused with nomothetic (universal) knowledge, we shall not achieve the aims of science, however closely we imitate the methods of the natural and mathematical sciences'.

Jaccard & Dittus (1990, cited in Krahé, 1992) argue that it's untrue that a strictly idiographic approach is directly opposed to the identification and development of universal laws of human behaviour. The idiographic researcher, like the nomothetic, is interested in explaining behaviour, and to do this both seek a general theoretical framework that specifies the constructs that should be focused upon and the types of relationships expected among these concepts. The essential difference between the two approaches is that one applies the framework to a single person, while the other applies it to people in general. However, they share the same scientific aim. (For a more detailed discussion of the whole idiographic–nomothetic issue, see Gross, 1995.)

Traits vs situations

Most definitions of traits focus on their stability and permanency, which implies that an individual's behaviour is consistent over time and from one situation to another. Indeed, Baron & Byrne (1991) define personality as:

> 'The combination of those relatively enduring traits which influence behaviour in a predictable way in a variety of situations'.

> *Ask yourself ...*
>
> - According to the *fundamental attribution error* (FAE) and *actor–observer effect* AOE), how are we likely to judge the *consistency* of our own behaviour and others' respectively? (See Chapter 23.)

The FAE involves attributing other people's behaviour primarily to their dispositional qualities (including personality traits). We're therefore likely to regard their behaviour as more consistent (and hence more predictable) than our own, which we see primarily as a response to the situation (AOE).

Seeing behaviour as being caused primarily by personality traits (the *trait approach*) is usually opposed to what has become known as *situationism* (Mischel, 1968) – the view that behaviour is largely determined by situational factors.

The consistency controversy

Mischel (1968), a social learning theorist (see Chapter 35), sparked the 'consistency controversy' by declaring that he could find very little evidence of *intraindividual* or *cross-situation* consistency. In other words, the same person tends to behave inconsistently in different situations – the opposite of what personality theorists would predict. He argued that the average correlation between different behavioural measures designed to tap the same personality trait was typically between 0.1 and 0.2, often lower, while correlations between scores on personality tests designed to measure a given trait and measures of behaviour in various situations meant to tap the same trait rarely exceeded 0.3.

Box 42.2   Situationism

Mischel took these very low correlations to indicate the importance of the situation in determining behaviour (**situationism**). If people behave inconsistently, the usefulness of the trait concept disappears and we're left only with situational influences to account for the inconsistency of individual behaviour. The same person behaves differently in different situations, because different situations require different behaviour and are associated with different kinds of reinforcements. So, from this (rather extreme) situationist perspective, intraindividual **inconsistency** is exactly what we'd expect!

Tony Blair's pro-CND past is seen by some as incompatible with his current New Labour policies

---

Ask yourself ...

• Intuitively, does there seem to be anything wrong with situationism, at least in its extreme form? Surely different people behave differently even within the same situation and, conversely, aren't we recognisably the same person from one situation to another?

Evidence against situationism

Eysenck & Eysenck (1980) and Kline (1983) cite a number of studies which demonstrate consistency between scores on questionnaires and rating scales on the one hand, and behaviour on the other (average correlations of around 0.8). In addition, several writers have argued that to regard behaviour

as being caused *either* by situational factors *or* by personality traits is an oversimplification of a complex issue. Bowers (1973), Endler (1975) and Pervin & Lewis (1978) all advocate an *interactionist* position, which stresses the mutual influence of situational and dispositional variables:

$$\text{Behaviour} = \text{Person} \times \text{Situation}$$

For example, Bowers reviewed 11 studies covering a wide range of behaviour, including aggression in young boys, anxiety in students and resistance to temptation in children. He concluded that 13 per cent of the variance in participants' behaviour was due to *person variables*, ten per cent to situational variables, and 20 per cent to an interaction between the two. While this kind of research cannot determine whether personality or situation is more important, the results nevertheless clearly favour the interactionist position (Argyle, 1983).

The psychological situation

Mischel (1973) has moved towards a more interactionist position. But, in preference to traits, he talks about *social cognitive units* (or *person variables*), which incorporate a person's cognition, and the effect this has on his/her actions which are then assessed in relation to the situations in which they occur. They focus on what the person *does* (cognitively, affectively and behaviourally) as opposed to what the person *has* in terms of traits, and include cognitive activities, encoding strategies, expectancies, values, preferences and goals.

Mischel believes that the same situation can have different *meanings* for different individuals, depending on past learning experiences. This determines how we select, evaluate and interpret stimuli and, in turn, how particular stimuli affect our behaviour. It follows that situational factors on their own cannot account adequately for human behaviour because they don't exist objectively, independent of the actor. Based on a study of children's ability to resist temptation when looking at attractive sweets, Mischel (1973) concluded that:

> 'The results clearly show that what is in the children's heads – not what is physically in front of them – determines their ability to delay'.

So, the *psychological situation* constitutes a critical determinant of behaviour: the psychological meaning of a situation for the individual (how it's perceived) is a crucial factor in predicting behaviour and accounting for regularities in behaviour across situations (Krahé, 1992). Another sense in which the influence of situations cannot be defined objectively is that personality traits, in particular introversion – extroversion, dictate the choice of situations people expose themselves to (Eysenck & Eysenck, 1985: see Box 42.3, page 615).

Mischel & Shoda (1995, 1998) have developed these ideas into a *cognitive–affective person system* that accounts for both intraindividual consistency and predictable patterns of variability across situations. For example, a person may be shy in small groups but an excellent public speaker. This pattern of behaviour would be cross-situationally inconsistent if viewed in purely trait terms, but if the differences in the psychological situation are taken into account, it becomes meaningful and predictable. Speaking to a large audience doesn't require engaging personally with any one individual, whereas making conversation in small groups does.

Situational factors now represent a *moderating influence* on individual differences. This is a more sophisticated response to Mischel's critique of traits than pure situationism, or even 'mechanistic interactionism', in which behaviour is seen as a function of combined but independent situational and trait factors (Hampson, 1999). Hampson states that contemporary personality psychology isn't so much concerned with consistency as with *coherence*. This acknowledges that people do show cross-situational variability in their behaviour, but that this can be understood when other factors are taken into account.

The psychometric approach

Factor analysis

As we saw in Chapter 41, *factor analysis* (FA) is a statistical technique, based on correlation, which attempts to reduce large amounts of data (such as scores on personality questionnaires) to much smaller amounts. Essentially, the aim is to discover which test items correlate with one another and which don't, and then to identify the resulting correlation clusters (or factors). A fundamental issue is: what's the smallest number of factors which can adequately account for the variance between participants on the measures in question?

Eysenck prefers an *orthogonal* method of FA, which aims to identify a small number of powerful, independent (uncorrelated) factors. Cattell's preference is for an *oblique* method, which aims to identify a larger number of less powerful factors, which aren't independent (they're correlated to some degree).

Since it's possible to carry out a further FA of oblique factors, they're referred to as *first-order factors* and the resultant regrouping of the oblique factors as *second-order factors*. In fact, Cattell has discovered a small number of second-order factors which correspond closely to Eysenck's three major second-order factors (see below). Eysenck's second-order factors are referred to as *types* (what Cattell calls *surface traits*) and Cattell's first-order factors as *traits* (or *source traits*).

Table 42.2 *Differences between Eysenck and Cattell in their preferred method of factor analysis*

	Eysenck	Cattell
Preferred method of FA	Orthogonal	Oblique
Level of analysis	Second order	First order
Description of factors	Types ('surface traits')	Traits ('source traits')

Both Cattell and Eysenck believe that their own methods best reflect the psychological reality of personality, but there's no objective way of establishing that one is right and the other wrong. However, Cattell (1966) and Cattell & Kline (1977) argue that an orthogonal technique prevents the attainment of *simple structure*: each factor will correlate quite highly with a few other factors and very little or not at all with a large number of others. This makes each factor simple to interpret.

Guilford (1959), on the other hand, believes that a set of uncorrelated factors is more simple than a set of oblique or correlated ones (which is why Eysenck opts for an orthogonal technique). However, Kline (1981b) maintains that most factor analysts, in practice, prefer oblique factors.

Eysenck's type theory

What are 'types'?

The term 'type' was formerly used to describe people who belonged either to one group or category or another, so that it was impossible for a particular individual to be considered a member of both. For example, according to the ancient Greek theory of the 'Four Temperaments' or 'Four Humours' (Galen, second century AD), a person was either *choleric* (due to an excess of yellow bile), *sanguine* (due to an excess of blood), *melancholic* (due to an excess of black bile) or *phlegmatic* (due to an excess of phlegm). These four humours are included in the inner circle of Eysenck's diagram below.

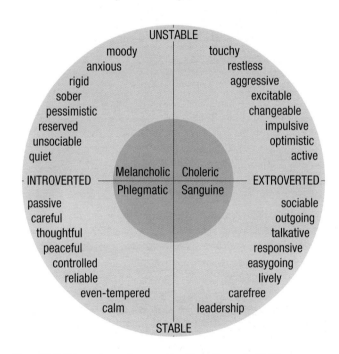

Figure 42.1 *Dimensions of personality (from Eysenck, 1965)*

According to Eysenck (1995), today the term 'type' is either not used at all or reserved for combinations of traits that are found to correlate. For example, extroversion is a type concept based on the observed correlations of sociability, liveliness, activity and so on. The search for a reliable and valid measurement of personality traits is only a first step: the traits we find aren't independent of each other but are correlated in certain patterns that suggest more complex entities that might be called types. But unlike Galen's four humours, Eysenck's types are *personality dimensions*, which represent continuums along which everyone can be placed.

Eysenck's dimensions in fact constitute the highest level of a hierarchy (Cattell's 'surface traits'), with a number of traits at the next level down (Cattell's 'source traits') and below that a set of habitual responses (typical ways of behaving) linked to a particular trait. At the lowest level is a specific response (a response on one particular occasion: see Figure 42.2, page 615).

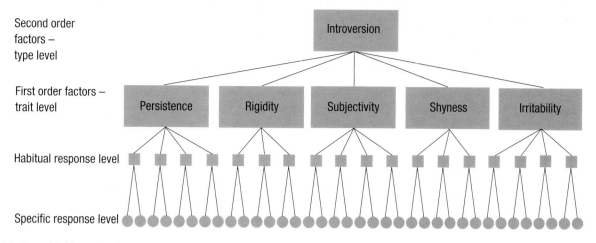

Figure 42.2 *Eysenck's hierarchical model of personality in relation to the introversion dimension (after Eysenck, 1953)*

Extroversion (E), neuroticism (N) and psychoticism (P)

Eysenck (1947) factor-analysed 39 items of personal data (including personality ratings) for each of 700 neurotic soldiers, screening them for brain damage and physical illness. Two orthogonal (uncorrelated) factors emerged: *introversion–extroversion* (E) and *neuroticism (emotionality)–stability* (N). These two dimensions are assumed to be normally distributed, so that most people will score somewhere in the middle of the scale, and very few at either extreme. 'Typical' introverts and extroverts are 'idealised extremes' (or ideal types).

The **typical introvert** is a quiet, retiring sort of person, introspective, fond of books rather than people; he's reserved and distant except to intimate friends. He tends to plan ahead, 'looks before he leaps' and distrusts the impulse of the moment. He doesn't like excitement, takes matters of everyday life with proper seriousness, and likes a well-ordered mode of life. He keeps his feelings under close control, seldom behaves in an aggressive manner, and doesn't lose his temper easily. He's reliable, somewhat pessimistic, and places great importance on ethical standards.

The **typical extrovert** is sociable, likes parties, has many friends, needs to have people to talk to, and doesn't like reading or studying by himself. He craves excitement, takes chances, often sticks his neck out, acts on the spur of the moment, and is generally an impulsive individual. He likes practical jokes, always has a ready answer, and generally likes change; he's carefree, easy-going, optimistic and likes to 'laugh and be merry'. He prefers to keep moving and doing things, tends to be aggressive and lose his temper quickly; altogether his feelings aren't kept under tight control and he's not always a reliable person.

As regards neuroticism, the typical high N scorer could be described as:

'... an anxious, worrying individual, moody and frequently depressed; he is likely to sleep badly and to suffer from various psychosomatic disorders. He is overly emotional, reacting too strongly to all sorts of stimuli and finds it difficult to get back on an even keel after each emotionally arousing experience'. (Eysenck, 1965)

By contrast, the typical low N scorer (stable) individual:

'... tends to respond emotionally only slowly and generally weakly and to return to baseline quickly after emotional arousal; he is usually calm, even-tempered, controlled and unworried'. (Eysenck, 1965)

Since the original 1947 study, the existence of E and N has been supported by further research involving literally thousands of participants. Exhaustive research in many parts of the world, by many different researchers, has confirmed the existence of E and N, as well as a third dimension, *psychoticism* (P) (Eysenck & Eysenck, 1985). This was originally uncovered in a 1952 study of psychiatric patients, but is less well established than the other two dimensions. Just as E and N are unrelated to each other, so they are both unrelated to P. According to Eysenck & Eysenck (1975):

'A high [P] scorer ... may be described as being solitary, not caring for people; he is often troublesome, not fitting in anywhere. He may be cruel and inhumane, lacking in feelings and empathy, and altogether insensitive. He is hostile to others, even his own kith and kin, and aggressive, even to loved ones. He has a liking for odd and unusual things, and a disregard for danger; he likes to make fools of other people, and to upset them'.

Unlike E and N, P isn't normally distributed – both normals and neurotics score low on P. Eysenck also believes that P overlaps with other psychiatric labels, in particular 'schizoid', 'psychopathic' and 'behaviour disorders'. The difference between normals and psychotics, as well as that between normals and neurotics, is one of degree only. However, Eysenck (1995) stresses that N and P only represent a *predisposition* ('diathesis'), unlike neurosis and psychosis which are actual psychological disorders. Under extreme stress, however, the predisposition can become a psychiatric illness (Claridge, 1985: see Chapter 44).

Personality questionnaires

The *Maudsley personality inventory* (MPI, 1959) measured both E and N. The *Eysenck personality inventory* (EPI) added a lie scale, which measures a person's tendency to give socially desirable answers (Eysenck & Eysenck, 1964: see Chapter 24). Finally, the *Eysenck personality questionnaire* (EPQ) added a P scale (Eysenck & Eysenck, 1975). There are also junior versions of these questionnaires for use with nine-year-olds and over.

The scales all comprise items of a 'yes/no' variety. They're intended primarily as research tools (as opposed to diagnostic tools for use in clinical settings) and, as such, they're generally regarded as acceptable, reliable and valid (Kline, 1981a; Shackleton & Fletcher, 1984). The main exception is the P scale, which Eysenck himself admits is psychometrically inferior to other scales.

A major way in which Eysenck has attempted to validate his scales is through *criterion analysis*. This involves giving the questionnaires to groups of individuals who are known to differ on the dimensions in question. For example, although the EPQ isn't meant to diagnose neurosis, we'd expect diagnosed neurotics to score very high on N compared with non-neurotics – and generally this is found to be the case.

The biological basis of personality

Eysenck attempts to explain personality differences in terms of the kinds of nervous system that individuals inherit:

■ As far as E is concerned, what's crucial is the balance between excitation and inhibition processes in the central nervous system (CNS), specifically the ascending reticular activating system (ARAS: see Chapter 4). Its main function is to maintain an optimum level of alertness or 'arousal'. It does this by enhancing the incoming sensory data to the cortex through the excitation of neural impulses, or by 'dampening them down' through inhibition.

Extroverts have a 'strong nervous system'. Their ARAS is biased towards the inhibition of impulses, with the effect of reducing the intensity of any sensory stimulation reaching the cortex (they're chronically *under-aroused*). For introverts, the bias is in the opposite direction: the intensity of any sensory stimulation reaching the cortex is increased (they're chronically *over-aroused*).

■ As far as N is concerned, it's the *reactivity* (or *lability*) of the sympathetic branch of the autonomic nervous system (ANS) that's crucial, in particular, differences in the limbic system, which controls the ANS (see Chapter 4, pages 60–61). The person who scores high on N has an ANS which reacts particularly strongly and quickly to stressful situations compared with less emotional or more stable individuals.

■ The biological basis of P is much more uncertain, but Eysenck (1980) has suggested that it may be related to levels of the male hormone, *androgen*, and/or other hormones (see Chapter 36).

Box 42.4 Evidence relating to biological differences between introverts and extroverts

- According to Eysenck (1967), extroverts become 'psychically fatigued' more easily (e.g. become bored more easily and persevere less) than introverts. According to Kline (1983), on long and tedious jobs extroverts should start better than introverts, do worse in the middle and then improve again towards the end, while introverts should work much more steadily throughout. These hypotheses were supported by Eysenck (1967, 1971) and Harkins & Green (1975), who found that introverts do better at vigilance tasks, which require prolonged periods of concentration.
- In real life, extroverts change jobs and sexual partners more frequently than introverts, are more likely to divorce, show less brand loyalty in shopping behaviour and move house more often (Eysenck, 1965; Eysenck & Eysenck, 1985).
- According to Eysenck (1970), introverts have lower pain thresholds and extroverts are more susceptible to the adverse effects of sensory deprivation. For example, one demonstration of the 'stimulus hunger' of extroverts is their willingness to go to great lengths to obtain a 'reward' of loud music or bright lights which introverts work hard to avoid.
- Claridge (1967) couldn't find a simple relationship between E and physiological arousal. Instead, there seems to be a complex interconnection between arousal and the individual's position on E and N.
- According to Hampson (1995), evidence for the role of the ARAS and arousal mechanisms in E is inconclusive, but great advances have been made since the mid-1980s in understanding the genetics of personality. As a result of large-scale twin, adoption and family resemblance studies, it's now widely concluded that about 50 per cent of the variation in self-report personality measures may be due to heredity (Loehlin *et al.*, 1988) (see Chapters 41 and 44).

Drugs and personality

Ask yourself ...

- In terms of introverted and extroverted behaviour, what should be the effect of (a) stimulant and (b) depressant drugs (see Chapter 8)?
- Who should be easier to sedate – introverts or extroverts?

According to Wilson (1976), we'd expect introverts to be more difficult to sedate using a drug such as sodium amytal because they're supposed to be more aroused. Claridge & Herrington (1963) in fact found that introverted neurotics (*dysthymics*) were more difficult to sedate than extroverted neurotics (*hysterics*), the latter being more easily sedated than normal participants. For the same reasons, regardless of an individual's normal position on the scale, *stimulant* drugs should shift behaviour in the direction of introversion, while *depressant* drugs (such as alcohol) should have the opposite effect.

Anxiolytic (anti-anxiety) drugs should increase emotional stability, *adrenergic* drugs (those which mimic the effects of adrenaline) should decrease it, *hallucinogens* should increase

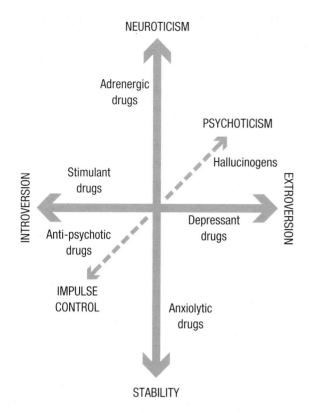

NEUROTICISM

Adrenergic
drugs

PSYCHOTICISM

Hallucinogens

Stimulant
drugs

INTROVERSION — EXTROVERSION

Anti-psychotic
drugs

Depressant
drugs

IMPULSE
CONTROL

Anxiolytic
drugs

STABILITY

Figure 42.3 *Drug addiction and personality (Eysenck, 1983). Source Eysenck, H.J. (1995) 'Trait theories of personality'. In S.E. Hampson & A.M. Coleman (Eds) Individual Differences and Personality. London, Longman*

psychotic behaviour and *anti-psychotic* drugs (narcoleptics) should decrease it (see Chapter 45). According to Eysenck (1995), empirical studies have, on the whole, supported these causal hypotheses. (See Figure 42.3, above.)

Personality and conditionability

From a strictly psychological point of view, the importance of the biological aspects of Eysenck's theory is how they're related to individual differences in *conditionability*. Because extroverts require a stronger stimulus to make an impact compared with the more easily stimulated introvert, and because the learning of S–R connections is best achieved by a strong and rapid build-up of excitation in the nervous system (which is characteristic of introverts), introverts should be more easily conditioned than extroverts.

Despite Eysenck's strong claims to the contrary, the evidence is equivocal: only about one half of the studies he reviewed in 1967 support his predictions. Eysenck seems to regard conditionability as a unitary trait, that is, if introverts are easily conditioned to one kind of stimulus, they'll also condition easily to a range of other stimuli. But such a general trait has never been demonstrated, and the experimental evidence mainly involves three conditioned responses – the GSR (galvanic skin response), the eye blink and simple verbal conditioning. According to Kline (1983), until such a general dimension is discovered, this part of the theory remains weak and, in addition, extrapolation from laboratory studies to real-life situations is dangerous. A way of testing this part of the theory in the real world is through applying it to criminality (see Chapter 46).

An evaluation of Eysenck's theory

■ One of its most serious weaknesses is the failure to produce any convincing evidence that introverts condition more easily than extroverts. Conditionability is a vital part of the overall theory, because it points 'inwards' towards the biological (including genetic) basis of personality and 'outwards' towards the socialisation experiences of different individuals (behaviour always being the product of an interaction between the nervous system and the environment).

■ Heim (1970) has criticised the EPI (and, by implication, the EPQ) because of its forced-choice ('yes/no') format. She argues that a few, simple yes/no questions can hardly be expected to do justice to the complexities of human personality, and she has criticised the lie scale for its lack of subtlety (see Chapter 3).

■ Validation of the scales has involved the use of *criterion groups*, such as groups of neurotics, who tend to score at the extreme ends of the scale. But can we assume that the scale is 'valid' for the majority of people who lie somewhere in the middle? This needs to be empirically tested rather than simply assumed.

■ Shackleton & Fletcher (1984) have highlighted the vast amount of research Eysenck's theory has generated:

'Whilst the theory as it now stands is not adequate, some aspects of it, maybe even most, may well survive the test of time'.

Indeed, E and N seem to have stood the test of time, in that they're both included in the 'big five' personality factors (see below).

Cattell's trait theory

As we've already seen, Cattell's factors are first-order, oblique, source traits, which he believed to be the fundamental dimensions of personality, the underlying roots or causes of clusters of behaviour (surface traits). Whereas surface traits may correspond to commonsense ways of describing behaviour and may sometimes be measured by simple observation, they're actually the result of interactions among the source traits. Valid explanations of behaviour must concentrate on source traits as the structural factors which determine personality.

Cattell identified three sources of data relevant to personality: L-data (L for 'life'), Q-data (Q for 'questionnaire') and T-data (T for 'tests').

Raymond B. Cattell (born 1905)

■ *L-data* refer to ratings by observers. Cattell regarded these as the best source, but he also recognised that they're notoriously difficult to obtain; great skill and time are needed to make accurate ratings.

■ *Q-data* refer to scores on personality questionnaires. His 16 factors (source traits) are measured by the widely used *Cattell 16 PF* (personality factor) *questionnaire*, which is intended for use with adults. As shown in Table 42.3 opposite, the first 12 factors are found in L-data and Q-data, while the last four (Q1–Q4) are based on Q-data only. There are versions of the 16 PF designed for children as young as four.

Cattell's scales aren't exclusively of the 'yes/no' variety (there may be three choices – yes/occasionally/no). Although intended mainly as a research instrument, the 16PF has been used in clinical work, as well as occupational selection and assessment. However, its validity as a diagnostic tool in a clinical setting has been seriously questioned.

■ *T-data* refer to objective tests specially devised to measure personality. For example, the objective–analytic (O–A) test battery measures, amongst other things, GSR, reaction time, body sway and suggestibility. T-data are objective, primarily in the sense that the purpose of the test is concealed from the participant.

Differences between Cattell and Eysenck

According to Cattell, some overlap between first-order (oblique) factors is to be expected. For example, an intelligent person (B-factor) is also likely to be shrewd and worldly (N-factor). Cattell also carried out a second-order FA of his 16 primary factors, which produced a number of surface traits. The two most important were *exvia–invia* and *anxiety*. These seem to correspond to Eysenck's E and N respectively (Figure 42.4, page 619). Others included *radicalism* (aggressive and independent), *tendermindedness* (sensitivity, frustration and emotionality) and *superego* (conscientious, conforming and preserving).

Cattell believes that there's a fundamental discontinuity between normals and, say, schizophrenics; that is, there's a *qualitative* difference between them (and not merely a *quantitative* one, as Eysenck maintains). For example, Q-data used with psychiatric patients produce 12 factors which discriminate psychotics as a group (e.g. paranoia, suicidal disgust, schizophrenia and high general psychosis); they score highly on these factors compared with normals. A second-order FA of Q-data from psychiatric patients yields three factors, one of which resembles Eysenck's P.

Cattell, much more than Eysenck, acknowledges how behaviour can fluctuate in response to situational factors. His definition of personality as that which 'determines behaviour in a defined situation and a defined mood' (Cattell, 1965) implies that behaviour is never totally determined by source traits. Although personality factors remain fairly stable over time, they constitute only one kind of variable influencing overt behaviour. Others include (a) *mood and state factors* (e.g. depression, arousal, anxiety, fatigue and intoxication); and (b) *motivational factors* (innate, biological drives and culturally acquired drives).

Table 42.3 *The 16 source traits measured by Cattell's 16 PF questionnaire (based on Cattell, 1965)*

Description	Name of trait	Description
Warm-hearted, outgoing, easygoing, sociable	**A** Affectia vs Sizia	Reserved, cool, detached, aloof
Abstract thinker, intellectual interests [high score]	**B** Intelligence	Concrete thinker, practically minded [low score]
Emotionally stable, calm, mature	**C** Ego strength vs Dissatisfied emotionality	Emotionally unstable, easily upset, immature
Assertive, aggressive, dominant, competitive	**E** Dominance vs Submissiveness	Submissive, modest, mild, accommodating
Happy-go-lucky, enthusiastic	**F** Surgency vs Desurgency	Pessimistic, subdued, sober, cautious, serious
Persevering, conscientious, moralistic [high score]	**G** Superego strength	Expedient, disregard for rules, law unto oneself [low score]
Adventurous, gregarious, uninhibited	**H** Parmia vs Threctia	Shy, timid, diffident, inhibited
Tender-minded, sensitive, gentle, clinging	**I** Premsia vs Harria	Tough-minded, self-reliant, realistic, no-nonsense
Suspicious, jealous, self-opinionated	**L** Protension vs Alexia	Trusting, adaptable, easy to get along with
Unconventional, imaginative, bohemian	**M** Autia vs Praxernia	Conformist, conventional, influenced by external realities
Shrewd, calculating, worldly	**N** Shrewdness vs Naivety	Simple, unpretentious, lacking insight
Insecure, worrying, self-reproaching [high score]	**O** Guilt proneness	Self-assured, confident, complacent, spirited [low score]
Liberal, free-thinking	**Q1** Radicalism vs Conservatism	Conservative, traditional
Preference for own decisions	**Q2** Self-sufficiency vs Group dependence	Group dependent, a follower
Controlled, socially precise [high score]	**Q3** Self-sentiment Strength	Undisciplined, careless of social rules [low score]
Relaxed, composed [high score]	**Q4** Ergic tension	Overwrought, tense, frustrated [low score]

Single- and multi-trait theories, and the 'big five'

Eysenck's and Cattell's theories are examples of *multi-trait theories*, but an influential *single-trait* theory is Rotter's (1966) *locus of control* (see Chapter 12). For a single-trait theory to be useful, it must identify a trait that determines a wide range of important behaviours (Hampson, 1995).

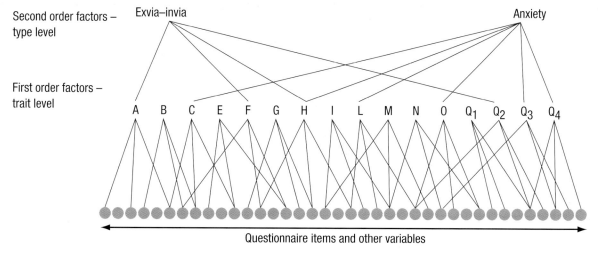

Figure 42.4 *The hierarchical organisation of personality resulting from a second-order analysis of the first-order 'source traits' (after Cattell, 1965)*

Multi-trait theories try to include all aspects of personality, and assume that individual differences can be described in terms of a particular profile on the same set of traits. According to Krahé (1992), despite its troubled history, 'the trait concept presents itself in remarkably good shape at the beginning of the '90s'. Since the 1980s, there's been a vast amount of research to discover a small but comprehensive number of basic trait dimensions which can account for the structure of personality and individual differences.

There's a growing consensus that personality can be adequately described by five broad constructs or factors, commonly referred to as the 'big five' (McCrae & Costa, 1989; Digman, 1990; Goldberg, 1993).

Table 42.4 *The 'big five' personality factors*

	Desirable traits	Undesirable traits
(I) Extroversion (corresponds to Eysenck's construct)	Outgoing, sociable, assertive	Introverted, reserved, passive
(II) Agreeableness	Kind, trusting, warm	Hostile, selfish, cold
(III) Conscientiousness	Organised, thorough, tidy	Careless, unreliable, sloppy
(IV) Emotional stability (or Neuroticism) (corresponds to Eysenck's construct).	Calm, even-tempered, imperturbable	Moody, temperamental, narrow.
(V) Intellect/openness to experience	Imaginative, intelligent, creative	Shallow, unsophisticated, imperceptive

While different versions of the 'big five' have been proposed, the five-factor model has provided a unified framework for trait research (Costa & McCrae, 1993). Although Eysenck (1991) continues to argue for a 'Giant Three' (E, N and P – a combination of factors II and III in the five-factor model), the differences seem quite trivial now compared with, say, the disagreement between Eysenck and Cattell's 16 source traits (Hampson, 1995). Nevertheless, there remains the fundamental problem of the meaning of the factors that are extracted

(Kline, 1993; Krahé, 1992). Ultimately, personality factors, however many, must be identified from their correlations with external criteria (Kline, 1993). According to Eysenck (1995), the system is still too new (except for E and N) for there to have been enough research to allow a proper evaluation. But Hampson (1999) believes that, at the end of the 1990s, the 'big five' remain pre-eminent as a description of normal personality.

Box 42.5 The stability of personality across the lifespan

According to Roberts & Delvecchio (2000), the consistency of personality increases from childhood to young adulthood, increases further still until about 30, then stabilises between 50 and 70. This was confirmed by Caspi (2000), who followed up a group of children from age three up to 21. Three-year-olds regarded as uncontrollable grew up to be impulsive, unreliable and antisocial, while those regarded as inhibited were more likely to grow up to be more depressed, unassertive and to have fewer sources of social support.

However, McCrae *et al.* (2000) suggest that some traits are more fluid that others. An international team of researchers looked at changes in the 'big five' between the ages of 14 and 30, in samples from Germany, Great Britain, Spain, the Czech Republic and Turkey. N, E and Openness to experience decreased over this period, but Agreeableness and Conscientiousness increased.

Kelly's personal construct theory

Kelly's personal construct theory (PCT) is an idiographic approach, stressing the uniqueness of each individual. It's also a *phenomenological approach*, that is, a view of the world through a person's own eyes and not an observer's interpretation or analysis.

Man the scientist

According to Kelly, we're all scientists in the sense that we put our own interpretation (or theories) on the world of events, and from these personal theories we produce hypotheses (predictions about future events). Every time we act, we're putting our hypotheses to the test and, in this sense, behaviour is the independent variable – it is the experiment. Depending on the outcome, our hypotheses are either validated or not, and this will determine the nature of our subsequent behavioural experiments (Fransella, 1981).

George A. Kelly (1905–1966)

Constructive alternativism

Although a real world of physical objects and events does exist, no one individual has the privilege of 'knowing' it: all we can do is place our personal constructs upon it. The better our constructs 'fit' the world generally, the better will be our control over our own, personal world. According to Kelly (1955), there's no way of getting 'behind' our interpretation of the world to check if it matches what the world is really like. All we have are our own interpretations, and so we necessarily see the world 'through goggles', which cannot be removed. However, these goggles or constructs *aren't* fixed once and for all. The person as scientist is constantly engaged in testing, checking, modifying and revising his or her unique set of constructs.

The repertory grid technique

Box 42.6 **Constructing a repertory grid (rep grid) (based on Kelly, 1955)**

The basic method involves the following steps:

- Write a list of the most important people in your life (*elements*).
- Choose three of these elements.
- Ask yourself, in what ways are two of these alike and different from the third?
  The descriptions given (e.g. 'My mother and girlfriend are affectionate, my father is not') constitute a *construct*, which is expressed in a *bipolar* way ('affectionate–not affectionate').
- This construct is applied to all the remaining elements. Remember, constructs are bipolar opposites (either affectionate or not affectionate).
- Then another set of three elements is selected and the whole process is repeated. It continues until either you've produced all the constructs you can (which is usually no more than 25 with one set of elements), or until a sufficient number has been produced as judged by the investigator.

All this information can be collated in the form of a grid, with the elements across the top and the constructs down the side, and a tick or cross indicating which pole of the construct is applicable (for example, a tick indicates 'affectionate' and a cross indicates 'not affectionate': see Table 42.5).

The *repertory grid test* ('rep grid') is an attempt to help individuals discover the fundamental constructs they use for perceiving and relating to others. It's used as a major research instrument, is very flexible, and can be used in different ways. It can be factor-analysed, which often reveals that many constructs overlap (they mean more or less the same thing). Probably between three and six major constructs cover most people's construct system.

The rep grid can be used nomothetically, as Bannister and Fransella have done with thought-disordered schizophrenics. Their *grid test of thought disorder* (Bannister & Fransella, 1967) contains standardised elements and constructs (supplied by the researcher), and the test has been standardised on large num-

Table 42.5 *Example of a rep grid (see Box 42.6)*

Constructs	Elements							
	Mother	**Father**	**Brother**	**Sister**	**Boyfriend**	**Girlfriend**	**Psychology lecturer**	**etc.**
Affectionate (✓) Non-affectionate (✗)	✓	✗	✗	✓	✗	✓	✓	
Intelligent (✓) Unintelligent (✗)								
Sense of humour (✓) No sense of humour (✗)								
etc.								

bers of similar patients so that an individual score can be compared with group norms. However, this is probably rather far removed from how Kelly intended the technique to be used.

The rep grid has also been used to study how patients participating in group psychotherapy change their perception of each other (and themselves) during the period of therapy: the group members themselves are the elements and a number of constructs are supplied (Fransella, 1970). Fransella (1972) has used this method extensively with people being treated for severe stuttering.

However, its uses aren't confined to clinical situations. Elements needn't be people at all, but can be occupations, religions, cars and so on. Shackleton & Fletcher (1984) argue that the rep grid stands on its own as a technique – you don't have to believe in Kelly's PCT in order to use it.

An evaluation of PCT

Bannister & Fransella (1980) and Fransella (1981) point out that PCT is deliberately stated in very abstract terms to avoid the limitations of a particular time and culture. It's an attempt to redefine psychology as a psychology of people and is 'content free'. As we noted earlier, PCT isn't so much a personality theory, more a total psychology. Kelly isn't concerned with separate subdivisions of psychology as dealt with in most textbooks. For example, the traditional concept of motivation can be dispensed with. We don't need concepts like drives, needs or psychic energy (see Chapter 9) to explain what makes people 'get up and go' – man is a form of motion and a basic assumption about life is that 'it goes on': 'It isn't that something makes you go on, the going on is the thing itself' (Kelly, 1962).

However, he implicitly assumes that we all seek a sense of order and predictability in our dealings with the external world – the over-riding goal of anticipating the future represents a basic form of motivation. We achieve this through behaving much like a research scientist. 'The scientist's ultimate aim is to predict and control ...' (see Chapter 3).

Various aspects of emotion are dealt with in terms of how an individual's construct system is organised and how it changes. For example, 'anxiety' is the awareness that what you're confronted with isn't within the framework of your existing construct system – you don't know how to construe it. For some, this approach is far too cognitive and rational, leaving the subjective experience (the 'gut feeling') that we call anxiety out of the picture (see Chapter 44).

Peck & Whitlow (1975) believe that Kelly trivialises important aspects of behaviour, including learning, emotion and motivation, and neglects situational influences on behaviour. PCT appears to place the person in an 'empty world'. However, they conclude by saying that:

'Personal construct theory constitutes a brave and imaginative attempt to create a comprehensive, cognitive, theory of personality'.

Humanistic theories

Humanistic theories (and Kelly's PCT) have their philosophical roots in *phenomenology* and *existentialism*, and some would say they're more 'philosophical' than 'psychological'. They're concerned with characteristics that are distinctively and uniquely human, in particular experience, uniqueness, meaning, freedom and choice. We have first-hand experience of ourselves as people, and Rogers' theory in particular is centred around the *self-concept*.

What Rogers and Maslow (see Chapter 9) have in common is their positive evaluation of human nature, a belief in the individual's potential for personal growth (*self-actualisation*). But while Maslow's theory is commonly referred to as a 'psychology of being' (self-actualisation is an end in itself and lies at the peak of his hierarchy of needs), Rogers' is a 'psychology of becoming' (it's the *process* of becoming a 'fully functioning person' that's of major importance and interest).

Rogers' self theory

As we saw in Chapter 2, Rogers (like Maslow) rejected the deterministic approach of psychoanalytic theory (see below) and behaviourism. Instead, humanistic theorists see behaviour as a response to the individual's perception/interpretation of external stimuli. As no-one else can know how we perceive, we're the best experts on understanding our own behaviour.

Rogers also sees human nature in a very positive and optimistic light:

'There is no beast in man; there is only man in man'.

The self

The *self* is an 'organised, consistent set of perceptions and beliefs about oneself'. It includes a person's awareness of 'what they are and what they can do' and influences both their perception of the world and their behaviour. We evaluate every experience in terms of self, and most human behaviour can be understood as an attempt to maintain consistency between our self-image and our actions (see Chapter 33).

However, this consistency isn't always achieved and our self-image (and related self-esteem) may differ quite radically from our actual behaviour and from how others see us. For example, a person may be highly successful and respected by others and yet regard him or herself as a failure! This illustrates what Rogers calls *incongruence*. Because incongruent experiences, feelings, actions and so on conflict with our (conscious) self-image (and because we prefer to act and feel in ways that are consistent with our self-image), they can be threatening. Consequently, we may deny them access to awareness (they may remain *unsymbolised*) through actual denial, distortion or blocking.

These *defence mechanisms* prevent the self from growing and changing, and widen the gulf between our self-image and reality (our actual behaviour or our true feelings). As the self-image becomes more and more unrealistic, so the incongruent person becomes more and more confused, vulnerable, dissatisfied and, eventually, seriously maladjusted. By contrast, the self-image of the congruent person is flexible and changes realistically as new experiences occur. When your self-image matches what you really think and feel and do, you're in the best position to self-actualise.

Box 42.7 **Two examples of a rigid and inflexible self-image**

Suppose that a young man's self-image requires that every woman he meets will find him irresistible and fall head-over-heels in love with him. He meets a woman whom he finds attractive, but she shows no interest in him (this represents *incongruence* between his self-image and his experience). How does he deal with the threat this represents for him? He might say, 'She's just playing hard to get' or 'She has no taste' or 'She must be crazy – thank goodness I found out before she fell hopelessly in love with me'.

At the opposite extreme is a young man who believes he's totally unattractive to women. If an attractive woman shows an interest in him, this will produce incongruence and hence threat, and he might deal with it by rationalising: 'She's just feeling sorry for me', or he might deliberately do something to sabotage the relationship and so remove the threat.

Development of the self-concept

Many of Rogers' therapeutic clients seemed to have learned during childhood that in order to obtain the love and acceptance of significant others (particularly parents), they have to feel and act in distorted or dishonest ways (*conditional positive regard*).

To maintain conditional positive regard, we develop *conditions of worth* (those conditions under which positive regard will be forthcoming) which become internalised. We perceive and are aware of those experiences that coincide with the conditions of worth, but distort or deny those that don't. This denial and distortion lead to a distinction between the *organism* (the whole of our possible experience, everything we do, feel and think) and the *self* (the recognised, accepted and acknowledged part of our experience). Ideally, the two would coincide, but for most of us they don't.

Corresponding to the need for positive regard is the need for *positive self-regard* (thinking of ourselves as good, lovable and worthy). To experience positive self-regard, our behaviour and experience must match our conditions of worth – but this can produce incongruence through the denial of our true thoughts and feelings. Since the need for positive regard and positive self-regard is so strong, these conditions of worth can supersede the values associated with self-actualisation. Consequently, we come to behave, think and feel in particular ways because others want us to, and many adult adjustment problems are bound up with an attempt to live by other people's standards instead of one's own.

The therapist in Rogers' client-centred therapy provides the client with *unconditional positive regard*. The therapist creates an atmosphere of total acceptance and non-judgemental support, regardless of what the client says or does, so that the client in turn comes to accept certain feelings and thoughts as his/her own, instead of denying, distorting and disowning them. Finally, positive self-regard is no longer dependent upon conditions of worth (see Chapter 45).

Psychodynamic theories

As we saw in Chapter 2, *psychodynamic* implies the active forces within the personality that motivate behaviour, in other words, the inner causes of behaviour, in particular the unconscious conflict between the id, ego and superego. Freud's was the first of this kind of theory and all psychodynamic theories stem, more or less directly, from Freud's psychoanalytic theory.

Ask yourself ...

- What do you already know about Freud's ideas? Psychoanalytic theory applies to motivation (Chapter 9), forgetting (Chapter 21), prejudice (Chapter 25), aggression (Chapter 29), and many aspects of development (see Chapters 35–38).

Freud's psychoanalytic theory

Freud believed that conflict within the personality is unavoidable, because the ego is being 'pulled' in two opposing directions by the id and the superego. The ego's solution comes in the form of *three* forms of compromise, namely *dreams*, *neurotic symptoms* and *defence mechanisms*.

Dreams

'A dream is a [disguised] fulfilment of a [suppressed or repressed] wish' (Freud, 1900; 1976a). It represents a compromise between forbidden urges and their repression. What we dream about and are conscious of upon waking is called the *manifest content*, while the meaning of the dream (the wish being fulfilled) is the *latent content*. The manifest content is often the product of the weaving together of certain fragments from that day's events (*day residues*) and the forbidden wish. It often appears disjointed, fragmentary and sometimes bizarre and nonsensical. *Dream interpretation* (a major technique involved in psychoanalysis) aims to make sense of the manifest content by 'translating' it into the underlying wish fulfilment.

CASE STUDY 42.1

An Oedipal dream reported by one of Freud's patients (from *The Interpretation of Dreams*, 1900; 1976a)

A 'typical example of a disguised Oedipus dream' is that of a man who dreamt that he had a secret liaison with a lady whom someone else wanted to marry. He was worried in case this other man might discover the liaison and the proposed marriage come to nothing. He, therefore, behaved in a very affectionate way to the man. He embraced him and kissed him.

Ask yourself ...

- How do you think Freud interpreted this dream?

Dreams come into being through *dream work* (controlled by the ego), which converts the underlying (latent) wish into the manifest content. It involves displacement, condensation and concrete representation:

- *Displacement* refers to the substitution of the real target of the dreamer's feelings by a person or object that then becomes the target for those feelings. The substitute is symbolically (unconsciously) linked to the true target, as in the example of one of Freud's patients who dreamed of strangling a little white dog which represented her sister-in-law, who had a very pale complexion and whom the dreamer had previously called 'a dog who bites' (Stevens, 1995). This is a crucial part of the *disguise* that conceals from the dreamer the true meaning of the dream.

  The sister-in-law/dog example shows how certain symbols will be peculiar to individual dreamers, but many dream symbols have a conventional meaning within a culture, particularly those that represent the penis (e.g. snakes, trees, trains, daggers, umbrellas), the vagina (e.g. small boxes, cupboards, ships and other vessels) and sexual intercourse (e.g. climbing ladders or stairs and entering tunnels).

- *Condensation* involves the same part of the manifest content representing different parts of the latent wish. For example, a king may represent not only the dreamer's father, but also authority figures or very wealthy and powerful people in general. So, more than one dream idea may be 'condensed' into a single manifest image.

The Nightmare *(Fuseli)*

- *Concrete representation* refers to the expression of an abstract idea in a very concrete way. For example, the concrete image of a king could represent the abstract notions of authority, power or wealth. This is sometimes called 'dramatisation' and is related to the use of symbols.

The importance of dream work is that it permits the expression of a repressed (and, therefore, forbidden and disturbing) wish, and at the same time allows the dreamer to go on sleeping. The compromise represented by dreaming takes the form of disguising the true nature of the dream (i.e. wish fulfilment), for if it were not disguised, the dreamer would wake up in a state of shock and distress. Hence, 'the dream is the guardian of sleep'.

Dream interpretation is also what Freud called the 'royal road to the unconscious': *reversing* the dream work and unravelling the wish from the manifest content can provide invaluable information about the unconscious mind in general, and about the dreamer's in particular.

Neurotic symptoms

Like dreams, neurotic symptoms are essentially the expression of a repressed wish (or memory) that's become disguised in very similar ways to dream work. The symptom may in some way symbolise the wish it's linked to, as in a patient who suffered from hysterical hand-twitching, which was related to her memories of being badly frightened while playing the piano (*displacement*). This same patient's hand-twitching was traced to two other memories (receiving a disciplinary strapping on the hands as a schoolgirl, and being forced to massage the back of a detested uncle: *condensation*). The symptom is often something 'physical', while the underlying cause is something 'mental' (*concrete representation*).

Most of Freud's patients were suffering from 'hysterical conversion neurosis' (or 'somatoform' disorders in current terminology): emotional energy is converted into a bodily form (such as paralysis, blindness, deafness, headaches and a whole variety of other 'physical' symptoms: see Chapter 44). The symptom deflects the patient's attention (and that of others) away from the repressed material: it's acceptable to consult a doctor about the symptom, but not about the unconscious wish. Freud & Breuer (1895) called these underlying wishes and memories *pathogenic* ('disease-producing') ideas, and Freud later concluded that all symptoms are caused by pathogenic ideas of a sexual nature (although not every dream).

Defence mechanisms

The ego defence mechanisms are, by definition, unconscious, and this is partly what makes them effective. They involve some degree of self-deception which, in turn, is related to their distortion of 'reality' (both internal and external). This prevents us from being overwhelmed by temporary threats or traumas, and can provide 'breathing space' in which to come to terms with conflict or find alternative ways of coping. As short-term measures, they're advantageous, necessary and 'normal', but as long-term solutions to life's problems they're usually regarded as unhealthy and undesirable (see Table 12.2, page 179). Many of the defences described in Table 42.5, page 624 (and others) were originally proposed or implied by Freud and later elaborated by his daughter, Anna (1936).

Levels of consciousness

According to Freud, thoughts, memories and other psychic material could operate at one of three levels: *conscious*, *preconscious* and *unconscious*. What we're consciously aware of at any one time represents the mere tip of an iceberg – most of our thoughts and ideas are either not accessible at that moment (preconscious) or are totally inaccessible (unconscious), unless special techniques such as free association and dream interpretation are used (see Chapter 45).

The ego represents the conscious part of the mind, together with some aspects of the superego (namely, those moral rules and values we're able to express in words: see Chapter 35). The unconscious comprises: (a) id impulses; (b) all repressed material; (c) the unconscious part of the ego (the part

Table 42.5 *Some major ego defence mechanisms*

Name of defence mechanism	Description	Example(s)
Repression	Forcing a threatening or distressing memory/feeling/wish out of consciousness and making it unconscious	A five-year-old child repressing its incestuous desire for the opposite-sex parent (see Chapter 35)
Displacement	Transferring our feelings from their true target onto a harmless, substitute target ('kicking the cat')	Frustration caused by problems at work expressed as domestic violence (see Chapter 29). Phobias (see Chapter 44)
Denial	Failing/refusing to acknowledge/perceive some aspect of reality	Refusing to accept that you have a serious illness, or that your partner is going off you (see Chapter 39)
Rationalisation	Finding an acceptable excuse (a 'cover story') for some really quite unacceptable behaviour/situation	'Being cruel to be kind'. 'I only did it because I love you'. (see Chapter 24)
Reaction-formation	Consciously feeling/thinking the opposite of your true (unconscious) feelings/thoughts	Being considerate/polite to someone you strongly dislike – even going out of your way to be nice to them
Sublimation	A form of displacement in which a (socially positive) substitute activity is found for expressing some unacceptable impulse	Playing sport to redirect aggressive urges (see Chapter 29)
Identification	Incorporating/introjecting another person into one's own personality – making them part of oneself	Identification with the aggressor (boys)/anaclitic identification (girls) (see Chapter 35)
Projection	Displacing your own unacceptable feelings/characteristics onto someone else	'I hate you' becomes (through reversal of subject/object) 'you hate me' (see Chapter 44)
Regression	Reverting to behaviour characteristic of an earlier stage of development	Losing your temper, comfort eating, sleeping more when depressed (see Chapter 44)
Isolation	Separating contradictory thoughts/feelings into 'logic-tight' compartments	Talking about some traumatic experience without any display of emotion – or even giggling about it (see Chapter 44)

involved in dream work, neurotic symptoms and defence mechanisms); and (d) part of the superego (for example, the vague feelings of guilt or shame which are difficult to account for). Freud depicted the unconscious as a dynamic force and not a mere 'dustbin' for all those thoughts and feelings which are too weak to force themselves into awareness. This is best illustrated by the process of repression (Thomas, 1985).

Psychic determinism

Much of our behaviour (and our thoughts and feelings) has *multiple* causes, some conscious, some unconscious. Freud called this *overdetermination*. By definition, we only know about the conscious causes, which we normally take to be the reasons for our actions. But if some of the causes are also unconscious, then the reasons we give for our behaviour can never tell the whole story (and the unconscious causes may be the more important). This means that we don't know ourselves as well as we'd like or as well as we think we do ('*irrational man*').

Overdetermination is one aspect of *psychic determinism*, the view that all behaviour is purposive or goal-directed and that everything we do, think and feel has a cause. It follows that so-called 'accidents' (things which 'just happen') do have a cause after all – and the cause may actually turn out to be the 'victim'. For instance, the 'accident-prone' person isn't an unfortunate victim of circumstances but is unconsciously bringing about the accidents – perhaps in an attempt to punish him/herself in some way. While not denying the existence of events which lie beyond people's control, Freud believed that it's more common for an 'accident' to be the consequence of our own, unconscious wishes and motives.

The psychopathology of everyday life

Another important way in which our everyday behaviour provides us with glimpses of the unconscious is what Freud called *Fehlleistungen* ('faulty achievements': Bettelheim, 1985), the all too common slips of the tongue ('Freudian slips'), slips of the pen, forgetting things (including words and people's names), leaving things behind and 'accidents'. Freud's translators used the term *parapraxes*.

Ask yourself ...

- Try and think of some examples of Freudian slips that have happened to you or that you've witnessed.
- How can you explain them?

Box 42.8 | **Some examples of parapraxes ('Freudian slips') (from *The Psychopathology of Everyday Life*, 1901, 1976b)**

1 A patient consulted me for the first time and from her history it became apparent that the cause of her nervousness was largely an unhappy married life. Without any encouragement she went into details about her marital troubles. She had not lived with her husband for about six months and she saw him last at the theatre, when she saw the play *Officer 606*. I called her attention to the mistake and she immediately corrected herself, saying that she meant to say *Officer 666* (the name of a recent popular play). I decided to find out the reason for the mistake, and as the patient came to me for analytic treatment, I discovered that the immediate cause of the rupture between herself and her husband was the disease which is treated by '606' [i.e. venereal disease].

2   I was to give a lecture to a woman. Her husband, upon whose request this was done, stood behind the door listening. At the end of my sermonising, which had made a visible impression, I said, 'Goodbye, sir!'. To the experienced person I thus betrayed the fact that the words were directed towards the husband; that I had spoken to oblige him.

3   While writing a prescription for a woman who was especially weighted down by the financial burden of the treatment, I was interested to hear her say suddenly, 'Please do not give me big bills, because I cannot swallow them'. Of course she meant to say pills.

An evaluation of Freud's theory
Empirical studies

There have been literally thousands of empirical studies of various aspects of Freud's theory. Two of the major reviews of this research have been carried out by Kline (1972, 1982) and Fisher & Greenberg (1977). They conclude that psychoanalytic theory cannot be accepted or rejected as a total package. As Fisher and Greenberg say:

'It is a complex structure consisting of many parts, some of which should be accepted, others rejected and the rest at least partially reshaped'.

Three basic kinds of study have been carried out:

- *validational* studies, which try to test directly various parts of the theory, mainly in the laboratory;
- those which try to investigate some of the underlying mechanisms involved, but which aren't direct tests of the theory (again mainly laboratory experiments);
- studies of the effects of psychoanalysis as therapy (see Chapter 45).

Fonagy (1981) asks whether it's conceivable that laboratory studies could 're-create' the clinical concepts and experience that Freud describes and, therefore, questions the usefulness of validational studies. He also queries the relevance of studies of treatment effectiveness as a way of 'testing' the theory – they're equivalent to the relevance of the effectiveness of aspirin to a theory of headaches!

Many validational studies have been concerned with Freud's theory of personality types, especially the oral and anal (see Chapter 35) and defence mechanisms, including repression (see Chapters 12 and 21). Fonagy (1981) believes that most relevant are studies which go beyond trying to replicate clinical phenomena, and which instead attempt to identify basic mechanisms or processes which may underlie unconscious phenomena.

Is the theory scientific?

Popper's criticism that Freud's theory is *unfalsifiable* and, therefore, unscientific, was discussed in Chapter 2 (see pages 17–18). However, it would be a serious mistake to regard reaction formation (the example used by Popper) as typifying Freudian theory, and the sheer volume of research suggests that Freudian theory cannot be dismissed as lightly as Popper and Eysenck would like on the grounds of it being 'unscientific'. According to Kline (1989), the view adopted by almost all experimental psychologists involved in the study of Freud's theory is that it should be seen as a collection of hypotheses. As Fisher & Greenberg (1977) argue, some of these hypotheses will turn out to be true, others false, when put to Popper's test of falsifiability.

Some hypotheses are undoubtedly more critical to the overall theory than others. For example, if no evidence could be found for repression, this would alter considerably the nature of psychoanalysis. But if it was found that the Oedipus complex was more pronounced in small as opposed to large families, the theory wouldn't be radically affected (Kline, 1989).

How valid is the case study method?

Although Freud often states or implies that his theories have been derived from his observations of his patients, he left us no direct record of the original data. He deliberately made no notes during therapy sessions, since this might interfere with the therapeutic relationship (see Chapter 45). He wrote them up several hours later, so that his case studies are *reconstructions* of what happened. He also reported on very few patients; only twelve are reported in depth and in some of these the details are incomplete (Stevens, 1995).

The case study relies on the reconstruction of childhood events, and, as used by Freud, is generally considered to be the least scientific of all empirical methods used by psychologists. It's open to many types of distortion and uncontrolled influences.

Box 42.9   The limitations of the case study method

Fisher & Greenberg (1977) point out Freud's tendency to select or emphasise material which supported particular interpretations. This form of bias is blatantly obvious in the case of Little Hans. As we saw in Chapter 35, Freud (1909) recognised that there was a problem of objectivity, because it was Little Hans' father actually conducting the psychoanalysis. But he goes on to say that this case was no different from the analysis of adults:

'For a psychoanalysis is not an impartial scientific investigation, but a therapeutic measure. Its essence is not to prove anything but merely to alter something'.

Freud seems to be digging a very large hole for himself! According to Storr (1987), the majority of psychoanalytic hypotheses are based on observations made in the course of psychoanalytic treatment, which cannot be regarded as a scientific procedure. Such observations are inevitably contaminated by the subjective experience and prejudice of the observer, however detached he/she tries to be, and so they cannot be regarded in the same light as observations made during, say, a chemistry or physics experiment.

How representative were Freud's patients?

One of the standard criticisms made of Freud's database is that his patients were mainly wealthy, middle-class Jewish females, living in Vienna at the turn of the century, making them highly unrepresentative of the population to whom his theories were generalised. If these people were also neurotic, how can we be sure that what Freud discovered about them is true of normal individuals? However, Freud regarded neurosis as *continuous* with normal behaviour, that is, neurotics are suffering only from more extreme versions of problems experienced by all of us (see Chapter 43).

More serious, perhaps, is the criticism that Freud studied only adults (with the very dubious exception of Little Hans), and yet he put forward a theory of personality *development*. How many steps removed were his data from his theory? According to Thomas (1985), the analyst interprets, through his or her theoretical 'lens', ostensibly symbolic material derived from the reported dreams, memories and so on of neurotics about apparent experiences stemming from their childhood one or more decades earlier. However, this in itself doesn't invalidate the theory, it merely makes the study of children all the more necessary.

Reification

Several writers have criticised terms like the id, ego and super-ego as bad metaphors. They don't correspond to any aspect of psychology or neurophysiology, and they encourage *reification*, that is, treating metaphorical terms as if they were 'things' or entities.

However, Bettelheim (1985) points out that much of Freud's terminology was mistranslated, and this has led to a misrepresentation of those parts of his theory. For example, Freud used the German terms *das Es* ('the it'), *das Ich* ('the I') and *das Über-Ich* ('the over-I'), which were intended to capture how the individual relates to different aspects of the self. The Latin terms *id*, *ego* and *superego* tend to depersonalise these, and give the impression that there are three separate 'selves' which we all possess! The Latin words (chosen by his American translator to give them greater scientific credibility) turn the concepts into cold technical terms which arouse no personal associations. Whereas 'the I' can only be studied from the inside (through introspection), the 'ego' can be studied from the outside (as behaviour). In translation, Freud's 'soul' became scientific psychology's 'psyche' or 'personality' (Bettelheim, 1985).

The nature of Freudian theory

As noted in Chapter 2, Freud's theory has great *hermeneutic strength*, that is, it provides methods and concepts which enable us to interpret and 'unpack' underlying meanings (Stevens, 1995). Stevens claims that:

> 'Although Freud wanted to create a nomothetic theory ... in effect he finished up with a set of "hermeneutic tools" – concepts and techniques that help us to interpret underlying meanings ...'.

There's no doubting the tremendous impact that Freud has had, both within psychology and outside. The *fertility* of psychoanalytic theory, in terms of the debate, research and theorising it has generated, makes it one of the richest in the whole of psychology. According to Kline (1989):

> ' ... Freudian theory is still a powerful intellectual force. To claim that it is dead, as do many experimental psychologists – at least by implication for it rarely influences their thinking – must be either ignorance or wishful thinking'.

Jung's analytical psychology

Structure of the personality and levels of consciousness

For Jung, the person is seen as a whole almost from the moment of birth. Personality isn't acquired piece by piece (the 'jigsaw' concept) through learning and experience, but is already there. So, instead of striving to achieve wholeness, our aim in life is to maintain it and to prevent the splitting or dissociation of the psyche into separate and conflicting parts. Jung saw the role of therapy as helping the patient recover this lost wholeness, and to strengthen the psyche so as to resist future dissociation.

The psyche comprises three major, interacting levels:

1 consciousness;
2 the personal unconscious;
3 the collective unconscious.

The distinction between 2 and 3 represents one of the major differences between Jung and Freud.

Consciousness

This is the only part of the mind known directly by the individual. It appears early in life through the operation of four basic functions: *thinking, feeling, sensing* and *intuiting*. In addition, there are two *attitudes* which determine the orientation of the conscious mind: *extroversion* and *introversion*.

Box 42.10 Extroversion and introversion, Jungian style

- The **extrovert's** libido (Jung's term for psychic energy as a whole or life-force) is directed **outwards** towards the objective world of physical objects, people, customs and conventions, social institutions and so on. Extroverts are preoccupied with **interpersonal** relationships, and are generally more active and outgoing.

- The **introvert's** libido is directed **inwards** towards the subjective world of thoughts and feelings, and they're preoccupied with **intrapersonal** matters, are introspective and withdrawn, and may be seen by others as aloof, reserved and antisocial.

Jung believed that a person is predominantly one or the other throughout life, although there may be occasional inconsistencies in different situations. So, for Jung, extroversion–introversion represents a **typology** of the 'either/or' variety while, as we saw above, Eysenck's 'adoption' of Jung's terms took the form of personality **dimensions**, with extreme extroversion at one end and extreme introversion at the other.

The development of consciousness is also the beginning of *individuation*, the process by which a person becomes psychologically 'in-dividual' (a separate, indivisible unit or whole). From this process emerges the ego, which refers to how the conscious mind is organised. It plays the essential role of 'gatekeeper to consciousness', selecting important sensations, feelings, ideas and so on, and allowing them through into conscious awareness (much as Freud's preconscious does). This prevents us from becoming overwhelmed by the mass of stimulation going on around (and inside) us. The ego provides a sense of identity and continuity, and is the central core of the personality.

The personal unconscious

The Freudian unconscious, in Jung's terms, is predominantly 'personal', that is, composed of the individual's particular and unique experiences which have been made unconscious through repression. For Jung, repressed material represents only one kind of unconscious content. The *personal unconscious* also includes things we've forgotten, as well as all those things we think of as being 'stored in memory' and which could become accessible by conscious recall (see Chapter 17).

Associated groups of feelings, thoughts and memories may cluster together to form a *complex*, a quite autonomous and powerful 'mini-personality' within the total psyche. The term is commonly used in everyday language, together with synonyms such as 'hang-up' (Hall & Nordby, 1973), and Freud's Oedipus complex illustrates this constellation of thoughts and feelings. Complexes often prevent complete individuation from taking place, and one aim of therapy is to free the patient from the grip of such complexes. In looking for the origin of complexes, Jung eventually turned to the collective unconscious.

The collective unconscious

This part of Jung's theory sets him apart from Freud probably more than any other. While Freud's id is part of each individual's personal unconscious and represents our biological inheritance, Jung believes that the mind (through the brain) has *inherited* characteristics which determine how a person will react to life experiences and what type of experiences these will be. Unlike Freud, Jung attached relatively little importance to our individual past in relation to the personal unconscious, but saw the evolutionary history of human beings as a species as being all-important in relation to the *collective* (or *racial*) *unconscious*.

The collective unconscious can be thought of as a reservoir of *latent* (or *primordial*) *images*. These relate to the 'first' or 'original' development of the psyche, stemming from our ancestral past, human, pre-human and animal (Hall & Nordby, 1973). These images are predispositions or potentialities for experiencing and responding to the world in the same way that our ancestors did. For example, we don't have to learn to fear the dark or snakes through direct experience, because we're naturally predisposed to develop such fears through the inheritance of our ancestors' fears.

Ask yourself ...

- Is there any evidence from the study of phobias which supports Jung's account of the collective unconscious? (See Box 44.2, page 647.)

These primordial images are also known as *archetypes* (a prototype or 'original model or pattern'). These are more like a photographic negative (which has to be developed through

experience) than an already developed and clearly recognisable photograph (Hall & Nordby, 1973); they are 'forms without content', potential ways of perceiving, feeling and acting. Jung identified a large number of archetypes, including birth, rebirth, death, power, magic, the hero, the child, the trickster, God, the demon, the wise old man, earth mother and the giant. He gave special attention to the *persona*, the *anima/animus*, the *shadow* and the *self*.

Box 42.11 The four major archetypes of the collective unconscious

The persona ('mask'): This is the outward face we present to the world, both revealing and concealing the real self. It allows us to play our part in social interaction, and to be accepted by others. It's the 'packaging' of the ego, the ego's PR man or woman, a kind of cloak between the ego and the objective world. It's very similar to the notion of a social role, which refers to the expectations and obligations associated with a particular social position. Jung describes it as the 'conformity' archetype.

Anima/animus: This refers to the unconscious mirror image of our conscious ('official') sex. If we're male, our anima is our unconscious female side, and if we're female, our animus is our unconscious male side. We all have qualities of the opposite sex – both biologically and psychologically – and in a well-adjusted person both sides must be allowed to express themselves in thought and behaviour.

The anima prefers all things vain, helpless, uncertain and unintentional; the animus prefers the heroic, the intellectual, the artistic and athletic. Jung believed that repression of the anima/animus is very common in Western culture, where the persona predominates. (This relates to androgyny: see Chapter 36.)

The shadow: This contains more of our basic animal nature than any other archetype and is similar to Freud's id. Like the id, it must be kept in check if we're to live in society but this isn't achieved easily and is always at the expense of our creativity and spontaneity, depth of feeling and insight. So, the shadow represents the source of our creative impulses, but also of our destructive urges. When the ego and shadow work harmoniously, the person is full of energy, both mentally and physically. The shadow of the highly creative person may occasionally overwhelm the ego, causing temporary insanity (confirming the popular belief that genius is akin to madness: see Chapter 44).

The self: This is the central archetype ('the archetype of archetypes'), which unites the personality, giving it a sense of 'oneness' and firmness. The ultimate aim of every personality is to achieve a state of selfhood and individuation (similar to self-actualisation). This is a life-long process, attained by very few individuals, Jesus and Buddha being notable exceptions. It is commonly represented as a mandala, an age-old symbol of wholeness and totality, found all over the world.

According to Brown (1961), there are three major sources of evidence for the collective unconscious:

- the 'extraordinary' similarity of themes in the mythologies of various cultures;
- the recurring appearance, in therapy, of symbols which have become divorced from any of the patient's personal

experiences, and which become more and more like the primitive and universal symbols found in myths and legends;

■ the content of fantasies of psychotics (especially schizophrenics), which are full of themes such as death and rebirth (similar to those found in mythology).

Brown argues that members of all cultures share certain common experiences, and so it's not surprising that they dream or create myths about archetypal themes.

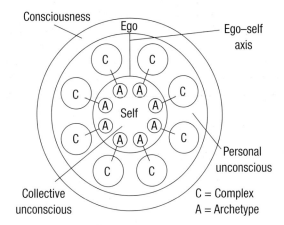

Figure 42.5 *Schematic diagram of Jung's model of the psyche (based on Stevens, 1990)*

Dream theory

Jung shared Freud's belief that dreams are the 'royal road to the unconscious', but he disagreed with Freud that all dreams are wish fulfilments. Rather, Jung saw dreams as an important way of attaining self-knowledge which, in turn (together with religious or spiritual experiences), is a path to achieving individuation.

The great function of dreams is to re-establish 'the total psychic equilibrium' and they're just as likely to point to the *future* (e.g. by suggesting a solution to a conflict) as to the past. He also believed that Freud's 'disguise' was far too elaborate, preferring to take dreams at face value. Dream symbols don't have a fixed meaning (as they very largely did for Freud), and Jung also advocated the study of *dream series*, that is, several dreams by the same individual recorded over a period of time.

Neurosis and therapy

Repression plays very little part in Jung's theory of neurosis; more important is the conflict between different parts of the personality which have developed unequally. Jungian therapy is much more concerned with future goals than past history, and the patient's present situation is the key to neurosis. Therapy aims to bring the patient into contact with the healing collective unconscious, largely through dream interpretation. Free association is also important, but the Jungian analyst, compared with the Freudian, plays a much more active role, and therapy is seen as a co-operative venture between patient and therapist (see Chapter 45).

CHAPTER SUMMARY

■ Experimental/'general' psychology is concerned with psychological processes common to all human beings ('**universal norms**'). Personality differences represent one kind of '**group norm**' and reflect the **nomothetic approach**. The **idiographic approach** is concerned with discovering **individual/idiosyncratic norms**.

■ Allport distinguished between **common** and **individual traits**. Individual traits can be **cardinal**, **central** and **secondary**. Most people possess a small number of central traits which compose the core of the personality.

■ The nomothetic–idiographic distinction is based on a **false dichotomy**. They are increasingly being seen as complementary and interdependent approaches, and even Allport argued that both should be used together in order to achieve the aims of science.

■ The **consistency controversy** was fuelled by Mischel, who rejected the **trait approach** in favour of **situationism**. **Interactionists** argue that all behaviour is the product of both personality and situational variables, and Mischel himself claims that it's the **psychological situation** that influences behaviour.

■ **Orthogonal FA** aims to identify a small number of powerful, uncorrelated factors (the method preferred by Eysenck), while **oblique FA** aims to identify a larger number of less powerful, correlated factors (preferred by Cattell).

■ Eysenck uses the term 'type' for sets of correlated traits or **personality dimensions**, specifically **introversion–extroversion** (E), **neuroticism–stability** (N), which are both normally distributed, and **psychoticism** (P), which isn't.

■ E, N and P are measured by the **Eysenck personality questionnaire** (EPQ). E and N are widely accepted as being reliable and valid, but there's much more doubt about P.

■ Extroverts are chronically **under-aroused**, while introverts are chronically **over-aroused**. Compared with low N scorers, the sympathetic branch of the ANS reacts particularly strongly to stressful situations in high N scorers. The biological basis of P is much more uncertain, but male hormones may be involved.

■ Introverts should be more easily **conditioned** than extroverts, but the evidence is equivocal. Eysenck assumes that conditionability is a unitary trait, but this has never been demonstrated and represents a weakness of the theory.

■ Cattell has identified a number of **second-order**, surface traits, including **exvia–invia** and **anxiety**, corresponding to E and N respectively. Cattell claims that with psychiatric patients, Q-data reveals a **qualitative** difference between normals and psychotics.

■ Compared with Eysenck, Cattell acknowledges the influence of situational factors on behaviour, as well as mood and state factors and motivational factors.

■ There's a growing consensus that personality can be adequately described by five broad constructs/factors (the '**big five**'), namely **extroversion**, **agreeableness**, **conscientiousness**, **neuroticism/emotional stability** and **intelligence/openness to experience**.

- Kelly's **personal construct theory** (PCT) is both idiographic and phenomenological. The underlying model is **man the scientist**. **Personal constructs** are designed to make the world more predictable and controllable.

- PCT is more a total psychology than a personality theory. It's often called a **cognitive** theory of personality and has been criticised for denying the subjective reality of emotional experience, as well as neglecting situational influences on behaviour.

- Like PCT, **humanistic theories** are rooted in **phenomenology** and **existentialism** and are concerned with uniquely human characteristics, including **self-actualisation**.

- The central concept in Rogers' theory is the **self**. Failure to maintain **consistency** between our self-image and our actions produces **incongruence**. Defence mechanisms may then be used, but these prevent the self from growing and changing, widening the gap between self-image and reality.

- To experience **positive self-regard**, our behaviour and experience must match our **conditions of worth**, but this can produce incongruence. The need for **positive regard** and positive self-regard are so strong that conditions of worth can supersede the values associated with self-actualisation.

- In **client-centred therapy**, the therapist provides **unconditional positive regard**, which enables the client to accept certain feelings and thoughts that are usually denied or distorted. In this way, **organismic values** gradually replace conditions of worth.

- Freud's **psychoanalytic theory** was the original **psychodynamic theory**, in which unconscious motivating forces play a central role. **Dreams**, **neurotic symptoms** and **defence mechanisms** represent three types of compromise through which the ego tries to meet the conflicting demands of the id and superego.

- Dreams consist of the **manifest content** and the **latent content** (the dream's meaning, namely, a **disguised wish fulfilment**). Dreams are created through **dream work**, with symbols playing a central role.

- Neurotic symptoms have a similar structure to dreams, which deflects the patient's attention away from the **pathogenic** ideas underlying the symptom.

- Defence mechanisms involve some degree of self-deception and distortion of reality which, in the short term, prevent us from being overwhelmed by anxiety. But as long-term solutions, they're unhealthy and undesirable.

- Our behaviour is **overdetermined** (one aspect of **psychic determinism**). The unconscious is revealed through **parapraxes**, including slips of the tongue ('Freudian slips').

- Freud's theories have generated a huge amount of empirical research. The most relevant studies are likely to be those which try to identify **mechanisms/processes** underlying unconscious phenomena.

- Psychoanalytic theory should be seen as a collection of hypotheses, some of which are more critical to the overall theory than others.

- Although Freud intended to produce a nomothetic theory, his work can be thought of as a set of **hermeneutic tools** that help to interpret underlying **meanings**. Although this kind of theory is difficult to test empirically, it has influenced our everyday understanding of ourselves.

- In Jung's **analytical psychology**, the Freudian unconscious is largely **personal**. It comprises much more than repressed material, including **complexes**.

- Complexes originate in the **collective/racial unconscious**, a reservoir of **primordial images** or **archetypes**, stemming from our ancestral past. Most important are the **persona**, **anima/animus**, the **shadow** and the **self**.

- Jungian **therapy** aims to bring the patient into contact with the healing collective unconscious, largely through dream interpretation.

Self-assessment questions

1 Critically assess the claim that everyone is unique.
2 Discuss the influence of personality traits **and** social situations on behaviour.
3 Describe and evaluate one psychometric **and** one non-psychometric theory of personality.

Web addresses

http://pmc.psych.nwu.edu/personality

http://galton.psych.nwu.edu/greatideas-html

pmc.psych.nwu.edu/personality.html

www.spsp.org/

www.ship.edu/~cgboeree/perscontents.html

www.wynja.com/personality/theorists.html

Further reading

Carver, C.S. & Scheier, M.F. (1992) *Perspectives on Personality* (2nd edition) Boston: Allyn and Bacon. A thorough, readable, comprehensive text covering all the major approaches.

Freud, S. (1976) *The Interpretation of Dreams*. Harmondsworth: Penguin (Pelican Freud Library). Generally regarded as Freud's finest work, originally published in 1900.

Chapter 43

Psychological Abnormality: Definitions and Classification

Introduction and overview

The emphasis in the preceding 42 chapters has been on normal

psychological processes and development. However, we've also

had occasion to qualify our discussion in two ways; first, by

considering examples of abnormality (which also often serve

to illuminate the normal); and second, by considering individ-

ual differences. This chapter brings these two issues together.

Also, two whole chapters have been devoted to discussing

abnormality in different ways: substance abuse (Chapter 8) and exceptional development (Chapter 40).

Clearly, normality and abnormality are two sides of one coin: each can only be defined in relation to the other. Also, implicit within this statement is the assumption that it's possible, and meaningful, to draw the line between normal and abnormal. Different criteria for defining normality/abnormality propose how and where the line can be drawn.

As we saw in Chapter 2, each of the major theoretical approaches discussed throughout this book – the neurobiological/biogenic, psychodynamic, behavioural, humanistic, cognitive approaches and so on – defines psychological abnormality, and advocates ways of dealing with it, in its particular way. These will be discussed together in Chapter 45. By focusing here on the concept of abnormality itself, and how psychiatrists have attempted to classify mental disorders (psychopathology: see Chapter 44), we shall be discussing the *medical model*. This sees abnormality as mental illness.

The concept of abnormality

Ask yourself ...

- Try to think of some examples of people behaving in 'odd' or 'strange' ways.
- What does 'odd' or 'strange' really mean here?
- Would this behaviour be sufficient grounds for labelling the person as 'abnormal'?

Abnormality as deviation from the average

This represents the literal sense of abnormality, whereby any behaviour which isn't typical or usual (that is, infrequent) is, by definition, abnormal: 'normal' is 'average'. However, this doesn't help to distinguish between atypical behaviour which is desirable (or, at least, acceptable) and that which is undesirable and unacceptable. For example, creative genius (such as Picasso's) and megalomania (such as Hitler's) are both statistically rare (and according to this criterion abnormal), but the former would be rated as much more desirable than the latter.

Also, there are certain types of behaviour and experience which are so common as to be normal in the statistical sense, but which are regarded as constituting psychological disorders (such as anxiety and depression). So, the statistical criterion appears to be neither necessary nor sufficient as a way of defining abnormality.

Abnormality as deviation from the norm

The statistical criterion is insufficient because it's essentially *neutral*; that is, deviation from the average is neither good nor bad, desirable nor undesirable. *Deviation from the norm*, however, implies not behaving or feeling as one *should*. 'Norm' has an 'oughtness' about it, such that particular behaviours are expected from us at particular times and in particular situations, and if those expectations aren't met or are positively 'transgressed', we and/or our behaviour may be judged 'bad' or 'sick'.

For example, many people regard homosexuality as abnormal, *not* because it's statistically less common than

heterosexuality, but because the 'normal' or 'natural' form of sexual behaviour in human beings is heterosexual. From a religious or moral perspective, homosexuality might be judged as 'bad', 'wicked', or 'sinful' (implying, perhaps, the element of choice). From a more biological or scientific perspective, it might be labelled 'sick', 'perverse', or 'deviant' (implying, perhaps, lack of choice).

Either way, even if it was found that a majority of men and women engaged in homosexual relationships (making *heterosexuality* abnormal according to the statistical criterion), these same people would still consider homosexuality a deviation from the norm and, therefore, abnormal. A further implication is that what's 'normal' is also 'desirable': unlike the statistical criterion, deviation from the norm doesn't allow for deviations which are also desirable.

Different kinds of norms

Within the same culture or society, a particular instance of behaviour may be considered normal or abnormal depending on the *situation* or *context*. For example, taking your clothes off is fine if you're about to step into a bath, but not if you're in the middle of a supermarket. However, *situational norms* aren't the only ones used to judge behaviour. *Developmental* (or age) *norms* dictate that, for instance, temper tantrums are perfectly normal in a two-year-old regardless of where they occur, but decidedly abnormal in a 32-year-old (even in the privacy of his/her own home). *Cultural norms* are discussed below in relation to the ideal mental health criterion.

Flagellants in the Philippines walk with bleeding wounds, during an Easter re-enactment of Christ's crucifixion

It's often far from obvious what norms are being broken when someone displays mental disorder: there's no law against being schizophrenic or having a panic attack, or being depressed, nor is it obvious what moral law or ethical principle is being broken in such cases. The kind of rule-breaking involved is discussed below in relation to the concept of mental illness.

Abnormality as deviation from ideal mental health

One way of 'fleshing out' the notion of desirability is to identify characteristics and abilities which people should possess for them to be considered normal. By implication, any lack or impoverishment of these characteristics and abilities constitutes abnormality or disorder.

Jahoda (1958) identified several ways in which mental health has been (or might be) defined, including:

- the absence of mental illness (clearly, a very negative definition);
- the ability to introspect, including the awareness of what we're doing and why;
- the capacity for growth, development and self-actualisation (as emphasised by Rogers and Maslow; see Chapters 9 and 42);
- integration of all the person's processes and attributes (e.g. balance between the id, ego and superego (Freud), and the achievement of ego identity (Erikson): see Chapters 37 –39);
- the ability to cope with stress (see Chapter 12);
- autonomy (a concept which appears in many theories, including those of Erikson and Gould: see Chapter 38);
- seeing the world as it really is (part of Erikson's concept of ego identity);
- environmental mastery: the ability to love, work and play, to have satisfying interpersonal relationships, and to have the capacity for adaptation and adjustment (Erikson's ego identity again, and Freud's *lieben* und *arbeiten* – love and work).

> ### Ask yourself ...
>
> - Is it possible to construct a list of ideals that everyone would agree with?
> - What's wrong with this approach to defining normality?

While many or all these criteria of mental health may seem valid and are intuitively appealing, their claim to be universal and absolute raises serious problems:

- According to these criteria, most of us would be considered maladjusted or disordered. For example, according to Maslow most of us don't achieve self-actualisation, so there's a fundamental discrepancy between these criteria and the statistical criterion (Mackay, 1975).
- Although many psychologists would accept these criteria, they're essentially *value judgements*, reflecting what's considered to be an ideal state of being human. By contrast, there's little dispute as to the precise nature of *physical health*. According to Szasz (1960), 'The norm is the structural and functional integrity of the human body', and if there are no abnormalities present, the person is considered to be in good health. Judgements about physical health don't involve making moral or philosophical decisions. 'What health is can be stated in anatomical and physical terms' (Szasz, 1960): ideal and statistical criteria tend to be roughly equivalent (Mackay, 1975).

- It follows that what's considered to be psychologically normal (and, hence, abnormal) depends upon the culture in which a person lives. Psychological normality and abnormality are culturally defined (unlike physical normality and abnormality which, Szasz believes, can be defined in universally applicable ways).

Oscar Wilde (1854–1900), the Irish writer, was imprisoned for homosexuality in 1895

CRITICAL DISCUSSION 43.1

Homosexuality – shifting definitions of abnormality

DSM-II (the second edition of the American Psychiatric Association's [APA] official classification of mental disorders, published in 1968) included homosexuality as a sexual deviation. In 1973, the APA Nomenclature Committee, under pressure from many professionals and gay activist groups, recommended that the category should be removed and replaced with 'sexual orientation disturbance'. This was to be applied to gay men and women who are 'disturbed by, in conflict with, or wish to change their sexual orientation'. The change was approved, but not without fierce protests from several eminent psychiatrists who maintained the 'orthodox' view that homosexuality is inherently abnormal.

When DSM-III was published in 1980, another new term, *ego-dystonic homosexuality* (EDH) was used to refer to someone who is homosexually aroused, finds this arousal to be a persistent source of distress, and wishes to become heterosexual. Since homosexuality itself was no longer a mental disorder, there was no inclusion in DSM-III of predisposing factors (as there was for all disorders). But they *were* included for EDH, namely, the individual homosexual's internalisation of society's negative attitudes (homophobia – fear of homosexuals – and *heterosexism* – anti-homosexual prejudice and discrimination). So, according to DSM-III, a homosexual is abnormal if s/he has been persuaded by society's prejudices that homosexuality is inherently abnormal, but at the same time it denied that homosexuality in itself is abnormal (Davison & Neale, 1994).

Not surprisingly, no such category as 'ego-dystonic heterosexuality' has ever been used (Kitzinger, 1990). When DSM-III was revised (DSM-III-R, 1987), the APA decided to drop EDH (which was rarely used). However, one of the many 'dustbin' categories, 'sexual disorder not otherwise specified', includes 'persistent and marked distress about one's sexual orientation'; this has been retained in DSM-IV (1994). ICD-10 (1992), the latest edition of the World Health Organisation's classification of diseases, also includes 'ego-dystonic sexual orientation' under 'disorders of adult personality and behaviour'.

In the UK up until the 1960s, homosexuality among consenting adults was illegal; in 1995 the age of consent was lowered to 18. Clearly, nothing has happened to homosexuality itself during the last 30 years or so. What has changed are attitudes towards it, which then became reflected in its official psychiatric and legal status. Homosexuality in itself is neither normal nor abnormal, desirable nor undesirable, and this argument can be extended to behaviour in general.

Abnormality as personal distress

From the perspective of the individual, abnormality is the subjective experience of intense anxiety, unhappiness, depression or a whole host of other forms that personal distress/suffering can take. While this may often be the only indication that anything is wrong (and may not necessarily be obvious to others), it may be a sufficient reason for seeking professional help. As Miller & Morley (1986) say:

> 'People do not come to clinics because they feel they have met some abstract definition of abnormality. For the most part they come because their feelings or behaviour cause them distress'.

However, the converse is also sometimes true: someone whose behaviour is obviously 'mad' as far as others are concerned may be oblivious of how others see them and may experience no subjective distress. This is sometimes referred to as lack of insight and is a feature of *psychosis* (see Table 43.4, page 639).

Abnormality as others' distress

If the person seen by others as behaving abnormally is the last to recognise that there's a problem, then others' concern may act as a counterbalance to his/her lack of insight. This suggests, as with all behaviour, that abnormality is *interpersonal* and not simply intrapersonal/intrapsychic. In other words, it takes place *between* people, in social situations, and isn't merely a reflection of an individual actor's personal qualities or characteristics (see Chapter 42).

From a practical and ethical perspective, this is a double-edged sword: others' distress may be both a 'blessing' (literally a life-saver, as in the case of someone who's unaware of the self-destructive nature of his/her drug abuse) and a curse (such as when a parent is distressed about a son or daughter's homosexuality, with which the person may feel perfectly comfortable). The former could be called *empathic concern*, where the 'helper' has an altruistic desire to reduce the other's distress, while in the latter, the helper's *personal distress* produces an egoistic desire to reduce his/her own distress (see Chapter 30). The question is, whose distress is the motive of the attempt to intervene?

Abnormality as maladaptiveness

Behaviour may be seen as abnormal if it prevents people from pursuing and achieving their goals, or doesn't contribute to their personal sense of well-being or prevents them from functioning as they would wish in their personal, sexual, social, intellectual and occupational lives. For example, drug abuse (or *substance-related disorder*) is defined mainly by how it produces social and occupational disability, such as poor work performance and serious marital arguments (see Chapter 8). Similarly, a fear of flying might prevent someone from taking a job promotion (Davison & Neale, 1994).

Although the emphasis here is on the *consequences* of the behaviour, such behaviours may be very distressing in themselves for the person concerned. For example, phobias are negative experiences, because they involve intense fear, regardless of any practical effects brought about by the fear.

Abnormality as unexpected behaviour

According to Davison & Neale (1994), it's abnormal to react to a situation or event in ways that couldn't be (reasonably) predicted, given what we know about human behaviour. For example, *anxiety disorders* are diagnosed when the anxiety is 'out of proportion to the situation'. The problem with this criterion is: who decided what's 'in proportion'? Is it just another form of deviation from the average, whereby what's reasonable or acceptable is simply how most people would be expected to behave? By this definition, *under-reacting* is just as abnormal as over-reacting, and yet only the latter is usually seen as a problem.

Abnormality as highly predictable/unpredictable behaviour

> *Ask yourself ...*
>
> * In light of the discussion of the *consistency controversy* in Chapter 42 (see pages 612–614), how might abnormality be defined in terms of the consistency of behaviour?

If we have generalised expectations about people's typical reactions to particular kinds of situation, then a person's behaviour is predictable to the extent that we know about the situation. However, not all situations are equally powerful influences on behaviour, and so cannot be used equally to predict a person's behaviour. It follows that it's normal for any individual's behaviour to be only *partially* predictable or consistent and, in turn, that it's abnormal for a person to display either *extremely* predictable or extremely unpredictable behaviour.

If people act so consistently that they seem to be unaffected by situations (including the other people involved), it's almost as if they're machines (or automatons). For example, someone suffering from *paranoid delusions* may see the world entirely in terms of others' harmful intentions.

This may, in turn, elicit certain kinds of responses in others, which may reinforce the delusions. According to Smith *et al.* (1986), people with behaviour disorders are unable to modify their behaviour in response to changing environmental requirements; their behaviour is maladaptive because it's inflexible and unrealistic. Equally, someone whose behaviour is very unpredictable is very difficult to interact with. People with *schizophrenia* are often perceived as embodying this kind of unpredictability, which is unnerving and unsettling – *for others*!

Abnormality as mental illness

Many writers (e.g. Maher, 1966) have pointed out that the vocabulary we use to refer to psychological disorder is borrowed from medical terminology: deviant behaviour is referred to as *psychopathology*, is classified on the basis of *symptoms*, the classification being called a *diagnosis*, the methods used to try to change the behaviour are called *therapies*, and these are often carried out in *mental* or *psychiatric hospitals*. If the deviant behaviour ceases, the patient is described as *cured*.

Other related terms are *syndrome*, *prognosis*, and *in remission*. This way of talking about psychological abnormality reflects the pervasiveness of a 'sickness' (or medical) model. Whether we realise it or not, when we think about abnormal *behaviour* we tend to think about it as if it were indicative of some underlying *illness*.

How valid is the medical model?

> *Ask yourself ...*
>
> - Try to formulate arguments for and against seeing abnormal behaviour as indicating mental illness.

Many defenders of the medical model have argued that it's more humane to regard a psychologically disturbed person as sick (or mad) than plain bad (it's more stigmatising to be regarded as morally defective: Blaney, 1975). However, when we label someone as sick or ill, we're removing from him/her all responsibility for his/her behaviour. Just as we don't normally hold someone responsible for having cancer or a broken leg, so 'mental illness' implies that something has *happened to* the person. S/he is a *victim* who is, accordingly, put in the care (and often the custody) of doctors and nurses who'll take over responsibility. (The attribution of blame and responsibility is relevant to understanding why certain types of victim are more or less likely to be helped: see Chapter 30.)

The stigma attached to mental illness may actually be *greater* than that attached to labels of 'bad', because our *fear* of mental illness is even greater than our fear of becoming involved in crime or other immoral activities. This, in turn, is based on our belief that while illness 'just happens to people' (i.e. we've no control over it), at least there's some degree of choice involved in criminal activity.

CRITICAL DISCUSSION 43.2

Is psychiatry value-free?

As we saw in relation to homosexuality (see Critical Discussion 43.1, page 632), norms change within the same culture over time. Hence, the criteria used by psychiatry to judge abnormality must be seen in a *moral context*, not a medical one (Heather, 1976). Psychiatry's claim to be an orthodox part of medical science rests upon the concept of mental illness, but far from being another medical speciality, psychiatry is a 'quasi-medical illusion' (Heather, 1976).

Similarly, Szasz (1962) argues that the norms from which the mentally ill are thought to deviate have to be stated in psychological, ethical and legal terms, and yet the remedy is sought in terms of medical measures. For this reason, Szasz believes that the concept of mental illness has replaced beliefs in demonology and witchcraft:

> *'Mental illness thus exists or is "real" in exactly the same sense in which witches existed or were real ...'.*

It also serves the same political purposes. Whenever people wish to exclude others from their midst, they attach to them stigmatising labels (e.g. 'foreigner', 'criminal', 'mentally ill') (Littlewood & Lipsedge, 1997). Unlike people suffering from physical illness, most people considered to be mentally ill (especially those 'certified' or 'sectioned' and so legally mentally ill) are so defined by *others* (relatives, friends, employers, police, and so on). They've upset the social order (by violating or ignoring social laws and conventions), and so society labels them as mentally ill and (in many cases) 'punishes' them by commiting them to a mental hospital (Szasz, 1974).

Diagnostic labelling as a form of control

As we noted earlier, people considered to be 'mentally ill' are often unpredictable, something that others find disturbing. Indeed, it's usually others who are disturbed by the patient's behaviour, rarely the patient (Laing, 1967). Attaching a diagnostic label represents a 'symbolic recapture' and this may be followed by a physical capture (hospitalisation, drugs, etc.: Szasz, 1974).

While medical diagnosis usually focuses only on the damaged or diseased parts of the body, psychiatric diagnosis describes the *whole person* – someone doesn't have schizophrenia but *is* schizophrenic. This represents a new and total identity, which describes not only the person but also how s/he should be regarded and treated by others. Psychiatric diagnosis, therefore, is a form of *action*. (We should note here that DSM-IV explicitly rejects the use of labels such as 'schizophrenic', and recommends instead 'an individual with schizophrenia'.)

What are schizophrenics doing wrong?

In what ways are schizophrenics, say, unpredictable, and what kinds of rules are they breaking? According to Scheff (1966), they're breaking *residual rules*, the 'unnameable' expectations we have regarding such things as 'decency' and 'reality'. These rules are themselves implicit, taken for granted and not articulated, which makes behaviour that violates them difficult to understand and also difficult to articulate. This is what makes it seem strange and frightening.

According to Becker (1963), psychiatric intervention is based, generally speaking, on middle-class values regarding decent, reasonable, proper behaviour and experience. These are then applied to working-class patients, who constitute the vast majority of the inmates of psychiatric hospitals.

Mental illness or problems in living?

Szasz (e.g. 1962) is probably the most radical critic of the concept of mental illness. He argues that the basic assumption made by psychiatrists is that 'mental illness' is caused by diseases or disorders of the nervous system (in particular, the brain), which are revealed in abnormal thinking and behaviour. If this is the case, it would be better to call them 'diseases of the brain' or neurophysiological disorders. This would then get rid of any confusion between physical, organic defects (which must be seen in an anatomical and physiological context) and 'problems in living' the person may have (which must be seen in an ethical and social context).

Szasz argues that the vast majority of cases of 'mental illness' are actually cases of problems of living. It's the exception rather than the rule to find a 'mentally ill' person who's actually suffering from some organic brain disease (such as in Alzheimer's disease, or alcoholic poisoning). This has traditionally been recognised by psychiatrists themselves, who distinguish between *organic* and *functional psychosis*. 'Functional' means that there's is no demonstrable physical basis for the abnormal behaviour and that something has gone wrong with how the person functions in the network of relationships which make up their world (Bailey, 1979).

However, many psychiatrists believe that medical science will, in time, identify the physical causes of functional disorders (which include schizophrenia and psychotic depression). Indeed, many claim that this point has already been reached (see Chapter 44). Yet according to Heather (1976), such evidence wouldn't cover all major categories of mental disorder (in particular, neurosis and personality disorder). Not even the most organically oriented psychiatrists would claim that these are bodily diseases in any sense!

adding to this list items which *aren't* illnesses in this sense. Agreeing with Szasz, Bailey maintains that:

- organic mental illnesses aren't mental illnesses at all but physical illnesses, in which mental symptoms are manifested and which aid diagnosis and treatment;
- functional mental illnesses aren't illnesses but disorders of psychosocial or interpersonal functioning (Szasz's 'problems in living'), in which mental symptoms are important in deciding the type of therapy the patient requires.

Diagnosis in general medicine and psychiatry

An important difference between diagnosis in general medicine and psychiatry is in the role of *signs* and *symptoms*. When doctors diagnose physical illnesses, they look for *signs* of disease (the results of objective tests, such as blood tests and X-rays, as well as physical examination) and *symptoms* (the patient's report of pain, and so on). They tend to attach more weight to the former. By contrast, psychiatrists are much more at the mercy of symptoms. Although psychological tests are the psychiatric equivalent of blood tests and X-rays, they're nothing like as reliable and valid (see Chapters 41 and 42) and, in practice, the psychiatrist will rely to a large extent on the patient's own description of the problem.

However, observation of the patient's behaviour, talking to relatives and others about the patient's behaviour and, increasingly, the use of brain-scanning techniques (such as CAT and PET: see below and Chapter 4) also contribute data regarding the signs of the illness. This is especially true in the case of serious disorders, such as schizophrenia. Nevertheless, the two major classification systems used by psychiatrists today, DSM and ICD, are based largely on the abnormal experiences and beliefs reported by patients, because we have no objective or biological markers for most neurotic or psychotic disorders (Frith & Cahill, 1995).

During the late 1970s, the American Psychiatric Association (APA) considered including a formal statement in DSM-III (1980) to the effect that mental disorders are a subset of medical diseases (Lilienfeld, 1995). While this proposal was eventually rejected, it sparked a storm of protests from psychologists, as well as many psychiatrists. The implication of the proposal was that the distinction between organic and functional disorders is invalid, and that all disorders are organic.

A major change that took place in DSM-IV (1994) compared with DSM-III-R (1987) was the removal of the category of 'organic mental disorders' and its replacement with 'delirium, dementia, amnestic and other cognitive disorders' (see Table 43.1, page 636). According to Davison & Neale (1994), the thinking behind this change is that the term 'organic' implies that the other major categories don't have a biological basis. Since research has shown the influence of biological factors through a whole range of disorders, it's now considered misleading to use the term 'organic'. To this extent, the concept of psychological abnormality is even more medicalised than it's ever been. However, ICD retains a separate category for organic disorders.

Box 43.1 **Does the concept of mental illness make sense?**

If, in most cases, it's *not* the brain that's diseased, in what sense can we think of the mind as being diseased? For Szasz, it's only in a *metaphorical* sense that we can attribute disease to the mind. In a literal sense, it's logically impossible for a non-spatial, non-physical mind to be suffering from a disorder of a physicochemical nature (unless, of course, we identify the mind with the brain: see Chapter 49). Szasz doesn't deny that the problem behaviours that mental health professionals see as indicative of mental illness are often strange, irritating and deviant. They may also be distressing for the person concerned, but they're *not* a symptom of underlying brain disease.

According to Bailey (1979), medicine began by classifying such things as syphilis and tuberculosis as illnesses, all sharing the common feature of a state of disordered structure and/or functioning of the human body as a physicochemical machine. The mistake was to keep

The classification of mental disorders

A brief history

An integral part of the medical model is the classification of mental disorder and the related process of diagnosis. All systems of classification stem from the work of Kraepelin, who published the first recognised textbook of psychiatry in 1883. Kraepelin claimed that certain groups of symptoms occur together sufficiently often for them to be called a 'disease' or syndrome. In other words, there's an underlying physical cause, just as a physical disease may be attributed to a physiological dysfunction (Davison & Neale, 1994). He regarded each mental illness as distinct from all others, with its own origins, symptoms, course and outcome.

Kraepelin (1896) proposed two major groups of serious mental diseases: *dementia praecox* (the original term for schizophrenia), caused by a chemical imbalance, and *manic–depressive psychosis* (caused by a faulty metabolism). His classification helped to establish the organic nature of mental disorders, and formed the basis for the *Diagnostic and Statistical Manual of Mental Disorders* (DSM), the APA's official classification system, and the *International Classification of Diseases* (ICD) (Chapter 5: 'Mental and behavioural disorders') published by the World Health Organisation.

DSM-I was published in 1952, DSM-II in 1968, followed by DSM-III (1980), DSM-III-R (1987) and DSM-IV (1994). Mental disorders were included in ICD for the first time in 1948 (ICD-6) and ICD-10 was published in 1992. Table 43.1 shows the major categories of both ICD-10 and DSM-IV. Table 43.2 (page 638) shows ten major categories, with examples of specific disorders based on both classification schemes.

Kraepelin's classification is also embodied in the 1983 Mental Health Act (in England and Wales). The Act identifies three major categories of mental disturbance/disorder, namely, *mental illness* (neurosis and psychosis, the latter subdivided into organic and functional), *personality disorder* (including psychopathy), and *mental impairment*.

Comparing DSM-IV and ICD-10

Broad similarities and differences

Table 43.1 shows how the two systems overlap. One of the major differences between them is the number of major categories. Most differences arise because DSM-IV uses a larger number of discrete categories to classify disorders that appear under a smaller number of more general categories in ICD-10. However, this is also reversed in one instance, as shown in Figure 43.2 (see page 637).

Neither system actually uses the term 'mental illness'. Instead, they use the term *mental disorder*, which is defined by DSM-IV as:

> *'A clinically significant behaviour or psychological syndrome or pattern that occurs in a person and that is associated with present distress (a painful symptom) or disability (impairment of one or more important areas of functioning) or with a significantly increased risk of suffering death, pain, disability, or an important loss of freedom. In addition, this syndrome or pattern must not be merely an expectable response to a particular event, for example, the death of a loved one'.* (APA, 1994)

Table 43.1 *The major categories of mental disorder as identified by DSM-IV and ICD-10*

DSM-IV	ICD-10
1 Delirium, dementia, amnestic and other cognitive disorders	**1** Organic, including symptomatic, mental disorders
2 Schizophrenic and other psychotic disorders	**2** Schizophrenia, schizotypal and delusional disorders
3 Substance-related disorders	**3** Mental and behavioural disorders due to psychoactive substance use
4 Mood disorders	**4** Mood (affective) disorders
5 Anxiety disorders	**5** Neurotic, stress-related and somatoform disorders
6 Somatoform disorders	
7 Dissociative disorders	
8 Adjustment disorders	
9 Disorders usually first diagnosed in infancy, childhood or adolescence including mental retardation – Axis II)*	**6** Behavioural and emotional disorders with onset usually occurring in childhood and adolescence
	7 Disorders of psychological development
	8 Mental retardation
10 Personality disorders (Axis II)*	**9** Disorders of adult personality and behaviour
11 Sexual and gender identity disorders	
12 Impulse control disorders not elsewhere classified	
13 Factitious disorders	
14 Sleep disorders	**10** Behavioural syndromes associated with physiological disturbances and physical factors
15 Eating disorders	
16 Other conditions that may be a focus of clinical attention	**11** Unspecified mental disorder

* see Table 43.3

'Mental disorder' is used by ICD-10:

> *' ... to imply the existence of a clinically recognisable set of symptoms or behaviour associated in most cases with distress and with interference with personal functions'.* (WHO, 1992)

Although we noted earlier that DSM-IV has become more organic in its approach, Cooper (1994) argues that only a few psychiatric diagnoses are associated with disturbed anatomy or physiology. Use of the term 'disorder' avoids the need to debate the meaning or value of 'disease' or 'illness'.

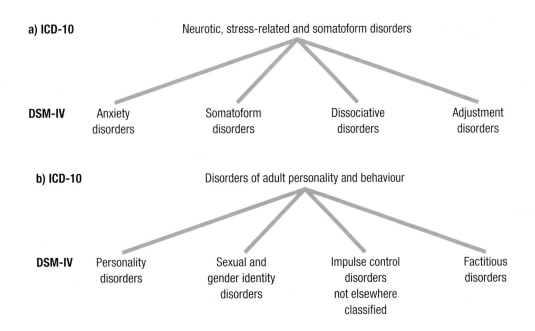

Figure 43.1 *Two examples of how a general ICD-10 category incorporates three or more DSM-IV categories*

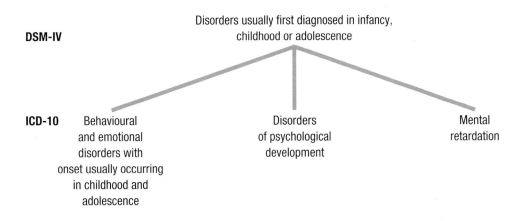

Figure 43.2 *An example of how a general DSM-IV category incorporates three ICD-10 categories*

Multi-axial classification

DSM-IV

One of the major changes which was made in DSM-III (1980) compared with DSM-II (1968) was the introduction of a *multi-axial system* of classification. Whereas DSM-II required only a simple diagnostic label (e.g. 'schizophrenia' or 'anxiety neurosis'), DSM-III (and, similarly, DSM-III-R and DSM-IV) instructed the psychiatrist to evaluate the patient on five different axes, which represent different areas of functioning (see Table 43.3, page 638).

The inclusion of the axes reflects the assumption that most disorders are caused by the *interaction* of biological, psychological and sociological factors. Instead of simply placing someone in a single clinical category (e.g. schizophrenia), the patient is assessed much more broadly, giving a more global and in-depth picture. While axes 1–3 are compulsory, 4 and 5 are optional. An important change made in DSM-IV compared with DSM-III-R was the 'return' of most developmental disorders to Axis I, with the exception of mental retardation.

ICD-10

According to Cooper (1994), it's often assumed that ICD-10 has only a single axis. However, although it doesn't have separate axes in the way that DSM has, built into the groupings of the disorders are broad types of *aetiology* (causal factors), such as organic causes, substance use and stress.

When ICD-10 was being constructed, it was agreed that, because of the incomplete and often controversial state of knowledge about the aetiology of most psychiatric disorders, the classification would be worked out on a *descriptive* basis. This implies, strictly, that disorders should be grouped according to similarities and differences of symptoms and signs, so that a particular disorder should occur only in one place. But it soon became clear that this wouldn't appeal to clinicians, who like to be able to give prominence to aetiology wherever possible (hence, the inclusion of the broad types of aetiology within the categories). Although this makes ICD-10 impure from a *taxonomic* (classificatory) point of view, it's much more likely to be used by clinicians (Cooper, 1994). In DSM-IV, assumptions about causation *aren't* used in making a diagnosis (it's *atheoretical*).

Table 43.2 *Major categories of mental disorder, with examples, based on DSM-IV and ICD-10*

Organic mental disorders: Delirium. Dementia due to: Alzheimer's disease; Creutzfeldt–Jakob disease (human version of BSE: 'mad cow disease'); HIV; Huntington's chorea; Parkinson's disease. Brain infections. Brain tumours. Brain damage

Schizophrenia and related psychotic disorders: Schizophrenia: paranoid; hebephrenic (disorganised); catatonic; simple; undifferentiated. Schizotypal disorder. Delusional disorder (paranoia). Schizophreniform disorder. Schizoaffective disorder. Brief reactive psychosis

Psychoactive substance use disorders: Intoxication, harmful use/abuse, dependence, withdrawal state re: alcohol; amphetamines; caffeine (and other stimulants); cannabis (cannabinoids); cocaine; hallucinogens; inhalants/volatile solvents; tobacco (nicotine); opioids; sedatives/hypnotics/anxiolytics; phencyclidine

Mood (affective) disorders: Depressive disorder (unipolar); manic disorder (bipolar 1); bipolar 2 disorders; mood disorder with seasonal pattern (seasonal affective disorder/SAD); mood disorder with postpartum onset (postnatal depression); premenstrual dysphoric disorder (premenstrual disorder/PMD); dysthymic disorder; cyclothymic disorder

Neurotic disorders: Anxiety disorders. Phobic anxiety disorders. Obsessive-compulsive disorders. Panic disorder. Dissociative disorders: dissociative amnesia (psychogenic amnesia); dissociative fugue (psychogenic fugue); dissociative identity disorder (multiple personality disorder); depersonalisation. Somatoform disorders. Hypochondriasis. Post-traumatic stress disorder

Disorders of infancy, childhood and adolescence: Autistic disorder. Attention-deficit/disruptive behaviour disorders: hyperkinetic disorder; conduct disorder. Separation anxiety disorder. Elective mutism. Tic disorders (e.g. Tourette's disorder). Enuresis. Encopresis. Stuttering. Disorders of speech and language. Specific developmental disorders of scholastic skills. Learning disorders

Mental retardation: Mild/Moderate/Severe/Profound. Associated with: genetic (e.g. chromosome) abnormalities; gross disease of the brain; antenatal damage; perinatal damage; postnatal damage; malnutrition

Personality disorders (disorders of adult personality): Antisocial (psychopathic). Paranoid. Schizoid (schizotypal). Anxious/avoidant. Dependent. Obsessive–compulsive. Emotionally unstable. Histrionic. Narcissistic. Pathological gambling. Pyromania. Kleptomania. Trichotillomania. Factitious disorder

Eating and sleeping disorders: Anorexia nervosa. Bulimia nervosa. Insomnia. Hypersomnia. Sleepwalking (somnambulism). Sleep (night) terrors

Sexual and gender identity disorders: Sexual desire disorders. Sexual arousal disorders. Paraphilias: exhibitionism; fetishism; voyeurism; paedophilia; frotteurism; transvestism; sexual sadism; sexual masochism. Transsexualism

Neurosis and psychosis

Both systems have dropped the traditional distinction between neurosis and psychosis, although ICD-10 retains the term 'neurotic' and DSM-IV retains the term 'psychotic'. According to Gelder *et al.* (1989, 1999), there are four major reasons for getting rid of the distinction:

- There are exceptions to all the criteria used to distinguish them (see Table 43.4, page 639).
- Disorders included under the broad categories of 'neurosis' or 'psychosis' have little in common.

- It's less informative to classify a disorder as neurotic or psychotic than to classify it as a particular disorder within that very broad category (e.g. 'schizophrenic' is more informative than 'psychotic').
- DSM-III wanted to remove the psychoanalytic influence in the way 'neurotic' was used and understood (based on Freud's theories: see Chapters 42 and 45). But in everyday psychiatric practice they're convenient terms for disorders which cannot be given more precise diagnoses, and also the terms are still in general use (as in 'antipsychotic drugs' and when referring to symptoms).

Table 43.4 (page 639) implies that psychosis is a very much more serious form of mental disorder than neurosis. According to Frith & Cahill (1995), psychosis is the technical term for what the layperson calls madness. In contrast to the symptoms of neurosis, psychotic symptoms (in particular delusions, hallucinations, passivity experiences and thought disorder) are outside the normal realm of experience and, as such, are outside our commonsense powers of understanding and empathy. It's these aspects of psychotic symptoms that isolate the person in 'a world of their own'.

Table 43.3 *The five axes of DSM-IV*

Axis I: Clinical syndromes (diagnostic category) **and other conditions that may be a focus of clinical attention**	This lists all mental disorders and the criteria for rating them, except personality disorders and mental retardation. 'Other conditions' may include problems related to abuse or neglect, academic problems, and 'phase of life' problems
Axis II: Personality disorders; mental retardation	These life-long, deeply ingrained, inflexible and maladaptive traits and behaviours may occur quite independently of Axis I clinical syndromes
Axis III: General medical conditions	Any medical condition that could affect the patient's mental state. For example, how might heart disease/diabetes/cancer affect mood and cognitive abilities, as well as response to treatment?
Axis IV: Psychosocial and environmental problems	Stressful events that have occurred within the previous year (e.g. divorce, death of parent or spouse), which could be contributory factors and/or which might influence the course of treatment. Rated on a scale of 1–7 (7 indicates 'catastrophic')
Axis V: Global assessment of functioning	How well has the patient performed during the previous year, in social relationships, leisure activities, and at work? On the global assessment of functioning scale, 0 denotes 'persistent danger', 100 denotes 'superior functioning'

Table 43.4 *The major criteria for making the traditional distinction between neurosis and psychosis*

Neurosis	Psychosis
Only part of the personality is involved/affected	The whole personality is involved/affected
Contact with reality is maintained	Contact with reality is lost, e.g. hallucinations and delusions represent the inability to distinguish between subjective experience and external reality
Neurotics have *insight* (that is, recognise they have a problem)	Psychotics *lack* insight
Neurotic symptoms/behaviour can be seen as an exaggeration of 'normal' behaviour (the difference is *quantitative*)	Psychotic symptoms/behaviour are *discontinuous* with 'normal' behaviour (the difference is *qualitative*)
Often begins as response to a stressor	There's usually *no* precipitating cause
The neurotic disturbance is related to the patient's previous personality (the premorbid personality)	The psychotic disturbance *isn't* related to the patient's premorbid personality
Treated mainly by *psychological* methods	Treated mainly by *physical* (somatic) methods

Schizophrenia is by far the commonest of the psychoses: the lifetime risk of having a schizophrenic breakdown is 0.5–2 per cent, compared with 0.6–1.1 per cent for affective psychosis, and, despite powerful drugs, about two-thirds of schizophrenics suffer recurring episodes. Delusions are by far the commonest of the psychotic symptoms. According to Jasper (1962, quoted in Frith & Cahill, 1995):

> *'Since time immemorial, delusion has been taken as the basic characteristic of madness. To be mad was to be deluded'.*

The use of diagnostic criteria

Both DSM and ICD have introduced explicit operational criteria for diagnosis (based on Spitzer *et al.*'s, 1978, *Research Diagnostic Criteria*). For each disorder, there's a specified list of symptoms, all or some of which must be present, for a specified period of time, in relation to age and gender, stipulation as to what other diagnoses mustn't be present, and the personal and social consequences of the disorder. The aim is to make diagnosis more reliable and valid (see below) by laying down rules for the inclusion or exclusion of cases.

Cultural influences on mental disorder

Cooper (1994) asks whether the *social consequences* should be included among the defining features of a disorder itself, especially within an internationally used system such as ICD, since the social environment of individuals varies so widely between cultures:

> *'The same symptoms and behaviour that are tolerated in one culture may cause severe social problems in another culture,*

and it is clearly undesirable for diagnostic decisions to be determined by cultural and social definitions'.

Cooper seems to be saying that definitions of normality/abnormality are *culturally relative* (see the earlier discussion of abnormality as deviation from the norm). But he also implies that it's possible to diagnose mental disorders *independently* of cultural norms, values and worldviews. This raises the fundamental question as to whether mental disorders exist in some objective sense. Just as modern medicine is based on the assumption that physical illness is the same throughout the world, and that definition, classification, causation and diagnosis are largely unaffected by cultural factors, so biologically orientated psychiatrists argue that organic psychoses, in particular schizophrenia and depression, are also 'culture free'.

CRITICAL DISCUSSION 43.3

Is schizophrenia culture free?

During the 1970s and 1980s, psychiatrists and clinical psychologists became increasingly interested in 'cultural psychiatry'. According to Berry *et al.* (1992), the central issue in the cross-cultural study of mental disorder is whether phenomena such as schizophrenia are:

- *absolute*: found in all cultures in precisely the same form;
- *universal*: present in some form in all cultures, but subject to cultural influence;
- *culturally relative*: unique to particular cultures and understandable only in terms of those cultures.

Of these three possibilities, only the first corresponds to a 'culture-free' view of abnormality. Berry *et al.* reject this view of abnormality, on the grounds that:

> ' ... *cultural factors appear to affect at least some aspects of mental disorders, even those that are so closely linked to human biology'.*

Universality is a more likely candidate for capturing the objective (biological) nature of mental disorder. Schizophrenia is the most commonly diagnosed mental disorder in the world, and of the major disorders, the largest number of culture-general symptoms has been reported for schizophrenia (WHO, 1973, 1979; Draguns, 1980, 1990).

However, according to Brislin (1993), there are at least three possible ways in which culture-specific factors can influence schizophrenia: (i) the form that symptoms will take, (ii) the precipitatory factory involved in the onset of the illness, and (iii) the prognosis.

(i) When schizophrenics complain that their minds are being invaded by unseen forces, in North America and Europe these forces keep up to date with technological developments. So, in the 1920s, these were often voices from the radio; in the 1950s, they often came from TV, in the 1960s it was satellites in space, and in the 1970s and 1980s spirits were transmitted through microwave ovens. In cultures where witchcraft is considered common, the voices or spirits would be directed by unseen forces under the control of demons.

(ii) Day *et al.* (1987) studied schizophrenia in nine different locations in the USA, Asia, Europe and South America. Acute schizophrenic attacks were associated with stressful events 'external' to the patients (such as losing one's job, unexpected death of spouse), which tended to cluster within a two- to three-week period before the onset of obvious symptoms. Some events could only be understood as stressful if the researchers had considerable information about the cultural background of the sample.

(iii) Lin & Kleinman (1988) found that the prognosis for successful treatment of schizophrenia was better in non-industrialised than industrialised societies. The former provide more structured, stable, predictable and socially supportive environments that allow schizophrenic patients to recover at their own pace and to be reintegrated into society.

A large number of studies have found that, in a wide range of non-Western cultures, there are apparently unique ways of 'being mad' (Berry *et al.*, 1992), that is, there are forms of abnormality that aren't easily accommodated by the categories of ICD or DSM. These *culture-bound syndromes* (CBSs) or 'exotic' disorders are first described in, and then closely or exclusively associated with, a particular population or cultural area, with the local, indigenous name being used.

For example, *Koro*, *jinjin bemar*, *suk yeong*, *suo-yang* (usually just 'Koro') refers to an acute panic/anxiety reaction to the belief, in a man, that his penis will suddenly withdraw into his abdomen, or in a women that her breasts, labia or vulva will retract into her body. This is reported in south-east Asia, south China and India (Finerman, 1994). These disorders are 'outside' the mainstream of abnormality as defined by, and 'enshrined' within, the classification systems of Western psychiatry, which determines the 'standard'. The underlying assumption is that mental disorders in the West are culturally neutral, that they can be defined and diagnosed *objectively*, while only CBSs show the influence of culture (Fernando, 1991).

At the same time, these (and other) cross-cultural studies suggest that the *concept* of mental disorder isn't merely an expression of Western values, but represents a basic human way of perceiving certain behaviour as evidence of abnormal psychological processes. According to Price & Crapo (1999):

'*... mental disorders occur in all cultures ... all cultures appear to label some specific behaviours in a way that is similar to the categories and definitions used by Western psychiatry ...*'.

Problems with the classification of mental disorder

One of the most famous studies criticising basic psychiatric concepts and practices is that of Rosenhan (1973).

KEY STUDY 43.1

On being sane in insane places (Rosenhan, 1973)

Eight psychiatrically 'normal' people (a psychology student, three psychologists, a paediatrician, a psychiatrist, a painter–decorator and a housewife) presented themselves at the admissions offices of twelve different psychiatric hospitals in the USA, complaining of hearing voices saying 'empty', 'hollow' and 'thud' (auditory hallucinations). These symptoms, together with their names and occupations, were the only falsification of the truth that was involved at any stage of the study.

All eight pseudo-patients were admitted (in eleven cases with a diagnosis of 'schizophrenia', in the other 'manic depression'), after which they stopped claiming to hear voices. They were eventually discharged with a diagnosis of '*schizophrenia* (or manic depression) *in remission*' (i.e. without signs of illness). The only people to have been suspicious of their true identity were some of their 'fellow' patients. It took between seven and 52 days (average 19) for them to convince the staff that they were well enough to be discharged.

In a second experiment, members of a teaching hospital were told about the findings of the original study, and were warned that some pseudo-patients would be trying to gain admission during a particular three-month period. Each member of staff was asked to rate every new patient as an impostor or not. During the experimental period, 193 patients were admitted, of whom 41 were confidently alleged to be impostors by at least one member of staff, 23 were suspected by one psychiatrist, and a further 19 were suspected by one psychiatrist and one other staff member. All were genuine patients.

Ask yourself ...

- What conclusions can you draw about psychiatric diagnosis from Rosenhan's study?
- Are there any features of the study that would make generalisation difficult?

Rosenhan's study was intended to test the hypothesis that psychiatrists can't reliably tell the difference between people who are genuinely mentally ill and those who aren't. Since reliability is a necessary prerequisite for validity, the implications of Rosenhan's results for the traditional psychiatric classification of mental disorders are very serious indeed.

Reliability

Diagnosis is the process of identifying a disease and allocating it to a category on the basis of symptoms and signs. Clearly, any system of classification will be of little value unless psychiatrists can agree with one another when trying to reach a diagnosis (*inter-rater/inter-judge reliability*) and represents a fundamental requirement of any classification system (Gelder *et al.*, 1989, 1999).

Early studies consistently showed poor diagnostic reliability. Psychiatrists varied widely in the amount of information they elicited at interview, and in their interpretation of that information, and variations were found between groups of psychiatrists trained in different countries. For example, the US–UK Diagnostic Project (Cooper *et al.*, 1972) showed American and British psychiatrists the same videotaped clinical interviews and asked them to make a diagnosis. New York psychiatrists diagnosed schizophrenia twice as often, while the London psychiatrists diagnosed mania and depression twice as often. (This led some wit to recommend that American schizophrenics should cross the Atlantic for a cure – presumably, the same advice should be given to British manic–depressives!) However, New York was thought not to be typical of North America.

The 'international pilot study of schizophrenia' (WHO, 1973) compared psychiatrists in nine countries – Columbia, the former Czechoslovakia, Denmark, England, India, Nigeria, Taiwan, USA and the former USSR. It found substantial agreement between seven of them, the exceptions being the USA and the USSR which both seemed to have unusually broad concepts of schizophrenia (thus confirming, after all, Cooper *et al.*'s results).

Improving reliability

Agreement between psychiatrists can be improved if they're trained to use standardised interview schedules, such as the present state examination (PSE; Wing *et al.*, 1974) and Endicott & Spitzer's (1978) schedule of affective disorders and schizophrenia (SADS). These are intended to:

- specify sets of symptoms which must be enquired about; and
- define the symptoms precisely and give instructions on rating their severity.

As we noted earlier, both DSM and ICD use explicit operational criteria in making a diagnosis, so that diagnosis may be more objective and hence more reliable. These are basically rules for deciding whether a particular patient is to be included within a particular diagnostic category or excluded from it.

There have undoubtedly been improvements in reliability since the publication of DSM-III (1980), aided by the use of 'decision trees' and computer programs that lead the psychiatrist through the tree (Holmes, 1994). However, problems remain:

- Specifying a particular number of symptoms from a longer list that must be evident before a particular diagnosis can be made seems very arbitrary. For example, DSM-IV insists on depressed mood plus four other symptoms to be present to diagnose major depression (see Table 44.1, page 650). But why four? (Pilgrim, 2000).
- The reliability of Axes 1 and 2 may not always be as high in everyday practice as they are when psychiatrists know that they're taking part in a formal reliability study (Davison & Neale, 1994).
- There's still room for *subjective interpretation* on the part of the psychiatrist. For instance, the elevated mood must be 'abnormally and persistently elevated' in order to diagnose mania. Likewise, assessment on Axis 5 requires comparison between the patient and an 'average person'. These examples beg all sorts of questions (Davison & Neale, 1994).

As far as ICD-10 is concerned, Okasha *et al.* (1993) found higher reliability compared with both ICD-9 and DSM-III-R, and Sartorius *et al.* (1993) concluded that ICD-10's clinical guidelines were suitable for widespread international use and showed good reliability. ICD-10 is expected to remain in use for about 20 years (twice as long as its predecessors) (Costello *et al.*, 1995).

Validity

This is much more difficult to assess than reliability, because for most disorders there's no absolute standard against which diagnosis can be compared. However much we improve reliability, this is no guarantee that the patient has received the 'correct' diagnosis (Holmes, 1994).

Predictive validity

The primary purpose of making a diagnosis is to enable a suitable programme of treatment to be chosen. Treatment cannot be selected randomly, but is aimed at eliminating the underlying cause of the disorder (where it's known). But in psychiatry there's only a 50 per cent chance of predicting correctly what treatment a patient will receive on the basis of diagnosis (Heather, 1976). Bannister *et al.* (1964) analysed statistically the relationship between diagnosis and treatment in 1000 cases, and found that there simply was no clear-cut connection. One reason for this seems to be that factors other than diagnosis may be equally important in deciding on a particular treatment.

For example, not only are black people in the UK more likely to be diagnosed as schizophrenic or compulsorily admitted to psychiatric hospital, they're also more likely to be given major tranquillisers or electroconvulsive therapy (ECT) than whites (Fernando, 1988). All ethnic minorities are less likely to be referred for psychotherapy than indigenous whites, and similar differences have been reported between working-class and middle-class groups. Women are also more likely to be diagnosed as psychiatrically ill than men (Winter, 1999: see Chapters 44 and 47). Winter (1999) believes that one viable explanation for these differences is that:

> '… general practitioners and psychiatrists, who are predominantly white, middle class and male, may be biased against, or insufficiently sensitive to the cultural and social situations of, black, working-class or female clients …'.

While Kraepelin originally believed that schizophrenia had a chronic, deteriorating course (i.e. patients would just become steadily worse), it seems that outcomes are extremely variable. They depend largely on socioeconomic factors, with about a 25 per cent chance of complete recovery. Response to treatment is also difficult to predict (see Chapter 45: Winter, 1999).

However, Falek & Moser (1975) found that agreement between doctors regarding angina, emphysema and tonsillitis (diagnosed without a definitive laboratory test) was no better (and sometimes actually worse) than that for schizophrenia. Clare (1980) argues that the nature of physical illness is not as clear-cut as the critics of the medical model claim. While agreeing with criticisms of psychiatric diagnosis, he believes they should be directed at psychiatrists and not the process of diagnosis in general.

Construct validity

According to Mackay (1975):

> 'The notion of illness implies a relatively discrete disease entity with associated signs and symptoms, which has a specific cause, a certain probability of recovery and its own treatments. The various states of unhappiness, anxiety and confusion which we term 'mental illness' fall far short of these criteria in most cases'.

According to Pilgrim (2000), calling madness 'schizophrenia', or misery 'depression' merely technicalises ordinary judgements. What do we add by calling someone who communicates unintelligibly 'schizophrenic'?

Similarly, Winter (1999) argues that:

'... *diagnostic systems are only aids to understanding, not necessarily descriptions of real disease entities* ...'.

Conclusions: To classify or not to classify?

Ask yourself ...

- Do you think it's scientifically valid – and ethically acceptable – to categorise people in terms of mental disorders?

According to Gelder *et al.* (1989), classifications are needed in psychiatry, as in medicine, to aid communication about the nature of patients' problems, prognosis and treatment, and so that research can be conducted with comparable groups of patients. They believe that critics of psychiatric classification are usually psychotherapists who believe that: (i) allocating a patient to a diagnostic category detracts from understanding his/her unique personality difficulty, and (ii) individual patients don't fit neatly into the available categories.

Categories vs dimensions

Traditionally, the classification of mental disorders has been categorical. Abnormality is assumed to differ *qualitatively* from normality, so that a person either belongs in a particular category or doesn't. But some researchers have argued that the most appropriate system for diagnosing and assessing mental disorders is *dimensional*; that is, abnormality and normality are only *quantitatively* different (involving a *continuum* of severity: Lilienfeld, 1998).

These two approaches mirror the important difference between psychiatry and psychology. According to Pilgrim (2000), diagnosis is a medical task that creates a simple dichotomy between the sick and the well: 'Is this person suffering from a mental disorder or not?' (and by extension, if 'yes', 'which one?'). By contrast, psychologists assume a *continuity* between normal and abnormal: 'How do we account for this person's actions and experience in this particular context?'.

The categorical system adopts a *nomothetic* approach: it emphasises the *similarities* between people (what all schizophrenics, for example, have in common). Its critics consider that an *idiographic* approach is more appropriate (see Chapter 42). Davison & Neale (1994) and Holmes (1994) agree that whenever we classify, we lose information about the *uniqueness* of the individual. What matters is whether the lost information is relevant which, in turn, depends on the purposes of the classification system (Davison & Neale, 1994).

Gelder *et al.* (1989) believe that:

'*The use of classification can certainly be combined with consideration of a patient's unique qualities, indeed it is important to combine the two because these qualities can modify prognosis and need to be taken into account in treatment*'.

The multi-axial approach of DSM can be regarded as a way of providing a much more detailed and rounded picture of the patient than was ever possible prior to 1980.

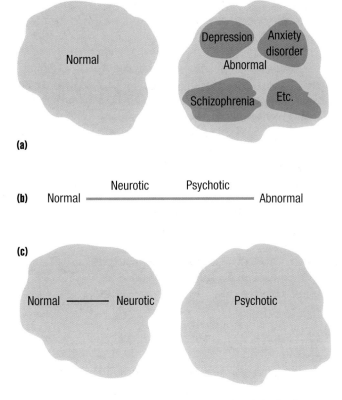

Figure 43.3 *Representations of (a) the categorical and (b) the dimensional views of abnormality. (c) combines (a) & (b)*

CHAPTER SUMMARY

- Abnormality as **deviation from the average** defines abnormality as not behaving in the way that most people do. But this fails to distinguish between atypical behaviour that's desirable and undesirable.

- **Deviation from the norm** defines abnormality as not behaving or feeling as one is **expected** to. But it's not obvious what norms are being broken in the case of mental disorder.

- The **deviation from ideal mental health** criterion identifies several definitions of mental health. But these involve **value judgements** about ideal states that are culturally defined (unlike physical health).

- Abnormality as **personal distress/suffering** defines abnormality in terms of subjective experiences. **Other people's distress** may act as a counterbalance to the lack of insight shown by some people with a mental disorder.

- Abnormality as **maladaptiveness** focuses on the **consequences** of abnormal behaviour for the individual, especially being prevented from achieving one's goals.

- Abnormality as **unexpected behaviour** means over-reacting to something, but under-reacting could be considered just as abnormal. Behaviour that's **highly consistent/predictable** or **highly inconsistent/unpredictable** may be considered abnormal.

- The way we talk about psychological disorder reflects the **medical model**. Critics argue that the norms from which the mentally ill are thought to deviate are expressed in moral, psychological and legal terms, not medical ones, yet the solution takes the form of medical treatment.

- According to Scheff, schizophrenics are breaking **residual rules**, which tend to reflect middle-class values regarding 'decency' and 'reality'.

- Szasz rejects the concept of mental illness, which refers either **neurophysiological disorders** or, more often, **problems in living**. This corresponds to the distinction between **organic** and **functional psychosis**.

- An integral part of the medical model is the **classification** of mental disorder and the related process of **diagnosis**. All systems of classification stem from Kraepelin's identification of dementia praecox (schizophrenia) and manic–depressive psychosis.

- **DSM-IV** uses a larger number of discrete categories to classify mental disorders that appear under a smaller number of wider categories in **ICD-10**.

- DSM uses a **multi-axial system** of classification, representing different areas of functioning: **clinical syndromes** (Axis I); **personality disorders/mental retardation** (Axis II); **general medical conditions** (Axis III); **psychosocial and environmental problems** (Axis IV) and **global assessment of functioning** (Axis V).

- ICD doesn't have separate axes in the way that DSM does, but broad types of **aetiology** are built into the categories of mental disorder. DSM-IV makes no assumptions about aetiology and is atheoretical.

- Both DSM and ICD have dropped the traditional distinction between **neurosis** and **psychosis**. Psychosis is a much more serious form of mental disorder, due to loss of contact with reality, and is **qualitatively different** from 'normal' behaviour.

- The cross-cultural study of schizophrenia tries to determine whether it's **absolute** ('culture free'), **universal** or **culturally relative**. Culture can influence the form of symptoms, precipitating events for the onset of symptoms, and prognosis.

- **Culture-bound syndromes** (CBSs) are seen as falling outside mainstream classifications of disorder, implying that Western mental disorders are objective and uninfluenced by cultural factors. However, all cultures seem to have the concept of mental disorder.

- Inter-rater/judge **reliability** has been improved in more recent versions of both DSM and ICD by the use of standardised interview schedules and explicit diagnostic criteria. But there's still room for subjective interpretation.

- **Validity** is more difficult to assess in the absence of absolute standards. For a diagnosis to be considered valid, it should allow prediction of treatment and recovery, as well as implying the cause(s) of the disorder.

- Psychotherapists using an **idiographic** approach criticise the use of psychiatric classification (which adopts a **nomothetic**, **categorical** approach), and psychologists prefer a **dimensional** approach. But these two approaches aren't mutually exclusive.

Self-assessment questions

1 Critically assess attempts to distinguish psychological normality and abnormality.

2 Describe and evaluate ICD and DSM as ways of classifying psychological abnormality.

3 Discuss research into the reliability and validity of any **one** approach to the classification of psychological abnormality.

Web addresses

http://www.who.ch

http://www.psych.org/main.html

http://www.apa.org/science/lib.html

http://mentalhelp.net/prof.htm

http://www.sterling.holycross.edu/departments/psychology/

http://www.mind.org.uk

Further reading

Davison, G.C. & Neale, J.M. (1994) *Abnormal Psychology* (6th edition). New York: John Wiley and Sons. An excellent reference text, which also adopts a critical approach to all aspects of abnormal psychology. Equally relevant to Chapters 44 and 45.

Lilienfeld, S.O. (1995) *Seeing Both Sides: Classic Controversies in Abnormal Psychology*. Pacific Grove, CA: Brooks/Cole Publishing Company. A unique approach, in which each of 19 controversial issues is represented by two readings that present opposing viewpoints, with the author previewing and discussing the debate, and offering a balanced synthesis. An exceptional book.

Littlewood, R. & Lipsedge, M. (1997) *Aliens and Alienists: Ethnic Minorities and Psychiatry* (3rd edition) London: Routledge. Considered by many to be a classic text on the links between racism, mental disorder and the psychiatric treatment of ethnic minorities.

Chapter 44

Psychopathology

Introduction and overview

As we saw in Chapter 43, the classification of mental disorders is an integral part of the *medical model*. ICD-10 and DSM-IV identify several general categories of mental disorder, within each of which are found a number of specific disorders. This chapter samples some of the disorders which, both historically and currently, have attracted most research interest – and often the most debate and controversy, both within and outside psychiatry.

Anxiety disorders is a category in DSM-IV subsumed by the ICD-10 category *neurotic, stress-related and somatoform disorders*. These include *phobic disorders* (*phobic anxiety disorders* in ICD-10), *obsessive–compulsive disorder* (OCD), and *post-traumatic stress disorder* (PTSD).

Eating disorders is a DSM-IV category subsumed by ICD-10's *behavioural syndromes associated with physiological disturbances and physical factors*. Two major eating disorders are *anorexia nervosa* and *bulimia nervosa*.

Of all the disorders identified in ICD-10 and DSM-IV, *schizophrenia* is the most serious. Kraepelin (1913) called the disorder *dementia praecox* (senility of youth), believing that it occurred early in adult life and was characterised by a progressive deterioration or dementia. However, Bleuler (1911) observed that it also began in later life, and wasn't always characterised by dementia. Bleuler coined the word schizophrenia to refer to a splitting of the mind's various functions, in which the personality loses its unity.

Mood (or *affective*) *disorders* involve a prolonged and fundamental disturbance of mood and emotions. At one extreme is *manic disorder* (or *mania*), and at the other is *depressive disorder*. Mania usually occurs in conjunction with depression (*bipolar disorder*). The term *unipolar* is reserved for the occurrence of depression on its own. (The term *manic–depressive* refers to *both* the unipolar and bipolar forms of affective disorder.)

Anxiety disorders

Of all forms of psychological distress, emotional disturbances are perhaps the most common (Lilienfeld, 1998), and '… fear is a core emotion in psychopathology' (LeDoux, 1998). While *anxiety* (a brooding fear of what might happen) was a central feature of Freud's psychoanalytic theory (LeDoux, 1998), many psychologists have argued that *fear* is a fundamentally *adaptive reaction* to stressors (specifically, threat), since it increases alertness and vigilance (see Chapter 7). It's generally considered abnormal only when it's disproportionate to objective circumstances. Fear probably evolved as an alarm signal to warn organisms of potential danger. But some people tend to feel afraid even when there's no (objective) threat present (i.e. anxiety). These 'false alarms' are what we call anxiety disorders.

For example, people with panic disorder experience sudden surges of extreme terror, even in perfectly safe environments. As Lilienfeld says:

'… it is this mismatch between the severity of individuals' emotional reactions and of objective stressors that makes panic disorder psychopathological …'.

Ask yourself …

- While this might seem like a perfectly reasonable way of distinguishing normal from abnormal anxiety, can you see any flaws in the argument?
- How does it relate to the *categorical/dimensional* approaches discussed in Chapter 43? (See page 642.)

Phobic disorders

A *phobia* is an extreme, *irrational* fear of some specific object or situation. Typically, the patient acknowledges that the object of fear is harmless, but the fear is experienced nonetheless (this is the irrational element). Trying to avoid the feared object or situation at all costs can interfere with the person's normal functioning, and distinguishes a phobia from a milder fear or mere dislike of something. Attempts to hide the phobia from others may induce further anxiety, guilt and shame.

Box 44.1	Some examples of the variety of phobias

Acrophobia: high places
Algophobia: pain
Anthropophobia: men
Aquaphobia: water
Arachnophobia: spiders
Astraphobia: storms, thunder, lightning
Belonophobia: needles
Claustrophobia: enclosed spaces
Cynophobia: dogs
Hematophobia: blood
Nycotophobia: darkness
Ophidiophobia: snakes
Pathophobia: disease
Pyrophobia: fire
Thanatophobia: death
Xenophobia: strangers

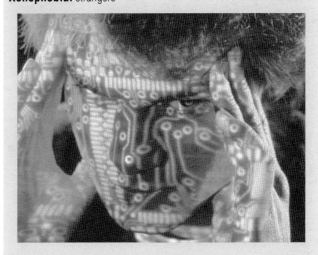

Technophobia is a feeling of fear or frustration experienced by people unfamiliar with modern digital and computer technology

As Box 44.1 shows, almost anything may become the object of a phobia, but some phobias are much more common than others. DSM-IV identifies three categories of phobia: agoraphobia, social phobia, and specific phobias.

Agoraphobia

This is the most common of all phobias (accounting for about 60 per cent of all phobic patients), and occurs predominantly in women (while most other phobias tend to be fairly evenly divided between the sexes). While agoraphobia is commonly defined as fear of open spaces, the *primary* fear is leaving the safety and security of home and/or companions. Fear of being in public places is *secondary* but, significantly, this is what the patient is usually aware of. It often centres on a fear of finding oneself in a situation from which escape is difficult, or where help is unavailable in the event of a panic attack (which often accompanies agoraphobia). Indeed, nearly all researchers agree that all cases of agoraphobia stem from fear of panic attacks (Lilienfeld, 1998). Mitchel (1982) sees agoraphobia as a form of *separation anxiety* (see Chapter 32).

Social phobia

This was identified in the UK in 1970, but not included in DSM until 1980 (Menninger, 1995). It's an intense and excessive fear of being observed by other people, such as when eating or drinking in public, talking to members of the opposite sex, or having to speak or write in front of others. These are all examples of *performance* social phobia. *Limited interactional* social phobia involves feeling anxious only in specific situations (such as when interacting with an authority figure), while *generalised* social phobia arises in most social situations.

The underlying fear is of acting in a way that's embarrassing or humiliating for the self or others. Like agoraphobia, most social phobics are women, and the problem typically begins in adolescence.

Having to make a speech in front of any kind of audience is likely to induce some degree of anxiety in most people. As a social phobia, anxiety over public speaking is an intense and excessive fear of being exposed to scrutiny by other people; it's an example of performance social phobia

Specific phobias

Most phobias fall into this category (see Box 44.1), and definitions of phobias usually attempt to define specific phobias. Generally, these are less disruptive than agoraphobia or social phobias. They can develop at any time of life, although some are quite common in childhood (such as cynophobia and nycotophobia), while 'illness and injury' phobias (and thanatophobia) tend to occur in middle age.

CASE STUDY 44.1

Popeye phobia

A three-year-old girl suddenly developed recurrent bronchitis, which got worse when she attended nursery school. The trouble was traced to the slippers of a boy in the same class. Every time the girl saw them she began to retch and cough, and became upset. The slippers sported a picture of Popeye, the cartoon sailor man. Even the mention of his name induced coughing. The girl had seen a Popeye cartoon at her friend's house and became frightened of it. Following behaviour therapy (see Chapter 45), the girl recovered.

(Based on Murray, 1997.)

Explaining phobias

> **Ask yourself ...**
>
> - How would Freud account for phobias (see Chapter 43)?
> - How would learning theory explain them (see Chapter 11)?

According to Freud, phobias are the *surface* expression of a much deeper conflict between the id, ego and superego, originating in childhood (as in Little Hans's fear of horses: see Chapter 35, pages 508–509). Phobias are (conscious) expressions of (unconscious) unacceptable wishes, fears and fantasies that have been *displaced* from their original, internal source onto some external object or situation that can be easily avoided.

Behaviourist critics of Freud's explanation pointed out that Hans's phobic response only occurred in the presence of a large horse pulling a heavily loaded cart at high speed, and that the phobia developed *after* Hans had witnessed a terrible accident involving a horse pulling a cart at high speed. As we saw in Chapter 11, phobias can be *classically conditioned*, and Wolpe (1969) argued that this is how *all* phobias arise. Some phobics (but not all) trace their phobias to some traumatic experience (often in childhood), and the *resistance to extinction* of some phobias is also consistent with the conditioning explanation.

According to Mowrer's (1947) *two-process/two-factor theory*, phobias are *acquired* through classical conditioning (factor 1) and *maintained* through *operant* conditioning (factor 2): *avoidance* of the phobic stimulus and the associated reduction in anxiety is *negatively reinforcing*. By contrast, Rachman's (1984) *safety signal hypothesis* sees avoidance as being motivated by *positive* feelings of safety.

However, the fact that some phobics *cannot* recall any traumatic experiences, and that extreme trauma doesn't inevitably lead to a phobia developing, is inconsistent with the conditioning explanation. We also saw in Chapter 11 that certain classes of stimuli (such as snakes) can more easily be made a conditioned response than others (such as flowers).

Box 44.2 Preparedness

Rosenhan & Seligman (1984) propose an *interaction* between biological and conditioning factors that *predisposes* us to acquire phobias of certain classes of stimuli. According to the concept of *preparedness/prepared conditioning*, we're genetically prepared to fear things that were sources of danger in our evolutionary past (see Gross *et al.*, 2000).

Hugdahl & Ohman (1977) have shown that in laboratory experiments, people without pre-existing phobias can be conditioned more easily to snakes than flowers. However, snakes have a negative 'reputation' or social status, while flowers are generally viewed positively and are completely non-threatening. So, although preparedness as an explanation for direct conditioning may not be valid, preparedness for *observational* and *instructional learning* is possible (Murray & Foote, 1979; Rachman, 1977).

Obsessive–compulsive disorder (OCD)

Obsessions are recurrent, unwanted, intrusive thoughts or images that don't feel voluntarily controlled, and which are experienced as morally repugnant or intensely distressing. They mostly have sexual, blasphemous or aggressive themes (see Case Study 44.2). For example, it's not uncommon for deeply religious people to have repeated blasphemous thoughts, such as 'God doesn't exist', or for caring parents to have thoughts of harming their children. These obsessions are resisted by being ignored or suppressed, or by 'neutralising' them with some other thought or action (Shafran, 1999); these may include compulsions.

Compulsions are actions which the victim feels compelled to repeat over and over again, according to rituals or rules. Obsessions and compulsions are often related, the latter representing an attempt to counteract the former. For example, compulsive handwashing may be an attempt to remove the obsessive preoccupation with contamination by dirt or germs, either as agent or victim. While the person recognises that the compulsive act is unreasonable and excessive, it's also seen as purposeful. The function of compulsive acts is to prevent a dreaded event and reduce distress. Many patients find the need to perform the compulsion distressing in itself, and are frustrated by the time it takes to complete it 'correctly' and how it interferes with normal social and work functioning.

Shafran (1999) gives the example of a man who was obsessed with the thought that he'd contracted AIDS from sitting next to someone who looked unkempt. In response to this, he repeatedly checked his body for signs of illness and washed his hands whenever he had an intrusive image of this person. When outside, he'd continually check around him to see if there were any discarded tissues that might carry the HIV virus. This became so laborious that he stayed indoors for much of the time. Any interruption to the checking and washing resulted in the entire routine starting again.

Obsession without the compulsion (Sutherland, 1976)

An example of an obsession occurring without compulsive behaviour is sexual jealousy, an extreme case of which is described by Stuart Sutherland in *Breakdown* (1976). Sutherland was a well-known British experimental psychologist who'd been happily married for several years when his wife suddenly revealed she'd been having an affair (but had no wish to end their marriage). At first, he was able to accept the situation, and found that the increased honesty and communication actually improved their marriage.

However, after asking his wife for further details of the affair, he became obsessed with vivid images of his wife in moments of sexual passion with her lover, and he couldn't remove these thoughts from his mind, day or night. Finally, he had to leave his teaching and research duties, and it was only after several months of trying various forms of therapy that he managed to reduce the obsessive thoughts sufficiently to be able to return to work.

Once regarded as a rare disorder, OCD now occupies a central position in clinical psychology and psychiatry (Tallis, 1994, 1995). In the US, OCD is the fourth most common disorder, and in the UK, an estimated one to one-and-a-half million people suffer from it. OCD affects slightly more females than males, and it usually begins in early adulthood.

Explaining OCD

Psychoanalytic explanations

According to *psychoanalytic theory*, obsessions are *defence mechanisms* (see Chapter 42, pages 623–624, and Chapter 45, page 668) that serve to occupy the mind and displace more threatening thoughts. Laughlin (1967), for example, sees the intrusion of obsessive thoughts as preventing the arousal of anxiety, by acting as a more tolerable substitute for a subjectively less acceptable thought or impulse. However, it's hard to see what obsessive thoughts of killing someone (one of the more common kinds of obsession) are a more tolerant substitute for.

Behavioural explanations

A *behavioural* explanation would see OCD as a way of reducing anxiety. If an obsession induces anxiety, then any compulsive behaviour that alleviates the anxiety should be more likely to occur (through negative reinforcement: e.g. Rachman & Hodgson, 1980). Since the compulsion only provides *temporary* relief from anxiety, when it starts to increase again the person is motivated to repeat the compulsive act. Paradoxically, compulsions (as well as avoidance and trying to suppress the obsession) serve to *increase* the frequency of the obsession. As Shafran (1999) says:

'These obsessions subsequently increase the compulsive behaviour, leaving the person trapped in the vicious obsession–compulsion cycle …'.

However, this can only account for OCD's *maintenance* – not how it developed in the first place. The *superstition hypothesis* might be more relevant here.

Rachman and Hodgson's account explicitly proposed that it's normal for people to have intrusive thoughts. For example, it's been shown that 90 per cent of non-patients have unwanted, intrusive thoughts with the same content as those of people diagnosed with OCD (including the impulse to disrupt a peaceful gathering and to jump in front of an approaching train). However, non-patients can dismiss their obsessions more easily, they experience them less often, and they're less distressed by them (Shafran, 1999).

Cognitive–behavioural explanations

According to *cognitive–behavioural theory* (e.g. Beck, 1976), 'normal' obsessions become abnormal when people interpret the occurrence and content of unwanted intrusive thoughts as indicating that they may be/have been/come to be *responsible* for harm or its prevention (Salkovskis, 1985; Salkovskis *et al.*, 1998). Lopatka & Rachman (1995) showed that in a high-responsibility condition, people with checking compulsions had stronger urges to check, experienced greater discomfort, and made higher estimates of the probability of harm, than those in a low-responsibility condition.

Another interpretation with specific implications for treatment (and which is closely linked to perceived responsibility for harm) is 'thought–action fusion' (TAF) (Rachman, 1993). This involves appraising intrusive thoughts as equivalent to actions. For example, one woman believed that if she had an image of her daughter lying dead, then it was as though she were 'tempting fate' and increasing the chances that her daughter would die. TAF involves two components:

- *likelihood TAF:* the belief that thinking about an unacceptable or disturbing event makes it more likely to *actually* happen;
- *moral TAF:* interpreting the obsessive thoughts and forbidden actions as *morally* equivalent. The person feels that his/her unacceptable thoughts, images and impulses are (almost) as bad as the event (e.g. 'Only a wicked mother would have thoughts about harming her child.').

According to Nieboer (1999), what Rachman calls TAF can be attributed to Freud (1909): patients with OCD had difficulties distinguishing thoughts from actions. As we saw earlier, Freud believed that obsessions are defensive psychological responses (that develop during the anal–sadistic stage: see Chapter 35). Attempts to prevent compulsive behaviour would, at best, produce *symptom substitution* (see Chapter 45) and, at worst, cause psychotic breakdown. By contrast, Rachman's 'version' of TAF has implications for the origin, maintenance and treatment of OCD, which are wholly different from those drawn by Freud (Shafran & Salkovskis, 1999).

Post-traumatic stress disorder (PTSD)

During World War I, many soldiers experienced *shell shock* (a shock-like state which followed the traumatic experiences of prolonged combat). In World War II, *combat fatigue* (or 'traumatic neurosis') was used to describe a similar reaction, characterised by terror, agitation or apathy, and insomnia.

Following the Vietnam War, the syndrome was renamed *post-traumatic stress disorder* (PTSD) and first appeared by that name in DSM-III (1980). The term describes an anxiety disorder which occurs in response to an extreme psychological or physical trauma outside the range of normal human experience (Thompson, 1997). Apart from war, such traumas include a physical threat to one's self or family, witnessing other people's deaths, and being involved in natural or human-made disasters. Examples include the Hillsborough football tragedy, the *Herald of Free Enterprise* cross-channel ferry disaster, and the Paddington rail disaster.

While Freud considered that at the root of many neurotic disorders is the inability to remember bad experiences (see Chapter 45), the opposite is true in the case of PTSD. As Brewin (1998) says:

> *'The curse of perpetual reminiscence is a cardinal feature of post-traumatic stress disorder (PTSD), in which sufferers attempt to avoid but cannot prevent vivid, emotionally arousing images repeatedly intruding into their waking or sleeping minds …'.*

Research has pointed to the fact that intrusive memories are also important in depression. Reynolds & Brewin (1997) compared matched samples of patients with PTSD and depression. While PTSD patients were a little more likely to have intrusive memories (which are also somewhat more vivid and frequent), they are otherwise very similar. Both groups were likely to experience very vivid and highly distressing memories on average several times per week and lasting several minutes (up to an hour). Also for both groups, they're mostly accompanied by physical sensations and a feeling of reliving the event. One of the few differences was that PTSD patients were more likely to report feeling helpless and to have a *dissociative experience*, such as feeling they were leaving their body or seeing themselves as an object in their memory.

PTSD may occur immediately following a traumatic experience or weeks, months and even years later. In the Vietnam War, there were relatively few cases of shell shock or combat fatigue, but on their return to the US, soldiers found it more difficult adjusting to civilian life than those who fought in the two World Wars.

As well as the symptoms described in Box 44.5, Vietnam veterans felt extreme guilt at having survived, while so many of their comrades hadn't. This is also common among survivors of disasters, as are exaggerated startle responses to unexpected stimuli.

Explaining PTSD

Unlike other anxiety disorders, the causes of PTSD are largely, if not exclusively, *environmental*. While phobias or OCD tend not to have common background factors, all PTSD sufferers share the experience of having been involved in a profoundly traumatising event.

Sufferers tend to show classically conditioned responses to stimuli present at the time of the event (e.g. Charney *et al.*, 1993). But since not everyone exposed to the traumatic event develops PTSD, other factors must be involved, such as individual differences in people's appraisal of events as stressors (see Chapter 12), and the *recovery environment* (such as family support and support groups).

The return of memories many years after the traumatic event suggests that keeping busy with socially valued life roles enables a person to *avoid* processing the traumatic memories. But this prevents the memories from becoming integrated into the individual's world-view. In conditioning terms, thinking about the traumatic event would lead to *extinction* of the responses associated with it.

Biological explanations

According to Butler (1996), PTSD can be seen as the breakdown of the normal stress response.

Ask yourself ...

- Remind yourself of how the normal stress response works (see Chapter 12, pages 173–175). Why do you think Butler (1996) describes PTSD as 'too much of a good thing'?

When stress becomes overwhelming, too much adrenaline and noradrenaline produce confusion, and impair learning and memory. Repeated adrenaline rushes seem to progressively sensitise brain chemistry, provoking even greater floods of adrenaline at lower thresholds. For example, one study cited by Butler found that those with childhood histories of physical or sexual abuse were significantly more likely to develop PTSD after combat in Vietnam than those who were without such histories.

Years after the trauma, the nervous systems of PTSD sufferers remain always on alert (as manifested in the startle responses and general emotional reactivity). Butler cites a study of Vietnam veterans who were injected with *yohimbine*, a psychoactive drug from South America that stimulates secretion of noradrenaline. While non-traumatised control participants reported a little heart-pounding, nine of the 15 veterans suffered panic attacks and six had full-blown flashbacks. Yohimbine temporarily disables alpha-2 receptors – brain cell structures which slow the release of adrenaline to the brain. Other research shows that PTSD patients have 40 per cent fewer alpha-2 receptors than normal controls.

The brains of PTSD sufferers release *endorphins* (natural opiates with pain-killing properties: see Chapter 4) far above normal levels, causing a *drop* in pain sensitivity. This over-activation of a natural anaesthetic response, in the face of something rationally known not to be dangerous (such as watching a movie about Vietnam) may partly explain the numbness reported by some.

Research suggests that moments of overwhelming terror can do lasting damage to the hippocampus (see Chapter 17). Butler (1996) cites three studies using MRI scans which found significant reductions in the size of the hippocampus of traumatised people, including women with histories of prolonged child sexual abuse. Those with the the smallest hippocampi displayed the most intense PTSD symptoms, including dissociation, that is, the tendency to 'space out', feel detached from one's body, and have unpredictable lapses of memory. This hippocampal damage may well be caused by an over-*reduction* in cortisol levels (see Chapter 12), which occurs after prolonged stress. Low cortisol levels are associated with brain cell death in the innermost section of the the hippocampus (the *dentate gyrus*), thought to contribute to creativity and the recall of long-term memories.

CRITICAL DISCUSSION 44.1

The positive side of PTSD

Some researchers have described PTSD as continuous with normal adaptive behaviour, rather than a distinctly abnormal reaction (Brewin *et al.*, 1996; Williams & Joseph, 1999). '*Post-traumatic growth*' (Tedeschi, 1999; Tedeschi & Calhoun, 1996; Tedeschi *et al.*, 1998) describes these positive changes in the areas of perception of self, relationships with others, and philosophy of life.

The underlying principle is a *changed perspective*. For example, having had sight of death, survivors emerge sadder but wiser. It's this wisdom that prompts survivors to redefine their philosophy of life: it's no longer taken for granted (Joseph *et al.*, 1993), and everyday existence is consequently valued in a new way.

This is consistent with Seligman & Csikszentmihalyi's (2000) call for the expansion of psychology into a science of optimal human functioning – at both the individual and social/community levels. As Linley (2000) puts it:

'From being a discipline with a primarily pathological focus, psychology can expand … to embrace the pinnacles of human attainment … psychology can show individuals and their societies how they may flourish, both in the face of and absence of adversity, so that genuine fulfilment might be achieved'.

Mood (affective) disorders

Manic disorder (mania)

Mania is a sense of intense euphoria or elation. A characteristic symptom is a 'flight of ideas': ideas come rushing into the person's mind with little apparent logical connection, and there's a tendency to pun and play with words. Manics have a great deal of energy and rush around, usually achieving little and not putting their energies to good use. They need little sleep and may appear excessively conceited (having 'grandiose ideas' or delusions). They display disinhibition, which may take the form of a vastly increased sexual appetite (usually out of keeping with their 'normal' personality), or going on spending sprees and building up large debts.

As we saw in the *Introduction and overview*, mania usually occurs in conjunction with depression (*bipolar disorder*), but in the rare cases in which mania occurs alone, 'bipolar' is also used (*unipolar* refers to episodes of depression alone: see below). Most patients with mania eventually develop a depressive disorder (Gelder *et al.*, 1999). '*Manic–depressive*' refers to both the unipolar and bipolar forms of affective disorder. Bipolar disorder is much less common than unipolar, occurring in fewer than 10 per 1000, usually before age 50. Each episode lasts about three months (Gelder *et al.*, 1999).

Depressive disorder

Depression represents the complete reverse of mania. The depressed person experiences a general slowing down and loss of energy and enthusiasm for life. Unipolar depressive disorder may begin at any time from adolescence onwards, with the average age of onset being the late 20s. With treatment, each episode lasts two to three months, six months or longer if untreated. It affects 20–30 men per 1000, but 40–90 per 1000 women (see Critical Discussion 44.2, page 651). About ten per cent of patients eventually commit suicide (Gelder *et al.*, 1999).

Table 44.1 *Symptoms of clinical depression (major depressive disorder) (based on Spitzer* et al., *1978)*

In order to be said to be suffering from clinical depression, a person should have experienced a number of the following symptoms together over a period of time.

A	Persistent low mood (for at least two weeks)

plus

B	At least five of the following symptoms:

1 Poor appetite or weight loss, or increased appetite or weight gain (change of 1 lb [450 g] a week over several weeks or 10 lb [4.5 kg] in a year when not dieting).
2 Sleep difficulty, or sleeping too much.
3 Loss of energy, fatiguability or tiredness.
4 Body slowed down or agitated (not mere subjective feeling of restlessness or being slowed down, but observable by others).
5 Loss of interest or pleasure in usual activities, including social contact or sex.
6 Feelings of self-reproach, excessive or inappropriate guilt.
7 Complaints or evidence of diminished ability to think or concentrate such as slowed thinking or indecisiveness.
8 Recurrent thoughts of death or suicide, or any suicidal behaviour.

Endogenous vs exogenous depression

A distinction that's deeply embedded within psychiatric thinking is that between *endogenous* ('from the inside') and *reactive* (or 'exogenous', from the outside) depression. The former was intended to denote depression arising from biochemical disturbances in the brain, while the latter was seen as being caused by stressful life experiences. These were also classified as psychotic and neurotic depression respectively, implying that the former is much more serious (see Table 43.4, page 639).

However, the distinction is controversial. According to Gelder *et al.* (1999), both types of cause are present in every case, and there appears to be a gradation of severity of the disorder, rather than distinct patterns. Indeed, Champion (2000) believes that endogenous depression can no longer be defined in terms of the absence of external causes, but by the *presence* of more severe symptoms.

Gender differences

In England, a woman is about 40 per cent more likely to be admitted to a psychiatric hospital than a man. However, as in other countries, rates of hospitalisation rise rapidly among the elderly and women outnumber men by 2:1 in the elderly population (75 and over). When admission rates for other categories of disorder are taken into account (such as the very similar rates between males and females for schizophrenia), it's depression that contributes most to the high overall rate of treated mental illness among women (Cochrane, 1995). While there are no sex differences in the rate of bipolar disorder (Strickland, 1992), women are two to three times more likely to be diagnosed with unipolar disorder than men (Williams & Hargreaves, 1995).

CRITICAL DISCUSSION 44.2

Are women naturally disposed towards depression?

A popular and widely held view is that women are naturally more emotional than men, and so are more vulnerable to emotional upsets. Hormonal fluctuations associated with the menstrual cycle, childbirth, the menopause and oral contraceptives have all been proposed as the mechanism which might account for the sex difference (Cochrane, 1995). Cochrane believes that there's no evidence that biochemical or physiological changes involved in the menopause, for example, have any direct effect on psychological functioning. But while the hormonal changes of the menstrual cycle may not be sufficient on their own to cause clinical depression, they may tend to reactivate memories and feelings from a previous period of major depression (caused by other factors) (Williams & Hargreaves, 1995).

According to Callaghan & O'Carroll (1993), there's some evidence that one in ten women who've just given birth is sufficiently depressed to need medical or psychological help (*mood disorder with post-partum onset/post-natal depression*). However, no specific causal hormonal abnormality has been identified, and social factors may be just as important as physical ones, such as her adjustment to a new role and the attention being diverted from her to the baby.

Hormonal changes cannot explain why the discrepancy in the female/male rates of depression is so large or why only *some* women are affected. One study found that when women who've recently given birth are compared with a sample of non-pregnant women of the same age, depression rates were very similar (8.7 and 9.9 per cent respectively) (Cooper *et al.*, 1988, cited in Cochrane, 1995). Not only does the risk of depression not increase following childbirth, it seems to be good for you!

Cochrane identifies a number of *non-biological explanations* of women's greater susceptibility to depression:

- Girls are very much more likely to be abused, particularly sexually, than boys, and victims of abuse are at least twice as likely to suffer clinical depression in adulthood as non-victims. Abuse alone could account for the female–male difference in the incidence of depression.

- A woman's acceptance of the traditional female gender role involves accepting that she'll have relatively little control over her life (see Chapter 36). This may contribute to *learned helplessness*, which has been used to account for the development of depression (see Chapter 12).

- The female–male difference in the rate of depression is at its greatest between the ages of 20 and 50, during which time marriage, childbearing, motherhood and the 'empty nest' syndrome will be experienced by a majority of women. Although women are increasingly becoming part of the labour force, being a full-time mother (especially of young children) and wife, and not having paid employment outside the home, are increasingly being seen as risk factors for depression, especially if they lack an intimate, confiding relationship (Brown & Harris, 1978: see Chapter 38).

- Cochrane (1983) argues that depression may be seen as a coping strategy that's available to women, in contrast to those of men (including alcohol and drugs and their work). Not only is it more acceptable for women to admit to psychological symptoms, but these may represent a means of changing an intolerable situation. But Callaghan & O'Carroll (1993) warn that:

'Unhappiness about their domestic, social, and political circumstances lies at the root of many women's concerns. This unhappiness must not be medicalised and regarded as a "female malady" ...'.

Explanations of depression

In addition to the causal factors discussed in Critical Discussion 44.2, all the major theoretical approaches have attempted to explain depression. Probably the most influential of these – both currently and in recent years – has been the *cognitive model*, especially Beck's (1963) *cognitive triad* of depression. Because his form of *cognitive–behaviour therapy* is mainly intended to treat depression, this – and other cognitive explanations – will be discussed in Chapter 45.

The role of genetic factors

Parents, siblings and children of severely depressed patients have a higher risk of affective disorders (10–15 per cent) than the general population (one to two per cent). Concordance for bipolar disorder is the same among MZs (identical twins) reared together or apart (about 70 per cent), compared with 23 per cent for DZs. Adoption studies confirm the importance of genetic factors: the natural parents of adoptees with a bipolar disorder have a higher rate of affective disorder than do natural parents of adoptees without a bipolar disorder (Gelder *et al.*, 1999).

> **Box 44.6 Other risk factors for depression**
>
> - There's strong evidence for an abnormality of 5-HT (i.e. serotonin) function, and *noradrenergic* function: see Chapters 4 and 45). (Gelder *et al.*, 1999).
> - Tebartz *et al.* (2000) found that depressed people have an enlarged amygdala (which is known to play a role in emotional information processing: see Chapter 4). The amygdalae of female patients were significantly larger than those of males.
> - Chronically (naturally occurring) low levels of cholesterol are associated with depressive symptoms and suicide, even when age, energy intake, alcohol consumption and the presence of chronic disease are controlled (Steegmans *et al.*, 2000).

Culture and depression

While there are an estimated 340 million people worldwide affected by depressive disorders (making it the most common of all mental disorders: Lyddy, 2000), Price & Crapo (1999) point out that various researchers have denied the presence of native concepts of depression among groups as diverse as the Nigerians, Chinese, Canadian Inuit, Japanese, Malaysians, and the Hopi Native Americans. Price and Crapo ask:

> '*If depression, as currently defined in Western culture and psychiatric diagnosis, is not found in non-Western cultures, how do we know that "depression" is not merely a Western folk concept, analogous to other culture-specific conditions such as* koro, kayak-angst, amok *or susto?'*.

According to Kaiser *et al.* (1998), DSM-IV recognises the vital role of culture in the expression and diagnosis of disorders. It encourages clinicians to keep cultural considerations in mind when assessing patients on each of the five axes. In the section dealing with depression, conditions which appear most often in specific cultures are outlined, as well as cultural variations in the manifestation of symptoms. For example, in some cultures people tend to present with *somatic* complaints (such as aches and pains), while in others *affective* symptoms are more common (such as sadness). The task of the clinician is to take the norms of the individual patient's cultural reference group into account, while at the same time avoiding cultural stereotypes (Kaiser *et al.*, 1998).

Ask yourself ...

- How does this discussion of cultural aspects of depression relate to the discussion in Chapter 43 of whether schizophrenia is culture-free? (See Critical Discussion 43.3, page 639.)

Schizophrenia

As we noted in the *Introduction and overview*, what we now call schizophrenia was originally called *dementia praecox* ('senility of youth') by Kraepelin (1896), who believed that the typical symptoms (namely, delusions, hallucinations, attention deficits and bizarre motor activity) were due to a form of mental deterioration which began in adolescence. But Bleuler (1911) observed that many patients displaying these symptoms *didn't* go on deteriorating, and that illness often began much later than adolescence. Consequently, he introduced the term 'schizophrenia' instead (literally 'split mind' or 'divided self') to describe an illness in which 'the personality loses its unity'.

According to Clare (1976), the diagnosis of schizophrenia in the UK relies greatly on Schneider's (1959) *first-rank symptoms*.

Table 44.2 *Schneider's (1959) first-rank symptoms of schizophrenia*

Passivity experiences and **thought disturbances**: *thought insertion* (thoughts are inserted into one's mind from outside and are under external influence), *thought withdrawal* (thoughts are removed from one's mind and are externally controlled), and *thought broadcasting* (thoughts are broadcast to/otherwise made known to others). External forces may include the Martians, the Communists, and the Government.

Auditory hallucinations (in the third person): *hallucinatory voices* are heard discussing one's thoughts or behaviour as they occur (a kind of running commentary), arguing about oneself (or using one's name), or repeating one's thoughts out loud/anticipating one's thoughts. They're often accusatory, obscene and derogatory, and may order the patient to commit extreme acts of violence. They're experienced as alien or under the influence of some external source, and also in the light of concurrent delusions (e.g. the voice of God or the devil: see below). The hallucinations of patients with *organic* psychoses are predominantly *visual*.

Primary delusions: *false beliefs* (incompatible with reality, usually of *persecution* or *grandeur*) held with extraordinary conviction, impervious to other experiences or compelling counter argument/contradictory evidence. The patient may be so convinced of their truth that they act on the strength of their belief, even if this involves murder and rape (as in the case of Peter Sutcliffe, the 'Yorkshire Ripper').

Schneider's first-rank symptoms are *subjective experiences*, which can only be inferred on the basis of the patient's verbal report. Slater & Roth (1969) regard hallucinations as the *least* important of all the major symptoms, because they aren't exclusive to schizophrenia (this is also true of delusions: see below). Slater and Roth identify four additional symptoms, which are *directly observable* from the patient's behaviour. (See Table 44.3 on page 653.)

Varieties of schizophrenia

Simple schizophrenia

This often appears during late adolescence, and has a slow, gradual onset. The main symptoms are gradual social withdrawal and difficulty in making friends, aimlessness and

Table 44.3 *Major symptoms of schizophrenia (based on Slater & Roth, 1969)*

Thought process disorder: the inability to keep to the point, being easily distracted/side-tracked. In *clang associations* (e.g. 'big', 'pig', 'twig'), words are 'thrown together' based on their sound rather than their meaning; this produces an apparently incoherent jumble of words ('*word salad*'). Also, the inability to finish a sentence, sometimes stopping in the middle of a word (*thought blocking*), inventing new words (*neologisms*) and interpreting language (e.g. proverbs) literally.

Disturbance of affect: events/situations don't elicit their usual emotional response (*blunting*), there's a more pervasive, generalised absence of emotional expression (as in minimal inflection in speech, and lack of normal variation in facial/bodily movements used to convey feelings: *flattening of affect*), loss of appropriate emotional responses (e.g. laughing/getting angry for no apparent reason, changing mood very suddenly, giggling when given some bad news: *incongruity of affect*).

Psychomotor disorders: muscles in a state of semi-rigidity (*catalepsy*), grimacing of facial muscles, limb twitching, stereotyped behaviours (such as constant pacing up and down), or assuming a fixed position for long periods of time, even several years in extreme cases (*catatonic stupor*).

Lack of volition: inability to make decisions or carry out a particular action, loss of will power or drive, loss of interest in what's going on and affection for friends/family.

idleness, blunting of affect, loss of volition and drive, and a decline in academic or occupational performance. Such people may become drifters or tramps, and are often regarded by others as idle and 'layabouts', but there are no major psychotic symptoms as in the other types of schizophrenia. Only ICD actually distinguishes this type, which is still used in some countries.

Hebephrenic (disorganised) schizophrenia

This is probably the nearest thing to many people's idea about what a 'mad' or 'crazy' person is like, and is normally diagnosed only in adolescents and young adults. Mood is shallow and inappropriate, thought is disorganised, and speech is incoherent. Delusions and hallucinations are fleeting and fragmentary, and behaviour is irresponsible, unpredictable, silly or mischievous, childish or bizarre and sometimes may be violent (if, for example, the patient is approached while hallucinating).

Catatonic schizophrenia

The patient may alternate between extremes such as *hyperkinesis* (hyperactivity) and stupor (a marked reduction of spontaneous movements and activity), or *automatic obedience* ('command automatism') and *negativism* (apparently motiveless resistance to all instructions/attempts to be moved or doing the opposite of what's asked). There may be episodes of apparently purposeless motor activity combined with a dreamlike (*oneroid*) state with vivid scenic hallucinations. Other characteristics are *mutism*, *posturing* (the voluntary assumption of inappropriate and bizarre postures) and *waxy flexibility* (maintenance of the limbs and body in externally imposed positions).

Paranoid (paraphrenic) schizophrenia

This is dominated by relatively stable, often *paranoid delusions* (although *delusions of grandeur* are also quite common), usually accompanied by auditory hallucinations. But in other respects, the patient is less disturbed (the personality is better preserved) than in the other kinds. It's the most *homogeneous* type, that is, paranoid schizophrenics are more alike than those in other categories.

Undifferentiated (atypical)

This category is meant to accommodate patients who cannot be easily placed elsewhere, that is, psychotic conditions that meet the general diagnostic criteria for schizophrenia, but which don't conform to any of the main types of schizophrenia (due to either insufficient or overlapping symptoms).

With the possible exception of paranoid, these 'sub-categories' are of doubtful validity. Some patients present symptoms of one sub-group at one time, then those of another sub-group later, and catatonic symptoms are much less common now than 50 years ago. The sub-groups cannot be clearly distinguished in clinical practice (Gelder *et al.*, 1999), which relates to the issue of reliability and validity of psychiatric diagnosis (see Chapter 43, pages 640–642).

Broah Schizophrene by Brian Charnley
This is one of a number of pictures in which the artist set out to depict some of the delusions and hallucinations which he himself was experiencing while suffering from schizophrenia. These included the feeling that other people had access to all his thoughts

Theories of schizophrenia

Is schizophrenia a brain disease?

Not only is schizophrenia one of the most serious forms of mental disorder but, as we saw in Chapter 43, it has become the focus for the whole controversy surrounding the *medical model*. Remember, Szasz distinguishes between neurological disorders and problems in living, leaving no room for 'mental illness'. So, is there evidence to suggest that schizophrenia is a neurological disorder?

When Kraepelin first identified dementia praecox, he was convinced that it was a physical disease like any other. The neuropathological changes associated with *general paralysis of the insane* (caused by syphilis) and *Alzheimer's disease* had just been discovered, and he expected that similar 'markers' would be found for schizophrenia and manic–depressive illness.

However, schizophrenia was categorised as a functional psychosis up until 1978 when, according to Gershon & Rieder (1992), the then new CT scan (see Chapter 4) was used for the first time to study the brains of chronic schizophrenics (by Johnstone *et al.* at the Clinical Research Centre in Middlesex, England). It revealed that chronic schizophrenics show an increase in the size of the lateral cerebral ventricles (the fluid-filled spaces in the middle of the brain), and other X-ray evidence confirmed that there was less brain tissue (especially in the medial temporal lobe). This was subsequently confirmed by MRI scans which, along with postmortem examinations, also revealed that schizophrenics have smaller hippocampi and part of their limbic system is also smaller. Gershon and Rieder also cite research which has shown reduced blood flow in the frontal cortex of schizophrenics, implying decreased neuronal activity. Postmortems also show that certain groups of neurons are organised in an abnormal way, or are connected differently, compared with non-schizophrenics.

All these differences are found when patients first develop symptoms (and may even precede the onset of symptoms), which suggests that they're *not* the result of being ill for a long time or of medication (Harrison, 1995). Also, these differences don't progress over time, nor is there any evidence of neural scar tissue (*gliosis*) that's normally found in degenerative disorders (such as Alzheimer's and Huntington's). This suggests a neurodevelopmental disorder, that is, a failure of brain tissue to develop normally, such as failure of neuronal growth or neuronal connections, or a disturbance in the 'pruning' of neurons that normally takes place between three and 15 years of age (Gershon & Rieder, 1992: see Chapters 4 and 37).

However, the differences are only apparent if a group of schizophrenics is compared with a group of non-schizophrenics: no-one can yet diagnose schizophrenia in an individual based *solely* on a brain scan or looking down a microscope (Harrison, 1995). Even if this could be done, the more fundamental question as to why some people develop these disorders and others don't would remain unanswered. The cognitive and affective abnormalities involved in psychosis are so severe that it's reasonable to expect brain abnormalities to be involved (Frith & Cahill, 1995), but the data are largely *correlational*.

Ask yourself ...

- How do psychologists interested in individual differences try to separate the effects of variables (potential causes of those differences) that are correlated?
- How could these methods be applied here? (See Chapter 41.)

The biochemical theory of schizophrenia

According to the *dopamine hypothesis*, the direct cause of schizophrenic symptoms is an excess of the neurotransmitter dopamine. The evidence for this hypothesis comes from three main sources:

- postmortems on schizophrenics show unusually high levels of dopamine, especially in the limbic system (Iversen, 1979);
- anti-schizophrenic drugs (such as chlorpromazine) are thought to work by binding to dopamine receptor sites, that is, they inhibit the ability of the dopamine receptors to respond to dopamine, thus reducing dopamine activity (see Chapter 45);
- high doses of amphetamines and L-dopa (used in the treatment of Parkinson's disease), both of which enhance the activity of dopamine, can sometimes produce symptoms very similar to the psychomotor disorders seen in certain types of schizophrenia. Dopamine-containing neurons are concentrated in the basal ganglia and frontal cortex, which are concerned with the initiation and control of movement; degeneration of the dopamine system produces Parkinson's disease (see Chapter 4).

Overall, the evidence is inconclusive (Lavender, 2000). For example, there's no consistent difference in dopamine levels between drug-free schizophrenics and normals, nor is there any evidence of higher levels of other metabolites indicating greater dopamine activity (Jackson, 1986). Even if such evidence did exist, this could just as easily be a *result* of schizophrenia as its cause, and if dopamine *were* found to be a causative factor, this might only be *indirect* (for example, abnormal family circumstances give rise to high levels of dopamine which, in turn, trigger the symptoms (Lloyd *et al.*, 1984).

It's unlikely that any problems with dopamine production/receptivity will prove to be the basic biochemical abnormality underlying all forms of schizophrenia – although it may play a crucial role in some forms (Jackson, 1990). According to Lavender (2000):

> '... if schizophrenia is not a clearly identifiable syndrome but an umbrella term covering a range of symptoms with unclear onset, course, and outcome, then it is obvious that much of the work investigating a specific biological basis will inevitably be inconclusive. So far, this appears to be the case'.

As Bentall (1990) argues, perhaps the time has come to concentrate on specific symptoms, before trying to find the biochemical cause(s).

The genetic theory of schizophrenia

As with intelligence (see Chapter 41), *family resemblance studies* confound genetic and environmental influences. In other words, there's no way of telling whether the correlation between the risk of developing schizophrenia and degree of family resemblance/blood tie is due to the greater genetic similarity or the greater similarity of environments. The two major alternative designs, *twin* and *adoption studies*, both face problems of their own. For example, they presuppose that schizophrenia is a distinct syndrome which can be reliably diagnosed by different psychiatrists (but see Chapter 43).

Twin studies

Ask yourself ...

- What conclusions can you draw fom Table 44.4 (opposite)?

As Table 44.4 shows, there's a wide variation in the concordance rate for schizophrenia in different studies, for both MZs and DZs, suggesting that different countries use different criteria for diagnosing schizophrenia (see Chapter 43). By the same token, if the highest concordance rate for MZs is 69 per cent (using a 'broad' criterion), this still leaves plenty of scope for the role of environmental factors. If schizophrenia were totally genetically determined, then we'd expect to find 100 per cent concordance rate for MZs: if one member of an MZ pair has schizophrenia, the other twin should also have it in every single case. In fact, most diagnosed cases *don't* report a family history (Frith & Cahill, 1995).

Nevertheless, the average concordance rate for MZs is five times higher than that for DZs (50 per cent and ten per cent, respectively: Shields, 1976, 1978). A more precise estimate for the relative importance of genetic and environmental factors comes from studies where MZs reared apart are compared with MZs reared together: according to Shields (1976, 1978), the concordance rates are quite similar for the two groups, suggesting a major genetic contribution.

Box 44.7 The equal environments assumption

Twin studies are based on the *equal environments assumption*:

- MZs aren't treated more similarly than same-sex DZs; or

- if they are, this doesn't increase MZs' similarity for the characteristic in question relative to same-sex DZs.

(This assumption therefore applies to the study of intelligence, too.)

According to Lilienfeld (1995), this assumption has stood up surprisingly well to careful empirical scrutiny. For example, researchers have identified MZs and DZs whose *zygosity* has been misclassified (i.e. MZs mistaken for DZs and vice versa). If similarity of rearing were the key factor underlying the greater concordance for MZs, then *perceived* zygosity (as opposed to actual zygosity) should be the best predictor of concordance. However, twin similarity in personality and cognitive ability is related much more closely to *actual* than perceived zygosity (Scarr and Carter-Saltzman, 1979).

Also, the greater similarity in parental rearing for MZs seems to be due largely or entirely to the fact that MZs elicit more similar reactions from their parents (Lytton, 1977). It seems, therefore, that the greater similarity of MZs is a *cause*, rather than an effect, of their more similar parental treatment.

Adoption studies

In many ways, adoption studies provide the most unequivocal test of genetic influence, because they allow the clearest separation of genetic and environmental factors. For example, Heston (1966) studied 47 adults born to schizophrenic mothers and

Table 44.4 *Concordance rates for schizophrenia for identical (MZ) and non-identical (DZ) twins (based on Rose et al., 1984)*

Study	'Narrow' concordance *		'Broad' concordance*	
	% MZs	% DZs	% MZs	% DZs
Rosanoff et al. (1934); USA (41 MZs, 53 DZs)	44	9	61	13
Kallmann (1946); USA (174 MZs, 296 DZs)	59	11	69	11–14
Slater (1953) England (37 MZs, 58 DZs)	65	14	65	14
Gottesman & Shields (1966); England (24 MZs, 33 DZs)	42	15	54	18
Kringlen (1968); Norway (55 MZs, 90 DZs)	25	7	38	10
Allen et al. (1972); USA (95 MZs, 125 DZs)	14	4	27	5
Fischer (1973); Denmark (21 MZs, 41 DZs)	24	10	48	20

* 'Narrow' is based on attempts to apply a relatively strict set of criteria when diagnosing schizophrenia. 'Broad' includes borderline schizophrenia, schizoaffective psychosis, and paranoid with schizophrenia-like features.

separated from them within three days of birth. As children, they'd been reared in a variety of circumstances, though not by the mother's family. They were compared (average age 36) with controls who were matched for circumstances of upbringing, but where mothers hadn't been schizophrenic: five of the experimental group but none of the controls were diagnosed as schizophrenic.

Rosenthal *et al.* (1971) began a series of studies in 1965 in Denmark, which has national registers of psychiatric cases and adoptions. They confirmed Heston's findings, using children separated from schizophrenic mothers, on average at six months.

The major study (Kety *et al.*, 1975) uses a different design. Two groups of adoptees were identified, 33 who had schizophrenia and a matched group who didn't. Rates of disorder were compared in the biological and adoptive families of the two groups of adoptees – the rate was greater among the biological relatives of the schizophrenic adoptees than among those of the controls, a finding which supports the genetic hypothesis. Further, the rate of schizophrenia wasn't increased among couples who adopted the schizophrenic adoptees, suggesting that environmental factors weren't of crucial importance (Gelder *et al.*, 1989). The reverse situation was studied by Wender *et al.* (1974), who found no increase among adoptees with normal biological parents but with a schizophrenic adoptive parent. Gottesman & Shields (1976, 1982), reviewing adoption studies, conclude that they show a major role for heredity.

A crucial assumption made when evaluating the results of adoption studies is *random placement* (see Chapter 41), that is, adoptees are placed with parents who are no more similar to their biological parents than by chance. Rose *et al.* (1984) consider selective placement to be the rule (rather than random placement) and so a major, if not fatal, stumbling block of adoption studies. However, Lilienfeld (1995) believes the random placement assumption is largely or entirely warranted.

Conclusions: the nature and nurture of schizophrenia

Perhaps the most reasonable conclusion is that there is converging evidence, from multiple sources, implicating genetic factors in the aetiology of schizophrenia. Its heritability seems to be comparable to that of any medical condition known to have a major genetic component, such as diabetes, hypertension, coronary artery disease and breast cancer (Lilienfeld, 1995). However, the precise mode of inheritance remains controversial (Frith & Cahill, 1995; Lilienfeld, 1995). The most popular current view is the 'multifactorial' (*polygenic*) model: a number of genes are involved which determine a predisposition, which then requires environmental factors to trigger the symptoms of the illness. This is referred to as a *diathesis* (i.e. predisposition) *–stress model*.

Zubin & Spring (1977), for example, claim that what we probably inherit is a degree of vulnerability to exhibiting schizophrenic symptoms. Whether or not we do depends on environmental stresses which may include viral infections during pregnancy (especially influenza A), severe malnourishment during pregnancy, birth injury or difficult birth, being born in winter, as well as 'critical life events' (see Chapter 38).

Laing and existential psychiatry

During the 1950s and 1960s, several British psychiatrists, notably R. D. Laing, Cooper and Esterson, united in their rejection of the medical model of mental disorder. Like Szasz, they denied the existence of schizophrenia as a disease entity and instead saw it as a metaphor for dealing with people whose behaviour and experience fail to conform to the dominant model of social reality. They thus spearheaded the *antipsychiatry movement* (Graham, 1986). Heather (1976) identifies three major landmarks in the development of Laing's thought, corresponding to the publication of three major books:

- In *The Divided Self* (1959), Laing tried to make sense of schizophrenia by 'getting inside the head' of a schizophrenic, trying to see the world as the schizophrenic sees it. This *existentialist analysis* retained the categories of classic psychiatry, but proceeded from the assumption that what the schizophrenic says and does are intelligible if you listen carefully enough. Laing found a *split* in the schizophrenic's relationship with the world and with the self: s/he experiences an intense form of *ontological insecurity*, making everyday events a threat to his/her very existence.
- In *Self and Others* (1961), Laing proposed the *family interaction model*. Schizophrenia can only be understood as

something which takes place *between* people (not *inside* them, as maintained by Laing's earlier psychoanalytic model). To understand individuals we must study not individuals but interactions between individuals, and this is the subject matter of *social phenomenology* (see Chapter 22). The family interaction model was consistent with research in America, especially that of Bateson *et al.* (1956), which showed that schizophrenia arises within families which use 'pathological' forms of communication, in particular contradictory messages (*double-binds*). For example, a mother induces her son to give her a hug, but when he does she tells him 'not to be such a baby'. Laing & Esterson (1964) presented eleven family case histories (in all of which one member becomes a diagnosed schizophrenic), in order to make schizophrenia intelligible in the context of what happens within the patient's family and, in so doing, to further undermine the disease model of schizophrenia.

- In *The Politics of Experience* (1967), two new models were presented. The *conspiratorial model* maintains that schizophrenia is a label, a form of violence perpetrated by some people on others. The family, GP and psychiatrists conspire against schizophrenics in order to preserve their definition of reality (the *status quo*). They treat schizophrenics as if they were sick, imprisoning them in mental hospitals, where they're degraded and invalidated as human beings. According to the *psychedelic model*, the schizophrenic is an exceptionally eloquent critic of society, and schizophrenia is 'itself a natural way of healing our own appalling state of alienation called normality'. Schizophrenia is seen as a voyage into 'inner space', a 'natural healing process'. Unfortunately, the 'natural sequence' of schizophrenia is very rarely allowed to occur because, says Laing, we're too busy treating the patient.

Eating disorders

In the past 30 years, eating disorders have become widespread in Western industrialised societies. This may be related to the overabundance of food, but it's likely to be influenced by societal norms that link attractiveness to being thin (APA, 1994). Indeed, the popular and scientific assumption is that the preoccupation with thinness and dieting rampant in Western societies is a direct cause of eating disorders. However, according to Fedoroff & McFarlane (1998):

'... it is well established that eating disorders are multidetermined and that culture is only one of many factors that contribute to the development of eating disorders ...'.

Furthermore:

'... cultural factors can only be understood as they interact with the psychology and biology of the vulnerable individual ... a culture cannot cause a disorder ...'.

Anorexia nervosa

Anorexia nervosa (AN) (literally, 'nervous lack of appetite') usually begins in adolescence (16–17) after the patient (90–95 per cent of whom are female) has become over-concerned about 'puppy fat' and has begun to diet. This dieting often masquerades as 'vegetarianism' (Lipsedge, 1997b) and progresses to a relentless attempt to achieve what is in fact an abnormally low body weight. AN seems to be increasing, with one to two per cent of schoolgirls and students affected. Up to one third also describe episodes of uncontrollable overeating (*binge-eating/bulimia nervosa*: see below). There's also evidence of an increase in cases of AN among males (Seligmann *et al.*, 1994). Where the age of onset is 8–14, about 25 per cent are boys (Frude, 1998).

An anorexic patient's painting of how she sees herself at 'normal' weight – obese, ugly and resentful (from Crisp, 1980)

Amenorrhoea is an important symptom of AN, which often occurs early in the develoment of the disorder. In about 20 per cent of cases, it precedes any obvious weight loss, and some patients seek help for this rather than their AN. Depression, lability of mood, social withdrawal, and lack of sexual interest are all common. Some patients have signs that are secondary to the low food intake, including constipation, low blood pressure, bradycardia (slow heart rate), sensitivity to cold and hypothermia (Gelder *et al.*, 1999). Those whose dieting progresses to AN (the vast *minority*) are more likely to have low self-esteem, and prevalence is increased among groups for whom weight and physical appearance are particularly relevant, such as ballet students and models (see Critical Discussion 44.3, page 659). Anorexics (or *anorectics*) are more likely to die than non-patients, both from the effects of starvation and suicide. According to the Eating Disorders Association (EDA), anorectics have the highest mortality rate of any mental disorder – between 13 and 20 per cent (Waterhouse & Mayes, 2000).

Among those with improved weight and menstrual function, some continue to have abnormal eating habits, some become overweight, and some develop bulimia. The most useful predictor of poor outcome is a long history of AN at the time when the patient is fist seen by a doctor (Gelder *et al.*, 1999).

Bulimia nervosa

As noted earlier, it's been known for some time that anorectics show bulimic features, but *bulimia nervosa* (BN) (from *bous* meaning 'ox' and *limos* meaning 'hunger') was only identified and named as a distinct disorder in 1979. The clear overlap between BN patients and the bulimic sub-group of AN patients has led some researchers to question whether these are really separate disorders (Mitchell & McCarthy, 2000). However, BN sufferers tend to be older, less likely to come from middle or upper class backgrounds, more likely to have been overweight in the past and engage in self-destructive or antisocial, impulsive behaviours (such as shoplifting, drug abuse, or deliberate self-harm). According to Russell (1979), BN is more intractable to treat, and patients have a poorer prognosis. It affects one to two per cent of females aged 15–40 (Gelder *et al.*, 1999).

- The disturbance does not occur exclusively during episodes of anorexia nervosa.

Specific types:
- *Purging type:* These individuals regularly purge after binge eating via self-induced vomiting or abuse of laxatives.
- *Non-purging type:* These individuals do not engage in self-induced vomiting or laxative abuse. Some may use compensatory methods of dieting and exercising.

Depression is common (mainly secondary to the eating disorder), and there is considerable lability of mood. It's not uncommon for sufferers to contemplate suicide after binging, or to actually attempt suicide. While denial is a common feature of AN, BN sufferers are usually well aware that they have a serious problem and require help (Mitchell & McCarthy, 2000). Also, the balance between the various characteristic behaviours means that bulimics are usually of normal weight (they don't 'look' bulimic – unlike anorectics).

The much publicised English anorectic twins, Samantha and Michaela Kendall. Despite receiving treatment in the USA, Samantha eventually died. Michaela died three years later

Episodes of bulimia may be precipitated by stressful events, the breaking of self-imposed dietary rules, or planned. It's the extreme lack of control over eating that distinguishes BN from AN. The binge initially provides pleasurable relief from the urge to eat and other kinds of tension. But this is soon followed by guilt and disgust. Repeated vomiting causes potassium depletion, which induces weakness, cardiac arrythmia (irregular

heart rhythms) and renal damage. Urinary infections and epileptic seizures may also occur (Gelder *et al.*, 1999). Tooth enamel becomes eroded by the gastric acid brought up by vomiting.

> *Ask yourself ...*
>
> - Based on these criteria for diagnosing AN and BN, do you think they represent exaggerations of 'normal' eating/dieting behaviours, or are they qualitatively different?

Explaining eating disorders

The quotes from Fedoroff & McFarlane (1998) at the beginning of this section imply that all the major theoretical perspectives have something to contribute to explaining the origins of both AN and BN. However, the recent – and ongoing – public debate about eating disorders, together with the claim that they may be a Western *culture-bound syndrome* (CBS) (e.g. DiNicola, 1990), suggests that explanations at the cultural (rather than the individual) level may be the place to start.

Are eating disorders universal?

While many studies have found evidence of common symptomatology as described by DSM and ICD in non-Western societies, others have proposed that some symptoms *don't* appear in some non-Western cultures. For example, an intense fear of fatness and body image disturbance aren't typical of AN patients in Hong Kong and India, and their reasons for refusing food are more likely to be linked to somatic symptoms, such as abdominal bloating and fullness. They're also much less likely to display bulimic symptoms. In non-Western countries, weight loss is often achieved purely by dietary restriction, rather than purging behaviours (Federoff & McFarlane, 1998).

Although emaciation, food refusal and amenorrhoea are universal symptoms of AN, it's important to evaluate symptoms in their cultural context. For example, is fasting a culturally sanctioned expression of religious piety (as in Middle Eastern countries), or is it a symptom of an underlying disorder? All the screening and diagnostic instruments have been developed in Europe and North America, and are based directly on Western concepts of abnormal eating. Consequently, patients who don't fit the model, but who may well be showing cultural diversity in the expression of a psychiatric disorder, will be ignored (Kleinman, 1987). This makes the detection of reliable cross-cultural differences very difficult.

Subcultural differences

According to Federoff & McFarlane (1998), the majority of the evidence from surveys and clinical reports indicates that the prevalence of AN and BN in non-white groups is lower than among whites. An interesting exception to this consistent finding is described in Key Study 44.1 (page 659).

KEY STUDY 44.1

BN among Asian and non-Asian girls in England (Mumford & Whitehouse, 1988; Mumford *et al.*, 1991)

Mumford and colleagues compared 204 Asian and 355 white schoolgirls in the North of England. Those whose self-report measures indicated a possible eating disorder were interviewed. 3.4 per cent of the Asian girls and 0.8 per cent of the white girls met the DSM-III-R (1987) criteria for BN.

Contrary to expectations, Asian girls from traditional families were *more* likely to develop an eating disorder than those from more Westernised families. The researchers suggest that the tensions of living in a traditional Asian family within a Western culture might be responsible.

Francesco Scavullo and the V girls. Sophie Dahl (second from the left) and her fuller figure colleagues demonstrate that thinness is not the only ideal/desirable body shape

Mumford *et al.* (1992) also found that English-speaking girls in Lahore, Pakistan, showed similar rates of BN to white schoolgirls in England. Significantly, the Pakistani girls lived in an area where there were many advertisements for slimming clinics and 'keep fit' clubs. They were also from upper social classes and were more likely to have adopted Western lifestyles and values.

The sociocultural hypothesis

Although (as previously noted) cultural factors aren't solely responsible for the development of eating disorders, Federoff & McFarlane (1998) acknowledge that:

'The convergence of evidence from numerous studies strongly indicates that sociocultural factors play a pivotal role in the development of eating disorders in Western societies ...'.

Ask yourself ...

* What kind of evidence would support the sociocultural hypothesis?
* What specific cultural factors would you expect to be particularly influential?

The sociocultural hypothesis is supported by reports of the emergence of eating disorders in developing countries, and evidence of their occurrence among immigrants from those countries who relocate to Western societies. As developing societies become more industrialised, there's greater exposure to Western attitudes and habits, including those relating to weight and body shape.

According to Lee (1993), Chinese in Hong Kong are changing from a traditional low-fat, high-fibre diet to a more Westernised, fast-food diet. Obesity is becoming more commonplace among adolescents, as are advertisements for weight-loss clinics and fitness clubs. The incidence of AN and BN is increasing in Japan as the influence of American culture on Japanese society becomes greater (Federoff & McFarlane, 1998).

If fast-food is a characteristic of Western culture, so is the preferred or 'ideal' appearance of women.

CRITICAL DISCUSSION 44.3

Can you catch anorexia from *Vogue* magazine?

In June 2000, the British government held a 'super-waif summit' to debate the causes of eating disorders. In prosperous Western societies, where food is abundant, thinness is a status symbol for women. Slimmer physiques reflect upward social mobility, and fat is generally degraded and stigmatised.

Taking *Playboy* centrefolds and Miss America contestants as representing the Western ideal of feminine beauty, Garner *et al.* (1980) found that ideal shape became progressively slimmer from 1959 to 1978. But at the same time, the actual weight and size of the female population has been *increasing*; this merely adds to the pressure on women to lose weight. This obsession with thinness is so widespread that a moderate degree of body dissatisfaction is now normative among Western women (Rodin *et al.*, 1985).

It's widely believed that the female preference for thinness is influenced by its glorification and glamorisation by the media, especially perhaps in women's magazines such as *Vogue*. A recent report by the British Medical Association claims that media images have a major impact on women's perceptions of their bodies, and calls for more 'Sophie Dahls than Kate Mosses' (*Nursing Times*, 2000).

According to Freeman (2000), who was hospitalised for four years with AN as a teenager, the media *aren't* the cause of eating disorders. But the current culture of skinniness legitimises the anorectic's belief that she's too fat and so on. As serious a problem as AN and BN are, the EDA regards *obesity* is the number one eating disorder among young girls –

and the population as a whole. According to figures for 1998, 17 per cent of British men and 21 per cent of women are clinically obese (Waterhouse & Mayes, 2000).

Interestingly, May 2000's *Marie Claire* published two different covers, one showing a thin Pamela Anderson, the other a curvaceous Sophie Dahl. Sixty-five per cent of readers bought the Dahl cover. It appears that sales of Barbie (in real terms 5 ft 8 in tall and a size 8) are falling, and the supermarket chain Tesco approached Mattel, Barbie's manufacturer, to produce her in a size 14/16 (Robinson, 2000).

Superimposed on these cultural factors are individual and family influences, which are the focus of psychodynamic, cognitive and genetic models (see Gross *et al.*, 2000; Mitchell & McCarthy, 2000). Since only a minority of females develop eating disorders, these other factors must play a part.

CHAPTER SUMMARY

- While **fear** evolved as an **adaptive** mechanism, **anxiety** often occurs in the absence of any external threat.

- A **phobia** is an extreme, irrational fear. Most common is **agoraphobia**, followed by **social** phobias and **specific** phobias. **Preparedness** may help explain why some phobias are more easily aquired than others.

- **Obsessions** are recurrent, intrusive thoughts and feelings, often accompanied by **compulsions**, which are repetitive, ritualised behaviours. Their function is to prevent a dreaded event and reduce distress.

- Skinner's **superstition hypothesis** tries to explain how **obsessive-compulsive disorder** (OCD) develops. Other, more cognitive explanations include Rachman's **thought–action fusion** (TAF) interpretation.

- **Body dysmorphic disorder** (BDD) has much in common with OCD. Intrusive thoughts focus on a particular party of the body which the patient finds defective, and compulsion-like behaviours commonly also occur.

- Symptoms of **post-traumatic stress disorder** (PTSD) include both defensive **avoidance/repression** and **flashbacks**.

- PTSD can be seen as a breakdown of the normal stress response. Excessive production of **endorphins** may explain the numbness, and **adrenaline** and **noradrenaline** are thought to destroy cells in the **hippocampus**.

- **Mood (affective) disorders** can be **bipolar** or **unipolar**. The traditional distinction between **endogenous/psychotic** and **reactive/neurotic depression** is controversial and causation is no longer implied when a diagnosis of clinical depression is made.

- The higher rate of depression among women is more likely to be due to **non-biological** than hormonal factors. **Cultural factors** are important in both the expression and diagnosis of depression.

- **Schizophrenia** is one of the most serious of all mental disorders. Schneider's **first-rank symptoms** are **subjective experiences**, while Slater and Roth's four additional symptoms are **directly observable** from the patient's behaviour.

- Differences between the brains of schizophrenics and non-schizophrenics aren't sufficient on their own to allow diagnosis, and evidence for the **dopamine hypothesis** is inconclusive.

- **Twin studies** point towards a major genetic contribution, although the concordance rate for MZs is far from 100 per cent. A crucial feature of twin studies is the **equal environments assumption**, which appears to be justified. **Adoption studies** also support the genetic theory.

- However, **environmental factors** trigger the symptoms (the **diathesis–stress model**). There's no clear-cut evidence as to what the environmental triggers are.

- **Anorexia nervosa** (AN) and **bulimia nervosa** (BN) have many symptoms in common. But bulimics are usually of normal weight, are older, are less likely to come from middle/upper class backgrounds, and engage in self-destructive or antisocial behaviours.

- AN and BN are occurring more frequently in developing cultures as they become more industrialised/Westernised, which includes changes in diet and attitudes towards desirable physical appearance. While there's much support for the **sociocultural hypothesis**, other **individual** factors are needed to provide a complete account.

Self-assessment questions

1 Discuss theory and research into **one or more** anxiety disorder.
2 Critically assess the role of cultural factors in **two or more** mental disorders.
3 Describe and evaluate **one or more** explanations of schizophrenia.

Web addresses

http://www.mentalhealth.com

http://www.nimh.hih.gov/publicat/ocd.htm

http://www.long-beach.va.gov.ptsd/stress.html

http://www.trauma-pages.com

http://www.mentalhealth.com

http://www.bbc.co.uk/health/features/eating-disorders.shtml

http://www.psycom.net/depression.central

http://www.gene.ucl.ac.uk/users/dcurtis/lectures/pgenfunc.html

www.edauk.com

http://rcpsych.ac.uk/public/help/anor/anor-frame.htm

http://mentalhelp.net/factsfam/anorexai.htm

http://www.priory-hospital.co.uk/htm/bulimi.htm

http://www.edreferral.com/bulimia_nervosa.htm

Further reading

Gelder, M., Mayou, R. & Geddes, J. (1999) *Psychiatry* (2nd edition) Oxford: Blackwell. Although written for psychiatry students, this is a rich source of information for psychologists.

Champion, L. & Power, M. (Eds) (2000) *Adult Psychological Problems: An Introduction* (2nd edition) Hove: Psychology Press. Separate chapters, by different authors, on all the major disorders, plus very useful introductory chapter describing the main psychological models.

Chapter 45

Treatments and Therapies

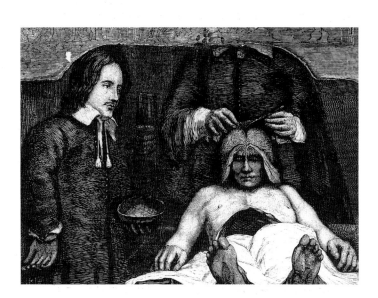

Introduction and overview

As Chapters 43 and 44 have shown, the study of psychological abnormality involves a convergence of psychiatry (a branch of medicine) and abnormal psychology, the latter defined as the scientific study of the causes of abnormal behaviour/mental disorders. In this chapter, the focus is on the *application* of what we know about abnormality in an attempt to help people with psychological problems. The two professional branches of the discipline of psychology whose goals are the maintenance and generation of mental health are *clinical psychology* and (the more recent) *counselling psychology* (Powell, 1995).

Both clinical and counselling psychology draw on the same research findings and range of theoretical approaches that have recurred throughout this book. They also both adopt the *scientist–practitioner model* of helping: the professional helper is guided by, and operates within the framework of, general scientific methods when assessing alternative treatments/therapies (Dallos & Cullen, 1990: see Chapter 3).

While clinical psychologists have traditionally been more influenced by *behavioural approaches* (based on classical and operant conditioning), counselling psychologists (as well as trained counsellors, who may not be psychologists) have been more influenced by the *humanistic approach*. A third, overlapping, professional group are *psychotherapists*; their methods reflect (to varying degrees) the influence of Freud's *psychoanalysis*.

Classifying treatments and therapies

The relationship between theory and therapy

Where theory has grown out of clinical practice (that is, work with psychiatric patients), theory and therapy are intimately connected (as in Freud's psychoanalysis, and Rogers's client-centred therapy). But behavioural therapies aren't always derived directly from learning theory, which is sometimes unable to account for therapeutic outcomes and certain aspects of abnormal behaviour. Some forms of therapy aren't directly related to any particular theory (e.g. psychodrama and transactional analysis) and, in practice, treatment is often *eclectic*, that is, it combines different techniques from different approaches.

Dimensions along which treatments can be placed

■ What most *psychological treatments* have in common is a rejection of the *medical model* (see Chapters 43 and 44). For example, although Freud distinguished between 'symptoms' and 'underlying pathology', the latter is conceived in psychological terms (not genetic or biochemical) and he was concerned with the individual and not the 'disorder'. Although he used diagnostic labels, he did so for linguistic convenience rather than as an integral part of his theories. He focused on understanding his patients' problems in their life context, rather than on clinical labelling (Mackay, 1975).

■ One aspect of 'technique' which is profoundly important in the therapeutic relationship is whether or not the therapist makes suggestions and gives advice to the patient (or client). In *directive therapies*, concrete suggestions are made and clients are often instructed to do certain things (such as 'homework' in between sessions, or specific exercises under the therapist's supervision). For example, *behaviour therapy* concentrates directly upon changing people's behaviour (and any desired changes in thoughts and feelings will 'look after themselves'). By contrast, *cognitive–behaviour therapy* (CBT) is aimed directly at thoughts and feelings: clients are instructed to talk to themselves in different ways, to give themselves instructions for behaviour, to write down their distressing and negative thought patterns, and so on.

■ *Non-directive therapies* concentrate on making sense of what's going on in the relationship between therapist and client, and on understanding the meanings of the client's experiences (as in psychoanalysis and client-centred therapy). These are more difficult to describe than directive therapies, because the therapist plays a more *passive* role:

'... listen[ing] and tak[ing] part with the client in exploring and experiencing what is going on between them'. (Oatley, 1984)

■ *Individual therapies* are conducted between a therapist and a client, while *group therapies* involve several clients at a time, with one or more therapists or leaders. Most of the major approaches described in this chapter are individual but some less well-known therapies are, by definition, group therapies (e.g. psychodrama, encounter groups and therapeutic communities). We should also note that psychodynamic and client-centred therapies may be individual or group, but they'll be described here in their individual form.

A major development in psychotherapy in the late 1970s and early 1980s was the emergence of *family therapies* and *marital/couple therapy*, reflecting the growing awareness by therapists of the important role played by the client's relationships in the development and maintenance of their problems (Dryden, 1984). This change seems to have been inspired by Laing's family interaction model of schizophrenia (see Chapter 44), which has been applied to less 'serious' problems that commonly occur in families and between partners. Generally, where the problem is seen as *interpersonal*, family, marital/couple or group therapy is likely to be recommended. But where the problem is seen as 'residing' within the client (*intrapsychic*), individual therapy would be recommended.

What is psychotherapy?

The term 'psychotherapy' is sometimes used to refer to all psychological treatments (as opposed to biological or somatic ones). For example, Holmes & Lindley (1989) define it as:

'The systematic use of a relationship between therapist and patient – as opposed to pharmacological or social methods – to produce changes in cognition, feelings and behaviour'.

Similarly:

'Psychotherapy is distinguished from such other forms of psychiatric treatment as the use of drugs, surgery, electric shock treatment and insulin coma treatment'. (Freedman *et al.*, 1975)

'Psychotherapy' (or 'psychodynamic therapy': see Chapter 2) is also used to refer to those methods based, directly or indirectly, on Freud's psychoanalysis. This approach is also known as *insight therapies* (or 'talking cures').

In the UK, the tradition has been to contrast psychotherapy with behaviour therapy, while in the US psychotherapy is used more broadly to include behavioural psychotherapy as well as 'psychodynamic therapy'. However, the UK Council for Psychotherapy (UKCP) has a behavioural psychotherapy section (members of which include the British

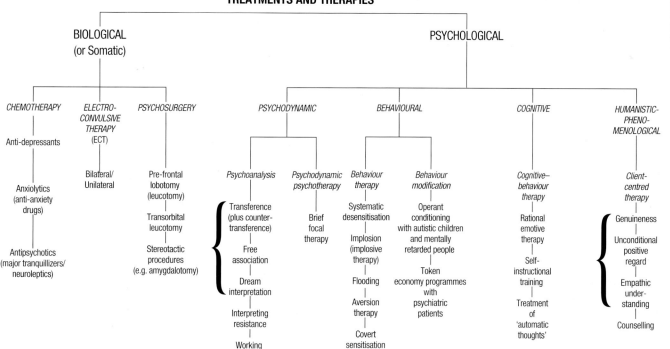

TREATMENTS AND THERAPIES

Figure 45.1 *Major approaches to treatment and therapy*

Association for Behavioural and Cognitive Psychotherapy), as well as a psychoanalytic and psychodynamic psychotherapy section. Other sections include humanistic and integrative psychotherapy, and family, marital and sexual therapy. In 1994, there were 73 member organisations of the UKCP. Special members include the British Psychological Society (BPS) and the Royal College of Psychiatrists, and the British Association for Counselling is an affiliated organisation (Pokorny, 1994).

Ask yourself ...

• Looking back at Chapter 43, try to identify (or infer) any principles (or specific details) that would be used by different theoretical approaches in the treatment of mental disorder. (You might find Chapter 4 useful too.)

Biological (somatic) therapies

Chemotherapy

This involves the use of *psychotropic drugs*, that is, drugs designed to affect mainly mental symptoms. Gelder *et al.* (1999) divide these into six groups, according to their primary actions (see Box 45.1). Several also have secondary actions (e.g. antidepressants also reduce anxiety). The focus here will be on the *antidepressants*, *anxiolytics* and *antipsychotics*.

Box 45.1 **Major categories of psychotropic drugs (Based on Gelder *et al.*, 1999)**

Anxiolytics: reduce anxiety. Because they have a general calming effect, they're sometimes called *minor tranquillisers*. In larger doses, they cause drowsiness (and so are sometimes called *sedatives*).

Hypnotics: promote sleep. Many are of the same type as drugs used as anxiolytics.

Antipsychotics: control delusions, hallucinations and psychomotor excitement in psychoses. They're sometimes called *major tranquillisers* because of their calming effect, and *neuroleptics*, because of their neurological side-effects, such as those resembling Parkinson's disease.

Mood-stabilising drugs: used to prevent the recurrence of affective disorders. One of these is *lithium carbonate* (Lithane or Lithonate), used to treat *bipolar mood disorder*.

Antidepressants: relieve the symptoms of depressive disorders, but don't elevate the mood of non-depressed people. Also used to treat anxiety disorders, including OCD.

Psychostimulants: elevate mood, but are used mainly for treating hyperactivity in children.

Antidepressants

The main difference between various kinds of antidepressants is in their side-effects, rather than their effectiveness or speed of action (Gelder *et al.*, 1999). They all increase 5-HT (serotonin) function, and many also increase noradrenaline function (see Chapter 44). Most can be given just once per day, but they usually 'kick in' only after 10–14 days. They should be withdrawn slowly: sudden cessation can cause restlessness, insomnia, anxiety and nausea.

Monoamine oxidase inhibitors (MAOIs)

Iproniazid was originally used in 1952 as a treatment for tuberculosis – it elevated patients' moods (without, incidentally, affecting the disease). Iproniazid and related drugs (e.g. *phenelzine* or Nardil) inhibit the activity of an enzyme known as monoamine oxidase (MAO), and gradually increase the activity levels of neurons that utilise noradrenaline (a monoamine) and 5-HT (see Chapter 4).

These are generally less effective than tricyclics when used to treat severe depression, and no more effective for mild depression. They're seldom the first choice of treatment, because of their side-effects (including cerebral haemorrhage) and dangerous interactions with other drugs and foodstuffs (although *reversible* MAOIs are safer).

Tricyclics

These are so-named because their basic chemical structure includes three carbon rings. *Imipramine* (Tofranil) and *amitryptyline* were the first to be introduced and are still used as a standard for comparing other antidepressants. They seem to act by blocking the reuptake of dopamine and noradrenaline, but some also block the reuptake of serotonin, others block serotonin alone, and some have no known effect on any of these systems (Hamilton & Timmons, 1995). They're effective in the treatment of both mild and severe depression, and are the first choice of drug in the latter.

However, they have many side-effects, including toxic effects on the cardiovascular system. As a result, they're gradually being replaced by modified tricyclics (such as *lofepramine* and *trazedone*) which cause fewer side-effects (Gelder *et al.*, 1999).

Specific serotonin reuptake inhibitors (SSRIs)

These 'second generation' drugs selectively inhibit the reuptake of serotonin into presynaptic neurons, that is, they make more serotonin available (see Chapter 4). Examples include *paroxetine* and *fluoxetine* (Prozac). They seem to be as effective as tricyclics in treating mild depression, and they're safer for patients with glaucoma and in overdose. Prozac has rapidly become the most commonly prescribed antidepressant medication (Costello *et al.*, 1995), having been taken by more than 38 million people (Boseley, 1999) since its introduction in 1988.

CRITICAL DISCUSSION 45.1

The Prozac (or 'vitamin P') controversy

In January 2000, the patent of Prozac's manufacturer (Eli Lilly) expired, meaning that cheap generic versions of the drug are set to flood the international market. This will make 'vitamin P' (as it's been called in the US) available to those who couldn't previously afford it. This is especially significant given that the World Health Organisation (WHO) predicts that depression will become the leading form of ill health across the globe, with an estimated one in three people being affected by 2010 (Munro, 2000b). This would mean 18 million depressed people in the UK alone (see Chapter 44). According to Munro:

'Drugs like Prozac are firmly entrenched in both professional and public minds as the treatment of choice for depression. There is a growing concern that the widespread use of antidepressants is blocking the development of other forms of treatment, such as cognitive therapy. Such a trend could be exacerbated by the increased affordability of fluoxetine.'

Some feel that an overemphasis on medication has grown from aggressive marketing by drug companies. With Prozac, people for the first time were going to their doctors *asking* for antidepressants (and by name). Prozac was marketed as a wonder drug (Baker, in Munro, 2000), and its biggest selling-pitch has been that it's almost impossible to kill yourself with an overdose. But since its launch in 1988 in the US (and in the UK shortly afterwards), there's been a spate of disturbing accounts of violence and suicide committed by people prescribed the drug by their doctors. Victims and families of killers have sued Eli Lilly in 200 court cases (Boseley, 1999).

According to Healy (in Boseley, 1999), about 250,000 people worldwide taking Prozac have attempted suicide (because of the drug), and about 25,000 will have succeeded. Eli Lilly knew as long ago as 1979 that Prozac can produce in some people a strange, agitated state of mind that can trigger an unstoppable urge to commit murder or suicide. This is a recognised psychiatric disorder called *akathisia*, which has long been associated with antipsychotic drugs (such as chlorpromazine). But while these drugs take away the will to do anything about the suicidal/violent feelings, Prozac doesn't!

Ask yourself ...

- Another aspect of the controversy surrounding Prozac is its use as a 'designer drug'. Kramer (1993) advocates that *everyone* could benefit from taking it, since it makes people more assertive and playful, and improves relationships. Kramer believes that in the near future, we'll be able to change our 'self' as easily as we change our clothes ('cosmetic psychopharmacology').
- Even if this were possible, do you think it's right?

How effective are antidepressants?

What this question usually means is: how much more effective are antidepressants than *placebos* ('dummy drugs', usually inert sugar pills). Fisher & Greenberg (1995) looked at 15 separate reviews of the literature relating to antidepressants, plus two large-scale *meta-analyses* ('studies of studies': see Box 45.8, page 678). Overall, the effectiveness of antidepressants appears to be modest, with a high relapse rate (over 60 per cent) amongst those who respond positively to the drugs but are then taken off them. Their benefits also tend to wane after a few months, even while they're still being taken.

Fisher and Greenberg also discuss the *methodology* of drug trials. In a classic *double-blind design*, neither the patient nor the researcher knows whether the patient is receiving a drug or a placebo. But when the (*inactive*) placebo doesn't produce as many bodily sensations as the drug, participants soon learn to discriminate between them. For example, imipramine causes dry mouth, tremor, sweating and constipation. These side-effects could be used by those administering the drug/placebo to identify the 'ons' and the 'offs', and they might convey their resulting expectations as to the effects of the drug/placebo to the participants.

For these reasons, *active* placebos (such as atropine), which *do* produce side-effects, are sometimes used. Thomson (cited in Fisher & Greenberg, 1995) compared 68 studies conducted between 1958 and 1972 which had used an inert placebo with seven which had used atropine. The antidepressant was found to be superior to the placebo in 59 per cent of the former, but in only 14 per cent (one study) of the latter.

Depressed people selected for clinical trials usually aren't representative of depressed people as a group. They're moderately depressed, not actively suicidal, and free from other physical and psychiatric illness (Fisher & Greenberg, 1995; Lyddy, 2000). Nevertheless, assigning a depressed person to a placebo condition when there's an effective treatment available is *ethically* problematic.

Khan *et al.* (2000) studied the potential risk to depressed patients assigned to placebo treatment by examining data from 45 antidepressant clinical trials. The overall incidence of suicide/attempted suicide was low, with no significant difference in risk between active treatments and placebo groups. Interestingly, placebo patients reported substantial symptom reduction (though less than the active treatment groups), and there was a positive correlation between the length of the trial and reduction in symptoms – regardless of the form of treatment group.

According to Fisher & Greenberg (1995), this isn't surprising, since a response to a placebo is just as biological (i.e. 'real') as a response to an antidepressant. The brain apparently responds in equivalent ways to both talk and drug treatment. Far from being extraneous or less of a biological reality than a chemical agent, placebos have been shown to produce certain effects usually thought to be confined to drugs. For example, they show *dose-level effects* (the larger the dose, the greater the impact), addictions and toxic effects.

Because it's impossible to eliminate placebo effects totally, it's impossible to demonstrate that psychotropic drugs have an independent, 'pure' biological impact. Fisher and Greenberg conclude by saying:

'… Administering a drug is not simply a medical (biological) act. It is, in addition, a complex social act whose effectiveness will be mediated by such factors as the patient's expectations of the drug and reactions to the body sensations created by that drug, and the physician's friendliness and degree of personal confidence in the drug's power …'.

Anxiolytics

These are used most appropriately to reduce severe anxiety. They should be prescribed for a short time only (usually a few days, seldom more that two to three weeks), because they can

result in tolerance and dependence. Withdrawal effects are reported in people using them for more than six months the *withdrawal syndrome* includes apprehension and anxiety, tremor, and muscle twitching (see Chapter 8). *Chlordiazepoxide* (marketed as Librium) and *diazepam* (Valium) appeared in the early 1960s, quickly becoming the most widely prescribed drugs of their time. In 1989, for example, there were 21 million prescriptions in the UK alone (Rassool & Winnington, 1993).

Chlordiazepoxide and diazepam are *benzodiazepines* (other examples being temazepam and flurazepam). They were initially called 'minor tranquillisers' (as opposed to the antipsychotic, major tranquillisers), but this terminology became unpopular and they're now simply called *anti-anxiety drugs*. They act by facilitating the activity of GABA (see Chapter 4). As well as anxiolytic, sedative and hypnotic effects (see Chapter 8), they have muscle-relaxant and anti-convulsant properties (Gelder *et al.*, 1999).

Antipsychotics

Antipsychotics (or major tranquillisers) such as *chlorpromazine* were originally developed to calm patients facing surgery, and they proved highly effective in reducing the incidence of death from surgical shock. Chlorpromazine (Largactil) and related *phenothiazines* were soon used with psychiatric patients (starting in the early 1950s). They revolutionised psychiatry by allowing the most disturbed schizophrenic patients to live outside a psychiatric hospital, or to reduce their average length of stay. However, many critics have called these drugs 'pharmacological straitjackets'.

They are effective in treating the acute, *positive* symptoms of schizophrenia, such as hallucinations, excitement, thought disorder and delusions, and they seem to work by blocking the D2 receptor for dopamine. However, they don't touch the *negative* symptoms (emotional blunting, slowness of speech and movement, lack of motivation, social withdrawal: see Tables 44.2 and 44.3, pages 652–653).

- *Extrapyramidal* (EP): *acute dystonia* (involuntary muscle contraction), *akathisia* (inner restlessness, agitation and pacing), *Parkinsonism* (shuffling gait, tremor, expressionless face, etc.), and *tardive dyskinesia* (chewing and sucking movements, grimacing, akathisia);
- *Anticholinergic*: dry mouth, blurred vision, low blood pressure (which may cause fainting attacks), constipation, glaucoma;
- *Neurolepticmalignant syndrome*: fluctuating levels of consciousness, hyperthermia, muscular ('lead pipe') rigidity, autonomic disturbances (such as unstable blood pressure, urinary incontinence, and tachycardia. While this is rare, it can be life-threatening, and can occur with *any* antipsychotic drug, at any dose, at any time (Hutton, 1998).

(Based on Gelder *et al.*, 1999)

The newer, 'atypical' antipsychotic drugs, such as *clozapine* and *riperidone,* are less likely to cause EP symptoms and may also treat the negative symptoms of schizophrenia. Clozapine is also the first atypical drug shown to be effective in treating patients who have failed to respond to 'typical' antipsychotics such as chlorpromazine (*Effective Health Care*, 1999; Gelder *et al.*, 1999).

Electroconvulsive therapy

In 1938, Cerletti and Bini, two Italian doctors, first gave an electric shock to the brain of a psychiatric patient, on the assumption that if a grand mal epileptic fit is induced (artificially), this should reduce or eliminate the symptoms of schizophrenia. Electroconvulsive therapy (ECT) started to be used widely in the US from the early 1940s. Ironically, it was found to be more effective for severe depression than schizophrenia, and is now used mainly with depressive patients.

The procedure

The patient is made comfortable on a bed, clothes loosened and shoes and dentures removed. Atropine is given as a routine pre-anaesthetic medication (to dry up salivary and bronchial secretions) and then thiopentone, a quick-acting anaesthetic, followed by a muscle relaxant. A 70–150 volt shock lasting 0.04–1.00 second is then given through electrodes placed on the temples, producing a generalised convulsion lasting for up to a minute (detected by facial and limb twitching). Typically, two to three treatments per week are given for three to four weeks.

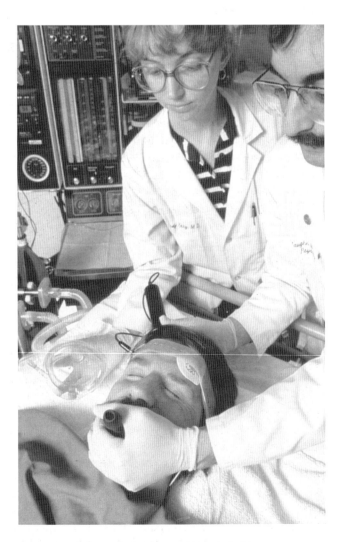

ECT as it is carried out today. Despite the technical improvements, ECT is a highly controversial treatment

Many psychiatrists believe that for severe depression, *bilateral* ECT (one electrode on each side of the head) is preferable, as it acts more quickly and fewer treatments are needed. In *unilateral* ECT, an electrode is applied to the *non-dominant* hemisphere side (the right side for most people) to reduce the side-effects, particularly memory disruption (Benton, 1981).

Side-effects

Memory disruption includes retrograde amnesia and impaired ability to acquire new memories (see Chapter 17). But because depression is associated with impaired memory function, it's unclear to what extent ECT itself is responsible (Benton, 1981). The patient is normally confused for up to 40 minutes following treatment, but recall of events prior to treatment gradually returns (although some degree of memory loss may persist for several weeks).

The mortality rate is now quite low (between 3.6 and 9 per 100,000 treatments (a figure very similar to that resulting from anaesthesia for minor surgery). This makes it one of the safest medical treatments there is, and when the number of suicides resulting from depression are taken into account, ECT emerges as very low risk indeed.

However, the possibility of death is only one of the objections made to ECT by MIND (the National Association for Mental Health) and PROMPT (Protect the Rights of Mental Patients in Therapy) in the UK, and NAPA (Network Against Psychiatric Assault) in the USA. The main objections are *ethical* (see Chapter 48). For example, since we don't know how ECT works (and whether it works), it shouldn't be used at all. Despite the objections, ECT seems to be enjoying a revival (Twombly, 1994).

How effective is ECT?

> *Ask yourself...*
>
> * Based on methods used in clinical drug trials, how do you think the effectiveness of ECT might be assessed?
> * Does this raise similar ethical problems to clinical drug trials?

Sackeim (1989) reviewed controlled comparisons of real and sham (simulated or 'dummy') ECT. In simulated ECT, the patient undergoes all aspects of the ECT procedure except that no electrical current is passed through the brain (so no seizure is produced). He concluded that real ECT is significantly more effective than sham ECT. Although bilateral is slightly more effective than unilateral, bilateral produces greater memory deficits. Sackeim also concluded that ECT is more effective than antidepressant drugs, and probably the most effective available treatment for depression. However the use of medication following ECT can help to prevent relapse.

Breggin (1991) is an outspoken critic of all physical treatments for mental problems. He presents two case histories to support his claim that ECT is capable of producing profound brain damage, and points out that elderly women are the most likely to receive it. It invariably causes acute organic brain syndrome or delirium, and severe, long-term deficits in cognitive and emotional functioning. ECT 'works' by causing brain damage: the patient suffers *anosognosia*, a condition in

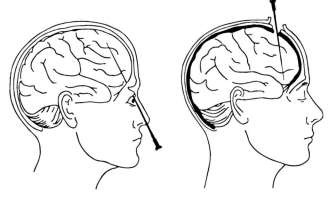

which the patient denies his or her psychological and physical difficulties (rather like 'treating' prolonged depression by being permanently drunk). Any beneficial effects are short lived, and the evidence that it reduces suicide risks is weak.

How does ECT work?

Benton (1981) identifies three explanations of how ECT works:

- Patients come to see ECT as a *punishment* which extinguishes their undesirable behaviour. However, equally unpleasant but subconvulsive shocks (which don't produce a convulsion) *aren't* effective. This is inconsistent with the 'punishment' explanation.
- *Memory loss* allows the restructuring of the patient's view of life. However, unilateral ECT is intended to *minimise* memory disruption but is also effective in reducing depression.
- The shock produces a wide range of *biochemical changes* in the brain (e.g. the stimulation of neurotransmitters, including noradrenaline and endorphins: Lilienfeld, 1995). This effect is more widespread than that produced by antidepressant drugs.

While there's no generally accepted explanation for how ECT works, this isn't a reason for not using it: many medical treatments fall into this category (e.g. the use of aspirin in the treatment of headaches: Benton, 1981). Clare (1980) argues that because it's relatively quick and easy to administer, ECT is much abused and overused.

Psychosurgery

Psychosurgery was pioneered by Moniz, a Portuguese professor of neurology. He was so impressed by the tranquillising effects of lesions to the frontal lobes of monkeys, that in 1935 he performed the first *prefrontal lobotomies* (or *leucotomies*) on human schizophrenics. Between 1935 and 1949, Moniz performed about 100 such operations, in which tissue connecting the frontal lobes of the cortex with subcortical brain areas is cut on both sides of the cortex (see Figure 45.2). (Moniz was awarded the Nobel Prize for Medicine in 1949, and was later shot in the spine by one of his lobotomised patients, confining him to a wheelchair for the rest of his life.)

Freeman & Watts (1942) pioneered psychosurgery in the USA, and it's been estimated that 40–50,000 prefrontal lobotomies have been performed in the US alone since the late 1930s. They modified Moniz's technique by inserting a scalpel either into burr holes drilled through the patient's temple, or through the eye socket (*transorbital leucotomy*: see Figure 45.2). Although their so-called 'standard leucotomy' was far from standardised anatomically, and despite unacceptable side-effects, the procedure was widely used in the UK and other countries (Gelder *et al.*, 1989). For example, in the UK, about 10,000 operations were carried out between 1942 and 1952, two-thirds of which involved schizophrenics and about one-quarter depressives, with the latter responding much more favourably.

Ask yourself ...
- However effective it might be, should psychosurgery *ever* be used?

Figure 45.2 *The drawing on the left shows the technique used by Freeman and Watts (transorbital leucotomy), a modification of Moniz's classical prefrontal lobotomy/leucotomy (shown on the right)*

Side-effects of psychosurgery included apathy, lethargy, epilepsy, intellectual impairment, aggressiveness and personality changes, as well as death. As it became clear that the frontal cortex has complex connections with the hypothalamus, temporal cortex, hippocampus, amygdala and mammillary bodies (see Chapter 4), the surgical approach became directed to some of these connections, rather than to the frontal lobe itself.

Box 45.4 Modern forms of psychosurgery

Today, the older 'blind' operations have been replaced by *stereotactic procedures*, which allow only very small amounts of brain tissue to be destroyed in very precise locations ('*fractional operations*'). For example, *amygdalotomy* involves bilateral lesions in the amygdala (destroying the neural circuit connecting the amygdala and the hypothalamus), usually in the treatment of abnormal, intractable aggression.

This is perhaps the most controversial of all psychosurgical techniques, partly because the patient isn't usually suffering, partly because it's often used with mentally retarded aggressive patients (so informed consent is unlikely to be given), and partly because, although the surgery has a 'marked calming effect' in 95 per cent of cases, it cannot entirely eliminate episodes of terror and outbursts of violence.

(Based on Gelder *et al.*, 1989)

Does psychosurgery work and should it ever be used?

In 1968, there were 38,000 leucotomies performed worldwide, but this figure dropped substantially during the 1970s. In England, the 500 operations performed in 1970 dropped to 62 in 1980, and a mere 18 in 1991 (Taylor, 1992). Since the 1950s and the widespread use of antipsychotic drugs, schizophrenics have rarely been treated in this way. In England and Wales, the use of psychosurgery is governed by the 1983 Mental Health Act, which endorses it only as a last resort, requiring the patient's consent. Though rare in the UK, it's still used in other countries, especially Australia and the US (Taylor, 1992).

Due to the lack of controlled evaluations, assessments of psychosurgery's effectiveness must be based on follow-up studies of patients who've undergone the procedure. But it's impossible to determine how much improvement would have taken place without surgery (Gelder *et al.*, 1989). While some improvements have been reported:

> '... *this intervention is rightfully viewed as a treatment of very last resort, given the permanence of psychosurgery and the poorly understood ways in which it works'.* (Davison & Neale, 1994)

Even with modern stereotactic procedures, serious side-effects still occur, and they should only ever be used if all other forms of treatment are considered inappropriate, or have been tried and failed (Gelder *et al.*, 1989).

Psychoanalysis and other psychodynamic approaches

Freud's model of psychological disorder

In Chapter 42, *neurotic symptoms* were described as compromises between the opposing demands made on the ego by the id and the superego. Symptoms (along with dreams and defences) are expressions of the inevitable conflict which arises from these opposing demands and are, at the same time, attempts to deal with it.

When a person experiences anxiety, the ego is signalling that it fears being overwhelmed by an all-powerful id (*neurotic anxiety*) or superego (*moral anxiety*), and so must mobilise its defences. Anxiety is the hallmark of most neurotic disorders, but except in 'free-floating anxiety', it becomes redirected or transformed in some way (depending on which particular defence is used). Consequently, the resulting symptom makes it even less likely that the true nature of the problem (i.e. the underlying conflict) will be spotted. *Phobias*, for example, involve *repression* (as do all neuroses) plus *displacement* and *projection* (see Chapter 44). Little Hans (see Chapter 35) had a phobia of being bitten by a horse, which could be explained in terms of:

- repressing his jealous anger and hatred felt towards his father;
- projecting these feelings onto his father, thus seeing him as a threatening, murderous man; and
- displacing this perception of his father onto a 'safer' target, namely, horses.

As we noted in Chapter 42, Freud believed that phobic objects symbolically represent the object for which they're a substitute.

Neuroses are *maladaptive solutions* to the individual's problems. They don't help resolve the conflict, but merely help to *avoid* it (both in thought and behaviour), and the neurotic's behaviour usually creates its own distress and unhappiness – this is the *neurotic paradox*.

Ask yourself...

- Try to explain neurotic behaviours (and the neurotic paradox) in *learning theory* (i.e. conditioning) terms.

So, in summary, psychoneurotic symptoms are indicative of deep-seated, unresolved, unconscious conflicts, usually of a sexual and/or aggressive nature, stemming from childhood feelings, memories, wishes and experiences. However, these defences aren't effective ways of dealing with the conflict, and they create their own distress and anxiety.

The aims of psychoanalysis

The goals of psychoanalysis can be stated in very broad, abstract terms, such as '... a far-reaching and radical restructuring of the personality ...' (Fonagy, 1995) and as attempts to provide the client with insight, self-knowledge and self-understanding. More specifically, the basic goal of psychoanalysis is to make 'the unconscious conscious', to undo unsatisfactory defences and, through a 'therapeutic regression' (Winnicott, 1958), to re-experience repressed feelings and wishes, which have been frustrated in childhood, in a safe context, and to express them, as an adult, in a more appropriate way, 'with a new ending' (Alexander & French, 1946).

Therapeutic techniques

The role of the analyst

In classical psychoanalysis, the analyst is meant to remain faceless and 'anonymous', not showing any emotion or revealing any personal information. Instead:

> '...*The doctor should be opaque to his patients and, like a mirror, should show them nothing but what is shown to him'.* (Freud, 1912, quoted in Jacobs, 1992)

With the analyst as an 'ambiguous object' or 'blank screen', the patient is able to project and displace repressed feelings, in particular those concerning parents (*transference*). This process is aided by the client lying on a couch, with the analyst sitting behind, out of the client's (analysand's) field of vision. Jacobs notes that, in practice, Freud often became personally involved in the therapeutic conversation and would explain his thinking to the patient (see below).

Sigmund Freud's couch (Freud Museum Publications Ltd)

Transference and counter-transference

Transference typically goes through a *positive* phase of emotional attachment to the analyst, followed by a *negative* and critical phase. According to Freud, this reflects working through the ambivalence experienced in the patient's childhood relationship with his/her parents (Stevens, 1995). According to Thomas (1990), transference has become so central to the theory and practice of psychoanalysis, that many analysts believe that making interpretations about transference is what distinguishes psychoanalysis from other forms of psychotherapy. When attention is focused on the transference and what's happening in the here and now, the historical reconstruction of childhood events and the search for the childhood origins of conflicts may take second place.

The related process of *counter-transference* refers to the therapist's feelings of irritation, dislike or sexual attraction towards the client. Thomas (1990) maintains that:

'... *In Freud's time, counter-transference feelings... were considered to be a failing on the part of the analyst. These feelings were to be controlled absolutely ... Now, counter-transference is considered an unavoidable outcome of the analytic process, irrespective of how well prepared the analyst is by analytic training and its years of required personal analysis ... most modern analysts are trained to observe their own counter-transference feelings and to use these to increase their understanding of the patients' transference and defences'.*

Interpretation and resistance

To enable the client to understand the transference and how it relates to childhood conflicts, the analyst must *interpret* it, that is, tell the client what it means in relation to what's already been revealed about the client's childhood experiences. Because this is likely to be painful and distressing, clients show *resistance*. This may take the form of 'drying up' when talking, changing the subject, dismissing some emotionally significant event in a very flippant way, even falling asleep or arriving late for therapy. All forms of resistance require interpretation.

The working alliance

As important as the analyst's anonymity may be the *'working alliance'* with the client. According to Jacobs (1984), this consists of two adults co-operating to understand the 'child' in the client. The analyst adopts a quiet, reflective style, intervening when s/he judges the client to be ready to make use of a particular interpretation. This is an art, and *doesn't* involve fitting the client into psychoanalytic theory, as some critics suggest (Jacobs, 1984).

Two other major techniques used to reveal the client's unconscious mind are *dream interpretation* (see Chapter 42) and *free association*, in which the client says whatever comes to mind, no matter how silly, irrelevant or embarrassing it may seem. These may both lead to resistance which, like transference, will in turn be interpreted by the analyst.

Box 45.5 The concept of cure: How do you know when to stop?

According to Jacobs (1984), the goals of therapy are limited by what clients consciously want to achieve and are capable of achieving, together with their motivation, ego strength, capacity for insight, ability to tolerate the frustration of gradual change, financial cost and so on. These factors, in turn, determine how a cure is defined and assessed.

In practice, psychoanalysis ranges from *psychoanalytical first aid* (Guntrip, 1968) or symptom relief, to different levels of more intense work. However, Storr (1966) believes that symptom relief is an inappropriate way of perceiving 'cure', partly because symptom analysis is only the *start* of the analytic process, and also because a majority of clients don't have clear-cut symptoms anyway. Similarly, Fonagy (2000) says that:

'... *Symptom change as a sole indicator of therapeutic benefit must indeed be considered crude in relation to the complex interpersonal processes that evolve over the many hundreds of sessions ...'.*

Freud himself recognised that psychoanalysis was only likely to be successful if the patient is voluntary, open to change, acknowledges that there's a problem and is neurotic rather than psychotic (the latter being unable to form a positive transference). Even if the patient possesses these characteristics, fresh neuroses or even the return of the original one cannot be ruled out. Analysis never really ends.

According to Fonagy (2000), evidence from a significant number of before–after studies suggest that psychoanalysis is consistently helpful to patients with milder (neurotic) disorders, and somewhat less consistently so for groups with more severe disorders. Other, less well controlled studies, suggest that longer intensive treatments tend to have better outcomes than shorter, non-intensive treatments. The impact of psychoanalysis is evident not just in relation to symptoms, but as measured by patient's work performances and reductions in healthcare costs.

Psychodynamic psychotherapy

In the UK, classic psychoanalysis requires the client to attend 3–5 sessions per week for several years (Fonagy, 2000) which, for many people, is far too expensive, as well as too time consuming.

In a modified form of analysis, therapist and client meet once or twice weekly for a limited period. There may be a 'contract' for a specified number of weeks as opposed to the open-ended arrangement of classic analysis. For example, Malan (1976) uses *brief focal therapy* (one session per week for about 30 weeks), in which the focus is on fairly specific psychological problems (such as a single conflict area or relationship in the client's current life). Although all the basic techniques of psychoanalysis may be used, there's considerably less emphasis on the client's past, and client and therapist usually sit in armchairs facing each other. This form of psychotherapy is practised by many clinical psychologists (as well as psychiatrists and social workers), who haven't received a full-blown psychoanalytic training (Fonagy, 1995; Fonagy & Higgitt, 1984). Fonagy (2000) cites evidence supporting the effectiveness of brief dynamic psychotherapy.

Behavioural approaches

Models of psychological disorder

According to the behavioural model, *all* behaviour, whether adaptive or maladaptive, is acquired by the same principles of classical and/or operant conditioning (see Chapter 11).

The medical model is completely rejected, including any distinction between 'symptoms' and underlying pathology. According to Eysenck (1960), if you 'get rid of the symptom ... you have eliminated the neurosis'. But according to Freud, if treatment tackles only the symptoms and not the underlying conflict, *new* neurotic symptoms will replace those which are removed (*symptom substitution*).

However, this is increasingly being seen as an oversimplification and misunderstanding of what behaviour therapy involves. Wachtel (1989), for example, argues that in some ways all theories and therapies make assumptions about 'symptoms as manifestations of some underlying problem'. What distinguishes different approaches is the view taken of the *nature* of those underlying problems, and how much change is needed for the problem to be remedied. He calls for an integration between the two approaches which, in practice, is already happening.

Behavioural technology vs behavioural analysis

According to Mackay (1975), some behaviour therapists (e.g. Eysenck, Rachman and Marks) try to discover which techniques are most effective with particular diagnostic groups. This *nomothetic* approach is called *behavioural technology*. Others (e.g. Yates and Meyer) believe that therapists should isolate the stimuli and consequences that are maintaining the inappropriate behaviour in each individual case, and that, accordingly, any treatment programme should be derived from such a 'behavioural analysis' (or 'functional analysis'). This *idiographic* approach is called *behavioural psychotherapy*.

Part of the functional analysis is an emphasis on *current* behaviour–environment contingencies, in contrast to the Freudian emphasis on *past* (particularly early childhood) events, and unconscious (and other internal) factors. Psychological problems are *behavioural* problems, which need to be *operationalised* (described in terms of observable behaviours) before we attempt to change them.

Classical conditioning, phobias and preparedness

According to Eysenck & Rachman (1965), the case of Little Albert (see Chapter 11) exemplifies how *all* phobias are acquired (i.e. through *classical conditioning*):

> '*Any neutral stimulus, simple or complex, that happens to make an impact on an individual at about the time a fear reaction is evoked, acquires the ability to evoke fear subsequently ... there will be generalisation of fear reactions to stimuli resembling the conditioned stimulus*'. (Wolpe & Rachman, 1960)

One of the problems with this explanation is that some phobias are easier to induce in the laboratory than others (in participants who don't already have them), and it's well known that certain naturally occurring phobias are more common than others. These findings are consistent with Seligman's (1970) concept of *preparedness* (see Chapters 11 and 44).

The persistence of phobias

Even more difficult for the classical conditioning model to explain is the *persistence* of naturally occurring phobias (that is, their failure to extinguish).

> ### Ask yourself...
> - How can *operant conditioning* help to explain the persistence of phobias? (See Chapter 44, page 646.)

The persistence of neurotic behaviour may also be accounted for in terms of what Freud (1926) called *secondary gain*. This refers to the attention and sympathy the neurotic receives from other people, which (unintentionally) positively reinforces it.

Behaviour therapy

Behaviour therapy refers to techniques based on *classical conditioning*, developed by psychologists such as Eysenck and Wolpe. Wolpe (1958) defined behaviour therapy as 'the use of experimentally established principles of learning for the purpose of changing unadaptive behaviour'.

Systematic desensitisation

The case of Little Peter (see Chapter 11) represents the earliest example of any kind of behavioural treatment, and the methods used to remove his phobia of animals were later called *systematic desensitisation* (SD) by Wolpe (1958). It represents a form of *counter-conditioning*, and the key principle in SD is that of *reciprocal inhibition*, according to which:

> '*... if a response inhibitory of anxiety can be made to occur in the presence of anxiety-evoking stimuli it will weaken the bond between these stimuli and the anxiety*'. (Wolpe, 1969)

In other words, it's impossible for someone to experience two opposite emotions (e.g. anxiety and relaxation) at the same time. Accordingly, a patient with a phobia is first taught to relax through deep muscle relaxation, in which different muscle groups are alternately relaxed and tensed (alternatively, hypnosis or tranquillisers might be used). So, relaxation and fear of the object or situation 'cancel each other out' (this is the 'desensitisation' part of the procedure).

The '*systematic*' part of the procedure involves a graded series of contacts with the phobic object (usually by imagining it), based on a *hierarchy* of possible forms of contact from the least to the most frightening. Starting with the *least* frightening form of contact, the patient, while relaxing, imagines the object (e.g. the word 'spider' on a printed page) until this can be done without feeling any anxiety at all. Then, and only then, the next most feared contact will be dealt with, in the same way, until the *most* frightening contact can be imagined with no anxiety (e.g. a large, hairy spider running all over your body).

Wolpe used imagination, because some of his patients' fears were so abstract (e.g. fear of criticism or failure) that it was impractical to confront them using real-life situations. He also believed that the ability to tolerate stressful imagery is generally followed by a reduction in anxiety in related real-life situations. Between sessions, patients are usually instructed to put themselves in progressively more frightening real-life situations. These 'homework assignments' help to move their adjustment from imagination to reality (Davison & Neale, 1994).

An evaluation of SD

Rachman & Wilson (1980) and McGlynn *et al.* (1981) believe that SD is definitely effective, although it's most effective for the treatment of specific phobias (e.g. animal phobias) as opposed to, say, agoraphobia (see Chapter 44), and for patients who are able to learn relaxation skills and have sufficiently vivid imaginations to be able to conjure up the sources of their fear. A limitation of SD is that some patients may have difficulty *transferring* from the imaginary stimulus to real-life situations.

There's some debate as to whether or not either relaxation or the use of a hierarchy of contact situations is actually necessary at all. According to Wilson & Davison (1971), for example, relaxation might be merely a useful way of encouraging a frightened person to confront what they're afraid of, which would otherwise be avoided. According to Marks (1973), SD works *not* because of the inhibiting effect of relaxation on anxiety (reciprocal inhibition), but because of the *exposure* to the feared situation; this seems to represent the generally accepted view among psychologists. Exposure is especially effective if it allows the person to disprove his or her predictions that something awful will happen if they come into contact with the feared object or situation, and graded exposure helps to build up the person's confidence to be able to cope with the exposure (Williams & Hargreaves, 1995).

Implosion (implosive therapy) and flooding

The essence of *implosion* is to expose the patient to what, in SD, would be at the top of the hierarchy. Instead of gradual exposure accompanied by relaxation, the patient is 'thrown in at the deep end' right from the start. This is done by getting the patient to imagine their most terrifying form of contact (the big, hairy spider let loose, again) with vivid verbal descriptions by the therapist (*stimulus augmentation*) to supplement the patient's vivid imagery. How is it meant to work?

■ The patient's anxiety is maintained at such a high level that eventually some process of *exhaustion* or *stimulus satiation* takes place – the anxiety level can only go down!
■ *Extinction* occurs by preventing the patient from making the usual escape or avoidance response (Mowrer, 1960). Implosion (and flooding), therefore, represents a form of 'forced reality testing' (Yates, 1970).

Flooding is exposure that takes place *in vivo* (e.g. with an actual spider). Marks *et al.* (1971) compared SD with flooding, and found flooding to be superior. Gelder *et al.* (1973) compared SD with implosion and found no difference.

Ask yourself...
• What conclusions can you draw from these findings?

The findings described above suggest that it's *in vivo* exposure which is crucial, and several researchers consider flooding to be more effective than implosion. Emmelkamp & Wessels

(1975) and Marks *et al.* (1981) used flooding with agoraphobics very successfully, and other studies have reported continued improvement for up to nine years after treatment without the appearance of 'substitute' problems. Wolpe (1973) forced an adolescent girl with a fear of cars into the back of a car and drove her around continuously for four hours. Her fear reached hysterical heights but then receded and, by the end of the journey, had completely disappeared. Marks (1981), in a review of flooding studies, found it to be the most universally effective of all the techniques used to treat phobias.

Ask yourself...
• Do you think that flooding is an ethically acceptable method of treating phobias?

Aversion therapy

In *aversion therapy*, some undesirable response to a particular stimulus is removed by associating the stimulus with another, aversive, stimulus. For example, alcohol is paired with an emetic drug (which induces severe nausea and vomiting), so that nausea and vomiting become a conditioned response to alcohol.

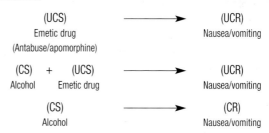

Patients would, typically, be given warm saline solution containing the emetic drug. Immediately before the vomiting begins, they're given a four-ounce glass of whisky which

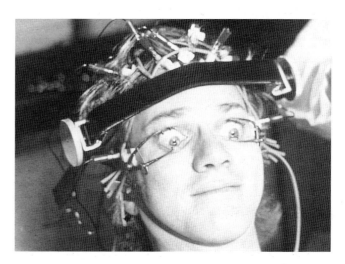

Malcolm McDowell in a scene from Clockwork Orange. *His eyes are clamped open, forcing him to watch a film portraying acts of violence and sadism, as part of aversion therapy. He'd earlier been given an emetic drug, so that extreme nausea and violence will become associated*

they're required to smell, taste and swill around in the mouth before swallowing. (If vomiting hasn't occurred, another straight whisky is given and, to prolong nausea, a glass of beer containing emetic.) Subsequent treatments involve larger doses of injected emetic, or increases in the length of treatment time, or a widening range of hard liquors (Kleinmuntz, 1980). Between trials, the patient may sip soft drinks to prevent generalisation to all drinking behaviour and to promote the use of alcohol substitutes. Meyer & Chesser (1970) found that about half their alcoholic patients abstained for at least one year following treatment, and that aversion therapy is better than no treatment at all.

More controversially, aversion therapy has been used with homosexuals, fetishists, male transvestites and sado-masochists, and Marks *et al.* (1970) reported desired changes for up to two years after treatment. In a typical treatment, slides of nude males are presented to male homosexuals, and then quickly followed by electric shocks. The conditioned response to the slides is intended to generalise to homosexual fantasies and activities outside the treatment sessions. More recently, attempts have been made to replace homosexual responses with heterosexual ones, by showing slides of naked females: any sexual response will terminate the shock.

CRITICAL DISCUSSION 45.2

Aversion therapy as a form of heterosexism

According to Davison & Neale (1994), several psychologists have argued that the social pressures on homosexuals to become 'straight' make it difficult to believe that the small minority of people who consult therapists for help in changing sexual preference are acting from choice.

The very fact that *change-of-orientation* treatments exist can be seen as condoning heterosexism. Clinicians work to develop procedures and study their effects only if they're concerned about the problem which their techniques are intended to remedy. The therapeutic literature contains relatively little material on helping homosexuals develop as individuals without this involving a change of sexual orientation. This contrasts with the many books and articles on how best to discourage homosexual behaviour and replace it by heterosexuality.

One very radical proposal is that therapists shouldn't help homosexuals become straight, even when such treatment is requested. But this, in turn, raises basic questions about limiting the options available to clients and, in refusing such treatment, aren't therapists making *value judgements*, just as they are when they agree to it? Isn't it the professional responsibility of therapists to meet the needs expressed by their clients? However, a client's request for a certain kind of treatment has never been sufficient justification for providing it (Davison & Neale, 1994).

In fact, there's been a dramatic reduction in the use of aversion therapy with homosexuals since the mid-1970s. (See Chapter 48 for a discussion of more general ethical issues relating to therapies.)

Covert sensitisation

Covert sensitisation (Cautela, 1967) is a variant of aversion therapy, which also includes elements of SD. 'Covert' refers to the fact that both the behaviour to be removed and the aversive stimulus to be associated with it are *imagined* by the patient, who has to visualise the events leading up to the initiation of the undesirable behaviour: just as this happens, s/he has to imagine nausea or some other aversive sensation.

'Sensitisation' is achieved by associating the undesirable act with an exceedingly disagreeable consequence (Kleinmuntz, 1980). The patient may also be instructed to rehearse an alternative 'relief' scene in which, for example, the decision not to drink is accompanied by pleasurable sensations. This is generally preferred to aversion therapy on humanitarian grounds, but is no more effective than aversion therapy (Gelder *et al.*, 1989).

Behaviour modification

Behaviour modification refers to techniques based on *operant conditioning*, developed by psychologists such as Ayllon and Azrin to build up appropriate behaviour (where it didn't previously exist), or to increase the frequency of certain responses and decrease the frequency of others.

According to Baddeley (1990), most behavioural programmes follow a broadly similar pattern involving a series of steps:

- **Step 1**. Specify the behaviour to be changed. It's important to choose small, measurable, achievable goals.
- **Step 2.** The goal should be stated as specifically as possible.
- **Step 3.** A *baseline rate* should be measured over a period of several days, that is, how the person 'normally' behaves with respect to the selected behaviour. This may involve detailed observation, which can suggest hypotheses as to what's maintaining that behaviour.
- **Step 4.** Decide on a *strategy*. For example, *selectively reinforce* non-yelling behaviour (through attention) and ensure that yelling behaviour is *ignored*.
- **Step 5.** *Plan treatment*. It's essential that everyone coming into contact with the patient behaves in accordance with the chosen strategy.

A design which is commonly used to check the effectiveness of treatment is the *AB–AB design*, where A is the baseline condition and B is the experimental treatment. So, if treatment is working, the level of yelling should be reduced during the initial B-phase (compared with the initial A-phase), and should increase again when treatment is stopped (the second A-phase). When treatment is reintroduced (second B-phase), yelling should once more reduce.

- **Step 6.** *Begin treatment.*
- **Step 7.** *Monitor progress.*
- **Step 8.** *Change* the programme if necessary.

Operant conditioning with special groups

Even under optimum conditions, autistic children never achieve the creative use of language and broad range of social skills of normal children (Thomas, 1985: See Chapter 40). However, Lovaas (1977) believe that many therapeutic gains can be retained at home (and even some modest improvements shown) if parents have been trained to the shaping techniques such as those described in Key Study 45.1 (see Chapter 11).

KEY STUDY 45.1

Shaping speech in autistic children (Lovaas *et al.*, 1967)

Lovaas *et al.* pioneered operant conditioning with autistic children who normally had little or no normal speech. They used a *shaping* technique:

- Verbal approval was paired with a piece of food whenever the child made eye contact, or merely attended to the therapist's speech or behaviour (which is also unusual for autistic children). This reinforces attention and associates a positive social gesture with food, so that verbal approval eventually becomes a conditioned reinforcer.
- The child was reinforced with food and praise whenever it made any kind of speech sound, or even tried to imitate the therapist's actions.
- Once this occurred without prompting, the therapist gradually withheld reinforcement until the child successfully imitated complete actions or uttered particular vowel or consonant sounds, then syllables, then words and, finally, combinations of words.

Sometimes, hundreds or even thousands of reinforcements were necessary before the child began to label objects appropriately or imitate simple phrases. Even when children have received extensive training, they're likely to regress if returned to a non-supportive institutional setting.

There are many striking examples of successful modification programmes with the mentally retarded, both adults and children. In one large-scale study, Matson *et al.* (1980) reported substantial improvements in the eating behaviour of profoundly impaired adults. They used peer and therapist modelling (see below), social reinforcement, verbal prompts to shape eating, the use of utensils, table manners, and so on. Reinforcers included going to meals early, and having one's own table-mat. There was a significant improvement in the treated group even four months after the end of treatment, compared with an untreated control group.

Azrin & Foxx (1971) and Foxx & Azrin (1973) produced a toilet-training 'package' in which:

- the client is taken to the toilet every half hour and given extra fluids, sweets, biscuits, praise and attention when it's used successfully;
- the client is strapped into a chair for half an hour, away from other people, if they have an accident. This *isn't* a punishment procedure, but '*time out*', that is, a time away from positive reinforcement.

As with speech training in autistic children, there are problems of generalising from hospital-based improvement to the home situation. But if parents continue the programme at home, there can be short- and long-term benefits.

A form of behaviour often displayed by autistic and mentally retarded individuals is self-mutilation by biting, scratching, head banging and so on, all of which can be life-threatening. This has been treated successfully by using operant techniques (e.g. Bull & LaVecchio, 1978).

The token economy

The *token economy* (TE) is based on the principle of *secondary reinforcement*. Tokens (secondary or *conditioned* reinforcers) are given for socially desirable/acceptable behaviours as they occur, and can then be exchanged ('cashed in') later on for certain 'primary' reinforcers.

The TE was introduced by Ayllon & Azrin (1968), who set aside an entire ward of a psychiatric hospital for a series of experiments in which reinforcements were provided for activities such as making beds and combing hair, and withheld for withdrawn or bizarre behaviour. The participants were 45 female chronic schizophrenic patients, with an average 16 years of hospitalisation. Some screamed for long periods, some were mute, many were incontinent, and a few were assaultive. Most no longer ate with cutlery, and some buried their faces in the food.

They were systematically reinforced for their ward work and self-care by receiving plastic tokens that could later be exchanged for special privileges (e.g. listening to records, going to movies, renting a private room, extra visits to the canteen). The entire life of each patient was, as far as possible, controlled by this regime.

If the introduction of chlorpromazine and other antipsychotic drugs in the 1950s marked a revolution in psychiatry, the introduction of TE programmes during the 1960s was, in its way, equally revolutionary. This was partly because it drew attention to the ways in which nursing (and other) staff were inadvertently maintaining the psychotic, 'mad' behaviour of many chronic schizophrenics by giving them attention, thus reinforcing unwanted behaviour.

Evaluating the TE

Two main advantages of the TE are:

- Tokens can be given *immediately* after some desirable behaviour occurs, thereby 'bridging' very long delays between the target response and the primary reinforcer. This is especially important when it's impractical or impossible to deliver the primary reinforcer immediately following the behaviour.
- Tokens make it easier to give consistent and effective reinforcers when dealing with a group of individuals.

According to Davison & Neale (1994):

'These regimes have demonstrated how even markedly regressed adult hospitalised patients can be significantly affected by systematic manipulation of reinforcement contingencies, that is, rewarding some behaviour to increase its frequency or ignoring other behaviour to reduce its frequency ...'.

Since the 1960s, hundreds of carefully controlled experiments have shown that various psychiatric patient behaviours can be brought under control by manipulating reward and punishment contingencies. According to Holmes (1994), one of the most impressive tests of the effectiveness of the TE is a study by Paul & Lentz (1977).

A comparison of TE, milieu therapy, and custodial care (Paul & Lentz, 1977)

Eighty-four chronic psychiatric patients, matched for age, gender, socioeconomic status, symptoms and length of hospitalisation, were randomly assigned to one of three treatment conditions:

Social learning/token economy

While acceptable behaviour was reinforced by giving the patient tokens, learning took place, specifically through modelling, shaping, prompting and instructions. Inappropriate behaviour wasn't reinforced. This regime embraced all aspects of the patients' lives. Like money, the tokens were a necessity – they bought meals. They could also be used to rent better sleeping quarters (e.g. a single room cost 22 tokens), obtain passes to leave the hospital, buy recreation time (e.g. TV, piano), and various luxuries/privileges (e.g. staying up later). These all had to be 'earned'.

Milieu therapy

The entire hospital became a 'therapeutic community' (Jones, 1953), with all its ongoing activities and personnel a part of the treatment programme. Social interaction and group activities were encouraged, so that through group pressure, patients were directed towards normal functioning. They were treated as responsible human beings, and expected to participate in their own readjustment (as well as that of fellow patients), including participation in decision making about the running of the ward. Staff impressed on them their positive expectations and praised them for doing well.

Custodial care (routine hospital management)

This included the use of antipsychotic drugs. Patients were alone for all but five per cent of their waking hours, with only occasional recreational, occupational, individual and group therapies.

The study lasted for 4½ years, with an 18-month follow-up. Throughout the entire six-year period, patients were assessed at regular six-monthly intervals, using structured interviews and behavioural observation. The objectives of both the TE and milieu therapy were to teach self-care, housekeeping, communication and vocational skills, to reduce symptomatic behaviour, and to release patients into the community.

Both social learning/TE and milieu therapy reduced some symptoms (such as bizarre motor behaviours). They were also both successful in increasing interpersonal, vocational, housekeeping and self-care skills (TE being the more successful). But both were equally unsuccessful in reducing cognitive distortions (delusions, hallucinations and incoherent speech) and hostile behaviour.

Over ten per cent of patients in the TE and seven per cent of those in milieu therapy were able to leave the hospital to live independently (e.g. in halfway houses), compared with none in custodial care. Those from the TE did significantly better at staying there. However, most of those who lived independently continued to manifest many signs of mental disorder, and failed to gain employment or participate in 'normal' social activities. The numbers of patients remaining on antipsychotic drugs dropped dramatically for those in both the milieu and TE groups.

According to Davison & Neale (1994), considering how poorly these patients had been functioning before the study began, the results are remarkable. However, since modelling and other social learning techniques were combined with the TE, the results shouldn't be accepted as demonstrating the effectiveness of the TE as such.

Although the changes brought about don't represent a cure, behavioural interventions can help to reverse the effects of institutionalisation, fostering social skills such as assertiveness in people who've been reinforced by hospital staff for passiveness and compliance (Davison & Neale, 1994). However, there's been very little increase in the use of TEs, despite continuing evidence of their effectiveness (Paul & Menditto, 1992).

Box 45.6 Some problems with TEs

- The control of behaviours has to be transferred from tokens to social reinforcers, both within and, ultimately, outside the hospital. The former is normally achieved by gradually 'weaning' patients off the tokens, and the latter by transferring patients to halfway houses and other community live-in arrangements. But there tends to be a high re-hospitalisation rate for such patients.

- Tokens may work by encouraging staff to observe behaviour systematically – not because the tokens act as reinforcers of the patient's behaviour (Gelder et al., 1989). Indeed, Burgio et al. (1983) found that selectively reinforcing *staff* for verbal interaction with residents produced a reliable improvement in the *residents'* behaviour. As with other successful behavioural interventions, the reason for the effectiveness of TE programmes may be quite unrelated to learning theory principles (Fonagy & Higgitt, 1984). This relates to *process research* (see text below).

- *Ethical problems* arise, because it's often necessary to deprive patients of some amenity before it can be earned with tokens. If this amenity is something that the patient should have by right (e.g. food), there's clearly an ethical difficulty. With some amenities (e.g. watching TV), it's difficult to decide whether they're a right or a privilege (Gelder et al., 1989).

- Ayllon and Azrin adopted the policy of giving visitors conducted tours, with the clients as guides. In some TEs, clients have the option of leaving the programme without penalty, and suggesting or negotiating changes in the contingencies used. Another precaution is to inform clients clearly of their legal and moral rights, and to instruct clients and staff to report any infringements of those rights. According to Martin & Pear (1992), the ethics of a TE will ultimately be judged on the basis of how effectively and humanely the transfer to the natural environment is carried out.

- Baddeley (1990) argues that when used in an educational setting (e.g. in a home for emotionally disturbed children), a TE can instil a highly mercenary approach to learning (TEs lead to token learning). For example, children may only read or indulge in any educational activity if directly rewarded for it. This may be effective within the confines of the TE itself, but will be inappropriate outside, where learning operates on a more indirect, long term and less immediate reward system.

Cognitive–behaviour therapy

Model of psychological disorder

According to Mahoney (1974) and Meichenbaum (1977), many (if not most) clinical problems are best described as disorders of thought and feeling. Since behaviour is to a large extent controlled by the way we think, the most logical and effective way of trying to change maladaptive behaviour is to change the maladaptive thinking which lies behind it. Beck (1993) defines *cognitive–behaviour therapy* (CBT) as:

'… the application of the cognitive model of a particular disorder with the use of a variety of techniques designed to modify the dysfunctional beliefs and faulty information processing characteristic of each disorder …'.

CBT is derived from various sources, including behaviour therapy and psychoanalysis, which define and operationalise cognition in different ways. However, the attempt to change cognition (*cognitive restructuring*) is always a means to an end, that end being 'lasting changes in target emotions and behaviour' (Wessler, 1986).

Rational emotive therapy

Ellis (1962, 1973) argues that *irrational thoughts* are the main cause of all types of emotional distress and behaviour disorders. Irrational thinking leads to a self-defeating internal dialogue of negative self-statements, and these are seen as 'covert' behaviours which are subject to the same principles of learning as overt behaviour. Phobias, for example, are linked to *catastrophising self-statements* and, as with other disorders, the aim of therapy is to replace these irrational, unreasonable beliefs and ideas with more reasonable and realistic ones.

In its simplest form, patients are told to look on the bright side, stop worrying, pull themselves together and so on. As Walker (1984) observes, 'rational' shouldn't be taken too literally, as sometimes counterproductive thoughts and beliefs may be replaced by more positive and helpful but equally irrational ones. For instance, it's not necessarily more rational to be an optimist than a pessimist, but it's usually more productive and should be encouraged in depressed patients.

Ellis (1962) identified eleven basic irrational beliefs or ideas which tend to be emotionally self-defeating, and which are commonly associated with psychological problems. These include, 'I must be loved and accepted by absolutely everybody', and 'I must be excellent in all possible respects and never make mistakes – otherwise I'm worthless'. In *rational emotive therapy* (RET), patients are challenged to prove that they're worthless because they make mistakes, or to say exactly how making mistakes makes one a worthless person. Patients may be explicitly directed to practise certain positive/optimistic statements, and are generally urged to 'look for the "musts" when they experience inappropriate emotions' (Wessler, 1986).

Self-instructional training

According to Meichenbaum (1977), neurotic behaviour is due, at least partly, to *faulty internal dialogues* (internal speech), in which the patient is failing to self-instruct successfully. The underlying rationale for *self-instructional therapy* (SIT) is a study by Meichenbaum & Goodman (1971). Impulsive and hyperactive children were trained to administer self-instructions for tasks on which they'd previously made frequent errors, first by talking aloud, then covertly, without talking, but still moving their lips and, finally, by talking covertly without any lip movements. This 'silent speech' is the essence of verbal thought (see Chapter 34).

Patients are made aware of the maladaptive nature of their self-statements, and are then helped to develop coping skills in the form of coping self-statements, relaxation and plans for behaviour change. For example, a patient might write down a strategy for dealing with a particular social interaction (e.g. asking someone to dance at a club) and then role-play it with a continuous commentary of self-statements before actually doing it 'for real'.

Wolpe (1978) argues that these techniques aren't very useful in cases of severe anxiety, because many strong neurotic fears are triggered by objects and situations which the patient *knows* are harmless – this is why phobias are irrational! So, Wolpe has used a technique called *thought stopping* (mainly with OCD patients), in which the patient is told to dwell on their obsessive thoughts and, while this is happening, the therapist shouts 'Stop!'. The patient then repeats the command out loud, and eventually repeats it subvocally (in thought only). (Covert sensitisation is a form of self-instruction or self-training: see above.)

Treatment of 'automatic thoughts'

Beck (1963) believes that *depressives* see themselves as victims. The key elements in depression are negative thoughts about oneself, the world and the future (the *cognitive triad* of depression), and these thoughts seem to come automatically and involuntarily. The source of such thoughts are logical errors based on faulty 'data' and, once negative thinking has been identified, it can be replaced by collecting evidence against it. Accordingly, Beck sees the client as a colleague of the therapist who researches verifiable reality (Wessler, 1986).

For example, if a client expresses the negative thought, 'I'm a poor father because my children aren't better disciplined', Beck would take the second part of the statement and seek factual evidence about its truth. He'd also focus on the evaluative conclusion that one is a poor father because one's children sometimes misbehave. In these and other ways, clients are trained to distance themselves from things, to be more objective, to distinguish fact from fiction and fact from evaluation, to see things in proportion, and not to see things in such extreme terms. Beck's cognitive therapy is less confrontational than RET.

An evaluation of Beck's approach

It's generally agreed that Beck's has been the most influential of the cognitive models of depression (Champion, 2000), although it's also been criticised for underemphasising social factors (Champion & Power, 1995). Beck (1993) has reviewed

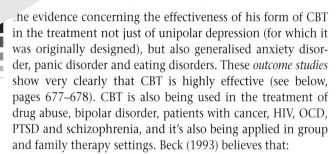

The evidence concerning the effectiveness of his form of CBT in the treatment not just of unipolar depression (for which it was originally designed), but also generalised anxiety disorder, panic disorder and eating disorders. These *outcome studies* show very clearly that CBT is highly effective (see below, pages 677–678). CBT is also being used in the treatment of drug abuse, bipolar disorder, patients with cancer, HIV, OCD, PTSD and schizophrenia, and it's also being applied in group and family therapy settings. Beck (1993) believes that:

> 'The very broad application of the theory and strategies bolsters the claim of cognitive therapy as a robust system of psychotherapy'.

Client-centred therapy

Model of psychological disorder

As we saw in Chapter 42, when a person is aware of a lack of congruence between their experience and self-concept, threat, anxiety or depression is experienced. Because of our need for positive regard, we may behave in ways which are discordant with the values of our self, and feeling threatened, anxious or depressed is the price we pay. Denial and distortion are used as defences against these unpleasant feelings, and as a result our self-concept becomes increasingly incongruent with reality. This, in turn, increases anxiety and makes the need for defences all the greater, creating a vicious circle.

Threat, anxiety or depression may interfere with the person's life in a less serious (neurotic) way, or it may be so great as to defy denial and distortion, leading to the disintegration of personality (psychosis). However, Rogers regards individuals as unique, and human personality is so complex that no diagnostic labelling of persons can ever be fully justified. Indeed, Rogers rejected all diagnostic labelling.

The aims of therapy

Client-centred therapy (CCT) is a process whereby individuals have the opportunity to reorganise their subjective world, so as to integrate and actualise the self. The key process, therefore, is facilitation of the experience of becoming a more autonomous, spontaneous and confident person (Graham, 1986).

People have an inherent tendency towards self-actualisation, but the conditions for facilitating its development reside in the relationship between the client and the therapist. The word 'client' is used to emphasise the person's self-responsibility (while 'patient' implies the opposite), and 'client-centred' implies that the client is encouraged to direct the whole therapeutic process – any changes which occur during therapy are brought about by the client.

The therapeutic process

The therapist's main task is to create a therapeutic atmosphere in which clients can become fully integrated again. This can only be achieved if clients *reduce* their *conditions of worth*, and *increase* their *unconditional positive self-regard*. The therapist's job is to create a situation in which clients can change themselves, and this is aided by an emotionally warm, accepting, understanding and non-evaluative relationship in which the

person is free from threat and has the freedom to be 'the self that he really is' (Graham, 1986).

There are three particularly significant qualities to the relationship, or therapist attitudes, which must be effectively communicated to the client.

Box 45.7 **The three therapist attitudes central to CCT**

Genuineness (authenticity or congruence): The therapist must show him/herself to be a real person, with feelings which should be expressed where appropriate. The client needs to feel that the therapist is emotionally involved, and not hiding behind a facade of professional impersonality: the therapist must be 'transparent'. This is the most important of the three qualities or attitudes.

Unconditional positive regard: The therapist must show complete acceptance of, and regard for, the client as a separate person in his/her own right. The therapist must deeply and genuinely care for clients as they are now, in a non-judgemental way.

Empathic understanding: The therapist must try to enter the client's inner world through genuine, attentive listening, which involves intense concentration. This may involve restating what the client says as a way of trying to clarify its emotional significance (rather than its verbal content). This requires the therapist to be sensitive to what's currently going on in the client's mind, and to meanings just below the level of awareness.

Thorne (1984) believes empathic understanding is the most 'trainable' of the three therapist attitudes, but is also remarkably rare. He also proposes *tenderness* as a fourth therapist attitude.

If these therapeutic conditions are established, clients will talk about themselves more honestly. This will re-establish congruence, which will be sufficient to produce changes in behaviour (Fonagy & Higgitt, 1984).

Evaluating CCT

Unlike most other humanistic therapists, Rogers has attempted to validate his therapy empirically (and has encouraged others to do so). A form of assessment used by Rogers is the *Q-sort*, which comprises a number of cards with statements referring to the self (e.g. 'I am a domineering person'). The client is asked to arrange them in a series of ten piles, ranging from 'very characteristic of me' to 'not at all characteristic of me' (describing the *self-image*), and the process is repeated so as to describe the *ideal self* (see Chapter 33). The two Q-sorts are then correlated to determine the discrepancy between self-image and ideal self – the lower the correlations, the greater the discrepancy. The whole procedure is repeated at various intervals during the course of therapy.

One way of assessing the importance of the three qualities or therapist attitudes is to train people to do so, and to give them transcripts or tape-recordings of therapy sessions which they then have to rate. Truax & Mitchell (1971) found that therapists who were rated high were much more likely to be associated with desirable changes in their clients, and low-rated therapists actually worsened their clients' conditions. But others have found that the therapist's personal characteristics are likely to be no more important than any specific techniques used.

An evaluation of therapy: Is it effective?

This deceptively simple-sounding question really comprises two interrelated questions:

1 Does it work? This is related to *outcome research.*
2 How does it work? This is related to *process research.*

Each question, in turn, comprises several other overlapping questions. *Outcome questions* include:

- Is psychotherapy (in general) effective?
- Is any one kind of psychotherapy more effective than another?
- What constitutes a satisfactory outcome?
- How should change be measured (and for how long after the end of treatment)?
- How much and what kind of change is necessary for a judgement of improvement to be made?

Process questions include:

- What are the necessary components of effective therapy?
- What are the mechanisms by which change is brought about (what are the 'active ingredients') ?
- Are different therapies effective because of the particular techniques and tools they use, or are there common factors that apply to all therapies?

Despite the close connection between them, researchers tend to focus on *either* outcome *or* process questions. Psychotherapy research began by concentrating on outcome, in the form of Eysenck's much-cited 1952 review article, in which he challenged what had up to that time been taken for granted about the effectiveness of psychoanalysis.

KEY STUDY 45.3

The effectiveness of psychotherapy (Eysenck, 1952)

Eysenck reviewed five studies of the effectiveness of psychoanalysis, and 19 studies of the effectiveness of 'eclectic' (mixed) psychotherapy. He concluded that only 44 per cent of psychoanalytic patients and 64 per cent of those who received the 'mixed' therapy improved. However, since roughly 66 per cent of patients improve *without* any treatment (*spontaneous remission*), Eysenck concluded that psychoanalysis in particular, and psychotherapy in general, simply don't work – they achieve nothing which wouldn't have happened anyway without therapy!

Outcome research

According to Eysenck (1992), the *outcome problem* had never been properly addressed by clinical psychologists prior to his article, which showed *only* that the available evidence wasn't sufficient to prove that psychoanalysis (and psychotherapy in general) was instrumental in bringing about recovery. It *didn't* suggest that it was ineffective (which is how many others interpreted his conclusions). Nevertheless, if it can be shown that psychoanalysis does *no better* than placebo treatments (see below) or no treatment at all (which the 1952 article showed):

'... then clearly the theory on which it is based was wrong. Similarly, if there were no positive effects of psychoanalysis as a therapy, then it would be completely unethical to apply this method to patients, to charge them money for such treatment, or to train therapists in these unsuccessful methods ...'. (Eysenck, 1992)

By 1960, Eysenck was arguing that behaviour therapy is the only kind of therapy worth rational consideration and he inspired an enormous amount of research on therapy outcomes (Oatley, 1984).

A re-assessment of Eysenck's conclusions

- If the many patients who drop out of psychoanalysis are excluded from the 44 per cent quoted by Eysenck (they cannot legitimately be counted as 'failures' or 'not cured'), the figure rises to 66 per cent.
- Bergin (1971) reviewed some of the studies included in Eysenck's review and concluded that, by choosing different criteria of 'improvement', the success rate of psychoanalysis could be raised to 83 per cent. He also cited studies which showed only a 30 per cent spontaneous remission rate.
- One of the two studies which Eysenck used to establish his spontaneous remission rate of 66 per cent was conducted by Landis (1938). Landis compared patients who'd received psychotherapy ('experimental group') with a control group who'd been hospitalised for 'neurosis' in state mental hospitals. Landis himself pointed out a number of differences between his psychotherapy group and the hospital patient controls, concluding that these differences

'all argue against the acceptance of [this] figure ... as a truly satisfactory baseline ...'.

- Bergin & Lambert (1978) reviewed 17 studies of untreated 'neurotics' and found a median spontaneous remission rate of 43 per cent. They also found that the rate of spontaneous remission varies a great deal depending on the disorder: generalised anxiety and depression, for example, are much more likely to 'cure themselves' than phobias or OCD. Similarly, Rachman & Wilson (1980) argue that:

'... the early assumption of uniformity of spontaneous remission rates among different disorders is increasingly difficult to defend'.

- Garfield (1992) argues that both the quantity and quality of psychotherapy research have increased since the time of Eysenck's 1952 article, especially since the 1970s, but Eysenck doesn't refer to this in his 1992 article.

Other outcome research

A review by Luborsky *et al.* (1975) concluded that all types of therapy are equally effective. Smith & Glass (1977) reviewed 400 studies of a wide variety of therapies (including psychodynamic, CCT, SD and eclectic) and concluded that all were more effective than no treatment. For example, the 'average' client who'd received therapy scored more favourably on the outcome measures than 75 per cent of those in the untreated control groups.

Smith *et al.* (1980) extended the 1977 study to include 475 studies (an estimated 75 per cent of the published literature). Strict criteria for accepting a study included the comparison of a treated group (given a specified form of therapy) with a second group (drawn from the same population) that were either given no therapy, put on a waiting list or given some alternative form of therapy. As with the 1977 results, the effectiveness of therapy was shown to be highly significant: the average client was better off than 80 per cent of the control groups on the outcome measures. Although different therapies had different kinds of effects, overall:

> 'Different types of psychotherapy (verbal or behavioural, psychodynamic, client-centred, or systematic desensitisation) do not produce different types or degrees of benefit'. (Smith et al., 1980)

Box 45.8 **Meta-analysis**

A distinctive feature of the Smith & Glass (1977) and Smith et al. (1980) studies is their use of meta-analysis (MA), a 'study of studies'. Lilienfeld (1995) defines MA as:

'... a procedure for aggregating and averaging the results of a large number of studies. Unlike the 'voting' method, meta-analysis allows researchers to consider the magnitude of findings and yield an overall measure of effect size – that is, an index of the magnitude of the effects of a treatment ... averaged across all studies ...'.

Effect size is essentially an indicator of the extent to which people who receive psychotherapy improve relative to those who don't: the greater the difference between these two groups, the greater the effect size. The 'voting method' (a term coined by Smith and Glass) simply involves adding up all the studies that support the effectiveness of psychotherapy and all those that don't – a result is counted as a 'hit' provided the difference between the two totals is statistically significant. But lumping together all the positive findings and all the negative findings obscures statistically significant results that are very large and those that are very small. As a result, it provides only a crude and often misleading summary of a body of literature (Lilienfeld, 1995). All outcome studies prior to Smith & Glass (1977) used the 'voting method'.

Another advantage of MA is that it allows researchers to examine whether certain variables are correlated with effect size, such as how experienced the therapist is and the age of clients. In this way, they can determine not only the overall effectiveness of psychotherapy (outcome research), but also what factors, if any, influence its effectiveness (process research).

Process research

Ask yourself...

- Based on the earlier discussion of specific treatment methods, try to formulate some questions relevant to process research (i.e. how they work).

■ Do relaxation and graded exposure to the feared object/situation make SD an effective means of removing phobias?

■ Are tokens an essential part of the TE, which successfully reduces the psychotic behaviour of schizophrenic patients?
■ Are the three therapist attitudes necessary if clients are to develop positive self-regard and to achieve congruence?

These are all questions about process. According to Kazdin & Wilcoxin (1976), the crucial ingredients of therapy (whatever techniques are involved) are:

■ the patient is influenced to expect success; and
■ the patient's self-concept changes, whereby s/he comes to believe (through supervised practice) that the previously feared object or situation can be coped with.

The patient's expectations of success relate to the crucial and controversial issue of the placebo effect.

The placebo effect

As we saw when discussing antidepressant drugs (see pages 664–665), a placebo denotes an inactive/inert substance, designed to take account of the psychological (as opposed to pharmacological) influences on physiological change (such as the expectation of improvement). So, in drug trials, the placebo condition is the control condition.

However, in psychotherapy, the expectancy is part of the treatment (Mair, 1992). Is it possible to devise a placebo control in psychotherapy research which is inactive in a way that's equivalent to taking a sugar pill? Even non-placebo controls (such as delayed treatment or no treatment conditions) will produce expectations specific to that particular condition (e.g. disappointment and rejection respectively) (Barkham & Shapiro, 1992).

If client expectations of success are one of the main 'active ingredients' or components involved in psychotherapy, then if a placebo has the capacity to inspire client expectations, making psychotherapy–placebo comparisons may underestimate the actual effectiveness of psychotherapy (Lilienfeld, 1995). Indeed, according to Frank (1989), if therapy effects don't exceed those of placebos (a conclusion drawn by, for example, Prioleau et al., 1983), this is because the placebo is psychotherapy:

> 'As a symbolic communication that combats demoralisation by inspiring the patient's hopes for relief, administration of a placebo is a form of psychotherapy. It is therefore not surprising that placebos can provide marked relief in patients who seek psychotherapy'. (Mair, 1989, quoted in Mair, 1992)

The role of non-specific factors

Cordray & Bootzin (1983) argue that one of the major ingredients involved in psychotherapy's effectiveness are the non-specific factors shared by most, or even all, therapies. The main proponent of this view is Frank (1973), who argues that psychotherapy has much in common with faith healing and other similar techniques. Far from being a derogatory comparison, Frank believes that the success of psychotherapy can be traced largely or entirely to four non-specific factors/components.

Frank's (1973) four non-specific factors/components involved in therapy

According to Frank, all psychotherapies:

- prescribe clearly delineated roles for therapist and client, with the former defined as 'expert' possessing unique healing skills. This raises the client's hopes that help will be forthcoming;
- involve settings designed to be associated with the alleviation of psychological distress (a 'designated place of healing'), e.g. carpeted rooms with scholarly books and journals and prominently displayed diplomas;
- provide a convincing theoretical rationale for making sense of the client's problems. This instils a sense of confidence in clients and reassures them that their problems aren't incomprehensible or unique;
- include therapeutic rituals (prescribed tasks or procedures, such as SD and free association) that further enhance the client's faith in the therapist and the therapeutic rationale. These are akin to the ceremonial rituals of faith healers; they cultivate the impression that something deeply significant and mysterious is taking place.

Above all, these factors help to combat demoralisation, the universal malady that brings people to therapy. Most individuals who voluntarily seek treatment experience low self-esteem, despair, helplessness, alienation and a profound sense of incompetence. All psychotherapies alleviate demoralisation by raising hopes and expectations of improvement, and by instilling feelings of confidence and self-worth (Mair, 1992).

Bandura (1977a) has integrated a number of findings into the proposal that the central element in psychological therapy is the cognitive change towards *self-efficacy*, the 'conviction that one can successfully execute a behaviour to produce a specified outcome' (see Chapter 35). This is brought about best through actual experience in facing previously feared or avoided situations.

The results of studies, like those of Smith & Glass (1977) and Smith *et al.* (1980), which claimed that differences in the effectiveness of various therapies are negligible, support Frank's argument. But other outcome studies have shown that the more active, structured, *directive therapies* work best (at least for certain types of disorder): they're more heavily 'saturated' with Frank's non-specific factors than are other psychotherapies (Lilienfeld, 1995).

Conclusions

The whole concept of 'cure' is highly complex, and is itself defined differently from different theoretical and therapeutic perspectives (see Box 45.5, page 669). The crux of Eysenck's (1952) review is how the effectiveness of psychotherapy should be assessed. He used Denker's (1946) criteria, namely:

- return to work and ability to carry on well in economic adjustments for at least five years;
- complaint of no further or very slight difficulties; and
- making successful social adjustments.

These are all fairly tangible indicators of improvement. Even more so is the behaviour therapist's criterion that cure is

achieved when patients no longer manifest the original maladaptive behaviour (e.g. the fear of spiders is eliminated). If these more stringent (or more easily measured) criteria of actual behaviour change are required before the therapist can be viewed as successful, then behaviour therapists do seem to be more effective than psychoanalysts or humanistic therapists (with cognitive approaches falling in between the two) (Rachman & Wilson, 1980; Shapiro & Shapiro, 1982).

But psychoanalytic therapists may answer the question 'Does therapy work?' by saying it's misleading, like asking whether friendship 'works'. It's an activity that people take part in, which is important to them, affects, moves, even transforms them (Oatley, 1984).

Because Eysenck is interested in comparing recovery rates (measured statistically), his assessment of the effects of therapy is purely *quantitative*. Psychoanalysts and those practising CCT are likely to be much more concerned with the *qualitative* aspects of therapy (such as the nature of the therapeutic process, and the role of the relationship between client and therapist). There are different kinds of questions one can ask when trying to assess the effects of psychotherapy.

According to Lilienfeld (1995), the question 'Is psychotherapy effective?', although remarkably complex in some respects, may actually be too simple in others. As Paul (1966) observes, what we need to ask is 'What treatment, by whom, is most effective for this individual, with that specific problem, and under which set of circumstances?' This is to do with matching client, therapy and setting and, according to Wilson & Barkham (1994), is a question that still haunts psychotherapy research and disturbs therapists.

CHAPTER SUMMARY

- Both **clinical** and **counselling psychology** adopt the **scientist–practitioner model** of helping, but they've been more influenced by behavioural and humanistic approaches respectively.
- Treatments and therapies differ according to whether they're **somatic** or **psychological**, **directive** or **non-directive**, **individual** or **group**.
- The term '**psychotherapy**' is sometimes used to refer to all non-somatic treatments, and sometimes to psychodynamic approaches/insight therapies.
- Major groups of **antidepressant drugs**, include **MAOIs**, **tricyclics**, and **SSRIs**, including fluoxetine (Prozac).
- Chlordiazepoxide (Librium) and diazepam (Valium) are widely prescribed **anxiolytics**. They belong to the **benzodiazepines**.
- **Antipsychotic drugs** (major tranquilliers/neuroleptics) revolutionised the treatment of schizophrenia and other psychotic disorders. But they only treat the **positive symptoms** of schizophrenia, and cause serious side-effects.
- **Electroconvulsive therapy** (ECT) is now used mainly with depressive patients. While it's probably more effective than antidepressants, its benefits are only short term, and it may cause long-term cognitive and emotional deficits.
- Although modern **stereotactic procedures** are much more precise than earlier **prefrontal lobotomies/leucotomies**, the use of **psychosurgery** remains extremely controversial. In the UK, it's used only as a last resort.

- According to Freud, **neuroses** involve the use of defences in an attempt to combat anxiety, but they're self-defeating, creating their own distress.
- The aims of **psychoanalysis** include providing insight. The analyst remains anonymous, which facilitates **transference**. **Interpreting** transference is a distinctive feature of psychoanalysis, as is the analyst's **countertransference**.
- The client's **resistance** to interpretations of transference must itself be interpreted. **Free association** and **dream interpretation** are other major techniques.
- **Psychodynamic psychotherapy** represents a modified form of psychoanalysis. **Brief focal therapy** deals with a specific area of difficulty in a much shorter period of time than classical psychoanalysis.
- **Behaviour therapy** and **modification** refer to techniques based on **classical** and **operant conditioning** respectively. Both see adaptive and maladaptive behaviour as being acquired in the same way, and both reject the medical model.
- Eysenck and Rachman see the case of Little Albert as a model of how all phobias are acquired. But this can only account for the initial learning of phobias (through **classical conditioning**), not for their persistence (which occurs through **negative reinforcement**).
- According to Wolpe, the key principle in **systematic desensitisation** (SD) is **reciprocal inhibition**. It appears that neither relaxation nor the use of a hierarchy is necessary, and the 'active ingredient' seems to be **exposure** to the feared object/situation.
- **Implosion** (implosive therapy) is supplemented by the therapist's **stimulus augmentation**. Both implosion and **flooding** represent forms of '**forced reality testing**'. Flooding is thought to be the most effective of all treatments for phobias.
- **Aversion therapy** is particularly controversial when used with homosexuals. **Covert sensitisation** is aversion therapy that takes place in the patient's imagination, and is preferable on humanitarian grounds.
- Lovaas pioneered **operant conditioning** with autistic children in an attempt to teach them to use speech. **Behaviour modification** has been used successfully-with mentally retarded adults and children, both to reduce self-mutilation and to teach toilet training.
- Ayllon and Azrin pioneered the **token economy** (TE), based on the principle of **secondary reinforcement**.
- Tokens may be effective because of the way they change **staff** behaviour and attitudes, which is contrary to what learning theory principles would predict. TEs also raise some very basic **ethical** issues.

- **Cognitive–behaviour therapy** (CBT) is based on the view that clinical disorders involve **faulty thoughts/cognitions**, which then produce maladaptive behaviour. **Cognitive restructuring** is a means to the end of changing emotions and behaviour.
- According to Ellis's **rational emotive therapy** (RET), **irrational thoughts** are the main cause of all types of emotional/behaviour disorders. Meichenbaum's **self-instructional training** (SIT) claims that neurotic behaviour is due to **faulty internal dialogues**.
- Beck's **cognitive therapy** aims to help clients understand the **cognitive triad** of depression. Therapy involves training in being more objective, separating fact from evaluation, and seeing things in less extreme ways.
- According to Rogers, threat, anxiety and depression are responses to a lack of congruence between our experience and self-concept. We may defend against these feelings, setting up a vicious circle, which may manifest itself in a neurotic or psychotic way.
- The aim of **client-centred therapy** (CCT) is to allow the natural tendency towards self-actualisation to develop through the therapist's **genuineness/authenticity**, **unconditional positive regard** and **empathic understanding**.
- Evaluating the effectiveness of therapy involves both **outcome** and **process research**. Eysenck's landmark article claimed that recovery from neurosis following psychotherapy is no greater than the rate of **spontaneous remission**.
- Both the quantity and quality of subsequent outcome research have increased, showing psychodynamic therapies in a much more favourable light. One important improvement is the use of **meta-analysis**.
- Unlike drug trials, in psychotherapy it may be impossible to devise an inactive **placebo control**. If therapy effects don't exceed those of placebos, this is because the placebo itself raises hopes of improvement.
- Frank identifies four **non-specific factors** responsible for the success of psychotherapy. They help to combat demoralisation, the common factor shared by all those who seek therapeutic help. Related to this is Bandura's concept of **self-efficacy**.

Self-assessment questions

1 Discuss the use of any **two** biological (somatic) therapies in the treatment of mental disorders.
2 Discuss the use of any **two** psychological therapies in the treatment of mental disorders.
3 Critically consider the effectiveness of psychotherapy.

Web addresses

ttp://www.breggin.com

http://www.mentalhealth.com

http://www.noah.cuny.edu/illness/mentalhealth/cornell/tests/ect.html

http://neurosurgery.mgh.harvard.edu.psysurg.htm

http://lcweb.gov/lexico/liv/p/Psychosurgery.html

http;//mentalhealth.com

http://psychcentral.com

http://fox.klte/~Kerosfi/psychotherapy

http://www.discoveryhealth.com

http://www.apsa.org

http://www.aapsa.org

http://www.divpsa.org

http://mindstreet.com.cbt.html

http://www.beckinstitute.org

www.metonia.org

www.samaritans.org.uk

Further reading

Dryden, W. & Feltham, C. (Eds) (1992) *Psychotherapy and its Discontents.* Buckingham: Open University Press. A collection of original articles, in which eight distinguished critics of psychotherapy outline their views, with a response from eight psychotherapists, followed by a rebuttal of the response. The critics include Eysenck, Sutherland and Masson.

Dryden, W. & Rentoul, R. (Eds) (1991) *Adult Clinical Problems: A Cognitive–Behavioural Approach.* London: Routledge. A detailed account of how cognitive–behavioural therapies can be applied to a wide range of disorders.

Chapter 46 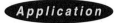 *Application*

Criminological Psychology

Introduction and overview

N ot surprisingly, many of the questions we've discussed about the causes of behaviour have also been applied to crime and criminal behaviour. While psychology is one of the disciplines contributing to *criminology* (others being law, sociology, anthropology, economics, geography, politics, statistics and psychiatry), *criminological* (or *forensic*) *psychology* attempts to apply psychological principles to the criminal justice system (Harrower, 1998).

Defined in this way, the present chapter clearly overlaps with Chapter 21, which looked specifically at aspects of *cognitive psychology* (in particular memory and face recognition) in relation to the law. The two chapters are complementary. By discussing research into eyewitness testimony and face recognition, we were looking in Chapter 21 at one half of the 'crime–victim' equation. Here, the focus is on the person committing the crime, rather than on the witness (although witnesses aren't necessarily victims).

Because crime is a form of social deviancy, definitions and perceptions of crime overlap with the criteria discussed in Chapter 43 for defining psychological abnormality. Also, one theory of criminal behaviour holds that it reflects a particular type of personality disorder (see Chapter 44). Discussion of moral development (see Chapter 35), gender (Chapter 36), adolescence (Chapter 37), and personality (Chapter 42) are all highly relevant to any attempt to understand and explain criminal behaviour.

The Division of Criminological and Legal Psychology was recognised by the British Psychological Society in 1977.

Who commits crime?

Ask yourself ...

- Think of a criminal and what comes to mind (i.e. what's your stereotype of a criminal)?
- Are different types of crime likely to be committed by different kinds of criminal (in terms of age, gender, social-class background etc.)?

According to Hollin (1999), the strongest evidence relevant to predicting who'll commit crime comes from *longitudinal studies*. For example, Loeber *et al.* (1995) investigated predictive factors for the onset of conduct disorder, itself an established risk factor for later delinquency, in 177 males aged 8–17. They were followed up for six years, and data were collected on a range of psychological, psychiatric and social factors. Parental substance abuse, low socio-economic status (SES), and the child's resistance to discipline were important factors in eventual progression to diagnosed conduct disorder.

Longitudinal studies have helped illuminate our understanding of many criminological issues, including the relationship between *age and crime*, predictors of *juvenile delinquency*, and patterns of *adult crime*.

Age and offending

Delinquency rates for both males and females consistently increase from about age eight, peaking at 16–17, then rapidly declining into the late teens and early twenties. But is this due to increasing *prevalence* (more young people committing crimes) or a rise in *incidence* (young offenders committing more offences as they get older)? While these are difficult to separate, it's generally agreed that the rise in offending rates with age reflect increasing prevalence (Hollin, 1999).

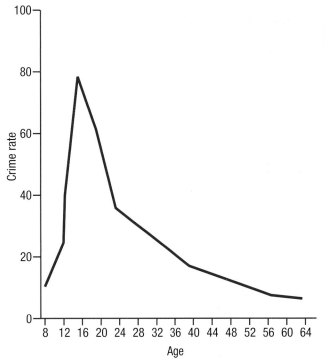

Figure 46.1 *The relationship between age and crime (from Hollin, 1999)*

'Crime rate' refers to prevalence, in terms of the percentage of people of specific ages who commit offences. As Figure 46.1 shows, about 20 per cent of twelve-year-olds, 80 per cent of 16-year-olds, 20 per cent of 36-year-olds, and eight per cent of 52-year-olds commit crime.

Although juveniles commit a lot of crime, most is relatively trivial, including a large number of *status offences* (which apply only to young people, such as truancy, under-age drinking, driving a motor vehicle under age) as opposed to *index* (or *notifiable*) *offences* (serious offences, such as murder, rape and sexual assault, burglary, arson and robbery, which are criminal acts *regardless* of age). Young people commit both types, but status offences are much more common (Hollin, 1999).

A defaced, grafittied statue of Winston Churchill

The age–crime relationship also shows that most crime is 'adolescence-limited' (Moffitt, 1993); that is, most young people 'grow out' of delinquency by the time they're 18. So, what is it about being a teenager that makes criminal behaviour so much more likely than at any other age?

Box 46.1   Risk-taking and delinquency

According to Hendry (1999), risk-taking has been one of the attributes of youth since adolescence became recognised as a distinct period of the lifespan (see Chapter 37). But it's an ill-defined concept. Is it part of the psychological make-up of youth, a necessary rite of passage en route to the acquisition of adult skills and self-esteem?

Whatever the answer to these questions risk-taking and delinquency can be seen as interrelated.

The desire to identify with the peer group, especially in mid-adolescence (Coleman & Hendry, 1999) requires adherence to particular types of behaviour and roles, which imposes a group conformity even when antisocial activities are involved. Paradoxically, many juvenile crimes may reflect underlying *values* that are generally approved and encouraged by society (such as acquiring material possessions). 'Inappropriate' behaviours (such as drug and alcohol use, smoking, and sexual behaviour) may be 'used' to identify with adult patterns of behaviour (Hendry, 1999).

Boys comprise the biggest proportion of juvenile offenders and enter the criminal justice system earlier than girls, and many juvenile crimes are *gendered* (such as joy-riding, a very 'male' crime). In the US at least, young men are much more likely than young women to have several sexual partners, use alcohol and marijuana, drive recklessly, and engage in physically violent behaviour. They're consequently much more likely to die as a result of accidental injuries, homicides and suicides than young women. While black female teenagers are about four times more likely to be murdered than their white counterparts, black males are about eight times more likely to die this way than theirs (Sonenstein, 1999).

Predictors of long-term offending

According to Hollin (1999), the most widely cited longitudinal study in the UK is the Cambridge Study in Delinquent Development. This began in 1961 with 411 males, aged eight to nine, and is still in progress, with over 90 per cent of the sample intact as they pass into their 40s. They've been repeatedly tested and interviewed throughout this period, and parents, peers and teachers have also been interviewed. A vast amount and range of data have been gathered, dealing with parental child-rearing practices, economic factors, school behaviour and much more. Summary reports have been published by Farrington & West (1990) and Farrington (1995).

About 20 per cent were actually convicted as juveniles, 33 per cent were convicted up to the age of 25, and self-reported delinquency matched official records reasonably well.

KEY STUDY 46.1

The Cambridge Study in Delinquent Development (Farrington & West, 1990; Farrington, 1995)

The most important distinguishing characteristics, observed at age eight to ten, of later delinquents (measured by convictions and self-report) fell into six main categories:

- antisocial childhood behaviour, including troublesomeness in school, dishonesty and aggression;
- hyperactivity/impulsivity/attention-deficit, including poor concentration, restlessness, daring, and psychomotor impulsivity;
- low intelligence and poor academic record;
- family criminal record, including convicted parents, delinquent older siblings, and siblings with behavioural problems;
- family poverty, including low family income, large family size and poor housing;
- poor parental child-rearing behaviour, including harsh and authoritarian discipline, poor supervision, parental conflict and separation from parents.

The intensity and severity of these personal and social disadvantages in childhood appear to be predictive of chronic offending in adolescence and adulthood. Over and above these factors, the age of first conviction, the school attended, employment, and moving to a more prosperous area were all related to patterns of criminal activity in adolescence.

In two independent studies, Elander *et al.* (2000a) confirmed that hyperactivity is a significant risk factor in boys, and Elander *et al.* (2000b) found that late-onset criminals (first conviction after age 22) were likely to have had a history of childhood and adolescent antisocial behaviour, major mental illness in adulthood, or both. Late-onset criminals are also more likely to be female.

By 18, the long-term offenders had adopted a lifestyle characterised by heavy drinking, sexual promiscuity, drug use, and minor crimes involving cars or group violence and vandalism. They were highly unlikely to have any formal qualifications, had unskilled manual jobs, and were often unemployed.

By 32, they were unlikely to be home-owners (and to be residentially mobile), had low paid jobs, tended to have physically assaulted their partners, and used a wide range of drugs. They had an extensive list of fines, probation and prison sentences. Overall, this was a socially dysfunctional existence. They committed more crimes while unemployed, and these were for financial gain – theft, burglary and fraud.

The formation of close relationships in early adulthood was related to a decrease in offending: those who were married were less likely to offend than those who weren't, provided their partners weren't convicted offenders. But compared with non-offenders, they were more likely to have divorced or separated from their wives and children, and to have more conflict with their wives/partners (see Chapter 32).

However, there was still considerable overlap between offenders and non-offenders: not all the convicted men displayed these characteristics. Neither a disadvantaged background nor 'social failure' (Farrington, 1990) inevitably leads to crime, but it massively increases the risk of criminal behaviour (the 'good boys from bad backgrounds' phenomenon: Farrington & West, 1990).

Crime and gender

According to Heidensohn (1996):

'Sex differences in criminality are so sustained and so marked as to be, perhaps, the most significant feature of recorded crime'.

Lyon (1998) observes that 84 per cent of recorded crime is committed by men, who comprise 96 per cent of the prison population in England and Wales. One-third of men born in 1953 had been convicted of an offence by the age of 30. Similarly, Harrower (1998) maintains that:

'Probably the most significant feature of both recorded and self-reported crime is that more males than females commit offences, particularly violent crimes, in spite of claims that women are becoming more violent in the 1990s … or that, because of their inherent deviousness, they have always been more criminal but have simply been able to conceal it …'.

Until recently, the 'maleness' of crime was taken as an accepted fact. In contrast to the 'ordinariness' of male crime, the few early studies of female offenders focused on their extraordinariness, as odd or ill creatures deviating from the norm (Lyon, 1998). In the 1970s, feminist perspectives began to develop in criminology, and the neglect of gender (especially women) was highlighted.

Women and crime

According to Lloyd (1995) in a book called *Doubly Deviant, Doubly Damned*:

'… when women commit violent crimes they are seen to have breached two laws: the law of the land which forbids violence and natural law which says women are passive carers not active aggressors'.

CRITICAL DISCUSSION 46.1

Women and violence

Throughout the years of heated debate concerning Myra Hindley's release from prison, there seems to have been an implicit assumption that to have committed her crimes, she must be especially evil *because ('ordinary') women don't commit (are incapable of) such crimes.*

Pearson (1998, in *When She Was Bad: How Women Get Away With Murder*) tries to demolish the cherished myth that women aren't naturally aggressive. Pearson (a woman) blames feminists and society as a whole for refusing to see women as dangerous and destructive. We cannot bring ourselves to recognise the reality of female aggression and violence. So, we find excuses for it, such as battered women syndrome, or premenstrual tension, or we see female killers (including Hindley and Rose West) as always junior accomplices of violent men.

According to Smith (1998), the myth that Pearson tries to demolish only tells half the story. There's also a terror that women are innately more cruel than men, a sentiment summed up in Kipling's 'the female of the species is more deadly than the male'.

It's been suggested that the criminal justice system is more 'chivalrous' (i.e. lenient) towards females, so that the gender difference in violent crime isn't in fact as large as official figures would make it seem (Harrower, 1998: see text below). But at the same time, there have been numerous cases in Britain of men killing their wives for trivial reasons, being found guilty of manslaughter and walking free after five or six years in prison, while women who kill their husbands tend to be convicted of murder and receive a life sentence (Smith, 1998). This injustice has led to the overturning of verdicts in celebrated cases like that of Sara Thornton, who was initially convicted of her husband's murder. She successfully argued that the court should have taken into account the cumulative effect of her husband's violence towards her, and she was released from jail.

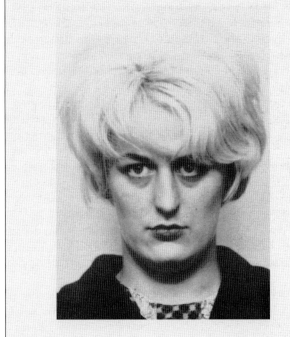

Myra Hindley

Criminology has notoriously ignored the fact of gender, preferring to offer universal theories of crime based on research with males (Harrower, 1998: see below, pages 686–689, and Chapter 47).

Gender bias in the criminal justice system

According to Lyon (1998), there's considerable evidence that men and women are treated differently by the criminal justice system. Ideas and attitudes about what constitutes 'normal' male and female behaviour affect how female offenders are treated. Lyon gives three examples:

- Hedderman & Gelsthorpe (1997) examined 13,000 cases of men and women convicted of shoplifting, violence and drug offences during 1991. For virtually every type of offence, women are treated more leniently than men. They also interviewed 200 magistrates about what they thought were the main influences on their decision-making. Women were considerably more likely than men to be discharged even when circumstances appeared to be entirely comparable. Magistrates were reluctant to fine women, especially those with dependent children, were more likely to define women offenders as troubled rather than troublesome, and to see their crimes as motivated by need rather than greed.

■ A high proportion of female offenders have themselves been the victims of crime (see Critical Discussion 46.1). Belknap (1996) found that prior victimisation, prostitution, running away and drug offences, and subsequent imprisonment were interrelated. Morris *et al.* (1994) surveyed large numbers of female prisoners in England and Wales, and almost half reported either being physically abused as children or the victims of domestic violence as adults. Another third reported sexual abuse. Similar findings were reported by HM Chief Inspector of Prisons (1997).

Some very young women become involved in prostitution through relationships with adults who offer accommodation and introduction to drug habits. The Children's Society (Lyon & Coleman, 1996) estimated that at least 5000 children under 16 are used for prostitution in Britain, and the number of girls of 16 or under who were convicted (1989–1994) rose by almost 80 per cent.

■ The most common female crimes are theft and property-related crimes, with a rising incidence of drug-related offences and crimes of violence against the person. Women are more likely to be in prison for the first time (about 70 per cent are 'first timers'), and are less likely to re-offend on release than males (under 50 per cent of female young offenders re-offend within two years, compared with 80 per cent of male young offenders).

Female prisoners are more likely to suffer from depression, to self-harm, abuse drugs or alcohol, seek medical help, and be prescribed (and often depend on) medication compared with male prisoners. They're also more likely to be imprisoned far from home, and to be adversely affected by custody. Most have dependent children, for whom many retain considerable responsibility. Women in prison are also more likely to be charged with breaking prison rules and other discipline-related offences.

Women (especially black women) appear to face greater discrimination than men on release from prison in relation to finding housing and employment. Because they constitute a tiny minority of the prison population as a whole (four per cent), women offenders may be regarded as unnatural or pathologically deviant (Lyon, 1998).

Men and crime

Feminist criminologists have helped to promote the view that 'masculinity' itself should be examined more closely in order to understand why so many young men commit offences – and are also the victims of crime (see Box 46.1). While at one time 'gender' was a 'code word' for women and femininity, it now refers to men and masculinity. Because of men's domination of all aspects of crime and the criminal justice system, it's only recently that their gender and the construction of their

masculinity have been considered valid areas for study in their own right.

> ### Ask yourself ...
>
> • Why is it that males are much more likely to commit crimes than females? (See Chapters 36 and 50.)

According to Lyon (1998), two major explanations of the male domination of crime are *biological determinism* and *social constructionism*. Are men born to take risks, challenge authority, become violent and commit crimes? Or do they learn these behaviours, and is crime the context in which their masculine identity develops and is affirmed?

As Wilson & Herrnstein (1985) point out:

> 'Crime is an activity disproportionately carried out by young men living in large cities. There are old criminals, and female ones, and rural and small town ones, but to a much greater degree than would be expected by chance, criminals are young urban males'.

Over 80 per cent of all offenders are male, and this pattern is repeated internationally. So what is it about the cultural history and social construction of *masculinity* which ensures that so many young males become involved in crime (Harrower, 1998)? According to Lyon (1998), a new research focus on masculinity and crime seeks to challenge popular images of young men as yobs and thugs, and to question their 'natural ' involvement in offending. She also argues that:

> '... gender and crime can only be fully explored within the context of culture and society taking account of key variables such as race, class, family, economic circumstances and individual differences'.

Theories of criminal behaviour

If, as we've seen, not all males commit crime and some females do, then there must be factors over and above gender that make people more likely engage in this sort of behaviour. Similarly, not all boys growing up in disadvantaged circumstances become adolescent or adult offenders. So, although being an urban male significantly increases your chances of committing crime, psychologists want to know what other influences are involved. In Hollin's (1997) terms:

> '... while the findings of the longitudinal surveys are important in describing the conditions associated with the onset of criminal behaviour, they also demand an explanation of how they cause delinquent behaviour. In other words, we still await a grand theory to explain the process by which the interaction between the young person and his or her environmental circumstances culminate in criminal behaviour'.

In the meantime, we can draw on existing psychological theories, which may be applicable to criminal behaviour, without being theories of criminal behaviour as such.

Ask yourself ...

- How would Freud explain criminal behaviour? (See Chapter 35, pages 506–509.)
- How would Kohlberg explain criminal behaviour? (See Chapter 35, pages 511–514.)
- How would *social learning theorists* (such as Bandura) explain criminal behaviour? (See Chapter 29, pages 425–429, and Chapter 35, pages 516–517.)
- How could Bowlby's *maternal deprivation hypothesis* help to explain criminal behaviour? (See Chapter 32, pages 470–471.)
- What methods would *behaviour geneticists* use to assess the influence of genetic factors on criminal behaviour? Based on studies of intelligence (see Chapter 41, pages 600–602) and schizophrenia (see Chapter 44, pages 654–656), what would you expect the relative influence of genetic and environmental factors to be?

Personality and criminality

According to Furnham & Heaven (1999), many studies have shown conclusively that personality factors are related to a wide range of antisocial, criminal and delinquent behaviours. The vast majority of this research has been cross-sectional and has looked for links between criminal behaviour and the personality dimensions originally investigated by Eysenck, namely introversion–extroversion (E), neuroticism–emotional stability (N), and psychoticism (P) (see Chapter 42, pages 615–616).

Eysenck's personality theory

E, N and conditionability

For Eysenck, the criminal is a neurotic extrovert (someone who scores high on both N and E). N is linked to crime through *anxiety* (Eysenck & Eysenck 1970). High anxiety functions very much like a drive, which multiplies with habit, so, someone who engages in delinquent behaviour is likely to persist in that behaviour if they're also high N scorers. The high E scorer is stimulus-hungry, engages in thrill-enhancing behaviours, and is more difficult to *condition*. Because 'conscience' is nothing more than a series of conditioned anxiety responses (see Chapter 35), the neurotic extrovert is undersocialised and has an underdeveloped conscience.

Cochrane (1974) reviewed a number of studies in which prisoners and control groups were given EPI questionnaires. Although prisoners are generally higher on N, they're *not* higher on E and, indeed, several studies have shown criminals to be *less* extroverted (and so more introverted) than controls. However, Eysenck (1974) responded to these findings by claiming that the EPI largely measures the 'sociability' component of extroversion rather than the 'impulsivity' component, which is more relevant to conditionability. This represents a change in his earlier position, in which he equated 'sociability' (the capacity for socialisation) and 'conditionability'. Cochrane concludes that, at least in its original form, the theory has been discredited.

Even if prisoners were uniformly more extroverted and neurotic than non-prisoners, it could still be possible to explain these differences by reference to factors other than personality. For example, offenders who are caught (or found

guilty) might differ in certain significant ways from those who aren't (or who aren't found guilty), such as the nature of the offence and the 'offender's' social status.

Farrington (1992) argues that the exact role of N depends on whether you're referring to 'official' or self-reported delinquency. 'Official' offenders are most often characterised by high N and *low* E scores (agreeing with Cochrane's findings), whereas self-reported offenders are the reverse: low N and *high* E. However, both forms of delinquency are related to high P (see below).

Heather (1976) argues that:

'The notion that such a complex and meaningful social phenomenon as crime can ever be explained by appealing to the activity of individual nervous systems would be laughable were it not so insidious'.

What makes the theory insidious, he says, is that it 'places the fault inside individuals rather than in the social system where it almost always belongs' (see Chapter 50).

Psychoticism and crime

P is more strongly correlated with crime than either N or E (Eysenck & Eysenck, 1970, 1985; Eysenck & Gudjonsson, 1989). According to Furnham & Heaven (1999), it's well established that high P scorers are also aggressive, uncaring, troublesome, inhumane, insensitive to others' needs and feelings, tend to not experience guilt, prefer strange and unusual things, and appear foolhardy (Eysenck & Eysenck, 1970). Howarth (1986) found that high P scorers are impulsive, tend to be unco-operative, rigid and lacking sensitivity, and Claridge (1981) found a close association between P and overt aggressiveness and impulsivity.

Not surprisingly, in view of all these findings, P scores are well able to discriminate between criminals and non-criminals (Eysenck & Gudjonsson, 1989).

KEY STUDY 46.2

A longitudinal study of delinquency and personality (Heaven, 1996b)

Heaven studied 282 14-year-olds over a two-year period, measuring delinquency, E, P and self-esteem. The best longitudinal predictor of later delinquency was P, with E and low self-esteem both having little impact. Although the importance of P supports previous findings, the overall effect was quite small: the three factors accounted for just over 16 per cent of the variance in delinquency scores when first measured, and only six per cent two years later. So, over time, the impact of personality on the maintenance of delinquency scores seems to have been rather limited (Furnham & Heaven, 1999).

Heaven suggests that factors (dimensions or *domains*) such as E are too broad and insensitive to capture the full subtlety of developmental change. Lower-order factors (or *facets*), such as excitement-seeking, trust, impulsiveness and venturesomeness might capture these subtleties better. This conclusion was supported by a separate study involving delinquency and the 'big five' personality factors (Heaven, 1996a: see Chapter 42, page 619).

According to Furnham & Heaven (1999):

'Clearly much more work needs to be done on assessing the interaction between personality and external factors such as family life, peer pressure, group norms and so on. Indeed, evidence also suggests that physiological factors (e.g. heart rate) may be implicated in the personality–behaviour link … This kind of research needs to be undertaken increasingly if we are to achieve a much more comprehensive understanding of the psychology of criminality'.

Antisocial personality disorder (psychopathy)

Definitions and classification

'Psychopathy' was first included in the 1959 Mental Health Act, which defined it as:

'… a persistent disorder or disability of mind (whether or not including subnormality of intelligence) which results in abnormally aggressive or seriously irresponsible conduct on the part of the patient and requires or is susceptible to medical treatment'.

According to the 1983 Mental Health Act:

'Psychopathy means a persistent disorder or disability of mind (whether or not including significant impairment of intelligence) which results in abnormally aggressive or seriously irresponsible conduct on the part of the person concerned'.

Because it was felt strongly that those with psychopathic disorder should only be compulsorily detained if there was a reasonable prospect of response to treatment, the diagnostic criteria in the definition were separated (in the 1983 Act) from the susceptibility to treatment clause (Prins, 1995). These are contained in other sections of the Act, which made compulsory admission for treatment available only if it can be stated that medical treatment is likely to alleviate or prevent a deterioration in the individual's condition. According to Prins:

'This was an important proviso because it recognised the difficulties involved in treating psychopaths, but kept the door open for therapeutic optimism … It also serves to emphasise the fact that the term psychopathic disorder should be used sparingly and not as a "dustbin" label for those clients or patients who are merely difficult, unco-operative or unlikeable …'.

A working group was set up by the Department of Health and the Home Office (1992) to review the treatment options for individuals with psychopathic disorder, their appropriate location, and arrangements for treatment. The 1994 report called for considerably more research into the nature of the disorder, its classification and management.

The report also recommended replacing the term 'psychopathic disorder' with 'personality disorder'. In fact, DSM–IV uses the term '*antisocial personality disorder*' (APD), and ICD–10 refers to '*dissocial personality disorder*' (DPD).

Box 46.2 The major characteristics of antisocial personality disorder (APD)

Individuals diagnosed with APD:

- lack tender feelings and concern for others' feelings, so that relationships are shallow and unstable; sex is purely 'functional' (if male) and they're highly promiscuous;
- appear to have no family loyalty and commit their crimes alone; they're basically loners;
- have superficial charm and are often socially skilled; their charm can be very disarming and enables them to manipulate and exploit others for their own gain;
- behave callously, as in inflicting pain or degradation or acting cruelly towards others;
- act violently towards their marriage partners, and their children, whom they may also neglect, resulting in separation and divorce;
- are impulsive and fail to strive consistently towards a goal, lacking a purpose in life; this may be reflected in an unstable employment record;
- have low tolerance of frustration and a tendency towards violence, which often causes repeated criminal offences. This may begin with petty acts of delinquency, but progresses to callous, violent crimes. Their lack of guilt and failure to learn from experience result in behaviour that persists despite serious consequences and legal penalties;
- they commit a disproportionate number of violent crimes.

(Based on Gelder *et al.*, 1999; Prins, 1995)

According to Hart & Hare (1996), 50–80 per cent of adult male prison inmates meet the DSM criteria for APD. Mitchell & Blair (2000) argue that:

'Unless we desire to label almost all individuals who engage in antisocial behaviour as presenting with a psychiatric disorder, we must consider these diagnoses to be unsatisfactory'.

Hare has developed an alternative, arguably more successful, method for identifying individuals whose antisocial behaviour may reflect an actual disorder. This is the revised psychopathy checklist (PCL–R: Hare, 1991), which measures two distinct, but correlated factors:

- *factor 1:* affective and interpersonal characteristics, including superficial charm, pathological lying, manipulation, lack of empathy, shallow affect, and lack of guilt;
- *factor 2:* chronic and versatile antisocial lifestyle, including proneness to boredom, parasitic lifestyle, impulsivity, juvenile delinquency, and violation of release conditions.

Essentially, the psychopathic individual is someone with an emotional disorder who also has a high risk of antisocial behaviour.

PCL–R has proved very reliable and is very useful in *risk assessment*. For example, within three years of release, 80 per cent of those judged to be psychopathic (based on PCL–R) had violated the conditions of their release, compared with just 25 per cent of the non-psychopaths. A meta-analytic study by Hemphill *et al.* (1998) found that psychopathic offenders were three times more likely to re-offend and four times more likely to re-offend violently within a year of release, compared with non-psychopathic offenders.

What causes APD?

Display of the full disorder seems to involve a complex interaction between social environment and biological predispositions. In particular, social environment (such as SES) influences factor 2, while factor 1 is unrelated to SES. This suggests that biological make-up determines whether individuals show emotional difficulties. But these emotional factors are only *risk factors*: an adverse social environment provides the conditions needed for the disorder to develop (Mitchell & Blair, 2000).

> ### Ask yourself ...
>
> • Which explanation of *schizophrenia* mirrors this account of APD? (See Chapter 44, page 656.)

Like other forms of criminality (see Key Study 46.1), parental antisocial attitudes, inconsistent discipline, physical punishment, broken homes, childhood separations all predict high APD scores in adolescence (Forth, 1995). However, the quality of parenting *doesn't* influence the probability of conduct disorders in children who display the emotional difficulties associated with APD – but they do in most children (Wootton *et al.*, 1997).

Box 46.3 Emotional processing in APD individuals

The two main explanations of how emotional processing differs in APD individuals and 'normals' are (a) abnormalities in the experience of fear; and (b) a fundamental inability to empathise:

• As proposed by Eysenck (see text above, page 687), socialisation is achieved through *fear conditioning* (see also Chapter 11). Normally, individuals learn to avoid antisocial behaviour because they're 'frightened' of the consequences. Those with impaired fear cannot be socialised in this way, so they don't learn the usual avoidance responses. However, much of the literature fails to support punishment as an effective means of socialisation, stressing instead the importance of *empathy induction*.

• Sad, and possibly fearful, expressions may serve a similar function in humans to submissive postures (appeasement gestures) in non-humans (Blair, 1995: see Lorenz's theory of aggression in Chapter 29). APD individuals are less sensitive, specifically, to others' sadness and fear (as opposed to expressions of anger, for example), and so are more difficult to socialise. They don't seem to feel the same aversion to the thought of other people's pain as do 'normal' individuals (see Chapters 30 and 35).

The brain and APD

It appears that the *amygdala* (see Chapter 4) functions atypically from an early age in people with APD. It's long been known that the amygdala plays a crucial role in the processing

of emotion, especially fear. Just like people with APD, normal humans and non-humans suffering damage to this area don't show normal fear conditioning (see Box 46.3) or startle reflex potentiation/priming (LeDoux, 1998).

The amygdala has also been shown (using PET: see Chapter 4) to be involved in human emotional response to sad facial expressions (Blair *et al.*, 1999). But this response is absent in individuals with APD.

Can APD be treated?

Controversy surrounding APD rivals that which has always surrounded schizophrenia, and raises some of the same fundamental issues, such as reliability and validity (see Chapter 44). According to Smith (2000), 'Personality disorder is surely the greyest of grey areas', and the diagnosis, far from showing the way to treatment, is in fact extremely unhelpful for nurses and patients alike. Believing that patients have a personality disorder can excuse us from trying to establish meaningful and helpful interactions with them.

While the general consensus is that APD – and personality disorder in general – is notoriously resistant to treatment, schizophrenia, for example, was also once thought to be untreatable. Mitchell & Blair (2000) are confident that research in the near future may allow us to treat APD too.

Offender profiling

> ### Ask yourself ...
>
> • What does offender profiling mean?
> • Can you give any examples – fictional or real?

CASE STUDY 46.1

Adrian Babb, serial rapist

One Sunday afternoon in June, 1987, a 75-year-old woman was returning to her flat in a tower block. As she entered the lift, a young man stepped in with her. Once the lift door had closed, he pinned her to the wall and forced her to the rooftop. There he raped her.

A few months later, Canter, a criminological psychologist, was given details of this and a number of related assaults, all against elderly and often frail victims in tower blocks in the same area of Birmingham. The information indicated a small area of the city in which the offender was likely to be living, his domestic circumstances and likely criminal record. It also pointed out his lack of experience in committing crimes, and the consequent likelihood that he'd have left forensic evidence at one or more of the crime scenes.

One of the principles on which *offender profiling* is based is that the details of exactly *how* the crime was committed (the stock-in-trade of detectives) is fundamental – there are many ways of raping and killing. The common themes of aggressive control and violent assault can be played out with many variations. For example, this serial rapist responded to aspects of his victims' discomfort. When one victim complained of the cold concrete on her bare flesh, he put some of the clothing he'd removed from her on the floor beneath her. This was typical of his style of assault. By contrast, other rapists delight in demeaning and degrading their victims.

These details suggested that he'd be known as helpful and considerate by those who didn't know of his violent assaults. He turned out to be Adrian Babb, a well-regarded, 20-year-old swimming pool attendant. His fingerprint was found at the scene of one of his crimes, he pleaded guilty to seven rapes, and was sentenced to 16 years in prison.

(Based on Canter, 1994a)

According to Harrower (2000), *offender profiling* (or *criminal personality*, *psychological*, or *behaviour profiling*) is seen as the sexy speciality of forensic psychology largely as a result of Fitz (Robbie Coltrane) in *Cracker*. But the poetic licence allowed in that TV series hasn't been particularly helpful to psychology as a discipline.

The so-called Unabomber, the disgruntled academic finally caught by the FBI after many years of tracking him down

Robbie Coltrane (centre) as Fitz in a scene from Cracker. *But forensic psychology isn't all its cracked up to be*

A brief history

Harrower (1998) traces what's now called offender profiling (OP) to 1888, when a police surgeon (Thomas Bond) compiled a detailed description of Jack the Ripper. During World War II, Walter Langer, a psychiatrist, was asked to compile a profile of Hitler by the Office of Strategic Studies. He constructed a psychodynamic personality profile, which took considerable account of Hitler's parents' influence on him, especially his mother. The aim was to provide sufficient insight into his personality to allow an interrogation strategy to be developed should he be captured. He accurately predicted that Hitler would commit suicide if he faced defeat.

According to Brown (2000), OP began when the police and a psychologist, James Brussel, collaborated in apprehending a serial bomber in New York during the 1950s.

CASE STUDY 46.2

The 'mad bomber' (Brussel, 1968)

Brussel was asked to profile the kind of person who could be capable of carrying out the bombings. He produced a remarkably accurate profile, deriving his characteristics from deductions based on crime scene data and the psychodynamic interpretation of letters written by the bomber and slashes left on the underside of theatre seats (where the bombs were secreted).

For example, the letters were written in a stilted English, suggesting a grammatical style reminiscent of Eastern European immigrants. These groups had settled mainly in Connecticut. The duration and single-mindedness of the attacks suggested an obsessive and conformist personality.

George Metesky, Slavic by birth, was eventually arrested and charged, following investigative leads suggested by the profile. He was in his early 50s, living in Connecticut with two unmarried sisters. At the time of his arrest, he was wearing a conventional double-breasted suit, obsessively buttoned up.

(Based on Brown, 2000)

Further development of OP was undertaken by the FBI Behavioural Science Unit during the 1980s. In the UK, interest in OP developed sharply following the Peter Sutcliffe ('Yorkshire Ripper') case. This involved the setting up of sophisticated computer-based retrieval systems. Now, all good detectives operate through their own 'computer bases' (their brains), enabling them to form pictures based on stored experience (Prins, 1995: see below).

What exactly is OP?

According to Copson (1996), there's no universally accepted definition of OP. It's really a 'term of convenience' covering techniques in which the behaviour shown in a crime is used to draw inferences about the likely offender. For Turco (1993), OP involves:

> '... the preparation of a biographical "sketch" gathered from information taken at a crime scene, from the personal history and habits of a victim, and integrating this with known psychological theory'.

The resulting sketch can be used by police officers to reduce their list of suspects, or to offer a new line of enquiry. Traditionally, the only clues noted at crime scenes tended to be 'hard' evidence (such as blood stains). But OP also allows recognition of other, less visible clues, such as choice of victim, location, nature of the assault, what's said or not said to the victim and so on (Harrower, 1998: see Case Studies 46.1 and 46.2). According to Harrower:

> 'The overall aim of profiling is to narrow the field of investigation, drawing inferences about the offender's motivation and personality from evidence left at the crime scene ...'.

OP is most useful when the scene reflects psychopathology, such as sadistic assaults. Ninety per cent of profiling involves murder and rape, although it's also used in arson, burglary, robbery, obscene phone calls, and the new crime of stalking (see Box 46.5, page 692).

Current approaches

A distinction is commonly made between the American and British approaches (Brown, 2000; Harrower, 1998).

The American approach

In 1979, FBI investigators began interviewing a growing number of imprisoned serial killers and sex murderers (including Charles Manson and Ted Bundy). The 36 who were interviewed were classified as *organised* (24) or *disorganised* (12). The former planned their crimes, the victims were targeted, and the element of control was important. They were of average intelligence, socially and sexually competent, and had intimate partners. By contrast, the disorganised were impulsive, carried out unplanned attacks, made no attempt to conceal the bodies, may have known the crime scenes beforehand and/or the victims, were socially inadequate, and were loners. These descriptions provided theoretical models which would allow accurate profiles to be compiled based on examination of the crime scene (Harrower, 1998).

According to Ressler (one of the interviewers) *et al.* (1988), sex killers tend to be white, unmarried males, either unemployed or unskilled workers, with previous histories of psychiatric illness or alcoholism, dysfunctional family backgrounds, and a sexual interest in voyeurism, fetishism and pornography. Their crime scenes provided information which could then be used to identify them as organised or disorganised.

The FBI now trains profilers worldwide, but it doesn't consider profiles to be suitable in all investigations: they're most useful where there's some indication of psychopathology. According to Harrower (1998):

> 'The basis of the FBI's approach is that the crime scene and the offender's modus operandi will reveal indicators of individual pathology, which may fit into a pattern already observed from case studies of incarcerated offenders'.

Douglas *et al.* (1986) describe the FBI *four stages approach* as:

- *data assimilating*, in which as much information as possible is collected;
- *crime classification*, when the type of crime is identified;
- *crime reconstruction*, during which hypotheses about the behaviour of victims are generated;
- *profile generation*, describing demographic and physical characteristics of the likely perpetrator.

According to Holmes (1989), the aims of profiling within this approach are to:

- reduce the scope of an investigation by providing basic information regarding the core social and psychological variables of the offender's personality (e.g. race, age range, employment status and type, educational background, and marital status;
- allow some prediction of future offences and their location;
- provide a psychological evaluation of belongings found in the offender's possession (e.g. souvenirs, trophies from previous offences);
- provide strategies for interviewing offenders which can take account of individual differences, but profit from experience with offenders who've displayed a common pattern of offending.

The British approach

This is associated with Britton (1997) and Canter (1994a, b: see Case Study 46.1). Canter was originally approached by the Metropolitan Police in 1985 to advise whether psychology could contribute to criminal investigations. In 1986 he became involved in what was initially a serial rape investigation, but later developed into a notorious serial murder case. He helped secure the arrest of John Duffy, convicted in 1988 of two murders and five rapes, for which he was given seven life sentences. The accuracy of his description of Duffy astonished both the police and the media.

Canter's approach is much more rooted in psychological principles than the FBI's. Criminals, like other people, act consistently (but see Chapter 42), and analysis of their behaviour will reveal patterns which can offer clues as to how they live when they're not offending.

Box 46.4 Canter's approach to profiling

As indicated in Case Study 46.1, the criminal leaves 'psychological traces' or 'shadows' in committing a crime:

> '... tell-tale patterns of behaviour that indicate the sort of person he is. Gleaned from the crime scene and reports from witnesses, these traces are more ambiguous and subtle than those examined by the biologist or physicist ... They are more like shadows [which] ... can indicate where investigators

should look and what sort of person they should be looking for'. (Canter, 1994b)

In addition, we all operate within a social context, so there's an implicit *social* relationship between the offender and victim. This again will offer major clues to the pattern of the offender's life. Sensitive and detailed examination of victims' testimony can reveal speech patterns, interests, obsessions and ways of behaving which will also have occurred in the offender's daily life. For example, rapists may treat their victims as they treat most of the women in their lives – in the case of Adrian Babb, he actually showed consideration for their feelings, which reflected a generally considerate attitude to other people: see Case Study 46.1).

According to Boon & Davies (1992), Canter and his colleagues have found five aspects of the criminal and his behaviour to be particularly revealing: residential location, criminal biography, personal characteristics, domestic and social characteristics, and occupational and educational history. Geography is especially important: offenders will operate in areas they know and feel comfortable in (a relatively short distance from their homes).

An evaluation of profiling

Copson (1995) described 30 British profilers who worked for the police, including forensic psychologists and psychiatrists, clinical psychologists and academic psychologists. Detectives' expectations about the application of PO weren't always clear, and not all profiles were equally well regarded. Jackson & Bekerian (1997) detected an unfortunate 'war of experts' potentially breaking out between various academic profilers, and Stevens (1997) has argued for continued co-operation between detectives and academics, so that OP can become a systematised tool for use in criminal investigations.

OP has undoubted potential if used properly by trained professionals (Harrower, 1998). But how successful is it? Holmes (1989) cites FBI data claiming that 192 cases of profile construction (1981) resulted in 88 arrests, but this was believed to have contributed to an arrest in just 17 per cent of them. Others (e.g Oleson, 1996) point out that the FBI's methodology may be fundamentally flawed: there's no control group against which to compare the evidence obtained from offenders, no mention of the statistical techniques used to analyse the data, and much of the interview data is accepted at face value.

In the UK, Copson & Holloway (1997) surveyed detectives who'd worked on 184 cases in which OP had been used. They believed it had produced identification of offenders in less than three per cent of cases, and 'helped to solve' the crime in 16 per cent. They conclude that:

'Profiling can work very well, but certainly not in the way some practitioners, let alone dramatists, would have you believe. There is nothing in our findings to support the notion that complex offender characteristics can be predicted with any great accuracy. In fact, with some people you would be better off tossing a coin'.

According to Harrower (2000):

'... both training and practical experience are vital in developing profiling expertise, and productive liaison between the

police and psychologists is the way forward in order to achieve both investigative and clinical objectives'.

As she points out, the phenomenon of serial murder and the development of OP have clearly captured the public imagination – and a growing number of psychology students want to become forensic psychologists.

Box 46.5   Stalking and its management

Stalking has come to describe persistent attempts to impose on another person unwanted communications (by 'phone, e-mail, letters, or grafitti) or contact (via approaches, following or maintaining surveillance). Associated behaviours include sending unsolicited gifts, ordering or cancelling services on the victim's behalf (e.g. pizzas and electricity supply), and it can also involve threats, escalating to both physical and sexual violence (Mullen *et al.*, 2000).

The term was first used in the American media in the late 1980s to describe repeated intrusions upon the famous, usually by disordered fans. It then generalised, first to include harassment of women by ex-partners, and later to all forms of ongoing harassment that induces fear in the victim, regardless of the relationship.

Mullen *et al.* (1999) have proposed a typology of stalking with five categories. These aren't mutually exclusive, but it provides a clinically useful guide when assessing or considering future *management*, and it predicts the likely duration of the stalking.

Intimacy seekers invariably have serious psychopathology, and are sometimes psychotic. The initial aim of management is to bring their disorders under reasonable control through a combination of drugs and structured psychotherapy. Long-term cessation of stalking is improved if their social isolation can be decreased and their capacity for social interaction improved. They're indifferent to threats or the reality of fines or imprisonment.

Rejected stalkers are rarely mentally ill but are often inadequate, dependent, angry men with marked social and interpersonal problems. They're quite often substance abusers. They'll often desist when threatened with imprisonment, but may also benefit from therapy.

Incompetent stalkers are the easiest to manage. Telling them to stop is usually sufficient. Most have stopped before receiving psychiatric help, but there's a very high rate of recidivism. The only long-term solution is to improve their social skills and social networks.

Resentful stalkers are difficult to engage in therapy, and are often substance abusers. Their basic personality is often suspicious and sensitive, and they become resentful of therapists just as they have of others who've crossed their path in the past. But once engaged, they do respond.

Predatory stalkers are best seen as sex offenders. The right mix of legal punishment and therapeutic intervention will relieve both the victim and the stalker of the burden of this destructive behaviour.

The treatment of offenders

According to Honderich (1993), there are two distinct views (both implicit and explicit) as to why people commit crime:

■ The individual is a rational agent with free will: an individual's circumstances reflect his/her choices (see Chapter 49).

- We're all, to a greater or lesser degree, products of our environments.

Related to the 'free will' viewpoint are two policies:

- provide as few opportunities as possible for choosing a criminal act;
- when people are caught, make the consequences as painful as possible to deter them from future offending.

Based on the second view:

- if environmental conditions are implicated in the cause of the crime, then change is needed in the environment (primarily, in the social structure);
- the adverse effects on individuals resulting from the environment need to be addressed.

According to Hollin (1999), in practice these viewpoints and policies crystallise into the debate about the relative effectiveness of punishment and treatment in crime prevention (see Box 46.5).

Situational crime prevention

If crimes are the end result of criminals seizing the opportunity to make a personal, usually financial, gain, then why not look at the opportunity as well as the criminal (Hollin, 1999)? This is exactly the approach of *situational crime prevention*: analysing and changing the environment in an effort to prevent crime.

Ask yourself ...

- Think of some practical ways in which situational crime prevention could be achieved (see Chapter 21, page 317).

The most straightforward way is to *reduce the opportunity for successful crime*, by removing and protecting the target. For example, replacing 'phone coin boxes with cards, introducing night transport systems to ensure safety of late night workers, and installing more car alarms, immobilisers and home security systems.

In addition, *increasing the risk of detection* can be achieved through formal surveillance in places where there's opportunity for crime. For example, increased police presence at football matches and city centres at pub-emptying times, CCTV, electronic 'tagging' of offenders, and neighbourhood watch schemes.

Ask yourself ...

- Can you see any potential problems with situational crime prevention – both practical and ethical?

When offenders are *deterred* from committing a criminal act, is crime actually being reduced or merely *displaced* onto other victims, times and situations? There are also civil liberties issues relating to tagging, CCTV, and other forms of surveillance.

Deterrance is also found in the harsh punishment approach (from fines to 'life sentences').

Punitive prison regimes

Ask yourself ...

- Do you believe that offenders should be punished, rather than rehabilitated?
- Are your reasons moral, as opposed to pragmatic (such as what is most likely to prevent re-offending)?
- Are punishment and rehabilitation necessarily mutually exclusive?

Reconviction rates (*recidivism*) of people discharged from prisons in England and Wales are 54–70 per cent (Lloyd *et al.*, 1994), depending on the type of offender, length of follow-up, and so on. *Punishment-oriented regimes* seek to reduce these figures, by making the experience of prison so aversive as to deter ex-prisoners from re-offending. These include the 'short, sharp shock' (introduced in the UK in the 1980s), and 'boot camps', an American concept involving a short period of incarceration in a strict military environment, with a rigid daily schedule of hard labour, drill and ceremony, and physical training (Mackenzie & Souryal, 1995).

Mackenzie & Shaw (1990) found that compared with offenders sentenced to traditional prisons, those who went to boot camp were more positive about their prison experiences and their futures, and held more prosocial attitudes. Mackenzie & Souryal (1995) also reported a range of positive outcomes for the boot-camp group, such as being drug free, physically healthy, believing that the regime had helped them, and an overall positive effect on their families. However, those sent to boot camp had been convicted of non-violent crimes, and had less serious criminal histories (Hollin, 1999).

Evidence regarding recidivism is very mixed. But there's little evidence that the military regime would successfully change future behaviour if the 'criminogenic needs of the offenders are not being addressed' (Mackenzie *et al.*, 1995).

According to Farrington (1995), findings from longitudinal studies (see Key Study 46.1) point to the need for strategies to improve young people's academic achievement, interpersonal skills, parental child-rearing practices, and to reduce poverty.

Treatment programmes

There's a vast literature on *therapeutic approaches*, especially with young offenders (e.g. Hollin & Howells, 1996), but the principles apply to young and adult offenders alike. Most major therapeutic approaches discussed in Chapter 45 have been used with offenders (and see Box 46.5), including psychodynamic psychotherapy, behaviour therapy, social skills training and cognitive–behaviour therapy.

Several *multimodal* (mixed or 'eclectic') programmes have also been used, in which several methods are combined. For example, aggression replacement training (Glick & Goldstein, 1987; Goldstein & Glick, 1996) combines structured learning training (including social skills and social problem-solving training), anger control, and moral education (see Chapter 35).

Does treatment work?

There are hundreds of outcome studies, using different types of intervention, conducted in different settings, and using different measures of 'success'. As with outcome studies in the treatment of mental disorder, *meta-analytic studies* allow general conclusions to be drawn (see Chapter 45). According to Hollin (1999):

- Overall, there's a ten per cent reduction in recidivism when treated offenders are compared with no-treatment controls. But this figure conceals tremendous variability between different programmes.
- The best results will be obtained with medium to high-risk offenders, using structured/focused/directive approaches (in practice, this usually means behavioural methods that incorporate a cognitive component).
- Treatment in the community has a stronger effect on delinquency than residential programmes.

CHAPTER SUMMARY

- **Longitudinal studies** help us understand the relationship between **age and crime**, with delinquency peaking at 16–17 years. This reflects increasing **prevalence** and a very high **crime rate** at this age.
- Most juvenile crimes are **status offences** (as opposed to **index/notifiable offences**). Also, most crime is 'adolescence-limited', which can be explained partly in terms of the greater **risk-taking** of adolescents, and partly in terms of **peer group pressure**.
- Several childhood factors have been shown to predict later offending, including, **low intelligence/poor school record**, a **family criminal record**, **family poverty**, and **poor parental child-rearing practices**.
- Although neither a disadvantaged background nor 'social failure' inevitably leads to crime, they massively increase the risks of criminal behaviour.
- Most crimes, especially violent crimes, are committed by males. This has led to a view of women who commit murder as **doubly deviant**, breaking both the law of the land and the 'natural law' relating to women's 'nature'.
- There's considerable evidence of **gender bias** and **gender differences** in the **criminal justice system**. These are apparent in sentencing, the link between committing crime and being the victim of crime, the kind of crimes committed, and behaviour inside prison and following release.
- Two extreme explanations of male domination of crime are **biological determinism** and **social constructionism**. All the major theoretical perspectives within psychology as a whole have been/can be applied to criminal behaviour.
- **Personality factors** (or **domains**), such as **N**, **E** and especially **P** are related to a wide range of antisocial, criminal and delinquent behaviours. However, more specific **facets** may be more valid predictors of developmental change.

- **Antisocial personality disorder** (APD) or **psychopathy** has long been implicated in criminal behaviour, especially violent crimes. One very controversial aspect of APD is its **treatability**.
- At the heart of APD seems to lie an **emotional disorder**, which represents a **risk factor** for the development of the full disorder. For antisocial behaviour to occur, there needs to be an adverse social environment.
- **Offender profiling** (OP) has been used to investigate a variety of crimes. But it's most useful when the crime scene reflects psychopathology, as in (serial) murder and rape.
- There are differences in the approaches used by the FBI and by British forensic psychologists, who place more emphasis on **psychological principles**. An important example is that offenders will tend to operate close to where they live.
- **Situational crime prevention** involves both reducing the opportunity for successful crime and increasing the risk of detection. But criminals may simply **displace** their offences onto other victims, places and times.
- **Punitive prison regimes** may help to reduce recidivism rates among less serious criminals, while **treatment programmes** are most successful with medium to high-risk offenders.
- A wide variety of treatments and therapies has been used, including **multimodal** approaches. **Structured** methods used in **non-residential settings** seem to be the most effective.

Self-assessment questions

1 Discuss the role of age **and** gender as influences on criminal behaviour.
2 Critically assess the relationship between crime and personality.
3 Describe and evaluate psychological research into crime prevention.

Web addresses

www.bps.org.uk/publications/jLC_1.cfm

www.nene.ac.uk/lrs/Subjects/Psychology/crim.html

www.ozemail.com.au/~dwillsh/

www.oklahoma.net/~jnichols/forensic.html

www.abfp.com

flash.lakeheadu.ca/~pals/forensics/

Further reading

Harrower, J. (1998) *Applying Psychology to Crime*. London: Hodder & Stoughton. A clearly written account of all the issues covered in this chapter. Also relevant to Chapter 21.

Hollin, C.R. (1999) Crime and crime prevention. In D. Messer & F. Jones (Eds) *Psychology and Social Care*. London: Jessica Kingsley. A brief but detailed discussion of the field by one of its major British researchers.

Seven

Issues and Debates

Chapter 47

Bias in Psychological Theory and Research

Introduction and overview

Mainstream academic psychology, modelling itself on classical, orthodox, natural science (such as physics and chemistry), claims to be *objective*, *unbiased*, and *value-free*. Collectively, these aims form the *positivist* view of science, or *positivism* (see Chapter 3). As applied to the study of humans, this implies that it's possible to study people as they 'really are', without the psychologist's characteristics influencing the outcome of the investigation in any way.

This chapter shows that a view of psychology as unbiased and value-free is mistaken. Two major forms of bias, *sexism* and *ethnocentrism* (which relate to gender and culture respectively) permeate much psychological theory and research.

Much of the chapter's content is relevant to the topic of prejudice and discrimination. As we saw in Chapter 25, prejudice and discrimination can be understood as characteristics of individuals or of social groups, institutions and even whole societies. With bias in psychological theory and research, it's sometimes individual psychologists, and sometimes 'psychology as a whole' that are guilty of bias.

Gender bias: Feminist psychology, sexism and androcentrism

Not surprisingly, most of the criticism of mainstream psychology regarding its gender bias has come from feminist psychology, which Wilkinson (1997) defines as:

> '... *psychological theory and practice which is explicitly informed by the political goals of the feminist movement'*.

While feminism and feminist psychology can take a variety of forms, two common themes are the valuation of women as worthy of study in their own right (not just in comparison with men), and recognition of the need for social change on behalf of women (Unger & Crawford, 1996).

Feminist psychology is openly political and sets out to challenge the discipline of psychology for its inadequate and damaging theories about women, and for its failure to see power relations as central to social life (Unger & Crawford, 1992). More specifically, it insists on exposing and challenging the operation of male power in psychology:

> '*Psychology's theories often exclude women, or distort our experience by assimilating it to male norms or man-made stereotypes, or by regarding "women" as a unitary category, to be understood only in comparison with the unitary category "men" ... Similarly, psychology [screens out] ... the existence and operation of social and structural inequalities between and within social groups'*. (Wilkinson, 1991)

Psychology obscures the social and structural operation of male power by concentrating its analysis on people as individuals (*individualism*). Responsibility (and pathology) are located within the individual, to the total neglect of social and political oppression. By ignoring or minimising the social context, psychology obscures the mechanisms of oppression. For example, the unhappiness of some women after childbirth is treated as a problem in individual functioning (with possible hormonal causes), thus distracting attention away from the difficult practical situation in which many new mothers find themselves (Wilkinson, 1997: see Critical Discussion 44.2, page 651).

Box 47.1 Some major feminist criticisms of psychology

- Much psychological research is conducted on all-male samples, but then either fails to make this clear or reports the findings as if they applied equally to women and men.
- Some of the most influential theories within psychology as a whole are based on studies of males only, but are meant to apply equally to women and men.
- If women's behaviour differs from men's, the former is often judged to be pathological, abnormal or deficient in some way (*sexism*). This is because the behaviour of men is, implicitly or explicitly, taken as the 'standard' or norm against which women's behaviour is compared (*androcentrism* – male-centredness, or the *masculinist bias*).
- Psychological explanations of behaviour tend to emphasise biological (and other internal) causes, as opposed to social (and other external) causes (*individualism*). This gives (and reinforces) the impression that psychological sex differences are inevitable and unchangeable. This reinforces widely held stereotypes about men and women, contributing to the oppression of women (another form of *sexism*).
- Heterosexuality (both male and female) is taken, implicitly or explicitly, as the norm, so that homosexuality is seen as abnormal (*heterosexism*).

Ask yourself ...

- Try to think of (at least) one example for each of the five major criticisms of psychological theory and research made in Box 47.1. Regarding the fourth point, how does this relate to attribution theory as discussed in Chapter 23?

The feminist critique of science

In many ways, a more fundamental criticism of psychology than those listed in Box 47.1 is feminists' belief that scientific enquiry itself (whether this be within psychology or not) is biased.

Psychology's claims to be a science are based on its methods (especially the experiment), and the belief that it's a value-free discipline (see Chapter 3). But can scientific enquiry be neutral, wholly independent of the value system of the human scientists involved? According to Prince & Hartnett (1993):

> '*Decisions about what is, and what is not, to be measured, how this is done, and most importantly, what constitutes legitimate research are made by individual scientists within a sociopolitical context, and thus science is ideological'*.

Many feminist psychologists argue that scientific method is gender-biased. For example, Nicolson (1995) identifies two major problems associated with adherence to the 'objective' investigation of behaviour for the way claims are made about women and gender differences:

- The experimental environment takes the individual 'subject's *behaviour*', as distinct from the 'subject' herself, as the unit of study. Therefore, it becomes deliberately blind to the behaviour's *meaning*, including its social, personal and cultural contexts. As a result, claims about gender differences in competence and behaviour are attributed to *intrinsic* qualities (either the product of 'gender role socialisation' or biology) as opposed to *contextual* qualities. This is another reference to *individualism* (see Box 47.1).

- Experimental psychology, far from being context-free, takes place in a very specific context which typically disadvantages women (Eagly, 1987). In an experiment, a woman becomes anonymous, stripped of her social roles and the accompanying power and knowledge she might have achieved in the outside world. She's placed in this "strange", environment, and expected to respond to the needs of (almost inevitably) a male experimenter who's in charge of the situation, with all the social meaning ascribed to gender power relations.

The belief that it's possible to study people 'as they really are', removed from their usual sociocultural contexts (in a 'de-contextualised' way), is completely invalid:

'Psychology relies for its data on the practices of socialised and culture-bound individuals, so that to explore 'natural' or 'culture-free' behaviour (namely that behaviour unfettered by cultural, social structures and power relations) is by definition impossible'. (Nicolson, 1995)

Feminist psychologists offer a critical challenge to psychological knowledge on gender issues by drawing on other disciplines, such as sociology. According to Giddens (1979), for example:

'There is no static knowledge about people to be "discovered" or "proved" through reductionist experimentation, and thus the researcher takes account of context, meaning and change over time'.

Ask yourself ...

- Do you agree with Nicolson's claim that all human behaviour is 'culture-bound'? What about 'instinctive' behaviours, such as eating, drinking and sex: does culture play a part here too? If so, in what ways? (These questions are equally relevant to the section on culture bias.)

Some practical consequences of gender bias

According to Kitzinger (1998), questions about sex differences (and similarities) aren't just scientific questions, they're also highly *political*. Some answers to these questions have been used to keep women out of universities, or to put them in mental hospitals. Other answers have been used to encourage women to go on assertiveness training courses, or to argue that women should have all the same rights and opportunities as men. In other words, the science of sex differences research is always used for political reasons:

'However much psychologists may think or hope or believe that they are doing objective research and discovering truths about the world they are always influenced ... by the social and political context in which they are doing their research'. (Kitzinger, 1998)

Celia Kitzinger, lesbian feminist psychologist

For Prince & Hartnett (1993), scientific psychology has *reified* concepts such as personality and intelligence (treating abstract or metaphorical terms as if they were 'things' or entities):

'... and the scientific psychology which "objectively" and "rationally" produced means of measuring these reifications has been responsible for physical assaults on women such as forced abortions and sterilisations'.

Between 1924 and 1972, more than 7500 women in the state of Virginia alone were forcibly sterilised, in particular, 'unwed mothers, prisoners, the feeble-minded, children with discipline problems'. The criterion used in all cases was mental age as measured by the Stanford–Binet intelligence test (Gould, 1981).

Having convinced society that intelligence 'exists' in some objective way, and having produced a means of measuring it, psychologists could then promote and justify discrimination against particular social groups. Another example of the use of intelligence tests to justify blatant discrimination (although not specifically against women) involved the army alpha and beta tests, which influenced the passing of the 1924 Immigration Restriction Act in the USA (see Chapter 41, page 596, and Gross, 1999).

CRITICAL DISCUSSION 47.1

Psychology's influence on immigration policy in the USA

Debates in Congress leading to passage of the Immigration Restriction Act (1924) continually made reference to data from the army alpha and beta tests. *Eugenicists* (who advocate 'selective breeding' in humans in order to 'improve' genetic stock) lobbied for immigration limits and for imposing harsh quotas against nations of inferior stock. In short, Southern and Eastern Europeans, who scored lowest on the army tests, should be kept out. The eugenicists battled and won one of the greatest victories of scientific racism in American history. 'America must be kept American', proclaimed President Coolidge as he signed the bill.

Throughout the 1930s, Jewish refugees, anticipating the Holocaust, sought to emigrate, but were refused admission. Estimates suggest that the quotas barred up to six million Southern, Central and Eastern Europeans between 1924 and 1939:

> 'We know what happened to many who wished to leave, but had nowhere to go. The paths to destruction are often indirect, but ideas can be agents as sure as guns and bombs'. (Gould, 1981)

(From Gould, 1981)

In the 1993 preface to *In a Different Voice* (1982), Gilligan says that at the core of her work on moral development in women and girls (see Chapter 35, page 514) was the realisation that within psychology, and in society at large, 'values were taken as facts'. She continues:

> 'In the aftermath of the Holocaust ... it is not tenable for psychologists or social scientists to adopt a position of ethical neutrality or cultural relativism ... Such a hands-off stance in the face of atrocity amounts to a kind of complicity'.

While the example she gives is clearly extreme, it helps to illustrate the argument that not only do psychologists (and other scientists) have a responsibility to make their values explicit about important social and political issues, but failure to do so may (unwittingly) contribute to prejudice, discrimination and oppression. These considerations are as relevant to a discussion of the ethics of psychological research as they are to gender (and culture) bias, and are discussed in more detail in Chapter 48.

The masculinist bias and sexism: A closer look

Box 47.1 (page 698) identified the masculinist bias (*androcentrism*) and sexism as two major criticisms of mainstream psychology made by feminist psychologists. While each of these can take different forms, emphasis here will be given to (a) the argument that men are taken as some sort of standard or norm, against which women are compared and judged, and (b) gender bias in psychological research.

The male norm as the standard

According to Tavris (1993):

> 'In any domain of life in which men set the standard of normalcy, women will be considered abnormal, and society will debate woman's "place" and her "nature". Many women experience tremendous conflict in trying to decide whether to

be 'like' men or "opposite" from them, and this conflict is itself evidence of the implicit male standard against which they are measuring themselves. This is why it is normal for women to feel abnormal'.

Tavris gives two examples of why it's normal for women to feel abnormal. First, in 1985, the American Psychiatric Association proposed two new categories of mental disorder for inclusion in the revised (third) edition of the Diagnostic and Statistical Manual of Mental Disorders (DSM-III-R: see Chapter 43). One was masochistic personality. In DSM-II, this was described as one of the psychosexual disorders, in which sexual gratification requires being hurt or humiliated. The proposal was to extend the term so that it became a more pervasive personality disorder, in which one seeks failure at work, at home, and in relationships, rejects opportunities for pleasure, puts others first (thereby sacrificing one's own needs) plays the martyr, and so on.

While not intended to apply to women exclusively, these characteristics are associated predominantly with the female role. Indeed, according to Caplan (1991), it represented a way of calling psychopathological the behaviour of women who conform to social norms for a 'feminine woman' (the 'good wife syndrome').

In short, such a diagnostic label was biased against women, and perpetuated the myth of women's masochism. The label was eventually changed to 'self-defeating personality disorder', and was put in the appendix of DSM-III-R.

Ask yourself ...

- If you were proposing a parallel diagnosis for men who conform to social norms for a 'masculine man', what characteristics would this have to include, and what would you call it? Could you justify including sadism in the diagnostic criteria for conformist men?

Tavris's second example of why it's normal for women to feel abnormal concerns causal attributions made about men's and women's behaviours. When men have problems, such as drug abuse, and behave in socially unacceptable ways, as in rape and other forms of violence, the causes are looked for in their upbringing. Women's problems, however, are seen as the result of their psyches or hormones. Explaining women's problems in this way is another form of individualism, with the further implication that it could have been different for men (they are the victims of their childhood, for example), but not for women ('that's what women are like'). (But see Chapter 46.)

The 'mismeasure of woman'

According to Tavris, the view that man is the norm and woman is the opposite, lesser or deficient (the problem) constitutes one of three currently competing views regarding the 'mismeasure of woman' (meant to parallel Gould's, 1981, *The Mismeasure of Man*, a renowned critique of intelligence testing: see above and Chapter 41). It's the view that underpins so much psychological research designed to discover why women aren't 'as something' (moral, intelligent, rational) as men (what Hare-

Mustin & Maracek, 1988 call alpha-bias: see below, page 702). It also underlies the enormous self-help industry: women consume millions of books and magazines advising them how to become more beautiful, independent and so on. Men, being 'normal', feel no need to 'fix' themselves in corresponding ways (Tavris, 1993).

Box 47.2 A demonstration of the 'mismeasure of woman'

Wilson (1994) maintains that the reason 95 per cent of bank managers, company directors, judges and university professors in Britain are men is that men are 'more competitive', and because 'dominance is a personality characteristic determined by male hormones'.

Wilson also argues that women in academic jobs are less productive than men: 'objectively speaking, women may already be over-promoted'. Women who do achieve promotion to top management positions 'may have brains that are masculinised'.

The research cited by Wilson to support these claims comes partly from the psychometric testing industries which provide 'scientific' evidence of women's inadequacies, such as (compared with men) their 'lack' of mathematical and spatial abilities. Even if women are considered to have the abilities to perform well in professional jobs says Wilson, they have personality defects (in particular, low self-esteem and lack of assertiveness) which impede performance:

'These differences [in mental abilities, motivation, personality and values] are deep-rooted, based in biology, and not easily dismantled by social engineering. Because of them we are unlikely to see the day when the occupational profiles of men and women are the same'.

(From Wilson, 1994, and Wilkinson, 1997)

Ask yourself ...

- Try to identify examples of individualism in Box 47.2.
- Can you formulate some arguments against Wilson's claims?

Box 47.3 Examples of gender bias at each stage of the research process

- **Question formulation**: It's assumed that topics relevant to white males are more important and 'basic' (e.g. the effects of TV violence on aggression in boys: see Chapter 29), while those relevant to white females, or ethnic minority females or males, are more marginal, specialised, or applied (e.g. the psychological correlates of pregnancy or the menopause).

- **Research methods and design**: Surprisingly often, the sex and race of the participants, researchers, and any stooges/confederates who may be involved, aren't specified. Consequently, potential interactions between these variables aren't accounted for. For example, men tend to display more helping behaviour than women in studies involving a young, female confederate 'victim' (see Chapter 30). This could be a function of either the sex of the confederate or an interaction between the confederate and the participant, rather than sex differences between the participants (which is the conclusion usually drawn).

- **Data analysis and interpretation**: Significant sex differences may be reported in very misleading ways, because the wrong sorts of comparisons are made. For example:

  '"The spatial ability scores of women in our sample is significantly lower than those of men, at the 0.01 level". You might conclude from this that women cannot or should not become architects or engineers. However, "Successful architects score above 32 on our spatial ability test ... engineers score above 31 ... twelve per cent of women and 16 per cent of men in our sample score above 31; eleven per cent of women and 15 per cent of men score above 32". What conclusions would you draw now?' (Denmark et al., 1988)

- **Conclusion formulation**: Results based on one sex only are then applied to both. This can be seen in some of the major theories within developmental psychology, notably Erikson's psychosocial theory of development (1950: see Chapters 37 and 38), Levinson et al.'s (1978) Seasons of a Man's Life (see Chapter 38), and Kohlberg's theory of moral development (1969: see Chapter 35). These all demonstrate beta-bias (Hare-Mustin & Maracek, 1988), and are discussed further below.

(Based on Denmark et al., 1988)

Sexism in research

The American Psychological Association's Board of Social and Ethical Responsibility set up a Committee on Nonsexist Research, which reported its findings as *Guidelines for Avoiding Sexism in Psychological Research* (Denmark et al., 1988). This maintains that gender bias is found at all stages of the research process:

- question formulation;
- research methods and design;
- data analysis and interpretation, and
- conclusion formulation.

The principles set out in the *Guidelines* are meant to apply to other forms of bias too: those concerned with race, ethnicity, disability, sexual orientation and socio-economic status.

Sexism in theory

Gilligan (1982) gives Erikson's theory of lifespan development (based on the study of males only) as one example of a sexist theory, which portrays women as 'deviants'. In one version of his theory, Erikson (1950) describes a series of eight universal stages, so that, for both sexes, in all cultures, the conflict between identity and role confusion (adolescence) precedes that between intimacy and isolation (young adulthood). In another version, he acknowledges that the sequence is different for a female, who postpones her identity as she prepares to attract the man whose name she'll adopt, and by whose status she'll be defined (Erikson, 1968). For women, intimacy seems to go along with identity: they come to know themselves through their relationships with others (Gilligan, 1982).

A symbol of Western plenty in the midst of Third World poverty

Despite his observation of sex differences, the sequence of stages in Erikson's psychosocial theory remains unchanged (see Table 38.1, page 545). As Gilligan points out:

> *'Identity continues to precede intimacy as male experience continues to define his [Erikson's] life-cycle concept'.*

Similarly, Kohlberg's (1969) six-stage theory of moral development was based on a 20-year longitudinal study of 84 boys, but he claims that these stages are universal (see Chapter 35). Females rarely attain a level of moral reasoning above stage three ('Good boy–nice girl' orientation), which is supposed to be achieved by most adolescents and adults. This leaves females looking decidedly morally deficient.

Like other feminist psychologists, Gilligan argues that psychology speaks with a 'male voice', describing the world from a male perspective and confusing this with absolute truth (*beta-bias*). The task of feminist psychology is to listen to women and girls who speak in a 'different voice' (Gilligan, 1982; Brown & Gilligan, 1992). Gilligan's work with females has led her to argue that men and women have qualitatively different conceptions of morality (but see Chapter 35). By stressing the *differences* between men and women (an *alpha-biased* approach), Gilligan is attempting to redress the balance, created by Kohlberg's beta-biased theory.

Ask yourself ...

- In what ways is Freud's psychoanalytic theory (especially the psychosexual stages of development) sexist (or what Grosz, 1987, calls 'phallocentric')?
- Repeat this exercise for Levinson *et al.*'s theory of adult development, and any other theory you're familiar with.

Culture bias

In discussing gender bias, several references have been made to cultural bias. As we noted earlier, Denmark *et al.*'s (1988) report on sexism is meant to apply equally to all other major forms of bias, including cultural (see Box 47.3). Ironically, many feminist critics of Gilligan's ideas have argued that women aren't a cohesive group who speak in a single voice, a view which imposes a false sameness upon the diversity of women's voices across differences of age, ethnicity, (dis)ability, class and other social divisions (Wilkinson, 1997).

Ask yourself ...

- Before reading on, ask yourself what's meant by the term 'culture'. How is it related to 'race', 'ethnicity' and 'subcultures'?

Cross-cultural psychology and ethnocentrism

According to Smith & Bond (1998), cross-cultural psychology studies *variability* in behaviour among the various societies and cultural groups around the world. For Jahoda (1978), its additional goal is to identify what's *similar* across different cultures, and thus likely to be our common human heritage (the *universals* of human behaviour).

Cross-cultural psychology is important because it helps to correct *ethnocentrism*, the strong human tendency to use our own ethnic or cultural groups' norms and values to define what's 'natural' and 'correct' for everyone ('reality': Triandis, 1990). Historically, psychology has been dominated by white, middle-class males in the USA. Over the last century, they've enjoyed a monopoly as both the researchers and the 'subjects' of the discipline (Moghaddam & Studer, 1997). They constitute the core of psychology's *First World* (Moghaddam, 1987).

Box 47.4 Psychology's First, Second and Third Worlds

- The USA, the *First World* of psychology, dominates the international arena and monopolises the manufacture of psychological knowledge, which it exports to other countries around the globe, through control over books and journals, test *manufacture* and distribution, training centres and so on.
- The *Second World* countries comprise Western European nations and Russia. They have far less influence in shaping psychology around the world, although, ironically, it's in these countries that modern psychology has its philosophical roots (see Chapter 3). Just as the countries of the Second World find themselves overpowered by American popular culture, they also find themselves overwhelmed by US-manufactured psychological knowledge.
- *Third World* countries are mostly importers of psychological knowledge, first from the USA but also from the Second World countries with which they historically had colonial ties (such as Pakistan and England). India is the most important Third World 'producer' of psychological knowledge, but even there most research follows the lines established by the US and, to a lesser extent, Western Europe.

(From Moghaddam & Studer, 1997)

Margaret Washburn and Mary Calkins; if these women are not household names, it is because psychological literature's treatment of women psychologists has kept them invisible

According to Moghaddam *et al.* (1993), American researchers and participants:

> ' ... have shared a lifestyle and value system that differs not only from that of most other people in North America, such as ethnic minorities and women, but also the vast majority of people in the rest of the world'.

Yet the findings from this research, and the theories based upon it, have been applied to *people in general*, as if culture makes no difference. An implicit equation is made between 'human being' and 'human being from Western culture' (the *Anglocentric* or *Eurocentric* bias).

When members of other cultural groups have been studied, they've usually been *compared* with Western samples, using the behaviour and experience of the latter as the 'standard'. As with androcentrism, it's the failure to acknowledge this bias which creates the misleading and false impression that what's being said about behaviour can be generalised without qualification.

Cross-cultural psychologists *don't* equate 'human being' with 'member of Western culture', because for them, cultural background is the crucial *independent variable*. In view of the domination of First World psychology, this distinction becomes crucial. At the same time, cross-cultural psychologists consider the search for universal principles of human behaviour as quite valid (and is consistent with the 'classical' view of science: see page 698 and Chapter 3).

What is culture?

Herskovits (1955) defines culture as 'the human-made part of the environment'. For Triandis (1994):

> 'Culture is to society what memory is to individuals. In other words, culture includes the traditions that tell 'what has worked' in the past. It also encompasses the way people have

learned to look at their environment and themselves, and their unstated assumptions about the way the world is and the way people should act'.

The 'human-made' part of the environment can be broken down into *objective* aspects (such as tools, roads and radio stations) and *subjective* aspects (such as categorisations, associations, norms, roles and values). This allows us to examine how subjective culture influences behaviour (Triandis, 1994). While culture is made by humans, it also helps to 'make' them: humans have an interactive relationship with culture (Moghaddam *et al.*, 1993).

Much cross-cultural research is actually based on 'national cultures', often comprising a number of subcultures, which may be demarcated by religion (as in Northern Ireland), language (Belgium), or race (Malaysia and Singapore). However, such research often fails to provide any more details about the participants than the name of the country (national culture) in which the study was carried out. According to Smith & Bond (1998), when this happens, we pay two 'penalties':

- When we compare national cultures, we can lose track of the enormous diversity found within many of the major nations of the world, and differences found between any two countries might well also be found between carefully selected subcultures within those countries.
- There's the danger of implying that national cultures are unitary systems, free of conflict, confusion and dissent. This is rarely the case.

How do cultures differ?

Definitions of culture such as those above stress what different cultures have in common. To evaluate research findings and theory that are culturally biased, it's even more important to consider how cultures differ from each other. Triandis (1990) identifies several cultural syndromes, which he defines as:

> ' ... a pattern of values, attitudes, beliefs, norms and behaviours that can be used to contrast a group of cultures to another group of cultures'.

Box 47.5 Three major cultural syndromes used to contrast different cultures

- **Cultural complexity** refers to how much attention people must pay to time. This is related to the number and diversity of the roles that members of the culture typically play. More industrialised and technologically advanced cultures, such as Japan, Sweden and the USA, are more complex in this way. (The concept of time also differs between cultures: see Chapter 18, page 268.)
- **Individualism–collectivism** refers to whether one's identity is defined by personal choices and achievements (the autonomous individual: *individualism*) or by characteristics of the collective group to which one is more or less permanently attached, such as the family, tribal or religious group, or country (*collectivism*). While people in every culture display both, the relative emphasis in the West is towards individualism, and in the East towards collectivism. Broadly, capitalist politico-economic systems are associated with individualism, while socialist societies are associated with collectivism.

- **Tight cultures** expect their members to behave according to clearly defined norms, and there's very little tolerance of deviation from those norms (see the criteria of normality/abnormality in Chapter 43). Japan is a good example of a tight culture, and Thailand an example of a **loose culture**.

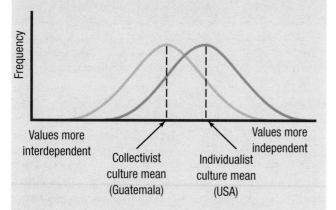

Figure 47.1 *Hypothetical distributions of interdependent/independent value scores in a collectivist and an individualist national culture (from Smith & Bond, 1998)*

(Based on Smith & Bond, 1998; Triandis, 1990, 1994)

The emic–etic distinction

Research has to begin somewhere and, inevitably, this usually involves an instrument or observational technique rooted in the researcher's own culture (Berry, 1969). These can be used for studying both cross-cultural differences and universal aspects of human behaviour (or the 'psychic unity of mankind').

> *Ask yourself ...*
>
> - Try to identify some behaviours (both normal and abnormal) which can be considered to have both universal (common to all cultures) and culture-specific features.

The distinction between culture-specific and universal behaviour is related to what cross-cultural psychologists call the *emic–etic distinction*, first made by Pike (1954) to refer to two different approaches to the study of behaviour. The *etic* looks at behaviour from outside a particular cultural system, the *emic* from the inside. This derives from the distinction made in linguistics between phon*etics* (the study of universal sounds, independently of their meaning) and phon*emics* (the study of universal sounds as they contribute to meaning: see Chapter 19, pages 278–279).

'Etics' refers to culturally general concepts, which are easier to understand (because they're common to all cultures), while 'emics' refers to culturally specific concepts, which include all the ways that particular cultures deal with etics. It's the emics of another culture that are often so difficult to understand (Brislin, 1993).

The research tools that the 'visiting' psychologist brings from 'home' are an emic for the home culture, but when they are assumed to be valid in the 'alien' culture and are used to

compare them, they're said to be an *imposed etic* (Berry, 1969). Many attempts to replicate American studies in other parts of the world involve an imposed etic: they all assume that the situation being studied has the same meaning for members of the alien culture as it does for members of the researcher's own culture (Smith & Bond, 1998).

The danger of imposed etics is that they're likely to involve imposition of the researcher's own cultural biases and theoretical framework. These simply may not 'fit' the phenomena being studied, resulting in their distortion. A related danger is *ethnocentrism* (see page 702).

CRITICAL DISCUSSION 47.2

Intelligence as an imposed etic

Brislin (1993) gives the example of the concept of intelligence. The etic is 'solving problems, the exact form of which hasn't been seen before', a definition which at least recognises that what constitutes a 'problem' differs between cultures. However, is the emic of 'mental quickness' (as measured by IQ tests, for example: see Chapter 41) universally valid? Among the Baganda people of Uganda, for example, intelligence is associated with slow, careful, deliberate thought (Wober, 1974). Nor is quick thinking necessarily a valid emic for all schoolchildren within a culturally diverse country like the USA (Brislin, 1993).

Psychologists need to adapt their methods, so that they're studying the same processes in different cultures (Moghaddam *et al.*, 1993). But how do we know that we're studying the same processes? What does 'same' mean in this context? For Brislin (1993), this is the problem of *equivalence*. The very experience of participating in psychological testing will be strange and unfamiliar to members of non-Western cultures (Lonner, 1990). Even if measures are adapted for use in other cultures, psychologists should be aware that simply being asked to do a test may be odd for some people (Howat, 1999). For a detailed discussion of different kinds of equivalence, see Gross (1995).

Advantages of cross-cultural research

It may now seem obvious (almost 'common sense') to state that psychological theories must be based on the study of people's behaviours from all parts of the world. However, it's important to give specific reasons and examples in support of this argument.

Box 47.6   Major advantages of cross-cultural research

- **Highlighting implicit assumptions:** Cross-cultural research allows investigators to examine the influence of their own beliefs and assumptions, revealing how human behaviour cannot be separated from its cultural context.
- **Separating behaviour from context:** Being able to stand back from their own cultural experiences allows researchers to appreciate the impact of situational factors on behaviour. They're thus less likely to make the fundamental attribution error (see Chapter 23), or to use a 'deficit model' to explain the performances of minority group members.

- **Extending the range of variables:** Cross-cultural research expands the range of variables and concepts that can be explored. For example, people in individualist and collectivist cultures tend to explain behaviour in different ways, with the latter less likely to make dispositional attributions (see Chapter 23).
- **Separating variables:** Cross-cultural research allows the separation of the effects of variables that may be confounded within a particular culture. For example, studying the effects of TV on school achievement is very difficult using just British or American samples, since the vast majority of these families owns (at least) one TV set!
- **Testing theories:** Only by conducting cross-cultural research can Western psychologists be sure whether their theories and research findings are relevant outside of their own cultural contexts. For example, Thibaut and Kelley's exchange theory of relationships (see Chapter 28), and Sherif *et al.*'s 'Robber's Cave' field experiment on intergroup conflict (see Box 25.x) have all failed the replication test outside of North American settings.

(Based on Rogoff & Morelli, 1989; Brislin, 1993; Moghaddam *et al.*, 1993, and Smith & Bond, 1998)

Cross-cultural versus cultural psychology

Several criticisms have been made of cross-cultural psychology, mainly from *cultural psychologists*, for whom mind is embedded in a sociohistorical process that shapes and creates 'multiple realities' (Shweder, 1990). Instead of trying to identify universal 'laws' of psychological functioning (a major goal of cross-cultural psychology), cultural psychologists adopt a relativistic approach and stress the *uniqueness* of different cultures (as in *indigenous* psychology). While cross-cultural psychology is an outgrowth of 'mainstream' psychology (see Chapter 3), with an emphasis on natural scientific methods, cultural psychology can be seen as a rejection of mainstream psychology, favouring the use of qualitative and ethnographic approaches (Martin, 1998: see Coolican, 1999).

Conclusions

This chapter has considered many different examples of how mainstream psychology is biased and, therefore, much less objective and value-free than is required by the positivist view of science it has traditionally modelled itself on. While gender and culture bias are often discussed separately, this chapter has shown that they're actually quite closely related. Despite its shortcomings, Moghaddam & Studer (1997) believe that cross-cultural psychology is one of the avenues through which minorities have begun to have their voices heard in psychology and that:

'... there has been a demand that psychology make good its claim to being the science of humankind by including women and non-whites as research participants'.

CHAPTER SUMMARY

- A **positivist** study of people implies an objective, value-free psychology, in which the psychologist's characteristics have no influence on the investigation's outcome. However, **sexism** and **ethnocentrism** pervade much psychological theory and research.
- **Feminist psychologists** challenge mainstream psychology's theories about women, who are either excluded from research studies or whose experiences are assimilated to/matched against male norms (**androcentrism/the masculinist bias**).
- Male power and social and political oppression are screened out through **individualism**, thus playing down the social context. This reinforces popular gender stereotypes, contributing to women's oppression.
- Feminist psychologists also challenge psychology's claim to be an objective, value-free science. Decisions about what constitutes legitimate research are made by individual scientists within a sociopolitical context, making science ideological.
- Scientific method itself is gender-biased, concentrating on the 'subject's' behaviour, rather than its meaning, and ignoring contextual influences. These typically include a male experimenter who controls the situation.
- Using psychometric test results, Wilson argues that men and women differ in terms of mental abilities, motivation, personality, and values, which are based in biology. This demonstrates **alpha-bias**.
- According to Denmark *et al.*, gender bias is found at all stages of the **research process**. The last stage (conclusion formulation) is related to **theory construction**. Levinson *et al.*'s, Erikson's, and Kohlberg's theories are based on all-male samples and describe the world from male perspectives (**beta-bias**).
- **Cross-cultural psychology** is concerned with both behavioural **variability** between cultural groups and behavioural **universals**. It also helps to correct **ethnocentrism**.
- American researchers and participants share lifestyles and value systems which differ from those of both most other North Americans and the rest of the world's population. Yet the research findings are applied to **people in general**, disregarding culture's relevance (the **Anglocentric/Eurocentric bias**).
- **Culture** is the human-made part of the environment, comprising both **objective** and **subjective** aspects. When cross-cultural researchers compare national cultures, they fail to recognise the great diversity often found **within** them.
- Different cultures can be assessed in terms of **cultural complexity**, **individualism–collectivism**, and considering whether they are **tight** or **loose**. The relative emphasis in the West is towards the former, and in the East towards the latter.
- The distinction between culture-specific and universal behaviour corresponds to the **emic–etic distinction**. When Western psychologists study non-Western cultures, they often use research tools which are emic for them but an **imposed etic** for the culture being studied.

- Only by doing cross-cultural research can Western psychologists be sure that their theories and research findings are relevant outside their own cultural contexts.
- Cross-cultural psychology is an outgrowth of mainstream psychology, adopting a natural scientific approach. **Cultural psychologists** reject this approach in favour of qualitative and ethnographic methods, stressing the **uniqueness** of cultures.

Self assessment questions

1 'While psychologists claim to study "human beings", their theories and research studies in fact apply only to a very limited sample of the world's population.'
   Critically consider the view that psychological theory **and/or** research studies are culturally biased.
2 Critically consider the view that psychological theory **and/or** research studies are gender-biased.

Web addresses

http://www.vix.com/men/articles/genderbiastest.html

http://www.millisecond.com/seandr/psych/BuchResp.html

http://www.iupui.edu/~anthkb/ethnocen.htm

http://www.nova.edu/ssss/FemMed/fmp.html

Further reading

Cole, M. (1996) *Cultural Psychology: A Once and Future Discipline.* Cambridge, MS: Harvard University Press. A scholarly but very readable account of the field by one of its leading figures.

Segall, M.S., Dasen, P.R., Berry, J.W. & Poortinga, Y.H. (1999) *Human Behaviour In Global Perspective: An Introduction to Cross-Cultural Psychology* (2nd edition.). Needham Heights, MA: Allyn & Bacon. Second edition of one of the 'classics' in the field.

Treew, K. & Kremer, J. (Eds) (1998) *Gender & Psychology.* London: Arnold. A collection of original chapters on a wide range of psychological topics, including feminism.

Chapter 48

Ethical Issues in Psychology

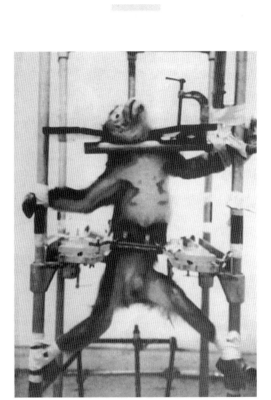

Introduction and overview

One of psychology's unique features is that people are both the investigators and the subject matter (see Chapter 3). This means that the 'things' studied in a psychological investigation are capable of thoughts and feelings. Biologists and medical researchers share this problem of subjecting living, sentient things to sometimes painful, stressful or strange and unusual experiences in the name of furthering science.

Just as Orne (1962) regards the psychological experiment as primarily a *social situation* (which raises questions of objectivity: see Chapter 3), so every psychological investigation is an *ethical situation* (raising questions of propriety and responsibility). Similarly, just as *methodological* issues permeate psychological research, so do *ethical* issues. For example, the aims of psychology as a science (see Chapters 1 and 3) concern what's *appropriate* as much as what's *possible*. Social psychology's use of stooges to deceive naïve participants (see Chapters 26, 27, 29 and 30), and the surgical manipulation of animals' brains in physiological psychology (Chapters 4 and 9) are further examples of the essential difference between the study of the physical world and that of living subjects. What psychologists can and cannot do is determined by the effects of the research on those being studied, as much as by what they want to find out.

However, psychologists are practitioners as well as scientists and investigators. They work in practical and clinical settings, where people with psychological problems require help (see Chapters 1 and 45). Whenever the possibility of changing people arises, ethical issues also arise, just as they do in medicine and psychiatry. This chapter looks at the ethical issues faced by psychologists as scientists/investigators, both of humans and non-humans, and as practitioners.

Codes of conduct and ethical guidelines

While there are responsibilities and obligations common to both the scientist and practitioner roles, there are also some important differences. These are reflected in the codes of conduct and ethical guidelines published by the major professional bodies for psychologists, the British Psychological Society (BPS) and the American Psychological Association (APA).

The *Code of Conduct for Psychologists* (BPS, 1985: see Figure 48.1) applies to both research and practice, and there are additional documents designed for the two areas separately. The *Ethical Principles for Conducting Research with Human Participants* (BPS, 1990, 1993) and the *Guidelines for the Use of Animals in Research* (BPS and the Committee of the Experimental Psychological Society, 1985) obviously apply to the former, while, for example, the *Guidelines for the Professional Practice of Clinical Psychology* (BPS, 1983) apply to the latter.

> ### Ask yourself ...
>
> - Do you think it's necessary for psychologists to have written codes of conduct and ethical guidelines?
> - What do you consider to be their major functions?

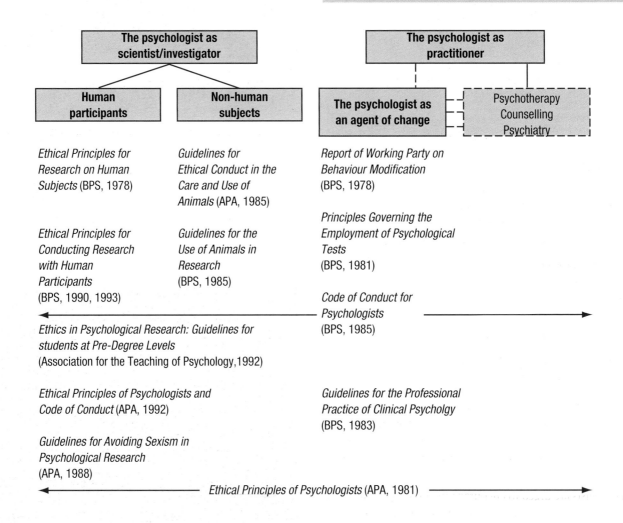

Figure 48.1 *Major codes of conduct/ethical guidelines published by the British Psychological Society (BPS) and the American Psychological Association (APA)*

According to Gale (1995), the fact that both the BPS and APA codes are periodically reviewed and revised indicates that at least some aspects don't depend on absolute or universal ethical truths. Guidelines need to be updated in light of the changing social and political contexts in which psychological research takes place. For example, new issues, such as sexual behaviour in the context of AIDS, might highlight new ethical problems. Information revealed by participants can create conflict between the need to protect individuals and the protection of society at large. For instance, in spite of the confidentiality requirement, should a researcher inform the sexual partner of an HIV-infected participant? As Gale (1995) points out:

'One consequence of such breaches of confidentiality could be the withdrawal of consent by particular groups and the undermining of future research, demonstrating ... how one ethical principle fights against another'.

More importantly, changing views about the nature of individual rights will call into question the extent to which psychological research respects or is insensitive to such rights.

One of the earliest formal statements of ethical principles published by the BPS was the *Ethical Principles for Research on Human Subjects* (1978). The *Ethical Principles* (1990, 1993) refers to 'participants' instead. Gale (1995) believes that this change of wording reflects a genuine shift in how the individual is perceived within psychology, from object (probably a more accurate term than 'subject') to person.

This change can be partly attributed to the influence of feminist psychologists, who've also helped to bring about the removal of sexist language from BPS and APA journals as a matter of policy (see Chapter 47).

Psychologists as scientists/investigators

Human participants

The *Ethical Principles for Conducting Research with Human Participants* (BPS, 1990, 1993, for the rest of this chapter abbreviated to '*Ethical Principles*') identifies several guiding principles. Some of the most important issues addressed are:

- consent/informed consent
- deception
- debriefing
- protection of participants.

The introduction to the *Ethical Principles* (1993) states that:

'Psychological investigators are potentially interested in all aspects of human behaviour and conscious experience. However, for ethical reasons, some areas of human experience and behaviour may be beyond the reach of experiment, observation or other forms of psychological investigation. Ethical guidelines are necessary to clarify the conditions under which psychological research is acceptable'. [paragraph 1.2]

Psychologists are urged to encourage their colleagues to adopt the Principles and ensure they're followed by all researchers whom they supervise (including GCSE, A/AS level, undergraduate and postgraduate students):

'In all circumstances, investigators must consider the ethical implications and psychological consequences for the participants in their research. The essential principle is that the investigation should be considered from the standpoint of all participants; foreseeable threats to their psychological well-being, health, values or dignity should be eliminated'. [paragraph 2.1]

Consent and informed consent

According to the *Ethical Principles*:

'Participants should be informed of the objectives of the investigation and all other aspects of the research which might reasonably be expected to influence their willingness to participate – only such information allows informed consent to be given [paragraph 3.1] ... Special care needs to be taken when research is conducted with detained persons (those in prison, psychiatric hospital, etc.), whose ability to give free informed consent may be affected by their special circumstances'. [paragraph 3.5]

> **Ask yourself ...**
>
> - You may recall that in Perrin & Spencer's (1981) British replication of Asch's conformity experiment (see Chapter 26, page 384), some of the participants were young offenders on probation, with probation officers as stooges. According to paragraph 3.5, would this be acceptable today?

'Investigators must realise that they often have influence over participants, who may be their students, employees or clients: this relationship must not be allowed to pressurise the participants to take part or remain in the investigation'. [paragraph 3.6]

In relation to paragraph 3.6., it's standard practice in American universities for psychology students to participate in research as part of their course requirements. So, while they're free to choose which research to participate in, they're *not* free to opt out.

Psychologists participating in naturalistic non-experimental research

Box 48.1 **Is there more to informed consent than being informed?**

Although *informed consent* clearly requires being informed of the procedure, participants won't have full knowledge until they've actually experienced it. Indeed, there's no guarantee that the investigators fully appreciate the procedure without undergoing it themselves. In this sense, it's difficult to argue that full prior knowledge can ever be guaranteed. How much information should be given beforehand? How much information can young children, elderly people, infirm or disabled people, or those in emotional distress be expected to absorb?

However, there's more to informed consent than just this 'informational' criterion. The status of the experimenter, the desire to please others and not let them down, the desire not to look foolish by withdrawing after the experiment is already under way, all influence the participant and seem to detract from truly choosing freely in a way that is assumed by the *Ethical Principles*.

(Based on Gale, 1995)

Deception

The *Ethical Principles* states that:

'Intentional deception of the participants over the purpose and general nature of the investigation should be avoided whenever possible. Participants should never be deliberately misled without extremely strong scientific or medical justification. Even then there should be strict controls and the disinterested approval of independent advisors'. [paragraph 4.2]

The decision that deception is necessary should be taken only after determining that alternative procedures (which avoid deception) are unavailable. Participants must be debriefed at the earliest opportunity (see Critical Discussion 48.1, page 711).

Debriefing

According to Aronson (1988):

'The experimenter must take steps to ensure that subjects leave the experimental situation in a frame of mind that is at least as sound as it was when they entered. This frequently requires post-experimental "debriefing" procedures that require more time and effort than the main body of the experiment'.

Where no undue suffering is experienced, but participants are deceived regarding the real purpose of the experiment:

'The investigator should provide the participant with any necessary information to complete their understanding of the nature of the research. The investigator should discuss with the participants their experience of the research in order to monitor any unforeseen negative effects or misconceptions'. [paragraph 5.1]

However:

'Some effects which may be produced by an experiment will not be negated by a verbal description following the research. Investigators have a responsibility to ensure that participants receive any necessary debriefing in the form of active intervention before they leave the research setting'. [paragraph 5.3]

Ask yourself ...

- Active intervention is more like a 'therapeutic' measure than just 'good manners'. Can you give examples of this second type of debriefing from both Milgram's and Zimbardo *et al.*'s experiments. (See Chapter 27.)

Protection of participants

'Investigators have a primary responsibility to protect participants from physical and mental harm during the investigation. Normally, the risk of harm must be no greater than in ordinary life, i.e. participants should not be exposed to risks greater than or additional to those encountered in their normal life styles'. [paragraph 8.1]

Debriefing represents a major means of protecting participants where emotional suffering has occurred. They must also be protected from the stress that might be produced by disclosing confidential information without participants' permission. If participants have been seriously deceived, they have the right to witness destruction of any such records they don't wish to be kept. Results are usually made anonymous as early as possible by use of a letter/number instead of name (Coolican, 1994).

Ethical issues arising from the study of social influence

As we noted in Chapter 27, Milgram's obedience experiments have been criticised on ethical grounds, and they're often held up as examples of how psychological research with human participants *shouldn't* be done. They undoubtedly helped highlight the ethical dimension of psychological research, and to define specific principles, such as those discussed above. Milgram's and other experiments in the area of social influence are among the most controversial in the whole of psychology, and for all these reasons are often cited in the context of the ethics of research.

Ask yourself ...

- Are there any features of Milgram's experimental procedure which you'd consider unethical? One way of approaching this is to ask yourself what you'd have found objectionable/unacceptable, either during or after the experiment, if you'd been one of his participants.

Protection from harm

One of Milgram's fiercest critics was Baumrind (1964), who argued that the rights and feelings of Milgram's participants had been abused, and that inadequate measures had been taken to protect them from stress and emotional conflict. While not denying that his participants did experience stress and conflict, Milgram defended himself by arguing that Baumrind's criticism assumes that the experimental outcome was *expected* – inducing stress *wasn't* an intended and deliberate effect of the experimental procedure. As Milgram (1974) noted:

'*Understanding grows because we examine situations in which the end is unknown. An investigator unwilling to accept this degree of risk must give up the idea of scientific enquiry*'.

In other words, an experimenter cannot know what the results are going to be before the experiment is conducted.

We might accept Milgram's claim that there was no reason to believe that participants would need protection. However, once he observed the degree of distress in his first experiment, should he have continued with the research programme (17 more experiments)? To justify this, Milgram would have pointed out that:

■ At whatever shock level the experiment ended, the participant was reunited with the unharmed Mr Wallace, and informed that no shock had been delivered. In an extended discussion with Milgram, obedient participants were assured that their behaviour was entirely normal, and that the feelings of conflict and tension were shared by others. Disobedient participants were supported in their decision to disobey the experimenter. This was all part of a thorough debriefing or 'dehoaxing', which happened as a matter of course with every participant (see Critical Discussion 48.1).

■ The experimenter didn't *make* the participant shock the learner (as Baumrind had claimed). Milgram began with the belief that every person who came to the laboratory was free to accept or reject the demands of authority. Far from being passive creatures, participants are active, choosing adults.

An APA ethics committee investigated Milgram's research shortly after its first publication in 1963 (during which time Milgram's APA membership was suspended). The committee eventually judged it to be ethically acceptable (Colman, 1987). In 1965, Milgram was awarded the prize for outstanding contribution to social psychological research by the American Association for the Advancement of Science.

According to Zimbardo (1973), the ethical concerns are even more pronounced in his own prison simulation experiment (see Chapter 27, pages 398–399) than in Milgram's experiments:

'*Volunteer prisoners suffered physical and psychological abuse hour after hour for days, while volunteer guards were exposed to the new self-knowledge that they enjoyed being powerful and had abused this power to make other human beings suffer. The intensity and duration of this suffering uniquely qualify the Stanford prison experiment for careful scrutiny of violations of the ethics of human experimentation*'.

Savin (1973) argued that the benefits resulting from Zimbardo *et al.*'s experiment didn't justify the distress, mistreatment and degradation suffered by the participants – the end *didn't* justify the means.

Ask yourself ...

• How could Zimbardo *et al.* defend themselves against this criticism in a way that Milgram couldn't?

Their experiment was due to last for two weeks, but when it was realised just how intense and serious the distress, mistreatment and degradation were, it was ended after six days. However, it could be asked why it wasn't stopped even sooner!

Deception and informed consent

According to Vitelli (1988), almost all conformity and obedience experiments (and more than one-third of all social psychological studies) deceive participants over the purpose of the research, the accuracy of the information they're given, and/or the true identity of a person they believe to be another genuine participant (or experimenter). Deception is considered unethical for two main reasons:

■ It prevents the participant from giving informed consent, that is, agreeing to participate knowing the true purpose of the study and what participation will involve.

■ The most potentially harmful deception is involved in studies, like those of Milgram and Zimbardo *et al.*, in which participants learn (unsettling) things about themselves as people.

Ask yourself ...

• Given that it's important to understand the processes involved in conformity and obedience (the *end*), can deception be justified as a *means* of studying them?

• Identify the deceptions that were involved in the experiments of Asch (see Chapter 26), Milgram and Zimbardo *et al.* Do you consider any of these to be more serious/unethical than the others, and if so, why?

CRITICAL DISCUSSION 48.1

Can deception ever be justified?

• Most participants deceived in Asch's conformity experiments were very enthusiastic, and expressed their admiration for the elegance and significance of the experimental procedure (Milgram, 1992).

• In defence of his own obedience experiments, Milgram (1974) reported that his participants were all thoroughly debriefed. This included receiving a comprehensive report detailing the procedure and results of all the experiments, together with a follow-up questionnaire about their participation. More specifically, the 'technical illusions', as Milgram calls deception, are justified because in the end they're accepted and approved of by those exposed to them. He saw this, in turn, as justifying the *continuation* of the experiments, which is relevant to the issue of protection from harm discussed above.

• Christensen (1988) reviewed studies of the ethical acceptability of deception experiments and concluded that as long as deception isn't extreme, participants don't seem to mind. Christensen suggests that the widespread use of mild forms of deception is justified, first because no one is apparently harmed, and second, because there seem to be few, if any, acceptable alternatives.

• Krupat & Garonzik (1994) reported that university psychology students who'd been deceived at least once as research participants didn't find the experience less enjoyable or interesting as a result. They also said they'd be less upset if they were lied to or misled again in the future (compared with those who hadn't been deceived).

- Other researchers have defended Milgram's use of deception on the grounds that without it, he'd have found results which simply don't reflect how people behave when they're led to believe they're in real situations (Aronson, 1988). In some circumstances, then, deception may be the best (and perhaps the only) way to obtain useful information about how people behave in complex and important situations.

As far as Zimbardo *et al.*'s prison simulation study is concerned, the only deception involved surrounded the arrest of the prisoners at the start of the experiment. They weren't told this would happen, partly because final approval from the local police force wasn't given until minutes before they decided to participate, and partly because the researchers wanted the arrests to come as a surprise.

As Zimbardo (1973) admits, 'This was a breach, by omission, of the ethics of our own informed consent contract', which told participants of everything that was going to happen to them (as far as this could be predicted). It was signed by every one of them, thus giving their permission for invasion of privacy, loss of civil rights, and harassment. Approval for the study had also been officially sought and received, in writing, from the body that sponsored the research, the Psychology Department at Stanford University, and the University Committee of Human Experimentation. This Committee didn't anticipate the extreme reactions that were to follow.

Like Milgram, Zimbardo *et al.* held debriefing sessions (both group and individual). All participants returned post-experimental questionnaires several weeks, then several months, later, then at yearly intervals. Many submitted retrospective diaries and personal analyses of the effects of their participation:

'We are sufficiently convinced that the suffering we observed, and were responsible for, was stimulus bound and did not extend beyond the confines of that basement prison'. (Zimbardo, 1973)

Widening the ethical debate

Protecting the individual versus harming the group

Although 'protection of participants' is one of the specific principles included in the *Ethical Principles*, they're all designed to prevent any harm coming to the participant, or the avoidance of overt 'sins' (Brown, 1997).

However, Brown (1997) argues that formal codes focus too narrowly on risks to the individual participant, in the specific context of the investigation. They neglect broader questions about the risks to the group to which the participant belongs.

Ask yourself ...

- Re-read Chapter 47. Try to identify some fundamental values and biases that are potentially damaging to particular social groups.
- In what ways are these values/biases harmful to these groups?

Box 48.2 The ethics of ethical codes: Underlying assumptions

According to Brown (1997), a core assumption underlying ethical codes is that what psychologists do as researchers, clinicians, teachers and so on is basically harmless and inherently valuable, because it's based on 'science' (defined as positivism: see Chapter 3). Consequently, it's possible for a psychologist to conduct technically ethical research but still do great harm. For example, a researcher can adhere strictly to 'scientific' research methodologies, get technically adequate informed consent from participants (and not breach any of the other major prescribed principles), but still conduct research which claims to show the inferiority of a particular group. Because it's conducted according to 'the rules' (both methodological and ethical), the question of whether it's ethical in the broader sense to pursue such matters is ignored.

For example, neither Jensen (1969) nor Herrnstein (1971) was ever considered by mainstream psychology to have violated psychology's ethics by the questions they asked regarding the intellectual inferiority of African Americans (see Chapter 41). Individual black participants weren't harmed by being given IQ tests, and might even have found them interesting and challenging. However, Brown (1997) argues that the way the findings were interpreted and used:

' *... weakened the available social supports for people of colour by stigmatising them as genetically inferior, thus strengthening the larger culture's racist attitudes. Research ethics as currently construed by mainstream ethics codes do not require researchers to put the potential for this sort of risk into their informed consent documents'.*

Jensen's and Herrnstein's research (highlighted by Herrnstein and Murray, in *The Bell Curve*, 1994) has profoundly harmed black Americans. Ironically, the book has received much methodological criticism, but only black psychologists (such as Hilliard, 1995, and Sue, 1995) have raised the more fundamental question of whether simply conducting such studies might be ethically dubious. As Brown observes:

' *To ask this question about the risks of certain types of inquiry challenges science's hegemony as the source of all good in psychology'.*

Herrnstein and Murray, Rushton (1995), Brand (cited in Richards, 1996a) and others, like the Nazi scientists of the 1930s, claim that the study of race differences is a purely 'objective' and 'scientific' enterprise (Howe, 1997).

If it's thought unethical to deceive individual black or female participants about the purposes of some particular study, but ethically acceptable to use the results to support the claim that blacks or women are genetically inferior, then this narrow definition of ethics makes it an ineffective way of guiding research into socially sensitive issues (Howitt, 1991). Formal codes continue to focus narrowly on risks to the individual participant, in the specific context of the investigation, but neglect questions about the risks to the group to which the participant belongs:

'As long as research ethics avoid the matter of whether certain questions ethically cannot be asked, psychologists will conduct technically ethical research that violates a more general ethic of avoiding harm to vulnerable populations'. (Brown, 1997)

Protecting the individual versus benefiting society

If the questions psychologists ask are limited and shaped by the values of individual researchers, they're also limited and shaped by considerations of methodology (what it's possible to do, practically, when investigating human behaviour and experience). For example, in the context of intimate relationships (see Chapter 28), Brehm (1992) claims that, by its nature, the laboratory experiment is extremely limited in the kinds of questions it allows psychologists to investigate.

Conversely, and just as importantly, there are certain aspects of behaviour and experience which could be studied experimentally, although it would be unethical to do so, such as 'jealousy between partners participating in laboratory research' (Brehm, 1992). Indeed, for Brehm:

'All types of research in this area involve important ethical dilemmas. Even if all we do is to ask subjects to fill out questionnaires describing their relationships, we need to think carefully about how this research experience might affect them and their partner'.

So, what it may be *possible* to do may be *unacceptable*, but equally, what may be *acceptable* may not be *possible*. However, just as focusing on protection of individual participants can work to the detriment of whole groups (see above), so it can discourage psychologists from carrying out *socially meaningful* research (what Brehm, 1992, calls the *ethical imperative*) which, potentially, may improve the quality of people's lives. Social psychologists in particular have a *two-fold* ethical obligation, to individual participants and to society at large (Myers, 1994). This relates to discussion of psychology's *aims* as a science (see Chapters 1 and 3). Similarly, Aronson (1992) argues that social psychologists are:

'... obligated to use their research skills to advance our knowledge and understanding of human behaviour for the ultimate aim of human betterment. In short, social psychologists have an ethical responsibility to the society as a whole'.

Talking about the aim of 'human betterment' raises important questions about basic values. It opens out the ethical debate in such a way that values must be addressed and recognised as part of the research process (something advocated very strongly by feminist psychologists: see above and Chapter 47).

Ask yourself ...

- Before reading on, try to think of some examples of how research findings you're familiar with might be used to benefit people in general. You may find it useful to focus on social psychology.

Box 48.3	An example of the benefits of social psychological research

In many bystander intervention studies (e.g. Latané & Darley, 1968: see Chapter 30), people are deceived into believing that an 'emergency' is taking place. Many of Latané and Darley's participants were very distressed by their experiences, especially those in the experiment in which they believed another participant was having an epileptic fit. Yet when asked to complete a post-experimental questionnaire (which followed a very careful debriefing), all said they believed the deception was justified and would be willing to participate in similar experiments again. None reported any feelings of anger towards the experimenter.

Beaman *et al.* (1978) built on these earlier experiments. They used a lecture to inform students about how other bystanders' refusals to help can influence both one's own interpretation of an emergency and feelings of responsibility. Two other groups of students heard either a different lecture or no lecture at all. Two weeks later, as part of a different experiment in a different location, the participants found themselves (accompanied by an unresponsive stooge) walking past someone who was slumped over or sprawled under a bike. Of those who'd heard the lecture about helping behaviour, 50 per cent stopped to offer help compared with 25 per cent who hadn't.

This suggests that the results of psychological research can be used to make us more aware of influences on behaviour, making it more likely that we'll act differently armed with that knowledge from how we might otherwise have done. In the case of bystander intervention, this 'consciousness-raising' is beneficial in a tangible way to the person who's helped. Being more sensitive to the needs of others, and feeling satisfied with having helped another person, may also be seen as beneficial to the helper.

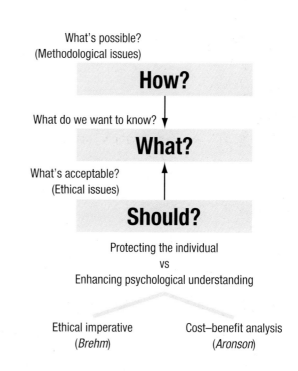

Figure 48.2 *Ethical and methodological constraints on the questions that psychologists can try to answer through the research process*

The 'double obligation dilemma'

The dilemma faced by social psychologists (regarding their obligations to society and individual participants) is greatest when investigating important areas such as conformity, obedience and bystander intervention (Aronson, 1992). In general, the more important the issue, (i) the greater the potential benefit for society, and (ii) the more likely an individual participant is to experience distress and discomfort. This is because the more important the issue, the more essential the use of *deception* becomes (see above, pages 711–712).

Psychologists want to know how people are likely to behave if they found themselves in that situation *outside* the laboratory. This raises several crucial *methodological* questions (such as experimental realism, external validity or mundane realism: see Chapters 3, 26 and 27). However, the key ethical issue hinges on the fact that the use of deception both contributes enormously (and perhaps irreplaceably) to our understanding of human behaviour (helping to satisfy the obligation to society), and at the same time significantly increases individual participants' distress (detracting from the responsibility to protect individuals).

Box 48.4 Some proposed solutions to the 'double obligation dilemma'

- Having accepted that, under certain circumstances, deception is permissible, most psychologists still advocate that it shouldn't be used unless it's considered essential (Milgram, 1992; Aronson, 1992). This is consistent with the BPS *Ethical Principles*.
- Aronson (1992) advocates a *cost–benefit analysis*: weighing how much 'good' (benefits to society) will derive from doing the research against how much 'bad' will happen to the participants.
- Milgram (1992) believes that if the experimental creation of stress or conflict were excluded on principle, and only studies which produced positive emotions were allowed, this would produce:

  '… *a very lopsided psychology, one that caricatured rather than accurately reflected human experience*'.

  Traditionally, the most deeply informative experiments in social psychology include those examining how participants resolve conflicts, such as Asch's studies of conformity (truth versus conformity: see Chapter 26), Latané and Darley's bystander intervention studies (getting involved in another's troubles versus not getting involved: see Chapter 30), and Milgram's own obedience experiments (internal conscience versus external authority: see Chapter 27).
- Two compromise solutions to the problem of not being able to obtain informed consent are *presumptive consent* (of 'reasonable people') and *prior general consent*. In the former, the views of many people are obtained about an experimental procedure's acceptability. These people wouldn't participate in the actual experiment (if it went ahead), but their views could be taken as evidence of how people in general would react to participation.

  Prior general consent could be obtained from people who might, subsequently, serve as experimental participants. Before volunteering to join a pool of research volunteers, people would be explicitly told that sometimes participants are misinformed about a study's true purpose and sometimes experience emotional stress. Only those

---

agreeing would be chosen (Milgram, 1992). This is a compromise solution, because people would be giving their 'informed consent' (a) well in advance of the actual study, (b) only in a very general way, and (c) without knowing what specific manipulations/deceptions will be used in the particular experiment in which they participate. It seems to fall somewhere between 'mere' consent and full 'informed consent' (and could be called *semi- or partially informed consent*).

Non-human (animal) subjects

The BPS Scientific Affairs Board published its *Guidelines for the Use of Animals in Research* (1985), in conjunction with the Committee of the Experimental Psychological Society. It offers a checklist of points which investigators should carefully consider when planning experiments with living non-humans. Researchers have a general obligation to:

'… *avoid, or at least to minimise, discomfort to living animals … discuss any future research with their local Home Office Inspector and colleagues who are experts in the topic … seek … Widespread advice as to whether the likely scientific contribution of the work … justifies the use of living animals, and whether the scientific point they wish to make may not be made without the use of living animals*'. [BPS, 1985]

This raises two fundamental questions: (a) how do we know non-humans suffer?, and (b) what goals can ever justify subjecting them to pain, suffering and even death?

How do we know that animals suffer?

Ask yourself …

- Identify examples of experiments involving animals in which they suffered pain and distress. Try to specify in *what ways* suffering occurred.

Box 48.5 Some criteria for judging animal suffering

- Disease and injury are generally recognised as major causes of suffering. Consequently, research such as Brady's (1958) 'executive monkey' experiments would probably not even be debated in the current climate (Mapstone, 1991). Brady attached pairs of monkeys to an apparatus which gave electric shocks, such that one monkey (the 'executive': see below) could prevent the shock by pressing a lever, but the other couldn't. The former developed ulcers and eventually died.
- Even if we're sure that animals aren't suffering physically, their confinement might cause mental suffering not affecting their external condition (Dawkins, 1980). For example, apparently healthy zoo and farm animals often show bizarre behaviours.
- We must find out about animal suffering by careful observation and experimentation. Because different species have different requirements, lifestyles, and, perhaps, emotions, we cannot assume that we know about their suffering or well-being without studying them species by species (Dawkins, 1980).

Drawing on the Institute of Medical Ethics (IME) Working Party's report (Haworth, 1992), Bateson (1986, 1992) has proposed criteria for assessing animal suffering, including:

- possessing receptors sensitive to noxious or painful stimulation, and
- having brain structures comparable to the human cerebral cortex.

Bateson (1992) tentatively concludes that insects probably don't experience pain, whereas fish and octopi probably do. However, the boundaries between the presence and absence of pain are 'fuzzy'.

An 'executive monkey'

Ask yourself ...

- Try to formulate arguments for and against the use of animals in research. This shouldn't be confined to psychological research, since much of the debate takes place in relation to medicine, pharmacology and so on.

How can we justify experiments with non-humans?

The question of whether or not animals suffer wouldn't arise if animals weren't being used in experiments in the first place. According to Gray (1987), the main justifications for animal experimentation are the *pursuit of scientific knowledge* and the *advancement of medicine*.

To justify the use of animals, especially when very stressful procedures are used, the research must be rigorously designed and the potential results must represent a significant contribution to our knowledge of medicine, pharmacology, biopsychology or psychology as a whole. This is a safeguard against distressing research being carried out for its own sake, or at the researcher's whim.

The *Guidelines* state that if the animals are confined, constrained, harmed or stressed in any way, the experimenter must consider whether the knowledge to be gained justifies the procedure. Some knowledge is trivial, and experiments mustn't be done simply because it's possible to do them. To take the executive monkeys experiments again (see Box 48.5), the medical justification (to discover why business executives develop

ulcers) was insufficient to justify their continuation. The monkeys' obvious suffering superseded even the combination of scientific and medical justification. However, there are other cases where, while the scientific justification may be apparent, the medical justification is much less so, such as Olds & Milner's (1954) experiments where animals' brains are stimulated via implantation of a permanent electrode (electrical self-stimulation of the brain/ES-SB: see Key Study 9.5, page 126).

Safeguards for animal subjects

Whatever practical application Olds and Milner's ES-SB experiments may have subsequently had (such as pain/anxiety relief in psychotics, epileptics and cancer patients), they don't seem to have been conducted with such human applications in mind. Can the scientific knowledge gained about ES-SB as a very powerful positive reinforcer on its own justify the rats' eventual 'sacrifice'? The very least required of researchers is that the minimum of suffering is caused, both during and following any surgical procedure and by any electric shock or food deprivation, the most objected-to treatments (Gray, 1987).

Box 48.6 Some safeguards for animal subjects

- Gray (1987) claims that food deprivation *isn't* a source of suffering, and that rats (the most commonly used experimental subjects in psychology) are either fed once a day when experimentation is over, or maintained at 85 per cent of their free-feeding (*ad lib*) body weight. Both are actually healthier than allowing them to eat *ad lib*. Electric shock may cause *some* but not *extreme* pain (based on observations of the animals' behaviour). The level permitted is controlled by the Home Office (HO) inspectors, who monitor implementation of The Animals (Scientific Procedures) Act (1986). The average level used in the UK is 0.68 milli-amperes, for an average of 0.57 seconds. This produces an unpleasant tickling sensation in humans.

- Procedures causing pain or distress are illegal, unless the experimenter holds an HO licence and relevant certificates. Even then, these procedures should be carried out only if there are no alternative ways of conducting the experiment. Similarly, it's illegal in the UK to perform any surgical or pharmacological procedure on vertebrates (or one invertebrate – the octopus) without an HO licence and relevant certification. Such procedures must be performed by experienced personnel.

- The *Guidelines* stress the importance of understanding species differences in relation to (i) caging and social environment, (ii) the stress involved in marking wild animals for identification or attaching them with radio transmitters, and (iii) the duration of food/drink deprivation. Field workers should disturb non-humans as little as possible. Even simple observation of animals in the wild can have marked effects on their breeding and survival.

- The number of animals used in laboratory experiments is declining. For example, in the UK, the Netherlands, Germany and several other European countries, the numbers have fallen by half since the 1970s (Mukerjee, 1997). However, the UK still uses approximately three million non-humans a year in experiments (85 per cent of which are mice, rats and other rodents), and a sharp rise in genome-related research is threatening to reverse this downward trend (Hawkes, 2000b). But putting this in perspective, over 700 million non-humans are killed for food every year (*Nursing Times*, 1996).

- The UK, Australia, Germany and several other countries require a utilitarian *cost–benefit analysis* (animal pain, distress and death versus acquisition of new knowledge and the development of new medical therapies for humans) to be performed before any animal experiment can proceed (Mukerjee, 1997; Rowan, 1997). Interestingly, most non-scientists also seem to perform some kind of cost-benefit analysis (Aldhous *et al.*, 1999: see Critical Discussion 48.2, page 717).

Despite these safeguards, the very existence of the 1986 Act condones the use of animals. Legally, the Act aims to spare animals 'unnecessary' pain and distress; implicitly, the law accepts that some research will involve suffering for the non-human subjects. Under the Act, applications for project licences have to say whether they've considered alternatives to using non-humans, and in granting the licence the Home Secretary must weigh up the likely benefit of the research against the adverse effects on the animal subjects. However, there's no remit to consider whether the proposed research is truly necessary (Seymour, 1996). Also, the Medicines Act (1968) requires that all new medicines undergo a range of tests on animals before they can be tested on humans (Lyall, 1993: see Box 48.7).

A list of 110 of British scientists has called for the Home Office to speed up the process of gaining approval for animal experiments: their complaint is that the procedure is so long-winded that foreign scientists will take all the prizes for medicine, biotechnology and drug research (Hawkes, 2000c). The list includes Blakemore (see Chapter 16), Gray (see below), Greenfield (see Chapters 7 and 8), and Iversen (see Chapter 4).

The medical justification argument

The strongest argument for animal experiments is undoubtedly the advancement of medical knowledge and treatments. However, scientific and ethical issues can easily become confused. Showing what's been achieved in a practical sense from such experiments represents only a minimum requirement for their justification. So, only if it can be convincingly shown, for example, that many drugs used in the treatment of human diseases (including anti-cancer drugs, AIDS treatments, anti-epileptic and antidepressant drugs: Green, 1994) have been developed using animals, and couldn't have been developed otherwise, can the ethical debate begin.

| Box 48.7 | Are animal experiments scientifically useful? |

The case for

- Animal experiments have played a crucial role in the development of modern medical treatments, and will continue to be necessary as researchers seek to alleviate existing ailments and respond to the emergence of new diseases.
- The causes of and vaccines for dozens of infectious diseases, including diphtheria, tetanus, rabies, whooping cough, tuberculosis, poliomyelitis, measles, mumps, and rubella, have been determined largely through animal experimentation. It's also led to the development of antibacterial and antibiotic drugs.

- Animal research has also been vital to areas of medicine, such as open-heart surgery, kidney disease and organ transplantation, diabetes, malignant hypertension, and gastric ulcers.
- There are no basic differences between the physiologies of laboratory animals and humans. Both control their internal biochemistry by releasing the same basic endocrine hormones (see Chapter 4), both send out similar chemical transmitters from neurons in the CNS and PNS (see Chapter 4), and both react in the same way to infection or tissue injury. Animal models of disease (see below) are intended to provide a means of studying a particular procedure (such as gene therapy for cystic fibrosis).

The case against

- Through genetic manipulation, surgical intervention, or injection of foreign substances, researchers produce diseases in laboratory animals that 'model' human diseases. However, evolutionary pressures have produced innumerable subtle differences between species, and the knock-on effect of applying a stimulus to one particular organ system on the animal's overall physiological functioning is often unpredictable and not fully understood.
- Important medical advances have been delayed because of misleading results from animal experiments. Cancer research is especially sensitive to physiological differences between species. Rats and mice, for example, synthesise about 100 times the recommended daily allowance of vitamin C believed to help the (human) body ward off cancer. Penicillin is toxic to guinea-pigs, while morphine stimulates cats (the opposite of the human response).
- The stress of handling, confinement, and isolation alters an animal's physiology, introducing a variable that makes extrapolating results to humans even more difficult. Laboratory stress can increase animals' susceptibility to infectious disease and certain tumours, as well as influencing hormone and antibody levels.
- Animal experiments to test the safety of drugs are confounded by the fact that tests on different species often produce conflicting results.

(Based on Barnard & Kaufman, 1997, Botting & Morrison, 1997, Mukerjee, 1997, and Sawyer, 1996)

Green (1994), Carlson (1992) and many other biopsychologists believe that the potential benefits of animal experiments is sufficient to justify their use.

Ask yourself ...

- What do you think of the claim that particular non-human species, namely those that are closest to us in an evolutionary sense, should be given 'special consideration' in the context of animal experiments?

CRITICAL DISCUSSION 48.2

Chimpanzees, AIDS and moral responsibility

What will become of several hundred research 'veterans' that are now considered to be of no further value to medical science? Their plight is a direct consequence of their genetic similarity to human beings, which makes them ideal models for the study of several diseases afflicting people worldwide, and the quest to find vaccines against them. During the 1970s, chimpanzees started to be used in large numbers in biomedical research in the USA. This came with the development of vaccines against hepatitis B, and later in a still unrealised search for a hepatitis C vaccine.

Some scientists lobbied for retirement facilities for the chimpanzees, but many began to seriously consider euthanasia as the only practical way to alleviate the crisis. Ironically, it was the AIDS epidemic in the mid-1980s which 'saved' the very chimpanzees that were 'used up'. Once again, they became 'surrogate human beings', this time in the development of HIV vaccines.

Yet by the mid-1990s, scientists began to turn to human volunteers for the initial testing of HIV vaccines, leaving large numbers of 'redundant' chimpanzees, which have a lifespan of up to 40 years. A report by the US National Research Council (1997) concluded that chimpanzees should be afforded special consideration, on ethical grounds, over other non-humans, and that euthanasia isn't an acceptable means of population control. This is consistent with one of the findings of a recent MORI poll conducted in the UK, namely that people are more likely to oppose experiments on monkeys than those on mice. Only those experiments designed to test or develop drugs to treat childhood leukaemia were seen as justifying monkeys' suffering (Aldhous *et al.*, 1999).

Wise (2000) argues that animals should have full rights under the law. Goodall describes Wise's book as the 'animals' Magna Carta' (Mee, 2000).

(Based on Mahoney, 1998)

Speciesism: Extending the medical justification argument

According to Gray (1991), while most people (both experimenters and animal rights activists) would accept the ethical principle that inflicting pain is wrong, we're sometimes faced with having to choose between different ethical principles, which may mean having to choose between human and non-human suffering. Gray believes that *speciesism* (discriminating against and exploiting animals because they belong to a particular [non-human] species: Ryder, 1990) is justified, and argues that:

'Not only is it not wrong to give preference to the interests of one's own species, one has a duty to do so'.

Such a moral choice involves establishing a calculus (Dawkins, 1990), which pits the suffering of non-humans against the human suffering which the former's use will alleviate. For Gray (1991):

'In many cases the decision not to carry out certain experiments with animals (even if they would inflict pain or suffering) is likely to have the consequence that more people will undergo pain or suffering that might otherwise be avoided'.

One of the problems associated with the prospeciesism argument is that medical advance may only become possible after extensive development of knowledge and scientific understanding in a particular field (Gray, 1991). In the meantime, scientific understanding may be the only specific objective that the experiment can readily attain. It's at this interim stage that the suffering imposed on experimental animals will far outweigh any (lesser) suffering eventually avoided by people, and this is at the core of the decisions that must be made by scientists and ethical committees.

Psychologists as practitioners

Clinical psychologists (as well as educational psychologists, psychotherapists, psychiatrists, social workers, nurses, counsellors and other professionals) are concerned with bringing about *psychological change*. It's in their capacity as agents of change that clinical psychologists face their greatest ethical challenges (see Chapter 1).

Ask yourself ...

* Consider some of the ethical issues faced by psychologists attempting to change other people's behaviour. Some are of a general nature, such as freedom versus determinism (see Chapter 49), others will overlap with ethical principles governing research (such as confidentiality and informed consent), and yet others may be specific to particular therapeutic approaches (see Chapter 45).

According to Fairbairn & Fairbairn (1987), clinical psychologists:

'... must decide how they will interact with those who seek their help; for example, whether in general they will regard them as autonomous beings with rights and responsibilities, or rather as helpless individuals, incapable of rational choice'.

Fairbairn and Fairbairn argue that two quite common beliefs likely to detract from an explicit consideration of professional ethics and values in psychological practice are (a) that psychology is a value-free science, and (b) that therapists should be value-neutral or 'non-directive'.

Psychology as value-free science

Central to clinical (and counselling) psychology is the *scientist–practitioner model* of helping (Dallos & Cullen, 1990). This sees clinical psychology as being guided by, and operating within, the framework of the general scientific method (see Chapters 3 and 45). If clinical psychologists view clinical psychology as having firm foundations in positivist science, they may disregard ethics because these aren't amenable to objective consideration. But even if the psychological knowledge used in clinical practice was always the result of the application of an objective scientific method, moral questions of an interpersonal kind are bound to arise *at the point at which it's applied* (Fairbairn & Fairbairn, 1987).

This distinction between possession of knowledge and its application ('science' versus 'technology') is fundamental to any discussion of ethics, because it's related to the notion of *responsibility*. Presumably, clinical psychologists *choose* which techniques to use with clients and how to use them. The mere existence (and even the demonstrated effectiveness) of certain techniques doesn't *in itself* mean that they must be used. Similarly, the kind of research which clinical psychologists consider worth doing (and which then provides the scientific basis for the use of particular techniques) is a matter of choice, and reflects views regarding the nature of people and how they can be changed (see Chapters 1 and 2).

Box 48.8 Criticisms of scientific behaviour therapy and modification

- Because of (rather than despite) its espoused status as a value-free, applied science, behaviour therapy and modification tend to devalue and thereby dehumanise their clients by treating people, for 'scientific' purposes, as if they were 'organisms' as opposed to 'agents', helpless victims of forces outside their control. This criticism also applies to medical psychiatry and classical psychoanalysis, except that both see the controlling forces as being internal (organic abnormalities or intrapsychic forces, respectively) as opposed to environmental contingencies (see Chapters 2 and 45).
- Clients soon come to believe that they're abnormal, helpless and also worthless, because this is part of the culture-wide stereotype of 'mental illness' (see Chapter 43). Negative self-evaluation and passivity characterise many, if not most, mental health clients, who think and behave like passive organisms. The solution lies in helping people recover, or discover, their agency.

(Based on Trower, 1987)

Therapists as value-neutral and non-directive

If psychology as a value-free science involves not regarding or treating clients fully as human beings, this second major issue is about the therapist or psychologist functioning as something less than a complete person within the therapeutic situation. Providing help and support in a non-directive, value-free way is a tradition for psychotherapists and counsellors (Fairbairn & Fairbairn, 1987). However, such an approach may seem to require remaining aloof and distant from the client which, in turn, may entail not treating the client with respect as a person, since this requires the therapist to recognise that the client is a person like him- or herself.

Ask yourself ...

- Do you believe that it's possible for therapists not to have any influence over their clients/patients?

The influence of the therapist

Adopting what's thought to be a value-free position in therapy may lead therapists to deny the importance or influence of their own moral values, which are often hidden in therapy. This kind of influence is much more subtle and covert than the coercion that can operate on hospitalised psychiatric patients, even voluntary ones. The in-patient is subjected to strong persuasion to accept the treatment recommendations of professional staff. As Davison & Neale (1994) observe:

'Even a "voluntary" and informed decision to take psychotropic medication or to participate in any other therapy regimen is often (maybe usually) less than free'.

CRITICAL DISCUSSION 48.3

Therapist influence in psychodynamic and behaviour therapy

The issue of the therapist's influence on the patient/client has been central to a long-standing debate between traditional (psychodynamic) psychotherapists and behaviour therapists (who are usually clinical psychologists by training: see Chapter 45). Psychotherapists regard behaviour therapy as unacceptable (even if it works), because it's manipulative and demeaning of human dignity. By contrast, they see their own methods as fostering the autonomous development of the patient's inherent potential, helping the patient to express his/her true self, and so on. Instead of influencers, they see themselves as 'psychological midwives', present during the 'birth', possessing useful skills, but there primarily to make sure that a natural process goes smoothly.

However, this is an exaggeration and misrepresentation of both approaches. For many patients, the 'birth' probably wouldn't happen at all without the therapist's intervention, and s/he undoubtedly influences the patient's behaviour. Conversely, behaviour therapists are at least partly successful because they establish active, co-operative relationships with their patients, who play much more active roles in the therapy than psychotherapists believe.

All therapists, of whatever persuasion, if they're at all effective, influence their patients. Both approaches comprise a situation in which one human being (the therapist) tries to act in a way that enables another human being to act and feel differently, and this is as true of psychoanalysis as it is of behaviour therapy.

(Based on Wachtel, 1977)

The crucial issue is the *nature* of the therapist's influence, rather than whether or not influence occurs. One ethical issue is whether the influence is exerted in a direction that is in the patient's interest, or in the service of the therapist's needs. Another is whether the patient is fully informed about the kind of influence the therapist wishes to exert, and the kind of ends being sought (the issue of *informed consent*). Therapist *neutrality* is a myth. Therapists influence their clients in subtle yet powerful ways. According to Davison & Neale (1994):

'Unlike a technician, a psychiatrist cannot avoid communicating and at times imposing his own values upon his patients. The patient usually has considerable difficulty in

finding the way in which he would wish to change his behaviour, but as he talks to the psychiatrist his wants and needs become clearer. In the very process of defining his needs in the presence of a figure who is viewed as wise and authoritarian, the patient is profoundly influenced. He ends up wanting some of the things the psychiatrist thinks he should want'.

In the above quotation, we can add 'psychologist' and 'psychotherapist' to 'psychiatrist'.

Freedom and behavioural control

While a behavioural technique such as systematic desensitisation is limited mainly to anxiety reduction, this can at least be seen as enhancing the patient's freedom, since anxiety is one of the greatest restrictions on freedom. By contrast, methods based on operant conditioning can be applied to almost any aspect of a person's behaviour. Those who use operant methods (such as the token economy) often describe their work rather exclusively in terms of behavioural control, subscribing to Skinner's (1971) view of freedom as an illusion (see Chapter 49, pages 726–727).

Wachtel (1977) believes that, when used in institutional settings (such as with long-term schizophrenic patients in psychiatric hospitals), the token economy is so subject to abuse that its use is highly questionable. It may be justifiable if it works, and if there's clearly no alternative way of rescuing a patient from an empty and destructive existence. But as a routine part of how society deals with deviant behaviour, this approach raises very serious ethical questions. One of these relates to the question of power. Like the experimental 'subject' relative to the experimenter, the patient is powerless relative to the institutional staff responsible for operating the token economy programme:

'Reinforcement is viewed by many – proponents and opponents alike – as somehow having an inexorable controlling effect upon the person's behaviour and rendering him incapable of choice, reducing him to an automaton or duly wound mechanism'. (Wachtel, 1977)

The alarming feature of the token economy is the reinforcing agent's power to deprive unco-operative patients physically of 'privileges' (see Box 45.6, page 674).

The abuse of patients by therapists

In recent years, there's been considerable criticism of psychotherapy (especially Freudian psychoanalysis), including its ethical shortcomings. Masson (1988) believes that there's an imbalance of power involved in the therapeutic relationship, and individuals who seek therapy need protection from the therapist's constant temptation to abuse, misuse, profit from and bully the client. The therapist has almost absolute emotional power over the patient, and Masson catalogues many examples of patients' emotional, sexual and financial abuse at their therapists' hands.

Not surprisingly, Masson's attack has stirred up an enormous controversy. Holmes (1992) agrees with the core of Masson's (1992) argument, namely that:

'No therapist, however experienced or distinguished, is above the laws of the unconscious, and all should have access to supervision and work within a framework of proper professional practice'.

However, in psychotherapy's defence, Holmes points out that exploitation and abuse are by no means confined to psychotherapy. Lawyers, university teachers, priests and doctors are also sometimes guilty (the case of Harold Shipman, the serial-killer doctor, being one, albeit rather extreme, example). All these professional groups have ethical standards and codes of practice (often far more stringent than the law of the land), with disciplinary bodies which impose severe punishments (usually expulsion from the profession). We shouldn't condemn an entire profession because of the transgressions of a small minority.

Conclusions

This chapter has considered the ethics of psychological research, with both human participants and animals subjects, as well as ethical issues arising from the psychologist's role as a professional involved in behaviour change. Discussion of ethical issues has, in various ways, struck at the heart of psychology itself, requiring us to ask what psychology is *for*. According to Hawks (1981), prevention rather than cure should be a primary aim of psychology, enabling people to cope by themselves, without professional help, thus 'giving psychology away' to people/clients. For Bakan (1967), the significant place in society of the psychologist is more that of the teacher than expert or technician.

CHAPTER SUMMARY

- Psychology's focus of study consists of **sentient** things. This makes every psychological investigation an **ethical situation**, with research determined as much by its effects on those being studied, as by what psychologists want to find out.

- The BPS's *Ethical Principles* identifies several guiding principles for research with human participants, including **consent/informed consent**, **deception**, **protection of participants**, **debriefing**, and **confidentiality**.

- Even if a participant has been fully informed about an experimental procedure, this doesn't guarantee **informed consent**.

- **Debriefing** must take place at the earliest opportunity following the use of **deception**, and an experimenter must ensure that participants leave the experimental situation in at least as positive a frame of mind as when they entered.

- The BPS and APA codes and guidelines are periodically revised in the light of changing social and political contexts. This indicates that there are **no absolute or universal ethical truths**.

- Ethical criticisms of Milgram's obedience experiments helped **trigger the debate** regarding the ethics of research within psychology as a whole.

- The distress that Milgram's participants experienced wasn't an intended or deliberate effect of the experimental procedure. Participants were thoroughly '**dehoaxed**' at the end of the experiment, and Milgram also argued that participants were free to obey or disobey.

- While deception is unethical if it prevents participants from giving informed consent, those who've been deceived generally approve of it retrospectively. Deception may sometimes be the best/only way of obtaining valuable insights into human behaviour.

- While ethical codes serve to protect individual participants, underlying assumptions may harm the **social groups** they represent. Formal codes neglect wider issues regarding the ethical acceptability of **socially sensitive research**.
- Psychological research must be **socially meaningful** (the **ethical imperative**). This applies particularly to the work of social psychologists.
- The dual obligation to individual participants and to society produces a dilemma regarding the use of deception. Three possible solutions are conducting a **cost–benefit analysis**, and obtaining either **presumptive consent** or **prior general consent**.
- While the physical suffering of experimental animals is obvious, mental suffering is less overt. The main justifications for animal experimentation are the **pursuit of scientific knowledge** and the **advancement of medicine**. Safeguards exist to minimise animals' pain and distress.
- The medical justification argument presupposes that medical benefits have actually resulted from animal experiments. However, scientific opinion is divided about this.
- According to **speciesism**, we're morally obliged to inflict pain on animals in order to reduce potential human suffering.
- Clinical psychologists and other **agents of change** are likely to neglect professional ethics, because of the twin beliefs that psychology is a value-free science (as embodied in the **scientist–practitioner model** of helping) and that therapists should be value-neutral/'non-directive'.
- However effective a particular technique may be, clinical psychologists still **choose** which techniques to use and what research is worth doing. **Behaviour therapy** and **modification** treat people as helpless organisms, resulting in low self-esteem and passivity.
- **Psychiatric in-patients** are subjected to **subtle coercion** to accept particular treatments, and therapists may exert an even more covert influence over their clients.
- **All** therapists, psychodynamic and behavioural alike, influence their clients/patients. The crucial issue is the **nature** of that influence.

- The **token economy** is often described in terms of **behavioural control**, and within institutions, staff have the **power** to deprive patients of 'privileges'. There's also a power imbalance between therapists and their clients. In both situations, abuse of power may occur.

Self-assessment questions

1 'Without research such as Milgram's, we would have no real understanding of how people behave in complex and important social situations.'
   To what extent can the use of deception be justified in social influence research studies?
2 'Researchers' only responsibility is the protection of their participants.'
   Discuss this view of the role of psychologists as investigators of human behaviour and experience, using examples from different areas of psychology.
3 Describe and evaluate arguments for and against the use of non-human animals in psychological research.
4 Discuss ethical issues faced by clinical psychologists and other agents of change.

Web addresses

http://www.bps/org.uk.charter/codofcon.htm

http://www.psy.herts.ac.uk/Docs/EthicalGuidelines.html

http://www.informin.co.uk/LM/LM119/LM119_AnimalExp. html

http://altweb.jhsph.edu/

http://www.aalas.org

http://www.apa.org/science/anguide.html

Further reading

Brown, L. (1997) 'Ethics in Psychology: Cui Bono?' In D. Fox & I. Prilleltensky (Eds) *Critical Psychology: An Introduction.* London: Sage. A view of ethics from a feminist perspective. Also relevant to Chapter 3.

Wise, R. (2000) *Rattling the Cage: Towards Legal Rights for Animals.* London: Profile Books. A serious argument by the Professor of Law at Harvard and other US universities.

Chapter 49

Free Will and Determinism, and Reductionism

Introduction and overview

As we saw in Chapter 3, any discussion of psychology's scientific status raises fundamental questions about the nature of the person or, at least, the image of the person that underlies major psychological theories (see Chapter 2), and which is implicit in much of the study of human behaviour. This chapter discusses two of these fundamental questions.

One question, debated by Western philosophers for centuries, is whether we choose to act as we do, or whether behaviours are caused by influences beyond our control (*free will* versus *determinism*). The other, which has a shorter history and is debated by philosophers of science, concerns the validity of attempts to explain complex wholes in terms of their constituent parts (*reductionism*). One example of this is the relationship between the mind (or consciousness) and the brain (the 'mind–body problem').

Free will and determinism

What is free will?

One way of approaching this question is to consider examples of behaviour where 'free will' (however defined) is clearly absent.

CASE STUDY 49.1

Tourette's disorder

Tim is 14 and displays a variety of twitches and tics. His head sometimes jerks and he often blinks and grimaces. Occasionally, he blurts out words, usually vulgarities. He doesn't mean to do it and is embarrassed by it, but he cannot control it. Because of his strange behaviour, most other children avoid him. His isolation and embarrassment are interfering with his social development. Tim suffers from a rare condition called Tourette's disorder.

(From Holmes, 1994)

Ask yourself ...

- What specific aspects of Tim's disorder are relevant to understanding the concept of 'free will'? If you think Tim lacks free will, what led you to this conclusion?
- Think of other behaviours (normal or abnormal) that demonstrate a lack of free will.

Intuition tells us that people have the ability to choose their own courses of action, determine their behaviour and, to this extent, they have *free will*. Simultaneously, though, this freedom is exercised only within certain physical, political, sociological and other environmental constraints. However, the positivistic, mechanistic nature of scientific psychology (see Chapter 3) implies that behaviour is *determined* by external (or internal) events or stimuli, and that people are passive responders. To this extent, people *aren't* free. *Determinism* also implies that behaviour occurs in a regular, orderly manner which (in principle) is totally predictable. For Taylor (1963), determinism maintains that:

> 'In the case of everything that exists, there are antecedent conditions, known or unknown, given which that thing could not be other than it is ... More loosely, it says that everything, including every cause, is the effect of some cause or causes; or that everything is not only determinate but causally determined'.

'Everything that exists' includes people and their thoughts and behaviours, so a 'strict determinist' believes that thought and behaviours are no different from (other) 'things' or events in the world. However, this begs the question of whether thoughts and behaviours are the same *kind of thing* or *event* as, say, chemical reactions in a test tube, or neurons firing in the brain. We don't usually ask if the chemicals 'agreed' to combine in a certain way, or if the neurons 'decided' to fire. Unless we were trying to be witty, we'd be guilty of *anthropomorphism* (attributing human abilities and characteristics to non-humans or things).

*This painting by Gustave Dore of the Old Testament story of Lot's wife being turned to stone (*The Rescue of Lot*) illustrates the human capacity for free will*

It's only *people* who can agree and make decisions. These abilities and capacities form part of our concept of a person, which, in turn, forms an essential part of 'everyday' or commonsense psychology (see Chapter 1). Agreeing and deciding are precisely the kinds of things we do *with our minds* (they're mental processes or events), and to be able to agree and make decisions, it's necessary to 'have a mind'. So, free will implies having a mind. However, having a mind *doesn't* imply free will: it's possible that decisions and so on are themselves *caused* (determined), even though they seem to be freely chosen.

Ask yourself ...

- Try to explain what someone means when s/he says: 'I had no choice but to ...' or 'You leave me no choice ...'. Can you interpret this in a way that's consistent with a belief in free will?

Different meanings of 'free will'

One of the difficulties with the free will versus determinism debate is the ambiguity of the concepts involved.

Having a choice

If we have choice, then we could behave differently given the same circumstances. This contrasts sharply with a common definition of determinism, namely that things could only have happened as they did, given everything that happened previously.

Not being coerced or constrained

If someone puts a loaded gun to your head and tells you to do something, your behaviour is clearly not free: you've been *forced* to act this way. This is usually where the philosophical debate about 'free will' begins, and is related to what James (1890) called *soft determinism* (see page 725).

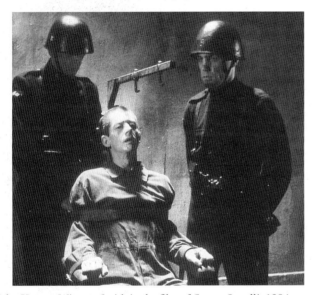

John Hurt as Winston Smith in the film of George Orwell's 1984

Voluntary behaviour

If 'involuntary' conveys reflex behaviour (such as the eye-blink response to a puff of air directed at the eye), then 'voluntary' implies 'free' (the behaviour isn't automatic). By definition, most behaviour (human and non-human) *isn't* reflex, nor is it usually the result of coercion. So is most behaviour free?

Box 49.1	Evidence for the distinction between voluntary and involuntary behaviour

Penfield's (1947) classic experiments involved stimulating the cortex of patients about to undergo brain surgery (see Chapter 4, page 49). Even though the cortical area being stimulated was the same as that which is involved when we normally ('voluntarily') move our limbs, patients reported feeling that their arms and legs were being moved passively, quite a different experience from initiating the movement themselves. This demonstrates that the subjective experience (*phenomenology*) of the voluntary movement of one's limbs cannot be reduced to the stimulation of the appropriate brain region (otherwise Penfield's patients shouldn't have reported a difference). Doing things voluntarily simply *feels* different from the same things 'just happening'.

Similarly, Delgado (1969) stimulated a part of the primary motor area in a patient's *left* hemisphere, causing the patient to form a clenched fist with his *right* hand. When asked to try to keep his fingers still during the next stimulation, the patient couldn't do it and commented, 'I guess, Doctor, that your electricity is stronger than my will'.

These examples support the claim that having free will is an undeniable part of our subjective experience of ourselves as people. The sense of self is most acute (and important and real for us) where moral decisions and feelings of responsibility for past actions are involved (Koestler, 1967). See text and Box 49.2 (page 724) for further discussion of free will and moral responsibility.

One demonstration of people's belief in their free will is *psychological reactance* (Brehm, 1966; Brehm & Brehm, 1981: see Chapter 9). A common response to the feeling that our freedom is being threatened is the attempt to regain or reassert it, which is related to the need to be free from others' controls and restrictions, to determine our own actions, and not be dictated to. A good deal of contrary (resistant) behaviour, otherwise known as 'bloody-mindedness' ('Don't tell me what to do!') seems to reflect this process (Carver & Scheier, 1992).

Similar to this need to feel free from others' control is *intrinsic motivation* or *self-determination* (Deci, 1980; Deci & Ryan, 1987). This refers to people's intrinsic interest in things, such that they don't need to be offered extrinsic incentives for doing them. Engaging in such activities is motivated by the desire for competence and self-determination.

So what happens if someone is offered an extrinsic reward for doing something which is already interesting and enjoyable in itself? Lepper *et al.* (1973) found that the activity loses its intrinsic appeal, and motivation is reduced (*the paradox of reward*). This has implications for accounts of moral development based on learning theory principles, especially operant conditioning (see Chapters 11 and 35).

Ask yourself ...

- How could you account for the 'paradox of reward' in terms of attributional principles, specifically, internal and external causes? (See Chapter 23.)

Deliberate control

Norman & Shallice (1986) define divided attention as an upper limit to the amount of processing that can be performed on incoming information at any one time. They propose three levels of functioning, namely *fully automatic processing*, *partially automatic processing*, and *deliberate control* (see Chapter 13, page 194). Deliberate control corresponds to free will.

Driving a car is a sensory–motor skill, performed by experienced drivers more-or-less automatically. It doesn't require deliberate, conscious control, unless some unexpected event disrupts the performance (such as putting your foot on the brake when there's an obstacle ahead: this is a 'rule of the game'). However, on an icy road this can be risky, since the steering wheel has a different 'feel' and the whole driving strategy must be changed. After doing it several times, this too may become a semi-automatic routine:

'But let a little dog amble across the icy road in front of the driver, and he will have to make a 'top-level decision' whether to slam down the brake, risking the safety of his passengers, or run over the dog. And if, instead of a dog, the jaywalker is a child, he will probably resort to the brake, whatever the outcome. It is at this level, when the pros and cons are equally balanced, that the subjective experience of freedom and moral responsibility arises'. (Koestler, 1967)

As we move downwards from conscious control, the subjective experience of freedom diminishes. According to Koestler:

'Habit is the enemy of freedom ... Machines cannot become like men, but men can become like machines'.

Koestler also maintains that the second enemy of freedom is very powerful (especially negative) emotion:

'When [emotions] are aroused, the control of decisions is taken over by those primitive levels of the hierarchy which the Victorians called "the Beast in us" and which are in fact correlated to phylogenetically older structures in the nervous system'.

The arousal of these structures results in 'diminished responsibility' and 'I couldn't help it' (Koestler, 1967).

Ask yourself ...

- In Koestler's quote above, (a) what does 'phylogenetically older structures' mean? and (b) what are the major 'primitive levels of the hierarchy' correlated with these structures? (See Chapter 4, pages 55–56.)

Why are psychologists interested in the concept of free will?

As noted in the *Introduction and overview*, the philosophical debate about free will and determinism is centuries old. It can be traced back at least to the French philosopher Descartes (1596–1650), whose ideas had a great influence on both science in general and psychology in particular (see Chapter 3). For much of its history as a separate, scientific discipline, psychology has operated as if there were no difference between natural, physical phenomena and human thought and behaviour (see Chapter 3, page 30).

During the period 1913–1956, psychology (at least in the USA) was dominated by behaviourism, Skinner being particularly influential. Skinner's beliefs about the influence of mental phenomena on behaviour, and those concerning free will, are discussed on pages 726–727.

Ask yourself ...

- Try to identify some (other) ways in which the issue of free will is relevant to psychological theory and practice. For example, how does the notion of free will relate to criteria for defining and diagnosing mental disorders? (See Chapter 43.)

Free will and psychological abnormality

Definitions of abnormality, and the diagnosis and treatment of mental disorders, often involve implicit or explicit judgements about free will and determinism. In a general sense, mental disorders can be seen as the partial or complete breakdown of the control people normally have over their thoughts, emotions and behaviours. For example, *compulsive* behaviour is, by definition, behaviour which a person cannot help but do: s/he is 'compelled' to do it. People are *attacked* by panic, *obsessed* by thoughts of germs, or become the *victims* of thoughts which are inserted into their mind from outside and are under external influence (see Chapter 44). In all these examples, things are happening to, or being done to, the individual (instead of the individual doing them), both from their own perspective and that of a psychologist or psychiatrist.

Being judged to have lost control (possession of which is usually thought of as a major feature of normality), either temporarily or permanently, is a legally acceptable defence in cases of criminal offences.

Box 49.2 Forensic psychiatry, diminished responsibility and the law

Forensic psychiatry deals with assessment and treatment of mentally disturbed offenders (see Chapter 46). The 1983 Mental Health Act has several clauses providing for the compulsory detention of prisoners (either while awaiting trial or as part of their sentences) in hospital. Psychiatrists, as expert witnesses, can play important roles in advising the Court about:

- fitness to plead;
- mental state at the time of the offence;
- diminished responsibility.

The defence of *diminished responsibility* (for murder) was introduced in England and Wales in the 1957 Homicide Act, largely replacing the plea of 'not guilty by reason of insanity', which was based on the 'McNaughton Rules' of 1843.

If accepted, there's no trial and a sentence of manslaughter is passed. If not accepted, a trial is held and the jury must decide whether the accused (at the time the crime was committed) was suffering from an abnormality of mind, and if so, whether it was such as to substantially impair his/her responsibility.

Peter Sutcliffe, the 'Yorkshire Ripper', was found guilty of the murder of 13 women and the attempted murder of seven others, despite his defence that he heard God's voice telling him to 'get rid' of prostitutes. In finding him guilty of murder, the jury didn't necessarily reject the defence's argument that he was suffering from paranoid schizophrenia, only that it didn't constitute a mental abnormality of sufficient degree to substantially impair responsibility for his acts. Sutcliffe was sentenced to 20 concurrent terms of life imprisonment, which he served initially in an ordinary prison before being sent to Broadmoor Special Hospital.

(Based on Gelder *et al.*, 1989, and Prins, 1995)

Free will and moral accountability

Underlying the whole question of legal (and moral) responsibility is the presupposition that people are, at least some of the time, able to control their behaviours and choose between different courses of action. How else could we ever be held responsible for any of our actions? In most everyday situations and interactions, we attribute responsibility, both to ourselves and others, unless we have reason to doubt it. According to Flanagan (1984):

'It seems silly to have any expectations about how people ought to act, if everything we do is the result of some inexorable causal chain which began millennia ago. "Ought", after all, seems to imply "can", therefore, by employing a moral vocabulary filled with words like "ought" and "should", we assume that humans are capable of rising above the causal pressures presented by the material world, and, in assuming this we appear to be operating with some conception of freedom, some notion of free will'.

Free will as an issue in major psychological theories

Most major theorists in psychology have addressed the issue of free will and determinism, including James, Freud, Skinner, and Rogers.

James and soft determinism

As we saw in Chapter 1, James pioneered psychology as a separate, scientific discipline. In *The Principles of Psychology* (1890), he devoted a whole chapter to the 'will', which he related to attention:

'The most essential achievement of the will ... when it is most "voluntary" is to attend to a different object and hold it fast before the mind ... Effort of attention is thus the essential phenomenon of will'.

For James, there was a conflict. Belief in determinism seemed to fit best with the scientific view of the world, while belief in free will seemed to be required by our social, moral, political, and legal practices, as well as by our personal, subjective experience (see above). His solution to this conflict was two-fold.

First, he distinguished between the scientific and non-scientific worlds. Psychology as a science could only progress by assuming determinism, but this doesn't mean that belief in free will must be abandoned in other contexts. So, scientific explanation isn't the only useful kind of explanation.

Second, he drew a further distinction between *soft* and *hard* determinism. According to *soft determinism*, the question of free will depends on the type(s) of cause(s) our behaviour has, not whether it's caused or not caused (the opposite of 'not caused' is 'random', not 'free'). If our actions have, as their immediate (proximate) cause, processing by a system such as *conscious mental life* (CML, which includes consciousness, purposefulness, personality and personal continuity), then they count as free, rational, voluntary, purposive actions.

According to *hard determinism*, CML is itself caused, so that the immediate causes are only part of the total causal chain which results in the behaviour we're trying to explain. Therefore, as long as our behaviour is caused at all, there's no sense in which we can be described as acting freely.

Freud and psychic determinism

Although in most respects their ideas about human behaviour are diametrically opposed, Freud and Skinner shared the fundamental belief that free will is an illusion. However, in keeping with their theories as a whole, their reasons are radically different.

Ask yourself ...

- Based on what you already know about Freud's psychoanalytic theory, try to identify those parts which are most relevant to his rejection of free will.

According to Strachey (1962):

'Behind all of Freud's work ... we should posit his belief in the universal validity of the law of determinism ... Freud extended the belief (derived from physical phenomena) uncompromisingly to the field of mental phenomena'.

Similarly, Sulloway (1979) maintains that all of Freud's work in science (and Freud saw himself very much as a scientist) was characterised by an abiding faith in the notion that all vital phenomena, including psychical (psychological) ones, are rigidly and lawfully determined by the principle of cause and effect. One major example of this was the extreme importance he attached to the technique of *free association*.

Box 49.3 How 'free' is Freud's 'free association'?

'Free association' is a misleading translation of the German '*freier Einfall*', which conveys much more accurately the intended impression of an uncontrollable 'intrusion' ('*Einfall*') by preconscious ideas into conscious thinking. In turn, this preconscious material reflects unconscious ideas, wishes and memories (what Freud was really interested in), since here lie the principal cause(s) of neurotic problems.

It's a great irony that 'free' association should refer to a technique used in psychoanalysis meant to reveal the *unconscious* causes of behaviour (see Chapter 45, page 668). It's because the causes of our thoughts, actions and supposed choices are unconscious (mostly *actively repressed*), that we think we're free. Freud's application of this general philosophical belief in causation to mental phenomena is called *psychic determinism* (see Chapter 42, page 624).

(Based on Sulloway, 1979)

For Freud, part of what 'psychic determinism' conveyed was that in the universe of the mind, there are no 'accidents'. No matter how apparently random or irrational behaviour may be (such as 'parapraxes' or 'Freudian slips'), unconscious causes can always account for them, and this also applies to hysterical symptoms and dreams. As Gay (1988) states, 'Freud's theory of the mind is ... strictly and frankly deterministic'. However:

- Freud accepted that true accidents, in the sense of forces beyond the victim's control (e.g. being struck by lightning), can and do occur, and aren't unconsciously caused by the victim.
- One of the aims of psychoanalysis is to 'give the patient's ego *freedom* to decide one way or another' (Freud, quoted in Gay, 1988), so therapy rests on the belief that people can

change. However, Freud saw the extent of possible change as being very limited (see Box 45.5, page 669).

■ One aspect of psychic determinism is *overdetermination*; that is, much of our behaviour has *multiple* causes, both conscious and unconscious. So, although our conscious choices, decisions and intentions may genuinely influence behaviour, they never tell the whole story (see Chapter 42, page 624).

■ Despite never having predicted in advance what choice or decision a patient would make, Freud maintained that these aren't arbitrary, and can be understood as revealing personality characteristics (Rycroft, 1966). What Freud often did was to explain his patients' choices, neurotic symptoms, and so on not in terms of causes (the *scientific* argument), but by trying to make sense of them and give them meaning (the *semantic* argument). Indeed, the latter is supported by the title of, arguably, his greatest book, *The Interpretation of Dreams* (1900) (as opposed to *The 'Cause' of Dreams*).

Skinner and the illusion of free will

Like Freud, Skinner sees free will as an illusion. However, while Freud focused on 'the mind', especially unconscious thoughts, wishes, and memories, Skinner's *radical behaviourism* eliminates all reference to mental or private states as part of the explanation of behaviour (including theories like Freud's!).

Although Skinner doesn't deny that pain and other internal states exist, they have no 'causal teeth' and hence no part to play in scientific explanations of (human) behaviour (Garrett, 1996). Free will (and other 'explanatory fictions') cannot be defined or measured objectively, nor are they needed for successful prediction and control of behaviour (for Skinner, the primary aims of a *science* of behaviour). It's only because the causes of human behaviour are often hidden from us in the environment, that the myth or illusion of free will survives.

Ask yourself ...

- Given what you know about Skinner's theory of operant conditioning and his 'analysis of behaviour', try to identify the causes of human behaviour which he believes are often hidden from us in the environment. (See Chapters 2 and 11.)

Skinner argues that when what we do is dictated by force or punishment, or by their threat (negative reinforcement), it's obvious to everyone that we're not acting freely. For example, when the possibility of prison stops us committing crimes, there's clearly no choice involved, because we know what the environmental causes of our behaviour are. Similarly, it may sometimes be very obvious which positive reinforcers are shaping behaviour (a bonus for working over-time, for example).

However, most of the time we're unaware of environmental causes, and it looks (and feels) as if we're behaving freely. Yet all this means is that we're free of punishments or negative reinforcement, and behaviour is still determined by the pursuit of things that have been positively reinforced in the past.

When we perceive others as behaving freely, we're simply unaware of their reinforcement histories (Fancher, 1996).

Box 49.4 The freedom myth and the rejection of punishment

In *Beyond Freedom and Dignity*, Skinner (1971) argued that the notion of 'autonomous man', upon which so many of Western society's assumptions are based, is both false and has many harmful consequences. In particular, the assumption that people are free requires that they're constantly exposed to punishment and its threat as a negative reinforcer (Fancher, 1996).

Ask yourself ...

- What *ethical* issues are raised by Skinner's advocacy of a utopian society like *Walden Two*?
- In what ways does this Utopia reflect Skinner's beliefs about the aims of a scientific psychology?

Skinner and moral responsibility

Clearly, Skinner's belief that free will is an illusion conflicts with the need to attribute people with free will if we're to hold them (and ourselves) morally (and legally) responsible for their behaviour. Skinner (1971) himself acknowledges that freedom and dignity are:

> ' ... essential to practices in which a person is held responsible for his conduct and given credit for his achievements'.

A makeshift game of roulette on the streets of Dili, East Timor. Where gambling is such a part of the culture, are individuals responsible for their behaviour?

However, Skinner equates 'good' and 'bad' with 'beneficial to others' (what's rewarded) and 'harmful to others' (what's punished) respectively, thus removing morality from human behaviour. For Skinner, 'oughts' aren't 'moral imperatives': they reflect practical, rather than moral, guidelines and rules. (Morea, 1990).

According to Garrett (1996), if we're rational, thinking creatures, capable of assessing ethical rules and principles, and evaluating the goodness of our lives, then we have all the freedom needed to reasonably prefer democratic to non- (or anti-) democratic forms of government (as expressed in *Walden Two* and *Beyond Freedom and Dignity*).

A further consequence of Skinner's rejection of the notion of 'autonomous man' is what Ringen (1996) calls *the behaviour therapist's dilemma*, which is closely related to some of the most fundamental ethical issues faced by psychologists as agents of change (see Chapter 48, pages 717–719).

Rogers, freedom and the fully functioning person

As we saw in Chapter 2, Rogers was perhaps the most influential *humanistic, phenomenological* psychologist. As such, he stressed the process of self-actualisation and the necessity of adopting the other person's perspective if we're to understand that person, and in particular, his/ her self-concept.

Understanding the self-concept is also central to Rogers' client-centred therapy (see Chapters 42 and 45). His experience as a therapist convinced him that real change does occur in therapy: people choose to see themselves and their life situations differently. Therapy and life are about free human beings struggling to become more free. Personal experience is important, but it doesn't imprison us. How we react to our experience is something we ourselves choose and decide (Morea, 1990).

Ask yourself ...

- According to Rogers, in what ways are individuals prevented from recognising their true feelings and behaviour?
- In what respect is Rogers' view of human beings a more optimistic one than, say, Freud's?

Rogers' deep and lasting trust in human nature didn't, however, blind him to the reality of evil behaviour:

'In my experience, every person has the capacity for evil behaviour. I, and others, have had murderous and cruel impulses ... feelings of anger and rage, desires to impose our wills on others ... Whether I ... will translate these impulses into behaviour depends ... on two elements: social conditioning and voluntary choice'. (Rogers, 1982, cited in Thorne, 1992)

By making the distinction between 'human nature' and behaviour, Rogers retains his optimistic view of human beings. However, this didn't exclude altogether a deterministic element in his later writings. In *Freedom to Learn for the eighties* (1983), he states that it's becoming clear from science that human beings are complex machines and not free, and determinism 'is the foundation stone of present-day science'. So how can this be reconciled with self-actualisation, psychological growth, and the freedom to choose?

One proposed solution is in the form of a version of soft determinism. Unlike neurotic and incongruent people whose defensiveness forces them to act in ways they'd prefer not to, the healthy, fully functioning person:

' ... not only experiences, but utilises, the most absolute freedom when he spontaneously, freely and voluntarily chooses and wills that which is absolutely determined'.

He seemed to mean that at the same time we choose our behaviour, it is also being determined by all the relevant conditions that exist. The open, responsive (fully-functioning) person is fully aware of all that's going on inside, and has an accurate grasp of existing external factors. This individual is free, but s/he will take a particular course of action: in the presence of all available stimuli there are certain behaviours that are most productive from both subjective and objective points of view. In this sense, there's no contradiction between free will and determinism: they coincide (Nye, 2000).

Reductionism

What is reductionism?

Together with positivism, mechanism, determinism, and empiricism, reductionism represents part of 'classical' science (see Chapter 3). Luria (1987) traces the origins of reductionism to the mid-nineteenth-century view within biology that an organism is a complex of organs, and the organs are complexes of cells. To explain the basic laws of the living organism, we have to study as carefully as possible the features of separate cells.

From its biological origins, reductionism was extended to science in general. For example, the properties of a protein molecule could be uniquely determined or predicted in terms of properties of the electrons or protons making up its atoms. Consistent with this view is Garnham's (1991) definition of reductionism as:

' ... the idea that psychological explanations can be replaced by explanations in terms of brain functioning or even in terms of physics and chemistry'.

Although reductionism's ultimate aim (according to its supporters) is to account for all phenomena in terms of microphysics, *any* attempt to explain something in terms of its components or constituent parts may be thought of as reductionist. A useful definition, which is consistent with this broader view, is that of Rose *et al.* (1984), for whom reductionism is:

'*... the name given to a set of general methods and modes of explanation both of the world of physical objects and of human societies. Broadly, reductionists try to explain the properties of complex wholes – molecules, say, or societies – in terms of the units of which those molecules or societies are composed*'.

Rose (1997) identifies four major types of reductionism (or different meanings of the term).

Box 49.6 Different meanings of reductionism

- **Reductionism as methodology:** This refers to the attempt to isolate variables in the laboratory in order to simplify the living world's enormous complexity, flux and multitude of interacting processes. This is the basis of the experiment, which reflects natural science's attempt to identify cause-and-effect relationships (see Chapter 3).
- **Theory reduction:** This refers to science's aim to capture as much of the world in as few laws or principles as possible. It's related to philosophical reductionism.
- **Philosophical reductionism:** This refers to the belief that because science is unitary, and because physics is the most fundamental of the sciences, ultimately all currently separate disciplines (including psychology) will be 'reduced' to physics (see the quotes from Garnham, 1991, above, and Crick, 1994, page 729).
- **Reductionism as ideology:** This refers to the very marked tendency in recent years to identify genes responsible for a whole range of complex human behaviours, including stress, anxiety, depression, personality, homosexuality, intelligence, alcoholism, criminality and violence.

(Based on Rose, 1997)

Rose calls the claim that there's a direct causal link between genes and behaviour, *neurogenetic determinism*. It involves a sequence of (false) assumptions and arguments, one of which is the dichotomy between genetic and environmental causes (or nature and nurture: see Chapter 50).

Ask yourself ...

- There are many examples of psychological theories and concepts which fit either or both of Garnham's and Rose *et al.*'s definitions. These can be found in all areas of psychology, but below are a few of the more 'obvious' examples. For each one, try to explain (a) why the theory or concept is reductionist, and (b) what the strengths and/or weaknesses of such an approach are.

  i According to *structuralism* (e.g. Wundt), perception is simply a series of sensations (see Chapter 3).
  ii According to Watson's *peripheralism*, thought consists of tiny movements of the vocal chords (see Chapter 18).

  iii Intelligence is a person's performance on a standardised intelligence test (his/her IQ score: see Chapter 41).
  iv Psychological sex differences are caused by biological factors (such as hormones: see Chapter 36).
  v According to Freud, personality development involves progress through a series of *psychosexual* stages (see Chapter 35).
  vi Schizophrenia is caused by an excess of the neurotransmitter, dopamine (see Chapter 44).
  vii According to Adorno *et al.*, anti-semitism (and other forms of racism) are symptomatic of the authoritarian personality (see Chapter 25).

The mind–body problem

Perhaps the oldest and most frequently debated example of reductionism is the *mind–body problem* (or the *problem of mind and brain*). Originally a philosophical issue, it continues to be discussed, often passionately, by neurophysiologists, biologists, neuropsychologists and psychologists in general.

While it's generally agreed that the mind (or consciousness) is a property of human beings (as is walking upright on two legs), and that without the human brain there'd be no consciousness, a 'problem' remains.

Box 49.7 The problem of the mind–brain relationship

- How can two 'things' be related when one of them is physical (the brain has size, weight, shape, density, and exists in space and time) and the other apparently lacks all these characteristics?
- How can something non-physical/non-material (the mind) influence or produce changes in something physical (the brain/body)?
- The 'classic' example given by philosophers to illustrate the problem is the act of deciding to lift one's arm. (This example also illustrates the exercise of [free] will: see text.) From a strictly scientific perspective, this kind of causation should be impossible, and science (including psychology and neurophysiology) has traditionally rejected any brand of *philosophical dualism*; that is, the belief in the existence of two essentially different kinds of 'substance', the physical body and the non-physical mind (see Box 49.8, page 729).

From an evolutionary perspective, could consciousness have equipped human beings with survival value unless it had causal properties (Gregory, 1981); that is, unless it could actually bring about changes in behaviour? Our subjective experiences tell us that our minds do affect behaviour, and that consciousness does have causal properties (just try lifting your arm). However, many philosophers and scientists from various disciplines haven't always shared the layperson's common-sense understanding.

While there are many theories of the mind–brain relationship, most aren't strictly relevant to the debate about reductionism. Box 49.8 and Figure 49.1 (see page 729) summarise most of the major theories, but emphasis will be given to reductionist approaches, especially as they impinge on psychological theories.

Box 49.8 **Some major theories of the mind–brain relationship**

- Theories fall into two main categories: *dualism* (which distinguishes between mind and brain), and *monism* (which claims that only mind or matter is real).
- According to Descartes' seventeenth-century dualist theory (which first introduced the mind–body problem into philosophy), the mind can influence the brain, but not vice versa. While *epiphenomenology* sees the mind as a kind of by-product of the brain (the mind has no influence on the brain), *interactionism* sees the influence as two-way.
- *Psychophysical parallelists* are dualists who believe that there's no mind–brain interaction at all: mental and neural events are merely perfectly synchronised or correlated.
- According to *mentalism/idealism*, only mental phenomena are real. *Phenomenological* theories, such as that of Rogers, and *constructionist* explanations of behaviour, have a mentalist 'flavour'.
- Most monist theories take one or other form of *materialism*.
- The *peripheralist* version of materialism is illustrated by Skinner's *radical behaviourism* (see Chapter 2). During the 1930s, Skinner denied the existence of mental phenomena (as had Watson, the founder of behaviourism). However, from 1945 he began to adopt a less extreme view, recognising their existence, but defining them as *covert/internal actions*, subject to the same laws of conditioning as overt behavioural events. This is a form of reductionism.
- *Centralist materialism* (or *mind–brain identity theory*) identifies mental processes with purely physical processes in the central nervous system. While it's logically possible that there might be separate, mental, non-physical phenomena, it just turns out that, as a matter of fact, mental states are identical with physical states of the brain. We are, simply, very complicated physico-chemical mechanisms.
- *Eliminative materialism* represents an extreme reductionist form of (centralist) materialism: see text below.

(Based on Flanagan, 1984; Gross, 1995, and Teichman, 1988)

Ask yourself ...

- Using your knowledge of biopsychology, try to relate the examples below to the theories outlined in Box 49.8 and Figure 49.1. Specifically, do these examples involve interactions between mind and brain, and, if so, in what direction is the influence taking place?
- **a** the effects of psychoactive drugs (see Chapters 8 and 45);
- **b** electrical stimulation of the brain (see Chapter 4);
- **c** Sperry's study of split-brain patients (see Chapter 4);
- **d** stress (see Chapter 12);
- **e** placebo effects (see Chapter 45).

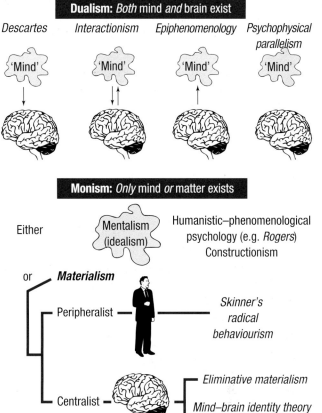

Figure 49.1 *An outline of the major theories of the mind–brain relationship*

Reductionist theories of the mind–brain relationship

As Box 49.8 shows, *eliminative materialism* is an extreme form of reductionist materialism. What makes it reductionist is the attempt to replace a psychological account of behaviour with an account in terms of neurophysiology. An example of this approach is Crick's (1994) *The Astonishing Hypothesis: The Scientific Search for the Soul*. According to Crick:

> '*You, your joys and your sorrows, your memories and your ambitions, your sense of personality and free will, are in fact no more than the behaviour of a vast assembly of nerve cells and their associated molecules*'.

But is this a valid equation to make? According to Smith (1994), the mind and brain problem is radically different from other cases of *contingent identity* (identical as a matter of fact) with which it's usually compared, such as 'a gene is a section of the DNA molecule'. What's different is reductionism, and the related issue of exactly what's meant by *identity*.

Box 49.9 **Different meanings of 'identity' relevant to the mind–brain relationship**

While it's generally agreed that we cannot have a mind without a brain, mind states and brain states aren't systematically correlated, and the neurophysiological and neurological evidence points towards *token identity.* For example, we cannot just assume that the same neurophysiological mechanisms will be used by two different people both engaged in the 'same' activity of reading (Broadbent, 1981). There are many ways that 'the brain' can perform the same task.

But it's precisely this kind of systematic correlation that mind–brain identity has been taken to imply, whereby whenever a mind state of a certain type occurs, a brain state of a certain type occurs (*type identity*). Token identity means that there must always be a place for an autonomous psychological account of human thought and action.

(Based on Harré *et al.*, 1985)

According to Penrose (1990), there's a built-in *indeterminacy* in the way individual neurons and their synaptic connections work (their responses are inherently unpredictable). Yet, despite this unpredictability at the level of the individual units or components, the system as a whole is predictable. The 'nervous system' (or subsystems within it) doesn't operate randomly, but in a highly organised, structured way.

Consciousness (see Chapter 7), intelligence (Chapter 41), and memory (Chapter 17) are properties of the brain as a system, *not* properties of the individual units, and they couldn't possibly be predicted from analysing the units. Instead, they 'emerge' from interactions between the units that compose the system (and so are called *emergent properties*). The whole is greater than the sum of its parts (Rose, 1997: see Chapter 15).

Can you be a materialist without being a reductionist?

According to Rose (1992):

> *'The mind is never replaced by the brain. Instead we have two distinct and legitimate languages, each describing the same unitary phenomena of the material world'.*

Rose speaks as a materialist and an *anti-reductionist*, who believes that we should learn how to translate between mind language and brain language (although this may be impossibly difficult: see Box 49.6). While most materialists are also reductionists, and vice versa, this isn't necessarily so. Freud, for example, was a materialist who believed that no single scientific vocabulary (such as anatomy) could adequately describe (let alone explain) all facets of the material world. He believed in the *autonomy of psychological explanation*.

The fact that there are different 'languages' for describing minds and brains (or different *levels of description* or *universes of discourse*) relates to the question of the relevance of knowing, say, what's going on inside our brains when we think or are aware. For Eiser (1994):

> *'The firing of neurons stands to thought in the same relation as my walking across the room (etc.) stands to my getting some coffee. It is absolutely essential in a causal or physical sense, and absolutely superfluous ... to the logic of the higher-order description. In short, I can accept that it happens, and then happily ignore it'.*

This explains how it's possible to be simultaneously a materialist (the brain is necessarily implicated in everything we do

and the mind doesn't represent a different kind of reality) *and* an anti-reductionist (we can describe and explain our thinking without having to 'bring my brain into it'). Two separate levels of description are involved.

Conclusions

Given psychology's intellectual and historical roots in philosophy and natural science, it's hardly surprising that psychological theories have contributed to the debate about free will versus determinism, and reductionism. The possession of free will is a fundamental aspect of our common sense concept of a person. Therefore, any theory calling itself psychological must have something to say about this issue.

Equally, belief (or not) in the independence of psychological from neurophysiological explanations of behaviour, is crucial to the survival of psychology itself as a separate discipline. According to Hegarty (2000), *psychoneuroimmunology* (which we discussed in Chapter 12 in relation to stress) offers a:

> *'... middle ground for mind–body monists and dualists to meet upon. Scientific research has given us insight into the complex realm of psychophysiology – the interface ... between body and mind and in which the emotions figure large ...'.*

CHAPTER SUMMARY

- Our intuitive belief in **free will** conflicts with the scientific belief in **determinism**. While free will implies having a mind, the things we do with our minds may themselves be determined.

- Free will is an ambiguous concept and can denote having a choice, not being coerced or constrained, voluntary behaviour, and deliberate control. The more automatic our behaviours, the weaker our subjective experience of freedom becomes.

- Stimulation of the brains of conscious patients' supports the view that free will is part of our experience of being a person. This is demonstrated by **psychological reactance** and **intrinsic motivation/self-determination**.

- Definitions of abnormality, and the diagnosis/treatment of mental disorders, often involve judgements about free will. **Diminished responsibility** is a legally acceptable defence (for murder).

- James distinguished between **soft** and **hard determinism**, the former allowing **conscious mental life** to be the immediate cause of behaviour.

- Freud extended the law of determinism to mental phenomena (**psychic determinism**). His concept of **overdetermination** allows the conscious mind a role in influencing behaviour, and he often tried to interpret the **meaning** of patients' thoughts and behaviours (rather than looking for causes).

- Skinner's radical behaviourism involves a rejection of **explanatory fictions**, such as free will and other mentalistic terms. The illusion of free will survives because the environmental causes of behaviour are often hidden from us.

- Rogers stressed self-actualisation, psychological growth and the freedom to choose. But he also argued that science shows people to be complex machines and not free. The fully functioning person chooses to act the way s/he must.

- Although the ultimate aim of **reductionism** is to account for all phenomena (including psychological) in terms of microphysics, **any** attempt to explain something in terms of its components is reductionist.

- Rose identifies **reductionism as methodology, theory reduction, philosophical reductionism** and **reductionism as ideology** (**neurogenetic determinism**).

- From a strictly scientific perspective, it should be impossible for a non-physical mind to influence the physical brain. However, from an evolutionary perspective, consciousness should be able to produce behaviour change.

- Theories of the mind–brain relationship are either **dualist** or **monist**. Dualist theories include Descartes' original dualism, **epiphenomenology**, **interactionism**, and **psychophysical parallelism**.

- Monist theories include **mentalism/idealism, peripheralist materialism** (such as Skinner's radical behaviourism) and **centralist materialism/mind–brain identity theory**.

- Skinner's definition of mental phenomena as covert/internal actions is reductionist, as is **eliminative materialism**. The latter confuses **type** with **token identity**.

- **Emergent properties** (such as intelligence and consciousness) reflect the activity of the brain **as a system**, and couldn't possibly be predicted from analysis of its components.

- While most materialists are also reductionists, some argue that psychology and neurophysiology constitute distinct **levels of description/universes of discourse**, which cannot replace each other. Freud, for example, believed in the **autonomy of psychological explanation**.

Self-assessment questions

1 Discuss the free will and determinism debate in relation to **two** theoretical approaches (e.g. those of Freud, Skinner).

2 Describe and evaluate arguments for and against reductionism as a form of explanation, using examples from psychological theory and research studies.

Web addresses

http://www.determinism.net

http://www.siu.edu/~philos/faculty/Manfedi/intro/freedom.html

http://www.ptproject.ilstu.edu/pt/fwdl.htm

http://cswww.essex.ac.uk/Research/FSS/MISC/reduction.html

Further reading

Rose, S. (1997) *Lifelines: Biology, Freedom, Determinism.* Harmondsworth: Penguin Books. A discussion of determinism and reductionism in the context of modern evolutionary theory, written by a leading antireductionist biologist.

Valentine, E.R. (1992) *Conceptual Issues in Psychology* (2nd edition). London: Routledge. Chapters on free will and determinism, the mind–body problem, consciousness and much more. Also useful for Chapter 3.

Chapter 50

Nature and Nurture

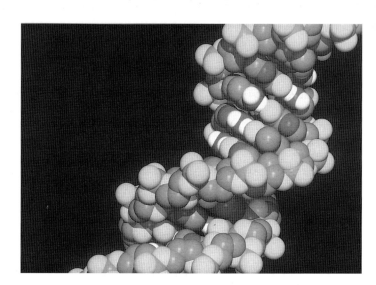

Introduction and overview

The debate concerning the influence of nature and nurture (or heredity and environment) on human development is one of the longest-running, and most controversial, both inside and outside psychology. It deals with some of the most fundamental questions that human beings (at least those from Western cultures) ask about themselves, such as 'How do we come to be the way we are?' and 'What makes us develop in the way we do?'.

These and similar questions have been posed (sometimes explicitly, sometimes implicitly) throughout this book in relation to a wide range of topics. These include perceptual abilities

(Chapter 16), language acquisition (Chapter 19), aggression (Chapter 29), attachment (Chapter 32), gender development (Chapter 36), intelligence (Chapter 41), and schizophrenia and depression (Chapter 44). In some of these examples, (such as language and perception) the focus of the debate is on an ability *shared by all human beings*, while in others (such as intelligence and schizophrenia) the focus is on *individual differences*.

In both cases, however, certain assumptions are made about the exact meaning of 'nature' and 'nurture', as well as about how they're related. By distinguishing different types of environment, such as *shared* and *non-shared*, it's easier to understand the relationship between nature and nurture, including *gene–environment correlation* and *gene–environment interaction*.

Nativism, empiricism and interactionism

Nativism is the philosophical theory according to which knowledge of the world is largely innate or inborn: nature (heredity) is seen as determining certain abilities and capacities. The French philosopher Descartes was a seventeenth-century nativist theorist who, as we noted in Chapter 3, had an enormous impact on science in general, including psychology. At the opposite philosophical extreme is *empiricism*, associated mainly with seventeenth-century British philosophers, and even more influential on the development of psychology. A key empiricist was Locke, who believed that at birth the human mind is a *tabula rasa* (or 'blank slate'). This is gradually 'filled in' by learning and experience.

Ask yourself ...

- Try to identify psychological (and other) theories which adopt an *extreme* position regarding the nature–nurture issue.
- Which particular features of the theories made you classify them in this way?

Nativism and empiricism are extreme theories in that they were trying to answer the question 'Is it nature or nurture?', as if only one or the other could be true. Early psychological theories tended to reflect these extremes, as in Gesell's concept of *maturation* and Watson's *behaviourism*.

Box 50.1   Gesell and Watson: two extreme viewpoints

According to Gesell (1925), one of the American pioneers of developmental psychology, *maturation* refers to genetically programmed patterns of change. The instructions for these patterns are part of the specific hereditary information passed on at the moment of conception (Bee, 2000). All individuals will pass through the same series of changes, in the same order, making maturational patterns *universal* and *sequential*. They're also 'relatively impervious to environmental influence'.

Gesell was mainly concerned with infants' psychomotor development (such as grasping and other manipulative skills), and locomotion, (such as crawling and walking). These abilities are usually seen as 'developing by themselves', according to a genetically determined timetable. Provided the baby is physically normal, practice or training aren't needed – the abilities just 'unfold'.

For Watson (1925), environmental influence is all-important (see Chapters 2 and 3), and human beings are completely malleable:

'Give me a dozen healthy infants, well-formed, and my own specialised world to bring them up in and I'll guarantee to take any one at random and train him to become any type of specialist I might select – a doctor, lawyer, artist, merchant-chief and, yes, even beggar-man and thief, regardless of his talents, penchants, abilities, vocations and race of his ancestors'.

Watson (1928) also claimed that there's no such thing as an inheritance of capacity, talent, temperament, mental constitution and character:

'The behaviourists believe that there is nothing from within to develop. If you start with the right number of fingers and toes, eyes, and a few elementary movements that are present at birth, you do not need anything else in the way of raw material to make a man, be that man genius, a cultured gentleman, a rowdy or a thug'.

Ask yourself ...

- Try to identify psychological theories and areas of research in which the process of maturation plays an important role. Examples are most likely to be found in developmental psychology.

The concept of maturation continues to be influential within psychology. Not only does maturation explain major biological changes, such as puberty (see Chapter 37) and physical aspects of ageing (see Chapter 39), but all stage theories of development assume that maturation underpins the universal sequence of stages. Examples include Freud's psychosexual theory (see Chapter 35), Erikson's psychosocial theory (see Chapters 37, 38 and 39), and Piaget's theory of cognitive development (see Chapter 34). Watson's extreme empiricism (or *environmentalism*) was adopted in Skinner's *radical behaviourism*, which represents a major model of both normal and abnormal behaviour (see Chapters 2 and 45).

Are nativism and empiricism mutually exclusive?

As noted in Box 50.1, maturationally-determined developmental sequences occur regardless of practice or training. However, as Bee (2000) points out:

'These powerful, apparently automatic maturational patterns require at least some minimal environmental support, such as adequate diet and opportunity for movement and experimentation'.

At the very least, the environment must be benign, that is, it mustn't be harmful in any way, preventing the ability or characteristic from developing. More importantly, the ability or characteristic cannot develop without environmental 'input'. For example, the possession of a language acquisition device (LAD) as proposed by Chomsky (1965: see Chapter 19) must be applied to the particular linguistic data provided by the child's linguistic community, so the child will only acquire *that* language (although it could just as easily have acquired *any* language). This is an undeniable fact about language acquisition, which Chomsky himself recognised.

Another example of the role of the environment involves vision. One of the proteins required for development of the visual system is controlled by a gene whose action is triggered only by visual experience (Greenough, 1991). So, some visual experience is needed for the genetic programme to operate. Although every (sighted) child will have some such experience under normal circumstances, examples like these tell us that maturational sequences don't simply 'unfold'. The system appears to be 'ready' to develop along particular pathways, but it requires experience to trigger the movement (Bee, 2000).

Another way of considering the interplay between nature and nurture is to look at Freud's and Piaget's developmental theories. Although maturation underlies the sequence of stages in both theories, the role of experience is at least as important.

| Box 50.2 | Nature and nurture in Freud's and Piaget's developmental theories |

For Freud it's not the sexual instinct itself that matters, but rather the reactions of significant others (especially parents) to the child's attempts to satisfy its sexual needs. Both excessive frustration and satisfaction can produce long-term effects on the child's personality, such as fixation at particular stages of development (see Box 35.1, page 507).

Although Freud is commonly referred to as an instinct theorist (suggesting that he was a nativist), his concept of an instinct was very different from the earlier view of unlearned, largely automatic (pre-programmed) responses to specific stimuli (based on non-human species: see Chapter 9). Instead of using the German word '*Instinkt*', he used '*Trieb*' (drive), which denotes a relatively undifferentiated form of energy capable of almost infinite variation through experience (see Box 2.2, page 15).

As a biologist, Piaget stressed the role of *adaptation* to the environment. This involves the twin processes of *assimilation* and *accommodation*, which in turn are related to (dis-)equilibrium (see Chapter 34). These mechanisms are part of the biological 'equipment' of human beings, without which their intelligence wouldn't change (the individual wouldn't progress through increasingly complex stages of development). However, the infant actively explores its environment and constructs its own knowledge and understanding of the world (the child as scientist: Rogoff, 1990). According to Piaget (1970), intelligence consists:

'... *neither of a simple copy of external objects nor of a mere unfolding of structures preformed inside the subject, but rather ... a set of structures constructed by continuous interaction between the subject and the external world*'.

Both Freud's and Piaget's theories demonstrate that:

'*There is a trade-off in nature between pre-specification, on the one hand, and plasticity, on the other, leading ultimately to the kind of flexibility one finds in the human mind*'. (Karmiloff-Smith, 1996)

Maturation is an example of what Karmiloff-Smith means by 'pre-specification', and *inborn biases* represent another example. For example, very young babies already seem to understand that unsupported objects will fall (move downward), and that a moving object will continue to move in the same direction unless it encounters an obstacle (Spelke, 1991: see Chapter 16). However, these 'pre-existing conceptions' are merely the beginning of the story. What then develops is the result of experience filtered through these initial biases, which constrain the number of developmental pathways that are possible (Bee, 2000).

According to Bee, no developmental psychologists today would take the 'Is it nature *or* nurture?' form of the debate seriously. Essentially, every facet of a child's development is a product of some pattern of interaction between the two. Until fairly recently, however, the theoretical pendulum was well over towards the nurture/environmental end of the continuum. In the last decade or so, there's been a marked swing back towards the nature/biological end, partly because of the impact of sociobiology and its more recent off-shoot evolutionary psychology (see Chapter 2).

Ask yourself ...

- Draw a diagram, representing a continuum, with 'extreme nativism' (nature) at one end and 'extreme empiricism' (nurture) at the other. Then place theories along the continuum to indicate the emphasis they give to either nature or nurture – or both. The theories can be drawn from any area of psychology. They're likely to include those identified in the first 'Ask yourself ...', but should also reflect the approaches discussed in Chapter 47. Some examples are given in Figure 50.3, page 736.

What do we mean by 'nature'?

In the *Introduction and overview*, we noted that some examples of the nature–nurture debate involve abilities or capacities common to all human beings (such as language and perception), while others involve individual differences (such as intelligence and schizophrenia). According to Plomin (1994), it's in the latter sense that the debate 'properly' takes place, and much of the rest of this chapter will reflect the 'individual differences' approach.

Within *genetics* (the science of heredity), 'nature' refers to what's typically thought of as inheritance, that is, differences in genetic material (chromosomes and genes) transmitted from generation to generation (from parents to offspring). The 'father' of genetics, Gregor Mendel (1865), explained the difference between different genes in terms of smooth and wrinkled seeds in garden peas. Similarly, modern human genetics focuses on genetic differences between individuals, reflecting the use of the word 'nature' by Galton, who coined the phrase nature–nurture in 1883 as it's used in the scientific arena (Plomin, 1994).

So, what are genes? Genes are the basic unit of hereditary transmission, consisting of large molecules of deoxyribonucleic acid (DNA). These are extremely complex chemical chains, comprising a ladder-like, double helix structure (discovered by Watson & Crick in 1953: see Figure 50.1).

The genes, which occur in pairs, are situated on the chromosomes, which are found within the nuclei of living cells. The normal human being inherits 23 pairs of chromosomes, one member of each pair from each parent. The twenty-third pair comprises the sex chromosomes, which are two Xs in females, and an X and a Y in males (see Chapter 36 and Figure 50.2).

The steps of the gene's double helix (or 'spiral staircase': Plomin, 1994) consist of four nucleotide bases (adenine, thymine, cytosine and guanine). These can occur in any order on one side of the double helix, but the order on the other side is always fixed, such that adenine always pairs with thymine, and cytosine always pairs with guanine. Taking just one member of each of the 23 pairs of chromosomes, the human *genome* comprises more than three billion nucleotide base pairs (Plomin, 1994). Two major functions of genes are *self-duplication* and *protein synthesis*.

Self-duplication

DNA copies itself by unzipping in the middle of the spiral staircase, with each half forming its complement: when a cell divides, all the genetic information (chromosomes and genes) contained within the cell nucleus is reproduced. This means that the 'offspring' cells are identical to the 'parent' cells (*mitosis*), but this process applies only to *non-gonadal* (non-reproductive) cells (such as skin, blood and muscle cells).

The reproductive (or germ) cells (ova in females, sperm in males) duplicate through *meiosis*, whereby each cell only contains half the individual's chromosomes and genes. Which member of a chromosome pair goes to any particular cell seems to be determined randomly. The resulting germ cells (*gametes*), therefore, contain 23 chromosomes, one of which will be either an X (female) or a Y (male). When a sperm fertilises an ovum, the two sets of chromosomes combine to form a new individual with a full set of 46 chromosomes.

Protein synthesis

The 'genetic code' was 'cracked' in the 1960s. Essentially, DNA controls the production of *ribonucleic acid* (RNA) within the cell nucleus. This 'messenger' RNA moves outside the nucleus and into the surrounding cytoplasm, where it's converted by ribosomes into sequences of amino acids, the building blocks of proteins and enzymes.

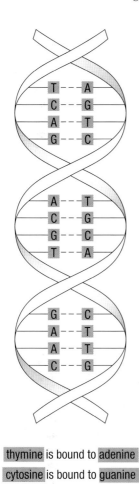

thymine is bound to adenine

cytosine is bound to guanine

Figure 50.1 *The structure of a DNA molecule represented schematically. This shows its double-stranded coiled structure and the complementary binding of nucleotide bases, guanine (G) to cytosine (C) and adenine (A) to thymine (T)*

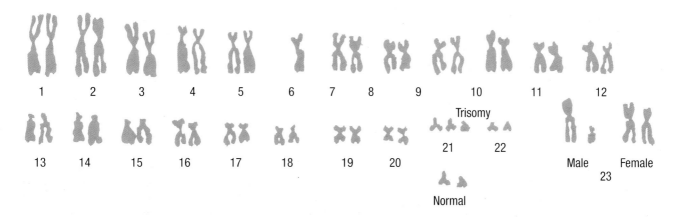

Figure 50.2 *A sample karyotype. The 21st chromosome has one too many chromosomes, a common problem. This is called a 'trisomy'. The 23rd chromosome pair is shown with both male and female versions. In a normal karyotype, only one such pair would be found*

Genes that code for proteins and enzymes are called *structural genes*, and they represent the foundation of classical genetics (Plomin, 1994). The first single-gene disorders discovered in the human species involved metabolic disorders caused by mutations (spontaneous changes) in structural genes. A much-cited example is phenylketonuria, which is discussed in relation to gene–environment interaction (see Chapter 41 and pages 738–739).

Most genes are *regulator* genes, which code for products that bind with DNA itself and serve to regulate other genes. Unlike the structural genes which are 'deaf' to the environment, the regulator genes communicate closely with the environment and change in response to it (Plomin, 1994).

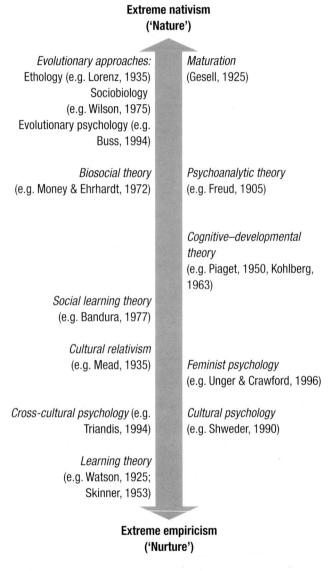

Figure 50.3 *A continuum representing the position of various psychological (and other) theories on the nature–nurture debate*

Neurogenetic determinism: Are there genes 'for' anything?

As noted in Box 49.6 (see page 728), several claims have been made in recent years about the discovery of genes 'for' a wide range of complex human behaviours (*reductionism as ideology*: Rose, 1997). Related to this is what Rose calls *neurogenetic*

determinism, the claim that there's a direct causal link between genes and behaviour. This involves the false assumption that causes can be classified as *either* genetic *or* environmental, and there are additional reasons for doubting the validity of neurogenetic determinism.

The phrase 'genes for' is a convenient, but misleading, shorthand used by geneticists. In the case of eye colour, for example (which, from a genetic point of view, is one of the more simple characteristics – or *phenotypes*), there's a difference in the biochemical pathways that lead to brown and to blue eyes. In blue-eyed people, the gene for a particular enzyme (which catalyses a chemical transformation *en route* to the synthesis of the pigment) is either missing or non-functional for some reason. A gene 'for blue eyes' now has to be reinterpreted as meaning 'one or more genes in whose absence the metabolic pathway that leads to pigmented eyes terminates at the blue-eye stage' (Rose, 1997).

As more is learned about the human genome, geneticists come to realise that many supposedly 'single-gene disorders' result from different gene mutations in different people. They may show a similar clinical picture, such as high blood cholesterol levels with an enhanced risk of coronary heart disease. However, the gene mutation, and hence the enzyme malfunction, that results in the disorder may be very different in each case. This also means that a drug which effectively treats the condition in one person may simply not work in another, whose cholesterol accumulation is caused by *different* biochemical factors (Rose, 1997).

Box 50.3   Is there more to heredity than DNA?

Cells not only inherit genes, they also inherit a set of instructions that tell the genes when to become active, in which tissue and to what extent. Without this 'epigenetic' instruction manual, multicellular organisms would be impossible. Every cell, whether a liver or skin cell, inherits exactly the same set of genes. However, the manual has different instructions for different cell types, allowing the cell to develop its distinctive identity. It seems that the instruction manual is wiped clean during the formation of germ cells, ensuring that all genes are equally available, until the embryo begins to develop specific tissues. However, there's evidence to suggest that changes in the epigenetic instruction manual can sometimes be passed from parent to offspring.

For example, pregnant women facing the brunt of the Nazi siege of the Netherlands at the end of World War II were reduced to near starvation. Some miscarried, but if they successfully gave birth, their babies appeared quite normal after a period of catch-up growth, and seemed no different from their better-nourished peers when tested at age 18. Many of these war babies now have children of their own (the grandchildren of the war-time pregnant mothers). Even girls who'd themselves been of normal weight at birth produced babies who were either underweight or grew into small adults, despite the post-war generation being well fed. Thus, there's a sort of 'sleeper effect', whereby the effects of starvation skipped a generation.

Such 'awkward' findings are very difficult for geneticists to explain. However, one possible explanantion is in the form of an epigenetic phenomenon called 'imprinting' (Reik, cited in Vines, 1998). Genes exist in pairs and they behave in exactly the same way regardless of which parent they come from. But in some cases an imprinted gene is activated only if it comes from the father, and in other cases only if it comes from the mother. Some sort of 'mark' must persist through the generations to tell the offspring's cells which genes to re-imprint. Whatever the precise mechanism by which they operate, the existence of imprinted genes demonstrates that not all genes are wiped totally clean of their epigenetic marks.

(Based on Ceci & Williams, 1999; Vines, 1998)

What do we mean by 'nurture'?

> *Ask yourself ...*
>
> * What do you understand by the term 'environment'? Try to identify different uses of the term and different 'levels' at which the environment exists.

When the term 'environment' is used in a psychological context, it usually refers to all those *post-natal* influences (or potential sources of influence) lying *outside/external* to the individual's body. These include other people, both members of the immediate family and other members of society, opportunities for intellectual stimulation, and the physical circumstances of the individual's life ('environs' or 'surroundings'). These influences are implicitly seen as impinging on a passive individual, who is *shaped* by them.

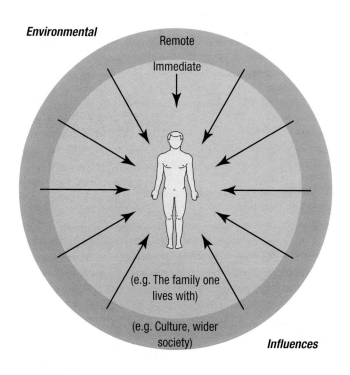

Figure 50.4 *Traditional, extreme behaviourist/environmentalist view of the environment as a set of external, post-natal influences acting upon a purely passive individual*

On all three counts, this view of the environment seems inadequate. It isn't just the individual person who's 'immersed in' or influenced by his/her environment, but during mitosis the specific location of any particular cell is constantly changing as the cluster of cells of which it's a part constantly grows. At an even more micro-level, the cell nucleus (which contains the DNA) has as its environment the cytoplasm of the cell.

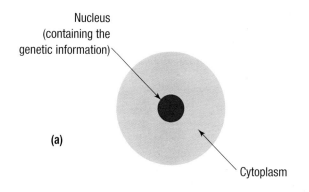

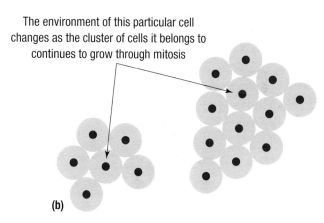

Figure 50.5 *For the nucleus of an individual cell, the environment is the surrounding cytoplasm (a). The specific location of any particular cell is constantly changing during mitosis (b)*

As we noted in Chapter 41, pre-natal non-genetic factors (such as the mother's excessive alcohol consumption during pregnancy) account for the largest proportion of biologically caused learning difficulties and lowered IQ. Finally, and most significantly, not only is 'nature' and 'nurture' a false dichotomy (see *Conclusions*), but it's invalid to regard the environment as existing independently of the individual (that is, objectively). Not only do people's environments influence them, but people make their own environments (Scarr, 1992: see Box 50.4, page 738). A way of thinking about how people do this is through the concept of *non-shared environments*, which is, in turn, related to *gene–environment correlation*.

Shared and non-shared environments

When the environment is discussed as a set of (potential) influences that impinge on the individual, it's often broken down into factors such as overcrowding, poverty, socioeconomic status (SES), family break-up, marital discord and so on. In studies of intelligence, for example, children are often compared in terms of these environmental factors, so that children from low SES groups are commonly found to have lower IQs than those from high SES groups (see Chapter 41).

When families are compared in this way, it's assumed that children from the same family will all be similarly and equally affected by those environmental factors (*shared environment*). For most characteristics, however, most children within the same family *aren't* very similar. In fact, they're often extremely varied in personality, abilities and psychological disorders. This observation is most striking when two adopted children are brought up in the same family: they're usually no more alike than any two people chosen at random from the general population (Plomin, 1996; Rutter & Rutter, 1992).

Dustin Hoffman as the autistic brother of Tom Cruise in Rain Man. *Both genetic and non-shared environmental factors are likely to have contributed to their different characteristics and abilities*

This substantial within-family variation *doesn't* mean that family environment is unimportant. Rather, as Plomin (1996) puts it:

> *'Environmental influences in development are doled out on an individual-by-individual basis rather than on a family-by-family basis'.*

In other words, differences between children growing up together is exactly what we'd expect to find, because it's the *non-shared environment* which has greater influence on development than the shared environment. Different children in the same family have different experiences. For example, Dunn & Plomin (1990) found that the ways in which parents respond differently to their different children (*relative differences*) are likely to be much more influential than the overall characteristics of the family (*absolute differences*). So, it may matter very little whether children are brought up in a home that's less loving or more punitive than average, whereas it may matter considerably that one child receives less affection or more punishment than his/her sibling. These findings imply:

> *'... that the unit of environmental transmission is not the family, but rather micro-environments within families'.* (Plomin & Thompson, 1987)

Gene–environment correlations

The concept of non-shared environments helps explain how the environment influences development, which is far more

sophisticated and useful than the original 'Is it nature or nurture?' question (see above). However, we need to understand the processes by which non-shared environments arise: *why* do parents treat their different children differently, and *how* do children in the same family come to have different experiences? In trying to answer these questions, psychologists and behaviour geneticists (see page 740) have, paradoxically, stressed the role of *genetic differences*. A major example of this approach is the concept of *gene–environment correlation*.

Box 50.4   Gene–environment correlations

Plomin *et al.* (1977) identified three types of gene–environment correlations:

- **Passive gene–environment correlations**: Children passively inherit from their parents environments that are correlated with their genetic tendencies. For example, parents who are of above average IQ are likely to provide a more intellectually stimulating environment than lower IQ parents.
- **Reactive gene–environment correlations**: Children's experiences derive from the reactions of other people to the children's genetic tendencies. For example, babies with a sunny, easy-going and cheerful disposition/temperament are more likely to elicit friendly reactions from others than miserable or 'difficult' babies (see Key Study 50.1, page 739). It's widely accepted that some children are easier to love (Rutter & Rutter, 1992). Similarly, aggressive children tend to experience aggressive environments, because they tend to evoke aggressive responses in others (see Chapter 29).
- **Active gene–environment correlations**: Children construct and reconstruct experiences consistent with their genetic tendencies. Trying to define the environment independently of the person is futile, since every person's experience is different. According to Plomin (1994):

> *'Socially, as well as cognitively, children select, modify and even create their experiences. Children select environments that are rewarding or at least comfortable, niche-picking. Children modify their environments by setting the background tone for interactions, by initiating behaviour, and by altering the impact of environments … they can create environments with their own propensities, niche-building'.*

Gene–environment interactions

As we've seen, the concept of gene–environment correlations is related to that of non-shared environments, which helps to explain how the environment exerts its influence. Another way of considering the environment's impact is to identify examples of *gene–environment interactions*.

Genetically speaking, *phenylketonuria* (PKU) is a simple characteristic. It's a bodily disorder caused by the inheritance of a single recessive gene from each parent. Normally, the body produces the amino acid phenylalanine hydroxylase which converts phenylalanine (a substance found in many foods, particularly dairy products) into tyrosine. But in the presence of the two recessive PKU genes, this process fails and phenylalanine builds up in the blood, depressing the levels of other amino acids. Consequently, the developing nervous system is deprived of essential nutrients, leading to severe mental retardation and, without intervention, eventually leading to death (see Chapter 40).

The relationship between what the child inherits (the two PKU genes – the *genotype*) and the actual signs and symptoms of the disease (high levels of phenylalanine in the blood, and mental retardation – the *phenotype*) appears to be straightforward, direct and inevitable: given the genotype, the phenotype will occur. However, a routine blood test soon after birth can detect the presence of the PKU genes, and an affected baby will be put on a low-phenylalanine diet. This prevents the disease from developing. In other words, an environmental intervention will prevent the phenotype from occurring. According to Jones (1993):

'[The] nature [of children born with PKU genes] has been determined by careful nurturing and there is no simple answer to the question of whether their genes or their environment is more important to their well-being'.

Ask yourself ...

- Try to identify some examples of gene–environment interactions that involve behaviour, as distinct from bodily diseases such as PKU. Two relevant areas are intelligence (Chapter 41) and schizophrenia (Chapter 44).

If there's no one-to-one relationship between genotype and phenotype in the case of PKU, it's highly likely that there'll be an even more complex interaction in the case of intelligence, certain mental disorders, personality and so on. One such example is *cumulative deficit*, which was discussed in Chapter 41 (see page 606). Another is the concept of *facilitativeness*.

According to Horowitz (1987, 1990), a highly *facilitative* environment is one in which the child has loving and responsive parents, and is provided with a rich array of stimulation.

When different levels of facilitativeness are combined with a child's initial *vulnerabilities/susceptibilities*, there's an interaction effect. For example, a *resilient* child (one with many protective factors and a few vulnerabilities) may do quite well in a poor environment. Equally, a *non-resilient* child may do quite well in a highly facilitative environment. Only the *non-resilient* child in a poor environment will do really poorly (see Figure 50.6).

This interactionist view is supported by a 30-year longitudinal study which took place on the Hawaiian island of Kanuai.

KEY STUDY 50.1

Werner's 'Children of the Garden Island'

Starting in 1955, Werner and her colleagues studied all of the nearly 700 children born on Kanuai in a given period, and followed them up at the ages of two, ten, 18 and 31–32. Werner became interested in a number of 'high risk'/'vulnerable' children, who, despite exposure before the age of two to four or more risk factors, went on to develop healthy personalities, stable careers and strong interpersonal relationships. These risk factors were: reproductive stress (either difficulties during pregnancy and/or during labour and delivery), and discordant and impoverished home lives, including divorce, uneducated, alcoholic or mentally disturbed parents.

As infants, these resilient children were typically described as 'active' 'affectionate', 'cuddly', 'easy-going', and 'even-tempered', with no eating or sleeping habits causing distress to their carers. These are all temperamental characteristics, which elicit positive responses from both family members and strangers. There were also environmental differences between the resilient and non-resilient children, such as smaller family size, at least two years between themselves and the next child, and a close attachment to at least one carer (relative or regular baby-sitter).

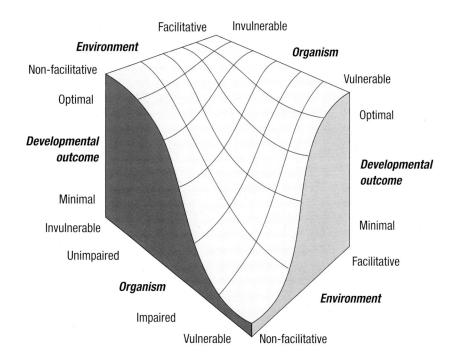

Figure 50.6 *Horowitz's model of the interaction of a child's environment with protective factors and vulnerabilities. The surface of the curve illustrates the level of a developmental stage, such as IQ or social skills. According to this model, if a low-birthweight child is reared in a poor environment, then it's likely that child will do less well than other children reared with a different combination of vulnerabilities and environment*

They also received considerable emotional support from outside the family, were popular with their peers, and had at least one close friend. School became a refuge from a disordered household.

Of the 72 children classified as resilient, 62 were studied after reaching their 30s. As a group, they seemed to be coping well with the demands of adult life. Three-quarters had received some college education, nearly all had full-time jobs and were satisfied with their work. According to Werner (1989):

> 'As long as the balance between stressful life events and protective factors is favourable, successful adaptation is possible. When stressful events outweigh the protective factors, however, even the most resilient child can have problems'.

Ask yourself ...

- In what ways can culture be thought of as an environmental influence on an individual's behaviour? Try to identify examples from different areas of psychology, but Chapter 47 might be a good place to begin.

Behaviour genetics and heritability

Behaviour genetics

According to Pike & Plomin (1999), 'Behaviour geneticists explore the origins of individual differences ... in complex behaviours'. More specifically, they attempt to quantify how much of the *variability* for any given trait (such as intelligence, aggressiveness or schizophrenia) can be attributed to (a) genetic

differences between people (*heritability*), (b) *shared environments*, and (c) *non-shared environments* (see above, pages 737–739). The heritability of intelligence was discussed in Chapter 41, as were the two major methods used by behaviour genetics, namely twin studies and adoption studies (also see Chapter 44).

If genetic factors are important for a trait, identical twins (MZs) will be more similar than non-identical twins (DZs). To the extent that twin similarity cannot be attributed to genetic factors, the *shared environment* is implicated. To the extent that MZs differ *within* pairs, *non-shared environmental* factors are implicated. Because adopted siblings are genetically unrelated to their adoptive family members, the degree of similarity between them is a direct measure of *shared environmental influence* (Pike & Plomin, 1999).

One interesting finding from behaviour genetic research is that the effects of a shared environment seem to decrease over time. In a ten-year longitudinal study of over 200 pairs of adoptive siblings, Loehlin *et al.* (1988) found that at an average age of eight, the correlation for IQ was 0.26. This is similar to other studies of young adoptive siblings, and suggests that shared environment makes an important contribution at this age. However, by age 18 the correlation was close to zero. According to Pike & Plomin (1999):

> 'These results represent a dramatic example of the importance of genetic research for understanding the environment. Shared environment is important for [general intelligence] during childhood when children are living at home. However, its importance fades in adolescence as influences outside the family become more salient'.

This conclusion might at first appear paradoxical, yet behaviour genetics provides the best available evidence for the importance of *nongenetic* factors in behavioural development (Plomin, 1995). For example, the concordance rate of MZs for schizophrenia is 40 per cent, which means that most pairs

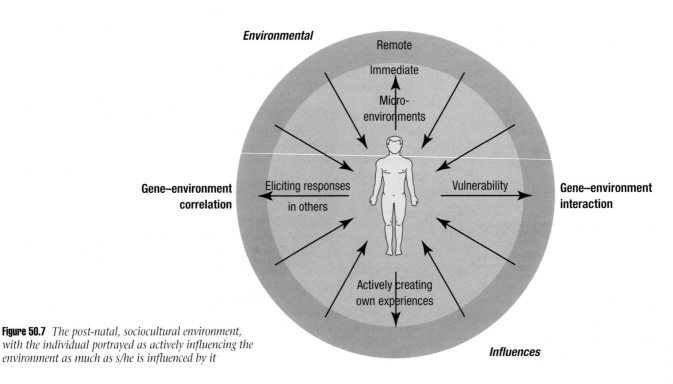

Figure 50.7 *The post-natal, sociocultural environment, with the individual portrayed as actively influencing the environment as much as s/he is influenced by it*

are *discordant* for diagnosed schizophrenia (see Chapter 44). While there can be no genetic explanation for this, 20 years ago the message from behaviour genetics research was that genetic factors play the major role. Today, the message is that these same data provide strong evidence for the importance of environmental factors as well as genetic factors (Plomin, 1995). Additionally, the data from twin studies are open to interpretation because not all MZs are equally identical. This is due to certain critical *environmental* factors.

Heritability

According to Ceci & Williams (1999), *heritability* is one of the most controversial concepts in psychology. As noted earlier, it's a statistical measure of the genetic contribution to differences between individuals, that is, it tells us what proportion of individual differences within a population (*variance*) can be attributed to genes. However, this *doesn't* mean that 'biology is destiny'. Indeed, as also noted above, behaviour genetics has helped confirm the importance of environmental factors, which generally account for as much variance in human behaviour as do genes (Plomin & DeFries, 1998). Even when genetic factors do have an especially powerful effect, as in PKU, environmental interventions can often fully or partly overcome the genetic 'determinants'.

According to Ceci & Williams (1999):

> *'Heritability estimates are highly situational: they are descriptions of the relative contributions of genes and environments to the expression of a trait in a specific group, place and time. Such estimates tell us nothing about the relative contributions if the group, place or time is changed'.*

Conclusions

According to Ceci & Williams (1999):

> *'Nearly all responsible researchers agree that human traits are jointly determined by both nature and nurture, although they may disagree about the relative contributions of each'.*

They also point out that not all biological influences on development are genetic: some are critical features of the intrauterine environment that are sometimes mistaken for genetic influences (see Box 50.5, and pages 583–584). So, 'biological' doesn't mean 'genetic', and just as importantly, 'environment' can refer to biological, psychological, social, and cultural influences.

In the 1950s, the extreme environmentalism of behaviourism dominated thinking about nature–nurture, but the 1960s saw the adoption of a more balanced view. The 1980s and 1990s saw psychology becoming much more accepting of genetic influence (Plomin, 1996). Plomin (1995) maintains that:

'Research and theory in genetics (nature) and in environment (nurture) are beginning to converge … the common ground is a model of active organism–environment interaction in which nature and nurture play a duet rather than one directing the performance of the other … It is time to put the nature–nurture controversy behind us and to bring nature and nurture together in the study of development in order to understand the processes by which genotypes become phenotypes'.

Similarly, Ceci & Williams (1999) conclude like this:

'The battle today seems more over the specific genetic and environmental mechanisms than over whether genes or environments matter'.

CHAPTER SUMMARY

- The **nature–nurture debate** concerns fundamental questions about the causes of human development, sometimes focusing on behaviours and abilities **shared by all human beings**, and sometimes on **individual differences**.

- **Nativists** see knowledge of the world as largely innate, whilst **empiricists** stress the role of learning and experience. These extreme viewpoints are reflected in early psychological theories, such as Gesell's **maturation** and Watson's **behaviourism**, respectively.

- The concept of maturation continues to be influential in psychology, as in biological processes such as puberty and ageing, and stage theories of development. Watson's **environmentalism** was adopted in Skinner's **radical behaviourism**.

- Nativism and empiricism aren't mutually exclusive. Not only must the environment be **benign**, but particular environmental input is often necessary. In both Freud's and Piaget's theories, experience is just as important as the underlying maturation.

- **Genetics** is the science of heredity. **Genes** are the basic units of hereditary transmission, responsible for **self-duplication** and **protein synthesis**. Self-duplication occurs through **mitosis** (in the case of non-reproductive cells) and **meiosis** (in the case of reproductive cells).

- **Neurogenetic determinism** makes the false assumption that causes can be classified as **either** genetic **or** environmental. Also, the phrase 'genes for' is a convenient but misleading shorthand for complex biochemical processes.

- Cells inherit genes along with an 'epigenetic' instruction manual, without which multicellular organisms would be impossible. Changes in the instruction manual may be passed from parent to offspring. Heredity may thus involve more than DNA.

- The term 'environment' is commonly used to refer to **post-natal** influences lying **outside** the body of a passive individual who's **shaped by them**. However, people also make their own environments, and for most characteristics, the **shared environment** seems to have little impact on development compared with the **non-shared environment**.

- The concept of non-shared environments helps explain **how** the environment influences development. Two ways in which non-shared environments arise are **gene–environment correlations** and **gene–environment interactions**.

- PKU illustrates the lack of a one-to-one relationship between **genotype** and **phenotype**. Other examples include **cumulative deficit** and Horowitz's concept of **facilitativeness**.

- **Behaviour genetics** attempts to quantify how much of the **variability** for any particular trait is due to **heritability**, **shared environments**, and **non-shared environments**.

- **Heritability estimates** describe the relative contributions of genes and environment for particular traits, in a specific population, at a particular place and time. They are measures of individual differences **within** groups, and can tell us nothing about **between**-group differences or particular individuals within a group.

- Human traits are determined by **both** nature **and** nurture. Where researchers may still disagree is over the **relative contributions** of each, and the specific genetic and environmental **mechanisms** involved.

Self-assessment questions

1 a Examine the assumptions made by **two** theories/theoretical approaches regarding the relationship between nature and nurture.

   b Assess the extent to which research evidence supports the view that nature and nurture interact.

2 'Instead of asking "how much does each contribute", we should be investigating *how* each contributes.'
   Discuss this view of the relationship between nature and nurture.

Web addresses

http://objana.com/frog/natnurt.html

http://genetics.nature.com

http://www.apa.org/releases/mother.html

http://www.learner.org/exhibits/personality/genes.html

Further reading

Ceci, S.J. & Williams, W. M. (1999, Eds.) *The Nature-Nurture Debate: The Essential Readings.* A collection of reprinted articles, each introduced by the editors.

Plomin, R. (1994) *Genetics and Experience: The Interplay Between Nature and Nurture.* Thousand Oaks, CA: Sage Publications. A detailed discussion of most of the issues covered in this chapter by a leading behaviour geneticist.

References

Abdulla, S. (1996) Illuminating our hardware. *The Times Higher,* 1 November, 18.

Abel, E.L. (1977) The relationship between cannabis and violence: A review. *Psychological Bulletin, 84,* 193–211.

Abernathy, E.M. (1940) The effect of changed environmental conditions upon the results of college examinations. *Journal of Psychology, 10,* 293–301.

Abraham, K. (1911) Notes on the psychoanalytical investigation and treatment of manic–depressive insanity and allied conditions. Originally written in 1911 and later published in E. Jones (Ed.) *Selected Papers of Karl Abraham, MD.* London: The Hogarth Press.

Abrahams, C. & Shanley, E. (1992) *Social Psychology for Nurses.* London: Edward Arnold.

Abrams, D. & Manstead, A.S.R. (1981) A test of theories of social facilitation using a musical task. *British Journal of Social Psychology, 20,* 271–278.

Abrams, D., Wetherell, M., Cochrane, S., Hogg, M.A. & Turner, J.C. (1990) Knowing what to think by knowing who you are: Self-categorisation and the nature of norm formation. *British Journal of Social Psychology, 29,* 97–119.

Abramson, L.Y. & Martin, D.J. (1981) Depression and the causal inference process. In J.M. Harvey, W. Ickes & R.F. Kidd (Eds) *New Directions in Attribution Research, Volume 3.* Hillsdale, NJ: Erlbaum.

Abramson, L.Y., Seligman, M.E.P. & Teasdale, J.D. (1978) Learned helplessness in humans: Critique and reformulation. *Journal of Abnormal Psychology, 87,* 49–74.

Adam, K. & Oswald, I. (1977) Sleep is for tissue restoration. *Journal of the Royal College of Physicians, 11,* 376–388.

Adam, K. & Oswald, I. (1983) Protein synthesis, bodily renewal and the sleep–wake cycle. *Clinical Science, 65,* 561–567.

Adams, J.A. (1976) Issues for a closed-loop theory of motor learning. In G.E. Stelmach (Ed.) *Motor Control: Issues and Trends.* London: Academic Press.

Adams, R.J. & Maurer, D. (1984) Detection of contrast by the new-born and two-month-old infant. *Infant Behaviour and Development, 7,* 415–422.

Adler, A. (1927) *The Practice and Theory of Individual Psychology.* New York: Harcourt Brace Jovanovich.

Adler, R. (2000) Pigeonholed. *New Scientist, 167*(2258), 389–341.

Adorno, T.W., Frenkel-Brunswick, E., Levinson, J.D. & Sanford, R.N. (1950) *The Authoritarian Personality.* New York: Harper & Row.

Ahmed, K. (1998) Island's youth pass TV test. *The Guardian,* 29 April, 6.

Ahuja, A. (2000) Drugs blow your mind. *The Times,* 15 June, 5.

Ainsworth, M.D.S. (1967) *Infancy in Uganda: Infant Care and the Growth of Love.* Baltimore, MD: Johns Hopkins University Press.

Ainsworth, M.D.S. (1989) Attachments beyond infancy. *American Psychologist, 44* (4) 709–716.

Ainsworth, M.D.S. & Wittig, B.A. (1969) Attachment and exploratory behaviour of 1-year-olds in a strange situation. In B.M. Foss (Ed.) *Determinants of Infant Behaviour, Volume 4.* London: Methuen.

Ainsworth, M.D.S., Bell, S.M.V. & Stayton, D.J. (1971) Individual differences in Strange Situation behaviour of one-year-olds. In H.R. Schaffer (Ed.) *The Origins of Human Social Relations.* New York: Academic Press.

Ainsworth, M.D.S., Blehar, M.C., Waters, E. & Wall, S. (1978) *Patterns of Attachment: A Psychological Study of the Strange Situation.* Hillsdale, NJ: Lawrence Erlbaum Associates Inc.

Aitchison, J. (1983) *The Articulate Mammal* (2nd edition). London: Hutchinson.

Aitchison, J. (1996) Wugs, woggles and whatsits. *Independent, Section 2,* 28 February, 8.

Ajzen, I. (1988) *Attitudes, Personality and Behaviour.* Milton Keynes: Open University Press.

Ajzen, I. (1991) The theory of planned behaviour. *Organisational Behaviour & Human Decision Processes, 50,* 179–211.

Ajzen, I. (1996) The directive influence of attitudes on behaviour. In P.M. Gollwitzer & J.A. Bargh (Eds) *The Psychology of Action.* New York: Guildford Press.

Ajzen, I. & Fishbein, M. (1970) The prediction of behaviour from attitudinal and normative beliefs. *Journal of Personality & Social Psychology, 6,* 466–487.

Ajzen, I. & Fishbein, M. (1977) Attitude–behaviour relations: A theoretical analysis and review of empirical research. *Psychological Bulletin, 84,* 888–918.

Ajzen, I. & Fishbein, M. (1980) *Understanding Attitudes and Predicting Social Behaviour.* Englewood Cliffs, NJ: Prentice-Hall.

Alcock, J.E. (1981) *Parapsychology: Science or Magic?* Oxford: Pergamon.

Aldersey-Williams, H. (1999) Gene genius? *The Independent on Sunday Magazine,* 10 January, 45–47.

Aldous, J. (1996) Developmental diversity, and converging paths: a commentary. *Journal of Social & Personal Relationships, 13,* 473–479.

Aldhous, P., Coghlan, A. & Copley, J. (1999) Let the people speak. *New Scientist, 162* (2187), 26–31.

Alexander, F. & French, T.M. (1946) *Psychoanalytic Therapy.* New York: Ronald Press.

Alibhai-Brown, Y. (2000) 'We are black men. That means we make babies'. *The Guardian,* 13 April, 8.

Allen, V. & Levine, J.M. (1968) Social support, dissent and conformity. *Sociometry, 31,* 138–149.

Allen, V.L. & Levine, J.M. (1971) Social support and conformity: The role of independent assessment of reality. *Journal of Experimental Social Psychology, 7,* 48–58.

Allport, D.A. (1980a) Patterns and actions: Cognitive mechanisms are content specific. In G. Claxton (Ed.), *Cognitive Psychology: New Directions.* London: Routlege, Kegan Paul.

Allport, D.A. (1980b) Attention and performance. In G. Claxton (Ed.) *Cognitive Psychology: New Directions*. London: Routledge & Kegan Paul.

Allport, D.A. (1989) Visual attention. In M. Posner (Ed.) *Foundations of Cognitive Science*. Cambridge, MA: MIT Press.

Allport, D.A. (1993) Attention and control. Have we been asking the wrong questions? A critical review of twenty-five years. In D.E. Meyer & S.M. Kornblum (Eds) *Attention and Performance, Volume XIV*. London: MIT Press.

Allport, D.A., Antonis, B. & Reynolds, P. (1972) On the division of attention: A disproof of the single-channel hypothesis. *Quarterly Journal of Experimental Psychology, 24*, 225–235.

Allport, F.H. (1924) *Social Psychology*. Boston: Houghton Mifflin.

Allport, G.W. (1935) Attitudes. In C.M. Murchison (Ed.) *Handbook of Social Psychology*. Worchester, MA: Clark University Press.

Allport, G.W. (1937) *Personality: A Psychological Interpretation*. New York: Holt, Rinehart & Winston.

Allport, G.W. (1947) *The Use of Personal Documents in Psychological Science*. London: Holt, Rinehart & Winston

Allport, G.W. (1954) *The Nature of Prejudice*. Reading, MA: Addison-Wesley.

Allport, G.W. (1955) *Theories of Perception and the Concept of Structure*. New York: Wiley.

Allport, G.W. (1960) *Personality and Social Encounter*. Boston: Beacon Press.

Allport, G.W. (1961) *Pattern and Growth in Personality*. New York: Holt Rinehart Winston.

Allport, G.W. (1968) The historical background of modern psychology. In G. Lindzey & E. Aronson (Eds) *Handbook of Social Psychology, Volume 1* (2nd edition). Reading, Mass: Addison-Wesley.

Allport, G.W. & Odbert, H.S. (1936) Trait names: A psycho-lexical study. *Psychological Monographs: General & Applied, 47,* (Whole No. 211).

Allport, G.W. & Pettigrew, T.F. (1957) Cultural influences on the perception of movement: The trapezoidal illusion among Zulus. *Journal of Abnormal & Social Psychology, 55,* 104–113.

Allport, G.W. & Postman, L. (1947) *The Psychology of Rumour*. New York: Holt, Rinehart & Winston.

Allport, G.W., Vernon, P.G. & Lindzey, G. (1951) *Study of Values*. Boston: Houghton-Mifflin.

Alsaker, F.D. (1992) Pubertal timing, overweight, and psychological adjustment. *Journal of Early Adolescence, 12,* 396–419.

Alsaker, F.D. (1996) The impact of puberty. *Journal of Child Psychology & Psychiatry, 37*(3), 249–258.

Altman, I. & Taylor, D.A. (1973) *Social Penetration: The Development of Interpersonal Relationships*. New York: Holt, Rinehart & Winston.

Altrocchi, J. (1980) *Abnormal Behaviour*. New York: Harcourt Brace Jovanovich.

Amato, P.R. (1993) Children's adjustment to divorce: Theories, hypotheses and empirical support. *Journal of Marriage & the Family, 55,* 23–28.

American Psychiatric Association (1952) *Diagnostic and Statistical Manual of Mental Disorders*. Washington: American Psychiatric Association.

American Psychiatric Association (1968) *Diagnostic and Statistical Manual of Mental Disorders* (2nd edition). Washington, D.C. American Psychiatric Association.

American Psychiatric Association (1980) *Diagnostic and Statistical Manual of Mental Disorders* (3rd edition). Washington, D.C. American Psychiatric Association.

American Psychiatric Association (1987) *Diagnostic and Statistical Manual of Mental Disorders* (3rd edition, revised). Washington, D.C. American Psychiatric Association.

American Psychiatric Association (1994) *Diagnostic and Statistical Manual of Mental Disorders* (4th edition). Washington: American Psychiatric Association.

American Psychological Association (1981) *Ethical Principles of Psychologists*. Washington, D.C.: American Psychological Association.

American Psychological Association (1982) *Ethical Principles in Conduct of Research with Human Participants*. Washington, D.C: American Psychological Association.

American Psychological Association (1985) *Guidelines for Ethical Conduct in the Care and Use of Animals*. Washington, D.C: American Psychological Association.

Amice, V, Bercovi, J., Nahoul, K., Hatahet, M., & Amice, J. (1989) Increase in H-Y antigen positive lymphocytes in hirsute women: Effects of cyproterone acetate and estradiol treatment. *Journal of Clinical Endocrinology & Metabolism, 68,* 58–62.

Amir, Y. (1969) Contact hypothesis in ethnic relations. *Psychological Bulletin, 71,* 319–342.

Amir, Y. (1994) The contact hypothesis in intergroup relations. In W.J. Lonner & R.S. Malpass (Eds) *Psychology and Culture*. Boston: Allyn & Bacon.

Anand, B.K. & Brobeck, J.R. (1951) Hypothalamic control of food intake in rats and cats. *Yale Journal of Biological Medicine, 24,* 123–140.

Ancona, L. & Pareyson, R. (1968) Contributo allo studio della a aggressione: la dinimica della obbedienza distructiva. *Archivio di Psicologia Neurologia e Psichiatria, 29,* 340–372.

Andersen, S.M. & Miranda, R. (2000) Transference: How past relationships emerge in the present. *The Psychologist, 13*(12), 608–609.

Anderson, A. (1978) 'Old' is not a four-letter word. *Across the Board*, May.

Anderson, C.A. & Ford, C.M. (1986) Affect of the game player: Short-term effects of highly and mildly aggressive video games. *Personality & Social Psychology Bulletin, 12,* 390–402.

Anderson, D.R., Lorch, E.P., Field, D.E., Collins, P.A. & Nathan, J.G. (1986) Television viewing at home: Age trends in visual attention and time with TV. *Child Development, 57,* 1024–1033.

Anderson, J.R. (1983) *The Architecture of Cognition* (2nd edition). Cambridge, Massachusetts: Harvard University Press.

Anderson, J.R. (1985) *Cognitive Psychology and its Implications*. New York: Freeman.

Anderson, J.R. (1995a) *Learning and Memory: An Integrated Approach*. Chichester: Wiley.

Anderson, J.R. (1995b) *Cognitive Psychology & its Implications*. New York: W.H. Freeman & Company.

Anderson, J.R. & Reder, L. (1979) An elaborate processing explanation of depth of processing. In L.S. Cermak & F.I.M. Craik (Eds), *Levels of Processing in Human Memory*. Hillsdale, New Jersey: Lawrence Erlbaum Associates Inc.

Anderson, L.D. (1939) The predictive value of infant tests in relation to intelligence at 5 years. *Child Development, 10,* 203–212.

Anderson, L.P. (1991) Acculturative stress: A theory of relevance to black Americans. *Clinical Psychology Review, 11,* 685–702.

Anderson, N.H. (1974) Cognitive algebra: Integration theory applied to social attribution. In L. Berkowitz (Ed.), *Advances in Experimental Social Psychology, Volume 7*. New York: Academic Press.

Anderson, T. & Magnusson, D. (1990) Biological maturation and the development of drinking habits and alcohol abuse among young males. A prospective longitudinal study. *Journal of Youth & Adolescence, 19,* 33–41.

Andreae, S. (1998) Desire: It starts in your genes, not in your jeans. *The Independent on Sunday, Real Life,* 15 November, 5.

Andrews, B. & Brewin, C.R. (2000) What did Freud get right? *The Psychologist, 13*(12), 605–607.

Annett, M. (1991) Laterality and cerebral dominance. *Journal of Child Psychology & Psychiatry, 32*(2), 219–232.

Annis, R.C. & Frost, B. (1973) Human visual ecology and orientation anisotropies in acuity. *Science, 182,* 729–731.

Anshel, M.H. (1996) Effects of chronic aerobic exercise and progressive relaxation on motor performance and affect following acute stress. *Behavioural Medicine, 21,* 186–196.

Antaki, C. (1984) Core concepts in attribution theory. In J. Nicholson & H. Beloff (Eds), *Psychology Survey 5.* Leicester: British Psychological Society.

Archer, J. (1976) Biological explanations of psychological sex differences. In B. Lloyd & J. Archer (Eds) *Exploring Sex Differences.* London: Academic Press.

Archer, J. (1992) Childhood gender roles: Social context and organisation. In H. McGurk (Ed.) *Childhood Social Development: contemporary perspectives.* Hove: Erlbaum.

Archer, J. (1996) Evolutionary Social Psychology. In M. Hewstone, W. Stroebe, & G.M. Stephenson (Eds) *Introduction to Social Psychology* (2nd edition). Oxford: Blackwell.

Archer, J. (1999) *The Nature of Grief: The Evolution and Psychology of Reactions to Loss.* London: Routledge.

Archer, J. & Lloyd, B. (1985) *Sex and Gender.* New York: Cambridge University Press.

Ardrey, R. (1966) *The Territorial Imperative.* New York: Atheneum.

Arendt, H. (1965) *Eichmann in Jerusalem: A Report on the Banality of Evil.* New York: Viking.

Argyle, M. (1983) *The Psychology of Interpersonal Behaviour* (4th edition). Harmondsworth: Penguin.

Argyle, M. (1987) *The Psychology of Happiness.* London: Methuen.

Argyle, M. (1988) *Bodily Communication* (2nd edition). London: Methuen.

Argyle, M. (1989) *The Social Psychology of Work* (2nd edition). Harmondsworth: Penguin.

Argyle, M. Alkema, F. & Gilmour, R. (1972) The communication of friendly and hostile attitudes by verbal and non-verbal signals. *European Journal of Social Psychology, 1,* 385–402.

Argyle, M. & Dean, J. (1965) Eye contact, distance and affiliation. *Sociometry, 28,* 289–364.

Argyle, M. & Henderson, M. (1984) The rules of friendship. *Journal of Social & Personal Relationships, 1,* 211–237.

Argyle, M., Henderson, M. & Furnham, A. (1985) The rules of social relationships. *British Journal of Social Psychology, 24,* 125–129.

Arkes, H.R. & Blumer, C. (1985) The psychology of sunk cost. *Organisational Behaviour & Human Decision Processes, 35,* 124–140.

Arkin, R., Cooper, H. & Kolditz, T. (1980) A statistical review of the literature concerning the self-serving bias in interpersonal influence situations. *Journal of Personality & Social Psychology, 48,* 435–448.

Arlin, P.K. (1975) Cognitive development in adulthood: A fifth stage? *Developmental Psychology, 11,* 602–606.

Arlin, P.K. (1977) Piagetian operations in problem finding. *Developmental Psychology, 13,* 297–298.

Armsby, R.E. (1971) A re-examination of the development of moral judgement in children. *Child Development, 42,* 1241–1248.

Armstrong, D.M. (1987) Mind–body problem: Philosophical theories. In R.L. Gregory (Ed.) *The Oxford Companion to the Mind.* Oxford: Oxford University Press.

Aronfreed, J. (1963) The effects of experimental socialisation: paradigms upon two moral responses to transgression. *Journal of Abnormal & Social Psychology, 66,* 437–438.

Aronfreed, J. (1969) The concept of internalisation. In D.A. Goslin (Ed.), *Handbook of socialisation theory and research.* Chicago: Rand McNally.

Aronfreed, J. & Reber, A. (1965) Internalised behavioural suppression and the timing of social punishment. *Journal of Personality & Social Psychology, 1,* 3–17.

Aronson, E. (1968) The process of dissonance. In N. Warren & M. Jahoda (Eds), *Attitudes.* Harmondsworth, Middlesex: Penguin.

Aronson, E. (1980) *The Social Animal* (3rd edition). San Francisco: W.H. Freeman.

Aronson, E. (1988) *The Social Animal* (5th edition). New York: Freeman.

Aronson, E. (1992) *The Social Animal* (6th edition). New York: Freeman.

Aronson, E. (2000) The jigsaw strategy: Reducing prejudice in the classroom. *Psychology Review, 7*(2), 2–5.

Aronson, E. & Carlsmith, J.M. (1963) Effect of the severity of threat on the devaluation of forbidden behaviour. *Journal of Abnormal & Social Psychology, 6,* 584–588.

Aronson, E. & Linder, D. (1965) Gain and loss of esteem as determinants of interpersonal attraction. *Journal of Experimental Social Psychology, 1,* 156–171.

Aronson, E. & Mills, J. (1959) The effect of severity of initiation on liking for a group. *Journal of Abnormal & Social Psychology, 59,* 177–81.

Aronson, E. & Osherow, N. (1980) Co-operation, prosocial behaviour and academic performance: Experiments in the desegregated classroom. In L. Bickman (Ed.), *Applied Social Psychology Annual, Volume 1.* Beverly Hills, California: Sage Publications.

Aronson, E., Bridgeman, D.L. & Geffner, R. (1978) The effects of a co-operative classroom structure on student behaviour and attitudes. In D. Bar-Tal & L. Saxe (Eds) *Social Psychology of Education.* New York: Wiley.

Aronson, E., Willerman, B. & Floyd, J. (1966) The effect of a pratfall on increasing attractiveness. *Psychonomic Science, 4,* 227–228.

Asch, S.E. (1946) Forming impressions of personality. *Journal of Abnormal & Social Psychology, 41,* 258–290.

Asch, S.E. (1951) Effect of group pressure upon the modification and distortion of judgements. In H. Guetzkow (Ed.) *Groups, Leadership and Men.* Pittsburgh, PA: Carnegie Press.

Asch, S.E. (1952) *Social Psychology.* Englewood Cliffs, NJ: Prentice Hall.

Asch, S.E. (1955) Opinions and social pressure. *Scientific American, 193,* 31–35.

Asch, S.E. (1956) Studies of independence and submission to group pressure: 1: A minority of one against a unanimous majority. *Psychological Monographs, 70,* Whole No. 416.

Aschoff, J. (1979) Circadian rhythms: General features and endocrinological aspects. In D.T. Krieger (Ed.) *Endocrine Rhythms.* New York: Raven Press.

Aschoff, J. & Wever, R. (1981) The circadian system in man. In J. Aschoff (Ed.) *Handbook of Behavioural Neurology, Volume 4.* New York: Plenum Press.

Aserinsky, E. & Kleitman, N. (1953) Regularly occurring periods of eye motility and concomitant phenomena during sleep. *Science, 118,* 273–274.

Aslin, R.N., Pisoni, D.B. & Jusczyk, P.W. (1983) Auditory development and speech perception in infancy. In P.H. Mussen (Ed.) *Handbook of Child Psychology* (4th edition). New York: Wiley.

Asperger, H. (1944) Die 'Autistischen Psychopathen' in Kindesalten. *Archiv für Psychiatric und Nervenkrankheiter, 117,* 76–136.

Association for the Teaching of Psychology (1992) Ethics in psychological research: Guidelines for students at pre-degree levels. *Psychology Teaching, 4–10, New Series, No 1*.

Atchley, R.C. (1982) Retirement: Leaving the world of work. *Annals of the American Academy of Political & Social Science, 464,* 120–131.

Atchley, R.C. (1985) *Social Forces and Ageing: An Introduction to Social Gerontology*. Belmont, California: Wadsworth.

Atchley, R.C. & Robinson, J.L. (1982) Attitudes towards retirement and distance from the event. *Research on Ageing, 4,* 288–313.

Atkinson, R.C. & Shiffrin, R.M. (1968) Human memory: A proposed system and its control processes. In K.W. Spence & J.T. Spence (Eds) *The Psychology of Learning and Motivation, Volume 2*. London: Academic Press.

Atkinson, R.C. & Shiffrin, R.M. (1971) The control of short-term memory. *Scientific American, 224,* 82–90.

Atkinson, R.C., Hilgard, E.R., & Atkinson, R.L. (1983) *Introduction to Psychology* (8th edition). New York: Harcourt Brace Jovanovich.

Atkinson, R.L., Atkinson, R.C., Smith, E.E. & Bem, D.J. (1990) *Introduction to Psychology* (10th edition). New York: Harcourt Brace Jovanovich.

Atkinson, R.L., Atkinson, R.C., Smith, E.E. & Bem, D.J. (1993) *Introduction to Psychology* (11th edition). London: Harcourt Brace Jovanovich.

Attie, I. & Brooks-Gunn, J. (1989) Development of eating problems in adolescent girls: A longitudinal study. *Developmental Psychology, 25,* 70–79.

Attneave, F. (1954) Some informational aspects of visual perception. *Psychological Review, 61,* 183–193.

Atwood, M.E. & Polson, P.G. (1976) A process model for water-jug problems. *Cognitive Psychology, 8,* 191–216.

Averill, J.R. (1994) In the Eyes of the Beholder. In P. Ekman & R.J. Davidson (Eds) *The Nature of Emotion: Fundamental Questions*. New York: Oxford University Press.

Ax, A.F. (1953) The physiological differentiation of fear and anger in humans. *Psychosomatic Medicine, 15,* 422–433.

Ayllon, T. & Azrin, N.H. (1968) *The Token Economy: A Motivational System for Therapy and Rehabilitation*. New York: Appleton Century Crofts.

Ayllon, T. & Haughton, E. (1962) Control of the behaviour of schizophrenic patients by food. *Journal of the Experimental Analysis of Behaviour, 5,* 343–352.

Azrin, N. H. & Foxx, R.M. (1971) A rapid method of toilet training the institutionalised retarded. *Journal of Applied Behaviour Analysis, 4,* 89–99.

Azrin, N.H. & Holz, W.C. (1966) Punishment. In W.K. Honig (Ed.) *Operant Behaviour: Areas of Research and Application*. New York: Appleton-Century-Crofts.

Baddeley, A.D. (1966) The influence of acoustic and semantic similarity on long-term memory for word sequences. *Quarterly Journal of Experimental Psychology, 18,* 302–309.

Baddeley, A.D. (1976) *The Psychology of Memory*. New York: Basic Books.

Baddeley, A.D. (1978) The trouble with levels: A re-examination of Craik and Lockhart's 'Framework for Memory Research'. *Psychological Review, 85,* 139–52.

Baddeley, A.D. (1981) The concept of working memory: A view of its current state and probable future development. *Cognition, 10,* 17–23.

Baddeley, A.D. (1982) Domains of recollection. *Psychological Review, 89,* 708–729.

Baddeley, A.D. (1984) Neuropsychological evidence and the semantic/episodic distinction. *Behavioural & Brain Sciences, 7,* 238–239.

Baddeley, A.D. (1986) *Working Memory*. Oxford: Oxford University Press.

Baddeley, A.D. (1990) *Human Memory*. Hove: Lawrence Erlbaum Associates.

Baddeley, A.D. (1995) Memory. In C.C. French & A.M. Colman (Eds) *Cognitive Psychology*. London: Longman.

Baddeley, A.D. (1996) Exploring the central executive. *Quarterly Journal of Experimental Psychology, 49A,* 5–28.

Baddeley, A.D. (1997) *Human Memory: Theory and Practice* (revised edition). East Sussex: Psychology Press.

Baddeley, A.D. (1999) *Essentials of Human Memory*. Hove: Psychology Press.

Baddeley, A.D. & Hitch, G. (1974) Working memory. In G.H. Bower (Ed.) *Recent Advances in Learning and Motivation, Volume 8*. New York: Academic Press.

Baddeley, A.D. & Warrington, E.H. (1970) Amnesia and the distinction between long- and short-term memory. *Journal of Verbal Learning & Verbal Behaviour, 9,* 176–189.

Baddeley, A.D., Thomson, N. & Buchanan, M. (1975) Word length and the structure of short-term memory. *Journal of Verbal Learning & Verbal Behaviour, 14,* 575–589.

Bahrick, L.E., Walker, A.S. & Neisser, U. (1981) Selective looking by infants. *Cognitive Psychology, 13,* 377–390.

Bailey, C.L. (1979) Mental illness – a logical misrepresentation? *Nursing Times,* May, 761–762.

Bailey, S. (1993) Fast forward to violence. *Criminal Justice Matters, 3,* 6–7.

Baillargeon, R. (1987) Object permanence in 3½- and 4½-month-old infants. *Developmental Psychology, 33,* 655–664.

Baittle, B. & Offer, D. (1971) On the nature of adolescent rebellion. In F.C. Feinstein, P. Giovacchini & A. Miller (Eds) *Annals of Adolescent Psychiatry*. New York: Basic Books.

Bakan, D. (1967) *On Method*. San Francisco: Jossey-Bass Inc.

Baker, A. (2000) 'Even as I bought it I knew it couldn't work'. In A. Baker (Ed.) *Serious Shopping: Essays in Psychotherapy and Consumerism*. London: Free Association Books.

Ball, S. & Nuki, P. (1996) Most under-11s watch violent videos. *Sunday Times,* 23 July, 1.

Baltes, M.M. & Baltes, P.B. (1986) *The Psychology of Control and Ageing*. Hillsdale, NJ: Erlbaum.

Baltes, P.B. (1983) Life-span developmental psychology: Observations on history and theory revisited. In R.M. Lerner (Ed.) *Developmental Psychology: Historical and Philosophical Perspectives*. Hillsdale, NJ: Erlbaum.

Baltes, P.B. (1987) Theoretical propositions of life-span developmental psychology: On the dynamics of growth and decline. *Developmental Psychology, 23,* 611–626.

Baltes, P.B. & Baltes, M.M. (1993) *Successful Ageing: Perspectives from the Behavioural Sciences*. Cambridge: Cambridge University Press.

Bandura, A. (1965) Influence of model's reinforcement contingencies on the acquisition of imitative responses. *Journal of Personality & Social Psychology, 1,* 589–595.

Bandura, A. (1969) *Principles of Behaviour Modification*. New York: Holt, Rinehart & Winston.

Bandura, A. (1971) *Social Learning Theory*. Englewood Cliffs, NJ: Prentice-Hall.

Bandura, A. (1973) *Aggression: A Social Learning Analysis*. London: Prentice Hall.

Bandura, A. (1974) Behaviour theory and models of man. *American Psychologist, 29,* 859–869.

Bandura, A. (1977a) Self-efficacy: Toward a unifying theory of behaviour change. *Psychological Review, 84,* 191–215.

Bandura, A. (1977b) *Social Learning Theory* (2nd edition). Englewood Cliffs, NJ: Prentice-Hall.

Bandura, A. (1984) Recycling misconceptions of perceived self-efficacy. *Cognitive Therapy & Research, 8,* 231–235.

Bandura, A. (1986) *Social Foundations of Thought and Action.* Englewood Cliffs, NJ: Prentice-Hall.

Bandura, A. (1989) Social cognitive theory. In R. Vasta (Ed.) *Six Theories of Child Development.* Greenwich: JAI Press.

Bandura, A. (1994) Social cognitive theory of mass communication. In J. Bryant & D. Zillman (Eds) *Media Effects: Advances in Theory and Research.* Hove: Erlbaum.

Bandura, A. & Walters, R. (1959) *Social Learning and Personality Development.* New York: Holt.

Bandura, A. & Walters, R. (1963) *Adolescent Aggression.* New York: Ronald Press.

Bandura, A., Ross, D. & Ross, S.A. (1961) Transmission of aggression through imitation of aggressive models. *Journal of Abnormal & Social Psychology, 63,* 575–582.

Bandura, A., Ross, D. & Ross, S.A. (1963) Imitation of film-mediated aggressive models. *Journal of Abnormal & Social Psychology, 66,* 3–11.

Banks, M.H. & Jackson, P.R. (1982) Unemployment and risk of minor psychiatric disorder in young people: Cross-sectional and longitudinal evidence. *Psychological Medicine, 12,* 789–798.

Bannister, D. (1963) The genesis of schizophrenic thought disorder: A serial invalidation hypothesis. *British Journal of Psychiatry, 109,* 680–688.

Bannister, D. (1965) The genesis of schizophrenic thought disorder: A retest of the serial invalidation hypothesis. *British Journal of Psychiatry, 111,* 377–382.

Bannister, D. & Agnew, J. (1976) The child's construing of self. In J.K. Coal & A.W. Landfield (Eds), *Nebraska Symposium on Motivation.* Lincoln, Nebraska: University of Nebraska Press.

Bannister, D. & Fransella, F. (1967) A grid test of schizophrenic thought disorder. Barnstaple: *Psychological Test Publications.* Also in *British Journal of Social & Clinical Psychology, 5,* 95–102.

Bannister, D. & Fransella, F. (1980) *Inquiring Man: The Psychology of Personal Constructs* (2nd edition). Harmondsworth: Penguin.

Bannister, D. & Mair, M.J.M. (1968) *The Evaluation of Personal Constructs.* London: Academic Press.

Bannister, D., Salmon, P. & Lieberman, D.M. (1964) Diagnosis–treatment relationships in psychiatry: A statistical analysis. *British Journal of Psychiatry, 110,* 726–732.

Banuazizi, A. & Mohavedi, S. (1975) Interpersonal dynamics in a simulated prison: A methodological analysis. *American Psychologist, 30,* 152–160.

Banyard, P. (1996) Psychology and advertising. *Psychology Review, 3*(1), 24–27.

Banyard, P. & Hayes, N. (1994) *Psychology: Theory and Applications.* London: Chapman & Hall.

Barber, B.K. & Buehler, C. (1996) Family cohesion and enmeshment: Different constructs, different effects. *Journal of Marriage & The Family, 58* (2), 433–441.

Bard, K.A. (1994) Developmental issues in the evolution of mind. *American Psychologist, 49,* 760.

Bard, P. (1928) A diencephalic mechanism for the expression of rage with special reference to the sympathetic nervous system. *American Journal of Physiology, 84,* 490–515.

Bargh, J.A. & Pietromonaco, P. (1982) Automatic information processing and social perception: The influence of trait information presented outside of conscious awareness on impression formation. *Journal of Personality & Social Psychology, 43,* 437–449.

Bargh, J.A., Chen, M., & Burrows, L. (1996) The automaticity of social behaviour: Direct effects of trait concept and stereotype activation on action. *Journal of Personality & Social Psychology, 71,* 230–244.

Barker, R., Dembo, T. & Lewin, K. (1941) Frustration and regression: An experiment with young children. *University of Iowa Studies in Child Welfare, 18,* 1–314.

Barkham, M. & Shapiro, D. (1992) Response to Paul Kline. In W. Dryden & C. Feltham (Eds) *Psychotherapy And Its Discontents.* Buckingham: Open University Press.

Barkow, J., Cosmides, L., & Tooby, J. (Eds) (1992) *The Adapted Mind: Evolutionary Psychology and the Generation of Culture.* New York: Oxford University Press.

Barnard, N.D. & Kaufman, S.R. (1997) Animal research is wasteful and misleading. *Scientific American,* February, 64–66.

Barnes-Gutteridge, W. (1974) *Psychology.* London: Hamlyn.

Baron, R.A. (1977) *Human Aggression.* New York: Plenum.

Baron, R.A. (1989) *Psychology: The Essential Science.* London: Allyn & Bacon.

Baron, R.A. & Byrne, D. (1991) *Social Psychology* (6th edition). Boston: Allyn and Bacon.

Baron, R.A. & Richardson, D.R. (1994) *Human Aggression* (2nd edition). New York: Plenum.

Baron, R.S. (1986) Distraction–conflict theory: Progress and problems. In L. Berkowitz (Ed.) *Advances in Experimental Social Psychology, Volume 19.* New York: Academic Press.

Baron-Cohen, S. (1987) Autism and symbolic play. *British Journal of Developmental Psychology, 5,* 139–148.

Baron-Cohen, S. (1988) Social and pragmatic deficits in autism: Cognitive or affective? *Journal of Autism & Developmental Disorders, 18,* 379–402.

Baron-Cohen, S. (1990) Autism: A specific cognitive disorder of 'mind-blindness'. *International Review of Psychiatry, 2,* 79–88.

Baron-Cohen, S. (1993) From attention–goal psychology to belief–desire psychology: The development of a theory of mind and its dysfunction. In S. Baron-Cohen, H. Tager-Flusberg, & D.J.Cohen (Eds) *Understanding other minds: Perspectives from Autism.* Oxford: Oxford University Press.

Baron-Cohen, S. (1995a) Infantile autism. In A.A. Lazarus & A.M. Colman (Eds) *Abnormal Psychology.* London: Longman

Baron-Cohen, S. (1995b) *Mindblindness: An Essay on Autism and Theory of Mind.* Cambridge, MA: MIT Press.

Baron-Cohen, S. (2000) Autism and 'theory of mind'. In J. Hartley & A. Branthwaite (Eds) *The Applied Psychologist* (2nd edition). Buckingham: Open University Press.

Baron-Cohen, S., Allen, J., & Gillberg, C. (1992) Can autism be detected at 18 months? The needle, the haystack, and the CHAT. *British Journal of Psychiatry, 161,* 839–843.

Baron-Cohen, S., Leslie, A.M., & Frith, U. (1985) Does the autistic child have a theory of mind? *Cognition, 21,* 37–46.

Barrett, M.D. (1986) Early semantic representations and early word usage. In S.A. Kuczaj & M.D. Barrett (Eds), *The Development of Word Meaning.* New York: Springer Verlag.

Barrett, M.D. (1989) Early language development. In A. Slater & G. Bremner (Eds) *Infant Development.* Hove: Erlbaum.

Barrett, R. & Robinson, B. (1994) Gay dads. In A.E. Gottfried & A.W. Gottfried (Eds) *Redefining Families.* New York: Plenum Press.

Bar-Tal, D. & Saxe, L. (1976) Perception of similarity and dissimilarity in attractive couples and individuals. *Journal of Personality & Social Psychology, 33,* 772–781.

Bartlett, D. (1998) *Stress: Perspectives and Processes.* Buckingham: Open University Press.

Bartlett, F.C. (1932) *Remembering.* Cambridge: Cambridge University Press.

Bartlett, F.C. (1958) *Thinking.* New York: Basic Books.

Bartlett, J.C. & Searcy, J. (1993) Inversion and configuration of faces. *Cognitive Psychology, 25,* 281–316.

748

References

Bass, E. & Davis, L. (1990) *The Courage to Heal: A Guide for Women Survivors of Child Sexual Abuse.* London: Cedar.

Bass, E. & Davis, L. (1993) *Beginning to Heal: A First Guide for Female Survivors of Child Sexual Abuse.* London: Cedar.

Bates, E., Benigni, L., Bretherton, I., Camaioni, L. & Volterra, V. (1979) *The Emergence of Symbols: Cognition and Communication in Infancy.* New York: Academic Press.

Bates, E., O'Connell, B. & Shore, C. (1987) Language and communication in infancy. In J.D. Osofsky (Ed.) *Handbook of Infant Development* (2nd edition). New York: Wiley.

Bateson, G., Jackson, D., Haley, J. & Weakland, J. (1956) Toward a theory of schizophrenia. *Behavioural Science, 1,* 251–264.

Bateson, P. (1986) When to experiment on animals. *New Scientist, 109* (14960), 30–32.

Bateson, P. (1992) Do animals feel pain? *New Scientist, 134* (1818), 30–33.

Batson, C.D. (2000) Altruism: Why do we help others? *Psychology Review, 7*(1), 2–5.

Batson, C.D. & Oleson, K.C. (1991) Current status of the empathy–altruism hypothesis. In M.S. Clark (Ed.) *Prosocial Behaviour. Review of Personality and Social Psychology, 12.* Newbury Park, CA.: Sage.

Baumeister, R.F. & Leary, M.R. (1995) The need to belong: Desire for interpersonal attachments as a fundamental human motivation. *Psychological Bulletin, 117,* 497–529.

Baumrind, D. (1964) Some thoughts on ethics of research: after reading Milgram's behavioural study of obedience. *American Psychologist, 19,* 421–423.

Baxter, B., Ninson, R.E., Wall, A-M., & Mckee, S.A. (1998) Incorporating culture into the treatment of alcohol abuse and dependence. In S.S. Kazarian & D.R. Evans (Eds) *Cultural Clinical Psychology: Theory, Research and Practice.* New York: Oxford University Press.

Baydar, N. & Brooks-Gunn, J. (1991) Effects of maternal employment and child-care arrangements on pre-schoolers' cognitive and behavioural outcomes. *Developmental Psychology, 27,* 932–945.

Bayley, N. (1969) *Bayley Scales of Infant Development.* New York: Psychological Corporation.

Beaman, A.L., Barnes, P.J., Klentz, B., & Mcquirk, B. (1978) Increasing helping rates through information dissemination: Teaching pays. *Personality & Social Psychology Bulletin, 4,* 406–411.

Beaumont, J.G. (1988) *Understanding Neuropsychology.* Oxford: Blackwell.

Beaumont, P. (1996) Thirtysomethings who won't grow up. *The Observer,* 19 May, 11.

Beck, A.T. (1963) Thinking and depression. *Archives of General Psychiatry, 9,* 324–333.

Beck, A.T. (1967) *Depression: Causes and Treatment.* Philadelphia: University of Philadelphia Press.

Beck, A.T. (1974) The development of depression: A cognitive model. In R.J. Friedman & M.M. Katz (Eds) *The Psychology of Depression: Contemporary Theory and Research.* New York: Wiley.

Beck, A.T. (1976) *Cognitive Therapy and the Emotional Disorders.* New York: International Universities Press.

Beck, A.T. (1993) Cognitive therapy: Past, present and future. *Journal of Consulting & Clinical Psychology, 61*(2), 194–198.

Beck, A.T. (1997) Cognitive therapy: Reflections. In J.K. Zeig (Ed.), *The Evolution of Psychotherapy: The Third Conference.* New York: Brunner/Mazel.

Beck, A.T. & Freeman, A. (1990) *Cognitive Therapy of Personality Disorders.* New York: Guilford Press.

Beck, A.T. & Weishaar, M.E. (1989) Cognitive therapy. In R.J. Corsini & D. Wedding (Eds) *Current Psychotherapies.* Itasca, ILL: Peacock.

Beck, A.T. & Young, J.E. (1978) College blues. *Psychology Today,* September, 80–92.

Beck, A.T., Rush, A.J., Shaw, B.F. & Emory, G. (1979) *Cognitive Therapy of Depression.* New York: Guilford Press.

Becker, H.S. (1963) *Outsiders: Studies in the Sociology of Deviance.* New York: Free Press.

Becker, M.H. (Ed.) (1974) The health belief model and personal health behaviour. *Health Education Monographs, 2,* 324–508.

Becker, M.H. (1984) Compliance with medical advice. In A. Steptoe & A. Mathews (Eds) *Health Care and Human Behaviour.* London: Academic Press.

Becker, M.H. & Rosenstock, I.M. (1984) Compliance with medical advice. In A. Steptoe & A. Mathews (Eds) *Health Care and Human Behaviour.* London: Acedemic Press.

Becker, M.H. & Rosenstock, I.M. (1987) Comparing social learning theory and the health belief model. In W.B. Ward (Ed.) *Advances in Health Education and Promotion.* Greenwich, CT: JAI Press.

Becker, M.H, Maiman, L.A., Kirscht, J.P., Haefner, D.P., & Drachman, R.H. (1977) The health belief model and prediction of dietary compliance: A field experiment. *Journal of Health & Social Behaviour, 18,* 348–366.

Bee, H. (1989) *The Developing Child* (5th edition). New York: Harper & Row.

Bee, H. (1992) *The Developing Child* (7th edition). New York: HarperCollins.

Bee, H. (1994) *Lifespan Development.* New York: HarperCollins.

Bee, H. (2000) *The Developing Child* (9th edition). Boston: Allyn & Bacon.

Bee, H. & Mitchell, S.K. (1980) *The Developing Person: A Lifespan Approach.* New York: Harper & Row.

Bekerian, D.A. & Bowers, J.M. (1983) Eye-witness testimony: Were we misled? *Journal of Experimental Psychology: Learning, Memory & Cognition, 9,* 139–145.

Bekerian, D.A. & Dennett, J.L. (1993) The cognitive interview technique: Reviewing the issues. *Applied Cognitive Psychology, 7,* 275–298.

Belknap, J. (1996) *The Invisible Woman: Gender, Crime and Justice.* Belmont, CA: Wadsworth.

Bell, S.M. & Ainsworth, M.D.S. (1972) Infant crying and maternal responsiveness. *Child Development, 43,* 1171–1190.

Bellur, R. (1995) Interpersonal attraction revisited: Cross-cultural conceptions of love. *Psychology Review, 1,* 24–26.

Beloff, J. (1987) Parapsychology and the mind–body problem. In R.L. Gregory (Ed.) *The Oxford Companion to the Mind.* Oxford: Oxford University Press.

Beloff, J. (1993) *Parapsychology: A Concise History.* London: Athlone Press.

Belsky, J. & Rovine, M.J. (1988) Nonmaternal care in the first year of life and the infant–parent attachment. *Child Development, 59,* 157–167.

Belson, W.A. (1978) *Television Violence and the Adolescent Boy.* Farnborough: Saxon House.

Bem, D.J. (1965) An experimental analysis of self-persuasion. *Journal of Experimental & Social Psychology, 1,* 199–218.

Bem, D.J. (1967) Self-perception: An alternative interpretation of cognitive dissonance phenomena. *Psychological Review, 74,* 183–200.

Bem, D.J. (1970) *Beliefs, Attitudes and Human Affairs.* Belmont, California: Brooks Cole.

Bem, D.J. (1972) Self-perception theory. In L. Berkowitz (Ed.) *Advances in Experimental Social Psychology, Volume 6.* New York: Academic Press.

Bem, D.J. & Allen, A. (1974) On predicting some of the people some of the time: A search for cross-situational consistencies in behaviour. *Psychological Review, 81,* 506–520.

Bem, S.L. (1974) The measurement of psychological androgyny. *Journal of Consulting & Clinical Psychology, 42* (2), 155–162.

Bem, S.L. (1984) Androgyny and gender schema theory: a conceptual and empirical integration. In R.A. Dienstbier (Ed.), *Nebraska Symposium on Motivation.* Lincoln, Nebraska: University of Nebraska Press.

Bem, S.L. (1985) Androgyny and gender schema theory: A conceptual and empirical integration. In T.B. Sonderegger (Ed.) *Nebraska Symposium on Motivation.* Nebraska, NE: University of Nebraska Press.

Bem, S.L. (1993) Is there a place in psychology for a feminist analysis of the social context? *Feminism & Psychology, 3*(2), 230–234.

Bender, M. (1995) The war goes on. *The Psychologist, 8,* 78–79.

Benedict, R. (1934) *Patterns of Culture.* Boston: Houghton Mifflin.

Benedict, R. (1954) Continuities and discontinuities in cultural conditioning. In W.E. Martin & C.B. Stendler (Eds), *Readings in Child Development.* New York: Harcourt Brace Jovanovich.

Bennett, M. (1993) Introduction. In M. Bennett (Ed.) *The Child as Psychologist: An Introduction to the Development of Social Cognition.* Hemel Hempstead: Harvester Wheatsheaf.

Bennett-Levy, J. & Marteau, T. (1984) Fear of animals: What is prepared? *British Journal of Psychology, 75,* 37–42.

Bennetto, J. (2000) 'The most dangerous message of all is the one that says all drugs are equally dangerous'. *The Independent,* 29 March, 3.

Benson, P.L., Karabenick, S.A. & Lerner, R.M. (1976) Pretty pleases: The effects of physical attractiveness, race and sex on receiving help. *Journal of Experimental & Social Psychology, 12,* 409–415.

Bentall, R. (Ed.) (1990) *Reconstructing Schizophrenia.* London: Routledge.

Bentall, R. (1998) Why there will never be a convincing theory of schizophrenia. In S. Rose (Ed.) *From Brains to Consciousness?: Essays on the New Sciences of the Mind.* Harmondsworth: Penguin.

Benton, D. (1981) ECT. Can the system take the shock? *Community Care,* 12 March, 15–17.

Bereiter, C. & Engelman, S. (1966) *Teaching Disadvantaged Children in The Pre-School.* Englewood Cliffs, NJ: Prentice-Hall.

Berger, H. (1929) Über das Elektrenkephalogramm des Menschen. *Archiv für Psychiatrie & Nervenkrankheiten, 87,* 527–570.

Bergin, A.E. (1971) The evaluation of therapeutic outcomes. In A.E. Bergin & S.L. Garfield (Eds) *Handbook of Psychotherapy and Behaviour Change: An Empirical Analysis.* New York: Wiley.

Bergin, A.E. (1980) Psychotherapy and religious values. *Journal of Consulting & Clinical Psychology, 48,* 642–645.

Bergin, A.E. & S.L. Garfield (Eds), *Handbook of Psychotherapy and Behaviour Change: An Empirical Analysis* (2nd edition). New York: Wiley.

Bergin, A.E. & Lambert, M.J. (1978) *The evaluation of therapeutic outcomes.* In A.E. Bergin and S.L. Garfield (Eds) *Handbook of Psychotherapy and Behaviour Change: an Empirical Analysis* (2nd edition). New York: Wiley.

Berko, J. (1958) The child's learning of English morphology. *Word, 14,* 150–177.

Berko, J. & Brown, R. (1960) Psycholinguistic research methods. In P.H. Mussen (Ed.) *Handbook of Research Methods in Child Development.* New York: Wiley.

Berkowitz, L. (1966) On not being able to aggress. *British Journal of Clinical & Social Psychology, 5,* 130–139.

Berkowitz, L. (1968) Impulse, aggression and the gun. *Psychology Today,* September, 18–22.

Berkowitz, L. (1969) The frustration–aggression hypothesis revisited. In L. Berkowitz (Ed.), *Roots of Aggression: A Re-examination of the Frustration–aggression Hypothesis.* New York: Atherton Press.

Berkowitz, L. (1978) Whatever happened to the frustration–aggression hypothesis? *American Behavioural Scientist, 21,* 691–708.

Berkowitz, L. (1989) The frustration–aggression hypothesis: an examination and reformation. *Psychological Bulletin, 106,* 59–73.

Berkowitz, L. (1990) On the formation and regulation of anger and aggression – a cognitive neoassociationistic analysis. *American Psychologist, 45,* 494–503.

Berkowitz, L. (1993) *Aggression: Its Causes, Consequences and Control.* New York: McGraw-Hill.

Berkowitz, L. (1995) A career on aggression. In G.G. Brannigan & M.R. Merrens (Eds) *The Social Psychologists: Research Adventures.* New York: McGraw-Hill.

Berkowitz, L. & Geen, R.G. (1966) Film violence and the cue properties of available targets. *Journal of Personality & Social Psychology, 3,* 525–530.

Berkowitz, L. & LePage, A. (1967) Weapons as aggression–eliciting stimuli. *Journal of Personality & Social Psychology, 7,* 202–207.

Berlin, B. & Kay, P. (1969) *Basic Colour Terms: Their Universality and Evolution.* Berkeley, CA: University of California Press.

Berlyne, D.E. (1960) *Conflict, Arousal and Curiosity.* London: McGraw-Hill.

Bernstein, B. (1961) Social class and linguistic development: A theory of social learning. In A.H. Halsey, J. Floyd & C.A. Anderson (Eds) *Education, Economy and Society.* London: Collier-Macmillan Ltd.

Berry, D.S. & Willingham, J.K. (1997) Affective traits, responses to conflict, and satisfaction in romantic relationships. *Journal of Research in Personality, 31,* 564–576.

Berry, J.W. (1969) On cross-cultural compatability. *International Journal of Psychology, 4,* 119–128.

Berry, J.W. (1994) *Cross-cultural health psychology.* Keynote address presented to the International Congress of Applied Psychology, Madrid (July).

Berry, J.W. (1998) Acculturation and Health: Theory and Research. In S.S. Kazarian & D.R. Evans (Eds) *Cultural Clinical Psychology: Theory, Research, and Practice.* New York: Oxford University Press.

Berry, J.W., Poortinga, Y.H., Segall, M.H. & Dasen, P.R. (1992) *Cross-Cultural Psychology.* Cambridge: Cambridge University Press.

Berscheid, E. (1985) Interpersonal attraction. In G. Lindzey & E. Aronson (Eds), *Handbook of Social Psychology* (3rd edition, Volume 2). New York: Random House.

Berscheid, E. & Walster, E.M. (1974) Physical attractiveness. In L. Berkowitz (Ed.) *Advances in Experimental Social Psychology, Volume 7.* New York: Academic Press.

Berscheid, E. & Walster, E.M. (1978) *Interpersonal Attraction* (2nd edition). Reading, MA: Addison-Wesley.

Berscheid, E., Dion, K., Hatfield, E. & Walster, G.W. (1971) Physical attractiveness and dating choice: A test of the matching hypothesis. *Journal of Experimental & Social Psychology, 7,* 173–189.

Bertenthal, B.I. & Fischer, K.W. (1978) Development of self-recognition in the infant. *Developmental Psychology, 14,* 44–50.

Besevegis, E. & Giannitsas, N. (1996) Parent–adult relations and conflicts as perceived by adolescents. In L. Verhofstadt-Deneve, I. Kienhorst & C. Braet (Eds) *Conflict and Development in Adolescence.* Leiden: DSWO Press.

Bestic, L. (1998) Sleep perchance to do more. *The Independent Review,* 29 December, 7.

Bettelheim, B. (1985) *Freud and Man's Soul.* London: Flamingo.

750

Bexton, W.H., Heron, W. & Scott, T.H. (1954) Effects of decreased variation in the sensory environment. *Canadian Journal of Psychology, 8,* 70.

Bickman, L. (1971) The effects of another bystander's ability to help on bystander intervention in an emergency. *Journal of Experimental Social Psychology, 7,* 367–379.

Bickman, L. (1974) The social power of a uniform. *Journal of Applied Social Psychology, 1,* 47–61.

Biederman, I. (1987) Recognition-by-components: A theory of human image understanding. *Psychological Review, 94,* 115–147.

Bierhoff, H.W. (1983) Wie hilfreich ist der Mensch? *Bild der Wissenschaft, 12,* 118–126.

Bierhoff, H.W. & Klein, R. (1988) Prosocial behaviour. In M. Hewstone, W. Stroebe, J.P. Codol & G.M. Stephenson (Eds) *Introduction to Social Psychology*. Oxford: Blackwell.

Billig, M. (1976) *Social Psychology and Intergroup Relations*. London: Academic Press.

Billig, M. (1978) *Fascists: A Social Psychological View of the National Front*. London: Harcourt Brave Jovanovich.

Billig, M. & Tajfel, H. (1973) Social categorisation and similarity in intergroup behaviour. *European Journal of Social Psychology, 3,* 27–52.

Binet, A. (1916) The development of intelligence in children (The Binet-Simon scale), translated from articles in *L'Annee psychologique* from 1905, 1908, and 1911 by Elizabeth Kile). Baltimore: Williams & Wilkins.

Binet, A. & Simon, TH. (1911) *A Method of Measuring the Development of the Intelligence of Young Children*. Lincoln, ILL: Courier Company.

Blackman, D.E. (1980) Images of man in contemporary behaviourism. In A.J. Chapman and D.M. Jones (Eds) *Models of Man*. Leicester: British Psychological Society.

Blackmore, S. (1996) Do you believe in psychic phenomena? Are they likely to be able to explain consciousness? *The Times Higher,* 5 April, V.

Blackmore, S. (1995) Parapsychology. In A.M. Colman (Ed.) *Controversies in Psychology*. London: Longman.

Blackmore, S. (1997) In search of the paranormal. *Psychology Review, 3*(3), 2–6.

Blackmore, S.J. (1988) Visions from the dying brain. *New Scientist, 5* May, 43–46.

Blair, R.J.R. (1995) A cognitive developmental approach to morality: Investigating the psychopath. *Cognition, 57,* 1–29.

Blair, R.J.R., Jones, L., Clark, F. & Smith, M (1997) The psychopathic individual: A lack of responsiveness to distress cues? *Psychophysiology, 34,* 192–198.

Blair, R.J.R., Morris, J.S., Frith, C.D., Perrett, D.I. & Dolan, R.J. (1999) Dissociable neural responses to facial expressions of sadness and anger. *Brain, 122,* 883–893.

Blakemore, C. (1988) *The Mind Machine*. London: BBC Publications.

Blakemore, C. & Cooper, G.F. (1970) Development of the brain depends on the visual environment. *Nature, 228,* 477–8.

Blaney, P. (1975) Implications of the medical model and its alternatives. *American Journal of Psychiatry, 132,* 911–914.

Blasi, A. (1980) Bridging moral cognition and moral action: a critical review of the literature. *Psychological Bulletin, 88,* 1–45.

Blau, P.M. (1964) *Exchange and Power in Social Life*. New York: Wiley.

Bleuler, E. (1911) *Dementia Praecox or the Group of Schizophrenias* (J. Avikin, trans.). New York: International University Press.

Bleuler, M.E. (1978) The long-term course of schizophrenic psychoses. In L.C. Wynne, R.L. Cromwell & S. Mathyse (Eds) *The Nature of Schizophrenia: New Approaches to Research and Treatment*. New York: Wiley.

Block, J. (1978) Review of H.J. Eysenck and S.B.G. Eysenck, The Eysenck Personality Questionnaire. In O. Buros (Ed.) *The Eighth Mental Measurement Yearbook*. Highland Park, NJ: Gryphon.

Block, J. (1979) Another look as sex differentiation in the socialisation behaviours of mothers and fathers. In F. Denmark & J. Sherman (Eds) *Psychology of Women: Future Directions of Research*. New York: Psychological Dimensions.

Bloom, B.S. (1964) *Stability and Change in Human Characteristics*. New York: Harcourt Brace Jovanovich.

Bloom, L. (1973) *One Word at a Time*. The Hague: Mouton.

Blundell, J.E. & Hill, A.J. (1995) Hunger and appetite. In Parkinson, B. & Colman, A.M. (Eds) *Emotion and Motivation*. London: Longman.

Blyth, D.A., Simmons, R.G., Bulcroft, R., Felt, D., Vancleave, E.F. & Bush, D.M. (1981) The effects of physical development on self-image and satisfaction with body–image for early adolescent males. *Research in Community & Mental Health, 2,* 43–73.

Boas, T, N., Coker, E. & Wakeling, A. (1992) Anorexia nervosa of late onset. *British Journal of Psychiatry, 160,* 257–260.

Boden, M. (1980) Artificial intelligence and intellectual imperialism. In A.J. Chapman & D.M. Jones (Eds) *Models of Man*. Leicester: British Psychological Society.

Boden, M. (1987a) *Artificial Intelligence and Natural Man* (2nd edition). Cambridge, MA: Harvard University Press.

Boden, M. (1987b) Artificial intelligence. In R. Gregory (Ed.), *Oxford Companion to the Mind*. Oxford: Oxford University Press.

Boden, M. (1993) The impact on philosophy. In D. Broadbent (Ed.) *The Simulation of Human Intelligence*. Oxford: Blackwell.

Bodmer, W.F. (1972) Race and I.Q.: The genetic background. In K. Richardson & D. Spears (Eds), *Race, Culture and Intelligence*. Harmondsworth, Middlesex: Penguin.

Bogardus, E.S. (1925) Measuring social distance. *Journal of Applied Sociology, 9,* 299–308.

Bogen, J.E. (1969) The other side of the brain. *Bulletin of the Los Angeles Neurological Societies, 34,* 3.

Bolles, R.C. (1967) *Theory of Motivation*. New York: Harper & Row.

Bolles, R.C. (1980) Ethological learning theory. In G.M. Gazda & R.J. Corsini (Eds) *Theories of Learning: A Comparative Approach*. Itaska, ILL.: Free Press.

Bond, C.F., JR. & Titus, L.J (1983) Social facilitation: A meta-analysis of 241 studies. *Psychological Bulletin, 94,* 265–292.

Bond, J., Coleman, P. & Peace, S. (Eds) (1993) *Ageing in Society: An Introduction to Social Gerontology*. London: Sage.

Bond, R.A. & Smith, P.B. (1996) Culture and conformity: A meta-analysis of studies using the Asch's (1952b, 1956) line judgement task. *Psychological Bulletin, 119,* 111–137.

Boon, J. & Davies, G. (1992) Fact and fiction in offender profiling. *Issues in Legal & Criminological Psychology, 32,* 3–9.

Booth, A. & Amato, P.R. (1994) Parental marital quality, parental divorce and relations with parents. *Journal of Marriage & The Family, 55,* 21–34.

Booth, T. (1975) *Growing up in Society*. London: Methuen.

Boring, E.G. (1923) Intelligence as the tests test it. *New Republic, 6* June, 35–37.

Boring, E.G. (1966) Introduction. In C.E.M. Hansel (Ed.) *ESP: A Scientific Evaluation*. New York: Scribners.

Borke, H. (1975) Piaget's mountains revisited: Changes in the egocentric landscape. *Developmental Psychology, 11,* 240–243.

Bornstein, M.H. (1976) Infants are trichromats. *Journal of Experimental Child Psychology, 19,* 401–419.

Bornstein, M.H. (1988) Perceptual development across the life-cycle. In M.H. Bornstein & M.E. Lamb (Eds) *Perceptual, Cognitive and Linguistic Development*. Hove: Erlbaum.

Bornstein, M.H. (1989) Sensitive periods in development: Structural characteristics and causal interpretations. *Psychological Bulletin, 105*, 179–197.

Boseley, S. (1999) They said it was safe. *The Guardian Weekend*, 30 October, 12–17.

Boseley, S. (2000) Study reveals teenage regrets over first sex. *The Guardian*, 5 May, 11.

Botting, J.H. & Morrison, A.R. (1997) Animal research is vital to medicine. *Scientific American*, 67–79, February.

Botwinick, J. (1978) *Ageing and Behaviour* (2nd edition). New York: Springer.

Bouchard, T.J. & McGue, M. (1981) Familial studies of intelligence: A review. *Science, 212*, 1055–1059.

Bouchard, T.J. & Segal, N.L. (1988) Heredity, environment and IQ. In *Instructor's Resource Manual* to accompany G. Lindzay, R. Thompson & B. Spring *Psychology* (3rd edition). New York: Worth Publishers.

Bouchard, T.J., Lykken, D.T., McGue, M., Segal, N.L. & Tellegen, A. (1990) Sources of human psychological differences: The Minnesota study of twins reared apart. *Science, 250*, 223–228.

Bourne, L.E., Dominowski, R.L. & Loftus, E.F. (1979) *Cognitive Processes*. Englewood Cliffs, NJ: Prentice-Hall.

Bousfield, W.A. (1953) The occurrence of clustering in the recall of randomly arranged associates. *Journal of General Psychology, 49*, 229–240.

Bower, B. (1994) Piecing together personality. *Science News, 145*, 152–154.

Bower, B. (1995) Deceptive appearances: Imagined physical defects take an ugly personal toll. *Science News, 148*, 40–41.

Bower, G.H. (1972) Mental imagery and associative learning. In L. Gregg (Ed.), *Cognition in Learning and Memory*. New York: Wiley.

Bower, G.H. (1975) Cognitive psychology: An introduction. In W. Estes (Ed.), *Handbook of Learning and Cognitive Processes, Volume 1*. Hillsdale, New Jersey: Lawrence Erlbaum Associates Inc.

Bower, G.H. & Karlin, M.B. (1974) Depth of processing pictures of faces and recognition memory. *Journal of Experimental Psychology, 103*, 751–757.

Bower, G.H. & Springston, F. (1970) Pauses as recoding points in letter series. *Journal of Experimental Psychology, 83*, 421–430.

Bower, G.H., Black, J.B. & Turner, T.J. (1979) Scripts in memory for text. *Cognitive Psychology, 11*, 177–220.

Bower, G.H., Clark, M., Lesgold, A. & Winzenz, D. (1969) Hierarchical retrieval schemes in recall of categorised word lists. *Journal of Verbal Learning & Verbal Behaviour, 8*, 323–343.

Bower, T.G.R. (1966) The visual world of infants. *Scientific American, 215*, 80–92.

Bower, T.G.R. (1971) The object in the world of the infant. *Scientific American, 225*, 38–47.

Bower, T.G.R. (1976) Repetitive processes in child development. *Scientific American, 235* (5), 38–47.

Bower, T.G.R. (1977) *The Perceptual World of the Child*. London: Fontana Paperbacks.

Bower, T.G.R. (1979) *Human Development*. San Francisco: W.H. Freeman.

Bower, T.G.R. & Wishart, J.G. (1972) The effects of motor skill on object permanence. *Cognition, 1*, 28–35.

Bower, T.G.R., Broughton, J.M. & Moore, M.K. (1970) Infant responses to approaching objects: An indicator of response to distal variables. *Perception & Psychophysics, 9*, 193–196.

Bowers, K. (1973) Situationism in psychology: An analysis and critique. *Psychological Review, 80*, 307–336.

Bowie, I. (1991) Eye structure: A functional view. *Nursing Standard, 5* (50), 54–55.

Bowlby, J. (1951) *Maternal Care and Mental Health*. Geneva: World Health Organisation.

Bowlby, J. (1953) *Child Care and the Growth of Love*. Harmondsworth: Penguin.

Bowlby, J. (1969) *Attachment and Loss. Volume 1: Attachment*. Harmondsworth: Penguin.

Bowlby, J. (1973) *Attachment and Loss. Volume 2: Separation*. Harmondsworth: Penguin.

Bowlby, J. (1977) The making and breaking of affectional bonds: 1. Aetiology and psychopathology in the light of attachment theory. *British Journal of Psychiatry, 130*, 201–210.

Bowlby, J. (1980) *Attachment and Loss. Volume 3: Loss, Sadness and Depression*. London: Hogarth Press.

Bowlby, J. (1988) *A Secure Base: Clinical Applications of Attachment Theory*. London: Tavistock/Routledge.

Bowlby, J., Ainsworth, M., Boston, M. & Rosenbluth, D. (1956) The effects of mother–child separation: A follow-up study. *British Journal of Medical Psychology, 24 (3 and 4)*, 211–247.

Bradbury, T.N. & Fincham, F.D. (1990) Attributions in marriage: Review and critique. *Psychological Bulletin, 107*, 3–33.

Braddick, O.J. (1974) A short range process in apparent motion. *Vision Research, 14*, 519–527.

Bradley, B.P. & Baddeley, A.D. (1990) Emotional factors in forgetting. *Psychological Medicine, 20*, 351–355.

Bradley, L.A. (1995) Chronic benign pain. In D. Wedding (Ed.) *Behaviour and Medicine* (2nd edition). St Louis, MO: Mosby-Year Book.

Bradshaw, J.L. & Wallace, G. (1971) Models for the processing and identification of faces. *Perception & Psychophysics, 9*, 443–448.

Brady, J.V. (1958) Ulcers in executive monkeys. *Scientific American, 199*, 95–100.

Braine, M.D.S. (1971) On two types of models of the internalisation of grammars. In D.I. Slobin (Ed.) *The Ontogenesis of Grammar*. New York: Academic Press.

Braine, M.D.S. (1976) Children's first word combinations. Monographs of the Society for Research in *Child Development, 41* (Whole No. 164).

Brainerd, C.J. (1978) Learning research and Piagetian theory. In L. Siegel & C.J. Brainerd (Eds), *Alternatives to Piaget: Critical Essays on the Theory*. New York: Academic Press.

Brainerd, C.J. (1978) Neo-Piagetian training experiments revisited: Is there any support for the cognitive–developmental stage hypothesis? *Cognition, 2*, 349–370.

Brainerd, C.J. (1983) Modifiability of cognitive development. In S. Meadows (Ed.) *Development of Thinking*. London: Methuen.

Brandon, S., Boakes, J., Glaser, D., & Green, R. (1998) Recovered memories of childhood sexual abuse: Implications for clinical practice. *British Journal of Psychiatry, 172*, 293–307.

Bransford, J.D., Franks, J.J., Morris, C.D. & Stein, B.S. (1979) Some general constraints on learning and memory research. In L.S. Cernak & F.I.M. Craik (Eds) *Levels of Processing in Human Memory*. Hillside, NJ: Erlbaum.

Breggin, P. (1991) *Toxic Psychiatry*. London: HarperCollins.

Brehm, J.W. (1956) Post-decision changes in the desirability of alternatives. *Journal of Abnormal & Social Psychology, 52*, 384–389.

Brehm, J.W. (1966) *A Theory of Psychological Reactance*. New York: Academic Press.

Brehm, S.S. (1992) *Intimate Relationships* (2nd edition). New York: McGraw-Hill.

Brehm, S.S. & Brehm, J.W. (1981) *Psychological Reactance: A Theory of Freedom and Control*. New York: Academic Press.

Brehm, S.S. & Kassin, S.M. (1996) *Social Psychology* (3rd edition). New York: Houghton Mifflin.

Brennen, T., Baguley, T., Bright, J., & Bruce, V. (1990) Resolving semantically induced tip-of-the-tongue states for proper nouns. *Memory & Cognition, 18,* 339–347.

Bretherton, I. (2000) Emotional availability: An attachment perspective. *Attachment & Human Development 2*(2), 233–241.

Breuer, J. & Freud, S. (1895) Studies on hysteria. In J. Strachey (Ed. and trans.) *Standard Edition of the Complete Psychological Works of Sigmund Freud (Volume 2)* London: Hogarth.

Brewer, M.B. & Kramer, R.M. (1985) The psychology of intergroup attitudes and behaviour. *Annual Review of Psychology, 36,* 219–243.

Brewer, W.F. (1974) There is no convincing evidence for operant or classical conditioning in adult humans. In W.B. Weimar & D.S. Palermo (Eds) *Cognition and the Symbolic Processes.* Hillsdale, NJ: Lawrence Erlbaum.

Brewin, C. (1998) Intrusive memories, depression, and PTSD. *The Psychologist, 11*(6), 281–283.

Brewin, C.R., Dalgleish, T., & Joseph, S. (1996) A dual representation theory of post-traumatic stress disorder. *Psychological Review, 103,* 670–686.

Brigham, J. & Malpass, R.S. (1985) The role of experience and contact in the recognition of faces of own- and other-race persons. *Journal of Social Issues, 41,* 139–155.

Brislin, R. (1981) *Cross-Cultural Encounters: Face-to-Face Interaction.* Elmsford, NY: Pergamon.

Brislin, R. (1993) *Understanding Culture's Influence on Behaviour.* Orlando, FL: Harcourt Brace Jovanovich.

British Broadcasting Corporation (1972) *Violence on Television: Programme Content and Viewer Perceptions.* London: BBC Publications.

British Psychological Society & The Committee Of The Experimental Psychological Society (1985) *Guidelines for the Use of Animals in Research.* Leicester: BPS.

British Psychological Society (1978) Ethical principles for research on human subjects. *Bulletin of the British Psychological Society, 31,* 48–49.

British Psychological Society (1983) *Guidelines for the Professional Practice of Clinical Psychology.* Leicester: British Psychological Society.

British Psychological Society (1985) A code of conduct for psychologists. *Bulletin of the British Psychological Society, 38,* 41–43.

British Psychological Society (1990) Ethical principles for conducting research with human participants. *The Psychologist, 3* (6), 269–272.

British Psychological Society (1993) Ethical principles for conducting research with human participants (revised). *The Psychologist, 6* (1), 33–35.

British Psychological Society (1995) *Recovered Memories: The Report of the Working Party of the British Psychological Society.* Leicester: British Psychological Society.

British Psychological Society (1999) Increase in depression. *The Psychologist, 12,* (6) 277.

Britton, P. (1997) *The Jigsaw Man.* London: Bantam Press.

Broad, W. & Wade, N. (1982) *Betrayers of the Truth: Fraud and Deceit in the Halls of Science.* London: Century Books.

Broadbent, D.E. (1954) The role of auditory localisation and attention in memory span. *Journal of Experimental Psychology, 47,* 191–196.

Broadbent, D.E. (1958) *Perception and Communication.* Oxford: Pergamon.

Broadbent, D.E. (1961) *Behaviour.* London: Eyre and Spottiswoode.

Broadbent, D.E. (1981) Non-corporeal explanations in psychology. In A.F. Heath (Ed.) *Scientific Explanation.* Oxford: Clarendon Press.

Broadbent, D.E. (1982) Task combination and selective intake of information. *Acta Psychologica, 50,* 253–290.

Brockner, J, & Rubin, Z. (1985) *Entrapment in Escalating Conflict.* New York: Springer-Verlag.

Brodbeck, A. & Irwin, O. (1946) The speech behaviour of infants without families. *Child Development, 17,* 145–146.

Brody, E.B. & Brody, N. (1976) *Intelligence: Nature, Determinants and Consequences.* New York: Academic Press.

Brody, H. (1995) The placebo response. In D. Wedding (Ed.) *Behaviour and Medicine* (2nd edition). St. Louis, MO: Mosby-Year Book.

Bromley, D.B. (1977) Speculations in social and environmental gerontology. *Nursing Times (Occasional Papers),* 53–56, 21 April.

Bromley, D.B. (1988) *Human Ageing: An Introduction to Gerontology* (3rd edition). Harmondsworth: Penguin.

Bronfenbrenner, U. (1960) Freudian theories of identification and their derivatives. *Child Development, 31,* 15–40.

Bronfenbrenner, U. & Ceci, S.J. (1994) Nature–nurture in developmental perspective: A bioecological theory. *Psychological Review, 101,* 568–586.

Brooks-Gunn, J. & Warren, M.P. (1985) The effects of delayed menarche in different contexts. Dance and non-dance students. *Journal of Youth & Adolescence, 14,* 285–300.

Brooks-Gunn, J., Attie, H., Burrow, C., Rosso, J.T. & Warren, M.P. (1989) The impact of puberty on body and eating concerns in athletic and non-athletic contexts. *Journal of Early Adolescence, 9,* 269–290.

Brown, B. & Grotberg, J.J. (1981) *Headstart: A Successful Experiment.* Courrier (Paris International Children's Centre).

Brown, G.W. & Harris, T.O. (1978) *Social Origins of Depression: A Study of Psychiatric Disorder in Women.* London: Tavistock.

Brown, H. (1985) *People, Groups and Society.* Milton Keynes: Open University Press.

Brown, H. (1996) Themes in Experimental Research on Groups from the 1930s to the 1990s. In M. Wetherell (Ed.) *Identities, Groups and Social Issues.* London: Sage, in association with the Open University.

Brown, J. (1999) Superwoman is feeling overworked and fed up. *Oxford Times (Business Supplement),* July/August, 11.

Brown, J. (2000) Psychology and policing. In J. Hartley & A. Branthwaite (Eds) *The Applied Psychologist* (2nd edition). Buckingham: Open University Press.

Brown, J.A. (1958) Some tests of the decay theory of immediate memory. *Quarterly Journal of Experimental Psychology, 10,* 12–21.

Brown, J.A.C. (1961) *Freud and the Post-Freudians.* Harmondsworth, Middlesex: Penguin.

Brown, J.A.C. (1963) *Techniques of Persuasion: From Propaganda to Brainwashing.* Harmondsworth: Penguin.

Brown, J.D. & Smart, S. (1991) The self and social conduct: Linking self-representations to prosocial behaviour. *Journal of Personality & Social Psychology, 60,* 368–375.

Brown, J.K. (1963) A cross-cultural study of female initiation rites. *American Anthropologist, 65,* 837–853.

Brown, K. (2000) How long have you got? *Scientific American Presents: The Quest to Beat Ageing, 11*(2), 8–15.

Brown, L.M. & Gilligan, C. (1992) *Meeting at the Crossroads: Women's Psychology and Girls' Development.* Cambridge, MA.: Harvard University Press.

Brown, L.S. (1997) Ethics in psychology: Cui bono? In D. Fox & I. Prilleltensky (Eds) *Critical Psychology: An Introduction.* London: Sage.

Brown, R. (1958) *Words and Things.* Glencoe, Illinois: Free Press.

Brown, R. (1965) *Social Psychology.* New York: The Free Press.

Brown, R. (1970) The first sentences of child and chimpanzee. In R. Brown, *Psycholinguistics.* New York: Free Press.

Brown, R. (1973) *A First Language: The Early Stages.* Cambridge, MA: Harvard University Press.

Brown, R. (1986) *Social Psychology:* The Second Edition. New York: Free Press.

Brown, R. & Kulik, J. (1977) Flashbulb memories. *Cognition, 5,* 73–99.

Brown, R. & Kulik, J. (1982) Flashbulb memories. In U. Neisser (Ed.) *Memory Observed.* San Francisco: Freeman.

Brown, R. & Lenneberg, E.H. (1954) A study in language and cognition. *Journal of Abnormal & Clinical Psychology, 49,* 454–462.

Brown, R. & McNeill, D. (1966) The 'tip-of-the-tongue' phenomenon. *Journal of Verbal Learning & Verbal Behaviour, 5,* 325–337.

Brown, R., Cazden, C.B. & Bellugi, U. (1969) The child's grammar from one to three. In J.P. Hill (Ed.) *Minnesota Symposium on Child Psychology, Volume 2.* Minneapolis: University of Minnesota Press.

Brown, R.J. (1988) Intergroup relations. In M. Hewstone, W. Stroebe, J.P. Codol & G.M. Stephenson (Eds), *Introduction to Social Psychology.* Oxford: Basil Blackwell.

Brown, R.J. (1996) Intergroup relations. In M. Hewstone, W. Stroebe & G.M. Stephenson (Eds) *Introduction to Social Psychology* (2nd edition). Oxford: Blackwell.

Brown, R.J. & Turner, J.C. (1981) Interpersonal and intergroup behaviour. In J.C. Turner & H. Giles (Eds) *Intergroup Behaviour.* Oxford: Blackwell.

Browne, J.A. & Howarth, E. (1977) A comprehensive factor analysis of personality questionnaire items: a test of twenty putative factor hypotheses. *Multivariate Behavioural Research, 12,* 399–427.

Brubaker, C. & Wickersham, D. (1990) Encouraging the practice of testicular self-examination: A field application of the theory of reasoned action. *Health Psychology, 9,* 154–163.

Bruce, V. (1982) Changing faces: visual and non-visual coding processes in face recognition. *British Journal of Psychology, 73,* 105–116.

Bruce, V. (1995) Perceiving and recognising faces. In I. Roth & V. Bruce, *Perception and Representation: Current Issues* (2nd edition). Buckingham: Open University Press.

Bruce, V. (1998) Fleeting images of shade: Identifying people caught on video. *The Psychologist, 11*(7), 331–337.

Bruce, V. & Green, P.R. (1990) *Visual Perception* (2nd edition). Hove: Erlbaum.

Bruce, V. & Young, A.W. (1986) Understanding face recognition. *British Journal of Psychology, 77,* 305–327.

Bruce, V. & Young, A. (1998) *In The Eye Of The Beholder: The Science of Face Perception.* Oxford: Oxford University Press.

Bruce, V., Burton, A.M. & Dench, N. (1994) What's distinctive about a distinctive face? *Quarterly Journal of Experimental Psychology, 47A,* 119–141.

Bruner, J.S. (1957) On perceptual readiness. *Psychological Review, 64,* 123–152.

Bruner, J.S. (1966) *Towards a Theory of Instruction.* Cambridge, Massachussets: Harvard University Press.

Bruner, J.S. (1975) The ontogenesis of speech acts. *Journal of Child Language, 2,* 1–21.

Bruner, J.S. (1978) Acquiring the uses of language. *Canadian Journal of Psychology, 32,* 204–218.

Bruner, J.S. (1983) *Child's Talk: Learning to Use Language.* Oxford: Oxford University Press.

Bruner, J.S.(1990) *Acts of Meaning.* Cambridge, MA: Harvard University Press.

Bruner, J.S. & Goodman, C.C. (1947) Value and need as organising factors in perception. *Journal of Abnormal & Social Psychology, 42,* 33–44.

Bruner, J.S. & Kenney, H. (1966) *The Development of the Concepts of Order and Proportion in Children.* New York: Wiley.

Bruner, J.S. & Postman, L. (1949) On the perception of incongruity. *Journal of Personality, 18,* 206–223.

Bruner, J.S. & Tagiuri, R. (1954) The perception of people. In G. Lindzey (Ed.) *Handbook of Social Psychology,* Volume 2. London: Addison Wesley.

Bruner, J.S., Busiek, R.D., & Minturn, A.L. (1952) Assimilation in the immediate reproduction of visually perceived figures. *Journal of Experimental Psychology, 44,* 151–155.

Bruner, J.S., Goodnow, J.J., & Austin, G.A. (1956) *A Study of Thinking.* New York: Wiley.

Bruner, J.S., Oliver, R.R. & Greenfield, P.M. (1966) *Studies in Cognitive Growth.* New York: Wiley.

Brunswik, E. (1952) The conceptual framework of psychology. In *The International Encyclopaedia of Unified Science, 1,* 10. Chicago, ILL: University of Chicago Press.

Brunswik, E. (1955) Representative design and probabilistic theory in a functional psychology. *Psychological Review, 62,* 193–217.

Brunswick, E. (1956) *Perception and the Representative Design of Psychological Experiments.* Berkeley, California: University of California Press.

Brussell, J.A. (1968) *Casebook of a Crime Psychiatrist.* London: New English Library.

Brussell, J.A. (1969) *Casebook of a Crime Psychiatrist.* London: New English Library.

Bryant, J. & Zillman, D. (Eds) (1994) *Media Effects: Advances in Theory and Research.* Hove: Erlbaum.

Bryden, M. & Saxby, L. (1985) Developmental aspects of cerebral lateralisation. In J. Obrzat & G. Hynd (Eds) *Child Neuropsychology, Volume 1: Theory and Research.* Orlando, FLA: Academic Press.

Bryne, D. & Griffitt, W. (1973) Interpersonal attraction. *Annual Review of Psychology, 24,* 317–336.

Buckhout, R. (1974) Eyewitness testimony. *Scientific American,* December, 23–31.

Bull, M. & LaVecchio, F. (1978) Behaviour therapy for a child with Lesch–Nyhan syndrome. *Developmental Medicine & Child Neurology, 20,* 368–375.

Bumpass, L.L., Sweet, J.A. & Cherlin, A. (1991) The role of cohabitation in declining rates of marriage. *Journal of Marriage & The Family, 53,* 913–927.

Burger, F. (1982) The 46-hour-a-week habit. *Boston Globe,* 2 May.

Burgio, L.D., Whitman, T.I., & Reid, D.H. (1983) A participative management approach for improving direct care staff performance in an institutional setting. *Journal of Applied Behaviour Analysis, 16,* 37–52.

Burke, M. (1999) Real men don't drink. *New Scientist, 164*(2214), 58–63.

Burks, B.S. (1928) The relative influence of nature and nurture upon mental development: A comparative study of foster parent–foster child resemblance and true parent–true child resemblance. *Yearbook of the National Society for the Study of Education, 27,* 219–316.

Burley, P.M. & McGuiness, J. (1977) Effects of social intelligence on the Milgram paradigm. *Psychological Reports, 40,* 767–770.

Burne, J. (1999) Don't worry, be happy. *The Guardian (Supplement),* 24 August, 8–9.

Burns, R.B. (1980) *Essential Psychology.* Lancaster: MTP Press.

Burnside, I.M., Ebersole, P. & Monea, H.E. (1979) *Psychological Caring Throughout the Lifespan.* New York: McGraw-Hill.

Burr, V. (1995) *An Introduction to Social Constructionism.* London: Routledge.

Burr, W.R. (1970) Satisfaction with various aspects of marriage over the life cycle: A random middle class sample. *Journal of Marriage & The Family, 32,* 29–37.

Burt, C. (1949) The structure of the mind: A review of the results of factor analysis. *British Journal of Educational Psychology, 19,* 110–11, 176–199.

Burt, C. (1955) The evidence for the concept of intelligence. *British Journal of Educational Psychology, 25,* 158–177.

Burt, C. (1958) The inheritance of mental ability. *American Psychologist, 13,* 1–15.

Burt, C. (1966) The genetic determination of differences in intelligence: A study of monozygotic twins reared together and apart. *British Journal of Psychology, 57,* 137–153.

Burton, A.M., Bruce, V. & Johnston, R.A. (1990) Understanding face recognition with an interactive activation model. *British Journal of Psychology, 81,* 361–380.

Burton, A.M., Wilson, S., Cowan, M., & Bruce, V. (1999) Face recognition in poor quality video: Evidence from security surveillance. *Psychological Science, 10,* 243–248.

Bushman, B. (1984) Perceived symbols of authority and their influence on compliance. *Journal of Applied Social Psychology, 14,* 501–508.

Bushnell, I.W.R., Sai, F., & Mullin, J.T. (1989) Neonatal recognition of the mother's face. *British Journal of Developmental Psychology, 7,* 3–15.

Buss, A.H. (1961) *The Psychology of Aggression.* New York: Wiley.

Buss, A.H. (1963) Physical aggression in relation to different frustrations. *Journal of Abnormal & Social Psychology, 67,* 1–7.

Buss, A.H. (1966) Instrumentality of aggression, feedback and frustration and determinants of physical aggression. *Journal of Personality & Social Psychology, 3,* 153–162.

Buss, A.H. (1992) Personality: primate heritage and human distinctiveness. In R.A. Zucker, A.I. Rabin, J. Aronoff, & S.J.Frank (Eds) *Personality Structure in the Life Course: Essays on Personality in the Murray Tradition.* New York: Springer.

Buss, A.H. & Plomin, R. (1984) *Temperament: Early Developing Personality* Traits. Hillsdale, NJ: Erlbaum.

Buss, D.M. (1987) Sex differences in human mate selection criteria: An evolutionary perspective. In C. Crawford, D. Krebs & M. Smith (Eds). *Sociobiology and Psychology: Ideas, Issues and Applications.* Hillside, NJ: Erlbaum.

Buss, D.M. (1988) The evolutionary biology of love. In R.J. Sternberg & M.L. Barnes (Eds) *The Psychology of Love.* New Haven, CT: Yale University Press.

Buss, D.M. (1989) Sex differences in human mate preferences: Evolutionary hypotheses tested in 37 cultures. *Behavioural & Brain Sciences, 12,* 1–49.

Buss, D.M. (1994) Mate preference in 37 cultures. In W.J. Lonner & R.S. Malpass (Eds) *Psychology and Culture.* Boston: Allyn & Bacon.

Buss, D.M. (1995) Evolutionary psychology: A new paradigm for psychological science. *Psychological Inquiry, 6,* 1–49.

Buss, D.M. (1999) *Evolutionary Psychology.* Boston, MA: Allyn & Bacon.

Butler, K. (1996) The biology of fear. *Family Therapy Networker, 20,* 39–45.

Butler, R. (1963) The life review: An interpretation of reminiscence in the aged. *Psychiatry, 26,* 65–76.

Butler, R.A. (1954) Curiosity in monkeys. *Scientific American,* February, 70–5.

Buunk, B. & Hupka, R.B. (1987) Cross-cultural differences in the elicitation of sexual jealousy. *Journal of Sexual Research, 23,* 12–22.

Buunk, B.P. (1996) Affiliation, attraction and close relationships. In M. Hewstone, W. Stroebe & G.M. Stephenson (Eds) *Introduction to Social Psychology* (2nd edition). Oxford: Blackwell.

Byrne, D. (1971) *The Attraction Paradigm.* New York: Academic Press.

Byrne, D. & Buehler, J.A. (1965) A note on the influence of propinquity upon acquaintanceships. *Journal of Abnormal & Social Psychology, 51,* 147–148.

Callaghan, P. & O'Carroll, M. (1993) Making women mad. *Nursing Times, 89,* 26–29.

Calvin, W.H. (1994) The emergence of language. *Scientific American,* October, 79–85.

Campbell, A. (1981) *The Sense of Well-Being in America.* New York: McGraw-Hill.

Campbell, A. & Muncer, S. (1994) Men and the meaning of violence. In J. Archer (Ed.) *Male Violence.* London: Routledge.

Campbell, B.A. & Church, R.M. (1969) (Eds) *Punishment and Aversive Behaviour.* New York: Appleton-Century-Crofts.

Campbell, D.T. (1967) Stereotypes and the perception of group differences. *American Psychologist, 22,* 817–829.

Campbell, J., Tyrell, D., & Zingaro, M. (1993) Sensation–seeking among water canoe and kayak paddlers. *Personality & Individual Differences, 14,* 489–491.

Campos, J.J., Langer, A. & Krowitz, A. (1970) Cardiac responses on the visual cliff in pre-locomotor human infants. *Science, 170,* 196–197.

Cannon, W.B. (1927) The James–Lange theory of emotions: A critical re-examination and an alternative theory. *American Journal of Psychology, 39,* 106–124.

Cannon, W.B. (1928) Neural organisation for emotional expression. In M.L. Reymert (Ed.) *Feelings and Emotions: The Wittenberg Symposium.* Worcester, MA: Clark University Press.

Cannon, W.B. (1929) *Bodily Changes in Pain, Hunger, Fear, and Rage.* New York: Appleton.

Cannon, W.B. & Washburn, A.L. (1912) An explanation of hunger. *American Journal of Physiology, 29,* 441–454.

Canter, D. (1994a) *Criminal Shadows.* London: HarperCollins.

Canter, D. (1994b) Not so elementary, dear Watson. *The Times Higher, 7* January, 17.

Caplan, P.J. (1991) Delusional dominating personality disorder (DDPD). *Feminism & Psychology, 1* (1), 171–174.

Capron, C. & Duyme, M. (1989) Assessment of effects of socio-economic status on IQ in full cross-fostering study. *Nature, 340,* 552–554.

Carlsmith, J.M., Collins, B.E. & Helmreich, R.L. (1966) Studies in forced compliance: 1. The effect of pressure for compliance on attitude change produced by face-to-face role playing and anonymous essay writing. *Journal of Personality & Social Psychology, 4,* 1–13.

Carlson, N.R. (1977) *Physiology of Behaviour.* Boston: Allyn & Bacon.

Carlson, N.R. (1987) *Discovering Psychology.* London: Allyn & Bacon.

Carlson, N.R. (1988) *Foundations of Physiological Psychology.* Boston: Allyn & Bacon.

Carlson, N.R. (1992) *Foundations of Physiological Psychology* (2nd edition). Boston: Allyn & Bacon.

Carlson, N.R. & Buskist, W. (1997) *Psychology: The Science of Behaviour* (5th edition). Needham Heights, MA.: Allyn and Bacon.

Carlson, N.R., Buskist, W., & Martin, G.N. (2000) *Psychology: The Science of Behaviour* (European Adaptation). Harlow: Pearson Education Ltd.

Carmichael, L., Hogan, P. & Walter, A. (1932) An experimental study of the effect of language on the reproduction of visually perceived forms. *Journal of Experimental Psychology, 15,* 1–22.

Carpenter, P. (1997) Learning Disability. In L. Rees, M. Lipsedge, & C. Ball (Eds) *Textbook of Psychiatry.* London: Arnold.

Carroll, D.W. (1986) *Psychology of Language.* Monterey, CA: Brooks/Cole Publishing Co.

Carroll, J.B. & Casagrande, J.B. (1958) The function of language classifications in behaviour. In E.E. Maccoby, T.M. Newcombe & E.L. Hartley (Eds) Readings in *Social Psychology* (3rd edition). New York: Holt, Rinehart & Winston.

Carstensen, L.L. (1992) Social and emotional patterns in adulthood: Support for socioemotional selectivity theory. *Psychology and Ageing, 7,* 331–338.

Carstensen, L.L. (1993) Motivation for social contact across the life span: A theory of socioemotional selectivity. In J. Jacobs (Ed.) *Nebraska Symposium on Motivation 1992, Developmental Perspectives on Motivation,* Volume 40. Lincoln: University of Nebraska Press.

Carstensen, L.L. (1996) Socioemotional selectivity: A life span developmental account of social behaviour. In M.R. Merrens & G.C. Brannigan (Eds) *The Developmental Psychologists: Research Adventures across the Life Span.* New York: McGraw-Hill.

Carstensen, L.L. & Turk-Charles, S. (1994) The salience of emotion across the adult life course. *Psychology & Ageing, 9,* 259–264.

Carter, J.R. & Neufeld, R.W.J. (1998) Cultural aspects of understanding people with schizophrenic disorders. In S.S. Kazarian & D.R.Evans (Eds) *Cultural Clinical Psychology: Theory, Research, and Practice.* New York: Oxford University Press.

Cartwright, S.A. (1851) Report on the Diseases and Physical Peculiarities of the Negro Race. *New Orleans Medicam & Surgical Journal,* May, 691–715.

Carver, C.S. & Scheier, M.F. (1981) *Attention and Self-Regulation: A Control Theory Approach to Human Behaviour.* New York: Springer-Verlag.

Carver, C.S. & Scheier, M.F. (1992) *Perspectives on Personality* (2nd edition). Boston: Allyn & Bacon.

Case, R. (1985) *Intellectual Development.* London: Methuen.

Caspi, A. (2000) The child is father of the man: Personality continues from childhood to adulthood. *Journal of Personality & Social Psychology, 78,* 158–172.

Caspi, A., Lynam, T.E., Moffitt, T.E. & Silva, P.A. (1993) Unravelling girls' delinquency: Biological, dispositional and contextual contributions to adolescent misbehaviour. *Developmental Psychology, 29,* 19–30.

Castles, A. & Coltheart, M. (1993) Varieties of develomental dyslexia. *Cognition, 47,* 149–180.

Cattell, R.B. (1963) Theory of fluid and crystallised intelligence: A critical experiment. *Journal of Educational Psychology, 54,* 1–22.

Cattell, R.B. (1965) *The Scientific Analysis of Personality.* Harmondsworth, Middlesex: Penguin.

Cattell, R.B. (1966) The scree test for the number of factors. *Multivariate Behavioural Research, 1,* 140–161.

Cattell, R.B. & Kline, P. (1977) *The Scientific Study of Personality and Motivation.* London: Academic Press.

Cautela, J.R. (1967) Covert sensitisation. *Psychology Reports, 20,* 459–468.

Cavanaugh, J.C. (1995) Ageing. In P.E. Bryant & A.M. Colman (Eds) *Developmental Psychology.* London: Longman.

Cave, S. (1998) *Applying Psychology to the Environment.* London: Hodder & Stoughton.

Ceci, S.J. & Williams, W.M. (Eds) (1999) *The Nature–Nurture Debate: The Essential Readings.* Oxford: Blackwell.

Cernoch, J.M. & Porter, R.H. (1985) Recognition of maternal axillary odors by infants. *Child Development, 56,* 1593–1598.

Chaiken, S. (1987) The heuristic model of persuasion. In M.P. Zanna, J.M. Olsen & C.P. Herman (Eds), *Social influence: The Ontario symposium,* Volume 5. Hillsdale, New Jersey: Lawrence Erlbaum Associates Inc.

Chaikin, A.L. & Darley, J.M. (1973) Victim or perpetrator? Defensive attribution of responsibility and the need for order and justice. *Journal of Personality & Social Psychology, 25,* 268–275.

Chalmers, D.J. (1997) The puzzle of conscious experience. *Scientific American Mysteries of the Mind, 7(1),* 30–37.

Champion, L. (2000) Depression. In L. Champion & M. Power (Eds) *Adult Psychological Problems: An Introduction* (2nd ed.) Hove: Psychology Press.

Champion, L.A. & Power, M.J. (1995) Social and cognitive approaches to depression: Towards a new synthesis. *British Journal of Clinical Psychology, 34,* 485–503.

Chapanis, N.P. & Chapanis, A. (1964) Cognitive dissonance – 5 years later. *Psychological Bulletin, 61 (1),* 1–22.

Chapman, L.J. (1967) Illusory correlation in observational report. *Journal of Verbal Learning & Verbal Behaviour, 6,* 151–155.

Chapman, L.J. & Chapman, J.P. (1969) Illusory correlation as an obstacle to the use of valid psychodiagnostic signs. *Journal of Abnormal Psychology, 74,* 271–280.

Chapman, R.S. (2000) Children's language learning: An interactionist perspective. *Journal of Child Psychology & Psychiatry, 41(1),* 33–54.

Charney, D.S., Deutsch, A.V., Krystal, J.H., Southwick, A.M. & Davis, M. (1993) Psychobiologic mechanisms of post-traumatic stress disorder. *Archives of General Psychaitry, 50,* 295–305.

Charter, D. (1995) 0.85 seeks 0.7 for 2.4. *The Times Higher, 11* August, 15.

Chaudhury, A. (1988) *How special is special?* Issue, Spring.

Cheng, P.W. (1985) Restructuring versus automaticity: Alternative accounts of skill acquisition. *Psychological Review, 92,* 414–423.

Cherry, E.C. (1953) Some experiments on the recognition of speech with one and two ears. *Journal of the Acoustical Society of America, 25,* 975–979.

Cherry, E.C. & Taylor, W.K. (1954) Some further experiments on the recognition of speech with one and two ears. *Journal of the Acoustical Society of America, 27* 554–559.

Cherry, F. & Byrne, D.S. (1976) Authoritarianism. In T. Blass (Ed.) *Personality Variables in Social Behaviour.* Hillsdale, NJ: Erlbaum.

Chisolm, K., Carter, M.C., Ames, E.W. & Morison, S.J. (1995) Attachment security and indiscriminately friendly behaviour in children adopted from Romanian orphanages. *Development & Psychopathology, 7,* 283–294.

Cho, K., Ennaceur, A., Cole, J.C. & Suh, C.K. (2000) Chronic jet-lag produces core defects. *Journal of Neuroscience, 20 (RC66),* 1–5.

Chomsky, N. (1957) *Syntactic Structures.* The Hague: Mouton.

Chomsky, N. (1959) Review of Skinner's verbal behaviour. *Language, 35,* 26–58.

Chomsky, N. (1965) *Aspects of the Theory of Syntax.* Cambridge, MA: MIT Press.

Chomsky, N. (1968) *Language and Mind.* New York: Harcourt Brace Jovanovich.

Chomsky, N. (1979) *Language and Responsibility.* Sussex: Harvester Press.

Christensen, L. (1988) Deception in psychological research: When is its use justified? *Personality & Social Psychology, 14,* 665–675.

Chua, S.E. & McKenna, P.J. (1995) Schizophrenia – a brain disease? A critical review of structural and functional cerebral abnormality in the disorder. *British Journal of Psychiatry, 166,* 563–582.

Cialdini, R.B. (1988) *Influence: Science and Practice.* Glenview, IL: Scott, Foresman.

Clamp, A.G. (2001) *Evolutionary Psychology.* London: Hodder & Stoughton (in press).

Clamp, A.G. & Russell, J. (1998) *Comparative Psychology.* London: Hodder & Stoughton.

Clare, A. (1976) What is schizophrenia? *New Society,* May 20, 410–412.

Clare, A. (1980) *Psychiatry in Dissent.* London: Tavistock.

Claridge, G. (1967) *Personality and Arousal*. Oxford: Pergamon Press.

Claridge, G. (1981) Psychoticism. In R. Lynn (Ed.) *Dimensions of Personality: Papers in Honour of H.J. Eysenck*. Oxford: Pergamon Press.

Claridge, G. (1985) *Origins of Mental Illness*. Oxford: Basil Blackwell.

Claridge, G. (1987) The continuum of psychosis and the gene. *British Journal of Psychiatry, 150,* 129–133 (correspondence).

Claridge, G. & Chappa, H.J. (1973) Psychoticism: A study of its biological basis in normal subjects. *British Journal of Social & Clinical Psychology, 12,* 175–187.

Claridge, G.S. & Herrington, R.N. (1962) Excitation-inhibition and the theory of neurosis: A study of the sedation threshold. In H.J. Eysenck (Ed.) *Experiments with Drugs*. New York: Pergamon Press.

Clark, K.E. & Miller, G.A. (1970) (Eds) *Psychology: Behavioural and Social Sciences Survey Committee*. Englewood Cliffs, NJ: Prentice Hall.

Clark, M.S., Millberg, S., & Erber, R. (1987) Arousal and state dependent memory: Evidence and some implications for understanding social judgements and social behaviour. In K. Fiedler & J.P. Forgas (Eds) *Affect, Cognition and Social Behaviour*. Toronto: Hogrefe.

Clark, M.S., Mills, J. & Corcoran, D. (1989) Keeping track of needs and inputs of friends and strangers. *Journal of Personality & Social Psychology, 15,* 533–542.

Clark, R.D. & Maass, A. (1988) The role of social categorisation and perceived source credibility in minority influence. *European Journal of Social Psychology, 18,* 381–394.

Clark, R.D. & Word, L.E. (1974) Where is the apathetic bystander? Situational characteristics of the emergency. *Journal of Personality & Social Psychology, 29,* 279–287.

Clarke, A. & Clarke, A. (1976) *Early Experience: Myth and Evidence*. London: Open Books.

Clarke, A. & Clarke, A. (1998) Early experience and the life path. *The Psychologist, 11*(9), 433–436.

Clarke, A. & Clarke, A. (2000) *Early Experience and the Life Path*. London: Jessica Kingsley.

Clarke, P.R.F. (1975) The medical model defended. *New Society,* January 9, 64–65.

Clarke, R. (1979) Assessment in psychiatric hospitals. *Nursing Times,* April 5, 590–592.

Clarke-Stewart, K.A. (1973) Interactions between mothers and their young children: Characteristics and consequences. *Monograph of the Society for Research into Child Development, 38* (6–7, Serial No. 153).

Clarke-Stewart, K.A. (1978) And daddy makes three: The father's impact on mother and young child. *Child Development, 49,* 446–478.

Clarke-Stewart, K.A. (1989) Infant day care: Maligned or malignant? *American Psychologist, 44,* 266–273.

Clarke-Stewart, K.A. (1991) A home is not a school. *Journal of Social Issues, 47,* 105–123.

Cloninger, C.R. (1987) Neurogenetic adaptive mechanisms in alcoholism. *Science, 236,* 410–416.

Clore, G.L. (1994) Why emotions require cognition. In P. Ekman & R.J. Davidson (Eds) *The Nature of Emotion: Fundamental Questions*. New York: Oxford University Press.

Clore, G.L. & Byrne, D.S. (1974) A reinforcement–affect model of attraction. In T.L. Huston (Ed.) *Foundations of Interpersonal Attraction*. New York: Academic Press.

Clore, G.L., Bray, R.M., Itkin, S.M. & Murphy, P. (1978) Interracial attitudes and behaviour at a summer camp. *Journal of Personality & Social Psychology, 36,* 706–712.

Cochrane, R. (1974) Crime and personality: Theory and evidence. *Bulletin of the British Psychological Society, 27,* 19–22.

Cochrane, R. (1983) *The Social Creation of Mental Illness*. London: Longman.

Cochrane, R. (1995) Women and depression. *Psychology Review, 2,* 20–24.

Cochrane, R. (1996) Marriage and madness. *Psychology Review, 3,* 2–5.

Cohen, F. & Lazarus, R. (1979) Coping with the stresses of illness. In G.C. Stone, F. Cohen & N.E. Ader (Eds) *Health Psychology: A Handbook*. San Francisco, CA: Jossey-Bass.

Cohen, G. (1975) Cerebral apartheid: A fanciful notion? *New Behaviour, 18,* 458–461.

Cohen, G. (1986) Everyday memory. In G. Cohen, M.W. Eysenck & M.E. Le Voi (Eds), *Memory: A Cognitive Approach*. Milton Keynes: Open University Press.

Cohen, G. (1990) Memory. In I. Roth (Ed.), *Introduction to Psychology, Volume 2*. Hove, E. Sussex/Milton Keynes: Open University/Lawrence Erlbaum Associates Ltd.

Cohen, G. (1993) Everyday memory and memory systems: The experimental approach. In G. Cohen, G. Kiss & M. Levoi (Eds) *Memory: Current Issues* (2nd edition). Buckingham: Open University Press.

Cohen, J. (1958) *Humanistic Psychology*. London: Allen & Unwin.

Cohen, J. (2000) Primate education. *Sunday Times Magazine, 13* August, 16–23.

Cohen, N.J. & Squire, L.R. (1980) Preserved learning and retention of pattern-analysing skills in amnesia: Dissociation of knowing how from knowing that. *Science, 210,* 207–210.

Cohen, S. & Taylor, L. (1972) *Psychological Survival: The Experience of Long-term Imprisonment*. Harmondsworth: Penguin.

Cohen, Y.A. (1964) *The Transition from Childhood to Adolescence: Cross-cultural Studies in Initiation Ceremonies, Legal Systems, and Incest Taboos*. Chicago: Aldine.

Colapinto, J. (2000) What the doctor ordered. *The Independent On Sunday Magazine,* 6 February, 8–13.

Colby, A. & Kohlberg, L. (Eds) (1987) *The Measurement of Moral Judgement*. New York: Cambridge University Press.

Colby, A., Kohlberg, L., Gibbs, J. & Lieberman, M. (1983) A longitudinal study of moral development. *Monographs of the Society for Research in Child Development, 48,* (1–2, Serial No. 200).

Cole, M. (1990) Cultural psychology: A once and future discipline? In J.J. Berman (Ed.) *Nebraska Symposium on Motivation: Cross-Cultural Perspectives*. Lincoln, NA: University of Nebraska Press.

Coleman, J.C. (1974) *Relationships in Adolescence*. London: Routledge & Kegan Paul.

Coleman, J.C. (1978) Current contradictions in adolescent theory. *Journal of Youth & Adolescence. 7,* 1–11.

Coleman, J.C. (Ed.) (1979) *The School Years*. London: Methuen.

Coleman, J.C. (1980) *The Nature of Adolescence*. London: Methuen.

Coleman, J.C. (1995) Adolescence. In P.E. Bryant & A.M. Colman (Eds) *Developmental Psychology*. London: Longman.

Coleman, J.C. & Hendry, L. (1999) *The Nature of Adolescence* (2nd edition). London: Routledge.

Coleman, J.C. & Roker, D. (1998) Adolescence. *The Psychologist, 11*(12), 593–596.

Collee, J. (1993) Symbol minds. *The Observer Life Magazine,* 26 September, 14.

Collins, A.M. & Loftus, E.F. (1975) A spreading-activation theory of semantic processing. *Psychological Review, 82,* 407–428.

Collins, A.M. & Quillian, M. (1969) Retrieval time for semantic memory. *Journal of Verbal Learning & Verbal Behaviour, 8,* 240–247.

Collins, A.M. & Quillian, M. R. (1972) How to make a language user. In E. Tulving & W. Donaldson (Eds) *Organisation of Memory*. New York: Academic Press.

Collins, H. (1994) *Times Higher Education Supplement,* 30 September, 18.

Collins, R. & Coltrane, S. (1985) *Sociology of Marriage and Family: Gender, Love and Property.* Chicago: Nelson Hall.

Collins, R. & Coltrane, S. (1995) *Sociology of Marriage and Family: Gender, Love and Property.* Chicago, ILL: Nelson Hall.

Collins, R.C. (1983) Headstart: An update on program effects. *Newsletter of the Society for Research in Child Development.* Summer, 1–2.

Collis, G.M. & Schaffer, H.R. (1975) Synchronisation of visual attention in mother–infant pairs. *Journal of Child Psychology & Psychiatry, 16,* 315–320.

Colman, A.M. (1987) *Facts, Fallacies and Frauds in Psychology.* London: Unwin Hyman.

Coltheart, M. & Jackson, M.E. (1998) Defining Dyslexia. *Child Psychology & Psychiatry Review, 3*(1), 12–16.

Coltheart, M., Masterson, J., Byng, S., Prior, M., & Riddoch, J. (1983) Surface dyslexia. *Quarterly Journal of Experimental Psychology, 35,* 469–495.

Comfort, A. (1977) *A Good Age.* London: Mitchell Beazley.

Compas, B.E., Hinden, B.R. & Gerhardt, C.A. (1995) Adolescent development: Pathways and processes of risk and resilience. *Annual Review of Psychology, 46,* 265–293.

Comstock, G. & Paik, H. (1991) *Television and the American Child.* New York: Academic Press.

Concar, D. (1994) Designing your own personality. *New Scientist, 141,* 22–26.

Condry, J. & Condry, S. (1976) Sex differences: A study in the eye of the beholder. *Child Development, 47,* 812–819.

Condry, J.C. & Ross, D.F. (1985) Sex and aggression: The influence of gender label on the perception of aggression in children. *Child Development, 56,* 225–233.

Conrad, C. (1972) Cognitive economy in semantic memory. *Journal of Experimental Psychology, 92,* 148–154.

Conrad, R. (1963) Acoustic confusions and memory span for words. *Nature, 197,* 1029–1030.

Conrad, R. (1964) Acoustic confusion in immediate memory. *British Journal of Psychology, 55,* 75–84.

Constanzo, P.R., Coie, J.D., Grumet, J.F. & Farnill, D. (1973) Re-examination of the effects of intent and consequence on children's moral judgements. *Child Development, 44,* 154–61.

Cook, E. (1997) Is marriage driving women mad? *Independent on Sunday, Real Life.* 10 August, 1–2.

Cook, S.W. & Selltiz, C.A.(1964) A multiple indicator approach to attitude measurement. *Psychological Bulletin, 62,* 36–55.

Cooley, C.H. (1902) *Human Nature and Social Order.* New York: Shocken.

Coolican, H. (1990) *Research Methods and Statistics in Psychology.* Sevenoaks: Hodder & Stoughton.

Coolican, H. (1994) *Research Methods and Statistics in Psychology* (2nd edition) London: Hodder & Stoughton.

Coolican, H. (1999) *Research Methods and Statistics in Psychology* (3rd edition). London: Hodder & Stoughton.

Coolican, H., Cassidy, T., Chercher, A., Harrower J., Penny, G., Sharp, R., Walley, M. & Westbury, T. (1996) *Applied Psychology.* London: Hodder & Stoughton.

Coon, D. (1983) *Introduction to Psychology* (3rd edition). St Paul, Minnesota: West Publishing Co.

Cooper, C. & Faragher, B. (1993) Psychological stress and breast cancer: the interrelationship between stress events, coping strategies and personality. *Psychological Medicine, 23,* 653–662.

Cooper, D. (1995) *NT Guide to Working With People Who Misuse Drugs.* Nursing Times Guides.

Cooper, G. (1994) Napoleon island to end TV exile. *Independent on Sunday,* 12 June, 7.

Cooper, G. (1996) The satisfying side of being home alone. *Independent,* 13 September, 3.

Cooper, J. & Fazio, R.H. (1984) A new look at dissonance theory. In L. Berkowitz (Ed.), *Advances in Experimental Social Psychology, Volume 15.* New York: Academic Press.

Cooper, J.E. (1994) Notes on unsolved problems. *In Pocket Guide to the ICD-10 Classification of Mental and Behavioural Disorders.* London: Churchill Livingstone.

Cooper, J.E. (1995) On the publication of the Diagnostic and Statistical Manual of Mental Disorders (4th edition). *British Journal of Psychiatry, 166,* 4–8.

Cooper, J.E., Kendell, R.E., Gurland, B.J., Sharpe, L., Copeland, J.R.M. & Simon, R. (1972) *Psychiatric Diagnosis in New York and London.* Oxford: Oxford University Press.

Cooper, P.J. (1995) Eating disorders. In A.A. Lazarus & A.M. Colman (Eds) *Abnormal Psychology.* London: Longman.

Cooper, R.S., Rotimi, C.N. & Ward, R. (1999) The puzzle of hypertension in African-Americans. *Scientific American, 253,* 36–43.

Coopersmith, S. (1967) *The Antecedents of Self Esteem.* San Francisco: Freeman.

Copson, G. (1995) Coals to Newcastle: A study of offender profiling. *Police Research Group Special Interest Paper 4.* London: Home Office.

Copson, G. (1996) At last some facts about offender profiling in Britain. *Forensic Update, 46, Division of Criminological & Legal Psychology.* Leicester: British Psychological Society.

Copson, G. & Holloway, K. (1997) *Offender Profiling.* Paper presented to the annual conference of the Division of Criminological & Legal Psychology, British Psychological Society (October).

Cordray, D.S. & Bootzin, R.R. (1983) Placebo control conditions: Tests of theory or of effectiveness. *Behavioural & Brain Sciences, 6,* 286–287.

Coren, S. & Girgus, J.S. (1978) *Seeing is Deceiving: The Psychology of Visual Illusions.* Hillsdale, NJ: Erlbaum.

Cornsweet, T.N. (1970) *Visual Perception.* New York: Academic Press.

Cornwell, T. (1997) Board tones down Ebonics policy. *Times Educational Supplement,* 31 January, 14.

Corrigan, R. (1978) Language development as related to stage-6 object permanence development. *Journal of Child Language, 5,* 173–189.

Corteen, R.S. & Dunn, D. (1974) Shock-associated words in a non-attended message: A test for momentary awareness. *Journal of Experimental Psychology, 102,* 1143–1144.

Corteen, R.S. & Wood, B. (1972) Autonomic responses to shock-associated words in an unattended channel. *Journal of Experimental Psychology, 94,* 308–313.

Cosmides, L. & Tooby, J. (1994) Beyond imitation and instinct blindness: Toward an evolutionary rigorous cognitive science. *Cognition, 50,* 41–77.

Costa, P.T. & McCrae, R.R. (1993) Bullish on personality psychology. *The Psychologist, 6* (7), 302–303.

Costello, T.W., Costello, J.T. & Holmes, D.A. (adapting author) (1995) *Abnormal Psychology.* London: HarperCollins.

Cottrell, N.B.(1968) Performance in the presence of other human beings: Mere presence, audience, and affiliation effects. In E.C. Simmel, R.A. Hope & G.A. Milton (Eds) *Social Facilitation and Imitative Behaviour.* Boston: Allyn & Bacon.

Cottrell, N.B., Wack, D.L., Sekerak, G.J., & Rittle, R.H. (1968) Social facilitation of dominant responses by the presence of others. *Journal of Personality & Social Psychology, 9,* 245–250.

Cox, T. (1978) *Stress.* London: Macmillan Education.

Craig, G.J. (1992) *Human Development* (6th edition). Englewood Cliffs, NJ: Prentice-Hall.

Craik, F.I.M. & Lockhart, R. (1972) Levels of processing. *Journal of Verbal Learning & Verbal Behaviour, 11,* 671–684.

Craik, F.I.M. & Tulving, E. (1975) Depth of processing and retention of words in episodic memory. *Journal of Experimental Psychology: General, 104,* 268–294.

Craik, F.I.M. & Watkins, M.J. (1973) The role of rehearsal in short-term memory. *Journal of Verbal Learning & Verbal Behaviour, 12,* 599–607.

Cramer, D. (1995) Special issue on personal relationships. *The Psychologist, 8,* 58–59.

Crandall, J.E. (1985) Effects of favourable and unfavourable conditions on the psi-missing displacement effect. *Journal of the American Association for Psychical Research, 79,* 27–38.

Crandell, L.E. & Hobson, R.P. (1999) Individual differences in young children's IQ: A social–developmental perspective. *Journal of Child Psychology & Psychiatry, 40*(3), 455–464.

Crawford, M. & Unger, R.K. (1995) Gender issues in psychology. In A.M. Colman (Ed.) *Controversies in Psychology.* London: Longman.

Crick, F. (1994) *The Astonishing Hypothesis: The Scientific Search for the Soul.* London: Simon & Schuster.

Crick, F. & Mitchison, G. (1983) The function of dream sleep. *Nature, 304,* 111–114.

Crisp, A.H. (1967) Anorexia nervosa. *Hospital Medicine, 1,* 713–718.

Crisp, A.H. (1983) Regular reviews: Anorexia nervosa. *British Medical Journal, 287,* 855–858.

Crocker, J., Thompson, L., McGraw, K. & Ingerman, C. (1987) Downward comparison, prejudice, and evaluation of others: Effects of self-esteem and threat. *Journal of Personality & Social Psychology, 52,* 907–916.

Cromer, R.F. (1974) The development of language and cognition: The cognition hypothesis. In B.M. Foss (Ed.) *New Perspectives in Child Development.* Harmondsworth: Penguin.

Cromer, R.F. (1980) Normal language development: Recent progress. In L.A. Hersov, M. Berger & A.R. Nicol (Eds), *Language and Language Disorders.* Oxford: Pergamon Press.

Crook, T. & Eliot, J. (1980) Parental death during childhood and adult depression: A critical review of the literature. *Psychological Bulletin, 87,* 252–259.

Crooks, R.L. & Stein, J. (1991) *Psychology: Science, Behaviour and Life* (2nd edition). London: Holt, Rinehart & Winston Inc.

Crowne, D.P. & Marlowe, D. (1964) *The Approval Motive.* New York: Wiley.

Croyle, R.T. & Cooper, J. (1983) Dissonance arousal: Physiological evidence. *Journal of Personality & Social Psychology, 45,* 782–791.

Crutchfield, R.S. (1954) A new technique for measuring individual differences in conformity to group judgement. *Proceedings of the Invitational Conference on Testing Problems,* 69–74.

Crutchfield, R.S. (1955) Conformity and character. *American Psychologist, 10,* 191–198.

Csikszentmihalyi, M. & Larson, R. (1984) *Being Adolescent: Conflict and Growth in the Teenage Years.* New York: Basic Books.

Cumberbatch, G. (1987) *The Portrayal of Violence on British Television.* London: BBC Publications.

Cumberbatch, G. (1997) Media violence: Science and common sense. *Psychology Review, 3,* 2–7.

Cumming, E. (1975) Engagement with an old theory. *International Journal of Ageing & Human Development, 6,* 187–191.

Cumming, E. & Henry, W.E. (1961) *Growing Old: The Process of Disengagement.* New York: Basic Books.

Curry, C. (1998) Adolescence. In K. Trew & J. Kremer (Eds) *Gender & Psychology.* London: Arnold.

Curtis, A. (1999) The psychology of pain. *Psychology Review, 5*(4), 15–18.

Curtiss, S. (1977) *Genie: A Psycholinguistic Study of a Modern-Day 'Wild Child'.* London: Academic Press.

Czeisler, C.A., Moore-Ede, M.C. & Coleman, R.M. (1982) Rotating shift work schedules that disrupt sleep are improved by applying circadian principles. *Science, 217,* 460–463.

Dacey, J.S. (1982) *Adolescents Today* (2nd edition). Glenview, Illinois: Scott, Foresman & Company.

Dale, P.S. (1976) *Language Development: Structure and Function* (2nd edition). New York: Holt, Rinehart & Winston.

Dalgleish, T. (1998) Emotion. In M Eysenck (Ed.) *Psychology: An Integrated Approach.* Harlow: Addison Wesley/Longman Ltd.

Dallos, R. & Cullen, C. (1990) Clinical psychology. In I. Roth (Ed.) *Introduction to Psychology, Volume 2.* Hove/E.Sussex/Milton Keynes: Open University Press/Lawrence Erlbaum Associates Ltd.

Dalton, K. (1997) Exploring the links: Creativity and psi in the Ganzfeld. *Proceedings of the 40th Annual Convention of the Parapsychological Association.* Hatfield, UK: University of Hertfordshire Press.

Daly, M. & Wilson, M. (1988a) *Homicide.* New York: Aldine de Gruyter Hawthorne.

Daly, M. & Wilson, M. (1988b) Evolutionary social psychology and family homicide. *Science, 28* October, 519–524.

Damon, W. & Hart, D. (1988) *Self-understanding in Childhood and Adolescence.* Cambridge: Cambridge University Press.

Damrosch, S. (1995) Facilitating Adherence to Preventive and Treatment Regimes. In D. Wedding (Ed.) *Behaviour and Medicine* (2nd edition). St. Louis, MO: Mosby Year Books.

Dana, C.L. (1921) The anatomic seat of the emotions: A discussion of the James–Lange theory. *Archives of Neurology & Psychiatry, 6,* 634.

Darley, J.M. (1991) Altruism and prosocial behaviour research: Reflections and prospects. In M.S. Clark (Ed.) *Prosocial Behaviour, Review of Personality & Social Psychology, 12.* Newbury Park: CA: Sage.

Darley, J.M. & Batson, C.D. (1973) From Jerusalem to Jericho: A study of situational and dispositional variables in helping behaviour. *Journal of Personality & Social Psychology, 27,* 100–108.

Darley, J.M. & Huff, C.W. (1990) Heightened damage assessment as a result of the intentionality of the damage causing act. *British Journal of Social Psychology, 29,* 181–188.

Darley, J.M. & Latané, B. (1968) Bystander intervention in emergencies: Diffusion of responsibility. *Journal of Personality & Social Psychology, 8,* 377–383.

Darlington, R.B. (1991) The long-term effects of model preschool programs. In L. Okagaki & R.J. Sternberg (Eds) *Directors of Development.* Hillsdale, NJ: Erlbaum.

Darwin, C. (1859) *The Origin of Species by Means of Natural Selection.* London: John Murray.

Darwin, C. (1871) *The Descent of Man and Selection in Relation to Sex.* London: John Murray.

Darwin, C. (1872) *The Expression of Emotion in Man and Animals.* London: John Murray.

Dasen, P.R. (1977) *Piagetian psychology: Cross-cultural Contributions.* New York: Gardner Press.

Dasen, P.R. (1994) Culture and cognitive development from a Piagetian perspective. In W.J. Lonner & R.S. Malpass (Eds) *Psychology and Culture.* Boston: Allyn & Bacon.

Dasen, P.R. (1999) Rapid social change and the turmoil of adolescence: A cross-cultural perspective. *World Psychology, 5.*

Dashiell, J.F. (1935) Experimental studies of the influence of social situations on the behaviour of individual human adults. In C. Murchison (Ed.) *Handbook of Social Psychology.* Worcester, Mass.: Clark University Press.

Datan, N., Rodeheaver, D. & Hughes, F. (1987) Adult development and ageing. *Annual Review of Psychology, 38,* 153–180.

Davey, G.C.L. (1983) An associative view of human classical conditioning. In G.C.L. Davey (Ed.) *Animal Models of Human Behaviour: Conceptual, Evolutionary, and Neurobiological Perspectives.* Chichester: Wiley.

Davidson, A.R. & Jaccard, J. (1979) Variables that moderate the attitude–behaviour relation: Results of a longitudinal survey. *Journal of Personality & Social Psychology, 37,* 1364–1376.

Davidson, R.J. (1994) Afterword. In P. Ekman & R.J. Davidson (Eds) *The Nature of Emotion: Fundamental Questions.* New York: Oxford University Press.

Davidson, R.J. & Ekman, P. (1994) Afterword: What Are The Minimal Cognitive Prerequisites for Emotion. In P. Ekman & R.J. Davidson (Eds) *The Nature of Emotion: Fundamental Questions.* New York: Oxford University Press.

Davies, D.L. (1956) Psychiatric illness in those enagaged to be married. *British Journal of Preventive & Social Medicine, 10,* 123–127.

Davies, E. & Furnham, A. (1986) Body satisfaction in adolescent girls. *British Journal of Medical Psychology, 59,* 279–288.

Davies, G. & Thasen, S. (2000) Closed-circuit television: How effective an identification aid? *British Journal of Psychology, 91,* 411–426.

Davies, J.C. (1969) The J-curve of rising and declining satisfactions as a cause of some great revolutions and a contained rebellion. In H.D. Graham & T.R. Gurr (Eds) *The History of Violence in America: Historical and Comparative Perspectives.* New York: Praeger.

Davies, T. (1994) Bless his cotton socks. *The Daily Telegraph,* 17 September, 42.

Davis, D., Cahan, S. & Bashi, J. (1977) Birth order and intellectual development: The confluence model in the light of cross-cultural evidence. *Science, 196,* 1470–1472.

Davis, J.A. (1959) A formal interpretation of the theory of relative deprivation. *Sociometry, 22,* 280–296.

Davis, K. (1940) Extreme isolation of a child. *American Journal of Sociology, 45,* 554–565.

Davis, K. (1947) Final note on a case of extreme isolation. *American Journal of Sociology, 52,* 432–437.

Davison, G. & Neale, J. (1994) *Abnormal Psychology* (6th edition). New York: Wiley.

Dawkins, M.S. (1980) The many faces of animal suffering. *New Scientist,* November 20.

Dawkins, M.S. (1990) From an animal's point of view: Motivation, fitness and animal welfare. *Behavioural & Brain Sciences, 13,* 1–9.

Dawkins, R. (1976) *The Selfish Gene.* Oxford: Oxford University Press.

Dawkins, R. (1989) *The Selfish Gene* (2nd edition). Oxford: Oxford University Press.

Day, R & Wong, S. (1996) Anomalous perceptual asymmetries for negative emotional stimuli in the psychopath. *Journal of Abnormal Psychology, 105,* 648–652.

Day, R., Nielsen, J., Korten *et al.* (1987) Stressful life events preceding the onset of schizophrenia: A cross-national study from the World Health Organisation. *Culture, Medicine & Psychiatry, 11,* 123–205.

de Bono, E. (1967) *The Use of Lateral Thinking.* Harmondsworth: Penguin.

De Bruxelles, S. (1999) Crash victim thinks wife is an imposter. *The Times,* 5 March, 7.

De Groot, A.D. (1965) *Thought and Choice in Chess.* The Hague: Mouton.

De Groot, A.D. (1966) Perception and memory versus thought: Some old ideas and recent findings. In B. Kleinmuntz (Ed.) *Problem-Solving: Research, Method and Theory.* New York: Wiley.

De Quervain, D.J.F., Roozendaal, B., Nitsch, R.M., McGaugh, J.L. & Hoch, C. (2000) Acute cortisone administration impairs retrieval of long-term declarative memory in humans. *Nature Neuroscience, 3,* 313–314.

DeValois, R.L. & Jacobs, G.H. (1984) Neural mechanisms of colour vision. In I. Darian-Smith (Ed.) *Handbook of Physiology,* Volume 3. Bethseda, MD: American Physiological Society.

de Villiers, P.A. & de Villiers, J.G. (1979) *Early Language.* Cambridge, MA: Harvard University Press.

Deaux, K. (1972) To err is humanising: But sex makes a difference. *Representative Research in Social Psychology, 5,* 20–28.

Deci, E.L. (1980) *The Psychology of Self-determination.* Lexington, MA.: D.C. Heath.

Deci, E.L. & Ryan, R.M. (1987) The support of autonomy and the control of behaviour. *Journal of Personality & Social Psychology, 53,* 1024–1037.

Deese, J. (1972) *Psychology as Science and Art.* New York: Harcourt Brace Jovanovich.

Delboeuf, J.L.R. (1892) Sur une nouvelle illusion d'optique. *Bulletin de L'Academie Royale de Belgique, 24,* 545–558.

Delgado, J.M.R. (1969) *Physical Control of the Mind.* New York: Harper & Row.

Dembroski, T. & Costa, P. (1987) Coronary prone behaviour: components of the Type A pattern and hostility. *Journal of Personality, 55,* 211–235.

Dement, W. (1972) *Some Must Watch While Some Must Sleep.* Stanford, California: Stanford Alumni Association.

Dement, W. & Kleitman, N. (1957) The relation of eye movements during sleep to dream activity: An objective method for the study of dreaming. *Journal of Experimental Psychology, 53* (5), 339–346.

Dement, W.C. (1960) The effects of dream deprivation. *Science, 131,* 1705–1707.

Dement, W.C. (2000) Tired of counting sheep? The world's greatest sleep expert on how to hit the snooze button. *The Independent on Sunday, Real Life,* 16 January, 1–2.

Dement, W.C. & Wolpert, E. (1958) The relation of eye movements, body motility and external stimuli to dream content. *Journal of Experimental Psychology, 55,* 543–553.

Denker, R. (1946) Results of treatment of psychoneuroses by the general practitioner: A follow-up study of 500 cases. *New York State Journal of Medicine, 46,* 356–364.

Denmark, F., Russo, N.F., Frieze, I.H. & Sechzer, J.A. (1988) Guidelines for Avoiding Sexism in Psychological Research: A report of the ad hoc committee on nonsexist research. *American Psychologist, 43*(7), 582–585.

Denney, N. & Palmer, A. (1981) Adult age differences on traditional problem-solving measures. *Journal of Gerontology, 36,* 323–328.

Dennis, W. (1960) Causes of retardation among institutional children: Iran. *Journal of Genetic Psychology, 96,* 47–59.

Denzin, N.K. (1995) Symbolic Interactionism. In J.A. Smith, R. Harré, & L.V. Langenhove (Eds) *Rethinking Psychology.* London: Sage.

Department of Health (1994) *Drugs: A Parents' Guide.* Central Print Unit.

Department of Health & Home Office (1994) *Report of the Department of Health and Home Office Working Group on Psychopathic Disorder.* London: Department of Health & Home Office.

Department of Health and Social Security (1983) *Mental Health Act, 1983.* London: HMSO.

Deregowski, J. (1968) Pictorial recognition in subjects from a relatively pictureless environment. *African Social Research 5,* 356–364.

Deregowski, J. (1969) Preference for chain-type drawings in Zambian domestic servants and primary school children. *Psychologia Africana, 82,* 9–13.

Deregowski, J. (1970) A note on the possible determinants of split representation as an artistic style. *International Journal of Psychology, 5,* 21–26.

Deregowski, J. (1972) Pictorial perception and culture. *Scientific American, 227,* 82–88.

Deregowski, J., Muldrow, E.S. & Muldrow, W.F. (1972) Pictorial recognition in a remote Ethiopian population. *Perception, 1,* 417–425.

Dermer, M. & Thiel, D.L. (1975) When beauty may fail. *Journal of Personality & Social Psychology, 31,* 1168–1176.

Deutsch, J.A. & Deutsch, D. (1963) Attention: Some theoretical considerations. *Psychological Review, 70,* 80–90.

Deutsch, J.A. & Deutsch, D. (1967) Comments on 'Selective attention: Perception or response?' *Quarterly Journal of Experimental Psychology, 19,* 362–363.

Deutsch, M. & Collins, M.E. (1951) *Interracial Housing: A Psychological Evaluation of a Social Experiment.* Minneapolis, MN: University of Minnesota Press.

Deutsch, M. & Gerard, H.B. (1955) A study of normative and informational social influence upon individual judgement. *Journal of Abnormal & Social Psychology, 51,* 629–636.

Deville-Almond, J. (2000) Man troubles. *Nursing Times, 96*(11), 28–29.

Devine, P.G. (1989) Stereotypes and prejudice: Their automatic and controlled components. *Journal of Personality & Social Psychology, 56,* 5–18.

Devine, P.G. & Zuwerink, J.R. (1994) Prejudice and guilt: The internal struggle to control prejudice. In W.J. Lonner & R.S. Malpass (Eds) *Psychology and Culture.* Boston: Allyn & Bacon.

Devlin Report (1976) *Report to the Secretary of State for the Home Development of the Departmental Committee on Evidence of Identification in Criminal Cases.* London: HMSO.

Dex, S. & Phillipson, C. (1986) Social policy and the older worker. In C. Phillipson & A. Walker (Eds) *Ageing and Social Policy: A Critical Assessment.* Aldershot: Gower.

Diagram Group (1982) *The Brain – A User's Manual.* New York: G.P. Putnams & Son.

Diamond, M. (1978) Sexual identity and sex roles. *The Humanist,* March/April.

Diamond, M. (1982) Sexual identity, monozygotic twins reared in discordant roles, and a BBC follow-up. *Archives of Sexual Behaviour, 11,* 181–186.

Diamond, M. & Sigmundson, H.K. (1997) Sex reassignment at birth. *Paediatric & Adolescent Medicine, 151,* 298–304.

Diamond, R. & Carey, S. (1986) Why faces are and are not special: An effect of expertise. *Journal of Experimental Psychology: General, 115,* 107–117.

Dicara, L.V. & Miller, N.E. (1968) Changes in heart rate instrumentally learned by curarised rats as avoidance responses. *Journal of Comparative & Physiological Psychology, 65,* 8–12.

Dicks, L. (2000) All for one! *New Scientist, 167*(2246), 30–35.

Diener, E. (1980) Deindividuation: The absence of self-awareness and self-regulation in group members. In P.B. Paulus (Ed.) *Psychology of Group Influence.* Hillsdale, NJ: Erlbaum.

Diener, E., Fraser, S.C., Beaman, A.L. & Kelem, R.T. (1976) Effects of deindividuation variables on stealing among Halloween trick-or-treaters. *Journal of Personality & Social Psychology, 33,* 178–183.

Dietch, J.T. (1995) Old age. In D. Wedding (Ed.) *Behaviour and Medicine* (2nd edition). St Louis, MO: Mosby-Year Book.

Digman, J.M. (1990) Personality structure: Emergence of the five-factor model. *Annual Review of Psychology, 41,* 417–440.

Dimatteo, M.R., Sherbourne, C., Hays, R., Ordway, L., Kravitz, R., McGlynn, E., Kaplan, S., & Rogers, W.H. (1993) Physicians' characteristics influence patients' adherence to medical treatment: Results from the medical outcomes study. *Health Psychology, 12,* 93–102.

DiNicola, V.F. (1990) Anorexia multiform: Self-starvation in historical and cultural context. *Transcultural Psychiatric Research Review, 27,* 245–286.

Dion, K.K. (1972) Physical attractiveness and evaluation of children's transgressions. *Journal of Personality & Social Psychology, 24,* 207–213.

Dion, K.K. & Berscheid, E. (1974) Physical attractiveness and peer perception among children. *Sociometry, 37,* 1–12.

Dion, K.K. & Dion, K.L. (1995) On the love of beauty and the beauty of love: Two psychologists study attraction. In G.G. Brannigan & M.R. Merrens (Eds) *The Social Psychologists: Research Adventures.* New York: McGraw-Hill.

Dion, K.L. & Dion, K.K. (1993) Gender and ethnocultural comparisons in styles of love. *Psychology of Women Quarterly, 17,* 463–473.

Dion, K.K., Berscheid, E. & Walster, E. (1972) What is beautiful is good. *Journal of Personality & Social Psychology, 24,* 285–290.

Dixon, N.F. (1971) *Subliminal Perception: The Nature of the Controversy.* London: McGraw Hill.

Dixon, N.F. (1981) *Preconscious Processing.* London: Wiley.

Dockrell, J., Grove, N., & Hasan, P. (1999) People with learning disabilities. In D. Messer & F. Jones (Eds) *Psychology and Social Care.* London: Jessica Kingsley.

Dodwell, P.C. (1995) Fundamental Processes in Vision. In R.L. Gregory & A.M. Colman (Eds) *Sensation and Perception.* London: Longman.

Dollard, J. & Miller, N.E. (1950) *Personality and Psychotherapy.* New York: McGraw Hill.

Dollard, J., Doob, L.W., Mowrer, O.H. & Sears, R.R. (1939) *Frustration and Aggression.* New Haven, CT: Harvard University Press.

Donaldson, M. (1978) *Children's Minds.* London: Fontana.

Donaldson, M. & McGarrigle, J.(1974) Some clues to the nature of semantic development. *Journal of Child Language, 1,* 185–194.

Donaldson, M. & Wales, R.J. (1970) On the acquisition of some relational terms. In J.R. Hayes (Ed.), *Cognition and the Development of Language.* New York: Wiley.

Donnerstein, E. & Berkowitz, L. (1981) Victim reactions in aggressive erotic films as a factor in violence against women. *Journal of Personality & Social Psychology, 41,* 710–724.

Donnerstein, E., Linz, D. & Penrod, S. (1987) *The Question of Pornography.* London: The Free Press.

Dorner, G. (1976) *Hormones and Brain Differentiation.* Amsterdam: Elsevier.

Douglas, J., Reissler, R.K., Burgess, A.W., & Hartman, C.R. (1986) Criminal profiling from crime scene analysis. *Behavioural Sciences & The Law, 4,* 401–421.

Douvan, E.A. & Adelson, J. (1966) *The Adolescent Experience.* New York: Wiley.

Dovidio, J.F. (1995) With a little help from my friends. In G.G. Brannigan & M.R. Merrens (Eds) *The Social Psychologists: Research Adventures.* New York: McGraw-Hill.

Dovidio, J.F., Allen, J.L. & Schroeder, D.A. (1990) Specificity of empathy–induced helping: Evidence for altruistic motivation. *Journal of Personality & Social Psychology, 59,* 249–260.

Dovidio, J.F., Piliavin, J.A., Gaertner, S.L., Schroeder, D.A. & Clark, R.D. (1991) The arousal: Cost–reward model and the process of intervention. In M.S. Clark (Ed.) *Prosocial Behaviour: Review of Personality and Social Psychology, 12.* Newbury Park, CA: Sage.

Dowd, J.J. (1975) Ageing as exchange: A preface to theory. *Journal of Gerontology, 30,* 584–594.

Dowd, M. (1984) Twenty years after the murder of Kitty Genovese, the question remains: Why? *The New York Times,* B1, B4.

Downing, D. (1988) *Daylight Robbery.* London: Arrow Books.

Drabman, R.S. & Thomas, M.H. (1974) Does media violence increase children's toleration of real-life aggression? *Developmental Psychology, 10,* 418–421.

Draguns, J. (1980) Psychological disorders of clinical severity. In H.C. Triandis & J. Draguns (Eds) *Handbook of Cross-Cultural Psychology,* Volume 6, *Psychopathology.* Boston: Allyn & Bacon.

Draguns, J. (1990) Applications of cross-cultural psychology in the field of mental health. In R. Brislin (Ed.) *Applied Cross-Cultural Psychology.* Newbury Park, CA: Sage.

Driver, J. (1996) Attention and segmentation. *The Psychologist, 9,* 119–123.

Dryden, W. (1984) Therapeutic arenas. In W. Dryden (Ed.), *Individual Therapy in Britain.* London: Harper & Row.

Duchene, P. (1990) Using biofeedback for childbirth pain. *Nursing Times, 86* (25), 56.

Duck, S. (Ed.) (1982) *Personal Relationships 4: Dissolving Personal Relationships.* London: Academic Press.

Duck, S. (1988) *Relating to Others.* Milton Keynes: Open University Press.

Duck, S. (1991) *Friends for Life* (2nd edition). Hemel Hempstead: Harvester Wheatsheaf.

Duck, S. (1992) *Human Relationships* (2nd edition). London: Sage.

Duck, S. (1995) Repelling the study of attraction. *The Psychologist, 8,* 60–63.

Duck, S. (1999) *Relating to Others* (2nd ed.) Buckingham: Open University Press.

Dugdale, N. & Lowe, C.F. (1990) Naming and stimulus equivalence. In D.E. Blackman & H. Lejeune (Eds) *Behaviour Analysis in Theory and Practice: Contributions and Controversies.* Hillsdale, NJ: Lawrence Erlbaum.

Dunbar, G., Lewis, V. & Hill, R. (1999) Control processes and road-crossing skills. *The Psychologist, 12*(8), 398–399.

Duncan, G. (1993) Economic deprivation and childhood development. Paper presented at the biennial meetings of the Society for Research in Child Development. New Orleans, April.

Duncan, H.F., Gourlay, N. & Hudson, W. (1973) *A Study of Pictorial Perception among Bantu and White Primary-school Children in South Africa.* Johannesburg: Witwatersrand University Press.

Duncan, J. (1979) Divided attention: The whole is more than the sum of its parts. *Journal of Experimental Psychology*: *Human Perception, 5,* 216–228.

Duncan, J. & Humphreys, G.W. (1992) Beyond the search surface: Visual search and attentional engagement. *Journal of Experimental Psychology*: *Human Perception & Performance, 18,* 578–588.

Duncan, S.L. (1976) Differential social perception and attribution of intergroup violence: Testing the lower limits of stereotyping of blacks. *Journal of Personality & Social Psychology, 34,* 590–598.

Duncker, K. (1926) A qualitative (experimental and theoretical) study of productive thinking (solving of comprehensible problems). *Journal of Genetic Psychology, 68,* 97–116.

Duncker, K. (1939) The influence of past experience upon perceptual properties. *American Journal of Psychology, 52,* 255–265.

Duncker, K. (1945) On problem-solving. *Psychological Monographs, 58* (Whole No. 270).

Dunn, J. (1993) *Young Children's Close Relationships: Beyond Attachment (Volume 4).* Newbury Park, CA: Sage.

Dunn, J. (1999) Making sense of the social world: Mindreading, emotion and relationships. In P.D. Zelazo, J.W. Astington, & D.R. Olson (Eds) *Developing Theories of Intention: Social Understanding and Self-control.* Mahwah, NJ: Lawrence Erlbaum.

Dunn, J. (2000) Siblings. *The Psychologist, 13*(5), 244–248.

Dunn, J. & Plomin, R. (1990) *Separate Lives: Why Siblings are so Different.* New York: Basic Books.

Durkin, K. (1985) *Television, Sex roles and Children.* Milton Keynes: Open University Press.

Durkin, K. (1995) *Developmental Social Psychology: From Infancy to Old Age.* Oxford: Blackwell.

Dutton, D.G. & Aron, A.P. (1974) Some evidence for heightened sexual attraction under conditions of high anxiety. *Journal of Personality & Social Psychology, 30,* 510–517.

Dutton, D.C. & Aron, A.P. (1989) Romantic attraction and generalised liking for others who are sources of conflict-based arousal. *Canadian Journal of Behavioural Science, 21,* 246–257.

Duval, S. & Wicklund, R.A. (1972) *A Theory of Objective Self-Awareness.* New York: Academic Press.

Dworetzky, J.P. (1981) *Introduction to Child Development.* St Paul, Minnesota: West Publishing Co.

Dyson, J. (1980) Sociopolitical influences on retirement. *Bulletin of the British Psychological Society, 33,* 128–130.

Eagly, A.H. (1983) Gender and social influence: A social psychological analysis. *American Psychologist,* September.

Eagly, A.H. (1987) *Sex Differences in Social Behaviour: A Social Role Interpretation.* Hillsdale, NJ.: Erlbaum.

Eagly, A.H. & Carli, L.L. (1981) Sex of researchers and sex-typed communication as determinants of sex differences in influencability: A meta-analysis of social influence studies. *Psychological Bulletin, 90,* 1–20.

Eagly, A.H. & Crowley, M. (1986) Gender and helping behaviour: A meta-analytic review of the social psychological literature. *Psychological Bulletin, 100,* 232–308.

Eagly, A.H. & Steffen, V.J. (1984) Gender stereotypes stem from the distribution of men and women into social roles. *Journal of Personality & Social Psychology, 46,* 735–754.

Eagly, A.H. & Wood, W. (1999) The origins of sex differences in human behaviour. *American Psychologist, 54,* 408–423.

Eaton, N. (1991) Expert systems in nursing. *Nursing Standard, 5* (38), 32–5.

Ebbinghaus, H. (1885) *On Memory.* Leipzig: Duncker.

Eckensberger, L.H. (1994) Moral development and its measurement across cultures. In W.J. Lonner & R.S. Malpass (Eds) *Psychology and Culture.* Boston: Allyn & Bacon.

Eckensberger, L.H. (1999) Socio-moral development. In D. Messer & S. Millar (Eds) *Exploring Developmental Psychology: From Infancy to Adolescence.* London: Arnold.

Eckensberger, L.H. & Zimba, R. (1997) The development of moral judgement. In J.W. Berry, P.R. Dasen & T.S. Saraswathi (Eds) *Handbook of Cross-cultural Psychology, Volume 2: Basic Processes and Human Development.* Boston: Allyn & Bacon.

Edley, N. & Wetherell, M. (1995) *Men in Perspective: Practice, Power and Identity.* Hemel Hempstead: Harvester Wheatsheaf.

Edwards, D. & Potter, J. (1992) *Discursive Psychology* London: Sage.

Edwards, G. (1986) The alcohol dependence syndrome: A concept as stimulus to enquiry. *British Journal of Addiction, 81,* 71–84.

Effective Health Care (1999) Drug treatments for schizophrenia. *Effective Health Care, 5,* 6.

Efran, M.G. (1974) The effect of physical appearance on the judgement of guilt, interpersonal attraction and severity of recommended punishment in a simulated jury task. *Journal of Experimental Research in Personality, 8,* 45–54.

Egan, J. (1998) Why can't dyslexics read? *Psychology Review, 5*(2), 12–15.

Ehntholt, K.A., Salkovskis, P.M. & Rimes, K.A. (1999) Obsessive–compulsive disorder, anxiety disorder and self-esteem: An exploratory study. *Behaviour Research & Therapy in Personality, 37,* 771–781.

Ehrenfels, C. von (1890) Über Gestaltqualitäten. Vierteljahrschrift für wissenschaftliche *Philosophie und Soziologie, 14,* 249–292.

Eimas, P.D. (1975) Speech perception in early infancy. In L.B. Cohen and P. Salapatek (Eds) *Infant Perception: From Sensation to Cognition, Volume 2.* New York: Academic Press.

Eisenberg, N. (1982) The development of reasoning regarding prosocial behaviour. In N. Eisenberg (Ed.) *The Development of Prosocial Behaviour.* New York: Academic Press.

Eisenberg, N. (1986) *Altruistic Emotion, Cognition and Behaviour.* Hillsdale, NJ.: Erlbaum.

Eisenberg, N. (1996) In search of the good heart. In M.R. Merrens & G.C. Brannigan (Eds) *The Developmental Psychologists: Research Adventures across the Life Span.* New York: McGraw-Hill.

Eisenberg, N., Miller, R.A., Shell, R., McNalley, S. & Shea, C. (1991) Prosocial development in adolescence: A longitudinal study. *Developmental Psychology, 27*(5), 849–857.

Eisenberg, N., Shell, R. Pasternack, J., Lennon, R. , Beller, R. & Mathy, R.M. (1987) Prosocial development in middle childhood: A longitudinal study. *Developmental Psychology, 23,* 712–718.

Eiser, J.R. (1983) From attributions to behaviour. In M. Hewstone (Ed.) *Attribution Theory: Social and Functional Extensions.* Oxford: Blackwell.

Eiser, J.R. (1994) *Attitudes, Chaos and the Connectionist Mind.* Oxford: Blackwell.

Eiser, J.R. & van der Pligt, J. (1988) *Attitudes and Decisions.* London: Routledge.

Ekman, P. (1986) *Telling Lies.* New York: Berkley Books.

Ekman, P. (1994) All emotions are basic. In P. Ekman & R.J. Davidson (Eds) *The Nature of Emotion: Fundamental Questions.* New York: Oxford University Press.

Ekman, P. & Friesen, W.V. (1975) *Unmasking the Face.* Englewood Cliffs, NJ: Prentice-Hall.

Ekman, P., Friesen, W.V. & Ellsworth, P. (1972) *Emotion in the Human Face: Guidelines for Research and an Integration of Findings.* New York: Pergamon.

Ekman, P., Friesen, W.V. & Simons, R.C. (1985) Is the startle reaction an emotion? *Journal of Personality & Social Psychology, 49,* 1416–1426.

Elander, J., Rutter, M., Siminoff, E., & Pickles, A. (2000b) Explanations for apparent late onset criminality in a high-risk sample of children followed-up in adult life. *British Journal of Criminality, 40,* 497–509.

Elander, J., Simonoff, E., Pickles, A., Holmshaw, J., & Rutter., M. (2000a) A longitudinal study of adolescent and adult conviction rates among children referred to psychiatric services for behavioural and emotional problems. *Criminal Behaviour & Mental Health, 10,* 40–59.

Elkind. D. (1967) Egocentrism in adolescence. *Child Development, 38,* 1025–1034.

Elkind, D. (1970) Erik Erikson's eight ages of man. *New York Times Magazine,* 5 April.

Elkind, D. (1971) *Children and Adolescents: Interpretative Essays on Jean Piaget.* New York: Oxford University Press.

Elkind, D. (1976) *Child Development and Education: A Piagetian Perspective.* Oxford: Oxford University Press.

Ellenberg, L. & Sperry, R.W. (1980) Lateralised division of attention in the commissurotomised and intact brain. *Neuropsychologia, 18,* 411–418.

Elliott, B.J. & Richards, M.P.M. (1991) Children and divorce: Educational performance before and after parental separation. *International Journal of Law & The Family, 5,* 258–278.

Elliot, C. D., Murray, D.J. & Pearson, L.S. (1979) *British Ability Scales.* Slough: National Foundation for Educational Research.

Elliot, C.D. (1990) *Differential Ability Scales: Introduction and Technical Handbook.* San Antonio, TX: The Psychological Corporation.

Ellis, A. (1958) *Rational Psychotherapy.* California: Institute for Rational Emotive Therapy.

Ellis, A. (1962) *Reason and Emotion in Psychotherapy.* Secaucus, NJ: Lyle Stuart (Citadel Press).

Ellis, A. (1973) *Humanistic psychotherapy.* New York: McGraw Hill.

Ellis, A. (1984) Rational–emotive therapy. In R. Corsini (Ed.) *Current Psychotherapies* (3rd edition). Itasca, Il: Peacock.

Ellis, A. (1987) The impossibility of achieving consistently good mental health. *American Psychologist, 42,* 364–375.

Ellis, A. (1989) The impossibility of achieving consistently good mental health. *American Psychologist, 42,* 364–375.

Ellis, A. (1993) Reflections on rational–emotive therapy. *Journal of Consulting & Clinical Psychology, 61,* 199–201.

Ellis, A. (1997) The evolution of Albert Ellis and rational emotive behaviour therapy. In J.K. Zeig (Ed.) *The Evolution of Psychotherapy: The Third Conference.* New York: Brunner/Mazel.

Ellis, H.D. & Young, A.W. (1990) Accounting for delusional misidentifications. *British Journal of Psychiatry, 157,* 239–248.

Ellis, H.D., Davies, G.M, & Shepherd, J.W. (1978) A critical examination of the Photofit system for recalling faces. *Ergonomics, 21,* 297–307.

Ellsworth , P.C. (1994) Levels of thought and levels of emotion. In P. Ekman & R.J. Davidson (Eds) *The Nature of Emotion: Fundamental Questions.* New York: Oxford University Press.

Emmelkamp, P.M.G. (1982) *Phobic and Obsessive–compulsive Disorders.* New York: Plenum.

Emmelkamp, P.M. (1994) Behaviour therapy with adults. In A.E. Bergin & S.L. Garfield (Eds) *Handbook of Psychotherapy and Behaviour Change* (4th edition). New York: Wiley.

Emmelkamp, P.M.G. & Wessels, H. (1975) Flooding in imagination versus flooding in vivo: A comparison with agoraphobics. *Behaviour Research & Therapy in Personality, 13,* 7–15.

Empson, J. (1989) *Sleep and Dreaming.* London: Faber and Faber.

Empson, J. (1993) *Sleep and Dreaming* (2nd, revised edition) Hemel Hempstead: Harvester Wheatsheaf.

Endicott, J. & Spitzer, R.L. (1978) A diagnostic interview: The schedule for affective disorders and schizophrenia. *Archives of General Psychiatry, 35,* 837–844.

Endler, N.S. (1975) A person–situation interaction model of anxiety. In C.D. Spielberger & I.G. Sarason (Eds) *Stress and Anxiety, Volume 1.* Washington, DC.: Hemisphere.

Engel, G.L. (1962) *Psychological Development in Health and Disease.* Philadelphia: Saunders.

Engel, G.L. (1977) The need for a new medical model: A challenge for bio-medicine. *Science, 196,*129–135.

Engel, G.L (1980) The clinical application of the biopsychosocial model. *American Journal of Psychiatry, 137,* 535–544.

Ericsson, K.A. & Charness, N. (1994) Expert performance: its structure and acquisition. *American Psychologist, 49,* 725–747.

Eriksen, C.W. (1990) Attentional search of the visual field. In D. Brogan (Ed.) *Visual Search.* London: Taylor & Francis.

Eriksen, C.W. & Yeh, Y.Y. (1987) Allocation of attention in the visual field. *Journal of Experimental Psychology: Human Perception and Performance, 11,* 583–597.

Erikson, E.H. (1950) *Childhood and Society.* New York: Norton.

Erikson, E.H. (1963) *Childhood and Society* (2nd edition). New York: Norton.

Erikson, E.H. (1968) *Identity: Youth and Crisis*. New York: Norton.

Erikson, E.H. (1980) *Identity and the Life Cycle*. New York: Norton.

Erikson, M. (1968) The inhumanity of ordinary people. *International Journal of Psychiatry, 6*, 278–279.

Erlenmeyer-Kimling, L. & Jarvik, L.F. (1963) Genetics and intelligence: A review. *Science, 142*, 1477–1479.

Eron, L.D. & Huesmann, L.R. (1985) The role of television in the development of prosocial and antisocial behaviour. In D. Olweus, M. Radke-Yarrow, & J. Block (Eds) *Development of Antisocial and Prosocial Behaviour*. Orlando, FL: Academic Press.

Esgate, A. (1999) No longer different? *The Psychologist, 12*(5), 254.

Esterson, A. (1993) *Seductive Mirage: An Exploration of the Work of Sigmund Freud*. Chicago and La Salle, Ill.: Open Court.

Estes, W.K. (1970) *Learning Theory and Mental Develoment*. New York: Academic Press.

Etzioni, A. (1968) A model of significant research. *International Journal of Psychiatry, 6*, 279–280.

Evans, C. (1987a) Parapsychology: A History of Research. In R.L. Gregory (Ed.) *The Oxford Companion to the Mind*. Oxford: Oxford University Press.

Evans, C. (1987b) Extra-sensory perception. In R.L. Gregory (Ed.) *The Oxford Companion to the Mind*. Oxford: Oxford University Press.

Evans, J. St. B.T. & Over, D.E. (1996) *Rationality and Reasoning*. Hove: Psychology Press.

Eysenck, H.J. (1947) *Dimension of Personality*. London: RKP.

Eysenck, H.J. (1952) The effects of psychotherapy: An evaluation. *Journal of Consulting Psychology, 16*, 319–324.

Eysenck, H.J. (1953) The logical basis of factor analysis. In D.N. Jackson & S. Messick (Eds) *Problems in Human Assessment*. New York: McGraw-Hill.

Eysenck, H.J. (1954) *The Psychology of Politics*. London: Routledge & Kegan Paul.

Eysenck, H.J. (Ed.) (1960) *Behaviour Therapy and the Neuroses*. Oxford: Pergamon.

Eysenck, H.J. (1965) *Fact and Fiction in Psychology*. Harmondsworth: Penguin.

Eysenck, H. J. (1967) *The Biological Basis of Personality*. Springfield, Ill.: C.C. Thomas.

Eysenck, H.J. (1970) *Crime and Personality*. London: Paladin.

Eysenck, H.J. (1971) *Race, Intelligence and Education*. London: Temple-Smith.

Eysenck, H.J. (1973) Personality and the maintenance of the smoking habit. In W. Dunn (Ed.) *Smoking Behaviour*. Washington, DC: Winston

Eysenck, H.J. (1974) Crime and personality reconsidered. *Bulletin of the British Psychological Society, , 27*, 23–24.

Eysenck, H.J. (1976) The learning theory model of neurosis: A new approach. *Behaviour Research & Therapy in Personality, 14*, 251–267.

Eysenck, H.J. (1980) The biosocial model of man and the unification of psychology. In A.J.Chapman & D.M. Jones (Eds) *Models of Man*. Leicester: British Psychological Society.

Eysenck, H.J. (1985) *Decline and Fall of the Freudian Empire*. Harmondsworth: Penguin.

Eysenck, H.J. (1991) Dimensions of personality: 16, 5 or 3? Criteria for a taxonomic paradigm. *Personality & Individual Differences, 8*, 773–790.

Eysenck, H.J. (1992) The outcome problem in psychotherapy. In W. Dryden & C. Feltham (Eds) *Psychotherapy and its Discontents*. Buckingham: Open University Press.

Eysenck, H.J. (1995) Trait Theories of Personality. In S.E. Hampson & A.M. Colman (Eds) *Individual Differences and Personality*. London: Longman.

Eysenck, H.J. & Eysenck, M.W. (1985) *Personality and Individual Differences: A Natural Science Approach*. New York: Plenum.

Eysenck, H.J. & Eysenck, S.B.G. (1964) *EPI Manual*. London: University of London Press.

Eysenck, H.J. & Eysenck, S.B.G. (1975) *Manual of the Eysenck Personality Questionnaire*. London: Hodder & Stoughton.

Eysenck, H.J. & Gudjonsson, G. (1989) *The Causes and Cures of Criminality*. New York: Plenum Press.

Eysenck, H.J. & Rachman, S. (1965) *The Cause and Cure of Neurosis*. London: RKP.

Eysenck, H.J. & Sargent, C. (1993) *Explaining the Unexplained: Mysteries of the Paranormal*. New York: Avery.

Eysenck, H.J. & Wakefield, J.A. (1981) Psychological factors as predictors of marital satisfaction. *Advances in Behaviour Research & Therapy in Personality, 3*, 151–192.

Eysenck, H.J. & Wilson, G.D. (1973) (Eds) *The Experimental Study of Freudian Theories*. London: Methuen.

Eysenck, M.W. (1979) Depth, elaboration and distinctiveness. In L.S. Cermak & F.I.M. Craik (Eds), *Levels of Processing in Human Memory*. Hillsdale, New Jersey: Lawrence Erlbaum Associates Inc.

Eysenck, M.W. (1982) *Attention and Arousal: Cognition and Performance*. Berlin: Springer.

Eysenck, M.W. (1984) *A Handbook of Cognitive Psychology*. London: Lawrence Erlbaum Associates.

Eysenck, M.W. (1986) Working memory. In G. Cohen, M.W. Eysenck & M.A. Le Voi (Eds) *Memory: A Cognitive Approach*. Milton Keynes: Open University Press.

Eysenck, M.W. (1993) *Principles of Cognitive Psychology*. Hove: Erlbaum.

Eysenck, M.W. (1995) Attention. In C.C. French & A.M. Colman (Eds) *Cognitive Psychology*. London: Longman.

Eysenck, M.W. (1997a) Doing two things at once. *Psychology Review, 4* (1), 10–12.

Eysenck, M.W. (1997b) Absent-mindedness. *Psychology Review, 3*, 16–18.

Eysenck, M.W. & Eysenck, H. J.(1980) Mischel and the concept of personality. *British Journal of Psychology, 71*, 191–204.

Eysenck, M.W. & Eysenck, M.C. (1980) Effects of processing depth, distinctiveness and word frequency on retention. *British Journal of Psychology, 71*, 263–74.

Eysenck, M.W. & Keane, M.J. (1990) *Cognitive Psychology: A Student's Handbook*. Hove: Lawrence Erlbaum Associates Ltd.

Eysenck, M.W. & Keane, M.J. (1995) *Cognitive Psychology: A Student's Handbook* (3rd edition). Hove: Erlbaum.

Eysenck, S. & Eysenck, H.J. (1970) Crime and personality: An empirical study of the three-factor theory. *British Journal of Criminology, 10*, 225–239.

Ezard, J. (2000) UK's work burden grows fastest in Europe. *The Guardian*, 21 June, 7.

Fagot, B.I. (1985) Beyond the reinforcement principle: Another step toward understanding sex-role development. *Developmental Psychology, 21*, 1091–1104.

Fairbairn, G. & Fairbairn, S. (1987) Introduction. In S. Fairbairn & G. Fairbairn (Eds) *Psychology, Ethics and Change*. London: Routledge & Kegan Paul.

Fairbairn, R. (1952) *Psychoanalytical Studies of the Personality*. London: Tavistock.

Falek, A. & Moser, H.M. (1975) Classification in schizophrenia. *Archives of General Psychiatry, 32*, 59–67.

Fancher, R.E. (1979) *Pioneers of Psychology*. New York: Norton.

Fancher, R.E. (1996) *Pioneers of Psychology* (3rd edition). New York: Norton.

Fantz, R.L. (1961) The origin of form perception. *Scientific American, 204* (5), 66–72.

Faraday, A. (1972) *Dream Power*. London: Pan Books.

Farber, S.L. (1981) *Identical Twins Reared Apart*. New York: Basic Books.

Farina, A. (1992) The stigma of mental disorders. In A.G. Miller (Ed.) *In the Eye of the Beholder*. New York: Praeger.

Farr, R. (1998) From collective to social representations: Aller et retour. *Culture & Psychology, 4*, 275–296.

Farr, R.M. & Moscovici, S. (Eds) (1984) *Social Representations*. Cambridge: Cambridge University Press.

Farrar, M.J. (1992) Negative evidence and grammatical morpheme acquisition. *Developmental Psychology, 28*, 90–98.

Farrington, D.P. (1990) Implications of criminal career research for the prevention of offending. *Journal of Adolescence, 13*, 93–113.

Farrington, D.P. (1992) Juvenile delinquency. In J. Coleman (Ed.) *The School Years: Current Issues in the Socialisation of Young People* (2nd edition). London: Routledge.

Farrington, D.P. (1995) The development of offending and antisocial behaviour from childhood: key findings from the Cambridge Study in delinquent development. *Journal of Child Psychology & Psychiatry, 36*, 929–964.

Farrington, D.P. & West, D.J. (1990) The Cambridge Study in delinquent development: A long-term follow-up of 411 London males. In H.T. Kerner & G. Kaiser (Eds) *Criminality: Personality, Behaviour, and Life History*. Berlin: Springer-Verlag.

Fazio, R.H. (1986) How do attitudes guide behaviour? In R.M. Sorrentino & E.T. Higgins (Eds) *Handbook of Motivation and Cognition: Foundations of Social Behaviour*. New York: Guilford.

Fazio, R.H. & Zanna, M.D. (1978) Attitudinal qualities relating to the strength of the attitude–behaviour relation. *Journal of Experimental Social Psychology, 14*, 398–408.

Fazio, R.H. & Zanna, M.D. (1981) Direct experience and attitude-behaviour consistency. In L. Berkowitz (Ed.), *Advances in Experimental Social Psychology, Volume 14*. New York: Academic Press.

Fazio, R.H., Zanna, M.P. & Cooper, J. (1977) Dissonance and self-perception: An integrative view of each theory's major domain of application. *Journal of Experimental & Social Psychology, 13*, 464–479.

Fechner, G.T. (1860) *Elemente der Psychophysik*. Leipzig: Bretkopf und Hartel.

Fedoroff, I.C. & McFarlane, T. (1998) Cultural aspects of eating disorders. In S.S. Kazarian & D.R. Evans (Eds) *Cultural Clinical Psychology: Theory, Research, and Practice*. New York: Oxford University Press.

Feighner, J.P., Robins, E., Guze, S.B., Woodruff, R.A., Winokur, G. & Munz, R. (1972) Diagnostic criteria for use in psychiatric research. *Archives of General Psychiatry, 26*, 57–63.

Felipe, N.J. & Sommer, R. (1966) Invasion of personal space. *Social Problems, 14*, 206–214.

Felmlee, D.H. (1995) Fatal attractions: Affection and disaffection in intimate relationships. *Journal of Social & Personal Relationships, 12*, 295–311.

Fennell, G., Phillipson, C. & Evers, H. (1988) *The Sociology of Old Age*. Milton Keynes: Open University Press.

Fenson, L., Dale, P.S., Reznick, J.S., Bates, E., Thal, D.J., & Pethick, S.J. (1994) Variability in early communicative development. *Monographs of the Society for Research in Child Development, 59* (5, Serial No. 242).

Fernando, S. (1988) *Race and Culture in Psychiatry*. London: Croom Helm.

Fernando, S. (1991) *Mental Health, Race and Culture*. London: Macmillan, in conjunction with MIND.

Ferster, C. (1965) Classification of behaviour pathology. In L. Krasner & L. Ullman (Eds) *Research in Behaviour Modification*. New York: Holt, Rinehart & Winston.

Ferster, C.B. & Skinner, B.F. (1957) *Schedules of Reinforcement*. New York: Appleton-Century-Crofts.

Feshbach, S. (1964) The function of aggression and the regulation of aggressive drive. *Psychological Review, 71*, 257–272.

Festinger, L. (1950) Informal social communication. *Psychological Review, 57*, 271–282.

Festinger, L. (1954) A theory of social comparison processes. *Human Relations, 7*, 117–140.

Festinger, L. (1957) *A Theory of Cognitive Dissonance*. New York: Harper & Row.

Festinger, L. & Carlsmith, J.M. (1959) Cognitive consequences of forced compliance. *Journal of Abnormal & Social Psychology, 58*, 203–210.

Festinger, L., Pepitone, A. & Newcomb, T. (1952) Some consequences of deindividuation in a group. *Journal of Abnormal & Social Psychology, 47*, 382–389.

Festinger, L., Schachter, S. & Back, K. (1950) *Social Pressures in Informal Groups: A Study of Human Factors in Housing*. Stanford, CA: Stanford University Press.

Firth, S. (1993) Cross-cultural perspectives on bereavement. In D. Dickenson & M. Johnson (Eds) *Death, Dying and Bereavement*. London: Sage (in association with the Open University).

Fischer, A., Fuchs, W. & Zinnecker, J. (1985) Jugenliche und Erwachsene '85. In *Jugenwerk der Deutschen Shell (Ed.) Arbeitsbericht und Dokumentation, Volume 5*. Leverskusen: Leske und Budrich.

Fischman, J. (1985) Mapping the mind. *Psychology Today*, September, 18–19.

Fishbein, H.D. (1984) *The Psychology of Infancy and Childhood: Evolutionary and Cross-cultural Perspectives*. Hillsdale, NJ: Lawrence Erlbaum.

Fishbein, M. (1967) Attitudes and the prediction of behaviour. In M. Fishbein (Ed.) *Readings in Attitude Theory and Measurement*. New York: Wiley.

Fishbein, M & Ajzen, I. (1974) Attitudes towards objects as predictors of single and multiple behavioural criteria. *Psychological Review, 81*, 59–74.

Fishbein, M. & Ajzen, I. (1975) *Belief, Attitude, Intention and Behaviour: An Introduction to Theory and Research*. Reading, MA: Addison-Wesley.

Fisher, R.P. & Geiselman, R.E. (1988) Enhancing eyewitness memory with the cognitive interview. In M.M. Gruneberg, P.E. Morris & R.N. Sykes (Eds) *Practical Aspects of Memory: Current Research and Issues. Volume 1: Memory in Everyday Life*. Chichester: John Wiley & Sons.

Fisher, S. & Greenberg, R. (1977) *The Scientific Credibility of Freud's Theories*. New York: Basic Books.

Fisher, S. & Greenberg, R. (Eds) (1980) *A Critical Appraisal of Biological Treatments for Psychological Distress: Comparisons with Psychotherapy and Placebo*. Hillsdale, NJ: Erlbaum.

Fisher, S. & Greenberg, R.P. (1995) Prescriptions for happiness? *Psychology Today, 28*, 32–37.

Fisher, S. & Greenberg, R.P. (1996) *Freud Scientifically Reappraised: Testing the Theories and the Therapy*. New York: Wiley.

Fiske, S.T. & Neuberg, S.L. (1990) A continuum of impression formation, from category-based to individuating processes: Influences of information and motivation on attention and interpretation. In L. Berkowitz (Ed.) *Advances in Experimental Social Psychology, Volume 23*. New York: Academic Press.

Fiske, S.T. & Taylor, S.E. (1991) *Social Cognition* (2nd edition). New York: McGraw-Hill.

Flanagan, O.J. (1984) *The Science of the Mind*. Cambridge, Mass.: MIT Press.

Flavell, J.H. (1971) First discussant's comments: What is memory development the development of? *Human Development, 14*, 272–278.

Flavell, J.H. (1977) *Cognitive Development*. Englewood Cliffs, New Jersey: Prentice-Hall.

Flavell, J.H. (1982) Structures, stages and sequences in cognitive development. In W.A. Collins (Ed.) *The Concept of Development: The Minnesota Symposia on Child Development, Volume 15*. Hillsdale, NJ: Erlbaum.

Flavell, J.H. (1986) The development of children's knowledge about the appearance–reality distinction. *American Psychologist, 41*, 418–425.

Flavell, J.H., Green, F.L. & Flavell, E.R. (1990) Developmental changes in young children's knowledge about the mind. *Cognitive Development, 5*, 1–27.

Flavell, J.H., Miller, P.H. & Miller, S.A. (1993) *Cognitive Development* (3rd edition). Englewood Cliffs, NJ.: Prentice-Hall.

Flavell, J.H., Shipstead, S.G., & Croft, K. (1978) What young children think you see when their eyes are closed. Unpublished report, Stanford University.

Fletcher, D. (1997) Boy raised as girl after surgical accident. *Daily Telegraph*, 15 March, 3.

Flowers, J.H., Warner, J.L. & Polansky, M.L. (1979) Response and encoding factors in ignoring irrelevant information. *Memory and Cognition, 7*, 86–94.

Fodor, J.A. (1983) *The Modularity of Mind*. Cambridge, Massachusetts: MIT Press.

Fodor, J.A. & Pylyshyn, Z.W. (1981) How direct is visual perception? Some reflections on Gibson's 'ecological approach'. *Cognition, 9*, 139–196.

Fodor, J.A. & Pylyshyn, Z.W. (1988) Connectionism and cognitive architecture: A critical analysis. *Cognition, 28*, 3–71.

Fogelman, K. (1976) *Britain's Sixteen-year-olds*. London: National Childrens' Bureau.

Folkard, S., Hume, K.I., Minors, D.S., Waterhouse, J.M. & Watson, F.L. (1985) Independence of the circadian rhythm in alertness from the sleep/wake cycle. *Nature, 313*, 678–679.

Folkman, S. & Lazarus, R.S. (1988a) Coping as a mediator of emotion. *Journal of Personality & Social Psychology, 54*, 466–475.

Folkman, S. & Lazarus, R.S. (1988b) *Manual for the Ways of Coping Questionnaire*. Palo Alto: Consulting Psychologists Press.

Fonagy, P. (1981) Research on psychoanalytic concepts. In F. Fransella, (Ed.), *Personality – Theory, Measurement and Research*. London: Methuen.

Fonagy, P. (1995) Psychoanalysis. In A.M. Colman (Ed.) *Applications of Psychology*. London: Longman.

Fonagy, P. (2000) The outcome of psychoanalysis: The hope of a future. *The Psychologist, 13*(12), 620–623.

Fonagy, P. & Higgitt, A. (1984) *Personality, Theory and Clinical Practice*. London: Methuen.

Fonagy, P., Steele, H., & Steele, M. (1991) Maternal representations of attachment during pregnancy predict the organisation of infant–mother attachment at one year of age. *Child Development, 62*, 891–905.

Fonagy, P., Steele, M., Steele, H., Higgitt, A., & Target, M. (1994) The Emmanuel Miller Memorial Lecture, 1992: The theory and practice of resilience. *Journal of Child Psychology & Psychiatry, 35*, 321–257.

Fontana, D. (1981a) Play. In D. Fontana (Ed.) *Psychology for Teachers* London: British Psychological Society/Macmillan Press.

Fontana, D. (1981b) Intelligence. In D. Fontana (Ed.), *Psychology for Teachers*. London: British Psychological Society/Macmillan Press.

Ford, K.M. & Hayes, P.J. (1998) On computational wings: Rethinking the goals of artificial intelligence. *Scientific American Presents, 9*(4), 78–83.

Ford, R. (1998) Study fails to link film violence to crime. *Times*, 8 January, 9.

Forth, A. (1995) Psychopathy in adolescent offenders: Assessment, family background and violence. *Issues in Criminological & Legal Psychology, 24*, 42–44.

Fortune, R. (1939) Arapesh warfare. *American Anthropologist, 41*, 22–41.

Fox, N.J. (1993) *Postmodernism, Sociology and Health*. Milton Keynes: Open University Press.

Foxx, R. & Azrin, N. (1973) *Toilet Training the Retarded*. Illinois: Research Press.

Frank, I.D. (1973) *Persuasion and Healing* (2nd edition). Baltimore: John Hopkins University Press.

Frank, I.D. (1989) Non-specific aspects of treatment: the view of a psychotherapist. In M. Shepherd & N. Sartorius (Eds) *Non-Specific Aspects of Treatment*. Toronto: Hans Huber.

Frankenhaeuser. F. (1975) Experimental approaches to the study of catecholamines and emotion. In L. Levi (Ed.) *Emotions: The Parameters and Measurement*. New York: Raven Press.

Frankenhauser, M. (1983) The sympathetic–adrenal and pituitary–adrenal response to challenge: Comparison between the sexes. In T.M. Dembroski, T.H. Schmidt & G. Blumchen (Eds) *Behavioural Bases of Coronary Heart Disease*. Basle: S. Karger.

Frankenhauser, M., Lundberg, U. & Chesney, M. (1991) *Women, Work and Health: Stress and Opportunities*. New York: Plenum.

Frankland, A. & Cohen, L. (1999) Working with recovered memories. *The Psychologist, 12*(2), 82–83.

Fransella, F. (1970) ... And then there was one. In D. Bannister (Ed.) *Perspectives in Personal Construct Theory*. London: Academic Press

Fransella, F. (1972) *Personal Change and Reconstruction: Research on a Treatment of Stuttering*. London: Academic Press.

Fransella, F. (1975) *Need to Change?* London: Methuen.

Fransella, F. (1981) Personal construct psychology and repertory grid technique. In F. Fransella (Ed.), *Personality – Theory, Measurement and Research*. London: Methuen.

Frean, A. (1994) Researchers study TV's arrival on media-free island. *The Times*, 6 June, 8.

Frean, A. (1995) Getting a kick from TV violence. *The Times*, 23 August, 31.

Freedman, A.M., Kaplan, H.I., & Sadock, B.J. (1975) *Comprehensive Textbook of Psychiatry, Volume 2*. Baltimore: Williams & Wilkins Co.

Freedman, J.L. (1963) Attidudinal effects of inadequate justification. *Journal of Personality, 31*, 371–385.

Freedman, J.L. (1965) Long-term behavioural effects of cognitive dissonance. *Journal of Experimental & Social Psychology, 1*, 145–55.

Freeman, C. (Ed.) (1995) *The ECT Handbook*. London: Gaskell.

Freeman, H. (2000) Thin end of the wedge. *The Guardian*, 21 June, 2.

Freeman, H. & Watts, J.W. (1942) *Psychosurgery*. Springfield, Ill.: Thomas.

Freud, A. (1936) *The Ego and the Mechanisms of Defence*. London: Chatto & Windus.

Freud, A. (1966) *Normality and Pathology in Childhood*. London: Hogarth Press.

Freud, A. & Dann, S. (1951) An experiment in group upbringing. *Psychoanalytic Study of the Child, 6*, 127–168.

Freud, S. (1891) *On Aphasia*. Translated by E. Stengel (1950). (New York) Image.

Freud, S. (1894) The defence neuropsychoses. In J. Strachey (Ed.) *The Standard Edition of the Complete Psychological Works of Sigmund Freud, Volume I*. London: The Hogarth Press, 1953.

Freud, S. (1899) Screen Memories: *Standard Edition of the Complete Psychological Works of Sigmund Freud, Volume III*. London: Hogarth Press.

Freud, S. (1900/1976a) *The Interpretation of Dreams*. Pelican Freud Library (4) Harmondsworth: Penguin.

Freud, S. (1901/1976b) *The Psychopathology of Everyday Life*. Pelican Freud Library (5) Harmondsworth: Penguin.

Freud, S. (1905/1977a) *Three Essays on the Theory of Sexuality*. Pelican Freud Library (7) Harmondsworth: Penguin.

Freud, S. (1909/1977b) *Analysis of a Phobia in a Five-year-old Boy*. Pelican Freud Library (8) Harmondsworth: Penguin.

Freud, S. (1914) *Remembering, Repeating and Working Through. The Standard Edition of Complete Psychological Works of Sigmund Freud, Volume XII*. London: Hogarth Press.

Freud, S. (1915) *Repression*. Standard Edition of the Complete Psychological Works of Sigmund Freud, Volume 14. London: Hogarth Press.

Freud, S. (1917) *Mourning and Melancholia*. London: The Hogarth Press.

Freud, S. (1920/1984) *Beyond the Pleasure Principle*. Pelican Freud Library (11). Harmondsworth: Penguin.

Freud, S. (1923/1984) *The Ego and the Id*. Pelican Freud Library (11). Harmondsworth: Penguin.

Freud, S. (1924) The passing of the Oedipus complex. In E. Jones (Ed.) *Collected Papers of Sigmund Freud, Volume 5*. New York: Basic Books.

Freud, S. (1926) Inhibitions, symptoms and anxiety. In *Standard Edition of the Complete Psychological Works of Sigmund Freud, Volume XX*. London: Hogarth Press.

Freud, S. (1933) *New Introductory Lectures on Psychoanalysis*. New York: Norton.

Freud, S. (1949) *An Outline of Psychoanalysis*. London: Hogarth Press.

Freud, S. & Breuer, J. (1895) *Studies on Hysteria*. Penguin Freud, Library, Volume 3. Harmondsworth: Penguin.

Friedman, M. & Rosenman, R.H. (1974) *Type A Behaviour and Your Heart*. New York: Harper Row.

Frijda, N.H. (1994) Varieties of affect: Emotions and episodes, moods, and sentiments. In P. Ekman & R. J. Davidson (Eds) *The Nature of Emotion: Fundamental Questions*. New York: Oxford University Press.

Frijda, N. & Jahoda, G. (1966) On the scope and methods of cross-cultural psychology. *International Journal of Psychology, 1*, 109–127.

Frisby, J.P. (1986) The computational approach to vision. In I. Roth & J.P. Frisby (Eds), *Perception and Representation*. Milton Keynes: Open University Press.

Frith, C. & Cahill, C. (1995) Psychotic disorders: Schizophrenia, affective psychoses and paranoia. In A.A. Lazarus & A.M. Colman (Eds) *Abnormal Psychology*. London: Longman.

Frith, U. (1985) Beneath the surface of developmental dyslexia. In K. Patterson, M. Coltheart, & J. Marshall (Eds) *Surface Dyslexia*. London: RKP.

Frith, U. (1989) *Autism: Explaining the Enigma*. Oxford: Basil Blackwell.

Frith, U. (1996) Cognitive explanations of autism. *Acta Paediatrics Supplement*, 416.

Frith, U. & Happé, F. (1994a) Autism: Beyond 'theory of mind'. *Cognition, 50*, 115–132.

Frith, U. & Happé, F. (1994b) Language and communication in the autistic disorders. *Philosophical Transactions of the Royal Society, Series B, 346*, 97–104.

Frith, U. & Snowling, M. (1983) Reading for meaning and reading for sound in autistic and dyslexic children. *Journal of Developmental Psychology, 1*, 329–342.

Frodi, A. (1975) The effect of exposure to weapons on aggressive behaviour from a cross-cultural perspective. *International Journal of Psychology, 10*, 283–292.

Fromant, S. (1988) Helping each other. *Nursing Times, 84* (36), 30–32.

Fromm, E. (1941) *Escape From Freedom*. New York: Farrar & Rinehart.

Fromm, E. (1962) *The Art of Loving*. London: Unwin Books.

Fromm, E. (1970) *The Crisis of Psychoanalysis – Essays on Freud, Marx and Social Psychology*. Harmondsworth: Penguin.

Fromm, E. (1977) *The Anatomy of Human Destructiveness*. Harmondsworth: Penguin.

Fromm-Reichman, F. (1948) Notes on the development of treatment of schizophrenics by psychoanalytic psychotherapy. *Psychiatry, 11*, 263–273.

Frost, J.A., Binder, J.R., Springer, J.A., Hemmeke, T.A., Bellgowan, P.S.F., Rao, S.M. & Cox, R.W. (1999) Language processing is strongly lateralised in both sexes: Evidence from functional MRI. *Brain, 122*, 199–208.

Frude, N. (1998) *Understanding Abnormal Psychology*. Oxford: Blackwell.

Frueh, T. & McGhee, P.E. (1975) Traditional sex-role development and amount of time spent watching television. *Developmental Psychology, 11*, 109.

Funk, S.C. (1992) Hardiness: A review of theory and research. *Health Psychology, 11*(5), 335–345.

Furnham, A. & Heaven, P. (1999) *Personality and Social Behaviour*. London: Arnold.

Furth, H.G. (1966) *Thinking Without Language*. New York: Free Press.

Gabrieli, J.D.E., Cohen, N.J., & Corkin, S. (1983) The acquisition of lexical and semantic knowledge in amnesia. *Society for Neuroscience Abstracts, 9*, 238.

Gadow, J.D. & Sprafkin, J. (1989) Field experiments of television violence: Evidence for an environmental hazard? *Paediatrics, 83*, 399–405.

Gadow, J.D. & Sprafkin, J. (1993) Television violence and children. *Journal of Emotional & Behavioural Disorders, 1*, 54–63.

Gaertner, S.L. & Dovidio, J.F. (1977) The subtlety of white racism, arousal, and helping. *Journal of Personality & Social Psychology, 35*, 691–707.

Gaertner, S.L. & Dovidio, J.F. (1986) The aversive form of racism. In J.F. Dovidio & S.L. Gaertner (Eds) *Prejudice, Discrimination and Racism*. Orlando, FL: Academic Press.

Gagné, R.M. (1970) *The Conditions of Learning* (2nd edition). New York: Holt, Rinehart & Winston.

Gagné, R.M. (1974) *Essentials of Learning for Instruction*. New York: Dryden Press.

Gahagan, J. (1984) *Social Interaction and its Management*. London: Methuen.

Gahagan, J. (1991) Understanding other people, understanding self. In J. Radford & E. Govier (Eds) *A Textbook of Psychology* (2nd edition). London: Routledge.

Gale, A. (1990) *Thinking about Psychology?* (2nd edition). Leicester: British Psychological Society.

Gale, A. (1995) Ethical issues in psychological research. In A.M. Colman (Ed.) *Psychological Research Methods and Statistics*. London: Longman.

Gallagher, M., Millar, R., Hargie, O. & Ellis, R. (1992) The personal and social worries of adolescents in Northern Ireland: Results of a survey. *British Journal of Guidance & Counselling, 30*(3), 274–290.

Gallup, G.G. (Jr) (1970) Chimpanzees: Self-recognition. *Science, 167*, 86–87.

Gallup, G.G. (1977) Self-recognition in primates. *American Psychologist, 32*, 329–338.

Gallup, G.G. (1998) Can animals empathise? Yes. *Scientific American Presents, 9*(4), 66, 68–71.

Garber, H.L. (1988) *The Milwaukee Project: Preventing Mental Retardation in Children at Risk.* Washington, DC: American Association on Mental Retardation.

Garcia, J. & Koelling, R.A. (1966) The relation of cue to consequence in avoidance learning. *Psychonomic Science, 4,* 123–124.

Garcia, J., Ervin, F.R. & Koelling, R.A. (1966) Learning with prolonged delay of reinforcement. *Psychonomic Science, 5*(3), 121–122.

Gardner, B.T. & Gardner, R.A. (1971) Two-way communication with an infant chimpanzee. In A. Schrier & F. Stollitz (Eds), *Behaviour of Non-human Primates, Volume 4.* New York: Academic Press.

Gardner, B.T. & Gardner, R.A. (1975) Evidence for sentence constituents in the early utterances of child and chimp. *Journal of Experimental Psychology: General, 104,* 244–267.

Gardner, B.T. & Gardner, R.A. (1980) Two comparative psychologists look at language acquisition. In K. Nelson (Ed.), *Children's Language, Volume 2.* New York: Gardner Press.

Gardner, H. (1983) *Frames of Mind: The Theory of Multiple Intelligences.* New York: Basic Books.

Gardner, H. (1985) *The Mind's New Science.* New York: Basic Books.

Gardner, H. (1987) Epilogue: Cognitive science after 1984. In Gardner, H. (1985) *The mind's new science.* New York: Basic Books.

Gardner, H. (1993) *Multiple Intelligences: The Theory in Practice.* New York: Basic Books.

Gardner, H. (1998) A multiplicity of intelligences. *Scientific American Presents: Exploring Intelligence, 9*(4), 18–23.

Gardner, R.A. & Gardner, B.T. (1969) Teaching sign language to a chimpanzee. *Science, 165*(3894), 664–672.

Gardner, R.A. & Gardner, B.T. (1978) Comparative psychology and language acquisition. Psychology: The state of the art. *Annals of the New York Academy of Sciences, 309,* 37–76.

Garfield, S. (1992) Response to Hans Eysenck. In W. Dryden & C. Feltham (Eds) *Psychotherapy and its Discontents.* Buckingham: Open University Press.

Garfield, S. & Bergin, A. (1994) Introduction and historical overview. In A. Bergin & S. Garfield (Eds) *Handbook of Psychotherapy and Behaviour Change.* Chichester: Wiley.

Garner, D.M., Garfinkel, P.E., Schwartz, D., & Thompson, M. (1980) Cultural expectations of thinness in women. *Psychological Reports, 47,* 483–491.

Garnham, A. (1988) *Artificial Intelligence: An Introduction.* London: Routledge, Kegan Paul.

Garnham, A. (1991) *The Mind in Action.* London: Routledge.

Garrett, R. (1996) Skinner's case for radical behaviourism. In W. O'Donohue & R.F. Kitchener (Eds) *The Philosophy of Psychology.* London: Sage.

Gatchel, R.J. (1995) *Stress and Coping.* In B. Parkinson & A.M. Colman (Eds) *Emotion and Motivation.* London: Longman.

Gathercole, S.E. & Baddeley, A.D. (1990) Phonological memory deficits in language-disordered children: Is there a causal connection? *Journal of Memory & Language, 29,* 336–360.

Gauker, C. (1990) How to learn language like a chimpanzee. *Philosophical Psychology, 3,* 31–53.

Gay, P. (1988) *Freud: A Life for our Time.* London: J.M. Dent & Sons.

Gaze, H. (1988) Stressed to the limit. *Nursing Times, 84*(36), 16–17.

Gazzaniga, M.S. (1967) The split-brain in man. *Scientific American, 221,* 24–29.

Gazzaniga, M.S. (1983) Right hemisphere language following brain bisection: A 2-year perspective. *American Psychologist, 38,* 525–537.

Gazzaniga, M.S. (1985) *The Social Brain: Discovering the Networks of the Mind.* New York: Basic Books.

Geen, R.G. (1990) *Human Aggression.* Milton Keynes: Open University Press.

Geen, R.G. (1995) Social motivation. In Parkinson, B. & Colman, A.M. (Eds) *Emotion and Motivation.* London: Longman.

Geen, R.G. & Berkowitz, L. (1966) Some conditions facilitating the occurrence of aggression after the observation of violence. *Journal of Personality, 35,* 666–676.

Geiselman, R.E., Fisher, R.P., Mackinnon, D.P. & Holland, H.L. (1985) Eyewitness memory enhancement in the police interview: Cognitive retrieval, mnemonics versus hypnosis. *Journal of Applied Psychology, 70,* 401–412.

Gelder, M., Gath, D. & Mayon, R. (1989) *The Oxford Textbook of Psychiatry* (2nd edition). Oxford: Oxford University Press.

Gelder, M., Mayou, R., & Geddes, J. (1999) *Psychiatry* (2nd edition). Oxford: Oxford University Press.

Gelman, R. (1978) Counting in the pre-schooler: What does and does not develop. In R.S. Siegler (Ed.) *Children's Thinking: What Develops?* Hillsdale, NJ: Erlbaum.

Gelman, R. (1979) Preschool thought. *American Psychologist, 34,* 900–905.

Gelman, R. & Baillargeon, R. (1983) A review of some Piagetian concepts. In J.H. Flavell & E.M. Markman (Eds) *Handbook of Child Psychology: Cognitive Development, Volume 3.* New York: Wiley.

Gerard, H.B., Wilhelmy, R.A. & Connolly, E.S. (1968) Conformity and group size. *Journal of Personality & Social Psychology, 8,* 79–82.

Gerbner, G. (1972) Violence in television drama: Trends and symbolic functions. In G.A. Comstock & E.A. Rubenstein (Eds) *Television and Social Behaviour, Volume 1, Media Content and Control.* Washington, DC: US Government Printing Office.

Gerbner, G. & Gross, L. (1976) Living with television: The violence profile. *Journal of Communication, 26,* 173–199.

Gerbner, G., Gross, L., Morgan, M. & Signorielli, N. (1980) The 'mainstreaming' of America: Violence profile No. II. *Journal of Communication, 30,* 10–29.

Gerbner, G., Gross, L., Signorielli, N. & Morgan, M. (1986) *Television's Mean World: Violence Profile No. 14–15.* Philadelphia: Annenberg School of Communications, University of Pennsylvania.

Gergen, K.J. (1973) Social psychology as history. *Journal of Personality & Social Psychology, 26,* 309–320.

Gergen, K.J. (1985) The social constructionist movement in modern psychology. *American Psychologist, 40,* 266–275.

Gergen, K.J. & Gergen, M.M. (1981) *Social Psychology.* New York: Harcourt Brace Jovanovich.

Gergen, K.J., Gergen, M.M. & Barton, W. (1973) Deviance in the dark. *Psychology Today, 7,* 129–130.

Gerrard, M., Gibbons, F.X., & Bushman, B.J. (1996) Relation between perceived vulnerability to HIV and precautionary sexual behaviour. *Psychological Bulletin, 119,* 390–409.

Gerrard, N. (1996) Autistic expression. *The Observer Review,* 15 December, 15.

Gerrard, N. (1997) Nicaragua's deaf children. *Observer Review,* 30 March, 5.

Gershon, E.S. & Rieder, R.O. (1992) Major disorders of mind and brain. *Scientific American, 267*(3), 88–95.

Geschwind, N. (1972) Language and the brain. *Scientific American, 226,* 76–83.

Geschwind, N. (1979) *The Brain.* San Francisco: Freeman.

Gesell, A. (1925) *The Mental Growth of the Preschool Child.* New York: Macmillan.

Gibbs, J.C. & Schnell, S.V. (1985) Moral development 'versus' socialisation. *American Psychologist, 40,* 1071–1080.

References

Gibson, E.J. & Walk, P.D. (1960) The visual cliff. *Scientific American, 202,* 64–71.

Gibson, E.J., Shapiro, F., & Yonas, A. (1968) Confusion matrices of graphic patterns obtained with a latency measure: A program of basic and applied research. (Final Report Project No. 5–1213, Cornell University).

Gibson, J.J. (1950) *The Perception of the Visual World.* Boston: Houghton Mifflin.

Gibson, J.J. (1966) *The Senses Considered as Perceptual Systems.* Boston: Houghton Mifflin.

Gibson, J.J. (1979) *The Ecological Approach to Visual Perception.* Boston: Houghton Mifflin.

Giddens, A. (1979) *Central Problems in Social Theory.* Basingstoke: Macmillan.

Gilbert, G.M. (1951) Stereotype persistence and change among college students. *Journal of Abnormal & Social Psychology, 46,* 245–254.

Gilbert, S.J. (1981) Another look at the Milgram obedience studies: The role of the graduated series of shocks. *Personality & Social Psychology Bulletin, 7,* 690–695.

Gilford, R. & Bengston, V. (1979) Measuring marital satisfaction in three generations: Positive and negative dimensions. *Journal of Marriage &The Family, 41,* 387–398.

Gilhooly, K. (1996) Working memory and thinking. *The Psychologist, 9,* 82.

Gillham, W.E.C. (1975) Intelligence: The persistent myth. *New Behaviour,* June 26, 433–435.

Gillham, W.E.C. (1978) Measurement constructs and psychological structure: Psychometrics. In A. Burton & J. Radford (Eds), *Thinking in Perspective.* London: Methuen.

Gillie, O. (1976) Pioneer of IQ fakes his research. *The Sunday Times,* 29 October, H3.

Gilligan, C. (1982) *In a Different Voice: Psychological Theory and Women's Development.* Cambridge, MA: Harvard University Press.

Gilligan, C. (1993) Letter to Readers (Preface). *In A Different Voice.* Cambridge, MA.: Harvard University Press.

Gilling, D. & Brightwell, R. (1982) *The Human Brain.* London: Orbis Publishing.

Gilovich, T. (1983) Biased evaluation and persistence in gambling. *Journal of Personality & Social Psychology, 44,* 1110–1126.

Ginsberg, H.P. (1981) Piaget and education: The contributions and limits of genetic epistemology. In K. Richardson & S. Sheldon (Eds) *Cognitive Development to Adolescence.* Milton Keynes: Open University Press.

Ginsberg, M.L. (1998) Computers, games and the real world. *Scientific American Presents, 9*(4), 84–89.

Glanzer, M. & Cunitz, A.R. (1966) Two storage mechanisms in free recall. *Journal of Verbal Learning & Verbal Behaviour, 5,* 928–935.

Glanzer, M. & Meinzer, A. (1967) The effects of intra-list activity on free recall. *Journal of Verbal Learning & Verbal Behaviour, 6,* 928–935.

Glassman, W.E. (1995) *Approaches to Psychology* (2nd edition). Buckingham: Open University.

Gleitman, H. (1981) *Psychology.* New York: Norton.

Gleitman, I.R. & Wanner, E. (1988) Current issues in language learning. In H.M. Bornstein & M.E. Lamb (Eds) *Developmental Psychology: An Advanced Textbook* (2nd edition). Hillsdale, NJ: Erlbaum.

Glick, B. & Goldstein, A.P. (1987) Aggression replacement training. *Journal of Counselling & Development, 65,* 356–367.

Glucksberg, S. & Cowan, N. (1970) Memory for non-attended auditory material. *Cognitive Psychology, 1,* 149–156.

Glucksberg, S. & Weisberg, R. (1966) Verbal behaviour and problem-solving: Some effects of labelling upon availability of novel functions. *Journal of Experimental Psychology, 71,* 659–664.

Godden, D. & Baddeley, A.D. (1975) Context-dependent memory in two natural environments: On land and under water. *British Journal of Psychology, 66,* 325–331.

Godden, D. & Baddeley, A.D. (1980) When does context influence recognition memory? *British Journal of Psychology, 71,* 99–104.

Goetsch, V.L. & Fuller, M.G. (1995) Stress and stress management. In D. Wedding (Ed.) *Behaviour and Medicine* (2nd edition). St. Louis, MO: Mosby-Year Book.

Goffman, E. (1963) *Stigma – Notes on the Management of Spoiled Identity.* Englewood Cliffs, N.J.: Prentice-Hall.

Goffman, E. (1968) *Asylums – Essay on the Social Situation of Mental Patients and Other Inmates.* Harmondsworth: Penguin.

Goffman, E. (1971) *The Presentation of Self in Everyday Life.* Harmondsworth: Penguin.

Goldberg, L.R (1993) The structure of phenotypic personality traits. *American Psychologist, 48,* 26–34.

Goldberg, S. (2000) *Attachment and Development.* London: Arnold.

Goldfarb, W. (1943) The effects of early institutional care on adult personality. *Journal of Experimental Education, 12,* 106–129.

Goldfarb, W. (1945) Effects of psychological deprivation in infancy and subsequent stimulation. *American Journal of Psychiatry, 102,* 18–33.

Goldin-Meadow, S. & Feldman, H. (1977) The development of a language-like communication without a language model. *Science, 197,* 401–403.

Goldman, R.J. & Goldman, J.D.G. (1981) How children view old people and ageing: a developmental study of children in four countries. *Australian Journal of Psychology, 3,* 405–418.

Goldman-Eisler, F. (1948) Breast-feeding and character formation. *Journal of Personality, 17,* 83–103.

Goldman-Eisler, F. (1951) The problem of 'orality' and its origin in early childhood. *Journal of Mental Science, 97,* 765–782.

Goldstein, A.P. & Glick, B. (1996) Aggression replacement training: methods and outcome. In C.R. Hollin & K. Howells (Eds) *Clinical Approaches to Working with Young Offenders.* Chichester: Wiley.

Goldstein, M.C. (1979) Pahari and Tibetan polyandry revisited. *Ethnology, 17,* 325–337.

Goldwyn, E. (1979) The fight to be male. *The Listener,* 24 May, 709–712.

Gollwitzer, P.M. (1993) Goal achievement: the role of intentions. In W. Stroebe & M. Hewstone (Eds) *European Review of Social Psychology, 4,* 141–185.

Golombok, S., Spencer, A. & Rutter, M. (1983) Children in lesbian and single-parent households: Psychosexual and psychiatric appraisal. *Journal of Child Psychology & Psychiatry, 24,* 551–572.

Golombok, S., Tasker, F., & Murray, C. (1997) Children raised in fatherless families from infancy: Family relationships and the socioemotional development of children of lesbian and single heterosexual mothers. *Journal of Child Psychology & Psychiatry, 38* (7), 783–791.

Goodall, J. (1965) Chimpanzees of the Gombe Stream Reserve. In I. DeVore, (Ed.) *Primate Behaviour: Field Studies of Monkeys and Apes.* New York: Holt, Rinehart & Winston.

Goodall, J. (1978) Chimp killings: Is it the man in them? *Science News, 113,* 276

Goodwin, R. (1995) Personal relationships across cultures. *The Psychologist, 8,* 73–75.

Gopnik, A. & Astington, J.W. (1988) Children's understanding of representational change and its relation to the understanding of false belief and the appearance–reality distinction. *Child Development, 59,* 26–37.

Gopnik, A. & Wellman, H.M. (1994) The theory theory. In L.A. Hirschfeld & S.A. Gelman (Eds) *Mapping the Mind*. Cambridge: Cambridge University Press.

Gordon, I.E. (1989) *Theories of Visual Perception*. Chichester: Wiley.

Gottesman, I. (1991) *Schizophrenia Genesis*. New York: W.H. Freeman.

Gottesman, I.I. & Shields, J. (1972) *Schizophrenia and Genetics: A Twin Study Vantage Point*. New York: Academic Press.

Gottesman, I.I. & Shields, J. (1976) A critical review of recent adoption, twin and family studies of schizophrenia: Behavioural genetics perspectives. *Schizophrenia Bulletin, 2*, 360–398.

Gottesman, I.I. & Shields, J.(1982) *Schizophrenia: The Epigenetic Puzzle*. Cambridge: Cambridge University Press.

Gottfredson. L.S. (1998) The General Intelligence Factor. *Scientific American Presents: Exploring Intelligence, 9*(4), 24–29.

Gottfried, A.W., Gottfried, A.E., Bathurst, K., & Guerin, D.W. (1994) *Gifted IQ: Early Developmental Aspects*. New York: Plenum Press.

Gottman, J.M. (1994) *What Predicts Divorce?* Hillsdale, NJ: Erlbaum.

Gould, R.L. (1978) *Transformations: Growth and Change in Adult Life*. New York: Simon & Schuster.

Gould, R.L. (1980) Transformational tasks in adulthood. In S.I. Greenspan & G.H. Pollock (Eds) *The Course of Life: Psychoanalytic Contributions Toward Understanding Personality Development, Volume 3: Adulthood and the Ageing Process*. Washington, DC: National Institute for Mental Health.

Gould, S.J. (1981) *The Mismeasure of Man*. Harmondsworth: Penguin.

Gouldner, A.W. (1960) The norm of reciprocity: A preliminary statement. *American Sociological Review, 25*, 161–178.

Graham, H. (1986) *The Human Face of Psychology*. Milton Keynes: Open University Press.

Grasha, A.F. (1983) *Practical Applications of Psychology* (2nd edition). Boston: Little, Brown & Co.

Gray, J.A. (1971) *The Psychology of Fear and Stress*. London: Weidenfeld & Nicolson.

Gray, J.A. (1975) *Elements of a Two-process Theory of Learning*. London: Academic Press.

Gray, J.A. (1987) The ethics and politics of animal experimentation. In H. Beloff & A.M. Colman (Eds) *Psychology Survey, No.6*. Leicester: British Psychological Society.

Gray, J.A. (1991) On the morality of speciesism. *The Psychologist, 4* (5), 196–198.

Gray, J.A. & Wedderburn, A.A. (1960) Grouping strategies with simultaneous stimuli. *Quarterly Journal of Experimental Psychology, 12*, 180–184.

Green, R. (1978) Sexual identity of 37 children raised by homosexual or transsexual parents. *American Journal of Psychiatry, 135*, 692–697.

Green, S. (1980) Physiological studies I and II. In Radford, J. & Govier, E. (Eds) *A Textbook of Psychology*. London: Sheldon Press.

Green, S. (1994) *Principles of Biopsychology*. Sussex: Lawrence Erlbaum Associates.

Greene, J. (1975) *Thinking and Language*. London: Methuen.

Greene, J. (1987) *Memory, Thinking and Language*. London: Methuen.

Greene, J. (1990) Perception. In I. Roth (Ed.) *Introduction to Psychology, Volume 2*. Milton Keynes: Open University Press.

Greenfield, P.M. & Smith, J.H. (1976) *The Structure of Communication in Early Language Development*. New York: Academic Press.

Greenfield, S. (1998) How might the brain generate consciousness? In S. Rose (Ed.) *From Brains to Consciousness?: Essays on the New Sciences of the Mind*. Harmondsworth: Penguin.

Greenhaigh, T. (2000) 'Jigsaw' E-fit system helps ensure that the face fits. *The Times Higher*, 31 March, 14.

Greenough, W.T. (1991) Experience as a component of normal development: Evolutionary considerations. *Developmental Psychology, 27*, 11–27.

Greenwald, A.G., Klinger, M.R., & Liu, T.J. (1989) Unconscious processing of dichoptically masked words. *Memory & Cognition, 17*, 35–47.

Greer, A., Morris, T. & Pettingdale, K.W. (1979) Psychological response to breast cancer: Effect on outcome. *The Lancet, 13*, 785–787.

Greer, S. & Morris, T. (1975) Psychological attributes of women who develop breast cancer: A controlled study. *Journal of Psychosomatic Research, 19*, 147–153.

Greer, S., Morris, T., Pettingale, K.W., & Haybittle, J.L. (1990) Psychological responses to breast cancer and fifteen year outcome. *Lancet, 335*, 49–50.

Gregor, A.J. & McPherson, D. (1965) A study of susceptibility to geometric illusions among cultural outgroups of Australian aborigines. *Psychologia, Africana, 11*, 490–499.

Gregory, R.L. (1966) *Eye and Brain*. London: Weidenfeld & Nicolson.

Gregory, R.L. (1970) *The Intelligent Eye*. London: Weidenfeld & Nicolson.

Gregory, R.L. (1972) Visual illusions. In B.M. Foss (Ed.) *New Horizons in Psychology, 1*. Harmondsworth: Penguin.

Gregory, R.L. (1973) *Eye and Brain* (2nd edition). New York: World Universities Library.

Gregory, R.L. (1980) Perceptions as hypotheses. *Philosophical Transactions of the Royal Society of London, Series B, 290*, 181–197.

Gregory, R.L. (1981) *Mind in Science*. Harmondsworth: Penguin.

Gregory, R.L. (1983) Visual illusions. In J. Miller (Ed.) *States of Mind*. London: BBC Productions.

Gregory, R.L (1987a) Paranormal. In R.L Gregory (Ed.) *The Oxford Companion to the Mind*. Oxford: Oxford University Press.

Gregory, R.L. (1987b) In defence of artificial intelligence – a reply to John Searle. In C. Blakemore & S. Greenfield (Eds), *Mindwaves*. Oxford: Blackwell.

Gregory, R.L. (1996) Twenty-five years after 'The Intelligent Eye'. *The Psychologist, 9*, 452–455.

Gregory, R.L. & Wallace, J. (1963) *Recovery from Early Blindness*. Cambridge: Heffer.

Griedd, J. et al.(1999) Brain development during childhood and adolescence: a longitudinal MRI study. *Nature Neuroscience, 2*, 861.

Griffit, W. & Veitch, R. (1974) Preacquaintance attitude similarity and attraction revisited: Ten days in a fallout shelter. *Sociometry, 37*, 163–173.

Griffiths, M. (1990) The cognitive psychology of gambling. *Journal of Gambling Studies, 6*, 31–42.

Griffiths, M. (1993) Are computer games bad for children? *The Psychologist, 6*, 401–407.

Griffiths, M.(1995) Technological addictions. *Clinical Psychology Forum, 76*, 14–19.

Griffiths, M. (1996) Nicotine, tobacco and addiction. *Nature, 384*, 18.

Griffiths, M. (1997a) Video games and aggression. *The Psychologist, 10*, 397–401.

Griffiths, M. (1997b) Selling hope: The psychology of the National Lottery. *Psychology Review, 4*(1), 26–30.

Griffiths, M. (1998) Violent video games: Are they harmful? *Psychology Review, 4*, 28–29.

Griffiths, M.D. (1999a) All but connected (Online relationships). *Psychology Post, 17*, 6–7.

Griffiths, M.D. (1999b) Internet addiction. *The Psychologist, 12*(5), 246–250.

Griffiths, M.D. (2000) Cyberaffairs: A new area for psychological research. *Psychology Review, 7*(1), 28–31.

Groome, D., Dewart, H., Esgate, A., Gurney, K., Kemp, R. & Towell, N. (1999) *An Introduction to Cognitive Psychology: Processes and Disorders*. London: Psychology Press.

References

Gross, A.E. & Crofton, C. (1977) What is good is beautiful. *Sociometry, 40,* 85–90.

Gross, M.U.M. (1993) *Exceptionally Gifted Children.* London: Routledge.

Gross, R. (1995) *Themes, Issues and Debates in Psychology.* London: Hodder & Stoughton.

Gross, R (1996) Psychology: *The Science of Mind and Behaviour* (3rd edition) London: Hodder & Stoughton.

Gross, R. (1999) *Key Studies in Psychology* (3rd edition). London: Hodder & Stoughton.

Gross, R. & McIlveen, R. (1996) *Abnormal Psychology.* London: Hodder & Stoughton.

Gross, R. & MCIlveen, R. (1999) *Therapeutic Approaches to Abnormal Behaviour.* London: Hodder & Stoughton.

Gross, R., Humphreys, P. & Petkova, B. (1997) *Challenges in Psychology.* London: Hodder & Stoughton.

Gross, R., McIlveen, R., Coolican, H., Clamp, A., & Russell, J. (2000) *Psychology: A New Introduction* (2nd edition). London: Hodder and Stoughton.

Grosz, E.A. (1987) Feminist theory and the challenge of knowledge. *Women's Studies International Forum, 10,* 475–480.

Gruendel, J.M. (1977) Referential overextension in early language development. *Child Development, 48,* 1567–1576.

Grusec, J.E. (1992) Social learning theory and developmental psychology: The legacies of Robert Sears and Albert Bandura. *Developmental Psychology, 28,* 776–786.

Grush, J.E. (1976) Attitude formation and mere exposure phenomena: A non-artifactual explanation of empirical findings. *Journal of Personality & Social Psychology, 33,* 281–290.

Guerin, B.J. (1993) *Social Facilitation.* Cambridge: Cambridge University Press.

Guilford, J.P. (1959) Three faces of intellect. *American Psychologist, 14,* 469–479.

Guilford, J.P. (1967) *The Nature of Human Intelligence.* New York: McGraw-Hill.

Guilford, J.P. (1982) Cognitive psychology's ambiguities: Some suggested remedies. *Psychological Review, 89,* 48–59.

Gunter, B. (1986) *Television and Sex-Role Stereotyping.* London: IBA and John Libbey.

Gunter, B. (1998) Telebuddies: Can watching TV make us more considerate? *Psychology Review, 4,* 6–9.

Gunter, B. (2000) Avoiding unsavoury television. *The Psychologist, 13*(4), 194–199.

Gunter, B. & Harrison, J. (1998) *Violence on Television: An Analysis of the Amount, Nature, Location and Origin of Violence in British Programmes.* London: Routledge.

Gunter, B. & McAleer, J.L. (1990) *Children and television – The One-Eyed Monster?* London: Routledge.

Gunter, B. & McAleer, J.L. (1997) *Children and Television – The One-Eyed Monster?* (2nd edition) London: Routledge.

Guntrip, H. (1968) *Schizoid phenomena: Object Relations and the Self.* London: Hogarth.

Gupta, U. & Singh, P. (1982) Exploratory study of love and liking and types of marriage. *Indian Journal of Applied Psychology, 19,* 92–97.

Gustafson, G. & Harris, K. (1990) Women's responses to young infants' cries. *Developmental Psychology, 26,* 144–152.

Guthrie, E.R. (1938) *Psychology of Human Conflict.* New York: Harper.

Gwiazda, J., Brill, S., Mohindra, I., & Held, R. (1980) Preferential looking acuity in infants from two to 58 weeks of age. *American Journal of Optometry & Physiological Optics, 57,* 428–432.

Haaga, D.A. & Beck, A.T. (1992) Cognitive therapy. In S. Pakyel (Ed.) *Handbook of Affective Disorders* (2nd edition). Cambridge: Cambridge University Press.

Haaga, D.A. & Davison, G.C. (1993) An appraisal of rational–emotive therapy. *Journal of Consulting & Clinical Psychology, 61,* 215–220.

Haber, R.N. & Hershenson, M. (1980) *The Physiology of Visual Perception.* New York: Holt, Rinehart & Winston.

Haigh, J. (1995) Inferring gamblers' choice of combinations in the National Lottery. *Bulletin – The Institute of Mathematics and Its Applications, 31,* 132–136.

Haith, M.M. (1990) Progress in the understanding of sensory and perceptual processes in early infancy. *Merrill-Palmer Quarterly, 36,* 1–26.

Hall, C.S. (1966) *The Meaning of Dreams.* New York: McGraw-Hill.

Hall, C.S. & Lindzey, G. (1957) *Theories of Personality.* New York: Wiley.

Hall, C.S. & Nordby, V.J. (1973) *A Primer of Jungian Psychology.* New York: Mentor.

Hall, E.T. (1959) *The Silent Language.* New York: Doubleday.

Hall, E.T. (1966) *The Hidden Dimension.* Gaeden City, NY: Doubleday & Company.

Hall, G.S. (1904) *Adolescence.* New York: Appleton & Co.

Halligan, P.W.(1995) Drawing attention to neglect: The contribution of line bisection. *The Psychologist, 8,* 257–264.

Halloran, J.D. & Croll, P. (1972) Television programmes in Great Britain. In G.A. Comstock & E.A. Rubenstein (Eds) *Television and Social Behaviour, Volume 1, Media Content and Control.* Washington, DC: US Government Printing Office.

Hamilton, D.L. & Gifford, R.K. (1976) Illusory correlation in interpersonal perception: A cognitive basis of stereotypic judgements. *Journal of Experimental Social Psychology 12,* 392–407.

Hamilton, L. W. & Timmons, C.R. (1995) Psychopharmacology. In D. Kimble & A. M. Colman (Eds) *Biological Aspects of Behaviour.* London: Longman.

Hamilton, V.L. (1978) Obedience and responsibility: A jury simulation. *Journal of Personality & Social Psychology, 36,* 126–146.

Hammersley, R. (1999) Substance use, abuse and dependence. In D. Messer & F. Jones (Eds) *Psychology and Social Care.* London: Jessica Kingsley Publishers.

Hampson, P.J. (1989) Aspects of attention and cognitive science. *Irish Journal of Psychology, 10,* 261–275.

Hampson, P.J. & Morris, P.E. (1996) *Understanding Cognition.* Oxford: Blackwell.

Hampson, S. (1995) The construction of personality. In S.E. Hampson & A.M. Colman (Eds) *Individual Differences and Personality.* London: Longman.

Hampson, S. (1999) Personality. *The Psychologist, 12*(6), 284–288.

Hanlon, M. (1999a) How to live longer. *The Independent on Sunday, Science,* 23 November, 55–56.

Hanlon, M. (1999b) Tribe who can't tell the difference between blue, green and purple. *The Express,* 18 March, 38–39.

Hansel, C.E.M. (1980) *ESP and Parapsychology: A Critical Evaluation.* Buffalo, N.Y: Prometheus.

Happé, F. (1994a) *Autism: An Introduction to Psychological Theory.* London: UCL Press.

Happé, F. (1994b) An advanced test of theory of mind: Understanding of story characters' thoughts and feelings by able autistic, mentally handicapped and normal children and adults. *Journal of Autism & Developmental Disorders, 24,* 129–154.

Happé, F. (1999) Why success is more interesting than failure. *The Psychologist, 12*(11), 540–545.

Harari, H. & McDavid, J.W. (1973) Teachers' expectations and name stereotypes. *Journal of Educational Psychology, 65,* 222–225.

Hardy, L. (1989) Sport psychology. In A.M. Colman & J.G.Beaumont (Eds) *Psychology Survey 7.* Leicester: British Psychologcal Society.

Hare, R.D. (1991) *Manual for the Hare Psychopathy Checklist – Revised*. Toronto: Multi-Health Systems.

Hare-Mustin, R. & Maracek, J. (1988) The meaning of difference: Gender theory, post-modernism and psychology. *American Psychologist, 43*, 455–464.

Hargreaves, D., Molloy, C. & Pratt, A. (1982) Social factors in conservation. *British Journal of Psychology, 73*, 231–234.

Hargreaves, D.J. (1986) Psychological theories of sex-role stereotyping. In D.J. Hargreaves & A.M. Colley (Eds) *The Psychology of Sex Roles*. London: Harper & Row.

Harkins, S. & Green, R.G. (1975) Discriminability and criterion differences between extroverts and introverts during vigilance. *Journal of Research in Personality, 9*, 335–340.

Harkins, S.G. & Jackson, J.M. (1985) The role of evaluation in eliminating social loafing. *Personality & Social Psychology Bulletin, 11*, 456–465.

Harlow, H.F. (1949) Formation of learning sets. *Psychological Review, 56*, 51–65.

Harlow, H.F. (1953) Mice, monkeys, men and motives. *Psychological Review, 60*, 23–32.

Harlow, H.F. (1959) Love in infant monkeys. *Scientific American, 200*, 68–74.

Harlow, H.F. & Harlow, M.K. (1962) Social deprivation in monkeys. *Scientific American, 207*(5), 136.

Harlow, H.F. & Suomi, S.J. (1970) The nature of love – simplified. *American Psychologist, 25*, 161–168.

Harlow, H.F. & Zimmerman, R.R. (1959) Affectional responses in the infant monkey. *Science, 130*, 421–432.

Harlow, H.F., Harlow, M.K. & Meyer, D.R. (1950) Learning motivated by a manipulation drive. *Journal of Experimental Psychology, 40*, 228–234.

Harlow, H.F., Harlow, M.K. & Suomi, S.J. (1971) From thought to therapy: Lessons from a primate laboratory. *American Scientist, 59*, 74–83.

Harré, R. (1983) *Personal Being*. Oxford: Blackwell.

Harré, R. (1985) The language game of self-ascription: A note. In K.J. Gergen & K.E. Davis (Eds) *The Social Construction of the Person*. New York: Springer-Verlag.

Harré, R. (1989) Language games and the texts of identity. In J. Shotter & K.J. Gergen (Eds) *Texts of Identity*. London: Sage.

Harré, R. & Secord, P.F. (1972) *The Explanation of Social Behaviour*. Oxford: Blackwell.

Harré, R., Clarke, D., & De Carlo, N. (1985) *Motives and Mechanisms: An Introduction to the Psychology of Action*. London: Methuen.

Harris, M. (1998) Perception. In P. Scott & C. Spencer (Eds) *Psychology: A Contemporary Introduction*. Oxford: Blackwell.

Harris, M.G. & Humphreys, G.W. (1995) Computational theories of vision. In R.L. Gregory & A.M. Colman (Eds) *Sensation and Perception*. London: Longman.

Harris, S.L., Handleman, J.S, Gordon, R., Kristoff, B. & Fuentes, F. (1991) Changes in cognitive and language function of preschool children with autism. *Journal of Autism & Developmental Disorder, 21*, 281–290.

Harrison, P. (1995) Schizophrenia: A misunderstood disease. *Psychology Review, 2*(2), 2–6.

Harrower, J. (1998) *Applying Psychology to Crime*. London: Hodder & Stoughton.

Harrower, J. (2000) Cracker it ain't. *Psychology Review, 6*(3), 14–15.

Hart, S.D. & Hare, R.D. (1996) Psychopathy and antisocial personality disorder. *Current Opinion in Psychiatry, 9*, 129–132.

Hartley, J. & Allen, C. (2000) Counselling at work. In J. Hartley & A. Branthwaite (Eds.) *The Applied Psychologist* (2nd edition). Buckingham: Open University Press.

Hartley, J. & Branthwaite, A. (1997) Earning a crust. *Psychology Review, 3*(3), 24–26.

Hartley, J. & Branthwaite, A. (2000) Prologue: The roles and skills of applied psychologists. In J Hartley & A Braithwaite (Eds) *The Applied Psychologist* (2nd edition). Buckingham: Open University Press.

Hartley-Brewer, J. (2000) Geniuses 'made with hard work, not born'. *The Guardian*, 15 April, 6.

Hartup, W.W. (1989) Social relationships and their developmental significance. *American Psychologist, 44*, 120–126.

Hartup, W.W., Laursen, B., Stewart, M.I, & Eastensen, A. (1988) Conflict and the friendship relations of young children. *Child Development, 59*, 1590–1600.

Haskins, R. (1989) Beyond metaphor: The efficacy of early childhood education. *American Psychologist, 44*, 274–282.

Hassett, J. & White, M. (1989) *Psychology in Perspective* (2nd edition). Cambridge: Harper and Row.

Haste, H., Markoulis, D. & Helkama, K. (1998) Morality, wisdom and the life span. In A. Demetriou, W. Doise & C. van Lieshout (Eds) *Life-Span Developmental Psychology*. Chichester: John Wiley & Sons Ltd.

Hastie, R. & Park, B. (1986) The relationship between memory and judgement depends on whether the judgement task is memory based or on-line. *Psychological Bulletin, 93*, 258–268.

Hatfield, E., Traupmann, J. & Walster, G.W. (1978) Equity and extramarital sexuality. *Archives of Sexual Behaviour, 7*, 127–142.

Hatfield, E., Walster, G.W. & Traupmann, J. (1978) Equity and premarital sex. *Journal of Personality & Social Psychology, 37*, 82–92.

Hattenstone, S. & Brockes, E. (2000) 'I'm not Crybaby Soo-Fi any more'. *The Guardian*, 7 July, 2–3.

Havighurst, R.J. (1964) Stages of vocational development. In H. Borrow (Ed.) *Man in a World of Work*. Boston: Houghton Mifflin.

Havighurst, R.J., Neugarten, B.L. & Tobin, S.S. (1968) Disengagement and patterns of ageing. In B.L. Neugarten (Ed.) *Middle Age and Ageing*. Chicago: University of Chicago Press.

Hawkes, N. (1998) Tongue-twisters. *The Times*, 23 February, 15.

Hawkes, N. (2000a) Scientists seek more animal test freedom. *The Times*, 13 June, 10.

Hawkes, N. (2000b) Second rise in animal experiments. *The Times*, 24 July, 6.

Hawkins, L.H. & Armstrong-Esther, C.A. (1978) Circadian rhythms and night shift working in nurses. *Nursing Times*, May 4, 49–52.

Hawkins, S.A. & Hastie, R. (1990) Hindsight: Biased judgements of past events after the outcomes are known. *Psychological Bulletin, 107*, 311–327.

Hawks, D. (1981) The dilemma of clinical practice – Surviving as a clinical psychologist. In I. McPherson & M. Sutton (Eds) *Reconstructing Psychological Practice*. London: Croom Helm.

Haworth, G. (1992) The use of non-human animals in psychological research: the current status of the debate. *Psychology Teaching*, 46–54. New Series, No.1.

Hay, D.C. & Young, A.W. (1982) The human face. In A.W. Ellis (Ed.) *Normality and Pathology in Cognitive Functions*. London: Academic Press.

Hayes, K.H. & Hayes, C. (1951) Intellectual develpment of a house-raised chimpanzee. *Proceedings of the American Philosophical Society, 95*, 105–109.

Hayes, K.J. & Hayes, C. (1952) Imitation in a home-raised chimpanzee, *Journal of Comparative Physiology & Psychology. 45*, 450–459.

Hayes, N. (1998) *Foundations of Psychology* (2nd edition). Surrey: Nelson.

Haynes, R.B., Sackett, D.L., & Taylor, D.W. (Eds) (1979) *Compliance in Health Care.* Baltimore: John Hopkins University Press.

Hayslip, B. & Panek, P.E. (1989) *Adult Development and Ageing.* New York: Harper & Row.

Hayward, S. (1998) Stress, health and psychoneuroimmunology. *Psychology Review, 5*(1), 16–19.

Hazan, C. & Shaver, P.R. (1987) Romantic love conceptualised as an attachment process. *Journal of Personality & Social Psychology, 52*(3), 511–524.

Heard, D. & Lake, B. (1997) *The Challenge of Attachment for Caregivers.* London: Routledge.

Hearnshaw, L.S. (1979) *Cyril Burt: Psychologist.* London: Hodder & Stoughton.

Hearold, S. (1986) A synthesis of 1043 effects of television on social behaviour. In G. Comstock (Ed.) *Public Communication and Behaviour.* New York: Academic Press.

Heather, N. (1976) *Radical Perspectives in Psychology.* London: Methuen.

Heaven, P. (1996a) Personality and self-reported delinquency: analysis of the 'Big Five' personality dimensions. *Personality & Individual Differences, 20,* 47–54.

Heaven, P. (1996b) Personality and self-reported delinquency: a longitudinal analysis. *Journal of Child Psychology & Psychiatry, 37,* 747–751.

Heavey, L., Pring, L., & Hermelin, B. (1999) A date to remember: The nature of memory in savant calendrical calculators. *Psychological Medicine, 29,* 145–160.

Hebb, D.O. (1949) *The Organisation of Behaviour.* New York: Wiley.

Heber, R. & Garber, H. (1975) The Milwaukee Project: A study of the use of familial retardation to prevent cultural retardation. In B.Z. Friedlander, G.M. Sterrit & G.E. Kirk (Eds) *Exceptional Infant, Volume 3: Assessment and Intervention.* New York: 0Brunner/Mazel.

Heber, R., Dever, R.B., & Conry, R.J. (1968) The influence of environmental and genetic variables on intellectual development. In H.J.Prehm, L.J.Hamerlynck, & J.E.Crosson (Eds) *Behavioural Research in Mental Retardation.* Eugene: University of Oregon Press.

Hedderman, C. & Gelsthorpe, L. (1997) Understanding the sentencing of women. *Home Office Research Study 170.* London: Home Office.

Hediger, H. (1951) *Wild Animals in Captivity.* London: Butterworth.

Hegarty, J. (2000) Psychologists, doctors and cancer patients. In J. Hartley & A. Branthwaite (Eds) *The Applied Psychologist* (2nd edition). Buckingham: The Open University Press.

Heidensohn, F. (1996) *Women and Crime* (2nd edition). Basingstoke: Macmillan.

Heider, E. (1972) Universals in colour naming and memory. *Journal of Experimental Psychology, 93,* 10–20.

Heider, E. & Oliver, D. (1972) The structure of the colour space in naming and memory for two languages. *Cognitive Psychology, 3,* 337–354.

Heider, F. (1946) Attitudes and cognitive organisation. *Journal of Psychology, 21,* 107–112.

Heider, F. (1958) *The Psychology of Interpersonal Relations.* New York: Wiley.

Heider, F. & Simmel, M. (1944) An experimental study of apparent behaviour. *American Journal of Psychology, 57,* 243–259.

Heim, A. (1970) *Intelligence and Personality – Their Assessment and Relationship.* Harmondsworth: Penguin.

Heim, A. (1975) *Psychological Testing.* London: Oxford University Press.

Held, R. (1965) Plasticity in sensory-motor systems. *Scientific American, 213*(5), 84–94.

Held, R. & Hein, A. (1963) Movement-produced stimulation in the development of visually guided behaviour. *Journal of Comparative & Physiological Psychology, 56,* 607–613.

Heller, R.F., Saltzstein, H.D. & Caspe, W.B. (1992) Heuristics in medical and non-medical decision-making. *Quarterly Journal of Experimental Psychology, 44A,* 211–235.

Hemphill, J.F., Hare, R.D., & Wong, S. (1998) Psychopathy and recidivism: A review. *Legal & Criminological Psychology, 3,* 139–170.

Henderson, M. (2000) Short exercise helps heart as much as sport. *The Times,* 29 August, 10.

Hendrick, C. & Constanini, A. (1970) Effects of varying trait inconsistency and response requirements on the primacy effect on impression formation. *Journal of Personality & Social Psychology, 15,* 158–164.

Hendrick, S.S., Hendrick, C. & Adler, N.L. (1986) Romantic relationships. Love, satisfaction and staying together. *Journal of Personality & Social Psychology, 54,* 980–988.

Hendry, L.B. & Kloep, M. (1999) Adolescence in Europe – an important life phase? In D. Messer & S. Millar (Eds) *Exploring Developmental Psychology: From Infancy to Adolescence.* London: Arnold.

Hendry, L.B. (1999) Adolescents and society. In D. Messer & F. Jones (Eds) *Psychology and Social Care.* London: Jessica Kingsley.

Hendry, L.B., Shucksmith, J., Love, J.G. & Glendinning, A. (1993) *Young People's Leisure and Lifestyles.* London: Routledge.

Hepworth, J.T. & West, S.G. (1988) Lynchings and the economy: A time series analysis of Hovland and Sears (1940). *Journal of Personality & Social Psychology, 55,* 239–247.

Hering, E. (1878) *Zur Lehre vom Lichtsinne.* Berlin: Springer.

Herkowits, M.J. (1955) *Man and His Works: The Science of Cultural Anthropology.* New York: Alfred K. Knopf.

Hermelin, B., Pring, L., Buhler, M., Wolff, S., & Heaton, P. (1999) A Visually Impaired Savant Artist: Interacting Perceptual and Memory Representations. *Journal of Child Psychology & Psychiatry, 40*(7), 1129–1139.

Heron, W. (1957) The pathology of boredom. *Scientific American, 196,* 52–69.

Herrnstein, R.J. (1971) IQ. *Atlantic Monthly,* September, 43–64.

Herrnstein, R.J. & Murray, C. (1994) *The Bell Curve: Intelligence and Class Structure in American Life.* New York: Free Press.

Hershenson, M., Munsinger, H. & Kessen, W. (1965) Preference for shapes of intermediate variability in the newborn human. *Science, 147,* 630–631.

Herskovits, M.J. (1955) *Cultural Anthropology.* New York: Knopf.

Hess, E.H. (1956) Space perception in the chick. *Scientific American,* July, 71–80.

Hess, R.D. & Shipman, V. (1965) Early experience and the socialisation of cognitive modes in children. *Child Development, 36,* 860–886.

Heston, L.L. (1966) Psychiatric disorders in fosterhome-reared children of schizophrenic mothers. *British Journal of Psychiatry, 122,* 819–825.

Heston, L.L. (1970) The genetics of schizophrenia and schizoid disease. *Science, 167,* 249–256.

Hetherington, A.W. & Ranson, S.W. (1942) The relation of various hypothalamic lesions to adiposity in the rat. *Journal of Comparative Neurology, 76,* 475–499.

Hetherington, E.M. (1967) The effects of familial variables on sex-typing, on parent–child similarity, and on imitation in children. In J.P. Hill (Ed.) *Minnesota Symposium on Child Psychology, Volume 1.* Mineapolis, MN: University of Minnesota Press.

Hetherington, E.M. (1989) Coping with family transitions: Winners, losers and survivors. *Child Development, 60,* 1–14.

Hetherington, E.M. & Baltes, P.B. (1988) Child psychology and life-span development. In E.M. Hetherington, R. Lerner, & M. Perlmutter (Eds) *Child Development in Life-Span Perspective.* Hillsdale, NJ: Erlbaum.

Hetherington, E.M. & Stanley-Hagan, M. (1999) The adjustment of children with divorced parents: A risk and resiliency perspective. *Journal of Child Psychology & Psychiatry, 40*(1), 129–140.

Hetherington, E.M., Cox, M. & Cox, R. (1978) The aftermath of divorce. In M.H. Stevens & M. Mathews (Eds), *Mother/child, Father/child Relationships.* Washington DC: National Association for the Education of Young Children.

Hewstone, M. & Brown, R.J. (1986) Contact is not enough: An intergroup perspective on the contact hypothesis. In M. Hewstone & R.J. Brown (Eds) *Contact and Conflict in Inter–group Encounters.* Oxford: Blackwell.

Hewstone, M. & Fincham, F. (1996) Attribution theory and research: Basic issues and applications. In M. Hewstone, W. Stroebe & G.M. Stephenson (Eds) *Introduction to Social Psychology* (2nd edition). Oxford: Blackwell.

Hewstone, M., Stroebe, W. & Stephenson, G.M. (1996) *Introduction to Social Psychology* (2nd edition). Oxford: Blackwell.

Highfield, R. (1999) Unique view through eyes of blind man who sees colour. *Daily Telegraph,* 23 November, 17.

Hilgard, E.R. (1974) Towards a neo-dissociationist theory: Multiple cognitive controls in human functioning. *Perspectives in Biology and Medicine, 17,* 301–316.

Hilgard, E.R., Atkinson, R.L. & Atkinson, R.C. (1979) *Introduction to Psychology* (7th edition). New York: Harcourt Brace Jovanovich.

Hill, C.Y., Rubin, Z. & Peplau, A. (1976) Breakups before marriage: The end of 103 affairs. *Journal of Social Issues, 32,* 147–167.

Hill, E. & Williamson, J. (1998) Choose six numbers, any numbers. *The Psychologist, 11*(1), 17–21.

Hill, P. (1993) Recent advances in selected aspects of adolescent development. *Journal of Child Psychology & Psychiatry, 34*(1), 69–99.

Hilliard, A.G. (1995) The nonscience and nonsense of the bell curve. *Focus: Notes from the Society for the Psychological Study of Ethnic Minority Issues,* 10–12.

Hilton, D.J. & Slugoski, B.R. (1986) Knowledge-based causal attribution: The abnormal conditions focus model. *Psychological Review, 93,* 75–88.

Hinde, R.A. (1974) *Biological Bases of Human Social Behaviour.* New York: McGraw Hill.

Hinde, R.A. (1982) *Ethology.* London: Fontana.

Hinton, J. (1975) *Dying.* Harmondsworth, Middlesex: Penguin.

Hiroto, D.S. & Seligman, M.E.P. (1975) Generality of learned helplessness in man. *Journal of Personality & Social Psychology, 31,* 311–327.

Hirsch, H. (1995) *Genocide and the Politics of Memory.* Chapel Hill, NC: The University of North Carolina Press.

Hiscock, J. (1996) Schools recognise 'Black English'. *The Daily Telegraph,* 21 December, 12.

Hitch, G.J. (1980) Developing the concept of working memory. In G. Claxton (Ed.) *Cognitive Psychology: New Directions.* London: Routledge & Kegan Paul.

HM Inspector Of Prisons (1997) *Women In Prison: A Thematic Review.* London: Home Office.

Hobbes, T. (1651) *Leviathan.* London: Dent, 1914.

Hobson, J.A. (1988) *The Dreaming Brain.* New York: Basic Books.

Hobson, J.A. (1989) Dream Theory: A New View of the Brain–Mind. *The Harvard Medical School Mental Health Letter, 5,* 3–5.

Hobson, J.A. (1995) Sleeping and dreaming. In D. Kimble & A.M. Colman (Eds) *Biological Aspects of Behaviour.* London: Longman.

Hobson, J.A. & McCarley, R.W. (1977) The brain as a dream state generator: An activation–synthesis hypothesis of the dream process. *American Journal of Psychiatry, 134,* 1335–1348.

Hochberg, J.E. (1970) Attention, organisation and consciousness. In D.I. Mostofsky (Ed.) *Attention: Contemporary Theory and Analysis.* New York: Appleton Century Crofts.

Hochberg, J.E. (1971) Perception. In J.W. Kling & L.A. Riggs (Eds) *Experimental Psychology.* New York: Holt.

Hochberg, J.E. (1978) Art and perception. In E.C. Carterette & H. Friedman (Eds) *Handbook of Perception, Volume 10.* London: Academic Press.

Hock, M., Taylor, C.B.H., Klein, N., Eibeu, R., Schatschneider, C., & Mercuri-Minich, N. (1994) School-age outcomes in children with birth weights under 750 g. *The New England Journal of Medicine, 331,* 753–759.

Hocket, C.D. (1960) The origins of speech. *Scientific American, 203,* 88–96.

Hodges, B. (1974) Effect of volume on relative weighting in 'impression' formation. *Journal of Personality & Social Psychology, 30,* 378–381.

Hodges, J. & Tizard, B. (1989) Social and family relationships of ex-institutional adolescents. *Journal of Child Psychology & Psychiatry, 30,* 77–97.

Hodgkin, J. (1988) Everything you always wanted to know about sex. *Nature, 331,* 300–301.

Hodson, P. (2000) Could it be his hormones? *The Independent Review,* 20 April, 8.

Hoffman, L.W. (1974) Effects of maternal employment on the child: A review of the Research. *Developmental Psychology, 10,* 204–228.

Hoffman, M.L. (1970) Conscience, personality and socialisation techniques. *Human Development, 13,* 90–126.

Hoffman, M.L. (1975) Altruistic behaviour and the parent–child relationship. *Journal of Personality & Social Psychology, 31,* 937–943.

Hoffman, M.L. (1976) Empathy, role taking, guilt and development of altruistic motives. In T. Lickona (Ed.), *Moral Development and Behaviour.* New York: Holt, Rinehart & Winston.

Hofling, K.C., Brotzman, E., Dalrymple, S., Graves, N. & Pierce, C.M. (1966) An experimental study in the nurse–physician relationships. *Journal of Nervous & Mental Disorders, 143,* 171–180.

Hogg, M.A. (1992) *The Social Psychology of Group Cohesiveness: From Attraction to Social Identity.* London: Harvester Wheatsheaf.

Hogg, M.A. (1993) Group cohesiveness: A critical review and some new directions. *European Review of Social Psychology, 4,* 85–111.

Hogg, M.A. & Abrams, D. (1988) *Social Identifications: A Social Psychology of Intergroup Relations and Group Processes.* London: Routledge.

Hogg, M.A. & Abrams, D. (2000) Social Psychology. In Carlson, N.R., Buskist, W. & Martin, G.N., *Psychology: The Science of Behaviour* (European Adaptation). Harlow: Pearson Education Limited.

Hogg, M.A. & Hains, S.C. (1996) Intergroup relations and group solidarity: Effects of group identification and social beliefs on depersonalised attraction. *Journal of Personality & Social Psychology, 70,* 295–309.

Hogg, M.A. & Hardie, E.A. (1991) Social attraction, personal attraction, and self-categorization: A field study. *Personality & Social Psychology Bulletin, 17,* 175–180.

Hogg, M.A. & Vaughan, G.M. (1995) *Social Psychology: An Introduction.* Hemel Hempstead: Prentice Hall/Harvester Wheatsheaf.

Hogg, M.A. & Vaughan, G.M. (1998) *Social Psychology: An Introduction* (2nd edition). Hemel Hempstead: Prentice Hall/Harvester Wheatsheaf.

Hohmann, G.W. (1966) Some effects of spinal cord lesions on experienced emotional feelings. *Psychophysiology, 3,* 143–156.

Holahan, C.K. (1988) Relation of life goals at age 70 to activity participation and health and psychological well-being among Terman's gifted men and women. *Psychology & Ageing, 3,* 286–291.

Holahan, C.K. & Sears, R.R. (1995) *The Gifted Group in Later Maturity.* Stanford, CA: Stanford University Press.

Hollander, E.P. & Willis, R.H. (1964) Conformity, independence and anticonformity as determiners of perceived influence and attraction. In E.P. Hollander (Ed.), *Leaders, Groups and Influence.* New York: Oxford University Press.

Hollin, C. (1997) Adolescent predictors of adult offending. *Psychology Review, 3*(4), 21–25.

Hollin, C. (1999) Crime and crime prevention. In D. Messer & F. Jones (Eds) *Psychology and Social Care.* London: Jessica Kingsley.

Hollin, C.R. & Howells, K. (Eds) (1996) *Clinical Approaches to Working with Young Offenders.* Chichester: Wiley.

Hollin, C. & Howells, K. (1997) Controlling violent behaviour. *Psychology Review, 3,* 10–14.

Holmes, D.S. (1994) *Abnormal Psychology* (2nd edition). New York: HarperCollins.

Holmes, J. (1992) Response to Jeffrey Masson. In W. Dryden & C. Feltham (Eds) *Psychotherapy and its Discontents.* Buckingham: Open University Press.

Holmes, J. (1993) *John Bowlby and Attachment Theory.* London: Routledge.

Holmes, J. & Lindley, R. (1989) *The Values of Psychotherapy.* Oxford: Oxford University Press.

Holmes, R. (1989) *Profiling Violent Crimes.* Newbury Park, CA: Sage.

Holmes, T.H. & Rahe, R.H. (1967) The social readjustment rating scale. *Journal of Psychosomatic Research, 11,* 213–218.

Holt, R.R. (1967) Individuality and generalisation in the psychology of personality. In R.R. Lazarus & E.M. Opton (Eds) *Personality.* Harmondsworth: Penguin.

Holtgraves, T. & Skeel, J. (1992) Cognitive biases in playing the lottery: Estimating the odds and choosing the numbers. *Journal of Applied Social Psychology, 22,* 934–952.

Homans, G.C. (1961) *Social behaviour: Its Elementary Forms.* New York: Harcourt Brace Jovanovich.

Homans, G.C. (1974) *Social Behaviour: Its Elementary Forms* (2nd edition). New York: Harcourt Brace Jovanovich.

Honderich, T. (1993) *How Free Are You? The Determinism Problem.* Oxford: Oxford University Press.

Honorton, C. (1985) Meta-analysis of psi Ganzfeld research: A response to Hyman. *Journal of Parapsychology, 49,* 51–91.

Honorton, C. (1992) The Ganzfeld novice: Four predictors of initial psi performance. *Proceedings of the 35th Annual Convention of the Parapsychological Association.*

Honorton, C., Berger, R.E., Varvoglis, M.P., Quant, M., Derr, P., Schechter, E.I., & Ferrari, D.C. (1990) Psi Communication in the Ganzfeld: Experiments with an automated testing system and a comparison with a meta-analysis of earlier studies. *Journal of Parapsychology, 54,* 99–139.

Honzik, M.P., MacFarlane, H.W. & Allen, L. (1948) The stability of mental test performance between two and eighteen years. *Journal of Experimental Education, 17,* 309–324.

Hopson, B. & Scally, M. (1980) Change and development in adult life: Some implications for helpers. *British Journal of Guidance & Counselling, 8,* 175–187.

Horgan, J. (1993) Eugenics revisited. *Scientific American,* June, 92–100.

Horgan, J. (1995) The new social Darwinists. *Scientific American,* October, 150–157.

Horn, J.L. (1982) The ageing of human abilities. In B. Wolman (Ed.) *Handbook of Developmental Psychology.* Englewood Cliffs, NJ: Prentice-Hall.

Horn, J.L. & Cattell, R.B. (1967) Age differences in fluid and crystallised intelligence. *Acta Psychologica, 26,* 107–129.

Horn, J.L. & Cattell, R.B. (1982) Whimsy and misunderstanding of Gf–Gc theory: A comment on Guilford. *Psychology Bulletin, 91,* 623–633.

Horn, J.M., Loehlin, J.L. & Willerman, L. (1979) Intellectual resemblance among adoptive and biological relatives: The Texas adoption project. *Behaviour Genetics, 9,* 177–207.

Horne, J. (1988) *Why We Sleep: The Functions of Sleep in Humans and Other Mammals.* Oxford: Oxford University Press.

Horney, K. (1924) On the genesis of the castration complex in women. *International Journal of Psychoanalysis, v,* 50–65.

Horowitz, F.D. (1987) *Exploring Developmental Theories: Towards a Structural/behavioural Model of Development.* Hillsdale, NJ: Erlbaum.

Horowitz, F.D. (1990) Developmental models of individual differences. In J. Colombo & J. Fagan (Eds) *Individual Differences in Infancy: Reliability, Stability, Predictability.* Hillsdale, NJ: Erlbaum.

Horowitz, M.J., Wilner, B.A., & Alvarez, M.A. (1979) Impact of event scale: A measure of subjective distress. *Psychosomatic Medicine, 41,* 209–218.

Horton, M. (1999) Prejudice and discrimination: Group approaches. In D. Messer & F. Jones (Eds) *Psychology and Social Care.* London: Jessica Kingsley Publishers.

Horwood, L.J. & Fergusson, D.M. (1999) A longitudinal study of maternal labour force participation and child academic achievement. *Journal of Child Psychology & Psychiatry, 40*(7), 1013–1024.

Houston, J.P., Hammen, C., Padilla, A. & Bee, H. (1991) *Invitation to Psychology* (3rd edition). London: Harcourt Brace Jovanovich.

Hovland, C.I. & Janis, I.L. (1959) *Personality and Persuasibility.* New Haven, CT: Yale University Press.

Hovland, C.I. & Sears, R.R. (1940) Minor studies in aggression, VI: Correlation of lynchings with economic indices. *Journal of Psychology, 2,* 301–310.

Hovland, C.I., Janis, I.L. & Kelley, H.H. (1953) *Communication and Persuasion: Psychological Studies of Opinion Change.* New Haven, CT: Yale University Press.

Hovland, C.I., Lumsdaine, A.A. & Sheffield, F.D. (1949) *Experiments in Mass Communication.* Princeton, NJ: Princeton University Press.

Howard, J.W. & Rothbart, M. (1980) Social categorisation and memory for ingroup and outgroup behaviour. *Journal of Personality & Social Psychology, 38,* 301–310.

Howarth, E. (1980) What does Eysenck's psychoticism scale really measure? *British Journal of Psychology, 77,* 223–227.

Howarth, E. (1986) What does Eysenck's psychoticism scale really measure? *British Journal of Psychology, 77,* 223–227.

Howat, D. (1999) Social and cultural diversity. *Psychology Review, 5*(3), 28–31.

Howe, M. (1980) *The Psychology of Human Learning.* London: Harper & Row.

Howe, M. (1989) The strange achievements of idiots savants. In A.M. Colman & J.G. Beaumont (Eds), *Psychology Survey, No. 7.* Leicester: British Psychological Society.

Howe, M. (1990) *The Origins of Exceptional Abilities.* Oxford: Blackwell.

Howe, M. (1995) Hothouse tots: Encouraging and accelerating development in young children. *Psychology Review, 2,* 2–4.

Howe, M. (1997) *IQ in Question: The Truth about Intelligence.* London: Sage.

Howe, M. (1998) Can IQ change? *The Psychologist, 11*(2), 69–71.

Howe, M. (1999) *Genius Explained*. Cambridge: Cambridge University Press.

Howe, M. & Griffey, H. (1994) *Give Your Child a Better Start*. London: Michael Joseph.

Howe, M., Davidson, J.W., & Sloboda, J.A. (1998) Innate talents: Reality or myth? *Behaviour & Brain Sciences, 21*(3), 399–407.

Howes, C. (1996) The earliest friendships. In W.M. Bukowski, A.F. Newcomb, & W.W. Hartup (Eds) *The Company They Keep: Friendship in Childhood and Adolescence*. Cambridge: Cambridge University Press.

Howes, D. & Solomon, R.L. (1950) A note on McGinnies' emotionality and perceptual defence. *Psychological Review, 57,* 229–234.

Howie, D. (1952) Perceptual defence. *Psychological Review, 59,* 308–315.

Howitt, D. (1991) *Concerning Psychology: Psychology Applied to Social Issues*. Milton Keynes: Open University Press.

Howitt, D. & Owusu-Bempah, J. (1994) *The Racism of Psychology: Time for Change*. Hemel Hempstead: Harvester Wheatsheaf.

Howlin, P.A. (1981) The effectiveness of operant language training with autistic children. *Journal of Autism & Developmental Disorders, 11,* 89–106.

Hoyenga, K.B. & Hoyenga, K.T. (1979) *The Question of Sex Differences*. Boston: Little Brown.

Hrdy, S.B. (1977) *The Langurs of Abu*. Cambridge, Massachusetts: Harvard University Press.

Hrdy, S.B. (1999) *Mother Nature*. London: Chatto & Windus.

Hubel, D.H. (1979) The brain. *Scientific American,* September, 38–47.

Hubel, D.H. & Wiesel, T.N. (1959) Receptive fields of single neurons in the cat's striate cortex. *Journal of Physiology, 148,* 579–591.

Hubel, D.H. & Wiesel, T.N. (1962) Receptive fields, binocular interaction and functional architecture in the cat's visual cortex. *Journal of Physiology, 160,* 106–154.

Hubel, D.H. & Wiesel, T.N. (1965) Receptive fields of single neurons in the two non-striate visual areas, 18 and 19 of the cat. *Journal of Neurophysiology, 28,* 229–289.

Hubel, D.H. & Wiesel, T.N. (1968) Receptive fields and functional architecture of monkey striate cortex. *Journal of Physiology, 195,* 215–243.

Hubel, D.H. & Wiesel, T.N. (1977) Functional architecture of the macaque monkey visual cortex. *Proceedings of the Royal Society of London,* Series B, 198, 1–59.

Hubel, D.H. & Wiesel, T.N. (1979) Brain mechanisms of vision. *Scientific American, 241,* 150–162.

Hudson, W. (1960) Pictorial depth perception in sub-cultural groups in Africa. *Journal of Social Psychology, 52,* 183–208.

Hudson, W. (1962) Pictorial perception and educational adaptation in Africa. *Psychologica Africana, 9,* 226–239.

Huesmann, L.R. & Eron, L.D. (1984) Cognitive processes and the persistence of aggressive behaviour. *Aggressive Behaviour, 10,* 243–251.

Huesmann, L.R. & Eron, L.D. (Eds) (1986) *Television and the Aggressive Child: A Cross-National Comparison*. Hove: Erlbaum.

Huesmann, L.R., Eron, L.D., Klein, R., Brice, P. & Fischer, P. (1983) Mitigating the imitation of aggressive behaviours by changing children's attitudes about media violence. *Journal of Personality & Social Psychology, 44,* 899–910.

Hugdahl. K. & Ohman, A. (1977) Effects of instruction on acquisition of electrodermal response to fear relevant stimuli. *Journal of Experimental Psychology, 3,* 608–618.

Hull, C.L. (1943) *Principles of Behaviour*. New York: Appleton, Century Crofts.

Hume, D. (1757) *Four Dissertations, IV: Of the Standard of Taste*. London: Millar.

Humphrey, N. (1986) *The Inner Eye*. London: Faber & Faber.

Humphrey, N. (1993) Introduction. In N. Humphrey (1986) *The Inner Eye*. London: Vintage.

Humphreys, G.W. & Riddoch, M.J. (1987) *To See But Not to See – A Case Study of Visual Agnosia*. London: Erlbaum.

Hunt, E. & Agnoli, A. (1991) The Whorfian hypothesis: A cognitive psychological perspective. *Psychological Review, 98,* 377–389.

Hunt, J. McVicker (1961) *Intelligence and Experience*. New York: Ronald Press.

Hunt, J. McVicker (1969) Has compensatory education failed? Has it been attempted? *Harvard Educational Review, 39,* 278–300.

Hunter, I.M.L. (1964) *Memory, Facts and Fallacies* (2nd edition). Harmondsworth: Penguin.

Huston, A.C. (1983) Sex-typing. In E.M. Hetherington (Ed.) *Socialisation, Personality and Social Development*. New York: Wiley.

Hutchins, E. (1980) *Culture and Inference: A Trobriand Case Study*. Cambridge, MA: Harvard University Press.

Hutt, C. (1972) *Males and Females*. Harmondsworth: Penguin.

Hutton, A. (1998) Mental health: Drug update. *Nursing Times, 94,* February, 11.

Hyde, J.S. & Linn, M.C. (1988) Gender differences in verbal ability: A meta-analysis. *Psychological Bulletin, 104,* 53–69.

Hyde, J.S., Fennema, E. & Lamon, S. (1990) Gender differences in mathematics performance: A meta-analysis. *Psychological Bulletin, 107,* 139–155.

Hyde, T.S. & Jenkins, J.J. (1973) Recall for words as a function of semantic, graphic and syntactic orienting tasks. *Journal of Verbal Learning & Behaviour, 12,* 471–480.

Hyman, R. (1985) The Ganzfeld psi experiment: A critical appraisal. *Journal of Parapsychology, 49,* 3–49.

Hyman, R. & Honorton, C. (1986) A joint communique: the psi Ganzfeld controversy. *Journal of Parapsychology, 50,* 351–364.

Ickes, W.J. & Barnes, R.D. (1977) The role of sex and self-monitoring in unstructured dyadic interactions. *Journal of Personality & Social Psychology, 35,* 315–330.

Illman, J. (1977) ECT: Therapy or trauma? *Nursing Times,* August 11, 1226–1227.

Imperato-McGinley, J., Peterson, R., Gautier, T. & Sturla, E. (1979) Androgens and the evolution of male-gender identity among pseudohermaphrodites with 5-alpha-reductase deficiency. *New England Journal of Medicine, 300,* 1233–1237.

Inhelder, B. & Piaget, J. (1958) *The Growth of Logical Thinking*. London: Routledge & Kegan Paul.

Insko, C.A., Drenan, S., Solomon, M.R., Smith, R., & Wade, T.G. (1983) Conformity as a function of the consistency of positive self-evaluation with being liked and being right. *Journal of Experimental Social Psychology, 19,* 341–358.

Isaacs, W., Thomas, J. & Goldiamond, I. (1960) Application of operant conditioning to reinstate verbal behaviour in psychotics. *Journal of Speech & Hearing Disorders, 25,* 8–12.

Israels, H. & Schatzman, M. (1993) The seduction theory. *History of Psychiatry, 4,* 32–59.

Ittelson, W.H. (1952) *The Ames Demonstrations in Perception*. Princeton, NJ: Princeton University Press.

Iversen, L.L. (1979) The chemistry of the brain. *Scientific American, 241,* 134–149.

Iwao, S. (1993) *The Japanese woman: Traditional Image and Changing Reality*. New York: Free Press.

Iwasa, N. (1992) Postconventional reasoning and moral education in Japan. *Journal of Moral Education, 21*(1), 3–16.

Izard, C. (1977) *Human Emotions*. New York: Plenum Press.

Jackendoff, R. (1993) *Patterns in the Mind: Language and Human Nature*. Hemel Hempstead: Harvester-Wheatsheaf.

Jackson, G. (1992) Women and psychology – What might that mean? Paper presented at Annual Conference, Association for the Teaching of Psychology, July.

Jackson, H.F. (1986) Is there a schizotoxin? A critique of the evidence of the major contender – dopamine. In N. Eisenberg & D. Glasgow (Eds) *Current Issues in Clinical Psychology (Volume 5)*. Aldershot, UK: Gower.

Jackson, H.F. (1990) Biological markers in schizophrenia. In R.P. Bentall (Ed.) *Reconstructing schizophrenia*. London: Routledge.

Jackson, J. & Bekerian, D. (Eds) (1997) *Offender Profiling: Theory, Research and Practice*. Chichester: Wiley.

Jackson, S., Cicogani, E. & Charman, L. (1996) The measurement of conflict in parent–adolescent relationships. In L. Verhofstadt-Deneve, I. Kienhorst & C. Braet (Eds) *Conflict and Development in Adolescence*. Leiden: DSWO Press.

Jacobs, M. (1984) Psychodynamic therapy: The Freudian approach. In W. Dryden (Ed.), *Individual Therapy in Britain*. London: Harper & Row.

Jacobs, M. (1992) *Freud*. London: Sage Publications.

Jahoda, G. (1954) A note on Ashanti names and their relationship to personality. *British Journal of Psychology, 45*, 192–195.

Jahoda, G. (1966) Geometric illusions and environment: A study in Ghana. *British Journal of Psychology, 57*, 193–199.

Jahoda, G. (1978) Cross-cultural perspectives. In H. Tajfel & C. Fraser (Eds) *Introducing Social Psychology*. Harmondsworth: Penguin.

Jahoda, G. (1980) Theoretical and system approaches in cross-cultural psychology. In H.C. Triandis & W.W. Lambert (Eds) *Handbook of Cross-Cultural Psychology*, Volume 1, *Perspectives*. Boston, MA: Allyn & Bacon.

Jahoda, M. (1958) *Current Concepts of Positive Mental Health*. New York: Basic Books.

James, W. (1884) What is an emotion? *Mind, 9*, 188–205.

James, W. (1890) *The Principles of Psychology*. New York: Henry Holt & Company.

James, W. (1902) The Varieties of Religious Experience. New York: Longmans Green.

Janis, I. (1971) *Stress and Frustration*. New York: Harcourt Brace

Janis, I. (1982) *Groupthink: Psychological Studies of Policy Decisions and Fiascos* (2nd edition). Boston, MA: Houghton-Mifflin.

Janis, I. & Feshbach, S. (1953) Effects of fear-arousing communication. *Journal of Abnormal & Social Psychology, 48*, 78–92.

Janis, I. & Terwilliger, R.T. (1962) An experimental study of psychological resistance to fear-arousing communication. *Journal of Abnormal & Social Psychology, 65*, 403–410.

Janis, I.L, Kaye, D., & Kirschner (1965) Facilitating effects of 'eating-while-reading' on responsiveness to persuasive communications. *Journal of Personality & Social Psychology, 1*, 181–186.

Jankowiak, W.R. & Fischer, E.F. (1992) A cross-cultural perspective on romantic love. *Ethnology, 31*, 149–155.

Janz, N.K. & Becker, M.H. (1984) The health belief model: A decade later. *Health Education Quarterly, 11*, 1–47.

Jaroff, L. (1993) Lies of the mind. *Time, 142*(23), 56–61.

Jarvis, M. (1994) Attention and the information processing approach. *Psychology Teaching, New Series (No. 3)*. December, 12–22.

Jellinek, E.M. (1946) Phases in the drinking history of alcoholics. *Quarterly Journal of Studies on Alcohol, 7*, 1–88.

Jellinek, E.M. (1952) The phases of alcohol addiction. *Quarterly Journal of Studies on Alcohol, 13*, 673–684.

Jellinek, E.M. (1960) *The Disease Concept of Alcoholism*. New Haven: CT: Hillhouse Press.

Jellison, J.M. & Oliver, D.F. (1983) Attitude similarity and attraction: An impression management approach. *Personality & Social Psychology Bulletin, 9*, 111–115.

Jenkins, J.G. & Dallenbach, K.M. (1924) Oblivescence during sleep and waking. *American Journal of Psychology, 35*, 605–612.

Jenkins, J.J. (1974) Remember that old theory of memory? Well, forget it! *American Psychologist, 29*, 785–795.

Jenness, A. (1932) The role of discussion in changing opinion regarding matter of fact. *Journal of Abnormal & Social Psychology, 27*, 279–96.

Jensen, A. (1969) How much can we boost IQ and scholastic achievement? *Harvard Educational Review, 39*, 1–23.

Jensen, A.R. (1980) *Bias in Mental Testing*. London: Methuen.

Jewett, J. (1998) Unpublished D.Clin. Psych. Research thesis, University College, London.

Jodelet, D. (1980) Les fous mentales au village. Unpublished doctoral dissertation. Ecoles des hautes studes in science sociales, Paris.

Joffe, H. (1996) AIDS research and prevention: A social representation approach. *British Journal of Medical Psychology, 69*, 169–190.

Johansson, G. (1975) Visual motion perception. *Scientific American, 14*, 76–89.

Johnson, D.W. & Johnson, R. (1985) Classroom conflict: Controversy over debate in learning groups. *American Education Research Journal, 22*, 237–256.

Johnson, J.H. & Sarason, I.G. (1978) Life stress, depression and anxiety: Internal/external control as a moderator variable. *Journal of Psychosomatic Research, 22*, 205–208.

Johnson, M.H. (2000) How babies' brains work. *The Psychologist, 13*(6), 298–301.

Johnson, M.H., Dziurawiec, S., Ellis, H., & Morton, J. (1991) Newborns' preferential tracking of face-like stimuli and its subsequent decline. *Cognition, 40*, 1–19.

Johnson, R.D. & Downing, L.E. (1979) Deindividuation and valence of cues: Effects on prosocial and antisocial behaviour. *Journal of Personality & Social Psychology, 37*, 1532–1538.

Johnson-Laird, P.N., Herrman, D.J. & Chaffin, R. (1984) Only connections: A critique of semantic networks. *Psychological Bulletin, 96*(2), 292–315.

Johnston, D.K. (1988) Adolescents' solutions to dilemmas in fables: Two moral orientations – two problem-solving strategies. In C. Gilligan, J.V. Ward & J.M. Taylor (Eds) *Mapping the Moral Domain*. Cambridge, MA: Harvard University Press.

Johnston, W.A. & Dark, V.J. (1986) Selective attention. *Annual Review of Psychology, 37*, 43–75.

Johnston, W.A. & Heinz, S.P. (1978) Flexibility and capacity demands of attention. *Journal of Experimental Psychology: General, 107*, 420–435.

Johnston, W.A. & Heinz, S.P. (1979) Depth of non-target processing in an attention task. *Journal of Experimental Psychology, 5*, 168–175.

Johnston, W.A. & Wilson, J. (1980) Perceptual processing of non-targets in an attention task. *Memory & Cognition, 8*, 372–377.

Jonas, K., Eagly, A.H. & Stroebe, W. (1995) Attitudes and persuasion. In M. Argyle & A.M. Colman (Eds) *Social Psychology*. London: Longman.

Jones, E.E. & Davis, K.E. (1965) From acts to dispositions: The attribution process in person perception. In L. Berkowitz (Ed.) *Advances in Experimental Social Psychology, Volume 2*. New York: Academic Press.

Jones, E.E. & Nisbett, R.E. (1971) *The Actor and the Observer: Divergent Perceptions of the Causes of Behaviour*. Morristown, NJ: General Learning Press.

Jones, E.E. & Sigall, H. (1971) The bogus pipeline: a new paradigm for measuring affect and attitude. *Psychological Bulletin, 76,* 349–364

Jones, E.E., Caputo, C., Legant, P. & Marecek, J. (1973) Behaviour as seen by the actor and as seen by the observer. *Journal of Personality & Social Psychology, 27*(2), 154–164.

Jones, E.E., Davis, K.E. & Gergen, K. (1961) Role playing variations and their informational value for person perception. *Journal of Abnormal & Social Psychology, 63,* 302–310.

Jones E.E., Rock, L., Shaver, K.G., Goethals, G.R. & Wand, L.M. (1968) Patterns of performance and ability attribution: An unexpected primacy effect. *Journal of Personality & Social Psychology, 10,* 317–340.

Jones, F. (1998) Risk taking and everyday tasks. *The Psychologist, 12*(2), 70–71.

Jones, F., Harris, P., & Crispin, C. (2000) Catching the sun: An investigation of sun-exposure and skin protective behaviour. *Psychology, Health & Medicine, 5,* 131–141.

Jones, G.V. (1979) Analysing memory by cuing: Intrinsic and extrinsic knowledge. In N.S. Sutherland (Ed.) *Tutorial Essays in Psychology: a Guide to Recent Advances, Volume 2.* Hillsdale, NJ.: Erlbaum.

Jones, H. (1993) Altered images. *Nursing Times, 89*(5), 58–60.

Jones, J. (1995) New breed of non-parents turn back on family. *Observer,* 16 April.

Jones, J.G. & Hardy, L. (1990) *Stress and Performance in Sport.* Chichester: John Wiley & Sons.

Jones, K.L., Smith, D.W., Ulleland, C.N., & Streissguth, A. (1973) Patterns of malformation in offspring of chronic alcoholic mothers. *Lancet, 1,* 1267–1271.

Jones, M. (1953) *The Therapeutic Community.* New York: Basic Books.

Jones, M. (2000) What goes up must come down. *The Psychologist, 13*(7), 350–352.

Jones, M. C. (1924) The elimination of children's fears. *Journal of Experimental Psychology, 7,* 382–390.

Jones, M.C. (1925) A laboratory study of fear: The case of Peter. *Pedagogical Seminary, 31,* 308–315.

Jones, S. (1993) *The Language of the Genes.* London: Flamingo.

Joseph, S., Williams, R., & Yule, W. (1993) Changes in outlook following disaster: The preliminary development of a measure to assess positive and negative responses. *Journal of Traumatic Stress, 6,* 271–279.

Jost, A. (1970a) Hormonal factors in the development of the male genital system. In E. Rosenberg & C.A. Paulsen (Eds), *The Human Testis.* New York: Plenum Press.

Jost, A. (1970b) Hormonal factors in sexual differentiation. *Philosophical Transactions of the Royal Society of London, B259,* 119–130.

Jourard, S.M. (1966) An exploratory study of body accessibility. *British Journal of Social & Clinical Psychology, 5,* 221–231.

Jourard, S.M. (1971) *Self-disclosure: An Exploratory Analysis of the Transparent Self.* New York: Wiley Interscience.

Jouvet, M. (1967) Mechanisms of the states of sleep: A neuropharmacological approach. *Research Publications of the Association for the Research in Nervous and Mental Diseases, 45,* 86–126.

Joynson, R.B. (1972) The return of mind. *Bulletin of the British Psychological Society, 25,* 1–10.

Joynson, R.B. (1974) *Psychology and Common Sense.* London: RKP.

Joynson, R.B. (1980) Models of man: 1879–1979. In A.J. Chapman & D.M. Jones (Eds) *Models of Man.* Leicester: British Psychological Society.

Judd, J (1997) Working mothers need not feel guilty. *Independent on Sunday,* 27 November, 5.

Juel-Nielsen, N. (1965) Individual and environment: A psychiatric and psychological investigation of monozygous twins raised apart. *Acta Psychiatrica et Neurologica Scandinavia (Suppl. 183).*

Jung, C.G. (1963) *Memories, Dreams, Reflections.* London: Collins/RKP.

Jung, C.G. (1964) (Ed.) *Man and his Symbols.* London: Aldus-Jupiter Books.

Kagan, J. (1971) *Change and Continuity in Infancy.* New York: Wiley.

Kagan, J., Kearsley, R. & Zelago, P. (1978) *Infancy: Its Place in Human Development.* Cambridge, MA: Harvard University Press.

Kagan, J., Kearsley, R.B. & Zelago, P.R. (1980) *Infancy – Its Place in Human Development.* (2nd edition). Cambridge, Massachusetts: Harvard University Press.

Kagan, J., Reznick, J.S. & Snidman, N. (1990) The temperamental qualities of inhibition and lack of inhibition. In M. Lewis & S.M. Miller (Eds) *Handbook of Developmental Psychopathology.* New York: Plenum Press.

Kahneman, D. (1973) *Attention and Effort.* Englewood Cliffs, NJ: Prentice-Hall.

Kahneman, D. & Henik, A. (1979) Perceptual organisation and attention. In M. Kubovy & J.R. Pomerantz (Eds) *Perceptual Organisation.* Hillsdale, NJ: Erlbaum.

Kahneman, D. & Tversky, A. (1984) Changing views of attention and automaticity. In R. Parasuraman, D.R. Davies & J. Beatty (Eds) *Varieties of Attention.* New York: Academic Press.

Kaiser, A.S., Katz, R., & Shaw, B.F. (1998) Cultural Issues in the Management of Depression. In S.S. Kazarian & D.R. Evans (Eds) *Cultural Clinical Psychology: Theory, Research, and Practice.* New York: Oxford University Press.

Kalish, R.A. (1975) *Late Adulthood: Perspectives on Human Development.* Monterey, California: Brooks-Cole.

Kalish, R.A. (1979) The new ageism and the failure models: A polemic. *Gerontologist, 19,* 398–402.

Kalish, R.A. (1982) *Late Adulthood: Perspectives on Human Development* (2nd edition). Monterey, CA: Brooks-Cole.

Kalnins, I.V. & Bruner, J.S. (1973) The coordination of visual observation and instrumental behaviour in early infancy. *Perception, 2,* 307–314.

Kamin, L.J.(1969) Predictability, surprise, attention and conditioning. In B.A. Campbell & R.M. Church (Eds) *Punishment and Aversive Behaviour.* New York: Appleton-Century-Crofts.

Kamin, L.J. (1974) *The Science and Politics of IQ.* Potomac, MD: Lawrence Erlbaum Associates.

Kaminer, H. & Lavie, P. (1991) Sleep and dreaming in Holocaust survivors: Dramatic decrease in dream recall in well-adjusted survivors. *Journal of Nervous & Mental Diseases, 179,* 664–669.

Kanizsa, A. (1976) Subjective contours. *Scientific American, 234,* 48–52.

Kanner, A.D., Coyne, J.C., Schaefer, C. & Lazarus, R.S. (1981) Comparison of two modes of stress measurement: Daily hassles and uplifts versus major life events. *Journal of Behavioural Measurement, 4,* 1–39.

Kanner, L. (1943) Autistic disturbance of affective contact. *Nervous Child, 12,* 17–50.

Karau, S.J. & Williams, K.D. (1995) Social loafing: Research findings, implications, and future directions. *Current Directions in Psychological Science, 4,* 134–139.

Karlins, M., Coffman, T.L. & Walters, G. (1969) On the fading of social stereotypes: Studies in three generations of college students. *Journal of Personality & Social Psychology, 13,* 1–16.

Karmiloff-Smith, A. (1996) The connectionist infant: Would Piaget turn in his grave? *Society for Research in Child Development Newsletter,* Fall, 1–2 and 10.

Karmiloff-Smith, A. (2000) Why babies' brains are not Swiss army knives. In H. Rose & S. Rose (Eds) *Alas, Poor Darwin: Arguments Against Evolutionary Psychology.* London: Jonathan Cape.

References

Karniol, R. (1978) Children's use of intention cues in evaluating behaviour. *Psychological Bulletin, 85,* 76–85.

Karraker, K.H., Vogel, D.A. & Lake, M.A. (1995) Parents' gender–stereotyped perceptions of newborns: The eye of the beholder revisited. *Sex Roles, 33(9/10),* 687–701.

Kastenbaum, R. (1979) *Growing Old – Years of Fulfilment.* London: Harper & Row.

Katona, C. (1940) *Organising and Memorising.* New York: Columbia University Press.

Katz, D. (1960) The functional approach to the study of attitudes. *Public Opinion Quarterly, 24,* 163–204.

Katz, D. & Braly, K. (1933) Racial stereotypes of one hundred college students. *Journal of Abnormal & Social Psychology, 28,* 280–290.

Katz, J.S. (1993) Jewish perspectives on death, dying and bereavement. In D. Dickenson & M. Johnson (Eds) *Death, Dying and Bereavement.* London: Sage (in association with the Open University).

Kazdin, A.E. & Wilcoxin, L.A. (1976) Systematic desensitisation and nonspecific treatment effects: A methodological evaluation. *Psychological Bulletin, 83,* 729–758.

Keasey, C.B. (1978) Children's developing awareness and usage of intentionality and motives. In C.B. Keasey (Ed.), *Nebraska Symposium on Motivation, Volume 25.* Lincoln: University of Nebraska Press.

Keegan, P. (1999) In the line of fire. *The Guardian (G2),* 1 June, 2–3.

Keeney, T.J., Cannizzo, S.R., & Flavell, J.H. (1967) Spontaneous and induced verbal rehearsal in a recall task. *Child Development, 38,* 953–966.

Keesey, R.E. & Powley, T.L. (1975) Hypothalamic regulation of body weight. *American Scientist, 63,* 558–565.

Kelley, H.H. (1950) The warm–cold variable in first impressions of people. *Journal of Personality, 18,* 431–439.

Kelley, H.H. (1967) Attribution theory in social psychology. In D. Levine (Ed.) *Nebraska Symposium on Motivation, Volume 15.* Lincoln, NE: Nebraska University Press.

Kelley, H.H. (1972) Causal schemata and the attribution process. In E.E. Jones, D.E. Kanouse, H.H. Kelley, S. Valins & B. Weiner (Eds) *Attribution: Perceiving the Causes of Behaviour.* Morristown, NJ: General Learning Press.

Kelley, H.H. (1973) The processes of causal attribution. *American Psychologist, 28,* 107–128.

Kelley, H.H. (1983) Perceived causal structures. In J.M.F. Jaspars, F.D. Fincham & M. Hewstone (Eds) *Attribution Theory and Research: Conceptual, Developmental and Social Dimensions.* London: Academic Press.

Kellogg, W.N. & Kellogg, L.A. (1933) *The Ape and the Child.* New York: McGraw Hill.

Kelly, G.A. (1955) *A Theory of Personality – The Psychology of Personal Constructs.* New York: Norton.

Kelly, G.A. (1962) Europe's matrix of decision. In M.R. Jones (Ed.) *Nebraska Symposiom on Motivation.* Lincoln, NA: University of Nebraska Press

Kelman, H. & Lawrence, L. (1972) Assignment of responsibility in the case of Lt. Calley: Preliminary report on a national survey. *Journal of Social Issues, 28(1),* 177–212.

Kelman, H.C. (1958) Compliance, identification and internalisation: Three processes of attitude change. *Journal of Conflict Resolution, 2,* 51–60.

Kelman, H.C. & Hovland, C.I. (1953) Reinstatement of the communication in delayed measurement of opinion change. *Journal of Abnormal & Social Psychology, 48,* 327–335.

Kempermann, G. & Gage, F.H. (1999) New nerve cells for the adult brain. *Scientific American, 280(5),* 38–43.

Kendell, R.E. (1975) *The Role of Diagnosis in Psychiatry.* Oxford: Blackwell.

Kendell, R.E. (1983) The principles of classification in relation to mental disease. In M. Shepherd & O.L. Zangwill (Eds), *Handbook of Psychiatry: 1, General Psychopathology.* Cambridge: Cambridge University Press.

Kenny, U. (1998) Cult or cure: the AA backlash. *Independent on Sunday, Real Life,* 10 May, 4.

Kenrick, D.T. (1994) Evolutionary social psychology: From sexual selection to social cognition. *Advances in Experimental Social Psychology,, 26,* 75–121.

Kent, L. *et al.* (1999) Comorbidity of autistic spectrum disorders in children with Down's syndrome. *Developmental Medical & Child Neurology, 41(3),* 154–158.

Kephart, W.M. (1967) Some correlates of romantic love. *Journal of Marriage & The Family, 29,* 470–474.

Keppel, G. & Underwood, B.J. (1962) Proactive inhibition in short-term retention of single items. *Journal of Verbal Learning & Verbal Behaviour, 1,* 153–161.

Kerckhoff, A.C. (1974) The social context of interpersonal attraction. In T.L. Huston (Ed.) *Foundations of Interpersonal Attraction.* New York: Academic Press.

Kerckhoff, A.C. & Davis, K.E. (1962) Value consensus and need complementarity in mate selection. *American Sociological Review, 27,* 295–303.

Kerig, P.K., Cowan, P.A., & Cowan, C.P. (1993) Marital quality and gender differences in parent–child interaction. *Developmental Psychology, 29(6),* 931–939.

Kerr, N.L. (1983) Motivation losses in small groups: a social dilemma analysis. *Journal of Personality & Social Psychology, 45,* 819–828.

Kestenbaum, G.I. & Weinstein, L. (1985) Personality, psychopathology and developmental issues in male adolescent video game use. *Journal of the American Academy of Child Psychiatry, 24,* 325–337.

Kety, S.S. (1975) Biochemistry of the major psychoses. In A. Freedman, H. Kaplan & B. Sadock (Eds) *Comprehensive Textbook of Psychiatry.* Baltimore: Williams & Wilkins.

Kety, S.S., Rosenthal, D., Wender, P.H. & Schulsinger, F. (1968) The types and prevalence of mental illness in the biological and adoptive families of adopted schizophrenics. In D. Rosenthal & S.S. Kety (Eds) *The Transmission of Schizophrenia.* Elmsford, NY: Pergamon Press.

Kety, S.S. Rosenthal, D., Wender, P.H., Schulsinger, F. & Jacobson, B. (1975) Mental illness in the biological and adoptive families of adoptive individuals who have become schizophrenic. In R.R. Fieve, D. Rosenthal & H. Bull (Eds) *Genetic Research in Psychiatry.* Baltimore: Johns Hopkins University Press.

Khan, A., Warner, H.A., & Brown, W.A. (2000) Symptom reduction and suicide risk in patients treated with placebos in antidepressant clinical trials. *Archives of General Psychiatry, 57,* 311–317.

Kilham, W. & Mann, L. (1974) Level of destructive obedience as a function of transmitter and executant roles in the Milgram obedience paradigm. *Journal of Personality & Social Psychology, 29,* 696–702.

Kimball, R.K. & Hollander, E.P. (1974) Independence in the presence of an experienced but deviant group member. *Journal of Social Psychology, 93,* 281–292.

Kimble, D.P. (1988) *Biological Psychology.* New York: Holt, Rinehart & Winston.

Kimura, D. (1993) Sex differences in the brain. *Scientific American, 267(3),* September, 80–87 (Special issue).

Kintsch, W. & Buschke, H. (1969) Homphones and synonyms in short-term memory. *Journal of Experimental Psychology, 80,* 403–407.

Kirby, R. & Radford, J. (1976) *Individual Differences*. London: Methuen.

Kitzinger, C. (1990) Heterosexism in psychology. *The Psychologist, 3(9)*, 391–392.

Kitzinger, C. (1998) Challenging gender biases: Feminist psychology at work. *Psychology Review, 4*(3), 18–20.

Kitzinger, C. & Coyle, A. (1995) Lesbian and gay couples: Speaking of difference. *The Psychologist, 8*, 64–69.

Kitzinger, C., Coyle, A., Wilkinson, S. & Milton, M. (1998) Towards lesbian and gay psychology. *The Psychologist, 11*(11), 529–533.

Klaus, H.M. & Kennell, J.H. (1976) *Maternal infant bonding*. St Louis: Mosby.

Klaus, R.A. & Gray, S.W. (1968) The early training project for disadvantaged children: A report after five years. *Monographs of the Society for Research in Child Development 33*(4) (Serial No. 120).

Klein, M. (1950) *Contributions to Psychoanalysis*. London: Hogarth Press.

Kleinman, A. (1987) Anthropology and psychiatry. The role of culture in cross-cultural research on illness. *British Journal of Psychiatry, 151,* 447–454.

Kleinman, A. & Kleinman, J. (1985) Somatisation: The interconnections in Chinese society among culture, depressive experiences and the meanings of pain. In A. Kleinman & B. Good (Eds) *Culture and Depression: Studies in the Anthropology and Cross-cultural Psychiatry of Affect and Disorder.* Berkeley: University of California Press.

Kleinmuntz, B. (1980) *Essentials of Abnormal Psychology* (2nd edition). London: Harper & Row.

Kleitman, N. (1927) Studies on the physiology of sleep; V; Some experiments on puppies. *American Journal of Physiology, 84,* 386–395.

Kleitman, N. (1963) *Sleep and Wakefulness* (2nd edition). Chicago: University of Chicago Press.

Kline, P. (1972) *Fact and Fantasy in Freudian Theory*. London: Methuen.

Kline, P. (1981a) The work of Eysenck and Cattell. In F. Fransella (Ed.), *Personality Theory, Measurement and Research.* London: Methuen.

Kline. P. (1981b) Personality. In D. Fontana (Ed.) *Psychology for Teachers.* British Psychological Society/Macmillan Press.

Kline, P. (1982) Personality and individual assessment. In A.J. Chapman & A. Gale (Eds) *Psychology and People: A Tutorial Text.* London: BPS/Macmillan Press.

Kline, P. (1983) *Personality – Measurement and Theory*. London: Hutchinson.

Kline, P. (1988) *Psychology Exposed*. London: Routledge.

Kline, P. (1989) Objective tests of Freud's theories. In A.M. Colman and J.G. Beaumont (Eds) *Psychology Survey No. 7.* Leicester: British Psychological Society.

Kline, P. (1993) Comments on 'Personality traits are alive and well'. *The Psychologist, 6*(7), 304.

Kline, P. (1995) Personality tests. In S.E. Hampson & A.M. Colman (Eds) *Individual Differences and Personality.* London: Longman.

Kline, P. (1998) Psychoanalytic perspectives. *Psychology Review, 5*(1), 10–13.

Kline, P. & Storey, R. (1977) A factor analytic study of the oral character. *British Journal of Social & Clinical Psychology, 16,* 317–328.

Kloep, M. & Hendry, L.B. (1999) Challenges, risks and coping in adolescence. In D. Messer & S. Millar (Eds) *Exploring Developmental Psychology: From Infancy to Adolescence.* London: Arnold.

Kloep, M. & Tarifa, F. (1993) Albanian children in the wind of change. In L.E. Wolven (Ed.) *Human Resource Development.* Hogskolan: Ostersund.

Kluckhohn, C. & Murray, H.A. (1953) Personality formation: The determinants. In C. Kluckhohn, H.A. Murray & D.M. Schneider (Eds) *Personality in Nature, Society and Culture* (2nd edition) New York: Knopf.

Klüver, H. & Bucy, P. (1937) 'Psychic blindness' and other symptoms following bilateral temporal lobectomy in Rhesus monkeys. *American Journal of Physiology,* San Diego, CA: Edits.

Kobasa, S. (1979) Stressful life events, personality, and health: An inquiry into hardiness. *Journal of Personality & Social Psychology, 37,* 1–11.

Kobasa, S. (1986) How much stress can you survive? In M.G. Walraven & H.E. Fitzgerald (Eds) *Annual Editions: Human Development, 86/87.* New York: Dushkin.

Kobasa, S., Maddi, S., & Kahn, S. (1982) Hardiness and health: a prospective study. *Journal of Personality & Social Psychology, 42,* 168–177.

Koestler, A. (1967) *The Ghost in the Machine*. London: Pan.

Koestler, A. (1970) *The Act of Creation*. London: Pan Books.

Koffka, K. (1935) *The Principles of Gestalt Psychology*. New York: Harcourt Brace and World.

Kohlberg, L. (1963) The development of children's orientations toward a moral order: 1. Sequence in the development of moral thought. *Human Development, 6,* 11–33.

Kohlberg, L. (1966) A cognitive–developmental analysis of childrens' sex-role concepts and attitudes. In E.E. Maccoby (Ed.), *The Development of Sex Differences.* Stanford, CA: Stanford University Press.

Kohlberg, L. (1969) Stage and sequence: The cognitive developmental approach to socialisation. In D.A. Goslin (Ed.) *Handbook of Socialisation Theory and Research.* Chicago: Rand McNally.

Kohlberg, L. (1975) The Cognitive–Developmental Approach to Moral Education. *Phi Delta Kappa,* June, 670–677.

Kohlberg, L. (1976) Moral stages and moralisation. In T. Likona (Ed.), *Moral Development and Behaviour.* New York: Holt, Rinehart & Winston.

Kohlberg, L. (1978) Revisions in the theory and practice of moral development. *Directions for Child Development, 2,* 83–88.

Kohlberg, L. (1981) *Essays on moral development, Volume 1*. New York: Harper & Row.

Kohlberg, L. (1984) *Essays on Moral Development: The Psychology of Moral Development, Volume 2.* New York: Harper & Row.

Kohlberg, L. & Nisan, M. (1987) A longitudinal study of moral judgement in Turkish males. In A. Colby & L. Kohlberg (Eds) *The Measurement of Moral Judgement.* New York: Cambridge University Press.

Kohlberg, L. & Ullian, D.Z. (1974) Stages in the development of psychosexual concepts and attitudes. In R.C. Van Wiele (Ed.) *Sex Differences in Behaviour.* New York: Wiley.

Kohler, I. (1962) Experiments with goggles. *Scientific American, 206,* 67–72.

Kohler, I. (1964) The formation and transformation of the visual world. *Psychological Issues, 3,* 28–46/116–133.

Köhler, W. (1925) *The Mentality of Apes*. New York: Harcourt Brace.

Köhler, W. (1947) *Gestalt Psychology*. New York: Liveright.

Kohn, M. (1998) Survival of the chattiest. *The Independent on Sunday,* 5 April, 44–45.

Kohn, M. (1999) It's good news for sea anemones. *The Independent on Sunday,* 31 January, 12.

Kolers, P.A. (1972) *Aspects of Motion Perception*. New York: Pergamon Press.

References

Koluchova, J. (1972) Severe deprivation in twins: A case study. *Journal of Child Psychology & Psychiatry, 13,* 107–114.

Koluchova, J. (1991) Severely deprived twins after 22 years observation. *Studia Psychologica, 33,* 23–28.

Kotelchuk, M. (1976) The infant's relationship to the father: experimental evidence. In M.E. Lamb (Ed.) *The Role of the Father in Child Development.* New York: Wiley.

Kraepelin, E. (1896) Dementia Praecox (trans.). In J. Cutting & M. Shepherd (Eds) (1987) *The Clinical Routes of the Schizophrenia Concept.* Cambridge: Cambridge University Press

Kraepelin, E. (1913) *Clinical Psychiatry: A Textbook for Physicians:* (translated by A. Diffendorf). New York: Macmillan.

Krahé, B. (1992) *Personality and Social Psychology: Towards a Synthesis.* London: Sage.

Kramer, P. (1993) *Listening to Prozac.* New York: Viking.

Kraus, A.S. & Lilienfeld, A.M. (1959) Some epidemiological aspects of the high mortality rate in the young widowed group. *Journal of Chronic Diseases, 10,* 207–217.

Krebs, D. & Adinolfi, A. (1975) Physical attractiveness, social relations and personality style. *Journal of Personality & Social Psychology, 31,* 245–253.

Krebs, D. & Blackman, R. (1988) *Psychology: A First Encounter.* New York: Harcourt Brace Jovanovich.

Kreitman, N. (1961) The reliability of psychiatric diagnosis. *Journal of Mental Science, 107,* 876–886.

Kreitman, N., Sainsbury, P. & Morrissey, J. (1961) The reliability of psychiatric assessment: An analysis. *Journal of Mental Science, 107,* 887–908.

Kremer, J. (1998) Work. In K. Trew & J. Kremer (Eds) *Gender & Psychology.* London: Arnold.

Kroger, J. (1985) Separation–individuation and ego identity status in New Zealand university students. *Journal of Youth & Adolescence, 14,* 133–147.

Kroger, J. (1996) *Identity in Adolescence: The Balance between Self and Other* (2nd edition). London: Routledge.

Kruger, A.C. (1992) The effect of peer and adult–child transactive discussions on moral reasoning. In M. Gauvain & M. Cole (Eds) *Readings on the Development of Children.* New York: W.H. Freeman & Company.

Kruglanski, A.W. (1977) The place of naive contents in a theory of attribution: Reflections on Calder and Zuckerman's critiques of the endogenous–exogenous partition. *Personality & Social Psychology Bulletin, 3,* 592–605.

Kruglanski, A.W. (1979) Causal explanation, teleological expansion: On radical particularism in attribution theory. *Journal of Personality & Social Psychology, 37,* 1447–1457.

Krupat, E. & Garonzik, R. (1994) Subjects' expectations and the search for alternatives to deception in social psychology. *British Journal of Social Psychology, 33,* 211–222.

Kübler-Ross, E. (1969) *On Death and Dying.* London: Tavistock/Routledge.

Kuhn, D., Nash, S.C. & Brucker, J.A. (1978) Sex role concepts of two- and three-year-olds. *Child Development, 49,* 445–451.

Kuhn, H.H. (1960) Self attitudes by age, sex and professional training. *Sociology Quarterly, 1,* 39–55.

Kuhn, H.H. & McPartland, T.S. (1954) An empirical investigation of self attitudes. *American Sociological Review, 47,* 647–652.

Kuhn, T.S. (1962) *The Structure of Scientific Revolutions.* Chicago: University of Chicago Press.

Kuhn, T.S. (1970) *The Structure of Scientific Revolutions* (2nd edition) Chicago: Chicago University Press.

Kulik, J.A. & Brown, R. (1979) Frustration, attribution of blame and aggression. *Journal of Experimental Social Psychology, 15,* 183–194.

Kulik, J.A. & Mahler, H.I.M. (1989) Stress and affiliation in a hospital setting: Pre-operative room-mate preferences. *Personality & Social Psychology Bulletin, 15,* 183–193.

Kuppens, M., de Wit, J., & Stroebe, W. (1996) Angstaanjagenheid in gezondheids-voorlichting: Een dual process analyse. *Gedrag en Gezondheid, 24,* 241–248.

Kurdek, L.A. (1994) The nature and correlates of relationship quality in gay, lesbian and heterosexual cohabiting couples: A test of the individual difference, interdependence, and discrepancy models. In B. Greene & G.M. Herek (Eds) *Lesbian and Gay Psychology: Theory, Research and Clinical Applications.* London: Sage.

Kurtines, W. & Greif, E.B. (1974) The development of moral thought: Review and evaluation of Kohlberg's approach. *Psychological Bulletin, 81*(8), 453–470.

Kurucz, J. & Feldmar, G. (1979) Prosopo-affective agnosia as a symptom of cerebral organic disease. *Journal of the American Geriatrics Society, 27,* 225–230.

LaPiere, R.T. (1934) Attitudes versus action. *Social Forces, 13,* 230–237.

LaBerge, D. (1983) Spatial extent of attention to letters and words. *Journal of Experimental Psychology: Human Perception & Performance, 9,* 371–379.

Labouvie-Vief, G. (1979) *Does Intelligence Decline with Age?* Bethesda, Maryland: National Institute of Health.

Labouvie-Vief, G. (1980) Beyond formal operations: uses and limits of pure logic in life-span development. *Human Development, 22,* 141–161.

Labouvie-Vief, G. (1985) Intelligence and cognition. In J.E. Birren & K.W. Schaie (Eds) *Handbook of the Psychology of Ageing* (2nd edition). New York: Van Nostrand Reinhold.

Labov, W. (1970) The logic of non-standard English. In F. Williams (Ed.) *Language and Poverty.* Chicago: Markham.

Labov, W. (1973) The boundaries of words and their meanings. In C.J.N. Bailey & R.W. Shuy (Eds) *New Ways of Analysing Variations in English.* Washington, DC: Georgetown University Press.

Lacey, H. (1998) She's leaving home. *Real Life: Independent on Sunday,* 31 May.

Lachman, R., Lachman, J.L., & Butterfield, E.C. (1979) *Cognitive Psychology and Information Processing.* Hillsdale, NJ: Lawrence Erlbaum Associates.

Lachman, S.J. (1984) Processes in visual misperception: Illusions for highly structured stimulus material. *Paper presented at the 92nd annual convention of the American Psychological Association,* Toronto, Canada.

Laing, R.D. (1959) *The Divided Self: An Existential Study of Sanity and Madness.* London: Tavistock.

Laing, R.D. (1961) *Self and Others.* London: Tavistock.

Laing, R.D. (1967) *The Politics of Experience and the Bird of Paradise.* Harmondsworth, Penguin.

Laing, R.D. (1972) *Knots.* Harmondsworth: Penguin.

Laing, R.D. & Esterson, A. (1964) *Sanity, Madness and the Family* London: Tavistock.

Laird, J.D. (1974) Self-attribution of emotion: The effects of facial expression on the quality of emotional experience. *Journal of Personality & Social Psychology, 29,* 475–486.

Lakoff, G. (1987) *Women, Fire and Dangerous Things: What Categories Reveal About The Mind.* Chicago, ILL: University of Chicago Press.

Lamb, M.E. (1977) Father–infant and mother–infant interaction in the first year of life. *Child Development, 48,* 167–181.

Lamb, M.E. (1979) The changing American family and its implications for infant social development: The sample case of maternal employment. In M. Lewis & L.A. Rosenblum (Eds) *The Social Network of the Developing Infant.* New York: Wiley.

Lamb, M.E., Sternberg, K.J., Hwang, P. & Broberg, A (Eds) (1992) *Child Care in Context.* Hillsdale, NJ: Erlbaum.

Lamb, M.E., Thompson, R.A., Gander, W. & Charnov, E.L. (1985) *Infant–Mother Attachment: The Origins and Significance of Individual Differences in Strange Situation Behaviour.* Hillsdale, NJ: Erlbaum.

Lambert, M.J., Shapiro, D.A. & Bergin, A.E. (1986) The effectiveness of psychotherapy. In S.L. Garfield & A.E. Bergin (Eds) *Handbook of Psychotherapy and Behaviour Change* (3rd edition). New York: Wiley.

Lambert, W.W., Solomon, R.L. & Watson, P.D. (1949) Reinforcement and extinction as factors in size estimation. *Journal of Experimental Psychology, 39,* 637–641.

Lambie, J. (1991) The misuse of Kuhn in psychology. *The Psychologist, 4*(1), 6–11.

Land, E.H. (1964) The retinex. *American Scientist, 52,* 247–64.

Land, E.H. (1977) The retinex theory of colour vision. *Scientific American, 237,* 108–128.

Lander, K. (2000) Big Brother's watching ... who? *The Psychologist, 13*(9), 468.

Landis, C. (1938) Statistical evaluation of psychotherapeutic methods. In S.E. Hinde (Ed.) *Concepts and Problems of Psychotherapy.* London: Heineman.

Lange, C. (1885) Om Sindsbevaegelser. et psychko. fysiolog. studie. English translation in K. Dunlap (Ed.) *The Emotions.* London: Hafner, 1967.

Langer, E.J. (1975) The illusion of control. *Journal of Personality & Social Psychology, 32,* 311–328.

Langlois, J. & Roggman, L. (1990) Attractive faces are only average. *Psychological Science, 1,* 115–121.

Langlois, J., Roggman, L. & Riser-Danner, L. (1990) Infants' differential social responses to attractive and unattractive faces. *Developmental Psychology, 26,* 153–159.

Langlois, J.H., Roggman, L.A., Casey, R.J., Ritter, J.M., Rieser-Danner, L.A., & Jenkins, V.Y. (1987) Infant preferences for attractive faces: rudiments of a stereotype. *Developmental Psychology, 23,* 363–369.

Larsen, K.S. (1974) Conformity in the Asch experiment. *Journal of Social Psychology, 94,* 303–304.

Larsen, K.S. (1982) Cultural conditions and conformity: The Asch effect. *Bulletin of the British Psychological Society, 35,* 347.

Larsen, K.S., Triplett, J.S., Brant, W.D. & Langenberg, D. (1979) Collaborator status, subject characteristics and conformity in the Asch paradigm. *Journal of Social Psychology, 108,* 259–263.

Larson, P.C. (1981) Sexual identification and self-concept. *Journal of Homosexuality, 7,* 15–32.

Lashley, K. (1926) Studies of cerebral function in learning: VII The relation between cerebral mass, learning and retention. *Journal of Comparative Neurology, 41,* 1–48.

Lashley, K. (1929) *Brain Mechanisms and Intelligence: A Quantitative Study of Injuries to the Brain.* Chicago, Illinois: University of Chicago Press.

Lashley, K. S. (1950) In search of the engram. *Proceedings from Social Experimental Biology, 4,* 454–82. Reprinted in F.A. Beach, D.O. Hebb, C.T. Morgan & H.W. Nissen (Eds), *The Neuropsychology of Lashley.* New York: McGraw-Hill.

Laswell, H.D. (1948) The structures and function of communication in society. In L. Bryson (Ed.), *Communication of Ideas.* New York: Harper.

Latané, B. & Darley, J.M. (1968) Group inhibitions of bystander intervention in emergencies. *Journal of Personality & Social Psychology, 10,* 215–221.

Latané, B. & Darley, J.M. (1970) *The Unresponsive Bystander: Why Does He Not Help?* New York: Appleton-Century-Croft.

Latané, B. & Nida, S. (1980) Social impact theory and group influence: A social engineering perspective. In P. Paulus (Ed.) *The Psychology of Group Influence.* Hillsdale, NJ: Lawrence Erlbaum.

Latané, B. & Rodin, J. (1969) A lady in distress: Inhibiting effects of friends and strangers on bystander intervention. *Journal of Experimental Social Psychology, 5,* 189–202.

Latané, B. & Wolf, S. (1981) The social impact of majorities and minorities. *Psychological Review, 88,* 438–453.

Latané, B., Nida, S. & Williams, D.W. (1981) The effects of group size on helping behaviour. In J.P. Rushton & R.M. Sorrentino (Eds) *Altruism and Helping Behaviour.* Hillsdale, NJ: Erlbaum.

Latané, B., Williams, K. & Harkins, S.G.(1979) Many hands make light work: The causes and consequences of social loafing. *Journal of Personality & Social Psychology, 37,* 822–832.

Lau, R.R. & Russell, D. (1980) Attributions in the sports pages. *Journal of Personality & Social Psychology, 39,* 29–38.

Lauer, J. & Lauer, R. (1985) Marriages made to last. *Psychology Today.* June, 22–26.

Laughlin, H.P.(1967) *The Neuroses.* Washington, DC: Butterworth.

Laurance, J. (2000) Young cocaine users run higher risk of strokes. *The Independent,* 13 May, 5.

Lauritsen, M., Mors, O., Mortensen, P.B., & Ewald, H. (1999) Infantile autism and associated autosomal chromosome abnormalities: A register-based study and a literature survey. *Journal of Child Psychology & Psychiatry, 40*(3), 335–345.

Lavender, T. (2000) Schizophrenia. In L. Champion & M. Power (Eds) *Adult Psychological Problems: An Introduction* (2nd edition). Hove: Psychology Press.

Laville, S. (1998) Curry and causing trouble – just like the average woman. *The Evening Standard,* 27 March, 5.

Lawson, E.A. (1966) Decisions concerning the rejected channel. *Journal of Experimental Psychology, 18,* 260–265.

Lazar, I. & Darlington, R. (1982) Lasting effects of early education: A report from the Consortium for Longitudinal Studies. *Monographs of the Society for Research in Child Development, 47* (2–3, Serial No. 195).

Lazarus, A.A. (1976) *Multimodal Behaviour Therapy.* New York: Springer.

Lazarus, A.A. (1977) *Behaviour Therapy and Beyond.* New York: McGraw Hill.

Lazarus, R.S. (1966) *Psychological Stress and the Coping Process.* New York: McGraw-Hill.

Lazarus, R.S. (1982) Thoughts on the relations between emotion and cognition. *American Psychologist, 37,* 1019–1024.

Lazarus, R.S. (1999) *Stress and Emotion: A New Synthesis.* London: Free Association Books.

Lazarus, R.S. & Folkman, S. (1984) *Stress, Appraisal, and Coping.* New York: Springer.

Lazarus, R.S. & McCleary, R.A. (1951) Automatic discrimination without awareness: A study of subception. *Psychological Review, 58,* 113–122.

Le Bon, G. (1895) *The Crowd: A Study of the Popular Mind.* London: Unwin.

LeDoux, J.E. (1994) Emotion-specific physiological activity: Don't forget about CNS physiology. In P. Ekman & R. J. Davidson (Eds) *The Nature of Emotion: Fundamental Questions.* New York: Oxford University Press.

LeDoux, J.E. (1998) *The Emotional Brain: The Mysterious Underpinnings of Emotional Life.* New York: Simon & Schuster.

Le Voi, M. (1993) Parallel distributed processing and its application in models of memory. In G. Cohen, G. Kiss & M. Le Voi, *Memory: Current Issues* (2nd edition). Buckingham: Open University Press.

Lea, S.E.G. (1984) *Instinct, Environment and Behaviour.* London: Methuen.

Leahy, A.M. (1935) Nature – nurture and intelligence. *Genetic Psychology Monograph, 17*, 235–308.

Leake, J. (2000) Screen games are linked to violence. *The Sunday Times*, 6 August, 28.

Lee, A. (1996) St. Helena study shows benefit of television. *The Times*, 3 August, 7.

Lee, D.N. & Lishman, J.R. (1975) Visual proprioceptive control of stance. *Journal of Human Movement Studies, 1*, 87–95.

Lee, K., Cameron, C.A., Xu, F., Fu, G. & Board, J. (1997) Chinese and Canadian children's evaluations of lying and truth telling: Similarities and differences in the context of pro- and antisocial behaviours. *Child Development, 68*, 924–934.

Lee, L. (1984) Sequences in separation: A framework for investigating endings of the personal (romantic) relationship. *Journal of Social & Personal Relationships, 1*, 49–74.

Lee, S. (1993) How abnormal is the desire for slimness? A survey of eating attitudes and behaviour among Chinese undergraduates in Hong Kong. *Psychological Medicine, 23*, 437–451.

Leekam, S. (1993) Children's understanding of mind. In M. Bennett (Ed.) *The Child as Psychologist: An Introduction to the Development of Social Cognition*. Hemel Hempstead, Herts.: Harvester Wheatsheaf.

Leff, J. (1981) *Psychiatry Around the Globe: A Transcultural View*. New York: Dekker.

Lefkowitz, M.M., Eron, L.D., Walder, L.O. & Huesmann, L.R. (1972) Television violence and child aggression: A follow-up study. In G.A. Comstock & E.A. Rubenstein (Eds) *Television and Social Behaviour, Volume 3. Television and Adolescent Aggressiveness*. Washington, DC: US Government Printing Office.

LeFrancois, G.R. (1983) *Psychology*. Belmont, CA: Wadsworth Publishing Co.

Legge, D. (1975) *An Introduction to Psychological Science*. London: Methuen.

Lemyre, L. & Smith, P.M. (1985) Intergroup discrimination and self-esteem in the minimal group paradigm. *Journal of Personality & Social Psychology, 62*, 99–105.

Lenneberg, E.H. (1960) Review of speech and brain mechanisms by W. Penfield and L. Roberts. In R.C. Oldfield & J.C. Marshall (Eds), *Language*. Harmondsworth: Penguin.

Lenneberg, E.H. (1967) *Biological Foundations of Language*. New York: Wiley.

Lenneberg, E.H. & Roberts, J.M. (1956) *The Language of Experience, Memoir 13. Indiana*: University of Indiania, Publications in Anthropology & Linguistics.

Lepper, M.R. & Greene, D. (1978) Overjustification research and beyond: Towards a means–end analysis of intrinsic and extrinsic motivation. In M.R. Lepper & D. Greene (Eds), *The Hidden Costs of Reward*. Hillsdale, New Jersey: Lawrence Erlbaum Associates Inc.

Lepper, M.R., Greene, D., & Nisbett, R.E. (1973) Undermining children's intrinsic interest with extrinsic reward: A test of the overjustification hypothesis. *Journal of Personality & Social Psychology, 28*, 129–137.

Lerner, M.J. (1965) The effect of responsibility and choice on a partner's attractiveness following failure. *Journal of Personality, 33*, 178–87.

Lerner, M.J. (1980) *The Belief in a Just World: A Fundamental Delusion*. New York: Plenum

Leslie, A.M. (1987) Pretence and representation: The origins of 'theory of mind'. *Psychological Review, 94*, 412–426.

Leslie, A.M. (1994) Pretending and believing: Issues in the theory of ToMM. *Cognition, 50*, 211–238.

Leslie, A.M. & Roth, D. (1993) What autism teaches us about metarepresentation. In S. Baron-Cohen, H. Tager-Fusberg, & D.J. Cohen (Eds) *Understanding other Minds: Perspectives from Autism*. Oxford: Oxford University Press.

Levenson, R.W. (1994) The Search for Autonomic Specificity. In P. Ekman & R.J. Davidson (Eds) *The Nature of Emotion: Fundamental Questions*. New York: Oxford University Press.

Levenson, R.W., Ekman, P. & Friesen, W.V. (1990) Voluntary facial action generates emotion-specific autonomic nervous system activity. *Psychophysiology, 27*, 363–384.

Levenson, R.W., Ekman. P., Heider, K. & Friesen, W.V. (1992) Emotion and autonomic nervous system activity in the Minangkabau of West Sumatra. *Journal of Personality & Social Psychology, 62*, 972–988.

Levin, I.P. & Gaeth, G.J. (1988) How consumers are affected by the framing of attribution information before and after consuming the product. *Journal of Consumer Research, 15*, 374–378.

Levine, N.E. (1988) *The Dynamics of Polyandry: Kinship, Domesticity and Population in the Tibetan Border*. Chicago: University of Chicago Press.

Levine, R., Sato, S., Hashimoto, T. & Verma, J. (1995) Love and marriage in 11 cultures. *Journal of Cross-Cultural Psychology, 26*, 554–571.

Levinger, G. (1980) Toward the analysis of close relationships. *Journal of Experimental Social Psychology, 16*, 510–554.

Levinger, G. & Clark, J. (1961) Emotional factors in the forgetting of word associations. *Journal of Abnormal & Social Psychology, 62*, 99–105.

Levinson, D.J. (1986) A conception of adult development. *American Psychologist, 41*, 3–13.

Levinson, D.J., Darrow, D.N., Klein, E.B., Levinson, M.H. & McKee, B. (1978) *The Seasons of a Man's Life*. New York: A.A. Knopf.

Levy, B. & Langer, E. (1994) Ageing free from negative stereotypes: Successful memory in China and among the American deaf. *Journal of Personality & Social Psychology, 66*, 989–997.

Levy, J., Trevarthen, C. & Sperry, R.W. (1972) Perception of bilateral chimeric figures following hemispheric disconnection. *Brain, 95*, 61–78.

Levy, R. (1996) Improving memory in old age through implicit self-stereotyping. *Journal of Personality & Social Psychology, 71*, 1092–1107.

Levy, S., Stroessner, S. & Dweck, C. (1998) Stereotype formation and endorsement: The role of implicit theories. *Journal of Personality & Social Psychology, 74*, 16–34.

Levy-Agresti, J. & Sperry, R.W. (1968) Differential perceptual capacities in major and minor hemispheres. *Proceedings of the National Academy of Sciences, 61*, 1151.

Lewin, R. (1991) Look who's talking now. *New Scientist*, 27 April, 48–52.

Lewis, M. (1990) Social knowledge and social development. *Merrill-Palmer Quarterly, 36*, 93–116.

Lewis, M. & Brooks-Gunn, J. (1979) *Social Cognition and the Acquisition of Self*. New York: Plenum.

Lewontin, R. (1976) *Race and Intelligence*. In N.J. Block & G. Dworkin (Eds) *The IQ Controversy: Critical Readings*. New York: Pantheon.

Ley, P. (1981) Professional non-compliance: a neglected problem. *British Journal of Clinical Psychology, 20*, 151–154.

Ley, P. (1989) Improving patients' understanding, recall, satisfaction and compliance. In A. Broome (Ed.) *Health Psychology*. London: Chapman & Hall.

Leyens, J.P. & Codol, J.P. (1988) Social cognition. In M. Hewstone, W. Stroebe, J.P. Codol & G.M. Stephenson (Eds) *Introduction to Social Psychology*. Oxford: Blackwell.

Leyens, J.P. & Dardenne, B. (1996) Basic concepts and approaches in social cognition. In M. Hewstone, W. Stroebe & G.M.

Stephenson (Eds) *Introduction to Social Psychology* (2nd edition). Oxford: Blackwell.

Liebert, R.M. & Baron, R.A. (1972) Some immediate effects of televised violence on children's behaviour. *Developmental Psychology, 6,* 469–475.

Liebert, R.M. & Sprafkin, J. (1988) *The Early Window: Effects of Television on Children and Youth.* New York: Pergamon Press.

Light, P. (1986) Context, conservation and conversation. In M. Richards & P. Light (Eds) *Children of Social Worlds.* Cambridge: Polity Press.

Light, P. & Gilmour, A. (1983) Conservation or conversation? Contextual facilitation of inappropriate conservation judgements. *Journal of Experimental Child Psychology, 36,* 356–363.

Light, P., Buckingham, N. & Robbins, A.H. (1979) The conservation task as an interactional setting. *British Journal of Educational Psychology, 49,* 304–310.

Likert, R. (1932) A technique for the measurement of attitudes. *Archives of Psychology, 22,* 140.

Lilienfeld, S.O. (1995) *Seeing Both Sides: Classic Controversies in Abnormal Psychology.* Pacific Grove, CA: Brooks/Cole Publishing Co.

Lilienfeld, S.O. (1998) *Looking into Abnormal Psychology: Contemporary Readings.* Pacific Grove, CA: Brooks/Cole Publishing Co.

Lin, E. & Kleinman, A. (1988) Psychopathology and clinical course of schizophrenia: A cross-cultural perspective. *Schizophrenia Bulletin, 14,* 555–567.

Linder, D.E., Cooper, J. & Jones, E.E. (1967) Decision freedom as a determinant of the role of incentive magnitude in attitude change. *Journal of Personality & Social Psychology, 6,* 245–254.

Lindsay, W.R. (1982) The effects of labelling: Blind and non-blind ratings of social skills in schizophrenic and non-schizophrenic control subjects. *American Journal of Psychiatry, 139,* 216–219.

Linley, A. (2000) Transforming psychology: The example of trauma. *The Psychologist, 13*(7), 353–355.

Linville, P.W. & Jones, E.E. (1980) Polarised appraisals of outgroup members. *Journal of Personality & Social Psychology, 38,* 689–703.

Linville, P.W., Fischer, G.W., & Salovey, P. (1989) Perceived distributions of the characteristics of ingroup and outgroup members: empirical evidence and a computer simulation. *Journal of Personality & Social Psychology, 57,* 165–188.

Lippmann, W. (1922) *Public Opinion.* New York: Harcourt.

Lipsedge, M. (1997a) Addictions. In L. Rees, M. Lipsedge, & C. Ball (Eds) *Textbook of Psychiatry.* London: Arnold.

Lipsedge, M. (1997b) Eating disorders. In L.Rees, M. Lipsedge, & C. Ball (Eds) *Textbook of Psychiatry.* London: Arnold.

Lipsitt, L.P. (1977) The study of sensory and learning processes of the newborn. *Clinics in Perinatology, 4,* 163–186.

Littlewood, R. (1992) Psychiatric diagnosis and racial bias: Empirical and interpretive approaches. *Social Science & Medicine, 34,* 141–149.

Littlewood, R. & Lipsedge, M. (1989) *Aliens and Alienists: Ethnic Minorities and Psychiatry.* London: Unwin Hyman.

Littlewood, R. & Lipsedge, M. (1997) *Aliens and Alienists: Ethnic Minorities and Psychiatry* (3rd edition). London: Routledge.

Llewellyn-Smith, J. (1996) Courses for gifted childten are often 'a waste of time'. *The Sunday Telegraph,* 5 September, 8.

Lloyd, A. (1995) *Doubly Deviant, Doubly Damned: Society's Treatment of Violent Women.* Harmondsworth: Penguin.

Lloyd, C., Mair, G., & Hough, M. (1994) *Explaining Reconviction Rates: A Critical Analysis.* London: HMSO.

Lloyd, P., Mayes, A., Manstead, A.S.R., Meudell, P.R. & Wagner, H.L. (1984) *Introduction to Psychology – An Integrated Approach.* London: Fontana.

Locke, J. (1690) *An Essay Concerning Human Understanding.* New York: Mendon (reprinted, 1964).

Locke, S.E. (1982) Stress, adaptation and immunity: Studies in humans. *General Hospital Psychiatry, 4,* 49–58.

Locksley, A., Ortiz, V. & Hepburn, C. (1980) Social categorisation and discriminatory behaviour: Extinguishing the minimal intergroup discrimination effect. *Journal of Personality & Social Psychology, 39,* 773–783.

Loeber, R., Green, S.M., Keenan, K., & Lahey, B.B. (1995) Which boys will fare worse? Early predictors on the onset of conduct disorder in a six-year longitudinal study. *Journal of the American Academy of Child & Adolescent Psychiatry, 34,* 499–509.

Loehlin, J.C. (1989) Partitioning environmental and genetic contributions to behavioural development. *American Psychologist, 44,* 1285.

Loehlin, J.C., Willerman, L. & Horn, J.M. (1988) Human behaviour genetics. *Annual Review of Psychology, 39,* 101–133.

Loftus, E.F. (1975) Leading questions and the eyewitness report. *Cognitive Psychology, 1,* 560–572.

Loftus, E.F. (1979) Reactions to blatantly contradictory information. *Memory & Cognition, 7,* 368–374.

Loftus, E.F. (1980) *Memory.* Reading, MA: Addison and Wesley.

Loftus, E.F. (1984) Expert testimony on the eyewitness. In G.L. Wells & E.F. Loftus (Eds), *Eyewitness Testimony: Psychological Perspectives.* Cambridge: Cambridge University Press.

Loftus, E.F. (1997) Creating false memories. *Scientific American,* September, 50–55.

Loftus, E.F. & Loftus, G. (1980) On the permanence of stored information in the human brain. *American Psychologist, 35,* 409–420.

Loftus, E.F. & Palmer, J.C. (1974) Reconstruction of automobile destruction: An example of the interaction between language and memory. *Journal of Verbal Learning & Verbal Behaviour, 13,* 585–589.

Loftus, E.F. & Zanni, G. (1975) Eyewitness testimony: The influence of wording on a question. *Bulletin of the Psychonomic Society 5,* 86–88.

Loftus, E.F., Freedman, J.L. & Loftus, G.R. (1970) Retrieval of words from subordinate and superordinate categories in semantic hierarchies. *Psychonomic Science, 21,* 235–236.

Loftus, E.F., Miller, D.G. & Burns, H.J. (1978) Semantic integration of verbal information into a visual memory. *Journal of Experimental Psychology, 4*(1), 19–31.

Loftus, G. (1974) Reconstructing memory: The incredible eyewitness. *Psychology Today,* December, 116–119.

Loftus, G. & Loftus, E.F. (1983) *Mind at Play: The Psychology of Video Games.* New York: Basic Books.

Logan, G.D. (1988) Toward an instance theory of automatisation. *Psychological Review, 95,* 492–527.

Logie, R.H. (1995) *Visuo-Spatial Working Memory.* Hove: Lawrence Erlbaum.

Logie, R.H. (1999) Working memory. *The Psychologist, 12*(4), 174–178.

Logie, R.H., Wright, R. & Decker, S. (1992) Recognition memory performance and residential burglary. *Applied Cognitive Psychology, 6,* 109–123.

Logothetis, N.K. (1999) Vision: A window on consciousness. *Scientific American, 281*(5), 44–51.

Lonner, W. (1990) An overview of cross-cultural testing and assessment. In R. Brislin (Ed.) *Applied Cross-Cultural Psychology.* Newbury Park, CA: Sage.

Lopatka, C. & Rachman, S. (1995) Perceived responsibility and compulsive checking: An experimental analysis. *Behaviour Research & Therapy, 33,* 673–684.

References

Lord, C.G., Ross, L., & Lepper, M.R. (1979) Biased assimilation and attityude polarisation: The effects of prior theories on subsequently considered evidence. *Journal of Personality & Social Psychology, 37*, 2098–2107.

Lorenz, K. (1935) The companion in the bird's world. *Auk, 54*, 245–273.

Lorenz, K.Z. (1966) *On Aggression*. London: Methuen.

Lott, A.J. & Lott, B.E. (1974) The role of reward in the formation of positive interpersonal attitudes. In T. Huston (Ed.) *Foundations of Interpersonal Attraction*. New York: Academic Press.

Lovaas, O.I. (1977) *The Autistic Child: Language Development Through Behaviour Modification*. New York: Halste Press.

Lovaas, O.I. (1987) Behavioural treatment and normal educational and intellectual functioning in young autistic children. *Journal of Consulting & Clinical Psychology, 55*, 3–9.

Lovaas, O.I., Freitas, L., Nelson, K. & Whalen, C. (1967) The establishment of imitation and its use for the development of complex behaviour in schizophrenic children. *Behaviour Research & Therapy in Personality, 5*, 171–81.

Lowe, G. (1995) Alcohol and drug addiction. In A.A. Lazarus & A.M. Colman (Eds) *Abnormal Psychology*. London: Longman.

Lowe, G. (2000) Catching the rays. *The Psychologist, 13*(8), 415.

Luborsky, L., Singer, B. & Luborsky, L. (1975) Comparative studies of psychotherapies: Is it true that 'everyone has won and all must have prizes'? *Archives of General Psychiatry, 32*, 995–1008.

Lucas, A. (1998) Randomised trial of early diet in preterm babies and later intelligence quotient. *British Medical Journal, 317*, 1481–1486.

Luchins, A.S. (1942) Mechanisation in problem-solving: The effect of Einstellung. *Psychological Monographs, 54* (Whole No. 248).

Luchins, A.S. (1957) Primacy–recency in impression formation. In C. Hovland (Ed.), *The order of presentation in persuasion*. New Haven, Connecticut: Yale University Press.

Luchins, A.S. & Luchins, E.H. (1959) *Rigidity of Behaviour*. Eugene, OR: University of Oregon Press.

Lumsden, C.J. & Wilson, E.O. (1983) *Promethean Fire*. Cambridge, MA: Harvard University Press.

Luria, A.R. (1968) *The Mind of a Mnemonist*. New York: Basic Books.

Luria, A.R. (1973) *The Working Brain: An Introduction to Neuropsychology* (translated by B. Haigh). New York: Basic Books.

Luria, A.R. (1975) *The Man with a Shattered World*. Harmondsworth, Middlesex: Penguin.

Luria, A.R. (1980) *Higher Cortical Functions in Man* (2nd edition, revised). New York: Basic Books.

Luria, A.R. (1987) Reductionism. In R.L. Gregory (Ed.) *The Oxford Companion to the Mind*. Oxford: Oxford University Press.

Luria, A.R. & Yudovich, F.I. (1971) *Speech and the Development of Mental Processes in the Child*. Harmondsworth: Penguin.

Lyall, J. (1993) Animal rites. *Nursing Times, 89*(10), 18–19.

Lyddy, F. (1999) Memory and one of its seven sins. *The Psychologist, 12*(9), 458.

Lyddy, F. (2000) Depression: The state of the disorder. *The Psychologist, 13*(8), 414–415.

Lyon, C.M. (1995) Helping children with challenging behaviour. *Nursing Standard, 10*(1), 33–35.

Lyon, J. (1998) Crime. In K. Trew & J. Kremer (Eds) *Gender & Psychology*. London: Arnold.

Lyon, J. & Coleman, C. (1996) *Understanding and Working with Young Women in Custody*. Brighton: TSA (Crown Copyright).

Lyons, J. (1970) *Chomsky*. London: Fontana.

Lytton, H. (1977) Do parents create, or respond to, differences in twins? *Developmental Psychology, 13*, 456–459.

Lytton, H. & Romney, D.M. (1991) Parents' differential socialisation of boys and girls: A meta-analysis. *Psychological Bulletin, 109*, 267–296.

Maccoby, E.E. (1980) *Social Development – Psychological Growth and the Parent–Child Relationship*. New York: Harcourt Brace Jovanovich.

Maccoby, E.E (1990) Gender and relationships: A developmental account. *American Psychologist, 45*, 513–520.

Maccoby, E.E. & Jacklin, C.N. (1974) *The Psychology of Sex Differences*. Stanford, CA: Stanford University Press.

Mackay, D. (1975) *Clinical Psychology: Theory and Therapy*. London: Methuen.

Mackay, D. (1984) Behavioural psychotherapy. In W. Dryden (Ed.), *Individual Therapy in Britain*. London: Harper & Row.

MacKay, D.C. & Newbigging, P.L. (1977) The Poggendorf and its variants do arouse the same perceptual processes. *Perception & Psychophysics, 21*, 26–32.

Mackay, D.G. (1973) Aspects of the theory of comprehension, memory and attention. *Quarterly Journal of Experimental Psychology, 25*, 22–40.

Mackenzie, D.L. & Shaw, J.W (1990) Inmate adjustment and change during shock incarceration: The impact of correctional boot camp programs. *Justice Quarterly, 7*, 125–150.

Mackenzie, D.L. & Souryal, C. (1995) A 'Machiavellian' perspective on the development of boot camp prisons: A debate. Unpublished symposium presentation.

Mackenzie, D.L., Brame, R., McDowall, D., & Souryal, C. (1995) Boot camp prisons and recidivism in eight states. *Criminology, 33*, 327–357.

Mackintosh, N.J. (1978) Cognitive or associative theories of conditioning: implications of an analysis of blocking. In S.H. Hulse, M. Fowler, & W.K. Honig (Eds) *Cognitive Processes in Animal Behaviour*. Hillsdale, NJ: Lawrence Erlbaum.

Mackintosh, N.J. (1984) In search of a new theory of conditioning. In G. Ferry (Ed.), *The Understanding of Animals*. Oxford: Blackwell and New Scientist.

Mackintosh, N.J. (1995) Classical and operant conditioning. In N.J. Mackintosh & A.M. Colman (Eds) *Learning and Skills*. London: Longman.

MacNamara, J. (1982) *Names for Things*. Cambridge, Massachusetts: Bradford MIT Press.

Maddison, D. & Viola, A. (1968) The health of widows in the year following bereavement. *Journal of Psychosomatic Research, 12*, 297.

Maddox, G.L. (1964) Disengagement theory: A critical evaluation. The *Gerontologist, 4*, 80–83.

Maes, J.B (1998) *Miracle Sleep Cure*. Thorsons.

Maes, S. & Elderen, van T. (1998) Health psychology and stress. In M.W. Eysenck (Ed.) *Psychology: An Integrated Approach*. London: Longman.

Magnusson, D., Stattin, H. & Allen, V.L. (1985) Biological maturation and social development: A longitudinal study of some adjustment processes from mid-adolescence to adulthood. *Journal of Youth & Adolescence, 14*, 267–283.

Maher, B.A. (1966) *Principles of Psychopathology: An Experimental Approach*. New York: McGraw-Hill.

Mahler, M. (1975) *The Psychological Birth of the Human Infant*. London: Hutchinson.

Mahoney, J. (1998) Mates past their prime. *Times Higher Educational Supplement*, 25 September, 18.

Mahoney, M.J. (1974) *Cognition and Behaviour Modification*. Cambridge, Massachusetts: Ballinger.

Maier, N.R.F. (1931) Reasoning in humans II: The solution of a problem and its appearance in consciousness. *Journal of Comparative Psychology, 12*, 181–194.

Maier, S.F. & Seligman, M.E.P. (1976) Learned helplessness: Theory and evidence. *Journal of Experimental Psychology: General, 105*, 3–46.

Main, M. (1991) Metacognitive knowledge, metacognitive monitoring, and singular (coherent) versus multiple (incoherent) models of attachment: Findings and directions for future research. In C.M. Murray Parkes, J.M. Stephenson-Hinde & P. Marris (Eds) *Attachment Across the Life-Cycle*. London: Routledge.

Main, M. (1995) Recent studies in attachment. In S. Goldberg, R. Muir, & J. Kerr (Eds) *Attachment theory: Social, Developmental, and Clinical Perspectives*. Hillsdale, NJ: The Analytic Press.

Main, M. & Weston, D.R. (1981) The quality of the toddler's relationship to mother and to father: Related to conflict behaviour and the readiness to establish new relationships. *Child Development, 52*, 932–940.

Main, M., Kaplan, N. & Cassidy, J. (1985) Security in infancy, childhood and adulthood: A move to the level of representation. In I. Bretherton & E. Waters (Eds) *Growing Points of Attachment: Theory and Research*. Chicago: University of Chicago Press.

Mair, K. (1992) The myth of therapist expertise. In W. Dryden & C. Feltham (Eds) *Psychotherapy and its Discontents*. Buckingham: Open University Press.

Major, B. (1980) Information acquisition and attribution processes. *Journal of Personality & Social Psychology, 39*, 1010–1023.

Malan, D. (1976) *Toward the Validation of Dynamic Psychotherapy*. New York: Plenum.

Malan, D., Heath, E.S., Bacal, H.A. & Balfour, F.H.G. (1975) Psychodynamic changes in untreated neurotic patients. *Archives of General Psychiatry, 32*, 110–126.

Malinowski, B. (1929) *The Sexual Life of Savages*. New York: Harcourt Brace Jovanovich.

Mandler, G. (1962) Emotion. In Brown, R. (Ed.) *New Directions in Psychology*. New York: Holt, Rinehart & Winston.

Mandler, G. (1967) Organisation and memory. In K.W. Spence & J.T. Spence (Eds) *The Psychology of Learning and Motivation (Volume 1)*. New York: Academic Press.

Mandler, G. (1984a) *Mind and Body: The Psychology of Emotion and Stress*. New York: Norton.

Mandler, G. (1984b) Representation and recall in infancy. In M. Moscovitch (Ed.) *Infant Memory*. New York: Plenum Press.

Mandler, J.M. & Johnson, N.S. (1977) Remembrance of things parsed: Story structure and recall. *Cognitive Psychology, 9*, 111–151.

Mann, L. (1969) *Social Psychology*. New York: Wiley.

Manstead, A.S.R. & Semin, G.R. (1980) Social facilitation effects: Mere enhancement of dominant responses? *British Journal of Social & Clinical Psychology, 19*, 19–36.

Manthorpe, J. (1994) Life changes. *Nursing Times, 90*(18), 66–67.

Mapstone, E. (1991) Special issue on animal experimentation. *The Psychologist, 4*(5), 195.

Maquet, P., Peters, J-M., Arts, J., Delfiore, G., Degueldre, C., Luxen, A. & Franck, G. (1996) Functional neuroanatomy of human rapid-eye-movement sleep and dreaming. *Nature, 383*, 163–166.

Maranon, G. (1924) Contribution à l'etude de l'action emotive de l'adrenaline. *Revue Française d'Endocrinologie, 2*, 301–325.

Maratsos, M.P. (1983) Some current issues in the study of the acquisition of grammar. In J.H. Flavell & E.M. Markman (Eds) *Cognitive Development, Volume 3*. New York: Wiley.

Marcel, A. & Patterson, K. (1978) Word recognition and production: reciprocity in clinical and normal studies. In J. Requin (Ed.) *Attention and Performance, Volume VII*. Hillsdale, NJ.: Erlbaum.

March, P. & Doherty, C. (1999) Dying and bereavement. In D. Messer & F. Jones (Eds) *Psychology and Social Care*. London: Jessica Kingsley Publishers.

Marcia, J.E. (1966) Development and validation of ego identity status. *Journal of Personality & Social Psychology, 3*, 551–558.

Marcia, J.E. (1967) Ego identity status: Relationship to change in self-esteem, general maladjustment and authoritarianism. *Journal of Personality, 35*, 118–133.

Marcia, J.E. (1968) The case history of a construct: Ego identity status. In E. Vinacke (Ed.), *Readings in General Psychology*. New York: Van Nostrand–Reinhold.

Marcia, J.E. (1980) Identity in adolescence. In J. Adelson (Ed.) *Handbook of Adolescent Psychology*. New York: Wiley.

Marcia, J.E. (1998) Peer Gynt's life cycle. In E. Skoe & A. von der Lippe (Eds). *Personality Development in Adolescence: A Cross National and Lifespan Perspective*. London: Routledge.

Marcus, D.E. & Overton, W.F. (1978) The development of cognitive gender constancy and sex-role preferences. *Child Development, 49*, 434–444.

Marks, I.M. (1973) The reduction of fear: Towards a unifying theory. *Journal of the Canadian Psychiatric Association, 18*, 9–12.

Marks, I.M. (1978) Exposure treatments: conceptual issues. In W.S. Agras (Ed.) *Behaviour Modification*. Boston: Little Brown.

Marks, I.M. (1981) Space phobia: pseudo-agoraphobic syndrome. *Journal of Neurology, Neorosurgery & Psychiatry, 44*, 387–391.

Marks, I.M. (1987) *Fears, Phobias and Rituals: Panic, Anxiety and their Disorders*. New York: Oxford University Press.

Marks, I.M., Gelder, M. & Bancroft, J. (1970) Sexual deviants two years after electric aversion. *British Journal of Psychiatry, 117*, 173–185.

Marks, M. & Folkard, S. (1985) Diurnal rhythms in cognitive performance. In J. Nicholson & H. Beloff (Eds) *Psychology Survey 5*. Leicester: British Psychological Society.

Markus, H. (1975) The effect of mere presence on social facilitation: an unobtrusive test. *Journal of Experimental Social Psychology, 14*, 289–397.

Markus, H. (1978) The effect of mere presence on social facilitation: An unobtrusive test. *Journal of Experimental Social Psychology, 14*, 389–397.

Markus, H. & Nurius, P. (1986) Possible selves. *American Psychologist, 41*, 954–969.

Marr, D. (1976) Early processing of visual information. *Philosophical Transactions of the Royal Society of London, B275*, 483–524.

Marr, D. (1982) *Vision: A Computational Investigation into the Human Representation and Processing of Visual Information*. San Francisco, CA: W.H. Freeman.

Marr, D. & Hildreth, E. (1980) Theory of edge detection. *Proceedings of the Royal Society of London, B, 207*, 187–217.

Marr, D. & Nishihara, K.H. (1978) Representation and recognition of the spatial organisation of three-dimensional shapes. *Proceedings of the Royal Society of London, B, 200*, 269–924.

Marris, P. (1958) *Widows and their Families*. London, RKP.

Marrone, M (1998) *Attachment and Interaction*. London: Jessica Kingsley Publishers.

Marsh, P., Rosser, E., & Harré, R (1978) *The Rules of Disorder*. London: RKP.

Marshall, G. & Zimbardo, P. (1979) Affective consequences of inadequately explaining physiological arousal. *Journal of Personality & Social Psychology, 37*, 970–988.

Marsland, D. (1987) *Education and Youth*. London: Falmer.

Martin, C.L. (1991) The role of cognition in understanding gender effects. *Advances in Child Development & Behaviour, 23*, 113–149.

Martin, G. (1998) Psychology and culture: Two major paradigms. *Psychology Teaching, New Series (6)*, 21–23.

Martin, G. & Pear, J. (1992) *Behaviour Modification: What It Is and How To Do It* (4th edition). Englewood Cliffs, NJ: Prentice-Hall.

Martin, N. (1999) Autism and theory of mind research. *The Psychologist, 12*(10), 516–517.

Martin, N. (2000a) Jet lag and sleep loss. *The Psychologist, 13*(80), 414.

Martin, N. (2000b) Personality across a lifetime. *The Psychologist, 13*(6), 308–309.

Martin, P. (1999) Sleep keeps us alert and intelligent. A lack of it can spell disaster. So why aren't we getting enough? *The Sunday Times Magazine,* 17 January, 35–40.

Martin, P. (2000) Spell bound. The *Sunday Times Magazine,* 23 July, 46–53.

Marvin, R.S. (1975) Aspects of the pre-school child's changing conception of his mother. Cited in Morris, C.G. (1988) *Psychology: An Introduction* (6th edition). Englewood Cliffs, NJ: Prentice Hall.

Masheter, C. (1997) Former spouses who are friends: Three case studies. *Journal of Social & Personal Relationships, 14,* 207–222.

Maslach, C. (1978) Emotional consequences of arousal without reason. In C.E. Izard (Ed.) *Emotions and Psychopathology.* New York: Plenum Publishing Company.

Maslach. C. (1979) Negative emotional biasing of unexplained arousal. *Journal of Personality & Social Psychology, 37,* 953–969.

Maslach, C. & Jackson, S.E. (1981) The measurement of experienced burnout. *Journal of Occupational Behaviour, 2,* 99–113.

Maslach, C., Santee, R.T. & Wade, C. (1987) Individuation, gender role, and dissent: Personality mediators of situational forces. *Journal of Personality & Social Psychology, 53,* 1088–1093.

Maslach, C., Stapp, J. & Santee, R.T. (1985) Individuation: Conceptual analysis and assessment. *Journal of Personality & Social Psychology, 49,* 729–738.

Maslow, A. (1954) *Motivation and Personality.* New York: Harper & Row.

Maslow, A. (1968) *Towards a Psychology of Being* (2nd edition). New York: Van Nostrand Reinhold.

Maslow, A. (1970) *Motivation and Personality* (2nd edition). New York: Harper & Row.

Maslow, C., Yoselson, K. & London, M. (1971) Persuasiveness of confidence expressed via language and body language. *British Journal of Social & Clinical Psychology, 10,* 234–240.

Mason, M.K. (1942) Learning to speak after six and one half years of silence. *Journal of Speech & Hearing Disorders, 7,* 295–304.

Massaro, D.W. (1989) *Experiemntal Psychology: An Information Processing Approach.* New York: Harcourt Brace Jovanovich.

Masson, J. (1984) *The Assault on Truth: Freud's Suppression of the Seduction Theory.* London: Faber & Faber.

Masson, J. (1988) *Against Therapy: Emotional Tyranny and the Myth of Psychological Healing.* New York: Athaneum.

Masson, J. (1992) The tyranny of psychotherapy. In W. Dryden & C. Feltham (Eds) *Psychotherapy and its Discontents.* Buckingham: Open University Press.

Matson, J.L., Ollendick, T.H., & Adkins, J. (1980) A comprehensive dining program for mentally retarded adults. *Behaviour Research & Therapy, 18,* 107–112.

Maunsell, J.H.R. & Newsome, W.T. (1987) Visual processing in monkey extrastriate cortex. *Annual Review of Neuroscience, 10,* 363–401.

Mayer, J. (1955) Regulation of energy intake and the body weight: The glucostatic theory and the lipostatic hypothesis. *Annals of the New York Academy of Sciences, 63,* 15–43.

Mayer, J. & Marshall, N.B. (1956) Specificity of gold thioglucose for ventromedial hypothalamic lesions and obesity. *Nature, 178,* 1399–1400.

Maykovich, M.K. (1975) Correlates of racial prejudice. *Journal of Personality & Social Psychology, 32,* 1014–1020.

Maylor, E.A. (1994) Ageing and the retrieval of specialised and general knowledge: Performance of ageing masterminds. *British Journal of Psychology, 85,* 105–114.

Mazzoni, G.A.L., Loftus, E.L., Seitz, A., & Lynn, S.J. (1999) Changing beliefs and memories through dream interpretation. *Applied Cognitive Psychology, 13,* 125–144.

McArthur, L.A. (1972) The how and why of why: Some determinants and consequences of causal attribution. *Journal of Personality & Social Psychology, 22,* 171–193.

McCall, R.B. (1975) *Intelligence and Heredity.* Homewood, Illinois: Learning Systems Co.

McCall, R.B., Applebaum, M.I. & Hogarty, P.S. (1973) Developmental changes in mental test performance. Monographs for the Society of Research in *Child Development, 38,* (3, Whole No. 150).

McCann, J.J. (1987) Retinex theory and colour constancy. In R.L. Gregory (Ed.) *Oxford Companion to the Mind.* Oxford: Oxford University Press.

McCarley, R.M. (1983) REM dreams, REM sleep and their isomorphism. In M.H. Chase & E.D. Weitzman (Eds), *Sleep Disorders: Basic and Clinical Research, Volume 8* (published as book). New York: Spectrum.

McCauley, C. & Stitt, C.L. (1978) An individual and quantitative measure of stereotypes. *Journal of Personality & Social Psychology, 36,* 929–940.

McClelland, D.C. (1958) Methods of measuring human motivation. In J.W. Atkinson (Ed.) *Motives in Fantasy, Action and Society.* Princeton, NJ: Van Nostrand.

McClelland, D.C. & Atkinson, J.W. (1948) The projective expression of need: I. The effect of different intensities of the hunger drive on perception. *Journal of Psychology, 25,* 205–222.

McClelland, D.C., Atkinson, J., Clark, R. & Lowell, E. (1953) *The Achievement Motive.* New York: Appleton-Century-Croft.

McCloskey, M. & Zaragoza, M. (1985) Misleading information and memory for events: Arguments and evidence against memory impairment hypothesis. *Journal of Experimental Psychology: General, 114,* 3–18.

McCormick, L.J. & Mayer, J.D. (1991) Mood-congruent recall and natural mood. *Poster presented at the annual meeting of the New England Psychological Association, Portland, ME.*

McCrae, R.R. & Costa, P.T. (1989) More reasons to adopt the five-factor model. *American Psychologist, 44,* 451–452.

McCrae, R.R., Costa, P.T., Ostendorf, F. *et al.* (2000) Nature over nurture: Temperament, personality and lifespan development. *Journal of Personality & Social Psychology, 78,* 173–186.

McCrone, J. (1999) Left brain, right brain. *New Scientist, 163*(2193), 26–30.

McCrone, J. (2000) Rebels with a cause. *New Scientist, 165*(2222), 22–27.

McCrystal, C. (1997) Now you can live forever, or at least for a century. *The Observer,* 15 June, 3.

McDougall, W. (1908) An *Introduction to Social Psychology.* London: Methuen.

McFadden, M. & Sneddon, I. (1998) Sexuality. In K. Trew & J. Kremer (Eds) *Gender & Psychology.* London: Arnold.

McGarrigle, J. & Donalson, M. (1974) Conservation accidents. *Cognition, 3,* 341–350.

McGeoch, J.A. (1936) Studies in retroactive inhibition. VIII: Retroactive inhibition as a function of the length and frequency of the interpolated task. *Journal of Experimental Psychology, 19,* 674–693.

McGeoch, J.A. (1942) *The Psychology of Learning.* New York: Spectrum.

McGinn, C. (1987) Could a machine be conscious? In C. Blakemore & S. Greenfield (Eds), *Mindwaves.* Oxford: Blackwell.

McGinnies, E. (1949) Emotionality and perceptual defence. *Psychological Review, 56,* 244–251.

McGlone, F., Park, A. & Roberts, C. (1996) *Relative values.* Family Policy Studies Centre: BSA.

McGlone, J. (1980) Sex differences in human brain asymmetry: A critical survey. *Behaviour & Brain Sciences, 3,* 215–227.

McGlynn, F.D., Mealiea, W.L. & Landau, D.L. (1981) The current status of systematic desensitisation. *Clinical Psychology Review, 1,* 149–179.

McGuire, A.M. (1994) Helping behaviours in the natural environment: Dimensions and correlates of helping. *Personality & Social Psychology Bulletin, 20,* 45–56.

McGuire, W.J. (1968) Personality and susceptibility to social influence. In E.F. Borgatta & W.W. Lambert (Eds) *Handbook of Personality: Theory and Research.* Chicago, ILL: Rand-McNally.

McGuire, W.J. (1969) The nature of attitudes and attitude change. In G. Lindzey & E. Aronson (Eds) *Handbook of Social Psychology, Volume 3* (2nd edition). Reading, MA: Addison-Wesley.

McGurk, H. (1975) *Growing and changing.* London: Methuen.

McIlroy, A.J. (1994) Screen test for children of St. Helena. *The Daily Telegraph,* 19 September, 9.

McIlveen, R. (1995) 'Goofing off' in groups: The psychology of 'social loafing'. *Psychology Review, 1*(3), 16–18.

McKinnon, J.A. (1979) Two semantic forms: neuro-psychological and psychoanalytic descriptions. *Psychoanalysis & Contemporary Thought, 2,* 25–76.

McLeod, J. (2000) Do firefighters suffer from stress? In J. Hartley & A. Branthwaite (Eds) *The Applied Psychologist* (2nd edition). Buckingham: Open University Press.

McLeod, P., Driver, J., Dienes, Z. & Crisp, J. (1991) Filtering by movement in visual search. *Journal of Experimental Psychology: Human Perception & Performance, 17,* 55–64.

McNally, R.J. & Reiss, S. (1982) The preparedness theory of phobias and human safety-signal conditioning. *Behaviour Research & Therapy in Personality, 20,* 153–159.

McNeill, D. (1966) The creation of language. In R.C. Oldfield & J.C. Marshall (Eds), *Language.* Harmondsworth: Penguin.

McNeill, D. (1970) *The Acquisition of Language.* New York: Harper & Row.

McNeill, J.E. & Warrington, E.K. (1993) Prosopagnosia: A face-specific disorder. *Quarterly Journal of Experimental Psychology, 46A,* 1–10.

McShane, R. (2000) Calming influence or chemical cosh? *Nursing Times, 96*(3), 28–29.

Mead, G.H. (1925) The genesis of the self and social control. *International Journal of Ethics, 35,* 251–273.

Mead, G.H. (1934) *Mind, Self and Society.* Chicago: University of Chicago Press.

Mead, M. (1928) *Coming of Age in Samoa.* Harmondsworth: Penguin.

Mead, M. (1930) *Growing up in New Guinea.* Harmondsworth: Penguin.

Mead, M. (1935) *Sex and Temperament in Three Primitive Societies.* New York: Dell.

Mead, M. (1949) *Male and Female: A Study of the Sexes in a Changing World.* New York: Dell.

Meadows, S (1986) *Understanding Child Development.* London: Hutchinson.

Meadows, S. (1988) Piaget's contribution to understanding cognitive development: An assessment for the late 1980's. In K. Richardson & S. Sheldon (Eds), *Cognitive Development to Adolescence.* Hove: Lawrence Erlbaum.

Meadows, S. (1993) *The Child as Thinker: The Acquisition and Development of Cognition in Childhood.* London: Routledge.

Meadows, S. (1995) Cognitive development. In P.E. Bryant & A.M. Colman (Eds) *Developmental Psychology.* London: Longman.

Medawar, P.B. (1963) *The Art of the Soluble.* Harmondsworth: Penguin.

Meddis, R. (1975) *The Sleep Instinct.* London: RKP.

Meddis, R. (1979) The evolution and function of sleep. In D.A. Oakley & H.C. Plotkin (Eds) *Brain, Behaviour and Evolution.* London: Methuen.

Medvedev, Z.A. (1975) Ageing and longevity: New approaches and new perspectives. *The Gerontologist, 15,* 196–201.

Mee, B. (2000) We'll see you in court. *The Independent on Sunday,* 21 May, 9–12.

Meeus, W.H.J & Raaijmakers, Q.A.W. (1986) Administrative obedience: Carrying out orders to use psychological–administrative violence. *European Journal of Social Psychology, 16,* 311–324.

Megargee, E.I. (1966) Uncontrolled and overcontrolled personality types in extreme antisocial aggression. *Psychological Monographs: General and Applied* (Whole No. 611).

Megargee, E.I. & Mendelsohn, G.A. (1962) A cross validation of twelve MMPI indices of hostility and control. *Journal of Abnormal & Social Psychology, 65,* 431–438.

Mehrabian. A. (1972) Nonverbal communication. In J. Cole (Ed.) *Nebraska Symposium on Motivation, Volume 19.* Lincoln, NE: University of Nebraska Press.

Meichenbaum, D. (1976) Towards a cognitive therapy of self-control. In G. Schawrtz & D. Shapiro (Eds) *Consciousness and Self-Regulation: Advances in Research.* New York: Plenum Publishing Co.

Meichenbaum, D. (1977) *Cognitive Behaviour Modification: An Integrative Approach.* New York: Plenum.

Meichenbaum, D.H. & Goodman, J. (1971) Training impulsive children to talk to themselves: A means of developing self-control. *Journal of Abnormal Psychology, 77,* 115–126.

Meilman, P.W. (1979) Cross-sectional age changes in ego identity status during adolescence. *Developmental Psychology, 15,* 230–231.

Melhuish, E.C. (1982) Visual attention to mothers' and strangers' faces and facial contrast in one-month-olds. *Developmental Psychology, 18,* 299–333.

Melhuish, E.C. (1993) Behaviour Measures: A measure of love? An overview of the assessment of attachment. *Association of Child Psychology & Psychiatry Review & Newsletter, 15,* 269–275.

Melton, A.W. & Irwin, J.M. (1940) The influence of degree of interpolated learning on retroactive inhibition and the overt transfer of specific responses. *American Journal of Psychology, 53,* 173–203.

Melton, L. (2000) Rhythm and blues. *New Scientist, 166* (2241), 28–31.

Meltzoff, A. & Moore, M. (1977) Imitation of facial and manual gestures by human neonates. *Science, 198,* 75–78.

Meltzoff, A. & Moore, M. (1983) Newborn infants imitate adult facial gestures. *Child Development, 54,* 702–709.

Meltzoff, A. & Moore, M. (1992) Early imitation within a functional framework: The importance of person identity, movement and development. *Infant Behaviour & Development, 15,* 479–505.

Memon, A. & Wright, D.B. (1999) Eyewitness testimony and the Oklahoma bombing. *The Psychologist, 12*(6), 292–295.

Mendel, G. (1865) Versuche über Pflanzenhybriden [Experiments in plant hybridisation]. *Verhandlungen des Naturs – Forschunden Vereines in Bruenn, 4,* 3–47.

Mendel, G. (1866) Versuche über Pflanzenhybriden [Experiments in plant hybridisation]. *Verhandlungen des Naturs – Forschunden Vereines in Bruenn, 4,* 3–47.

Menninger, W.W. (Ed.) (1995) *Fear of Humiliation – Integrated Treatment of Social Phobia and Comorbid Conditions.* N.J.: Jason Aronson.

Messer, D. (1995) Seeing and pulling faces. *The Psychologist, 8,* 77.

Messer, D. (2000) Language acquisition. *The Psychologist, 13*(3), 138–143.

Meyer, J.P. & Pepper, S. (1977) Need compatibility and marital adjustment in young married couples. *Journal of Personality & Social Psychology, 35*, 331–342.

Meyer, V. & Chesser, E.S. (1970) *Behaviour Therapy in Clinical Psychiatry*. Harmondsworth: Penguin.

Middleton, W., Moylan, A., Raphael, B., Burnett, P., & Martinek, N. (1993) An international perspective on bereavement-related concepts. *Australian and New Zealand Journal of Psychiatry, 27*, 457–463.

Midgley, C. (1998) TV violence has little impact on children, study finds. *The Times*, 12 January, 5.

Miell, D. (1990) Issues in Social Psychology. In I. Roth (Ed.) *Introduction to Psychology, Volume 2*. Hove: Lawrence Erlbaum/Open University.

Mikula, G. (1994) Perspective-related differences in interpretations of injustive by victims and victimizers: A test with close relationships. In M.J. Lerner & G. Mikula (Eds) *Injustice in Close Relationships: Entitlement and the Affectional Bond*. New York: Plenum.

Milavsky, J.R., Kessler, R.C., Stipp, H. & Rubens, W.S. (1982) *Television and Aggression: A Panel Study*. New York: Academic Press.

Miles. T.R. (1967) On defining intelligence. In S. Wiseman (Ed.) *Intelligence and Ability*. Harmondsworth: Penguin.

Milgram, S. (1963) Behavioural study of obedience. *Journal of Abnormal & Social Psychology, 67*, 391–398.

Milgram, S. (1965) Liberating effects of group pressure. *Journal of Personality & Social Psychology, 1*, 127–134.

Milgram, S. (1969) The lost-letter technique. *Psychology Today, 3*(3), June, 30–33.

Milgram, S. (1974) *Obedience to Authority*. New York: Harper & Row.

Milgram, S. (1992) *The Individual in a Social World* (2nd edition). New York: McGraw-Hill.

Miller, D.T. & Ross, M. (1975) Self-serving biases in the attribution of causality: Fact or fiction? *Psychological Bulletin, 82*, 213–225.

Miller, E. & Morley, S. (1986) *Investigating Abnormal Behaviour*. London: Erlbaum.

Miller, E. & Morris, R. (1993) *The Psychology of Dementia*. Chichester: Wiley.

Miller, G.A. (1956) The magical number seven, plus or minus two: Some limits on our capacity for processing information. *Psychological Review, 63*, 81–97.

Miller, G.A. (1962) *Psychology: The Science of Mental Life*. Harmondsworth: Penguin.

Miller, G.A. (1968) *The Psychology of Communication – Seven Essays*. Harmondsworth: Penguin.

Miller, G.A. (1969) Psychology as a means of promoting human welfare. *American Psychologist, 24*, 1063–1075.

Miller, G.A. (1978) The acquisition of word meaning. *Child Development, 49*, 999–1004.

Miller, G.A. & McNeill, D. (1969) Psycholinguistics. In G. Lindzey & E. Aronson (Eds) *The Handbook of Social Psychology, Volume 3*. Reading, MA: Addison-Wesley.

Miller, G.A. & Selfridge, J.A. (1950) Verbal context and the recall of meaningful material. *American Journal of Psychology, 63*, 176–185.

Miller, I. & Norman, W. (1979) Learned helplessness in humans: A review and attribution theory model. *Psychological Bulletin, 86*, 93–118.

Miller, N.E. (1941) The frustration–aggression hypothesis. *Psychological Review, 48*, 337–342.

Miller, N.E. (1948) Theory and experiment relating psychoanalytic displacement to stimulus-response generalisation. *Journal of Abnormal & Social Psychology, 43*, 155–178.

Miller, N.E. (1978) Biofeedback and visceral learning. *Annual Review of Psychology, 29*, 373–404.

Miller, N.E. & Dicara, L.V. (1967) Instrumental learning of heart-rate changes in curarised rats: Shaping and specificity to discriminative stimulus. *Journal of Comparative & Physiological Psychology, 63*, 12–19.

Miller, W.R., Rosellini, R.A. & Seligman, M.E.P. (1977) Learned helplessness and depression. In J.D. Maser & M.E.P. Seligman (Eds) *Psychopathology: Experimental Models*. San Francisco: W.H. Freeman.

Mills, J. & Clark, M.S. (1980) 'Exchange in communal relationships.' (Unpublished manuscript.)

Milner, A.D. & Goodale, M.A. (1996) The visual brain in action, *Oxford Psychology Series, 27*. Oxford: Oxford University Press.

Milner, B. (1971) Interhemispheric differences in the localisation of psychological processes in man. *British Medical Bulletin, 27*, 272–277.

Milner, B., Corkin, S. & Teuber, H.L. (1968) Further analysis of the hippocampal amnesic syndrome: 14-year follow-up study of H.M. *Neuropsychologia, 6*, 215–234.

Minard, R.D. (1952) Race relations in the Pocohontas coalfield. *Journal of Social Issues, 8*, 29–44.

Minsky, M. (1975) A framework for representing knowledge. In P.H. Winston (Ed.), *The Psychology of Computer Vision*. New York: McGraw Hill.

Miranda, F.S.B., Caballero, R.B., Gomez, M.N.G. & Zamorano, M.A.M. (1981) Obediencia a la antoridad. *Pisquis, 2*, 212–221.

Mischel, W. (1968) *Personality and Assessment*. New York: Wiley.

Mischel, W. (1969) Continuities and change in personality. *American Psychologist, 24*, 1012–1018.

Mischel, W. (1973) Toward a cognitive social learning reconceptualisation of personality. *Psychological Review, 80*, 252–283.

Mischel, W. & Mischel, H.N. (1976) A cognitive social learning approach to morality and self-regulation. In T. Lickona (Ed.) *Moral Development and Behaviour: Theory, Research and Social Issues*. New York: Holt, Rinehart & Winston.

Mischel, W. & Shoda, Y. (1995) A cognitive–affective system theory of personality: Reconceptualising situations, dispositions, dynamics and invariance in personality structure. *Psychological Review, 102*, 246–268.

Mischel, W. & Shoda, Y. (1998) Reconciling processing dynamics and personality dispositions. *Annual Review of Psychology, 49*, 229–258.

Misselbrook, D. & Armstrong, D. (2000) How do patients respond to presentation of risk information? A survey in General Practice of willingness to accept treatment for hypertension (cited in Ogden, 2000).

Mistry, J. & Rogoff, B. (1994) Remembering in cultural context. In W.J. Lonner & R.S. Malpass (Eds) *Psychology and Culture*. Boston: Allyn & Bacon.

Mita, T.H., Dermer, M. & Knight, J. (1977) Reversed facial images and the mere exposure hypothesis. *Journal of Personality & Social Psychology, 35*, 597–601.

Mitchel, R. (1982) *Phobias*. Harmondsworth: Penguin.

Mitchell, A. (1999) Liquid genius. *New Scientist, 161*(2177), 26–30.

Mitchell, D. & Blair, J. (2000) Psychopathy. *The Psychologist, 13*(7), 356–360.

Mitchell, J. & McCarthy, H. (2000) Eating disorders. In L. Champion & M. Power (Eds) *Adult Psychological Problems: An Introduction* (2nd edition). Hove: Psychology Press.

Mitchell, J. (1974) *Psychoanalysis and Feminism*. Harmondsworth: Penguin.

Mitchell, P. (1997) *Introduction to Theory of Mind: Children, Autism and Apes*. London: Arnold.

Moddia, B. (1996) Sold short. *Nursing Times, 92*(18), 26–30.

Moerk, E.L. (1989) The LAD was a lady, and the tasks were ill-defined. *Developmental Review, 9*, 21–57.

Moerk, E.L. & Moerk, C. (1979) Quotations, imitations and generalisations: Factual and methodological analyses. *International Journal of Behaviour Development, 2*, 43–72.

Moffit, T.E. (1993) Adolescence-limited and life-course-persistent antisocial behaviour: A developmental taxonomy. *Psychological Review, 100*, 674–701.

Moghaddam, F.M. (1987) Psychology in the Three Worlds: As reflected by the crisis in social psychology and the move towards indigenous Third World Psychology. *American Psychologist, 42*, 912–920.

Moghaddam, F.M. (1998) *Social Psychology: Exploring Universals Across Cultures*. New York: W.H. Freeman & Co.

Moghaddam, F.M. & Studer, C. (1997) Cross-cultural psychology: The frustrated gadfly's promises, potentialities and failures. In D. Fox & D. Prilleltensky (Eds) *Critical Psychology: An Introduction*. London: Sage.

Moghaddam, F.M., Taylor, D.M. & Wright, S.C. (1993) *Social Psychology in Cross-cultural Perspective*. New York: W.H. Freeman & Co.

Mollon, P. (1998) *Remembering Trauma: A Psychotherapist's Guide to Memory and Illusion*. Chichester: John Wiley & Sons.

Mollon, P. (2000) *Freud and False Memory Syndrome*. Cambridge: Icon Books.

Money, J. (1971) Sexually dimorphous behaviour, normal and abnormal. In N. Kretchner & D.N. Walcher (Eds), *Environmental Influences on Genetic Expression*. Washington DC: US Government Printing Office.

Money, J. (1974) Prenatal hormones and postnatal socialisation in gender identity differentiation. In J.K. Cole & R. Dienstbier (Eds) *Nebraska Symposium on Motivation*. Lincoln: University of Nebraska Press.

Money, J. & Erhardt, A. (1972) *Man and Woman, Boy and Girl*. Baltimore, MD: The Johns Hopkins University Press.

Money, J., Hampson, J.G. & Hampson, J.L. (1957) Imprinting and the establishment of gender role. *Archives of Neurology & Psychiatry, 77*, 333–336.

Montgomery, P. (1993) Paid and unpaid work. In J. Kremer & P. Montgomery (Eds) *Women's Working Lives*. Belfast: HMSO.

Moore, C. & Frye, D. (1986) The effect of the experimenter's intention on the child's understanding of conservation. *Cognition, 22*, 283–298.

Moran, A. (2000) Improving sporting abilities: training concentration skills. In J. Hartley & A. Branthwaite (Eds) *The Applied Psychologist* (2nd edition). Buckingham: Open University Press.

Moray, N. (1959) Attention in dichotic listening: Affective cues and the influence of instructions. *Quarterly Journal of Experimental Psychology, 11*, 56–60.

Morea, P. (1990) *Personality: An Introduction to the Theories of Psychology*. Harmondsworth: Penguin.

Moreno, J.L. (1953) *Who Shall Survive?* (2nd edition). New York: Beacon.

Morgan, C. & Averill, J.R. (1992) True feelings, the self, and authenticity: A psychosocial perspective. In D.D. Franks & V. Gecas (Eds) *Social Perspectives on Emotion, Volume 1*. Greenwich, CT: JAI.

Morgan, C.D. & Murray, H.A. (1935) A method for investigating fantasies. *Archives of Neurological Psychiatry, 34*, 289–306.

Morgan, H. (2000) The new physics through a Jungian perspective. In E. Christopher & H. Solomon (Eds) *Jungian Thought in the Modern World*. London: Free Association Press.

Morgan, M.J. (1969) Estimates of length in a modified Müller–Lyer figure. *American Journal of Psychology, 82*, 380–384.

Morland, J. (1970) A comparison of race awareness in northern and southern children. In M. Goldschmid (Ed.) *Black Americans and White Racism*. Monterey, CA: Brooks/Cole.

Morris, A., Wilkinson, C., Tisi, A., Woodrow, J., & Rockley, A. (1994) *Managing the Needs of Female Prisoners*. London: Home Office.

Morris, C.D., Bransford, J.D. & Franks. J.J. (1977) Levels of processing versus transfer appropriate processing. *Journal of Verbal Learning & Verbal Behaviour, 16*, 519–533.

Morris, P.E. (1978) Models of long-term memory. In M.M. Gruneberg & P.E. Morris (Eds), *Aspects of Memory*. London: Methuen.

Morris, P.E., Tweedy, M. & Gruneberg, M.M. (1985) Interest, knowledge and the memorising of soccer scores. *British Journal of Psychology, 76*, 415–425.

Morris, R.L. (1989) Parapsychology. In A.M. Colman & J.G. Beaumont (Eds) *Psychology Survey, 7*. Leicester: British Psychological Society.

Morselli, E. (1886) Sulla dismorfofobia e sulla tafefobia. *Bolle Tino della R Accademia di Genova, 6*, 110–119.

Morton, J. (1970) A functional model for memory. In D.A. Norman (Ed.) *Models of Human Memory*. New York: Academic Press.

Moruzzi, G. & Magoun, H.W. (1949) Reticular formation and activation of the EEG. *Electroencephalography & Clinical Neurophysiology, 1*, 455–473.

Moscovici, S. (1961) *La Psychoanalyse: Son Image et Son Public*. Paris: Presses Universitaires de France.

Moscovici, S. (1976a) *La Psychoanalyse: Son Image et Son Public* (2nd edition). Paris: Presses Universitaires de France.

Moscovici, S. (1976b) *Social Influence and Social Change*. London: Academic Press.

Moscovici, S. (1980) Towards a theory of conversion behaviour. In L. Berkowitz (Ed.) *Advances in Experimental Social Psychology, 13*, 209–239.

Moscovici, S. (1981) On social representations. In J.P. Forgas (Ed.) *Social Cognition: Perspectives on Everyday Understanding*. London: Academic Press.

Moscovici, S. (1982) The coming era of representations. In J-P Codol & J.P. Leyens (Eds) *Cognitive Analysis of Social Behaviour*. The Hague: Martinus Nijhoff.

Moscovici, S. (1984) The phenomenon of social representations. In R.M. Farr & S. Moscovici (Eds) *Social Representations*. Cambridge: Cambridge University Press.

Moscovici, S. (1985) Social influence and conformity. In G. Lindzey & E. Aronson (Eds) *Handbook of Social Psychology* (3rd edition). New York: Random House.

Moscovici, S. & Faucheux, C. (1972) Social influence, conforming bias and the study of active minorities. In L. Berkowitz (Ed.) *Advances in Experimental Social Psychology, Volume 6*. New York: Academic Press.

Moscovici, S. & Hewstone, M. (1983) Social representations and social explanations: From the 'näive' to the 'amateur' scientist. In M. Hewstone (Ed.) *Attribution Theory: Social and Functional Extensions*. Oxford: Blackwell.

Moscovici, S. & Lage, E. (1976) Studies in social influence III: Majority versus minority influence in a group. *European Journal of Social Psychology, 6*, 149–174.

Moscovici, S. & Zavalloni, M. (1969) The group as a polariser of attitudes. *Journal of Personality & Social Psychology, 12*, 125–135.

Moskovitz, S. (1983) *Love Despite Hate – Child Survivors of the Holocaust and their Adult Lives*. New York: Schocken.

Moskovitz, S. (1985) Longitudinal follow-up of child survivors of the Holocaust. *American Academy of Child Psychiatry, 24,* 401–407.

Motluck, A. (1999) Jane behaving badly. *New Scientist, 164*(2214), 28–33.

Mowrer, O.H. (1947) On the dual nature of learning – a reinterpretation of 'conditioning' and 'problem-solving'. *Harvard Educational Review, 17,* 102–148.

Mowrer, O.H. (1950) *Learning Theory and Personality Dynamics.* New York: Ronald Press.

Mowrer, O.H. (1960) *Learning Theory and Behaviour.* New York: John Wiley.

Moyer, K.E. (1976) *The Psychobiology of Aggression.* New York: Harper & Row.

Much, N. (1995) Cultural psychology. In J.A. Smith, R. Harré, & L. Van Langenhove (Eds) *Rethinking Psychology.* London: Sage.

Mukerjee, M. (1997) Trends in animal research. *Scientific American, 63,* February.

Muldoon, O. & Reilly, J. (1998) Biology. In K. Trew & J. Kremer (Eds) *Gender & Psychology.* London: Arnold.

Mullen, P.E., Pathe, M., & Purcell, R. (2000) Stalking. *The Psychologist, 13*(9), 454–459.

Mullen, P.E., Pathe, M., Purcell, R., & Stuart, G. (1999) A study of stalkers. *American Journal of Psychiatry, 156,* 1244–1249.

Muller, H.J. & Maxwell, J. (1994) Perceptual integration of motion and form information: Is the movement filter involved in form discrimination? *Journal of Experimental Psychology: Human Perception & Performance, 20,* 397–420.

Mumford, D.B. & Whitehouse, A.M. (1988) Increased prevalence of bulimia nervosa among Asian schoolgirls. *British Medical Journal, 297,* 718.

Mumford, D.B., Whitehouse, A.M., & Choudry, I.Y. (1992) Survey of eating disorders in English-medium schools in Lahore, Pakistan. *International Journal of Eating Disorders, 11,* 173–184.

Mumford, D.B., Whitehouse, A.M., & Platts, M. (1991) Sociocultural correlates of eating disorders among Asian schoolgirls in Bradford. *British Journal of Psychiatry, 158,* 222–228.

Mummendey, A. (1996) Aggressive behaviour. In M. Hewstone, W. Stroebe & G.M. Stephenson (Eds) *Introduction to Social Psychology* (2nd edition). Oxford: Blackwell.

Mummendey, A. & Otten, S. (1989) Perspective specific differences in the segmentation and evaluation of aggressive interaction sequences. *European Journal of Social Psychology, 19,* 23–40.

Mundy-Castle, A.C. & Nelson, G.K. (1962) A neuropsychological study of the Kuysma forest workers. *Psychologia Africana, 9,* 240–272.

Munro, R. (2000) Cheap and cheerful. *Nursing Times, 96*(3), 16.

Munroe, R.H., Shimmin, H.S, & Munroe, R.L. (1984) Gender understanding and sex-role preference in four cultures. *Developmental Psychology, 20,* 673–682.

Munsinger, H. (1975) The adopted child's IQ: A critical review. *Psychological Bulletin, 82,* 623–659.

Murdock, B.B. (1962) The serial position effect in free recall. *Journal of Experimental Psychology, 64,* 482–488.

Murphy, G. (1947) *Personality: A Bio-social Approach to Origins and Structure.* New York: Harper & Row.

Murray, E.J. & Foote, F. (1979) The origins of fear of snakes. *Behaviour Research & Therapy in Personality, 17,* 489–493.

Murray, H.A. (1938) *Explorations in Personality.* New York: Oxford University Press.

Murray, I. (1997) Popeye phobia was no laughing matter. *The Times,* 4 August, 3.

Murray, I. & Whitworth, D. (1999) TV a threat to toddlers, doctors say. *Times,* 5 August, 1.

Murstein, B.I. (1972) Physical attractiveness and marital choice. *Journal of Personality & Social Psychology, 22,* 8–12.

Murstein, B.I. (1976) The stimulus–value–role theory of marital choice. In H. Grunebaum & J. Christ (Eds) *Contemporary Marriage: Structures, Dynamics and Therapy.* Boston: Little, Brown.

Murstein, B.I. (1978) *Exploring Intimate Lifestyles.* New York: Springer.

Murstein, B.I. (1986) *Paths to Marriage.* Beverly Hills, CA: Sage.

Murstein, B.I. (1987) A clarification and extension of the SVR theory of dyadic parting. *Journal of Marriage & The Family, 49,* 929–933.

Murstein, B.I. & MacDonald, M.G. (1983) The relation of 'exchange orientation' and 'commitment' scales to marriage adjustment. *International Journal of Psychology, 18,* 297–311.

Murstein, B.I., MacDonald, M.G. & Cereto, M. (1977) A theory of the effect of exchange orientation on marriage and friendship. *Journal of Marriage & The Family, 39,* 543–548.

Myers, D.G. (1990) *Exploring Psychology.* New York: Worth.

Myers, D.G. (1994) *Exploring Social Psychology.* New York: McGraw-Hill.

Myers, D.G. (1998) *Psychology* (5th edition). New York: Worth.

Myers, D.G. & Lamm, H. (1975) The group polarisation phenomenon. *Psychological Bulletin, 83,* 602–627.

Myers, L.B. (2000) Deceiving others or deceiving themselves? *The Psychologist, 13*(8), 400–403.

National Institute of Mental Health (1982) *Television and Behaviour: Ten Years of Scientific Progress and Implications for the Eighties, Volume 1.* Washington, DC: US Government Printing Office.

Navon, D. (1977) Forest before trees: The precedence of global features in visual perception. *Cognitive Psychology, 9,* 353–383.

Navon, D. (1984) Resources – A theoretical soup stone? *Psychological Review, 91,* 216–234.

Navon, D. & Gopher, D. (1979) On the economy of the human processing system. *Psychological Review, 86,* 214–255.

Naylor, T. (1988) What happens if the drugs really don't work? *The Independent on Sunday, Real Life,* 1 February, 3.

Neisser, U. (1964) Visual search. *Scientific American, 210,* 94–102.

Neisser, U. (1967) *Cognitive Psychology.* New York: Appleton Century Crofts.

Neisser, U. (1976) *Cognition and Reality.* San Francisco, CA: W.H. Freeman.

Neisser, U. (1979) The concept of intelligence. In R.J. Sternberg & D.K. Detterman (Eds), *Human Intelligence: Perspectives on its Theory and Measurement.* New Jersey: Norwood.

Neisser, U. (1982) *Memory Observed.* San Francisco, CA: Freeman.

Neisser, U. & Becklen, R. (1975) Selective looking: Attending to visually specified events. *Cognitive Psychology, 7,* 480–494.

Nelson, K. (1973) Structure and strategy in learning to talk. *Monographs of the Society for Research in Child Development, 38,* 149.

Nelson, K. (1977) Facilitating children's syntax acquisition. *Developmental Psychology, 13,* 101–107.

Nelson, S.A. (1980) Factors influencing young children's use of motives and outcomes as moral criteria. *Child Development, 51,* 823–829.

Nelson, T.O. & Vining, S.K. (1978) Effect of semantic versus structural processing on long-term retention. *Journal of Experimental Psychology: Human learning & memory, 4,* 198–209.

Nesselroade, J.R., Schaie, K.W. & Batter, P.B. (1972) Ontogenetic and generational components of structural and quantitative change in adult behaviour. *Journal of Gerontology, 27,* 222–228.

Neugarten, B.L. (1965) Personality and patterns of ageing. *Gawein, 13,* 249–256.

Neugarten, B.L. (1975) The future of the young-old. *The Gerontologist, 15,* 4–9.

Neugarten, B.L. & Havighurst, R.J. (1969) Disengagement reconsidered in a cross national context. In R.J. Havighurst (Ed.), *Adjustment to Retirement*. Assess, Netherlands: Van Gorcum.

Neugarten, B.L. & Neugarten, D.A. (1987) The changing meanings of age. *Psychology Today, 21*, 29–33.

Neugarten, B.L., Moore, J.W. & Lowe, J.C. (1965) Age norms, age constraints and adult socialisation. *American Journal of Sociology, 70*, 710–717.

New Scientist (1999) Desperate remedies. *New Scientist, 164*(2214), 34–36.

Newcomb, T.M. (1943) *Personality and Social Change*. New York: Holt, Rinehart & Winston.

Newcomb, T.M. (1947) Autistic hostility and social reality. *Human Relations, 1*, 69–86.

Newcomb, T.M. (1953) An approach to the study of communication. *Psychological Review, 60*, 393–404.

Newcomb, T.M. (1961) *The Acquaintanceship Process*. New York: Holt, Rinehart & Winston.

Newcomb, T.M. (1978) The acquaintance process: Looking mainly backwards. *Journal of Personality & Social Psychology, 36*, 1075–1083.

Newell, A. (1973) Production systems: Models of control structures. In W.G. Chase (Ed.), *Visual Information Processing*. New York: Academic Press.

Newell, A. & Simon, H.A. (1972) *Human Problem-Solving*. Englewood Cliffs, NJ: Prentice-Hall.

Newell, A., Shaw, J.C. & Simon, H.A. (1958) Elements of a theory of human problem-solving. *Psychological Review, 65*, 151–166.

Newman, H.H., Freeman, F.N. & Holzinger, K.J. (1937) Twins: *A Study of Heredity and the Environment*. Chicago, ILL: University of Chicago Press.

Newson, E. (1994) Video violence and the protection of children. *Psychology Review, 1*, 2–6.

Newstead, S. (1995) Language and thought: The Whorfian hypothesis. *Psychology Review, 1*, 5–7.

NFER-Nelson (1996) *British Ability Scales (BAS II)*. NFER-Nelson.

Nicholson, J. (1977) *Habits*. London: Macmillan.

Nicholson, J. (1993) *Men and Women: How Different Are They?* (2nd edition). Oxford: Oxford University Press.

Nicholson, J.M., Fergusson, D.M. & Horwood, L.J. (1999) Effects on later adjustment of living in a stepfamily during childhood and adolescence. *Journal of Child Psychology & Psychiatry, 40*(3), 405–416.

Nicolson, P. (1995) Feminism and psychology. In J.A. Smith, R. Harré, & L. Van Langenhove (Eds) *Rethinking Psychology*. London: Sage.

Nieboer, R. (1999) Bridging the gap. Letter, *The Psychologist, 12*(8), 385.

Nisbett, R.E. (1972) Hunger, obesity and the ventromedial hypothalamus. *Psychological Review, 79*, 433–453.

Nisbett, R.E. & Borgida, E. (1975) Attribution and the psychology of prediction. *Journal of Personality & Social Psychology, 32*, 923–943.

Nisbett, R.E. & Ross, L. (1980) *Human Inference: Strategies and Shortcomings of Social Judgement*. Englewood Cliffs, New Jersey: Prentice-Hall.

Nisbett, R.E. & Wilson, T. (1977) Telling more than we can know: Verbal reports on mental processes. *Psychology Review, 84*, 231–259.

Nisbett, R.E., Caputo, C., Legant, P. & Maracek, J. (1973) Behaviour as seen by the actor and as seen by the observer. *Journal of Personality & Social Psychology, 27*, 154–165.

Nolan, J. & Markham, R. (1998) The accuracy–confidence relationship in an eyewitness task: Anxiety as a modifier. *Applied Cognitive Psychology, 12*, 43–54.

Norman, D.A. (1968) Toward a thoery of memory and attention. *Psychological Review, 75*, 522–536.

Norman, D.A. (1969) Memory while shadowing. *Quarterly Journal of Experimental Psychology, 21*, 85–93.

Norman, D.A. (1976) *Memory and Attention* (2nd edition). Chichester: Wiley.

Norman, D.A. (1981) Categorisation of action slips. *Psychological Review, 88*, 1–15.

Norman, D.A. & Bobrow, D.G. (1975) On data-limited and resource-limited processes. *Cognitive Psychology, 7*, 44–64.

Norman, D.A. & Shallice, T. (1980) *Attention to Action: Willed and Automatic Control of Behaviour (CHIP Report 99)*. San Diego, California: University of California.

Norman, D.A. & Shallice, T. (1986) Attention to action: Willed and automatic control of behaviour. In R.J. Davidson, G.E. Schwartz & D. Shapiro (Eds) *The Design of Everyday Things*. New York: Doubleday.

Norton, C. (1999) Maternal instinct 'is extinct for one woman in five'. *The Independent*, 27 October, 7.

Norton, C. (2000a) Brains can fight breast cancer. *Independent on Sunday*, 16 April, 12.

Norton, C. (2000b) Rate of teenage pregnancies is highest for nearly a decade. *The Independent*, 29 March, 12.

Nursing Times (1996) *Nursing Times, 92*(5), 27.

Nursing Times (2000) Doctors fear that magazines get fat on thin images. *Nursing Times, 96*(23), 10–11.

Nuttall, N. (1996) Missing ingredient may control gluttons' appetite. *The Times*, 4 January, 3.

Nye, R.D. (2000) *Three Psychologies: Perspectives form Freud, Skinner, and Rogers* (6th edition). Belmont, CA: Wadsworth/Thomson Learning.

O'Connell, S. (2000) Pain? Don't give it another thought. *The Independent Review*, 16 June, 8.

O'Connor, N. & Hermelin, B. (1988) Low intelligence and special abilities. *Journal of Child Psychology & Psychiatry, 29*(4), 391–396.

O'Grady, M. (1977) Effects of subliminal pictorial stimulation on skin resistance. *Perceptual & Motor Skills, 44*, 1051–1056.

O'Leary, K.D. & Wilson, G.T. (1975) *Behaviour Therapy: Application and Outcome*. Englewood Cliffs, NJ: Prentice-Hall.

Oakes, P.J. & Turner, J.C. (1980) Social categorisation and intergroup behaviour: Does minimal intergroup discrimination make social identity more positive? *European Journal of Psychology, 10*, 295–301.

Oakes, P.J., Haslam, S.A. & Turner, J.C. (1994) *Stereotyping and Social Reality*. Oxford: Blackwell.

Oakhill, J.V. (1984) Why children have difficulty reasoning with three-term series problems. *British Journal of Developmental Psychology, 2*, 223–230.

Oakley, D.A. (1983) The varieties of memory: A phylogenetic approach. In A.R. Mayes (Ed.) *Memory in Humans and Animals*. Wokingham: Van Nostrand.

Oatley, K. (1981) The self with others: The person and the interpersonal context in the approaches of C.R. Rogers and R.D. Laing. In Fransella, F. (Ed.), *Personality – Theory, Measurement and Research*. London: Methuen.

Oatley, K. (1984) *Selves in Relation: An Introduction to Psychotherapy and Groups*. London: Methuen.

O'Brien, M., Huston, A.C., & Risley, T.R. (1983) Sex-typed play of toddlers in a day care centre. *Journal of Applied Developmental Psychology, 4*, 1–9.

Ochert, A. (2000) I think, therefore I die. *The Times Higher*, 31 March, 22.

Ochse, R. & Plug, C. (1986) Cross-cultural investigation of the validity of Erikson's theory of personality development. *Journal of Personality & Social Psychology. 50*, 1240–1252.

Offer, D. (1969) *The Psychological World of the Teenager*. New York: Basic Books.

Offer, D. & Offer, J.B. (1975) *From Teenage to Young Manhood: A Psychological Study*. New York: Basic Books.

Offer, D., Ostrov, E., Howard, K.I. & Atkinson, R. (1988) *The Teenage World: Adolescents' Self-Image in Ten Countries*. New York: Plenum Press.

Offer, D, Rostov, E. & Howard, K.I. (1981) *The Adolescent: A Psychological Self-portrait*. New York: Basic Books.

Ogden, J. (2000) *Health Psychobiology: A Textbook* (2nd edition). Buckingham: Open University Press.

Ogden, J., Boden, J., Caird, R. *et al.* (2000) You're depressed; No I'm not: GPs' and patients' different models of depression. *British Journal of General Practice, 49*, 123–124.

Ogg, M.A. & Hardie, E.A. (1991) Social attraction, personal attraction and self-categorisation: A field study. *Personality & Social Psychology Bulletin, 17*, 175–180.

Ohman, A., Erikkson, A. & Olofsson, C. (1975 a) One-trial learning and superior resistance to extinction of autonomic responses conditioned to potentially phobic stimuli. *Journal of Comparative & Physiological Psychology 88*, 619–627.

Ohman, A., Erixson, G. & Lofberg, L. (1975 b) Phobias and preparedness: phobic and neutral pictures as conditioned stimuli for human autonomic responses. *Journal of Abnormal Psychology, 84*, 41–45.

Okashs, A., Sadek, A., Al-Haddad, M.K., & Abdel-Mawgould, M. (1993) Diagnostic agreement in psychiatry: A comparative study between ICD-9 and DSM-III-R. *British Journal of Psychiatry, 162*, 621–626.

Olds, J. (1956) Pleasure centres in the brain. *Scientific American*, October, 105–106.

Olds, J. (1958) Self-stimulation of the brain. *Science, 127*, 315–23.

Olds, J. (1962) Hypothalmic substrates of reward. *Physiological Review, 42*, 554–604.

Olds, J. & Milner, P. (1954) Positive reinforcement produced by electrical stimulation of the septal area and other regions of the rat brain. *Journal of Comparative & Physiological Psychology 47*, 419–427.

Oleson, J. (1996) Psychological profiling: Does it actually work? *Forensic Update, 46*, 11–14.

Oliner, S.P. & Oliner, P.M. (1988) *The Altruistic Personality: Rescuers of Jews in Nazi Europe*. New York: Free Press.

Olson, J.M. & Ross, M. (1988) False feedback about placebo effectiveness: Consequences for the misattribution of speech activity. *Journal of Experimental Social Psychology, 24*, 275–291.

Olson, R.K. & Attneave, F. (1970) What variables produce similarity grouping? *American Journal of Psychology, 83*, 1–21.

Ono, T., Squire, L.R., Raichle, M.E., Perrett, D.I., & Fukuda, M. (Eds) (1993) *Brain Mechanisms of Perception and Memory: From Neurons to Behaviour*. New York: Oxford University Press.

Ora, J.P. (1965) *Characteristics of the volunteer for psychological investigation*. Office of Naval Research, Contract 2149 (03), Technical Report 27.

Orne, M.T. (1962) On the social psychology of the psychological experiment: with particular reference to demand characteristics and their implications. *American Psychologist, 17*, 776–783.

Orne, M.T. & Holland, C.C. (1968) On the ecological validity of laboratory deceptions. *International Journal of Psychiatry, 6*, 282–293.

Ornstein, R. (1975) *The Psychology of Consciousness*. Harmondsworth: Penguin.

Ornstein, R. (1986) *The Psychology of Consciousness* (2nd edition, revised). Harmondsworth: Penguin.

Osgood, C.E. (1966) Dimensionality of the semantic space for communication via facial expression. *Scandinavian Journal of Psychology, 7*, 1–30.

Osgood, C.E. & Tannenbaum, P.H. (1955) The principle of congruity in the prediction of attitude change. *Psychological Review, 62*, 42–55.

Osgood, C.E., Suci, G.J. & Tannenbaum, P.H. (1957) *The Measurement of Meaning*. Urbana, Illinois: University of Illinois Press.

Oswald, I. (1966) *Sleep*. Harmondsworth: Penguin.

Oswald, I. (1969) Human brain protein, drugs and dreams. *Nature, 223*, 893–897.

Oswald, I. (1974) *Sleep* (2nd edition). Harmondsworth: Penguin.

Oswald, I. (1980) Sleep as a restorative process: Human clues. *Progress in Brain Research, 53*, 279–288.

Owen, L. & Stoneman, C. (1972) Education and the Nature of Intelligence. In D. Rubinstein & C. Stoneman (Eds) *Education for Democracy* (2nd edition) Harmondsworth: Penguin.

Owen, W. (1990) After Hillsborough. *Nursing Times, 86*(25), 16–17.

Oxendine, J.B. (1970) Emotional arousal and motor performance. *Quest, 13*, 23–30.

Ozonoff, S., Pennington, B.F., & Rogers, S.J. (1991) Executive function deficits in high-functioning autistic children: Relationship to the theory of mind. *Journal of Child Psychology & Psychiatry, 32*, 1081–1106.

Packard, V. (1957) *The Hidden Persuaders*. New York: McKay.

Page, D.C., Mosher, R., Simpson, E.M. *et al.* (1987) The sex-determining region of the human Y chromosome encodes a finger protein. *Cell, 51*, 1091–1104.

Pagel, M. (1995) Speaking your mind. *Times Higher*, 7 July, 17–18.

Paivio, A. (1969) Mental imagery in associative learning and memory. *Psychological Review, 76*, 241–263.

Paivio, A. (1971) *Imagery and Verbal Processes*. New York: Holt, Rinehart & Winston.

Paivio, A. (1986) *Mental Representations: A Dual Coding Approach*. Oxford: Oxford University Press.

Palermo, D.S. (1971) Is a scientific revolution taking place in psychology? *Psychological Review, 76*, 241–263.

Pallanti, S., Quercioli, L. & Pazzagli, A. (1999) Effects of clozapine on awareness of illness and cognition in schizophrenia. *Psychiatry Research, 86*, 239–249.

Palmer, J.A., Honorton, C., & Utts, J. (1988) *Reply to the National Research Council Study on Parapsychology*. Research Triangle Park, NC: Parapsychological Association Inc.

Palmer, S.E. (1975) The effects of contextual scenes on the identification of objects. *Memory & Cognition, 3*, 519–526.

Palmore, E. (1977) Facts on ageing. *The Gerontologist, 17*, 315–320.

Paludi, M.A. (1992) *The Psychology of Women*. Dubuque, IA: Wm. C. Brown.

Panskepp, J. (1994) The basics of basic emotion. In P. Ekman & R.J. Davidson (Eds) *The Nature of Emotion: Fundamental Questions*. New York: Oxfored University Press.

Papez, J.W. (1937) A proposed mechanism of emotion. *Archives of Neurology & Psychiatry, 38*, 725–743.

Parfit, D. (1987) Divided minds and the nature of persons. In Blakemore, C. & Greenfield, S. (Eds) *Mindwaves*. Oxford: Blackwell.

Parke, R.D. (1978) Perspectives on father–infant interaction. In J.D. Osofsky (Ed.), *Handbook of infancy*. New York: John Wiley & Sons.

Parke, R.D. (1981) *Fathering*. London: Fontana.

Parke, R.D. & Collmer, C.W. (1975) Child abuse: An interdisciplinary analysis. In E.M. Hetherington (Ed.) *Review of*

Child Development Research, Volume 5. Chicago, ILL.: University of Chicago Press.

Parke, R.D., Berkowitz, L., Leyens, J.P., West, S.G. & Sebastian, R.J. (1977) Some effects of violent and non-violent movies on the behaviour of juvenile delinquents. In L. Berkowitz (Ed.) *Advances in Experimental Social Psychology, Volume 10*. New York: Academic Press.

Parkes, C.M. (1970) The first year of bereavement: A longitudinal study of the reaction of London widows to the death of their husbands. *Psychiatry, 33*, 444–467.

Parkes, C.M. (1975) *Bereavement – Studies of Grief in Adult Life.* Harmondsworth: Penguin.

Parkes, C.M. (1993) Bereavement as a psychosocial transition: Processes of adaptation to change. In M.S. Stroebe, W. Stroebe & R.O. Hansson (Eds) *Handbook of Bereavement: Theory, research and intervention*. New York: Cambridge University Press.

Parkes, C.M. (1995) Attachment and bereavement. In T. Lundin (Ed.) *Grief and Bereavement: Proceedings from the Fourth International Conference on Grief and Bereavement in Contemporary Society*, Stockholm, 1994. Stockholm: Swedish Association for Mental Health.

Parkes, C.M. & Weiss, R.S. (1983) *Recovery From Bereavement*. New York: Basic Books.

Parkes, C.M., Benjamin, B. & Fitzgerald, R.G. (1969) Broken heart: A statistical study of increased mortality among widowers. *British Medical Journal, 1*, 740–743.

Parkin, A.J. (1987) *Memory and Amnesia: An Introduction*. Oxford: Blackwell.

Parkin, A.J. (1993) *Memory: Phenomena, Experiment and Theory*. Oxford: Blackwell.

Parkin, A.J. (2000) *Essential Cognitive Psychology*. Hove: Psychology Press.

Parkin, A.J., Lewinson, J. & Folkard, S. (1982) The influence of emotion on immediate and delayed retention: Levinger and Clark reconsidered. *British Journal of Psychology, 73*, 389–393.

Parkinson, B. (1987) Emotion – Cognitive Approaches. In H. Beloff and A.M. Colman (Eds), *Psychology Survey, No. 6*. Leicester: British Psychological Society.

Parrott, A. (1997) Ecstatic but memory depleted? *The Psychologist, 10*, 265.

Pascual-Leone, J. (1980) Constructive problems for constructive theories: The current relevance of Piaget's work and a critique of information-processing simulation psychology. In R.H. Kluwe & H. Spads (Eds) *Developmental Models of Thinking*. New York: Academic Press.

Patel, K. (1994) Memory of Freud may be forgotten in court. *Times Higher Education Supplement*, May 20

Patterson, F.G. (1978) The gestures of a gorilla: Language acquisition in another pongid. *Brain and Language, 5*, 72–97.

Patterson, F.G. (1980) Innovative uses of language by a gorilla: A case study. In K. Nelson (Ed.), *Children's Language, Volume 2*. New York: Gardner Press.

Patterson, F.G. & Linden, E. (1981) *The Education of Koko*. New York: Holt, Rinehart & Winston.

Paul, G.L. (1966) *Insight Versus Desensitisation in Psychotherapy: An Experiment in Anxiety Reduction*. Stanford, CA: Stanford University Press.

Paul, G.L. & Lentz, R.J. (1977) *Psychosocial treatment of chronic mental patients: Milieu versus social learning programs*. Cambridge, MA.: Harvard University Press.

Paul, G.L. & Menditto, A.A. (1992) Effectiveness of inpatient treatment programs for mentally ill adults in public psychiatric facilities. *Applied & Preventative Psychology: Current Scientific Perspectives, 1*, 41–63.

Pavlov, I.P. (1927) *Conditioned Reflexes*. Oxford: Oxford University Press.

Payne, D. (2000) Shock study triggers call to ban ageist slur. *Nursing Times, 96(18)*, 13.

Pearson, P. (1998) *When She Was Bad: How Women Get Away With Murder*. London: Virago.

Peck, D. & Whitlow, D. (1975) *Approaches to Personality Theory*. London: Methuen.

Peck, R.C. (1968) Psychological developments in the second half of life. In B.L. Neugarten (Ed.) *Middle age and Ageing*. Chicago, ILL: University of Chicago Press.

Peek, L. (2000) One in six girls now reaches puberty aged 8. *The Times*, 19 June, 3.

Peele, S. (1989) *The Diseasing of America: Addiction Treatment out of control*. Lexington, MA: Lexington Books.

Penfield, W. (1947) Some observations on the cerebral cortex of man. *Proceedings of the Royal Society, 134*, 349.

Penfield, W. (1958) The role of the temporal cortex in recall of past experiences and interpretation of the present. In W. Penfield (Ed.), *Neurological Bases of Behaviour*. Boston: Little Brown.

Penfield, W. & Roberts, L. (1959) *Speech and Brain Mechanisms*. Princeton: Princeton University Press.

Penny, G. (1996) Health Psychology. In H. Coolican *Applied Psychology*. London: Hodder & Stoughton.

Penrod, S. (1983) *Social Psychology*. Englewood Cliffs, NJ: Prentice-Hall.

Penrose, R. (1987) Minds, machines and mathematics. In C. Blakemore & S. Greenfield (Eds) *Mindwaves*. Oxford: Blackwell.

Penrose, R. (1990) *The Emperor's New Mind*. Oxford: Oxford University Press.

Peplau, L.A. (1981) What homosexuals want in relationships. *Psychology Today, 15* (March), 28–38.

Peplau, L.A. (1982) Research on homosexual couples: An overview. *Journal of Homosexuality, 8*, 3–8.

Peplau, L.A. (1991) Lesbian and gay relationships. In J.C. Gonsiorek & J.D. Weinrich (Eds) *Homosexuality: Research Implications for Public Policy*. London: Sage.

Perret, D.J., May, K.A. & Yoshikawa, S. (1994) Facial shape and judgements of female attractiveness. *Nature, 368*, 239–242.

Perrin, S. & Spencer, C. (1981) Independence or conformity in the Asch experiment as a reflection of cultural and situational factors. *British Journal of Social Psychology, 20*, 205–209.

Perry, D.G. & Bussey, K. (1979) The social learning theory of sex differences: Imitation is alive and well. *Journal of Personality & Social Psychology, 37*, 1699–1712.

Perry, M. (2000) Dead men walking. *Nursing Times, 96(11)*, 29–30.

Persaud, R. (1994) Just what the doctor ordered? *The Times Higher*, 20 May, 21.

Pervin, L.A. & Lewis, M. (1978) *Perspective in Interactional Psychology*. New York: Plenum Press.

Petersen, A.C. (1988) Adolescent development. *Annual Review of Psychology, 39*, 583–607.

Petersen, A.C. & Crockett, L. (1985) Pubertal timing and grade effects on adjustment. *Journal of Youth & Adolescence, 14*, 191–206.

Petersen, A.C., Sarigiani, P.A. & Kennedy, R.E. (1991) Adolescent depression: Why more girls? *Journal of Youth & Adolescence, 20*, 247–271.

Peterson, C. & Seligman, M.E.P. (1984) Causal explanations as a risk factor for depression: Theory and evidence. *Psychological Review, 91*, 347–374.

Peterson, L.R. & Peterson, M.J. (1959) Short-term retention of individual items. *Journal of Experimental Psychology, 58*, 193–198.

Petitto, L.A. (1988) 'Language' in the prelinguistic child. In F.S. Kessell (Ed.) *The Development of Language and Language*

794

Researchers: Essays in Honour of Roger Brown. Hillsdale, NJ: Erlbaum.

Petit-Zeman, S. (2000) Mmm, guilt-free chocolate. *The Times,* 18 July, 10.

Petkova, B. (1995) New views on the self: Evil women – witchcraft or PMS? *Psychology Review, 2*(1), 16–19.

Pettigrew, T.F. (1958) Personality and sociocultural factors in intergroup attitudes: A cross-national comparison. *Journal of Conflict Resolution, 2,* 29–42.

Pettigrew, T.F. (1959) Regional difference in antinegro prejudice. *Journal of Abnormal & Social Psychology, 59,* 28–56.

Pettigrew, T.F. (1971) *Racially Separate or Together?* New York: McGraw Hill.

Pettito, L.A. & Seidenberg, M.S. (1979) On the evidence from linguistic abilities in signing apes. *Brain and Language, 8,* 162–183.

Petty, R.E. & Cacioppo, J.T. (1981) *Attitudes and Persuasion; Classic and Contemporary Approaches.* Dubuque, Iowa: Brown.

Phillips, D.P. (1986) Natural experiments on the effects of mass media violence on fatal aggression: Strengths and weaknesses of a new approach. In L. Berkowitz (Ed.) *Advances in Experimental Social Psychology,* Volume 19. New York: Academic Press.

Phillips, H. (2000) They do it with mirrors. *New Scientist, 166*(2243), 26–29.

Phillips, J.L. (1969) *The Origins of Intellect: Piaget's Theory.* San Francisco: W.H. Freeman.

Piaget, J. (1932) *The Moral Judgement of the Child.* London: Routledge & Kegan Paul.

Piaget, J. (1950) *The Psychology of Intelligence.* London: Routledge & Kegan Paul.

Piaget, J. (1951) *Play, Dreams and Imitation in Children.* London: RKP.

Piaget, J. (1952) *The Child's Conception of Number.* London: Routledge & Kegan Paul.

Piaget, J. (1963) *The Origins of Intelligence in Children.* New York: Norton.

Piaget, J. (1970) Piaget's theory. In P.H. Mussen (Ed.) Carmichael's *Manual of Child Psychology* (3rd edition), *Volume 1.* New York: Wiley.

Piaget, J. (1972) Intellectual evolution from adolescence to adulthood. *Human Development, 15,* 1–21.

Piaget, J. (1973) *The Child's Conception of the World.* London: Paladin.

Piaget, J. & Inhelder, B. (1956) *The Child's Conception of Space.* London: RKP.

Piaget, J. & Inhelder, B. (1969) *The Psychology of the Child.* London: Routledge & Kegan Paul.

Piaget, J. & Szeminska, A. (1952) *The Child's Conception of Number.* London: Routledge & Kegan Paul.

Pike, A. & Plomin, R. (1999) Genetics and development. In D. Messer & S. Millar (Eds) *Exploring Developmental Psychology: From Infancy to Adolescence.* London: Arnold.

Pike, K.L. (1954) Emic and etic standpoints for the description of behaviour. In K.L. Pike (Ed.) *Language in Relation to a Unified Theory of the Structure of Human Behaviour.* Glendale, CA: Summer Institute of Linguistics.

Pilgrim, D. (2000) Psychiatric diagnosis: More questions than answers. *The Psychologist, 13*(6), 302–305.

Piliavin, I.M., Piliavin, J.A. & Rodin, S. (1975) Costs, diffusion and the stigmatised victim. *Journal of Personality & Social Psychology, 32,* 429–438.

Piliavin, I.M., Rodin, J. & Piliavin, J.A. (1969) Good Samaritanism: An underground phenomenon? *Journal of Personality & Social Psychology, 13,* 289–299.

Piliavin, J.A. & Charng, H.W. (1990) Altruism: A review of recent theory and research. *American Sociological Review, 16,* 27–65.

Piliavin, J.A. & Piliavin, I.M. (1972) Effects of blood on reactions to a victim. *Journal of Personality & Social Psychology, 23,* 353–362.

Piliavin, J.A., Dovidio, J.F., Gaertner, S.L. & Clark, R.D. (1981) *Emergency Intervention.* New York: Academic Press.

Piliavin, J.A., Piliavin, I.M., Loewenton, E.P., McCauley, C. & Hammond, P. (1969) On observers' reproductions of dissonance effects: The right answers for the wrong reasons? *Journal of Personality & Social Psychology, 13,* 98–106.

Pine, K. (1999) Theories of cognitive development. In D. Messer & S. Millar (Eds) *Exploring Developmental Psychology: From Infancy to Adolescence.* London: Arnold.

Pinel, J.P.J. (1993) *Biopsychology* (2nd edition). Boston: Allyn & Bacon.

Pineo, P.C. (1961) Disenchantment in the later years of marriage. *Journal of Marriage & Family Living, 23,* 3–11.

Pinker, S. (1994) *The Language Instinct: How the Mind Creates Language.* New York: Morrow.

Pinker, S. (1997a) *How the Mind Works.* New York: Norton.

Pinker, S. (1997b) Why they kill their newborns. *New York Times Magazine,* 2 November, 52–54.

Piven, J. & Folstein, S. (1994) The genetics of autism. In M.L. Bauman & T.L. Kemper (Eds) *The Neurobiology of Autism.* Baltimore: John Hopkins University Press.

Place, U.T. (1956) Is consciousness a brain process? *British Journal of Psychology, 47,* 44–51

Plant, S. (1999) *Writing on Drugs.* London: Faber & Faber.

Pleck, J.H. (1999) Balancing work and family. *Scientific American Presents, 10*(2), 38–43.

Plomin, R. (1988) The nature and nurture of cognitive abilities. In R.J. Sternberg (Ed.) *Advances in the Psychology of Human Intelligence, Volume 4.* Hillsdale, NJ: Erlbaum.

Plomin, R. (1994) *Genetics and Experience: The Interplay Between Nature and Nurture.* Thousand Oaks, CA: Sage.

Plomin, R. (1995) Genetics and children's experiences in the family. *Journal of Child Psychology & Psychiatry, 36,* 33–68.

Plomin, R. (1996) Nature and nurture. In M.R. Merrens & G.C. Brannigan (Eds) *The Developmental Psychologists: Research Adventures across the Life Span.* New York: McGraw-Hill.

Plomin, R. & DeFries, J.C. (1980) Genetics and intelligence: Recent data. *Intelligence, 4,* 15–24.

Plomin, R. & DeFries, J.C. (1998) The genetics of cognitive abilities and disabilities. *Scientific American,* May, 62–69.

Plomin, R. & Loehlin, J.C. (1977) Genotype–environment interaction and correlation in the analysis of human behaviour. *Psychological Bulletin, 84,* 309–322.

Plomin, R. & Loehlin, J.C.(1989) Direct and indirect IQ heritability estimates: A puzzle. *Behavioural Genetics, 19,* 331–342

Plomin, R. & Thompson, R. (1987) Life-span developmental behavioural genetics. In P.B. Baltes, D.L. Featherman & R.M. Lerner (Eds) *Life-Span Development and Behaviour, Volume 8.* Hillsdale, NJ: Erlbaum.

Plomin, R., DeFries, J.C., & Loehlin, J.C. (1977) Genotype–environment interaction and correlation in the analysis of human behaviour. *Psychological Bulletin, 84,* 309–322.

Plotkin, H. (1995) *The Nature of Knowledge.* London: Penguin.

Plunkett, K. (1981) Psycholinguistics. In B. Gilliam (Ed.), *Psychology For Today* (2nd edition). Sevenoaks: Hodder & Stoughton.

Plutchik, R. (1980) *Emotion: A Psychobioevolutionary Synthesis.* New York: Harper & Row.

Plutchik, R. (1986) *Emotion: A psychoevolutionary synthesis.* New York: Harper & Row.

Plutchik, R. & Ax, A.F. (1967) A critique of determinants of emotional state by Schachter and Singer (1962). *Psychophysiology, 4,* 79–82.

Poggio, T. & Koch, C. (1987) Synapses that compute motion. *Scientific American, 255*, 46–92.

Pokorny, M. (1994) Appendix A: Structure of the United Kingdom Council for Psychotherapy and list of its member organisations. In P. Clarkson & M. Pokorny (Eds) *The Handbook of Psychotherapy.* London: Routledge.

Polanyi, M. (1958) *Personal Knowledge.* London: RKP.

Pollak, J.M. (1979) Obsessive–compulsive personality: A review. *Psychological Bulletin, 86*, 225–241.

Pollitt, E. & Gorman, K.S. (1994) Nutritional deficiencies as developmental risk factors. In C.A. Nelson (Ed.) *The Minnesota Symposia on Child Development, Volume 27.* Hillsdale, NJ: Erlbaum.

Pomerantz, J. & Garner, W.R. (1973) Stimulus configuration in selective attention tasks. *Perception and Psychophysics, 14*, 565–569.

Pomerantz, J. & Schwaitzberg. S.D. (1975) Grouping by proximity: Selective attention measures. *Perception & Psychophysics, 18*, 355–361.

Popper, K. (1945) *The Open Society and its Enemies.* London: RKP.

Popper, K. (1950) Indeterminism in quantum physics and in classical physics. *British Journal of Philosophy and Science, 1*, 117–133/173–195.

Popper, K. (1959) *The Logic of Scientific Discovery.* London: Hutchinson.

Popper, K. (1968) *Conjecture and Refutations: The Growth of Scientific Knowledge.* New York: Harper & Row.

Popper, K. (1972) *Objective Knowledge: An Evolutionary Approach.* Oxford: Oxford University Press.

Poskocil, A. (1977) Encounters between blacks and white liberals: The collision of stereotypes. *Social Forces, 55*, 715–727.

Posner, M.I. (1980) Orienting of attention. *Quarterly Journal of Experimental Psychology, 32*, 3–25.

Posner, M.I. & Petersen, S.E. (1990) The attention system of the human brain. *Annual Review of Neuroscience, 13*, 25–42.

Posner, M.I., Nissen, M.J. & Ogden, W.C. (1978) Attended and unattended processing modes: The role of set for spatial location. In H.L. Pick & I.J. Saltzman (Eds) *Modes of Perceiving and Processing Information.* Hillsdale, NJ: Erlbaum.

Posner, M.I., Snyder, C.R.R. & Davidson, B.J. (1980) Attention and the detection of signals. *Journal of Experimental Psychology: General, 109*, 160–174.

Postman, L., Bruner, J.S. & McGinnies, E. (1948) Personal values as selective factors in perception. *Journal of Abnormal & Social Psychology, 43*, 142–154.

Potter, J. (1996) Attitudes, social representations and discursive psychology. In M. Wetherell (Ed.) *Identities, Groups and Social Issues.* London: Sage, in association with the Open University.

Potter, J. & Wetherell, M.S. (1987) *Discourse and Social Psychology: Beyond Attitudes and Behaviour.* London: Sage.

Povinelli, D.J. (1998) ... Maybe not. *Scientific American Presents, 9*(4), 67, 72–75.

Povinelli, D.J., Nelson, K.E. & Boysen, S.T. (1990) Inferences about guessing and knowing by chimpanzees (*Pan troglodytes*). *Journal of Comparative Psychology, 104*, 203–210.

Povinelli, D.J., Nelson, K.E. & Boysen, S.T. (1992) Comprehension of role reversal in chimpanzees: Evidence of empathy? *Animal Behaviour, 43*, 633–640.

Powell, G.E. (1995) Clinical and counselling psychology. In A.M. Colman (Ed.) *Applications of Psychology.* London: Longman.

Powell, J. (2000) Drug and alcohol dependence. In L. Champion & M. Power (Eds) *Adult Psychological Problems: An Introduction* (2nd edition). Hove: Psychology Press.

Powell, R.A. & Boer, D.P. (1994) Did Freud mislead patients to confabulate memories of abuse? *Psychological Reports, 74*, 1283–1298.

Powell, S.D. (1999) Autism. In D. Messer & S. Millar (Eds) *Exploring Developmental Psychology: From Infancy to Adolescence.* London: Arnold.

Power, M. (2000) Freud and the unconscious. *The Psychologist, 13*(12), 612–614.

Pratkanis, A. & Aronson, E. (1991) *Age of Propaganda: Everyday Uses and Abuses of Persuasion.* New York: Freeman.

Pratkanis, A., Eskenazi, J., & Greenwald, A.G. (1990) What you expect is what you believe (but not necessarily what you get): On the influence of subliminal self-help audiotapes. Paper presented at Western Psychological Association, Los Angeles, CA. (April).

Premack, D. (1971) Language in chimpanzee? *Science, 172*, 808–822.

Premack, D. (1976) *Intelligence in Ape and Man.* Hillsdale, New Jersey: Lawrence Erlbaum Associates Inc.

Premack, D. & Woodruff, G. (1978) Does the chimpanzee have a theory of mind? *Behavioural & Brain Sciences, 4*, 515–526.

Prentice-Dunn, S. & Rogers, R.W. (1983) Deindividuation in aggression. In R.G. Geen & E.I. Donnerstein (Eds) *Aggression: Theoretical and Empirical Reviews, Volume 2.* New York: Academic Press.

Price, R.A. & Vandenberg, S.G. (1979) Matching for physical attractiveness in married couples. *Personality & Social Psychology Bulletin, 5*, 398–400.

Price, W.F. & Crapo, R.H. (1999) *Cross-Cultural Perspectives in Introductory Psychology* (3rd edition). Belmont, CA: Wadsworth Publishing Company.

Price-Williams, D. (1966) Cross-cultural studies. In B.M. Foss (Ed.), *New Horizons in Psychology, 1.* Harmondsworth, Middlesex: Penguin.

Prince, J. & Hartnett, O. (1993) From 'psychology constructs the female' to 'females construct psychology'. *Feminism & Psychology, 3*(2), 219–224.

Pring, L. & Hermelin, B. (1997) Naïve savant talent and acquired skill. *Autism, 1*, 199–214.

Pringle, Kellmer, M. (1986) *The Needs of Children* (3rd edition) London: Hutchinson.

Prins, H. (1995) *Offenders, Deviants or Patients?* (2nd edition). London: Routledge.

Prioleau, L., Murdock, M. & Brody, N. (1983) An analysis of psychotherapy versus placebo studies. *Behaviour & Brain Sciences, 6*, 273–310.

Putnam, H. (1975) The meaning of meaning. In H. Putnam (Ed.) *Mind, Language and Reality: Philosophical Papers of Hilary Putnam, Volume 2.* Cambridge: Cambridge University Press.

Quattrone, G.A. (1982) Overattribution and unit formation: When behaviour engulfs the person. *Journal of Personality & Social Psychology, 42*, 593–607.

Quattrone, G.A. (1986) On the perception of a group's variability. In S. Worchel & W. Austin (Eds) *The Psychology of Intergroup Relations, Volume 2.* New York: Nelson-Hall.

Quiery, N. (1998) Parenting and the family. In K. Trew & J. Kremer (Eds) *Gender & Psychology.* London: Arnold.

Quinton, D. & Rutter, M. (1988) *Parental Breakdown: The Making and Breaking of Intergenerational Links.* London: Gower.

Rabbitt, P.M.A. (1967) Ignoring irrelevant information. *American Journal of Psychology, 80*, 1–13.

Rachman, S. (1977) The conditioning theory of fear-acquisition: A critical examination. *Behaviour Research & Therapy in Personality, 15*, 375–387.

Rachman, S. (1978) *Fear and Courage.* San Francisco: W.H. Freeman.

Rachman, S. (1984) Agoraphobia – a safety signal perspective. *Behaviour Research & Therapy, 22*, 59–70.

Rachman, S. (1993) Obsessions, responsibility and guilt. *Behaviour Research & Therapy, 31*, 793–802.

Rachman, S. & Hodgson, R. (1980) *Obsessions and Compulsions*. New York: Prentice Hall.

Rachman, S. & Wilson, G. (1980) *The Effects of Psychological Therapy*. Oxford: Pergamon.

Radford, J. (1980) Intelligence. In J. Radford & E. Govier (Eds) *A Textbook of Psychology*. London: Sheldon Press.

Rafal, R.D. & Posner, M.,I. (1987) Deficits in human visual spatial attention following thalamic lesions. *Proceedings of the National Academy of Sciences, 84*, 7349–7353.

Raichle, M.E. (1994) Visualising the mind. *Scientific American, 269*, 36–42.

Rainey, N. (1998) Old age. In K. Trew & J. Kremer (Eds) *Gender & Psychology*. London: Arnold.

Ramachandran, V.S (1998) The Unbearable Likeness of Being. *The Independent on Sunday*, 22 November, 22–24.

Ramachandron, V.S. & Anstis, S.M. (1986) The perception of apparent motion. *Scientific American, 254*, 80–87.

Ramachandran, V.S & Blakeslee, S. (1998) *Phantoms in the Brain*. London: Fourth Estate.

Ramey, C.T. & Ramey, S. (1992) Effective early intervention. *Mental Retardation, 30*, 337–345.

Ramsay, R. & de Groot, W. (1977) A further look at bereavement. Paper presented at EATI conference, Uppsala. Cited in P.E. Hodgkinson (1980) Treating abnormal grief in the bereaved. *Nursing Times*, 17 January, 126–128.

Rank, S.G. & Jacobson, C.K. (1977) Hospital nurses' compliance with medication overdose orders: a failure to replicate. *Journal of Health & Social Behaviour, 18*, 188–193.

Rao, K.R. & Palmer, J. (1987) The anomaly called psi: Recent research and criticism. *Behaviour & Brain Sciences, 10*, 539–643.

Raphael, B. (1984) *The Anatomy of Bereavement*. London: Hutchinson.

Rassool, G.H. & Winnington, J. (1993) Using psychoactive drugs. *Nursing Times, 89*, 38–40.

Rathus, S.A. (1984) *Psychology* (3rd edition). London: Holt, Reinhart & Winston.

Rathus, S.A. (1990) *Psychology* (4th edition). New York: Holt, Rinehart & Winston.

Rayment, T. (2000) The innocent outcast. *The Sunday Times Magazine*, 18 June, 31–36.

Reason, J. (1979) Actions not as planned: The price of automatisation. In G. Underwood & R. Stevens (Eds) *Aspects of Consciousness: Volume 1, Psychological Issues*. London: Academic Press.

Reason, J. (1984) Absent-mindedness. In J. Nicholson & H. Beloff (Eds) *Psychology Survey 5*. Leicester: British Psychological Society.

Reason, J. (1992) Cognitive underspecification: Its variety and consequences. In B.J. Baars (Ed.) *Experimental Slips and Human Error: Exploring the Architecture of Volition*. New York: Plenum Press.

Reason, J. (2000) The Freudian slip revisited. *The Psychologist, 13*(12) 610–611.

Reason, J. & Mycielska, K. (1982) *Absentmindedness: The Psychology of Mental Lapses and Everyday Errors*. Englewood Cliffs, NJ: Prentice-Hall.

Reason, P. & Rowan, J. (Eds.,1981) *Human Inquiry: A Sourcebook of New Paradigm Research*. Chichester: Wiley.

Reber, A.S. (1985) *The Penguin Dictionary of Psychology*. Harmondsworth: Penguin.

Rebok, G.W. (1987) *Life Span Cognitive Development*. New York: Holt, Rinehart, Winston.

Rechtschaffen, A. & Kales, A. (1968) A manual of standardised terminology, techniques, and scoring system for sleep stages of human subjects. *National Institute of Health Publication 204*. Washington, DC: US Government Printing Office.

Rechtschaffen, A., Bergmann, B.M., Everson, C.A., Kushida, C.A. & Gilliland, M.A. (1989b) Sleep deprivation in the rat: X. Integration and discussion of the findings. *Sleep, 12*, 68–87.

Rechtschaffen, A., Bergmann, B.M., Everson, C.A., Kushida, C.A. & Gilliland, M.A. (1989a) Sleep deprivation in the rat: 1. Conceptual issues. *Sleep, 12*, 1–4.

Rechtschaffen, A., Gilliland, M., Bergmann, B. & Winter, J. (1983) Physiological correlates of prolonged sleep deprivation in rats. *Science, 221*, 182–184.

Reedy, M.N. (1983) Personality and ageing. In D.S. Woodruff & J.E. Birren (Eds) *Ageing: Scientific Perspectives and Social Issues* (2nd edition). Monterey, CA: Brooks/Cole.

Rees, M.I., Fenton, I., Williams, N.M. *et al.* (1999) Autosome search for schizophrenia susceptibility genes in multiply affected families. *Molecular Psychiatry, 4*, 353–359.

Regan, D.T. & Totten, J. (1975) Empathy and attribution: Turning observers into actors. *Journal of Personality & Social Psychology, 32*, 850–856.

Reich, B. & Adcock, C. (1976) *Values, Attitudes and Behaviour Change*. London: Methuen.

Reisenzein, R. (1983) The Schachter theory of emotion: Two decades later. *Psychological Bulletin, 94*, 239–264.

Rescorla, R.A. (1967) Pavlovian conditioning and its proper control procedures. *Psychological Review, 74*, 71–80.

Rescorla, R.A. (1968) Probability of shock in the presence and absence of CS in fear conditioning. *Journal of Comparative & Physiological Psychology 66*, 1–5.

Resnick, L., Levine, J. & Teasley, S. (Eds) (1991) Perspectives on socially shared cognition. Washington, DC: American Psychological Association.

Ressler, R.K., Burgess, A.W., & Douglas, J. (1988) *Sexual Homicide: Patterns and Motives*. Lexington: Lexington Books.

Rest, J. (1983) Morality. In J.H. Flavell & E. Markman (Eds) *Handbook of Child Psychology, Volume 3*. New York: Wiley.

Rest, J., Turiel, E. & Kohlberg, L. (1969) Level of moral development as a determinant of preference and comprehension of moral judgement made by others. *Journal of Personality, 37*, 225–252.

Restle, F. (1957) Discrimination of cues in mazes: A resolution of the 'place versus response' question. *Psychological Review, 64*, 217–228.

Restle, F. (1974) Critique of pure memory. In R. Solso (Ed.), *Theories in Cognitive Psychology: The Loyola Symposium*. New York: Wiley.

Reyner, L.A. & Horne, J.A. (2000) Early morning driven sleepiness: Effectiveness of 200mg caffeine. *Psychophysiology, 37*, 251–256.

Reynolds, M. & Brewin, C. (1997) A comparison of intrusive autobiographical memories in depression and post-traumatic stress disorder. Manuscript submitted for publication.

Rheingold, H.L. (1961) The effect of environmental stimulation upon social and exploratory behaviour in the human infant. In B.M. Foss (Ed.) *Determinants of Infant Behaviour, Volume 1*. London: Methuen.

Rheingold, H.L. (1969) The effect of a strange environment on the behaviour of infants. In B.M. Foss (Ed.), *Determinants of Infant Behaviour, Volume 4*. London: Methuen.

Rheingold, H.L. & Eckerman, C.O. (1973) Fear of a stranger – a critical examination. In H.W. Reese (Ed.), *Advances in Child Development and Behaviour, Volume 8*. New York: Academic Press.

Rice, M. (1989) Children's language acquisition. *American Psychologist, 44*, 149–156.

Richards, A. & Wolpert, L. (1997) The insiders' story. *Independent on Sunday Review,* 27 September, 44–45.

Richards, G. (1996a) Arsenic and old race. *Observer Review,* 5 May, 4.

Richards, G. (1996b) *Putting Psychology in its Place.* London: Routledge.

Richards, M.P.M. (1995) The International Year of the Family – family research. *The Psychologist, 8,* 17–20.

Richardson, J.T.E. (1974) Imagery and free recall. *Journal of Verbal Learning & Verbal Behaviour, 13,* 709–713.

Richardson, K. (1991) *Understanding Intelligence.* Milton Keynes: Open University Press.

Riegel, K.F. (1976) The dialectics of human development. *American Psychologist, 31,* 689–700.

Riesen, A.H. (1947) The development of visual perception in man and chimpanzee. *Science, 106,* 107–108.

Riesen, A.H. (1965) Effects of early deprivation of photic stimulation. In S. Oster & R. Cook (Eds), *The Biosocial Basis of Mental Retardation.* Baltimore: Johns Hopkins University Press.

Riley, V. (1981) Neuroendocrine influences on immunity and neoplasia. *Science, 211,* 1100–1109.

Ringen, J. (1996) The behaviour therapist's dilemma: Reflections on autonomy, informed consent, and scientific psychology. In W. O'Donohue & R.F. Kitchener (Eds) *The Philosophy of Psychology.* London: Sage Publications.

Rips, L.J., Shoben, E.H. & Smith, E.E. (1973) Semantic distance and the verification of semantic relations. *Journal of Verbal Learning & Verbal Behaviour, 12,* 1–20.

Rivers, W.H.R. (1901) Vision. In A.C. Haddon (Ed.) *Reports of the Cambridge Anthropological Expedition to the Torres Straits, Volume 2, Part 1.* Cambridge: Cambridge University Press.

Rivers, W.H.R. (1906) *The Todas.* New York: Macmillan.

Roberts, B.W., & DelVecchio, W.F. (2000) The rank-order consistency of personality traits from childhood to old age: A quantitative review of longitudinal studies. *Psychological Bulletin, 126,* 3–25.

Roberts, R. & Newton, P.M. (1987) Levinsonian studies of women's adult development. *Psychology & Ageing, 39,* 165–174.

Robertson, J. & Robertson, J. (1971) Young children in brief separation: A fresh look. *Psychoanalytic Study of the Child, 26,* 264–315

Robertson, J. & Robertson J. (1967–73) *Film Series, Young Children in Brief Separation: No 3 (1969): John, 17 months, 9 days in a Residential Nursery.* London: Tavistock.

Robinson, J.O. (1972) *The Psychology of Visual Illusions.* London: Hutchinson.

Robinson, K. (2000) Big women, the battle is over at last. The *Independent on Sunday,* 14 November, 3.

Robinson, L. (1997) Black adolescent identity and the inadequacies of western psychology. In J. Roche & S. Tucker (Eds) *Youth in Society.* London: Sage.

Rock, I. (1983) *The Logic of Perception.* Cambridge, MA: MIT Press.

Rock, I. (1984) *Perception.* New York: W.H. Freeman.

Rodin, D.I. & Nelson, R.D. (1989) Evidence for Consciousness-Related Anomalies in Random Physical Systems. *Foundations of Physics, 19*(12), 1499–1514.

Rodin, J., Silberstein, L.R., & Striegel-Moore, R.H. (1985) Women and weight: A normative discontent. In T.B. Sonderegger (Ed.) *Nebraska Symposium on Motivation: Volume 32, Psychology and Gender.* Lincoln: University of Nebraska Press.

Rogers, C.R. (1942) *Counselling and Psychotherapy: Newer Concepts in Practice.* Boston: Houghton Mifflin.

Rogers. C.R. (1951) *Client-centred Therapy – Its Current Practices, Implications and Theory.* Boston: Houghton Mifflin.

Rogers, C.R. (1959) A theory of therapy, personality and interpersonal relationships as developed in the client-centred framework. In S. Koch (Ed.) *Psychology: A Study of Science, Volume III, Formulations of the Person and the Social Context.* New York: McGraw-Hill.

Rogers, C.R. (1961) *On Becoming a Person.* Boston: Houghton Mifflin.

Rogers, C.R. (1969) *Freedom to Learn: A View of What Education Might Become.* Columbus, OH: Charles E. Merrill.

Rogers, C.R. (1970) *Encounter Groups.* New York: Harper & Row.

Rogers, C.R. (1983) *Freedom to Learn in the '80s.* Columbus, OH: Charles Merrill.

Rogers, J., Meyer, J. & Mortel, K. (1990) After reaching retirement age physical activity sustains cerebral perfusion and cognition. *Journal of the American Geriatric Society, 38,* 123–128.

Rogers, L., Resnick, M.D., Mitchell, J.E. & Blum, R.W. (1997) The relationship between socioeconomic status and eating-disordered behaviours in a community sample of adolescent girls. *International Journal of Eating Disorders, 22,* 15–23.

Rogoff, B. (1990) *Apprenticeship in Thinking: Cognitive Development in Social Context.* New York: Oxford University Press.

Rogoff B. & Morelli, G. (1989) Perspectives on children's development from cultural psychology. *American Psychologist, 44,* 343–348.

Rokeach, M. (1948) Generalised mental rigidity as a factor in ethnocentrism. *Journal of Abnormal & Social Psychology, 43,* 254–278.

Rokeach, M. (1960) *The Open and Closed Mind.* New York: Basic Books.

Rokeach, M. (1968) *Beliefs, Attitudes and Values.* San Francisco: Jossey-Bass.

Roker, D., Player, K. & Coleman, J. (1998) Exploring adolescent altruism: British young people's involvement in voluntary work and campaigning. In M. Yates & J. Youniss (Eds) *Community Service and Civil Engagement in Youth: International Perspectives.* Cambridge: Cambridge University Press.

Rollman, G.B. (1998) Culture and pain. In S.S. Kazarian & D.R. Evans (Eds) *Cultural Clinical Psychology: Theory, Research, and Practice.* New York: Oxford University Press.

Rolls, B.J., Wood, R., Rolls, E.T., Lind, H., & Ledingham, J.G. (1980) Thirst following water deprivation in humans. *American Journal of Physiology, 239,* 476–482.

Rolls, E.T. & Rolls, B.J. (1982) Brain mechanisms involved in feeding. In L.M. Barker (Ed.) *The Psychobiology of Human Food Selection.* Westport, CT: AVI Publishing Company.

Rorer, L.G. (1998) Attacking arrant nonsense forthrightly. *Contemporary Psychology, 43,* 597–600.

Rosch, E. (1973) Natural categories. *Cognitive Psychology, 4,* 328–350.

Rose, H. (2000) Colonising the social sciences? In H. Rose & S. Rose (Eds) *Alas, Poor Darwin: Arguments Against Evolutionary Psychology.* London: Jonathan Cape.

Rose, M. & Fletcher, G.J.O.(1985) Attribution and social perception. In G. Lindzey & E. Aronson (Eds) *Handbook of Social Psychology,* Volume 2 (3rd edition). New York: Random House.

Rose, P. & Platzer. H. (1993) Confronting prejudice. *Nursing Times, 89*(31), 52–54.

Rose, S. (1976) *The Conscious Brain.* Harmondsworth: Penguin.

Rose, S. (1992) *The Making of Memory: From Molecule to Mind.* London: Bantam Books.

Rose, S. (1997) *Lifelines: Biology, Freedom, Determinism.* Harmondsworth: Penguin.

Rose, S. (2000) Escaping evolutionary psychology. In H. Rose & S. Rose (Eds) *Alas, Poor Darwin: Arguments Against Evolutionary Psychology.* London: Jonathan Cape.

Rose, S., Lewontin, R.C., & Kamin, L.J. (1984) *Not in our Genes: Biology, Ideology and Human Nature.* Harmondsworth: Penguin.

Rose, S.A. & Blank, M. (1974) The potency of context in children's cognition: an illustration through conservation. *Child Development, 45,* 499–502.

Rosen, B. (1980) Moral dilemmas and their treatment. In B. Munsey (Ed.) *Moral Development, Moral Education and Kohlberg.* Birmingham, Alabama: Religious Education Press.

Rosenberg, M. (1965) *Society and the Adolescent Self-image.* Princeton, New Jersey: Princeton University Press.

Rosenberg, M.J. & Hovland, C.I. (1960) Cognitive, affective, and behavioural components of attitude. In M.J. Rosenberg, C.I. Hovland, W.J. McGuire, R.P. Abelson & J.W. Brehm (Eds) *Attitude Organisation and Change: An Analysis of Consistency Among Attitude Components.* New Haven, CT: Yale University Press.

Rosenblatt, P.C. (1993) The social context of private feelings. In M.S. Stroebe, W. Stroebe & R.O. Hansson (Eds) *Handbook of Bereavement: Theory, Research and Intervention.* New York: Cambridge University Press.

Rosenblum, L.A. & Harlow, H.F. (1963) Approach–avoidance conflict in the mother surrogate situation. *Psychological Reports, 12,* 83–85.

Rosenhan, D.L. (1973) On being sane in insane places. *Science, 179,* 365–369.

Rosenhan, D.L. & Seligman, M.E. (1984) *Abnormal Psychology.* New York: Norton.

Rosenman, R.H., Brand, R.J., Jenkins, C.D., Friedman, M., Strauss, R. & Wurm, M. (1975) Coronary heart disease in the Western Collaborative Group Study. *Journal of the American Medical Association, 233,* 872–877.

Rosenman, R.H., Friedman, M., Straus, R., Wurm, M., Kositichek, R., Hahn, W. & Werthessen, N.T. (1964) A predictive study of coronary heart disease. *Journal of the American Medical Association, 189,* 103–110.

Rosenthal, A.M. (1964) *Thirty-Eight Witnesses.* New York: McGraw-Hill.

Rosenthal, D., Wender, P.H., Kety, S.S. & Welner, J. (1971) The adopted-away offspring of schizophrenics. *American Journal of Psychiatry, 128,* 307–311.

Rosenthal, R. (1966) *Experimenter Effects in Behavioural Research.* New York: Appleton-Century-Crofts.

Rosenthal, R. & Fode, K.L. (1963) The effects of experimenter bias on the performance of the albino rat. *Behavioural Science, 8,* 183–189.

Rosenthal, R. & Jacobson. L. (1968) *Pygmalion in the Classroom: Teacher Expectation and Pupils' Intellectual Development.* New York: Holt.

Rosenthal, R. & Lawson, R. (1964) A longitudinal study of the effects of experimenter bias on the operant learning of laboratory rats. *Journal of Psychiatric Research, 2,* 61–72.

Rosenthal, R. & Rosnow, R.L. (1966a) *The Volunteer Subject.* New York: Wiley.

Rosenthal, R. & Rosnow, R.L. (1966b) Volunteer subjects and the results of opinion change studies. *Psychological Reports, 19,* 1183.

Rosnow, I. (1985) Status and role change through the life cycle. In R.H. Binstock & E. Shanas (Eds) *Handbook of Ageing and the Social Sciences* (2nd edition). New York: Van Nostrand Reinhold.

Rosnow, R.L. & Rosenthal, R. (1997) *People Studying People: Artifacts and Ethics in Behavioural Research.* New York: W.H. Freeman.

Ross, L. (1977) The intuitive psychologist and his shortcomings. In L. Berkowitz (Ed.) *Advances in Experimental Social Psychology, Volume 10.* New York: Academic Press.

Ross, L. & Nisbett, R.E. (1991) *The Person and the Situation: Perspectives of Social psychology.* New York: McGraw-Hill.

Roth, I. (1986) An introduction to object perception. In I. Roth & J.P. Frisby (Eds) *Perception and Representation.* Milton Keynes: Open University Press.

Roth, I. (1995) Object recognition. In I. Roth & V. Bruce (Eds) *Perception and Representation: Current Issues* (2nd edition). Buckingham: Open University Press.

Rothbart, M., Evans, M. & Fulero, S. (1979) Recall for confirming events: Memory processes and the maintenance of social stereotyping. *Journal of Experimental Social Psychology, 15,* 343–355.

Rotter, J. (1966) Generalised expectancies for internal versus external control of reinforcement. *Psychological Monographs, 30*(1), 1–26.

Rotter, J., Seerman, M. & Liverant, S. (1962) Internal versus external locus of control of reinforcement: A major variable in behaviour theory. In N.F. Washburne (Ed.), *Decisions, Values and Groups.* New York: Pergamon Press.

Roussea, J.J. (1762) *Emile* (republished 1955). New York: Dutton, Everyman's Library.

Rowan, A.N. (1997) The benefits and ethics of animal research. *Scientific American,* 64–66, February.

Rowan, J. (1978) *The Structured Crowd.* London: Davis Poynter.

Royal College of Psychiatrists (1987) *Drug scenes: A report on drugs and drug dependence by the Royal College of Psychiatrists.* London: Gaskell.

Rubin, E. (1915) *Synsoplevede Figurer.* Kobenhaun: Gyldendalske Boghandel.

Rubin, J.Z., Provenzano, F.J. & Luria, Z. (1974) The eye of the beholder: Parents' views on sex of newborns. *American Journal of Orthopsychiatry, 44,* 512–519.

Rubin, Z. (1973) *Liking and Loving.* New York: Holt, Rinehart & Winston.

Rubin, Z. & McNeil, E.B. (1983) *The Psychology of Being Human* (3rd edition). London: Harper & Row.

Rubinstein, J.L. & Howes, C. (1979) Caregiving and infant behaviour in day care and in homes. *Developmental Psychology, 15,* 1–24.

Ruble, D.N. (1984) Sex-role development. In M.C. Bornstein & M.E. Lamb (Eds) *Developmental Psychology: An Advanced Text.* Hillsdale, NJ: Erlbaum.

Rubovits, P.C. & Maehr, M.L. (1973) Pygmalion in black and white. *Journal of Personality & Social Psychology, 25,* 210–218.

Ruch, J.C. (1984) *Psychology: The Personal Science.* Belmont, CA: Wadsworth Publishing Co.

Rufford, N. (2000) Genes will make us live for 1,200 years. *The Sunday Times,* 25 June, 9.

Rumbaugh, D.M. & Savage-Rumbaugh, S. (1994) *Language and Apes.* APA Psychology teacher Network.

Rumbaugh, D.M., Gill, T.V. & Glaserfeld, E. (1973) Reading and sentence completion by a chimpanzee. *Science, 182,* 731–733.

Rumbaugh, D.M., Warner, H. & Von Glaserfeld, E. (1977) The Lana project: Origin and tactics. In D.M. Rumbaugh (Ed.) *Language Learning by a Chimpanzee: The LANA Project.* New York: Academic Press

Rumelhart, D.E. (1975) Notes on a schema for stories. In D.G. Bobrow & A. Collins (Eds), *Representation and Understanding: Studies in Cognitive Science.* New York: Academic Press.

Rumelhart, D.E. & Norman, D.A. (1983) Representation in memory. In R.C. Atkinson, R.J. Herrstein, B. Lindzey & R.D. Luce (Eds), *Handbook of Experimental Psychology.* Chichester: Wiley.

Rumelhart, D.E. & Norman, D.A. (1985) Representation of knowledge. In M.M. Aitkenhead & J.M. Slack (Eds), *Issues in Cognitive Modelling.* London: Lawrence Erlbaum Associates Ltd.

Rumelhart, D.E., Hinton, G.E. & McClelland, J.L. (1986) A general framework for parallel distributed processing. In D. Rumelhart, J.L. McClelland & the PDP Research Group (Eds), *Parallel Distributed Processing: Volume 1.* Foundations. Cambridge, Massachusetts: MIT Press.

Runciman, W.G. (1966) *Relative Deprivation and Social Justice*. London: Routledge & Kegan Paul.

Rushton, J.P. (1980) *Altruism, Socialisation and Society*. Englewood Cliffs, New Jersey: Prentice Hall.

Rushton, J.P. (1995) *Race, Evolution and Behaviour*. New Brunswick, NJ: Transaction Publishers.

Rushton, W.A.H. (1987) Colour vision: Eye mechanism. In R. Gregory (Ed.), *The Oxford Companion to the Mind*. Oxford: Oxford University Press.

Russell, G.F.M. (1979) Bulimia nervosa: an ominous variant of anorexia nervosa. *Psychological Medicine, 9,* 429–448.

Russell, J. (1984) *Explaining Mental Life: Some Philosophical Issues in Psychology*. London: Macmillan Press.

Russell, J., Saltmarsh, R., & Hill, E. (1999) What do executive factors contribute to the failure on false belief tasks by children with autism? *Journal of Child Psychology & Psychiatry, 40*(6), 859–868.

Rutter, M. (1981) *Maternal Deprivation Reassessed* (2nd edition). Harmondsworth: Penguin.

Rutter, M. (1989) Pathways from childhood to adult life. *Journal of Child Psychology & Psychiatry, 30,* 23–25.

Rutter, M. (and the English and Romanian Adopteer (ERA) study team) (1998) Developmental catch-up, and deficit following adoption after severe global early privation. *Journal of Child Psychology & Psychiatry, 39*(4), 465–476.

Rutter, M. & Rutter, M. (1992) *Developing Minds: Challenge and Continuity across the Life Span*. Harmondsworth: Penguin.

Rutter, M. & Yule, W. (1975) The concept of specific reading retardation. *Journal of Child Psychology & Psychiatry, 16,* 181–197.

Rutter, M., Graham, P., Chadwick, D.F.D. & Yule, W. (1976) Adolescent turmoil: Fact or fiction? *Journal of Child Psychology & Psychiatry, 17,* 35–56.

Rutter, M., Silberg, J., O'Connor, T., & Siminoff, E. (1999) Genetics and child psychiatry, II: Empirical research findings. *Journal of Child Psychology & Psychiatry, 40*(1), 19–55.

Ryan, J. (1972) IQ – the illusion of objectivity. In K. Richardson & D. Spears (Eds), *Race, Culture and Intelligence*. Harmondsworth: Penguin.

Ryan, R.M. & Lynch, J.H. (1989) Emotional autonomy versus detachment: revisiting the vicissitudes of adolescence and young adulthood. *Child Development, 60,* 340–356.

Rycroft, C. (1966) Introduction: Causes and Meaning. In C. Rycroft (Ed.) *Psychoanalysis Observed*. London: Constable & Co. Ltd.

Ryder, R. (1990) Open reply to Jeffrey Gray. *The Psychologist, 3,* 403.

Ryder, R. (1991) Sentientism: A comment on Gray and Singer. *The Psychologist,* May, 201.

Ryle, G. (1949) *The Concept of Mind*. London: Hutchinson.

Sachs, J. & Truswell, L. (1976) Comprehension of two-word instructions by children in the one-word stage. *Journal of Child Language, 5,* 17–24.

Sackheim, H.A. (1982) Hemispheric asymmetry in the expression of positive and negative emotions. *Archives of Neurology, 39,* 210–218.

Sackeim, H.A. (1989) The efficacy of electroconvulsive therapy in the treatment of major depressive disorder. In S. Fisher & R.P. Greenberg (Eds) *The Limits of Biological Treatments for Psychological Distress: Comparisons with Therapy and Placebo*. Hillsdale, NJ.: Lawrence Erlbaum.

Sacks, O. (1985) *The Man who Mistook his Wife for a Hat and Other Clinical Tales*. New York: Summit Books.

Sacks, O. (1995) *An Anthropologist on Mars*. London: Picador.

Sacks, O. (1998) Foreword. In V.S. Ramachandran & S. Blakeslee, *Phantoms in the Brain*. London: Fourth Estate.

Saegert, S.C., Swap, W. & Zajonc, R.B. (1973) Exposure context and interpersonal attraction. *Journal of Personality & Social Psychology, 25,* 234–242.

Salamé, P. & Baddeley, A.D. (1982) Disruption of short-term memory by unattended speech: Implications for the structure of working memory. *Journal of Verbal Learning & Verbal Behaviour, 21,* 150–164.

Salapatek, P. (1975) Pattern perception in early infancy. In L.B. Cohen & P. Salapatek (Eds) *Infant Perception: From Sensation to Cognition, Volume 1. Basic Visual Processes*. London: Academic Press.

Salkovskis, P.M. (1985) Obsessional–compulsive problems: A cognitive–behavioural analysis. *Behaviour Research & Therapy, 23,* 571–583.

Salkovskis, P.M., Forrester, E., & Richards, C. (1998) Cognitive–behavioural approach to understanding obsessional thinking. *British Journal of Psychiatry (Supplement 35),* 53–63.

Salkovskis, P.M., Westbrook, D., Davis, J., Jeavons, A. & Gledhill, A. (1997) Effects of neutralising on intrusive thoughts: An experiment investigating the etiology of obsessive–compulsive disorder. *Behaviour Research & Therapy, 35,* 211–219.

Salomon, G. (Ed.) (1997) *Distributed Cognitions: Psychological and Educational Considerations*. Cambridge: Cambridge University Press.

Samuel, J. & Bryant, P. (1984) Asking only one question in the conservation experiment. *Journal of Child Psychology & Psychiatry, 25,* 315–318.

Sanders, G.S., Baron, R.S., & Moore, D.L. (1978) Distraction and social competence as mediators of social facilitation. *Journal of Experimental Social Psychology,, 14,* 291–303.

Sanford, R.N. (1937) The effects of abstinence from food upon imaginal processes. A further experiment. *Journal of Psychology, 3,* 145–159.

Sangiuliano, I. (1978) *In Her Time*. New York: Morrow.

Santrock, J.W. (1986) *Psychology: The Science of Mind and Behaviour*. Dubuque, IA: William C. Brown.

Sapir, E. (1929) The study of linguistics as a science. *Language, 5,* 207–214.

Sarbin, T.R. & Mancuso, J.C. (1980) *Schizophrenia: Medical Diagnosis or Moral Verdict?* New York: Pergamon.

Sartorius, N., Kaelber, C.T. & Cooper, J.E. (1993) Progress toward achieving a common language in psychiatry. Results from the field trials accompanying the clinical guidelines of mental and behavioural disorders in ICD-10. *Archives of General Psychiatry, 50,* 115–124.

Savage, R., & Armstrong, D. (1990) Effect of a general practitioner's consulting style on patients' satisfaction: a controlled study. *British Medical Journal, 301,* 968–970.

Savage-Rumbaugh, E.S. (1990) Language as a cause-effect communication system. *Philosophical Psychology, 3,* 55–76.

Savage-Rumbaugh, E.S., Murphy, J., Seveik, R.A., Williams, S., Brakke, K. & Rumbaugh, D.M. (1993) Language comprehension in ape and child. *Monographs of the Society for Research in Child Development, 58,* 3–4.

Savage-Rumbaugh, E.S., Rumbaugh, D.M. & Boysen, S.L. (1978) Symbolic communication between two chimpanzees (Pan troglodytes). *Science, 201,* 641–644.

Savage-Rumbaugh, E.S., Rumbaugh, D.M. & Boysen, S.L. (1980) Do apes use language? *American Scientist, 68,* 49–61.

Savickas, M.L. (1995) Work and adjustment. In D. Wedding (Ed.) *Behaviour and Medicine* (2nd edition). St Louis, MO: Mosby-Year Book.

Savin, H.B. (1973) Professors and psychological researchers: conflicting values in conflicting roles. *Cognition, 2*(1), 147–149.

Sawyer, L. (1996) … Or An Abomination? *Nursing Times, 92*(5), 28.

Sayers, J. (1982) *Biological Politics: Feminist and Anti-feminist Perspectives*. London: Tavistock.

Scarr, S. (1984) *Mother Care/Other Care*. New York: Basic Books.

Scarr, S. (1992) Developmental theories for the 1990s: Development and individual differences. *Child Development, 63,* 1–19.

Scarr, S. (1998) American child care today. *American Psychologist, 53*(2), 95–108.

Scarr, S. & Carter-Saltzman, L. (1979) Twin method: Defence of a critical assumption. *Behavioural Genetics, 9,* 527–542.

Scarr, S. & Thompson, W. (1994) Effects of maternal employment and nonmaternal infant care on development at two and four years. *Early Development & Parenting, 3*(2), 113–123.

Scarr, S. & Weinberg, R.A. (1976) IQ test performance of black children adopted by white families. *American Psychologist, 31,* 726–739.

Scarr, S. & Weinberg, R.A. (1978) The influence of 'family background' on intellectual attainment. *American Sociological Review, 43,* 674–692.

Scarr, S. & Weinberg, R.A. (1983) The Minnesota adoption studies – genetic difference and malleability. *Child Development, 54,* 260–267.

Scarr-Salapatek, S. (1971) Social class and IQ. *Science, 174,* 28–36.

Scarr-Salapatek, S. (1976) An evolutionary perspective on infant intelligence – species patterns and individual variations. In M. Lewis (Ed.), *Origins of Intelligence*. New York: Plenum.

Schachter, D.L. (1986) Amnesia and crime. *American Psychologist, 41,* 186–195.

Schachter, J. (1957) Pain, fear, and anger in hypertensives and normotensives: A psychophysiologic study. *Psychosomatic Medicine, 19,* 17–29.

Schachter, S. (1951) Deviation, rejection and communication. *Journal of Abnormal & Social Psychology, 46,* 190–207.

Schachter, S. (1959) *The Psychology of Affiliation: Experimental Studies of the Sources of Gregariousness*. Stanford, CA: Stanford University Press.

Schachter, S. (1964) The interaction of cognitive and physiological determinants of emotional state. In L. Berkowitz (Ed.) *Advances in Experimental Social Psychology, Volume 1*. New York: Academic Press.

Schachter, S. (1971) *Emotion, Obesity and Crime*. New York: Academic Press.

Schachter, S. & Singer, J.E. (1962) Cognitive, social and physiological determinants of emotional state. *Psychological Review, 69,* 379–399.

Schachter, S. & Wheeler, L. (1962) Epinephrine, chlorpromazine and amusement. *Journal of Abnormal & Social Psychology, 65,* 121–128.

Schachter, S., Goldman, R., & Gordon, A. (1968) The effects of fear, food deprivation, and obesity on eating. *Journal of Personality & Social Psychology, 10,* 107–116.

Schaffer, D.R. (1985) *Developmental Psychology – Theory, Research and Applications*. Monterey, CA: Brooks Cole Publishers.

Schaffer, H.R. (1966) The onset of fear of strangers and the incongruity hypothesis. *Journal of Child Psychology & Psychiatry, 7,* 95–106.

Schaffer, H.R. (1971) *The Growth of Sociability*. Harmondsworth: Penguin.

Schaffer, H.R. (1996a) *Social Development*. Oxford: Blackwell.

Schaffer, H.R. (1996b) Is the child father to the man? *Psychology Review, 2*(3), 2–5.

Schaffer, H.R. (1977) *Mothering*. London: Fontana/Open Books.

Schaffer, H.R. (1989) In A. Slater & G. Bremner (Eds) *Infant Development*. Hove & London: Lawrence Erlbaum.

Schaffer, H.R. (1998) Deprivation and its effects on children. *Psychology Review, 5*(2), 2–5.

Schaffer, H.R. & Emerson, P.E. (1964) The development of social attachments in infancy. *Monographs of the Society for Research in Child Development, 29* (Whole No. 3).

Schaffer, L.H. (1975) Multiple attention in continuous verbal tasks. In P.M.A. Rabbitt and S. Dormi (Eds), *Attention and Performance, Volume 5*. London: Academic Press.

Schaie, K.W. & Hertzog, C. (1983) Fourteen-year cohort-sequential analysis of adult intellectual development. *Developmental Psychology, 19,* 531–543.

Schaie, K.W. & Labouvie-Vief, G. (1974) Generational versus autogenetic components of change in adult cognitive behaviour: A fourteen year cross-sequential study. *Developmental Psychology, 101,* 305–320.

Schaie, K.W. & Strother, C.R. (1968) The effect of time and cohort differences upon age changes in cognitive behaviour. *Multivariate Behaviour Research, 3,* 259–294.

Schank, R.C. (1975) *Conceptual Information Processing*. Amsterdam: North-Holland.

Schank, R.C. (1982) *Dynamic Memory*. New York: Cambridge University Press.

Schank, R.C. & Abelson, R.P. (1977) *Scripts, Plans, Goals and Understanding*. Hillsdale, New Jersey: Lawrence Erlbaum Associates Inc.

Scheer, S.D. & Unger, D.G. (1995) Parents' perceptions of their adolescence – implications for parent–youth conflict and family satisfaction. *Psychological Reports, 76*(1), 131–136.

Scheerer, M. (1963) Problem solving. *Scientific American, 208*(4), 118–128.

Scheff, T.J. (1966) *Being Mentally Ill: A Sociological Theory*. Chicago: Aldine Press.

Scherer, K.R. (1994) Toward a Concept of 'Modal Emotions'. In P. Ekman & R. J. Davidson (Eds) *The Nature of Emotion: Fundamental Questions*. New York: Oxford University Press.

Schiff, N., Duyme, M., Dumaret, A., Stewart, J., Tomkiewicz, S. & Feingold, J. (1978) Intellectual status of working-class children adopted early into upper-middle-class families. *Science, 200,* 1503–1504.

Schiffman, R. & Wicklund, R.A. (1992) The minimal group paradigm and its minimal psychology. *Theory & Psychology, 2,* 29–50.

Schifter, D.E. & Ajzen, I. (1985) Intention, perceived control and weight loss: An application of the theory of planned behaviour. *Journal of Personality & Social Psychology, 49,* 843–851.

Schlenker, B.R. (1980) *Impression Management*. Monterey, CA: Brooks/Cole.

Schlenker, B.R. (1982) Translating action into attitudes: an identity-analytic approach to the explanation of social conduct. In L. Berkowitz (Ed.) *Advances in Experimental Social Psychology, (Volume 15)*. New York: Academic Press.

Schlitz, M.J. & Honorton, C. (1992) Ganzfeld psi performance within an artistically gifted population. *Journal of the American Society for Psychical Research, 86,* 83–98.

Schlosberg, H.S. (1941) A scale for the judgement of facial expression. *Journal of Experimental Psychology, 29,* 497–510.

Schlossberg, N.K. (1984) Exploring the adult years. In A.M. Rogers & C.J. Scheirer (Eds) *The G. Stanley Hall Lecture Series (Volume 4)*. Washington, DC: American Psychological Association.

Schlossberg, N.K., Troll, L.E. & Leibowitz, Z. (1978) *Perspectives on Counselling Adults: Issues and Skills*. Monterey, CA: Brooks/Cole.

Schmidt, H. (1969) Precognition of a quantum process. *Journal of Parapsychology, 33,* 99–108.

Schmiedler, G.R. (1997) Psi-conducive experimenters and psi-permissive ones. *European Journal of Parapsychology, 13,* 83–94.

Schmitt, B.H., Gilovich, T., Goore, N., & Joseph, L. (1986) Mere presence and socio-facilitation: one more time. *Journal of Experimental Social Psychology, 22,* 242–248.

Schneider, D.J. (1995) Attribution and Social Cognition. In M. Argyle & A.M. Colman (Eds) *Social Psychology.* London: Longman

Schneider, K. (1959) *Clinical Psychopathology.* New York: Grune & Stratton.

Schneider, W. & Fisk, A.D. (1982) Degree of consistent training: Improvements in search performance and automatic process development. *Perception & Psychophysics, 31,* 160–168.

Schneider, W. & Shiffrin, R.M. (1977) Controlled and automatic human information processing: I. Detection, search and attention. *Psychological Review, 84,* 1–66.

Schroeder, D.A., Penner, L.A., Dovidio, J.F. & Piliavin, J.A. (1995) *The Psychology of Helping and Altruism: Problems and Puzzles.* New York: McGraw-Hill.

Schroth, M. (1995) A comparison of sensation-seeking among different groups of athletes and non-athletes. *Personality & Individual Differences, 18,* 219–223.

Schuchter, S.R. & Zisook, S. (1993) The course of normal grief. In M.S. Stroebe, W. Stroebe & R.O. Hansson (Eds) *Handbook of Bereavement: Theory, Research and Intervention.* New York: Cambridge University Press.

Schueller, G.H. (2000a) Hey! Good looking. *New Scientist, 166*(2243), 30–34.

Schueller, G.H. (2000b) Thrill or chill. *New Scientist, 166*(2236), 20–24.

Schulman, A. (1974) Memory for words recently classified. *Memory and Cognition, 2,* 47–52.

Schurz, G. (1985) Experimentelle Überprufung des Zusammenhangs zwischen Persönlichkeitsmerkmalen und der Bereitschaft der destruktiven Gehorsam gegenüber Autoritaten. *Zeitschrift für Experimentelle und Augewandte Psychologie, 32,* 160–177.

Schwartz, G.E., Weinberger, D.A. & Singer, J.A. (1981) Cardiovascular differentiation of happiness, sadness, anger, and fear following imagery and exercise. *Psychosomatic Medicine, 43,* 343–364.

Scodel, A. (1957) Heterosexual somatic preference and fantasy dependence. *Journal of Consulting Psychology, 21,* 371–374.

Scollon, R. (1976) *Conversations With a One-Year-Old.* Honolulu: University of Hawaii Press.

Scott, C. (1987) Paranormal phenomena: The problem of proof. In R.L Gregory (Ed.) *The Oxford Companion to the Mind.* Oxford: Oxford University Press.

Scroth, M. (1995) A comparison of sensation-seeking among different groups of athletes and non-athletes. *Personality & Individual Differences, 18,* 219–223.

Searle, J.R. (1980) Minds, brains and programs. *The Behaviour & Brain Sciences, 3,* 417–457.

Searle, J.R. (1987) Minds and brains without programs. In C. Blakemore and S. Greenfield (Eds), *Mindwaves.* Oxford: Blackwell.

Sears, R.R., Maccoby, E.E. & Levin, H. (1957) *Patterns of Child Rearing.* New York: Harper & Row.

Secord, P.F. & Backman, C.W. (1964) *Social Psychology.* New York: McGraw Hill.

Segal, M.W. (1974) Alphabet and attraction: An unobtrusive measure of the effect of propinquity in the field setting. *Journal of Personality & Social Psychology, 30,* 654–657.

Segall, M.H. (1994) A cross-cultural research contribution to unravelling the nativist–empiricist controversy. In W.J. Lonner & R.S. Malpass (Eds) *Psychology and Culture.* Boston: Allyn & Bacon.

Segall, M.H., Campbell, D.T. & Herskovits, M.J. (1963) Cultural differences in the perception of geometrical illusions. *Science, 139,* 769–771.

Segall, M.H., Campbell, D.T. & Herskovits, M.J. (1966) *The Influence of Culture on Visual Perception.* Indianapolis: Bobbs-Merrill.

Segall, M.H., Dasen, P.R., Berry, J.W. & Poortinga, Y.H. (1990) *Human Behaviour in Global Perspective: An Introduction to Cross-Cultural Psychology.* New York: Pergamon.

Segall, M.H., Dasen, P.R., Berry, J.W., & Poortinga, Y.H. (1999) *Human Behaviour in Global Perspective: An Introduction to Cross-Cultural Psychology* (2nd edition). Needham Heights, MA: Allyn & Bacon.

Seidenberg, M.S. & Petitto, L.A. (1987) Communication, symbolic communications and language: Comment on Savage-Rumbaugh, McDonald, Sevcik, Hopkins and Rupert (1986). *Journal of Experimental Psychology: General, 116,* 279–287.

Selfridge, O.G. (1959) Pandemonium: A paradigm for learning. *Symposium on the Mechanisation of Thought Processes.* London: HMSO.

Selfridge, O.G. & Neisser, U. (1960) Pattern recognition by machine. *Scientific American, 203,* 60–8.

Seligman, M.E.P. (1970) On the generality of the laws of learning. *Psychology Review, 77,* 406–418.

Seligman, M.E.P. (1971) Phobias and preparedness. *Behaviour Therapy, 2,* 307–320.

Seligman, M.E.P. (1972) *Biological Boundaries of Learning.* New York: Academic Press.

Seligman, M.E.P. (1973) Fall into hopelessness. *Psychology Today, 7,* 43–47.

Seligman, M.E.P. (1974) Depression and learned helplessness. In R.J. Friedman & M.M. Katz (Eds) *The Psychology of Depression: Contemporary Theory and Research.* Washington, D.C: Winston-Wiley.

Seligman, M.E.P. (1975) *Helplessness: On Depression, Development and Death.* San Francisco: W.H. Freeman.

Seligman, M.E.P. (1992) Wednesday's children. *Psychology Today, 25,* 61.

Seligman, M.E.P. & Csikszentmihalyi, M. (2000) Positive psychology: An introduction. *American Psychologist, 55,* 5–14.

Seligman, M.E.P. & Maier, S.F. (1967) Failure to escape traumatic shock. *Journal of Experimental Psychology, 74,* 1–9.

Seligman, M.E.P., Maier, S.F. & Solomon, R.L. (1971) Unpredictable and uncontrollable aversive events. In F.R. Brush (Ed.), *Aversive Conditioning and Learning.* New York: Academic Press.

Seligmann, J., Rogers, P., & Annin, P. (1994) The pressure to lose. *Newsweek, 123,* 60–61.

Sellen, A.J. & Norman, D.A. (1992) The psychology of slips. In B.J. Baars (Ed.) *Experimental Slips and Human Error: Exploring the Architecture of Volition.* New York: Plenum Press.

Selye, H. (1936) A syndrome produced by diverse nocuous agents. *Nature, 138,* 32.

Selye, H. (1956) *The Stress of Life.* New York: McGraw-Hill.

Selye, H. (1976) *The Stress of Life* (revised edition). New York: McGraw-Hill.

Selye, H. (1980) The stress concept today. In I.L. Kutash (Ed.) *Handbook on Stress and Anxiety.* San Francisco: Jossey-Bass.

Senatore, V., Matson, J.L & Kazdin, A.E. (1982) A comparison of behavioural methods to teach social skills to mentally retarded adults. *Behaviour Therapy, 13,* 313–324.

Sergent, J. (1984) An investigation into component and configurational processes underlying face recognition. *British Journal of Psychology, 75,* 221–242.

Serpell, R.S. (1976) *Culture's Influence on Perception.* London: Methuen.

Serpell, R. S. (1979) How specific are perceptual skills? A cross-cultural study of pattern reproduction. *British Journal of Psychology, 70,* 365–380.

Serpell, R. S. (1994) The cultural construction of intelligence. In W.J. Lonner & R.S. Malpass (Eds) *Psychology and Culture*. Boston: Allyn & Bacon.

Seymour, J. (1995) Counting the cost. *Nursing Times 91*(22), 24–27.

Seymour, J. (1996) Beastly dilemmas. *Nursing Times, 92*(5), 24–26.

Shackleton, V.J. & Fletcher, C.A. (1984) *Individual Differences – Theories and Applications*. London: Methuen.

Shaffer, H.J., Stein, S.A., Gambino, B., & Cummings, T.N. (Eds) (1989) *Compulsive Gambling: Theory, Research and Practice*. Lexington, MA: Lexington Books.

Shaffer, L.H. (1975) Multiple attention in continuous verbal tasks. In P.M.A. Rabbitt & S. Dornic (Eds) *Attention and Performance (Volume V)*. London: Academic Press

Shafran, R. (1999) Obsessive compulsive disorder. *The Psychologist, 12*(12), 588–591.

Shafran, R. & Salkovskis, P. (1999) The safe hands of Dr. Freud? Letter, *The Psychologist, 12*(10), 487.

Shah, A. & Frith, U. (1983) An islet of ability in autistic children: a research note. *Journal of Child Psychology & Psychiatry, 24*, 613–620.

Shah, A. & Frith, U. (1993) Why do autistic individuals show superior performance on the Block Design test? *Journal of Child Psychology & Psychiatry, 34*, 1351–1364.

Shallice, T. (1982) Specific impairments of planning. *Philosophical Transactions of the Royal Society of London, 13298*, 199–209.

Shallice, T. & Warrington, E.K. (1970) Independent functioning of verbal memory stores: A neurophysiological study. *Quarterly Journal of Experimental Psychology, 22*, 261–273.

Shanab, M.E. & Yahya, K.A. (1978) A cross-cultural study of obedience. *Bulletin of the Psychonomic Society, 11*, 267–269.

Shapiro, C.M., Bortz, R., Mitchell, D., Bartel, P. & Jooste, P. (1981) Slow-wave sleep: A recovery period after exercise. *Science, 214*, 1253–1254.

Shapiro, D.A. & Shapiro, D. (1982) Meta-analysis of comparative therapy outcome studies: A replication and refinement. *Psychological Bulletin, 92*, 581–604.

Shatz, M. (1994) *A Toddler's Life: Becoming a Person*. New York: Oxford University Press.

Shatz, M. & Gelman, R. (1973) The development of communication skills: Modification in the speech of young children as a function of the listener. *Monographs of the Society for Research in Child Development, 38*, No.152.

Shavitt, S. (1990) The role of attitude objects in attitude functions. *Journal of Experimental Social Psychology, 26*, 124–128.

Shea, J.D. (1985) Studies of cognitive development in Papua New Guinea. *International Journal of Psychology, 20*, 33–61.

Sheehy, G. (1976) *Passages – Predictable Crises of Adult Life*. New York: Bantam Books.

Sheehy, G. (1996) *New Passages*. New York: HarperCollins.

Sheeran, P., Abraham, C., & Orbell, S. (1999) Psychological correlates of heterosexual condom use: a meta-analysis. *Psychological Bulletin, 125*, 90–132.

Sheridan, C.L. & King, R.G. (1972) Obedience to authority with an authentic victim. *Proceedings of the 80th Annual Convention, American Psychological Association, 7*(1), 165–166.

Sherif, M. (1935) A study of social factors in perception. *Archives of Psychology, 27*, Whole No. 187.

Sherif, M. (1936) *The Psychology of Social Norms*. New York: Harper & Row.

Sherif, M. (1966) *Group Conflict and Co-operation: Their Social Psychology*. London: RKP.

Sherif, M., Harvey, O.J., White, B.J., Hood, W.R. & Sherif, C.W. (1961) *Intergroup Conflict and Co-operation: The Robber's Cave Experiment*. Norman, OK: University of Oklahoma Press.

Sherif, M. & Hovland, C.I. (1961) *Social Judgement: Assimilation and Contrast in Communication and Attitude Change*. New Haven, Connecticut: Yale University Press.

Sherif, M. & Sherif, C. (1969) *Social Psychology*. New York: Harper & Row.

Sherrington, C.S. (1900) Experiments on the value of vascular and visceral factors for the genesis of emotion. *Proceedings of the Royal Society, 66*, 390–403.

Sherrington, C.S. (1906) *The Integrative Action of the Nervous System*. London: Constable.

Shields, J. (1962) *Monozygotic Twins Brought Up Apart and Brought Up Together*. London: Oxford University Press.

Shields, J. (1976) Heredity and environment. In H.J. Eysenck & G.D. Wilson (Eds), *Textbook of Human Psychology*. Lancaster: MTP.

Shields, J. (1978) Genetics. In J.K. Wing (Ed.), *Schizophrenia – Towards a New Synthesis*. London: Academic Press.

Shiffrin, R.M. & Schneider, W. (1977) Controlled and automatic human information processing: II. Perceptual learning, automatic attending and a general theory. *Psychological Review, 84*, 127–190.

Shortliffe, E.H. (1976) *Computer-Based Medical Consultations: MYCIN*. New York: American Elsevier.

Shotland, R.L. & Straw, M.K. (1976) Bystander response to an assault: When a man attacks a woman. *Journal of Personality & Social Psychology, 34*, 990–999.

Shotter, J. (1975) *Images of Man in Psychological Research*. London: Methuen.

Showalter, E. (1998) Sex, lies and therapy. *The Independent on Sunday, Section 2*, 5 April, 5.

Shuey, A. (1966) *The Testing of Negro Intelligence*. New York: Social Science Press.

Shulman, H.G. (1970) Encoding and retention of semantic and phonemic information in short-term memory. *Journal of Verbal Learning & Verbal Behaviour, 9*, 499–508.

Shulman, P. (2000) Design for living. *Scientific American Presents: The Quest to Beat Ageing, 11*(2), 18–21.

Shuren, J.E., Brott, T.G., Schefft, B.K., & Houston, W. (1996) Preserved colour imagery in an achromatopsic. *Neuropsychologia, 34*, 485–589.

Shweder, R.A. (1990) Cultural psychology: What is it? In J.W. Stigler, R.A. Shweder & G. Herdt (Eds) *Cultural Psychology*. Cambridge: Cambridge University Press.

Shweder, R.A. (1991) *Thinking Through Cultures: Expeditions in Cultural Psychology*. Cambridge, MA: Harvard University Press.

Shweder, R.A., Mahapatra, M. & Miller, J.G. (1987) Culture and moral development. In J. Kagan & S. Lamb (Eds) *The Emergence of Morality in Young Children*. Chicago: University of Chicago Press.

Siann, G. (1985) *Accounting for Aggression – Perspectives on Aggression and Violence*. London: Allen & Unwin.

Siddique, C.M. & D'Arcy, C. (1984) Adolescence, stress and psychological well-being. *Journal of Youth & Adolescence, 13*, 459–474.

Siegler, R.S. (1976) Three aspects of cognitive development. *Cognitive Psychology, 4*, 481–520.

Siegler, R.S. (1989) How domain-general and domain-specific knowledge interact to produce strategy choices. *Merrill-Palmer Quarterly, 35*, 1–26.

Siffre, M. (1975) Six months alone in a cave. *National Geographic*, March, 426–435.

Sigall, H. & Landy, D. (1973) Radiating beauty: Effects of having a physically attractive partner on person perception. *Journal of Personality & Social Psychology, 28*, 218–224.

Sigall, H. & Ostrove, N. (1975) Beautiful but dangerous: Effects of offender attractiveness and nature of crime on juridic judgement. *Journal of Personality & Social Psychology, 31*, 410–414.

Silva, P.A., McGee, R., & Williams, S. (1985) Some characteristics of 9-year-old-boys with general reading backwardness or specific reading retardation. *Journal of Child Psychology & Psychiatry, 26*, 407–421.

Silverman, I. (1971) Physical attractiveness and courtship. *Sexual Behaviour*, September, 22–25.

Simeon, D., Hollander, E., Stein, D.J., Cohen, L. & Aronowitz, B. (1995) Body dysmorphic disorder in the DSM-IV field trial for obessive–compulsive disorder. *American Journal of Psychiatry, 152*, 1207–1209.

Simmons, J.Q. & Lovaas, O.I. (1969) Use of pain and punishment as treatment techniques with childhood schizophrenia. *American Journal of Psychotherapy, 23*, 23–26.

Simmons, R. & Rosenberg, S. (1975) Sex, sex roles and self-image. *Journal of Youth & Adolescence, 4*, 229–256.

Simmons, R.G. & Blyth, D.A. (1987) *Moving into Adolescence: The Impact of Pubertal Change and School Context.* New York: Aldine de Gruyter.

Simon, H.A. (1979) Information-processing theory of human problem solving. In W. Estes (Ed.), *Handbook of Learning and Cognitive Processes, Volume 5.* Hillsdale, NJ: Lawrence Erlbaum Associates Inc.

Simons, R.L. (1996) The effects of divorce on adult and child adjustment. In R.L. Simons (Ed.) *Understanding Differences Between Divorced and Intact Families: Stress, Interaction, and Child Outcomes.* Thousand Oaks, CA: Sage.

Simpson, J.A., Campbell, B., & Berscheid, E. (1986) The association between romantic love and marriage: Kephart (1967) twice revisited. *Personality & Social Psychology Bulletin, 12*, 363–372.

Simpson, M. (2000) Creative life in a scientific world. In E. Christopher & H. McF. Solomon (Eds) *Jungian Thought in the Modern World.* London: Free Association Books.

Sims, A.C.P. & Gray, P. (1993) The media, violence and vulnerable viewers. Document presented to the Broadcasting Group, House of Lords.

Sinclair-de-Zwart, H. (1969) Developmental Psycholinguistics. In D. Elkind & J. Flavell (Eds) *Handbook of Learning and Cognitive Processes, Volume 5.* Hillsdale, NJ: Erlbaum.

Singer, D. (1989) Children, adolescents and television – 1989. *Paediatrics, 83*, 445–446.

Singer, J.E., Brush, C.A. & Liblin, J.C. (1965) Some aspects of deindividuation: Identification and conformity. *Journal of Experimental Social Psychology, 1*, 356–378.

Singer, W. (1998) Consciousness from a neurobiological perspective. In S. Rose (Ed.) *From Brains to Consciousness?: Essays on the New Sciences of the Mind.* Harmondsworth: Penguin.

Singh, D. (1993) Adaptive significance of female attractiveness: The role of waist to hip ratio. *Journal of Personality & Social Psychology, 65*, 293–307.

Sinha, D. (1997) Indigenising psychology. In J.W. Berry, Y.H. Poortinga & J. Pandey (Eds) *Handbook of Cross-cultural Psychology* (2nd edition), *Volume 1.* Boston: Allyn & Bacon.

Sistrunk, F. & McDavid, J.W. (1971) Sex variable in conforming behaviour. *Journal of Personality & Social Psychology, 2*, 200–207.

Skeels, H.M. (1966) Adult status of children with contrasting early life experiences. *Monographs of the Society for Research in Child Development, 31*, (Whole No. 3).

Skeels, H.M. & Dye, H.B. (1939) A study of the effects of differential stimulation on mentally retarded children. *Proceedings of the American Association of Mental Deficiency, 44*, 114–136.

Skinner, B.F. (1938) *The Behaviour of Organisms.* New York: Appleton-Century-Crofts.

Skinner, B.F. (1948a) Superstition in the pigeon. *Journal of Experimental Psychology, 38*, 168–172.

Skinner, B.F. (1948b) *Walden Two.* New York: Macmillan.

Skinner, B.F. (1950) Are theories of learning necessary? *Psychological Review, 57*, 193–216.

Skinner, B.F. (1953) *Science and Human Behaviour.* New York: Macmillan.

Skinner, B.F. (1957) *Verbal Behaviour.* New York: Appleton-Century-Crofts.

Skinner, B.F. (1958) Teaching machines. *Science, 128*, 969–977.

Skinner, B.F. (1971) *Beyond Freedom and Dignity.* New York: Knopf.

Skinner, B.F. (1974) *About Behaviourism.* New York: Alfred Knopf.

Skinner, B.F. (1985) 'Cognitive science and behaviourism.' (Unpublished manuscript. Harvard University.)

Skinner, B.F. (1987) Skinner on behaviourism. In R.L. Gregory (Ed.) *The Oxford Companion to the Mind.* Oxford: Oxford University Press.

Skinner, B.F. (1990) Can psychology be a science of mind? *American Psychologist, 45*, 1206–1210.

Skodak, M. & Skeels, H. (1949) A final follow-up study of 100 adopted children. *Journal of Genetic Psychology, 75*, 85–125.

Skriver, J. (1996) Naturalistic decision-making. *The Psychologist, 9*, 321–322.

Skuse, D. (1984) Extreme deprivation in early childhood, I: Diverse outcome for three siblings from an extraordinary family. *Journal of Child Psychology & Psychiatry, 25*(4), 523–541.

Skuse, D. (1984) Extreme deprivation in early childhood II: Theoretical issues and a comparative review. *Journal of Child Psychology & Psychiatry, 25*(4), 543–572.

Slaby, R.G. & Frey, K.S. (1975) Development of gender constancy and selective attention to same–sex models. *Child Development, 46*, 839–856.

Slater, A. (1989) Visual memory and perception in early infancy. In A. Slater & G. Bremner (Eds) *Infant Development.* Hove: Erlbaum.

Slater, A. (1994) Perceptual development in infancy. *Psychology Review, 1*, 12–16.

Slater, A. & Morison, V. (1985) Shape constancy and slant perception at birth. *Perception, 14*, 337–344.

Slater, E. & Roth, M. (1969) *Clinical Psychiatry* (3rd edition). London, Ballière Tindall and Cassell.

Sloane, R., Staples, F., Cristol, A., Yorkston, N. & Whipple, K. (1975) *Psychotherapy Versus Behaviour Therapy.* Cambridge, MA: Harvard University Press.

Slobin, D.I. (1975) On the nature of talk to children. In E.H. Lenneberg & E. Lenneberg (Eds) *Foundations of Language Development, Volume 1.* New York: Academic Press.

Slobin, D.I. (1979) *Psycholinguistics* (2nd edition). Glenview, ILL: Scott, Foresman and Company.

Slobin, D.I. (1986) *The Cross-Linguistic Study of Language Acquisition.* Hillsdale, NJ: Erlbaum.

Sloboda, J.A., Davidson, J.W., & Howe, M.J.A. (1994a) Is everyone musical? *The Psychologist, 7*, 349–354.

Sloboda, J.A., Davidson, J.W., & Howe, M.J.A. (1994b) Musicians: Experts not geniuses. *The Psychologist, 7*, 363–364.

Sloboda, J., Hermelin, B., & O'Connor, N. (1985) An exceptional musical memory. *Music Perception, 3*, 155–170.

Sluckin, W. (1965) *Imprinting and Early Experiences.* London: Methuen.

Slugoski, B. & Hilton, D. (2000). Conversation. In W.P. Robinson & H. Giles (Eds) *Handbook of Language and Social Psychology* (2nd edition). Chichester: Wiley.

Smail, D. (1987) Psychotherapy and 'change': Some ethical considerations. In S. Fairbairn and G. Fairbairn (Eds), *Psychology, Ethics and Change*. London: RKP.

Smart, J.J.C. (1959) Sensations and brain processes. *The Philosophical Review, 68*, 141–156.

Smith, A.D. (1998) Ageing of the brain: Is mental decline inevitable? In S. Rose (Ed.) *From Brains to Consciousness: Essays on the New Sciences of the Mind*. Harmondsworth: Penguin.

Smith, C. & Lloyd, B.B. (1978) Maternal behaviour and perceived sex of infant. *Child Development, 49*, 1263–1265.

Smith, C.U.M. (1994) You are a group of neurons. *The Times Higher Educational Supplement,* 27 May, 20–21.

Smith, D.E., Wesson, D.R., Buxton, M.E., Seymour, R., & Kramer, H.M. (1978) The diagnosis and treatment of the PCP abuse syndrome. In R.C. Peterson & R.C. Stillman (Eds) *Phencyclidine (PCP) Abuse: An Appraisal*. NIDA Research Monographs, 21, DHEW Publication. Washington, DC: US Government Printing Office.

Smith, E.M., Brown, H.O., Toman, J.E.P. & Goodman, L.S. (1947) The lack of cerebral effects of D-tubo-curarine. *Anaesthesiology, 8*, 1–14.

Smith, H.B., Bruner, J.S. & White, R.W. (1956) *Opinions and Personality*. New York: John Wiley.

Smith, J. (1998) What happens when girl beats boy. *The Independent on Sunday,* 30 August, 13.

Smith, J.A., Harré, R., & Van Langenhove, L. (1995) Introduction. In J.A.Smith, R. Harré, & L. Van Langenhove (Eds) *Rethinking Psychology*. London: Sage.

Smith, J.R., Brooks-Gunn, J. & Klebanov, P.K. (1997) Consequences of living in poverty for young children's cognitive and verbal ability and early school achievement. In G.J. Duncan & J. Brooks-Gunn (Eds), *Consequences of Growing Up Poor*. New York: Russell Sage Foundation.

Smith, K.R. & Zick, C.D. (1996) Risk of mortality following widowhood: Age and sex differences by mode of death. *Social Biology, 43*, 59–71.

Smith, M. (2000) Is there such a thing as a personality disorder? *Nursing Times, 96*(18), 16.

Smith, M.L. & Glass, G.V. (1977) Meta-analysis of psychotherapeutic outcome studies. *American Psychologist, 32*, 752–760.

Smith, M.L., Glass, G.V. & Miller, T.I. (1980) *The Benefits of Psychotherapy*. Baltimore: Johns Hopkins University Press.

Smith, P.B. (1995) Social influence processes. In M. Argyle & A.M. Colman (Eds) *Social Psychology*. London: Longman.

Smith, P.B. & Bond, M.H. (1993) *Social Psychology across Cultures: Analysis and perspectives*. Hemel Hempstead: Harvester Wheatsheaf.

Smith, P.B. & Bond, M.H. (1998) *Social Psychology Across Cultures* (2nd edition). Hemel Hempstead: Prentice Hall Europe.

Smith, P.K. (1990) Ethology, sociobiology and developmental psychology: In memory of Niko Tinbergen and Konrad Lorenz. *British Journal of Developmental Psychology, 8*(2), 187–196.

Smith, P.K. (1995) Social development. In P. E. Bryant & A.M.Colman (Eds) *Developmental Psychology*. London: Longman.

Smith, P.K. & Cowie, H. (1988) *Understanding Children's Development*. Oxford: Basil Blackwell.

Smith, P.K. & Cowie, H. (1991) *Understanding Children's Development* (2nd edition). Oxford: Basil Blackwell.

Smith, P.K. & Daglish, L. (1977) Sex differences in parent and infant behaviour in the home. *Child Development, 48*, 1250–1254.

Smith, P.K., Cowie, H. & Blader, M. (1998) *Understanding Children's Development* (3rd edition). Oxford: Blackwell.

Smith, R.E., Sarason, I.G. & Sarason, B.R. (1986) *Psychology – The Frontiers of Behaviour* (3rd edition). New York: Harper & Row.

Smith, V.L. & Ellsworth, P.C. (1987) The social psychology of eyewitness accuracy: Misleading questions and communicator expertise. *Journal of Applied Psychology, 72*, 294–300.

Snaith, R.P. (1994) Psychosurgery: Controversy and enquiry. *British Journal of Psychiatry, 161*, 582–584.

Snarey, J.R. (1985) Cross-cultural universality of social-moral development: a critical review of Kohlbergian research. *Psychological Bulletin, 97*, 202–232.

Snarey, J.R. (1987) A question of morality. *Psychology Today,* June, 6–8.

Snarey, J.R., Reimer, R. & Kohlberg, L. (1985) Development of sociomoral reasoning among kibbutz adolescents: A longitudinal cross-cultural study. *Developmental Psychology, 21*(1), 3–17.

Snow, C.E. (1977) Mother's speech research: From input to interaction. In C.E. Snow and C.A. Ferguson (Eds) *Talking to Children: Language Input and Acquisition*. New York: Cambridge University Press.

Snow, C.E. (1983) Saying it again: The role of expanded and deferred imitations in language acquisition. In K.E. Nelson (Ed.) *Children's Language, Volume 4*. New York: Gardner Press.

Snowling, M. (1998) Dyslexia as a Phonological Deficit: Evidence and Implications. *Child Psychology & Psychiatry Review, 3*(1), 4–11.

Snyder, F.W. & Pronko, N.H. (1952) *Vision with Spatial Inversion*. Wichita, KS: University of Wichita Press.

Snyder, M. (1979) Self-monitoring processes. In L. Berkowitz (Ed.) *Advances in Experimental Social Psychology, Volume 18*. New York: Academic Press.

Snyder, M. (1987) *Public Appearance/Private Realities: The Psychology of Self-Monitoring*. New York: W.H. Freeman.

Snyder, M. (1995) Self-monitoring: Public appearances versus private realities. In G.G. Brannigan & M.R. Merrens (Eds) *The Social Psychologists: Research Adventures*. New York: McGraw-Hill.

Snyder, S. (1977) Opiate receptors and internal opiates. *Scientific American, 236*, 44–56.

Soal, S.G. & Bateman, F. (1954) *Modern Experiments in Telepathy*. London: Faber & Faber.

Sobanski, E. & Schmidt, M.H. (2000) Body dysmorphic disorder: A review of the current knowledge. *Child Psychology & Psychiatry Review, 5*(1), 17–24.

Sober, E. (1992) The evolution of altruism: Correlation, cost and benefit. *Biology & Philosophy, 7*, 177–188.

Sobesky, W. (1983) The effects of situational factors on moral judgements. *Child Development, 54*, 575–584.

Solms, M. (2000) Freudian dream theory today. *The Psychologist, 13*(12), 618–619.

Solomon, R.L. & Wynne, L.C. (1953) Traumatic avoidance learning: the outcomes of several extinction procedures with dogs. *Psychological Monograph, 67:* 4(354), 66–67.

Solomons, J. & George, C. (1999) The development of attachment in separated and divorced families: Effects of overnight visitation, parent and couple variables. *Attachment & Human Development, 1*(1), 2–33.

Solso, R.L. (1979) *Cognitive Psychology*. New York: Harcourt Brace Jovanovich.

Solso, R.L. (1995) *Cognitive Psychology* (4th edition). Boston: Allyn & Bacon.

Sommer, R. (1969) *Personal Space: The Behavioural Basis of Design*. Englewood Cliffs, NJ: Prentice-Hall.

Sonnerstein, F.L. (1999) Teenage American males: Growing up with risks. *Scientific American Presents, Men: The Scientific Truth about Their Work, Play, Health and Passions, 10*(2), 87–91.

Sowell, E.R. *et al.* (1999) In vivo evidence for post-adolescent brain maturation in frontal and striatal regions. *Nature Neuroscience, 2*, 859.

Sparrow, S.S. & Davis, S.M. (2000) Recent advances in the assessment of intelligence and cognition. *Journal of Child Psychology & Psychiatry, 41*(1), 117–131.

Spearman, C. (1904) General intelligence, objectively determined and measured. *American Journal of Psychology, 15,* 201–293.

Spearman, C. (1967) The doctrine of two factors. In S. Wiseman (Ed.), *Intelligence and Ability.* Harmondsworth: Penguin. (Original work published 1927.)

Speisman, J.C., Lazarus, R.S., Mordkoff, A.M. & Davidson, L.A. (1964) The experimental reduction of stress based on ego defence theory. *Journal of Abnormal & Social Psychology, 68,* 397–398.

Spelke, E.S., Zelazo, P., Kagan, J. & Kotelchuck, M. (1973) Father interaction and separation protest. *Developmental Psychology, 9,* 83–90.

Spelke, E.S. (1991) Physical knowledge in infancy: Reflections on Piaget's theory. In S. Carey & R. Gelman (Eds) *The Epigenesis of Mind: Essays on Biology and Cognition.* Hillsdale, NJ: Erlbaum.

Spelke, E.S., Hirst, W.C. & Neisser, U. (1976) Skills of divided attention. *Cognition, 4,* 215–230.

Spencer, C. & Perrin, S. (1998) Innovation and conformity. *Psychology Review, 5*(2), 23–26.

Sperling, G. (1960) The information available in brief visual presentation. *Psychological Monographs, 74* (Whole No. 498).

Sperling, G. (1963) A mode for visual memory tasks. *Human Factors, 5,* 19–31.

Sperling, G. & Speelman, R.G. (1970) Acoustic similarity and auditory short-term memory: Experiments and a model. In D.A. Norman (Ed.), *Models of Human Memory.* New York: Academic Press.

Sperling, H.G. (1946) 'An experimental study of some psychological factors in judgement', Master's thesis, New School for Social Research.

Sperry, R.W. (1943) The effect of 180 degree rotation in the retinal field of visuo-motor co-ordination. *Journal of Experimental Zoology, 92,* 263–279.

Sperry, R.W. (1964) The great cerebral commissure. *Scientific American, 210,* 42–52.

Sperry, R.W. (1968) Hemisphere deconnection and unity in conscious awareness. *American Psychologist, 23,* 723–733.

Sperry, R.W. (1974) Lateral specialisation in the surgically separated hemispheres. In F.O. Schmitt & F.G. Worden (Eds) *The Neurosciences: Third Study Program.* Cambridge, MA: MIT Press.

Sperry, R.W. (1982) Some effects of disconnecting the cerebral hemispheres. *Science, 217,* 1223–1226.

Sperry, R.W. & Gazzaniga, M.S. (1967) Language following surgical disconnection of the hemispheres. In F. Darley (Ed.), *Brain Mechanisms underlying Speech and Language.* New York: Grune and Stratton.

Sperry, R.W., Gazzaniga, M.S. & Bogen, J.E. (1969) Inter-hemispheric relationships: The neocortical commissures; syndromes of hemisphere disconnection. In P.J. Vinken & G.W. Bruyn (Eds) *Handbook of Clinical Neurology, Volume 4.* New York: Wiley.

Spitz, R.A. (1945) Hospitalism: An inquiry into the genesis of psychiatric conditions in early childhood. *Psychoanalytic Study of the Child, 1,* 53–74.

Spitz, R.A. (1946) Hospitalism: A follow-up report on investigation described in Vol. 1, 1945. *Psychoanalytic Study of the Child, 2,* 113–117.

Spitz, R.A. & Wolf, K.M. (1946) Anaclitic depression. *Psychoanalytic Study of the Child, 2,* 313–342.

Spitzer, R.L. (1975) On pseudoscience in science, logic in remission and psychiatric diagnosis: A critique of Rosenhan's 'On being sane in insane places'. *Journal of Abnormal Psychology, 84,* 442–452.

Spitzer, R.L. (1976) More on pseudoscience in science and the case for psychiatric diagnosis. *Archives of General Psychiatry, 33,* 459–470.

Spitzer, R.L., Endicott, J. & Robins, E. (1978) Research diagnostic criteria: Rationale and reliability. *Archives of General Psychiatry, 35,* 773–782.

Spitzer, R.L., Skodal, A.E., Gibbon, M. & Williams, J.B.W. (Eds) (1981) *DSM-III Case Book.* Washington, DC: American Psychiatric Association.

Sprecher, S., Aron, A., Hatfield, E. & Cortese, A. (1994) Love: American style, Russian style and Japanese style. *Personal Relationships, 1,* 349–369.

Sroufe, L.A. & Waters, E. (1977) Attachment as an organisational construct. *Child Development, 48,* 1184–1199.

Staats, A.W. & Staats, C.K. (1963) *Complex Human Behaviour.* New York: Holt Rinehart & Winston.

Stahlberg, D. & Frey, D. (1988) Attitudes, 1: Structure, measurement and functions. In M. Hewstone, W. Stroebe, J.P. Codol & G.M. Stephenson (Eds) *Introduction to Social Psychology.* Oxford: Blackwell.

Stainton Rogers, R., Stenner, P., Gleeson, K. & Stainton Rogers, W. (1995) *Social Psychology: A Critical Agenda.* Cambridge: Polity Press.

Stampfl, T. & Levis, D. (1967) Essentials of implosive therapy. *Journal of Abnormal Psychology, 72,* 496–503.

Stanovich, K.E. (1986) Cognitive processes and the reading problems of learning disabled children: Evaluating the assumption of specificity. In J.K. Torgensen & B.Y.L. Wong (Eds) *Psychological and Educational Perspectives on Learning Disabilities.* San Diego, CA: Acadmic Press.

Stanovich, K.E. (1998) Refining the phonological core deficit model. *Child Psychology & Psychiatry Review, 3*(1), 17–21.

Stanovich, K.E. & Siegel, L.S. (1994) The phenotypic performance profile of reading-disabled children: A regression-based test of the phonological-core variable-difference model. *Journal of Educational Psychology, 86,* 24–53.

Stattin, H. & Klackenberg, G. (1992) Family discord in adolescence in the light of family discord in childhood. Paper presented at Conference Youth – TM, Utrecht.

Stattin, H. & Magnusson, D. (1990) *Pubertal Maturation in Female Development.* Hillsdale: Erlbaum.

Stayton, D.J. & Ainsworth, M.D.S. (1973) Individual differences in infant response to brief, everyday separations as related to other infant and maternal behaviours. *Developmental Psychology, 9,* 226–235.

Stayton, D.J., Ainsworth, M.D.S. & Main, M.B. (1973) Development of separation behaviour in the first year of life: Protest, following and greeting. *Developmental Psychology, 9,* 213–225.

Steegmans, P.H.A., Hoes, A.W., Bak, A.A., van der Does, E., & Grobbee, D.E. (2000) Higher prevalence of depressive symptoms in middle-aged men with low serum cholesterol levels. *Psychosomatic Medicine, 62,* 205–211.

Steele, H., Steele, M., & Fonagy, P. (1995) Assocations among attachment classifications of mothers, fathers and infants. *Child Development, 67,* 541–555.

Stein, B.S., Morris, C.D. & Bransford, J.D. (1978) Constraints on effective elaboration. *Journal of Verbal Learning & Verbal Behaviour, 17,* 707–714.

Stein, J. & Fowler, S. (1985) Effects of nonocular occlusion on visuomotor perception and reading in dyslexic children. *Lancet, ii,* 69–73.

Steiner, I.D. (1972) *Group Processes and Productivity.* New York: Academic Press.

Stephan, C.W. & Langlois, J. (1984) Baby beautiful: Adult attributions of infant competence as a function of infant attractiveness. *Child Development, 55,* 576–585.

Stephan, W.G. (1978) School desegregation: An evaluation of predictions made in Brown vs. the Board of Education. *Psychological Bulletin, 85,* 217–238.

Stephenson, G.M. (1988) Applied social psychology. In M. Hewstone, W Stroebe, J.P. Codol & G.M. Stephenson (Eds), *Introduction to Social Psychology.* Oxford: Basil Blackwell.

Sternberg, E. (2000) *The Balance Within: The Science Connecting Health and Emotions.* New York: W.H. Freeman.

Sternberg, E. & Gold, P.W. (1997) The mind–body interaction in disease. *Scientific American Mysteries of the Mind, 7*(1), 8–15.

Sternberg, R.J. (1979) The nature of mental abilities. *American Psychologist, 34,* 214–230.

Sternberg, R.J. (1985) *Beyond IQ: A Triarchic Theory of Human Intelligence.* Cambridge: Cambridge University Press.

Sternberg, R.J. (1986) A triangular theory of love. *Psychological Review, 93,* 119–135.

Sternberg, R.J. (1987) Intelligence. In R. Gregory (Ed.), *The Oxford Companion to the Mind.* Oxford: Oxford University Press.

Sternberg, R.J. (1988a) *The Triarchic Mind: A New Theory of Human Intelligence.* New York: Viking.

Sternberg, R.J. (1988b) Triangulating love. In R.J. Sternberg & M.L. Barnes (Eds) *The Psychology of Love.* New Haven, CT: Yale University Press.

Sternberg, R.J. (1990) *Metaphors of Mind.* Cambridge: Cambridge University Press.

Sternberg, R.J. (1995) Intelligence and cognitive styles. In S.E. Hampson & A.M. Colman (Eds) *Individual Differences and Personality.* London: Longman.

Sternberg, R.J. (1998) How intelligent is intelligence testing? *Scientific American Presents: Exploring Intelligence, 9*(4), 12–17.

Sternberg, R.J. (2000) In search of the zippeump-a-zoo. *The Psychologist, 13*(5), 250–255.

Sternberg, R.J. & Grigorenko, E. (Eds) (1997) *Intelligence, Heredity and Environment.* New York: Cambridge University Press.

Stevens, J. (1997) Standard investigatory tools and offender profiling. In J. Jackson & D. Bekerian (Eds) *Offender Profiling: Theory, Research and Practice.* Chichester: Wiley.

Stevens, R. (1995) Freudian Theories of Personality. In S.E. Hampson & A.M. Colman (Eds) *Individual Differences and Personality.* London: Longman.

Stewart, V.M. (1973) Tests of the 'carpentered world' hypothesis by race and environment in America and Africa. *International Journal of Psychology, 8,* 83–94.

Stokes, P. (1999) Horror film boys convicted of stabbing friend. *Daily Telegraph,* 7 August, 5.

Stoner, J. A. F. (1961) A comparison of individual and group decisions involving risk. Unpublished master's thesis, Massachusetts Institute of Technology.

Stones, E. (1971) *Educational Psychology.* London: Methuen.

Storms, M.D. (1973) Videotape and the attribution process: Reversing actors' and observers' points of view. *Journal of Personality & Social Psychology, 27,* 165–175.

Storr, A. (1966) The concept of cure. In C. Rycroft (Ed.), *Psychoanalysis Observed.* London: Constable.

Storr, A. (1968) *Human Aggression.* Harmondsworth: Penguin.

Storr, A. (1987) Why psychoanalysis is not a science. In C. Blakemore and S. Greenfield (Eds), *Mindwaves.* Oxford: Blackwell.

Stouffer, S.A., Suchman, E.A., DeVinney, L.C., Starr, S.A. & Williams, R.M. (1949) *The American Soldier: Adjustment During Army Life, Volume 1.* Princeton, NJ: Princeton University Press.

Strachey, J. (1962–1977) Sigmund Freud: A sketch of his life and ideas. This appears in each volume of the Pelican Freud Library: originally written for the *Standard Edition of the Complete Psychological Works of Sigmund Freud,* 1953–1974. London: Hogarth Press.

Stratton, G.M. (1896) Some preliminary experiments on vision. *Psychological Review, 3,* 611–617.

Strickland, B.R. (1992) Women and depression. *Current Directions in Psychological Science, 1,* 132–135.

Stroebe, M.S. & Stroebe, M. (1993) The mortality of bereavement: A review. In M.S. Stroebe, W. Stroebe & R.O. Hansson (Eds) *Handbook of Bereavement: Theory, Research and Intervention.* New York: Cambridge University Press.

Stroebe, M.S., Stroebe, W. & Hansson, R.O. (1993) Contemporary themes and controversies in bereavement research. In M.S. Stroebe, W. Stroebe & R.O. Hansson (Eds) *Handbook of Bereavement: Theory, Research and Intervention.* New York: Cambridge University Press.

Stroebe, W. (2000) *Social Psychology and Health* (2nd edition). Buckingham: Open University Press.

Stroop, J.R. (1935) Studies of interference in serial verbal reactions. *Journal of Experimental Psychology, 18,* 643–662.

Stuart-Hamilton, I. (1994) *The Psychology of Ageing: An Introduction* (2nd edition). London: Jessica Kingsley.

Stuart-Hamilton, I. (1997) Adjusting to later life. *Psychology Review, 4*(2), 20–23, November.

Stuttaford, T. (2000) Healthy children grow up sooner. *The Times,* 19 June, 3.

Sue, D., Sue, D. & Sue, S. (1994) *Understanding Abnormal Behaviour* (4th edition). Boston: Houghton Mifflin.

Sue, S. (1995) Implications of the Bell curve: Whites are genetically inferior in intelligence? *Focus: Notes from the Society for the Psychological Study of Ethnic Minority Issues,* 16–17.

Sulloway, F.J. (1979) *Freud, Biologist of the Mind: Beyond the Psychoanalytic Legend.* New York: Basic Books.

Sumner, W.G. (1906) *Folkways.* Boston: Ginn.

Suomi, S.J. (1982) Biological foundations and developmental psychobiology. In C.B. Kopp and J.B. Krakow (Eds), *Child Development in a Social Context.* Reading, Massachusetts: Addison-Wesley.

Suomi, S.J. & Harlow, H.F. (1972) Depressive behaviour in young monkeys subjected to vertical chamber confinement. *Journal of Comparative & Physiological Psychology, 80,* 11–18.

Suomi, S.J. & Harlow, H.F. (1972) Social rehabilitation of isolate-reared monkeys. *Developmental Psychology, 6,* 487–496.

Surrey, D. (1982) 'It's like good training for life'. *Natural History, 91,* 71–83.

Sutherland, P. (1992) *Cognitive Development Today: Piaget and his Critics.* London: Paul Chapman Publishing.

Sutherland, S.N. (1976) *Breakdown.* London: Weidenfeld & Nicolson.

Sutton, S.R., McVey, D., & Glanz, A. (1999) A comparative test of the theory of reasoned action and the theory of planned behaviour in the prediction of condom use intentions in a national sample of English young people. *Health Psychology, 18,* 72–81.

Swensen, C.H. (1983) A respectable old age. *American Psychologist, 46,* 1208–1221.

Sylva, K. (1996) Education: Report on the Piaget–Vygotsky centenary conference. *The Psychologist, 9,* 370–372.

Szasz, T.S. (1962) *The Myth of Mental Illness.* New York: Harper & Row.

Szasz, T. (1974) *Ideology and Insanity.* Harmondsworth: Penguin.

Szymanski, K. & Harkins, S.G. (1987) Social loafing and self-evaluation with a social standard. *Journal of Personality & Social Psychology, 53,* 891–897.

Taddonio, J.L. (1976) The relationship of experimenter expectancy to performance on ESP tasks. *Journal of Parapsychology, 40,* 107–114.

Tagiuri, R. (1969) Person perception. In G. Lindzey and E. Aronson, (Eds), *Handbook of Psychology, Volume 2.* Reading, Massachusetts: Addison-Wesley.

Tajfel, H. (1969) Social and cultural factors in perception. In G. Lindzey & E. Aronson (Eds) *Handbook of Social Psychology, Volume 3.* Reading, MA: Addison-Wesley.

Tajfel, H. (Ed.) (1978) *Differentiation Between Social Groups: Studies in the Social Psychology of Intergroup Relations.* London: Academic Press.

Tajfel, H. (1981) *Human Group and Social Categories.* Cambridge: Cambridge University Press.

Tajfel, H. & Billig, M. (1974) Familiarity and categorisation in inter-group behaviour. *Journal of Experimental Social Psychology, 10,* 159–170.

Tajfel, H. & Turner, J. (1979) An integrative theory of intergroup conflict. In G.W. Austin and S. Worchel, (Eds), *The Social Psychology of Intergroup Relations.* Monterey, California: Brooks Cole.

Tajfel, H. & Turner, J.C. (1986) The social identity theory of Intergroup Behaviour. In S. Worchel & W. Austin (Eds) *Psychology of Intergoup Relations.* Chicago: Nelson-Hall.

Tajfel, H., Billig, M.G. & Bundy, R.P. (1971) Social categorisation and intergroup behaviour. *European Journal of Social Psychology, 1,* 149–178.

Tallis, F. (1994) Obsessive-compulsive disorder. *The Psychologist, 7,* 312.

Tallis, F. (1995) *Obsessive-Compulsive Disorder: A Cognitive and Neuropsychological Perspective.* Chichester: Wiley.

Tanaka, J.W. & Farah, M.J. (1993) Parts and wholes in face recognition. Quarterly *Journal of Experimental Psychology, 46A,* 225–246.

Tanner, J.M. (1978) *Fetus into Man: Physical Growth from Conception to Maturity.* Cambridge, MA: Harvard University Press.

Tanner, J.M. & Whitehouse, R.H. (1976) Clinical longitudinal standards for height, weight, height velocity, weight velocity and stages of puberty. *Archives of Disorders in Childhood, 51,* 170–179.

Targ, R. & Puthoff, H. (1974) Information transmission under conditions of sensory shielding. *Nature, 251,* 602–607.

Targ, R. & Puthoff, H. (1977) *Mind-reach.* New York: Delacorte.

Tavris, C. (1993) The mismeasure of woman. *Feminism & Psychology, 3*(2), 149–168.

Taylor, D.M. & Porter, L.E. (1994) A multicultural view of stereotyping. In W.J. Lonner & R.S. Malpass (Eds) *Psychology and Culture.* Boston: Allyn & Bacon.

Taylor, G. (1993) Challenges from the margins. In J. Clarke (Ed.) *A Crisis in Care.* London: Sage.

Taylor, J. (1992) A questionable treatment. *Nursing Times, 88*(40), 41–43

Taylor, P.F. & Kopelman, M.D. (1984) Amnesia for criminal offences. *Psychological Medicine 14,* 581–588.

Taylor, R. (1963) *Metaphysics.* Englewood Cliffs, NJ: Prentice-Hall.

Taylor, S.E. (1981) A categorisation approach to stereotyping. In D.L. Hamilton (Ed.) *Cognitive Processes in Stereotyping and Intergroup Behaviour.* Hillsdale, NJ: Erlbaum.

Taylor, S.E., Peplau, L.A. & Sears, D.O. (1994) *Social Psychology* (8th edition). Englewood Cliffs, NJ: Prentice-Hall.

Teasdale, J. (1988) Cognitive vulnerability to persistent depression. *Cognition & Emotion, 2,* 247–274.

Tebartz, van Elst, L., Woermann, F., Lemieux, L., & Trimble, M.R. (2000) Increased amygdala volumes in female and depressed humans. A quantitative magnetic resonance imaging study. *Neuroscience Letters, 281,* 103–106.

Tedeschi, J.T. & Rosenfield, P. (1981) Impression management theory and the forced compliance situation. In J.T. Tedeschi (Ed.), *Impression Management Theory and Social Psychological Research.* New York: Academic Press.

Tedeschi, J.T., Schlenker, B.R. & Bonoma, T.V. (1971) Cognitive dissonance: Private ratiocination or public spectacle? *American Psychologist, 26,* 685–695.

Tedeschi, R.G. (1999) Violence transformed: Post-traumatic growth in survivors and their societies. *Aggression & Violent Behaviour, 4,* 319–341.

Tedeschi, R.G. & Calhoun, L.G.(1996) The Post-traumatic Growth Inventory: Measuring the positive legacy of trauma. *Journal of Traumatic Stress, 9,* 455–471.

Tedeschi, R.G., Park, C.L., & Calhoun, L.G. (1998) Post-traumatic growth: Conceptual issues. In R.G. Tedeschi, C.L.Park, & L.G.Calhoun (Eds) *Post-traumatic Growth: Positive Changes in the Aftermath of Crisis.* Mahwah, NJ: Lawrence Erlbaum.

Teichman, J. (1988) *Philosophy and the Mind.* Oxford: Blackwell.

Teigen, K.H. (1994) Variants of subjective probabilities: Concepts, norms and biases. In G. Wright & P. Aytan (Eds) *Subjective Probability.* Chichester: John Wiley.

Teitelbaum, P.H. (1955) Sensory control of hypothalamic hyperphagia. *Journal of Comparative & Physiological Psychology 48,* 156–163.

Teitelbaum, P. (1967) Motivation and control of food intake. In C.F. Code (Ed.), *Handbook of Physiology: Alimentary Canal, Volume 1.* Washington, DC: American Physiological Society.

Teitelbaum, P. (1971) The encephalisation of hunger. In E. Stellar and J.M. Sprague (Eds), *Progress in Physiological Psychology, Volume 4.* London: Academic Press.

Teitelbaum, P. & Epstein, A.N. (1962) The lateral hypothalamic syndrome: Recovery of feeding and drinking after hypothalamic lesions. *Psychological Review, 67,* 74–90.

Teitelbaum, P. & Stellar, E. (1954) Recovery from the failure to eat produced by hypothalamic lesions. *Science, 120,* 894–895.

Teixeira, J.M.A. (1999) Association between maternal anxiety in pregnancy and increased uterine artery resistance index: Cohort based study. *British Medical Journal, 318*(7177), 153–157.

Temoshok, L. (1987) Personality, coping style, emotions and cancer: Towards an integrative model. *Cancer Surveys, 6,* 545–567 (Supplement).

Terman, L. (1921) In symposium: Intelligence and its measurement. *Journal of Educational Psychology, 12,* 127–133.

Terman, L. (1925) *Mental and Physical Traits of a Thousand Gifted Children: Volume 1, Genetic studies of genius.* Stanford, CA: Stanford University Press.

Terman, L. (1954) The discovery and encouragement of exceptional talent. *American Psychologist, 9,* 221–238.

Terman, L. & Merrill, M.A. (1937) *Measuring Intelligence.* London: Harrap.

Terman, L. & Ogden, M.H. (1959) *Genetic Studies of Genius (Volume 4): The Gifted Group at Midlife.* Stanford, CA: Stanford University Press.

Terrace, H.S. (1979) *Nim.* New York: Knopf.

Terrace, H.S. (1987) Thoughts without words. In C. Blakemore & S. Greenfield (Eds), *Mindwaves.* Oxford: Basil Blackwell.

Thibaut, J.W. & Kelley, H.H. (1959) *The Social Psychology of Groups.* New York: Wiley.

Thomas, A. & Chess, S. (1977) *Temperament and Development.* New York: Brunner/Mazel.

Thomas, J.C. (1974) An analysis of behaviour in the 'hobbit–orcs' problem. *Cognitive Psychology, 28,* 167–178.

Thomas, K. (1990) Psychodynamics: The Freudian approach. In I. Roth (Ed.) *Introduction to Psychology*. Hove: Lawrence Erlbaum Associates Ltd.

Thomas, R. (1999) Lack of sleep leaves night-owl Britons retarded. *The Observer*, 21 March, 1.

Thomas, R.M. (1985) *Comparing Theories of Child Development* (2nd edition). Belmont, CA: Wadsworth Publishing Company.

Thompson, C. (1943) 'Penis envy' in women. *Psychiatry, 6*, 123–125.

Thompson, L.A., Detterman, D.K., & Plomin, R. (1991) Associations between cognitive abilities and scholastic achievement: Genetic overlap but environmental differences. *Psychological Science, 2*, 158–165.

Thompson, P. (1980) Margaret Thatcher – a new illusion. *Perception, 9*, 483–484.

Thompson, S.B.N. (1997) War experiences and post-traumatic stress disorder. *The Psychologist, 10*, 349–350.

Thorndike, E. L. (1898) Animal intelligence: An experimental study of the associative processes in animals. *Psychological Review Monograph Supplement 2* (Whole No. 8).

Thorndike, E.L. (1911) *Animal Intelligence*. New York: Macmillan.

Thorne, B. (1984) Person-centred therapy. In W. Dryden (Ed.), *Individual Therapy in Britain*. London: Harper & Row.

Thorne, B. (1992) *Rogers*. London: Sage Publications.

Thornhill, R. & Wilmsen-Thornhill, N. (1992) The evolutionary psychology of men's coercive sexuality. *Behaviour & Brain Sciences, 15(2)*, 363–375.

Thurstone, L.L. (1928) Attitudes can be measured. *American Journal of Sociology, 33*, 529–554.

Thurstone, L.L. (1935) *The Vectors of the Mind*. Chicago: University of Chicago Press.

Thurstone, L.L. (1938) Primary mental abilities. *Psychometric Monographs, No. 1*.

Thurstone, L.L. (1940) Current issues in factor analysis. *Psychological Bulletin, 37*, 189–236.

Thurstone, L.L.(1947) *Multiple Factor Analysis*. Chicago: University of Chicago Press.

Tillman, W.S. & Carver, C.S. (1980) Actors' and observers' attributions for success and failure: A comparative test of predictions from Kelley's cube, self-serving bias and positivity bias formulations. *Journal of Experimental Social Psychology, 16*, 18–32.

Tinbergen, N. (1951) *The Study of Instinct*. Oxford: Clarendon Press.

Tipper, S.P. & Driver, J. (1988) Negative priming between pictures and words: Evidence for semantic analysis of ignored stimuli. *Memory & Cognition, 16*, 64–70.

Titchener, E.B. (1903) *Lectures on the Elementary Psychology of Feeling and Attention*. New York: Macmillan.

Tizard, B. (1977) *Adoption: A Second Chance*. London: Open Books.

Tizard, B. & Hodges, J. (1978) The effects of early institutional rearing on the development of eight-year-old children. *Journal of Child Psychology & Psychiatry, 19*, 99–118.

Tizard, B. & Phoenix, A. (1993) *Black, White or Mixed Race?* London: Routledge.

Tizard, B. & Rees, J. (1974) A comparison of the effects of adoption, restoration to the natural mother and continued institutionalisation on the cognitive development of four-year-old children. *Child Development, 45*, 92–99.

Tizard, B., Joseph, A., Cooperman, O. & Tizard, J. (1972) Environmental effects on language development: A study of young children in long-stay residential nurseries. *Child Development, 43*, 337–358.

Tizard, J. & Tizard, B. (1971) Social development of 2-year-old children in residential nurseries. In H.R. Schaffer (Ed.), *The Origins of Human Social Relations*. London: Academic Press.

Tobin-Richards, M.H., Boxer, A.M. & Petersen, A.C. (1983) The psychological significance of pubertal change: Sex differences in perceptions of self during early adolescence. In J. Brooks-Gunn & A.C. Petersen (Eds) *Girls at Puberty: Biological and Psychosocial Perspectives*. New York: Plenum.

Tolman, E.C. (1948) Cognitive maps in rats and man. *Psychological Review, 55*, 189–208.

Tolman, E.C. & Honzik, C.H. (1930) Introduction and removal of reward and maze-learning in rats. *University of California Publications in Psychology, 4*, 257–275.

Tolman, E.C., Ritchie, B.F., & Kalish, D. (1946) Studies in spatial learning, 1: Orientation and the short-cut. *Journal of Experimental Psychology, 36*, 13–25.

Tomlinson-Keasey, C. (1985) *Child Development: Psychological, Sociocultural, and Biological Factors*. Chicago: Dorsey Press.

Trabasso, T. (1977) The role of memory as a system in making transitive inferences. In R.V. Kail & J.W. Hagen (Eds) *Perspectives on the Development of Memory and Cognition*. Hillsdale, NJ: Erlbaum.

Traupmann, J., Hatfield, E. & Wexer, P. (1983) Equity and sexual satisfaction in dating couples. *British Journal of Social Psychology, 22*, 33–40.

Tredre, R. (1996) Untitled article. *Observer Life*, 12 May, 16–19.

Treisman, A.M. (1960) Contextual cues in selective listening. Quarterly *Journal of Experimental Psychology, 12*, 242–248.

Treisman, A.M. (1964) Verbal cues, language and meaning in selective attention. *American Journal of Psychology, 77*, 206–219.

Treisman, A.M. (1988) Features and objects: The fourteenth Bartlett memorial lecture. *Quarterly Journal of Experimental Psychology, 40A*, 201–237.

Treisman, A.M. & Geffen, G. (1967) Selective attention: Perception or response. *Quarterly Journal of Experimental Psychology, 19*, 1–18.

Treisman, A.M. & Gelade, G. (1980) A feature-integration theory of attention. *Cognitive Psychology, 12*, 97–136.

Treisman, A.M. & Riley, J.G.A. (1969) Is selective attention selective perception or selective response?: A further test. *Journal of Experimental Psychology, 79*, 27–34.

Treisman, A.M. & Sato, S. (1990) Conjunction search revisited. *Journal of Experimental Psychology*: *Human Perception & Performance, 16*, 459–478.

Treisman, A.M. & Schmidt, H. (1982) Illusory conjunctions in the perception of objects. *Cognitive Psychology, 14*, 107–141.

Trew, K. (1998) Identity and the self. In K. Trew & K. Kremer (Eds) *Gender & Psychology*. London: Arnold.

Triandis, H. (1990) Theoretical concepts that are applicable to the analysis of ethnocentrism. In R.W. Brislin (Ed.) *Applied Cross-Cultural Psychology*. Newbury Park, CA.: Sage.

Triandis, H. (1994) *Culture and Social Behaviour*. New York: McGraw-Hill.

Triplett, N. (1898) The dynamogenic factors in pacemaking and competition. *American Journal of Psychology, 9*, 507–533.

Triseliotis, J. (1980) Growing up in foster care and after. In J. Triseliotis (Ed.), *New Developments in Foster Care and Adoption*. London: RKP.

Trivers, R.L. (1971) The evolution of reciprocal altruism. *Quarterly Review of Biology, 46*, 35–57.

Troscianko, T. (1987) Colour vision: Brain mechanisms. In R. Gregory (Ed.), *The Oxford Companion to the Mind*. Oxford: Oxford University Press.

Trower, P. (1987) On the ethical bases of 'scientific' behaviour therapy. In S. Fairbairn & G. Fairbairn (Eds), *Psychology, Ethics and Change*. London: RKP.

Trowler, P. (1988) *Investigating the Media*. London: Unwin Hyman Limited.

Troy, M. & Sroufe, L.A. (1987) Victimisation among preschoolers: the role of attachment relationship theory. *Journal of the American Academy of Child & Adolescent Psychiatry, 26,* 166–172.

Truax, C. & Mitchell, K. (1971) Research on certain therapist interpersonal skills in relation to process and outcome. In A.E. Bergin & S.L. Garfield (Eds), *Handbook of Psychotherapy and Behaviour Change: An Empirical Analysis.* New York: Wiley.

Tulving, E. (1962) Subjective organisation in free recall of unrelated words. *Psychological Review, 69,* 344–354.

Tulving, E. (1968) Theoretical issues in free recall. In T.R. Dixon & D.L. Horton (Eds) *Verbal Behaviour and General Behaviour Theory.* Englewood Cliffs, NJ: Prentice-Hall.

Tulving, E. (1972) Episodic and semantic memory. In E. Tulving & W. Donaldson (Eds) *Organisation of Memory.* London: Academic Press.

Tulving, E. (1974) Cue-dependent forgetting. *American Scientist, 62,* 74–82.

Tulving, E. (1979) Relation between encoding specificity and levels of processing. In L.S. Cermak & F.I.M. Craik (Eds), *Levels of Processing in Human Memory.* Hillsdale, New Jersey: Lawrence Erlbaum Associates Inc.

Tulving, E. (1983) *Elements of Episodic Memory.* London: ClarendonPress/Oxford University Press.

Tulving, E. (1985) How many memory systems are there? *American Psychologist, 40,* 385–398.

Tulving, E. & Pearlstone, Z. (1966) Availability versus accessibility of information in memory for words. *Journal of Verbal Learning & Verbal Behaviour, 5,* 389–391.

Tulving, E. & Psotka, J. (1971) Retroactive inhibition in free recall: Inaccessibility of information available in the memory store. *Journal of Experimental Psychology, 87,* 1–8.

Tulving, E. & Thompson, D.M. (1973) Encoding specificity and retrieval processes in episodic memory. *Psychological Review, 80,* 352–373.

Turco, R. (1993) Psychological profiling. *International Journal of Offender Therapy & Comparative Criminology, 34*(2), 147–154.

Turiel, E. (1966) An experimental test of the sequentiality of developmental stages in the child's moral judgements. *Journal of Personality & Social Psychology, 3,* 611–618.

Turiel, E. (1978) Distinct conceptual and developmental domains: Social convention and morality. In C.B. Keasey (Ed.), *Nebraska Symposium on Motivation, Volume 25.* Lincoln, Nebraska: Nebraska University Press.

Turing, A.M. (1936) On computable numbers, with an application to the Entscheidungsproblem. *Proceedings of the London Mathematical Society, Series 2 (42),* 230–265.

Turing, A.M. (1950) Computing machinery and intelligence. *Mind, 59,* 433–460.

Turnbull, C. (1961) *The Forest People.* New York: Simon & Schuster.

Turnbull, C. (1989) *The Mountain People.* London: Paladin.

Turnbull, S.K. (1995) The middle years. In D. Wedding (Ed.) *Behaviour and Medicine* (2nd edition). St. Louis, MO: Mosby-Year Book.

Turner, J.C. (1982) Towards a cognitive redefinition of the social group. In H. Tajfel (Ed.), *Social Identity and Intergroup Relations.* Cambridge: Cambridge University Press.

Turner, J.C. (1985) Social categorisations and the self-concept: A social cognitive theory of group behaviour. In E.J. Lawler (Ed.), *Advances in Group Processes: Theory and Research, Volume 2.* Greenwich, Connecticut: JAI Press.

Turner, J.C. (1991) *Social Influence.* Milton Keynes: Open University Press.

Turner, J.C., Hogg, M.A., Oakes, P.J., Reicher, S.D. & Wetherell, M.S. (1987) *Rediscovering the Social Group: A Self-categorisation Theory.* Oxford: Blackwell.

Turner, J.S. & Helms, D.B. (1989) *Contemporary Adulthood* (4th edition). Fort Worth, FL: Holt, Rinehart & Winston.

Turner, L.H. & Solomon, R.L. (1962) Human traumatic avoidance learning. *Psychological Monographs, 76,* 40.

Turner, M. (1999) Annotation: Repetitive behaviour in autism: A review of psychological research. *Journal of Child Psychology & Psychiatry, 40*(6), 839–849.

Turney, J. (1999) Human nature totally explained. *The Times Higher,* 12 March, 18.

Turpin, G. & Slade, P. (1998) Clinical and Health Psychology. In P. Scott & C. Spencer, *Psychology: A Contemporary Introduction.* Oxford: Blackwell.

Tversky, A. (1972) Elimination by aspects: A theory of choice. *Psychological Review, 79,* 281–299.

Tversky, A. & Kahneman, D. (1971) Belief in the law of small numbers. *Psychological Bulletin, 76,* 105–110.

Tversky, A. & Kahneman, D. (1974) Judgement under uncertainty: Heuristics and biases. *Science, 185,* 1124–1131.

Tversky, A. & Kahneman, D. (1980) Causal schemas in judgements under uncertainty. In M. Fishbein (Ed.) *Progress in Social Psychology.* Hillsdale, NJ: Erlbaum.

Tversky, A. & Kahneman, D. (1986) Rational choice and the framing of decisions. *Journal of Business, 59,* 5251–5278.

Twombly, R. (1994) Shock therapy returns. *New Scientist,* 5 March, 21–23.

Tyerman, A. & Spencer, C. (1983) A critical test of the Sherifs' Robber's Cave experiment: Intergroup competition and co-operation between groups of well-acquainted individuals. *Small Group Behaviour, 14,* 515–531.

Tyler, T.R. & Cook, F.L. (1984) The mass media and judgement of risk: Distinguishing impact on personal and societal level judgement. *Journal of Personality & Social Psychology, 47,* 693–708.

Uhlig, R. (1996) Boy challenging dyslexia theory. *The Daily Telegraph,* 11 January, 19.

Ullmann, L.P. & Krasner, L. (1969) *A Psychological Approach to Abnormal Behaviour.* Englewood Cliffs, NJ: Prentice-Hall.

Ullmann, L.P. & Krasner, L.A. (1975) *A Psychological Approach to Abnormal Behaviour* (2nd edition). Englewood Cliffs, NJ: Prentice Hall.

Underwood, B.J. (1948) Retroactive and proactive inhibition after 5 and 48 hours. *Journal of Experimental Psychology, 38,* 29–38.

Underwood, B.J. (1957) Interference and forgetting. *Psychological Review, 64,* 49–60.

Underwood, G. (1974) Moray vs the rest: The effects of extended shadowing practice. *Quarterly Journal of Experimental Psychology, 26,* 368–372.

Unger, R. (1979) *Female and Male.* London: Harper & Row.

Unger, R. & Crawford, M. (1992) *Women and Gender: A Feminist Psychology.* New York: McGraw-Hill.

Unger, R. & Crawford, M. (1996) *Women and Gender: A Feminist Psychology* (2nd edition). New York: McGraw-Hill.

US Riots Commission (1968) *Report of the National Advisory Commission on Civil Disorder.* New York: Bantam Books.

Utts, J. & Josephson, B.D. (1996) Do you believe in psychic phenomena? Are they likely to be able to explain consciousness? *The Times Higher,* 5 April, v.

Vaidyanathan, P, & Naidoo, J. (1991) Asian Indians in Western countries: Cultural identity and the arranged marriage. In N. Bleichrodt & P. Drenth (Eds) *Contemporary Issues in Cross-Cultural Psychology.* Amsterdam: Swets & Zeitlinger.

Valentine, E.R. (1982) *Conceptual Issues in Psychology.* London: Routledge.

Valentine, E.R. (1992) *Conceptual Issues in Psychology.* (2nd edition). London: Routledge.

810

References

Valins, S. (1966) Cognitive effects of false heart-rate feedback. *Journal of Personality & Social Psychology, 4,* 400–408.

van Avermaet, E. (1988) Social influence in small groups. In M. Hewstone, W. Stroebe, J.P. Codol & G.M. Stephenson (Eds), *Introduction to Social Psychology.* Oxford: Basil Blackwell.

van Avermaet, E. (1996) Social influence in small groups. In M. Hewstone, W. Stroebe & G.M. Stephenson (Eds) *Introduction to Social Psychology* (2nd edition). Oxford: Blackwell.

Van Essen, D.C. (1985) Functional organisation of primate visual cortex. In A. Peters. & E.G. Jones (Eds) *Cerebral Cortex, Volume 2: Visual Cortex.* New York: Plenum Press.

Van Ijzendoorn, M.H. & Bakjermans-Kranenburg, M.J. (1996) Attachment representations in mothers, fathers, adolescents and clinical groups: A meta-analytic search for normative data. *Journal of Consulting & Clinical Psychology, 64,* 8–21.

Van Ijzendoorn, M.H. & De Wolff, M.S. (1997) In search of the absent father: Meta analyses of infant–father attachment: A rejoinder to our discussants. *Child Development, 68,* 604–609.

Van Ijzendoorn, M.H. & Kroonenberg, P.M. (1988) Cross-cultural patterns of attachment: A meta-analysis of the Strange Situation. *Child Development, 59,* 147–156.

Van Ijzendoorn, M.H. & Schuengel, C. (1999) The development of attachment relationships: Infancy and beyond. In D. Messer & S. Millar (Eds) *Exploring Developmental Psychology: From Infancy to Adolescence.* London: Arnold.

Van Langenhove, L. (1995) The theoretical foundations of Experimental Psychology and its alternatives. In J.A. Smith, R. Harré, & L. Van Langenhove (Eds) *Rethinking Psychology.* London: Sage.

Van Lehn, K. (1983) On the representation of procedures in repair theory. In H.P. Ginsburg (Ed.) *The Development of Mathematical Thinking.* London: Academic Press.

Vanneman, R.D. & Pettigrew, T.F. (1972) Race and relative deprivation in the urban United States. *Race, 13,* 461–486.

Vasagar, J. (2000) Drug-taking falling among teenagers. *The Guardian,* 2 June, 13.

Vaughn, B.E., Gove, F.L. & Egeland, B.R. (1980) The relationship between out-of-home care and the quality of infant-mother attachment in an economically disadvantaged population. *Child Development, 51,* 1203–1214.

Veale, D., Boocock, A., Goumay, K., Dryden, W., Shah, F,. Willson, R., & Walburn, J. (1996) Body dysmorphic disorder: A survey of fifty cases. *British Journal of Psychiatry, 169,* 196–201.

Veitia, M.C. & McGahee, C.L. (1995) Ordinary addictions: Tobacco and alcohol. In D. Wedding (Ed.) *Behaviour and Medicine* (2nd edition). St. Louis. MO: Mosby Year Books.

Vernon, M.D. (1955) The functions of schemata in perceiving. *Psychological Review, 62,* 180–192.

Vernon, P.E. (1950) The hierarchy of ability. In S. Wiseman (Ed.), *Intelligence and Ability.* Harmondsworth: Penguin.

Vernon, P.E. (1969) *Intelligence and Cultural Environment.* London: Methuen.

Vernon, P.E. (1971) *The Structure of Human Abilities.* London: Methuen.

Vernon, P.E. (1979) *Intelligence: Heredity and Environment.* San Francisco: W.H. Freeman.

Vines, G. (1998) Hidden inheritance. *New Scientist, 160*(2162), 26–30.

Vines, G. (1999) The gene in the bottle. *New Scientist, 164*(2214), 38–43.

Vitelli, R. (1988) The crisis issue reassessed: An empirical analysis. *Basic & Applied Social Psychology, 9,* 301–309.

Vivian, J. & Brown, R. (1995) Prejudice and intergroup conflict. In M. Argyle & A.M. Colman (Eds) *Social Psychology.* London: Longman.

Vivian, J., Brown, R.J. & Hewstone, M. (1994) 'Changing attitudes through intergroup contact: The effects of membership salience.' (Unpublished manuscript, Universities of Kent and Wales, Cardiff.)

Von Senden, M. (1960) *Space and Sight: The Perception of Space and Shape in the Congenitally Blind Before and After Operations* (P. Heath, trans.). London: Methuen. (Original work published 1932.)

Von Wright, J.M., Anderson, K. & Stenman, U. (1975) Generalisation of conditioned GSRs in dichotic listening. In P.M.A. Rabbitt & S. Dornic (Eds), *Attention and Performance, Volume 1.* London: Academic Press.

Vygotsky, L. (1962) *Thought and Language.* Cambridge, MA: MIT Press (originally published in 1934).

Vygotsky, L.S. (1978) *Mind in Society.* Cambridge, MA: Harvard University Press.

Vygotsky, L.S. (1981) The genesis of higher mental functions. In J.V. Wertsch (Ed.) *The Concept of Activity in Soviet Psychology.* Armonk, NY: Sharpe.

Wachtel, P.L. (1977) *Psychoanalysis and Behaviour Therapy: Toward an Integration.* New York: Basic Books.

Wachtel, P.L. (1989) Preface to the paperback edition. In *Psychoanalysis and Behaviour Therapy.* New York: Basic Books.

Wada, J. & Rasmussen, T. (1960) Intracarotid injection of sodium amytal for lateralisation of cerebral speech dominance. *Journal of Neurosurgery, 17,* 266–282.

Wade, C. & Tavris, C. (1990) *Psychology* (2nd edition). New York: Harper & Row.

Wade, C. & Tavris, C. (1993) *Psychology* (3rd edition). New York: HarperCollins.

Wade, C. & Tavris, C. (1994) The longest war: Gender and culture. In W.J. Lonner & R.S. Malpass (Eds) *Psychology and Culture.* Boston: Allyn & Bacon.

Wade, C. & Tavris, C. (1999) *Invitation to Psychology.* New York: Longman.

Wadeley, A. (1996) Subliminal perception. *Psychology Review, 3*(1), September.

Wagenaar, W.A. (1988) *Paradoxes of Gambling Behaviour.* Hove: Lawrence Erlbaum.

Waldrop, M.F. & Halverson, C.F (1975) Intensive and extensive peer behaviour: Longitudinal and cross-sectional analysis. *Child Development, 46,* 19–26.

Walker, L.J. (1984) Sex differences in the development of moral reasoning: A critical review. *Child Development, 55,* 677–691.

Walker, L.J. (1989) A longitudinal study of moral reasoning. *Child Development, 60,* 157–166.

Walker, L.J. (1995) Sexism in Kohlberg's moral psychology? In W.M. Kurtines & J. Gewirtz (Eds) *Moral Development: An Introduction.* Needham Heights, MA: Allyn & Bacon.

Walker, L.J. (1996) Is one sex morally superior? In M.R. Merrens & G.C. Brannigan (Eds) *The Developmental Psychologists: Research Adventures Across the Life Span.* New York: McGraw-Hill.

Walker, L.J., DeVries, B. & Trevathan, S.D. (1987) Moral stages and moral orientations in real-life and hypothetical dilemmas. *Child Development, 58,* 842–858.

Walker, M.B. (1992) *The Psychology of Gambling.* Oxford: Butterworth Heinemann.

Walker, R., Findlay, J.M., Young, A.W., & Lincoln, N.B. (1996) Saccadic eye movements in object-based neglect. *Cognitive Neuropsychology, 13,* 569–615.

Walker, S. (1984) *Learning Theory and Behaviour Modification.* London: Methuen.

Walley, M. & Westbury, T. (1996) Sport psychology. In H. Coolican, *Applied Psychology.* London: Hodder & Stoughton.

Walster, E. (1966) The assignment of responsibility for an accident. *Journal of Personality & Social Psychology, 5,* 508–516.

Walster, E. (1970) The effect of self-esteem on liking for dates of various social desirabilities. *Journal of Experimental & Social Psychology, 6,* 248–253.

Walster, E., Aronson, E. & Abrahams, D. & Rottman, L. (1966) Importance of physical attractiveness in dating behaviour. *Journal of Personality & Social Psychology, 4,* 508–516.

Walster, E.H., Walster, G.W. & Berscheid, E. (1978) *Equity Theory and Research.* Boston, Massachusetts: Allyn and Bacon.

Walters, G.D. (1999) *The Addiction Concept: Working hypothesis or self-fulfilling prophecy.* Needham Heights, MA: Allyn & Bacon.

Walton, G.E., Bower, N.J.A. & Bower, T.G.R. (1992) Recognition of familiar faces by newborns. *Infant Behaviour & Development, 16,* 233–253.

Wark, P. & Ball, S. (1996) Death of innocence. *Sunday Times,* 23 June, 12.

Warren, S. & Jahoda, M. (Eds). (1973) *Attitudes* (2nd edition). Harmondsworth, Middlesex: Penguin.

Warrington, E.K. & Saanders, H.I. (1971) The fate of old memories. *Quarterly Journal of Experimental Psychology, 23,* 432–442.

Warrington, E.K. & Weiskrantz, L. (1968) New method of testing long-term retention with special reference to amnesic patients. *Nature, 217,* 972–974.

Warrington, E.K. & Weiskrantz, L. (1970) Amnesic syndrome: Consolidation or retrieval? *Nature, 228,* 628–630.

Wason, P.C. (1960) On the failure to eliminate hypotheses in a conceptual task. *Quarterly Journal of Experimental Psychology, 12,* 129–140.

Wason, P.C. (1983) Realism and rationality in the selection task. In J. Evans (Ed.) *Thinking and Reasoning: Psychological Approaches.* London: Routledge & Kegan Paul.

Waterhouse, R. & Mayes, T. (2000) Unhealthy obsession. *The Sunday Times,* 25 June, 16.

Waterhouse, R., Macaskill, M., & Boztas, S. (2000) Young people are drinking to 'get trolleyed' like never before. And trouble is often close behind. *The Sunday Times,* 23 July, 23.

Waters, E. (1978) The reliability and stability of individual differences in infant–mother attachments. *Child Development, 49,* 483–494.

Waters, E., Wippman, J & Sroufe, L.A. (1979) Attachment, positive affect and competence in the peer group: Two studies in construct validation. *Child Development, 50,* 821–829.

Watson, J.B. (1913) Psychology as the behaviourist views it. *Psychological Review, 20,* 158–177.

Watson, J.B. (1919) *Psychology from the Standpoint of a Behaviourist.* Philadelphia: J.B. Lippincott.

Watson, J.B. (1924) *Behaviourism.* New York: J.B. Lippincott.

Watson, J.B. (1925) *Behaviourism.* New York: Norton.

Watson, J.B. (1928) *Psychological Care of Infant and Child.* New York: Norton.

Watson, J.B. & Rayner, R. (1920) Conditioned emotional reactions. *Journal of Experimental Psychology, 3,* 1–14.

Watson, J.D. & Crick, F.H.C. (1953) Molecular structure of nucleic acid: A structure for deoxyribose nucleic acid. *Nature, 171,* 737–738.

Watson, O.N. & Graves, T.D. (1966) Quantitative research in proxemic behaviour. *American Anthropologist, 68,* 971–985.

Watts, J. (2000) Dare to be different, Japanese are urged. *The Guardian,* 21 January.

Waugh, N.C. & Norman, D.A. (1965) Primary memory. *Psychological Review, 72,* 89–104.

Weatherley, D. (1961) Anti-semitism and expression of fantasy aggression. *Journal of Abnormal & Social Psychology, 62,* 454–457.

Webb, W.B. (1975) *Sleep: The Gentle Tyrant.* Englewood Cliffs, NJ: Prentice-Hall.

Webb, W.B. (1982) Sleep and biological rhythms. In Webb, W.B. (Ed.) *Biological Rhythms, Sleep and Performance.* Chichester: John Wiley & Sons.

Webb, W.B. & Bonnett, M.H. (1979) Sleep and dreams. In M.E. Meyer (Ed.) *Foundations of Contemporary Psychology.* New York: Oxford University Press.

Webster, C.D., McPherson, H., Sloman, L., Evans, M.A., & Kuchar, E. (1973) Communicating with an autistic boy by gestures. *Journal of Autism & Childhood Schizophrenia, 3,* 337–346.

Wechsler, D. (1944) *The Measurement of Adult Intelligence* (3rd edition). Baltimore: Williams & Wilkins.

Wechsler, D. (1958) *The Measurement and Appraisal of Adult Intelligence* (4th edition). Baltimore: Williams & Wilkins.

Wechsler, D. (1974) *Wechsler Intelligence Scale for Children.* New York: Psychological Corporation.

Wechsler, D. (1989) *Wechsler Preschool and Primary Scale of Intelligence* (revised edition). San Antonio, TX: The Psychological Corporation.

Wechsler, D. (1991) *Wechsler Intelligence Scale for Children* (3rd edition) *Manual.* San Antonio, TX: The Psychological Corporation.

Wechsler, D. (1997) *Wechsler Adult Intelligence Scale* (3rd edition) *Manual.* San Antonio, TX: The Psychological Corporation.

Weinberg, R. (1989) Intelligence and IQ: Landmark issues and great debates. *American Psychologist, 44,* 98–104.

Weiner, B. (1986) *An Attributional Theory of Motivation and Emotion.* New York: Springer-Verlag.

Weiner, B. (1992) *Human Motivation: Metaphors, Theories and Research.* Newbury Park, CA: Sage.

Weinman, J. (1995) Health Psychology. In A.M. Colman (Ed.) *Controversies in Psychology.* London: Longman.

Weinstein, N. (1983) Reducing unrealistic optimism about illness susceptibility. *Health Psychology, 2,* 11–20.

Weinstein, N. (1984) Why it won't happen to me: Perceptions of risk factors and susceptibility. *Health Psychology, 3,* 431–457.

Weisfeld, G. (1994) Aggression and dominance in the social world of boys. In J. Archer (Ed.) *Male Violence.* London: Routledge.

Weiskrantz, L. (1956) Behavioural changes associated with ablation of the amygdaloid complex in monkeys. *Journal of Comparative & Physiological Psychology, 49,* 381–391.

Weiskrantz, L. (1982) Comparative aspects of studies of amnesia. *Philosophical Transactions of the Royal Society. London B, 298,* 97–109.

Weiskrantz, L. (1986) *Blindsight: A Case Study and Implications.* Oxford: Oxford University Press.

Weiskrantz, L. (1988) *Thought Without Language.* Oxford: Oxford University Press.

Weiss, J.M. (1972) Psychological factors in stress and disease. *Scientific American, 226,* 104–113.

Weiss, R.S. (1993) Loss and recovery. In M.S. Stroebe, W. Stroebe & R.O. Hansson (Eds) *Handbook of Bereavement: Theory, Research and Intervention.* New York: Cambridge University Press.

Weisstein, N. (1993) Psychology constructs the female; or, The fantasy life of the male psychologist (with some attention to the fantasies of his friend, the male biologist and the male anthropologist). *Feminism & Psychology, 3(2),* 195–210.

Wellman, H.M. (1990) *The Child's Theory of Mind.* Cambridge, MA: MIT Press.

Wells, G.L. (1993) What do we know about eyewitness identification? *American Psychologist, 48,* 553–571.

Wells, G.L. & Harvey, J.H. (1977) Do people use consensus information in making causal attributions? *Journal of Personality & Social Psychology, 35,* 279–293.

Wender, P.H., Rosenthal, D., Kety, S.S., Schulsinger, F., & Welner, J. (1974) Crossfostering: A research strategy for clarifying the role of genetic and experiential factors in the aetiology of schizophrenia. *Archives of General Psychiatry, 30*, 212–228.

Werner, E.E. (1989) Children of the Garden Island. *Scientific American*, April, 106–111.

Wessler, R.L. (1986) Conceptualising cognitions in the cognitive-behavioural therapies. In W. Dryden & W. Golden (Eds) *Cognitive–Behavioural Approaches to Psychotherapy*. London: Harper & Row.

Westermarck, E.R. (1894) *The History of Human Marriage (3 Volumes)*. New York: Macmillan.

Weston, D. & Turiel, E. (1980) Act–rule relations: Children's concepts of social rules. *Developmental Psychology, 16*, 417–424.

Wetherell, M. (1982) Cross-cultural studies of minimal groups: Implications for the social identity theory of intergroup relations. In H. Tajfel (Ed.) *Social Psychology and Intergroup Relations*. Cambridge: Cambridge University Press.

Wetherell, M. (1987) Social identity and group polarisation. In J.C. Turner, M.A. Hogg, P.J. Oakes, S.D. Reicher & M. Wetherell, *Rediscovering the Social Group: A Self-Categorisation Theory*. Oxford: Blackwell.

Wetherell, M. (1996) Group conflict and the social psychology of racism. In M. Wetherell (Ed.) *Identities, Groups and Social Issues*. London: Sage, in association with the Open University.

White, G.L. (1980) Physical attractiveness and courtship process. *Journal of Personality & Social Psychology, 39*, 660–668.

White, R.W. (1959) Motivation reconsidered: The concept of competence. *Psychological Review, 66*, 297–333.

Whittell, G. (1996) Black American slang wins place in classroom. *The Times*, 21 December, 11.

Whorf, B.L. (1956) *Language, Thought and Reality*. Cambridge, MA: MIT Press.

Whyte, J. (1998) Childhood. In K. Trew & J. Kremer (Eds) *Gender & Psychology*. London: Arnold.

Whyte, W.W. (1956) *The Organisation Man*. New York: Simon and Schuster.

Wichstrom, L. (1998) Self-concept development during adolescence: Do American truths hold for Norwegians? In E. Skoe & A. von der Lippe (Eds) *Personality Development in Adolescence: A Cross National and Life Span Perspective*. London: Routledge.

Wickelgren, W.A. (1965) Acoustic similarity and retroactive interference in short term memory. *Journal of Verbal Learning & Verbal Behaviour, 4*, 53–61.

Wickelgren, W.A. (1973) The long and the short of memory. *Psychological Bulletin, 80*, 425–438.

Wickelgren, W.A. (1974) Single trace fragility theory of memory dynamics. *Memory & Cognition, 2*, 775–780.

Wickens, C.D. (1972) Characteristics of word encoding. In A. Melton & E. Martin (Eds) *Coding Processes in Human Memory*. Washington, DC: Winston.

Wickens, C.D. (1984) Processing resources in attention. In R. Parasuraman & D.R. Davies, (Eds), *Varieties of Attention*. London: Academic Press.

Wickens, C.D. (1992) *Engineering Psychology and Human Performance* (2nd edition). New York: HarperCollins.

Wicker, A.W. (1969) Attitude versus actions: The relationship of verbal and overt behavioural responses to attitude objects. *Journal of Social Issues, 25*(4), 41–78.

Wicklund, R.A. (1975) Objective self-awareness. In L. Berkowitz (Ed.) *Advances in Experimental Social Psychology, Volume 8*. New York: Academic Press.

Wilding, J.M. (1982) *Perception: From Sense to Object*. London: Hutchinson.

Wiemann, J.M. & Giles, H. (1988) Interpersonal communication. In M. Hewstone, W. Stroebe, J.P. Codol, & G.M. Stephenson (Eds) *Introduction to Social Psychology*. Oxford: Blackwell.

Weiner, B. (1995) *Judgements of Responsibility*. New York: Guildford.

Wilkinson, S. (1989) The impact of feminist research: Issues of legitimacy. *Philosophical Psychology, 2*(3), 261–269.

Wilkinson, S. (1991) Feminism & psychology: From critique to reconstruction. *Feminism & Psychology, 1*(1), 5–18.

Wilkinson, S, (1997) Feminist psychology. In D. Fox & D. Prilleltensky (Eds) *Critical Psychology: An Introduction*. London: Sage.

Williams, A. (1998) *'Doctor I Can't Sleep'*. Amberwood Publishing.

Williams, B. (1999) Unpublished D. Clin. Psych. Research thesis, South Thames (Salomons) University.

Williams, J.E. & Best, D.L. (1994) Cross-cultural views of women and men. In W.J. Lonner & R.S. Malpass (Eds) *Psychology and Culture*. Boston: Allyn & Bacon.

Williams, J.M.G. & Hargreaves, I.R. (1995) Neuroses: Depressive and anxiety disorders. In A.A. Lazarus & A.M. Colman (Eds) *Abnormal Psychology*. London: Longman.

Williams, K, Harkins, S.G. & Latané, B. (1981) Identifiability as a deterrant to social loafing: Two cheering experiments. *Journal of Personality & Social Psychology, 40*, 303–311.

Williams, P. (2000) 'Soon we won't relate to each other in person at all'. *The Independent on Sunday,* 16 January, 12.

Williams, R. & Joseph, S. (1999) Conclusions: An integrative psychosocial model of post-traumatic stress disorder. In W. Yule (Ed.) *Post-traumatic Stress Disorders: Concepts and Therapy*. Chichester: Wiley.

Williams, T.M. (Ed.) (1986) *The Impact of Television: A National Experiment in Three Communities*. New York: Academic Press.

Williams, W.M. & Ceci, S.J. (1997) Are Americans becoming more or less alike? Trends in race, class, and ability differences in intelligence. *American Psychologist, 52*, 1226–1235.

Willis, R.H. (1963) Two dimensions of conformity–nonconformity. *Sociometry, 26*, 499–513.

Wilson, E.O. (1975) *Sociobiology – The New Synthesis*. Cambridge, MA: Harvard University Press.

Wilson, E.O. (1978) *On Human Nature*. Cambridge, Massachusetts: Harvard University Press.

Wilson, G. (1994) Biology, sex roles and work. In C. Quest (Ed.) *Liberating Women from Modern Feminism*. London: Institute of Economic Affairs, Health & Welfare Unit.

Wilson, G.D. (1976) Personality. In H.J. Eysenck & G.D. Wilson (Eds) *A Textbook of Human Psychology*. Lancaster: MTP.

Wilson, G.T. & Davison, G.C. (1971) Processes of fear reduction in systematic desensitisation: Animal studies. *Psychological Bulletin, 76*, 1–14.

Wilson, G.T., O'Leary, K.D., Nathan, P.E. & Clark, L.A. (1996) *Abnormal Psychology: Integrating Perspectives*. Needham Heights, MA.: Allyn and Bacon.

Wilson, J.E. & Barkham, M. (1994) A practitioner–scientist approach to psychotherapy process and outcome research. In P. Clarkson & M. Pokorny (Eds) *The Handbook of Psychotherapy*. London: Routledge.

Wilson, J.Q. & Herrnstein, R.J. (1985) *Crime and Human Nature*. New York: Touchstone.

Wimmer, H. & Perner, J. (1983) Beliefs about beliefs: representation and constraining function of wrong beliefs in young children's understanding of deception. *Cognition, 13*, 103–128.

Winch, R.F. (1955) The theory of complementary needs in mate selection: A test of one kind of complementariness. *American Sociological Review, 20*, 52–56.

Winch, R.F. (1958) *Mate Selections: A Study of Complementary Needs.* New York: Harper.

Wing, J.K., Cooper, J.E. & Sartorius, N. (1974) *Measurement and Classification of Psychiatric Symptoms.* Cambridge: Cambridge University Press.

Wing, L. (1988) The continuum of autistic characteristics. In E. Schopler & G. Mesibor (Eds) *Diagnosis and Assessment in Autism.* New York: Plenum Press.

Wing, L. (1997) The history of ideas on autism: legends, myths and reality. Autism: *The International Journal of Research & Practice, 1,* 13–23.

Wing, L. & Gould, J. (1979) Severe impairments of social interaction and associated abnormalities in children: Epidemiology and classification. *Journal of Autism & Developmental Disorders, 9,* 11–29.

Wingfield, A. & Byrnes, D. (1972) Decay of information in short-term memory. *Science, 176,* 690–692.

Winner, E. (1996) The rage to master: The decisive role of talent in the visual arts. In K.A. Ericsson (Ed.) *The Road to Excellence: The Acquisition of Expert Performance in ther Arts and Sciences.* Hillsdale, NJ: Lawrence Erlbaum Associates.

Winner, E. (1998) Uncommon talents: Gifted children, prodigies and talents. *Scientific American Presents, 9*(4), 32–37.

Winnicott, D.W. (1958) *Through Paediatrics to Psychoanalysis.* London: Hogarth Press.

Winson, J. (1997) The meaning of dreams. *Scientific American Mysteries of the Mind, Special Issues, 791,* 58–67 (originally published November, 1990).

Winter, D.A. (1999) Psychological problems: Alternative perspectives on their explanation and treatment. In D. Messer & F. Jones (Eds) *Psychology and Social Care.* London: Jessica Kingsley.

Wise, S. (2000) *Rattling the Cage: Towards Legal Rights for Animals.* Profile Books.

Wishner, J. (1960) Reanalysis of 'impressions of personality'. *Psychological Review, 67,* 96–112.

Witkin, H.A., Dyk, R.B., Faterson, H.F., Goodenough, D.R. & Karp, S.A. (1962) *Psychological Differentiation.* London: Wiley.

Wittgenstein, L. (1953) *Philosophical Investigations.* Oxford: Blackwell.

Wittgenstein, L. (1961) *Tractatus Logico-Philosophicus* (translated by D.F. Pears & B.F. McGuinness). London: Routledge & Kegan Paul (originally published in 1921).

Wober, J.M., Reardon, G. & Fazal, S. (1987) *Personality, Character Aspirations and Patterns of Viewing Among Children.* London: IBA Research Papers.

Wober, M. (1974) Towards an understanding of the Kiganda concept of intelligence. In J.W. Berry & P.R. Dasen (Eds) *Culture and Cognition.* London: Methuen.

Wolf, S. & Wolff, H.G. (1947) *Human Gastric Function.* New York: Oxford University Press.

Wolkowitz, O.M., Bertz, B., Weingartner, H., Beccaria, L., Thompson, K., & Liddle, R.A. (1990) Hunger in humans induced by MK-329, a specific peripheral-type cholecystokinin receptor antagonist. *Biological Psychiatry, 28,* 169–173.

Wollen, K.A., Weber, A. & Lowry, D.H. (1972) Bizareness versus interaction of mental images as determinants of learning. *Cognitive Psychology, 3,* 518–523.

Wollheim, R. (1971) *Freud.* London: Fontana.

Wolpe, J. (1958) *Psychotherapy by Reciprocal Inhibition.* Stanford, CA: Stanford University Press.

Wolpe, J. (1969) For phobia: A hair of the hound. *Psychology Today, 3,* 34–37.

Wolpe, J. (1969) *The Practice of Behaviour Therapy.* Oxford: Pergamon Press.

Wolpe, J. (1973) *The Practice of Behaviour Therapy.* New York: Pergamon Press.

Wolpe, J. (1978) Cognition and causation in human behaviour and its therapy. *American Psychologist, 33,* 437–446.

Wolpe, J. & Rachman, S. (1960) Psychoanalytic evidence: A critique based on Freud's case of Little Hans. *Journal of Nervous & Mental Disease, 131,* 135–145.

Wolpe, J. & Wolpe, D. (1981) *Our Useless Years.* Boston: Houghton-Mifflin.

Wood, D.J., Bruner, J.S. & Ross, G. (1976) The role of tutoring in problem-solving. *Journal of Child Psychology & Psychiatry, 17,* 89–100.

Wood, J.T. & Duck, S. (1995) *Understanding Relationship Processes 6: Understudied Relationships: Off the Beaten Track.* Thousand Oaks, CA: Sage.

Woodcock, A., Stenner, K., & Ingham, R. (1992) Young people talking about HIV and AIDS: Interpretations of personal risk of infection. Health Education Research: *Theory & Practice, 7,* 229–247.

Woodruff, G. & Premack, D. (1979) Intentional communication in the chimpanzee: The development of deception. *Cognition, 7,* 333–362.

Woods, B. (1998) *Applying Psychology to Sport.* London: Hodder & Stoughton.

Woodworth, R.S. (1918) *Dynamic Psychology.* New York: Columbia University Press.

Woodworth, R.S. (1938) *Experimental Psychology.* New York: Holt.

Word, C.O., Zanna, M.P. & Cooper, J. (1974) The non-verbal mediation of self-fulfilling prophecies in interracial interaction. *Journal of Experimental Social Psychology, 10,* 109–120.

World Health Organisation (1973) *Report of the International Pilot Study of Schizophrenia, Volume 1.* Geneva: WHO.

World Health Organisation (1979) *Schizophrenia: An Initial Follow-up.* Chichester: Wiley.

World Health Organisation (1992) *The ICD-10 Classification of Mental and Behavioural Disorders: Clinical Descriptions and Diagnostic Guidelines.* Geneva: WHO.

Wright, D.B. (1993) Recall of the Hillsborough disaster over time: Systematic biases of 'flashbulb' memories. Applied *Cognitive Psychology, 7,* 129–138.

Wundt, W. (1874) *Grundzuge der Physiologischen Psychologie.* Leipzig: Engelmann.

Wundt, W. (1897) *Outlines of Psychology* (Trans. C. H. Judd). Leipzig: Wilhelm Engelmann.

Wynn, V.E. & Logie, R.H. (1998) The veracity of long-term memory: Did Bartlett get it right? *Applied Cognitive Psychology, 12,* 1–20.

Yam, P. (1998) Intelligence Considered. *Scientific American Presents: Exploring Intelligence, 9*(4), 6–11.

Yarbus, A.L. (1967) *Eye Movements and Vision* (B. Haigh, trans). New York: Plenum.

Yates, A.J. (1970) *Behaviour Therapy.* New York: Wiley.

Yin, R.K. (1969) Looking at upside-down faces. *Journal of Experimental Psychology, 81,* 141–145.

Yip, A. (1999) Same-sex couples. *Sociology Review, 8*(3), 30–33.

Young, A.W. & Bruce, V. (1998) Pictures at an exhibition: The science of the face. *The Psychologist, 11*(3), 120–125.

Young, A.W., de Haan, E.H.F., Newcombe, F., & Hay, D.C. (1990) Facial neglect. *Neuropsychologia, 28,* 391–415.

Young, A.W., Hay, D.C. & Ellis, A.W. (1985) The faces that launched a thousand slips: Everyday difficulties and errors in recognising people. *British Journal of Psychology, 76,* 495–523.

Young, A.W., Hellawell, D.J. & Hay, D.C. (1987) Configurational information in face perception. *Perception, 16,* 747–759.

Young, A.W., Newcombe, F., De Haan, E.H.F., Small, M. & Hay, D.C. (1993) Face perception after brain injury: Selective impairments affecting identity and expression. *Brain, 116*, 941–959.

Young, S. (1994) Brain cells hit the big time. *New Scientist,* February, 23–27.

Yuille, J.C. & Cutshall, J.L. (1986) A case study of eyewitness memory of a crime. *Journal of Applied Psychology, 71,* 291–301.

Zaidel, E. (1978) Auditory language comprehension in the right hemisphere following cerebral commissurotomy and hemispherectomy. In A. Caramassa & E. Zuriff (Eds), *Acquisition and Language Breakdown: Parallels and Divergences.* Baltimore, Maryland: Johns Hopkins University Press.

Zaidel, E. (1983) A response to Gazzaniga. *American Psychologist, 38,* 542–546.

Zajonc, R.B. (1965) Social facilitation. *Science, 1429,* 269–274.

Zajonc, R.B. (1968) Attitudinal effects of mere exposure. *Journal of Personality & Social Psychology, Monograph Supplement 9, Part 2,* 1–27.

Zajonc R.B. (1980a) Feeling and thinking: Preferences need no inferences. *American Psychologist, 35,* 151–175.

Zajonc, R.B. (1980b) Compresence. In P. Paulus (Ed.) *Psychology of Group Influence.* Hillsdale, NJ: Lawrence Erlbaum.

Zajonc, R.B. (1984) On the primacy of affect. *American Psychologist, 39,* 117–123.

Zajonc, R.B. (1989) Styles of explanation in social psychology. *European Journal of Social Psychology, 19,* 345–368.

Zajonc, R.B. & Markus, G.B. (1975) Birth order and intellectual development. *Psychological Review, 82,* 74–88.

Zajonc, R.B., Marcus, H.M. & Wilson, W.R. (1974) Exposure effects and associative learning. *Journal of Experimental Social Psychology, 10,* 248–263.

Zajonc, R.B., Shaver, P., Tarvis, C. & Van Kreveld, D. (1972) Exposure, satiation and stimulus discriminability. *Journal of Personality & Social Psychology, 21,* 270–280.

Zajonc. R.B., Swap, W.C., Harrison, A. & Roberts, P. (1971) Limiting conditions of the exposure effect: Satiation and relativity. *Journal of Personality & Social Psychology, 18,* 384–391.

Zanna, M.P. & Cooper, J. (1974) Dissonance and the pill: An attribution approach to studying the arousal propensities of dissonance. *Journal of Personality & Social Psychology, 29,* 703–709.

Zborowski, M. (1952) Cultural components in response to pain. *Journal of Social Issues, 8,* 16–30.

Zebrowitz, L.A. (1990) *Social Perception.* Milton Keynes: Open University Press.

Zeki, S. (1978) Uniformity and diversity of structure and function in rhesus monkey prestriate visual cortex. *Journal of Physiology, 277,* 273–290.

Zeki, S. (1980) The representation of colours in the visual cortex. *Nature, 284,* 412–418.

Zeki, S. (1992) The visual image in mind and brain. *Scientific American, 267,* 43–50.

Zeki, S. (1993) *A Vision of the Brain.* Oxford: Blackwell.

Zeldow, P.B. I(1995) Psychodynamic Formulations of Human Behaviour. In D. Wedding (Ed.) *Behaviour and Medicine* (2nd edition). St. Louis, MO: Mosby Year Book.

Zigler, E. & Styfco, S.J. (1993) Using research and theory to justify and inform Head Start expansion. Social Policy Report, *Society for Research in Child Development, 7*(2), 1–21.

Zilboorg, G. & Henry, G.W. (1941) *A History of Medical Psychology.* New York: Norton.

Zillman, D. (1978) Attribution and misattribution of excitatory reactions. In J.H. Harvey, W. Ickes & R.F. Kidd (Eds) *New Directions in Attribution Research, Volume 2.* New York: Erlbaum.

Zillman, D. (1982) Transfer of excitation in emotional behaviour. In J.T. Cacioppo & R.E. Petty (Eds) *Social Psychophysiology: A Sourcebook.* New York: Guilford Press.

Zillman, D. & Bryant, J. (1974) Effect of residual excitation on the emotional response to provocation and delayed aggressive behaviour. *Journal of Personality & Social Psychology, 30,* 782–791.

Zillman, D. & Bryant, J. (1984) Effects of massive exposure to pornography. In M.N. Malamuth & E. Donnerstein (Eds) *Pornography and Sexual Aggression.* New York: Academic Press.

Zimbardo, P.G. (1969) The human choice: Individuation, reason, and order versus deindividuation, impluse, and chaos. In W.J. Arnold & D. Levine (Eds) *Nebraska Symposium on Motivation.* Lincoln: University of Nebraska Press.

Zimbardo, P.G. (1973) On the ethics of intervention in human psychological research with special reference to the 'Stanford Prison Experiment'. *Cognition, 2*(2), 243–255.

Zimbardo, P.G. (1992) *Psychology and Life* (13th edition). New York: Harper Collins.

Zimbardo, P.G. & Leippe, M. (1991) *The Psychology of Attitude Change and Social Influence.* New York: McGraw-Hill.

Zimbardo, P.G.& Ruch, F.L. (1973) *Psychology and Life.* New York: Scott Foreman.

Zimbardo, P.G. & Weber, A.L. (1994) *Psychology.* New York: HarperCollins.

Zimbardo, P.G., Banks, W.C., Craig, H. & Jaffe, D. (1973) A Pirandellian prison: The mind is a formidable jailor. *New York Times Magazine,* 8 April, 38–60.

Zinberg, D.S. (1997) Ebonics unleashes tongues. *The Times Higher Education Supplement,* 14 February, 14.

Zubin, J. & Spring, B. (1977) Vulnerability – a new view of schizophrenia. *Journal of Abnormal Psychology, 86,* 103–126.

Zuckerman, A. (1979) *Sensation-seeking: Beyond the Optimal Level of Arousal.* New York: Wiley.

Zuckerman, M. (1978) Actions and occurrences in Kelley's cube. *Journal of Personality & Social Psychology, 36,* 647–656.

Index

Author index

Subject index

Page numbers in bold indicate
definitions of words/concepts.